The Routledge Handbook of Hospitality Marketing

This handbook analyzes the main issues in the field of hospitality marketing by focusing on past, present and future challenges and trends from a multidisciplinary global perspective. The book uniquely combines both theoretical and practical approaches in debating some of the most important marketing issues faced by the hospitality industry.

Parts I and II define and examine the main hospitality marketing concepts and methodologies. Part III offers a comprehensive review of the development of hospitality marketing over the years. The remaining parts (IV–IX) address key cutting-edge marketing issues such as innovation in hospitality, sustainability, social media, peer-to-peer applications, Web 3.0 etc. in a wide variety of hospitality settings. In addition, this book provides a platform for debate and critical evaluation that enables the reader to learn from the industry's past mistakes as well as future opportunities.

The handbook is international in its constitution as it attempts to examine marketing issues, challenges and trends globally, drawing on the knowledge of experts from around the world. Because of the nature of hospitality, which often makes it inseparable from other industries such as tourism, events, sports and even retail, the book has a multidisciplinary approach that will appeal to these disciplines as well as others including management, human resources, technology, consumer behavior and anthropology.

Dogan Gursoy is the Taco Bell Distinguished Professor in the School of Hospitality Business Management at Washington State University, USA and the Editor-in-Chief of the *Journal of Hospitality Marketing & Management*. His research has been published broadly in refereed Tier I journals such as *Annals of Tourism Research*, *Journal of Travel Research*, *Tourism Management*, *International Journal of Hospitality Management* and *Journal of Hospitality & Tourism Research*. He has also developed and designed the "Hotel Business Management Training Simulation" (www. hotelsimulation.com), a virtual management training game where participants are divided into teams and assigned the task of running 500-room hotels in a competitive virtual marketplace.

The Routledge Handbook of Hospitality Marketing

Edited by Dogan Gursoy

Routledge
Taylor & Francis Group

LONDON AND NEW YORK

First published 2018
by Routledge
2 Park Square, Milton Park, Abingdon, Oxon OX14 4RN

and by Routledge
711 Third Avenue, New York, NY 10017

Routledge is an imprint of the Taylor & Francis Group, an informa business

British Library Cataloguing-in-Publication Data
A catalogue record for this book is available from the British Library

Library of Congress Cataloging-in-Publication Data
Names: Gursoy, Dogan, editor.
Title: The Routledge handbook of hospitality marketing / edited by Dogan Gursoy.
Description: New York : Routledge, 2018. | Includes bibliographical references and index.
Identifiers: LCCN 2017012476 (print) | LCCN 2017037030 (ebook) |
ISBN 9781315445526 (Master ebook) | ISBN 9781315445519 (Web pdf) |
ISBN 9781315445502 (epub3) | ISBN 9781315445496 (Mobipocket) |
ISBN 9781138214668 (hardback : alk. paper)
Subjects: LCSH: Hospitality industry–Marketing.
Classification: LCC TX911.3.M3 (ebook) | LCC TX911.3.M3 R68 2018 (print) |
DDC 647.94068/8–dc23
LC record available at https://lccn.loc.gov/2017012476

ISBN: 978-1-138-21466-8 (hbk)
ISBN: 978-1-315-44552-6 (ebk)

Typeset in Bembo
by Out of House Publishing

Contents

Contents

Contents

Figures

Tables

Tables

Contributors

James Brian Aday, PhD, is an assistant professor in the Department of Hospitality and Tourism Management, College of Business, San Francisco State University.

Pia A. Albinsson is Associate Professor in Marketing in the Walker College of Business at Appalachian State University, Boone, NC, USA. She obtained her PhD in Business Administration from New Mexico State University in 2009. Her research interests include collaborative and green consumption, consumer activism and advertising effectiveness.

Blake H. Bai is a PhD student in School of Hospitality and Tourism at the Auckland University of Technology, Auckland, New Zealand. Research interests include technology innovation, consumer behavior and cultural influence in hospitality and tourism.

Adela Balderas-Cejudo is a research fellow at the Oxford Institute of Population Ageing, University of Oxford, professor at Cámara Bilbao University Business School and assistant professor for the Bachelor's degree in Gastronomy and Culinary Arts, Basque Culinary Center, University of Mondragon, Spain. Dr. Balderas has a PhD in Business Administration. Her doctoral thesis is on Senior Tourism. She has a Masters in Marketing, an Executive MBA and a Masters in Career Coaching. She also specialized in professional coaching at the University of New York. A consultant in marketing and business skills, Dr. Balderas has a wealth of teaching experience at the undergraduate and graduate levels. She is a lecturer at Esic Business and Marketing School, and is currently director of a Master's program at Basque Culinary Center, University of Mondragon and is a consultant for different international hotel chains in the hospitality industry. Dr. Balderas is a visiting professor and lecturer at the University of Salamanca (Spain), College of Economics at the University of Xiamen (China), and lecturer at the University of Regensburg (Germany) and University of Northumbria (United Kingdom) for the International Hospitality Management module.

Albert Barreda is an assistant professor in the Department of Hospitality Leadership at Missouri State University. He completed his PhD degree in the Rosen College of Hospitality Management at the University of Central Florida. He earned his Master's degree in Hospitality and Tourism Management from the Isenberg School of Management at the University of Massachusetts, Amherst, MA. His research focuses on revenue management, vacation ownership, strategic intuition, branding structure, hospitality bankruptcy, corporate finance and information technology. Dr. Barreda's research has been presented in major industry and research conferences around the world including: Macau, China; Taichung, Taiwan; Portugal, Europe; Seoul, South Korea;

London, United Kingdom; Hong Kong; and the United States of America. He is the author of several refereed papers in leading academic journals including *Tourism Management, Computers in Human Behavior, Journal of Vacation Marketing, Journal of Relationship Marketing* and others. He has also received several awards for his research contributions, and has consulting experience in the areas of hotel investment, and market research for hospitality and tourism organizations.

Jeff Beck is an associate professor in the School of Hospitality Business at Michigan State University, where he teaches courses in marketing, sales and revenue management. His research interests include revenue management, sales and ethics in hospitality. Beck is currently the chair of a scientific paper review committee for the ICHRIE annual conference, and an associate editor for the *Journal of Hospitality & Tourism Research*. He has extensive experience in the hospitality industry, including ten years with Marriott Lodging. He earned his Bachelor's degree in Marketing from the Kelley School of Business at Indiana University, and his advanced degrees from Purdue University.

Stefanie Benjamin is an assistant professor in the Department of Retail, Hospitality & Tourism Management at the University of Tennessee, Knoxville, TN. She obtained her PhD in Educational Foundations and Inquiry from the University of South Carolina in 2015 and is the author of various published journal papers on tourism. Her research interests are focused on cultural and historical landscapes in relation to heritage tourism in the US South, with special attention devoted to power, politics, and collective memory. She has work experience in marketing and in providing services for consumers in the retail, entertainment and hotel industry. She is also a certified qualitative researcher, as a professional improvisation actor.

Kemal Birdir is a full-time professor in the Department of Tourism Management at Mersin University, Turkey. He obtained a Master's degree in 2013 and completed his PhD thesis on Hospitality Human Resources Management. His research interests include tourism management and hospitality management.

Edward C. Bolden is the Educational Research and Assessment Specialist in University Technology at Case Western Reserve University. He received his PhD in Evaluation and Measurement from Kent State University, where he serves as an adjunct instructor and conducts research with faculty from the Hospitality Management program. His area of research interest is applied statistics and research design.

Robert Bosselman is a full professor and a department chair in the Department of Apparel, Events, & Hospitality Management, College of Human Sciences at Iowa State University, Ames, IA, USA.

Natalya Brown is an associate professor in the Nipissing University School of Business and Department of Political Science, Philosophy and Economics. Her research interests include eco-tourism and the adoption of sustainable practices by small and medium-sized tourism establishments.

Bidisha Burman is an Associate Professor in Marketing in the College of Business at Mary Washington University, Fredericksburg, VA, USA. She obtained her PhD in Marketing from Louisiana State University in 2004. Her research interests include pricing, green/sustainability marketing, services marketing, judgment and decision-making, and advertising effectiveness.

Eun-Kyong (Cindy) Choi is an assistant professor in the Department of Nutrition and Hospitality Management at the University of Mississippi. Her research is centered on social media marketing, service recovery and customer behavior in the hospitality industry.

Baris Civak is a research assistant. He has undergraduate and graduate degrees in tourism management. He is currently studying for a doctorate in the field of tourism management. He has conducted studies and publications within this field on yield management, online distribution channel management, front office management, organization theory and accessible tourism. Since 2013, he has continued his academic career at Anadolu University, Faculty of Tourism.

Ali Dalgıç is a research assistant and PhD candidate in the Department of Tourism Management at Mersin University. He completed his Master of Science degree in Management in December 2013. His research interests include event management, alternative tourism and special interest tourism.

Giacomo Del Chiappa, PhD, is Associate Professor of Marketing at the Department of Economics and Business, University of Sassari (Italy), and associate researcher at CRENoS. His research is related to destination governance and branding, consumer behaviour and digital marketing.

S. Emre Dilek is an assistant professor in the Department of Gastronomy and Culinary Arts, School of Tourism and Hotel Management at Batman University, Batman, Turkey. In 2012 he completed his Master's thesis, titled *Green Marketing Applications in Tourism Businesses: A Field Research*. In this thesis, the relationship between tourism and the environment was questioned, and the concept of green marketing and green marketing related implementations in tourism were researched. In 2016 he completed his PhD thesis, titled *Evaluation of Moral Responsibility of Tourism Regarding Animals in the Context of Meta-Criticism*. This study conducted a critical analysis by introducing areas where animals are commodified in the tourism industry. His research interests tourism sociology, tourism and animal ethics, philosophy and green marketing.

Murat Emeksiz has undergraduate, graduate and PhD degrees in tourism management. He executed a national project on small and medium-sized hospitality businesses from 2005 to 2007. He has published articles in the *International Journal of Hospitality Management* and the *Journal of Hospitality Marketing & Management*. He has conducted studies and produced publications in the areas of yield management, convention and event management, small tourism businesses, individual outdoor activities, sustainable urban tourism and small tourism regions. Since 1995, his academic career has continued at the Faculty of Tourism, Anadolu University.

Precious Chikezie Ezeh is a PhD candidate in the Department of Marketing at Nnamdi Azikiwe University, Awka, Anambra State, Nigeria. He has a Master's of Science (MSc), Bachelor of Science (BSc), Post Graduate Diploma (PGD), and Higher National Diploma (HND) in Marketing. Ezeh is a lecturer at Federal University Gusau, Zamfara State, Nigeria in the Department of Business Administration. He has spent over 15 years in hospitality management and as a management trainer. He has lectured in Hospitality Marketing as a part-time lecturer at Federal Polytechnic Oko, Anambra State, Nigeria, in the Departments of Marketing and Hospitality Management, and Tourism. Ezeh has co-authored and published four books on marketing, written over ten articles, and presented numerous papers on hotel management at many conferences. Ezeh's research interest is on the marketing of services (hotel and finance). Ezeh is a member of many international and national professional bodies, including the Hospitality and Tourism Management Association of Nigeria, which he joined in 2009. He is a consultant to many hotels in Nigeria.

Lawrence Hoc Nang Fong is an assistant professor in the Faculty of Business Administration at the University of Macau. His research interests include social media marketing, technology adoption and online consumer behaviour in the fields of hospitality and tourism.

Anestis Fotiadis, PhD, is a member of the academic teaching and research staff at Zayed University, Abu Dhabi, United Arab Emirates. His research and teaching is related to rural tourism, small-scale sports event management, and sustainable development.

Ladan Fotouhnezhad is a market analyst at the Business Strategy and Marketing Department of Sarava Pars, Iran. She is an MBA Marketing graduate from UKM University, Kuala Lumpur, Malaysia. She graduated in 2013 from UKM and is a peer reviewer for Elsevier journals. Her research interests include advertising and the hospitality industry, as well as entrepreneurship.

Irene Gil-Saura is Full Professor in Marketing and Chair in the Department of Marketing at the University of Valencia, Spain. Her research is centered on services marketing, consumer behavior and retailing. Her articles have appeared in many journals, such as *Tourism Management*, *Industrial Marketing Management*, *International Journal of Hospitality Management*, *International Journal of Contemporary Hospitality Management*, *The Service Industries Journal*, *Annals of Tourism Research*, *Journal of Vacation Marketing* and *Journal of Hospitality Marketing & Management*.

W.K. Athula C. Gnanapala is a senior lecturer in the Department of Tourism Management, Faculty of Management Studies, Sabaragamuwa University of Sri Lanka. Dr. Gnanapala obtained his first degree, a BSc in Tourism Management, from the Sabaragamuwa University of Sri Lanka in 1997, followed by an MSc in Management at the University of Sri Jayewardenapura. He obtained his doctoral degree in Tourism Management from the Xiamen University, China.

Ozan Güler is a research assistant in the Department of Tourism Management at Mersin University, Turkey. He obtained a Master's degree in 2013 and is writing up his PhD thesis on consumer behavior. His research interests include tourism marketing and gastronomy.

Dogan Gursoy is the Taco Bell Distinguished Professor in the School of Hospitality Business Management at Washington State University and the Editor-in-Chief of the *Journal of Hospitality Marketing & Management*. His research interests include services management, hospitality and tourism marketing, tourist behavior, travelers' information search behavior, community support for tourism development, cross-cultural studies, consumer behavior, involvement and generational leadership. His research has been published broadly in refereed Tier I journals such as *Annals of Tourism Research*, *Journal of Travel Research*, *Tourism Management*, *International Journal of Hospitality Management* and *Journal of Hospitality & Tourism Research*. He has also developed and designed the "Hotel Business Management Training Simulation" (www.hotelsimulation.com/), a virtual management training game where participants are divided into teams and assigned the task of running 500-room hotels in a competitive virtual marketplace.

C. Michael Hall is a professor in the Department of Management, Marketing and Entrepreneurship at the University of Canterbury, New Zealand; docent, Department of Geography, University of Oulu, Finland; and a visiting professor at Linneaus University, Kalmar, Sweden.

Serhat Harman obtained his Bachelor's degree in Tourism Management from Canakkale Onsekiz Mart University in 2004. He received a Master's degree from Canakkale Onsekiz Mart University, Institute of Social Sciences, in 2007. Harman received his PhD from Canakkale Onsekiz Mart University, Institute of Social Sciences in 2007. He is working as an associate professor at Batman University. His research focuses on different aspects of tourist behavior.

Cindy Yoonjoung Heo is an assistant professor at Ecole hôtelière de Lausanne, Switzerland (HES-SO/University of Applied Sciences Western Switzerland). Her research interests include the strategic elements of revenue management, consumer behavior and sharing economy. Her academic articles have appeared in *Annals of Tourism Research, Tourism Management* and the *International Journal of Hospitality Management.*

Aaron Hsiao is a lecturer in the Department of Tourism, Sport and Hotel Management at Griffith University, Australia. His research focuses on cross-cultural management, organisational citizenship behaviour, and internal marketing. He is also developing an interest in work-integrated learning (WIL).

Yinghua Huang is an assistant professor in the Department of Hospitality Management at San José State University. She received her PhD in Hotel and Restaurant Administration from Oklahoma State University. Her research interests include destination marketing, place attachment, service management and research methods.

Myunghee Mindy Jeon is an associate professor at Salem State University. Her research interests are focused in the areas of lodging management and tourism, more specifically hospitality information technology, social media, customer behavior, and resident quality of life in tourism destinations.

Ana Isabel Jiménez-Zarco is Associate Professor of Innovation and Marketing at the Open University of Catalonia, Spain. Her main research interests include tourism, product innovation, and brand image. Professor Jiménez-Zarco has published in *Tourism Management* and *Computers in Human Behavior,* and in other journals.

Dan Jin is a Master's student at the School of Hospitality and Tourism Management, Purdue University, Indiana, USA. Her research interests include hospitality service failure and hospitality technology.

Hyun-Woo Joung is an assistant professor at the Department of Nutrition and Hospitality Management, University of Mississippi. His main research interests are generational differences in restaurant service management and human resource management.

Erhan Kaya is currently Vice President of Business Development and Marketing at Hotel Linkage, a leading name within the US hospitality industry; its R&D office is located in Istanbul, Turkey. His undergraduate, graduate and MBA degrees are in tourism management. He has been working in the travel industry for almost 20 years. He has expertise is yield management and online travel technologies, with a passion for internet and technology.

Bona Kim is an assistant professor in the Department of Business and Tourism at Mount Saint Vincent University, Canada. She obtained her PhD in Hotel & Tourism Management from the Hong Kong Polytechnic University. Her research interests include sensory marketing, hospitality management, tourism experience, tourist well-being, pilgrimage and religious tourism.

Chloe S. Kim is a PhD candidate in the School of Hospitality and Tourism at Auckland University of Technology, Auckland, New Zealand. Her research interests include social media marketing and customer relationship management in hospitality and tourism, with her work portfolio including brand development for hospitality businesses.

Eojina Kim is an assistant professor in the Department of Hospitality and Tourism Management, Pamplin College of Business, Virginia Tech, Blacksburg, VA, USA.

Peter B. Kim is an associate professor in the School of Hospitality and Tourism at the Auckland University of Technology, Auckland, New Zealand. He obtained his PhD in Hospitality and Tourism Management from Virginia Tech University. His research interests include service management and marketing and strategic human resource management.

Bonnie J. Knutson is a professor in the School of Hospitality Business, Michigan State University. Dr. Knutson has had countless articles published in industry and academic publications, authored *M³: Membership Marketing in the Millennium* and is editor-emeritus of the *Journal of Hospitality and Leisure Marketing*. She has been named a MSU Distinguished Faculty and a MSU Distinguished Alumni. Dr. Knutson has also received the Hospitality Business Alumni Association Lifetime Academic Achievement Award, the esteemed Withrow Award for teaching and research in the Broad College of Business, and the prestigious Golden Key Teaching Excellence Award for outstanding instruction and dedication to students.

Mehmet Ali Köseoglu joined the School of Hotel and Tourism Management, Hong Kong Polytechnic University as assistant professor in 2016. He teaches strategic management in the hospitality industry. He has teaching experience from the USA, Turkey and Kuwait. His research interests are strategic management and bibliometric analysis. His research has been published in top-tier journals such as *Annals of Tourism Research, International Journal of Hospitality Management, Journal of Travel & Tourism Marketing, International Journal of Contemporary Hospitality Management, Anatolia, Business Research Quarterly* and *Scientometric*.

Drita Kruja is Professor of Services Marketing and Marketing Research in the Management & Marketing Department at the European University of Tirana, Albania. She is involved in a wide range of academic and scientific activities, which are mainly related to marketing and tourism problems.

Gang Li is an associate professor in the School of Information Technology at Deakin University, Australia.

Shaowu Liu is a postdoctoral researcher in the Advanced Analytics Institute at the University of Technology Sydney, Australia.

Isabel Llodrà-Riera is Coordinator of Cibersociety at Fundació Balear d'Innovació i Tecnologia, Spain. Her research interests fall in the areas of social media and tourism, and she has published in *Tourism Management* and *International Journal of Quality and Service Sciences*, among other journals.

Steve Lui is the Director, IT Field Services West/Hawaii Region, for Hilton Hotels Corporation. Mr. Lui is also an industry lecturer in the Department of Hospitality and Tourism Management, College of Business, San Francisco State University.

Emily (Jintao) Ma is an associate professor in the Department of Hospitality & Tourism Management at the University of Massachusetts, Amherst, USA. Her research interests include organizational behavior in hospitality and tourism contexts, and employee and customer experience in hospitality and tourism organizations.

Thomas A. Maier is Associate Professor of Hospitality Management at the School of Management, University of San Francisco, San Francisco, CA, USA. He has published in hospitality peer-reviewed journals on hotel and restaurant revenue management. His work has been presented at several domestic and international conferences, including the Cornell University Hospitality Research and EYEFOR Travel Inc., North American Travel Distribution Summits.

Colin Mang is an adjunct professor in the School of Business at Nipissing University. His research interests include consumer adoption of new technologies, including tablets and smartphones.

María Pilar Martínez-Ruiz is Associate Professor of Marketing at the Marketing Department, University of Castilla-La Mancha, Spain. Her research interests fall in the areas of tourism, retailing and ICT. Professor Martínez-Ruiz has published in *Tourism Management, European Journal of Marketing* and in other journals.

Felix Mavondo works at the Monash Business School Department of Marketing, Monash University. Professor Mavondo has extensively published his research and is on the editorial board of several marketing, management and tourism journals. He often acts as an ad hoc reviewer for most of the top marketing and tourism journals. Professor Mavondo's current research interests include sustainable tourism, dynamic capabilities and supply chain management, and strategic marketing.

Richard G. McNeill has been a professor at Northern Arizona University (NAU), W.A. Franke College of Business, School of Hotel and Restaurant Management in Flagstaff, Arizona since fall 1989. He teaches international business, marketing and sales. Additionally, he consults with the hospitality industry, specializing in the convergence of marketing/sales/revenue management in the digital era to generate top-line revenue. Dr. McNeill holds a doctorate (Ed.D) from Arizona State University, specializing in educational leadership, organization, and policy studies. He has been a member of the Hospitality Sales and Marketing Association since the 1980s. Dr. McNeill holds two of this association's certifications: Certified Hospitality Marketing Executive and Certified Hospitality Sales Executive. Additionally, he is a member of the American Marketing Association. Dr. McNeill was the lead co-author of a 2006 hospitality text: *Selling Hospitality: A Situational Approach*. Most recently, he completed the draft of his next book (working title): *Hospitality Selling Today: TraDigital Convergence and Collaboration*. He is the author of numerous hospitality sales and marketing articles and conference proceedings.

Simon Milne is Professor of Tourism in the School of Hospitality and Tourism at the Auckland University of Technology, Auckland, New Zealand. He obtained his PhD in Economic Geography from Cambridge University. His research interests include links between technology, customer satisfaction, and tourism economic development.

Sergio Moreno Gil is Director of Institutional Relations at UNESCO Chair of Tourism Planning and Sustainable Development, Universidad de Las Palmas de Gran Canaria, Spain. In the past, he has worked for Hilton Hotels in Germany, TUI Group Spain and as a visiting researcher at the World Tourism Research Centre (UoC – Canada). Dr. Moreno is an external expert advisor for the European Commission on tourism projects. He has written more than 20 books and book chapters, and 30 international papers.

Adina Letiția Negrușa serves as an associate professor at the Faculty of Business at Babeş-Bolyai University, Romania. She obtained her PhD in Management in 2004 and her research interests relate to hospitality and tourism management and managing the innovation process.

Rosemarie Neuninger works in the Department of Marketing at the University of Otago. Her research specializes in the application of qualitative and quantitative research methods. She has a background in investigating consumer behavior and decision-making in different product categories. Her research interests also include sustainable food production, food and beverage marketing, and business practices.

Frank Ohara is the Chair and associate professor in the Department of Finance at the School of Management, University of San Francisco, San Francisco, CA, USA. With over 15 years' financial management and administrative experience in the computer manufacturing and financial services industries, he brings extensive knowledge of corporate financial reporting and analysis as well as financial case and statement analysis to the university.

Fevzi Okumus is a professor within the Hospitality Services Department at the University of Central Florida's Rosen College of Hospitality Management. He was the founding Chair of the Hospitality Services Department from 2007 to 2013. He received his PhD in Strategic Hotel Management from Oxford Brookes University, UK. His research areas include strategy implementation, strategic human resources management, corporate social responsibility, competitive advantage, knowledge management, crisis management, destination marketing, information technology and developing countries. He has widely published in leading journals. He has an h-index of 28 and his publications have received over 3,300 citations. He is the Editor-in-Chief of the *International Journal of Contemporary Hospitality Management* (IJCHM) and also serves on the editorial boards of 21 international journals. He is a frequent speaker at international conferences.

Nuray Selma Özdipçiner has received her Bachelor's and Master's degrees from the marketing department at Marmara University. She received her doctorate from the tourism business department at Adnan Menderes University. She has been working at Pamukkale University since 1994. Her research interests are tourism marketing, health tourism and consumer behavior.

Linda Piper is an assistant professor at the Nipissing University School of Business and a PhD candidate. Her research interests include ecotourism, sustainable tourism and corporate social responsibility.

Girish Prayag is a Senior Lecturer in Marketing in the Department of Management, Marketing and Entrepreneurship at the University of Canterbury, New Zealand. He received his PhD in Tourism Management from the University of Waikato (New Zealand). His research interests are related to the emotional experiences of tourists, tourism market segmentation, organizational resilience, and destination marketing.

Shangzhi (Charles) Qiu is a PhD candidate in the School of Hospitality and Tourism Management at Purdue University, Indiana, USA. His research interests include cross-cultural consumer behavior, consumer irrational decisions and health tourism.

Roya Rahimi joined the Business School at the University of Wolverhampton as a lecturer in 2014. She teaches across tourism, hospitality and events subject areas. Her research interests are CRM, relationship marketing, organizational culture, human resource management, gender equality and tourism higher education. Her work has been published in top-tier journals such as *Annals of Tourism Research, Journal of Tourism & Hospitality Research, Journal of Travel & Tourism Marketing, International Journal of Contemporary Hospitality Management* and *Anatolia*. Her work has also been presented at various international conferences and appears in book chapters published by Routledge, CABI, Emerald and IGI. She sits on the editorial board of the *Journal of Hospitality and Tourism Technology* and *European Management Review*, and also serves as reviewer for a number of leading journals. In 2016, Rahimi received the Valene L. Smith Prize for the best presented paper at the International Conference of Service Quality in Hospitality & Tourism in Isfahan.

Haywantee Ramkissoon is an associate professor and Director of the Tourism Research Cluster at Curtin Business School, and Senior Research Fellow at Monash University. She holds two doctoral degrees in Tourism and Applied Environmental Psychology. Ramkissoon publishes in leading tourism journals such as *Annals of Tourism Research, Tourism Management, Journal of Travel Research, Journal of Sustainable Tourism* and *Tourism Analysis*. She is the book review editor for *Current Issues in Tourism* and is the research note editor for *Journal of Hospitality Marketing & Management*. Ramkissoon serves on 14 editorial boards of high-quality journals in her field.

J.R. Brent Ritchie holds the Professorship of Tourism Management in the Haskayne School of Business at the University of Calgary. He also serves as Chair of the University's World Tourism Education and Research Centre. Dr. Ritchie, who was the Founding Chair of the United Nations World Tourism Organization's Tourism Education and Science Council, is the recipient of numerous awards recognizing his extensive contributions to research and publication in the field. They include the TTRA Lifetime Achievement Award and the UNWTO Ulysses Prize.

Olga Rivera-Hernáez has a degree in Economics and Business Administration from the University of Deusto, and a PhD in Economics and Business Administration from the Autonomous University of Madrid. She is Professor of Organization and Corporate Policy and her research activity is centered on business competitiveness and innovation, knowledge management and organizational learning, communities of practice, transformation and change management. Dr. Rivera belongs to the Deusto research team on Innovation and Organization Management in the Knowledge Society, a team that she launched in 1995 and led until 2009. In recent years, and after her role as Deputy Minister of Quality, Research and Health Innovation in the Basque Government, she has implemented these lines of research in the socio-health sector, and in the silver economy. She has published dozens of articles in international indexed publications, most recently focused on senior tourism and active and healthy aging.

Veronica Rozalia Rus is a lecturer at the Faculty of Business, Babeş-Bolyai University, Romania. She obtained her PhD in Cybernetics and Economic Statistics in 2009 and her research interests relate to decision support systems and hospitality information systems.

María-Eugenia Ruiz-Molina is Associate Professor in the Marketing Department of University of Valencia, where she earned her PhD in Business Administration and Management. She has also been a lecturer at several universities: Universitat Jaume I in Castellón, Polytechnical University of Valencia, University at Albany and the Virtual University of Catalonia (Universitat Oberta de Catalunya). Her research interests focus on services marketing, consumer behavior and retailing.

Chris Ryan is a professor and Director of the China-New Zealand Tourism Research Unit, the University of Waikato Management School, Hamilton, New Zealand.

Maja Šerić is an assistant professor in the Department of Marketing at the University of Valencia in Spain. Her research is focused on integrated marketing communications, brand equity and hospitality marketing. Her papers have been published in a number of hospitality and tourism leading journals, such as the *International Journal of Hospitality Management*, *International Journal of Contemporary Hospitality Management*, *Journal of Hospitality Marketing & Management*, *Tourism Management*, *International Journal of Tourism Research*, *Journal of Destination Marketing & Management*, *Journal of Vacation Marketing* and others.

Gaunette Sinclair-Maragh is an associate professor in the School of Hospitality and Tourism Management at the University of Technology, Jamaica. She holds a PhD in Business Administration with a specialization in Hospitality and Tourism Management from Washington State University in the USA. Her research interests include tourism planning and development, destination marketing, attraction management and event planning management.

Soma Sinha Roy is an assistant professor in the discipline of Marketing Management at Amity University Kolkata, India. She obtained her PhD from the Indian Institute of Technology, Kharagpur, India in 2015. Her research interests include customer delight, services marketing, consumer behavior and brand management. Besides teaching, she is interested in research and publications.

Ercan Sirakaya-Turk is a professor and the Associate Dean for Research, Grants, Graduate and International Programs in the College of Hospitality, Retail and Sports Management at the University of South Carolina. Dr. Sirakaya-Turk was the founding Editor-in-Chief for *e-Review of Tourism Research*, the online tourism research bulletin; since 2015, he has been the Editor-in-Chief of the journal of *Tourism Analysis*. He teaches tourism, marketing, tourism economics and advanced research methods classes while overseeing faculty grants, research, graduate and international programs of four departments in his college. His current research focuses around destination branding, tourist behavior, associative networks and sustainable tourism.

Lisa Slevitch is currently an associate professor in the School of Hotel and Restaurant Administration at the College of Human Sciences at Oklahoma State University. Her research interests are in the areas of hospitality marketing and management, particularly in the field of determinants of customer satisfaction, consumer behavior and sustainability. Her articles have been published in the *International Journal of Hospitality Management*, *International Journal of Contemporary Hospitality Management*, *Cornell Hospitality Quarterly* and other reputable hospitality and tourism journals. Dr. Slevitch is an active member of professional and academic hospitality associations. Currently, she serves on the Board of International Society of Travel and Tourism Educators.

Inna Soifer is an instructor in the Kemmons Wilson School of Hospitality and Resort Management at the University of Memphis. With over a decade of experience in the hospitality industry, she teaches lodging management and event planning courses.

Marios Sotiriadis is a visiting professor at the University of South Africa, South Africa and at University of Ningbo, China. Formerly he was a professor in the Tourism Business Management Department, TEI of Crete, and a tutor at the Hellenic Open University, Greece. He received his PhD in Tourism Management from the University of Nice Sophia-Antipolis, Nice, France. He is the author of nine books and monographs, three distance learning manuals and three e-learning materials on aspects of tourism marketing and management. He has undertaken a variety of research and consultancy projects (e.g., feasibility studies, business plans, marketing research and plans, and human resources projects) for both public and private organizations of the tourism and travel industry. His research and writing interests include tourism destination and businesses marketing and management. His articles have been published by international journals and presented at conferences.

Vishnee Sowamber is a sustainable development strategist at LUX* Resorts & Hotels group, who offers expertise and provides leadership-level support for sustainability. She holds an MBA, a BSc in Tourism & Hospitality Management, and is in her final year of Bachelor of Laws (LLB). She has very strong leadership skills which drive decision-making in strategic reviews (projects such as Global Reporting Initiative, integrated annual report, the Stock Exchange of Mauritius Sustainability Index, carbon offsetting, energy efficiency projects; water optimization, waste management, corporate social responsibility projects management in collaboration with various national and international bodies). She undertakes a range of activities concerned with sustainable development policy making and strategy, which include drafting guidance, making recommendations, reviewing policy and procedure, and researching new initiatives.

Liang (Rebecca) Tang is an associate professor in the Department of Apparel, Events, & Hospitality Management, College of Human Sciences, Iowa State University, Ames, IA, USA.

Valentin Toader is a lecturer at the Faculty of Business, Babeş-Bolyai University, Romania. He obtained his PhD in International Economic Relations in 2008, focusing on the economics of tourism and macroeconomics. Between 2011 and 2013, he was the regional coordinator on an interregional project promoting innovation in rural tourism – Innovative and Responsible Tourism Territories (www.iartterritories.com).

Andrew R. Walls, PhD, is an associate professor in, and the Department Chair of the Department of Hospitality and Tourism Management, College of Business, San Francisco State University.

Chuhan (Renee) Wang is a PhD candidate in Hospitality Management at the University of South Carolina, Columbia, USA. She received her Bachelor's degree in Hospitality and Tourism Management from the cooperative program of Tianjin University of Commerce and Florida International University. She received her Master's degree in Hospitality and Tourism Management from Virginia Tech, Virginia, USA where she was a teaching assistant while also interning at a local winery as the Marketing Director Assistant. She also worked on campus for the President of Virginia Tech and the Inn at Virginia Tech for three years. She received various academic scholarships and won a research grant from the Office of the Vice President for Research at the University of South Carolina. She has attended and presented several academic papers at national and international conferences such as the Graduate Conference and TTRA. She teaches introductory courses on tourism, hospitality, and tourism and hospitality marketing. Her research interests mainly focus on social media and digital marketing, hotel emerging technology and big data analysis.

Saerom Wang is a PhD student at the School of Hospitality and Tourism Management at Purdue University, Indiana, USA. She obtained her M.S. from the School of Hospitality and Tourism Management at Sejong University, Republic of Korea. Her research interests include hospitality marketing, social media in tourism marketing and consumer behavior.

James Arthur Williams is an assistant professor in the Department of Retail, Hospitality & Tourism Management, University of Tennessee, Knoxville, TN. He obtained his PhD in Hospitality Management from Iowa State University in 2012 and is the author of several published journal papers, as well as a bestselling memoir, *From Thug to Scholar: An Odyssey to Unmask my True Potential*. His research interests are in transformational leadership, soft skills, emotional intelligence, mentorship and hospitality pedagogy. He is an actor and former professional arena football player and held leadership roles in lodging, the United States Air Force, banking, manufacturing, sales and education.

Lu Zhang is an assistant professor in the School of Hospitality Business, Michigan State University. Her research interests center on topics related to digital marketing such as online reviews (e.g., how customers process online reviews) and m-commerce (e.g., last-minute booking using mobile devices).

Introduction

Dogan Gursoy

Hospitality marketing refers to all marketing activities and efforts directed towards the increase of revenues in the hospitality industry (Nunkoo, Gursoy, and Ramkissoon, 2013). The hospitality industry offers complex hospitality experiences to its customers within a very competitive global marketplace and encompasses numerous sectors such as lodging, food and beverage, cruise, entertainment, etc. In view of this, the planning, design and management of marketing activities to attract hospitality customers is considered to be a focal challenge for hospitality businesses in a globalized and highly competitive market (Gursoy, Saayman, and Sotiriadis, 2015). Despite its segmentation as an industry, there are key marketing issues and challenges that are pertinent to all subsectors within the hospitality industry (Xu and Gursoy, 2015). These key marketing issues and challenges can prove critical for the success of any hospitality business, no matter what subsector of the industry the business may focus upon (Jiang, Ramkissoon, and Mavondo, 2016). Ignoring these key marketing issues and challenges can have detrimental effects.

Over the past 50 years, the field of hospitality marketing has witnessed a tremendous growth in the amount of information and knowledge generated by both academics and practitioners (Gursoy, Uysal, Sirakaya-Turk, Ekinci, and Baloglu, 2014). The main reason for this tremendous growth is that hospitality marketing researchers and practitioners have been trying to understand complex decision-making processes of hospitality consumers and the factors that may influence those processes, because understanding consumer behavior is the core of marketing (Ladeira, Santini, Araujo, and Sampaio, 2016). Hospitality marketers need to understand the reasons for hospitality consumers' purchase and consumption behaviors of products and services as well as the ways they purchase and consume them so that they can develop effective marketing strategies to attract those customers (Ong, 2015).

As the field of hospitality marketing experiences maturity and scientific sophistication, it is important that we as hospitality researchers and practitioners fully understand the breadth and depth of existing knowledge that can help us explain, understand, monitor and predict concepts and constructs related to hospitality marketing (Tresidder, 2015). *The Routledge Handbook of Hospitality Marketing* carefully examines marketing issues that are raised in the contemporary hospitality marketing literature and are faced by hospitality businesses in their everyday operations. Defining key marketing concepts and issues and exploring the type of impacts they may have on the success of hospitality businesses can enable us to set the stage for a better understanding of the supply and demand issues the industry is facing today. Furthermore, examining the current key trends and issues such as sustainability and innovation and then focusing on future trends within the industry can provide critical insights into the successful development and implementation of marketing strategies and activities within the hospitality industry.

The Routledge Handbook of Hospitality Marketing examines key contemporary marketing concepts, issues and challenges that affect numerous sectors in the industry within a multi-disciplinary global perspective. The handbook addresses cutting-edge marketing issues such as innovation in hospitality, sustainability, social media, peer-to-peer applications, experience marketing, etc. The handbook is international in its nature as it attempts to examine marketing issues, challenges and trends from around the world, drawing on the knowledge and expertise of experts from around the world. By compiling and presenting critical research topics that capture a variety of concepts and constructs used in the hospitality marketing field, *The Routledge Handbook of Hospitality Marketing* aims to be a go-to resource for credible hospitality marketing knowledge.

This handbook aims at bridging the gap in the contemporary hospitality marketing literature by carefully examining both theoretical and practical hospitality marketing issues and challenges. The unique feature of this handbook is that it combines both theoretical and practical approaches in debating some of the most important marketing issues faced by the industry. We know that this handbook will help the researchers and practitioners in our field to refer to and locate hospitality marketing knowledge with minimal effort.

Hospitality consumers' decision-making process

Hospitality consumers' decision-making process is influenced by both psychological and non-psychological variables (García de Leaniz and Rodríguez Del Bosque Rodríguez, 2015). Psychological variables, such as attitudes, beliefs and intentions, are internal to the consumer whereas non-psychological variables, such as time, price of a product and characteristics of a consumer, are the external causes of this process (Chen and Yuan, 2016). While the external and internal factors that may influence hospitality consumers' decision-making process have received significant attention from both hospitality researchers and practitioners, the globalization and digital revolution that have taken place in the recent decades present exceptional challenges and opportunities when it comes to planning, developing, managing and marketing hospitality offerings and experiences (Lu and Gursoy, 2015). Recent advancements in online technology have been influencing not only those critical internal and external forces revolving around the decision-making process of hospitality consumers but also the way that consumers purchase those hospitality products and services (Aday and Phelan, 2015; Choi, Fowler, Goh, and Yuan, 2015). These external and internal forces, and the impacts of rapidly evolving online technology on those forces, are critical subjects for hospitality marketing managers and researchers to identify and also to investigate because this knowledge can help marketing managers to identify the stage or the point of the decision-making process the marketing efforts should be directed towards (Hanks, Line, and Mattila, 2015).

The consumer decision-making process received a lot of interest from marketing researchers during the second half of the last century. A substantial body of literature has emerged in a short time in this field. The early 1960s saw remarkable advancements in the theory of consumer behavior (Sirakaya and Woodside, 2005). The pioneering comprehensive models of consumer behavior appeared during this time to provide an extensive description and systematic framework of the entire buying process (Sirakaya and Woodside, 2005). The most influential early models of consumer behavior, what Gilbert (1991) calls the "Grand Models of Consumer Behavior," were developed by Nicosia (1966), Engel, Kollat and Blackwell (1968) and Howard and Sheth (1969). Although the grand models of consumer behavior were very useful for understanding the decision-making process of consumers, they carried some shortcomings in terms of their applicability to service-dominated purchases such as purchase of hospitality products. Gilbert (1991) commented that their focus on the purchase of goods rather than on both that of goods and services and their sole consideration of individual purchase rather than both individual and group purchases are the two main shortcomings.

Differentiating futures of hospitality products

Most hospitality products and services are bought, used and evaluated in the form of experiences (Lu and Gursoy, 2015). Furthermore, customers of hospitality products and services desire a series of services that allow multiple options and experience opportunities. For hospitality customers, the product is the total experience, covering the entire amalgam of all aspects and components of the experience encounter, including attitudes and expectations. Hospitality customers generally perceive and evaluate their consumption as an experience, even though various services might be offered by different departments. In fact, their consumption experience consists of a structured series of services and providers/producers, which operate separately. From the supply side, the hospitality offering is definitely a series of experiences achieved through a combination of a diverse array of products and services (Middleton et al., 2009).

Since the production, delivery, consumption and evaluation of experiences differ from those of other products, marketing strategies utilized by hospitality businesses to communicate with hospitality consumers, and the decision-making strategies used by hospitality consumers, tend to be different from the strategies utilized to purchase other products. First, hospitality products and services are mostly intangible. That is, they are mainly composed of experiences and performances. Consumers cannot try them before purchasing. In addition, in most cases, there is no tangible product to take home except for memories, souvenirs, pictures and receipts. Second, they are heterogeneous. There can be substantial differences between producers in the production and delivery of a hospitality product, which can significantly increase the possibility of receiving an experience that does not meet expectations. Third, individuals consume most hospitality products at different locations to where they live. Fourth, most hospitality products tend to be expensive. Fifth, the decision-making process for hospitality products can take much longer than for many other tangible products because of the high perceived risk associated with hospitality purchases, mainly due to the amount of time, effort and money required to purchase those products (Lu, Gursoy, and Lu, 2016). Consequently, hospitality consumers go through a decision-making process that is very complex.

The Routledge Handbook of Hospitality Marketing

Our vision for this handbook is to create an international platform for balanced academic hospitality marketing research with practical applications for the hospitality industry, in order to foster synergetic interaction between academia and industry. More than 90 prominent scholars in the field of hospitality marketing contributed to this handbook. The collection of topics presented in this handbook represents an unprecedented scholarly attempt to cover a large number of both conceptual and practical topics not regularly found in standard hospitality marketing texts. Contributors to this handbook provide in–depth coverage of each conceptual and practical topic so that each chapter can serve as a trusted source of reference that can provide essential knowledge and references on the respective topic for hospitality academics and practitioners. It is our strong believe that the topics included in this handbook will appeal to both hospitality researchers and practitioners. It is our sincere hope that these chapters will contribute to knowledge and theory of hospitality marketing as distinct, multifaceted fields approached through the administrative disciplines, the liberal arts and the social sciences. Furthermore, this handbook provides an outlet for innovative studies that can make a significant contribution to the understanding, practice and education of hospitality marketing. We strongly believe that each chapter included in this handbook will make a significant contribution to the dissemination of knowledge while serving as a unique forum for both industry and academia.

The Routledge Handbook of Hospitality Marketing aims to consider and analyze the main issues and challenges in the field of hospitality marketing by focusing on the past, present and future issues, challenges and trends from a multidisciplinary global perspective. This handbook starts by defining and examining the main hospitality marketing concepts and methodologies, and then provides a comprehensive review of the development of hospitality marketing over the years. The handbook then focuses on key current issues and provides a platform for debate and critical evaluation that will enable the reader to learn from past mistakes as well as future opportunities. Because of the nature of hospitality, which often makes it inseparable from other industries such as tourism, events, sports and even retail, *The Routledge Handbook of Hospitality Marketing* is multidisciplinary in nature with aspects borrowed from other disciplines such as management, human resources, technology, consumer behavior and anthropology.

This handbook has the following specific objectives: (i) to identify, define and analyze the application of the main hospitality marketing concepts, methodologies, issues and challenges; (ii) to provide a comprehensive review of the development of hospitality marketing over the years; (iii) to explore the adoption and implementation of various hospitality marketing approaches in various hospitality contexts and sectors; (iv) to examine current key marketing trends, issues and challenges that affect numerous sectors in the industry; (v) to address cutting-edge marketing issues such as innovation in hospitality, sustainability, social media, peer-to-peer applications, etc.; and (vi) to identify future trends and issues within a multidisciplinary global perspective. The handbook concludes by providing marketing implications and recommendations for hospitality businesses to enable them to successfully create and manage marketing strategies and actions.

The handbook includes 49 chapters written by leading researchers in the field of hospitality marketing. The book is divided into nine themes, each theme exploring marketing issues that are of critical importance for hospitality organizations. Part I provides a historical overview of hospitality marketing and provides definitions of various marketing concepts. It also provides a critical review of consumer behavior in hospitality marketing. Part II focuses on research methodologies utilized in the field of hospitality marketing and their evolution over the years. Part III provides an overview of various hospitality marketing approaches, functions and strategies. Part IV examines issues related to consumer behavior in hospitality. It includes chapters on a critical review of hospitality consumer behavior; customer motivations, attitudes and beliefs; relationship marketing and loyalty; marketing hospitality products to customers from diverse generations; marketing strategies to build up customer trust; hospitality product distribution; and psychology of pricing. Part V examines the impact of culture on hospitality marketing. Part VI focuses on sustainability and environmental issues that may affect hospitality marketing. Part VII covers hospitality marketing issues related to innovation while Part VIII focuses on the impact of the internet and technology on hospitality marketing. Part IX explores issues to do with the key area of change and the future of hospitality marketing

As the editor of the handbook, I acknowledge the fact that we may have left out some critical topics and/or concepts. For the sake of simplicity and functionality, we have focused on the topics that are most critical for hospitality marketing researchers and practitioners. Thus, the list of topics included in this handbook is neither complete nor exhaustive in it its coverage of hospitality marketing topics. For this, I apologize. My goal is to simply provide a list of the most critical hospitality marketing topics in one place in order to create a credible source of information for the hospitality researchers of today and the future, which practitioners could use as a point of departure for their research initiatives and business endeavors.

Contributors to this handbook have spent countless hours working to provide in-depth coverage of each conceptual and practical topic so that each chapter can serve as a trusted source of reference that can provide essential knowledge and references on the respective topic to hospitality academics and practitioners. I would like to express my sincere gratitude and thanks to all the contributors who graciously volunteered their time and effort to put this amazing handbook together.

I also would like to thank our colleagues and the researchers in the field of hospitality marketing who have created both the theoretical and practical knowledge on the topics included in this handbook; you have given us reasons to initiate a project like this one. You are a true inspiration and source of this handbook's birth, and I hope that you will find this handbook useful. As the editor, I extend my sincere thanks to the publisher Routledge and their highly skilled staff members for making this project a reality.

References

Aday, J.B. and Phelan, K.V., 2015. Competitive advantage or market saturation: An in-depth comparison of flash-sale sites through content analysis. *Journal of Hospitality Marketing & Management*, 24(3), pp. 287–313.

Chen, H.S. and Yuan, J., 2016. A journey to save on travel expenses: The intentional buying process of consumers on opaque-selling websites. *Journal of Hospitality Marketing & Management*, 25(7), pp. 820–840.

Choi, E.K., Fowler, D., Goh, B. and Yuan, J.J., 2015. Social media marketing: Applying the uses and gratifications theory in the hotel industry. *Journal of Hospitality Marketing & Management*, 25(7), pp. 771–796.

Engel, J.F., Kollat, D.T. and Blackwell, R.D., 1968. A model of consumer motivation and behavior. *In* J.F. Kollat, R.D. Blackwell and J.F. Engel (Eds.), *Research in consumer behavior*, Holt, Rinehart and Winston, Inc., New York, NY, pp. 3–20.

García de Leaniz, P.M. and Rodríguez Del Bosque Rodríguez, I., 2015. Exploring the antecedents of hotel customer loyalty: A social identity perspective. *Journal of Hospitality Marketing & Management*, 24(1), pp. 1–23.

Gilbert, D.C., 1991. Consumer behavior in tourism. *In* C.P. Cooper (Ed.), *Progress in tourism, recreation and hospitality management*, Vol. 3, Belhaven Press, Lymington, Hants, UK, pp. 78–105.

Gursoy, D., Saayman, M. and Sotiriadis, M.D. (Eds.), 2015. *Collaboration in tourism businesses and destinations: A handbook*. Emerald Group Publishing, Bingley, UK.

Gursoy, D., Uysal, M., Sirakaya-Turk, E., Ekinci, Y. and Baloglu, S., 2014. *Handbook of scales in tourism and hospitality research*, CABi, Boston, MA.

Hanks, L., Line, N.D. and Mattila, A.S., 2016. The impact of self-service technology and the presence of others on cause-related marketing programs in restaurants. *Journal of Hospitality Marketing & Management*, 25(5), pp. 547–562.

Howard, J.A. and Sheth, J.N., 1969. The theory of buying behavior. *Journal of Marketing*, 40, pp. 67–76.

Jiang, Y., Ramkissoon, H. and Mavondo, F., 2016. Destination marketing and visitor experiences: The development of a conceptual framework. *Journal of Hospitality Marketing & Management*, 25(6), pp. 653–675.

Ladeira, W.J., Santini, F.D.O., Araujo, C.F. and Sampaio, C.H., 2016. A meta-analysis of the antecedents and consequences of satisfaction in tourism and hospitality. *Journal of Hospitality Marketing & Management*, 25(8), pp. 975–1009.

Lu, A.C.C. and Gursoy, D., 2015. A conceptual model of consumers' online tourism confusion. *International Journal of Contemporary Hospitality Management*, 27(6), pp. 1320–1342.

Lu, A.C.C., Gursoy, D. and Lu, C.Y.R., 2016. Antecedents and outcomes of consumers' confusion in the online tourism domain. *Annals of Tourism Research*, 57, pp. 76–93.

Nicosia, F.M., 1966. *Consumer decision process: Marketing and advertising implications*. Prentice Hall, Englewood Cliffs, NJ.

Nunkoo, R., Gursoy, D. and Ramkissoon, H., 2013. Developments in hospitality marketing and management: Social network analysis and research themes. *Journal of Hospitality Marketing & Management*, 22(3), pp. 269–288.

Ong, B.S., 2015. Attitudes, perceptions, and responses of purchasers versus subscribers-only for daily deals on hospitality products. *Journal of Hospitality Marketing & Management*, 24(2), pp. 180–201.

Sirakaya, E. and Woodside, A.G., 2005. Building and testing theories of decision making by travellers. *Tourism Management*, 26(6), pp. 815–832.

Tresidder, R., 2015. Experiences marketing: A cultural philosophy for contemporary hospitality marketing studies. *Journal of Hospitality Marketing & Management*, 24(7), pp. 708–726.

Xu, X. and Gursoy, D., 2015. A conceptual framework of sustainable hospitality supply chain management. *Journal of Hospitality Marketing & Management*, 24(3), pp. 229–259.

Part I
Hospitality marketing concepts

1
Hospitality marketing
A historical perspective

S. Emre Dilek and Serhat Harman

Introduction

The aim of marketing activities is to create customer value and unique customer experiences. This is also true of marketing activities in the hospitality industry (Maier and Prusty, 2016). Hospitality marketing should be undertaken professionally, depending on the different characteristics of the hospitality industry. Thus, marketing managers in the hospitality industry must understand the nature of hospitality marketing, including from a historical perspective.

Marketing is thought to have become an academic discipline in the first half of the twentieth century (Bartels, 1988). Marketing services had emerged as a sub-field of the marketing of physical goods by the 1980s (Kozak and Andreu, 2006). Academic interest in the marketing of hospitality and tourism services had developed by the end of the 1980s. Today, successful hospitality marketing is a vital force within the hospitality industry and also impacts on tourism destinations.

Following the second half of the twentieth century, studies focusing on hospitality marketing and hospitality marketing practices have begun to appear. The development of hospitality marketing should first be analyzed by situating the appearance and evolution of the discipline of marketing within its historical context (Enrique Bigné, 1996; Kozak and Andreu, 2006).

This chapter consists of two main parts. In the first part, the nature of hospitality, and the definitions and characteristics of hospitality marketing are presented. Hospitality marketing mix is then explained. In the second part of the chapter, a periodization is suggested and a discussion of the historical perspectives of hospitality marketing is presented based on the suggested periodization.

Hospitality marketing

Tourism is a complex phenomenon and consists of different sub-sectors. Tourism is the total system of all the people and organizations that collaborate in order to provide touristic experiences to travellers, who each travel for different purposes and stay overnight at destinations. Hospitality is one of the major components of the tourism system (Goeldner and Ritchie, 2009, p. 154). The hospitality industry covers both the food services sector and the accommodation/lodging sector. Satisfying the basic needs of travellers, such as providing meals and a safe bed/room, was initially the major aim of early hospitality providers. In contemporary society, however, hospitality is more than this; it also includes providing unique experiences to guests and creating value for customers. Thus, hospitality marketing covers all marketing efforts made in order to create unique value and experiences for guests. Before examining historical perspectives of hospitality marketing, we should define the nature of hospitality and the characteristics of hospitality marketing.

Nature of hospitality

The word 'hospitality' in English refers to accommodation and food services (Oh and Pizam 2008, p. 4). However, brief studies such as those by King (1995), Jones (1996), Lashley (2000) and Oh and Pizam (2008) indicate that the term hospitality has a deeper meaning and refers to more than just accommodation and food services. According to Lashley (2000), hospitality has three domains; these are social, private and commercial domains. The private domain refers to the learning of the behaviours of being a host and of being a guest, and the mutual understanding of the other party's needs and wants (Oh and Pizam, 2008). The social domain also refers to the mutual understanding of the social and cultural values of both sides (guest and host); in other words, converting strangers into friends (Selwyn, 2000; Oh and Pizam, 2008). The commercial domain covers all types of economic relationships between the host and the guest (Lashley, 2000).

King's (1995) seminal work entitled "What is hospitality?" provides a deep and clear understanding of the term. King (1995) points out that hospitality has four main characteristics. These are: it is conferred by a host on a guest who is on a trip away from home; the host and guest come together in an interactive manner; it includes both tangible and intangible factors; the host provides security, and psychological and physiological comfort.

The historical roots of hospitality date back to ancient times. For example, there are references in ancient Greek and Roman sources to the mobility of soldiers and traders, and their need for a safe place to sleep and eat. There are also Bible references to the old nature of hospitality, shaped by travellers staying overnight in inns (Weissinger, 2000). In the nineteenth century, the introduction of the railroads had a significant impact on commercial accommodation. By the twentieth century, various types of accommodation facilities were part of the hospitality industry, including motels and luxury hotels (Weissinger, 2000).

It is possible to say that today, the scope of the hospitality industry is limitless. For example, in 2016 Euromonitor International forecasted US$550 billion of revenue for the European hospitality industry (Statista, 2016). Another report by the American Hotel and Lodging Association indicated that in 2015, the US lodging sector created 1.9 million jobs, generated US$176 billion in 2015, and is comprised of nearly 5 million guestrooms (AHLA, 2016).

Definition of marketing

Marketing deals with customers more than any other business function. Customers' needs and wants are key to the philosophy of marketing. Different marketing associations and scholars use different definitions of marketing. For example, Kotler and Armstrong (2014, p. 27) define marketing as "the process by which companies create value for customers and build strong customer relationships in order to capture value from customers in return". According to Middleton et al. (2009, p. 24), on the other hand, marketing is the process of achieving voluntary exchanges between two parties (buyer and seller), while marketing management includes all the decisions for the facilitating of this exchange process. Furthermore, the American Marketing Association (AMA) defines marketing as "the activity, set of institutions, and processes for creating, communicating, delivering, and exchanging offerings that have value for customers, clients, partners, and society at large" (AMA, 2016); this definition was approved by AMA in 2013. Each of these marketing definitions have a point in common; the term 'customer value'.

Before a customer buys a product or service, there are some costs that the customer faces by choosing a specific product or service, as well as some benefits. Customer value is a concept that is strongly related to the perceived costs and benefits of a product or service. According to Kotler and Armstrong (2014, p. 35), customer value is the "customer's evaluation of the difference between all the benefits and the costs of a marketing offer relative to those competing". It is clear, therefore, that in order to create customer value, the company must first understand what customers really want and how they can satisfy these wants before their competitors do.

What is hospitality marketing?

The historical roots of modern marketing theory go back to the first half of the twentieth century (Middleton, 2000). In the early days of marketing theory, marketing scholars and their studies focused on the sales and distribution of consumer goods. With the development of the world economy, and the service industry in particular, however, marketing studies began to focus on how to facilitate the exchange of services. Lovelock and Wright (1999, p. 5) define a service as "an act or performance offered by one party to another". The service production process can occur alongside the provision of physical goods and the service performance can be intangible. Others define a service as an intangible product that is sold or purchased in the marketplace (Reid and Bojanic, 2006, p. 9). When talking about hospitality marketing, marketing efforts should be expanded to include the marketing of services, which in turn requires a number of different marketing implications and an extensive marketing mix. Kotler, Bowen and Makens (2014, p. 13) point out that hospitality marketing includes the marketing of tangible products, services and experiences. This means that, in the hospitality industry, understanding customer experiences and the social, physiological and personal domains underlying the formation of such experiences is very important (Tresidder, 2015). Thus, there is a need for the definition of hospitality marketing to include a customer experience domain. We can therefore define hospitality marketing as the process by which hospitality companies create value for customers and memorable customer experiences, and build strong customer relationships in order to capture value from customers in return. This means that hospitality marketing efforts must focus on very different aspects of marketing practices.

Hospitality marketing studies cover various topics adapted from marketing theory. Line and Runyan's (2012) work examined hospitality marketing articles published in scholarly journals. Their findings indicate that the main research topics found in hospitality marketing journals are the marketing environment, consumer perceptions and characteristics, marketing functions management, planning and strategies, electronic marketing, public relations, internal marketing, demand and pricing, and marketing research. Similarly, Oh, Kim and Shin's (2004) study indicates that the most widely researched topics are the marketing environment, consumer behaviour, marketing functions, and marketing research. Nunkoo, Gursoy and Ramkissoon (2013) analyzed recent developments in hospitality marketing journals. They found that the main topics or themes are consumer behaviour in restaurants, tourist behaviour, website management/social media/technology adoption, festivals, events, exhibitions, destination management and marketing, hospitality finance and revenue management, and human resources, among other topics.

Every year, millions of people travel for different purposes, including pleasure, business, visiting friends and relatives, and so on. When people are away from home and staying overnight in their target destinations, they have needs and wants that are more than simply their basic needs and wants, such as food and accommodation. A traveller or guest needs to be comfortable, as they would in their own home, and to have memorable experiences. Here, therefore, it can be said that hospitality marketing deals with the customer's needs and wants when they are away from home. Indeed, in this very dynamic and increasingly fragmented market, hospitality marketing efforts are particularly vital for hospitality business owners.

Characteristics of hospitality marketing

Dealing with a mixture of physical goods, services and experiences means that a number of characteristics are brought to hospitality marketing efforts. We must first examine the characteristics of hospitality marketing based on its service nature; this is a widely discussed topic in hospitality marketing studies.

Intangibility is one of the main characteristics of hospitality marketing. This refers to not being able to test, feel, hear or smell the products of hospitality companies before purchasing them (Morrison, 1989, p. 27; Kotler and Armstrong, 2014, p. 39). Inseparability means that both customers and employers are part of the service performance (Lovelock and Wright, 1999, pp. 10–11). For example, in hotels and restaurants, guests are highly involved in the service production process. Variability is another characteristic of hospitality marketing; this refers to the fact that the quality of service or service performance is highly variable due to the subjective nature of customers' evaluations (Kotler and Armstrong, 2014, p. 41). This also limits quality control in hospitality marketing. In addition, hospitality services cannot be stored for future sales; they are consumed as they are produced (Morrison, 1989, p. 30).

Hospitality services are interdependent with other services in the tourism industry; indeed, all service performance stages are interdependent (Middleton and Clarke, 2000, p. 47). A tourist evaluates all of the services received at the destination, or in a particular hotel or restaurant. Thus, a service culture must be developed by the firm. The distribution of services is different to the distribution of physical goods (Morrison, 1989, p. 31). In the distribution of physical goods, goods are transferred to the sale point or to customers, whereas in hospitality marketing, customers must reach the service points. The pricing of hospitality products is another important aspect of hospitality marketing. The pricing of services is more difficult than the pricing of goods because determining the fixed and variable costs can be difficult.

Hospitality experiences are multifaceted and include the consumption of various goods and services, such as food and beverages, accommodation, the aesthetic appeal of the service point or the entire tourist destination. Creating memorable touristic experiences therefore requires more detailed marketing efforts (Tresidder, 2015, p. 711). Customers should be treated like royalty during the consumption of services in order for memorable hospitality experiences to be created. In the communication of messages, meanwhile, the authenticity of the service should be stressed. Customer interpretation of perceived service performance should be thoroughly examined.

Marketing mix in hospitality

Service providers use a number of marketing tools to satisfy customers' needs and wants. The term 'marketing mix' refers to the combination of marketing tools employed to satisfy customers' needs, but is defined somewhat differently by different scholars. Morrison (1989, p. 17) defines marketing mix as "controllable factors (activities in an organization's direct control) that are used to satisfy the needs of specific customer groups". On the other hand, Kotler, Bowen and Makens (2014, p. 110) accept that the main component of marketing mix is the marketing strategy, and define marketing as a "set of controllable, tactical marketing tools that firms intend to produce the response it wants in the target market". Here we can understand that the term marketing covers all of the tools a firm employs to meet the needs of target markets. These tools can be grouped under four headings: Products, Price, Place, and Promotion (Kotler and Armstrong, 2014, p. 76).

In hospitality businesses, as explained above, it is mostly services that are produced; some critics therefore point out that the 4Ps of the marketing mix (Product, Price, Place, and Promotion) is only relevant for physical goods. In terms of hospitality services, they have pushed marketing scholars to search for new marketing elements in order to cover service marketing efforts. A new definition of marketing mix has been suggested, called the 4Cs of service marketing. This marketing mix includes Customer Value, Customer Cost, Communication, and Convenience. Customer Value corresponds to Product, Customer Cost to Price, Communication to Promotion, and lastly, Convenience corresponds to Place (Middleton and Clarke, 2000, p. 89).

Based on the characteristics of hospitality marketing, marketing mix in the context of hospitality has been expanded to 7Ps by some (Middleton and Clarke, 2004, p. 94) and even to 8Ps by others (Morrison, 1989, p. 18). According to Morrison (1989), marketing mix in the context of hospitality should include: Product, Price, Place, Promotion, Packaging, People, Programming, and Partnerships. Middleton and Clarke (2004), on the other hand, suggest that hospitality marketing mix should include: Product, Price, Place, Promotion, People, Process, and Physical Evidence. These elements are briefly explained below:

Product refers to all of the elements on offer to customers, including physical goods and intangible services. Product also includes some visual elements, such as staff behaviour, uniforms, equipment, furniture, buildings and so on (Morrison, 1989, p. 235).

Price is a tool that fixes the terms of voluntary exchange between customers that are willing to buy and service producers that want to sell (Middleton and Clarke, 2004, p. 138).

Place refers to all of the efforts made to make products available to customers. In hospitality marketing, however, Place can include all of the efforts made to facilitate travellers reaching the service point.

Promotion is the mixture of tools used to communicate with target markets (Morrison, 1989, p. 295). It includes advertising, personal selling, sales promotions, merchandising, and public relations.

People includes all of the human interactions that take place during the service performance. This includes visitors, employees, and the host community (Middleton and Clarke, 2004, p. 95).

Process refers to the service delivery process. This includes all of the activities and procedures started by designing the service offer and finished by the performance of the service (Middleton and Clarke, 2004, pp. 98–99).

Physical Evidence refers to all of the efforts made to affect the sensory impressions of customers. This includes environmental factors such as atmosphere as well as the signage for the service point (Booms and Bitner, 1981).

Historical development of hospitality marketing

As with production itself, people have been engaged in marketing throughout history, whether they are aware of it or not. Marketing is nearly as old as civilization and business (Wearne and Morrison, 2011, p. 2). Bartering was used in trade before the invention of money. And the invention of money changed the way of trade and business as well as the social and cultural structure. Trade and business could then expand to ever-wider geographical areas, from within local towns to other cities and even further afield to other countries. With the system of money, merchants could attempt to expand their markets to overseas territories. In other words, after money supplanted simple bartering, markets could grow, which resulted in the expansion of the movements of goods to market. In this way, the development of marketing began in the early twentieth century (Bartels, 1976).

Indeed, Bartels (1962) claims that the term 'marketing' was first used between 1906 and 1911, while Bussiere (2000) states that the term was first used in the *American Economic Review* in 1897, and Shaw (1995) states it was used in the *American Encyclopedic Dictionary* in 1896 (Tadajewski and Jones, 2008). It can therefore be said that the term marketing was used in the early 1900s. Bartels also points out that universities played a significant role in the development of marketing (Bartels, 1988), and that the first course on the subject – albeit under a different term and discussed in terms of distributive industries, trade, commerce or mercantile institutions – was offered by E.D. Jones in 1902 at the University of Michigan (Tadajewski and Jones, 2008).

These developments demonstrate that the term marketing was not used by institutions before the 1900s. As with the development of marketing and the evolution of hospitality, we cannot declare exactly when professional hospitality marketing efforts started. So we may term this period the 'nihilistic stage'. This stage begins with the leisured elites of ancient Greece and Rome, the re-emergence of tourism during the Renaissance, and the development of spas and Grand Tours in the seventeenth and eighteenth centuries (Arva and Kuruvilla, 2012), and ends with the first organized tour or first modern mass tourism activity arranged by Thomas Cook in 1841 (Towner, 1995; Walton, 2010). Therefore, from its beginnings to the emergence of Thomas Cook, tourism activities and hospitality marketing has almost never been institutionalized; this period is referred to as the pre-modern era.

The development of the concept of marketing corresponds with the 'institutionalization stage' of hospitality marketing (from 1841 to 1950). This term refers to the modern era of McDonaldization, when society changed due to increasing industrialization (Ritzer, 1983). Following the Industrial Revolution, the hospitality industry and hospitality marketing began to develop based upon the following social and economic changes: increasing leisure time, the right to paid holidays, technological developments, increasing levels of income and education, urbanization, population increases, social insurance, tourism consciousness, freedom of travel, trade-unions, etc.

The post-modern or Disneyization era followed after the 1950s, when dramatic social, economic, environmental, and cultural changes continued quarter on quarter (Urry, 1995). During this time, post-modern approaches to marketing began to develop, which also affected hospitality marketing. Alternative types of tourism were presented to tourists alongside customized tourism; this stage is therefore known as the 'customizing stage'.

The 'coexistence stage' refers to the current era, in which modern and post-modern values coexist. Ritzer and Liska (1997) have called this stage McDisneyization, as the post-modern fantasy (Disneyization) and the rules of efficiency (McDonaldization) coexist within the same products and services. Hospitality marketing now depends upon customer experiences.

Nihilistic stage (pre-modern)

The nihilistic stage refers to the pre-modern era of hospitality marketing that developed in parallel with the development of the hospitality industry. While hospitality is not a new phenomenon, hospitality marketing is more recent. Hospitality has existed in various forms for as long as *homo sapiens* have lived in settlements (Baum, 2011, p. 23), whereas hospitality marketing began with

Thomas Cook's first organized tour in 1841. Hospitality confers the idea of providing safety for travellers and merchants, and dates back to ancient times (Durant, 1935, 1939; White, 1970; Gray and Liguori, 1980; Heal, 1990), whereas hospitality marketing is commercial and dates from the *hotel garni*, elegant rented apartments, at the beginning of the twentieth century (Medlik, 1972). During the nihilistic stage, therefore, when someone wanted to visit a foreign town, they could expect accommodation and guides free of charge from local residents (Urry, 1995). Therefore, we cannot discuss commercial hospitality marketing during the nihilistic stage as it simply did not exist.

Institutionalization stage (modern/McDonaldization)

From 1841 to 1950, following the process of industrialization, hospitality marketing emerged as the global tourism industry began to develop. During this time, the concept of marketing was constantly changing due to changes in the products and services offered to tourists, which in turn was because of changes in their needs and wants. Social, cultural, and economic conditions developed and changed year-by-year during this time.

By the 1950s, the discipline of marketing had changed. The first decade of the twentieth century is known as the 'period of discovery' in the discipline of marketing, whereas 1910–1920 is known as the 'conceptualization period', 1920–1930 as the 'period of integration', 1930–1940 as the 'development period', and 1940–1950 as the 'reappraisal period' (Bartels, 1976).

By 1950, this development had influenced the discipline of hospitality marketing. The revolution in manufacturing that saw the rise of the Fordist organization of production, mass production, and mass consumption also affected the service industries and tourism. This led to mass consumption by tourists, the collective gaze of tourists, increasing demand for undiscerned, standardized products and services that offer familiarity to tourists, dependence on economies of scale and low prices, which in turn led to increasing numbers of tourists (Shaw and Williams, 2004). This understanding of hospitality has led to the commercialization of hospitality, causing hospitality marketing to be discussed in commercial terms. This modern era of hospitality marketing, known as McDonaldization, refers to the institutionalization of hospitality marketing.

Customizing stage (post-modern/Disneyization)

By the 2000s, hospitality marketing had become an important field in tourism studies (Li and Petrick, 2008). In fact, O'Leary et al. (2004) state that hospitality marketing is the most popular topic in this academic field, and accounted for more than one-fifth (over 145 papers) of the 723 papers reviewed. Dev, Buschman and Bowen et al. (2010) report that hospitality marketing-related articles published by *Cornell Hospitality Quarterly* accounted for eight of the total number of 119 articles (6.7%) in the 1960s, 14 of 141 articles (10%) in the 1970s, 41 of 398 articles (10.3%) in the 1980s, 91 of 778 articles (11.7%) in the 1990s, and 95 of 524 articles (18.1%) in the 2000s. This suggests that the place of hospitality marketing within tourism studies has progressed since the 1950s. This progress has led to deep discussions within hospitality marketing, and the hospitality marketing field completed its institutionalization. In later years, during the post-modern era of the emotionalization/Disneyization of tourism (Bryman, 1999) or the post-Fordist organization of production, the hospitality marketing paradigm has developed into various niche fields depending on social, environmental, cultural, economic, and technological transformations. Consequently, the focus shifted to psychographic factors rather than sociological factors to explain the different purchasing habits and decisions of people in post-modern societies (Baker,

2000; Arva and Kuruvilla, 2012). Thus, the development of hospitality marketing turned towards the organization of personally identifiable production in what is known as the 'customizing stage', from 1950 to today.

This stage has been evaluated by Dev, Buschman and Bowen (2010) under the following six categories relating to different decades: promotion (1960s), product development and market research (1970s), revenue management and brand development (1980s), customer satisfaction and loyalty (1990s), internet marketing comes-of-age (2000s), and data-driven marketing (2010s). On the other hand, Li and Petrick (2008) distinguish between three categories: relationship orientation, network approach, and service-dominant logic. In addition, the stages of hospitality marketing development may be categorized depending on the occurrence of hotel brands by decades (see Table 1.1).

As can be seen in Table 1.1, from the 1800s to 2000s, the number of hotel brands has rapidly increased all over the world, particularly after the 1960s. This is why the period after the 1960s is known as the post-modern or Disneyization era; the customizing stage. In other words, the idea of hospitality was commercialized, which led to the rise of hospitality marketing. As the internet has become more widespread, internet-driven hospitality marketing types have emerged in the hospitality industry. E-marketing (1974), database marketing (1981), mobile marketing (1985), relationship marketing (1986), niche marketing (1989), and social media marketing (2005) are some of the dramatic transformations that have happened year-by-year (Scopus, 2016). As a result of these changes and transformations, the most important element of hospitality marketing has become the experience-driven approach.

Coexistence stage (modern + post-modern/McDisneyization)

The coexistence stage can be defined as the combination of the modern and post-modern approaches to hospitality marketing. As consumption habits continue to change, the approach taken to hospitality marketing must also change. Marketing experts have pointed out these changes and argue that they bring to light concepts such as fantasy, virtual reality, aesthetic value, and authenticity, which affect individual purchasing behaviours (Arva and Kuruvilla, 2012). This is more than simply noticing either modern or post-modern hospitality marketing mixes; rather, the two approaches – and their respective rules of efficiency and aesthetic value or fantasy – can coexist within the same products and services.

This situation has triangulated in the 2010s with the increasing use of the internet and social media, and the corresponding changes in marketing communications (Dev, Buschman and Bowen, 2010). This means that the coexistence stage has generally been dominated by the data-driven approach to hospitality marketing. The increasing number of social media channels and the effectiveness of these channels means that tourism businesses can, and must, better understand their customers' needs and demands. If a customer is concerned about the environment, the hotel that will appeal to that customer is one that has given information about its environmentally friendly practices via social media. Besides this, hotels must combine marketing, architecture, and engineering to develop new products that meet customers' concerns about sustainability, authenticity, and the aesthetic.

The example above refers to two issues that have arisen during the coexistence stage of hospitality marketing: (1) tourism businesses should pay attention to the specialized needs of customers when developing new products or services; (2) they should provide information to customers via the internet and social media. If they fail to do this, they will fail to catch the spirit of the age, which may damage their hospitality marketing mix and their data-driven marketing communication.

Table 1.1 Hotel brand introductions by decade

1960s	1970s	1980s	1990s	2000s
Affinia	Adam's Mark	Amanresort	AC	Aloft
Arabella	Brittania	AmericInn	Americas Best Value	Anantara
Barcelo	Budgetel	AmeriHost	Baymont	Andaz
Camino Real	Caesar Park	Ayres	Beaches	Azimut
Dedeman	Concorde	City Lodge	Candlewood Suites	Bulgari
Delta	CrestDays Inn	Clarion	FiestaAmericana Grand	Domina
Doubletree	Dunfey	Comfort	Four Points	Element
Econolodge	Dusit	Conrad	Gloria	Hard Rock
Four Seasons	FiestaAmericana	Copthorne	Great Wolf	Heliopark
Golden Tulip	Gaylord	Country Inn	Holiday Inn Express	HNA
Harrah's	Hyatt House	Courtyard	Trump	Home Inns
Hyatt Regency	Ibis	Crowne Plaza	Jumeriah	Home2Suites
La Quinta	ITC	Embassy Suites	Katerina	Hyatt Place
Mandarin Oriental	JAL	Fairfield Inn	Mainstay Suites	Indigo
Maritim	Knights Inn	Formule 1	Malmaison	Maxima
Mercure	Le Meridien	Grand Hyatt	Millennium	Mgallery
Motel 6	Lotte	Hampton Inn	Radisson SAS	Missoni
New Otani	Mövenpick	Hawthorne Suites	Sarovar	One
Novotel	Orient Express (1883)	Homewood Suites	Springhill Suites	Pullman
Okura	Red Lion	InnSuites Boutique	Staybridge Suites	Radisson Blu
Outrigger	Red Roof Inn	Jinjiang	Studio 6	Rezidor
Park Royal	Residence Inn	Jinling	The Luxury Collection	Rocco Forte
Rodeway Inn	Rosewood	Joie de Vivre	TownePlace	Wynn
SAS	Shangri La	Kimpton	W	
Sofitel	Sonesta	Marco Polo	Wingate	
Southern Sun	Super 8	Microtel		
Stouffer	Trust House Forte	Morgans		
Thistle		New Century		
Woodfin		Omni		
		Pan Pacific		
		Park Hyatt		
		Park Inn		
		Pestana		
		Protea		
		Regent		
		Renaissance		
		Sandals		
		Scandic		
		Sleep Inn		
		Sun International		
		Swissotel		
		Toyoko Inn		
		Trident		
		Warwick		
		Waterford		
		Wyndham		

1900–1959				
Americana	Hilton	Marriott	Quality Courts	Sands
Ashok	Hiway House	Oberoi	Ramada	Sheraton
Best Western	Holiday Inn	Othon	Radisson	Statler
Ciga	HowardJohnson	Peninsula	Ritz-Carlton	Steigenberg
Club Med	Hyatt		Riu	Taj
Dan	Inter Continental		RockResorts	Travelodge
Fairmont	Loews		St. Regis	WesternInternational

1800s				
Carlton	Harvey House	Langham	Ritz	Vier Jahreszeiten
Claridge's	Kempinski	NH	Savoy	Waldorf=Astoria

Source: Dev, Buschman and Bowen (2010) "Hospitality Marketing: A Retrospective Analysis (1960–2010) and Predictions (2010–2020)," *Cornell Hospitality Quarterly* 51(4), 465. Reproduced with permission.

Conclusion

Hospitality marketing is the process by which hospitality businesses create value for customers and memorable customer experiences, and build strong customer relationships in order to capture value from customers in return. This definition highlights how satisfying customers' needs and wants is the starting point of hospitality marketing, which is followed by efforts to create customer value and unique experiences. Services provided by hospitality businesses have historical roots going back to ancient times. In ancient times, food and safe accommodation would be the main needs of travellers. Today, however, the needs and wants of travellers are more complicated and various. The philosophy of hospitality marketing has therefore been transformed into a mixture of experiential and relational forms.

Hospitality marketing has had to adapt to new consumer behaviours that have emerged due to social changes and transformations. As consumption habits and modes of production in all sectors, including in hospitality, have changed, products and services have correspondingly changed, reflecting the shift from the nihilistic stage to the coexistence stage. Approaches to hospitality marketing have also gone from the general to the specific. The slogans used in new hospitality marketing in this coexistence stage include participation, edutainment, fantasy, personalization, and fun (Arva and Deli-Gray, 2011). According to Dev, Buschman and Bowen (2010), a rise in promotion could be seen during the 1960s, whereas the 1970s were a decade in which product development and market research were prevalent. Brand management was the focus of the 1980s, whereas customer satisfaction and loyalty dominated the 1990s, internet marketing was the theme of the early 2000s, and data-driven marketing rose to prominence in the 2010s.

The literature review in this chapter gave a brief overview of the historical development of hospitality marketing using the process of periodization. Our proposition for the periodization of hospitality marketing is based on the commercialization of the industry. This commercialization has changed consumption habits and forms of production. Certainly, other periodization propositions are possible based on different criteria. The business environment continues to dynamically change, and in the decades to come there may be further changes in consumption habits and production forms; this will necessitate a new proposition for the periodization of hospitality marketing.

References

AHLA (American Hotel & Lodging Association) (2016) *Lodging Industry Trends 2015.* www.ahla.com/uploadedFiles/_Common/pdf/Lodging_Industry_Trends_2015.pdf (Accessed 6 October 2016).
AMA (American Marketing Association) (2016) *Definition of Marketing.* www.ama.org/AboutAMA/Pages/Definition-of-Marketing.aspx (Accessed 19 September 2016).
Arva, H.L. and Kuruvilla, S.J. (2012) "A Global Perspective on the Development of Tourism Marketing," *The Indore Management Journal* 3(4), 31–41.
Arva, L. and Deli-Gray, Z. (2011) "New Types of Tourism and Tourism Marketing in The Post-Industrial World," *Applied Studies in Agribusiness and Commerce* 5, 33–37.
Baker, A. (ed.) (2000) *Serious Shopping: Essays in Psychotherapy and Consumerism,* London: Free Association Books.
Bartels, R. (1962) *The Development of Marketing Thought,* Homewood, IL: Irwin.
Bartels, R. (1976) *The History of Marketing Thought* (2nd edition), Columbus, OH: GRID Inc.
Bartels, R. (1988) *The History of Marketing Thought* (3rd edition), Columbus, OH: Publishing Horizons.
Baum, T. (2011) *Hospitality Management* (Vol. 1), London: Sage Publications.
Booms, B.H. and Bitner, M.J. (1981) "Marketing Strategies and Organization Structures for Service Firms," in J.H. Donnelly and W.R. George (eds.) *Marketing of Services,* Chicago: American Marketing Association, 47–51.

Bryman, A. (1999) "The Disneyization of Society," *The Sociological Review* 47(1), 25–47.

Bussière, D. (2000) "Evidence of a marketing periodic literature within the American Economics Association: 1895-1936," *Journal of Macromarketing* 20(2), 137–143.

Dev, C.S., Buschman, J.D. and Bowen, J.T. (2010) "Hospitality Marketing: A Retrospective Analysis (1960–2010) and Predictions (2010–2020)," *Cornell Hospitality Quarterly* 51(4), 459–469.

Durant, W. (1935) *The Story of Civilization: Part I Our Oriental Heritage*, New York: Simon and Schuster.

Durant, W. (1939) *The Story of Civilization: Part II The Life of Greece*, New York: Simon and Schuster.

Enrique Bigné Alacañiz, J. (1996) "Tourism and Marketing in Spain: Analysis of The Situation and Future Perspectives," *The Tourist Review* 51(1), 34–40.

Goeldner, C.R. and Ritchie, J.R.B. (2009) *Tourism: Principles, Practices, Philosophies*, Hoboken, NJ: John Wiley & Sons. Inc.

Gray, W.S. and Liguori, S.C. (1980) *Hotel and Motel Management and Operations*, Englewood Cliffs, NJ: Prentice Hall.

Heal, F. (1990) *Hospitality in Early Modern England*, Oxford: Clarendon Press.

Jones, P. (1996) "Hospitality Research – Where Have We Got To?" *International Journal of Hospitality Management* 15(1), 5–10.

King, C.A. (1995) "What is Hospitality?" *International Journal of Hospitality Management* 14(3), 219–234.

Kotler, P.T. and Armstrong, G. (2014) *Principles of Marketing* (15th edition), Harlow, UK: Pearson.

Kotler, P.T., Bowen, J.T. and Makens, J. (2014) *Marketing for Hospitality and Tourism* (6th edition), Pearson New International Edition, Harlow, UK: Pearson.

Kozak, M. and Andreu, L. (eds.) (2006) *Progress in Tourism Marketing*, Oxford: Elsevier.

Lashley, C. (2000) "Towards a Theoretical Understanding," in C. Lashley and A. Morrison (eds.) *In Search of Hospitality: Theoretical Perspectives and Debates*, Oxford: Butterworth-Heinemann, 1–17.

Li, X.R. and Petrick, J.F. (2008) "Tourism Marketing in an Era of Paradigm Shift," *Journal of Travel Research* 46(3), 235–244.

Line, N.D. and Runyan, R.C. (2012) "Hospitality Marketing Research: Recent Trends and Future Directions," *International Journal of Hospitality Management* 31(2), 477–488.

Lovelock, C. and Wright, L. (1999) *Principles of Marketing and Management*, New York: Prentice-Hall.

Maier, T.A. and Prusty, S. (2016). "Managing Customer Retention in Private Clubs Using Churn Analysis: Some Empirical Findings," *Journal of Hospitality Marketing & Management* 25(7), 797–819.

Medlik, S. (1972) *Profile of the Hotel and Catering Industry*, London: Heinemann.

Middleton, G. (2000) "A Preliminary Study of Chefs' Attitudes and Knowledge of Healthy Eating in Edinburgh's Restaurants," *International Journal of Hospitality Management* 19(4), 399–412.

Middleton, V.T. and Clarke, J.R. (2000) *Marketing in Travel and Tourism* (2nd edition), London: Butterworth-Heinemann.

Middleton, V.T. and Clarke, J.R. (2004) *Marketing in Travel and Tourism* (3rd edition), London: Elsevier Butterworth-Heinemann.

Middleton, V.T., Fyall, A., Morgan, M. and Ranchhod, A. (2009) *Marketing in Travel and Tourism* (4th edition), Oxford: Routledge.

Morrison, A. M. (1989) *Hospitality and Travel Marketing*, New York: Delmar Publishers.

Nunkoo, R., Gursoy, D. and Ramkissoon, H. (2013) "Developments in Hospitality Marketing and Management: Social Network Analysis and Research Themes," *Journal of Hospitality Marketing & Management* 22(3), 269–288.

O'Leary, J.T., Lehto, X.Y., Cheng, C. K. and Oh, Y.–J. (2004) "A Synthesis of Tourism Research Topics," *10th Anniversary Meeting of International Symposia on Society and Resource Management*, Keystone Resort, CO.

Oh, H. and Pizam, A. (eds.) (2008) *Handbook of Hospitality Marketing Management*, Oxford, UK: Elsevier.

Oh, H., Kim, B.Y. and Shin, J.H. (2004) "Hospitality and Tourism Marketing: Recent Developments in Research and Future Directions," *International Journal of Hospitality Management* 23(5), 425–447.

Reid, R.D. and Bojanic, D.C. (2006) *Hospitality Marketing Management* (4th edition), Hoboken, NJ: John Wiley & Sons Inc.

Ritzer, G. (1983) "The McDonaldization of Society," *Journal of American Culture* 6(1), 100–107.

Ritzer, G. and Liska, A. (1997) "McDisneyization and Post-Tourism: Complementary Perspectives on Contemporary Tourism," in C. Rojek and J. Urry (eds.) *Touring Cultures: Transformations of Travel and Theory*, New York: Routledge, 96–109.

Scopus (2016) Searches of Scopus Database according to Article Title, Abstract, Keywords. www.scopus.com/ [Accessed 19 Sep 2016].

Selwyn, T. (2000) "An Anthropology of Hospitality," in C. Lashley and A. Morrison (eds.) *In Search of Hospitality: Theoretical Perspectives and Debates*, Oxford, UK: Butterworth-Heinemann, 18–37.

Shaw, E.H. (1995) "The first dialogue on macromarketing," *Journal of Macromarketing* 15(1), 7–20.

Shaw, G. and Williams, A. (2004) "From Lifestyle Consumption to Lifestyle Production: Changing Patterns of Tourism Entrepreneurship," in R. Thomas (ed.) *Small Firms in Tourism: International Perspective*, Oxford: Elsevier, 99–114.

Statista (2016) *Hospitality Industry in Europe*. www.statista.com/markets/420/travel-tourism-hospitality/ (Accessed 4 October 2016).

Tadajewski, M. and Jones, D.G.B. (eds.) (2008) *History of Marketing Thought* (Vol. 1), London: Sage Publications.

Towner, J. (1995) "What is Tourism's History?" *Tourism Management* 16(5), 339–343.

Tresidder, R. (2015) "Experiences Marketing: A Cultural Philosophy for Contemporary Hospitality Marketing Studies," *Journal of Hospitality Marketing & Management* 24(7), 708–726.

Urry, J. (1995) *Consuming Places*, London: Psychology Press.

Walton, J.K. (2010) "Thomas Cook," in R. Butler and R. Russell (eds.) *Giants of Tourism*, Wallingford: CABI, 81–92.

Wearne, N. and Morrison, A. (2011) *Hospitality Marketing* (3rd edition), New York: Routledge.

Weissinger, S. S. (2000) *Hotel/Motel Operations: An Overview* (2nd edition), New York: Delmar Thomson Learning.

White, A. (1970) *Palaces of the People: A Social History of Commercial Hospitality*, New York: Taplinger.

2

A critical review of hospitality marketing concepts

Gaunette Sinclair-Maragh

Introduction

Marketing is described as an exchange process where two or more parties give something of value to satisfy their needs (Boone & Kurtz, 1992). This exchange process is paramount as it involves the transfer of volume, which should leave both parties satisfied (Kotler, 2000). The practice of marketing emerged and evolved through five significant eras (Tosun, Okumus & Fyall, 2008). The period between 1880 and 1930 is described as the production/manufacturing era (Tosun, et al., 2008), where it was believed that as long as the product is good it will sell itself. Emphasis was placed on the production of good quality products, which assumedly will be purchased by consumers.

Subsequent to 1930, there have been several changes which allow consumers to have more buying choices. These changes include global competition, product availability and accessibility, vast information and more spending power/disposable income. With an increase in the production of the same and similar products by several manufacturers and the changing needs of consumers, the focus consequently changed to influencing consumers to buy the product. This resulted in the product concept, where the emphasis was on distributing the products to the consumer. Companies became very aggressive in their selling techniques through personal selling and the use of advertisements to influence consumer buying behavior, with the aim of convincing them to purchase the product.

There was a subsequent change to the marketing orientation of these companies as it became more obvious that marketing is a different concept and practice from selling. This led to the marketing era in the 1940s (Tosun et al., 2008). Being influenced by issues such as decline in personal incomes and reduction in consumer demand for products, there was a shift from the seller's market to the buyer's market due to the plethora of available products. This was driven by the principle of supply and demand, and the overabundance of products created the need for consumer orientation. With this concept, the needs of consumers were determined and then products were designed to satisfy their needs. Marketing then took on new dimensions, including philosophies that relate to the wellbeing of the general society, making responsible marketing decisions and being socially responsible. This led to the advent of the societal marketing concept by the late 1970s (Gronroos, 1978).

The marketing concepts described as marketing management philosophies emerged within the manufacturing industry and have been adopted by the service industry. Although extensive studies have been conducted to advance knowledge on these concepts and to guide the marketing functions of organizations, the literature remains sparse regarding their application to the hospitality industry, which is an important service economy in many countries.

The purpose of this review is to critically analyze the five hospitality marketing concepts, namely, production, product, selling, marketing and societal marketing, by examining their application to tourism destinations and hospitality businesses. This has become necessary since the use of these philosophies is fairly new to the hospitality industry when compared to the manufacturing industry (Morrison, 2010).

The following section will explore the five marketing concepts and examine their applicability to tourism destinations and hospitality businesses. For the purpose of this analysis, the term 'visitors' is operationalized as consumers of a destination's tourism products and the term 'guests' as consumers of hospitality products.

Marketing concepts in hospitality

Marketing concepts are philosophies that hospitality businesses use to assess their customers before making decisions to satisfy their needs better than their competitors. These concepts emerged first as the production philosophy within the manufacturing industry during the 1920s. Since then, the production philosophy has evolved into other marketing philosophies which have been respectively applied as the product, selling, marketing and societal marketing orientations.

Current hospitality organizations can employ these concepts at any given stage of the business operation. Tosun et al. (2008) find that the hospitality industry in Turkey has the tendency to employ the marketing philosophies in the order of product concept followed by the market/customer concept, manufacturing concept, selling concept and then societal marketing concept. The following will review the five marketing concepts as applied to hospitality businesses.

Production concept

This philosophy, also known as the manufacturing concept, is the oldest of the five concepts. It suggests that visitors or guests prefer goods and services that are widely available, making them easily accessible and inexpensive. Customers' needs and wants are not the primary focus of this market orientation (Morrison, 2010). It is generally used by companies who want to achieve high production efficiency and low costs as well as mass distribution (Kotler, 2000). It is also based on another premise that businesses should focus on increasing their production capacity as consumers will always purchase the product (Tosun et al., 2008).

Prior to the 1950s, an era of the beginning of capitalism, businesses focused on efficiency issues relating to production and manufacturing. Say's Law was used to guide production. This law proposes that "supply will create its own demand." This means that once a product is made, people will purchase it, especially if it is at a low cost. This principle was also applicable to the hospitality industry as during the 1920s, which was an era of economic prosperity, many hotels were constructed and renovated due to readily available financing and capital. At that time, travel was encouraged as there was an increase in spending power. Hotels were able to provide accommodation to the increased number of persons traveling. In 1927, the world's largest hotel at that time, Chicago's Hotel Steven (now Chicago Hotel), opened with 3000 rooms (Rushmore &

Baum, 2002). Having an abundance of hotel rooms creates demand for the service, and costs remain affordable for travelers.

The hotels operated based on volume and applied economies of scale practices to attain low operating costs, which resulted in low selling price. These hotels aimed at efficient operations through compact facilities and fewer guest services. Many of them were located in areas where there were several restaurant chains; hence, they did not have to provide a lot of food and beverage services. Low operating costs allow hotels to pass on savings to guests by selling rooms at a low price.

The application of the production concept continues in current hospitality operations. Several hotels and motels offer the European plan, where only the room is charged for, or the bed and breakfast plan; other meals and amenities have to be paid for by the guests. This is suitable for guests who are traveling for business purposes and short stays.

The focus of the production concept is on production and profitability and not on the needs of customers. Additionally, it is most effective when hospitality businesses operate in a very high growth market (Bhasin, 2016). It is the preferred concept by hospitality organizations that operate in the overseas market. Their intention is to widen the market base and ultimately increase market share. Quer, Claver and Andreu (2007) explain that Spanish hotel companies engage in international expansion because they face difficulty growing in their own country. They therefore expand into new emerging tourist destinations in other countries to increase their overall market share. In this case, the production concept is being applied as a corporate growth strategy. Not only does it increases market share but also profitability.

The production concept also enables the efficient use of resources when operating in the overseas market. McDonald's Corporation benefits from the standardized theme, menu, signage and logo, service standard, and production and delivery processes used among its restaurants in the overseas market. Despite their location around the world, each McDonald's fast food restaurant uses the same resources. Through operation efficiency they are able to derive economies of scale (Bowie & Buttle, 2013). Standardization, especially as it relates to fast food restaurants, allows for volume purchasing, reduction in stock levels and easier training procedures (Bowie & Buttle, 2004). Service procedures are on a flow chart, which allows for greater efficiency in achieving the tasks. All of these allow the restaurant chain to benefit from low operation cost. Similarly, budget hotels tend to use consistent structures and standardized products, which give them brand consistency. Their blueprint would already have been tried and proven and is easy to duplicate in other locations.

Another feature of the production concept is that it is used especially in developing countries where visitors want to obtain the product and not necessarily the features (Kotler, 2000). This is evident in the mass tourism product offered by many tropical destinations. This tourism product, labeled as leisure, pleasure or holiday tourism, is characterized by the sun, sand and sea offerings. It is the main motivation for travel by the majority of visitors who want to enjoy the beach and corresponding water activities. Destination features such as culture and heritage, flora and fauna, and other special interests, attractions and events are not their primary reason for travel. For instance, the majority of visitors to Jamaica, an island destination in the Caribbean region (Sinclair-Maragh & Gursoy, 2015), travel for the leisure/pleasure/holiday tourism (Jamaica Tourist Board, 2015).

Due to the demand for this type of product in Jamaica, there is a strong focus on this form of mass tourism by consecutive governments and tourism planners. The emphasis is on developing and expanding the tourism industry by facilitating the construction of more hotels. This will provide additional room capacity to meet market demand and growth. In addition, these properties are constructed on the beachfront or in very close proximity to the sea/beach in an all-inclusive setting where the guests have access to all services and amenities (Sinclair-Maragh, 2014). The concept of beachfront hotels or resorts is not unique to Jamaica but is characteristic of the Caribbean region as well as countries in other tropical destinations such as the Pacific region. Mass tourism contributes to the economic development of these destinations as it is a revenue generator through large sales volume. Tosun et al. (2008) point out that variables such as overall sales volume as well as revenue and occupancy ratio are predictors of the production concept. These are also associated with mass tourism, justifying this form of tourism as an example of the production concept.

Some destinations, particularly in their initial stage of development, employ the production concept to increase the number of visitors. For instance, Turkey applied this philosophy to its marketing activities to increase its market share (Tosun et al., 2008). Cuba, another country in the Caribbean region, is aiming at improving its economy through tourism. Although American tourism is banned under the US trade embargo (Hamre, 2016), the restored diplomatic relations between the United States of America (USA) and Cuba in 2015 has relaxed the travel restrictions (Gross, 2016). In order to accommodate more visitors from the USA, Cuba is increasing its accommodation sector with the building of large hotels and resorts (Cuba Business Report, 2016). Although Cuba is not a new destination, as prior to the 1959 Revolution it was renowned for its white sandy beaches, it now has to prepare for the expected increase in American visitors (Cuba Journal, 2016). The destination planners may have to apply the production concept in this initial stage of redevelopment to motivate American travelers who desire low cost but good quality hospitality/tourism products.

Tosun et al. (2008) indicate that the profile of customers and their location are strongly related to the production concept. This explains the use of this concept in Caribbean tourism, which is described as a mono-product concentrated on sun, sand and sea (Vincenzo, 2005). The majority of visitors have a preference for this tourism product and travel to the region for this experience. They are usually accommodated in a hotel located on the beachfront. In sync with the production concept, the assumption is that visitors always want this form of tourism and so little or no consideration is given to their future needs.

Product concept

The product concept assumes that visitors or guests focus on the quality within a product. The premise is that they desire quality, performance and innovative features. Hospitality organizations, therefore, have to constantly improve existing products rather than develop new ones. These businesses should not make new changes frequently as they can lose their competitive advantage. The drawback in applying this concept is that they would have sacrificed creativity and innovation by constantly improving existing new products and not developing new ones.

Fundamentally, hospitality businesses such as hotel companies need to provide added value to potential customers through innovative products that they would not normally get from their competitors (Frehse, 2006). An assessment of small to medium-sized hotels in alpine tourism destinations in Europe by Pikkemaat and Peters (2006) shows a low degree of innovation in all areas of the hotel value chain. The researchers point out that innovation is a very important business strategy in tourism. Through innovative features, hospitality businesses can differentiate their offerings. These should be difficult to imitate or recreate and provide unique functions so that they can remain for a long period of time. This is supported by the resource base view, which stipulates that for a product to remain competitive it must be inimitable and unique as well as rare and unsubstitutable (Barney, 1991).

Orfila-Sintes, Crespí-Cladera and Martínez-Ros (2005) find that the higher category hotels in the Balearic Islands are more innovative than the lower category ones. One possible reason for this is that higher category hotels have to maintain their market position and competitiveness. They therefore add value to their guests' experience through innovative products and features, as desired by that market segment. This market segment would also be able to pay the associated cost.

Another feature of the product concept is that it is used by hotels during periods of economic decline to maintain market share. Between 2001 and 2005, hotels in Spain had to rethink their product offering and employ differentiation strategies. Some of them partnered with wineries to offer tours and wine tasting. According to Vila, Enz and Costa (2011), innovation should be a part of an organization's culture in order to achieve sustainability.

Although the product concept assumes that visitors or guests have a preference for products that are better in quality and have innovative features, some may prefer a product that is simple and easy to use. What is important is that their needs must be constantly assessed to determine what new products to provide and when to provide them. Companies using the product philosophy tend to ignore customers' needs and focus on product improvement (Tosun et al., 2008). This can result in marketing myopia which, according to Reid and Bojanic (2009), can cause hospitality organizations to become complacent and miss opportunities that can be of future benefit. This will eventually characterize the business and become its orientation. It is, however, important to note that although product improvement is necessary, it must be done in consensus with visitors.

Selling concept

This marketing management philosophy suggests that organizations should "sell what they make rather than make what the market wants" (Kotler, 2000, p. 11). It focuses on the need of the seller to obtain profit through increased sales volume. Overall, there is no understanding of the market and consequently of the needs of the customer, neither is this concept geared at building and maintaining customer relationships. The selling concept assumes that customers will not purchase the product or enough of the product on their own, and therefore rely on aggressive promotions from hospitality organizations. This marketing philosophy became very popular in the 1950s when the supply of products was greater than the demand. Businesses had to ensure that the products they supplied were sold (Bowie & Buttle, 2004).

Based on the premise that consumers' buying behavior must be influenced, this concept requires promotional tools to stimulate buying. This is achieved in particular by changing their inert buying motive tendencies (Mascarenhas, 2007). Organizations push their sales through various techniques and strategies which focus on the guests purchasing the product. These include advertising, sales promotion and personal selling (Belch & Belch, 2003) and other persuasive selling tactics such as probing and sales pitch. Even if customers do not like the product, once they are influenced or persuaded, they will make the purchase. Customers also tend to forget about any initial dissatisfaction they may have and purchase the product. In achieving the selling objectives, hospitality organizations usually establish sales volume targets to be accomplished by their sales force.

The selling concept is usually used for products that are not normally purchased. These include products that are not considered for satisfying individuals' basic needs. Hospitality goods and services fall in this category as persons tend to travel, take vacations or visit attractions when they have the spending power or adequate disposable income to do so. The selling concept is also used for products that are unsought and those that may not be known until they are promoted, for example, certain restaurants and airlines (Kotler, Keller, Koshy & Jha, 2012).

With the selling concept, there are usually single transactions with customers who are normally unknown (Tosun et al., 2008), hence there is no customer-connectivity or loyalty on either side. Managers' performance is also based on short-term financial measures (Morrison, 2010). The sustainability of this marketing management philosophy is questionable since the focus is on selling rather than on the customer. There is no consideration of loyalty and return customers to ensure the longevity of the relationship. Although higher market share is achieved through persuasive selling to a mass of people, this will not be a long-term gain.

The selling concept is successfully used by hotels and airlines in their yield management endeavor (Ladeira, Santini, Araujo & Sampaio, 2016). Hotel rooms and airline seats are perishable in nature. During low season these businesses tend to use the selling strategy to ensure that they have full occupancy. It is important to derive full revenue on a daily basis through maximized room and seat occupancy, respectively (Salehi-Esfahani, Ravichandran, Israeli & Bolden, 2016). This is because the revenue for rooms and seats not sold yesterday or for unoccupied seats on a previous flight would have been lost; it cannot be regained in the current period.

Selling was once thought to be synonymous with marketing (Tosun et al., 2008); however, there is a distinction. Selling is the push factor to encourage customers to purchase the product while marketing is the pull factor which gets the customer to the provider of the product. Selling has an inward focus on business while marketing has an outward focus on the customer. With selling, profit is realized through sales volume while for marketing, profit is achieved through customer satisfaction.

Marketing concept

The marketing philosophy, otherwise called customer orientation, focuses on the needs of the customer (Kotler, 2000). This philosophy guides the selling efforts of hospitality businesses and is based on the pillars of efficiency, effectiveness and social responsibility, as well as the target market, customer needs, integrated marketing and profitability. The marketing concept is grounded on the premise that an organization needs to be more effective than its competitors in creating, delivering and communicating customer value to its selected target customers (Kotler, 2000). Customers of hospitality products want to see the products meet their wants and needs more than the competition. If hospitality businesses are able to satisfy them with the desired goods and services, then there is the propensity for profitability through sustained market share.

As used in the hospitality industry, the marketing concept requires that guests or visitors be the focal area of importance. This necessitates that particular attention be given to them. Many hospitality businesses have realized the importance of doing this and consequently implemented programs geared towards improving customer experience and satisfaction. This includes sending them birthday cards, acknowledging them on their special occasions, and remembering their names when they visit, as well as their likes and dislikes. These have actually become traditional customer-oriented practices by some hotels.

Hotels and airline companies have embarked on loyalty programs where guests and passengers, respectively, are recognized for their commitment to the entities through loyalty points and frequent flier programs among other initiatives. In September 2016, Marriott International acquired Starwood Hotels and Resorts Worldwide, Incorporation. Starwood's guests will be able to transfer their membership status to the Marriot's reward program (e-Hotelier, 2016), thereby maintaining their customer status and accumulation of reward points.

Hilton Worldwide Holdings Incorporation recognized the importance of satisfying customers. They led the way in opening the first airport hotel in 1959 to meet the demand of that segment of travelers requiring accommodation in close proximity to the airport. Over the years, they continued to improve their offerings to meet customers' expectations. For instance, the Lady Hilton Hotel concept was designed to provide distinct amenities for female guests. Through their customer experience strategy, the Hilton Worldwide Holdings Incorporation relaunched their loyalty programme to better focus on the experiences of customers rather than the mere collection of reward points. For instance, they have increased the number of premium rooms for guests to purposefully use their reward points to upgrade to that room category (Marketing Week, 2011).

Having 13 brands across the world, it is important for this multinational hotel company to maintain its market share. Agarwal, Krishna Erramilli and Dev (2003) posit that market orientation positively influences the performance of hotels operating in international markets. Hilton Worldwide Holdings recognized that negative customer experiences will have bad implications for their business and so the marketing philosophy is emphasized to maintain its market position. In meeting the guests' expectations, the hotel company anticipates good financial health (Marketing Week, 2011). In support, Sandvik and Sandvik (2003) emphasize that long-term customer satisfaction is among the key variables for achieving profitability. Likewise, Grissemann, Plank and Brunner-Sperdin (2013) posit that customer orientation is an important factor in enhancing both financial and non-financial performance of hotels.

In essence, marketing orientation suggests that hospitality businesses identify the market segments whose needs they can successfully satisfy, and further develop the 4Ps of the marketing mix (product, price, place and promotion) to satisfy customers (Enz, 2010). Marketing orientation is a viable option to sustain the operations of hospitality businesses. Webster (1988) points out that this concept was very instrumental in giving dominance to American businesses in the world's economy. However, the shift to strategic planning meant that the focus of many companies moved away from the use of the marketing concept. When these businesses were faced with the reality of losing their market positons, they subsequently returned to the application of the marketing concept (Burman, Albinsson & Hyatt, 2016). Sin, Alan, Heung and Yim (2005) confirm that market orientation has a positive and significant relationship with the marketing performance and financial performance of a hotel. Grissemann et al. (2013) also find that customer orientation is a key factor in enhancing the business performance of hotels.

Societal marketing

Societal marketing is a new orientation of marketing (Prosenak & Mulej, 2007). This marketing philosophy is based on the premise that hospitality businesses should determine the needs, wants and interests of their target market so as to satisfy their needs more than the competitors in a way that will be beneficial not only to the customer but by extension the wider society. This marketing practice embraces societal welfare as a primary objective and suggests that hospitality entities should not only focus on the traditional outcomes of profit and customer satisfaction in their marketing plans but also on societal wellbeing. In doing so, these entities will take into consideration both quantitative and qualitative objectives, where the former relates to revenue, sales and profits and the latter pertains to consumer and societal benefits. This is reinforced by Prosenak and Mulej (2007), who posit that organizations need to use a holistic marketing approach to develop innovative products while simultaneously being socially responsible.

The societal marketing concept underpins the principles of corporate social responsibility, responsible tourism and sustainable development. Societal marketing relates to social responsibility since the latter focuses not only on existing generations but also on future ones. Societal marketing is also related to sustainable development as marketing decisions must focus on long-term effects. It is a means of acting in the best interest of society in terms of preservation of the environment through pollution management, recycling of waste material, resource conservation and poverty alleviation. Royal Caribbean has demonstrated its thrust in this regard by designing ships so that waste material can be properly managed and disposed (Morrison, 2010). Some hotels have implemented environmental management programs; others have even employed Environmental Officers (Morrison, 2010).

Hotel companies, while offering hospitality services, are being responsible to the environment through green hospitality services (Mohammed, Guillet, Schuckert & Law, 2016). According to Menaktole and Jachai (2007), consumers in India have a preference for lodgings that have adopted green practices. It is believed that despite the consumers' unwillingness to pay for these services, these hotels can achieve competitive advantage from implementing and executing green practices. Green marketing will become an important business strategy in promoting the implementation of environmental programs (McDaniel & Rylander, 1993).

Hospitality organizations may experience resistance in executing this marketing philosophy from stockholders and shareholders whose interests are in the return on their investments. Even employees can be judgmental of the level of interest and spending on projects external to the organization and consequently resist this marketing practice. There is also the discourse surrounding the ethics of societal marketing as it is sometimes claimed not to be philanthropic or altruistic but a means of deriving increased market share and revenue.

A notion of the societal marketing concept is that there has to be a shift from the profit orientation of businesses in the industry to social, economic and environmental sustainability priorities (Tresidder, 2015). In this way, a sustainable tourism marketing approach will be realized. This type of marketing leads to a better quality of life for all stakeholders (Jamrozy, 2007). Payne and Dimanche (1996) purport that there should be a code of conduct for the tourism industry in terms of how it provides for local environments and community needs. As indicated by Buhalis (2000), destination marketing practices should not only include strategic objectives but also the sustainability of local resources. This ethical stance should be incorporated into the planning and decision-making processes if sustainability is to be achieved.

For tourism to be sustained it has to adopt societal marketing strategies (Ryan, 1991). Societal marketing is a new genre of marketing (Prosenak & Mulej, 2007). It is a holistic approach to marketing in terms of including the social wellbeing of its guests and that of the general society. Hospitality businesses need to use a holistic marketing approach to develop innovative products and simultaneously be socially responsible.

Conclusion

There is no doubt regarding the symbiotic relationship between tourism/hospitality and marketing. Although the marketing concepts emerged within the manufacturing industry, they have been successfully adopted by the hospitality industry. Despite being applied in distinct eras since the 1920s in the manufacturing industry, they are being used at various stages of the life cycle of a destination or hospitality business. This is because their principles differ. The production concept suggests that buyers prefer goods that are cheap and easily available. Hospitality businesses respond through mass distribution of the product. The product concept suggests that consumers prefer products that are innovative and of high quality. This is important in providing value-added features to visitors or guests. While the selling concept converts products into cash through persuasion and coercion, the marketing concept provides solutions to customers' needs and aims to achieve competitive advantage. Societal marketing extends the marketing platform by not only satisfying customers' needs but to include the welfare of the general society.

Marketing concepts are used depending on the company's management, orientation, philosophies and values. Apart from these micro-environmental factors that are directly linked to business operation, the application of these concepts also depends on general macro-environmental parameters and opportunities such as political, economic, socio-cultural, technological and environmental factors, popularly known as the PESTE factors. Hospitality businesses can begin with any of the marketing orientations, depending on the organization's management culture and operating conditions.

References

Agarwal, S., Krishna Erramilli, M., & Dev, C. S. (2003). Market orientation and performance in service firms: Role of innovation. *Journal of Services Marketing*, 17(1), 68–82.

Barney, J. (1991). Firm resources and sustained competitive advantage. *Journal of Management*, 17(1), 99–120.

Belch, G. E., & Belch, M. A. (2003). *Advertising and promotion: An integrated marketing communications perspective*. McGraw-Hill.

Bhasin, H. (2016). Production concept. *Marketing 91*. Retrieved on October 15, 2016 from www.marketing91.com/production-concept.

Boone, L. E., & Kurtz, D. L. (1992). *Contemporary marketing*. Dryden Press.

Bowie, D., & Buttle, F. (2004). *Hospitality marketing: An introduction*. Routledge.

Bowie, D., & Buttle, F. (2013). *Hospitality marketing*. Taylor & Francis.

Buhalis, D. (2000). Marketing the competitive destination of the future. *Tourism Management*, 21(1), 97–116.

Burman, B., Albinsson, P. A., & Hyatt, E. (2016). One night or many? Effects of amenity charge transparency on consumer reaction. *Journal of Hospitality Marketing & Management*, 25(8), 1010–1033.

Cuba Business Report (2016). Great expectations – the tourists are coming. *Cuba Business Report: Economic News and Business Development in Cuba*. Retrieved on October 3, 2016 from www.cubabusinessreport.com/great-expectations-the-tourists-are-coming.

Cuba Journal (2016). Cuba's 2016 mid-year tourism figures show continued strength. Retrieved on October 6, 2016 from http://cubajournal.co/cubas-2016-mid-year tourism-figures-show-continued-strength.

e-Hotelier (2016). Marriott completes Starwood acquisition to create world's largest hotel company. Retrieved on October 1, 2016 from http://ehotelier.com/global/2016/09/23/marriott-completes starwood-acquisition-create-worlds-largest-hotel-company/#.V-Wxca4z-Ec.email.

Enz, C. A. (2010). *The Cornell School of Hotel Administration handbook of applied hospitality strategy*. Sage.

Frehse, J. (2006). Innovative product development in hotel operations. *Journal of Quality Assurance in Hospitality & Tourism*, 6 (3–4), 129–146.

Grissemann, U., Plank, A., & Brunner-Sperdin, A. (2013). Enhancing business performance of hotels: The role of innovation and customer orientation. *International Journal of Hospitality Management*, 33, 347–356.

Gronroos, C. (1978). A service-orientated approach to marketing of services. *European Journal of Marketing*, 12(8), 588–601.

Gross, M. (2016). A record breaking 3.1 million tourists visited Cuba in 2015. Retrieved on October 6, 2016 from www.travelandleisure.com/articles/tourists-visited cuba-in-2015.

Hamre, J. (2016). Surge of Americans tests limits of Cuba's tourism industry. Retrieved on October 6, 2016 from www.reuters.com/article/us-cuba-usa-tourism-idUSKCN0V40DP.

Jamaica Tourist Board (2015). Annual travel statistics. Retrieved October 16, 2016 from www.jtbonline.org.

Jamrozy, U. (2007). Marketing of tourism: A paradigm shift toward sustainability. *International Journal of Culture, Tourism and Hospitality Research*, 1(2), 117–130.

Kotler, P. (2000). *Marketing management*. Prentice Hall.

Kotler, P., Keller, K. L., Koshy, A., & Jha, M. (2012). Analyzing consumer markets. *Marketing management* (14th ed.). Pearson.

Ladeira, W. J., Santini, F.D.O., Araujo, C. F., & Sampaio, C. H. (2016). A meta-analysis of the antecedents and consequences of satisfaction in tourism and hospitality. *Journal of Hospitality Marketing & Management*, 25(8), 975–1009.

Marketing Week (2011). Case study: Hilton Worldwide. Retrieved October 8, 2016 from www.marketing-week.com/2011/11/02case-study-hilton-worldwide.

Mascarenhas, O. A. J. (2007). *Responsible marketing: Concepts, theories, models, strategies and cases*. Royal Publishing Company.

McDaniel, S. W., & Rylander, D. H. (1993). Strategic green marketing. *Journal of Consumer Marketing*, 10(3), 4–10.

Menaktole, K., & Jachai, V. (2007). Exploring consumer attitude and behavior towards green practices in the lodging industry in India. *International Journal of Contemporary Hospitality*, 19(5), 364–377.

Mohammed, I., Guillet, B. D., Schuckert, M., & Law, R. (2016). An empirical investigation of corporate identity communication on Hong Kong hotels' websites. *Journal of Hospitality Marketing & Management*, 25(6), 676–705.

Morrison, A. M. (2010). *Hospitality and travel marketing* (4th ed.). Delmar Publishers.

Orfila-Sintes, F., Crespí-Cladera, R., & Martínez-Ros, E. (2005). Innovation activity in the hotel industry: Evidence from Balearic Islands. *Tourism Management*, 26(6), 851–865.

Payne, D., & Dimanche, F. (1996). Towards a code of conduct for the tourism industry: An ethics model. *Journal of Business Ethics*, 15(9), 997–1007.

Pikkemaat, B., & Peters, M. (2006). Towards the measurement of innovation: A pilot study in the small and medium-sized hotel industry. *Journal of Quality Assurance in Hospitality & Tourism*, 6(3–4), 89–112.

Prosenak, D., & Mulej, M. (2007). *How can marketing contribute to increase of well-being in transitional (and other) societies?* In Snoj, B. & Milfelner, B. (eds.), 1st International Scientific Marketing Theory Challenges in Transitional Societies Conference. September 20–21, Maribor: University of Maribor, Faculty of Economics and Business, 127–133.

Quer, D., Claver, E., & Andreu, R. (2007). Foreign market entry mode in the hotel industry: The impact of country-and firm-specific factors. *International Business Review*, 16(3), 362–376.

Reid, R. D., & Bojanic, D. C. (2009). *Hospitality marketing management*. John Wiley and Sons.

Rushmore, S., & Baum, E. (2002). Growth and development of the hotel-motel industry. *The Appraisal Journal*, 70(2), 148–162.

Ryan, C. (1991). Tourism and marketing: A symbiotic relationship? *Tourism Management*, 12(2), 101–111.

Salehi-Esfahani, S., Ravichandran, S., Israeli, A., & Bolden III, E. (2016). Investigating information adoption tendencies based on restaurants' user-generated content utilizing a modified information adoption model. *Journal of Hospitality Marketing & Management*, 25(8), 925–953.

Sandvik, I. L., & Sandvik, K. (2003). The impact of market orientation on product innovativeness and business performance. *International Journal of Research in Marketing*, 20(4), 355–376.

Sin, L. Y., Alan, C. B., Heung, V. C., & Yim, F. H. (2005). An analysis of the relationship between market orientation and business performance in the hotel industry. *International Journal of Hospitality Management*, 24(4), 555–577.

Sinclair-Maragh, G. M. (2014). Resort-based or resource-based tourism? A case study of Jamaica. *Emerald Emerging Markets Case Studies*, 4(2), 1–19.

Sinclair-Maragh, G., & Gursoy, D. (2015). Imperialism and tourism: The case of developing island countries. *Annals of Tourism Research*, 50, 143–158.

Tosun, C., Okumus, F., & Fyall, A. (2008). Marketing philosophies: Evidence from Turkey. *Annals of Tourism Research*, 35(1), 127–147.

Tresidder, R. (2015). Experiences marketing: A cultural philosophy for contemporary hospitality marketing studies. *Journal of Hospitality Marketing & Management*, 24(7), 708–726.

Vila, M., Enz, C., & Costa, G. (2011). Innovative practices in the Spanish hotel industry. *Cornell Hospitality Quarterly*, 53(1), 75–85.

Vincenzo, Z. (2005). Caribbean tourism and development: An overview. *European Centre for Development Policy Management*. Discussion Paper No. 65.

Webster, F. E. (1988). The rediscovery of the marketing concept. *Business Horizons*, 31(3), 29–39.

3

A critical review of market segmentation, target marketing and positioning in hospitality marketing

Precious Chikezie Ezeh

Introduction

The process of segmentation, targeting and positioning (STP) is fundamental to effective strategic marketing (Tanford and Malek, 2015). Every organization is geared to STP because of its numerous advantages. Most scholars have shown that STP strategy should be a sequential phenomenon, where an organization has to segment first and target second before positioning, but Bowen (1998) argues that the segmentation process is no longer a sequential process; it is an integrative process due to technological advancement. Bowen (1998) views segmenting and targeting as a two-step process, while Kotler, Bowen, and Makens (1999) view it as a three-step process, but I would argue that it is a holistic concept. Kotler (1989) developed the four steps of market segmentation strategy as the 4Ps of Probing, Partitioning, Prioritizing, and Positioning. Probing entails analyzing the market; Partitioning commences when you begin to provide different products to different clusters of your customers due to their uniqueness; Prioritizing is ranking the segments you want to focus on because you have a potentially superior advantage for satisfying them; finally, Positioning, involves pinpointing the competitive options in each segment that you are going to target

Kotler, Bowen, and Makens (1999) state that Segmentation involves a three-step process of market segmenting, market targeting, and market positioning.

- The first step is dividing a market into special groups of buyers who might require separate marketing mixes. The primary basis on which a company segments its market is through demographic, geographic, psychographic and behaviouristic segmentation.
- The second step is market targeting, which is the evaluation of the attractiveness of each segment and the selection of one or more of the market segments. Targeting decisions can then be made based on the range of identified segments. In order to choose the most appropriate target markets, it is necessary to understand what different segments want and the extent to which the organization can meet those wants. Bowen (1998) argues that before the introduction of computerized segmentation programs, the steps of segmenting and targeting were two distinct

processes, i.e., marketers first identified the segments and then looked for the segments that would be the most profitable in the long term for the organization; but following the introduction of computerized methods, these steps are now often combined.

- The third step is market positioning; once a company has chosen its target market, it must decide what positions to occupy in those segments. A product's position is the place the product occupies in consumers' minds relative to competing products. Bowen (1998) categorizes the positioning task into three steps identifying a set of possible competitive advantages on which to build a position; selecting the right competitive advantages; and effectively communicating and delivering the chosen position to a carefully selected target market. Positioning refers to the way in which an organization tries to communicate its value proposition to its target market in order to convince customers that it has a distinct offer. In effect, positioning is about the way in which the organization tries to build and communicate its competitive advantage.

Following this introduction, the rest of the chapter focuses on discussing STP, followed by a conclusion.

Market segmentation

The term "market segmentation" was introduced into the marketing literature in 1956 by Wendell R. Smith in an article entitled, "Product Differentiation and Market Segmentation" (Kotler, 1989). Since then, many scholars have defined the concept of segmentation in different ways. Market segmentation entails picking out specific bases for dividing the market and developing descriptions of the segments identified. In order to segment a market, it is important to understand who the customers are, what they buy, where they are, why they buy and how they buy in order be grouped together; we conceptualize this as the W^4H (Who, What, Where, Why and How) of segmenting.

Market segmentation is concerned with the process of identifying different groups of customers who are similar in ways that are relevant to marketing. It can be seen as a process of dividing the heterogeneous market into different homogeneous groups of consumers who have common needs and wants. Market segmentation is equally a process of identifying subsets of consumers who have unique, homogenous demand characteristics. Weinstein (2004, p. 4) offered the following definition: "Segmentation marketing means knowing your customers, giving them exactly what they want or may want, building strong relationships with channel affiliates and co-marketing partners, and communicating via highly targeted promotional media." Therefore, when the marketing mix is being applied to specific target markets, rather than the population at large, the organization is gearing towards a market segmentation strategy.

In fast-changing and hypercompetitive markets with a lot of business organization 'casualties', segmentation becomes paramount. Marketing is focused on customer orientation, which is the process of identifying and satisfying customers' needs and wants at a profit. Therefore, applying a customer orientation focus to a specific target market is known as market segmentation. Myers (1996) argued that market segmentation is the most important strategic concept in marketing and has aided the survival and growth of many firms. A company's quality goods or services are arguably no longer the main factor for the survival of the business; rather, it is the compatibility of its product with the targeted market.

Hospitality guests vary in their expectations and requirements. Therefore, hospitality managers should identify subsets of hospitality guests who share similar needs, and design goods or services in a way that will satisfy the targeted guests in order to compete more effectively against competitors. A study carried out by Ezeh (2015) provides a significant example; the study shows that hotel guests in Awka, Anambra state, Nigeria are more interested in "steady electric power supply, steady water supply, availability of night clubs/program, nearness to other hotels, and availability of commercial sex workers" which is are unique concerns compared to those of more developed areas. Therefore, hotel managers in Awka, Anambra state, Nigeria should segment based on those identified variables in order to compete effectively.

Weinstein (2004) posited that segmentation-based marketing is a proof of sound business strategy and value creation in any organization. Bowie and Buttle (2004) equally stated that there is a broad consensus that segmentation is the starting point for developing effective marketing strategies. Therefore, segmentation should be a strategic option of every business enterprise. Business organizations must focus on target markets and niches that exhibit similar needs and wants. Companies must satisfy discerning customers who can choose from a lot of products that are in the marketplace.

Bases for segmentation of hotels

Regardless of the primary basis of segmentation (i.e., demographics, geography, psychographics, or behavior), motivations, attitudes, and beliefs are important factors that identify and distinguish market segments. Equally, many scholars have segmented particular markets using different criteria, which shows that there is no known single way of segmenting a market. MacKay and Fesenmaier (1998) segment the getaway market into five segments: precontemplators, contemplators, ready for action, active and maintainers. They explained the segments as follows:

- Precontemplators are those that are not in the market for a getaway trip;
- Contemplators are those that would consider a getaway trip;
- Ready for action are those who have decided to take a getaway trip;
- Active are those that take a getaway trip; and
- Maintainers are always in the market for a getaway trip.

In their study on fast food restaurants, Grazin and Olsen (1997) identified three groups of consumer: non-users, light users, and heavy users. Oh and Jeong (1996) took a different approach to segmenting the fast food market, categorizing consumers into the following groups: neat service seeker, convenience seeker, classic diner, and indifferent diner. Loker and Perdue (1992) segmented the nonresident summer travel market into six segments: naturalists, nondifferentiators, family/friend oriented, excitement/escape, pure excitement seekers and escapists. Legolierel (1998) segmented tourists based on expenditure-based segmentation. Oyewole (2010) segmented the countries of the world into nine market segments: heavy travelers, heavy spenders (HH); heavy travelers, medium spenders (HM); heavy travelers, light spenders (HL); medium travelers, heavy spenders (MH); medium travelers, medium spenders (MM); medium travelers, light spenders (ML); light travelers, heavy spenders (LH); light travelers, medium spenders (LM); and light travelers, light spenders (LL). Arimond, Achenreiner and Elfessi (2003) identified five segments in their study on the Wisconsin rural tourism market: attraction enthusiasts, outdoor recreationists, friends and family visitors, special event attendees, and nature sightseers. Ibrahim and Gill (2005) suggested four potential niche markets: recreational, sports, culture, and ecotourism that can be promoted in the repositioning of the destination.

Nicholls and Roslow (1989) argued that a hotel can be segmented based on sleeping facilities, eating, meeting, and entertaining. They stated that the *sleeping facilities* may be single, twin, double, or king-sized, while *eating* may be waiter-service dining, cafeteria style, self-service, snacking, quick service, raw bar, ethnic menus, or eating facilities being available for breakfast, lunch, dinner, and, perhaps, in-between times. For *meeting*, he suggested that the hotel needs to provide space to accommodate individuals and organizations for various purposes such as conferences, banquets, outings, and celebrations. For *entertainment*, a traveler away from home frequently has spare time, idle time, or forced social time. The hotel provides a way of meeting this need on site with fun and recreation, nightclubs, discos, swimming, sports facilities, spas, and fitness centers.

Primary basis of segmentation

Researchers have shown different ways of segmenting markets, which proves that there is no one correct way in which to segment a market. Kotler (1989) divided segmentation variables into four major areas: Demographic, Psychographic, Geographic, and Behaviouristic. Beane and Ennis (1987) added Benefit, Purchase Occasion, Usage Incidence, User Status, Usage Rate, and Image Segmentation.

1. *Demographic segmentation*: The process of using the primary variables of age, gender, family life cycle, and ethnicity to segment the markets. Club 24 in Awka, Anambra state, Nigeria, for example, uses age and lifestyle stage variables to attract young singles interested in a vibrant nightlife. Demography is the distribution of population according to age, gender, educational qualification, family size, etc.
2. *Psychographic segmentation*: Dividing buyers into different groups based on social class, lifestyle, and personality characteristics. Psychographic and lifestyle segmentation are based on personality traits, attitudes, motivations, and mental activities. People in the same demographic group may have very significantly different psychographic profiles.
3. *Geographic segmentation*: The division of markets according to geographical boundaries, such as countries, provinces/states, regions, cities, or neighborhoods. In the past, for most destination marketing organizations (DMOs), market segmentation was often limited to understanding the more lucrative international tourist market. In Nigeria, many hospitality organizations are segmented based on international, national, regional, state, or street hotels.
4. *Behaviour segmentation*: It divides the market into groups based on the various types of buying behaviour. Common bases include *usage rate* (light, medium, and heavy), *user status* (former users, non-users, potential users, first-time users, and regular users of a product), *loyalty status* (many people stay in five-star hotels as much for the status it confers on them as for the additional comfort), *buyer-readiness stage*, and *occasions*. On special occasions, people are prepared to pay more for special treatment; so many restaurants now have deals for children's birthday parties, while hotels and cruise liners have special honeymoon suites.
5. *Benefit segmentation*: It divides customers based on the benefits they desire, such as education, entertainment, luxury, or low cost. Customers weigh different features of a service, and these are evaluated to form the basis of benefit segmentation. A benefit segmentation study should attempt to do three things: (1) determine the benefits people look for in a product; (2) determine the kinds of people looking for each benefit; and (3) determine the proximity of existing brands to these benefit needs.
6. *Purchase Occasion segmentation*: Consumers are grouped based on the reasons or times they purchase a product. Beer drinkers might be classified as heavy drinkers who are trying to escape, drinkers seeking social acceptance, or drinkers who have one beer when dining out. The hotel bar would look for a new occasion or use for which consumption of its product might be appropriate.

7. *Usage Incidence segmentation*: This is an extension of benefit segmentation and purchase incidence segmentation. Segments are based on the reasons why a product is used and the occasions on which the product is used. Usage incidence segmentation attempts to find out how people are using a product by identifying the "need states" of the consumer. It goes beyond the obvious answers to try to find out the true reasons for using the product and, therefore, the benefits sought or gained.

8. *User Status segmentation*: This divides consumers according to their use of a product (but not the amount of the product they use). Consumers may be non-users, ex-users, potential users, first-time users, or regular users. Marketing messages will be different depending on the segment one is tailoring the message towards. Beane and Ennis (1987) argue that an advertisement to a non-user would probably be informational and about the product class in general while a regular user might be told of the merits of one product versus that of a competitor.

9. *Usage Rate segmentation*: This is separate from usage status segmentation in that only users are considered. Usage rate segmentation divides consumers into light, medium, and heavy user groups. One of the things that makes usage rate segmentation so popular is that many companies can use it. Also, many market research firms and syndicated services can supply data regarding product usage rates based on several demographic and geographic characteristics.

10. *Image segmentation*: This area involves consumers' self-image or self-concept and its relationship to the image of the product. Segmentation based on self-image or self-concept does not easily fit into one of Kotler's four categories. It is really a combination of the psychographic and behaviouristic aspects of the consumer.

Bowie and Buttle (2004) argue that hotel and lodging companies segment according to the *purpose of travel*, into the following categories:

- *Business*
- *Non-business* (variously defined as leisure, holiday, personal, or social)
- *Visiting friends and relatives (VFR)*.

Business customers tend to:

- Be less price-sensitive, since the employer generally meets hospitality and travel expenses
- Be more likely to stay for one night, or only a few, on each trip
- Be more frequent, or regular, users of hotel accommodation
- Stay at establishments that are within a reasonable (10–30 minutes) travel time of their place of work – hence the higher demand for business accommodation close to commercial, industrial, and retail areas
- Be less seasonal – business travel patterns are less dependent upon weather and holiday schedules.

Leisure customers tend to:

- Be much more price-sensitive than business travelers, since they are paying for the accommodation out of their own taxed income
- Be more likely to stay longer on each trip – short breaks are normally at least a couple of days, two-week holidays are common, and longer holiday periods are not unusual

- Be less frequent users of hotel accommodation (unless they are also business travelers)
- Stay at establishments that are close to leisure amenities and tourist attractions – hence the demand for cultural, rural and seaside resort hotels
- Be much more seasonal, both in terms of climate and the time of year.

Visiting friends and relatives customers

From an accommodation demand perspective, this segment does not generate significant volumes of business for hotels since people tend to stay in the homes of their friends and relatives. This market is more important to tourism establishments in the day-visitor leisure and recreation sectors, and to restaurants and bars.

The benefits of segmentation

Bowie and Buttle (2004), and Hsu and Powers (2002) stated the following benefits of market segmentation:

1. Segmentation is cost-effective because the firm will target only those that want to buy a particular hospitality product.
2. Segmentation enables a company to design and develop the hospitality offer to satisfy customers more effectively.
3. Segmentation improves profitability by maximizing customer satisfaction, and generating repeat and recommended sales.
4. Fundamentally, segmentation ties the operation and all its marketing activities to some recognizable group or groups of consumers who can be expected to respond in a similar way to a marketing appeal.
5. A segmented marketing strategy's operators and marketers have a clear reference group to use as a benchmark for making decisions.
6. Segmentation allows the selection of consumer groups that offer the best profit potential at various times.
7. The process of analyzing markets by segment may reveal a group that is not served or an under-served segment.

Hsu and Powers (2002) argued that market segmentation not only helps us understand what people want in a product, it also gives a good idea of the price they are willing to pay and where they want to be served. Therefore, segmentation offers an opportunity to make more effective use of promotional media by identifying those that can reach the target markets effectively (Chen and Yuan, 2015). Bowie and Buttle (2004) listed some difficulties for effective segmentation in hospitality firms: the costs of carrying out marketing research; the lack of flexibility in hospitality products; the additional costs of developing and communicating separate offers for different target markets; the complexity of constantly changing consumer behavior; and finally the problem of targeting different and often incompatible target markets who use the premises at the same time.

The segmentation process (Bowie and Buttle, 2004)

Bowie and Buttle (2004) argued that the process of segmentation involves the following stages: (1) specify the market; (2) establish segmentation criteria; (3) generate segmentation variables;

(4) develop and evaluate market segment profiles; (5) evaluate the company's competences to serve selected segments effectively.

1. *Specification*: The market to be served or segmented needs to be clearly identified, forming a broad definition of consumers' needs and wants in the sector. Hospitality guests are mostly influenced by their environment.
2. *Establish segmentation criteria*: A set of criteria needs to be developed against which the various segmentation opportunities can be evaluated for market attractiveness. According to Kotler (1980), useful segments must be: measurable, accessible, and substantial. A segment must be easy to measure in order to determine its size, location, and content. Segments must be accessible through some kind of marketing vehicle. If they are not, how can you communicate the relative benefits of your product to that segment? Finally, the segment must be of substantial size to warrant attention. A segment should be large enough to warrant a special marketing program. Bowie and Buttle (2004) argued that segmented markets should be discrete, measurable, of a profitable size, accessible, and compatible.
   - Discrete – can the segment be described as having a unique set of shared requirements and expectations requiring a specific marketing program?
   - Measurable – can the market size be measured in terms of value and/or volume, growth rates, and market share of current players?
   - Profitable size – does the segment have sufficient profit potential to justify the investment? Through careful analysis, companies can often identify smaller, more profitable 'niche' markets within larger market segments. For single-unit hospitality companies, the market will primarily be focused on the company's micro-environment and depends upon the local characteristics of demand and existing/potential competitors.
   - Accessible – can the segment be reached via distribution and marketing communication channels? There is no point in targeting a segment if the company cannot communicate with potential consumers.
   - Compatible – marketers should ensure that any new target markets are compatible with existing target markets.
3. *Generate segmentation variables*: Segmentation variables provide the basis for classifying consumers into different market segments. Bowie and Buttle (2004) segmented hospitality variables into purpose of visit; geo-demographics; buyer, user and lifestyle characteristics; price – poor and rich lodgers; and time.
4. *Develop market segment profiles based on segmentation variables*: Detailed market segment profiles by Bowie and Buttle (2004) included the size of the market in terms of value and volume; customer purchase details (frequency of visit, average room/food/bar spend, number in party); consumer characteristics (benefits sought, price sensitivity); and accessibility/responsiveness to marketing programs.
5. *Evaluate the company's competencies*: The company needs to ensure that it has the competencies and resources to serve and satisfy the segment's needs and wants profitably.

Targeting

Effective target marketing requires marketers to identify and profile distinct groups of buyers who differ in their needs and preferences, and to select one or more market segments to target (Kotler and Keller, 2006). Business travelers are more critical judges of service quality than leisure travelers (Callan, 1996; Griffin, Shea, and Weaver, 1996; Ostrowski, O'Brien, and Gordon, 1994). In their study on the differences between frequent and infrequent business travelers, Weaver and

Oh (1993) found that good quality towels, free newspapers, in-room safes, and fax machines are facilities that are significantly more important to frequent business travelers. Ananth, DeMicco, Moreo, and Howey (1992) found that early dining hours, extra blankets, non-smoking rooms, night light in bathroom, and grab bars in the bathroom are attributes that are more important to mature travelers than younger travelers.

The basic range of targeting strategies

There are various ways in which a segment can be targeted; these strategies are Undifferentiated, Differentiated, Focused, and Customized.

1. *Undifferentiated*: This is when an organization serves an entire marketplace with a single marketing mix which does not distinguish between sub-segments of the market. Equally, it may be the case that the cost of segmenting the market and producing a set of different marketing mixes is not commercially justifiable for the organization.
2. *Differentiated*: This is when an aggregate marketplace, such as hospitality industry, is organized into a number of segments, each of which is targeted with a tailored or special marketing mix. This may arise when a company has been able to identify a commercially valid basis upon which an aggregate market can be broken down into segments.
   Focused: This is when a choice is made to target a small subset of the segments of a multi-segment marketplace with a single marketing mix that best suits the needs of that segment. This approach to segmentation is where a company breaks a market down into a set of segments but chooses to target a small subset of available segments or, in some cases, only a single segment. A focused approach may take a number of different forms: Single segment concentration, Selective specialization, Product specialization, and Market specialization.
   a. *Single segment concentration* – when an organization concentrates only on a single segment in the market and supplies products tailored specifically to the needs of those customer groups. This approach is often described as niche marketing. It is potentially highly profitable, because the organization focuses all its efforts on a particular segment of the market where it has a strong differential advantage. At the same time there are risks associated with this approach, because if the segments were to disappear or a new competitor enters the market, the organization could be vulnerable to a significant loss of business.
   b. *Selective specialization* – instead of the organization concentrating only on one segment it chooses to operate in several (possibly unrelated) segments. This approach to targeting is less focused than single segment specialization, but probably less risky.
   c. *Product specialization* – the organization that concentrates on supplying a particular product type to a range of customer groups is pursuing a product specialization strategy. This approach to market targeting may be particularly appropriate for organizations with particular strengths or knowledge in relation to a given technology or product.
   d. *Market specialization* – rather than concentrating on a particular product, the organization chooses to specialize in meeting the needs of a particular customer group. This strategy may be most suitable where knowledge of the customer group's particular needs is a particularly important basis for establishing a competitive advantage. Most hotels pursue this type of approach in relation to high net-worth individuals – they seek to provide a range of different hospitality products to meet the needs of the high net-worth customers.
3. *Customized*: This is when an organization tailors their marketing mix to the individual's specific needs. Some markets lend themselves more naturally to a customized approach, especially

those that are in service sectors involving a high degree of human interface. In the hospitality industry, customized targeting is most in evidence as part of a hybrid strategy in which a distinct set of services is offered to a particular segment and then the service is customized to individuals within that segment.

Positioning

Bowen (1998) posits that a product's position is the way the product is defined by consumers on important attributes, that is, the place the product occupies in consumers' minds relative to competing products. Consumers are exposed to an excess of information about products and services; they cannot re-evaluate products every time they make a buying decision. To simplify buying decision making, consumers organize products into categories – they "position" products and companies in their minds (Kotler, Bowen, and Makens, 1999). Understanding of positioning can help marketers manage their market and product. If they have an undesirable position, the research validating their unfavourable position will often provide insight into what needs to be done to gain a more favourable position (Bowen, 1998).

Whatever position is decided upon, it must satisfy some basic tests of its likely effectiveness. Jobber (2004) identifies a set of four such tests, namely:

1. *Clarity* – is the basis of the position clear and straightforward to grasp?
2. *Credibility* – can the position be justified and validated by the evidence available?
3. *Consistency* – is the essence of the position communicated consistently over time in all elements of the marketing mix?
4. *Competitiveness* – does the position result in benefits to the customers that are demonstrably superior to those provided by its competitors?

Summary

This chapter outlined the key principles underpinning the STP strategy, and defined the bases for segmenting the market. The chapter then went on to evaluate the different methods of segmentation linked to consumers' characteristics. STP was identified as a key step towards organizational survival.

References

Ananth, M., DeMicco, F.J., Moreo, P.J. and Howey, R.M. (1992) "Marketplace lodging needs of mature travellers", *The Cornell Hotel and Restaurant Quarterly*, Vol. 33, No. 4, pp. 12–24.

Arimond, G., Achenreiner, G. and Elfessi, A. (2003) "An innovative approach to tourism market segmentation research: An applied study", *Journal of Hospitality & Leisure Marketing*, Vol. 10, No. 3/4, pp. 25–56.

Beane, T.P. and Ennis, D.M. (1987) "Market segmentation: A review", *European Journal of Marketing*, Vol. 21, No. 5, pp. 20–42.

Bowen, J.T. (1998) "Market segmentation in hospitality research: No longer a sequential process", *International Journal of Contemporary Hospitality Management*, Vol. 10, No. 7, pp. 289–296.

Bowie, D. and Buttle, F (2004) *Hospitality Marketing: An Introduction*, Elsevier Butterworth-Heinemann, Burlington, MA.

Callan, R.J. (1996) "An appraisement of UK business travellers' perceptions of important hotel attributes", *Hospitality Research Journal*, Vol. 19, No. 4, pp. 113–127.

Chen, H.S. and Yuan, J. (2015) "A journey to save on travel expenses: The intentional buying process of consumers on opaque-selling websites", *Journal of Hospitality Marketing & Management*, Vol. 25, No. 7, pp. 820–840.

Datta, Y (1996) "Market segmentation: An integrated framework", *Long Range Planning,* Vol. 29, No, 6, pp. 797–811.

Ezeh, P.C. (2015) "Conceptual framework on the factors that influence the acceptance of a hotel". Unpublished paper.

Grazin, K.L. and Olsen, J.E. (1997) "Market segmentation for fast-food restaurants in an era of health consciousness", *Journal of Restaurant & Foodservice Marketing,* Vol. 2, No. 2, pp. 1–20.

Griffin, R.K., Shea, L. and Weaver, P. (1996) "How business travellers discriminate between mid-priced and luxury hotels: An analysis using a longitudinal sample", *Journal of Hospitality and Leisure Marketing,* Vol. 4, No. 2, pp. 63–74.

Hsu, C.H.C. and Powers, T. (2002) *Marketing Hospitality,* 3rd ed. John Wiley & Sons, Inc., New York.

Ibrahim, E.E. and Gill, J. (2005) "A positioning strategy for a tourist destination, based on analysis of customers' perceptions and satisfactions", *Marketing Intelligence & Planning,* Vol. 23, No. 2, pp. 172–188.

Jobber, D. (2004) *Principles and Practice of Marketing,* 4th ed., McGraw-Hill International, London.

Kotler, P. (1989) "From mass marketing to mass customization", *Planning Review,* Vol. 17, No. 5, pp. 10–47.

Kotler, P. (1980) *Principles of Marketing,* Prentice-Hall, Englewood Cliffs, NJ.

Kotler, P. and Keller, K. (2006) *Marketing Management,* 12th ed., Pearson Prentice Hall, Englewood Cliffs, NJ.

Kotler, P., Bowen, J.T. and Makens, J.C. (1999) *Marketing for Hospitality and Tourism,* 2nd ed., Prentice-Hall, Upper Saddle River, NJ.

Legolierel, P (1998) "Toward a market segmentation of the tourism trade: Expenditure levels and consumer behavior instability", *Journal of Travel & Tourism Marketing,* Vol. 7, No. 3, pp. 19–39.

Loker, L.E. and Perdue R.R. (1992) "A benefit based segmentation of a nonresident summer travel market", *Journal of Travel Research,* Vol. 31, No. 1, pp. 30–35.

MacKay, K.J. and Fesenmaier, D.R. (1998) "A process approach to segmenting the gateway travel market", *Journal of Travel & Tourism Marketing,* Vol. 7, No. 3, pp. 1–39.

Myers, C.S. (1996) "Trust, commitment and values shared in long-term relationships in the services marketing industry", Master's thesis submitted to the University of Nevada, Las Vegas.

Nicholls, J.A.F. and Roslow, S. (1989) "Segmenting the hotel market", *FIU Hospitality Review,* Vol. 7, No. 1, pp. 39–47.

Oh, H. and Jeong, M. (1996) "Improving marketers' predictive power of customer satisfaction on expectation–based target market levels", *Hospitality Research Journal,* Vol. 19, No. 4, pp. 65–85.

Ostrowski, P.L., O'Brien, T.V. and Gordon, G.L. (1994) "Determinants of service quality in the commercial airline industry: Differences between business and leisure travelers", *Journal of Travel & Tourism,* Vol. 3, No. 1, pp. 19–46.

Oyewole, P (2010) "Country segmentation of the international tourism market using propensity to travel and to spend abroad", *Journal of Global Marketing,* Vol. 23, 152–168,

Tanford, S. and Malek, K. (2015) "Segmentation of reward program members to increase customer loyalty: The role of attitudes towards green hotel practices", *Journal of Hospitality Marketing & Management,* Vol. 24, No. 3, pp. 314–343.

Weaver, P.A. and Oh, H.C. (1993) "Do American business travelers have different hotel service requirements?", *International Journal of Contemporary Hospitality Management,* Vol. 5, No. 3, pp. 16–21.

Weinstein, A. (2004) *Handbook of Market Segmentation: Strategic Targeting for Business and Technology Firms,* 3rd ed., The Haworth Press, Inc., Binghamton, NY.

Part II
Hospitality marketing methodologies

4

A critical review of hospitality marketing statistical techniques and applications

Edward C. Bolden, III

Research in hospitality marketing

This section will explore the three major approaches to research in hospitality marketing: quantitative, qualitative, and mixed methods. Each of these approaches has been utilized in various ways and has been published in recent hospitality marketing literature, so this chapter provides a brief overview of how each of these has been applied in the published research. A brief review of each of the three types is included, followed by a more in-depth look into quantitative analysis and the statistical techniques most commonly used in the hospitality marketing literature.

Quantitative research

Quantitative research involves the collection and analysis of numerical or statistical data, gathered through objective measurements (Dimitrov, 2009). Numerical data are generated from direct measurements and observations, as well as polls, surveys, or questionnaires. This use of measurable, transformable data is applied to make comparisons and identify patterns in the defined variables. This method is widely considered to be more structured than qualitative methods, and typically involves a larger sample population (hence, quantity). Statistical applications and techniques will be the main focus for much of this chapter, so they will not be discussed in detail here.

Most hospitality marketing research is quantitative in nature, where variables such as consumer spending, advertising expenditures, and ratings such as service quality and attitudes are all numerical. In fact, more than 70 percent of articles published in the *Journal of Hospitality Marketing & Management* over the past several years comprise quantitative research and statistical analysis of numerical variables. Ultimately, the appeal of quantitative methods lies in the ability to report reliable and valid conclusions because the data are objective measurements. The weakness of this approach is the amount of detail to be collected, often leaving the question of "why?" unanswered.

Qualitative research

Qualitative research, on the other hand, collects data from fewer subjects that provides a more in-depth examination of participants (Merriam & Tisdell, 2016). This research approach focuses on the quality of information provided (hence, qualitative), rather than just numbers. The details and richness of data collected via this method is the strength of qualitative research. The two main weaknesses of this approach, conversely, lie in the extensive time commitment required and potential concerns with the reliability of the data collected. It takes substantially more time to collect and analyze qualitative data than it does quantitative data, particularly when the sample sizes increase.

The most common qualitative research applications in hospitality marketing include interviews, focus groups, and observations. Patrons and customers are frequently subjects of interviews with the purpose of collecting detailed information. Focus groups and observations often provide invaluable information on marketing techniques, approaches, and effectiveness, while observations serve to validate consumer behavior. Case studies and ethnographic approaches, while still under the umbrella of qualitative research, are extremely rarely used in hospitality marketing due to the limited information that can be collected relevant to the discipline; however, focus groups and interviews are extremely common data collection methods in both hospitality and marketing.

Qualitative research is appealing in hospitality marketing because it enables researchers to explore behaviors, attitudes, and opinions that cannot be collected through closed-ended survey questions or an exploration of industry metrics. Researchers can focus on information that underlies behaviors and attitudes through asking questions as simple as "why?" It is qualitative data that typically informs development of both theories and quantitative data collection instruments. Qualitative data has its place within the hospitality marketing literature, but it is often overshadowed when implemented independently; much more frequently some qualitative methods are combined with a quantitative approach to constitute a mixed methods design.

Mixed methods research

Mixed methods research combines both quantitative and qualitative components into one research study. The application of mixed methods is appealing because it enables the researcher to balance the strengths of each approach, while hoping to minimize weaknesses or critiques of each through triangulation of information collected (Creswell & Plano Clark, 2011). Thus, the researcher is able to maximize the validity and reliability of the qualitative information when supplemented with quantitative data, while being able to better describe or explain that data using the qualitative information. This approach is particularly sound when the data are used effectively to supplement each other, where the sources are used to triangulate the data.

This approach is particularly attractive in hospitality marketing, where there is widespread appeal to collecting quantitative data for comparison or theory testing, but also incorporating the richness of qualitative information. For example, it is easy to find useful data in the hospitality industry such as money spent, customer numbers, or demographic characteristics. Incorporating qualitative information allows research subjects to provide detail not evident in the numbers, such as why they responded the way they did, and what factors impacted their decision, or their thought processes. Mixed methods approaches could be more widely utilized than they are to overcome some weaknesses evident in each method independently.

Statistical techniques and applications

The following review of statistical techniques and applications is not intended to provide you with all you need to know to implement a certain technique. Instead, the purpose is to provide a brief overview of each technique and how it has been applied in the hospitality marketing literature. For more details and information on any of these techniques, please see the list of further reading. Therefore, an overview of the techniques will be presented within the context of hospitality marketing research.

Comparing groups

There is a lot of interest in hospitality marketing in comparing groups on a number of variables, whether it be their habits, preferences, or behaviors. Determining where there are differences between groups, or even levels of a certain variable, is a staple of hospitality marketing research as businesses look to define whom they can best target, on whom they may be missing out, and how different groups compare with each other on a wide range of possible variables.

How researchers compare groups depends primarily on two main factors: (1) the types of variables involved, and (2) the number of groups that are to be compared. Variables that are categorical (e.g., race/ethnicity, type of employment, region of origin) have discrete categories and are treated differently from variables that are continuous (e.g., age, income, or miles traveled), when the possibilities range from zero to infinity. How these two types of variables can be compared, or the analysis that is appropriate, is explained in detail within the appropriate sections below.

Chi-Square

Chi-Square tests are used when both variables to be compared are categorical, where the focus is on the number of people in categories rather than mean scores on some dimension (Aron & Aron, 2003). For example, a researcher could look at travelers' region of origin (i.e., Northeast, Midwest, Southeast, Southwest, and Northwest) and how those travelers compare on type of employment (i.e., full-time, part-time, unemployed). Here, the analysis explores the frequencies within each of the possible groupings and applies a Chi-Square test to determine if the frequencies represent a pattern or association between variables.

Chi-Square tests are used rarely in the hospitality marketing literature. Often, they are replaced with analyses of continuous variables. Continuous variables are derived from subscale scores—typically generated from individual scale items—allowing for a more summative approach to data analysis and easier interpretation of results. While there is nothing incorrect about this approach, many demographic variables are reported without considering the representation of groups. Analyses such as the Chi-Square test could inform researchers of a biased sample, where they may find an association between variables due to sampling issues. Ultimately, the Chi-Square analysis would inform the researcher of an uneven distribution between groups, which may shed light on potential bias in the analysis.

t-test

The t-test is used when there is a single continuous variable compared between two groups or levels of a categorical variable. In other words, the t-test compares means of two groups. The strength of the t-test is its simplicity; however, it is also an extremely limited statistical analysis because the researcher is limited to testing only two groups on one variable. It is a very simple test to conduct, even by hand, but lacks the ability to fit the needs of most researchers in comparing three or more groups. Thus, there is no mention of using a *t*-test as a primary analysis upon review of more than two years of literature in hospitality marketing journals.

Much like the Chi-Square analysis, this is not seen as frequently in the hospitality marketing literature due to the complexity of many variables for which data is collected. Most often, a researcher is looking at comparing multiple groups, leading the *t*-test to be obsolete in favor of more appropriate methods. Frequently, researchers will employ an analysis of variance to test two groups, which provides the same result (Hinkle, Wiersma, & Jurs, 2003). The *t*-test is most frequently used in the literature as a follow-up test, comparing multiple means as a way of establishing statistical significance.

ANOVA family

The analysis of variance (ANOVA) is a family of procedures for testing variability among the means of multiple groups (Aron & Aron, 2003). The ANOVA family is the most frequently used analysis for comparing groups because it allows more than two groups or levels of an independent variable to be compared on one continuous variable (Dimitrov, 2009). Using the ANOVA family is appealing because there is no limit to the number of groups that can be compared, the researcher can compare the groups on multiple variables simultaneously (i.e., MANOVA), and the researcher can also account for repeated measurements and other variables that allow for more control in the analysis (i.e., ANCOVA). Providing all of the possible analyses within the ANOVA family is outside the scope of this work; however, the appeal to hospitality marketing for several of these will be discussed.

The ANOVA family is widely used in hospitality marketing because of the ability to make comparisons between group means, to explore multiple dependent variables, and to exert some control over certain variables. The adaptability of these tests lead them to be widely used across all domains of research. Within hospitality marketing, variations of ANOVA have been applied in cases from the simple, such as comparing temporal orientations on vacation categories (Loda & Amos, 2014), to the complex, such as examining the effects of culture, customer loyalty, and restaurant pricing on customer complaints (Kim, Lee, & Mattila, 2014).

While variations of ANOVA are used often in the literature, rarely do they exist as the sole analysis in a research publication. In most cases, particularly in the hospitality marketing literature, these analyses are part of a larger instrument design research project that involves descriptive statistics and an exploration of instrument reliability (e.g., Ong, 2015). As expected, there are also instances when these analyses are paired with other techniques such as factor analytic or multiple regression techniques (e.g., Chen & Chen, 2014; Miao, 2014). The ability for variations of ANOVA to meet the many needs of statistical analysis lead it to be a very widely used technique in hospitality marketing and beyond.

Exploring relationships among variables

Another technique common in hospitality marketing is the exploration of relationships among variables. Relationships are explored at a basic level using correlational analysis, or the statistical value representing the degree of relatedness between two variables. Often, this is taken a step further, where the relationship between variables is used to predict one variable from the other, called regression. In regression analysis, multiple variables can be explored to determine which of a set of variables most strongly predicts the variable of choice. A breakdown of correlational and regression analyses follows.

Correlational analysis

The relationship between two variables is measured by the extent to which they co-relate, or how changes in one variable are met with changes in the other (Dimitrov, 2009). The correlation coefficient is the value that represents the strength and direction of the relationship between two variables (Hinkle, Wiersma, & Jurs, 2003). There are multiple correlation coefficients, with Pearson's r and Spearman's rho (ρ) being the most common. The values of the coefficients range from −1 to 1, with negative values representing an inverse relationship between variables and higher absolute values suggesting a stronger relationship between them. The single coefficient effectively summarizes the direct relationship between two variables, which is foundational in advanced applications such as linear regression and structural equation modeling.

Correlations are often used in hospitality marketing to explore the extent to which variables are related. Most often, this is only a stepping stone before applying one of the more advanced techniques such as regression, factor analysis, and structural equation modeling, which are discussed in the following sections. Ultimately, those more advanced techniques rely on the tenets of correlational analysis to define relationships among more than two variables. Correlation values are reported frequently in the hospitality marketing literature, but rarely does this analysis approach exist independent of other statistical applications.

Regression

Regression is the process of applying the statistical relationships between variables with the intention of estimation (Fox, 2016). Though this approach is widely used in prediction and forecasting metrics, the researcher is exploring the pattern within the data and its ability to accurately estimate the value of one variable based on its relationship with other variables. Regression analyses range from simple, including only one independent variable, to multiple, where there are two or more independent variables. Simple regression informs the researcher about how much the independent variable can predict the dependent variable. Multiple regression relies on the correlations between each of the variables to explore the complex relationship of multiple variables at once. The alternative to multiple regression analysis would be a sequential interpretation of correlation values that may be impacted by the presence of additional variables, whereas multiple regression allows us to explore these all at once.

Regression has been used in hospitality marketing in many contexts; often to explore impacts of attitudes on behaviors. For example, Lo, Wu, and Tsai (2015) used regression to assess the impact of service quality on positive emotions after a spa experience. Similarly, Abubakar and Mavondo (2014) predicted customer satisfaction and positive word-of-mouth ratings from variables related to the environment and emotions. Given the large number of variables that can be considered in the hospitality industry, there are many ways in which regression analyses have been applied. Industries continually strive to use data to approach marketing in a strategic fashion, and the implementation of regression analyses is an extremely powerful tool when used appropriately. Determining predictors of customer satisfaction and behavior are integral parts of a strategic business approach that is rooted in research.

Path models

Path models are an extension of multiple regression, analyzing the relationships between variables in a way that focuses on causality and the determination of effect based on the inter-relationships of the variables (Olobatuyi, 2006). Path analysis is also an integral part of structural equation modeling, which will be discussed in the following section. The path analysis approach is appealing because it allows the researcher to account for the relationships among multiple variables that, in turn, serve as predictors in one single model. Therefore, researchers can formulate and test the impact multiple variables have on each other and on an outcome, which is not possible using just multiple regression techniques. Path analyses are similar to confirmatory factor analyses in the way that they are tested, which is by determining fit between the model and the data.

Path analysis has been used in hospitality marketing research as an extension of multiple regression analyses to address direct and indirect impacts of independent variables, particularly customer perceptions and satisfaction. Liat, Mansori, and Huei (2014) explored the effects of perceived service quality, corporate image, and customer satisfaction on customer loyalty. Path analysis has also been applied to explore the relationships between argument quality, source credibility, and information usefulness to predict information adoption (Salehi-Esfahani, Ravichandran, Israeli, & Bolden, 2016), as well as perceptions related to price, quality, value, and satisfaction, and their relationships with repurchase intention and word-of-mouth communication (Oh, 1999). Path analysis has demonstrated utility within hospitality marketing; however, path analysis most often exists within the context of more advanced structural equation models.

Factor analysis techniques

Factor analysis relies on examining the correlations between multiple variables to establish a lesser number of underlying variables termed "factors" (Thompson, 2004). Ultimately, through the exploration of relationships among variables, factor analysis seeks to combine variables in a meaningful way to identify or generate underlying factors. Factor analysis can be exploratory or confirmatory in nature, depending on the investigation and any existing, hypothesized theory. Exploratory factor analysis (EFA) is used where there is no theory predicting how variables organize into factors, as the analysis explores the underlying structure of the relationships. In contrast, confirmatory factor analysis (CFA) is used to test how well the data fit the theorized model of inter-variable relationships.

Hospitality marketing has seen both exploratory and confirmatory factor analyses become prominent within the literature. As researchers continue developing instruments to assess opinions and attitudes, they continue to be subject to exploratory analyses. Morosan (2015) used EFA to explore factors from a set of items and encountered three main sources of influence: online, print, and destination marketing organization media. Confirmatory analyses are most often used a) to confirm a theory of underlying factors based on previous research, or b) as a follow-up to EFA techniques. For example, Triantafillidou and Siomkos (2014) used CFA to verify the structure of a scale proposed by other researchers, providing validation before conducting other analyses using their data.

Both EFA and CFA results are typically used in addition to other analyses, such as regression, to test further hypotheses based on the factors uncovered or validated. There are times as well that exploratory and confirmatory analyses are presented within the same publication, such as by Abubakar and Mavondo (2014). Most often in the research, factor analyses are included as part of establishing a structural equation model (e.g., Prayag, Khoo-Lattimore, & Sitruk, 2015) or within a regression application (e.g., Ganglmair-Wooliscroft & Wooliscroft, 2014). Exploratory and confirmatory factor analyses provide researchers with a powerful technique to explore inter-relationships between variables that become extremely useful when combined with other analyses.

Structural Equation Modeling

Structural Equation Modeling (SEM) is yet a further extension of multiple regression and factor analysis that allows the researcher to explore relationships of unobserved, latent variables (Schumacker & Lomax, 2015). This is done by combining the techniques of confirmatory factor analysis, path analysis, and regression techniques to establish how the observed variables relate to latent variables, and then how latent variables relate to each other. Path and confirmatory factor analyses fall under the umbrella of structural equation models (Kline, 2011); however, they are most frequently referred to by their more specific names. The ability for SEM to model complex data structures lead it to be an increasingly used tool across many areas of research.

The strengths of this advanced technique lie in its ability to account for so many variables simultaneously, testing the extent to which the data align with the theorized model. These complex inter-relationships can be calculated much quicker using computer-based programs, leading the theory and analyses to become increasingly complex without calculation limits. Unfortunately, the sample size must increase with the complexity of the model, leading to difficulty collecting enough data to reliably test hypotheses. These complex relationships also involve a substantial amount of estimation and SEM is often criticized for being an under-developed statistical technique without clear agreement on when a model and data align.

Hospitality marketing has seen an increase in the use of SEM over the past several years, employing the analysis to meet the needs of testing increasingly complex theories and inter-relationships among variables. The variety of applications of SEM range from exploring the relationships between customer satisfaction, customer delight, attitudinal loyalty, and behavioral loyalty (Kim, Knutson, & Vogt, 2014) to the exploration of utilitarian value and hedonic value as they influence destination image with a moderator of processing fluency (Tang & Jang, 2014). Researchers continue to apply SEM methodology to test increasingly advanced theories and relationships among variables in hospitality management.

Summary of techniques in current research

Trends

Over the past several years, the use of statistics in hospitality marketing research has become increasingly more advanced. While there is still the need for, and publication of, articles covering theoretical bases using descriptive statistics and some of the more simple analysis, training and software advances make it much easier to explore more complex interactions among variables. Theories and measurements have become more sophisticated and the statistical analysis techniques have adapted to accommodate testing these theories. As such, multiple regression, factor analyses, and structural equation modeling are becoming more common in the hospitality marketing literature.

Some notable approaches that have been used in recent publications include an economic model function estimation, efficiency analysis, and qualitative approaches including content analysis, multi-relational approach, and a consensus map. These research approaches are more common in other subject areas, but have been applied in a way to help contribute to knowledge in hospitality marketing. There are multiple techniques used in the marketing research that are used frequently, such as factor analyses and SEM; however, there continues to be innovative approaches and novel research applications within the hospitality marketing literature. When it comes to application of research and statistical techniques, there is always a tool that is considered most appropriate based on the research questions.

While research in general has become increasingly complex, researchers do still achieve success in publishing both qualitative and basic quantitative research designs. This occurs most often in under-researched areas of hospitality marketing and serve to lay the foundation for expansion of theories and incorporation of additional measurements. Though the trend can be summarized as an increasing complexity of statistical techniques, there is still the need for more basic approaches to form the foundation upon which increasingly detailed and multifaceted investigations can be built.

Evaluation of techniques

This chapter was intended to provide evidence of the diversity of statistical analyses applied within the hospitality marketing literature. Throughout this section, several popular analyses—and a few more rarely used techniques—were summarized through the lens of current research interests and publications. Overall, there has been an increased interest in some advanced statistical techniques such as multiple regression and structural equation modeling due to the advances in technology and the development of more sophisticated theories. Taken together, these advanced techniques have been applied to meet the changing needs of researchers, as they explore the relationships among more and more variables in the hope of validating theory.

Most importantly, these methods have been widely implemented with integrity. Throughout the process of reviewing the articles, the respective researchers are consistently successful at making the case for implementing a certain method and outlining why it was the most appropriate. Hospitality marketing research consumers, more than many other research areas, are consistently reminded of the fidelity with which techniques are applied when presented with strong cases for research. Providing a critical review of statistical techniques applied in the hospitality marketing literature proves to be a much easier task when the methods are explained as thoroughly, applied as diligently, and interpreted as accurately as they have been in the past several years of research.

Future directions and recommendations

The past five to ten years have brought more advanced statistical applications and methodologies to hospitality marketing, and research as a whole, as technology and education make such analyses more available and applicable to hypothesis testing. As more researchers are exposed to and trained in these methods, it allows for a more comprehensive approach to testing theories. Within the domain of hospitality marketing, there continue to be researchers applying leading-edge techniques to answer their questions, and that trend is likely to continue. It is evident that hospitality marketing will continue to contribute to developing even more advanced techniques as theory and research become increasingly more complex.

In the coming years, the interconnectivity between individuals and institutions is expected to continue increasing, leading to an overwhelming amount of data available for analysis. Making these connections between hospitality consumers, service providers, and researchers would provide an abundance of data around which research questions could be developed, theories could be contrived, and hypotheses could be tested. Data and metrics never before collected can become increasingly available and analyzed in a meaningful way, such as the recent windfall of social networking data and the resulting approach of social network analysis. Social network analysis could be particularly powerful from a customer interaction and marketing perspective, if employed correctly, and could become a promising area of research for those in hospitality as a whole.

The primary recommendation is for hospitality marketing researchers to continue evolving and applying the advanced techniques to their research when appropriate. Stemming from that, researchers ought to continue letting theory guide their investigations and explorations rather than applying an advanced analysis for its own sake. Though there has been an influx of advanced statistical techniques published in the literature over the past several years, there is still a place for more basic approaches, qualitative, and mixed-method analyses, such as in theory generation and early exploration. Researchers must lay the foundation upon which more advanced techniques become applicable by developing strong, testable hypotheses rooted in theory and demonstrating basic relationships between variables before moving to the complex analyses of structural equation or regression modeling.

In addition, hospitality marketing researchers should keep their focus on the reader, providing useful interpretations for research consumers and the workforce at large. As the analyses become more convoluted, the explanations and interpretations of the results must be meaningful to those who apply the research in everyday experience. Research is conducted to inform practice, so those in the hospitality industry and marketing sector should be able to contrive best practices from research. This can only be the case if those conducting and leading the research are able to explain their findings and report their results in a way that can be consumed and deemed useful to those in practice.

Summary

The aim of this chapter was to provide a brief background of research types and common statistical approaches utilized in the hospitality marketing literature. A review of quantitative, qualitative, and mixed methods research was supplemented by a description of how each has been applied to hospitality marketing exploration. Within the quantitative domain, statistical techniques and applications ranging from a basic comparison of groups to structural equation modeling was provided. Within each, a brief review of the technique and how it has been utilized in relevant hospitality marketing literature has been provided. Lastly, a review of the techniques has been provided and recommendations have been presented.

Overall, there has been an increase in the complexity of research, and accompanying statistical analysis, in the hospitality marketing literature. Statistical analyses and theory development have evolved together to provide a more comprehensive examination of the hospitality marketing discipline. Researchers continue to apply statistical techniques to best meet the needs of the research, implementing and interpreting analyses with fidelity to contribute to meaningful literature. The sole caveat is that researchers should continue appealing to the research consumer, providing an interpretation that can be useful to the practicing hospitality marketing professional.

References

Abubakar, B. & Mavondo, F. (2014) Tourism destinations: Antecedents to customer satisfaction and positive word-of-mouth. *Journal of Hospitality Marketing & Management* 23, 833–864.

Aron, A. & Aron, E. N (2003) *Statistics for Psychology*, Third edition, Upper Saddle River, NJ: Prentice Hall.

Chen, W. J. & Chen, M. L. (2014) Factors affecting the hotel's service quality: Relationship marketing and corporate image. *Journal of Hospitality Marketing & Management* 23, 77–96.

Creswell, J. W. & Plano Clark, V. L. (2011) *Designing and Conducting Mixed Methods Research*, Second edition, Thousand Oaks, CA: Sage.

Dimitrov, D. M. (2009) *Quantitative Research in Education: Intermediate and Advanced Methods*, Oceanside, NY: Whittier Publications, Inc.

Fox, J. (2016) *Applied Regression Analysis and Generalized Linear Models*, Third edition, Thousand Oaks, CA: Sage.

Ganglmair-Wooliscroft, A. & Wooliscroft, B. (2014) "Part of me": National parks integration into the extended self of domestic tourists. *Journal of Hospitality Marketing & Management* 23, 360–379.

Hinkle, D. E., Wiersma, W., & Jurs, S. G. (2003) *Applied Statistics for the Behavioral Sciences*, Fifth edition, Belmont, CA: Cengage Learning.

Kim, M., Knutson, B. J., & Vogt, C. A. (2014) Posttrip behavioral differences between first-time and repeat guests: A two-phase study in a hospitality setting. *Journal of Hospitality Marketing & Management* 23, 722–745.

Kim, M. G., Lee, C. H., & Mattila, A. S. (2014) Determinants of customer complaint behavior in a restaurant context: The role of culture, price level, and customer loyalty. *Journal of Hospitality Marketing & Management* 23, 885–906.

Kline, R. (2011) *Principles and Practice of Structural Equation Modeling*, Third edition, New York, NY: Guilford.

Liat, C. B., Mansori, S., & Huei, C. T. (2014) The associations between service quality, corporate image, customer satisfaction, and loyalty: Evidence from the Malaysian hotel industry. *Journal of Hospitality Marketing & Management* 23, 314–326.

Lo, A., Wu, C., & Tsai, H. (2015) The impact of service quality on positive consumption emotions in resort and hotel spa experiences. *Journal of Hospitality Marketing & Management* 24, 155–179.

Loda, M. D. & Amos, C. (2014) Temporal orientation and destination selection. *Journal of Hospitality Marketing & Management* 23, 907–919.

Merriam, S. B. & Tisdell, E. J. (2016) *Qualitative Research: A Guide to Design and Implementation*, Fourth edition, San Francisco, CA: Jossey-Bass.

Miao, L. (2014) Emotion regulation at service encounters: Coping with the behavior of other customers. *Journal of Hospitality Marketing & Management* 23, 49–76.

Morosan, C. (2015) The influence of DMO advertising on specific destination visitation behaviors. *Journal of Hospitality Marketing & Management* 24, 47–75.

Oh, H. (1999) Service quality, customer satisfaction, and customer value: A holistic perspective. *Hospitality Management* 18, 67–82.

Olobatuyi, M. E. (2006) *A User's Guide to Path Analysis*, New York, NY: University Press.

Ong, B. S. (2015) Attitudes, perceptions, and responses of purchasers versus subscribers-only for daily deals on hospitality products. *Journal of Hospitality Marketing & Management* 24, 180–201.

Prayag, G., Khoo-Lattimore, C., & Sitruk, J. (2015) Casual dining on the French Riviera: Examining the relationship between visitors' perceived quality, positive emotions, and behavioral intentions. *Journal of Hospitality Marketing & Management* 24, 24–46.

Salehi-Esfahani, S., Ravichandran, S., Israeli, A., & Bolden, E. (2016) Investigating information adoption tendencies based on restaurants' user-generated content utilizing a modified information adoption model. *Journal of Hospitality Marketing & Management* 25, 925–953.

Schumacker, R. E. & Lomax, R. G. (2015) *A Beginner's Guide to Structural Equation Modeling*, Fourth edition, New York, NY: Routledge.

Tang, L. R. & Jang, S. S. (2014) Information value and destination image: Investigating the moderating role of processing fluency. *Journal of Hospitality Marketing & Management* 23, 790–814.

Thompson, B. (2004) *Exploratory and Confirmatory Factor Analysis: Understanding Concepts and Applications*, Washington, DC: American Psychological Association.

Triantafillidou, A. & Siomkos, G. (2014). Consumption experience outcomes: Satisfaction, nostalgia intensity, word-of-mouth communication and behavioural intentions. *Journal of Consumer Marketing*, 31, 526–540.

Further reading

Aron, A. & Aron, E. N (2003) *Statistics for Psychology*, Third edition, Upper Saddle River, NJ: Prentice Hall.

Creswell, J. W. & Plano Clark, V. L. (2011) *Designing and Conducting Mixed Methods Research*, Second edition, Thousand Oaks, CA: Sage.

Dimitrov, D. M. (2009) *Quantitative Research in Education: Intermediate and Advanced Methods*, Oceanside, NY: Whittier Publications, Inc.

Fox, J. (2016) *Applied Regression Analysis & Generalized Linear Models*, Third edition, Thousand Oaks, CA: Sage.

Hinkle, D. E., Wiersma, W., & Jurs, S. G. (2003) *Applied Statistics for the Behavioral Sciences*, Fifth edition, Belmont, CA: Cengage Learning.

Kline, R. (2011) *Principles and Practice of Structural Equation Modeling*, Third edition, New York, NY: Guilford.

Merriam, S. B. & Tisdell, E. J. (2016) *Qualitative Research: A Guide to Design and Implementation*, Fourth edition, San Francisco, CA: Jossey-Bass.

Olobatuyi, M. E. (2006) *A User's Guide to Path Analysis*, New York, NY: University Press.

Schumacker, R. E. & Lomax, R. G. (2015) *A Beginner's Guide to Structural Equation Modeling*, Fourth edition, New York, NY: Routledge.

Thompson, B. (2004) *Exploratory and Confirmatory Factor Analysis: Understanding Concepts and Applications*, Washington, DC: American Psychological Association.

5

Qualitative marketing methodology

Rosemarie Neuninger

Introduction

The American Marketing Association formally defines marketing research as "the function that links the consumer, customer, and public to the marketer through information" (American Marketing Association, 2004). Businesses use marketing research to monitor their performance, particularly concerning the 4Ps: price, place, promotion, and products. Marketing research is also conducted in the scholarly community to obtain an academic understanding of the behavior of marketers and consumers. The main aim is to identify how the different elements in the marketing mix influence consumer behavior. A business might study the attitudes, behaviors, media consumption, and lifestyles of existing and potential customers. Based on the information that is gathered, the organization will be able to identify and define market-driven opportunities and problems as well as to develop and assess marketing actions (Hair et al., 2013). To gather information, two distinct types of approaches are generally applied: *qualitative* or *quantitative*. The differences between these two types of research methodologies manifest in the type and method of data collection, type of analysis, and even the underlying research philosophies. This chapter will focus on qualitative hospitality marketing methodologies and their application to hospitality research.

This chapter is organized as followed: first, a brief description is provided of the qualitative and quantitative paradigms, together with a discussion of their main differences. Second, a general introduction is given on the nature of qualitative research. Third, the strengths of qualitative research methodologies are discussed, with a particular focus on applications to the hospitality sector. Fourth, a general overview is provided of the different approaches to qualitative research in hospitality. The chapter closes with future directions.

The underlying paradigms of qualitative and quantitative research

A detailed consideration of the different philosophical approaches that underpin qualitative and quantitative research is beyond the scope of this chapter, as these have been extensively considered in the literature (Denzin and Lincoln, 2005; Keegan, 2009; Hennink et al., 2011;

Slevitch, 2011; Tracy, 2013; Creswell, 2014). This section presents the most meaningful distinctions between the qualitative and quantitative paradigms.

The researcher's paradigms (way of understanding reality, constructing knowledge, and gathering information about the world) differ in their underlying ontology (assumed nature of reality), epistemology (nature of knowledge), methodology (aims of scientific investigation), and methods (research techniques and tools) (Slevitch, 2011). The qualitative paradigm is based on interpretivism, while the quantitative paradigm is based on positivism. The ontological view of interpretivists is that reality and knowledge are "constructed and reproduced through communication, interaction, and practice" (Tracy, 2013: 62). Furthermore, interpretivists believe that reality and the individual who observes it (the researcher) cannot be separated. Positivists, in contrast, believe that there is a single independent reality (Tracy, 2013) which can be discovered, measured, and understood (O'Dwyer and Bernauer, 2013). Interpretivists' epistemology aims to "understand people's lived experience from the perspective of people themselves" where reality is socially constructed and people's experiences cannot be separated from the "social, cultural, historical or personal context" (Hennink et al., 2011: 14–15). Positivists, on the other hand, believe that the researcher can observe facts of reality and objectively measure them with minimal disturbance (Hennink et al., 2011: 15). Finally, as pointed out by Slevitch (2011: 75), "methodologies determine methods." Hence, the researcher's philosophical position will determine the choice of tools to collect data.

Despite long debates about which paradigm is superior, the modern view is that the purpose of both methodologies is to discover new knowledge (Carter and Little, 2007; O'Dwyer and Bernauer, 2013) and that both methodologies are credible (Walle, 1997). Slevitch (2011: 78) suggested that it should be left to the researcher to decide "which paradigm reflects his or her set of personal beliefs", and to let that dictate the researcher's selection of methods. Braun and Clarke (2006: 80), on the contrary, pointed out that "what is important is that the theoretical framework and methods match what the researcher wants to know and that they acknowledge these, and recognize them as decisions". Furthermore, it has been suggested that some research questions are more suitable to qualitative research design, while others are more appropriate for a quantitative design (O'Dwyer and Bernauer, 2013). Overall, it appears that rather than continuing to compare the different paradigms point-by-point, researchers should focus on selecting the most appropriate method that will best address the research question and that will allow them to successfully and efficiently achieve project milestones in a timely manner (Richards and Morse, 2013). In this chapter, we adopt the interpretivist paradigm and emphasize its usefulness in the field of hospitality.

The main characteristics of qualitative research

This section will start with a brief overview of some of the main characteristics of qualitative research and contrast them to quantitative research. Qualitative research has its origin in anthropology (Chacko and Nebel, 1990), sociology, the humanities, and philosophy (Creswell, 2014). Its application started to grow in the early 1960s (Bryman and Burgess, 1999). However, it was not until the late 1970s and in the 1980s that qualitative research started to become very popular in developed countries (Keegan, 2009). It was more recently still that the advantages and importance of qualitative research methods in hospitality-related studies have gained greater prominence (Taylor and Edgar, 1996; Walsh, 2003; Sandiford and Seymour, 2007; Slevitch, 2011). Today, qualitative research is an essential methodology in many disciplines, including hospitality.

Qualitative research applies an inductive reasoning or 'bottom-up' approach. That is to say, the research begins by making specific observations. Following this, the researcher formulates the right research question(s), which is vital to gather the right data (Boeije, 2010). The next step involves selecting a suitable research method and obtaining ethical approval from the responsible human ethics committee. Participants are generally recruited from the community and based on their suitability to contribute to the topic of investigation. Prior to commencing the study, additional written consent from each participant is usually required.

The main aim of qualitative research is to obtain a deep understanding of *why* people behave the way they do, *how* opinions and attitudes are formed, *how* people are affected by the events that go on around them, and to understand *how* and *why* cultures and practices have developed in the way they have. With this approach, the opinions and behaviors of a small proportion of the population are collected in a relatively short amount of time. Different methods, such as in-depth interviews, focus groups, observation, ethnography (Krueger and Casey, 2015), online interviews and online focus groups (Mann and Stewart, 2000), and more recently, netnography (Kozinets, 2010), are used to collect qualitative data. Qualitative research is typically conducted in a natural setting and the moderator uses no pre-determined responses. Qualitative data includes text, image, video or audio data. This approach requires a skilled and experienced researcher to collect and analyze the required data.

Qualitative research methods focus on generating a 'thick description' of context, which requires interpretation. With this approach, researchers describe "social phenomena in terms of the meaning people bring to them" (Boeije, 2010: 11). The data analysis is completed either manually or by using different types of software packages. When completing the analysis manually, typically thematic analysis is applied. Thematic analysis is "a method for identifying, analysing and reporting patterns (themes) within data" (Braun and Clarke, 2006: 79). The data is interpreted by using a coding system to identify themes and patterns and to then discover relationships among the themes and patterns. Braun and Clarke (2006) suggested six key stages for conducting thematic analysis: familiarization with the data, generating initial codes, searching for themes among codes, reviewing themes, defining and naming themes. Themes are "co-constructed between the respondents and researchers' interpretation of reality" (Lugosi et al., 2016: 84). The results give insight and understanding into opinions, values, and behaviors of people in a social context and enable academics and practitioners to develop meaningful theories. Data analysis can also be completed by using computer-aided qualitative data analysis software (CAQDAS) (Tracy, 2013; Silver, 2014). Software packages such as HyperRESEARCH, ATLAS.ti, NVivo, Quirkos, XSight, web QDA, and Saturate are among the most popular programs used in qualitative analysis. These software packages offer the researcher tools (e.g., transcribing, content analysis, coding, and text interpretation) that assist with the analysis.

In contrast to qualitative research, quantitative research is concerned with numerical data, e.g., from customer surveys and questionnaires, where the researcher has pre-determined the response opinions. A deductive reasoning or 'top-down' approach is applied. In this case, the researcher begins with the theory and then narrows the research down to testable hypotheses. The data is collected in a structured way to generate reliable statistical results, which are used to draw conclusions and to make recommendations. The sentiments of a large statistically representative sample of the population are collected and analyzed by statistical modeling, to recommend a final course of action. Lastly, the data is used to support conclusions. The remainder of this chapter concentrates on hospitality research that lends itself predominantly to qualitative rather than quantitative methods.

Strengths of the application of qualitative research methods in hospitality

Qualitative research methods have various strengths from which researchers in the hospitality industry can benefit. The hospitality sector is a broad construct (Ottenbacher et al., 2009), and thus different areas within hospitality may be amenable to different degrees to various qualitative research methods. The first strength is that qualitative research allows researchers to generate exploratory and preliminary insights about phenomena, which might be difficult to achieve with quantitative research (Hair et al., 2013). Qualitative research may also enable researchers to formulate hypotheses for a subsequent quantitative study or to better understand and interpret quantitative data (Chacko and Nebel, 1990). A second strength is that qualitative approaches are suitable to investigate problems that are not clear-cut and that may be difficult to investigate with the common quantitative research methods such as surveys, which struggle to uncover detail beyond short pre-determined statements (Kwortnik Jr, 2003). For instance, managers are able to learn about how different individuals think and feel about a particular topic and to investigate leadership, managerial, and behavioral issues (Chacko and Nebel, 1990). Furthermore, important issues related to hospitality managers, employees and consumers/guests might be investigated in-depth by using a qualitative method. Pullman et al. (2005) pointed out that the best way to understand how consumers feel about a hotel is by analyzing their sources of written comments. Walsh (2003: 69) furthermore suggested that "nothing is more useful to understand phenomena being studied than to be unobtrusively 'hanging out' at a site, interviewing employees and guests, and observing operations".

There is a growing body of literature demonstrating how different research topics within the hospitality industry have been investigated using qualitative research methods. Previous studies explored, for example: work and family issues to understand the turnover problem in hotels (O'Neill, 2012); hotel workers' positive and negative features of their current work experience (Boon, 2007); whether service quality dimensions are pertinent to the hotel industry (Ramsaran-Fowdar, 2007); what guests consider to be a hotel's design highlights and failures (Pullman and Robson, 2007); how work and leisure operate as allies (Boon, 2006); and the relationship with customer loyalty in the hotel industry (Bowen and Chen, 2001). The complexity and open-ended nature of these research topics dictated that they could be investigated best using qualitative research techniques.

The use of the different qualitative research methods in hospitality

In this section, the most common qualitative research methods that have been applied to investigate hospitality related topics are reviewed. The three most common methods are discussed: (1) in-depth interviews, (2) focus groups, and (3) ethnography. Data collection methods are presented in such a form that the details of each method and their limitations are outlined, along with examples highlighting their unique benefits to different areas of the hospitality industry. Different studies have been selected to illustrate the way in which the data has been collected and analyzed.

In-depth interviews

In-depth interviews are used to investigate topics that require an in-depth and detailed understanding of individuals' attitudes, perceptions, and behaviors. This method is particularly useful for investigating topics that are too complex for a group discussion. In-depth interviews involve a one-to-one and face-to-face interaction between the interviewer (who asks the questions) and the interviewee (who answers the questions), and the conversation is audio/video-recorded (Johnson and Rowlands, 2012). In some cases, phone or Internet interviewing might be applied (Glanz et al., 2007). The interview questions can be either structured, semi-structured or unstructured (Bryman and Burgess, 1999). In each case, before the interview takes place the researcher needs to carefully plan the questions. Additionally, it is important that the participant doesn't simply answer 'yes' or 'no' and that a dialogue is established. Each interview can take from up to 30 minutes to more than an hour. The interview begins with an 'icebreaker' question and then moves on to the relevant questions. For the interview to be successful, it is not only important to have an experienced interviewer but also to select carefully the participants. Participants should be knowledgeable about the topic that is being investigated so that they can contribute to the study. When ending the interview the participant is usually rewarded with some form of incentive (e.g., cash or vouchers) for taking part in the study. After having completed all the interviews, the researcher begins with the data analysis by listening to each of the audio recordings and transcribing them. The analysis will proceed according to the qualitative analysis discussed earlier in this chapter. For a full description of the interview methods and best practices, see Gubrium et al. (2012).

Previous studies in the hospitality industry have applied in-depth interviews to understand how hospitality operators understand service (Crawford, 2013); to investigate present and future managers' perspectives about the hospitality industry (Pizam and Shani, 2009); to investigate how chefs and restaurateurs perceive the Michelin star system in Europe (Johnson et al., 2005); to understand the views of executives on developing healthier menu options in restaurants (Glanz et al., 2007); and to understand consumers' motivations for hospitality purchases (Kwortnik Jr, 2003). The application of in-depth interviews was ideal for investigating these topics. For instance, Johnson et al. (2005) used semi-structured in-depth interviews with chefs at Michelin-starred restaurants to identify the perceived factors contributing to their success, as well as the challenges they faced despite their rating success. The authors found semi-structured interviews to be the most appropriate method for a number of reasons. Due to the individual specialized nature of each restaurant, and the stature of the chefs, routine questionnaires might have been hard to formulate and were not likely to gain an enthusiastic response. The authors felt they needed to gain the trust of their subjects, particularly when discussing sensitive business information. Structured interviews also gave the researchers the opportunity to ask follow-up questions and to gain deep insights into the subjects. More recently, Lugosi et al. (2016) investigated the experiences of parents and carers whose children were consumers within the hospitality sector. The researchers found semi-structured interviews suitable for their work, as they allowed the identification of themes, which did not fit within a rigid pre-determined framework. Furthermore, they did not need to strictly categorize their subjects, e.g., by sex or ethnic origin, but found that their subjects' identities intersected with different issues to different degrees.

Limitations of in-depth interviews

In-depth interviews have various limitations. Some of these limitations are common to all qualitative methods. For example, in-depth interviews are costly and they require an experienced interviewer. Another disadvantage is that the results might not be reliable and generalizable to the population. Finally, data interpretation is conducted by the researcher and is very subjective, which can bias the results of the study.

Other limitations are unique to the interview method. Participants may feel intimidated or trapped when sitting alone with the interviewer. In-depth interviews typically take a long time and the participant may get exhausted and run out of ideas. The researcher might have to conduct a large number of interviews to obtain credibility.

Focus groups

The application of focus groups has been discussed in the literature extensively (Fern, 2001; Lindlof and Taylor, 2011; Cater and Low, 2012; Krueger and Casey, 2015). A focus group is conducted with a group of people to capture in-depth insights. Participants are selected and recruited carefully, as they should share homogeneous characteristics related to the topic that is being investigated. The successful application of this research method is highly dependent on the interaction of the participants as well as the interaction with the facilitator (Cater and Low, 2012). The facilitator must create a relaxed and open environment where participants can feel comfortable to interactively and spontaneously talk about their opinions, beliefs, attitudes, and perceptions in regard to an issue, idea, product or service. Their talk demonstrates "a kind of 'chaining' or 'cascading' effect in which each person's turn of the conversation links to, or tumbles out of, the topics and expressions that came before it" (Lindlof and Taylor, 2011: 183). This group effect reveals insightful information that cannot be obtained when conducting one-to-one interviews. Each session typically lasts for approximately one and a half hours and, as with interviews, participants may be given an incentive for participating in the study. Researchers generally conduct three to four focus-group sessions with similar types of participants (Krueger and Casey, 2015). During each session, a skilled facilitator leads each session using a set of pre-prepared open-ended questions and takes notes. Each focus group is video- and audio-recorded and the facilitator must take notes during each session. The standard group discussion comprises five to eight people, but the size may vary from as few as four to as many as 12 (Krueger and Casey, 2015). However, Krueger and Casey (2015) recommend not conducting focus groups with more than ten people as these are difficult to control and will also limit people expressing their opinions. After the discussions, the researcher analyzes each of the groups to identify patterns and themes. If new information is still generated after conducting the third or fourth focus groups, then it is recommended to continue conducting further groups until saturation is reached, i.e., when further discussion produces no more useful information (Krueger and Casey, 2015). The data analysis should proceed as discussed earlier in this chapter.

The focus-group method has been applied in a number of hospitality-related topics: for example, to investigate consumers' perceptions of wine awards (Neuninger et al., 2017); the attitudes of hospitality students about working in hospitality (O'Neill, 2012); and adolescents' awareness and use of menu labels in restaurants (Evans et al., 2016). Focus groups are very suitable for generating insights from an interactive group discussion. For example, in the study by Neuninger et al. (2017), the authors used four focus groups to explore an under-investigated topic. By using this method, the researchers were able to obtain more insights into wine consumers' perceptions, feelings, and thinking than would be obtained from quantitative research methods such as surveys or questionnaires. Also, the method gathered a wider range of viewpoints than is possible with interviews or ethnographic methods. Their findings showed that wine awards might have unexpected effects on consumers, the opposite to those the retailers intended. The study on menus (Evans et al., 2016) investigated the use of menu labels to improve healthy eating by adolescents using five focus groups. The authors identified the attributes used by the adolescents to make purchase decisions and gathered suggestions for replacing unfamiliar information, e.g., caloric intake, with familiar information, e.g., exercise equivalents. This study illustrates the benefit of using focus groups in hospitality settings; suggestions and insights about what concepts the target market does and does not respond to can be gained even if the researcher has no prior indication of what these might be. Thus, these examples show that focus groups are a suitable research method to investigate unexplored topics and for gathering information that might be otherwise fairly difficult to obtain.

Limitations of focus groups

In addition to the general limitations of qualitative research, focus groups have some extra limitations. First, focus groups are a group discussion and are highly dependent on participant turnout and their sharing of thoughts. Also, some participants may feel embarrassed or shy about expressing their real opinions in front of others. Therefore, a highly skilled moderator is required to ensure that that the discussion can occur without a dominant participant taking over and that the discussion does not go off-track. A third disadvantage is that focus groups collect only the opinions of a group and will therefore not obtain the in-depth responses of single individuals as would be obtained with in-depth interviews. In addition, each focus-group session is limited by time, during which only a limited amount of questions can be answered.

Ethnography

Ethnography has its roots in the disciplines of anthropology and sociology (Carson et al., 2001). One of the main characteristics of ethnographic methods is that the ethnographer is required to live closely beside and among cultures to collect 'rich' data and to then develop 'thick description' (Elliott and Jankel-Elliott, 2003). Anthropologist Bronislaw Malinowski (1888–1942) established the participant observation method with his research conducted in the Trobriand Island in the South Pacific (Malinowski, 2014). The main aim of ethnographic work is to generate an in-depth understanding of the "shared patterns of behaviors, language, and actions of an intact cultural group in a natural setting over a prolonged period of time" (Creswell, 2014: 14) and to tell a "credible, rigorous, and authentic story" (Fetterman, 2010: 1). According to Grbich (2013: 41), ethnography is suitable when the researcher is interested in investigating a culture (a group of people typically with common elements of location/language/purpose) and its operations, rituals, and belief systems. Furthermore, one of the major strengths of conducting ethnographic work is that the culture that is studied can be described in detail in terms of their belief systems, values, behaviors, and interconnections. Rather than testing a pre-formed hypothesis, ethnographic research usually uses "grounded theory" (Grbich, 2013: 41). Grounded theory consists of field research (in particular, observations as they occur in real life) and is applied when there is little or poor knowledge of an area. It is used to generate theories that are based on observations. Ethnographic research draws upon a variety of research techniques including participant observation, in-depth interviews (structured and unstructured), questionnaires, focus groups, mapping, photography, and video documentation (Adams, 2012). According to Adams (2012), ethnographic work entails conducting long-term fieldwork (six months to two years or more), which is completed once sufficient, convincing, and significant information has been collected. Ethnography is a process which requires the researcher to build a sense of 'intimacy' and 'trust' with the participants (Fetterman, 2010). In ethnographic research, researchers create a 'deep understanding' of the research topic through adopting *emic* and *etic* perspectives. Tracy (2013: 35–36) describes *emic* as "a perspective in which behavior is described from the actor's point of view" while *etic* is "a perspective in which behavior is described according to externally derived, non-culture specific criteria." However, this type of qualitative research method appears to be applied less in hospitality than in other areas (Lugosi, 2009).

Despite the limited presence of ethnographic research in hospitality management, some studies have attempted to apply this research method to understand and to interpret human behavior in the hospitality environment. Such studies have typically aimed at understanding the culture within restaurants and placing restaurants within the wider culture (Whyte, 1948; Marshall, 1986; Cheang, 2002; Erickson, 2004; Fonseca, 2005; Seymour and Sandiford, 2005; Sandiford and Seymour, 2007; Spradley and Mann, 2008). The study by Seymour and Sandiford (2005) used participant observation and semi-structured interviews over a specific period of time. One of the authors worked as a full-time staff member at the restaurant being studied while conducting the ethnographic fieldwork. This study shows the usefulness of qualitative research methods to obtain insights into how employees think and feel about the work of emotion management. Such an approach allows gradual data accumulation rather than a single 'snapshot' that would arise from the application of other research methods such as surveys or experiments. In another study by Sandiford and Seymour (2007), the authors also applied ethnographic research. One of the authors investigated customer and worker interactions in the restaurant where she worked. She conducted participant observation, took field notes, interviewed customers and managers, surveyed customers and analyzed comment cards, analysed quality audit reports, and compared her findings with other restaurants. The application of the ethnographic approach enabled the researchers to place the results in their correct cultural context.

Limitations of ethnography

There are various limitations involved in conducting ethnographic research. First, compared to any other qualitative research methods, ethnographic research is tremendously time-consuming. The fieldwork is lengthy, as the researcher is required to be part of the culture or group for the duration of the fieldwork. Another limitation is that it is often difficult to gain access to the group that is to be investigated. More than for other methods, the results are subjective and open to misinterpretation and observer bias. Due to the long time-scale, organizing the data and the results in a coherent way is often difficult. Lastly, it is difficult to replicate ethnographic studies for the purpose of validation.

Future directions for the application of qualitative research in hospitality

Increasingly, hospitality businesses are developing an online presence using social media (e.g., Facebook, Twitter, Instagram) and review sites (e.g., TripAdvisor and Google) to increase their reputation. People who participate in these online communities interact with each other primarily via the Internet for multiple reasons (e.g., to make friendships, play online games, to make complaints, to give advice, and to make decisions based on the recommendations of others). They frequently use platforms such as Facebook for 'check-ins' and to provide reviews of hospitality businesses. Reviews on Facebook take the form of a 'star' rating and users are also able to provide a written review and to express their sentiment. This feature can be beneficial for a brand, provided the reviews are positive, as these reviews are available on the Internet to a multitude of people and institutions. However, when providing these ratings and writing feedback, consumers are able to express both positive and negative emotions. According to Erickson (2004), an individual's sharing of negative emotions in the virtual world, as a consequence of bad experiences, can potentially be damaging for an organization. Typically, individuals complain about poor-quality products and services. Potential customers might read such comments and be put off by this negative information. Hence, companies would be wise to monitor on a regular basis what has been said about their product, services, and brand. In doing so, these companies need to pay particular attention to the emotional tone of social media discussions (Jalonen, 2014). This can be achieved by both quantitative and qualitative methods.

Netnography (online ethnography) is an innovative qualitative approach that originated as a result of the increased online development of social networking technologies (netware) (Mkono, 2013). Kozinets (1997: 470) defines netnography "as a written account of on-line cyberculture, informed by the methods of cultural anthropology. Cyberculture refers to a culture that is mediated by contemporary computerized communications technology (i.e., 'the Internet')." This qualitative method was developed in marketing and consumer research, and is used to conduct online fieldwork to study cultures and communities. Netnography has been found to be useful to gain deep insights (Mkono, 2013). The application of this method could be particularly useful for the hospitality industry to monitor their organizations, to develop better strategies, and to understand their consumers and employees, as well as for scholars to study the hospitality industry within the broader online culture.

In summary, there is a growing use of qualitative methods for understanding consumers' and employees' experiences in the hospitality industry. Qualitative methods can offer deeper insights than quantitative data. Thus, the hospitality industry and academics can greatly benefit from the increased use of qualitative research methods, in particular, online methods and social media monitoring. They will allow academics to draw in-depth conclusions about hospitality and its place in society. Businesses, on the other hand, will be able to identify and to more easily address problems and discontent among employees and potential customers.

References

Adams, M. A. 2012. Ethnographic methods. *In:* Dwyer, L., Gill, A. & Seetaram, N. (eds.) *Handbook of research methods in tourism: Quantitative and qualitative approaches.* Cheltenham, UK; Northampton, Massachusetts. Edward Elgar Publishing.

American Marketing Association. (2004). *Marketing research* [Online]. Available at: www.ama.org/AboutAMA/Pages/Definition-of-Marketing.aspx [Accessed June 14, 2016].

Boeije, H. 2010. *Analysis in qualitative research.* London. Sage Publications.

Boon, B. 2006. When leisure and work are allies: The case of skiers and tourist resort hotels. *Career Development International,* 11, 594–608.

Boon, B. 2007. Working within the front-of-house/back-of-house boundary: Room attendants in the hotel guest room space. *Journal of Management & Organization,* 13, 160–174.

Bowen, J. T. & Chen, S.-L. 2001. The relationship between customer loyalty and customer satisfaction. *International Journal of Contemporary Hospitality Management,* 13, 213–217.

Braun, V. & Clarke, V. 2006. Using thematic analysis in psychology. *Qualitative Research in Psychology,* 3, 77–101.

Bryman, A. & Burgess, R. G. 1999. *Qualitative research.* London; Thousand Oaks, California. Sage Publications.

Carson, D., Gilmore, A., Perry, C. & Gronhaug, K. 2001. *Qualitative marketing research.* London; Thousand Oaks, California; New Delhi. Sage Publications.

Carter, S. M. & Little, M. 2007. Justifying knowledge, justifying method, taking action: Epistemologies, methodologies, and methods in qualitative research. *Qualitative Health Research,* 17, 1316–1328.

Cater, C. & Low, T. 2012. Focus groups. *In:* Dwyer, L., Gill, A. & Seetaram, N. (eds.) *Handbook of research methods in tourism: Quantitative and qualitative approaches.* Cheltenham, UK; Northampton, Massachusetts. Edward Elgar Publishing.

Chacko, H. E. & Nebel, E. C. 1990. Qualitative research: Its time has come. *Journal of Hospitality & Tourism Research,* 14, 383–391.

Cheang, M. 2002. Older adults' frequent visits to a fast-food restaurant: Nonobligatory social interaction and the significance of play in a "third place". *Journal of Aging Studies,* 16, 303–321.

Crawford, A. 2013. Hospitality operators' understanding of service: A qualitative approach. *International Journal of Contemporary Hospitality Management,* 25, 65–81.

Creswell, J. W. 2014. *Research design: Qualitative, quantitative, and mixed methods approaches.* Thousand Oaks, California. Sage Publications.

Denzin, N. K. & Lincoln, Y. S. 2005. *The Sage handbook of qualitative research.* Thousand Oaks, California. Sage Publications.

Elliott, R. & Jankel-Elliott, N. 2003. Using ethnography in strategic consumer research. *Qualitative Market Research: An International Journal*, 6, 215–223.

Erickson, K. 2004. To invest or detach? Coping strategies and workplace culture in service work. *Symbolic Interaction*, 27, 549–572.

Evans, A. E., Weiss, S. R., Meath, K. J., Chow, S., Vandewater, E. A. & Ness, R. B. 2016. Adolescents' awareness and use of menu labels in eating establishments: Results from a focus group study. *Public Health Nutrition*, 19, 830–840.

Fern, E. F. 2001. *Advanced focus group research*. Thousand Oaks, California; London; New Delhi. Sage Publications.

Fetterman, D. M. 2010. *Ethnography: Step-by-step*. Los Angeles, California. Sage Publications.

Fonseca, V. 2005. Nuevo Latino: Rebranding Latin American cuisine. *Consumption, Markets and Culture*, 8, 95–130.

Glanz, K., Resnicow, K., Seymour, J., Hoy, K., Stewart, H., Lyons, M. & Goldberg, J. 2007. How major restaurant chains plan their menus: The role of profit, demand, and health. *American Journal of Preventive Medicine*, 32, 383–388.

Grbich, C. 2013. *Qualitative data analysis: An introduction*. London; Thousand Oaks, California. Sage Publications.

Gubrium, J. F., Holstein, J. A., Marvasti, A. B. & McKinney, K. D. 2012. *The SAGE handbook of interview research: The complexity of the craft*. 2nd ed. Thousand Oaks, California. Sage Publications.

Hair, J. J. F, Wolfinbarger, M., Bush, R. & Ortinau, D. 2013. *Essentials of marketing research*. New York. McGraw-Hill.

Hennink, M. M., Bailey, A. & Hutter, I. 2011. *Qualitative research methods*, London; Thousand Oaks, California. Sage Publications.

Jalonen, H. 2014. Negative emotions in social media as a managerial challenge. *European Conference on Management, Leadership & Governance*, 2014. Academic Conferences International Limited. Klagenfurt, Austria, 128–135.

Johnson, C., Surlemont, B., Nicod, P. & Revaz, F. 2005. Behind the stars: A concise typology of Michelin restaurants in Europe. *Cornell Hotel and Restaurant Administration Quarterly*, 46, 170–187.

Johnson, J. M. & Rowlands, T. 2012. The interpersonal dynamics of in-depth interviewing. *In:* Gubrium, J. F., Holstein, J. A., Marvasti, A. B. & McKinney, K. D. (eds.) *The Sage handbook of interview research: The complexity of the craft*. 2nd ed. London; New Delhi; Singapore. Sage Publications.

Keegan, S. 2009. *Qualitative research: Good decision making through understanding people, cultures and markets*. London. Kogan Page Publishers.

Kozinets, R. V. 1997. "I want to believe": A netnography of the X-Philes' subculture of consumption. *Advances in Consumer Research*, 24, 470–475.

Kozinets, R. V. 2010. *Netnography: Doing ethnographic research online*. Los Angeles, California; London. Sage Publications.

Krueger, R. & Casey, M. A. 2015. *Focus groups: A practical guide for applied research*. New Delhi; Singapore. Sage Publications.

Kwortnik Jr, R. J. 2003. Clarifying "fuzzy" hospitality-management problems with depth interviews and qualitative analysis. *Cornell Hospitality Quarterly*, 44, 117–129.

Lindlof, T. R. & Taylor, B. C. 2011. *Qualitative communication research methods*. Thousand Oaks, CA. Sage Publications.

Lugosi, P. 2009. Ethnography, ethnographers and hospitality research: Communities, tensions and affiliations. *Tourism and Hospitality Planning & Development*, 6, 95–107.

Lugosi, P., Robinson, R. N., Golubovskaya, M. & Foley, L. 2016. The hospitality consumption experiences of parents and carers with children: A qualitative study of foodservice settings. *International Journal of Hospitality Management*, 54, 84–94.

Malinowski, B. 2014. *Argonauts of the Western Pacific: An account of native enterprise and adventure in the archipelagos of Melanesian New Guinea*. Abingdon, Oxon; New York. Routledge.

Mann, C. & Stewart, F. 2000. *Internet communication and qualitative research: A handbook for researching online*. London. Sage Publications.

Marshall, G. 1986. The workplace culture of a licensed restaurant. *Theory, Culture & Society*, 3, 33–47.

Mkono, M. 2013. Using net-based ethnography (netnography) to understand the staging and marketing of "authentic African" dining experiences to tourists at Victoria Falls. *Journal of Hospitality & Tourism Research*, 37, 184–198.

Neuninger, R., Mather, D. & Duncan, T. 2017. Consumer's scepticism of wine awards: A study of consumers' use of wine awards. *Journal of Retailing and Consumer Services*, 35, 98–105.

O'Dwyer, L. & Bernauer, J. 2013. *Quantitative research for the qualitative researcher*. Los Angeles. Sage Publications.

O'Neill, J.W. 2012. Using focus groups as a tool to develop a hospitality work-life research study. *International Journal of Contemporary Hospitality Management*, 24, 873–885.

Ottenbacher, M., Harrington, R. & Parsa, H. 2009. Defining the hospitality discipline: A discussion of pedagogical and research implications. *Journal of Hospitality & Tourism Research*, 33, 263–283.

Pizam, A. & Shani, A. 2009. The nature of the hospitality industry: Present and future managers' perspectives. *Anatolia*, 20, 134–150.

Pullman, M., McGuire, K. & Cleveland, C. 2005. Let me count the words: Quantifying open-ended interactions with guests. *Cornell Hotel and Restaurant Administration Quarterly*, 46, 323–343.

Pullman, M. & Robson, S. 2007. Visual methods: Using photographs to capture customers' experience with design. *Cornell Hotel and Restaurant Administration Quarterly*, 48, 121–144.

Ramsaran-Fowdar, R. R. 2007. Developing a service quality questionnaire for the hotel industry in Mauritius. *Journal of Vacation Marketing*, 13, 19–27.

Richards, L. & Morse, J. 2013. *Readme first for a user's guide to qualitative methods*. Thousand Oaks, California. Sage Publications.

Sandiford, P. J. & Seymour, D. 2007. A discussion of qualitative data analysis in hospitality research with examples from an ethnography of English public houses. *International Journal of Hospitality Management*, 26, 724–742.

Seymour, D. & Sandiford, P. 2005. Learning emotion rules in service organizations: Socialization and training in the UK public-house sector. *Work, Employment & Society*, 19, 547–564.

Silver, C. 2014. *Using software in qualitative research: A step-by-step guide*. London. Sage Publications.

Slevitch, L. 2011. Qualitative and quantitative methodologies compared: Ontological and epistemological perspectives. *Journal of Quality Assurance in Hospitality & Tourism*, 12, 73–81.

Spradley, J. P. & Mann, B. E. 2008. *The cocktail waitress: Woman's work in a man's world*. Long Grove, Illinois. Waveland Press.

Taylor, S. & Edgar, D. 1996. Hospitality research: The emperor's new clothes? *International Journal of Hospitality Management*, 15, 211–227.

Tracy, S. J. 2013. *Qualitative research methods: Collecting evidence, crafting analysis, communicating impact*. Chichester, West Sussex, UK. Wiley-Blackwell.

Walle, A. H. 1997. Quantitative versus qualitative tourism research. *Annals of Tourism Research*, 24, 524–536.

Walsh, K. 2003. Qualitative research: Advancing the science and practice of hospitality. *Cornell Hospitality Quarterly*, 44, 66.

Whyte, W. F. 1948. *Human relations in the restaurant industry*. New York. McGraw-Hill.

Further reading

Altinay, L., Paraskevas, A., & Jang, S. 2016. *Planning research in hospitality and tourism*. 2nd ed. Abingdon, Oxon; New York. Routledge. This book provides a concise and clear approach to planning a research project in hospitality and tourism.

Belk, R. W. 2007. *Handbook of qualitative research methods in marketing*. Cheltenham. Edward Elgar Publishing. This book discusses qualitative research methods in marketing.

Berg, B. L. 2012. *Qualitative research methods for the social sciences*. 8th ed. Boston. Pearson. This book is a guide to data collection, organization, and analysis strategies in the social sciences.

Corti, L. 2014. *Managing and sharing research data: A guide to good practice*. Los Angeles. Sage Publications. This book is about managing and sharing research data. It includes case studies and practical activities.

Denzin, N. K. & Lincoln, Y. S. 2013. *The landscape of qualitative research*. 4th ed. Thousand Oaks, California. Sage Publications. In this book a detailed description of the different scientific paradigms underlying qualitative research for advanced readers is presented.

Pan, B., MacLaurin, T. & Crotts, J. C. 2007. Travel blogs and the implications for destination marketing. *Journal of Travel Research*, 46(1), 35–45. This reading discusses travel blogs.

Phillimore, J. & Goodson, L. 2004. *Qualitative research in tourism: Ontologies, epistemologies and methodologies* (Vol. 14). London. Routledge. This book discusses the philosophies underpinning qualitative research and how these can be used.

Salmons, J. 2015. *Qualitative online interviews: Strategies, design, and skills.* 2nd ed. Thousand Oaks, California. Sage Publications. This book describes in detail online interviews.

Schreier, M. 2012. *Qualitative content analysis in practice.* London; Thousand Oaks, California. Sage Publications. This reading provides a step-by-step discussion of content analysis.

Urquhart, C. 2012. *Grounded theory for qualitative research: A practical guide.* London. Sage Publications. This book is for first-time researchers discussing grounded theory.

6

Quantitative marketing methodology and methods

Lisa Slevitch

Quantitative marketing methodology and methods

Terms such as *methodology* and *methods* are quite commonly used interchangeably in spite of the fact that these two terms have very distinct meanings. Methodologies represent philosophical positions; methods exemplify research tools or techniques appropriate within that specific methodological orientation (Slevitch 2011). As Guba and Lincoln (1994) state, any scientific inquiry is grounded in certain *ontology* (assumptions concerning the nature of reality) and *epistemology* (assumptions of what is knowledge), which determine a certain *methodology* (the principles regulating scientific investigation) as well as *research methods* (techniques or tools regarding the practical implementation of the study). The theory of science postulates that *what we believe about reality determines what we take as legitimate knowledge and how we acquire it, which in return, defines our principles of scientific investigation, which sequentially define the research techniques we apply* (Guba & Lincoln 1994, p. 6).

Quantitative methodology comes from *positivism*, characterized by a realist orientation and grounded in the assumptions that objective reality exists independent of human perception and can be described as it really is (Sale et al. 2002). Quantitative epistemology states that the investigator and the investigated are independent entities and postulates that facts can be separated from values (Slevitch 2011). Consequently, researchers can achieve truth to the extent that their work corresponds to how things really are, and achieve validity through correspondence between the data and the independently existing reality that the data reflects (Guba & Lincoln 1994).

Therefore, scientific phenomena can be investigated in terms of generalizable causal effects that permit prediction, and the goal of scientific inquiry should be to measure and analyze causal relationships among variables with a purpose of generalization (Denzin & Lincoln 1994). Quantitative methodology can be characterized as *experimental* or *manipulative* as it purports that questions and hypotheses are proposed, then tested and confirmed while preventing outcomes from being inappropriately influenced (Guba & Lincoln 1994; Slevitch 2011).

Given that objectivity and generalization are the main goals, sample size is critical in quantitative methodology as a large sample ensures better representativeness and generalizability of findings. Quantitative methodology necessitates methods grounded in statistical analysis, inferential statistics, hypothesis testing, mathematical analysis, experimental and quasi-experimental design randomization, blinding, structured protocols, and questionnaires with a limited range of predetermined responses (Lee 1999).

Quantitative research methods are usually associated with the following activities:

- Development of theories, models, and hypotheses
- Designing measurement instruments (i.e. scales)
- Experimental control and manipulation of variables
- Collection of empirical data
- Modeling and analysis of data

In quantitative research, causal relationships are typically examined by manipulating variables hypothesized to influence the phenomena in question while controlling other variables relevant to the experimental outcomes. A fundamental principle in quantitative research is that correlation does not imply causation, although some academics, i.e. Granger (1969), suggest that a series of correlations can imply a degree of causality as a spurious relationship may exist for variables between which some covariance is found. Associations among variables can be examined among combinations of continuous and categorical variables using statistical methods.

According to Yoo et al. (2011) and Morosan et al. (2014), hospitality marketing research mostly utilizes the following quantitative methods: descriptive data analysis, general significance of difference tests, causal modeling techniques, multivariate statistical methods, and other statistical methods, such as correspondence analysis, multi dimensional scaling, and time series analysis. Hospitality marketing is no exception from general marketing in terms of rules for selecting the appropriate method of analysis. Typically, two major factors should be considered: (1) whether the variables in question are dependent or interdependent and, (2), whether the data are metric, measured by interval or ratio scales, or non-metric, measured by ordinal scales. The dependent variables are those which can be explained or predicted by other variables, while interdependent variables are those which cannot be explained uniquely by each other (Baker 2003). Most hospitality marketing variables tend to be interdependent, i.e. marketing mix variables such as price, promotion, distribution, and product are all connected to each other.

Since hospitality marketing research often involves either dependent or interdependent variables, the major groups of methods can be divided into the following categories:

1. *General significance of differences tests.* A group of tests that allows differences to be examined between a certain sample result and some expected population value, or two or more sample results.
2. *Multivariate techniques.* Various techniques examining the relationships and patterns that stem from interaction and interdependence among main variables at the same time.
3. *Regression and forecasting techniques.* Regression assesses the relationships among a set of variables in question. Forecasting methods are used to predict sales, demand, etc.
4. *Causal modeling.* Includes two main analytical models for testing causal hypotheses: path analysis and Structural Equation Modeling (SEM). Path analysis assumes perfect measurement of the observed variables and models the structural relationships between the variables. SEM assesses both measurement and the causal relationships, i.e. structural components of a system.
5. *Simulation techniques.* Often used in situations requiring complex modeling which is not amenable to analytical solutions. The importance of the simulation technique in marketing is that it offers a form of laboratory experimentation by permitting the researcher to change selected individual variables in turn while holding all the others constant.

6. *Artificial intelligence techniques.* There are two main models in this set of techniques: Expert System – involving user intervention to accommodate changes within the model, and Neural Network, a tool that is more flexible than Expert System tool, allowing 'retraining' via addition of new input and output data.

Although the sets of methods above do not include the entirety of the quantitative methods used in hospitality marketing research, they represent the most frequently used techniques and can be characterized as the most relevant and appropriate to cope with most hospitality marketing problems in terms of research and analysis.

General significance of differences tests

Tests for statistical significance of differences are used to determine the probability that what we think is a relationship between variables is a random occurrence. They also tell us the probability of making an error if we assume that the relationship exists. The most common of such tests are *chi-square goodness-of-fit test, Kolmogorov-Smirnov test* (both non-parametric), and *t-tests* and *z-tests* (parametric). For nominal data, when a variable falls into two or more categories and the aim is to determine whether the observed number of cases in each cell corresponds to the expected number, chi-square goodness-of-fit is used as a test for statistical significance (Churchill & Iacobucci 2009). Kolmogorov-Smirnov test is the ordinal counterpart to the chi-square goodness-of-fit test.

T-tests are parametric tests for statistical significance with interval and ratio data. T-tests can be used in several different types of statistical analysis:

- to examine whether there are differences between two groups on the same variable (based on the mean value of that variable for each group);
- to determine whether a group's mean value is greater or less than some standard;
- to test whether the same group has different mean scores on different variables.

T-test has a distribution that approaches the normal distribution, particularly if the sample size is greater than 30 (Churchill & Iacobucci 2009). The normal curve is distributed about a mean of zero, with a standard deviation of one. A t-score can fall along the normal curve either plus or minus some standard deviation units from the mean. To achieve statistical significance, the t-score must fall far from the mean and be quite different from the value of the mean of the distribution, showing only a low probability of occurring randomly if there is no relationship between the variables in question.

When testing a hypothesis about two means, the t-test should be used when the variance is unknown and the z-test should be applied if the variance is known. One of the common issues with t-tests is that it is possible to have differences that are small but statistically significant due to a very large sample size. In a similar sample of a smaller size, the differences would not be enough to be statistically significant.

When more than two means are compared, *analysis of variance* (ANOVA) is frequently applied (Baker & Hart 2008). The ANOVA approach is based on a procedure that uses variances to determine whether the means are different. The procedure entails comparing the variance between group means versus the variance within groups as a way of determining whether the groups are all part of one larger population or separate populations with different characteristics. ANOVA assesses the importance of one or more factors by comparing the response variable means at the different factor levels. ANOVA requires data from approximately normally distributed populations with equal variances between factor levels. However, ANOVA procedures work quite well even if the normality assumption has been violated, unless one or more of the distributions are highly skewed, or if the variances are quite different. In such cases, transformations of the original dataset are recommended to correct these violations (Churchill & Iacobucci 2009). As for applications in hospitality marketing research, significance of differences tests are often used in experimental and quasi-experimental studies as well as research involving hypotheses testing. For examples see Chan (2013), Kim et al. (2013), or Zheng et al. (2016).

Multivariate methods

Multivariate methods are predominant techniques in hospitality marketing (Yoo et al. 2011; Morosan et al. 2014). One of the major reasons for such popularity is the ability to analyze complex interrelated or interdependent data. There are six main multivariate methods used in hospitality marketing research: factor analysis; cluster analysis; latent analysis; multidimensional scaling; conjoint analysis; and correspondence analysis.

Factor analysis

Factor analysis is a popular technique which allows for the reducing of a large number of variables into a few interpretable constructs or dimensions (Churchill & Iacobucci 2009). The method examines and distinguishes patterns in the data with the view to lessening data into factors, which can be very helpful for analyzing data from smaller samples or making decisions about segmentation, behavioral patterns, product or service attributes, dimensions of image, etc. The main hurdles of factor analysis are determining how many factors to extract and the labeling of the emerging factors. An example of factor analysis application in hospitality research can be found in Dotson and Clark (2004) or Beldona et al. (2012).

Cluster analysis

Cluster analysis refers to techniques that discern clusters in a particular data set. Cluster analysis is an exploratory tool which aims at sorting different items into groups in a way that the degree of association between two items in the same cluster is maximal (high homogeneity) and is minimal for items in different clusters (high heterogeneity). Geometrically, the points within a cluster should be close together, while different clusters should be far apart (Baker 2003).

Cluster analysis is similar to factor analysis in the sense that both are data reduction techniques and can present output data in a graphical multidimensional format to make it easier to understand and analyze. Cluster analysis is often used for segmentation or for grouping products, brands, customers, cities, etc. One of the main limitations of cluster analysis is that it does not have any goodness-of-fit measures or tests of significance, and often various clustering methods produce dissimilar results. Examples of how cluster analysis can be applied in hospitality settings can be found in Ruiz-Molina et al. (2013) and Denizci Guillet et al. (2015).

Latent analysis

Latent analysis is a technique relatively similar to factor analysis. It can be used as a tool to investigate causal systems involving both manifest variables and latent factors with discrete components (Baker & Hart 2008). Similar to factor analysis, latent analysis aims to extract important factors and show how variables relate with these factors. Additionally, latent analysis can classify respondents into typologies and in that way it is analogous to cluster analysis. The main advantage of latent analysis is that it could be used for examining causal models involving latent variables.

Latent analysis is appropriate for the examination of data with discrete components because it attempts to explain the observed association between the manifest variables by introducing one or more other variables. The main proposition of latent analysis is that the observed association between two or more manifest categorical variables is due to the mixing of heterogeneous groups. In this sense, latent analysis can be viewed as a data 'unmixing' procedure analogous to the factor-analytic model. Latent analysis has been primarily applied for segmentation research, consumer behavior analysis, and market structure analysis. See Díaz and Koutra (2013) for more details.

Multidimensional scaling

Multidimensional scaling is a technique that is often considered an alternative to factor analysis because it can display the structure of distance-like data as a geometrical picture. It enables easy comprehension of the results because the relationships among the variables are visualized and can be assessed (Baker 2003). Multidimensional scaling is mainly concerned with the representation of differences or similarities among data items. Generally, multidimensional scaling aims at detecting underlying dimensions that enable explaining observed similarities or dissimilarities as distances between the investigated items. In factor analysis, the similarities between items (variables) are stated in the correlation matrix. In multidimensional scaling, analysis is based on the similarity or dissimilarity matrix, in addition to correlation matrices.

The advantage of multidimensional scaling relative to factor or cluster analyzes is its capability to show the complete structure of all variables in question, even from attitudinal (non-metric) data. Multidimensional scaling has been used for such hospitality marketing problems as determining marketing mix, sales and market share, market segmentation, brand positioning, etc. Application of this method in hospitality research can be found in Jackson and Singh (2015) and Wong and Wu (2013).

Conjoint analysis

Conjoint analysis is a technique concerned with the joint effects of two or more independent variables on the ordering of a dependent variable (Baker 2003). Similar to multidimensional scaling, conjoint analysis is often used when psychological judgments, i.e. customer preferences, and product/service attributes are involved. The popularity of conjoint analysis in marketing research stems from its ability to assess the evaluations individuals place on the different attributes of a given product or service. New product design and testing, modifications to existing products, price–value relationships, attitude measurement, promotional congruence testing, and ranking are the tasks where conjoint analysis is frequently employed. See Arenoe et al. (2015) for more information.

Correspondence analysis

Correspondence analysis is a graphical technique for representing multidimensional tables (Baker & Hart 2008). It is designed to analyze tables containing some measure of correspondence between the rows and columns. Correspondence analysis displays the relationships between the rows and columns of a cross-tabulation table and can be employed to scale a matrix of non-negative data to represent points (rows or columns) in a lower dimensional space. The results provide information which is similar in nature to that produced by factor analysis as they examine the structure of variables included in the table. Correspondence analysis can be used for analyzing binary, discrete and/or continuous data. This technique is particularly useful to identify market segments, track brand image, position a product against its competition, and determine who respondents in a survey most closely resemble. See Baloglu and Pekcan (2006) for an example.

Regression and forecasting techniques

Multiple regression

Regression analysis is concerned with the nature and strength of relationships between two or more variables. The purpose of regression is to make predictions about values of the dependent variable based on the values of independent variable(s) (Speed 1994). Regression provides measures of association and can provide better understanding of the implicit relationships among various independent and dependent variables.

Generalized linear models (GLM)

GLMs are methods which model data as linear relationships because those can be easily described mathematically. Even in cases when relationships are non-linear, it is possible to apply linear methods by using transformations which approximate non-linear relationships to linear ones (Baker & Hart 2008). The techniques that fall under the GLM umbrella include:

- Ordinary least-squares regression
- Logistic regression
- Log-linear modeling

Ordinary least-squares (OLS) regression

OLS can be presented in simple or multiple form. Simple OLS regression portrays the relationship between two variables using a line, which is computed using the least-squares method and provides a line of best fit that can be expressed through the following equation:

$$Y = \alpha + \beta X + \varepsilon$$

where Y is the value of the dependent variable that is being predicted or explained, α is the constant or intercept, β is the slope for independent variable X that is explaining the variance in Y, and ε represents random error.

Multivariate OLS regression is used when there are more than two variables. A multiple OLS regression model with k variables can be expressed by the following equation: $Y = \alpha + \beta_1 X_1 + \beta_2 X_2 + \beta_3 X_3 + \beta_4 X_4 + \cdots + \beta_k X_k + \varepsilon$, where dependent variable Y is regressed by k-number of independent variables X.

OLS regression can be used to model response (dependent) variables measured on an interval scale (i.e. continuous variables such as age, performance, price, etc.). Explanatory variables (independent variables) can be continuous, ordered, or unordered categorical data. See Yang and Cai (2016) for an example.

Logistic regression

Logistic regression is used to model a binary variable (i.e male–female) when the data are not linear as binary response variables have a non-linear S-shaped distribution (Baker, 2003). Such distribution can be modeled using a linear equation after a transformation. As with OLS regression, any number of explanatory variables (interval or categorical) can be used. The same basic form of the model and considerations apply to the data as with multiple OLS regression. Similar to multivariate OLS, a logistic regression can be represented as:

$$Y = \alpha + \beta_1 X_1 + \beta_2 X_2 + \beta_3 X_3 + \beta_4 X_4 + \ldots + \beta_k X_k + \varepsilon$$

The only difference is in the interpretation of the parameters. See Stylos and Vassiliadis (2015) for how this method is applied in hospitality marketing.

Log-linear modeling

The log-linear model is analogous to the OLS and logistic regression models and is often used to model categorical data (i.e. data in the form of contingency tables). The traditional method of analyzing such data is to use the chi-square statistic as part of the cross-tabs procedure, which can only deal with two variables and cannot model the data to provide predictions.

Log-linear technique makes use of the linear model and a transformation involving the natural log. Similar to OLS and logistic regression, the form of model is a linear combination:

$$\ln \text{(cell count)} = \alpha + \beta_1 X_1 + \beta_2 X_2 + \beta_3 X_3 + \beta_k X_k$$

Log-linear analysis makes it possible to assess the overall fit of the model. Parameters from the model are similar to the other models, but are interpreted somewhat differently due to the log-linear transformation. See Yim et al. (2014) for more details.

Discriminant analysis (DA)

Discriminant analysis also uses a linear equation to predict dependent variables, but unlike regression analysis when the parameters are used to minimize the sum of squares, in DA the parameters are selected in a way as to maximize the ratio of variance between group means to variance within groups.

DA aims to model the difference between the classes of data. Additionally, discriminant analysis has continuous independent variables and a categorical dependent variable. DA has been successfully used in hospitality marketing for predicting brand loyalty, consumer innovators, preferences of products or services, etc. See Prayag (2012) for an example of DA application.

Forecasting methods

Generally, forecasting methods can be split into three categories: qualitative techniques, time series analysis, and causal models (Chambers et al. 1979). Those techniques are primarily used to forecast demand, sales, repeat purchases, etc. In hospitality marketing research, the most commonly used forecasting technique is the time series analysis, which relies on historical data and analyzes time series data in order to extract meaningful statistics and other characteristics of the data. The main premise of time series forecasting is to examine the past observations of a time series to develop an appropriate model which describes the inherent structure of the series. Then, the obtained model can be used to project future values for the series. The most frequently used time series models are the Autoregressive Integrated Moving Average (ARIMA) model and Seasonal ARIMA. Tanford and Suh (2013) provide a good example of how time series can be applied in the hospitality field.

Causal modeling

In hospitality marketing research, causal relationships are frequently examined, employing path analysis and structural equation modeling techniques. Those two techniques became primary approaches for testing causal hypotheses regarding social and behavioral phenomena as both methods allow researchers to test theories and concepts involving latent variables at the observation level (Hair et al. 2012).

Path analysis (PA)

Path analysis is a method for studying and graphically expressing patterns of causal relationships among sets of variables. One of the advantages of PA is that it allows the direct and indirect effects of variables to be examined. PA assumes that the relationships among the variables are linear and additive. Direct effects or path coefficients are represented by regression weights. Indirect effects can be assessed when an independent variable affects a dependent variable through a third variable. In such cases, the indirect effect can be computed as the product of the respective path coefficients. It should be noted that PA cannot deduce causal relationships from the values of the correlation coefficients alone. PA should combine the quantitative information given by the correlations with available qualitative information on causal relations (Baker 2003). For examples of PA application, see Karatepe (2011) and Kuruüzüm et al. (2009).

Structural equation modeling (SEM)

The structural equation modeling technique is frequently used to test theories and concepts involving causal models with observable (manifest) and unobservable (latent) variables. SEM simultaneously evaluates both the measurement and causal/structural components of the system in question as it compares reproduced correlations to the original correlations. SEM acknowledges that measures in the model can be imperfect, measurement errors as well as residuals can be correlated, and that reciprocal causation is a possibility (Baker 2003). Additionally, a priori theory is required for SEM analysis.

There are two major SEM approaches: covariance-based and partial least squares method. Covariance-based SEM estimates model parameters in a way so that the discrepancy between the estimated and sample covariance matrices is minimized. Partial least squares SEM maximizes the explained variance of the endogenous latent variables. It does so by estimating partial model relationships in an iterative sequence of ordinary least-squares regressions and estimates latent variable scores as exact linear combinations of their associated manifest variables and treats them as perfect substitutes for the manifest variables. In this way, the scores indicate the variance that can explain the endogenous latent variables.

Because partial least squares SEM evaluates models by a series of OLS regressions, it relaxes the assumption of multivariate normality (Hair et al. 2012). Many uses of SEM in hospitality research can be seen in such areas as consumer behavior, new product or service adoption, marketing strategy, organizational decision-making, and advertising. See Castellanos-Verdugo et al. (2009) and Leonidou et al. (2013) for application examples.

Simulation techniques

Time/cost concerns, time availability, and problems associated with field experimentation often lead to simulation methods being used as a source of information. In such instances, it is often desirable to construct a model of a situation and obtain relevant information through the manipulation of this model referred to as simulation. The idea behind simulation is to create a complex model to look like a real process or system and then experiment with this model with an aim of obtaining knowledge about the real system. Simulations are particularly useful for studying complex marketing systems (Gupta et al. 2010).

According to Doyle and Fenwick (1976), marketing simulations can be divided into three categories:

1. Computer models of the behavior of marketing system components
2. Computer models of the effect of different marketing instruments on demand
3. Marketing games

In hospitality marketing research, simulation techniques have been primarily used in the educational and training sphere (Feinstein & Parks 2002), for projecting demand and sales (Zakhary et al. 2011), and deriving simulation datasets (Yoo et al. 2011).

Lisa Slevitch

Artificial intelligence (AI)

Artificial intelligence models are somewhat similar to simulation techniques. AI techniques attempt to represent, understand, and analyze human reasoning in a range of situations (Baker 2003). The two most common AI methods are expert systems and neural networks.

Expert systems

Expert system are computer programs which contain human expertise or knowledge that can be used to generate reasoned advice or instructions. The knowledge base is usually represented as a set of IF... THEN... rules and the expert system algorithm matches together appropriate combinations of rules in order to generate conclusions. One of the variations of the expert system method is the association rule (AR) method (Ahmad et al. 2012). As Chen (2015) states, ARs are created by identifying associations or correlations of interest in a large dataset. The AR method was originally developed to detect frequent item sets appearing synchronously in market baskets. To illustrate, if a consumer who purchases product X regularly buys product Y as well, then a relationship exists between the two products. Chen further states that the AR method can identify synchronous relationships relative to two measures: support and confidence. For the rule "if X, then Y" (X → Y), in the transaction set D, *support* (sup(X → Y)) identifies the proportion of patterns occurring in transaction set D. *Confidence* (conf(X → Y)) represents the strength of the rule as the proportion of transactions containing X that includes Y too. Consequently, sup(X → Y) = P(X ∩ Y) and conf(X → Y) = P(Y | X). With the minimum support threshold and minimum confidence threshold, the ARs can be formulated to distinguish between strong and weak rules (Chen & Wu 2005). To determine whether a particular hospitality marketing domain is appropriate for expert systems methods, see the checklist provided in Baker (2003). The biggest issue related to the effectiveness and applicability of expert system methods is the construction and validation of the knowledge base.

A number of studies have applied the AR method to examine customer preferences (Chen & Chang 2013) and explore customer behavior (Huang & Hsueh 2010). Additionally, the AR method was used in research on pricing, advertising appeals, choice of promotional techniques, promotion evaluation, strategic positioning, assessment of sales, brand management, marketing planning, etc. (Curry & Moutinho 1991). Expert systems and particularly the AR method remain novel in hospitality marketing research. Nevertheless, those methods slowly gain interest and use (see Chen 2015 for a good example).

Neural networks

Neural networks were developed to provide abilities to bypass the strictness of expert systems and to develop fuzzy logic decision-making tools (Baker & Hart 2008). Similar to expert systems, neural networks employ structured input and output data to establish patterns that resemble human decision-making. Input data are compared to relative output data for many data points. The relationships between the input data and output data help to establish a pattern that signifies the decision-making style in question. Establishing patterns from data points removes the requirement to build rules supporting decision-making. One of the important features of neural networks is their capability of retraining, which is done through the addition of new input and output data. That is an improvement over expert systems that require user involvement to adjust for variable changes within the model.

One of the important advantages of neural networks is that neural networks can utilize intuitive, trial-and-error thinking marketing researchers typically need. Another important feature of neural networks is synthesis of psychometric and econometric analyses as the best qualities of both can be used. One of the weaknesses of neural networks is accuracy, but it has the ability to learn from increased input/output facts and the ability to address data that other decision-support systems cannot handle logically (Baker 2003).

Neural networks have been successfully applied in such marketing areas as consumer behavior, market segmentation, pricing modeling, and strategy planning (Curry & Moutinho 1991). Though used rarely, neural networks methods have been successfully applied in hospitality marketing research. For example, Mikulić et al. (2012) and Deng et al. (2008) used neural network methods to determine critical quality components in hospitality products and services. Analogously, Golmohammadi et al. (2011) used this method to conduct importance analysis of travel attributes. Huarng et al. (2012) used a neural networks approach to forecast tourism demand while Youn and Gu (2010) used it to predict lodging firm failures.

Emerging methods and future directions

When describing marketing discipline frontiers in the third millennium, Achrol and Kotler (2012) identified the following emergent paradigms that were likely to impact the methods used in hospitality marketing research:

- Consumer sensations and sense-making
- Neurophysiology of consumer behavior and sensory experiences
- Products and services as sensory experiences

The authors explain that the core of marketing is the process of consumption built upon three pillars: satisfaction, value, and utility. At the heart of consumption reside consumers' needs and satisfaction, which are a product of complex experiences filtered through our senses. The senses help us comprehend and experience the world around us and they include the visual (perceptual); auditory and olfactory, taste, touch and feel (tactile and haptic sense); limb position and motion (proprioception and kinesthesis); and whole-body orientation and motion (vestibular sense). The big question yet to be fully answered is: "What does it mean to say that 'we experience' something, and that the experience is satisfactory?" That is the primary challenge of the new millennia marketing research, particularly in the consumer behavior area.

A complete understanding of consumer experiences has not been achieved in the field of hospitality. The majority of hospitality experiences are conveyed through self-reported feedback tools such as surveys or interviews. But self-reporting techniques tend to produce unreliable results (Zaltman 2003). Often respondents cannot truly express their perceptions because people do not think in linear, hierarchical ways. Instead, they experience it as a whole, involving complex interactions of various factors on a conscious and subconscious level. As Zaltman states, consumers cannot plausibly explain their thinking and behavior because 95% of thinking is taking place in the unconscious mind. Additionally, consumers do not primarily think in words as only a small portion of the brain's neural activity surfaces in language. Thus, this is why self-reported feedback does not provide a complete picture of customer experiences.

Many researchers believe that understanding consumer behavior and consumption experiences is inextricably linked to neurophysiological methods (Zaltman 2003; Lindstrom 2008; Achrol & Kotler 2012). The quest for understanding experiences as customer sensations and sense-making has propelled the shift from the cognitive to neurological domain in marketing research. As a result, the field of neuromarketing has been quickly established and the UK's *Journal of Consumer Behavior* devoted a special issue in 2008 to this topic.

Capturing neurophysiological responses to different experiences calls for tools allowing the examination of various cellular mapping networks located in specific areas of the brain. Mobile EEG (electroencephalography), PET, and MRI devices allow the capturing of neurological responses in different parts of the brain and are capable of capturing the complexity of sensory experiences. Another tool that is capable of capturing complex responses is based in neurobiochemistry and captures hormonal reactions to different stimuli (Koc & Boz 2014). Incorporating such devices and methods in marketing research is challenging as it requires certain neurological and technical expertise but more and more attempts are being made to include neurophysiological tools in modern marketing research, particularly in experimental studies (Isabella et al. 2015).

Though the need for neurophysiological methods in hospitality research has been recognized (Seric et al. 2015), only a few studies have employed such methods (Koc & Boz 2014). Therefore, there are opportunities for hospitality researchers to be pioneers in applying neurophysiological methods and to bring hospitality marketing up to speed with the general marketing discipline.

References

Achrol, R. S. & Kotler, P. (2012). "Frontiers of the Marketing Paradigm in the Third Millennium," *Journal of the Academy of Marketing Science* 40, 1, 35–52.

Ahmad, A., Dey, L. & Halawani, S. M. (2012) "A Rule-Based Method for Identifying the Factor Structure in Customer Satisfaction," *Information Sciences* 198, 118–129.

Arenoe, B., Van Der Rest, J. P. I. & Kattuman, P. (2015). "Game Theoretic Pricing Models in Hotel Revenue Management: An Equilibrium Choice-Based Conjoint Analysis Approach," *Tourism Management* 51, 96–102.

Baker, M. & Hart, S. (2008) *The Marketing Book*, Oxford: Butterworth-Heinemann.

Baker, M. J. (2003) *The Marketing Book*, Oxford: Butterworth-Heinemann.

Baloglu, S. & Pekcan, Y. A. (2006) "The Website Design and Internet Site Marketing Practices of Upscale and Luxury Hotels in Turkey," *Tourism Management* 27, 1, 171–176.

Beldona, S., Lin, K. & Yoo, J. (2012). "The Roles of Personal Innovativeness and Push vs Pull Delivery Methods in Travel-Oriented Location-Based Marketing Services," *Journal of Hospitality and Tourism Technology* 3, 2, 86–95.

Castellanos-Verdugo, M., Oviedo-García, M. A. M., Roldán, J. L. & Veerapermal, N. (2009) "The Employee-Customer Relationship Quality: Antecedents and Consequences in the Hotel Industry," *International Journal of Contemporary Hospitality Management* 21, 3, 251–274.

Chambers, J. C., Mullick, T. K. & Smith, D. D. (1979) "How to Choose the Right Forecasting Technique," *Harvard Business Review*, July-August, 45–74.

Chan, E. (2013). "Managing Green Marketing: Hong Kong Hotel Managers' Perspective," *International Journal of Hospitality Management* 34, 442–461.

Chen, L. F. (2015) "Exploring Asymmetric Effects of Attribute Performance on Customer Satisfaction Using Association Rule Method," *International Journal of Hospitality Management* 47, 54–64.

Chen, L. S. & Chang, P. C. (2013) "Extracting Knowledge of Customers' Preferences in Massively Multiplayer Online Role Playing Games," *Neural Computing and Applications* 23, 6, 1787–1799.

Chen, M. C. & Wu, H. P. (2005) "An Association-Based Clustering Approach to Order Batching Considering Customer Demand Patterns," *Omega* 33, 4, 333–343.

Churchill, G. A. & Iacobucci, D. (2009) *Marketing Research: Methodological Foundations*, Mason, OH: South-Western Cengage Learning.

Curry, B. & Moutinho, L. (1991) "Expert Systems and Marketing Strategy: An Application to Site Location Decisions," *Journal of Marketing Channels* 1, 1, 23–27.

Deng, W. J., Chen, W. C. & Pei, W. (2008) "Back-Propagation Neural Network Based Importance–Performance Analysis for Determining Critical Service Attributes," *Expert Systems with Applications* 34, 2, 1115–1125.

Denizci Guillet, B., Guo, Y. & Law, R. (2015). "Segmenting Hotel Customers Based on Rate Fences through Conjoint and Cluster Analysis," *Journal of Travel & Tourism Marketing* 32, 7, 835–851.

Denzin, N. K. & Lincoln, Y. S (1994) "Introduction: Entering the Field of Qualitative Research." *In:* Denzin, N. &. Lincoln, Y. (eds.) *Handbook of Qualitative Research,* Thousand Oaks, CA: Sage Publications, pp. 1–17.

Díaz, E. & Koutra, C. (2013) "Evaluation of the Persuasive Features of Hotel Chains Websites: A Latent Class Segmentation Analysis," *International Journal of Hospitality Management* 34, 338–347.

Dotson, M. & Clark, J. D. (2004). "The Impact of Promotions on Hotel Decision Choice: A Demographic Study," *Journal of Hospitality & Leisure Marketing* 11, 2–3, 81–95.

Doyle, P. & Fenwick, I. (1976) "Sales Forecasting—Using a Combination of Approaches," *Long Range Planning* 9, 3, 60–64.

Feinstein, A. H. & Parks, S. J. (2002) "Simulation Research in the Hospitality Industry," *Developments in Business Simulation and Experiential Learning* 29, 45–57.

Golmohammadi, A., Shams Ghareneh, N., Keramati, A. & Jahandideh, B. (2011) "Importance Analysis of Travel Attributes Using a Rough Set-Based Neural Network: The Case of Iranian Tourism Industry," *Journal of Hospitality and Tourism Technology* 2, 2, 155–171.

Granger, C. W. J. (1969) "Investigating Causal Relations by Econometric Models and Cross-Spectral Methods," *Econometrica: Journal of the Econometric Society* 37, 3, 424–438.

Guba, E. G. & Lincoln, Y. S. (1994) "Competing Paradigms in Qualitative Research." *In:* Denzin, N. K. & Lincoln, Y. S. (eds.) *Handbook of Qualitative Research,* Thousands Oaks, CA: Sage, pp. 105–117.

Gupta, A., Singh, K. & Verma, R. (2010) "Simulation: An Effective Marketing Tool," *Simulation* 4, 11, 8–12.

Hair, J. F., Sarstedt, M., Ringle, C. M. & Mena, J. A. (2012) "An Assessment of the Use of Partial Least Squares Structural Equation Modeling in Marketing Research," *Journal of the Academy of Marketing Science* 40, 3, 414–433.

Huang, C. F. & Hsueh, S. L. (2010) "Customer Behavior and Decision Making in the Refurbishment Industry: A Data Mining Approach," *Journal of Civil Engineering and Management* 16, 1, 75–84.

Huarng, K. H., Hui-Kuang Yu, T., Moutinho, L. & Wang, Y.C. (2012) "Forecasting Tourism Demand by Fuzzy Time Series Models," *International Journal of Culture, Tourism and Hospitality Research* 6, 4, 377–388.

Isabella, G., Mazzon, J. A. & Dimoka, A. (2015) "Culture Differences, Difficulties, and Challenges of the Neurophysiological Methods in Marketing Research," *Journal of International Consumer Marketing* 27, 5, 346–363.

Jackson, L. A. & Singh, D. (2015) "Environmental Rankings and Financial Performance: An Analysis of Firms in the US Food and Beverage Supply Chain," *Tourism Management Perspectives* 14, 25–33.

Karatepe, O. M. (2011) "Customer Aggression, Emotional Exhaustion, and Hotel Employee Outcomes: A Study in the United Arab Emirates," *Journal of Travel & Tourism Marketing* 28, 3, 279–295.

Kim, S., Wang, K. & Ahn, T. H. (2013) "Which Endorser and Content Are Most Influential in Korean Restaurant Promotions?" *International Journal of Hospitality Management* 33, 208–218.

Koc, E. & Boz, H. (2014) "Psychoneurobiochemistry of Tourism Marketing," *Tourism Management* 44, 140–148.

Kuruüzüm, A., Ipekçi Çetin, E. & Irmak, S. (2009) "Path Analysis of Organizational Commitment, Job Involvement and Job Satisfaction in Turkish Hospitality Industry," *Tourism Review* 64, 1, 4–16.

Lee, T. W. (1999) *Using Qualitative Methods in Organizational Research,* Thousands Oaks, CA: Sage.

Leonidou, L. C., Leonidou, C. N., Fotiadis, T. A. & Zeriti, A. (2013) "Resources and Capabilities as Drivers of Hotel Environmental Marketing Strategy: Implications for Competitive Advantage and Performance," *Tourism Management* 35, 94–110.

Lindstrom, M. (2008) *Buyology: Truth and Lies About Why We Buy,* New York: Doubleday.

Mikulić, J., Paunović, Z. & Prebežac, D. (2012) "An Extended Neural Network-Based Importance-Performance Analysis for Enhancing Wine Fair Experience," *Journal of Travel & Tourism Marketing* 29, 8, 744–759.

Morosan, C. T., Bowen, J. & Atwood, M. (2014) "The Evolution of Marketing Research," *International Journal of Contemporary Hospitality Management* 26, 5, 706–726.

Prayag, G. (2012) "Paradise for Who? Segmenting Visitors' Satisfaction with Cognitive Image and Predicting Behavioural Loyalty," *International Journal of Tourism Research* 14, 1, 1–15.

Ruiz-Molina, M., Gil-Saura, I. & Seric, M. (2013) "The Use of ICT in Established and Emerging Tourist Destinations: A Comparative Analysis in *Hotels," Journal of Hospitality and Tourism Technology* 4, 2, 96–118.

Sale, J. E. M., Lohfeld, L. H. & Brazil, K. (2002) "Revisiting the Quantitative-Qualitative Debate: Implications for Mixed-Methods Research," *Quality and Quantity* 36, 1, 43–53.

Seric, N., Jurisic, M. & Petricevic, D. (2015) "Neuromarketing Potential for Tourist Destination Brand Positioning," *Tourism in South East Europe,* 3, 429–439.

Slevitch, L. (2011) "Qualitative and Quantitative Methodologies Compared: Ontological and Epistemological Perspectives," *Journal of Quality Assurance in Hospitality & Tourism* 12, 1, 73–81.

Speed, R. (1994) "Regression Type Techniques and Small Samples." *In*: Hooley, G. J. and Hussey, M. K. (eds.) *Quantitative Methods in Marketing*, London: Academic Press, pp. 89–104.

Stylos, N. & Vassiliadis, C. (2015) "Differences in Sustainable Management Between Four and Five-Star Hotels Regarding the Perceptions of Three-Pillar Sustainability," *Journal of Hospitality Marketing & Management* 24, 8, 791–825.

Tanford, S. & Suh, E. (2013) "How Restaurant Variety Indirectly Impacts Gaming for Different Casino Worth Segments," *International Journal of Contemporary Hospitality Management* 25, 3, 328–345.

Wong, I. A. & Wu, J. S. (2013) "Understanding Casino Experiential Attributes: An Application to Market Positioning," *International Journal of Hospitality Management* 35, 214–224.

Yang, Z. & Cai, J. (2016) "Do Regional Factors Matter? Determinants of Hotel Industry Performance in China," *Tourism Management* 52, 242–253.

Yim, E. S., Lee, S. & Kim, W. G. (2014) "Determinants of a Restaurant Average Meal Price: An Application of the Hedonic Pricing Model," *International Journal of Hospitality Management* 39, 11–20.

Yoo, M., Lee, S. & Bai, B. (2011) "Hospitality Marketing Research from 2000 to 2009: Topics, Methods, and Trends," *International Journal of Contemporary Hospitality Management* 23, 4, 517–532.

Youn, H. & Gu, Z. (2010) "Predicting Korean Lodging Firm Failures: An Artificial Neural Network Model Along With a Logistic Regression Model," *International Journal of Hospitality Management* 29, 1, 120–127.

Zakhary, A., Atiya, A. F., El-Shishiny, H. & Gayar, N. E. (2011) "Forecasting Hotel Arrivals and Occupancy Using Monte Carlo Simulation," *Journal of Revenue & Pricing Management* 10, 4, 344–366.

Zaltman, G. (2003) *How Customers Think: Essential Insights into the Mind of the Market*, Boston, MA: Harvard Business Press.

Zheng, T., Farrish, J. & Kitterlin, M. (2016) "Performance Trends of Hotels and Casino Hotels through the Recession: An ARIMA with Intervention Analysis of Stock Indices," *Journal of Hospitality Marketing & Management* 25, 1, 49–68.

7

Questionnaire survey design in hospitality marketing

Yinghua Huang

Introduction

Questionnaire surveys are the most common method for data collection in hospitality and tourism research (Ballantyne, Packer, & Axelsen, 2009; Dolnicar, Grün, & Yanamandram, 2013). Researchers use questionnaires to investigate consumer behaviors, opinions, perceptions, and attitudes, such as destination loyalty, satisfaction, service quality, and revisit intention (Baloglu & Love, 2005; Chi & Qu, 2008; Dolnicar & Grün, 2013). Questionnaire design, therefore, is at the heart of many empirical studies, determining the quality of data collected and the reliability and validity of research results (Krosnick & Presser, 2010).

A substantial amount of research has examined the theoretical and methodological issues associated with questionnaire design and best practices in different contexts. Previous studies have demonstrated that small design differences in questionnaires can lead to significant changes in the research findings (Dolnicar et al., 2013; Krosnick, 1999). For example, methodological research literature has revealed that the length, question/response format, visual layout, question wording, disclosure of survey progress, questionnaire distribution mode, and other features of the questionnaire design influence data quality (Chang & Krosnick, 2010; Cole, 2005; Dolnicar et al., 2013; Vicente & Reis, 2010). In recent decades, scholars have been seeking to find the best strategies to develop "good" questionnaires that can ensure high data quality and strong response rates. Despite the popularity of questionnaire design research in social science literature, remarkably little research in the field of hospitality and tourism has discussed how to improve questionnaire design (Cole, 2005; Keegan & Lucas, 2005; Litvin & Kar, 2001). This phenomenon calls for a greater awareness of questionnaire design among hospitality and tourism researchers.

This chapter seeks to provide a state-of-the-art review of questionnaire design research in the marketing, hospitality, and tourism literature to identify important themes and topics related to designing a questionnaire. First, it will introduce satisficing theory to explain the cognitive process of answering a questionnaire and the crucial role of questionnaire design in producing reliable results. Second, it provides a step-by-step procedure for designing a questionnaire based on the literature. Then, both conventional wisdom and primary methodological debates of questionnaire design are discussed. Finally, this chapter identifies emerging issues and research directions for questionnaire design in the hospitality and tourism literature.

Satisficing theory and questionnaire design

Questionnaires are not only a tool for gathering information, but are also "a conversation with a purpose" between the researcher and respondent (Bingham & Moore, 1934; Krosnick & Presser, 2010). While the researcher asks a question and the respondent answers it through a questionnaire, we consider the process to be a conversation that involves cognitive efforts (Moroney & Cameron, 2016). The literature describes respondents' cognitive process of answering a questionnaire in four steps: (1) Trying to comprehend the intent of the question; (2) Searching memories to retrieve the relevant information; (3) Integrating all related information to form a summary judgment; (4) Translating judgment into the supplied responses (Krosnick & Presser, 2010; Tourangeau, Rips, & Rasinski, 2000). If the respondent performs these four steps thoroughly and accurately, the researchers consider the respondent to be optimizing.

Krosnick (1999) proposed satisficing theory to explain why people sometimes don't optimize their effects in responding to questionnaires, and proposed two alternatives to optimizing that respondents can apply: strong satisficing and weak satisficing. Strong satisficing occurs when the respondent responds based on steps 1 and 4 but omits the memory retrieval process and the summary judgment process. For example, a respondent who just looks through the wording of the question and picks a response completely arbitrarily employs strong satisficing. On the other hand, the respondent may employ the weak satisficing strategy by engaging in the four cognitive steps, but only doing so superficially. For example, respondents may not consider a question's meaning thoroughly, may not search their memories comprehensively, may formulate judgment less than carefully, and/or may select a response without precision.

Satisficing theory conceptualizes optimizing and strongly satisficing as two ends of a continuum of cognitive effort, while weak satisficing occurs to varying degrees between the ends. The theory proposes three factors that determine when and which strategy the respondent will choose to answer a question: (1) question difficulty, (2) respondent ability, and (3) motivation. When the respondent's cognitive ability or motivation is lower, the person is more likely to satisfice in a survey. When a question is more difficult to understand or to answer, the respondent is also more likely to employ cognitive shortcuts to answer it. Since it is hard for researchers to manipulate respondents' cognitive ability or motivation throughout the survey process, reducing question difficulty is the only way to minimize respondents' satisficing behavior. In other words, a well-designed questionnaire should be easy for respondents to comprehend and respond to and should motivate the respondents to optimize their cognitive effects and improve the quality of responses (Krosnick & Presser, 2010; Vannette & Krosnick, 2014).

Steps of questionnaire design

Designing a questionnaire is a complex process. Researchers have provided various recommendations for the steps of questionnaire development. Stehr-Green et al. (2003) introduced eight steps for developing a questionnaire. First, identify the hypotheses about the research problem. Second, specify the information needed to test the proposed hypotheses.

Third, figure out the information necessary for conducting the study and to investigate the confounding factors. Fourth, write the questions for collecting information needed. Fifth, format the questions in a questionnaire. Sixth, pretest the questionnaires. Seventh, modify and double-check the questionnaire. Finally, train administrators to distribute and collect the questionnaire. Based on an extensive literature review, this chapter summarizes the common suggestions found in the literature for the questionnaire design process below.

Step 1: Identify what information to collect, based on the research questions.

Step 2: Develop questions and measurement items based on existing literature or expert insights. The researcher can either adopt questions from an existing questionnaire verified by previous studies, or generate new questions and measurement items using interviews, focus groups, or other techniques.

Step 3: Decide how to distribute the questionnaire, then design the questionnaire layout and question format accordingly. Previous studies have indicated that different questionnaire distribution modes, such as web-based survey, paper-and-pencil questionnaire, telephone interview, have an influence on the quality of data collection (Chang & Krosnick, 2010; Cole, 2005; Dolnicar et al., 2013). For example, symbols and graphics can be appropriate question formats for web-based and paper-and-pencil surveys; however, they are not good options for telephone interviews (Chang & Krosnick, 2010; Krosnick & Presser, 2010). Therefore, researchers should consider distribution modes before designing the question formats and layout.

Step 4: Choose an appropriate question response format. There are a variety of question formats available for different research questions. Table 7.1 presents some examples of popular question formats used in the hospitality and tourism literature. Previous studies indicate that question formats have impacts on research results (Dolnicar & Grün, 2013; King, Meiselman, & Carr, 2013). Therefore, researchers need to choose the response format carefully.

Step 5: Pilot the questionnaire, and test the reliability and validity. It is wise to invite experts to examine the questionnaire and administer the questionnaire to a small sample of the relevant population. Through expert review, some problems such as question wording, ordering, logic, layout issues, and time for completion can be fixed. After the pretest data collection, researchers should conduct item analysis and factor analysis to evaluate the measurement scales.

Step 6: Revise the questionnaire and amend measurement scales until sufficient reliability and validity are demonstrated.

Step 7: Finalize the questionnaire and prepare a protocol for administering the questionnaire.

Key considerations of questionnaire design

This section presents a number of key issues about questionnaire design based on a review of the literature. First, the conventional wisdom about questionnaire wording and ordering is discussed. Then, this section highlights the popular topics that have drawn the attention of researchers in the past. These key issues include choosing open-ended questions or closed questions, question response formats, scale labeling, the option of "Don't Know," and web-based questionnaire design.

Table 7.1 Popular question formats and examples

Question Formats	Examples
Fill-in-the-blank	If you won $1,000 and were not going to get the money for 1 week, what is the smallest amount of money you would accept today rather than having to wait 1 week? *See Weatherly, Derenne, & Terrell (2011)*
Open-ended question	What images and characteristics come to your mind when you think of the following destinations as an association convention destination? *See Baloglu & Love (2005)*
Agree/Disagree (A/D) Likert-type scale	Eureka Springs has safe and secure environment. Strongly Disagree 1 2 3 4 5 6 7 Strongly Agree *See Chi & Qu (2008)*
Item-specific scale	
a. Bipolar scale	a. How much do you favor or oppose avoiding "fast food"? Strongly Oppose Somewhat Oppose Slightly Oppose Neither Favor Nor Oppose Slightly Favor Somewhat Favor Strongly Favor *See Tourangeau, Couper, & Conrad (2007)*
b. Unipolar scale	b. How often do you feel sad? Constantly, very often, somewhat often, rarely, or never? *See Saris et al. (2010)*

Semantic differential format

As a holiday destination, I would describe Antarctica as:

	Very	Moderately	Slightly	Neither	Slightly	Moderately	Very	
Unsafe	□	□	□	□	□	□	□	Safe
Inexpensive	□	□	□	□	□	□	□	Expensive

See Dolnicar & Grün (2013)

Check all that apply (CATA)

Please think of the laundry detergent brand named "Radiant," and pick any of the following attributes that are associated with it.

□ Get clothes very clean
□ Whitens whites
□ Attractively priced
□ Noticeably freshens clothes and bed linen
See Dolnicar, Rossiter, & Grün (2012)

Force-choice full binary format

I think McDonald's is

	Yes	No
Yummy	□	□
Cheap	□	□

See Dolnicar, Grün, & Leisch (2011)

Conventional wisdom

Previous research provides extensive recommendations about question design. The common suggestions are as follows:

1. Include a brief and friendly cover letter to explain the survey purpose and give clear instructions (Keegan & Lucas, 2005; Ravichandran & Arendt, 2008).
2. Select words that are in frequent use in popular discourse, which have only one primary definition, with a smaller number letters and that are easy to pronounce. Technical jargon, slang, notation, and abbreviations should be avoided in questions (Stehr-Green et al., 2003).
3. Each question item should just contain a single idea, and double-barreled questions should be avoided (Stehr-Green et al., 2003).
4. Avoid leading questions that press respondents toward an answer (Song, Son, & Oh, 2015).
5. Include filter questions, rather than asking questions that do not apply to a respondent (Kreuter et al., 2011; Krosnick & Presser, 2010).
6. Make response options exhaustive and mutually exclusive (Krosnick & Presser, 2010).
7. Place easy questions at the beginning of the questionnaire, and put questions on sensitive topics or that are hard to answer at the end (Ekman et al., 2007).
8. Demographic questions may be presented at the end to keep respondents engaged (Krosnick & Presser, 2010).

Open-ended vs. closed questions

When it comes to writing questions, the researcher needs to decide, first, whether to make the question open-ended or closed. Both types have advantages and limitations. Closed questions are very popular in hospitality and tourism research, and are used with bipolar or unipolar Likert-type scales, pick-any checklists, matching, ranking and so on (Dolnicar & Grün, 2013). Closed questions are easy to administer and analyze, and generally suit questions in which the universe of possible response categories is well known (Gehlbach, 2015; Song et al., 2015). In the absence of such common wisdom about response categories, closed questions can produce measurement error because they do not provide responses that suit participants' opinions (Gehlbach, 2015). For example, when asking numeric questions such as age, number of visits, and duration of a trip, open questions are preferable to closed questions (Krosnick & Presser, 2010; Stehr-Green et al., 2003).

Open-ended questions enable respondents to give answers based on their perspectives, which in turn adds richness to research findings. The open-ended format includes fill-in-the-blank, and full answers with multiple words or sentences. When researchers seek to explore opinions about a controversial topic, open-ended questions are recommended. However, coding responses to open-ended questions is more time-intensive and complex than coding close-response questions. Previous research has also found that open-ended questions are more likely to elicit "Don't Know" answers and non-responses than closed-response questions (Krosnick & Presser, 2010).

Response formats of closed questions

The literature reveals that different response formats have impacts on research reliability and validity (Dolnicar & Grün, 2013; King et al., 2013). This section focuses on the most popular question formats in hospitality and tourism literature. Examples of these popular formats are presented in Table 7.1.

1. Agree/Disagree (A/D) Likert-type scale format is dominant in the literature, because it can be used for any type of construct and because it streamlines questionnaire administration (Saris et al., 2010). Researchers can present the same A/D scale for a wide array of measurement statements. The researchers presume that responses on the A/D scale permit them to compare responses. For example, if a questionnaire presents the statement, "I am usually in good mood," with an A/D scale, researchers assume that respondents who answer "strongly agree" are happier than respondents who answer "strongly disagree."

A limitation of A/D scales is that respondents may disagree with a measurement item for various reasons, some of which violate the presumed relationship between the scale coding scheme and the nature of the measurement (Saris et al., 2010). In the example of "I am usually in good mood," the respondent could disagree with the statement for a number of reasons: (1) he is usually in a bad mood; (2) he usually feels neither good nor bad, and instead is generally affectless; or (3) he is always in a good mood, and "usually" does not reflect the universality sufficiently. The researcher assumes that the respondents who are never or rarely in a good mood will disagree with the statement; however, some respondents who are in a good mood may also disagree with the statement. Reflecting these complications, previous studies indicate that the A/D format has more measurement errors than the item-specific response format (Fowler, 1995; Saris et al., 2010). Another concern of using the A/D scale is acquiescence response bias. Previous studies show that some respondents are inclined to answer an A/D scale question by responding "agree," no matter whether the answer accurately reflects their opinion or not (Krosnick, 1999; Vannette & Krosnick, 2014). Therefore, researchers must be very careful about the wording of the measurement items when using the A/D scale format.

2. Item-specific (IS) format provides a scale demarcated with specific words for question responses. Rather than a single set of Agree/Disagree labeling, the IS response options vary from question to question. The researchers can choose either bipolar IS scale or unipolar scale. For example, a bipolar IS scale can be labeled "strongly satisfied, somewhat satisfied, slightly satisfied, neither satisfied nor dissatisfied, slightly dissatisfied, somewhat dissatisfied, strongly dissatisfied," and a unipolar scale can use "excellent, very good, good, fair, or bad." The IS format is considered to provide a much more direct way for respondents to answer than the A/D format, because it allows the researcher to choose the most appropriate words for measuring the underlying construct. In addition, the IS format helps to reduce acquiescence bias when words like "agree" and "yes" are not presented. As a result, the IS format has produced better data quality than the A/D format in previous studies (Krosnick & Presser, 2010; Saris et al., 2010).

3. Semantic differential format is similar to the bipolar IS scale. It offers a pair of contrasting adjectives, and asks the respondents to rate the attitude object on several itemized rating scales between the two bipolar extremes. For example, common pairs of opposed phrases include high quality–low quality, inexpensive–expensive, unsafe–safe, unfriendly–friendly. Friborg, Martinussen, and Rosenvinge (2006) compared the semantic differential format and Likert-type scale format, and found that the semantic differential format reduced the respondent acquiescence bias and fitted the data better. The researchers argued that using positive words only in the labeling, such as "5=true" and "1=not true," may cause acquiescence bias. The semantic differential format presents both positive and negative words and can help to minimize the acquiescence bias effectively (Billiet & McClendon, 2000; Friborg et al., 2006).

4. Check-all-that-apply (CATA) format lists all options and asks respondents to tick those that apply. Although this format is widely used in the industry, research shows that it usually produces incomplete, low-quality data (Dolnicar & Grün, 2013; Gehlbach, 2015). In particular with longer checklists, respondents tend to select more boxes toward the top of a list and ignore choices lower down on the list that might apply. The respondents would perform weak satisficing to this question, which is when they tick some choices at the beginning and feel happy enough to move onto the next question without examining the rest of the checklist. Therefore, this format is not recommended.

5. *Forced-choice binary format* requests respondents to answer each item presented with a choice between "Yes" or "No." Previous studies have provided mixed findings about the comparison between forced-choice and other formats. Some researchers have found that the forced-choice binary format provides more complete, high-quality data than other formats such as CATA and A/D scales (Dillman, Smyth, & Christian, 2014; Smyth et al., 2006). Dolnicar and Grün (2013) examined six different question formats for measuring destination image, and indicated that the forced-choice binary format performs better than other popular formats. However, other studies have found no advantage in forced-choice questions (Jaeger et al., 2014; Ray, 1990). Krosnick and Presser (2010) pointed out that the binary format with yes and no options may encourage acquiescence bias, which means the respondents are more likely to answer yes than no. The effect of the forced-choice binary format, therefore, is still under debate and warrants further investigation in the future.

Scale labeling

Scale labeling is a key issue in questionnaire design. A principle for scale labeling is to ensure that all possible response categories are labeled, with no overlapping among all labels (Krosnick & Presser, 2010). Dolnicar and Grün (2013) examined articles on destination image published in the top three tourism journals (*Journal of Travel Research, Tourism Management,* and *Annals of Tourism Research*) between 2002 and 2012. They found that 48% of publications adopted a 5-point scale, 40% used a 7-point scale, 6% applied a 6-point scale, 4% used a binary question format, and 2% used a 9-point scale. The 7-point-scale and 5-point-scale, therefore, are most popular among hospitality and tourism researchers.

The debate of scale labeling focuses on the question as to the optimal number of points on scales and how to use descriptors for the scale points. A number of methodological research studies have compared the effectiveness of 7-point-scale, 5-point-scale, and other scales with different numbers of points (Preston & Colman, 2000; Revilla et al., 2013), and argued that whether or not to add more rating points is subject to the refinement of people's mental representations of the underlying construct (Krosnick & Presser, 2010) and the format of the scale itself (Krosnick et al., 2015). Revilla et al. (2013) studied the effect of rating points for A/D scales, and revealed that 5 points are better than 7 or 11 points, because the 5-point A/D scale yields data that is of high quality. In another study comparing item-specific (IS) scales in a restaurant service context, Preston and Colman (2000) suggest that IS scales with 7, 9, or 10 points are generally better. In a recent report presented to the U.S. National Science Foundation, Krosnick et al. (2015) recommended 7-point scales for measuring bipolar constructs, and 5-point scales for measuring unipolar constructs. Taken as a whole, this chapter suggests that in choosing the number of scale points, researchers should consider respondents' cognitive capability, the scale format selected, and the polarity of the underlying construct.

Once the number of scale points is decided, the researcher needs to determine how to label the scale categories. There are two common practices: labeling the two end points with descriptors and using numbers to represent the remaining categories, or labeling all the points with words and not numbers. Recent studies suggest that the latter is preferred (Gehlbach, 2015; Tourangeau, Couper, & Conrad, 2007). The descriptive labels can help to clarify the meaning of the scale categories directly, while numerical labels add to respondent burden by adding one more step in the cognitive process as they need to interpret the number with the meaning of a specific scale category (Krosnick et al., 2015; Revilla et al., 2013).

The option of "Don't Know"

Another debate in questionnaire design is whether or not to offer the option of "Don't Know" (DK) or "Not Applicable" (NA). Some researchers suggest that including a DK/NA option in the questionnaire can help those respondents without any relevant information or clear opinion to express their true answer (Gilljam & Granberg, 1993). Ryan and Garland (1999) examined the value of the DK/NA option in tourism research, and recommended offering a DK/NA option to tourists because they might have just arrived at the tourism destination and feel they lack the knowledge to answer some questions. They also suggest including the DK/NA option in the pilot study stage and to analyze the patterns of the DK/NA option to identify any problems of question wording or cognitive difficulty.

A number of researchers, on the other hand, found that the DK/NA option does not improve the measurement process (Krosnick et al., 2002; McClendon & Alwin, 1993). Previous studies have revealed that the DK/NA option encourages respondent satisficing behavior and self-protection against sensitive questions (Hippler & Schwarz, 1989; Krosnick & Presser, 2010). People select the DK/NA option for various reasons: lacking in information, confusion about the question meaning, holding contradictory feelings about the question, avoiding efforts to think, hiding socially undesirable responses, and so on. Therefore, offering the DK/NA option actually does not provide much useful information for the researchers. Instead, it encourages those respondents who need more time to think or don't want to reveal their true opinions to pick a quick alternative.

Some researchers point out that respondents may volunteer to express "don't know" when the DK/NA option is not offered, so that the DK/NA option is not necessary. Krosnick et al. (2015) suggest, in their latest report to the National Science Foundation, that researchers should encourage respondents to provide substantive responses if they volunteer a "don't know" answer. Instead of simply giving the DK/NA option, the researchers can ask questions such as "why are you not sure about the question?" and "what is your best guess?" to elicit substantive responses.

Web survey design and interactivity

As internet technology advances, the web-based questionnaire has become an increasingly popular tool for data collection. Hung and Law (2011) reviewed publications in 30 tourism and hospitality journals between 1999 and 2008, and found that the number of studies using web-based surveys has increased exponentially. The most common benefits reported in the literature include low cost, convenience, and fast response time (Hung & Law, 2011; Schleyer & Forrest, 2000). The web-based questionnaire also enables researchers to minimize missing data and improve the response rate by creating attractive question appearance and interactivity (Dolnicar et al., 2013; Vicente & Reis, 2010). For example, researchers can incorporate various colors, visual presentation, audio and video content, and pop-up instructions to facilitate the response process. The "forced answer" feature enables the display of a missing data message, which alerts the respondent to complete all unanswered questions before submission.

Researchers have examined how visual presentation factors, layout, and interactive features of web surveys influence data quality (Dolnicar et al., 2013; Toepoel, Das, & van Soest, 2009a). Previous studies indicate that putting more questions on a screen helps to reduce the total survey time, but it produces more missing data and makes respondents feel less positive about the survey process (Lozar Manfreda, Batageli, & Vehovar, 2002; Vicente & Reis, 2010). Toepoel, Das, and van Soest (2009b) recommended that the optimal number of questions on a single screen may range from four to ten, so that respondents do not have to scroll to see any of the questions. In addition, web surveys offer new interactive formats for researchers to ask questions. Different from paper-and-pencil surveys, web surveys enable respondents to drag and drop favorite brands into an answer basket, express opinions by throwing balls in different bins on the computer screen, or even choose an avatar and play a game while taking a survey (Delavande & Rohwedder, 2008; Dolnicar et al., 2013). In a study on tourism and quality of life, Dolnicar et al. (2013) compared traditional and interactive question formats and their influences on data quality. They found that interactive questions improved the data quality and made the survey process easier and more fun for respondents. However, research on web survey interactivity and data quality is limited. Researchers need to further investigate the measurement validity of various interactive formats.

A number of previous studies compared the effectiveness of web survey and other survey distribution methods. Previous research suggests that web surveys have lower response rates than other survey modes such as mail and phone interviews (Heerwegh & Loosveldt, 2008; Vicente & Reis, 2010). Web surveys also suffer a higher coverage error, because not everyone in the study population has access to the internet (Cole, 2005). As a result, researchers are recommended to adopt multiple distribution modes for data collection, or to target the population of web users only (Dolnicar, Laesser, & Matus, 2009; Litvin & Kar, 2001). The decision of distribution modes depends on the subject population, research questions, and the research budget and time (Hung & Law, 2011).

The future of questionnaire design in hospitality marketing

This chapter has reviewed questionnaire design research in the marketing, hospitality, and tourism literature. Compared to the large body of questionnaire research in marketing journals, only a few studies on questionnaire design have been conducted in the tourism and hospitality-related context (Cole, 2005; Litvin & Kar, 2001; Ryan & Garland, 1999). Given the significant differences between tourism experience and other types of service, Dolnicar et al. (2013) call for more studies to be conducted within the tourism literature to verify the research findings of questionnaire design from the marketing literature. Researchers are encouraged to examine the issues of question formats, layout, survey modes, and other questionnaire features in tourism and hospitality settings, and to identify the best options for our domain of research.

When it comes to the best practices of questionnaire design and its effectiveness, the findings from the current literature are quite mixed (Krosnick & Presser, 2010; Krosnick et al., 2015). One reason is that the researchers used different criteria to evaluate data quality. Some studies may use non-response rate and item missing data, some may examine concurrent validity and reliability, and some may just access respondents' subjective opinions. Therefore, future research might adopt multiple criteria to evaluate questionnaire effectiveness, and compare the results with previous studies. In particular, regarding the selection of survey modes, most previous studies just compared a single mode versus another (Cole, 2005; Dolnicar et al., 2013). As a result, we do not have sufficient empirical evidence about the effectiveness of mixed survey modes, and future research should examine this issue and further explore how to combine different survey modes to optimize data quality. Moreover, the increasing popularity of social media and mobile devices enables researchers to distribute questionnaires through new channels, such as mobile applications, tablets, and other mobile devices. The challenges and opportunities related to this new mobile-based survey mode warrants further investigation.

References

Ballantyne, R., Packer, J., & Axelsen, M. (2009). Trends in tourism research. *Annals of Tourism Research*, 36(1), 149–152.

Baloglu, S., & Love, C. (2005). Association meeting planners' perceptions and intentions for five major US convention cities: The structured and unstructured images. *Tourism Management*, 26(5), 743–752.

Billiet, J., & McClendon, M. J. (2000). Modeling acquiescence in measurement models for two balanced sets of items. *Structural Equation Modeling*, 7, 608–628.

Bingham, W.V., & Moore, B.V. (1934). *How to interview* (Rev. ed.). New York: Harper.

Chang, L., & Krosnick, J. A. (2010). Comparing oral interviewing with self-administered computerized questionnaires: An experiment. *Public Opinion Quarterly*, 74(1), 154–167.

Chi, C. G. Q., & Qu, H. (2008). Examining the structural relationships of destination image, tourist satisfaction and destination loyalty: An integrated approach. *Tourism Management*, 29(4), 624–636.

Cole, S.T. (2005). Comparing mail and web-based survey distribution methods: Results of surveys to leisure travel retailers. *Journal of Travel Research*, 43(4), 422–430.

Delavande, A., & Rohwedder, S. (2008). Eliciting subjective probabilities in Internet surveys. *Public Opinion Quarterly*, 72(5), 866–891.

Dillman, D. A., Smyth, J. D., & Christian, L. M. (2014). *Internet, phone, mail, and mixed-mode surveys: The tailored design method* (4th ed.). Hoboken, NJ: John Wiley.

Dolnicar, S., & Grün, B. (2013). Validly measuring destination image in survey studies. *Journal of Travel Research*, 52(1): 3–14.

Dolnicar, S., Grün, B., & Leisch, F. (2011). Quick, simple and reliable: Forced binary survey questions. *International Journal of Market Research*, 53(2), 231–252.

Dolnicar, S., Grün, B., & Yanamandram, V. (2013). Dynamic, interactive survey questions can increase survey data quality. *Journal of Travel & Tourism Marketing*, 30(7), 690–699.

Dolnicar, S., Laesser, C., & Matus, K. (2009). Online versus paper format effects. In Dolnicar, S., Rossiter, J. R. & Grun, B. (2012). "Pick-any" measures contaminate brand image studies. *International Journal of Market Research*, 54 (6), 821–834.

Dolnicar, S., Rossiter, J. R., & Grün, B. (2012). "Pick-any" measures contaminate brand image studies. *International Journal of Market Research*, 54(6), 821–834.

Ekman, A., Klint, Å., Dickman, P. W., Adami, H. O., & Litton, J. E. (2007). Optimizing the design of web-based questionnaires—experience from a population-based study among 50,000 women. *European Journal of Epidemiology*, 22(5), 293–300.

Friborg, O., Martinussen, M., & Rosenvinge, J. H. (2006). Likert-based vs. semantic differential-based scorings of positive psychological constructs: A psychometric comparison of two versions of a scale measuring resilience. *Personality and Individual Differences*, 40(5), 873–884.

Fowler, F. J. (1995). Improving survey questions: Design and evaluation. *Applied Social Research Methods Series*, 38, 56–57.

Gehlbach, H. (2015). Seven survey sins. *The Journal of Early Adolescence*, 35(5–6), 883–897.

Gilljam, M., & Granberg, D. (1993). Should we take don't know for an answer? *Public Opinion Quarterly*, 57, 348–357.

Heerwegh, D., & Loosveldt, G. (2008). Face-to-face versus web surveying in a high-internet-coverage population: Differences in response quality. *Public Opinion Quarterly*, 72(5), 836–846.

Hippler, H. J., & Schwarz, N. (1989). "No-opinion" filters: A cognitive perspective. *International Journal of Public Opinion Research*, 1, 77–87.

Hung, K., & Law, R. (2011). An overview of Internet-based surveys in hospitality and tourism journals. *Tourism Management*, 32(4), 717–724.

Jaeger, S. R., Cadena, R. S., Torres-Moreno, M., Antúnez, L., Vidal, L., Gimenez, A., & Paisley, A. G. (2014). Comparison of check-all-that-apply and forced-choice Yes/No question formats for sensory characterisation. *Food Quality and Preference*, 35, 32–40.

Keegan, S. N., & Lucas, R. (2005). Hospitality to hostility: Dealing with low response rates in postal surveys. *International Journal of Hospitality Management*, 24(2), 157–169.

King, S. C., Meiselman, H. L., & Carr, B. T. (2013). Measuring emotions associated with foods: Important elements of questionnaire and test design. *Food Quality and Preference*, 28(1), 8–16.

Kreuter, F., McCulloch, S., Presser, S., & Tourangeau, R. (2011). The effects of asking filter questions in interleafed versus grouped format. *Sociological Methods & Research*, 40(1), 88–104.

Krosnick, J. A. (1999). Survey research. *Annual Review of Psychology*, 50(1), 537–567.

Krosnick, J. A., Holbrook, A. L., Berent, M. K., Carson, R. T., Hanemann, W. M., Kopp, R. J., Mitchell, R. C., Presser, S., Ruud, P. A., Smith, V. K., Moody, W. R., Green, M. C., & Conaway, M. (2002). The impact of "no opinion" response options on data quality: Non-attitude reduction or invitation to satisfice? *Public Opinion Quarterly*, 66, 371–403.

Krosnick, J. A., & Presser, S. (2010). Question and questionnaire design. *Handbook of Survey Research*, 2(3), 263–314.

Krosnick, J. A., Presser, S., Fealing, K. H., Ruggles, S., & Vannette, D. (2015). The future of survey research: Challenges and opportunities. *The National Science Foundation Advisory Committee for the Social, Behavioral and Economic Sciences Subcommittee on Advancing SBE Survey Research*. Retrieved 19 March 2016 from www.nsf.gov/sbe/AC_Materials/The_Future_of_Survey_Research.pdf.

Litvin, S. W., & Kar, G. H. (2001). E-surveying for tourism research: Legitimate tool or a researcher's fantasy? *Journal of Travel Research*, 39(3), 308–314.

Lozar Manfreda, K., Batagelj, Z., & Vehovar, V. (2002). Design of web survey questionnaires: Three basic experiments. *Journal of Computer-Mediated Communication*, 7(3). Retrieved March 19 2016 from www.websm.org/uploadi/editor/Lozar_2002_Design.doc.

McClendon, M. J., & Alwin, D. F. (1993). No-opinion filters and attitude measurement reliability. *Sociological Methods and Research*, 21, 438–464.

Moroney, W. F., & Cameron, J. (2016). The questionnaire as conversation: Time for a paradigm shift, or at least a paradigm nudge? *Ergonomics in Design: The Quarterly of Human Factors Applications*, 24(2), 10–15.

Preston, C. C., & Colman, A. M. (2000). Optimal number of response categories in rating scales: Reliability, validity, discriminating power, and respondent preferences. *Acta Psychologica*, 104(1), 1–15.

Ravichandran, S., & Arendt, S. W. (2008). How to increase response rates when surveying hospitality managers for curriculum-related research: Lessons from past studies and interviews with lodging professionals. *Journal of Teaching in Travel & Tourism*, 8(1), 47–71.

Ray, J. J. (1990). Acquiescence and problems with forced-choice scales. *The Journal of Social Psychology*, 130(3), 397–399.

Revilla, M. A., Saris, W. E., & Krosnick, J. A. (2013). Choosing the number of categories in agree–disagree scales. *Sociological Methods & Research*, doi: 0049124113509605.

Ryan, C., & Garland, R. (1999). The use of a specific non-response option on Likert-type scales. *Tourism Management*, 20(1), 107–113

Saris, W. E., Revilla, M., Krosnick, J. A., & Shaeffer, E. M. (2010). Comparing questions with agree/disagree response options to questions with item-specific response options. *Survey Research Methods*, 4(1), 61–79.

Schleyer, T., & Forrest, J. L. (2000). Methods for the design and administration of web-based surveys. *Journal of the American Medical Informatics Association*, 7(4), 416–425.

Smyth, J. D., Dillman, D. A., Christian, L. M., & Stern, M. J. (2006). Comparing check-all and forced-choice question formats in web surveys. *Public Opinion Quarterly*, 70(1), 66–77.

Song, Y., Son, Y. J., & Oh, D. (2015). Methodological issues in questionnaire design. *Journal of Korean Academy of Nursing*, 45(3), 323–328.

Stehr-Green, P. A., Stehr-Green J.K., & Nelson, A. (2003). Developing a questionnaire. *Focus on Field Epidemiology*, 2(2), 1–6.

Toepoel, V., Das, M., & van Soest, A. (2009a). Design of web questionnaires: The effect of layout in rating scales. *Journal of Official Statistics*, 25(4), 509–528.

Toepoel, V., Das, M., & van Soest, A. (2009b). Design of web questionnaires: The effects of the number of items per screen. *Field Methods*, 21(2), 200–213

Tourangeau, R., Couper, M. P., & Conrad, F. (2007). Color, labels, and interpretive heuristics for response scales. *Public Opinion Quarterly*, 71(1), 91–112.

Tourangeau, R., Rips, L. J., & Rasinski, K. A. (2000). *The psychology of survey response*. Cambridge: Cambridge University Press.

Vannette, D. L., & Krosnick, J. A. (2014). A comparison of survey satisficing and mindlessness. In Ie, A., Ngnoumen, C. T., & Lang. E. J. (eds.). *The Wiley Blackwell handbook of mindfulness* (pp. 312–327). New York: John Wiley & Sons.

Vicente, P., & Reis, E. (2010). Using questionnaire design to fight nonresponse bias in web surveys. *Social Science Computer Review*, 28(2), 251–267.

Weatherly, J. N., Derenne, A., & Terrell, H. K. (2011). Testing the reliability of delay discounting of ten commodities using the fill-in-the-blank method. *The Psychological Record*, 61(1), 113–126.

Part III
Hospitality marketing approaches, functions and strategies

8

The foundation of twenty-first-century hospitality marketing strategy

Bonnie J. Knutson

Some of my earliest memories are of working in our family's store. Like many others of my generation, I grew up in a family business. We had a small, neighborhood Italian grocery store that offered conventional packaged items and locally grown produce. What set our store apart from all other grocery stores, however, was its superior meats. People would come from far and wide just to buy the top-quality premium meat that my dad sold. He wouldn't even let choice grade in the store.

I was fortunate to have learned marketing at my dad's knee. Even though he only had an eighth-grade education, he instinctively knew that the most important real estate in marketing is the six inches between the consumer's ears. He would often tell me that marketing has nothing to do with our store itself, but had everything to do with how people think about our store. Little did either of us know that Al Ries and Jack Trout would encapsulate what my dad always believed in their benchmark book, *Positioning: The Battle for Your Mind*.[1] Their revolutionary approach showed that a business's marketing strategy must create a "position" in the consumer's mind that reflects the brand's strengths and weaknesses as well as those of its competitors.

Sitting on top of the mind's ladder

The goal of every hospitality brand should be to create TOMA. TOMA is an acronym that stands for Top-of-Mind-Awareness – i.e. where your brand is positioned on a ladder in the minds of its customers and prospective customers. When an executive wants to have lunch with business associates, what is the first place that comes to mind? When a bridesmaid wants to host a wedding shower, what is the first venue that she thinks about? When a new executive moves into town, what is the first club that he or she looks to join? Reaching the lofty TOMA goal is important because a person will buy the first thing that comes to mind 67% of the time.[2] This gives the top-ranked brand in its category a distinct competitive advantage.

The definitive work on ladders in the mind came from Al Ries and Jack Trout, in their classic book. Because we live in an over-communicated society, the cluttered mind has to organize information in such a way that it makes sense and can readily be retrieved. So we form mental categorical ladders with all possibilities neatly organized on their respective rungs. To manage the explosion of brands, products, and services, people categorize and rank each possibility in their minds. Visualize a series of ladders in your mind. Each ladder represents a different product category. Places to have Sunday breakfast with the children. Restaurants for a romantic candle-light dinner. Someplace to impress clients. A bed and breakfast for a weekend getaway. Hotels to host a large corporate meeting or conference. The most prestigious country club to join. Each rung on the mind's ladder represents a brand name or possibility where you can go to fulfill that particular need or want.

Some mental ladders have several steps.[3] Others have few. Still others have one. Take the notion of where to go for Sunday breakfast with the children. A family could go to IHOP, McDonald's, a local diner, or have brunch at an area hotel. They could even swing by Whole Foods and pick up ready-to-eat items to take home and eat on their deck. The question is, which alternative is on the top rung of the ladder? Which has TOMA? Where does your hospitality brand rank on its categorical ladder? Marketing is all about getting to the top rung in the consumer's mind.

A new definition

Marketing is known by many definitions. Conceptually, managers plan, organize, staff, motivate, and control. Managers also compete. At its core, marketing is a competitive process designed to result in consumers selecting your business over the countless other competitive alternatives available to them. With the unique nature of the increasingly competitive hospitality industry, it is critical that managers hone their marketing skills in order to successfully compete. To say that every hospitality brand lives in an unprecedented era of competition is an understatement. Operating costs have skyrocketed – products, labor, insurance, energy, and yes, even marketing. At the same time, the ability or willingness of consumers to absorb these rising costs in the form of increased prices, fewer choices, and less service has diminished. Every manager feels the squeeze.

Some may consider marketing to be research, advertising, or selling. While these are parts of marketing, they are not marketing in its true and contemporary sense. Marketing is actually the change agent for a hospitality organization. In the twenty-first century, marketing serves as a change agent because it focuses on the rapidly changing needs and wants of customers. It guides the organization to research, design, and develop strategies that respond to an increasingly unpredictable and competitive business environment. At its core, then, marketing is innovation. In other words, it anticipates change and makes adjustments to change; it is the change mechanism – the innovator – for the business.[4] While marketing is not the whole business, it is the heart of the business.

An interesting corollary says that, in essence, a hospitality business is really in the business of raising a customer's standard of living.[5] This notion addresses the social and psychological nature of any hospitality business, which helps to elevate guests to higher-order hospitality needs. By definition, human beings – i.e. consumers – are social creatures. They have a strong sense of community, of wanting to belong to something. Do you remember studying Abraham Maslow's hierarchy of needs? Maslow tells us that, once we have our basic survival needs met – food, water, shelter – we are motivated by our need to be a part of something larger than we are. We want to belong to a group or a community. So it is natural that people want to connect with brands that give them a sense of belonging to something special. Brands such as Harley-Davidson, Starbucks, Amazon, and even Oprah are classic examples.

A strong foundation will support a strong business. In the case of effective marketing, the foundation is built on a modern definition that can be applicable to all types of hospitality in all types of situations. Its underpinning comes from words in the American Marketing Association's revised 2013 definition: "Marketing is the activity, set of institutions, and processes for creating, communicating, delivering, and exchanging offerings that have value for customers, clients, partners, and society at large."[6] If we cull these words into a fresh definition for the contemporary hospitality industry, we can simply say that hospitality marketing is the process for making and keeping customers at a profit. Period. Embodied within this uncomplicated 13-word description is everything a hospitality enterprise has to do to grow and maintain an active, loyal, and profitable market. If I can adapt an aphorism from marketing authority Sergio Zeeman, hospitality marketing is simply selling more things to more people more often for more money at more profit.[7]

Positioning

There are many in the hospitality industry who think that the concept of positioning is a relatively new idea. It isn't. While the notion has been around for 40 years,[8] it really didn't become a lexicon in the business world until the early 1980s when Ries and Trout published their hallmark *Positioning* book. Since that time, positioning has been slowly but surely edging its way into the hospitality world, where today, it has been elevated to an essential principle in marketing.

But just exactly what is positioning and why is it so critical? Positioning has always been defined as, not what you do to the product or service, but what you do to the mind.[9] Over the years, it has come to mean two things. First, it is the total process by which marketers try to create a desirable image in the minds of their target markets. For hospitality, this process includes every detail from the appearance of the parking area to pricing to room design to the ease of navigating the website. Said another way, the process includes every – and I mean every – single touch point between the brand and the customer or prospective customer. Here's where the notion of focus enters the marketing picture.

Think of focus like a magnet. In magnets, all the magnetic domains (molecules) point in the same direction. These microscopic magnetic fields combine to create one large magnetic field so the magnet works; it attracts. The more the domains point in the same direction, the stronger the overall field. If, on the other hand, the domains are not aligned – i.e. they all don't point in the same direction – the material will not produce a magnetic field. It will not work; it will not attract; it just sits there.[10] It is the same with positioning. All the business's "domains" must point towards one clear positioning strategy in order to create a strong magnetic marketing field.

To illustrate, here are three examples showing how a brand image can be undermined by having one little marketing element out of focus. There was a new restaurant named America's Cup. It was a casual, mid-priced, young adult-orientated spot where you could get a good sandwich, tasty sides, and a cold drink. As you would expect, it had a nautical theme in décor, menu items, and promotions. The marketing thrust was definitely red, white, and blue. One day, when I walked in there for a quick lunch meeting, something was very out of sync. The servers were all dressed in brown pants and orange shirts! Brown and orange? In a nautical-themed restaurant? It just didn't fit. And it surely didn't support the brand image. When I asked the manager why the brown and orange, his answer was that he had them left over from another of his restaurants and he wanted to save money by re-using them. That decision was definitely not on strategy and did not strengthen his brand.

Then there is Chipotle. During 2015, it was rocked by an outbreak of E.coli in its restaurants. While management was praised for taking a pro-active stance on the problem, the negative publicity did not reinforce its image of fresh ingredients and sustainable food practices. Sales dropped and their stock price suffered.

Finally, there is the country club that wanted to position itself as the premier luxury club in its competitive area. Yet, when a member calls for a dinner reservation, the first question the receptionist asks is, "What is your member number?" According to the general manager, this procedure makes it easier on the staff. While it may be easier on the staff, this one decision undermines the club's marketing strategy. Is there anything in that member number question that says "premier" or "luxury"? I think not.

Each of these cases shows how one marketing faux pas can weaken an entire positioning strategy. There is an old saying that a successful marketing strategy is not doing one thing a thousand percent better, but doing a thousand things one percent better. You can readily understand why it is so important to have every single customer touch point in focus – i.e. supporting the hospitality brand's image, supporting its desired strategic position.

This is particularly important in the social media era. I'm often asked about the impact of user-generated social media on brand equity. Simply put, it diminishes your control of your brand's message. When you promote or advertise via traditional (old) media, you can significantly generate awareness, interest, and drive expectations, which can be enhanced if you integrate new media into your promotional strategy. But when consumers communicate with other consumers via social media channels, their comments can influence brand image, expectations, and even behaviors. It becomes word of mouth on steroids. While data differ across sources, the influence of social media in customer-to-customer communication cannot be denied. In general, about 70 percent of consumers place more value in user-generated comments (positive or negative) that in online content generated by businesses.[11] Simply put, 92 percent of consumers trust recommendations from others, even people they don't know, over branded content, and 70 percent say that online reviews are their second-most-trusted source. Nearly half also follow comments on blogs.[12]

The second thing positioning means is that a brand can only position itself on one thing. This is called the brand's attribute or differentiating characteristic. While it can differentiate on anything, it must differentiate on something. The business must be known for something that clearly sets it apart from its competitors. Some cases in point:

Absolut Vodka, a Swedish brand of vodka, uses advertising to separate it from its competitors. In a market segment that is pretty generic in product qualities (some vodka aficionados might disagree on this point), Absolut's fame is due to its long-running print advertising campaign that is based on the distinctive shape of its bottle. Started more than 35 years ago, the ads cleverly feature the Absolut bottle-shape in the center and a title such as *Absolut Manhattan* that features an aerial photo of Manhattan where Central Park is shown in the shape of the Absolut bottle.

Then there is the legendary Madonna Inn near San Luis Obispo, California. As an international landmark destination, the Madonna Inn redefines the unique resort category with its enchanting décor and 110 whimsical guestrooms, whose themes range from Krazy Dazy to Matterhorn to Yahoo.[13] There is also Dick's Last Resort, "known for its outrageous, surly, and energetic servers who dish out good grub, cold booze, and heaping helpings of sarcasm."[14] And who can hear the name *The Masters* and not think of Augusta?

Walmart is famous for its low prices. Newman's Own stands out because of its social consciousness, W Hotels stand apart as the original trendy hotel, Jennifer Lopez (J-Lo) is known for her beauty, Einstein for his mind, and the Kardashians for "keeping up with."

In marketing, the term *attribute* is widely used but rarely understood. Simply put, an attribute is a characteristic or distinctive feature of a business. While each hospitality business is a mixture of many characteristics, being known for one of these attributes is what makes it unique in the consumer's mind. Marilyn Monroe could have been an intellectual genius, but that wasn't what she was known for. What made her special was that she was the pinup beauty of her time. In the world of umbrellas, the Brigg is arguably the most famous, not for its design, its materials, or its price. Its claim to fame is the fact that it has been awarded the Royal Warrant as umbrella supplier to the Prince of Wales. Wouldn't you want to stay dry the same way as the royal family does? The same differentiation rules goes for Crest; it fights cavities. AFLAC; it has the duck. St. Andrews; it is the home of golf. And Ragu; it's Italian.

The thing that has changed the hospitality industry business the most over the past decade is the amazing proliferation of product choices in virtually every category imaginable. In the hotel sector alone, there are full-service, limited service, extended stay, resorts, boutiques, motels, bed and breakfasts, and the recently added Airbnb segment. Within each, there are luxury, mid-price, and economy. Then there are family, pet-friendly, adults-only, and all-inclusive. There is even a segment called flophouses. It is the same with restaurants. Common segments include fast food, fast casual, family, fine dining, buffet, pub, bar, and café or bistro. There are chains, regionals, and the independent "mom and pop" restaurants. More recently, food trucks and pop up restaurants are adding additional competition, along with the food service available in supermarkets, convenience-stores, and even department stores. The same is true for private clubs where there is the traditional country club category as well as more targeted niche club such as tennis, yacht, and fitness.

The only way a hospitality business can stand out among its competitors is to be known for something. Anything. If yours is a hotel, your strategy could be to position it as historic, such as the 1886 Crescent Hotel & Spa, that sits high above the Victorian village of Eureka Springs, Arkansas. It is a distinctive landmark hotel recognized by the National Trust for Historic Preservation and known as the symbol of hospitality in its region. If yours is a restaurant, it may be known as having the best ice cream in your market, like Tom's Ice Cream Bowl, which is tucked away in a residential neighborhood in Zanesville, Ohio. Maybe it could be positioned as having the largest wine selection, as is Bern's Steakhouse, in the SoHo district of New York City. I even knew of one club that was known for the special popovers it served in lieu of dinner rolls, which became the surrogate for having the best food in the area.

Peter Drucker once defined leadership as "thinking through the organization's mission, defining it and establishing it, clearly and visibly."[15] Jack Trout, also author of *Differentiate or Die*, said that in this age of killer competition, he would change the definition to "thinking through the organization's difference, defining it and establishing it, clearly and visibly."[16] I agree. The key, then, is to think through your brand's many features, find the attribute that makes it unique, and you'll have the key to develop the marketing strategy that will effectively build your brand position.

Four positioning quadrants

Developing a positioning strategy may seem like a difficult task. There are countless texts written about it. Industry magazines are full of articles about how this brand succeeded or that brand failed. There are also presentations at industry conferences, association meetings, seminars, webinars, as well as countless consultants. All of these sources are valuable and can provide significant insights into your marketing strategy. But the sheer numbers of available resources can make the process seem confusing and complicated. It's not. It's not because there are basically four – and only four – positioning strategies a brand can adopt. They are called the Four Strategic Quadrants of Marketing.[17] The objective is to identify which of the four strategies will yield the most effective marketing efforts and then build on it.

These four strategies are built around the intersection of two axes, both of which influence how any hospitality business can sell more products to more guests more often for more money and at more profit. The horizontal axis is anchored at one end by how early the brand was established – i.e. when the brand entered its market. The other end of the horizontal axis is anchored by how dependent the brand is on its attributes and image to distinguish it in the market. The vertical axis is anchored at one end by how succinctly the business meets the needs of its customers and, at the other end, by its credibility for consistently providing top quality over time. The intersection of these axes forms the four quadrants, giving us the four basic brand positioning strategies: First, Biggest, Best, or Different.

Be first

Strategy #1 is to position your brand as the original in its category. Being first simply means that the brand is the earliest one in the market seen to fulfill consumers' needs. This strategy communicates originality and expertise in the category. There is no substitute for being 'the real thing'; all others become merely derivatives. By being the original, you delegate competitors to a copycat position; i.e. this is akin to being a reproduction of a masterpiece. The classic example of this strategy is, of course, Coca-Cola. Born in Atlanta, Georgia, on May 8, 1886, pharmacist Dr. John Stith Pemberton created the syrup that would be teamed with carbonated water to produce the first drink giving consumers "a moment of refreshment for a very small amount of money" (https:/fee. org/articles/beautiful-together-through-advertising/). This simple strategy launched a global identity that now operates in more than 200 countries. Coca-Cola positions itself as the "real thing."

If a marketing strategy is to be positioned as the original; all competitors must therefore be copies. The beauty of being defined as the first or original is that, by definition, there can only be one brand in the category. Residence Inn is an example. The chain was launched in 1975 in Wichita, Kansas by Jack DeBoer as an extended stay concept, and was acquired by Marriott International in 1987. In reality, however, extended stays existed earlier in the form of cottages or hostels. But it took DeBoer to name and promote the category, thereby positioning Residence Inn as the original extended stay brand. Within any competitive set, then, there can only be one original beach resort, one original Italian pizza parlor, one original yacht club, one original winery, one original fitness club in a market. There can only be one St. Andrews, the home of golf.

If your brand is not really the original in a category, you can still claim that strategy by being perceived as being first. The key is staking a claim on a specific attribute of the brand and successfully promoting it. Consider Boston's famed Durgin-Park with its tagline that *We serve history*. While it certainly wasn't the original restaurant in the city, its history does go back to pre-revolutionary times when merchant Peter Faneuil (of Faneuil Hall fame) added a small dining room in his waterfront warehouse.[18] Maybe your hotel can lay claim to being the first to be a totally "green" property, or maybe the building is seen as "cool" because it was created by an internationally recognized young designer. In both of these cases, there is an attribute on which a marketing strategy can center on being seen as the original or first.

Be biggest

Strategy #2 is built on size or market penetration. Being number one communicates the credibility of becoming the leader in a category. It can often result from the fact that it was first and could establish a large base (i.e. market share) before serious competitors entered the fray. This strategy evolves over time with consistency in facilities, programs, and service quality. Consumers come to trust the brand and give trustworthiness to its message. In non-hospitality industries, Microsoft, Apple, and Home Depot are all cases in which their category leadership position allows them to embrace the biggest or number one strategy.

Here too, even though a brand may not be the leader in its category, it can still employ a market leader strategy by identifying a single attribute in which it can be perceived as having the biggest market share. Perhaps you have the biggest marina along the coastline, possibly your club boasts the largest membership in the area, or maybe your hotel ballroom can seat more people than any other venue in the city. Here again, only one brand can enjoy the position of biggest or market share leader in its attribute category. By default, then, all others in that market are positioned as inferior on that single attribute.

Be better

Strategy #3 establishes the hospitality brand as the best or better than all its competitors. Being better communicates having superior facilities, products, and service or the inferiority of the competition. By being the best, you can derive a "We're #1" strategy, much like Walmart does in the discount category, Southwest Airlines accomplishes in the low-cost airline class, and FedEx achieves when packages "absolutely, positively have to be there overnight."

Again, a brand can also be *perceived* as being better if it identifies a specific attribute and positions on it. For example, in 1978, Burger King launched its flamed broiled campaign as a positioning strategy against the market leader, McDonald's. In a similar vein, Wendy's classic 1984 "where's the beef?" campaign was designed to position it as a better value in the hamburger wars. And, again, only one hospitality brand can effectively claim the positioning strategy of being best or better in its category or perceived as best on a given attribute or characteristic.

Be different

But what if your brand is not the first, is not the biggest, or is not the best in the category in which it competes? What positioning strategy is left for it? Fortunately, there is a fourth, which we call Different. This is the strategy that most hospitality brands adopt. Being different communicates the benefit of having a unique attribute or benefit that is unlike any offerings currently available. There are examples such as Heart Attack Grill, with its differentiated hamburger experience, Pringles, with its tubular packaging, or Buffalo Wild Wings (BW3), with its saucy chicken wings. What unique attribute makes your hospitality brand different? The distinctive styles of pizza? The funky décor? A spectacular ocean view from every guest room balcony? A club that focuses on having great family/children's activities? Whichever characteristic your research and analysis identifies, embrace it and make sure all your marketing domains communicate that uniqueness.

About now, you may be thinking that your brand can fit into more than one of these four positioning quadrants. That's possible and may even be probable. After all, Walmart could readily position itself as being the first, being the biggest, being the best, and being different. The same might be said for brands like Starbucks, Nike, and Whole Foods. But each of these successful brands is smart enough to clearly position itself in only one of the quadrants. They know that, in this overly communicated and highly competitive business environment, their brand must be known for something that clearly sets it apart from its competitors. It must be the same for your hospitality business. So remember these three truisms: (1) Positioning means that a brand must establish a clear picture in the minds of consumers. (2) To achieve this, it must adopt a positioning strategy rooted in one of these four quadrants: first, biggest, best, and different. (3) While it can position itself on *many* of its attributes, it must select only *one*.

Porter's positioning power

Originally an engineer, Michael Porter became a noted economist specializing in business strategies to achieve and maintain a competitive advantage. In his 1980 classic, *Competitive Strategy: Techniques for Analyzing Industries and Competitors*, Porter offers three strategies that can overlay onto the four positioning quadrants.[19] His strategies are defined by two components. He calls one "strategic scope," which looks at the demand side of the equation – i.e. both the extent and composition of the target market. For any hospitality business, this means the number and size of the target markets from which you can draw. He calls the other the "strategic strength," which looks at the supply side. For your brand, this means analyzing your core competencies to find the best attribute on which to differentiate it among all its competitors.

In its simplest form, Porter believes that a brand can distinguish itself in one of three attribute areas. The first is price. But if it doesn't make sense to position your business as being the low cost, cheapest, or most expensive among its competitors, it could readily be positioned on value, prestige, or exclusivity – all of which are surrogates for price. Porter's second area is market segment, which can come into play if your mission is to attract only a narrow segment of the market. For example, a fitness club could target only serious, hard core strength-building members. While not a private club, this is the successful strategy adopted by *Curves*, the fitness venture designed for women who are uncomfortable working out in a more traditional gym. A restaurant might position itself as the trendy after-work lounge for young executives, much like the Entrepreneurs' Organization (EO) has done for entrepreneurs only. The EO is now a dynamic, global network of more than 20,000 business owners in 48 countries. Founded in 1987 by a group of young entrepreneurs, EO is the catalyst that enables entrepreneurs to learn and grow from each other, leading to greater business success and an enriched personal life. To a large extent, their success stems from the strategy to target a very narrow market.[20] Porter's third strategy centers on finding that element that is considered inimitable or so unique by consumers that they are willing to pay a premium to experience it. A notable example is Dinner-in-the-Sky. In 2006, a communications agency and a company that provided cranes for amusement park installations joined forces to develop this distinctive flying dinner table concept.[21]

You can see that overlaying these three strategies on the four quadrants can readily give you 12 potential approaches to establishing a succinct and effective position in the minds of consumers. It is important to remember, however, that you must do the work (translate work into research, analysis, and strategic planning) to find that single attribute on which your brand should be hung. One attribute. Only one. It is essential to remember, too, that a brand's position is the sum perception achieved in the mind of the current and prospective customer as a result of every communication the brand has with its target market – i.e. every consumer touch point.

Three functions of a hospitality marketer

Nearly half a century ago, business guru Theodore Levitt said that the purpose of business is to make and keep customers.[22] It might seem that his admonition is just plain common sense, not some cutting-edge revelation. On the other hand, competitive pressures are forcing some hospitality managers to believe that the purpose of any business is making money. The focus on skyrocketing operational costs, dwindling revenues, ROMIs (Returns on Marketing Investment), cost containment, and a series of sophisticated business school jargon has drawn attention away from the real purpose of business: *to make and keep customers*. No one is suggesting that revenues are not important. They are critical in an industry that lives on repeat business, loyalty, brand image, and cash flow. Without adequate revenues (and cash flow), a restaurant, a hotel, a club, or an entertainment venue "ain't no more."

As a hospitality business leader, you understand your facilities, products, programs and services; you understand managerial accounting, how to compute ROIs, and how to establish cost control procedures; and you understand how to manage your employees. Each of these functions is an essential support to the purpose of your brand; i.e. your customers. It is marketing that *focuses* a business on the value of making and keeping its customers. Therefore, you have to view marketing as a process with three major tasks.

Identify the demand

If you remember your basic economics courses, demand is the size of the market that is ready, willing, and able to buy by attracting customers who have the need/want and resources to buy. In other words, demand is simply finding the opportunities to increase market share. This function has two complementary parts. The first task is to pinpoint the number of potential customers that fit your target markets. The second task, of course, is to really understand the needs, wants, and expectations of current customers – i.e. their "hot buttons."

Influence the demand

In its essence, influencing demand is persuading people to pass up the competition and spend their time and money in your property. It is the function which we commonly think of when we hear the word marketing. Influencing is promoting your brand's benefits and experiences. It is developing programs, products, and services that your target market need, want, expect – and are willing to pay for. It is effectively communicating these benefits in ways and places that break through the clutter, are memorable, and will drive action. It is the sum total of all communication touch points between your brand and consumers. This is the part of marketing that sways people's choices through differentiation, brand building, and communicating.

Service the demand

We all know that the most powerful form of advertising is still word of mouth, or in today's electronic world, world of mouth. In the marketing field, it is called radial advertising. Radial advertising emanates from operations, of course. We also all know that past experience is the best predictor of future buying behavior because we all want to recreate the good experiences we have had. If, then, operations influence how many times people come to your restaurant for dinner, whether they make reservations for the annual New Year's Eve celebration in your ballroom, or where they choose to stay on vacation, shouldn't operations come under the marketing umbrella? In the new perspective of marketing, the answer is clearly yes. This is why the new AMA definition includes the notion of *delivering* and *value*.

The worst thing business ever did was structure an organizational chart that places the chief executive at the top of a pyramid with marketing branching out on one side and operations on the other. Visually, it separates the two functions. As a result, the value of servicing demand was never seen as an indispensable part of marketing. Times have changed, however, so the need to draw the *three* elements – identifying, influencing, and servicing – together under a single marketing philosophy is gaining prominence. Take a look at your organizational chart to make sure it reflects this new, unified reality.

Each of these three marketing responsibilities involves a variety of marketing tasks: research, positioning, packaging, differentiating, pricing, promotion, servicing, budgeting and analysis – all of which serve the purpose of increasing guest count and loyalty. In other words, you can adopt the mantra of the camp song we used to sing as children: *Make new friends (members), but keep the old; one is silver and the other gold.*[23]

Notes

1 Ries, Al and Trout, Jack. (2001) *Positioning: The Battle for Your Mind*. McGraw-Hill.
2 www.businessnorth.com/marketing.asp?RID=433
3 The maximum number of rungs on a mind's ladder is generally thought to be seven; three is considered to be typical. Marketing expert, Eloy Trevino, however, uses a "rule of two." He believes that, in any category, there is #1 and #2, then there is everyone else. Think of soft drinks where there is Coca-Cola and Pepsi, then everyone else. In discount stores, there is Walmart and Target, then everyone else. In ketchup, it is Heinz and Hunts and everyone else.
4 Knutson, Bonnie (2012) *Membership Marketing in the New Millennium*. Club Managers Association of America, pp. 2–4.
5 This theory is based on thoughts put forth by noted marketer, Phillip Kotler, in his book, *Principles of Marketing*. Prentice-Hall, 1996.
6 www.ama.org/AboutAMA/Pages/Definition-of-Marketing.aspx
7 Zeeman, Sergio and Brott, Armin. (2003) *The End of Advertising as We Know It*. John Wiley & Sons.
8 Trout, Jack. (1969) "'Positioning' is a game people play in today's me-too market place," *Industrial Marketing*, vol. 54, no. 6, pp. 51–55.
9 Trout, Jack. (1996) *The New Positioning*. McGraw-Hill, p. ix.
10 Graphics (How Magnets Work): http://science.howstuffworks.com/magnet1.htm
11 www.dmnews.com/dmnotes/10-stats-that-show-why-user-generated-content-works/article/444872/
12 www.adweek.com/socialtimes/why-influencer-marketing-is-the-new-content-king-infographic/618187
13 www.madonnainn.com/
14 www.dickslastresort.com/
15 www.word-gems.com/leadership.drucker.html
16 Trout, Jack. (2000) *Differentiate or Die*. John Wiley & Sons, p. 53.
17 Development of the 4-Quadrant Concept has been a collaborative effort led by Eloy Trevino, one of the most brilliant marketing strategists I've ever had the pleasure to work with. He is with Prophet and located in Chicago.
18 http://arkrestaurants.com/durgin_park/
19 Porter, Michael. (1980) *Competitive Strategy: Techniques for Analysing Industries and Competitors*. The Free Press.
20 www.eonetwork.org/
21 http://dinnerinthesky.com/#concept
22 www.rites-of-passage.com/images/Levitt_TheMarketingImagination.pdf
23 www.scoutsongs.com/lyrics/makenewfriends.html

9

Product/service management

Drita Kruja

Introduction

In the marketing world, the term *product* refers to any goods and services sold by a business. A good is a tangible item that can be touched, such as pizza. A service refers to an activity undertaken for another person, such as providing a place to sleep. The main product of the hospitality industry is service. Many hospitality businesses, such as restaurants, provide both goods and services. The goods are the food, while the services are identified as the cooking, presentation, and serving of that food (Reynolds and Chase 2014: 384).

Although different approaches are utilized by authors regarding the product offer, all agree on the point that the product is composed of a complex of tangible and intangible elements. The development of the marketing offer begins with the product/service; there is nothing to sell without the product concept. The basic functional solutions are simply delivered by the products to address consumer needs and wants, and should be designed to provide customer satisfaction to specified target markets. When examining the product element of the marketing mix, the key point that should be kept in mind is the complexity of the hospitality offering.

Besides the planned component, the product (particularly in relation to hospitality and travel products) also includes unplanned elements that can dramatically distort and disrupt the experience, leading to unplanned customer dissatisfaction or, for that matter, satisfaction (Kotler, Bowen and Makens 2014: 240).

This chapter explores the components of the hospitality service/product, product/benefit bundles, new product development, and the product life cycle. It presents two perspectives from which the product is viewed. The first focuses on that of the customer, which is represented by a bundle of benefits that will satisfy their needs and wants. The second is that of the firm and represents what it creates and offers to the customer. The chapter concludes that product planning should consider all of these aspects in order to come up with the "right" product.

Customer experience

The hospitality industry has been identified as being a business of people. The full range of features and characteristics that make up any hospitality experience are extremely wide and the use of a variety of services will vary from customer to customer. Each experience will be different due to the characteristics of services, both tangible and intangible.

The basic equation that captures all the components of the customer experience that must be effectively managed by those in the industry as per Ford, Sturman and Heaton (2012: 10) is:

Customer (guest) experience = service product + service setting + service delivery system

The service/product offering

Hospitality products are an output of the hotel and catering industry and can be defined as the set of satisfactions and dissatisfactions derived by a customer from their hospitality experience.

For example, Medlik and Ingram (2000) have identified five basic components of hotels that contribute to this experience:

- Location – geographical placement of a hotel in a particular village or town; its specific location offering convenience and easy access in an area free of noise and other disturbances; attractiveness of its surroundings.
- Facilities – the infrastructural and recreational facilities, such as bedrooms, restaurants, bars, conference rooms, swimming pools, tennis courts etc.
- Services – personal attention.
- Image – how the hotel is generally perceived by consumers.
- Price – expression of value provided by the hotel through its location, facilities and satisfaction derived by consumers from the use of the above elements of the service product.

Product benefit bundles

Consumers rarely purchase a single hospitality product in isolation. Customers search for a combination of benefits for the satisfaction of their needs and wants.

Products such as accommodation, food and drink offered by hospitality businesses are part of the larger tourism product, either through a tour operator or the customer experience of visiting the tourist destination.

A hospitality service/product is defined as a bundle of benefits comprised of the physical environment, the effects of service personnel and other customers (Bateson 2002). Customer satisfaction can be affected by external factors outside the control of hospitality operators.

For example, for a hotel visitor (business or leisure), the hotel product is a "bundle," which may itemized as:

- Initial experience and reactions in selecting from a brochure.
- Experience of the booking process.
- First impression on entering the hotel.
- Reception process on arrival.
- Standard of room and any en suite facilities.
- Experience of customer–staff interactions.
- Provision of meals and any ancillary services.
- Checking out process on leaving.
- Any follow up, such as online questionnaire of feedback, received subsequently.

(Middleton et al. 2009: 85)

This list serves to stress the point that individual products are composed of a series of elements that combine to satisfy the purchaser's needs. This helps marketing managers to increase their knowledge of products and improve their presentation and delivery to prospective customers.

The service/product offering consists of four elements: (1) a core product (benefit), (2) facilitating products/services, (3) supporting services/products, and (4) the augmented product (or extended product).

The core benefit

The core product is "what" the customer is fundamentally buying and is the main reason for the service purchase (Wirtz and Lovelock 2016). This consists of the very basic features and is the main reason for consumption. In hospitality, the core product (benefit) is the generic function that it provides for guests. For an operation, it is the reason for being in the market (Gronroos 1990). Hotels offer a place to sleep (accommodation and security), while a restaurant provides a place to eat (the provision of nourishment and a pleasant social experience). The core products are defined by the customer, not the business. If a resort hotel advertised as being for "rest and recuperation" is chosen by the customer, then R&R is the core product for that customer. Normally, the core product level is not the key for competition with other hospitality businesses.

Supplementary services

Delivery of the core product is usually accompanied by a variety of other service-related activities referred to as *supplementary services*. These augment the core product, facilitating its use, and reinforcing value-added enhancements that help customers to use it more effectively and add appeal to their overall experience. Core products tend to become commoditized as the industry matures and competition increases, so the search for competitive advantage often emphasizes supplementary services. Adding supplementary elements or increasing their level of performance should be done in ways that enhance the perceived value of the core product and enable the service provider to charge a higher price.

Supplementary services include facilitating and supporting services.

Facilitating services are an absolutely essential part of an operation. Without these, delivery of the core benefit becomes impossible. In a hotel, the absence of a front desk or housekeeping will make it unworkable. Similarly, in a restaurant, the kitchen provides a facilitating service; without it, the operation cannot function. For a resort, recreation facilities are an essential facilitating service and can be arranged in such a way that they can also be used to differentiate the operation from competitors. An example is a restaurant that not only has a kitchen but one that provides exceptional cuisine, or perhaps an open kitchen which displays the cooking process.

One of the most powerful facilitating services in lodging is the reservation system. Reservations (including appointments and check-in) represent a special type of order-taking that entitles customers to a specified unit of service – for example, an airline seat, restaurant table, or hotel room (Wirtz and Lovelock 2016).

Another facilitating service offered by most hotels and an increasing number of restaurants is information. Customers appreciate advice on how to get the most value from a service and how to avoid problems. Also, documentation may be required by customers for what has already taken place, such as the confirmation of reservations, receipts and tickets, or monthly summaries of account activity. Companies should ensure they provide timely and accurate information.

The most useful way to provide information is by using front-line employees, printed notices, brochures, and instruction books. Information can also be provided through videos or software-driven tutorials, touch-screen video displays, or through company websites. This service is intended to bind customers to the operation.

Supporting services are not essential to providing the core benefit, but are critical to *marketing* the operation. They are used to differentiate an operation from its competitors. For example, a restaurant is not a necessary component of a hotel, but its presence can be used to differentiate one property from another. For example, Marriott Hotels offer a variety of foodservices at each hotel location, whereas the company's Courtyard by Marriott properties offer only limited foodservice and its Fairfield Inns arm offers no foodservice. The availability of foodservice is used, then, to differentiate Marriott hotel products from one another and from other lodging products.

The location of the hotel will impact the range and scope of services offered. A remote country hotel may offer comprehensive in-house leisure facilities and entertainment whereas a city centre hotel may not need to offer such a range of facilities since guests will be more likely to leave the hotel to experience the city.

Supporting services/products offer a competitive advantage only if they are properly planned and implemented. They must meet or exceed customer expectations to achieve a positive effect (Kotler, Bowen and Makens 2014: 242).

Extended product/service

Hospitality companies can compete by making their service different from competitors through enhancements to the basic service. The core service is the basic market competency of the business, but it is insufficient as the basis for commercial success in a highly competitive market, one with low barriers to entry. Rapert and Wren (1998), and Kotler and Armstrong (2010) explain that to best satisfy customers, businesses in the hospitality industry must offer an extended product.

The goal of Starbucks is to serve the customer within three minutes from the back of the line to receiving their drink in their hand. This benchmark was based on market research which indicated that the three-minute standard was a key component in how current Starbucks customers defined "excellent service" (Wirtz and Lovelock 2016: 720).

Physical setting

The second component of the customer experience is the physical setting or environment (so-called servicescape) in which the experience takes place. Bitner (1992: 65) defines servicescape as "all of the objective physical factors that can be controlled by the firm to enhance (or constrain) employee and customer actions". Various studies over the years (Booms and Bitner 1982; Bitner 1986, 1990, 1992; Han and Ryu 2009; Harrell, Hutt and Anderson 1980; Kotler 1973; Kotler, Bowen and Makens 2014; Mehrabian and Russell 1974; Reimer and Kuehn 2005; Shostack 1977; Zeithaml, Parasuraman and Berry 1985; Wakefield and Blodett 1996; Wirtz and Lovelock 2016) have concluded that physical environment has the ability to influence human behavior in communicating the firm's image and purpose to customers, and also influencing the customer's ultimate satisfaction with the service, especially in high-contact, people-processing services such as the hospitality industry.

According to Hoffman and Bateson (2010), the environment and its accompanying atmosphere affect buyer behavior in three important ways:

1. *Cognitive response,* how people interpret cues.
2. *Emotional response,* greatly influences the individual's satisfaction level and intention to return.
3. *Physiological response,* affects both customer enjoyment and the ability of service providers to do quality work.

For example, at Starbucks the coffee and the products are important, but the key to the company's success has been its warm, inspiring, and welcoming environment; the design and provision of an experience that makes the company a part of the community or local culture.

Many hotels have a concept based upon a theme. For example, the Hyaat Regency Tamaya Resort and Spa in New Mexico is a thematic resort whose theme is the culture of the Tamyame, welcoming guests with outstretched arms. The architecture is reminiscent of a historic southwestern Pueblo community.

Elements of the physical environment

The physical environment for hospitality products includes facility exterior and interior, employees, and customers.

Facility exterior

The external architecture of the building, its surrounding environment, landscape, accessibility, parking facilities, size, age, quality of maintenance, signage, logo, and lighting are some key elements that influence initial customer impressions or attitudes and help to create a context for the services that will follow.

A hotel lobby could be considered one of the most important servicescapes because of its impact in guests forming their first impressions (Countryman and Jang 2006: 534). According to Siguaw and Enz (1999) and Dubé and Renaghan (2000), the architectural style and other public spaces are essential attributes that influence the purchase decision-making of the customer; creating value during their stay; and impacting the profitability and success of the hotel by increasing the average daily rate and occupancy.

Facility interior

Facility interior includes elements such as interior design, equipment used to serve the customer directly or used in the running of the business, signage, layout, air quality, and temperature (Hoffman and Bateson, 2010: 200). Bitner (1992), Wakefield and Blodgett (1996), and Han and Ryu (2009) have all found that the appearance of the interior design, style, layout, and decor play an important role in the perception of whether or not the environment looks appealing. The combination of all these internal factors creates an overall atmosphere that should be properly designed to attract potential customers.

Employees

The appearance, attitude, and behavior of employees can strengthen or weaken the impression created by a service environment (Lee and Ok 2016). The hotel staff should be provided with an appropriate uniform or something that identifies them with the hotel, such as a name badge that matches with the brand image and other elements of the physical environment. Some advice given to employees should include: check your appearance. Is your uniform clean? Is your hair combed and restrained so that it does not fall into the guests' food? Is your perfume or cologne, and makeup appropriate and not overbearing?

Customers

The atmosphere in the physical environment is strongly influenced by the appearance and behavior of the actual customers of the hospitality product. Future customers are hugely impacted by who or what they see and hear when they first visit the premises. If the environment and the behavior of the customers in terms of language, loudness, politeness, and sobriety are consistent with the expectations of such potential customers, they will feel comfortable and are likely to become patrons.

The service delivery system

Service delivery systems include the human components – possible interactions between the customer and the process within a service environment – the process for delivering the service, and its information technology (Goldstein et al. 2002; Johnston and Clark 2008; Smart, Maull, and Childe 1999).

Customers expect that employees will make them feel valued and important, and it is this treatment that will motivate patrons to use the service again. There are four stages of customer (guest) involvement in the delivery of hospitality products: pre-arrival, arrival, consumption (occupancy), and departure.

Pre-arrival stage

This includes everything the guest does before arriving at the hotel. When guests make reservations over the phone, the interaction with the receptionist creates the first impression of the hotel.

Arrival stage

The arrival stage includes everything that occurs when the guest arrives at the hotel, including unloading the luggage, getting it into the hotel, parking the car, and registering with reception.

The design, maintenance, and aesthetics of parking areas, grounds, and facilities, appropriateness of signage, and adequate lighting and security all add to the quality of the impressions generated (Mok, Sparks, and Kandampully 2013: 59). For guests who have not made reservations, this will be their first encounter with the hotel and its staff.

Consumption phase (occupancy stage)

The occupancy stage includes everything the guest does while staying at the hotel. Guests use room service, watch movies, eat in the hotel restaurant, buy drinks in the lounge, and use its recreational facilities. Sometimes the customers act as staff, for example, during breakfast they help themselves to the food available.

Departure stage

The departure stage includes all activities associated with leaving the hotel and settling the bill. It is important for front office staff to be efficient.

Information technology

The service industry has felt the indirect effect of the technology dislocation experienced by customers and is now increasingly encountering its direct effects. Information technology has altered the landscape radically over a relatively short period. It serves to enhance task-productivity of individual service employees and contributes to economies of scale through standardization and mass production techniques; customizing and integrating the customer's user process to adapt to the increasingly complex co-productive relationship; and to ensure that customers are less dependent upon their suppliers.

For example, the Sheraton Hotel offered an updated website. Julie Atkinson, Senior Vice President, Global Digital for Starwood Hotels & Resorts commented that:

> The refreshed Sheraton.com site reveals improved navigation and functionality that gives its visitors easy access to detailed and compelling property content, with the option to socialize across key networks.

> *(Sheraton Hotels & Resorts 2015)*

Additional benefits of the update include:

- Easier booking process with improved Find Reservation technology
- Accessible Search Again menus throughout the entire site
- Dynamic images and content to increase conversation and engage visitors as they search or book
- User-friendly updated maps with Add Location feature that offers property details while exploring the map.

> *(www.starwoodhotels.com/)*

New product development

Competition is strong and dynamic in the hospitality industry. In one form or another, new products can be the key to company growth and success. Developing new products or modifying existing ones is essential to meet changing customer needs and competitor actions. A new product is one that is new in any way for the company concerned. It can become "new" in many ways. A new idea can be turned into a new product and begin a new product life cycle. Existing products can become "new" products in a new market.

Idea generation

Idea generation is the brainstorming of the product development process. New ideas can come from the consumer, employees, research and development (R&D), and competitors.

Analyzing new and different views of the company's markets helps marketing managers spot opportunities that have not yet occurred to competitors or even to potential customers. Basic studies of present consumer behavior flag up opportunities, too.

When looking for ideas, the consumer's viewpoint is all-important. It may be helpful to consider the image held by potential customers of the firm and its product. Personal interviews; one or more focus groups, and ethnographic research approaches; advisory panels; analysis of consumer complaints or problems are important research techniques used to generate new product ideas. No one firm can always be first with the best new ideas. So, the search for ideas should include attention to what current and potential competitors are doing. Front-line employees should be used as a source for new ideas, because they are well-informed as to customer likes and dislikes. Other idea sources are trade magazines, shows, seminars, and conferences; government agencies; marketing research firms; universities; and inventors (Kotler, Bowen, and Makens 2014: 254). For example: many of the products and services of Starbucks are a direct result of suggestions from patrons or local employees. Customized CD music collections and the sale of sandwiches, gums, and chocolates were all the result of customer recommendations. The iced Starbucks, blended Starbucks, and Frappuccino were born from customers and baristas, rather than corporate headquarters.

When Marriott began its Fairfield Inn and Suites brand, it started simply as Fairfield Inn. Then, with marketing research (focus groups and surveys), the company found that its Fairfield Inn customers desired a luxury class room within the value hotel of the Fairfield line. Responding to this, Marriott changed the name to Fairfield Inn and Suites and added high class rooms and amenities such as a spa. Marriott has been highly successful in using marketing research to develop a segmentation strategy of targeting different customers with different needs by providing different products and options. The diverse offerings have helped it to appeal to an increasingly wide range of clients and win a greater portion of business.

Screening

A good new idea should eventually lead to a product and marketing mix that will give the firm a competitive advantage and hopefully one that will last. During the screening stage, companies attempt to avoid two types of errors – a "go error," which occurs when the firm continues to evaluate an idea that will not be successful, and "no go error," which occurs when the firm discards an idea that might lead to a successful new product. It is important that criteria for screening be neither too rigid nor too loose.

Two questions must be answered:

1. Is the idea compatible with the organization's mission and objectives (internal capabilities such as development, production, and marketing; financial needs, and competitive factors)?
2. Is the product initiative commercially feasible (market attractiveness, technical feasibility, financial attractiveness, and consistent with social and environmental concerns)?

(Cravens and Piercy 2009: 253)

Screening eliminates ideas that are not compatible or feasible for the business.

Concept development and testing

The purpose of concept testing is to obtain a reaction to the new product concept from a sample of potential buyers before it is developed. Concept testing uses market research, ranging from focus groups to surveys of potential customers, to compare two or more concepts. The product (good or service) can be described in words and visually (e.g., multimedia virtual buying environment). This helps to gain feedback from customers. If the results are positive this conveys that the new product idea fits customer needs. If the results are discouraging, it is best to eliminate the idea at this stage. The concept test is a useful way to evaluate the product idea very early in the development process.

Marketing strategy

Marketing strategy includes the target market, positioning strategy, and marketing program plans. At the same time, a tentative marketing mix is developed, including the label, brand name, advertising message, and distribution strategy.

Business analysis

At the business analysis stage the surviving ideas are evaluated according to the commercial feasibility, the organization's requirement for initial estimates of sales and costs, and profit projections. This analysis often requires detailed studies of markets and competition as well as costs and technical inputs. The marketer should continue to develop a product idea only if the forecast shows the organization can afford to make it a success. If the product clearly will not be able to meet organizational objectives on these measures, then investment in development can be shifted to products more likely to meet the stated objectives.

Product development

If business analysis results in favorable forecasts, the product concept is further developed, turning the idea on paper into a prototype model. The research and development (R&D) personnel create the prototype. At this stage the product's technical feasibility is determined. Sometimes this stage requires a large investment and takes a long time because the firm must first build a prototype and test it with consumers, then it may develop a revised version which will again be tested with consumers. This process may occur a number of times until the firm develops a product that meets its consumers' needs, or until the project is abandoned.

Test marketing

The test marketing stage of the new product process involves exposing actual products to prospective consumers under (controlled) realistic purchase conditions and in limited geographical areas to see if they will buy. At this stage, the organization can test variations in the product or marketing mix, including alternative names, prices, and advertising budgets or messages. Depending on the results of the test, the product can be introduced nationally, withdrawn, or sent back to the product development stage for modifications to the product or marketing program.

Customers completing taste tests (new menu) and questionnaires allow the company to distinguish between stated preferences and actual behavior. Test marketing is expensive and time-consuming. Also, it provides the competition with an opportunity to learn about the new product. This stage can be skipped if the costs of product development are low and management is already confident of its success. For products that are truly innovative, it may be risky to skip test marketing unless the product is clearly superior in value to existing alternatives.

Commercialization

A product idea that survives this far can finally be placed on the market. During this step the organization commits to marketing and starts full-scale production, distribution, and promotion.

At this time it may still need to make adjustments to the marketing mix. Commercialization does not have to be a headlong plunge into the marketplace. When the costs of marketing are high, the organization can choose to gradually roll it out, thus introducing the product city by city or region by region until the whole market is served.

Product life cycle (PLC)

A difference between expectations and usage experience may indicate a new product opportunity. A widely used concept in product planning is that of the product life cycle (PLC). Products, like people, have been viewed as having a life cycle. Competitors are always developing and copying new ideas and products – making existing products out-of-date more quickly than ever.

The product life cycle (PLC) describes the stages through which a new product class goes from beginning to the end in its availability within the marketplace.

There are five stages: new product development; introduction; growth; maturity; and decline. While it is true that all product classes will move through the five stages, the PLC does not predict how long a product class will stay in any given stage. It is important for marketers to understand the different stages of the product life cycle because different strategies are required for products at different stages.

Product development

According to Allen (2015), the product development stage is often referred to as "the valley of death" because the failure rate is high. During the development stage, sales are zero and the company's investment costs add up. The investment made by businesses at this stage includes the developing of prototypes and testing through market research to ensure that the new product will succeed in profitably satisfying customer needs.

Introduction stage

Introduction can be described as the pioneering stage of PLC. At this stage the new hospitality product is launched onto the marketplace, sometimes after a long period of development – for

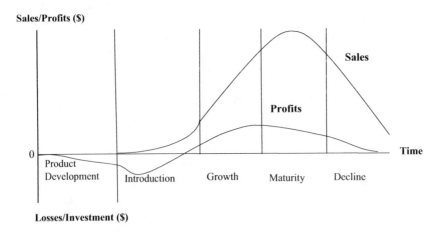

Figure 9.1 Product life cycle stages

example, the opening of a new restaurant. The innovators may be the only people aware of the new product, but they represent only a small percent of the population and the sales of the new product will be low. Usually during this period, profits will be negative because a lot of money has been spent on promotion to educate target markets about the new product and how it will benefit them. The marketing objective is to build primary demand and increase potential buyer awareness of the product and encourage them to try it. During this stage, the price can be high as a skimming strategy and serves the company in recovering the costs of development.

As the introduction proceeds, budgets will have to be rethought, staff skills developed further, and systems redesigned, because this is a learning phase wherein experience is the teacher (Kumar 2010: 63). For example, Starbucks has been aggressively expanding by entering newer markets and strengthening its position in countries in which it already has a presence. The stages of PLC are different. According to Thomas Yang, former Senior VP of International Marketing, Starbucks is at the introductory stage within international markets, allowing consumers to discover what the Starbucks experience is about. In contrast, the company has had a presence in North America since 1971 and is actually in the maturity stage of its product life cycle.

A successful introduction stage will lead to the growth stage.

Growth stage

The growth stage can be referred to as the golden period of the PLC. Early adopters begin to try the product as they obtain feedback from innovators, and begin influencing the early majority. The challenges of this stage include keeping up with demand and fending off competitors who are attracted to the market because of its growth in sales (more and more consumers are learning about the new product), and profits are also increasing rapidly, particularly in the early part of growth. Emphasizing its secondary demand – or demand for its brand – it lowers its prices or enhances brand image and spends additional promotional resources telling consumers why their product is better than that of competitors. Some companies make big strategy planning mistakes at this stage by not understanding the product life cycle. They see the big sales and biggest profit opportunities of the early market growth stage, but ignore the competition that will soon follow. When they realize their mistakes, it may be too late. It may be the right time to introduce the next round of product innovation, remembering the long lead-in times that can occur between a new hospitality idea and its implementation (Kumar 2010: 63). Marketing strategies are adopted by hospitality companies in the growth stage:

- Relationship marketing – continuous feedback from customers and staff
- Targeting new market segments, possibly with minor product modifications

(Bowie and Buttle 2013: 158)

Further, Reid and Bojanic (2009: 70) state that:

> Encouraging word-of-mouth recommendation continuing to educate consumers about the benefits of the product and starting to differentiate it from the competitors 'offerings'.

Maturity stage

A product is considered to be mature when it becomes familiar to the market. In the early part of the maturity stage, sales continue to increase, although at a decreasing rate. By the end of the stage, sales have begun to decline. Profits decline in the maturity stage and some companies cease their marketing efforts. Competition is very tough during maturity, and some competitors cut prices to attract or hold onto business. Innovation and outstanding guest relations achieved through the delivery of breakthrough service are some of the means of coping with competitive pressures in the maturity stage of the life cycle (Kumar 2010: 64). At this stage, brands have quite similar physical attributes and it is difficult for companies to differentiate their products. Promotional expenses in the maturity stage are often directed towards all types of sales promotions to keep consumers using the product and encourage brand-switching by consumers belonging to competitors. It is common to seek new markets for products in the maturity stage. In this stage, company strategy is to reduce overall marketing costs by improving promotional and distribution efficiency. Less-efficient companies cannot compete with this pressure and drop out of the market. This stage may continue for many years until a new product idea comes along.

Decline stage

The decline stage is the beginning of the end and occurs when sales and profits are steadily dropping. Frequently, products enter this stage not because the company has implemented the wrong strategy, but rather due to environmental changes (competition, technological advancement, or social value changes, etc.). Also, the hospitality industry is highly cyclical in nature and its performance (revenues, profits, etc.) depends upon economic growth. Brands that have developed strong consumer loyalty decline slower than those that have not been differentiated from their competitors. Advertising support for a product in this stage diminishes. The decline stage is often the most difficult for companies to address. Dropping a product is an emotional decision in that many individuals have committed time and effort to its early successes in the PLC.

References

Allen, K.R. (2015) *Launching new ventures: An entrepreneurial approach.* Boston, MA: Cengage Learning.
Bateson, J. (2002) Consumer performance and quality in services. *Managing Service Quality: An International Journal,* 12(4), pp. 206–209.
Bitner, M.J. (1986) Consumer responses to the physical environment in service settings. *Creativity in Services Marketing,* 43(3), pp. 89–93.
Bitner, M.J. (1990) Evaluating service encounters: The effects of physical surroundings and employee responses. *The Journal of Marketing,* 54(2), pp. 69–82.
Bitner, M.J. (1992) Servicescapes: The impact of physical surroundings on customers and employees. *The Journal of Marketing,* 56(2), pp. 57–71.
Booms, B.H. and Bitner, M.J. (1982) Marketing services by managing the environment. *Cornell Hotel and Restaurant Administration Quarterly,* 23(1), pp. 35–40.
Bowie, D. and Buttle, F. (2013) *Hospitality marketing.* 2nd ed. (e-book). London: Taylor & Francis.
Countryman, C.C. and Jang, S. (2006) The effects of atmospheric elements on customer impression: The case of hotel lobbies. *International Journal of Contemporary Hospitality Management,* 18(7), pp. 534–545.
Cravens, D.W. and Piercy, N. (2009) *Strategic marketing.* 9th ed. New York: McGraw-Hill.
Dubé, L. and Renaghan, L.M. (2000) Creating visible customer value. *Cornell Hospitality Quarterly,* 41(1), pp. 62–72.
Ford, R.C., Sturman, M. and Heaton, C. (2012) *Managing quality service in hospitality.* International Edition. London: Cengage.
Goldstein, S.M., Johnston, R., Duffy, J. and Rao, J. (2002) The service concept: The missing link in service design research? *Journal of Operations Management,* 20(2), pp. 121–134.
Gronroos, C. (1990) Relationship approach to marketing in service contexts: The marketing and organizational behavior interface. *Journal of Business Research,* 20(1), pp. 3–11.
Han, H. and Ryu, K. (2009) The roles of the physical environment, price perception, and customer satisfaction in determining customer loyalty in the restaurant industry. *Journal of Hospitality & Tourism Research,* 33(4), pp. 487–510.
Harrell, G.D., Hutt, M.D. and Anderson, J.C. (1980) Path analysis of buyer behavior under conditions of crowding. *Journal of Marketing Research,* 17, pp. 45–51.

Hoffman, K.D. and Bateson, J.E. (2010) *Services marketing: Concepts, strategies, & cases.* 4th ed. Mason, OH: Cengage Learning.

Johnston, R. and Clark, G. (2008) *Service operations management: Improving service delivery.* 3rd ed. Upper Saddle River, NJ: FT/Prentice Hall (Pearson Education).

Kotler, P. (1973) Atmospherics as a marketing tool. *Journal of Retailing*, 49(4), pp. 48–64.

Kotler, P. and Armstrong, G. (2010) *Principles of marketing.* Upper Saddle River, NJ: Pearson Education.

Kotler, P., Bowen, J.T. and Makens, J.C. (2014) *Marketing for hospitality and tourism.* 6th ed. Upper Saddle River, NJ: Pearson Prentice Hall.

Kumar, P. (2010) *Marketing of hospitality and tourism services.* 1st ed. New Delhi: Tata McGraw Hill Education.

Lee, J. and Ok, C.M. (2016). Hotel employee work engagement and its consequences. *Journal of Hospitality Marketing & Management*, 25(2), pp. 133–166.

Medlik, S. and Ingram, H. (2000) *The business of hotels.* 4th ed. Oxford: Butterworth Heinemann.

Mehrabian, A. and Russell, J.A.(1974)The basic emotional impact of environments. *Perceptual and Motor Skills*, 38(1), pp. 283–301.

Middleton, V.T., Fyall, A., Morgan, M. and Ranchhod, A. (2009) *Marketing in travel and tourism.* 4th ed. Oxford: Butterworth Heinemann.

Mok, C., Sparks, B. and Kadampully, J. (2013) *Service quality management in hospitality, tourism, and leisure.* New York: Routledge.

Rapert, M.I. and Wren, B.M. (1998) Service quality as a competitive opportunity. *Journal of Services Marketing*, 12(3), pp. 223–235.

Reid, R.D. and Bojanic, D.C. (2009) *Hospitality marketing management.* 5th ed. Hoboken, NJ: John Wiley and Sons.

Reimer, A. and Kuehn, R. (2005) The impact of servicescape on quality perception. *European Journal of Marketing*, 39(7/8), pp. 785–808.

Reynolds, S.J. and Chase, M.D. (2014) *Hospitality services.* 3rd ed. Tinley Park, IL: The Goodheart-Willcox Company, Inc.

Sheraton Hotels & Resorts. (2015) Sheraton Hotels & Resorts reveals new visual identity with launch of fully re-designed Sheraton.com. Available at: http://transformation.sheraton.com/pdf/Sheraton_Reveals_New_Visual_Identity.pdf.

Shostack, G.L.(1977) Breaking free from product marketing. *The Journal of Marketing*, 41, pp. 73–80.

Siguaw, J.A. and Enz, C.A.(1999) Best practices in hotel architecture. *The Cornell Hotel and Restaurant Administration Quarterly*, 40(5), pp. 44–49.

Smart, P.A., Maull, R.S. and Childe, S.J.(1999) A reference model of "operate" processes for process-based change. *International Journal of Computer Integrated Manufacturing*, 12(6), pp. 471–482.

Wakefield, K.L. and Blodgett, J.G.(1996) The effect of the servicescape on customers' behavioral intentions in leisure service settings. *Journal of Services Marketing*, 10(6), pp. 45–61.

Wirtz, J. and Lovelock, C. (2016) *Services marketing: People, technology, strategy.* 8th ed. New York: World Scientific.

Zeithaml, V.A., Parasuraman, A. and Berry, L.L. (1985) Problems and strategies in service marketing. *The Journal of Marketing*, 49(2), pp. 33–46.

Websites

Starwood Hotels and Resorts, www.starwoodhotels.com/

Further reading

Bitner, M.J. (1992) Servicescapes: The impact of physical surroundings on customers and employees. *The Journal of Marketing*, 56(2), pp. 57–71. (An extended treatment of servicescape.)

Wirtz, J. and Lovelock, C.(2016) *Services marketing: People, technology, strategy.* 8th ed. New York: World Scientific. (An extended treatment of supplementary and core services, Chapter 4.)

10

Distribution of hospitality products

Thomas A. Maier and Frank Ohara

Overview of online distribution system

The online distribution system is a network of computer-based reservation and technology systems made up of hotels, third-party travel intermediaries, airlines, and travel agencies. The distribution network composition includes: (1) global distribution systems, (2) search engines, (3) voice-property direct bookings, (4) social media platforms, and (5) channel management tactics.

Global distribution system

The global distribution system (GDS) originated from the airline and travel agent platform. That platform consisted of the hardware system connectivity provided by airlines to traditional brick and mortar travel agencies interested in booking air, hotel, and destination management activities for consumers. Systems used included: (1) Sabre, (2) Galileo, and (3) Amadeus. With today's complex hotel distribution network, GDS connectivity still plays a key role. GDS reservations or channels can account for 10–15% of total hotel rooms booked. Usually, higher end hotels (luxury-upper upscale) and leisure travelers generate a greater proportional share of rooms booked through these channels because of the personalized and curated travel planning requirements. However, rapidly changing smartphone technology has provided both content and easy-to-use booking platforms for travelers on the go.

Industry insights profile: Amadeus International Holdings SA (AMADF)

Amadeus is a leading transaction processor for the global travel and tourism industry, providing advanced technology solutions to our travel provider and travel agency customers worldwide. We act as an international network providing comprehensive real-time search, pricing, booking, ticketing and other processing solutions to travel providers and travel agencies through our Distribution business area, and we offer travel providers (today, principally airlines) an extensive portfolio of technology solutions which automate certain

Figure 10.1   Distribution network

mission-critical business processes, such as reservations, inventory management and other operational processes, through our IT Solutions business area. Our transaction-based pricing model allows our customers to convert certain fixed technology costs into variable costs that vary with passenger volumes; it also links our revenue to global travel volumes rather than travel spending, thus reducing the volatility of our operating results.

(MarketWatch 2016)

Search engine optimization

Given the rapidly changing technology entering the travel industry marketplace, customer search activity has moved to the forefront of electronic distribution marketing strategies. In addition to traditional electronic distribution channels, the driving force behind mobile commerce is the smartphone. Bolstered by the big data revolution, many search companies and industry heavy-weights, such as Google finder, Kayak, and Bing travel, have now entered the hotel distribution landscape with market advantage accumulated through customer user data and search behavior. Meta-search, paid search and ad placement are front and center across all major search and social media platforms in today's travel booking distribution network.

Consequently, strategic marketing strategy and human capital oversight is necessary to establish overarching customer segmentation and channel production goals to achieve desired room night production. Once these strategies and goals are in place, ongoing maintenance and monitoring of *various* consumer responses to search are necessary. This can be accomplished through various analytics platforms and processes. Currently debated by industry is the criticism of search optimization techniques and the return on investment, or ROI, associated with search engine content, analytics and paid ad investments. Those investments can be in the form of advanced analysis techniques, human capital resources, and paid search monitoring programs that give up-to-the-minute insight on customer behavior to search engine programming.

Table 10.1 Amadeus financial performance

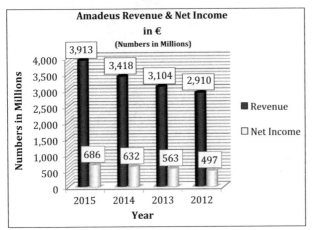

Paid search versus organic search

Driven by advanced technology and data analytics, both the magnitude and scope of paid search advertisement has continued to evolve rapidly. Major search engine providers (Google, Bing and Yahoo!) have entered the distribution landscape as direct consumer booking providers while also benefiting from increased demand in paid search advertising spots. This means that web page design and functionality takes on greater importance in terms of reaching targeted customers. Key search word and homepage design/layout is necessary to attain optimum page ranking in search engines. Ideal alignment of website design includes capabilities to align with web crawlers or spiders indexing particular set of pages (Paraskevas, 2011). An important component of paid search is the conversion rate of bookings attributed to paid search advertisements, meaning how much money is spent relative to number of rooms booked. Finding the most attractive keywords to both advertisers and consumers remains the key strategic consideration facing hoteliers in their quest to drive consumers to their direct booking channel.

Distribution industry profile: Travelport Worldwide Ltd.

They own and operate Galileo, Apollo, and Worldspan. Travelport Worldwide Ltd. is a Travel Commerce Platform providing distribution, technology, payment and other solutions for global travel and tourism industry. It is comprised of a Travel Commerce Platform, through which it facilitates travel commerce by connecting the world's leading travel providers with online and offline travel buyers in a proprietary business to business travel marketplace. In addition, Travelport has leveraged its domain expertise in the travel industry to design a pioneering B2B payment solution that addresses the needs of travel intermediaries to efficiently and securely settle travel transactions. Technology Services through which it provides critical IT services to airlines, such as shopping, ticketing, departure control and other solutions, enabling them to focus on their core business competencies and reduce costs. The company was founded in 2006 and is headquartered in Langley, the United Kingdom.

(MarketWatch 2016)

Table 10.2 Travelport financial performance

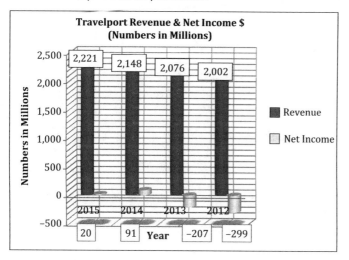

The Company's travel commerce platform, Air, provides real-time search, pricing, booking, change, payment and itinerary creation for travelers using the services of online and offline travel agencies for both leisure and business travel. Its Beyond Air portfolio includes distribution and merchandising solutions for hotel, car rental, rail, cruise-line and tour operators, payment solutions, advertising and other platform services. It also offers other platform services, including subscription services, processing services, business intelligence data services and marketing analytical tools to travel agencies, travel providers and other travel data users. It provides information technology (IT) solutions to airlines, such as pricing, shopping, ticketing, ground handling and other services.

(Reuters 2016)

Voice-property direct

The most traditional distribution channel in the travel and hotel industry in particular is the central reservation or direct booking channel. In fact, this remains the most profitable channel for hoteliers. The reason direct bookings are ideal for hoteliers is the potential elimination of third-party (OTA) commissions ranging from 18% to 25% per booking.

Given recent advances in smartphone capability and ease of use, hoteliers are enjoying a resurgence of direct bookings via "click to book" or "click to call" reservation tabs on hotel direct websites accessed via smartphones. The central reservations system is the lifeline of the hotel operation. The central reservation system is a major technology investment at both the unit and multi-unit levels. Usually, central reservation systems are part of an overall property management system. Included in the property management system would be inventory management, pricing, guest history, loyalty programming capabilities and accounting programs.

The costs of property management systems range from $500,000 to over $1 million per hotel unit. In most cases franchisee owners of major brands are required to use the proprietary systems of the brand. For independent hotel operators, third-party platforms may be

Table 10.3 Day in the life profile of a revenue manager

8:00	**Review previous day's revenues**
9:00	Update monthly, quarterly forecast
10:00	**Meeting with senior executives – quarterly forecast**
11:00	Make pricing adjustments – peak demand patterns
12:00	**Lunch meeting with third-party intermediaries – Expedia**
1:00	Review STR reports (occupancy, average rate and revpar indices)
2:00	**Meet with channel managers – discuss packaging promotion strategies**
3:00	Conference call with property-level General Managers to troubleshoot revenue shortfall areas
4:00	**Visit the central reservation department to offer insights on pricing strategy to reservation agents**

purchased in aggregate functionality or process-by-process configuration. Brand standards and requirements for the central reservation platform are set forth by their proprietary source booking codes, room type configurations, customer segmentation definitions and common settings among and between other branded hotels.

The most obvious benefit of direct bookings is the elimination of third-party commissions, thereby improving the net average rate to hoteliers. The centralized reservation process can also provide valuable information pertaining to travel patterns and seasonal fluctuations in business. The data insight from guest history databases housed in the central reservation platform affords revenue managers with credible data associated with customized pricing and inventory management needs.

Industry profile: A day in the life of ... a revenue manager

The role of revenue manager has become increasingly more important given the increase in global distribution activity. Typically, the key function of revenue managers is managing inventory, customer demand, and price. The role of hotel revenue managers has taken on greater levels of importance given the advancement of data analytics and competitive market environments. Revenue managers rely heavily on data collected through the property management system, central reservation platforms, past history, forecasts, social media sites, and STR reports (Smith Travel Research reports). The importance of mining past trends and predicting future demand remains a key function of the revenue manager. Setting prices and understanding demand fluctuations in the market can only be accomplished through regular and more advanced data collection methods. However, given the rise in prominence of online reservations and the global distribution system, business analytics are taking on greater levels of importance, requiring proper coordination between revenue managers and marketing executives. A typical day for a revenue manager is outlined in Table 10.3.

The key data collection needed by revenue managers occurs through property management, central reservation systems and other functional components associated with the property management system. They include: guest user profiles, rate controls and room type assignments, room categories, group room allocation (blocks) and interface capabilities with the global distribution networks. CRS (Central Reservation System) programming is the main source of hotel product information, including: address, mapping-directions, phone number, social media links, amenity offerings, key features and contact information. The central reservation system in particular houses the descriptive data necessary to process reservations. The central reservation system is the conduit for multiple channels and inventory availability across multiple distribution channels.

Revenue managers and market analysts manage demand and rate strategies through inventory restrictions and various other tactical maneuvers that include: (1) length of stay, (2) various arrival patterns, (3) rate changes (i.e., seasonal, weekend/weekday), (4) price-tiers (best available rate, rack rate, deluxe, standard) and (5) bed type (i.e., king, double queen, suite). Upwards of 20–25% of total rooms booked annually are channeled through the voice/direct-booking channel. Voice-direct channel bookings may vary by type of hotel (independent/branded), type of traveler (leisure/group), and boutique/economy classification. Guests booking direct usually represent those travelers with an emotional connection to the brand. Other reasons guests book direct or use voice reservations include:

- Over-informed guests who follow travel review sites and want clarification on the product
- Overwhelmed travelers that are unable to make a decision because of so much information online (ads, social review sites, OTA)
- Price-conscious consumers looking for the best deals
- Consumers avoiding cancellation fees associated with OTA channels
- Consumers looking for more personal experiences

Social media – digital marketing

Technology continues to change the way consumers book travel, especially through new and emerging platforms. The growing social media scene is especially important for Millennial generation travelers. Leading the social media revolution is continual advancement in mobile and smartphone technology. Almost one in five internet searches for hotel bookings is done on a mobile device. That includes scanning review sites, responding to selected influencers in their social circles and securing the booking on the go. Accordingly, hoteliers need to adapt their web design and test that it is configured in a way that is mobile and tablet ready. In this regard, room-booking "hotlinks" are essential.

Industry profile: A day in the life of … a digital channel marketer

The role of a digital marketing channel manager has continued to evolve with gains in technology and shifts in consumer bookings across multiple distribution channels. Typically, the key function of marketing channel managers is managing social media and online channels for opportunities to: (1) reinforce their brand message, (2) monitor competitors, (3) respond to negative reviews, (4) track paid search ads, (5) generate social media awareness and post interesting photos/activities, and (6) achieve budgeted room night demand and price. A typical day for a channel manager is outlined in Table 10.4.

Table 10.4 Day in the life profile of a digital channel marketer

Time	Activity
8:00	Review/post consumer messaging on social media sites (Instagram, Twitter, Facebook)
9:00	Update monthly promotions and product specials
10:00	Meeting with marketing director on current campaigns
11:00	Reach out to key influencers with opportunity for loyalty programming
12:00	Review consumer travel review sites (Yelp, TripAdvisor)
1:00	Review monthly financial reports (occupancy, average rate and revpar indices)
2:00	Meet with revenue managers – discuss packaging promotion strategie for short-term business needs
3:00	Conference call brand headquarters to discuss OTA paid search/ad placement and channel production returns
4:00	Meeting with Expedia market representative to go over hotel performance and channel productivity

Leading social mobile platforms ranging from search engines to user-generated blogs and travel review sites all offer opportunities for hoteliers to market customers across multiple channels. Perhaps the most rapidly expanding discipline of Hospitality Marketing is the convergence of smartphone technology and social media platform influences on travel bookings. The main social media platforms include:

- Facebook
- Instagram
- Twitter
- Foursquare
- Tumblr
- Pinterest

The key role for digital channel marketers is to increase brand loyalty while building customer demand. Digital marketing generates demand by creating awareness in the hotel product and persuading consumers to consider booking their hotel on a regular basis – ideally, booking the hotel through channel direct platforms. The channel manager must also interface on a regular basis with OTA market managers. OTA market managers are responsible for supporting hotels in representing their best position on each channel. Monitoring channel productivity, price and responsiveness are key functions associated with the marketing channel manager function. Of critical importance to channel marketing managers is cooperation and coordination with the revenue management department. By creating cooperative and ongoing dialogue between the revenue management and marketing departments, hoteliers can enhance the value of each department and more proactively take their revenue opportunities to the next level.

OTA – channel management/pricing

Online travel agencies provide consumers with convenience and travel site search options for travel-related bookings. They are classified into either: (1) merchant or (2) retail categories. Under the merchant model, Expedia, Orbitz and Travelocity are the primary players. In this business model the hotel is paid a net rate after the OTA intermediary takes their pre-negotiated commission rate for rooms booked through this online booking channel. As stated earlier, commission rates can range from 18% to 28%. They also have a pass through an 800-call central reservation system that handles upwards of 40% of all reservations with add-ons and travel booking assistance. On the other hand, in the retail model, paid room-booking commissions are based on a pre-negotiated percentage of the rate. In the retail model, the hotel pays commissions to the intermediary after the gross room rate is communicated to the property.

Academic scholars have asserted the importance of revenue management practices that emphasize market segmentation analysis and competitive positioning in order to fully grasp the costs of OTA commission models. They contend that effectively managing top-line growth by customer segment and OTA channel requires adequate reporting, recording guest history data and overall data management processes. In particular, the adequate recording of gross revenues and commissions is needed to adequately assess the contribution of net revenue per channel (Anderson 2010; Kimes 2016). Over the years, major hotel brands have attempted to minimize the impact of OTAs on their share of business and to minimize the effect of diluted rates attributable to commissions. Not only do OTAs dilute direct booking room nights from brands, they also create competitive market conditions and choice for consumers that impacts all hoteliers in a particular market, who risk losing their market share through the direct booking channel and one another. The scale and magnitude of the OTA market influence and insurmountable marketing prowess is unprecedented. OTAs have a marketing and technology scale unmatched by traditional hoteliers. The value proposition offered by OTAs in offering the best value to their guests is notable. Not only do they build customer loyalty, they also enjoy steady commission revenues and room inventory from brands. The OTA marketplace is divided into sub-categories such as opaque and non-opaque booking channels.

The opaque channels (Hotwire, Priceline.com)

Opaque channels exist to offer deep-discounts and price bidding opportunities to consumers. For hoteliers, this means offering distressed inventory for last-minute sales. Hoteliers drawing customers away from direct booking channels and training them to book away from the direct booking channel must exercise caution. Inconsistent messaging across distribution channels can yield lower net rates for hoteliers. The balance between distressed inventory sales and maintaining rate integrity is a complex process.

Table 10.5 Priceline financial profile

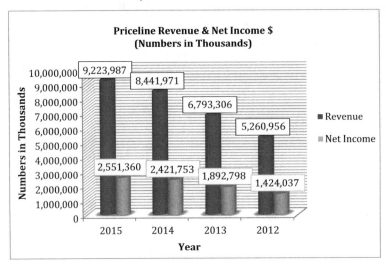

Opaque channel industry profile: Priceline.com

The Priceline Group, Inc. is an online travel company, which provides travel and related services. It offers accommodation reservations including hotels, bed and breakfasts, hostels, apartments, vacation rentals and other properties. The company provides services through Booking.com, priceline.com, agoda.com, KAYAK, rentalcars.com and OpenTable brands. Its priceline.com brand also offers consumers reservations for rental cars, airline tickets, vacation packages and cruises. The company also allows consumers to easily compare air-line ticket, hotel reservation and rental car reservation information from hundreds of travel websites at once through KAYAK. The Priceline Group was founded by Jay Scott Walker on July 18, 1997 and is headquartered in Norwalk, CT.

(MarketWatch 2016)

The non-opaque channels (Expedia, Orbitz, Travelocity)

The bulk of online bookings occurs across non-opaque channels. The commissions paid to OTAs usually ranges from 18% to 28% of the gross room rate charged. Although commission rates dilute revenues, non-opaque OTAs offer considerable opportunities to penetrate the market and gain new customers.

Despite the commission impact on net rates, non-opaque OTA channels offer hoteliers tre-mendous market penetration opportunities. Current industry debate remains with respect to offering distressed inventory through third-party intermediaries. Most independent operators and other hotel competitors seeking additional market share value the opportunity to secure more business at lower prices. The main goal for hoteliers managing non-opaque channels is offering room inventory when demand is low to try and boost occupancy rates without sacri-ficing their customer base and rate structures.

Table 10.6 Expedia financial profile

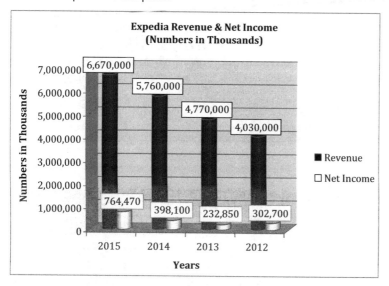

OTA industry profile: Expedia

Expedia, Inc. is an online travel company. The company provides travel products and services to leisure and corporate travelers, including travel agencies, tour operators, travel supplier direct websites and call centers, consolidators and wholesalers of travel products and services, large online portals and search websites, certain travel meta-search websites, mobile travel applications, social media websites, as well as traditional consumer ecommerce and group buying websites. It also offers travel and non-travel advertisers access to a potential source of incremental traffic and transactions through its various media and advertising offerings on its transaction-based websites.

(MarketWatch 2016)

For hotel operators, beyond the OTA relationship is the cohesiveness of property-level system components and functionality. This means that a competent information systems (IT) department should be a reliable resource for the operations team, and adequate investment in human capital is required in that regard because multiple property-level IT systems and web-based technology interfaces require constant monitoring and maintenance. This includes both systems hardware reporting and installation, but also ongoing training to ensure sales and marketing and reservations team members are up to speed on the benefits of the various systems in delivering more room revenue.

OTA industry profile: Orbitz

Orbitz Worldwide, Inc., incorporated on June 18, 2007, is an online travel company (OTC). The Company offers leisure and business travelers to research, plan and book a range of travel products and services, including hotels, flights, vacation packages, car rentals, cruises, travel insurance, destination services and event tickets. The Company's brand portfolio includes Orbitz and CheapTickets in the United States, ebookers in Europe and HotelClub and RatesToGo (collectively HotelClub) in Asia Pacific region. The Company also owns and operates Orbitz for Business (OFB), a corporate travel management company, and the Orbitz Partner Network (OPN), which delivers private label travel solutions to a range of partners.

(Reuters, 2016)

Expedia bought Orbitz in 2014 for $1.8 Billion. All data represented is before the purchase, when Orbitz was operating as a public company under the symbol OWW.

(Reuters, 2016)

Brand.com (hotel direct-booking site)

At the center of the current industry debate surrounding direct-hotel bookings and OTAs is the continual necessity and efforts of brands to move share away from OTAs. For the most part, the Brand.com or the hotel direct-booking channel is one of the highest yielding reservation channels available to hoteliers. Additionally, the Brand.com booking channel is strongly linked to the value proposition offered by current brands to franchisees. Embedded in the franchise royalty fees generated by brands are central reservation bookings and website services. Grassroot efforts are underway at the hotel-unit level to enhance customer interfaces with employees that are geared towards driving customers to the Brand.com booking channel.

Additionally, Brand.com direct bookings help solidify guest loyalty and overall brand allegiance. Continual usage effort designed to build return visitation initiatives on behalf of the brand or direct hotel booking channel requires marketing efforts geared towards cross-property (brand) utilization. Usually, midscale–economy chain hotels have a predominately higher proportion of rooms booked through these channels and offer a respectable return on franchise fee costs in order to drive loyalty members to the properties' direct-booking channels. With the prolific growth of OTAs, price transparency has changed the traveling consumers' selection

Table 10.7 Orbitz financial performance

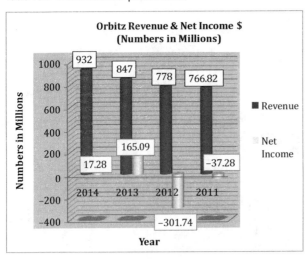

criteria and is shifting purchasing power away from brands and into the hands of consumers. Since travelers have taken more control of the pricing decision and selection criteria, this means that hotel operators have been forced to adapt their pricing strategies. Given consumers' greater control of their buying decisions, buying decisions center on price-value perceptions. As a result, price strategies and web-content/channel messaging coming from brands needs to be consistent across all distribution channels.

Distribution pricing strategy

Revenue management theory provides a foundational basis for pricing considerations in the distribution channel discussion. Researchers have indicated that the application of revenue management theory to the distribution landscape lies in four key dimensions:

- Inventory management control mechanisms
- Price optimization and yield
- Demand modeling and forecasting
- Interaction and interface with web-based consumers and OTAs.

They assert the importance of technology-driven system-level integration in order to properly manage the complex nature of the distribution system. Researchers believe that the onset of new data, technological advances and high-powered analytical tools afford hoteliers the opportunity to evaluate contribution margins by distribution channel. Multiple stakeholder groups, multiple application domains, social media channels, rate transparency and the interrelatedness of purchaser and supplier decision-making have made the management of various customer segments and purchasing channels highly variable. Given the complex nature of various distribution channels, application of dynamic pricing theory offers the best alignment of pricing approaches to meet the demands of highly variable hotel market booking channels. Revenue management theorists contend that hoteliers are moving towards price optimization models that have price sensitivity capabilities that balance revenue mix across multiple channels through predictive algorithms (Cross, Higbie and Cross 2009; Kimes, 2016; Anderson, 2010; Boyd and Bilegan 2003).

An effective distribution pricing strategy needs to be attractive enough to appeal to a multitude of customer segments. Today, distribution pricing decisions include a variety of tactics designed to maximize revenues. Theoretical pricing models concerning the process of adjusting prices dynamically in the context of limited capacity remain critical to hoteliers. The key distribution pricing decisions made by hoteliers need to take into account the following elements:

- Seasonal fluctuations in room demand
- Packaging and promoting various room types
- Pricing stratification across multiple segments
- Monitoring day-of-week demand patterns
- Having a keen awareness of customer loyalty goals and objectives
- Crafting strategic promotions by channel
- Incentivizing current and new customers to book at Brand.com
- How to reach targeted customer segments by channel.

With increased levels of customer activity across multiple distribution channels, hoteliers have both the opportunity and the burden to consistently message their targeted audience to retain market share. Through the use of packaging and product marketing, it is essential to target specific customer groups. When creating specific promotions and packaging of products together (hotel room, car or dinner), it is essential to target specific customers by specific channels. Targeted channel promotions need to take into account the contribution rate for each reservation by each channel. In this case, retained customer data becomes highly valuable in targeting unique users online.

Measuring distribution effectiveness

Given the continual and rapid technological evolution of smartphone and mobile social booking activity, mobile social booking platforms require effective website design and functionality support that requires more investment in human capital resources. In fact, revenue management researchers have argued the effect of hotel price offering on websites can favorably impact the consumer purchasing decision (Noone and Mattila, 2009).

Accordingly, other researchers have presented theories and frameworks for measuring web-effectiveness and cross-distribution channel pricing. The RCO2P model in particular is a useful tool for hoteliers to deepen their insight into customer perception of price, value and product alignment. In Maier and Thielbar's research they have constructed a four-part assessment tool to measure web-effectiveness across multiple distribution channels (Maier and Thielbar, 2012). Their model is based on (1) reach, (2) content, (3) consistency, and (4) price parity and measured the following.

- Reach – hotel representation and page sequencing across multiple OTA and direct booking channels based on their share of unique visitor traffic within the online hotel distribution marketplace. As such, a hotel that scored high in the reach key performance attribute is one that is represented across multiple online lodging travel intermediaries. It is believed that with this online customer behavior dynamic in mind, the financial impact of absence on a strong referrer site can unfavorably impact the effectiveness of a hotel's online distribution strategy.
- Consistency – customer confusion leads to negative externalities and potential lost business. Hotels which represent themselves across multiple referrer sites with the same presence and marketing message convert a greater share of online booking opportunities.
- Content – with diminishing search costs and the improved capability to search online, hotels must stay relevant with their content in order to stimulate Internet users. Stagnant content, particularly photos, represents a barrier to booking for a hotel. Simultaneously, virtual tours, social media interaction and multiple language options can be provided, so long as they don't inhibit the site performance (speed).
- Price parity – evaluating a hotel's ability to distribute the same price point across multiple online distribution sources and its own, alleviating customer confusion, controlling the dynamic nature of variable pricing over time, and the perception pricing of the hotel product relative to its features.

The ordinal scale scores of each of the aforementioned attributes are based on a 0.00 to 1.00 ordinal range. Each of the four attributes are weighted evenly in calculating the aggregate scores. Range 0.00–0.50 is *situation critical*. The hotel is missing opportunities for customer acquisition and perpetuating a reputation for customer confusion and poor price positioning controls. Range 0.50–0.75 is *situation at risk*. The hotel is taking advantage of certain components of effective online distribution but is missing the opportunity to differentiate themselves from competitors. Hotels in this range require corrective action in order to prevent the accumulation of customer ambivalence over time and lack of reach, content and consistency overall. Range 0.75–1.00 is

Table 10.8 Hotel price-parity

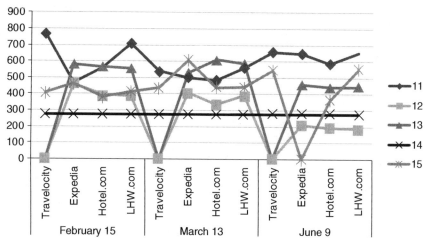

situation optimal and indicates whether hotels are on a progressive level of optimal customer acquisition and retention, continually replenishing their opportunities with a new customer base. The optimal hotel is represented across major referrer sites used by their origin markets and has represented their hotel consistently and relevantly with new brand content and creativity. Hotels in the optimal range attract a high quantity of relevant unique visitor traffic, and usually enjoy full market share or better.

Table 10.8 illustrates the application of the RCO2P index price-parity data measurement of price distribution across three distribution channels: Expedia, Travelocity and Brand.com (direct). In particular, only one of the five hotels monitored (14) exhibited price-parity across all three channels. In some cases, the absolute worst scenario occurred with luxury hotel (11) offering their highest rate on the Brand.com (direct channel) and encouraging consumers to book on OTA sites for better perceived value and price. Table 10.8 depicts a synopsis of five luxury hotels' price offerings across multiple channels including the Brand.com or direct channel (LHW.com). Results of the Maier and Thielbar study provide valuable insight into the lack of price-parity across all the channels. Of the five hotels, only luxury hotel 14 exhibits price-parity across all selected distribution channels. In fact, luxury hotel 11 exhibits the least effective distribution pricing strategy given the fact that they offer the highest price on their proprietary website, thus driving consumers to the third-party distribution channel with 18–25% commission rates.

A changing distribution landscape

Given the onset of mobile technology, consumers are more informed about price and product than ever before (Kuo, Chen and Boger, 2016). The online distribution platform has provided them with rate transparency and shifted the purchasing power away from brands. Adding insult to injury, hoteliers now must compete with social media sites and major search engines (Google, Bing) for organic customer search and influencer activities. It is becoming increasingly more difficult to organically search the web for hotel rooms and airline bookings without paid search advertisements for OTAs and other travel intermediary sites prominently displaying ads on the consumer device. According to academic researchers, online booking channels have become more personalized, convenient and transparent in nature. This transparency has altered the traveling public's selection criteria and purchasing power, allowing consumers to take more control of the online dialogue and subsequent price–value relationship pertaining to product selection and loyalty (Estis, 2008).

For the future, the challenge facing hoteliers will be staying relevant across multiple distribution channels. Beyond staying relevant, they must also contend with a rapidly changing sharing services economy in hotel (Airbnb), restaurant and car (Uber/EATS) markets. Disruptive technological innovations will continue to influence the way consumers travel, dine and socially engage. A key focus area remains maintaining market share and mitigating intermediary influence on the net rates. Lastly, mobile messaging/mobile apps are set to garner top priority in terms of social messaging and millennial generation consumer behavior.

Summary

- The distribution landscape is changing rapidly and moving rapidly to smartphone and mobile device user interfaces reflective of the Millennial consumer wave.
- In order for hotels to remain relevant and drive business through direct booking channels, they should maintain their proprietary website with relevant photo content, use paid search, public relations, high-profile TV advertisement, video and multilingual resources.
- Improving presence with page sequencing and representing your product across all relevant third-party/social sites has taken on greater importance.
- Managing price-parity across all distribution channels requires regular and frequent monitoring and adjusting of prices to adequately reach the targeted customer segments through the highest yielding booking channel.
- Managing brand message, developing consumer response platforms and managing travel reviews requires adequate human capital and technological resources.

Check your knowledge

1. Compare and contrast a Brand.com website (www.marriott.com/default.mi) design with the property direct website design or homepage (www.marriott.com/hotels/travel/dendt-denver-marriott-city-center/). Do you see differences in content? Is the message to consumers consistent between both channels? If not, what are the differences?
2. Take a moment to go online and select a future date for a two-night hotel stay, Friday/Saturday stay. Select at least four distribution channels to search: Expedia, Travelocity, Brand.com (direct) and Priceline.com. Compare and contrast the rates for the same hotel across all distribution channels. Determine whether price-parity exists across all channels.
3. Which year-on-year Expedia revenue gain to net income is the highest percentage?
4. Visit Expedia, Travelocity and Brand.com (direct) for a Marriott hotel near you. Identify three factors that would set apart each website landing page.

References

Advances in Hospitality and Tourism Marketing and Management Conference. June 2011. "Urban hotels online distribution competency." Conference publication. Istanbul, Turkey.
Amadeus International Holdings SA (AMADF) "AMADF Stock News – Amadeus IT Group SAA Stock." *Seeking Alpha*. n.d. Web. 13 Oct. 2016. http://seekingalpha.com/symbol/AMADF.

Anderson, C. (2010) *Demand management*, Los Angeles, CA: Sage.

Boyd, E. and Bilegan, I. (2003) "Revenue management and e-commerce," *Management Science* 49, 1363–1386.

Cross, R.G., Higbie, J.A. and Cross, D.Q. (2009) "Revenue management's renaissance: A rebirth of the art and science of profitable revenue generation," *Cornell Hospitality Quarterly* 50, 56–81.

Estis, C. (2008). *Demystifying Distribution 2.0*. A TIG Global Special Report. HMSAI.

Expedia Inc. *EXPE Key Statistics*. MarketWatch, n.d. Web. 13 Oct. 2016. www.marketwatch.com/investing/stock/expe/profile.

Kimes, S. (2016) "The evolution of hotel revenue management," *Journal of Revenue and Pricing Management* 15, 247–251.

Kuo, C.M., Chen, H.T. and Boger, E. (2016) "Implementing city hotel service quality enhancements: Integration of Kano and QFD analytical models," *Journal of Hospitality Marketing & Management* 25(6), 748–770.

Maier, T. and Thielbar, J. (2012) "RCO2P: An analytics tool designed to improve lodging channel distribution effectiveness," Cornell Hospitality Research Summit, October 2012. Ithaca, NY. Conference publication.

MarketWatch (2016). Data of Amadeus IT Group., S.A. www.bolsamadrid.es/ing/aspx/Empresas/FichaValor.aspx?ISIN=ES0109067019&id=ing.

Noone, B.M. and Mattila, A.S. (2009) "Hotel revenue management and the Internet: The effect of price presentation strategies on customers' willingness to book," *International Journal of Hospitality Management* 28, 272–279.

Orbitz. *Reuters*. Thomson Reuters, n.d. Web. 13 Oct. 2016. www.reuters.com/finance/stocks/companyProfile?symbol=OWW.N.

Paraskevas, A. (2011) "Search engine marketing: Transforming search engines into hotel distribution channels," *Cornell Hospitality Quarterly* 52, 200–208.

Priceline Group Inc. *PCLN Key Statistics*. MarketWatch, n.d. Web. 13 Oct. 2016. www.marketwatch.com/investing/Stock/PCLN/profile?CountryCode=US.

Reuters (2016). Profile: Travelport Worldwide Ltd. www.reuters.com/finance/stocks/companyProfile?symbol=TVPT.N.

Travelport Worldwide Ltd. *TVPT Key Statistics*. MarketWatch, n.d. Web. 13 Oct. 2016. www.marketwatch.com/investing/stock/tvpt/profile.

Travelport Worldwide Ltd. *Reuters*. Thomson Reuters, n.d. Web. 13 Oct. 2016. www.reuters.com/finance/stocks/overview?symbol=TVPT.N.

Further reading

Hayes, D. and Miller, A. (2011) *Revenue Management for the Hospitality Industry*. Wiley and Sons (revenue management fundamentals).

Law, R. and Hsu, C.H. (2005) "Customers' perceptions on the importance of hotel web site dimensions and attributes," *International Journal of Contemporary Hospitality Management* 17(6), 493–503 (building effective hotel direct websites).

O'Connor, P. and Frew, A.J. (2004) "An evaluation methodology for hotel electronic channels of distribution," *International Journal of Hospitality Management* 23(2), 179–199 (measuring web distribution effectiveness).

Choi, S. and Kimes, S.E. (2002) "Electronic distribution channels' effect on hotel revenue management," *Cornell Hotel and Restaurant Administration Quarterly* 43(3), 23–31(price and length of stay booking patterns).

Paraskevas, A., Katsogridakis, I., Law, R. and Buhalis, D. (2011) "Search engine marketing: Transforming search engines into hotel distribution channels," *Cornell Hospitality Quarterly* 52(2), 200–208 (search engine optimization techniques).

Scharlar, A., Wöber, K.W. and Bauer, C. (2003) "An integrated approach to measure web site effectiveness in the European hotel industry." *Information Technology & Tourism* 6(4), 257–271 (measuring website attributes).

11

Financial marketing decisions in the hospitality industry

Albert Barreda

Financial marketing decisions in the hospitality industry

For marketers, planning, executing, and controlling marketing strategies lie at the center of any hospitality enterprise. However, before allocating resources, selecting among different marketing strategies, and assessing the after-effect of a marketing plan, hospitality marketers must have a solid comprehension of the financial impact of marketing decision-making, and a practical understanding of how financial methods might be utilized to assess and control marketing activities. A hospitality marketer should consider five main functional analyses to guarantee the feasibility of a marketing line of action: revenue analysis, cost control, profitability analysis, investment-decision analysis, and analysis of financing sources for hospitality organizations (Bierman and Smidt 2012). This chapter jointly covers the relevance of profitability and investment-decision analyses.

Financial marketing decisions provide hospitality organizations with a line of action in their attempt to attain expected goals (Downie 1997; Zheng et al. 2016). I have developed this chapter by considering that most of the final marketing strategies have a financial outcome in their formulation. Therefore, financial methods are imperative when developing marketing plans and when assessing the positive or negative outcomes of marketing actions. The author's goal is not to present a detailed discussion of the principles of accounting or finance but instead to present valuable information for the hospitality marketer regarding the financial implications of marketing decision-making.

This chapter contributes to the hospitality marketing literature by discussing how marketing activities impact the financial position of an organization, and by presenting important financial methods of analysis to model marketing strategies. Revenue analysis explores the benefits of forecasting the amount of consumers who will buy a product or service. Cost analysis explores the different cost concepts and technical analyses that affect the optimization of the performance of hospitality organizations. Profitability and investment-decision analyses explore the principal factors that need to be taken into consideration to explain the potential returns that a marketing project will generate after execution. Lastly, the analysis of financing sources explores the established sources of money in the hospitality industry. This chapter plans to serve as a reference or guidebook of financial methods for hospitality managers and marketers.

Examination of revenues

From a theoretical perspective, hospitality scholars have defined revenues as the inflow of assets, diminution of financial obligations, or an amalgamation of both resulting from selling services and hospitality products (Schmidgall 2011). Normally, in hospitality organizations, revenues mostly embrace food and beverage sales, room sales, and interest and dividends from investments and payments received from retail space for lease (DeFranco and Lattin 2006). Revenue analysis starts with a realistic assessment of the size of the market and the analysis of competitors. The next step is to forecast the sales opportunity on a quarterly or annual basis. A development of an accurate budget is a critical action in this step (Pereira 2016). The forecast might be built according to market segments (restaurant, hotels, cruises, flights, theme parks, etc.), identifying their psychographic and demographic variables. The forecast might also be expanded with a 30-day forecasting per location (state or country), and leading business accounts (direct booking, loyal, corporate, OTA, tour operators).

The sales estimate should exhibit the projected business dynamic in the first and following quarters of a fiscal year. Marketers must consider the analysis of historical data, the use of market research that helps experts to forecast potential revenues based on similar organizations and markets, and finally, the analysis of competitors. New and existing competitors impact the level of sales obtained by the hospitality enterprise. The purpose is not simply establishing the level of demand in a particular market but also revealing the level of demand for your particular product or service (Rao 2014).

Projecting total sales

For well-defined markets, it is important to determine:

> What amount/percentage of total industry sales revenues of products/services is achieved by our hospitality organization in a specific period?

Sales revenue is obtained by multiplying unit price and unit volume. For example, in the hotel sector:

Rooms revenue = room price × rooms sold

Rooms revenue in this case might decrease/increase by charging differential room rates or by selling more rooms. Differential pricing decisions in hotels are influenced by constrained and unconstrained demand. In hotels, for instance, constrained demand is when demand is lower than current room inventory (supply). Existing reservations reveal actual room sales. Unconstrained demand is defined as the amount of rooms that can be sold when there are no restrictions of room inventory. Under the definition of constrained demand (demand < supply), managers tend to decrease prices. Under the definition of unconstrained demand (demand > supply), managers tend to increase prices (Chen et al. 2015). Managers must determine the following: if unit price is decreased, how much additional volume is required to sustain the same level of revenues? Therefore, a main task to estimate future revenues is to consider the following parameters:

- *Historical data.* Historical data could be analyzed using different forecasting methods. If no historical data exist, the organization must start recording operation records immediately. Some records consist of products sold, prices, revenue by segment, etc. Two common forecasting methods are the regression approach and the Artificial Neural Network (ANN)

(Peng et al. 2014). The former approach clearly focuses on the causal relationships between demand and the elements influencing it. This is reasonable for the evaluation of marketing strategies because it provides various statistics to calculate reliability and validity (Chu 2014). The latter is another commonly used approach in hospitality and tourism demand forecasting (Claveria and Torra 2014) as it does not have the limitations of multiple regression analysis (Peng et al. 2014). Any approach that consider historical data as a basis for projecting the future has assumptions and limitations in the level of precision in forecasting (Pereira 2016).

- *Expert projections.* One effective approach to project sales revenue by product and segment is the use of human experience of senior sales associates, brand managers, and revenue managers. Their judgement is an informal and effective approach to forecasting sales (Seifert et al. 2015).
- *Consumer market surveys.* This is a primary method of forecasting future intentions to buy. Hospitality organizations ask consumers what and how much they are expecting to buy at various prices during a year. The most common consumer market survey methods are questionnaire-based (mailed, face-to-face, and web-based) and opinion-based. The latter consists of approaching consumers (travelers, tourists) and asking them for their opinions about specific hospitality and travel products (Mauri and Minazzi 2013). Although consumer surveys are more time-consuming, hospitality enterprises have the opportunity to project sales revenue based on market segment levels and sub-segment levels. This helps hospitality organizations to know the right mix of business that will come in the near future (Lasek et al. 2016).
- *Competition and market indicators.* Data on competitors, such as new market entrants, reconditioned properties and closures, is critical to estimate the effect of an increase or decrease in market supply. Hospitality organizations that provide data (e.g. Smith Travel Research) assists hospitality managers in reducing the gap from the past (historical data) to the future (prediction). The analysis of market data, market indicators, online data (Yang et al. 2014), market trends, and competitive sets allows hospitality organizations to assess the impact that these forces have on future market performance (Gunter and Önder 2015).

Examination of costs

The application of marketing strategies is influenced by the high fixed cost structure in several sectors of the hospitality industry, particularly in the lodging sector (Vij 2016; Singal 2015). Therefore, the examination of cost structure is strictly associated with the assessments of revenues discussed in the previous section (Sanjeev et al. 2012). After estimating revenue streams, the examination of costs must be wisely studied. In this section, I present several cost definitions, categories of costs, and various methods of cost behavior evaluation used in the hospitality industry.

Definition of costs

Estimating the costs associated with marketing activities is complex (Unegbu and Audu 2015: 22). This is also the case for other accounting research topics such as cost allocation, activity-based accounting, product costing, cost drivers, and cost variances (Park and Jang 2014). As managers execute strategies, costs are allocated to specific profit centers (rooms, bar, restaurant, telecommunications, spa, parking, etc.). For the manufacturing and retail industry, where management accounting has been initiated, the accounting methods are intended to center on efficiency control of manufacturing practices, including the activities and production periods and estimating total (direct and indirect) costs. Generally, cost allocation methods for the manufacturing and retail industries have focused on product-based methods (Öker and Adıgüzel 2016).

In the hospitality industry, the application and development of market-oriented methods are applied. These methods include activity-based costing (Pavlatos and Paggios 2009) and time-driven activity-based costing (Basuki and Riediansyaf 2014: 27). Activity-based costing (ABC) is viewed as one of the main accounting methods in the hospitality industry due to its straightforward two-stage method. As an alternative to considering cost centers for aggregating total costs, ABC methods consider activities. This technique does not require the allocation of a service area expense to a production area as in traditional methods. In essence, ABC methods require knowing what activities are conducted in the service areas (Patiar 2016). Time-driven activity-based costing (TDABC) connects overall ledger costs directly to organization areas rather than activities, assigning overhead and indirect expenses to services based on the actual work needed from the different areas of the organization. The TDABC method overcomes several ABC limitations (Öker and Adıgüzel 2016; Kaplan and Anderson 2003). Since the positive performance (profitability) of a hospitality organization is estimated according to the difference between departmental revenues and costs associated with the elaboration and delivery of hospitality services, a marketing plan must not be evaluated as successful without a reliable examination of costs.

Cost categories

Hospitality organizations have numerous categories of costs that should be selectively chosen and controlled. Because there are many different types of costs, they must be sensibly recognized when formulating and executing marketing strategies (Tsai et al. 2015). Hospitality marketers must understand the precise function of a marketing cost in the bottom line of the organization. Costs are categorized into numerous major types, several of which are helpful in developing the budget expense of the marketing activities to execute (O'Neill et al. 2008).

Fixed costs

Fixed costs are those costs that are stable over a period of time, normally one fiscal year, irrespective of the level of activity. These costs may increase or decrease in the long term, especially during periods of volatile inflation (Singal 2015). For instance, when food revenues increase by 10% or spa sales revenues decrease by 20%, the fixed costs do not change based on this activity. Examples of fixed costs include manager salaries, rent, interest expense, insurance expense, property, plant and equipment leases, and depreciation expense.

The finance literature mentions three types of fixed costs (Stevens et al. 2012; Schmidgall, 2002), including *committed fixed costs*, *capacity fixed costs*, and *discretionary fixed costs*. *Committed fixed costs* are related to specific payment programs for a period of time. *Capacity fixed costs* refer to the ability of the organization to provide unique products and services related to the industry sector in which the company is involved. For example, capacity fixed costs for a fine dining restaurant are costs related to capacity to prepare specific dedicated meal courses. *Discretionary fixed costs* do not influence in any aspect the current capacity of the hospitality organization. These costs may be controlled at the discretion of managers. Managers tend to control costs related to training, educational workshops, altruistic donations, and rewards for activities in order to meet expected budgets.

Variable and semi-variable costs

The changes in variable costs are closely associated with production. These costs fluctuate in direct proportion to variations in sales volume. For example, when restaurant sales rise by 8%, the cost of revenues is expected to rise by 8%. Food supplies and salaries and wages are common cases of costs that change with production. Other costs include semi-variable costs (commonly mixed costs) that vary with production but not in a direct way. These costs tend to include fixed and variable cost components (Tang et al. 2014). Hotel sales associates, for instance, receive a fixed salary (fixed component) and sales commissions based on the amount of sales (variable component).

Step costs

In hospitality organizations, a step cost does not vary proportionally with variations in production. These costs mainly vary based on a distinct discrete range of activities. Housekeeping salaries and property costs are common examples of step costs. For instance, when a fine dining restaurant supervisor is able to direct no more than ten waiters/waitresses, then the manager must add another restaurant supervisor upon including the eleventh restaurant waiter/waitress.

Period costs

Period costs are strictly related to the passage of time instead of transactional occurrences (Schmidgall 2002: 284). These costs are determined based on time intervals rather than pure transactions of products or services. Room selling expenses, marketing and promotional expenses, selling expenses, administrative expenses, rewards expenses, equipment rental expenses, and depreciation expenses, etc. are common examples of period costs. For example, when a hotel rents a reservation system, the rental expense is $1500 per month. Regardless of the amount of reservations the hotel experiences, the rental cost of the reservation system remains the same for each period of time.

Direct and indirect costs

Direct costs are characterized as being easy to trace to a particular service, product, activity, department, or division (Kotas 2014: 26). For example, if a restaurant prepares "Ceviche" (Peruvian cuisine), the cost of the fish, lemon, onion, and the cost of the chef are direct costs. These costs are distinctly traceable to the kitchen area and to each dish prepared. Indirect costs are not clearly traceable to a specific service, product, or division in the hospitality organization. For example, the cost to rent the restaurant property is not directly traceable to the kitchen, the restaurant floor, or to specific food items prepared.

Other costs include incremental costs, standard costs, sunk costs, opportunity costs, product costs, controllable and non-controllable costs, and differential costs. These costs are not the focus of discussion in this chapter.

Techniques of cost behavior assessment

Cost behavior techniques are useful to assess cost behavior in hospitality organizations. Assessing cost behaviors is important to be able to comprehend the financial implications of marketing activities. Every hospitality marketer must consider cost estimations for marketing projects before executing marketing efforts. There are several techniques used to analyze costs, and their applications vary from expert to expert. The ultimate goal of cost analysis is to understand the positive or negative impact of marketing initiatives. The cost analysis may be conducted through the use of the most common techniques presented in the literature:

Trend analysis technique

Commonly known as "scattergraph," programmable calculators have the capacity to display historical points of costs to detail projected points of costs in the future (Stevens et al. 2012: 105). A basic method of plotting historical costs of a particular cost component is valuable. The scattergraph technique projects cost data for several periods of time. This technique demands cost data to be mapped against specific activity variables, e.g. electricity costs versus level of room demand per month. A trend line is fitted by assessment, and fixed and variable cost components are established based on the total cost line (Harris and Mongiello 2006: 143).

Costs estimation technique

This technique requires a skilled marketer or group of marketers to evaluate marketing activities, establish adequate expenses, and reveal the nature of each cost in fixed and variable terms. Once costs are recognized as fixed or variable, total costs are estimated. To establish variable costs per unit, total variable costs are divided by the number of items produced. For example, common variable costs in hospitality organizations are food cost, beverage costs, cleaning supplies, room amenities, administration and general sales, marketing, and some management fees.

Statistical cost analysis technique (regression)

The statistical cost analysis technique provides relevant information in order to make sound marketing decisions. This technique is based on the fact that a cost (dependent variable) is expected to be the function of one or more variables. This technique is based on the fundamentals of regression and correlation analyses (Harrell 2015: 359). A regression line is fitted to monthly data considering the "method of least squares" with the purpose of establishing fixed and variable cost elements ($y = a + bx$) (Harris and Mongiello 2006). The advantage of statistical cost analysis over trend analysis, covered previously, is that in regression analysis, the dotted line (cost function) is computed instead of being assessed based on pure judgements. Statistical cost analysis is less subjective than trend analysis. According to Harris (1995), the "correlation coefficient" (r) and the "coefficient of determination" (r-squared) are considered to assess the level of relationship among the variables.

Percentage of total revenues technique

Several costs might be presented as a percentage of total revenues (Shieh et al. 2014: 35). Marketing expenses, for instance, are expressed as a percentage of total restaurant sales. Adequate revenue projections are a good basis for this cost analysis technique. The percentage of revenues technique indicates a linear correlation between revenues and the costs under consideration (Stevens et al. 2012). The main rationale of this technique is to show how a financial statement item associates historically to sales revenues, and then to consider that association to forecast the percentage of those financial items based on projected sales revenues (Barros 2005).

These four techniques presented have advantages and disadvantages, with distinct levels of precision and subjectivity. When hospitality marketers attempt to consider the use of any of these techniques, it is recommended to apply a method that initially is easy to apply and subsequently consider the use of more sophisticated techniques.

Hospitality profit assessment

The ultimate and possibly the supreme analysis in delineating the impact of a marketing strategy is the prospective profitability it represents for organizations (McDonald and Wilson 2016: 352). Preceding paragraphs have discussed the importance of examining revenues and costs associated with marketing activities in the hospitality arena. In this section, the author discusses analytical methods to guarantee profitable marketing strategies and to assist in the decision-making process of marketing efforts in hospitality organizations. A hospitality marketer must engage in the comprehension of break-even techniques, the identification of specific satisfactory levels of return on investment (ROI), the application of capital budgeting methods available to evaluate investment alternatives, and the source and utilization of funds before selecting and executing marketing activities.

Break-even analysis

The estimation of break-even levels for revenues, profits, and expenses of marketing activities for the performance of business organizations is critical (Sharma 2014). Marketing managers who want to make educated decisions that guarantee the continuous development of the company need to prepare flexible scenarios to determine not only the impact of projected sales and profits but also break-even thresholds of expenses of marketing activities.

Break-even analysis (BEA) is a technique applied to determine the volume or sales value needed to cover costs of production. It is the point where neither profits nor losses are made (Stewart and Mueller 2014). BEA considers that fixed costs remain constant at least in 12 months and that variable costs fluctuate based on volume (sales) at invariable selling prices. If this selling price fluctuates (high or low price), the break-even level will fluctuate as well (Alhabeeb 2012: 247).

Once fixed costs, variable costs per unit, units of production, and price per unit have been calculated, the general break-even formula can be built by:

$$0 \text{ (In)} = PU - VU - F$$

where:

0	=	Zero (no profit, no loss)
In	=	Income
P	=	Price Per Unit
U	=	Units Sold
V	=	Variable Cost / Unit
F	=	Fixed Cost
PU	=	Total Revenue (volume of units)
P − V	=	Contribution Margin
VU	=	Total Variable Costs

Other break-even formulas derive from the general formula. For instance, first, the formula the break-even (BE) point for Units Sold is expressed in the following manner:

$$BE \, Units \, Sold \, U = \frac{F}{(P - V)}.$$

Second, the formula for the BE point for Fixed Costs is expressed in the following manner:

$$BE \, Fixed \, Costs \, F = PU - VU$$

Third, the formula for the BE point for selling Price is expressed in the following manner:

$$BE \, selling \, Price \, P = \frac{F}{U} + V$$

And fourth, the formula for the BE point for Variable Costs is expressed in the following manner:

$$BE \, Variable \, Costs \, V = P - \frac{F}{U}$$

Note that all formulas are derived from the general formula presented initially. Applying basic algebra, the marketer can express other break-even formulas.

In a scenario in which a hotelier needs to know the number of room sales to break-even, the following data may be considered for analysis:

- 40-room Hotel
- Annual Fixed Costs F = 190,000
- Room Price P = US$50
- V per Room = US$20

$$\text{BE Units Sold U} = \frac{F}{(P-V)}.$$

$$\text{BE Units Sold U} = \frac{190,000}{(50-20)}$$

BE Units Sold = 6,333 rooms

Figure 11.1 presents an example of displaying BEA in a graph.

In Figure 11.1, point 1 represents the BE point in which the firm neither made a profit nor loss. Point 2 displays the area of profit after reaching the BE point. And point 3 displays the area of loss for failing to reach the BE point in which costs are covered.

Return on investment (ROI) and return on marketing investment (ROMI)

Hospitality marketing is experiencing change in the way that companies communicate with consumers (Hamid and McGrath 2015: 4). This new period of technological changes and new ways of communication demands innovative marketing instruments and techniques for assessment of return on investment (ROI) when planning and executing marketing strategies (Buhalis and Mamalakis 2015). ROI assessment is very valuable in establishing the health of marketing investments (Louzada et al. 2014: 71).

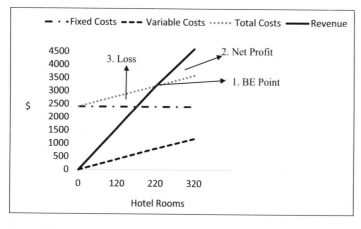

Figure 11.1   Break-even point graph

Specifically, ROI is how much of a solid and acceptable profit an investment generates after execution (Xiao et al. 2012). In essence, ROI represents the relationship between profit and the project that generates that profit, and is commonly considered in order to assess the results of marketing activities (Smyth and Lecoeuvre 2015).

ROI is broadly utilized by marketers (Mintz and Currim 2013), accountants (Tappura et al. 2015), financial experts, investors, and managers (McNulty et al. 2013: 209–221). ROI analysis is useful in defining the good condition of an investment; however, ROI alone is not a perfect indicator of the safety of the project, and only defines the significance of a project conveyed as a percentage (Stevens et al. 2012). In marketing and financial analysis, ROI is estimated by comparing the tangible profit generated by the project and the investment considered for that project. The following formula simply exemplifies the formula to calculate ROI:

ROI = Profit / Total Investment Costs

For example: Assuming a marketing project estimates to profit US$42,500 and to invest US$160,000, then the ROI is:

ROI = 27% = $42,500 / $160,000

Evaluating the benefits of marketing activities for the performance of the organization is still considered a controversial subject for scholars and industry experts. Current literature suggests that the return on investment (ROI) and marketing-specific investment (ROMI) are fundamental elements between the dynamics of marketing and finance (Smyth and Lecoeuvre 2015). There are still limited studies studying the gap between ROI and ROMI in different business sectors, especially in the hospitality industry.

The concept of ROI, previously explained, is considered to apply to any type of investments, including marketing-related activities in the retail, service, and manufacturing industries. The concept of ROMI is exclusively utilized to marketing-specific projects and activities (Stacey 2015). In essence, ROMI involves both marketing activities within the traditional ROI and the return on executing marketing strategies (Lenskold 2003). According to Smyth and Lecoeuvre (2015), ROMI presents one comparative means. The following formula displays the calculation of ROMI:

$$ROMI = \frac{Gross\, margin - Marketing\, investment}{Marketing\, investment}$$

where the gross margin = revenue − cost of goods − incremental expenses.

Manchanda et al. (2005) suggest that ROMI presents some concerns because of the limited accessible aggregate data. Even due to this limitation, the assumption is to apply ROMI as a reference alongside the use of other qualitative data to evaluate the potential of a marketing activity (Kahneman and Tversky 2000). Therefore, it is essential to evaluate marketing efforts, considering quantitative and qualitative approaches.

Capital budgeting process

Capital budgeting is essential for an efficient and productive hospitality marketing decision-making process (Jang et al. 2013). Hospitality marketing projects which require time to plan and execute must be based on the financial benefits that a specific project will generate (Seetanah and

Sannassee 2015). Capital budgeting consists of listing all the investment prospects available, ranking them according to profitability, and accepting all projects up to the level at which marginal benefits equal marginal costs (Stevens et al. 2012). Capital budgeting is the systematic practice of evaluating alternative projects in marketing, land, buildings, systems, and other long-term assets for future cash flows (Turner and Guilding 2013). Since marketing strategies generally require the hospitality organization to commit to a long-term course of action, precise analysis is required to ascertain the potential benefits (Ryu and Lee 2013).

The following framework has been put forward to identify and select potential investments in the capital decision-making process (Stevens et al. 2012: 108):

First: Classify a project.
Second: Recognize alternatives.
Third: Estimate relevant costs (cash outflows) and revenues (cash inflows) involved due to the project taken.
Fourth: Establish the alternative that presents the most attractive benefits (Accept/Reject stage).

Common methods of capital budgeting

Different capital budgeting techniques are used to assess investment alternatives before the accept/reject stage (Özer 1996: 20–24). The three common methods (net present value, internal rate of return, and payback period) will be briefly examined (Ryu and Lee 2013; Lohmann and Baksh 1993). The focus of these methods of analyzing projects is to select investments that augment the value of the enterprise's investment (Bierman and Smidt 2012: 2). These methods are also well applied in the hospitality industry (Arif et al. 2016; Turner and Guilding 2012).

Payback period

The payback period (PP), a non-time technique, assesses the number of periods (years) that it takes to recover the net investment (Bazargan et al. 2013: 54). The net investment is the cost of the investment project and net annual cash flows are the potential cash flows per year. The PP formula is:

$$\text{Payback Period} = \frac{\text{Net Investment outlay}}{\text{Net annual cash flow}}$$

For instance, if a hospitality enterprise executes a marketing plan that costs $200,000, and the strategic plan generates cash flow of $100,000 annually, then the payback period is 2.0 years. A project with a shorter PP among mutually exclusive alternatives is considered to be a more attractive project for selection. However, even when the project net investment is recovered in a shorter period of time (Brunzell et al. 2013), the PP does not reflect the cash flows after the payback period. There is no specific standard for an acceptable PP, and lastly, another concern is that PP does not consider the time value of cash flows as reflected in other capital budgeting techniques (net present value and internal rate of return) (Lohmann and Baksh 1993).

Net present value

Net present value (NPV), the most popular discounted cash-flow method (Karadag et al. 2009), is an improvement on the non-time techniques in that it overcomes the disadvantages presented by their limitations (Stevens et al. 2012). Bazargan et al. (2013) state that "The net present value is a metric that identifies the net cash flows of a project over a number of years discounted to today's cash values."

The estimation of NPV mainly requires a balance between cash outflows and future cash inflows in terms of time-adjusted cash values discounted at specific interest rates (Olawale et al. 2010: 1274). Commonly, the interest rate considered to discount projected cash flows is the cost of capital rate (Lunkes et al. 2015). Once NPV metrics have been estimated, positive NPV values are considered profitable since the time-adjusted internal rate of return of the project is superior than the cost of capital rate (Stevens et al. 2012). If the NPV value is negative, then the investment should not be considered (Karadag et al. 2009). The NPV is commonly calculated with the following formula (Sayadi et al. 2014):

$$NPV = \frac{C_1}{1+r} + \frac{C_2}{(1+r)^2} + \frac{C_3}{(1+r)^3} + \frac{C_4 \dots I_0}{(1+r)^n} - NI$$

$$NPV = \sum_{t=1}^{n} \frac{C_t}{(1+r)^t} - I$$

where:

NPV = Net present value of the project
C = Expected annual cash flows
i = Interest rate (cost of capital rate)
NI = Present value of the net investment
n = Investment in years

Internal rate of return

The internal rate of return (IRR) determines the growth of capital in relative terms and ascertains the growth percentage of gross capital per year (Pasqual et al. 2013). This index is merely the real return of the investment (Lunkes et al. 2015). It is generally known as the interest rate that discounts the prospect cash flows and makes them comparable to the original net investment (García-Suaza et al. 2014).

The IRR of an investment is the discount interest rate that produces an NPV of zero (Stevens et al. 2012). The IRR differs from the NPV technique because it reveals the prospective benefits of the project (Tang and Tang 2003). In essence, the IRR index reduces the complexity of the NPV and also reduces investments to a single number that marketers might utilize to decide whether an investment is profitable or not (Rossi 2015). The formula of IRR is represented as follows:

$$\sum_{t=1}^{n} \frac{C_t}{(1+r)^t} - I_0 = 0$$

where r = IRR.

Stevens et al. (2012: 115) state: "When NPV is positive, the IRR is greater than the cost of capital; when NPV is negative, the IRR is less than the cost of capital. If the IRR is greater than the firm's cost of capital, the investment is a positive one."

Because the IRR index is directly associated with the NPV index, it is well known among managers and therefore more instantly applied (Patrick and French 2016).

Sources of financing in the hospitality industry

In the hospitality industry, a pivotal function of marketing a project is obtaining legal and reliable sources for financing company activities (e.g. marketing plans, capital expenditures, etc.) through capital markets (stocks and bonds), retained earnings, bank loans, government sources, venture capitalists, and franchising (Muradoğlu and Sivaprasad 2014). For hospitality marketers, finding sources of money is critical for the execution of strategic marketing plans in order to finance the creation and marketing of strategic plans. A hospitality company might consider the following sources of financing activities in the hospitality industry (Arif et al. 2016: 180):

- Capital markets: Issuing common stocks, preferred stocks, and bonds.
- Retained earnings: Retaining earnings is an effective and low-cost source to fund projects including advertising and marketing projects (Serrasqueiro and Nunes 2014).
- Bank loans: Obtaining financing from banks is a common practice in hospitality and other industries. The lending periods include short-term, medium-term and long-term lending.
- Collection of receivables: Many hospitality enterprises raise funds from marketing activities and business-growth activities and also from their borrowers (Arif et al. 2016: 180).
- Government sources: Sometimes the government offers funds to organizations in cash grants and alternatives ways of support, as part of its commitment of assisting to improve the economy (Carter et al. 1997: 92).
- Venture capital: In the hospitality industry, venture capital is a method of funding projects in which financing is obtained from private investors (Campopiano et al. 2016). These investors generally determine the timing and form of investment, including their participation in the project (supervising, assessment, and hiring) (Abdulsaleh and Worthington 2013: 36).
- Franchising: This is a common accepted business practice in the hospitality industry (Ingram 2013). Franchising is a process of corporate growth that reduces financial risks for the franchisor (Yeung et al. 2016). In the hospitality industry, it has been an effective method to raising additional capital for growth in the past two decades (Alon et al. 2012).

Conclusions

This chapter has examined the financing aspects, including revenue analysis, cost analysis, and profitability analysis, that hospitality marketers usually consider when executing marketing activities. As hospitality marketers develop long-term marketing strategies, every organization must consider the financial benefits and expenses for executing marketing activities. Therefore, when hospitality marketers consider the financial analysis of their marketing strategies, they are able to guarantee the financial benefits that result from executing marketing strategies.

To ensure that the implementation of well-designed marketing activities maximizes the profitability of the hospitality organization, marketers must consider a detailed projection of revenues, a comprehensive estimation of project-related costs, and a realistic profitability analysis that includes financial analysis and capital budgeting methods.

References

Abdulsaleh, A. M. and Worthington, A. C. (2013) "Small and medium-sized enterprises financing: A review of literature," *International Journal of Business and Management* 8(14), 36.

Alhabeeb, M. J. (2012) "Break-even analysis," in *Mathematical Finance*, John Wiley & Sons, Inc.. doi: 10.1002/9781118106907.ch13.

Alon, I., Ni, L. and Wang, Y. (2012) "Examining the determinants of hotel chain expansion through international franchising," *International Journal of Hospitality Management* 31(2), 379–386.

Arif, T. M. H., Noor-E-Jannat, K. and Anwar, S. R. (2016) "Financial statement and competitiveness analysis: A study on tourism & hospitality industry in Bangladesh," *International Journal of Financial Research* 7(4), 180–189.

Barros, C. P. (2005) "Measuring efficiency in the hotel sector," *Annals of Tourism Research* 32(2), 456–477.

Basuki, B. and Riediansyaf, M. D. (2014) "The application of time-driven activity-based costing in the hospitality industry: An exploratory case study," *Journal of Applied Management Accounting Research* 12(1), 27–54.

Bazargan, M., Lange, D., Tran, L. and Zhou, Z. (2013) "A simulation approach to airline cost benefit analysis," *Journal of Management Policy and Practice* 14(2), 54–61.

Bierman Jr, H. and Smidt, S. (2012) *The Capital Budgeting Decision: Economic Analysis of Investment Projects*, Routledge.

Brunzell, T., Liljeblom, E. and Vaihekoski, M. (2013) "Determinants of capital budgeting methods and hurdle rates in Nordic firms," *Accounting & Finance* 53(1), 85–110.

Buhalis, D. and Mamalakis, E. (2015) "Social media return on investment and performance evaluation in the hotel industry context," in Tussyadiah, I., Inversini, A. (Eds.), *Information and Communication Technologies in Tourism*, Springer International Publishing, 241–253.

Campopiano, G., Minola, T. and Sainaghi, R. (2016) "Students climbing the entrepreneurial ladder: Family social capital and environment-related motives in hospitality and tourism," *International Journal of Contemporary Hospitality Management* 28(6), 1115–1136.

Carter, S., MacDonald, N. J. and Cheng, D. C. (1997) *Basic Finance for Marketers*, Food & Agriculture Organization of the United Nations.

Chen, C. M., Lin, Y. C. and Tsai, Y. C. (2015) "How does advertising affect the price elasticity of lodging demand? Evidence from Taiwan," *Tourism Economics* 21(5), 1035–1045.

Chu, F. L. (2014) "Using a logistic growth regression model to forecast the demand for tourism in Las Vegas," *Tourism Management Perspectives* 12, 62–67.

Claveria, O. and Torra, S. (2014) "Forecasting tourism demand to Catalonia: Neural networks vs. time series models," *Economic Modelling* 36, 220–228.

DeFranco, A. L. and Lattin, T. W. (2006) *Hospitality Financial Management*, Wiley.

Downie, N. (1997) "The use of accounting information in hotel marketing decisions," *International Journal of Hospitality Management* 16(3), 305–312.

García-Suaza, A. F., Guataquí, J. C., Guerra, J. A. and Maldonado, D. (2014) "Beyond the Mincer equation: The internal rate of return to higher education in Colombia," *Education Economics* 22(3), 328–344.

Gunter, U. and Önder, I. (2015) "Forecasting international city tourism demand for Paris: Accuracy of uni- and multivariate models employing monthly data," *Tourism Management* 46, 123–135.

Hamid, N. R. A. and McGrath, M. G. (2015) "The diffusion of internet interactivity on retail web sites: A customer relationship model," *Communications of the IIMA* 5(2), Article 4.

Harrell, F. (2015) *Regression Modeling Strategies: With Applications to Linear Models, Logistic and Ordinal Regression, and Survival Analysis*, Springer.

Harris, P. J. (1995) *Accounting and Finance for the International Hospitality Industry*, Butterworth-Heinemann.

Harris, P. J. and Mongiello, M. (2006) *Accounting and Financial Management: Developments in the International Hospitality Industry*, Routledge.

Ingram, H. (2013) "Franchising hospitality services," *International Journal of Contemporary Hospitality Management* 13(5), 267–268.

Jang, S. C. S., Tang, C. H. H., Park, K. and Hsu, L. T. (2013) "The marketing–finance interface–a new direction for tourism and hospitality management," *Tourism Economics* 19(5), 1197–1206.

Kahneman, D. and Tversky, A. (2000) "Prospect theory: An analysis of decision under risk," in Kahneman, D., Tversky, A. (Eds.), *Choices, Values, and Frames*, Cambridge University Press, 17–43.

Kaplan, R. S. and Anderson, S. R. (2003) "Time-driven activity-based costing," https://papers.ssrn.com/sol3/papers.cfm?abstract_id=485443.

Karadag, E., Cobanoglu, C. and Dickinson, C. (2009) "The characteristics of IT investment decisions and methods used in the US lodging industry," *International Journal of Contemporary Hospitality Management* 21(1), 52–68.

Kotas, R. (2014) *Management Accounting for Hotels and Restaurants*, Routledge.

Lasek, A., Cercone, N. and Saunders, J. (2016) "Restaurant sales and customer demand forecasting: Literature survey and categorization of methods," in Leon-Garcia, A. et al. (Eds.), *Smart City 360°*, Springer International Publishing, 479–491.

Lenskold, J. (2003) *Marketing ROI: The Path to Campaign, Customer, and Corporate Profitability*, McGraw-Hill.

Lohmann, J. R. and Baksh, S. N. (1993) "The IRR, NPV and Payback Period and their relative performance in common capital budgeting decision procedures for dealing with risk," *The Engineering Economist* 39(1), 17–47.

Louzada, L. M., Costa, A. L. and Giraldi, J. D. M. E. (2014) "Return on investment in sports marketing initiatives: A study focusing on a Brazilian soccer team," *International Journal of Business Administration* 5(5), 71–83.

Lunkes, R. J., Ripoll-Feliu, V., Giner-Fillol, A. and da Rosa, F. S. (2015) "Capital budgeting practices: A comparative study between a port company in Brazil and in Spain," *Journal of Public Administration and Policy Research* 7(3), 39–49.

Manchanda, P., Wittink, D. R., Ching, A., Cleanthous, P., Ding, M., Dong, X. J., … and Steenburgh, T. (2005) "Understanding firm, physician and consumer choice behavior in the pharmaceutical industry," *Marketing Letters* 16(3–4), 293–308.

Mauri, A. G. and Minazzi, R. (2013) "Web reviews influence on expectations and purchasing intentions of hotel potential customers," *International Journal of Hospitality Management* 34, 99–107.

McDonald, M. and Wilson, H. (2016) *Marketing Plans: How to Prepare Them, How to Profit from Them*, John Wiley & Sons.

McNulty, Y., De Cieri, H. and Hutchings, K. (2013) "Expatriate return on investment in the Asia Pacific: An empirical study of individual ROI versus corporate ROI," *Journal of World Business* 48(2), 209–221.

Mintz, O. and Currim, I. S. (2013) "What drives managerial use of marketing and financial metrics and does metric use affect performance of marketing-mix activities?," *Journal of Marketing* 77(2), 17–40.

Muradoğlu, Y. G. and Sivaprasad, S. (2014) "The impact of leverage on stock returns in the hospitality sector: Evidence from the UK," *Tourism Analysis* 19(2), 161–171.

O'Neill, J. W., Hanson, B. and Mattila, A. S. (2008) "The relationship of sales and marketing expenses to hotel performance in the United States," *Cornell Hospitality Quarterly* 49(4), 355–363.

Öker, F. and Adıgüzel, H. (2016) "Time-driven activity-based costing: An implementation in a manufacturing company," *Journal of Corporate Accounting & Finance* 27(3), 39–56.

Olawale, F., Olumuyiwa, O. and George, H. (2010) "An investigation into the impact of investment appraisal techniques on the profitability of small manufacturing firms in the Nelson Mandela Metropolitan Bay Area, South Africa," *African Journal of Business Management* 4(7), 1274–1280.

Özer, B. (1996) "An investment analysis model for small hospitality operations," *International Journal of Contemporary Hospitality Management* 8(5), 20–24.

Park, K. and Jang, S. (2014) "Hospitality finance and managerial accounting research: Suggesting an interdisciplinary research agenda," *International Journal of Contemporary Hospitality Management* 26(5), 751–777.

Pasqual, J., Padilla, E. and Jadotte, E. (2013) "Technical note: Equivalence of different profitability criteria with the net present value," *International Journal of Production Economics* 142(1), 205–210.

Patiar, A. (2016) "Costs allocation practices: Evidence of hotels in Australia," *Journal of Hospitality and Tourism Management* 26, 1–8.

Patrick, M. and French, N. (2016) "The internal rate of return (IRR): Projections, benchmarks and pitfalls," *Journal of Property Investment & Finance* 34(6).

Pavlatos, O. and Paggios, I. (2009) "Activity-based costing in the hospitality industry: Evidence from Greece," *Journal of Hospitality & Tourism Research* 33(4), 511–527.

Peng, B., Song, H. and Crouch, G. I. (2014) "A meta-analysis of international tourism demand forecasting and implications for practice," *Tourism Management* 45, 181–193.

Pereira, L. N. (2016) "An introduction to helpful forecasting methods for hotel revenue management," *International Journal of Hospitality Management* 58, 13–23.

Rao, R. S. (2014) "Emerging trends in hospitality and tourism," *International Journal of Research*, 1–8.

Rossi, M. (2015) "The use of capital budgeting techniques: An outlook from Italy," *International Journal of Management Practice* 8(1), 43–56.

Ryu, K. and Lee, J. S. (2013) "Examination of restaurant quality, relationship benefits, and customer reciprocity from the perspective of relationship marketing investments," *Journal of Hospitality & Tourism Research*, doi: 1096348013515919.

Sanjeev, G. M., Gupta, K. and Bandyopadhyay, R. (2012) "Financial challenges in the Indian hospitality industry," *Worldwide Hospitality and Tourism Themes* 4(2), 163–173.

Sayadi, A. R., Tavassoli, S. M. M., Monjezi, M. and Rezaei, M. (2014) "Application of neural networks to predict net present value in mining projects," *Arabian Journal of Geosciences* 7(3), 1067–1072.

Schmidgall, R. S. (2002) *Hospitality Industry Managerial Accounting* (5th ed.), Educational Institute of the American Hotel & Lodging Association.

Schmidgall, R. S. (2011) *Hospitality Industry Managerial Accounting* (7th ed.), Educational Institute of the American Hotel & Lodging Association.

Seetanah, B. and Sannassee, R. V. (2015) "Marketing promotion financing and tourism development: The case of Mauritius," *Journal of Hospitality Marketing & Management* 24(2), 202–215.

Seifert, M., Siemsen, E., Hadida, A. L. and Eisingerich, A. B. (2015) "Effective judgmental forecasting in the context of fashion products," *Journal of Operations Management* 36, 33–45.

Serrasqueiro, Z. and Nunes, P. M. (2014) "Financing behaviour of Portuguese SMEs in hotel industry," *International Journal of Hospitality Management* 43, 98–107.

Sharma, M. P. (2014) "Study of banking break even point: An innovative tool for banking industry," *International Journal of Innovative Research and Development* 3(11), 164–168.

Shieh, H. S., Hu, J. L. and Gao, L.Y. (2014) "Tourist preferences and cost efficiency of international tourist hotels in Taiwan," *International Journal of Marketing Studies* 6(3), 35–48.

Singal, M. (2015) "How is the hospitality and tourism industry different? An empirical test of some structural characteristics," *International Journal of Hospitality Management* 47, 116–119.

Smyth, H. and Lecoeuvre, L. (2015) "Differences in decision-making criteria towards the return on marketing investment: A project business perspective," *International Journal of Project Management* 33(1), 29–40.

Stacey, E. C. (2015) *Measuring the Return on Marketing Investment*, Center for Measurable Marketing at NYU Stern.

Stevens, R. E., Loudon, D. L. and Wrenn, B. (2012) *Marketing Management: Text and Cases*, Routledge.

Stewart, M. G. and Mueller, J. (2014) "Cost-benefit analysis of airport security: Are airports too safe?" *Journal of Air Transport Management* 35, 19–28.

Tang, S. L. and Tang, J. H. (2003) "Technical note: The variable financial indicator IRR and the constant economic indicator NPV," *The Engineering Economist*, 48(1), 69–78.

Tang, Y. H., Amran, A. and Goh, Y. N. (2014) "Environmental management practices of hotels in Malaysia: Stakeholder perspective," *International Journal of Tourism Research* 16(6), 586–595.

Tappura, S., Sievänen, M., Heikkilä, J., Jussila, A. and Nenonen, N. (2015) "A management accounting perspective on safety," *Safety Science* 71, 151–159.

Tsai, Y. L., Dev, C. S. and Chintagunta, P. (2015) "What's in a brand name? Assessing the impact of rebranding in the hospitality industry," *Journal of Marketing Research* 52(6), 865–878.

Turner, M. J. and Guilding, C. (2012) "Factors affecting biasing of capital budgeting cash flow forecasts: Evidence from the hotel industry," *Accounting and Business Research* 42(5), 519–545.

Turner, M. J. and Guilding, C. (2013) "Capital budgeting implications arising from locus of hotel owner/operator power," *International Journal of Hospitality Management* 35, 261–273.

Unegbu, A. O. and Audu, M. A. (2015) "Service cost management in hospitality industry: Critical gaps analysis," *Journal of Emerging Trends in Economics and Management Sciences* 6(1), 22–30.

Vij, M. (2016) "The cost competitiveness, competitiveness and sustainability of the hospitality industry in India," *Worldwide Hospitality and Tourism Themes* 8(4), 432–443.

Xiao, Q., O'Neill, J. W. and Mattila, A. S. (2012) "The role of hotel owners: The influence of corporate strategies on hotel performance," *International Journal of Contemporary Hospitality Management* 24(1), 122–139.

Yang, Y., Pan, B. and Song, H. (2014) "Predicting hotel demand using destination marketing organization's web traffic data," *Journal of Travel Research* 53(4), 433–447.

Yeung, R. M., Brookes, M. and Altinay, L. (2016) "The hospitality franchise purchase decision making process," *International Journal of Contemporary Hospitality Management* 28(5), 1009–1025.

Zheng, T., Farrish, J. and Kitterlin, M. (2016) "Performance trends of hotels and casino hotels through the recession: An ARIMA with intervention analysis of stock indices," *Journal of Hospitality Marketing & Management* 25(1), 49–68.

Further reading

Carter, S., MacDonald, N. J. and Cheng, D. C. (1997) *Basic Finance for Marketers*, Food & Agriculture Organization of the United Nations. (This book provides basic, practical knowledge and methods for marketers, unexperienced in the discipline of finance and accounting.)
Pearce, M. (2000) *Financial Analysis for Marketing Decisions*, Ivey Publishing. (A review of the common calculations in marketing.)
Stevens, R. E., Loudon, D. L. and Wrenn, B. (2012) *Marketing Management: Text and Cases*, Routledge. (Covers essential managerial elements of marketing.)

12

Marketing information management

Nuray Selma Özdipçiner

Introduction

Information, the key to productivity in modern times, has grown exponentially over time. The amount of information currently generated in a single day is almost equal to the amount of information previously produced in an entire century. Information has become a strategic and indispensable resource due to rapidly evolving information and communication technologies. Quick and easy access to all types of information has also changed the social structure, and companies need to be in line with the requirements of the information age (Ladeira et al., 2016).

The companies that initially only used technology have recognized over time that the use of technology alone is not enough to gain an advantage in an increasingly competitive environment. They have realized that more of their knowledge must be transformed into information so that the original sufficiency, performance and efficiency of their company can be maintained (MacMorrow, 2001). Currently, the acquisition and evaluation of information is considered to be an important organizational skill, and organizations in the information society drive profit by turning information into value (Goksel and Baytekin, 2008).

Development of information management

Toffler and Toffler have described society's transition into an information society as occurring in waves: the agrarian society, the industrial society and the information society (Toffler and Toffler, 1995). By transitioning from an industrial society to an information society, information has begun to play a key role in the success of organizations. Rapid change and uncertainty have made information the most important tool for organizations (Kocel, 1998). Currently, the value of commercial businesses is measured not by the real estate and fixed assets they possess, but rather by the information they produce and the applicability of this knowledge to everyday life (Little et al., 2002).

The revolution of information and communication began after the second half of the twentieth century, and it has accelerated ever since. Development of information management as a discipline and its definition as an organizational process for operations occurred in the late 1990s (Koza, 2008). During this period, various books, conferences and journals were produced on the subject (Little et al., 2002). Later, the concept of the information society emerged, along with the spread of information to society as a whole. The information society concept has often been used since the second half of the twentieth century, and various discussions have taken place on the subject. According to some scholars, as a natural consequence of the developments in information technology, the United States, Japan and Western European countries have transformed from industrial societies into information societies. The most valuable commodity in this new society is information. Traditional heavy industry was also replaced by information technology (Celik, 1998). The source of wealth and prosperity in the information economy is the production and distribution of information and experience (Laudon and Laudon, 2006).

Reasons for the emergence of information management

Information and technology are of critical importance in all sectors. Information systems are essential for organizing the flow of information and replicating the sources of information.

The drivers of information management are as follows (from *Cagdas Bilgi Sistemi ve Digital Işletmeler* (Anon. (2010)):

- A clear and increasing shift of assets towards information and non-tangible resources;
- The recognition of people as a major source of organizational information;
- Constantly accelerating changes in the market, in competition and in technology that require continuous learning;
- Increased awareness of innovation as the main component of the competitive structure and its relationship to the production of information, as well as implementation of the produced information;
- Growing importance of cross-border information transfer;
- Technological limitations and potential.

Concept and definition of information management

It is important to define information before defining its management. Data are the flow of processes and events acquired by an organization' systems (Laudon and Laudon, 2006). Information, on the other hand, is the processing of these data and making it significant and usable for decision-makers (Gupta, 1996); it is also the decisions and skills created by people interpreting the variety of information they have gained (Setzer, 2001).

There are two different types of information: a system-based type consisting of statistical data (information) and a type consisting of experience based on human consciousness, which is revealed in a more meaningful and holistic way by interpreting such data (knowledge) (Machlup, 1984; Beijerse, 2000). Creation of different information by bringing together and interpreting other information can be performed in the wisdom stage, which is the highest point in the concept of information (Odabas, 2005).

According to Broadbent, information management is based on two foundations. The first is the literal use of information in the organization; to realize this, the information should be effectively managed. The second foundation is the implementation of employees' qualifications, skills, talents, thoughts, ideas, intuition, connection, motivation and dreams in their jobs. These elements come in the form of tacit knowledge hosted in the individuals' brains. This tacit knowledge should be converted into explicit knowledge to be transferred and managed. If the tacit knowledge is not disclosed and used, this type of knowledge remains in the individuals' brains and cannot be accessed. Explicit knowledge contributes to the productivity of the organization and, if it remains tacit knowledge, it loses its impact, which has implications for the decision-making process (Broadbent, 1998; Awad and Ghaziri, 2004).

Information management has been defined by many scholars in the literature. Several definitions follow:

Parker (2000, p. 233) likened information to water and suggested that information comes from many sources, flows continuously and may be contaminated or lost during leakage or filtering. He also stated that information should be collected, treated, stored and distributed before being made available for use, and he emphasized the need to manage information: "flow of information must strictly be managed, if it will be delivered to those who need it, at the right time and in the right context or scope."

According to Malhotra (1998), "information management regulates the operation of data and information processing by information technologies and corporate operations that combine the people's creativity and innovative strength to work in synergy."

Rubin (2000, p. 19) argued that information management is "the implementation of information science in the organizations," in which information science is defined as "a science that studies qualifications and behavior of the information, the power affecting management of the flow of information and the means for processing the information, for optimal access and use."

According to Buckman (2004, p. 32), information management is "a systematic approach to ensure dissemination of information at the right time, to the right people so that the information would emerge and create value."

In summary, the concept of information management addresses, regardless of the medium (text, data archives, images, audio, animation, web pages, etc.), the selection, provision, regulation, use, protection, sorting and destruction of the information (Taylor, 1999). Information management has three different aspects based on information, technology and culture (Alavi and Leidner, 1999), and if these three factors intersect, organizations can reach a successful level of performance and optimal enterprise (Benbya et al., 2004).

Objectives and means of information management

As Alavi and Leidner (2001) stated, information management has three objectives. The first is to enable the visibility and accessibility of an organization's sources of information, such as documents, maps, files and plans. The second objective is to create an information-intensive cultural environment by supporting or encouraging studies of information sharing. The third is to create a communication environment in which people and systems interact and cooperate, resulting in the establishment of an information-sharing platform. Duffy (2001, p. 59) listed the objectives of information management as follows:

a. To benefit from intellectual capital, to encourage the transfer of information and to ensure information sharing;
b. To speed up the learning curve;
c. To speed up improvement;
d. To speed up the exchange of information;
e. To allow information to reach the right people, at the right time.

Information management is a management field that addresses intellectual capital as a controllable value. Institutional dynamics, management models and technology are the most important means used to manage the information. Such means must work together and in harmony to ensure that an organization can acquire data and information, develop the information acquired and transfer it to individuals performing specific tasks (Odabas, 2003). The means of information discovery and creation are as follows (Durst et al., 2013, p. 127):

a. Data mining (data cleaning, data analysis, integration of results and interpretation of the model).
b. Groupware and knowledge portals contribute to the creation of the information.
c. Knowledge maps can provide the staff with a descriptive visual model for the ideas, concepts and cognitive models within a common context. Concept maps are used for organizing large information sources, such as planning information sources, information implementation steps, informative concepts, expert networks or implementation communities (Eppler, 2008).
d. Means of information management (e.g., blogging, wikis, and video casting) help the development of communications products.

Information management system

Information management is a large and complex system that works in harmony and consists of technological tools and equipment, as well as various techniques, management types, and human and cultural infrastructure (Odabas, 2005). In summary, an information management system is the management of information, communication and human sources in the same environment in a consistent and orderly manner (Kim, 2000).

Implementation of an information management system

As a relatively new concept, information management still lacks a conclusive model supported by a majority consensus (Awad and Ghaziri, 2004). While some authors suggest a five-stage model for the process of information management, involving creation, acquisition, organization, access and use of the information (Soliman and Spooner, 2000), others suggest a four-stage model involving the creation/acquisition, conversion/organization, sharing/implementation and protection/storage of the information (Gold et al., 2001). Additionally, many other authors have suggested three-stage models, such as sharing, dissemination and use (Darroch and McNaughton, 2003); acquisition, sharing and implementation/evaluation (Bharadwaj et al., 2005); and acquisition, coding and dissemination/implementation (Pretorius and Steyn, 2005).

Although the information management processes stated by these authors are different in some aspects, four common themes are found: acquisition, conversion, implementation and protection of the information (Gold et al., 2001).

Acquisition of information

Information can be acquired either from internal activities or outside sources (Burman et al., 2016). At the organizational level, information is communicated within the structure of the company. During their relationships with the internal and external environments, companies acquire information and convert it into knowledge when necessary. They act by combining such knowledge with their own experiences, values and rules (Sena and Shani, 1999), which requires sharing personal experience and collaboration. Inter-organizational cooperation is a potential source of information and has critical importance in acquiring information. Sharing technology, personnel actions and the connections between the organization and its partners also helps in information acquisition (Gold et al., 2001).

Conversion of the information

Conversion of the information includes activities such as integration, combination, configuration and coordination (Kivijarvi, 2004). The main objective is to minimize the time between knowledge discovery and the corporate benefit from the information. The method for the organizations and businesses to convert their sources of knowledge into an advantage in the competitive environment is to identify and organize the information and to create information repositories (Ozdemirci and Aydin, 2007). Successful management of information depends on the ability to integrate information from thousands of individuals (Kivijarvi, 2004). The basis of competition is the power and ability to control the information generated and to use the correct information. The use of not only controlled information but also reproduced and unrestrainedly disseminated information hinders corporate activities. In this regard, information management should also organize the production of information and refine the information produced (Odabas, 2005).

Implementation of the information

What gives a company a competitive advantage is not abstract information, but rather its effective usage and implementation. Implementation of information is a company's use of the information under its control, in the fastest way, to accomplish its objectives. At this stage, the information is used, the results of this usage are evaluated and, if necessary, the information management processes are reorganized (Hauschild et al., 2001). Inapplicable and unshared information does not add value to the business. Portal, e-mail, instant messaging and searching technologies, chart data and office systems are used to share information (Laudon and Laudon, 2006). According to Kalling and Styhre (2003), information sharing is performed through interaction, collaboration, education and text distribution. The questions of what information and how much will be shared, and how, why and when it will be shared are extremely important for the survival of businesses. Since possessing knowledge indicates a very privileged power, sharing it may result in losing or increasing that power. In this context, the factors that influence and impede the sharing of information need the utmost attention (Koseoglu et al., 2011).

Protection of the information

Companies must keep and store the information acquired from their internal and external sources to use when necessary. Keeping this information minimizes the loss of information gained by the company. Organizations store information in memory systems in different ways. Such systems store information received from the brain in chip cards, hard disks, filing cabinets, libraries and data warehouses (Perez et al., 2002). Expert systems help companies to protect their acquired information through organizational processes and the implementation of cultural experiences (Laudon and Laudon, 2006). The protection of information is difficult due to its nature. Actions such as cooperation, useful codes of conduct and job design can be taken to protect the information. Companies may develop technologies that prevent and monitor access to vital information (Gold et al., 2001), and information management does not limit storage of the information to a particular location. Since users are indifferent to the location of the information they seek, the most important aspect for the user is the ability to access information in the fastest and most reliable way possible (Ozdemirci and Aydin, 2007).

Dimensions of an information management system

Implementation of information management involves several dimensions:

Information management strategy

An organization's information management strategy is based on the company's strategy. Its objective is to create, share and manage the relevant information assets that will help meet the tactical and strategic needs (www.knowledge-management-tools.net/). The design of information management varies based on the different cultural structures and business norms of organizations and companies. Therefore, in an organization, the business and information management strategies should be balanced, and these two processes should be implemented together (Ozdemirci and Aydin, 2007).

Organizational culture

The organizational culture reflects the employees' thoughts and feelings about the organization and describes their perception of the organization (Zaim, 2005), and it is a method used to mutually influence people. This culture affects the resistance shown to the organizational change of sharing all information (www.knowledge-management-tools.net/). By transferring the personnel's knowledge and experience to the system, the system can be maintained independent of individuals. Thus, mistakes can be corrected by other members of the system. In addition, it becomes easier to change personnel between departments (Drucker, 1999). However, organizational culture is entrenched in organizations and cannot be very easily changed. Over time, the culture becomes ingrained within the behaviors and habits of the employees. The employees keep the information and experience they have acquired to themselves. They believe this makes them powerful and secure in their jobs, so they do not want to share information with anyone (Awad and Ghaziri, 2004). A well-designed information management system enables the organization to monitor and evaluate the employees who share information and cooperate. Cultural changes that reward sharing, cooperation and production of values are a necessity and the result of this system (Ozdemirci and Aydin, 2007).

Organizational processes

Only the correct processes, environments and systems may enable the implementation of information management (www.knowledge-management-tools.net/). In this sense, an effective information management strategy includes processes such as providing technological systems, social and cultural elements, change and development, human resource management, and, in particular, rewarding motivation and voluntary participation in the process for all employees in an organization (Ozdemirci and Aydin, 2007).

Management and leadership

Based on its needs, each organization may create various manager positions and roles for information management. Managers are responsible for the order and continuity of their work groups so that they achieve the established task and objective. They are also responsible for providing the motivation necessary to achieve the group objectives and to organize internal and external environments for group performance. If information managers want to succeed, they should make decisions with a good knowledge of the economic, technological, social, political and ethical factors of society (O'Dell, 1998). In addition to selecting, keeping and using when necessary the right and required information for the company, managers are also responsible for converting the information into an easily understandable form (Jennex, 2008).

Technology

The objective of information management technologies is to create an environment for the exchange of information (Handzic, 2007). Preferred technologies should comply with the standards, should have lower costs than others, and should have continuous technical support and the longest possible warranty. In addition, the technological infrastructure to be established should be appropriate for the business volume of the organization. Computers and communication technologies should not only be used for storing information but also provide access to and ensure the regulation and safety of this information (Shanhong, 2002). Additionally, qualification of the personnel to use this technology is important. Employees who are competent in understanding the technological infrastructure and the information are required. People who have not received relevant training cannot be expected to produce information (Davenport and Prusak, 1998).

Politics

Implementation of long-term sustainable initiatives – including all corporate functions – can be costly. Information management also includes many changes that require a new budget, such as the renewal of the technological infrastructure, training staff, the provision, distribution, storage of information and making the information available for use as needed by the organization. Such activities should be considered an investment rather than an expenditure. In addition, they are not recurring investments.

Marketing information management

Organizations that want to establish a competitive advantage in the market obtain the information from the source (Drucker, 1992). Every day, managers are faced with changing environmental conditions. An intensely competitive environment has forced organizations to use innovative marketing activities to understand consumer needs and increase consumer satisfaction and retention (Noori and Salimi, 2005). As the management and marketing operations of organizations become more complicated over time, the importance of a marketing information system has increased twofold for managers, who have to make decisions quickly (Cakici and Gok, 2004; Yukselen, 2008). Because managers have to collect and analyze relevant information to plan marketing activities, marketing information systems have enabled quick reactions to customer requests (Li, 1995). Information systems can be the cornerstone of a new approach to marketing (Talvinen, 1995) and can be used as a tool for marketing information management. Therefore, management and system designers should be more aware of the need to integrate the marketing and management processes into existing systems in innovative ways (Talvinen, 1995). In marketing departments, marketing information management is required for activities such as developing new products, sales or demand forecasting, product screening, pricing strategy, sales profitability analysis, promotion strategies, computer operating budgets, advertising media selection, appointment of regional sales agents, customer credit approval, location of the facilities (warehouses, etc.), salespeople and delivery routes, determination of the economic order quantity, determination of reorder times (Lia et al., 2001) and customer lifetime value.

As in other industries, service industries have shown intense interest in this matter. For example, various authors in the literature have noted that information systems could bring potential benefits to the tourism and hotel industry in areas such as marketing planning, marketing reports, decision-making, time-saving, routine activities, sales activities and customer service, internal communication, market sentiment, consumer satisfaction, consumer information, providing cost savings in marketing, profitability, creating new products/services, sales promotion, and marketing research and productivity (Chatzipanagiotou and Coritos, 2010). Although the hotel industry was the first to use information technologies, the use of marketing information systems in this industry has a complicated and wide-ranging structure, ranging from operational activities to strategic decisions. Hotel managers have to address problems such as the changing demands of tourists, last-minute bookings and quality of service. A marketing information system provides significant market information to the hotel management and the capabilities to process and archive it. Therefore, it is important to make proactive efforts to develop marketing information systems. In this way, organizations can improve their customer information and satisfaction, as well as the quality of services and, more generally, produce a strategic marketing plan (Law and Jogaratnam, 2005).

In summary, marketing information management involves the generation and management of the information required to make rapid decisions and minimize risks. However, it should be noted that marketing information management is a sub-system of organization information management. Establishing a standalone system in the marketing department limits the realized information and organizational benefits.

Stages of marketing information management

The steps that organizations must pursue to create a marketing information management system (Tiwana, 1999; Barutcugil, 2002) can be summarized as follows:

Evaluation of the infrastructure

1. *Analysis of existing infrastructure.* First the infrastructure should be analyzed and the current situation defined.
2. *Association of information management and company strategy.* For successful implementation of information management practices, there should first be links between the business strategy, the information management strategy (Ozdemirci and Aydin, 2007) and the marketing strategy of the organization. To do so, a consumer-oriented framework should be created to show the importance of knowledge for the organization (Barutcugil, 2002). Creating such a structure is not a problem for the marketing department because the entire system is already consumer-oriented. The entire organization must be structured in the same way to support the marketing department.

Analysis, design and development of an information management system

3. *Designation of the information management infrastructure.* Focusing only on the consumer in each business process is not sufficient. The interaction between the processes should also be considered. The spontaneous operations of small organizations change as the organization grows; employees identify themselves with specialized business processes and do not want to share the information they have. The method for sharing the information with the whole organization should be defined. The impact of rapid information dissemination on the organization's performance is great; therefore, a common language and understanding should be created to determine where the information should be applied by using information technology, which provides a flow of information when needed (Barutcugil, 2002).
4. *Review of the current information assets and systems.* All information assets that are currently available in the organization should be reviewed, and the method to adapt them into the new system should be determined. Functionless information assets should be eliminated, and new information assets should be added to the system.
5. *Creation of an information management team.* When establishing the information management system, it is essential to create new roles and responsibilities in the organizational structure.

Such tasks can be designed in three stages, usually defined as high (strategic level), medium (process level) and lower level (information worker). Information workers work in the information creating, sharing and renewal processes. However, the tasks of organizing and presenting the data to benefit the organization belong to the manager, whose critical role is to facilitate the information management process (Barutcugil, 2002).

6. *Preparation of the information management project.* As each organization has a different structure, their information management systems will also be different. Therefore, each organization should create a system suitable to its organization (Tiwana, 1999). The creation and implementation of infrastructure for the information management system is usually executed through projects. The plans, including all details of the information management system, facilitate both the implementation and the control. The plans also include many details on sharing information with internal or external structures of organizations, addressing questions such as which information should be shared, when, how and with whom it should be shared.

7. *Development of the information management system.* The value of new information and goods or services based on the new information is inversely proportional to the contact time. Competitors discover and learn the new information in a very short time, and customers continue to demand products with a high information value. Continuous renewal of information is more important than the content of information. If you continuously obtain new information and reflect it in your goods and services, customer value increases. The way to develop the new information is by teaching because teaching is the best way to learn. In order to teach, the subject should be very well understood. This enables us to verify and reinforce the information and to correct our faults. During product development, organizations work together with consumers (Barutcugil, 2002).

Dissemination and implementation of information management

8. *Implementation of information management based on a plan.* This step requires a business culture based on trust. The best communication strategy should be produced by using the developing communication technologies. Next, the most important process for information organizations is to learn at the highest speed possible. The next step for an organization that has achieved all of this is to develop new information and to share it in the largest and most profitable way (Barutcugil, 2002). The plan for and implementation of information management should contain phases for these steps.

9. *Organizing change, the culture and the reward structure.* An information organization needs to become a learning organization. In this way, the company completely learns to quickly adapt to the change in the market and the uncertainty in the environment (Handzic, 2007). In hierarchical organizational structures, fear-based cultures dominate. In flatter and more open organizational structures, trust-based cultures that facilitate cooperation and common ownership are created. Trust is a prerequisite for information sharing, as it opens communication channels, encourages knowledge sharing and increases organizational learning (Barutcugil, 2002).

Evaluation of information management

10. *Performance evaluation.* One of the methods most widely used to evaluate the success of information systems is comprised of interdependent dimensions such as system quality, information quality, service quality, intended use, user satisfaction and net benefit (DeLone and

McLean, 2003). Evaluation of information management should be directed at both financial and competitive effects. Methods such as cost-benefit analysis, net current value and balanced scorecards can be used for evaluation (Tiwana, 1999).

Although this analysis demonstrates many benefits of information management, failures of information management cannot be denied. Some researchers state that the rate of failure in information management projects is 50%, while others state that this level is higher (Akhavan et al., 2005). Information management practices fail because of reasons such as a lack of measurable benefits and performance indicators, a lack of adequate management support, improper planning, design, coordination and evaluation, a lack of knowledge among managers and employees, problems with organizational culture and the wrong organizational structure (Frost, 2014).

References

Anon. (2010). *Cagdas Bilgi Sistemi ve Digital Işletmeler [Modern Information Sytem and Digital Administration]*, Anadolu Un. Acık Ogretim Fakultesi. Anatolia University. Open Source. [Online]. Available at: https://books.google.com.tr/books?id=suwDHLyRFb0C&printsec=frontcover&hl=tr#v=onepage&q&f=false. Accessed: 3.6.2016.

Akhavan, P., Jafari, M. & Fathian, M. (2005). Exploring failure-factors of implementing knowledge management systems in organizations, *Journal of Knowledge Management Practice*, 6(5), 1–8. [Online]. Available at: www.tlainc.com/jkmpv6.htm. Accessed: 4.7.2016.

Alavi, M. & Leidner, D. (1999). *Knowledge Management Systems: Issues, Challenges, and Benefits*. Communications of the Association for Information Systems, 1 (2nd ed.).

Alavi, M. & Leidner, D. (2001). Knowledge management and knowledge management systems: Conceptual foundations and research issues, *MIS Quarterly*, 25(1), 107–136.

Awad, E. & Ghaziri, H. (2004). *Knowledge Management*. International ed. Upper Saddle River, NJ: Pearson/Prentice Hall.

Barutcugil, İ. (2002) *Bilgi Yönetimi [Information Management]*. Istanbul: Kariyer Yayincilik.

Beijerse, R.P. (2000). Knowledge management in small and medium-sized companies: Knowledge management for entrepreneurs, *Journal of Knowledge Management*, 4(2), 162–174.

Benbya, H., Passiante, G. & Belbaly, N. A. (2004). Corporate portal: A tool for knowledge management synchronization, *International Journal of Information Management*, 24, 201–220.

Bharadwaj, S., Bhushan S. & Saxena, C. (2005). Knowledge management in global software teams, *Vikalpa*, 30(4), 65–75.

Broadbent, M. (1998). The phenomenon of knowledge management: What does it mean to the information profession? *Information Outlook*, 2(5): 23–36. [Online]. Available at: www.sla.org/pubs/serial /io/1998/may98/broadben.html. Accessed: 2.6.2016.

Buckman, H. (2004). *Building a Knowledge Driven Organization*. Boston: McGraw Hill.

Burman, B., Albinsson, P.A. & Hyatt, E. (2016). One night or many? Effects of amenity charge transparency on consumer reaction, *Journal of Hospitality Marketing & Management*, 25(8), 1010–1033.

Cakici, C. & Gok, T. (2004) Otel işletmeciliğinde pazarlama bilgi sistemi: yapılan bir araştırma ve sonuçları [Marketing information system in hotel management: A survey research and its results], *Oneri*, 6(22), 73–85.

Celik, A. (1998). Bilgi toplumu üzerine bazı notlar [Some notes on information society], *Hacettepe Universitesi Edebiyat Fakultesi Dergisi*, 15(1), 53–59.

Chatzipanagiotou, K.C. & Coritos, C.T. (2010). A suggested typology of Greek upscale hotels based on their MrkIS: Implications for hotels' overall effectiveness, *European Journal of Marketing*, 44(11/12), 1576–1611.

Darroch, J. & McNaughton, R.M. (2003). Beyond market orientation: Knowledge management and the innovativeness of New Zealand firms, *European Journal of Marketing*, 37(3–4), 572–593.

Davenport, T.H. & Prusak, L. (1998). *İş Dünyasında Bilgi Yönetimi, Kuruluşlar Ellerindeki Bilgiyi Nasıl Yönetirler? [Working Knowledge: Managing What Your Organisation Knows]*. Translation: Gunhan Gunay. Istanbul: Rota Yayınları.

DeLone, W.H. & McLean, E.R. (2003). DeLone and McLean model of information systems success: A ten-year update, *Journal of Management Information Systems*, 19(4), 9–30.

Drucker, P.F. (1992). *Gelecek İçin Yönetim* [*The 1990s and Beyond*]. Translation: Fikret Occan, Ankara: Iş bankasi yayinları.

Drucker, P.F. (1999). Yeni örgütün ortaya çıkışı [The emergence of new organization], *Bilgi Yönetimi* (Translation: Gündüz Bulut) Harvard Business Review, Dergisi'nden Secmeler, MESS, Istanbul, 11–28.

Duffy, J. (2001) Managing intellectual capital, *Information Management* 35(2), 59–64.

Durst, S., Edvardsson., I.R. & Bruns, G. (2013). Knowledge creation in small construction firms, *Journal of Innovation Management*, 1(1), 125–142.

Eppler, M.J. (2008) Knowledge maps: Typologies and application examples, *Knowledge Management Strategies: A Handbook of Applied Technologies*, Ed. K. Klinger, Hershey, NY: IGI Publishing, 116–142.

Frost, A. (2014). A synthesis of knowledge management failure factors. [Online]. Available at: www.knowledge-management-tools.net. Accessed: 30.6.2016.

Goksel, A.B. & Baytekin, E.P. (2008). Bilgi toplumunda isletmeler acısından onemli bir zenginlik entelektuel sermaye, halkla iliskiler acısından bir degerlendirme [An important wealth in the knowledge society in view of enterprises: The intellectual capital – an evaluation from PR perspective], *Istanbul Universitesi Iletisim Fakultesi Dergisi*, 31, 81–90.

Gold, A.H., Malhotra, A. & Segars, A.H. (2001). Knowledge management: An organizational capabilities perspectives, *Journal of Management Information Systems*, 8(1), 185–214.

Gupta, U.G. (1996) *Management Information Systems: A Managerial Perspective*. Berkeley, CA: West Group.

Handzic, M. (2007). *Knowledge Management: Through the Technology Glass*. London: World Scientific Publishing.

Hauschild, S., Stein, W. & Licht, T. (2001). Creating a knowledge culture, *The Mckinsey Quarterly*, 1, 74–81.

Jennex, E. (2008). *Knowledge Management: Concepts, Methodologies, Tools and Applications*. New York: Information Science Reference.

Kalling, T. & Styhre, A. (2003). *Knowledge Sharing in Organizations*. Malmo: Daleke Grafiska AB.

Kim, S. (2000). The roles of knowledge professionals for knowledge management, *INSPEL*, 34(1), 1–8.

Kivijarvi, H. (2004). Knowledge conversion in organizational context: A framework and experiments, *The 37th Hawaii International Conference on System Sciences*, 1–10. [Online]. Available at: http://ieeexplore.ieee.org/stamp/stamp.jsp?tp=&arnumber=1265582. Accessed: 17.6.2016

Kocel, T. (1998). *Isletme Yoneticiligi* [*Business Administration*]. Istanbul: Beta Basım Yayim.

Koseoglu, M., Gider, O. & Ocak, S. (2011). Bilgi paylasımı tutumunu etkileyen faktorler nelerdir? Bir kamu hastanesi ornegi [What are the factors affecting the knowledge sharing attitudes? A research on a state hospital], *Eskisehir Osmangazi Universitesi IIBF Dergisi*, 6(1), 215–243.

Kotler, P. (1997). *Marketing Management: Analysis, Planning, Implementation and Control*. Upper Saddle River, NJ: Prentice Hall.

Koza, M. (2008). *Bilgi Yönetimi* [*Knowledge Management*]. İstanbul: Kum Saati Yayın Dagıtım Ltd. Sti.

Ladeira, W.J., Santini, F.D.O., Araujo, C.F. & Sampaio, C.H. (2016). A meta-analysis of the antecedents and consequences of satisfaction in tourism and hospitality, *Journal of Hospitality Marketing & Management*, 25(8), 975–1009.

Laudon, K.C. & Laudon, J.P. (2006) *Management Information Systems: Managing The Digital Firm*. 10th Ed., Translation: Naralan, A., Ed. Horan, B. Upper Saddle River, NJ: Pearson Education Inc

Law, R. & Jogaratnam, G. (2005). A study of hotel information technology applications, *International Journal of Contemporary Hospitality Management*, 17(2), 170–180.

Li, E.Y. (1995). Marketing information systems in the top U.S. companies: A longitudinal analysis, *Information & Management*, 28, 13–31.

Lia, E.Y., McLeod, R.J. & Rogers, J.C. (2001). Marketing information systems in Fortune 500 companies: A longitudinal analysis of 1980, 1990, and 2000, *Information & Management*, 38, 307–322.

Little, S., Quintas, P. & Ray, T. (2002). *Managing Knowledge: An Essential Reader*. London: Sage Publications.

Machlup, F. (1984). *Knowledge: Its Creation, Distribution and Economic Significance, Volume III: The Economics of Information and Human Capital*, Princeton, NJ: Princeton University Press.

MacMorrow, N. (2001). Knowledge management: An introduction, *Annual Review of Information Science and Technology*, 35, 381–421.

Malhotra, Y. (1998). Knowledge management, knowledge organizations & knowledge workers: A view from the front lines, January 30, 1998. [Online]. Available at: www.brint.com/interview/maeil.htm.

Noori, B. & Salimi, M.H. (2005). A decision-support system for business-to-business marketing, *Journal of Business & Industrial Marketing*, 20(4/5), 226–236.

O'Dell, C. (1998). *If Only We Knew What We Know: The Transfer of Internal Knowledge and Best Practice*. San Francisco: Free Press.

Odabas, H. (2003). Kurumsal bilgi yönetimi [Organizational information management], *Turk Kutuphaneciligi*, 17(4), 357–368.

Odabas, H. (2005). Bilgi yönetim sistemi, bilgi çağı, bilgi yönetimi ve bilgi sistemleri [Information management system, information age, information management and information systems]. In Aktan, C. C. & Vural, I.Y. (Eds.), *Bilgi Cagi Bilgi Yonetimi ve Bilgi Sistemleri*. Konya: Cizgi Kitabevi, 1–11.

Ozdemirci, F. & Aydin, C. (2007). Kurumsal bilgi kaynakları ve bilgi yonetimi [Institutional knowledge sources and knowledge management], *Turk Kutuphaneciligi*, 21(2), 164–185.

Parker, S. (2000). Knowledge is like light – information is like water, *Information Development*, 16(4), 233–236.

Perez, M.P., Sanches, A., Carnicer, M.P. & Jimenez, M.J.V. (2002). Knowledge tasks and teleworking: A taxonomy model of feasibility adoption, *Journal of Knowledge Management*, 6(3), 272–284.

Pretorius, J.C. & Steyn, H. (2005). Knowledge management in project environments, *South African Journal of Business Management*, 36(3), 41–50.

Rubin, R.E. (2000). *Foundations of Library and Information Science*. New York: Neal-Schuman Publishers.

Sena, J. A. & Shani, (Rami) A.B. (1999). Intellectual capital and knowledge creation: Towards an alternative framework. In Liebowitz, J. (Ed.), *Knowledge Management Handbook*. Washington, D.C.: CRC Press, 8.1–8.16.

Setzer, V.W. (2001). Data, information, knowledge and competency. [Online]. Available at: www.ime.usp.br/~vwsetzer/data-info.html. Accessed: 12.9.2016.

Shanhong, T. (2002). Knowledge management in libraries in the 21st century. *IFLA Publications – Libraries in the Information Society*, 102, 88–93.

Soliman, F. & Spooner, K. (2000). Strategies for implementing knowledge management: Role of human resource management, *Journal of Knowledge Management*, 4(4), 337–345.

Talvinen, J.M. (1995). Information systems in marketing, *European Journal of Marketing*, 29(1), 8–26.

Taylor, A.G. (1999). *The Organization of Information*. Englewood, CO: Libraries Unlimited. Cited by: Tonta, Y. Bilgi yönetiminin kavramsal tanimi ve uygulama alanlari [Conceptual definition and application areas of knowledge management], *Kutuphaneciligin Destanı Sempozyumu* [The Legend of the Librarianship Symposium], 21–24 October 2004, Ankara. [Online]. Available at: http://yunus.hacettepe.edu.tr/~tonta/yayinlar/BilgiYonetimi.pdf. Accessed: 28.6.2016.

Tiwana, A. (1999). *The Knowledge Management Toolkit* (1st ed.). Upper Saddle River, NJ: Prentice Hall PTR.

Toffler, A. & Toffler, H. (1995). *Creating a New Civilization [Yeni Bir Uygarlık Yaratmak]* (Translation: Z. Dicleli). Istanbul: Inkilap Kitapevi.

Yukselen, C. (2008). *Pazarlama: Ilkeler, Yonetim, Ornek Olaylar [Marketing: Principles, Management, Case Studies]* (7th ed.). Ankara: Detay yayıncilik, 7. bsk.

Zaim, H. (2005). *Bilginin Artan Onemi ve Bilgi Yonetimi*. Istanbul: Işaret Yayınları.

13

Selling in the hospitality industry

Jeffrey A. Beck

Introduction

Within the promotional mix, personal selling is a key part of marketing strategy that relies heavily on the interaction between the salesperson and the client or prospective client for the purpose of creating, developing, and strengthening a business relationship. Personal selling is more important than other forms of promotion because of the interpersonal nature of the selling relationship. While advertising is the most common form of promotion, personal selling has an element of persuasion that advertising and other one-way forms of marketing communication do not exhibit. Therefore, personal selling involves oral and written communications between a salesperson and a prospective customer or customers for the purpose of informing them about, persuading them to purchase, and/or reminding them of the products or services the salesperson's hospitality organization has to offer.

As we look at the evolution of marketing as it pertains to hospitality, sales as an era of hospitality marketing progression began in the 1940s and progressed in the 1950s when franchising was initiated by Kemmons Wilson of Holiday Inn. At that point, sales in hospitality led to the development of marketing departments, greater understanding of consumer behavior, and a movement toward marketing activities that would provide potential clients, and sales activities that would close the sale. Marketing, then, became more of a strategic activity focused on brand development, and sales activities were tactical: let's get 'the heads in the beds'. As technology has evolved, the sales function of the hospitality industry has changed, foreshadowing many opportunities for reflection and empirical research in the hospitality research community.

Sales methods: A historical perspective

There appears to be five different periods in the evolution of selling and sales as a profession. These eras progressed from the 'snake oil salesman', who would misrepresent to achieve the sale, to the current day, where a collaborative approach that requires equal input from the customer and the salesperson is the norm. The development of these techniques moves from 'cronyism' to 'collaboration' (Harris, Ravid, Sverdlove, and Basuroy, 2016). Because of the various markets that hotels serve, different methodologies appear to be functional and in use by contemporary hotel sales professionals.

The evolution of sales as a profession in the United States appears to have begun in the late 1800s (Friedman, 2004). At that time, the salesperson tended to be an aggressive and adventurous individual who was essential to the development of new markets. The relationship between the customer and salesperson tended to be one of friendship; the salesperson would be more of an order taker. Unfortunately, the salesman took advantage of the relationship by acting as an expert. Economic times were prosperous; product differentiation was not required as competition was limited (Harris et al., 2016). During this era, ethics took a back seat to getting the sale; the new age of industrial management that required reports, quotas, and other pressures to produce sales made it necessary for salespeople to 'win at all costs' (Friedman, 2004). The sales function in hospitality was a 'promotional' approach; competition was also limited in the industry.

The salesman of this era could be known as a Controller. This period started just after the First World War and lasted until the mid-1960s. The salesman was a product expert. Companies like Ford Motor Company and National Cash Register trained salesmen to use a 'canned' presentation approach. Salespeople were taught to take control of the sales interaction. Manipulation occurred through emotional intimidation, jargon, and other tricks to win the sale. The sales function in hospitality began to take shape during this period. Although salesmen in hospitality were still order takers, it was recognized through expanding competition that the sales function must become specialized within the industry.

The evolution of sales methodologies in the modern era

A variety of sales methodologies were developed between the 1930s and 1950s. Many of the methodologies developed in the 1950s used a formula approach; a standardized technique that was meant to be followed in its entirety. These methodologies, some still taught in college classrooms, were designed using acronyms to help the sales professional remember each step of the process. These acronyms described an element of the sales process that was to lead the sales professional to outstanding performance (Finkelstein, 2013).

One of the first methods was the SELL technique, which guided the salesperson to tell the customer success stories that sold the customer on the benefits derived from the product or service. SELL was short for show, explain, lead to benefit, and let them talk. SELL was followed by ADAPT, which was designed to focus on the business problems of the prospect. The ADAPT method was a logical questioning system that was designed to ask assessment questions, discovery questions, activation questions, projection questions, and transition questions. The answers to these questions were then used to create a tailored presentation which would convince the prospect of the benefit of the salesperson's product or service (Ingram, Laforge, Avila, Schwepker, and Williams, 2008).

Many of these acronym techniques were used to help salespeople remember what type of question to ask, and when to ask them. The ARC technique was designed primarily for retail salespeople (Finkelstein, 2013). Salespeople asked the customer what they wanted, then worked to cross-sell and upsell to increase the size of the order. One of the most famous techniques is AIDA, short for attention, interest, desire, and action. This 'canned' approach is usually best used with commoditized products. While AIDA is still used in telemarketing situations, it has been modified to fit face-to-face situations as AIDCA, or attention, interest, desire, conviction, and action (Heller, 1999).

The next era of selling and sales techniques coincided with the evolution of the customer-centric marketing function. Products were differentiated from one another, and emphasis on the benefits a particular product had to offer was contrasted to the competition. The customer had more control over the sales process; the relationship was more of a partnership. This particular methodology was pioneered by Xerox Corporation, and became an easy to adapt method of professional sales for the hospitality industry. Focused on the idea of 'Need Satisfaction' selling, hospitality companies like Marriott and Hilton modified these techniques of 'feature–benefit' selling to fit the world of hospitality sales. Based on Xerox's original technique, hospitality sales was a five- to seven-step process that the salesperson would follow in order to achieve sales success. Developmental, this particular method required a phased approach; the next step in the process could not be approached until both salesperson and client agreed on the outcome of the previous step. These five to seven steps include prospect identification, prospect qualification, presentation and negotiation, closing the sale, and post-sales service. In many hospitality organizations, these techniques are still in use today. Many sales professionals believe that this was the dawn of professional selling (Harris et al., 2016). While more of a 'process' than other techniques of the past, unless salespeople truly knew and understood their customer's needs and what was of value, the presentation to a customer or prospect focused more on product features. Strategic selling was a methodology that assumed the salesperson had the basic selling skills for individual client interaction. The strategic selling methodology added techniques for planning and managing large and complex sales, such as business transient contracts, or B2B selling in the lodging industry.

The next phase of selling techniques and the sales process is the well-known consultative sales process. In this technique, the feature–benefit approach is secondary to the primary focus of understanding the customer's needs. Salespeople are trained at questioning techniques that help them to understand the unique needs of the customer. Some have called these techniques the 'hurt and rescue' approach (Finkelstein, 2013). The salesperson identifies the problem or problems that are hurting the customer, and then comes to the rescue by presenting features and benefits that appeal and are relevant to the customer (Rackham, 1988). The control in this sales relationship is a shared one; both salesperson and customer seek a mutually satisfactory outcome. As the hospitality industry has become more competitive, this method has become a standard. Many hospitality and tourism sales professionals, who have received training from the major lodging companies, have adopted these techniques with success. This method has also been called relationship selling, where the salesperson becomes an advocate for the customer within the hospitality organization.

Salespeople have done well at developing relationships with their customers. A new approach, 'CustomerCentric' selling, places emphasis on *how* customers use a product or service, rather than on what benefits are derived from the product or service (Bosworth and Holland, 2004). The premise of this technique, especially for non-commodity products and services, is that the customer is looking to solve a problem, achieve a goal, or satisfy a need through the sale. Interestingly, this technique moves away from focusing on users of the product or service, and toward the decision-makers. Further, this technique is designed to empower buyers, rather than sell to them (Bosworth and Holland, 2004).

Many customers have affinity toward a single brand. Therein lies the problem: a consultative approach tends to be one-sided. With many of the hospitality industry's business customers, long-term partnerships have been formed. With this strategic alliance, hospitality sales organizations and their customers realize that long-term success requires a relationship of trust that will contribute to long-term success, regardless of the economic climate (Eades and Sullivan, 2014). Thus, a selling method prevalent today is known as the collaborative technique. This method has three components of note: (1) A successful and trustworthy business relationship; (2) Both the buying and selling organizations need each other to succeed; and (3) There is an element of risk that could harm one or both of the collaborators. This approach makes it important for the selling organization to make it *easy for the customer to buy.*

The evolution of professional selling in an internet world

As previously stated, many of the techniques developed in the 1960s were still in use within hospitality organizations at the turn of the twenty-first century. Salespeople were (and in some organizations still are) using the step methodologies described earlier, focusing on a sales process controlled by the salesperson. The lack of data available to hospitality managers, along with the deeply embedded traditions of hospitality sales, prevented progression to new methodologies, training, and organization of the sales function (Rach, 2015).

Early models of selling services contended that customers of hospitality products often had direct interactions with various functions within the selling organization (Buttle, 1993). Therefore, the customer contact personnel responsible for these interactions became part of the sales process. Reservations agents, front desk personnel, sales coordinators and assistants, and catering service and sales staff all played an important role in selling the services of the property.

In the 'old school' of lodging sales, general managers and directors of sales developed their business wisdom for what business to accept and what prices to charge through experience. As one general manager put it, "I keep raising prices until people complain or occupancy goes down" (Beck and Knutson, 2006, p. 48). With the change of ownership structures in the past ten to fifteen years, more emphasis has been placed on the value of the hotel and the land it sits on. Subsequently, more focus has been placed on the metrics that demonstrate the unique selling position of the hotel, and the performance of the sales organization.

In this 'old school' approach, personality and human relations skills were viewed as the cornerstone to sales success. Personal appearance, demeanor, and social graces were the norm for the hospitality sales professional. During this time frame, the salesperson was more of an advocate for the customer. Conversations at sales meetings were more about what the customer was willing to pay, and less about what the property was capable of charging based on demand.

The confluence of the revenue management/customer relationship function and the sales function in hospitality has provided for disruption in how sales is viewed and managed by owners, asset managers, brands, and general managers (Beck, Knutson, Kim, and Cha, 2010).

With the increase of data, general managers, directors of sales, and other revenue leaders are able to measure the success of the sales effort by techniques used, customer value, and return on investment (Rach, 2015).

While the sales function was once the key method for driving revenue, it has become part of a unified approach which includes revenue management, customer relationship management, marketing, and operations. Three schools of thought have arisen with the evolution of this unified approach. The reorganization of the sales function, through clustered sales offices, has been the approach taken by some hospitality operators. The question is "What has been done to maximize revenue through the sales effort?" The sales function in this school of thought is also a revenue generator for the brand/franchisor that helps to support the franchisee for a fee.

The second school of thought focuses on the changes in the traditional buying process, based on the advent of technologies that allow for a portion of the process to be automated. The effect of this technological advance has allowed owners and operators of limited service properties to streamline the sales process, at the cost of not having trained sales personnel for times when human interaction is required. The third school of thought places the sales process secondary to the revenue management function. The sales function has become an 'internal intermediary' between the customer and the revenue management function. In this case, the role of the salesperson is reversed. The salesperson is more an advocate for the property than that of the customer, and must create value for the customer, in the form of a willingness to pay.

The selling process and social media

Social media has been proposed as having a role in the sales process (Andzulis, Panagopoulos, and Rapp, 2012). From the customer identification phase to service after the sale, the various tools of social media can have a positive impact on salespeople guiding the customer through the sales process. Hospitality marketers have relied on social media primarily as a presentation medium for demonstrating the value proposition of their property for leisure, business transient, and groups, but there are many other uses related to the sales process that are viable, and that warrant investigation by hospitality researchers.

Using the classification system developed by Kaplan and Haenlein (2010) and adapted by Andzulis et al. (2012), four categories of social media technologies have emerged as potential tools in the selling process. Collaborative projects, where content is created by many end users, may have utility in information gathering, needs discovery, presentation, and service follow-up. Blogs can be used for similar purposes; blogs can be very useful for monitoring comments based on posts in the development of lead generation. Shared content in communities such as YouTube and Facebook can be useful in internal sales support, and in demonstration of the value proposition. Social networking media such as LinkedIn and Twitter are valuable for referrals and laying the groundwork for future opportunities (Andzulis et al., 2012). Another classification that would fit within the world of hospitality sales would be the virtual game world, which consists of three-dimensional platforms with users as personalized avatars that interact with each other. Clearly, such platforms would be ideal for property tours, internal sales support, and salesforce development. A future research direction for hospitality sales research could use the Andzulis et al. social media sales process framework to identify the use and effectiveness of social media by sales organizations.

The changing nature of the buying process

Buttle (1993) asserted that most hotels' sales objective is to produce short-term sales revenues based on group room business. In Buttle's revised model of services selling, the sales team must 'tangibilize' the service through methods such as property tours, printed materials, videos, complementary offerings, and 'brag books'. What must be pointed out is that this revised model of selling services was developed at the dawn of the internet and before the advances of technology. The internet, through the simplicity of a Google search, can provide the materials, videos, and brag books (testimonials) for which the property was once the source.

According to research by Google and CEM, customers reported that they are 60 percent through the sales process before they contact a sales representative (Gillium, 2013). Hotel buyers are now able to go online to view (1) the items that 'tangibilize' the hotel, (2) price and availability, and (3) evaluations from other customers. Once that has occurred, they are then able to (4) book the property. Clearly, a more transactional buying process has been established, but sales personnel must change their role from information provider to information collector. Buying process information, along with client motivation information, becomes more important for achieving the sale (see Figure 13.1).

The advent of the electronic request for proposal (e-RFP) has become a great tool for the meeting planner, but has challenged sales personnel to keep up with the volume of e-RFPs sent to the property (Kovaleski, 2013). Many come from third-party meeting planning firms that specialize in site selection. Salespeople can spend anywhere from one half to one full hour responding to a single e-RFP. Sales and revenue leaders should insure that marketing communication

Figure 13.1 Valuable customer information for sales professionals

materials available to buyers are consistent across platforms, the most valuable marketing content should be private – in the hands of sales personnel – and sales analytic processes should be strengthened (Gillum, 2013).

The group selling organization

Several trends have begun to make the buying and selling of group business a transaction, rather than the relationship sale it has been for years (Lutz, 2011). In 2007, Marriott introduced Sales Force One, designed to streamline the sales process. With the many brands and on-property salespeople, there could be as many as fifteen different hotel sales representatives from as many hotels calling on one account. With the new structure, the number was reduced to one through the reorganization to cluster, or regional, sales offices.

This reorganization was the result of different buying processes; groups' needs had evolved. Some of these needs include: smaller, less complex meetings that are more transactional, and require less attention by a salesperson. Booking windows have shortened, suggesting that a 'one stop shop' mentality has become part of the small meeting group buying process. As was mentioned earlier, many buyers are taking advantage of the e-RFP process, which has been addressed through the cluster office manpower. Finally, many buyers are using third-party site selection companies, that do not require relationship building until toward the end of the buying process, should the property be selected as a viable candidate for the meeting or event (Lutz, 2011).

The outcome of these changes will require new training schemes of on-property personnel. If there is no on-property sales person, those staff members on property will be required to develop sales skills. Cluster sales coordinators will be less creative for the customer and hotel owner, finding the solution that is easiest, based on the electronic portfolio of hotels (Lutz, 2011). There has been at least one lawsuit filed by a hotel owner arguing that the best interest of the hotel owner is secondary to the brand. (Shapiro, 2011). This cluster style of sales management has also been unpopular with meeting planners; the personal relationships developed with on-property sales personnel in the past are no longer possible. Not all hotel brands have gone to this model; it may make for compelling research to determine the outcomes of such a reorganization compared to brands that have not reorganized.

Future research in hospitality selling

Recent research has studied the quality of relationships between the meeting planner and salesperson (Lee, Su, and Dubinsky, 2005; Kim and Qu, 2012). These studies focused on the characteristics of the salesperson, and the attitudes of the meeting planner. What has not been investigated is the effect the newly created cluster sales organization has on the relationship between the parties in the sales process. Future research could also consider the impact of e-RFP on the selling model proposed by Kim and Qu.

Empirical study on the relationship between the revenue manager and the sales manager would also be of merit. This could be expanded to include how this interaction impacts the relationship with the meeting planner as well. It could be that the transactional nature that appears to be evolving in the sales process may negatively affect relationship quality with planners. Further, changes in the buying process could be investigated in terms of their impact on the sales process in hospitality. The exploratory study by Beck and Knutson (2006) could be replicated, examining the changes in sales structure at limited service and full-service properties.

The impact of social media on the sales process is a research stream beginning to have an impact in the mainstream sales literature. The opportunities to investigate the impact of social media in hospitality selling could be of value to both the hospitality industry and the sales research literature. Finally, Rach (2015) proposes the need for new skill sets for salespeople in hospitality. Hospitality researchers interested in human resources, training, and organizational development issues may find this area to be of merit for investigation.

References

Andzulis, J., Panagopoulos, N. & Rapp, A. (2012). A review of social media and implications for the sales process. *Journal of Personal Selling and Sales Management*, 32(3), 305–316.

Beck, J. & Knutson, B. (2006). An exploratory study of sales managers' activities in lodging properties. *Journal of Hospitality and Leisure Marketing*, 15(1), 45–63.

Beck, J., Knutson, B.J., Kim, S. & Cha, J. (2010). Developing the dimensions of activities important to successful revenue management performance: an application to the lodging industry. *International Journal of Revenue Management*, 4(3/4), 268–283.

Bosworth, M.T. & Holland, J.R. (2004). *CustomerCentric Selling*. New York: McGraw-Hill.

Buttle, F.A. (1993). Selling services: A contingency model. *Journal of Services Marketing*, 7(3), 36–48.

Eades, K.M. & Sullivan, T.T. (2014). *The Collaborative Sale*. Hoboken, NJ: John Wiley & Sons.

Finkelstein, P. (2013). The history of sales methodologies: Why some work and some don't. Sales Essentials. Barrett.com.au. Retrieved from http://salesessentials.com. Accessed 1 October 2016.

Friedman, W.A. (2004). *Birth of a Salesman: The Transformation of Selling in America*. Cambridge, MA: Harvard University Press.

Gillium, S. (2013). The disappearing sales process. Retrieved from www.forbes.com/sites/gyro/2013/01/07/the-disappearing-sales-process/#34a9cfa025d9. Accessed 10 January 2016.

Harris, R. (2009). Selling in tough times: From 'cronyism' to collaboration (The 5 c's of selling). Retrieved from www.sitepronews.com/2009/03/19/selling-in-tough-times-from-"cronyism"...-to-collaboration-the-5-c's-of-selling. Accessed 1 October 2016.

Harris, M., Ravid, S.A., Sverdlove, R. & Basuroy, S. (2016). Intellectual property contracts: theory and evidence from screenplay sales. Retrieved from https://papers.ssrn.com/sol3/papers.cfm?abstract_id=2017802. Accessed 8 August 2017.

Heller, R. (1999). *Selling Successfully*. New York, NY: DK Publishing.

Ingram, T., Laforge, R., Avila, R., Schwepker, C. & Williams, W. (2008). *Professional Selling: A Trust-based Approach*, 4th edition. Mason, OH: Cengage Learning.

Kaplan, A. & Haenlein, M. (2010). Users of the world unite! The challenges and opportunities of social media. *Business Horizons*, 53(1), 59–68.

Kim, M. & Qu, H. (2012). A refined model of relationship selling between meeting planners and suppliers. *Journal of Travel and Tourism Marketing*, 29(2), 105–118.

Kovaleski, D. (2013). 4 tips for better RFPs. Retrieved from http://meetingsnet.com/tips-top/4-tips-better-rfps. Accessed 10 January 2016.

Lee, S., Su, H. & Dubinsky, A.J. (2005). Relationship selling in the meeting planner/hotel salesperson dyad. *Journal of Hospitality and Tourism Research*, 29(4), 427–447.

Lutz, D. (2011). The big gamble: Commoditizing group sales. Retrieved from: http://velvetchainsaw.com/2011/03/25/big-gamble-commoditizing-hotel-group-sales/. Accessed 10 January 2016.

Rach, L. (2015). *The Evolution of Sales: Perspectives and Realities Defining the Modern Sales Professional*. United States: Foundation of the Hospitality Sales & Marketing Association International.

Rackham, N. (1988). *Spin Selling*. New York, NY: McGraw–Hill.

Richardson Group (2016). *2016 Selling Challenges Study*. Retrieved from www.richardson.com/PageFiles/3/Richardson-2016-Sales-Challenges-Report-UK.pdf. Accessed 1 October 2016.

Shapiro, M.J. (2011). Lawsuit claims Marriott's sales initiative shows 'callous disregard' of hotel owner's interests. Retrieved from www.meetings-conventions.com/News/Hotels-and-Resorts/Lawsuit-Claims-Marriott-s-Sales-Initiative-Shows--Callous-Disregard--of-Hotel-Owners--Interests/. Accessed 1 October 2016.

14

Promotion in the hospitality industry

Ali Dalgıç, Ozan Güler and Kemal Birdir

Promotion

The role of promotion, which is one of the four Ps of the marketing mix (product, price, place and promotion), is to communicate with individuals, groups or organizations directly or indirectly in order to create awareness about a product/company and convincing them to purchase (Pride & Ferrell, 1991: 436; Kotler & Armstrong, 2012: 52; Ogden-Barnes & Minahan, 2015: 9). To obtain maximum benefit from promotional efforts, marketers must make every effort to thoroughly plan, implement, coordinate and control the communication process (Pride & Ferrell, 1991: 437). Companies need a purposive, planned, and integrable communication program rather than a slapdash and garish one since it is one of the pivotal agents in a company's efforts to build profitable customer relationships (Bowie & Buttle, 2004: 196; Kotler & Keller, 2012: 358). Building strong customer relationships requires much more than just developing a quality, affordable and available good or service. A successful product or service means nothing without precisely coordinated and integrated communication with the target groups.

As is well known, the most famous and global companies and brands, such as Coca-Cola, Ford Motor Company, MasterCard, American Express, Blackberry, Carlsberg, Starbucks, Johnson & Johnson, Shell, Procter & Gamble, etc., are still seeking new communication methods and platforms. The same situation is valid for the hospitality and tourism industry as well. Despite the familiarity and wealth of companies and brands in this industry, they spend millions of dollars on various promotion activities. According to iSpot.tv, Marriot International Inc., Choice Hotels International Inc., and Wyndham Worldwide Inc. spent $47.2 million, $29.9 million and $17.4 million, respectively, on TV advertising in the United States in 2015 (Skift, 2016a). Companies have revised and improved their promotion activities as consumers have become familiar with technological developments (Kotler, Bowen & Makens, 2010: 359). As customers have become well-informed and individualistic consumers, new fields have emerged that have shaped consumers'preferences and behaviors, such as social and digital media. The internet has changed almost everything, including marketing promotion methods (Kotler & Keller, 2012: 357), but has not changed the crucial importance of communication(McCabe & Foster, 2014: 398), and has created new marketing promotion

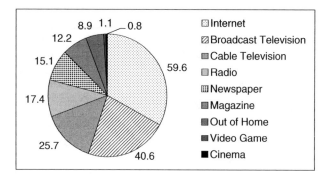

Figure 14.1   Advertising revenue market share ($ billions) by media – 2015

methods (Kotler & Keller, 2012: 357). When the 20-year advertising revenue growth of the internet is compared against radio, TV, newspaper and magazine, its growth curve is the most dramatic (IAB, 2016: 21). According to a survey conducted by PwC and Interactive Advertising Bureau (IAB), the internet is the leading source of advertising by $59.6 billion and internet advertising has experienced double-digit annual growth in every year except 2009; no other media has experienced double-digit growth in any year (IAB, 2016: 21–23). Figure 14.1 presents a pie chart prepared according to 2015 Internet Ad Revenue data gathered from IAB/PwC's Report.

Promotion mix/marketing communication mix

Promotion mix, also called marketing communication mix, involves the specific combination of advertising, sales promotion, personal selling, public relations-publicity and direct marketing tools that hospitality and tourism companies use in order to build a strong customer relationship (Kotler, Bowen & Makens, 2010: 358). In addition to these elements, companies could benefit from events and experiences, interactive marketing and word-of-mouth marketing in order to create brand awareness, positive brand judgments and feelings, and strong consumer loyalty (Kotler & Armstrong, 2012: 408; Kotler & Keller, 2012: 500).

1. **Advertising** – Introductory and paid form of nonpersonal presentations which are designed with the aim of leaving the target audience with a favorable impression by providing information on products or services (Pride & Ferrell, 1991: 446; Percy & Elliott, 2005: 4) via print media (newspapers and magazines), broadcast media (radio and television), network media (telephone, cable, satellite, wireless), electronic media (audiotape, videotape, videodisk, CD-ROM, web page), and display media (billboards, signs, posters) (Kotler & Keller, 2012: 500). According to statistics, while Walt Disney Company spent approximately US$2.1 billion on advertising in 2014 (Businessinsider, 2016), Hilton Hotels Worldwide invested US$269.1 million on advertising in the USA in 2012 (Statistica, 2016a). According to travel and hospitality advertising statistics in 2008, the top five advertisers in the travel industry were; Travelport Corporate Solutions, Inc., VacationsToGo.com, The Walt Disney Corporation, Best Western International, Inc., and Hilton Hotels Corporation (Nielsen, 2009).
2. **Sales Promotion** – A variety of immediate or short-term and mostly seasonal initiatives or materials to encourage trial or purchase of a product or service, including samples, coupons,

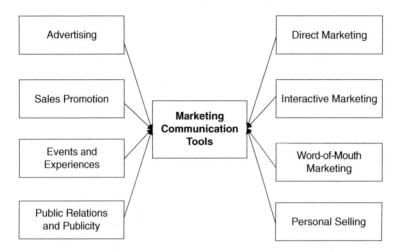

Figure 14.2   Marketing communication tools

premiums, demonstrations, contests, etc. (Pride & Ferrell, 1991: 448–449; Kotler & Keller, 2012: 500). For example, on the ninth anniversary of their maiden voyage, Virgin Blue Airlines gave away 1000 plane tickets for $9 each through their Twitter social media web page. In addition to this example, the hospitality industry offers a variety of special deals, hot deals, last-minute sales, early bird promotions, loyalty program promotions, try before you buy promotions, special day promotions, upgrade promotions etc.

3. **Events and experiences** – Company or sponsored-driven promotion activities aimed to create daily or special brand-related interactions with consumers via sports and entertainment organizations, festivals, street activities, etc. (Keller, 2009: 141; Kotler & Keller, 2012: 500). Hospitality companies could both be a sponsor or direct host for an event and thus could operate its promotion activities. For example, Turkish Airlines organized the World Golf Cup Amateur Series 2016 with 100 qualifying events in 61 countries worldwide. The company announced that the 100 lucky Grand Final qualifiers would be able to use Business Class flights with Turkish Airlines, stay in accommodation at the Grand Final Titanic Delux Belek Resort and play at the Regnum Carya Gold & Spa Resort Hotels. As can be seen, it is a great example of combination and cooperation of hospitality companies for an event which is seen as a smart promotion activity tool.

4. **Public relations and publicity** – Personal or nonpersonal activities aimed at protecting and strengthening the company image for employees or consumers, other firms, the government and the media via press kits, speeches, seminars, lobbying, etc. (Pride & Ferrell, 1991: 437; Kotler & Armstrong, 2012: 408; Kotler & Keller, 2012: 500). Hospitality companies are among the most assertive and successful campaigners in terms of P&R campaigns. KLM Royal Dutch Airlines' "happy to help" campaign scanned social media over the course of five days searching for passengers facing travel woes throughout the world, and responded with a creative and relevant campaign. JetBlue Airways' "chain letter of human goodness" campaign awarded one free JetBlue ticket to several deserving individuals involved in humanitarian efforts, thus aiming to enable people to fulfill a dream or make a meaningful humanitarian impact on the world.

5. **Direct marketing** – A promotion tool based on direct communications so as to get quick feedback about products or services and maintain a strong relationship with the target customers. The most common tools are face-to-face meetings, phone calls, e-mails or other internet channels (Kotler, Bowen & Makens, 2010: 358; Kotler & Keller, 2012: 500). Direct marketing is

also a successful tool for building favorable customer relationship management (CRM). Hotels, airline companies and travel agencies are the leading companies applying direct marketing strategies through TV, magazines, newspapers, social media, e-mails, mobile applications, catalogs and phone calls. Many people could get a phone call from travel agencies about new travel packages or come across a sales person from a travel agency that endeavors to sell a hotel's offer directly.

6. **Interactive marketing** – An online environment that provides both a comfortable and personal shopping experience for customers and an increase in customer awareness, customer satisfaction and sales, and lower costs for the companies via websites, blogs, online shopping, etc. (Kotler & Keller, 2012: 500). In the early 2000s, total spending on online advertising in the USA was approximately US$8 billion; however, it amounted to US$59.6 billion (34.7% mobile and 65.3% internet) in 2015, with an increase of 20.4% from 2014 (IAB, 2016; Statistica, 2016b). Social media advertising expenditures totaled US$10.9 billion in 2015 compared to US$7 billion in 2014, and in this context the leisure travel industry maintained its proportion with 9% in 2014 and 2015, and was ranked as the fourth major industry (IAB, 2016). Hospitality and tourism businesses use online and offline connections to steer guests to the main website and on-site communications, which help to direct customer behavior or achieve a required marketing outcome. As more consumers call for real-time information online, hospitality and tourism marketers are responding with advanced online marketing strategies. According to Think with Google, 65% of leisure travelers consult the web early in the travel process and 69% of business travelers determine their travel details by searching options online. As a striking example, Hampton Hotels, part of Hilton Worldwide, was chosen as the winner of Hotels Magazine's 2013 Social Hotel Awards with its "Hamptonality Campaign." The hotel reported that the video for this campaign had 3 million views in eight weeks and a 60% increase in Facebook fans since the launch of the campaign (Skift, 2016b). Interactive marketing is not limited to hotels' smart efforts. Airline companies such as WestJet (Christmas Miracle: real-time giving – over 45 million views on YouTube), KLM (Disney's Planes – over 2.9 million views on YouTube) and tour operators such as Thomas Cook (surprise wedding on a plane – over 2 million views on YouTube) provide great examples of successful interactive promotion campaigns.

7. **Word-of-mouth marketing** – Expresses customers' positive or negative post-purchasing evaluations regarding their consuming experiences through oral or written communication, or electronically (Keller, 2009: 141; Kotler & Keller, 2012: 500). Not only small businesses but also giants attach great importance to word-of-mouth (WoM) marketing due to its positive and negative outcomes. Companies should encourage their consumers to share their consumption experiences, whether satisfactory or dissatisfactory. Due to the service-oriented and intangible structure of the hospitality and tourism industry, having either positive or negative WoM is crucial, particularly electronic WoM, for companies which care about complaint management. Nowadays, social media tools such as Twitter, Facebook, Instagram, and online travel platforms TripAdvisor, Booking, Foursquare and so on are the leading platforms for sharing customers' consumption experience in depth. These comments and feedback significantly affect companies' image, reputation and profitability as a consequence. Taking into account the monthly total of 385 million comments from 340 million different visitors at TripAdvisor, the significance of WoM marketing becomes clear (TripAdvisor, 2016). Through WoM, customers not only share written but also visual feedback. Founder and author of the foodmarketingschool.com website, Karen Fewell, says that over 78 million images tagged with #foodporn and 173 million tagged with #food have been posted on Instagram.

8. **Personal selling** – Activities based on face-to-face interaction with purchasers (Pride & Ferrell, 1991: 447) in order to inform and persuade them (Pride & Ferrell, 1991: 447). Personal selling consists of personal efforts of employees such as sales presentations, sales meetings, fairs, trade shows, etc. (Kotler & Keller, 2012: 500). Hyatt Hotels Corporation developed an exclusive sales automation application (Envision) that allows their international and national sales force (NSF) to have direct access to all sales functions. In addition, Hyatt Hotels Corporation joins globally known travel fairs such as ITB, World Travel Market and Asia Luxury Travel Market, and organizes Hyatt fairs and sales calls in order to provide the hotels with face-to-face access to Hyatt's best existing and potential clients in the context of direct marketing efforts.

Due to changes in customer attitudes and behaviors, and technological and global developments, marketing communicators go beyond the traditional communication platforms and try to benefit from a variety of communication platforms at the same time (Kotler & Keller, 2012: 500). Table 14.1 presents a list of the numerous communication platforms available to marketing communicators.

Table 14.1 Common communication platforms

Advertising	Sales Promotion	Events and Experiences	Public Relations and Publicity	Direct and Interactive Marketing	Word of Mouth Marketing	Personal Selling
Print and broadcast ads	Contests, games, sweepstakes, lotteries	Sports	Press kits	Catalogs	Person to person	Sales presentations
Packaging – outer	Premiums and gifts	Entertainment	Speeches	Mailings	Chat rooms	Sales meetings
Packaging inserts	Sampling	Festivals	Seminars	Telemarketing	Blogs	Incentive programs
Cinema	Fairs and trade shows	Arts	Annual reports	Electronic shopping		Samples
Brochures and booklets	Exhibits	Causes	Charitable donations	TV shopping		Fairs and trade shows
Posters and leaflets	Demonstrations	Factory tours	Publications	Fax		
Directories	Coupons	Company museums	Community relations	E-mail		
Reprints of ads	Rebates	Street activities	Lobbying	Voice mail		
Billboards	Low-interest financing		Identity media	Company blogs		
Display signs	Trade-in allowances		Company magazine	Websites		
Point-of-purchase displays	Continuity programs					
DVDs	Tie-ins					

Source: Kotler & Keller (2012: 501).

Basic communication process and integrated marketing communication

Communication is the transmission of information and knowledge between a sender (source) and a receiver (audience). The source must convert its message into a series of signs that express ideas or concepts, which is called the coding process. Straight after this, the source must select the most effective and lucid medium of transmission out of the numerous communication platforms (Pride & Ferrell, 1991: 439–440). The process continues with checking whether the receiver gets the right message that the source coded, namely, a follow-up decoding process.

When the result of decoding is different from what is coded, noise emerges deriving from many agents such as mediums of transmission, signs, receivers etc. (Pride & Ferrell, 1991: 440). The last, but not least, feedback process involves the receiver's response to the message (Kalla, 2005: 303). Feedback varies greatly according to the type of communication. While during face-to-face situations verbal and nonverbal feedback could be immediate, mass communications situations provide slow and difficult feedback to recognize such as the level of sales volume or consumer attitudes and awareness (Pride & Ferrell, 1991: 441–442). Some hotels, restaurants and online booking companies even offer discounts in return for obtaining feedback.

Marketing communication represents the voice of the brand and has a pivotal role in effective communication with customers about the company's product/service offers. It is a complement to activities that aim to encourage, persuade and inform the company's target groups. Marketing communication aims to provide detailed information on products' operational features, and could provide much broader perspectives for customers such as how and why a product is used, by what kind of person, and where and when; customers can learn about who makes the product and what the company and brand stand for (Keller, 2001: 823). Integrated marketing communication is a marketing effort that is widely accepted and applied at different levels by contemporary companies and organizations, with the aim of brand creation and development (Madhavaram, Badrinarayanan & McDonald, 2005: 69; Kotler & Keller, 2012: 501). The American Association of Advertising Agencies (AAAA) defines integrated marketing communication as:

> a concept of marketing communication planning that recognizes the added value of a comprehensive plan that evaluates the strategic roles of a variety of communication disciplines, e.g. general advertising, direct response, sales promotion and public relations – and combines these disciplines to provide clarity, consistency and maximum communication impact.
>
> *(De Pelsmacker, Geuens, &Van den Bergh, 2001: 8)*

Integrated marketing communication fosters a company's communication skills and with its many promotion options accelerates and eases the process of product/service promotion and brand development (Madhavaram, Badrinarayanan & McDonald, 2005: 69).

In terms of hospitality and tourism companies, it is possible to state that communication channels and target audiences are numerous. Therefore, planning and managing this process is crucial (McCabe & Foster, 2014: 397). Accordingly, companies must plan and implement the most effective and practicable communication methods. To be one step ahead of the rivals, an effective marketing communication process should be followed, composed of six steps: "identify the target audience," "determine the communication objectives," "design the message," "select the communication channels," "select the message source" and "measure the communications' results" (Kotler & Armstrong, 2012: 415–420; Kotler & Keller, 2012: 362). Identifying the target audience could be specified as the beginning of the marketing communication process. The audience might be individuals, groups, special publics or the general public and the communicator's decision on "what will be said," "how it will be said," "when it will be said," "where it

173

will be said," and "who will say it" differs according to the type of the target audience. Hence, the first step of effective marketing communication begins with identifying the target audience properly (Kotler, Bowen & Makens, 2010: 362). In this context, market segmentation and branding strategies have great importance in the hospitality and tourism industry, particularly for hotels. Hotels have a variety of accommodation classes, such as top luxury, upper upscale, upscale, upper midscale, midscale and economy-budget. According to 2015 statistics, Marriott International has the highest number of brands in the list of chained-brand hotels, with 26 different brands under four market segments excluding midscale and economy. Accor Hotels, Wyndham Worldwide and Hilton Worldwide are the other companies that have more brands than others; however, Accor Hotels differs from the others with its 21 brands under all lodging segments (Wikipedia, 2016).

Following the determination of a target audience, the marketing communicator should decide what reaction is expected. According to target consumers' readiness states involving "awareness," "knowledge," "liking," "preference," "conviction" and "purchase," the communicator is supposed to develop objectives and design the messages (Kotler, Bowen & Makens, 2010: 362–363). The communicator should take three issues into account: "what to say" (message content), "how to say it logically" (message structure) and "how to say it symbolically" (message format) (Kotler, Bowen & Makens, 2010: 365). The message should get attention, hold interest, arouse desire and result in action (AIDA Model) from the target audiences (Kotler, Bowen & Makens, 2010: 362–365); namely, it should leave a favorable mark in the target audience's minds (Kotler, Keller, Brady, Goodman & Hansen, 2009: 696–697; Middleton, Fyall, Morgan & Ranchhod, 2009: 297). The designed message could be sent through personal communication channels (face-to-face, person to audience, over the telephone, through mail or e-mail, online chat etc.) and nonpersonal communication channels (media tools, atmospheres, events etc.) (Kotler, Bowen & Makens, 2010: 368; Kotler & Armstrong, 2012: 419–420).

The impact of the messages depends heavily on the other key factor, the source of the message. The credibility of the message source is quite important and the most important three factors that impact credibility are expertise, trustworthiness and likability (Kotler, Bowen & Makens, 2010: 370). Companies often use celebrities as spokespeople since attractive sources obtain higher attention and recall; however, it is a double-edged sword resulting from credibility issues (Kotler, Bowen & Makens, 2010: 370). For example, Turkish Airlines starred basketball player Kobe Bryant and football player Lionel Messi (approximately 150 million views on YouTube), football players Didier Drogba and Lionel Messi (approximately 65 million views on YouTube), English soccer team Manchester United (approximately 4 million views on YouTube), film-maker and Vine star, Zach King (approximately 3 million views on YouTube), food blogger İdil Tatari (approximately 4 million views on YouTube), leading golfers Rory McIlroy and Charl Schwartzel (approximately 1.5 million views on YouTube), movie stars Kevin Costner (approximately 160,000 views on YouTube) and Ben Affleck (approximately 300,000 views on YouTube) in filmed commercials. Hostelworld, which is an online hostel book engine, starred rapper 50 Cent (over 300,000 views on YouTube) and Lufthansa Airlines starred German soccer team FC Bayern Munich (over 500,000 views on YouTube. In addition to direct commercial campaigns, some companies prefer to use key testimonials to get some real benefits from the marketing efforts. For example, Mandarin Oriental Hotel Group has a page on their website called "Our Celebrity Fans" and introduces 29 exceptional personalities as their loyal fans and regular visitors such as Geoffrey Rush, Morgan Freeman, Lucy Liu, Christian Louboutin, Vanessa Mae, Bryan Ferry and so on.

Last but not the least, the communicator should evaluate the effectiveness of the marketing communication process. This involves evaluating whether the audience remembers the message, how many times they saw it, what aspects they remember, what are their feelings and emotions about the message and what kind of differences are there between past and present attitudes toward the product or company (Kotler, Bowen & Makens, 2010: 372; Kotler & Armstrong, 2012: 420).

Case study: Website launch contest creates 40% surge in visits

Background

During the economic downturn in late 2009, The Reefs in Bermuda opened a new spa and private residence club. The 64-room luxury resort, which has a high repeat guest rate, needed to both sell real estate and increase hotel stays by expanding its customer base. The Reefs was about to launch a new search engine optimized website for both the hotel and Club. Previously, they had two separate sites.

Objectives

- To increase web visits
- To generate top-of-mind awareness in past guests and new prospects of The Reefs' experience
- To expand The Reefs' database

Strategy

To launch the new site MP&A created an online contest that turned loyal guests into advocates and generated interest in the property among prospects and the media.

For February, the month of love, The Reefs created the "Show Your Love" contest and asked past guests to share a favorite experience in 500 words. Entries were narrowed to seven finalists, posted on the website and voted on by the public. Public voting provided an opportunity to expose the resort experience via strong testimonials to new prospects. A vacation giveaway to both the winning story and a randomly selected voter provided an incentive to past guests to enter and to the public to read the stories and vote.

Implementation

An integrated digital marketing campaign, including website, e-mail, social media and public relations, was designed by MP&A to communicate the contest from launch to the selections of both winners.

A contest icon was designed and used in all communications, including a button on the website home page. Communications included: landing page with entry form, finalist stories, voting form and rules; HTML e-mails; press releases to travel media; and messages on The Reefs' Facebook page and blog.

Building upon the month of love, messages focused on love of The Reefs and Bermuda such as proposals in the sand, destination weddings, honeymoons and family celebrations.

Results

With less than $4,000 and relying on email/database marketing, social media and public relations efforts, The Reefs exceeded its goals for the promotion. The contest generated 603 essay entries and 3,264 votes.

It also increased traffic to the new website. The month-long contest launch generated a 165% increase in website visits compared to 2009, and the first day of voting generated more than 3,000 contest-specific web visits and 50 new Facebook fans. Web visits were up nearly 40% for the contest period compared to the same time in 2009 and continue to trend ahead of previous years.

"Show Your Love" also succeeded in generating awareness [of] new prospects. During the contest, 60% of web visits were new and there were 229 new e-newsletter subscribers. PR resulted in several media placements including Caribbean Travel + Life, Bermuda.com and a feature article in Hilton Head Monthly (the winners' home town).

Within two weeks of the contest, 64 reservations [were] directly tracked to the campaign representing nearly $200,000 in room revenue.

Source: Madiganpratt (2016).

Establishing the total market communication budget

Achieving the targets of a marketing communication plan is a top priority for hospitality and tourism companies; however, determining how much to spend on marketing communication is one of the most difficult decisions for marketing communicators (Kotler, Bowen & Makens, 2010: 372; Kotler & Keller, 2012: 510). Spending on marketing expenditures varies substantially according to the type of industries and companies (Kotler & Keller, 2012: 510). On the other hand, a large budget does not mean guaranteed return, and sometimes small budgets could be adequate for the companies (Kotler, Bowen & Makens, 2010: 373). Four common methods that the hospitality and tourism companies could benefit from to set total communication budgets are (Kotler, Bowen & Makens, 2010: 372–374; Kotler & Keller, 2012: 510–512):

1. **Affordable method**: This frequently used method is based on the idea of "how big a marketing budget my company can afford," and for the companies which prefer this method promotion is seen as short term and the effect of promotion on sales is underestimated.
2. **Percentage–of-sale method**: As an easy and the most frequently used budgeting method, this method implies that the companies could set their promotion budget at a certain percentage of current or anticipated sales or of the sales price. Lack of conformity for long-term planning and remaining limited to only available funds are the major disadvantages of this method. Companies could miss the new market opportunities as the marketing budget is shaped by taking previous sales into account.
3. **Competitive-parity method**: Some companies set their communication budget using their rivals or competitors. The supporting arguments behind this method are twofold: competitors' budgets could represent an accurate perspective of the industry and this method prevents companies from going to promotion wars; however, both arguments are consistent with the realities due to companies differing from each greatly and the free market economy

being open to any kind of marketing wars. For small-sized hotels, the promotion expenditure is 2% of sales, a typical amount is approximately 4–5% of total sales (Boston Hospitality Review, 2015).

4. **Objective-and-task method**: The most logical budgeting method among others is based on three criteria: (1) defining specific objectives, (2) determining the tasks that must be followed to materialize objectives and (3) estimating the total promotion cost. The aspect that makes this method smart is that the companies must achieve harmony between dollars spent and the promotional results; however, this is not easy.

Conclusion

Promotion, which is the crucial element of the marketing mix, is of prime importance for the hospitality and tourism industry due to its service-oriented and intangible structure. The key characteristics of the industry have provided a basis for utilizing a great variety of communication platforms and promotion tools. Having investigated the promotion activities in the hospitality industry, it is evident that the accommodation companies, airline companies, travel agencies, food and beverage companies and others in the industry have great awareness and knowledge regarding the effectiveness of promotion activities. According to the objectives, target audience and the total market communication budget of companies, promotion tools have become diversified; however, currently, internet and TV are the leading platforms, accounting for approximately 90% of promotion activities. It is quite clear that thanks to the rapid development of the internet, innovative and inspiring media promotion tools have emerged and most businesses have turned their promotion efforts towards social and digital media.

The key issue in promotion efforts is improvement of the integrated marketing communication plan. As is clearly expressed in this chapter, each step of the integrated marketing plan calls for detailed and realistic evaluations. It does not make any sense to select the accurate communication channel irrespective of the target audience, main objectives and the budget. Besides, imponderable and unpredictable promotion efforts could result in unclear and confusing implications. Companies should take the future of the hospitality and tourism industry into consideration in relation to promotion activities. In an industry with severe competition and political uncertainty, each company should prepare an applicable and traceable promotion plan reflecting its short and long-term aims. As a result, it is expected that the hospitality and tourism companies which follow the market, attach importance to social, cultural and environmental developments and dominant trends, and which seek changes in customer attitudes and behaviors, have great potential to leave a positive impression on the target audience.

References

Bowie, D., & Buttle, F. (2004). *Hospitality Marketing: An Introduction*, Oxford: Butterworth Heinemann.

De Pelsmacker, P., Geuens, M., & Van den Bergh, J. (2001). *Marketing Communications (Supplementary chapter on Communicating with kids, teens and senior consumers)*, Harlow, Essex: Pearson Education.

Kalla, H. K. (2005). "Integrated Internal Communications: A Multidisciplinary Perspective". *Corporate Communications: An International Journal*, 10(4), 302–314.

Keller, K. L. (2001). "Mastering the Marketing Communications Mix: Micro and Macro Perspectives on Integrated Marketing Communication Programs". *Journal of Marketing Management*, 17(7–8), 819–847.

Keller, K. L. (2009). "Building Strong Brands in A Modern Marketing Communications Environment". *Journal of Marketing Communications*, 15(2–3), 139–155.

Kotler, P., & Armstrong, G. (2012). *Principles of Marketing*, Upper Saddle River, NJ: Pearson Education.

Kotler, P., & Keller, K. L. (2012). *Marketing Management*, Upper Saddle River, NJ: Pearson Education.

Kotler, P., Bowen, J. T., & Makens, J. C. (2010). *Marketing for Hospitality and Tourism*, 5/e, Upper Saddle River, NJ: Pearson Education.

Kotler, P., Keller, K., Brady, M., Goodman, M., & Hansen, T., (2009). *Marketing Management*, Harlow, Essex: Pearson Education Limited.

Madhavaram, S., Badrinarayanan, V., & McDonald, R. E. (2005). "Integrated Marketing Communication (IMC) and Brand Identity as Critical Components of Brand Equity Strategy: A Conceptual Framework and Research Propositions". *Journal of Advertising*, 34(4), 69–80.

McCabe, S., & Foster, C. (2014). "Marketing Communications in Tourism: A Review and Assessment of Research Priorities", in Scott McCabe (ed.) *The Routledge Handbook of Tourism Marketing*, Abingdon, Oxon: Routledge, 396–408.

Middleton, V. T., Fyall, A., Morgan, M., & Ranchhod, A. (2009). *Marketing in Travel and Tourism*, Oxford: Butterworth Heinemann.

Ogden-Barnes, S., & Minahan, S. (2015). *Sales Promotion Decision Making: Concepts, Principles, and Practice*, New York: Business Expert Press.

Percy, L., & Elliott, R. (2005). *Strategic Advertising Management*, New York: Oxford University Press.

Pride, W., & Ferrell, O. C. (1991). *Marketing: Concepts and Strategies*. 7th ed, Boston: Houghton Mifflin

Internet references

Boston Hospitality Review (2015). Digital Marketing Budgets for Independent Hotels. www.bu.edu/bhr/2015/08/25/digital-marketing-budgets-for-independent-hotels-continuously-shifting-to-remain-competitive-in-the-online-world/. Access Date: 9 October 2016.

Businessinsider (2016). Ten Companies That Spend The Most On Advertising. www.businessinsider.com/10-biggest-advertising-spenders-in-the-us-2015-7/#10. Access Date: 6 October 2016.

IAB (2016). Internet Advertising Revenue Report – 2015 Full Year Results. www.iab.com/wp-content/uploads/2016/04/IAB-Internet-Advertising-Revenue-Report-FY-2015.pdf. Access Date: 4 October 2016.

Madiganpratt (2016). Website Launch Contest Creates 40% Surge in Visits. http://madiganpratt.com/results.html. Access Date: 7 October 2016.

Nielsen (2009). Hospitality and Travel Advertising Report. www.nielsen.com/content/dam/corporate/us/en/newswire/uploads/2009/06/hospitality-08vs07-june-09.pdf. Access Date: 6 October 2016.

Skift (2016a). The Biggest Hotel Brands for TV Advertising. https://skift.com/2016/03/16/the-biggest-hotel-brands-for-tv-advertising-in-2015-in-the-u-s/. Access Date: 3 October 2016.

Skift (2016b). The Best Hotel Social Media Campaigns of 2013. https://skift.com/2013/10/21/the-best-hotel-social-media-campaigns-of-2013/. Access Date: 6 October 2016.

Statistica (2016a). Hilton Advertising Spending in USA (2016). www.statista.com/statistics/308920/hilton-advertising-spending-usa/. Access Date: 6 October 2016.

Statistica (2016b). Total Spending on Online Advertising in the U.S. www.statista.com/statistics/183816/us-online-advertising-revenue-since-2000/. Access Date: 4 October 2016.

TripAdvisor (2016). About TripAdvisor. www.tripadvisor.com.tr/pages/about_us.html. Access Date: 7 October 2016.

Wikipedia (2016). List of Chained-Brand Hotels. https://en.wikipedia.org/wiki/List_of_chained-brand_hotels. Access Date: 7 October 2016.

Further reading

Almeida, N. M., Silva, J. A., Mendes, J., & Oom do Valle, P. (2012) "The Effects of Marketing Communication on the Tourist's Hotel Reservation Process". *Anatolia*, 23(2), 234–250.

Baloglu, S., & Pekcan, Y. A. (2006) "The Website Design and Internet Site Marketing Practices of Upscale and Luxury Hotels in Turkey". *Tourism Management*, 27(1), 171–176.

Christou, E. (2011) "Exploring Online Sales Promotions in the Hospitality Industry". *Journal of Hospitality Marketing & Management*, 20(7), 814–829.

Goi, C. L. (2009) "A Review of Marketing Mix: 4Ps or More?" *International Journal of Marketing Studies*, 1(1), 2.

Hudson, S., & Thal, K. (2013) "The Impact of Social Media on the Consumer Decision Process: Implications for Tourism Marketing". *Journal of Travel & Tourism Marketing*, 30(1–2), 156–160.

Line, N. D., & Runyan, R. C. (2012) "Hospitality Marketing Research: Recent Trends and Future Directions", *International Journal of Hospitality Management*, 31(2), 477–488.

Litvin, S. W., Goldsmith, R. E., & Pan, B. (2008) "Electronic Word-Of-Mouth in Hospitality and Tourism Management". *Tourism Management*, 29(3), 458–468.

Mangold, W. G., & Faulds, D. J. (2009) "Social Media: The New Hybrid Element of the Promotion Mix". *Business Horizons*, 52(4), 357–365.

McCabe, S. (Ed.). (2014) *The Routledge Handbook of Tourism Marketing*, Abingdon, Oxon: Routledge.

Šerić, M. (2016) "Content Analysis of the Empirical Research on IMC from 2000 to 2015". *Journal of Marketing Communications*, 22, 1–39.

15

Advertising in the hotel industry

The influence of emotional appeals in advertising on consumers' purchase intention in the hotel industry

Ladan Fotouhnezhad

Introduction

The key difference between service marketing and marketing of goods and products was first highlighted by Shostack in a *Journal of Marketing* article (1977) called "Breaking Free from Product Marketing." Since that time, advertising scholars have been further exploring this topic to a great extent and since 1980, research in this area has experienced phenomenal growth. In order to move this body of research forward in an organized manner, Tripp and Stafford provided comprehensive reviews of the services advertising literature. Stafford's review (1988) focused on the question of whether or not professionals should advertise. After Stafford's review, Tripp (1997) prepared a conceptual review of the services advertising literature from 1980 to 1995. She examined the ten leading outlets for services research and reviewed seventy-seven articles. Ruiz and Sicilia (2004) and other scholars in their studies supported the assumption that different consumers react and behave differently in response to different advertising appeals.

On the other hand, the rational/emotional framework has been deliberated comprehensively in the marketing and advertising literature, most probably stemming from Copeland's innovative proposal which said that consumers purchase products for either rational or emotional reasons.

In this regard, a number of scholars have employed Pollay's (1983) complete list of forty-two rational and emotional appeals. Among them, Albers-Miller and Stafford (1999a) for example, defined emotional appeal as attracting customers by arousing their feelings and emotions or creating particular moods instead of offering realistic information or logical debate. They examined differences in the use of emotional and rational advertising appeals across experiential and utilitarian services in eleven culturally diverse countries, using Pollay's list (to see part of this list, please refer to Appendix 1).

The growing body of research has explained many aspects of service marketing in terms of emotional appeals, their categories and the fundamental differences between them. Yet, there are still some vague aspects which remain untouched, namely the examination of the rational/emotional framework in service marketing, or to be more specific in the hospitality sector for hotels, and also examining the effect of individuals' emotions in this context.

The purpose of this chapter is to shed some light on the effectiveness of emotional appeals in service marketing and hospitality, in particular the hotel industry, and to highlight their effect on consumers' purchase intention.

Why is advertising used in the hospitality industry?

Despite the richness of literature in the service marketing field of study, research on Direct to Customer Advertising (DTCA) remains primarily exploratory in nature and little is known about its effects on consumer behavior; as a case in point, the influence of these appeals on purchase intention. This has been a concern for many researchers such as Mortimer and Grierson (2010), who believe that although services advertising is beginning to gain recognition as an important area of academic research, little research has been undertaken on services advertising in the international environment.

What does this chapter explain about hospitality advertising?

Considering the content analyses in hospitality and hotel industry service marketing, it is known that Pollay identified forty-two appeals commonly found in product advertisements and classified these as either emotional or rational. Albers–Miller and Stafford (1999a) proposed that twenty-eight of these appeals were relevant to services and have utilized this shortened list to examine services advertising content. Their most substantial study examined utilitarian and experimental service advertisements across eleven culturally diverse countries. It was found that, overall and within each country, emotional appeals were being used for experiential services and rational appeals were used for utilitarian services. In this chapter, the scope is defined as testing the effect of emotional appeals by testing the influence of dominant emotional appeals in hotel advertising and its moderating factors: advertising theme (Informative versus Persuasive) and the trip mode contexts (Pleasure Trip versus Non-Pleasure Trip).

The vague aspects of Pollay's study, such as the answer to the questions "which appeals are more emotional?" and "which ones are more service related?" have been clarified, thanks to the efforts of Albers–Miller and Stafford. Following analysis of their study, it could be concluded that sixteen appeals in Pollay's list are emotional and service related. However, the extent of their influence is still unclear and questions still remain as to which appeals are dominant and how influential they are. In this chapter, these aspects will be examined through two case studies.

Objectives

With the above-mentioned issues in mind, the influence of emotional appeals in advertising on consumers' purchase intention in the hotel industry will be explained in this chapter. Thus, the dominant emotional appeals in hotel advertising and their effectiveness in terms of increasing purchase intention with the presence of moderating factors such as informativeness/persuasiveness of the advertising theme or trip mode (Pleasure/Non-Pleasure Trip) will be described thoroughly in this section.

Rational/emotional appeals

It is known that advertising is a complex form of communication that operates with objectives and strategies, leading to various types of impact on consumers' thoughts, feelings, and actions to induce positive consumer response (i.e., attitudes, brand recognition and recall).

Although direct-to-consumer (DTC) advertisers are increasingly using emotional appeals such as endorsers and humor, studies that examine impacts of such appeals on consumers' reactions to DTCA are scarce. Before going further, what is advertising appeal?

By definition, advertising appeal is a conscious attempt to motivate potential consumers toward some form of activity (such as gathering further information or purchasing) or to influence them to change their attitude or conception toward the advertised product.

Nevertheless, this topic is too vast to be examined thoroughly as a whole; hence, it has been reduced to a focus on rational/emotional frameworks. The rational/emotional framework has been deliberated comprehensively in the marketing and advertising literature, most probably stemming from Copeland's (1924) innovative proposal, which said that consumers purchase products for either rational or emotional reasons.

Rational appeal is defined as a "rationally oriented purchase stimulated by directly giving explanations of a product's advantages" (Lin, 2011, p. 2) and emotional appeal has been defined as attracting customers by arousing their feelings and emotions or creating particular moods instead of offering realistic information or logical debates.

Other investigations of the rational/emotional framework, such as Okazaki et al.'s (2010) exclusive review of seventy-five international studies from the advertising literature focusing on advertising appeals, show that the concepts of hard sell and soft sell, along with such related concepts as rational versus emotional appeals, direct versus indirect appeals, and degree of informativeness, have been the focus of attention of advertising scholars. Consequently, the informativeness/persuasiveness factors are moderating factors in case studies.

Informativeness/persuasiveness

In the informativeness/persuasiveness literature, most undergraduate advertising textbooks focus on discriminating between persuasive advertising and informative advertising; this is the reason to ask what the key differences are between informative and persuasive advertising.

Informativeness is defined as an appeal which mainly explains and gives information about the product's characteristics and the benefits that consumers receive by making the purchase; while persuasiveness is related to understanding, and consequently modifying, attitudes by influencing other people's minds.

Pleasure vs. non-pleasure trip mode

Most studies categorized the travel mode in terms of business trips vs. leisure trips without providing an unambiguous description of these categories. However, trip mode has always been considered as one of the personal factors such as gender, age, or income. Liu et al. (2012) continue that different patterns of travel (such as travelling as a family, with friends, or as a couple) or for different purposes, brings about different expectations of hotels for travelers and articulate that there are five trip modes available: business trip, trip as a couple, trip with friends, trip with family, and solo trip., A group of travelers with similar travel experiences or personal factors may have different expectations of factors of the same hotel in different trip modes. But this does not always hold true, since studies confirm that there are customers whose expectations of hotel factors do not change in any trip mode.

On the other hand, some researchers categorize the trip mode into only two groups, defined as "business travelers" and "leisure travelers." Business travelers use a hotel for business meetings, conference attendance, sales meetings, executive meetings and training sessions and have different expectations to "road warriors" and leisure travelers, who in turn may travel with children and have different expectations for a hotel than those who travel as couples or singles. The other differences between travelers may be based on demographic and/or psychographic characteristics.

In this chapter, however, the categorization of "trip mode" is simplified to "pleasure/non-pleasure trip modes" where "pleasure trip mode" is similar to the "leisure trip" definition, and every other category of travel, such as for health-related purposes, business, etc., are categorized as "non-pleasure trip."

Purchase intention

Intention is defined as "a subjective probability for an individual to engage in certain behavior" (Fishbein and Ajzen, 1975, p. 6). Expanding this definition to purchase intentions and consumers' willingness to exhibit purchase behavior, Hsu articulates that "purchase intention refers to certain transactional behaviors that occur after the consumers' make a general product evaluation and an emotional reaction reflecting their attitude towards an object" (Hsu, 1990, p. 16). The aim behind advertising is to convince consumers to purchase and repurchase the product over and over again.

Emotional appeals and purchase intention

Taking into consideration all the previous insights, a lingering question in this body of knowledge is: What is the effect of emotional appeals in advertising on consumers' purchase intention in the hotel industry?

As has been explained adequately earlier in this chapter, many researchers believe that different advertising appeals influence consumer judgment on product and purchase intentions. In addition, researchers have proposed that some emotional appeals draw the consumer's attention towards the ad, but only few of them affect the purchase decision. This supports the statement that "emotional appeals can affect the purchase intention," which can be illustrated in the framework shown in Figure 15.1.

However, to answer the above question satisfactorily, it should be broken down into two simpler questions:

I) What emotional appeals are dominant in hotel advertising?

II) Which emotional appeals are more effective in terms of increasing purchase intention?

In order to answer these two questions, case-study research was conducted. Case study I answers question I and case study II answers question II.

Figure 15.1 Emotional appeal/purchase intention relationship

Ladan Fotouhnezhad

Case study I

The dominant emotional appeals in hotel advertising

To answer question I in the above-mentioned framework, the experiment explained in this case study was designed in order to clarify which emotional appeals are dominant in hotel advertising.

By analyzing twenty-one articles on emotional/rational appeals, a total number of sixty-two appeals with somewhat different definitions were identified. However, an adequate number of previous studies in their content analysis have tried to generate different classifications of emotional appeals. The primary reference for most recent research in this framework is Pollay's list of forty-two advertising appeals, which is a comprehensive classification of all appeals employed in advertising. Thus, to maintain the use of a standard list which is accepted by marketing scholars, Pollay's list was chosen as the main reference for this study (Pollay's list as well as its definitions is available in Appendix 1). In another research study conducted by Albers-Miller and Stafford (1999a), an inspection of 944 advertisements in eleven countries shortened the list to twenty-eight appeals through the omission of appeals which were not relevant to the service industry in order to separate service-related and non-related appeals. Their study also consists of a dichotomous classification of all appeals into rational and emotional groups. Table 15.1 below shows the entire classifications. The highlighted column is the list of emotional appeals which are important for services, which consists of sixteen emotional, service-related appeals.

Albers-Miller and Stafford's classification

As there is great diversity in terms of hotel advertisements, based on the report of hotel-online. com, the top three hotel groups of 2015 were chosen as target hotels for assessment of their

Table 15.1 Albers-Miller and Stafford classification

No.	Emotional – service related	Emotional – not service related	Rational – service related	Rational – not service related
1.	Adventure	Youth	Effective	Cheap
2.	Affiliation	Modesty	Convenient	Technological
3.	Community	Nurturance	Natural	
4.	Dear	Family	Wisdom	
5.	Distinctive	Magic	Productivity	
6.	Enjoyment	Maturity	Tamed	
7.	Freedom	Humility	Independence	
8.	Morality	Frail	Healthy	
9.	Ornamental	Untamed	Durable	
10.	Plain	Casual	Modern	
11.	Popular	Sexuality	Safety	
12.	Relaxation	Succorance	Neat	
13.	Security			
14.	Status			
15.	Traditional			
16.	Vain			

184

advertisements (Panayotis, 2016). These three hotel groups consisted of InterContinental Hotel Group (IHG), which has the top spot in groups as Best Western retains the top spot in brands, followed by Hilton Worldwide in second place, and then Marriott International. The reason behind choosing more than one hotel group was to reduce the potential side-effects of other probable moderators such as brand loyalty or brand recognition of one hotel brand from a particular hotel group by the majority of respondents. The hotel groups were also selected from international well-known hotel groups so that cultural factors, which are outside the scope of this research, do not affect the respondents' judgments.

While there is no official source of hotel group commercials to hand, YouTube commercials were used as samples. After an extensive search for commercials of each hotel group, less than thirty commercials were identified. Some of the commercials were not usable due to their low quality. Consequently, to keep the quality and the number of commercials for all three groups equal, a YouTube channel of selected commercials was created for each hotel group by the author for further exploration.

The next stage was an inspection of hotel advertisements to find the dominant appeals. Coding using Pollay's list of definitions was completed by the author by watching each commercial a sufficient number of times in order to inspect the whole commercial to either find all the appeals from the list in Appendix 1 or to declare that the appeal does not exist in a specific commercial. Each commercial was inspected a minimum of five times. Simultaneously, although all commercials have both of the aspects of informativeness and persuasiveness, the dominant factor was coded for each commercial. The sixty commercials for three hotel groups were coded using the above-explained method. Three other experts reviewed the coding to inspect the accuracy of the coded appeals.

The next step in finding the dominant appeals was analyzing the data from the assessment of the advertisements. First of all, the total number of appeals was determined for each commercial. This analysis was useful in terms of finding the advertisements with the highest and lowest number of appeals; this information was used in the experiment design that will be explained further in the sections that follow.

Second, the replications of different appeals in the twenty commercials of each hotel group and also in all sixty commercials together was calculated. The appeals with a replication percentage higher that 10% were considered as dominant appeals in the commercials.

From this analysis, for InterContinental Hotel Group (IHG) the dominant appeals were Relaxation (22% replication) and Enjoyment (16%). On the other hand, for Hilton Worldwide commercials, the dominant appeals were Relaxation (15%) and Distinctiveness (13%), and for Marriott International the dominant appeal was Distinctiveness (13%). Considering all of the commercials together, Relaxation (14%), Distinctive (11%) and Enjoyment (11%) were the dominant emotional appeals in the sixty commercials (the definitions of these terms can be found at the end of the chapter). For further details on the list of appeals and their replication rates, please refer to Appendix 2.

Using this coding method, the results showed that 80% of InterContinental Hotel Group (IHG), 50% of Hilton Worldwide and 35% of Marriott International commercials were persuasive. The overall results suggest that 55% of all commercials were considered persuasive and the rest (45%) were coded as informative.

In conclusion, the framework can be expressed more clearly as the following:

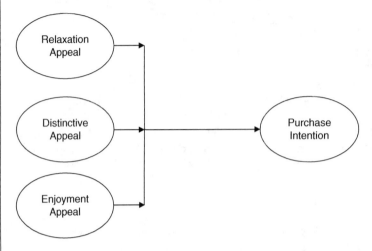

Figure 15.2 Dominant emotional appeals/purchase intention relationship

Case study II

The most effective emotional appeals for increasing purchase intention

Having the dominant emotional appeals in hand, and considering the "trip mode" as the context, hypotheses were generated (see Appendix 3) and tested in both pleasure and non-pleasure contexts to answer the below questions:

As trip mode has always been considered (Liu et al., 2012) as one of the personal factors such as gender, age or income, the next question will be:

I)   Is trip mode an effective element in paying attention to emotional factors of advertisement?

Analysis has also been conducted on the persuasiveness/informativeness of the commercials as persuasiveness/informativeness can moderate the influence of emotional appeals on purchase intention. Since informative advertising mostly depends on facts and information (although they might make use of persuasive methods too), the commercials which explicitly explain the amenities were coded as informative commercials.

On the other hand, persuasive advertising looks for appeals which target customers' emotions to get them to purchase the good or service (same). For this reason, any commercial which used story telling or showed the pleasure derived from using amenities by any means other than openly explaining such facilities (orally or in written format), were coded as persuasive commercials.

II) Does informativeness/persuasiveness of emotional advertisements affect consumers' purchase intention?

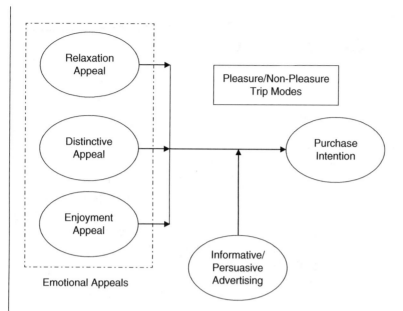

Figure 15.3 Dominant emotional appeals and purchase intentions in both trip mode contexts

Experiment design

In order to test the hypotheses, the first step was to choose the proper advertisement to be shown to the respondents. To permit the manipulation of visual and verbal cues, real hotel advertisements were used as stimuli in this study. To reduce the effects of other probable moderating/mediating variables which are out of the scope of the current research, as was explained above, three hotel groups were chosen for the selection of their commercials to be shown to respondents of the experiment: InterContinental Hotel Group (IHG), Hilton Worldwide, and Marriott International.

Among the twenty commercials from each hotel group, the selected commercials had to have the following features: (1) With the intention of testing commericals from all three hotel groups, three sets of commercials must be chosen. The source for each set was YouTube. (2) Very old commercials, ones with unacceptable quality and the commercials which had been designed for special occasions such as the World Cup were omitted from the list of commercials which had the potential to be chosen. (3) Each set had to contain at least one informative and one persuasive commercial in order to make comparisons and to check the effect of the moderating variable. With the aim of keeping the experiment as short as possible, it was decided to choose only one commercial from each category. (4) Commercials longer than ninety seconds were considered too long to be shown. Accordingly, any commercial longer than ninety seconds was omitted. (5) The commercials had to contain the dominant emotional appeals, which are Relaxation, Distinctive and Enjoyment. The commericals which lacked even one of the appeals were not eligible to be chosen. (6) The lower the number of total emotional appeals was, the better option the commercial would be, merely in terms of minimizing the subliminal influence of other emotional factors

Ladan Fotouhnezhad

on testing the effect of each dominant appeal. Having these criteria in mind, a list of commercials with an ascending total number of emotional appeals was generated

The above-mentioned criteria were the prerequisites. To choose the commercials which should be shown to audiences in the experiment, another analysis was conducted. For each hotel group, one analysis tested whether the top five appeals existed in each commercial. The second test took "Persuasiveness/Informativeness" and "duration of commercials" into consideration as well and prioritized commercials accordingly.

Two waves of pre-testing ensured that the selected target advertisements were acceptable. Five marketing experts examined the commercials to ensure they were understandable for audiences. The next step was to check the different devices used in the experiment for their sound and picture quality. The devices consisted of the same video projectors, a laptop computer and an iPad.

In order to run the experiment, a total number of 135 respondents chosen by the convenience sampling method participated in three sets of experiments. The questionnaire had a total of seventy-four items to test the hypotheses in five different sections.

Considering the commercials' viewing time and the time allocated to giving the necessary instructions, it took each respondent approximately fifteen to twenty minutes to complete the task. By omitting four unworkable answer sets, a total number of 131 questionnaires were usable.

For InterContinental Hotel Group (IHG), a total of forty-one respondents viewed the two commercials related to this hotel group. For Hilton Worldwide this number was forty-six and for Marriot International it was forty-four. The respondents answered the questions based on the pleasure and non-pleasure context. The statistics on how the answers based on these two contexts were distributed between the three hotel groups is summarized in Table 15.2.

Research findings

After manual data entry of the printed questionnaires, all data were transferred to one SPSS file for analysis. After detection of missing data and testing the validity and reliability of the data, a correlational analysis of demographic variables, purchase intention and test of significant differences was conducted. Testing the main effects and moderating effects was conducted afterwards, using the multiple regression analysis method. In the following, a summary is provided of the analyses which were conducted to answer a series of questions; these questions are repeated here in order to create a clear picture in readers' minds.

Table 15.2 Distribution of respondents' answers analysis

	Pleasure	Percentage	Non-Pleasure	Percentage	Total	Percentage
IHG	21	16%	20	15%	41	31%
Hilton	30	23%	16	12%	46	35%
Marriott	29	22%	15	11%	44	34%
Total	80	61%	51	39%	131	100%

Do emotional appeals in advertising affect consumers' purchase intention in the hotel industry?

Referring to the data analysis results in Appendix 4, it is obvious that answering this question without considering trip mode has many limitations. However, the great influence of emotional appeals in advertising is undeniable and this case study has proved it to be true in the hotel industry as well. In answering the next questions, the effect of emotional appeals will be expressed more clearly.

What emotional appeals are dominant in hotel advertising?

To answer this question, from the data provided in Appendix 4, it is obvious that Relaxation, Distinctive and Enjoyment are the dominant appeals (with a replication rate greater than 10%) and for this reason, they have been used as independent variables in the study.

Which emotional appeals are more effective in terms of increasing purchase intention?

According to hierarchical moderated regression analyses, the most influential appeals in the whole study were determined. Table 15.3 shows the effective dominant appeals in the pleasure trip context while Table 15.4 shows the results for the non-pleasure context.

The data supported the hypotheses for the pleasure trip context, showing that the Enjoyment appeal in informative commercials has the greatest influence and it has been repeated two more times for both persuasive commercial and its direct relationship with purchase intention. The next

Table 15.3 Effective dominant appeals in Pleasure trip context

No	Hypothesis	Trip mode	Independent variable	Moderating variable	Dependent variable	Standardized ß coefficients
13	H1Ea	Pleasure	Enjoyment	Informativeness	Purchase Intention	0.523**
4	H1R	Pleasure	Relaxation	–	Purchase Intention	0.444**
14	H1Eb	Pleasure	Enjoyment	Persuasiveness	Purchase Intention	0.355**
12	H1E	Pleasure	Enjoyment	–	Purchase Intention	0.272*
2	H1I	Pleasure	All	Informativeness	Purchase Intention	0.091**
3	H1P	Pleasure	All	Persuasiveness	Purchase Intention	0.033*
11	H1Dc	Pleasure	Distinctive	Both	Purchase Intention	0.005

Table 15.4 Effective dominant appeals in Non-Pleasure trip context

No	Hypothesis	Trip mode	Independent variable	Moderating variable	Dependent variable	Standardized ß coefficients
8	H2D	Non-Pleasure	Distinctive	–	Purchase Intention	0.437**
12	H2E	Non-Pleasure	Enjoyment	–	Purchase Intention	0.298**
6	H2Rb	Non-Pleasure	Relaxation	Persuasiveness	Purchase Intention	0.051*
13	H2Ea	Non-Pleasure	Enjoyment	Informativeness	Purchase Intention	0.042*

most influential appeal is Relaxation, and subsequently, merging all three emotional appeals as dimensions of dominant emotional appeal, it is the third significant contributor in both informative and persuasive commercials.

The last variable in this table was Distinctive, which did not affect purchase intention directly, but in persuasive advertising it was more powerful in comparison to informative advertising.

In contrast to the other trip context, Distinctive is the most influential factor for non-pleasure travelers when there is no moderator. In the same context, Enjoyment is next and again it has been repeated in informative commercials and in comparing the advertising theme it was more powerful again. Relaxation in persuasive commercials is another significant factor. Moreover, in comparing the two commercial themes, Distinctive was more powerful in the informative context.

To recap, it can be concluded that Enjoyment is the most powerful emotional appeal among all forms of appeal. As is shown in Table 15.4, β is usually high for this variable.

Does the informativeness/persuasiveness of emotional advertisements affect consumers' purchase intention?

Considering the results of the hierarchical moderated regression model analysis, it is clear that the advertising theme certainly affects the influence of emotional appeals on purchase intention in most cases, and informativeness influences the dominant appeal in the pleasure trip context.

When the three dominant appeals are merged as one independent variable, called "Dominant," the moderating role of the advertisement theme faded and Dominant appeals in the non-pleasure trip context were the most significant cases which were not influenced by moderators.

In addition, the influence of persuasiveness and informativeness when Dominant appeals were used in the pleasure context did not affect purchase intention and these moderators had no effect on dominant appeals in the pleasure context.

In a step-by-step explanation of this phenomenon, it is obvious that the Dominant and moderating variable (Informativeness) both had a separate effect on the dependent variable. By adding the moderator into the model, it can be seen that there is no moderating effect; but as the independent variable is not a statistically significant contributor, it means there is no relationship between dominant and purchase intention to be moderated by informativeness. However, when Dominant and Informativeness both interact as a new variable, the relationship becomes a significant contributor, which is a new finding.

Is trip mode an effective element in paying attention to the emotional factors of advertisement?

As all of the data analyses show, the two trip modes, and the results are different to a great extent, and the influence of trip mode is undeniable.

Conclusion

The above-mentioned interpretations of analyses and the results provide some general guidelines for advertising strategy. The study's findings coupled with the above issues suggest that advertising experts and marketing managers should consider their target market and their purpose of traveling as an influential factor in designing commercials and marketing campaigns in order to increase the purchase intention of their target audiences more significantly.

To achieve this goal, according to the profile of respondents, it has been proven that educated people prefer more informative advertising rather than persuasive advertising and in different trip mode contexts, their expectations differ to a great extent but are common in one fact: Enjoyment appeal in commercials is the most influential appeal in comparison to the other two variables for increasing purchase intention. Hence, it can be used as part of both pleasure and non-pleasure trip modes commercials to increase purchase intention.

From the test of significant differences, it has also been concluded that women are slightly more eager to purchase hotel services in comparison to men. This means that as the difference between men and women is significant in terms of their purchase intention, women might be influenced more easily (further studies are needed) and women are a better selection as target groups of hotel commercials in comparison to men.

For the pleasure trip target market of hotel, the Relaxation appeal is also another effective influential factor, while the Distinctive appeal is more preferable in the non-pleasure context. Since the difference between the influence of informative and persuasive commercials is not that significant, it might also be concluded that a commercial which has both aspects might be more successful in comparison to pure informative or persuasive commercials. However, to ensure the validity of this statement, further studies are needed.

Definition of the main terms

Emotional Appeal: Emotional appeal has been defined as attracting customers by arousing their feelings and emotions or creating particular moods instead of offering realistic information or through logical debate. In addition, it stimulates positive or negative emotions in consumers by inspiring their purchase intentions (Albers-Miller and Stafford, 1999a; Hetsroni, 2000; Kotler, 2003).For the three independent variables, the only available definitions are those put forward by Pollay, and hence, they are used here as well:

Relaxation Appeal: According to Pollay's definition, relaxation appeal is an appeal which can be defined by "Rest, retire, retreat, loaf, contentment, be at ease, be laid-back, vacations, holiday, to observe."

Distinctive Appeal: According to Pollay, distinctive appeal can be defined by the terms rare, unique, unusual, scarce, infrequent, exclusive, tasteful, elegant, subtle, esoteric and hand-crafted.

Enjoyment Appeal: According to Pollay, enjoyment appeal is a combination of feelings such as to have fun, laugh, to be happy, to celebrate, to enjoy games, parties, feasts and festivities, and to participate.

Informative Advertisement Theme: Informative advertising mostly depends on facts and information, although it might make use of persuasive methods too (Lister, 2013).

Persuasive Advertisement Theme: On the other hand, persuasive advertising looks for appeals which target customers' emotions to get them to purchase the good or service (Lister, 2013).

Pleasure Trip Context: Any trip for the sake of pleasure and not for purposes such as business, healthcare, education etc. can be considered as a pleasure trip. In the literature, it has also been termed leisure trip (Chu & Choi, 2000; Liu et al., 2012; Martínez-Garcia et al., 2012; Yavasa & Babakus, 2005).

Non-Pleasure Trip Context: In this research, non-pleasure trip is considered as a trip which has to be done for purposes other than pleasure. Business travelers who use a hotel for business meetings, conference attendance, sales meetings, executive meetings and training sessions are a group of this context's customers (Yavasa & Babakus, 2005) and others would be travelers for educational purposes, healthcare services etc. Unlike other studies, instead of categorizing in terms of leisure trip and business trip, a more generalizable term of "Non-Pleasure trip" mode was used.

Appendices

Appendix 1: Pollay's definition list of the sixteen service-related emotional appeals

Pollay's Appeals	Description
1. Adventure	Boldness, daring, bravery, courage, seeking adventure, thrills, or excitement
2. Affiliation	To be accepted, liked by peers, colleagues and community at large, to associate or gather with, to be social, to join, unite or otherwise bond in friendship, fellowship, companionship, co-operation, reciprocity, to conform to social customs, have manners, social graces and decorum, tact and finesse
3. Community	Relating to community, state, national publics, public spiritedness, group unity, national identity, society, patriotism, civic and community organizations or other social organizations
4. Dear	Expensive, rich, valuable, highly regarded, costly, extravagant, exorbitant, luxurious, priceless
5. Distinctive	Rare, unique, unusual, scarce, infrequent, exclusive, tasteful, elegant, subtle, esoteric, hand-crafted
6. Enjoyment	To have fun, laugh, be happy, celebrate, to enjoy games, parties, feasts and festivities, to participate
7. Freedom	Spontaneous, carefree, abandoned, indulgent, at liberty, uninhibited, passionate
8. Morality	Humane, just, fair, honest, ethical, reputable, principled, religious, devoted, spiritual
9. Ornamental	Beautiful, decorative, ornate, adorned, embellished, detailed, designed, styled
10. Plain	Unaffected, natural, prosaic, homespun, simple, artless, unpretentious
11. Popular	Commonplace, customary, well-known, conventional, regular, usual, ordinary, normal, standard, typical, universal, general, everyday
12. Relaxation	Rest, retire, retreat, loaf, contentment, be at ease, be laid-back, vacations, holiday, to observe
13. Security	Confident, secure, possessing dignity, self-worth, self-esteem, self-respect, peace of mind
14. Status	Envy, social status or competitiveness, conceit, boasting, prestige, power, dominance, exhibitionism, pride in ownership, wealth (including the sudden wealth of prizes), trend setting, to seek compliments
15. Traditional	Classic, historical, antique, legendary, time-honored, longstanding, venerable, nostalgic
16. Vain	Having a socially desirable appearance, being beautiful, pretty, handsome, being fashionable, well groomed, tailored, graceful, glamorous

Appendix 2: Emotional appeals analysis

IHG			Hilton			Marriot			Total		
Appeal	Repetition	%	Appeal	Repetition	%	Appeal	Repetition	%	Appeal	Repetition	Percentage
Relaxation	24	22%	Relaxation	25	15%	Distinctive	25	13%	Relaxation	66	14%
Enjoyment	17	16%	Distinctive	22	13%	Enjoyment	18	9%	Distinctive	54	11%
Popular	9	8%	Enjoyment	16	9%	Ornamental	18	9%	Enjoyment	51	11%
Security	9	8%	Affiliation	15	9%	Relaxation	17	9%	Affiliation	36	8%
Status	8	7%	Dear	15	9%	Affiliation	14	7%	Ornamental	35	7%
Adventure	7	6%	Security	13	8%	Dear	13	7%	Security	34	7%
Distinctive	7	6%	Popular	12	7%	Vain	13	7%	Dear	33	7%
Affiliation	7	6%	Ornamental	11	6%	Popular	12	6%	Popular	33	7%
Ornamental	6	6%	Adventure	10	6%	Security	12	6%	Adventure	26	5%
Dear	5	5%	Freedom	8	5%	Freedom	11	6%	Freedom	22	5%
Community	3	3%	Plain	8	5%	Traditional	11	6%	Status	21	4%
Freedom	3	3%	Vain	6	4%	Adventure	9	5%	Vain	21	4%
Vain	2	2%	Status	4	2%	Community	9	5%	Plain	14	3%
Morality	1	1%	Morality	2	1%	Status	9	5%	Community	13	3%
Plain	0	0%	Traditional	2	1%	Plain	6	3%	Traditional	13	3%
Traditional	0	0%	Community	1	1%	Morality	2	1%	Morality	5	1%
Total	108	100%	Total	170	100%	Total	199	100%	Total	477	100%

Appendix 3: List of hypotheses

The hypotheses that were tested in order to answer the research questions can be listed as below.

H1: In Pleasure trip mode, a Persuasive commercial will increase the effect of Emotional appeals on Purchase intention more than when the commercial is Informative.

H1I: In Pleasure trip mode, an Informative commercial will increase the effect of Emotional appeals on Purchase intention more than a Persuasive commercial.

H1P: In Pleasure trip mode, a Persuasive commercial will increase the effect of Emotional appeals on Purchase intention more than an Informative commercial..

H1R: In Pleasure trip mode, the Relaxation appeal in advertising influences the Purchase intention.

H1Ra: In Pleasure trip mode, the Informativeness of the commercial increases the effect of Relaxation appeal on Purchase intention.

H1Rb: In Pleasure trip mode, the Persuasiveness of the commercial increases the effect of Relaxation appeal on Purchase intention.

H1Rc: In Pleasure trip mode, the Persuasiveness of the commercial increases the effect of Relaxation appeals on Purchase intention more than the Informativeness of the commercial.

H1D: In Pleasure trip mode, the Distinctive appeal in advertising influences the Purchase intention.

H1Da: In Pleasure trip mode, the Informativeness of the commercial increases the effect of the Distinctive appeal on Purchase intention.

H1Db: In Pleasure trip mode, the Persuasiveness of the commercial increases the effect of the Distinctive appeal on Purchase intention.

H1Dc: In Pleasure trip mode, the Persuasiveness of the commercial will increase the effect of the Distinctive appeal on Purchase intention more in comparison to the Informativeness of the commercial.

H1E: In Pleasure trip mode, the Enjoyment appeal in advertising influences Purchase intention.

H1Ea: In Pleasure trip mode, the Informativeness of the commercial increases the effect of the Enjoyment appeal on Purchase intention.

H1Eb: In Pleasure trip mode, the Persuasiveness of the commercial increases the effect of the Enjoyment appeal on Purchase intention.

H1Ec: In Pleasure trip mode, the Persuasiveness of the commercial increases the effect of the Enjoyment appeal on Purchase intention more than the Informativeness of the commercial.

The same hypotheses can be generated for the Non-Pleasure trip mode. For instance:

H2: In Non-Pleasure trip mode, an Informative commercial will strengthen the effect of the Emotional appeal on Purchase intention to a greater extent than when the commercial is Persuasive.

Appendix 4: Summary of hypotheses' test results

Summary of Pleasure trip context hypotheses' test results

Appeals	Pleasure Trip Context			
Relaxation	H1R✓	H1Ra✗	H1Rb✗	H1Rc✗
Distinctive	H1D✓	H1Da✗	H1Db✗	H1Dc✗
Enjoyment	H1E✓	H1Ea✓	H1Eb✓	H1Ec✗

✓ The hypothesis is supported
✗ The hypothesis is rejected

Summary of Non-Pleasure context hypotheses' test results

	Non-Pleasure Trip Context			
Relaxation	H2R✗	H2Ra✗	H2Rb✓	H2Rc✗
Distinctive	H2D✓	H2Da✗	H2Db✗	H2Dc✓
Enjoyment	H2E✓	H2Ea✓	H2Eb✗	H2Ec✓

✓ The hypothesis is supported
✗ The hypothesis is rejected

Comparison between the two trip mode contexts

	Hypotheses			
Relaxation	HR✗	HRa✓	HRb✗	HRc✗
Distinctive	HD✓	HDa✓	HDb✓	HDc✓
Enjoyment	HE✓	HEa✓	HEb✗	HEc✓

✓ The results are same
✗ The results are different

References

Albers-Miller, N. D., & Stafford, M. R. (1999a). An international analysis of emotional and rational appeals in services vs goods advertising. *Journal of Consumer Marketing*, 16(1), 42–57.

Albers-Miller, N. D., & Stafford, M. R. (1999b). International services advertising: an examination of variation in appeal use for experiential and utilitarian services. *Journal of Services Marketing*, 13(4/5), 390–406.

Chu, R. K. S., & Choi, T. (2000). An importance-performance analysis of hotel selection factors in the Hong Kong hotel industry: a comparison of business and leisure travellers. *Tourism Management*, 21, 363–377.

Copeland, M. T. (1924). *Principles of Merchandising*. New York, NY: Arno Press.

Fishbein M., & Ajzen, I. (1975). *Belief, Attitude, Intention and Behavior Reading: An Introduction to Theory and Research*. Mass: Addison-Wesley.

Hetsroni, A. (2000). The relationship between values and appeals in Israeli advertising: a smallest space analysis. *Journal of Advertising*, 29(3), 55–68.

Hsu, S. J. (1990). *Management*. 10th ed. Taipei: Tunghua Publishing Co., Ltd.

Kotler, P. (2003). *Marketing Management*. 11th ed. Englewood Cliffs, NJ: Prentice Hall.

Lin, L.-Y. (2011). The impact of advertising appeals, advertising spokespersons and advertising attitudes on purchase intentions. *African Journal of Business Management*, 5(21), 8446–8457.

Lister, J. (2013). *What Are the Major Differences Between Informative and Persuasive Advertising?* Retrieved 2016.07.04, http://smallbusiness.chron.com/major-differences-between-informative-persuasive-advertising-25785.html

Liu, S., Law, R., Rong, J., Li, J., & Hall, J. (2012). Analyzing changes in hotel customers' expectations by trip mode. *International Journal of Hospitality Management*, 34, 359–371.

Martínez-Garcia, E., Ferrer-Rosell, B., & Coenders, G. (2012). Profile of business and leisure travelers on low cost carriers in Europe. *Journal of Air Transport Management*, 20, 12–14.

Mortimer, K., & Grierson, S. (2010). The relationship between culture and advertising appeals for services. *Journal of Marketing Communications*, 16(3), 149–162.

Okazaki, S., Mueller, B., & Taylor, C. R. (2010). Measuring soft-sell versus hard-sell advertising appeals. *Journal of Advertising*, 39(2), 5–20.

Panayotis, G. *MKG Hospitality,* Retrieved 2016.06.04, www.hotel-online.com/press_releases/release/global-hotel-ranking-2015-a-second-chinese-operator-climbs-into-the-top-10

Pollay, R. W. (1983). Measuring the cultural values manifest in advertising. *Current Issues and Research in Advertising*, 71–92.

Ruiz, S., & Sicilia, M. (2004). The impact of cognitive and/or affective processing styles on consumer response to advertising appeals. *Journal of Business Research*, 57, 657–664.

Shostack, G. L. (1977). Breaking free from product marketing. *Journal of Marketing*, 41(2), 73–80.

Stafford, D.C. (1988). Advertising in the professions: a review of the literature. *International Journal of Advertising*, 7(3), 189–220.

Tripp, C. (1997). Services advertising: an overview and summary of the research, 1980–1995. *Journal of Advertising*, 26(4), 21–38.

Yavasa, U., & Babakus, E. (2005). Dimensions of hotel choice criteria: congruence between business and leisure travelers. *Hospitality Management*, 24, 359–367.

Further reading

Protean Hospitality, viewed 2013, https://issuu.com/lbernste/docs/protean_hotel_brand_emotion_study_overview1

Albers–Miller, N. D., & Stafford, M. R. (1999a). An international analysis of emotional and rational appeals in services vs goods advertising. *Journal of Consumer Marketing*, 16(1), 42–57.

Albers–Miller, N. D., & Stafford, M. R. (1999b). International services advertising: an examination of variation in appeal use for experiential and utilitarian services. *Journal of Services Marketing*, 13(4/5), 390–406.

Pollay, R. W. (1983). Measuring the cultural values manifest in advertising. *Current Issues and Research in Advertising*, 71–92.

16

Public relations in hospitality marketing

W.K. Athula C. Gnanapala

Introduction

Tourism involves moving away from the usual living space, and destination selection is a crucial process that is influenced by many different factors. Therefore, accurate information is a key factor in the selection of a holiday destination by a tourist. Marketers need to have a proper mechanism to provide needed information quickly and effectively. Similarly, the believability of the information is critical for the tourist decision-making process. So, tourism marketers are required to use effective communication tools to stimulate the purchase decision of the tourists. As highlighted by Kotler and Armstrong (2012), it is vital for companies to adopt and maintain effective integrated marketing communications (IMC) to market their products. A company's IMC should carefully integrate many communication channels to deliver a clear, consistent and compelling message about the organization and its brands. Therefore, companies use diverse promotional strategies in their promotional mix, usually consisting of a specific blend of advertising, public relations, personal selling, sales promotion, and direct-marketing tools that the company uses to persuasively communicate customer value and build customer relationships (Kotler & Armstrong 2012). Also, as highlighted by the Chartered Institute of Marketing (2009), the promotional mix consists of the five variables of advertising, sales promotion, personal selling, public relations and direct marketing, and among these public relations is considered the most cost-effective promotional strategy.

PR and the company's public environment

Tourism is a multidisciplinary industry, and therefore involves many different stakeholders. A stakeholder may be a person, group or organization that has an interest or concern in an organization involved in this industry. Stakeholders can affect or be affected by an organization's ability to achieve its vision and objectives. The key stakeholders in the tourism and hospitality industry are suppliers (those who supply raw materials and other inputs), distributional channels (agents, tour operators, retailers and other global distributional channels), investors (owners, shareholders, banks and other financial institutions), government, employees, media, NGOs, religious and cultural organizations, and so on (Gunn 1994; Byrd 2001; Pavlovich 2003). Further,

Kotler and Armstrong (2012) and Kotler, Bowen and Makens (2010) highlight that the public is any group that has an actual or potential interest in, or impact on, an organization's ability to achieve its objectives, and suggested that there are seven types of publics (financial publics, media publics, government publics, citizen-action publics, local publics, general publics, and internal publics). A company can prepare effective marketing plans for those publics and individual consumers to obtain goodwill through favourable word of mouth, and so on.

The ultimate satisfaction and experiences of tourists mostly depends on the ability of tourism organizations to maintain good and cordial relationships with the key stakeholders who are directly and indirectly involved with and influence the tourist consumption process. The success and co-existence of these organizations/stakeholders also depend on their ability to share mutual benefits collaboratively. If one party fails to play their role in a responsible way, the entire industry may be negatively affected. The PR department of an organization has an ability to remove these barriers and shortcomings though maintaining mutual understanding, trust, and the promotion of effective relationships among the stakeholders.

Jafari (2000) called PR a form of reputation management which helps to maintain effective communication and relationships between an organization and its publics and helps to establish goodwill and mutual understanding. Further, Jafari (2000) highlighted that PR targets several groups to obtain their support and contributions to directly and indirectly achieve organizational goals and objectives. First, as the key internal public, the employees should receive information about the company's objectives, strategies and basic ethical guidelines, to understand the current situation of the organization with respect to achieving the said objectives. To provide better quality services to tourists, service encounter employees should be aware and conscious of their importance and the importance of their behaviour for the future wellbeing of the industry and the organization.

Second, the financial stakeholders such as banks, stockholders and other investors should find sufficient accurate information to confirm their investment decisions through regular reports, newsletters of annual stakeholder meetings, and so on. Third, suppliers, distributors and customers should be regularly informed by direct mail, press releases, and so on to keep them loyal. Fourth, local community pressure groups such as environmentalists, NGOs, and the community and religious organizations of the country or region in which company makes its products should receive honest and accurate information, otherwise they will oppose and protest against organizational decisions and operational activities. Fifth, the politicians, media managers and journalists who select and sometime even distort and distribute information to the public should be targets for PR.

The significance of PR over other promotional tools

Tourism marketers use various methods and strategies to reach, make aware, and persuade their target customer groups and other stakeholders to have favourable attitudes towards the organization. However, they have realized that communicating the message to the target audience effectively is not an easy task. The believability and trustworthiness of the messages may be questionable since the message sent to the customers through different means may differ. Further, the tools used by organizations to communicate with their publics are most probably one-way communications. The audience will receive only the filtered and controlled message and this may not touch one or a few senses of the human groups involved. Therefore, PR can play a vital role in overcoming these shortcomings since it touches all the senses of the target groups through third-party endorsements.

As highlighted by CIM (2009, p. 3), publicity is something that happens to a company and the results may be good or bad. PR involves a sustained attempt to develop the company reputation as a business, by using the media to help create desirable images. It is a way of keeping the business in the customers' minds. For Oliver (2010), PR focuses on building good relations with the company's various publics by obtaining favourable publicity, building up a good corporate image, and handling or heading off unfavourable rumours, stories and events.

In addition, Middleton, Fyall and Morgan (2009, p. 306) note that PR does not involve the actual purchase of media space, because the objective is to obtain favourable publicity for an organization and its products in the media through news reports, features and reviews.

Through PR activities a company should maintain healthy relationships with its diverse stakeholders as a network, not only for ensuring favourable publicity for its offerings, but also to enhance their corporate image. In contrast, other promotional activities, especially advertisements, can communicate only to a selected target audience through paid forms as non-personal presentations (Middleton et al. 2009; Kotler & Armstrong 2012). The other special feature of PR is building a corporate image based on positive publicity through a third-party endorsement; therefore, the credibility and believability must significantly exist at a higher level. As highlighted by Pizam (2005), PR by its very meaning connotes dealing with the public; however, the public who may have some relationship with hospitality or tourism organizations takes many different forms. As highlighted by Middleton et al. (2009), PR programmes are usually complementary activities to media advertising in tourism. However, the message given out through PR is more credible since it has come through a third party.

The British Institute of Public Relations defines PR as:

> the discipline which builds and maintains reputation, with the aim of earning understanding and support and influencing opinion and behaviour. It is the planned and sustained effort to establish and maintain goodwill and mutual understanding between an organisation and its publics.
>
> *(cited by Middleton et al. 2009, p. 306)*

This definition highlights two important areas. First, PR activities are aiming to build mutual understanding or trust between an organization and its publics, and second it targets a wider range of stakeholders and other communication and promotional tools, for example, advertisements or direct marketing.

PR tools

Pizam (2005) noted that customers, both current and potential, are the most obvious public group to help companies achieve their objectives. All public groups, though, act as a third party, therefore it is more important to develop effective programmes to raise awareness and educate them if we want them to act as ambassadors for tourism and hospitality organizations. Hence, the PR department must play an important role in improving the awareness of tourists and other stakeholders, in order to create positive attitudes towards the tourism and hospitality organization. The literature highlights the following as the key PR functions of the organizations (Pizam 2005; Kotler & Armstrong 2009; Middleton et al. 2009; Kotler et al. 2010):

A. Writing editorials and press releases
B. Lobbying and persuading
C. Corporate and business communications

D. Publicizing of products and services
E. Public affairs and community relations
F. Familiarization tours
G. Event management (trade fairs and exhibitions)
H. Stakeholder management
I. Crisis management

Hospitality marketers cannot fully control the message and the publicity that is received by customer groups and other publics through PR activities, since the message often goes through a third party. However, even though the publicity may be favourable or unfavourable from the marketing point of view, consumers will still receive more accurate and updated information this way. This is because tourists may receive more contradictory information through different sources, and therefore may be more confused and unable to make decisions, for example whether to travel and where to travel. Thus, a PR department can provide more up-to-date and accurate information quickly through credible sources. Its key responsibility, then, is to be prepared to face any crisis effectively.

The unique practices in hospitality marketing

PR practices in tourism

As highlighted by LaTour (2008, p. 175), the Hilton international definition of PR is 'the process by which we create a positive image and customer preferences through third-party endorsement'. Further, the authors argue that PR is neglected by hospitality marketers as a stepchild even though it is more important to reach targeted consumers more effectively. There are many arguments over paid media in this situation; first, advertising budgets often increase day by day even though the number of customers does not increase proportionately, and perhaps are stagnating or declining. Second, sales promotion and personal selling brings a larger cost from having to give short-term incentives to intermediaries and consumers to keep them with the company. In practice, consumers pay less attention to most of the marketing communication methods of companies; therefore, companies need other more cost-effective methods to reach target customer groups effectively, and PR can fill this gap if marketers use its tools strategically.

Thus, marketers have realized that PR is a most cost-effective promotional tool. For example, Kotler et al. (2010) highlight the creative use of news events, publications, social events, community relations and other PR techniques in distinguishing a company and its products from competitors. PR activities also exist at different levels of business organizations. Further, Kotler et al. (2010) highlight that only few decades ago the PR and marketing functions were handled by two different departments within a firm, while today these functions are integrated and function more effectively as one entity.

The success of the tourism and hospitality industry is dependent on its ability to build effective and long-lasting human interactions (Khoo-Lattimore, Yang & Lai 2016). Therefore, it is required to use methods that provide information to tourists though all of their five senses to create positive perceptions of the products and services offered by destinations and other suppliers. Tools such as familiarization tours; trade fairs and exhibitions; academic conferences and symposia; hosting and sponsoring major events (sports, political, cultural, and so on); films and documentaries – providing locations for filming; social media relations; and community relations and empowerment are identified as the most cost-effective PR techniques in tourism and hospitality marketing. These are now discussed.

Familiarization tours

Familiarization, or FAMIL, tours are considered as one of the most significant and cost-effective PR tools in promoting destinations and their hospitality products. Typically, travel agents, tour operators and media organizations will take part in these tours. In this model, the National Tourism Organizations (NTOs) and Destination Management Organizations (DMOs) invite these travel intermediaries and other key stakeholders to take part and get first-hand experience of the attractions and other resources in a location that is available to tourists. The main purpose of hosting travel agents, tour operators or media groups in a destination is to increase their knowledge and awareness about the destination.

During a FAMIL the participants collect information and experiences, and media representatives take photographs and prepare audiovisual programmes to create free publicity though their media channels. Once they return to their own country or region they make efforts to promote that destination though their tour packages, brochures, magazines, newspapers, radio, TV and other communication and promotional methods. Since the media representatives and journalists discuss their positive experiences with such evidence as high-quality photographs and films, believability is high.

Trade fairs and exhibitions

Trade fairs and exhibitions allow destinations to showcase their products to target customers and middlemen to create awareness of their products, and to educate and inspire the buying and selling efforts. The main advantage of attending trade fairs and exhibitions is the ability to meet different parties in one place physically and to exchange information. It allows the participants to clarify their doubts and make other queries, and therefore trade fairs and exhibitions are highly effective. As highlighted by Gnanapala (2016), trade fairs and exhibitions are the kinds of events that perform an effective marketing role in the tourism and hospitality industry, and the events bring tourists and other stakeholders to a one place where they can see, touch, listen, smell, and sometimes taste the goods in the exhibition.

Trade fairs and exhibitions thus bring advantages to a destination, and other tourism and hospitality organizations can see the competitive offerings, new trends, and market opportunities. The fairs may target the trade, consumers, or both. Tourism fairs and exhibitions are open to consumers/tourists and other travel intermediaries such as tour operators, travel agents, media organizations and other tourism-related professional bodies. Usually, the first few or last days are open only to industry people and media organizations, and the rest of the time the fairs are open to the public. The stakeholders come and observe, and clarify their queries with the representatives of companies. The respective organizations employ knowledgeable and friendly staff to provide answers to the participants. Tourism fairs and exhibitions are very colourful, and the facilities may be decorated nicely to get the attention of the audience. Satisfied people will buy tour packages and make business contracts, and further recommend these places and products to final consumers.

Academic conferences and symposia

Tourism-related academic conferences and symposia have become more popular in recent decades. The events are usually organized by universities and other academic institutions in collaboration with scientific and academic journals. The conferences provide an important channel for the exchange of information, and social and academic networking. They provide opportunities for academics, researchers, students and other interested parties to present their new scientific findings and to discuss and solve their academic and intellectual puzzles. Also, the symposium programme includes an excursion to a popular and attractive tourist resort of the country in which the conference is taking place.

A typical symposium will have keynote speeches by distinguished figures from the relevant field and thereby obtains favourable publicity. Also, the symposium will include panel and round-table discussions, workshops, and so on, relating to various issues and themes. The events provide a forum to present and discuss different scenarios, and therefore credibility and believability is high, since the facts are generated in a systematic and scientific way. Ultimately, the industry and the destination may obtain favourable publicity through national and international media channels.

Hosting and sponsoring major events (sports, political, cultural)

Major events help countries to enjoy another form of product placement in international markets. The hosting of major international events, such as sports, cultural and political events, help destinations to position themselves among international audiences and markets. For example, the recent Commonwealth Summit in Sri Lanka, the Cricket World Cup in India, the Olympic Games in Brazil, and the Football World Cup 2014 in Brazil obtained favourable publicity through major international media. The procession of the Temple of the Tooth Relic of Sri Lanka in August every year attracts many tourists, and obtains favourable publicity through national media channels. Such events help countries to develop effective marketing communication to exploit each potential marketing opportunity with press releases, feature articles, media interviews, websites and so on.

Film locations, films and documentaries

Countries that are rich in natural and cultural heritage will be selected as locations for international films and documentaries. Millions of people are exposed to the films every year, and the destinations too get favourable publicity. The films and video documentaries can be of two types: first, films produced by domestic producers and marketed in foreign countries through globally reputed media channels; second, foreign reputed film corporations and media organizations choose a specific country to produce their films and telecasts internally. Travel films which inspire and motivate people to travel and explore new destinations are a category of these. Famous travel movies such as *The Way, 180° South, Wild, Tracks, The Darjeeling Limited, Out of Africa, The Endless Summer, The Art of Travel, Hit the Road: India* helped the countries involved to position their countries as popular tourist destinations (IMDb nd; *The Telegraph* nd). Further, the documentaries produced by foreign media channels such as Discovery, Animal Planet, and National Geographic created amazing publicity about destinations such as Kenya, India, Thailand, Africa, Cambodia etc.

Further, countries can stimulate and attract tourists through world-famous films produced in those countries; for example, *The Bridge Over the River Kwai* and *Monkey Kingdom* were filmed in Sri Lanka. Also, the films *The Beach* and *The Lord of the Rings* have helped to promote tourism in Thailand and New Zealand. As highlighted by Bowie and Buttle (2004, 2011), destinations that actively promote themselves as ideal locations for film and television productions get positive publicity to increase tourist arrivals.

Social media and public relations

The usage of social media has increased dramatically in recent years due to its convenience and the wide usage of ICT equipment for day-to-day communications and other activities. As emphasized by Buhalis and Foerste (2015), advanced technology enables users to amalgamate information from various sources on their mobile devices, personalize their profile through applications and social networks, and interact dynamically with their context.

The main advantage of social media is the ability to provide information quickly in a more attractive and colourful way to the target customer through trusted personal sources. Further, it allows people to express and write down their actual feelings: the satisfaction or dissatisfaction; problems and difficulties; the delight and 'wow' feelings that are encountered though the holiday stay; and combine these with convincing photographs, video clips, and so on. Social media provides an online platform to discuss and share this information and experiences among the members of the network. Since the information/messages come though known credible and believable sources, there is a higher level of trustworthiness, and bulk information can be transferred quickly through tailor-made channels to focused individuals.

Tourists who visit a country or destination will write about their experiences or even the shortcomings of their experiences; however, destination managers cannot control the spreading of such information, even that which is negative. The only thing a destination can do is to provide quality services and experiences to satisfy or delight customers. The satisfied customers will then communicate their positive experiences to third parties. Tourism and hospitality marketers have realized that this is the way that social media can generate effective positive word-of-mouth marketing (Kotler et al. 2010; Gnanapala 2016). Therefore, it is vital to use social media platforms, designing the right message to the right customer groups through implementing successful marketing campaigns. As highlighted by Gnanapala (2016), Facebook, Twitter, YouTube, Podcasts and Travelshake are the best known and most effective social media networks for marketing in the tourism and hospitality industry.

In addition to these online booking platforms, virtual travel agencies and online travel guides provide different information from diverse parties for tourists to review and decide upon their next holiday destination. At the same time these sites, for example TripAdvisor, provide opportunities for tourists to write down their travel experiences, both satisfactory and unsatisfactory. The potential tourist can go through these comments and decide whether to go and where to go.

Community relations and empowerment

Community education and awareness is one of the most significant factors in this situation, but is mostly lacking in the tourism and hospitality industry (Pearce, Moscardo & Ross 1996; Timothy 2000; Chheang 2010). Effective PR activities can play a major role in the development of a positive relationship between the tourism organizations, e.g. hoteliers, and the local community, as well as among the tourism organizations, tourists and the local community in the destination area. It is noted that the local community, especially in developing countries, has more negative thoughts, attitudes and perceptions about the growth and development of the tourism industry. Based on these negative thoughts, a local community may think that tourism is an evil and try to avoid it, perhaps even engaging in sabotage activities. This negative perception has created many problems and issues in tourism.

One of these is the lack of understanding of tourism as a major social and economic activity, and therefore communities oppose and take actions against tourism through protesting, harassing, insulting and even kidnapping and killing tourists. These unfavourable situations ultimately impact on tourist satisfaction, or locals will not join the industry, and/or will not approve of their children selecting the tourism industry for their career path. Therefore, the tourism sector in developing countries, especially the hotel industry, has faced a threat to the attraction and retention of employees (United Nations Conference on Trade and Development 2003). PR activities can do a better job to educate and make communities sufficiently aware to change their mindset positively towards tourism development (Caywood 2004).

Tourism and hospitality organizations, for example hoteliers, make efforts to maintain good relationships with local communities through various PR activities such as recruiting employees from the surrounding area, purchasing some inputs and raw materials from locals, donations and

CRS activities in schools, supporting the poor and disabled, and supporting religious organizations (Nayomi & Gnanapala 2015). Also, government authorities use effective PR activities to change the traditional mindset in a paradigm shift towards a better understanding and awareness of the tourism industry and its potential benefits:

> For example, Heritance Kandalama, a Green Globe awarded five-star hotel, commenced its operations in 1994 beside the Kandalama Lake in a picturesque environment. While it was under construction there were many protests, and many parties claimed that the hotel would pollute the natural and the socio-cultural environment in the area. Finally, the company built an award winning environmental friendly hotel, and introduced many programs to deliver benefits to the local community through their CSR activities. As policy, the hotel recruits 70% of the employees within 25 km from the hotel, and its purchasing policy also targets the locals and buys a variety of fruits and vegetables from the local community, which helps to improve the living standard of the locals. The hotel also conducts capacity building such as empowerment programmes for local women, and has helped them to start their own small scale businesses targeting tourists. The hotel has appointed a community relations officer, and provides benefits for the local community like donations for schools, religious organizations, construction of roads and water and electricity supplies for rural villages, and provides houses for poor and disabled people etc. under their CSR activities. Therefore, the hotel maintains a healthy relationship with its immediate community, and since they are satisfied, positive word of mouth publicity has finally spread to all other stakeholders.
>
> *(Nayomi & Gnanapala 2015)*

An effective PR toolkit is necessary to develop combinations of the many different activities available for the promotion of destinations and their hospitality products and services. Therefore, the PR department and its professionals need to design strategies and programmes more carefully, and widen the breadth and depth of these activities. These PR activities will help organizations to achieve their communication objectives with minimum cost, effort and resources. The key feature of PR activities then, when compared with other promotional tools, is the ability of even a small tourism organization with a limited budget to have well-planned and organized PR programmes.

Further, the PR function provides a unique way of communicating and promoting a company and its offerings through building a higher visibility in the public space. Petrovici (2014) shows that PR represents a strategic form of communication, which focuses on gaining an audience's understanding and acceptance, as well as building good relationships between an organization and its public. However, the unique characteristics of the tourism and hospitality industry in relation to its service domain has raised major challenges in the race to identify and adopt the most efficient and cost-effective methods of promoting tourist products, building a positive image and increasing awareness about tourist destinations, to attract the tourists. Petrovici (2014) argues that the PR function fills this gap by providing credible and believable information through third-party endorsements.

Community relations and PR

Unlike other tangible products, the marketing of tourism involves many different stakeholders, and these are all part of the success of any marketing campaign. Hence, industry organizations need to be made aware of target customer groups through being provided the relevant information at the right time. As highlighted by Mathieson and Wall (2006), tourism is both an economic and social phenomenon as well as an agent of change. Tourism involves tourists, the destination and its people, and the routes and means by which they are brought together. PR can assist destinations and their tourism organizations to attract, build and maintain profitable relationships among all stakeholders.

Tourism development brings both benefits and negative impacts to a destination, and therefore stakeholders are more concerned about the activities and behaviours of tourism destinations and its key organizations (Inskeep 1991; Gunn & Var 2002; Hall 2008). Responsible organizations take more steps to manage the possible negative impacts on society and environment through maintaining healthy community relationships, providing benefits and other significant information. Mass travel also brings with it tourism development, and organizations need to develop strategies to mitigate the possible negative impacts. However, the question is whether those measures are communicated effectively or not. If not, there will be misunderstanding that may lead to the creation of more conflicts and issues. Sometime the organizations use commercial paid media to communicate, but the believability of this is usually at a very low level.

The PR function helps tourism and hospitality institutions to communicate with stakeholders more effectively through different media channels. As highlighted by L'Etang (2006), there is a mismatch and lack of association between theory and practice in relation to PR in the tourism industry. There are different reasons for this: first, the theory, models and concepts of PR have neither been developed nor applied widely in this industry, which continues to be *conceptually* dominated by marketing; and second, PR activities are so prevalent in the *practices* of the industry, and PR is the predominant activity in promotion and communication in the tourism industry (L'Etang 2006; Huertas 2008).

Huertas (2008) notes that PR activities are an essential component of tourism marketing and, therefore, both public and private sector tourism establishments maintain close relationships with media, and regularly produce press releases to obtain publicity and create and maintain a favourable image with their public. The problem is that, while government and large tourism organizations maintain very close and friendly contacts with media organizations, small-scale tourism establishments do not show an ability to maintain such close contacts with media and other key stakeholders, due to a lack of proper understanding of the management and marketing programmes they require.

Crisis management

Tourism is an industry that is highly sensitive to emotion; therefore it is vulnerable and can be affected by changes in economic, socio-cultural, political and natural environments, and by epidemics or natural disasters. A crisis is any situation that has the potential to affect long-term confidence in an organization or a product, or which may interfere with its ability to continue operating normally (PATA 2003; Malhotra & Venkatesh 2009; AlBattat & Mat Som 2013). The PR department of a tourism and hospitality organization also needs to manage the vulnerable situations that negatively affect the organization's day-to-day activities as well as its future. Therefore, crisis management is vitally important, and needs to have good management plans and practices in place. Middleton et al. (2009) identified a range of possible crisis situations that may be faced by hospitality and tourism organizations in the future.

During the last few decades, various vulnerable situations have negatively influenced tourist decisions and behaviour. Terrorist attacks such as the bombing in Egypt in 2006, Mumbai in 2006, London in 2005, the Bali attacks against tourists in 2005, and Madrid in 2004, Jakarta in 2003, Bali in 2002, the September 11 attacks against the USA, terrorist attacks in Sri Lanka, and recent terrorist attacks in Germany, France, and Belgium negatively affected the tourism industry. In addition, the tsunami disaster in South East Asia (2004), SARS and Bird Flu, and Foot and Mouth Outbreaks in Britain also had a negative influence on the tourism industry (Malhotra & Venkatesh 2009; Buultjens, Ratnayake & Gnanapala 2015a). These incidents, epidemics and events create negative perceptions and perceived fear among the tourists who travel to those destinations, since tourism is a highly sensitive industry. However, the reduction of tourist arrivals also creates a lot of issues and problems among affected destinations, and all stakeholders therefore face a lot of problems and issues (Floyd et al. 2004).

However, McKercher & Hui (2004) highlight the fact that tourists have relatively short memories; therefore, they tend to travel to such destinations when they feel that the destination is temporarily free from these hazards and other associated threats. The passing of time also shows that negative events and disasters do not have an everlasting impact on tourists' visitation (Malhotra & Venkatesh 2009; AlBattat & Mat Som 2013; Buultjens, Ratnayake & Gnanapala 2015b). For example, even severely affected destinations can again become popular tourist hotspots, such as Bali, Egypt, Sri Lanka, Mumbai, and the recent terrorist attack cities in Europe.

The literature suggests that the negative events which need an effective crisis management programme so that they can be addressed effectively (Middleton et al. 2009; Kotler et al. 2010) are the following:

A. Product defects and related issues
B. Industrial action and service failures
C. Epidemics, health and safety issues
D. Crimes against tourists
E. Natural disasters
F. Civil conflicts
G. Terrorist attacks and war

Crisis management is an important area of PR, and is the way of dealing with a situation wisely. Publicity is not healthy in certain situations, and may negatively influence tourist behavior and the image of the destination/organization. There are situations when things go wrong, sometimes due to management error, and sometimes due to events beyond management control, for example terrorist attacks, food poisoning in hotels and restaurant food, and other health and environmental hazards.

An effective crisis management programme will reduce the negative effects of these events. The PR activities of a company may have a strong impact on public awareness, at a much lower cost than advertising. The PR department can effectively handle these vulnerable situations to change the negative perceptions of the tourists. Under crisis management, a PR department needs to develop an immediate contingency plan to control the situation and build trust among the public about the competency of the destination organization. It needs to contact all relevant media sources and channels, and should provide real information and publicize the steps that have been taken to reduce the immediate effects of a disaster. If possible, it is important to invite media personnel to come and see the real situation and accurately report it. Here, the most important thing is to appoint a spokesperson to provide up-to-date information; otherwise there may be many contradictory sets of information and arguments. To mitigate this, an organization needs to maintain good relationships with close contact between its PR department and different medias, until the situation has returned to normal. Of assistance here, though, is the fact that in the present globalized digital world it is easier to disseminate information through electronic sources and other social media channels effectively.

Measuring the effectiveness of PR campaigns

Like any other activity, it is necessary to identify the effectiveness of the PR campaigns launched by a destination or any other business organization in the tourism and hospitality sector. The impact of PR activities can be evaluated through the process of establishing standards of measurement, defining what is excellence, and finally evaluating the outcomes based on defined standards (Michaelson & Stacks 2011; Michaelson, Wright & Stacks 2012). The founding professionals of PR argue that, for activities to be effective they must be a key senior manager duty, and must counsel action and behaviours, but also give evidence of its effectiveness (Dozier, Grunig & Grunig 1995; Grunig, Grunig & Dozier 2002; Michaelson & Stacks 2011).

However, it may be a difficult task to identify the exact contribution of each PR activity since these are an assortment of many different activities. Jafari (2000) notes that the effectiveness of a PR campaign can be measured in two ways: by counting the length and number of press articles and television reports, and by measuring the organization's image before and after a special PR campaign through conducting surveys with relevant target groups. However, the weakness of this method is that the image of a company is also influenced by other communications instruments, such as advertisements, sales promotions, direct marketing and even social media marketing.

Middleton et al. (2009) conclude that PR results should be evaluated against previously set objectives; however, this evaluation is not an exact science, as it may be more qualitative and subjective than quantitative and objective. They also suggested three possible methods to measure the outcomes of PR programmes. First, media content analysis can be conducted using word counts, popularity and the page-space received, and by counting the frequency of mentions of the organization's name, brands and logos. Second, an analysis can be conducted of the types of comments (favourable, neutral or unfavourable), the quality of the materials included, and the types of pages used (editorial, front cover, and so on). Third, a survey can be conducted to measure and identify the attitudes, awareness and perceptions of the target audience before and after the programme.

Financial and non-financial indicators can also be used to measure the effectiveness of PR campaigns (Stacks 2010). Non-financial indicators are defined as how stakeholders and stockholders perceive an organization's credibility, relationships, reputation, degree of trust and confidence (Stacks 2010; Michaelson & Stacks 2011). Finally, a PR campaign will only be a success if it has been planned, coordinated and measured against a desired set of results (CIM 2009, p. 5).

Organizations can obtain wider publicity though enhancing their image if they can use PR activities more effectively. Their use is also considered to be one of the most cost-effective promotional tools available to the tourism and hospitality industry. However, organizations and destinations do not currently fully utilize their capacity to promote their businesses. The industry will experience both favourable and unfavourable situations from time to time. The unfavourable situations cannot be managed effectively through other paid commercial sources (such as advertising), due to a lack of time, credibility and/or trustworthiness. Organizations can practise using diverse PR tools to obtain wider publicity though image building and third-party endorsements, and to handle any unfavourable situations through a proper crisis management programme. However, ultimate success is dependent on the ability of the PR department to develop, launch and monitor effective PR programmes. Effective PR activities create positive *word of mouth* publicity in the minds of different stakeholders, and it is the most powerful and effective promotional tool in the present tourism and hospitality business world for the task of ensuring effectiveness in the marketplace.

References

AlBattat, AR & Mat Som, AP 2013, 'Emergency Preparedness for Disasters and Crises in the Hotel Industry', *SAGE Open Journals*, July–September, pp. 1–10.

Bowie, D & Buttle, F 2004, *Hospitality Marketing: An Introduction*, Elsevier Butterworth-Heinemann, Burlington.

Bowie, D & Buttle, F 2011, *Hospitality Marketing: Principles and Practice*, 2nd edition, Elsevier, Amsterdam.

Buhalis, D & Foerste, M 2015, 'SoCoMo Marketing for Travel and Tourism: Empowering Co-creation of Value', *Journal of Destination Marketing and Management*, Vol. 4, no. 3, pp. 151–161.

Buultjens, J, Ratnayake, I & Gnanapala, WKAC 2015a, 'From Tsunami to Recovery: The Resilience of the Sri Lankan Tourism Industry' in BW Ritchie and K Campiranon (eds), *Tourism Crisis and Disaster Management in the Asia-Pacific*, CABI, Oxford.

Buultjens, J, Ratnayake, I & Gnanapala, WKAC 2015b, 'Post-Conflict Tourism Development in Sri Lanka: Implications for Building Resilience', *Current Issues in Tourism*, Vol. 19, no. 4, pp. 355–372.

Byrd, ET 2001, 'Stakeholders in Sustainable Tourism Development and Their Roles: Applying Stakeholder Theory to Sustainable Tourism Development', *Tourism Review*, Vol. 62, no. 2, pp. 6–13.

Caywood, CL 2004, *The Handbook of Strategic Public Relations and Integrated Communications*, Tata McGraw-Hill, New Delhi.

Chartered Institute of Marketing (CIM) 2009, *How to Achieve an Effective Promotional Mix*, CIM, Maidenhead, Berkshire.

Chheang, V 2010, 'Tourism and Local Community Development in Siem Reap', *Ritsumeikan Journal of Asia Pacific Studies*, Vol. 27, pp. 85–101.

Dozier, DM, with Grunig, LA & Grunig, JE 1995, *Manager's Guide to Excellence in Public Relations and Communication Management*, Lawrence Erlbaum, Mahwah, NJ.

Floyd, MF, Gibson, H, Pennington-Gray, L & Thapa, B 2004, 'The Effect of Risk Perceptions on Intentions to Travel in the Aftermath of September 11, 2001', *Journal of Travel and Tourism Marketing*, Vol. 15, no. 2–3, pp. 19–38.

Gnanapala, WKAC 2016, 'Destination Marketing Approaches for Wildlife Tourism', in JK Fatima (ed), *Wilderness of Wildlife Tourism*, Apple Academic Press, Waretown, NJ.

Grunig, LA, Grunig, JE & Dozier, DM 2002, *Excellent Public Relations and Effective Organizations: A Study of Communication Management in Three Countries*, Lawrence Erlbaum, Mahwah, NJ.

Gunn, CA 1994, *Tourism Planning: Basics, Concepts, Cases*, Taylor & Francis, New York.

Gunn, CA & Var, T 2002, *Tourism Planning: Basics, Concepts, Cases*, Routledge, New York.

Hall, CM 2008, *Tourism Planning: Policies, Processes and Relationships*, Pearson, Harlow.

Huertas, A 2008, 'Public Relations and Tourism: Fighting for the Role of Public Relations in Tourism', *Public Relations Review*, Vol. 34, pp. 406–408.

IMDb nd, *25 Best Travel Movies of All Time*. Available from: www.imdb.com /list/ls070653194/ (accessed 12 August 2016).

Inskeep, E 1991, *Tourism Planning: An Integrated and Sustainable Development Approach*, John Wiley & Sons, London.

Jafari, J 2000, *Encyclopaedia of Tourism*, Routledge, London.

Kotler, P & Armstrong, G 2009, *Principles of Marketing*, Pearson, Upper Saddle River, NJ.

Kotler, P & Armstrong, G 2012, *Principles of Marketing*, 14th edition, Pearson, Upper Saddle River, NJ.

Kotler, P, Bowen, JT & Makens, JC 2010, *Marketing for Hospitality and Tourism*, Pearson, Upper Saddle River, NJ.

Khoo-Lattimore, C, Yang, ECL & Lai, MY 2016, 'Comparing the Meanings of Food in Different Chinese Societies: The Cases of Taiwan and Malaysia', *Journal of Hospitality Marketing & Management*, Vol. 25, no. 8, pp. 954–974.

LaTour, K 2008, 'Advertising, Public Relations and Crisis Management', in H Oh and P Abraham (eds), *Handbook of Hospitality Marketing Management*, pp. 153–185, Butterworth Heinemann, Oxford.

L'Etang, J 2006, 'Public Relations in Sport, Health and Tourism', in J L'Etang & M Pieczka (eds), *Public Relations: Critical Debates and Contemporary Practice*, Lawrence Erlbaum, New Jersey.

McKercher, B & Hui, ELL 2004, 'Terrorism, Economic Uncertainty and oUtbound Travel from Hong Kong', in CM Hall, DJ Timothy & DT Duval (eds), *Safety and Security in Tourism: Relationships, Management and Marketing*, pp. 99–116, Haworth Press, New York.

Malhotra, R & Venkatesh, U 2009, 'Pre-crisis Period Planning: Lessons for Hospitality and Tourism', *Worldwide Hospitality and Tourism Themes*, Vol. 1, pp. 66–74.

Mathieson, A & Wall, G 2006, *Tourism – Change, Impacts, Opportunities*, Pearson, Essex.

Michaelson, D & Stacks, DW 2011, 'Standardization in Public Relations Measurement and Evaluation', *Public Relations Journal*, Vol. 5, pp. 7–8.

Michaelson, D, Wright, DK & Stacks, DW 2012, 'Evaluating Efficacy in Public Relations/Corporate Communication Programming: Towards Establishing Standards of Campaign Performance', *Public Relations Journal*, Vol. 6, no. 5, pp. 1–25.

Middleton, VTC, Fyall, A & Morgan, M 2009, *Marketing in Travel and Tourism*, Butterworth-Heinemann, Oxford.

Nayomi, G & Gnanapala, WKAC 2015, 'Socio-Economic Impacts on Local Community through Tourism Development with Special Reference to Heritance Kandalama', *Tourism, Leisure and Global Change*, Vol. 2, pp. 57–73.

Oliver, S 2010, *Public Relations Strategy*, Kogan Page, London.

Pavlovich, K 2003, 'The Evolution and Transformation of a Tourism Destination Network: The Waitomo Caves, New Zealand', *Tourism Management*, Vol. 24, no. 2, pp. 203–216.

PATA 2003, *Crisis: It Won't Happen to Us*, Pacific Asia Travel Association, Bangkok.

Pearce, PL, Moscardo, G & Ross, GF 1996, *Tourism Community Relationships*, Elsevier, Oxford.

Petrovici, A 2014, 'Public Relations in Tourism: A Research on the Perception of the Romanian Public Upon Responsible Tourism', *Procedia – Social and Behavioral Sciences*, Vol. 163, pp. 67–72.

Pizam, A 2005, *International Encyclopaedia of Hospitality Management*, Elsevier Butterworth-Heinemann, Oxford.

Stacks, DW 2010, *Primer of Public Relations Research*, Guilford, New York.

The Telegraph nd, *The Top 100 Films Inspired to Travel*. Available from: www.telegraph.co.uk/travel/lists/The-top-100-films-that-inspire-travel/ (accessed 4 August 2016).

Timothy, DJ 2000, 'Building Community Awareness of Tourism in a Developing Country Destination', *Tourism Recreation Research*, Vol. 25, no. 2, pp. 111–116.

United Nations Conference on Trade and Development 2003, *Sustainable Tourism: Contribution to Economic Growth and Sustainable Development*. Available from: http://unctad.org/meetings/en/SessionalDocuments/ciem5d2_en.pdf (accessed 25 July 2016).

Further reading

Caywood, CL 2004, *The Handbook of Strategic Public Relations and Integrated Communications*, Tata McGraw-Hill, New Delhi.

Dozier, DM, with Grunig, LA & Grunig, JE 1995, *Manager's Guide to Excellence in Public Relations and Communication Management*, Lawrence Erlbaum, Mahwah, NJ.

Grunig, LA, Grunig, JE & Dozier, DM 2002, *Excellent Public Relations and Effective Organizations: A Study of Communication Management in Three Countries*, Lawrence Erlbaum, Mahwah, NJ.

Huertas, A 2008, 'Public Relations and Tourism: Fighting for the Role of Public Relations in Tourism', *Public Relations Review*, Vol. 34, pp. 406–408.

Malhotra, R & Venkatesh, U 2009, 'Pre-crisis Period Planning: Lessons for Hospitality and Tourism', *Worldwide Hospitality and Tourism Themes*, Vol. 1, pp. 66–74. doi:10.1108/17554210910949896.

Michaelson, D & Stacks, DW 2011 'Standardization in Public Relations Measurement and Evaluation', *Public Relations Journal*, Vol. 5, pp. 7–8.

Middleton, VTC, Fyall, A & Morgan, M 2009, *Marketing in Travel and Tourism*, Butterworth-Heinemann, Oxford.

Oliver, S 2010, *Public Relations Strategy*, Kogan Page, London.

Stacks, DW 2010, *Primer of Public Relations Research*, Guilford, New York.

Wilcox, DL, Cameron, GT & Reber, BH 2015, *Public Relations: Strategies and Tactics*, Pearson, Harlow.

17

Online distribution channels and yield management in the hotel industry

Baris Civak, Erhan Kaya and Murat Emeksiz

Introduction

Online distribution channels are e-commerce platforms allowing hoteliers to sell rooms over the internet. In this aspect, online distribution channels may be described as virtual sales offices operating through the internet. This particular rapid development has recently led hoteliers to carry out their business through online channels. The fact that the internet is effective, efficient and budget friendly in this sense (Law, Leung and Buhalis 2009) has increased the importance of online distribution channels. The ratio of online distribution channels to total sales and their contribution to total revenue increase in a consistent way while the interaction between yield management (YM) and online distribution channels is reported to be high. Consequently, due to the elevated importance of online distribution channels and their impact on yield management practices, YM has become the business of selling the right room to the right customer through the right channel for the right price at the right time (Willie 2011; Civak 2016).

Online distribution channels

Distribution is one of the most critical factors for hotels under local competition (Buhalis 2001). Owing to electronic distribution channels, hoteliers have been able to sell their products far and near. A series of innovations in information and communication technologies have enabled them to benefit from this opportunity. With the penetration of the internet into all fields of life, information and communication technologies have developed dramatically (Guo et al. 2014), and booking systems have become online systems operating through the internet. People have started to make their travel reservations through the internet (Kim, Kim and Han 2007). Concurrently, online booking systems have allowed hoteliers to handle flexible rates better and increase their occupancy in accordance with YM with more dynamic pricing (Guo et al. 2013).

The channels through which online hotel bookings are made can be listed under two categories: direct and mediated distribution channels. Direct distribution channels are the platforms

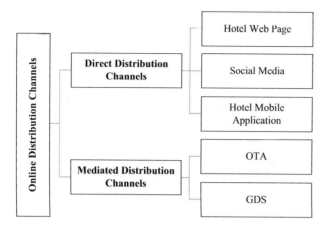

Figure 17.1 Online distribution channels

through which hotels perform their sales and bookings without using any intermediaries or paying any commission. Direct distribution channels are established with the integration of a booking engine onto a web page, social media accounts and a mobile application. However, mediated distribution channels rely on intermediaries to make their bookings. The difference between the two is in the commission paid by the hotelier. In direct sales, the hotel performs the booking without paying any commission while a booking is defined as a mediated sale when commission is paid. The mediated distribution channels that hoteliers can use to sell their rooms through online platforms are online travel agencies (OTA) and global distribution systems (GDS). Online distribution channels in the accommodation industry are illustrated in Figure 17.1.

Each online distribution channel is managed according to its properties since each has some characteristic advantages, and in order to benefit from these advantages properly, some specific strategies must be applied for each channel. For example, OTAs strongly contribute to the occupancy rates of hotels. GDSs also contribute to occupancy as well as being a profitable channel in terms of inbound customer profile. Although the number of reservations obtained from mobile and social media channels is relatively low, they promise to be significant sales channels in the future. On the other hand, hotel websites stand as the most important channel due to several advantages (Civak 2016).

Hotel websites

Hotel websites are situated at the core of digital strategies (Baloglu and Pekcan 2006) due to the direct and positive impact of website quality on customer satisfaction and buying intention (Bai, Law and Wen 2008). For this reason, many hotel enterprises develop their own websites in order to promote their products and services, enhance their customer relations and perform direct sales in response to increasing demand for online services (Zafiropoulos, Vrana and Paschaloudis 2006; Law, Qi and Buhalis 2010). Hotel websites are significant for three reasons. First, as a distribution channel, the cost of the reservations obtained through websites to the hotel is the lowest. Second, websites are effective for acquiring regular guests. Third, hoteliers can utilize the customer information obtained from bookings made through websites. Mediated channels do not share all the customer information with the hotel (Civak 2016).

In order to turn hotel website visitors from potential customers into purchasing customers, a booking engine must be integrated into the website. The reservations obtained in this way are the least costly since only the cost of installing the booking engine applies (Turkeyf Reservation Systems' website 2016). With the booking engine installed, hoteliers will save money on the commission fees charged by OTAs, and their websites will no longer serve as a catalogue only. At this point, hotel enterprises must install a duplex booking engine which can be integrated into a property management system (PMS). However, a point to take into consideration here is that the website must have a comprehensible, easy to access and user-friendly interface. Additionally, hotel enterprises must work on attracting potential customers to their websites. To address this point, hotels may offer promotions on their websites to gain regular customers. In particular, international chain hotels offer promotional codes to customers who visit their websites in order to add more customers to their loyalty programs and to cancel out the commission fee paid to the mediated channels (Civak 2016).

Social media accounts

Social media is described as an online platform where people with common interests can share their ideas, comments and opinions (Weber 2009). Social media has kept on expanding, especially since internet use has become widespread. Hoteliers conduct basic marketing activities, such as advertisement, presentation and promotions over social media platforms. Hotels have been able to obtain reservations directly through their accounts on some world-renowned social media platforms such as Facebook and Twitter by adding a booking engine.

The management of online distribution channels does not mean opening/closing sales or distributing prices only; hoteliers also sell experiences to their customers. Likewise, customers share experiences of their stay on social media, blog pages, forums and websites. The role of social media here is electronic word-of-mouth marketing. These comments may influence the buying behaviour of other potential customers either negatively or positively, and positive comments may constitute an advantage for lesser-known hotels (Vermeulen and Seegers 2009). It has been confirmed that hotel evaluation sites such as TripAdvisor have an impact on the buying behaviour of consumers (Casalo et al. 2015). Accordingly, it has been revealed that the brands in the 'best hotels' list are more preferable to those in the 'worst hotels' list. It has been noted that negative commenting is the most determining factor in the overall assessments (Kim, Lim and Brymer 2015). That is, social media comments have an effect on the marketing of the hotel. In the hotels which hold a good online reputation and are capable of managing this, the average room rates are likely to be higher (Diana-Jens and Ruibal 2015). Therefore, hoteliers must monitor the comments and build interaction with their customers.

Social media channels are very important for developing YM strategies since they also serve as data sources for the yield management department, because YM has become customer-oriented in principle. While social media provides information for pricing and promotion activities in the short term, it also provides information about customers to create a new market channel on a long-term basis (Noone, McGuire and Rohlfs 2011).

Hotels are not the sort of establishments that serve one nation only. Therefore, hotel-related comments and news are shared in many languages. Despite this, it is very difficult to monitor the comments and news shared in different languages and platforms, but the software developed under the name of *online reputation management tool* (ORMT) allows these platforms to be monitored in many languages (Vendesta's website 2015).

Hotel mobile booking applications

Today, mobile phones have turned into functional hand-sized computers and named as "smartphones" (Wang, Xiang and Fesenmaier 2014). Through several features, smartphones offer a wide range of opportunities to travellers. One of them is to be able to make reservations online. Hotel mobile booking applications, which can be defined as the best online booking tool, have become online distribution channels which allow customers to make bookings over the internet no matter where they are.

People who like using smartphones benefit from this convenience by installing hotels' or OTAs' mobile applications on their phones (Mo Kwon, Bae and Blum 2013). From the hoteliers' perspective, they use mobile booking applications developed in recent years to remain competitive and improve revenue. Furthermore, these applications have become a part of new marketing strategies for hotels. The rapid development of the use of mobile applications means that they are an attractive tool for hoteliers to elevate their image and reputation (Anuar, Musa and Khalid 2014).

Hoteliers are also able to update their rates and availability status automatically, and obtain reservations by integrating the mobile booking application into their booking systems. Although the number of mobile reservations obtained from social media is relatively low, it is predicted that this number will grow in the future (Civak 2016).

Global distribution systems

Airline operators established their own computerized reservation systems in order to facilitate their workflow; and these systems are now at the core of the distribution system on a global basis (Kaya 2008). Consequently, as understood from their name, GDSs have turned into giant organizations mediating the marketing of the hotels globally.

GDSs contribute to marketing activities worldwide with their systems allowing electronic booking in various sectors, such as air transportation, tourism or car rental. These systems can be dennoted as the first-generation GDS, and have changed with the development and expansion of the internet. Due to these distribution channels, known as online GDS today, the marketing and selling activities of hotels can be performed over the internet throughout the world. Although it is still not open to end users, the reservations obtained by travel agencies are defined as online since they are performed over the internet.

Online travel agencies

Websites called online travel agencies or third-party websites (Toh, Raven and DeKay 2011) are online distribution channels which sell hotel rooms on the internet for a certain amount of commission (Ling, Guo and Yang 2014). Alongside traditional travel agencies, some agencies have brought a new dimension to the hotel–agency relationship by implementing sales and reservations over the internet (Lee, Guillet and Law 2013). Some online travel agencies (for example, Booking.com) have penetrated into the sector with the aim of offering the best price (Law, Chan and Goh 2007), and commission-based sales are determined via mutual agreement between the agency and the hotelier. Research studies have recently shown that making reservations through OTAs is gainig popularity. By taking these new trends into consideration and making sales through online channels, hotels gain an advantage over their competitors (Inversini and Masiero 2014), because most online reservations are made through OTAs (Pan, Zhang and

Law 2013). However, hotels are facing financial problems due to the high commission fees paid to OTAs (Gazzoli, Gon Kim and Pallakurthi 2008). In order to eliminate the commission fee, hotels must focus on making sales through direct distribution channels (Toh et al. 2011; Tso and Law 2005). Nevertheless, hoteliers are not recommended to turn away from sales made through the OTA channel completely in order to exclude commission fees. Hotel managements improve their visibility thanks to OTAs (Ling et al. 2015).

OTAs are classified into three models according to their business models and principles (Law et al. 2007; Starkov and Price 2003):

- Merchant model
- Agency (commissionable) model
- Opaque model

In a *merchant model*, OTAs buy the hotel rooms for a certain price and add their commission to it. Hotels do not pay any commission. In an *agency model* where commission may apply, OTAs charge a certain percentage of fees as commission for the sales of hotel rooms. In this model, the hotel earns the same price as the direct sales price given on the hotel's website. For example, for a room sold through Expedia, a commission rate of 20% is paid to the agency. In an *opaque model*, an agreement is made between the OTA and the hotel, and the rooms are sold based on customer offer. The most popular one is Priceline Group. The offers obtained through this system are shared with the hotel management and the hotel may reject the offer as an option.

One of the most significant issues in the management of online distribution channels is *rate parity*, which stands for the different price applied to the same room on different channels. This is very important in terms of both agency–hotel relations and customer relations. It is noted that successful YM is not possible in the case of a different price being calculated for the same room on online distribution channels and particularly on OTAs. In order to overcome this, the room types must be configured properly on online channels. Each online channel has a unique configuration, and each room type must match correctly on online distribution channels. Another measure is to check the room inventory on a regular basis (Civak 2016).

Information technologies used in online distribution channel management

In hotel enterprises, information technologies are used in order to store customer information, lower the cost and to bring about some operational conveniences in the workflow (Camisón 2000). While information technologies give remarkable support to the hotel industry on an operational basis (Melián-González and Bulchand-Gidumal 2016), they also help hoteliers to take strategic decisions. The duty of the yield managers is to support the hoteliers to designate strategies by analysing the data on a staff level. Yield managers benefit from the technology to implement their role. In this sense, YM has a close relationship with information technologies. In fact, today, the realization of YM is quite difficult in the absence of information technologies. The role of information technologies is significant for obtaining and analysing data, and making demand-related deductions, since the use of technological innovations has become an asset to compete and succeed in the marketplace (Civak 2016). Hoteliers spend a large amount of money on e-commerce tools in order to maintain their present customers and attract potential customers. It has been determined that e-commerce expenditures have a dramatically positive impact on room revenue (Hua, Morosan and DeFranco 2015).

For the management of online distribution channels, without information technologies it seems primitive today to send price and availability information to online distribution channels and registering reservations and sales into the system. All these activities are managed easily, precisely, immediately and without interruption thanks to information technologies. Hotels are able to benefit from these technologies in line with their budget and requirements. A variety of new software is used in the management of online distribution channels, such as *rate shopper (RS), channel manager (CM), online reputation management tool (ORMT)* as well as property management system *(PMS), yield management system (YMS)* and *booking engine* (Civak 2016; Civak and Emeksiz, 2016).

Property management systems

Property management systems are "softwares that are composed of packages integrated into each other and some other integrated systems thereof allowing the management processes to be applied and managed over the computer, and producing operational, statistical and analytical data" (Kınay 2013: 1). In other words, they are computer applications related to the operational activities performed in hotels (Emeksiz and Yolal 2007). These activities are outlined as follows (DIA's website 2015):

- Reservation and registration
- Checking customer payments, checkout and booking status
- Occupancy and vacancy monitoring upon sales analyses
- Income and outcome analysis
- Checking daily, monthly and annual data with accounting integration

In order to implement YM, technically it is necessary to obtain, evaluate and utilize customer information. Collecting, processing and using customer information when necessary in the hotel sector facilitates the workflow while it allows hoteliers to know about their customers and accordingly establish marketing strategies. Collecting customer information is an intense process, and data is crucial for YM (Donaghy, McMahon and McDowell 1995). The utilization of information technologies for collecting data is significant in this process. Using PMS only will not be sufficient, because PMS merely stores the raw data. However, the analysis of the data is another process. Hotels cannot develop their plan and strategy with raw data. At this stage, they require a number of auxiliary systems to process raw data.

Yield management systems

Experienced staff is a must for the realization of YM in hotels. However, it is not possible for YM personnel to conduct all activities at the same time, such as monitoring the competitors, managing online channels, performing demand analysis and management, and examining customer comments for ensuring customer satisfaction (Emeksiz, Gursoy and Icoz 2006). Additionally, due to the staff structure in the organization, the YM department is supposed to conduct all these activities simultaneously and share opinions for strategic decision-making. While conducting and following up all these activities is easier in small-scale hotels, it may be challenging for YM departments in upscale ones, because the YM department or sales departments in the hotels do not have the time and resources to conduct these activities (Turkeyf Reservation Systems' website 2016). Therefore, handling these activities with the help of technology saves YM personnel from considerable secretarial work and helps them to focus on strategic decision-making. Saving time as well as labour costs and reducing the workload are some of the advantages of YMS. The benefits that YMS provides to hoteliers are listed below in more detail (Protel's website 2016):

- Ensures that price and availability is determined by the analysis of data obtained from many sources.
- Provides immediate increase and decrease in current prices on online channels according to the occupancy status of the hotel (when pre-determined).
- Ensures simultaneous price equality on all booking channels by updating the prices automatically, consistently and precisely with intersystem connections.
- Secures continuous monitoring of the expected risks with system alerts.
- System saves on work and time by choosing the most appropriate estimation model automatically.
- Directs booking personnel to offer a variety of prices and dates to increase revenue per room.
- Increases yield efficiency by offering the optimal pricing.

YMS calculates the optimal price by collecting the following data (Hotel Linkage's website 2015a):

- Occupancy status and average room price of the hotel
- Reservation trend of the hotel
- Hotel budget
- Estimated occupancy rate of the hotel
- Search rate of the hotel through booking engine
- Occupancy rates and prices of competitors
- Current market information obtained from demand-related trend reports
- Number of planes landing at the airport and number of flight tickets issued for the related destination
- Weather forecast
- Reviews on the hotel
- The popularity of the hotel on social media

Booking engines

A booking engine is a tool allowing the hotel to obtain reservations directly through its website, social media accounts and mobile reservation application. Technology consultants can design booking engines in accordance with the websites, mobile applications and social media accounts of hotels. What is significant in the booking engine technology is a solid security infrastructure. Additionally, the hotel may attain more efficiency from the booking engine with the presence of a CM. In the absence of CM technology, connecting a PMS to the booking engine provides a more convenient workflow.

Competitor analysis reports

The competitor analysis reports used for YM and the management of online distribution channels aim to compare daily, weekly or monthly prices and yield performance of the hotels. The main purpose is to compare a hotel's own performance to other hotels in the same region. These reports also provide market information on the average price and occupancy of the competitors. The tools that hoteliers use for this purpose are the rate shopper (RS) software and the reports provided by STR Global company (Civak 2016).

Rate shopper

One of the important components of YM is the status of the competitors. RS is a type of software that allows hotel management to monitor the prices of their competitors. In other words, price-searching software constitute a system that shares actual price information of the market with the hotels. They present price information to hoteliers on their competitors (both the prices on the hotel websites and online travel channels) on a daily or weekly basis. RS ensures prices optimization by being integrated with YMS. This system provides hotels with the following benefits (eRewMax's website 2015):

- Revision of the market simultaneously
- Constant monitoring of the prices of competitors
- The opportunity to monitor all channels to maintain the balance of room rates on sales channels
- The optimization of room rates

RS works by taking the following steps: The program is opened and competitors in the market are identified. Online sales spots through which competitors sell their rooms are listed, such as Booking.com, Expedia.com, HRS.com. Room types of the competitors and what rate is demanded for a specific date with the unit of currency are entered in the system, and then a daily electronic report is sent automatically to the email address given. This report includes the rates of the competitors within a 30-day period. The report may be received more than once during the day when required (Civak 2016).

STR Global reports

Hoteliers that require regional market information may register their rates and occupancy information into the system after becoming a member of the STR Global company network. Similarly, hotels that wish to compare their past performances to other hotels via the STR Global report may also register on the system. Without giving the names and contact information of rival hotels, their average occupancy and rate information is reported to the hotel. Thus, the hotel can see their average rate and occupancy performance in comparison to the competitors. The difference with RS is that STR Global report compares historical data while RS displays the future rates of the competitors. In this sense, the properties of the STR Global firm are as follows (STR Global's website 2016):

- Only data providers are present.
- Annual subscription.
- Displays the performance of the hotel according to the preferred rival hotel list.
- Allows for choosing four rival hotel groups.
- Chronologically compares occupancy, ADR and RevPAR information for 18 months.
- Sharing personal data is not allowed.
- Includes free market information.
- Allows the monitoring of group customer, short-term customer and contracted customer information by adding free market information.

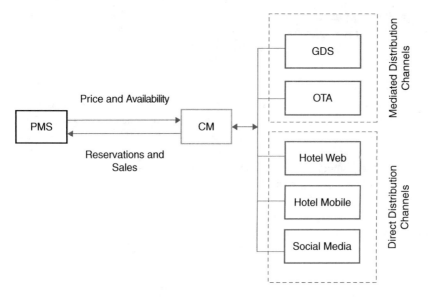

Figure 17.2   Channel manager

Channel manager

Channel manager (CM) is software that enables hotels to update their rates and occupancy information onto one online channel source while transferring the reservations and sales obtained from online channels to PMS. The CM tool builds dual communication with online channels. Having sent the rate and occupancy information to all online channels (OTA, GDS hotel web, social media and hotel mobile apps) through the CM, room availability is updated with bookings and sales obtained from online channels. The mode of operation of the CM is demonstrated in Figure 17.2.

Even though a hotel employs one person for entering price and availability onto online reservation channels and registering the bookings to the PMS, it is difficult to make necessary updates on time. For example, assuming that the reservation of five rooms is registered to online channels, it is unlikely that sales can be suspended in all other channels when they are being sold on one of them. If two more rooms are sold through another channel at the same time, seven rooms would be sold on the online distribution channels where five rooms had been already sold. If the hotel does not have any available room in the room inventory, this means that some rooms are sold above capacity. Hence, using a CM system in hotels where online sales are strongly preferred will ease the workflow and prevent possible errors. Using CM in hotels is now crucial, because online channel management can be tiring and time-consuming since it needs to be updated regularly. The easiest way to do this is to enter price, availability and promotional information in the panel of the CM tool (Hotel Channel Manager's website 2015). In this way, price equality will be ensured on all channels.

Online reputation management

Reputation reflects the impressions, thoughts, understanding and values that exist in people's minds about a particular company (Yalcin and Ene 2013). Within this context, online reputation may be defined as the negative or positive impressions that companies leave in people's minds through the internet.

It has been proven in a study that online reviews are effective for online sales, resulting in a 10% increase in sales (Ye et al. 2011). In this regard, it can be said that hotel reviews are highly important; because it is clear that negative hotel reviews influence the buying behaviour of consumers while positive reviews and numeric evaluations, such as grading out of 10 or from *excellent* to *very poor*, affect the buying decisions of the consumers positively (Sparks and Browning 2011). Nowadays, many customers who want to book a holiday package or book a hotel room online make reservations according to hotel reviews (Vermeulen and Seegers 2009). Customer reviews are the best way of influencing a hotel's reputation and marketing. Thus, social media must be monitored closely. By identifying the missing points and making amends; exploring customer reviews on social media or other channels and the yield management department and other departments responding to those comments, this may enhance customer satisfaction and improve the reputation of the hotel. In this sense, it can be concluded that social media, holiday and hotel reviews and websites, blog pages, forums, comparative analysis sites and news in the press have a huge impact on the sales and reputation of a hotel. Accordingly, the ORMT collects the hotel reviews made on the above-mentioned online platforms and allows them to be displayed, monitored and responded to on one screen (Civak 2016).

Reviews may also help hoteliers to make a self-evaluation, because the negative hotel reviews might present an opportunity to fix some mistakes. Likewise, positive reviews can build trust for customers. Hotels will be successful in this sense if they can manage their reputation on online platforms (Forbes' website 2015).

Search engine optimization

Another important issue for hotel websites is to be ranked near the top of a search result list displayed on the internet. If a traveller cannot see the website of the hotel in a specific destination in the top-ranked search results of a search engine, the chance of making sales through the hotel website lowers. Therefore, hotels have conducted some studies to increase their visibility with search engine optimization (SEO). The main purpose of these studies is to ensure that the website is placed near the top of the ranking list and accordingly sell rooms by their website being more salient to potential customers (Hotel Linkage's website 2015b). SEO is the process of listing websites as a result of a free product or service search on the internet. In other words, SEO can be defined as a cluster of strategies and metrics used for increasing the number of visitors by ensuring that a website is ranked near the top of search-engine search results (Parikh and Deshmukh 2013).

Prior to implementing SEO, it is essential to know about the competences of the customer, market and hotel. For SEO, it is better to choose five to ten key words which can represent the content correctly, because the optimization works according to possible searches made by users (Zilincan 2015). Technology consultancy companies describe SEO as dominating search engines (Hotel Runner's website 2015). It is possible that online distribution channel sales will improve with SEO activities. Therefore, performing SEO activities in all hotels, regardless of their capacity, will increase the chance of successfully marketing the hotel. These activities are usually performed by both marketing and technology departments in hotels, whereas in chain hotels, the headquarters conduct SEO activities (Civak 2016).

Figure 17.3 demonstrates how online channels can be managed effectively by means of information technologies. According to this figure, YMS makes price and availability suggestions to the yield management department by analysing the data collected through RS, PMS, ORMT

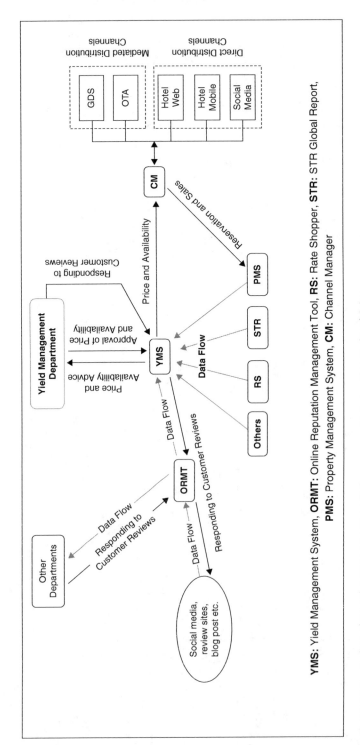

Figure 17.3 Online channel management cycle by means of information technologies

and other information tools. The yield management department enters a decision into the system, based upon the YMS's price and availability suggestions. CM obtains price and availability information from the registered YMS. CM sends the obtained price and availability information to online distribution channels simultaneously and without interruption. The reservations and sales obtained through online distribution channels appear on the PMS again by means of the CM. Thus far it is the sales part of the management of online distribution channels. Another part of the online channel management cycle is online customer reviews. The customer reviews on online platforms determined via the ORMT appear on the YMS, and the yield manager responds to the customer reviews via the YMS. Other departments see and respond to these reviews either via the ORMT or YMS by entering the system via an assigned password. In common practice, other departments respond to the reviews via ORMT. When systems communicate with each other in this way, system users can manage the online distribution channels of the hotels immediately and without interruption (Civak 2016).

References

Anuar, J., Musa, M. and Khalid, K. (2014). "Smartphone's Application Adoption Benefits Using Mobile Hotel Reservation System (MHRS) among 3 to 5-Star City Hotels in Malaysia," *Procedia-Social and Behavioral Sciences*, 130, 552–557.

Bai, B., Law, R. and Wen, I. (2008). "The Impact of Website Quality on Customer Satisfaction and Purchase Intentions: Evidence from Chinese Online Visitors," *International Journal of Hospitality Management*, 27(3), 391–402.

Baloglu, S. and Pekcan, Y. A. (2006). "The Website Design and Internet Site Marketing Practices of Upscale and Luxury Hotels in Turkey," *Tourism Management*, 27(1), 171–176.

Buhalis, D. (2001). "Tourism Distribution Channels: Practices and Processes," in D. Buhalis and E. Laws (eds.) *Tourism Distribution Channels: Practices, Issues and Transformations*, London: Thomson, 7–32.

Camisón, C. (2000). "Strategic Attitudes and Information Technologies in the Hospitality Business: An Empirical Analysis," *International Journal of Hospitality Management*, 19(2), 125–143.

Casalo, L. V., Flavian, C., Guinaliu, M. and Ekinci, Y. (2015). "Do Online Hotel Rating Schemes Influence Booking Behaviors?" *International Journal of Hospitality Management*, 49, 28–36.

Civak, B. (2016). *Otel Isletmelerinde Getiri Yonetimi ile Online Kanal Yonetimi ve Teknolojilerinin Etkilesimi* [Interaction of Yield Management with Online Channel Management and Its Technologies in Hotel Enterprises], (Master's thesis. Eskisehir: Anadolu University).

Civak, B. and Emeksiz M. (2016). "Online Distribution Channel Management and Technologies" in *6th AHTMM Conference Proceedings*, Guangzhou, 95.

Diana-Jens, P. and Ruibal, A. R. (2015). "Online Reputation and Its Impact on Hotel Pricing Strategies," *Cuadernos de Turismo*, 36, 453–456.

Donaghy, K., McMahon, U. and McDowell, D. (1995). "Yield Management: An Overview," *International Journal of Hospitality Managemet*, 14(2), 139–150

Emeksiz, M. and Yolal, M. (2007). *Konaklama Isletmelerinde Onburo Yonetimi: Getiri Yonetimi – Odalar Yonetimi – Bilgi Teknolojileri – Talep, Kapasite ve Fiyat Boyutlariyla* [Front Office Management: Yield Management – Room Division – Information Technologies – Demand, Capacity and Price Dimensions]. Ankara: Detay Yayıncılık.

Emeksiz, M., Gursoy, D. and Icoz, O. (2006). "A Yield Management Model for Five-Star Hotels: Computerized and Non-Computerized Implementation," *International Journal of Hospitality Management*, 25(4), 536–551.

Gazzoli, G., Gon Kim, W. and Palakurthi, R. (2008). "Online Distribution Strategies and Competition: Are The Global Hotel Companies Getting It Right?," *International Journal of Contemporary Hospitality Management*, 20(4), 375–387.

Guo, X., Ling, L., Yang, C., Li, Z. and Liang, L. (2013). "Optimal Pricing Strategy Based on Market Segmentation for Service Products Using Online Reservation Systems: An Application to Hotel Rooms," *International Journal of Hospitality Management*, 35, 274–281.

Guo, X., Zeng, X., Ling, L. and Yang, C. (2014). "Online Competition between Hotels and Online Travel Agencies: From the Perspective of Cash Back After Stay," *Tourism Management Perspective*, 12, 104–112.

Hua, N., Morosan, C. and DeFranco, A. (2015). "The Other Side of Technology Adoption: Examining the Relationships between E-Commerce Expenses and Hotel Performance," *International Journal of Hospitality Management*, 45, 109–120.

Inversini, A. and Masiero, L. (2014). "Selling Rooms Online: The Use of Social Media and Online Travel Agents," *International Journal of Contemporary Hospitality Management*, 26(2), 272–292.

Kaya, E. (2008). *Istanbul'da Bulunan Bes Yıldızlı Konaklama Isletmelerinde Getiri Yonetimi ve Elektronik Dagıtım Kanallari ile Etkilesimi* [A Yield Management Application in Five Star Hotels in Istanbul and Interaction with Electronic Distribution Channels], (Master's thesis. Istanbul: Istanbul University).

Kınay, H. (2013). *Otel Otomasyonlari* [Hotel Automations] (2nd ed.), Bursa: Ekin Yayinevi.

Kim, D. J., Kim, W. G. and Han, J. S. (2007). "A Perceptual Mapping of Online Travel Agencies and Preference Attributes," *Tourism Management*, 28(2), 591–603.

Kim, W. G., Lim, H. and Brymer, R. A. (2015). "The Effectiveness of Managing Social Media on Hotel Performance," *International Journal of Hospitality Management*, 44, 165–171.

Law, R., Chan, I. and Goh, C. (2007). "Where to Find the Lowest Hotel Room Rates on the Internet? The Case of Hong Kong," *International Journal of Contemporary Hospitality Management*, 19(6), 495–506.

Law, R., Leung, R. and Buhalis, D. (2009). "Information Technology Applications in Hospitality and Tourism: A Review of Publications from 2005 to 2007," *Journal of Travel and Tourism Marketing*, 26(5–6), 599–623.

Law, R., Qi, S. and Buhalis, D. (2010). "Progress in Tourism Management: A Review of Website Evaluation in Tourism Research," *Tourism Management*, 31(3), 297–313.

Lee, H. A., Guillet, B. D. and Law, R. (2013). "An Examination of The Relationship Between Online Travel Agents and Hotels: A Case Study of Choice Hotels İnternational and Expedia. Com," *Cornell Hospitality Quarterly*, 54(1), 95–107.

Ling, L., Dong, Y., Guo, X. and Liang, L. (2015). "Availability Management of Hotel Rooms under Cooperation with Online Travel Agencies," *International Journal of Hospitality Management*, 50, 145–152.

Ling, L., Guo, X. and Yang, C. (2014). "Opening the Online Marketplace: An Examination of Hotel Pricing and Travel Agency On-Line Distribution of Rooms," *Tourism Management*, (45), 234–243.

Melián-González, S. and Bulchand-Gidumal, J. (2016). "A Model that Connects Information Technology and Hotel Performance," *Tourism Management*, 53, 30–37.

Mo Kwon, J., Bae, J. I. and Blum, S. C. (2013). "Mobile Applications in the Hospitality Industry," *Journal of Hospitality and Tourism Technology*, 4(1), 81–92.

Noone, B. M., McGuire, K. A. and Rohlfs, K. V. (2011). "Social Media Meets Hotel Revenue Management: Opportunities, Issues and Unanswered Questions," *Journal of Revenue and Pricing Management*, 10(4), 293–305.

Pan, B., Zhang, L. and Law, R. (2013). "The Complex Matter of Online Hotel Choice," *Cornell Hospitality Quarterly*, 54(1), 74–83.

Parikh, A. and Deshmukh, S. (2013). "Search Engine Optimization," *International Journal of Engineering Research and Technology*, 2(11), 3–21.

Sparks, B. A. and Browning, V. (2011). "The Impact of Online Reviews on Hotel Booking Intentions and Perception of Trust," *Tourism Management*, 32(6), 1310–1323.

Starkov, M. and Price, J. (2003). "Online Travelers Prefer Booking Directly on the Hotel Website." [online] Available: www.archaeol.freeuk.com/EHPostionStatement.hthttp://cdn.hebsdigital.com/1492126425/cms/pressroom/apr_03_hebs_article_2003_booking_directly_vs_intermediaries.pdf (Accessed: 15 Nov 2016).

Toh, R. S., Raven, P. and DeKay, F. (2011). "Selling Rooms: Hotels vs. Third-Party Websites," *Cornell Hospitality Quarterly*, 52(2), 181–189.

Tso, A. and Law, R. (2005). "Analysing the Online Pricing Practice of Hotels in Hong Kong," *International Journal of Hospitality Management*, 24, 301–307

Vermeulen, I. E. and Seegers, D. (2009). "Tried and Tested: The Impact of Online Hotel Reviews on Consumer Consideration," *Tourism Management*, 30(1), 123–127.

Wang, D., Xiang, Z. and Fesenmaier, D. R. (2014). "Adapting to the Mobile World: A Model of Smartphone Use," *Annals of Tourism Research*, 48, 11–26.

Weber, L. (2009). *Marketing to the Social Web: How Digital Customer Communities Build Your Business*. Hoboken, NJ: John Wiley and Sons.

Willie, P. (2011). *A Comparative Study of the Hotel İndustry: Revenue Management Strategy in Canada and the United States* (Doctoral dissertation, Nova Southeastern University).

Yalcin, A. and Ene, S. (2013). "Online Ortamda Kurumsal Marka Imajının Marka Sadakati ile Iiskisi Uzerine Bir Arastirma [A Study on the Relationship between Online Brand Image and Online Brand Loyalty]," *Iktisadi ve Idari Bilimler Dergisi*, 34(1), 113–134.

Ye, Q., Law, R., Gu, B. and Chen, W. (2011). "The Influence of User-Generated Content on Traveler Behavior: An Empirical Investigation on the Effects of E-Word-Of-Mouth to Hotel Online Bookings," *Computers in Human Behavior*, 27(2), 634–639.

Zafiropoulos, C., Vrana, V. and Paschaloudis, D. (2006), "The Internet Practices of Hotel Companies: An Analysis from Greece," *International Journal of Contemporary Hospitality Management*, 18(2), 156–163

Zilincan, J. (2015). "Search Engine Optimization," In *CBU International Conference Proceedings*, 3, 506–510.

Internet references

crsturkeyf.com (2016). Turkeyf Reservation Systems official website. [online] http://crsturkeyf.com/for-hotels/revenue-yield-manager/?lang=tr (Accessed: 02 Jan. 2016).

crsturkeyf.com (2016). Turkeyf Reservation Systems official website. [online] http://crsturkeyf.com/for-hotels/webhotelier-booking-engine/?lang=tr (Accessed: 18 Dec. 2015).

dia.com (2015). DIA official website. [online] www.dia.com.tr/otel-yonetimi/# (Accessed: 26 Dec.2015)

erevmax.com (2015). eRewMax official website. [online] www.erevmax.com/ratetiger/hotel-rate-shopper.html (Accessed: 20 Sept. 2015)

forbes.com (2015). Forbes official website. [online] www.forbes.com/sites/susanadams/2013/03/14/6-steps-to-managing-your-online-reputation/ (Accessed: 27 Dec. 2015).

hotelchannelmanager.org (2015). Hotel Channel Manager official website. [online] http://hotelchannelmanager.org/ (Accessed: 26 Dec. 2015).

hotellinkage.com (2015a). Hotel Linkage official website. [online] www.hotellinkage.com/revenue-management-system/4590714835 (Accessed: 02 Jan. 2016).

hotellinkage.com (2015b). Hotel Linkage official website. [online] www.hotellinkage.com/seo/4586428750 (Accessed: 22 Dec. 2015)

hotelrunner.com (2015). Hotel Runner official website. [online] http://hotelrunner.com/tr/ozellikler/online-pazarlama-seo (Accessed: 22 Dec. 2015)

protel.com (2016). Protel official website. [online] www.protel.com.tr/opera-otel-yonetim-sistemi/gelir-yonetimi/ (Accessed: 02 Jan. 2016).

strglobal (2016). STR Global official website. [online] www.strglobal.com/products/star-program (Accessed: 23 Feb. 2016).

vendasta.com (2015). Vendesta official website. [online] www.vendasta.com/marketplace/reputation-management (Accessed: 27 Dec. 2015).

18

Internal marketing

Aaron Hsiao and Emily Ma

The concept of internal marketing

The concept of internal marking was first proposed by Berry et al. (1976) as a solution to the problem of delivering high service quality consistently. Internal marketing is defined as a "planned effort using a marketing-like approach to motivate, educate and coordinate internal customers (employees) towards creating satisfaction for external customers and ... increase these businesses' performance" (Turkoz and Akyol 2008: 149). The concept of internal marketing is based on the assumption that the organization is a market; therefore, it is possible to apply marketing inside the organization. Researchers have indicated the similarities between internal and external customers (e.g. Turkoz and Akyol 2008), and have indicated that everyone in an organization has a customer (Gronroos 1981). Internal customers of organizations must be happy before the organizations can effectively serve external customers (Berry 1980). Internal marketing views employees as internal customers, viewing jobs as internal products and services, and aims to design products and services to better meet the needs of these internal customers (Greene et al. 1994). Internal marketing is a coordinating philosophy that focuses on customer satisfaction and organizational productivity and effectiveness through constant improvement of employees' performance (Ahmed and Rafiq 2003).

Internal marketing involves a number of activities and researchers generally agree that it is a multi-dimensional construct. However, variations still exist with regard to the dimensions of internal marketing, particularly when applied in different contexts. For example, Rafiq and Ahmed (2000) suggested that internal marketing should contain nine dimensions (categories: (1) Inter-functional Coordination and Integration; (2) Job Satisfaction; (3) Empowerment; (4) Service Quality; (5) Employee Motivation; (6) Vision of the Organization; (7) Employee Development; (8) Strategic Reward; and (9) Senior Leadership. From the internal marketing perspective, job satisfaction refers to the necessity of an organization to have satisfied employees in order to have satisfied customers (George 1990). Empowerment is considered an essential part of internal marketing and is the process of enabling or authorizing an individual employee to think, behave, take action, control work and make decisions in autonomous ways (Kruja et al., 2016; Rafiq and Ahmed 1998). Rafiq and Ahmed (1998) further suggested that employees consider jobs as sources for self-actualization and development; therefore, internal marketing should seek to increase employees' motivation by treating jobs as internal products for employees. Internal marketing efforts and programmes should be imaginatively and sensitively created and implemented so that employees can believe in organizations' short and long-term visions (Foreman and Money 1995). Foreman and Money (1995) further suggested that employees must be well-trained and developed in order to effectively employ internal marketing. Strategic rewards help to motivate employees and achieve other goals of internal marketing. Senior leadership refers to the moral and intellectual ability of leaders to lead the organization and employees in the right direction (Ahmed and Rafiq 2003). Kaurav et al. (2015) also supported the nine-dimensional framework and according to this framework, inter-functional coordination and integration is the coordinated utilization of organizations' resources in order to create superior value for customers (Narver and Slater 1990).

A recent study by Narteh and Odoom (2015), however, suggested that internal marketing contains six dimensions: (1) Internal Communication; (2) Employee Training; (3) Corporate Culture; (4) Reward Systems; (5) Organizational Commitment; and (6) Empowerment. Internal communication is considered a necessary component of internal marketing as a means of achieving organizational objectives (Finney 2011). Training is an important internal marketing activity because it impacts on the overall competitiveness of an organization (Birdi et al. 2008). Training should cover multiple aspects such as leadership development, job responsibilities, business ethics, etc. and good training leads to job satisfaction and loyalty (Ladyshewsky 2007; Weber 2007). Corporate culture refers to organizations' core values that prescribe preferred norms and forms of employee behaviours (Papasolomou and Vrontis 2006). Corporate culture helps to foster employee commitment; once employees feel that they fit in well with their work environment, they perform well and tend to be more loyal. Researchers have repeatedly reported the importance of a fair reward system and suggest that salary satisfaction is positively associated with job satisfaction and performance (e.g. Awwad and Agti 2011). Organizational commitment refers to how employees identify with and are involved with an organization. Internal marketing shows that the management of the organization cares about employees, and therefore could foster organizational commitment (Ballantyne 2003), which has been proven to be positively associated with employee job satisfaction and organizational citizenship behaviour (Ma and Qu 2011). Empowerment is a practice whereby managers give employees the discretion to make decisions about job-related activities (Czaplewski et al. 2001). Empowerment is particularly important for hospitality organizations, where service employees often need to go the extra mile to meet and exceed customer expectations.

In hospitality contexts, Kim et al. (2016) proposed a five-dimensional framework for internal marketing, consisting of: welfare systems, training, compensation, communication and management support. Welfare systems refer to the benefits employees could obtain in addition to wages (Kim et al. 2001). Training offers opportunities for employees to enhance their knowledge and skills (Back et al. 2011). Compensation links employees' pay with their performance and is an important indicator of employee commitment. Management support is an important part of organizational culture, and can help facilitate a two-way information-flow between employees and leaders (Cooper and Cronin 2000). We will provide more details on this framework in the measurement section. Communication usually refers to a company's activities or efforts to share, deliver and exchange information, ideas, feelings and opinions among employees to achieve the company's goals (Back et al. 2011; Clampitt and Downs 1993; Kim et al. 2001).

Internal marketing and the service-profit chain

The importance of internal marketing has been well-acknowledged by researchers (e.g. Heskett and Schlesinger 1994; Kaurav et al. 2015; Schlesinger and Heskett 1991). Both internal customers (employees) and external customers need to be at the centre of management concern, and investment in employees can directly link to profitability (Heskett and Schlesinger 1994). According to the service-profit chain model (Heskett and Schlesinger 1994), internal marketing and customer satisfaction are closely linked. The service–profit–chain model established a relationship between employee satisfaction, loyalty, work performance and customer satisfaction, loyalty and profitability (Figure 18.1).

The service–profit–chain model starts with internal service quality, indicating the strategic roles played by internal marketing in an organization, because internal service quality is directly influenced by internal marketing efforts (Elsamen and Alshurideh 2012). Specifically, employee attitudes are influenced by internal service quality, which is greatly influenced by internal marketing efforts (Ieong and Lam 2016). Employees' attitudes further determine their performance and intention to stay with the current organization, which further impacts on customer satisfaction, loyalty and profitability. Revenue growth and profitability can further enhance internal service quality. Based on a case study on Sears, Rucci et al. (1998) found that a 5-point improvement in employee attitudes led to a 1.3-point improvement in customer satisfaction and a 0.5% improvement in revenue growth. Bang, Oh and Chung (2016) also claimed that good and effective internal marketing is a must for good and strong customer satisfaction. Service companies should: value investments in people as much as they value investments in machines and equipment; use technology to support front-line service employees; emphasize the importance of recruitment and training efforts for employees at all levels, no matter whether they are housekeepers or senior executives; and link performance with compensation for employees at all levels (Schlesinger and Heskett 1991).

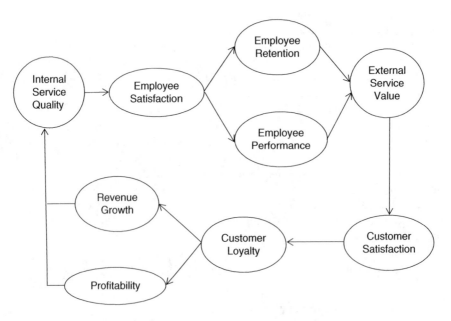

Figure 18.1 Service profit chain
Source: Adapted from Heskett and Schlesinger (1994).

Internal marketing in hospitality contexts

Internal marketing is particularly relevant and important for service organizations, such as hotels and restaurants, where employees play a critical role in service delivery (Kotler 1991). The current generation has witnessed a strong growth in the service sector globally. This accelerated growth is accompanied by stiff competition among service-intensive organizations, especially the hotel and restaurant industry. Selnes (2013) found that 67% of hospitality businesses fail in their first year of operation because employees are not capable of winning customers, which is a failure due to poor internal marketing. Akroush et al. (2013) found that organizations without effective internal marketing easily face low employee morale, motivation and high turnover. Therefore, internal marketing is an indispensable element of a business and organizations should treat employees as valuable assets and sources of competitive advantage (Agnihotri et al. 2016). Organizations have to pay special attention to internal marketing to employees so that they can be aware of the product and strategies of the organization and give a good service to customers (Bansal and Taylor 2015; Ennew, Binks and Chiplin 2015; Mathe and Slevitch 2013).

Good internal marketing activities can lead to a number of positive organizational and individual-level outcomes. Based on a study on a hospitality organization in the US, Hsu (2002) suggested that internal marketing plays a crucial role in increasing employees' commitment with the organization. The study further suggested that managers should share information with employees effectively and value their employees as organizational assets. The service-intensive nature of the hospitality industry means that service employees play critically important roles. As suggested by Lewis (1989), internal marketing helps to satisfy our internal customers (service employees). When our internal customers are satisfied, they will be motivated to satisfy our external customers. In addition, internal marketing also encourages the marketing orientation of employees, no matter whether they are service-contact employees or not. Proper internal marketing can encourage employees to go above and beyond expectations and eliminates sources of dissatisfaction. Bansal et al. (2001) explored the impact of internal marketing activities on external marketing outcomes and suggested that internal marketing activities can lead to internal customers' (employees') satisfaction, trust and loyalty to the organization, which further facilitate employees' extra-role behaviours to external customers, thus helping to create external customer satsifaction and loyalty.

Case study 1: Fairmont Hotels & Resorts

Fairmont is a Canadian luxury hotel brand established in 1907. Fairmont recognizes the critical roles played by internal marketing in achieving guest satisfaction and implements systematic internal marketing approaches (Fairmont.com 2016). Hudson (2016) suggested that internal marketing is the key to success for Fairmont. The internal marketing efforts started with attracting self-motivated, results-oriented employees, followed by extensive orientation and training processes to ensure employees are aware of the organizational culture and also equipped with sufficient knowledge and skills to serve customers. Fairmont also provides employees with further education opportunities through the E-Cornell online education programme (Fairmont.com 2016). Employees are empowered to achieve ultimate guest service outcomes and are encouraged to go the extra mile to satisfy customers.

Fairmont rewards good employee performance with benefits, incentives and compensations so that employee satsifaction can be enhanced and they are continually motivated to provide excellent service. This is consistent with a previous research finding that linking performance with employee compensations is critically important in motivating good employee performance (Schlesinger and Heskett 1991). Fairmont also recognizes good performance with awards such as the "Star of the Month" programme. Internal communications are handled seriously in the forms of newsletters, emails, posters, daily shift briefings, meetings and electronic signage, etc. to make sure all internal customers are aware of what is going on at Fairmont. Leaders take genuine care of subordinates. For example, managers would sit with new employees to discuss their career development plan. Fairmont now operates more than 130 hotels and residential properties globally (Fairmont.com 2016). It has won numerous awards over the journey and the most recent ones include the TripAdvisor – Travelers' Choice Awards, the AAA Five Diamond Rating and the World Luxury Hotel Awards (Fairmont.com 2016).

Case study 2: Shangri-La Hotels and Resorts

Hong Kong-based Shangri-La Hotels and Resorts is one of the largest Asian-based deluxe hotel groups in the region and owns and/or manages more than 90 hotels and resorts globally with a room inventory of over 38,000 (Shangri-la.com 2016). Shangri-La has been ranked as a top-tier hotel group as it has emphasized internal marketing practices throughout its operational process. The company has integrated service principles, service model, training style and career growth methods in different regions in order to maintain employee satisfaction in achieving a high level of service quality.

The key elements of internal marketing strategies for Shangri-La include organizational culture, management, employees and service. For the organizational culture and service, Shangri-La has its own service model, which is called "Shangri-La Hospitality", for achieving competitive advantage through the integration of five core organizational values: respect, humility, courtesy, helpfulness, and sincerity. This demonstrates the internal and external communicational efficiency of the organization by delivering clear information about company policies and goals (Shangri-la.com 2016).

In order to deliver outstanding employee performance, Shangri-La has developed a five-level organizational design to delegate authority to its employees. That is to say, it has a clear and organized system for its employees to follow separate instructions, exercise discretion, and a fund that employees can access without management consent to deal with customers' requests. This enhances a level of confidence as well as increasing the level of responsiveness in their employees so that they can make assured and prompt decisions. Shangri-La also requires training for all employees through the Shangri-La Academy and hotel training programmes. These programmes involve simulating work situations and scenarios with frequent mistakes and professional practices so that trainees learn to exercise the methods that are implemented at Shangri-La (Sutanto and Fandianto 2012).

Shangri-La practices equal opportunities and embraces diversity in the workplace. The aim of managing diversity is to build an environment that works for all individuals of the organization

(Thomas 2005). Complementing equal opportunity and affirmative action policies with managing diversity is probably the most effective way for organizations to maintain workplace harmony (Hsiao et al. 2015; Kirton and Greene 2005; Wrench et al. 2008). In terms of employee well-being, the hotel has introduced the Health Passport that was specifically created with the help of expert recommendations to offer educational information on strengthening individual health, enabling employees access to nutrition tips, a body/mass index chart, a workplace exercise guide and many more areas of support.

Shangri-La also promotes work–life balance to ensure that staff primarily focus on their health so that they are then are able to meet personal and business goals. Internal communications are actively practiced through the hotel's Voice Programme, whereby staff are encouraged to participate in the hotline service to offer ideas/recommendations for improving departments' communication and cooperation efficiency. The importance of organizational and management support has been well recognized in the hospitality literature (Colakoglu et al. 2010). Ehigie and Otukoya (2005) also found employee work outcomes were associated with how they perceived organizational support and fair interpersonal treatment. Bergen et al. (2005) suggested that with the right support, training and modelling behaviour, general staff will be able to develop successful work relationships and open communication. Implementing internal marketing approaches leads to a win–win situation: employees enhance their attitudes and behaviours, in turn increasing their productivity, while Shangri-La promotes the company image and builds closer relationships with its internal consumers.

Measurements for internal marketing

As mentioned earlier in the chapter, internal marketing involves a number of activities and is considered as a multi-dimensional construct. Inconsistencies are observed in internal marketing measurements. This section will focus on internal marketing measurements used in hospitality contexts.

Arnett et al. (2002) proposed a model for hotel employees' positive behaviours and empirically tested it on 860 employees in a Casino hotel. Internal marketing activities are treated as the starting point for employees' job satisfaction, pride and positive behaviours. In this study, internal marketing was measured from five dimensions, namely, role clarity, evaluation of reward systems, work environment, evaluation of management and organizational performance. Arnett et al. (2002: 92) also provided sample statements used to measure each dimension. For example, role clarity was measured using "I understand what my role is in the delivery of excellent customer service". Evaluation of reward system was measured using "High performers are rewarded". Work environment was measured as "I have the resources that I need to deliver excellent customer service". Evaluation of management was measured using "Managers take action quickly to correct employee problems" and organizational performance was measured using "This hotel provides better guest services than its rivals".

Keller et al. (2006) measured internal marketing as a four-dimensional construct, using 19 statements. The four dimensions are: Internal Job/Product, Internal Price, Internal Places, and Internal Promotion (Table 18.1).

Internal Job/Product means the basic-level needs of the employees. It also represents training needs, levels of responsibility, involvement in decision-making, career opportunities, basic relational and psychological support of co-workers and the working environment (Ahmed and

Table 18.1 Four-dimensional measurements of internal marketing

Dimensions of internal marketing	Statements of each dimension
Internal job/product	1. The HR department cares about my welfare. 2. My supervisor and colleagues admire and respect me. 3. The HR department will tell me how to work, and why. 4. My supervisor will let me know if I have done a great job. 5. My work environment is beneficial to my career development.
Internal price	6. The HR department often spends some time answering my questions. 7. The HR department helps me to solve my problems actively. 8. The HR department give me feedback on my demands on time. 9. The HR department will supply me with essential information quickly.
Internal place	10. My supervisor/colleagues discusses my work problems in private. 11. My supervisor/colleagues and I communicate freely. 12. My supervisor/colleagues share their work happiness with me. 13. We have good information-sharing. 14. The HR department has an effective information feedback system.
Internal promotion	15. The HR department has established a fair work atmosphere. 16. The HR department provides a harmonious work environment. 17. My supervisor/colleagues assure me they will assist me when needed. 18. My supervisor and colleagues often praise me behind my back. 19. My supervisor and colleagues will tell me good and useful news.

Source: Keller et al. (2006).

Table 18.2 Five-dimensional measurements of internal marketing

Dimensions of internal marketing	Statements of each dimension
Welfare systems (Back et al. 2011; Kim et al. 2001)	This organization offers good employee benefits. This organization has good welfare facilities. This organization offers good vacation systems. This organization has a good system for employees to take a leave of absence.
Training (Back et al. 2011; Lux et al. 1996)	This organization provides regular service training. There are enough training programs in this organization. Training sessions in this organization help me to understand customer needs.
Compensation (Foreman and Money 1995; Lux et al. 1996)	This organization fairly rewards employee performance. This organization establishes my pay linked to my performance. In this organization, those employees who develop a close relationship with customers are rewarded for their efforts.
Communication (Back et al. 2011; Clampitt and Downs 1993)	In this organization, I can express my opinions freely in a liberal atmosphere. The exchange of information in this organization is adequate. This organization provides adequate information on the requirements of my job.
Management support (Jaworski and Kohli 1993)	The management in this organization offers guidance in solving job-related problems. Two-way information flow across management levels is encouraged by the management in this organization. The management in this organization encourages open communication.

Source: Kim et al. (2016).

Rafiq 2003). Internal Price is defined by Burin (2011) as being associated with the costs that employees pay to work for the organization. These costs comprise opportunity costs, psychological costs and the emotional labour costs of working for organizations. Internal Place can be referred to as the work environment. It contains the organizational culture, values, assumptions, artefacts and every symbolic aspect of the organization (Ahmed and Rafiq 2003). Internal Promotion is a distribution process for explaining the management strategy to employees and serves to clarify their role in the development and success of the strategy. It also can be suggested as a form of internal communication which is concerned with channels, outlets or distribution methods needed to ensure that the internal product/job or service has been provided to the employees correctly (Owomoyela et al. 2013). All dimensions achieved a Cronbach's alpha of 0.80 or above.

In a recent study in hospitality contexts, Kim et al. (2016) measured internal marketing from five perspectives based on previous researchers' work. The five dimensions are: welfare systems training, compensation, communication and management support. A total of 16 items were used to measure the five dimensions. Details on the measurement scale are summarized in Table 18.2.

References

Agnihotri, R., Dingus, R., Hu, M. Y., and Krush, M. T. (2016) "Social Media: Influencing Customer Satisfaction in B2B Sales," *Industrial Marketing Management* 53, 172–180.

Ahmed, P. K., and Rafiq, M. (2003) *Internal Marketing: Tools and Concepts for Customer-Focused Management*, Oxford, UK: Butterworth Heinemann.

Akroush, M. N., Abu-ElSamen, A. A., Samawi, G. A., and Odetallah, A. L. (2013) "Internal Marketing and Service Quality in Restaurants," *Marketing Intelligence and Planning* 31(4), 304–336.

Arnett, D. B., Laverie, D. A., and McLane, C. (2002) "Using Job Satisfaction and Pride as Internal-Marketing Tools," *The Cornell Hotel and Restaurant Administration Quarterly* 43(2), 87–96.

Awwad, M. S., and Agti, D. A. M. (2011) "The Impact of Internal Marketing on Commercial Banks' Market Orientation," *International Journal of Bank Marketing* 29(4), 308–332.

Back, K. J., Lee, C. K., and Abbott, J. A. (2011) "Internal Relationship Marketing: Korean Casino Employees' Job Satisfaction and Organizational Commitment," *Cornell Hospitality Quarterly* 52(2), 111–124.

Ballantyne, D. (2003) "A Relationship-Mediated Theory of Internal Marketing," *European Journal of Marketing* 37(9), 1242–1260.

Bang, W. S., Oh, J. S., and Chung, K. H. (2016) "A Study on the Effect of Internal Marketing on Internal Service Quality: The Moderating Role of Self-Esteem," *The Korea Society of Management Information Systems Conference*, 102–108.

Bansal, H., Mendelson, M. B., and Sharma, B. (2001) "The Impact of Internal Marketing Activities on External Marketing Outcomes," *Journal of Quality Management* 6, 61–76.

Bansal, H. S., and Taylor, S. (2015) "Investigating the Relationship between Service Quality, Satisfaction and Switching Intentions," in *Proceedings of the 1997 Academy of Marketing Science (AMS) Annual Conference*, Coral Gables, FL: Springer International Publishing, 303–304.

Bergen, C. W. V., Soper, B., and Parnell, J. A. (2005) "Workforce Diversity and Organisational Performance," *Equal Opportunities International* 24(3/4), 1–16.

Berry, L. L. (1980) "Services Marketing is Different," *Business*, May/June, 24–30.

Berry, L. L., Hensel, J. S., and Burke, M. C. (1976) "Improving Retailer Capability for Effective Consumerism Response," *Journal of Retailing* 52(3), 3–14.

Birdi, K., Clegg, C., Patterson, M., Robinson, A., Stride, C. B., Wall, T. D., and Wood, S. J. (2008) "The Impact of Human Resource and Operational Management Practices on Company Productivity: A Longitudinal Study," *Personnel Psychology* 61(3), 467–501.

Burin, C. (2011) *The Perceived Influence of the Elements of Internal Marketing on the Brand Image of Staffing Agencies in South Africa*. Master's dissertation, Department of Business Management, University of Johannesburg.

Clampitt, P. G., and Downs, C. W. (1993) "Employee Perceptions of the Relationship between Communication and Productivity: A Field Study," *Journal of Business Communication* 30(1), 5–28.

Colakoglu, U., Culha, O., and Atay, H. (2010) "The Effects of Perceived Organisational Support on Employees'Affective Outcomes: Evidence from the Hotel Industry," *Tourism and Hospitality Management* 16(2), 125–150.

Cooper, J., and Cronin, J.J. (2000) "Internal Marketing: A Competitive Strategy for the Long-Term Care Industry," *Journal of Business Research* 48(3), 177–181.

Czaplewski, A. J., Ferguson, J. M., and Milliman, J. F. (2001) "Southwest Airlines: How Internal Marketing Pilots Success," *Marketing Management* 10(1), 4–17.

Ehigie, B., and Otukoya, O. (2005) "Antecedents of Organsational Citizenship Behavior in a Government-Owned Enterprise in Nigeria," *European Journal of Work and Organsational Psychology* 14, 389–399.

Elsamen, A. A., and Alshurideh, M. (2012) "The Impact of Internal Marketing on Internal Service Quality: A Case Study in a Jordanian Pharmaceutical Company," *International Journal of Business and Management* 7(19), 84–95.

Ennew, C. T., Binks, M. R., and Chiplin, B. (2015) "Customer Satisfaction and Customer Retention: An Examination of Small Businesses and Their Banks in the UK," in *Proceedings of the 1994 Academy of Marketing Science (AMS) Annual Conference*, Nashville, TN: Springer International Publishing.

Fairmont.com (2016) Retrieved June 3, 2016 from www.fairmont.com/about-us/

Finney, S. (2011) "Stakeholder Perspective on Internal Marketing Communication: An ERP Implementation Case Study," *Business Process Management Journal* 17(2), 311–331.

Foreman, S. K., and Money, A. H. (1995) "Internal Marketing: Concepts, Measurement and Application," *Journal of Marketing Management* 11, 755–768.

George, W. (1990) "Internal Marketing and Organisational Behaviour: A Partnership in Developing Conscious Employees at Every Level," *Journal of Business Research* 20(1), 63–70.

Greene, W., Walls, G., and Schrest, L. (1994) "Internal Marketing: The Key to External Marketing Success," *Journal of Services Marketing* 8(4), 5–13.

Gronroos, C. (1981) "Internal Marketing: An Integral Part of Marketing Theory," In: Donnelly, J.H. and George, W.R. (Eds.), *Marketing of Services*, 1st Edition, Orlando, FL: American Conference Proceedings, pp. 236–238.

Heskett, J. L., and Schlesinger, L. A. (1994) "Putting the Service-Profit Chain to Work," *Harvard Business Review* 72(2), 164–174.

Hsiao, A., Auld, C., and Ma, E. (2015) "Perceived Organizational Diversity and Employee Behaviour," *International Journal of Hospitality Management* 48, 102–112.

Hsu, S. H. (2002) *Internal Marketing in the Hospitality Industry: Communication Satisfaction and Organizational Commitment*, Michigan: Eastern Michigan University.

Hudson, S. (2016) *Internal Marketing Is the Key to Success at Fairmont.* Hotel Business Review. Retrieved June 3, 2016 from http://hotelexecutive.com/business_review/3994/internal-marketing-is-the-key-to-success-at-fairmont

Ieong, C.Y., and Lam, D. (2016) "Role of Internal Marketing on Employees' Perceived Job Performance in an Asian Integrated Resort," *Journal of Hospitality Marketing & Management*, 25(5), 589–612.

Jaworski, B. J., and Kohli, A. K. (1993) "Market Orientation: Antecedents and Consequences," *Journal of Marketing* 57(3), 53–70.

Kaurav, R. P. S., Paul, J., and Chowdhary, N. (2015) "Effect of Internal Marketing on Hotels: Empirical Evidence for Internal Customers," *International Journal of Hospitality and Tourism Administration* 16(4), 311–330.

Keller, S. B., Lynch, D. F., Ellinger, A. E., Ozment, J., and Calantone, R. (2006) "The Impact of Internal Marketing Efforts in Distribution Service Operations," *Journal of Business Logistics* 27(1), 109–137.

Kim, J., Song, H. J., and Lee, C. K. (2016) "Effects of Corporate Social Responsibility and Internal Marketing on Organizational Commitment and Turnover Intentions," *International Journal of Hospitality Management* 55, 25–32.

Kim, S. I., Cha, S. K., and Lim, J.Y. (2001) "A Correlational Study among Internal Marketing Factor, Nurse's Job Satisfaction, and Organizational Commitment in Hospital Nursing Organization," *Journal of Korean Public Health Nurse* 15(10), 42–55.

Kirton, G., and Greene, A.-M. (2005) *The Dynamics of Managing Diversity: A Critical Approach*, London: Elsevier.

Kotler, P. (1991) *Marketing Management: Analysis, Planning, Implementation and Control*, 7th Edition, Englewood Cliffs, NJ: Prentice-Hall Inc.

Kruja, D., Ha, H., Drishti, E., and Oelfke, T. (2016) "Empowerment in the Hospitality Industry in the United States," *Journal of Hospitality Marketing & Management* 25(1), 25–48.

Ladyshewsky, R. (2007) "A Strategic Approach to Integrating Theory to Practice in Leadership Development," *Leadership and Organization Development Journal* 28(5), 426–443.

Lewis, R. C. (1989) "Hospitality Marketing: The Internal Approach," *Cornell Hospitality Quarterly* 30, 40–45.

Lux, D. J., Jex, S. M., and Hansen, C. P. (1996) "Factors Influencing Employee Perceptions of Customer Service Climate," *Journal of Market-Focused Management* 1(1), 65–86.

Ma, E., and Qu, H. (2011). "Social Exchanges as Motivators of Hotel Employees' Organizational Citizenship Behavior: The Proposition and Application of a New Three-Dimensional Framework," *International Journal of Hospitality Management* 30(3), 680–688.

Mathe, K., and Slevitch, L. (2013). "An Exploratory Examination of Supervisor Undermining, Employee Involvement Climate, and the Effects on Customer Perceptions of Service Quality in Quick-Service Restaurants," *Journal of Hospitality and Tourism Research* 37(1), 29–50.

Narteh, B., and Odoom, R. (2015) "Does Internal Marketing Influence Employee Loyalty? Evidence from the Ghanaian Banking Industry," *Services Marketing Quarterly* 36(2), 112–135.

Narver, J. C., and Slater, S. F. (1990) "The Effect of a Market Orientation on Business Profitability," *Journal of Marketing* 54(4), 20–35.

Owomoyela, S. K., Ola, O. S. and Oyeniyi, K. O. (2013) "Investigating the Impact of Marketing Mix Elements on Consumer Loyalty: An Empirical Study on Nigerian Breweries PLC," *Interdisciplinary Business Research* 4(11), 485–486.

Papasolomou, I., and Vrontis, D. (2006) "Building Corporate Branding through Internal Marketing: The Case of the UK Retail Bank Industry," *Journal of Product and Brand Management* 15(1), 37–47.

Rafiq, M., and Ahmed, P. K. (2000) "Advances in the Internal Marketing Concept: Definition, Synthesis and Extension," *Journal of Services Marketing* 14(6), 449–462.

Rucci, A. J., Kirn, S. P., and Quinn, R. T. (1998) "The Employee-Customer-Profit Chain at Sears," *Harvard Business Review* 76(1), 82–97.

Schlesinger, L. A., and Heskett, J. L. (1991) "The Service-Driven Service Company," *Harvard Business Review* 69(5), 71–81.

Selnes, F. (2013) "An Examination of the Effect of Product Performance on Brand Reputation, Satisfaction and Loyalty," *Journal of Product and Brand Management* 2(4), 45–60.

Shangri-la.com (2016) Retrieved from www.shangri-la.com/corporate/about-us/employee/

Sutanto, E. M., and Fandianto, L. (2012) "Effectiveness Analysis of Shangri-La Academy Program Towards Employees Working Motivation at Shangri-La Hotel Surabaya," *Journal of Indonesian Economy and Business* 27(3), 406–417.

Thomas, K. M. (2005) *Diversity Dynamics in the Workplace*, 1st Edition, San Francisco: Wadsworth.

Turkoz, I., and Akyol, A. (2008) "Internal Marketing and Hotel Performance," *Anatolia: An International Journal of Tourism and Hospitality Research* 19(1), 149–177.

Weber, J. A. (2007) "Business Ethics Training: Insights from Learning Theory," *Journal of Business Ethics* 70(1), 61–85.

Wrench, J. S., Paltz, S. N., McCroskey, J. C., Berletch, N., Powley, C., and Wehr, A. (2008) "Organisational Coaching as Instructional Communication," *Human Communication: A Journal of the Pacific and Asian Communication Association* 11(3), 273.

19

Perceptual and relational approach to hotel brand equity

Measurement, criticism, and challenges

Maja Šerić and Irene Gil-Saura

Introduction

A great body of literature has emphasized the importance of research on the brand equity concept, as it represents the result of marketing communication activities (Keller 2009) and is a key driver of business success in hospitality (Prasad and Dev 2000). The concept is understood as the extra added value derived from consumers' perceptions of the brand name of a product or service (Yoo et al. 2000). A strong brand stimulates the attraction of all market players, hinders competitors' strategies, and allows differentiated positioning (Lemmink et al. 2003). Thereby, products and services with strong brand equity are strongly associated with outstanding marketing strategies and competitive advantage (Keller 2003, 2009). This is why brand equity has grown in importance among both practitioners and academics (Oliveira-Castro et al. 2008), with particularly strong relevance in the hotel environment (Bailey and Ball 2006).

Alongside this growing interest in the concept, a wide variety of approaches and methodologies appeared, which has led to disagreements concerning its conceptualization and measurement. Srivastava and Shocker (1991) have even initiated a debate on the redundancy of the notion, indicating that its definition is not necessary as it is equivalent to the idea of brand loyalty, attachment, positioning or competitive advantage. Accordingly, in the hospitality literature a certain confusion and questions have emerged regarding the meanings of the concept (Bailey and Ball 2006), the best way to measure it (Kim and Kim 2005; Hsu et al. 2012), and its main drivers and consequences (Šerić et al. 2016). Issues regarding the correct evaluation of the concept are still present, both in theory and practice (Lee et al. 2011).

Aaker (1991, p. 15) defined brand equity as "a set of brand assets and liabilities linked to a brand, its name and symbol that adds to or subtracts from the value provided by a product or service to a firm and/or to that firm's customers." Keller (1993, p. 8) suggested that brand equity can be understood as "the differential effect of brand knowledge on consumer response to the marketing of the brand." Yoo and Donthu (2001, p. 1) provided another brand equity conceptualization, defining the construct as "consumers' different response between a focal brand and an unbranded product when both have the same level of marketing stimuli and product attributes."

In the hotel context, brand equity is considered as "the favorable or unfavorable attitudes and perceptions that are formed and influence a customer to book at a hotel brand" (Prasad and Dev,

2000 p. 24). It also represents "the value that consumers and hotel property owners associate with a hotel brand, and the impact of these associations on their behavior and the subsequent financial performance of the brand" (Bailey and Ball 2006, p. 34). Although these definitions are valuable in defining the essence of the concept, to date there has been little agreement on which variables actually contribute to the development of hotel brand equity (Hsu et al. 2012). In their recent work on hotel customer-based brand equity, Šerić et al. (2016) noted that this aspect needs to be examined as a matter of priority. This chapter attempts to address this issue.

In the next section we will describe the variables that are most frequently employed to measure brand equity in hospitality. However, as the most common understanding of the concept has started to be questioned in recent years, we will also discuss some critical issues regarding hotel brand equity understanding and propose new calls for research and challenges.

Critical variables for measurement of hotel brand equity

The proposals of Aaker (1991) and Keller (1993) are the most referenced brand equity conceptualizations in the marketing literature, and they both approached the concept from the consumer perspective. This consumer-centered approach to brand equity research is useful as it provides guidelines for marketing strategies and highlights areas where research can be useful in the decision-making process (Keller 1993). This is why research on both brand equity in general and hotel brand equity in particular emphasizes a customer-based perspective.

While Aaker (1991) discussed four main brand equity dimensions, i.e. brand awareness, brand image, perceived quality, and brand loyalty, Keller (1993) measured the concept through brand awareness and brand image. In the hospitality marketing literature, Aaker's proposal is the most frequently referenced (e.g. Kim et al. 2003; Kim and Kim 2004, 2005; Kayaman and Arasli 2007; Lee and Kim 2009; Hyun and Kim 2011; Šerić and Gil-Saura 2012; Šerić et al. 2016). Therefore, brand awareness, brand image, perceived quality, and brand loyalty appear as the most employed variables in research on hotel brand equity.

In addition, we consider it necessary to examine the role of two other variables in brand equity creation, i.e., trust and commitment. These constructs have not been used in brand equity evaluation as frequently as those proposed by Aaker (1991). However, owing to their strong impact on customer loyalty in hospitality (e.g. Kim et al. 2001; Tideswell and Fredline 2004; Mattila 2006; Hsu et al. 2012; Leeman and Reynolds 2012), which, according to Aaker (1991), is the strongest component of brand equity, we believe that they might play an important role in the development of hotel brand equity.

Therefore, we identify the following variables that have an important role in hotel brand equity building: a) brand awareness; b) brand image; c) perceived quality; d) brand loyalty; e) brand trust; and f) brand commitment. Among them, we identify three perceptual variables (i.e., brand awareness, brand image, and perceived quality) and three relational variables (i.e., brand loyalty, brand trust, and brand commitment) (see Figure 19.1). In the following subsections we will explain how these variables can contribute to the development of brand equity and discuss how they have been examined in the hospitality literature.

Perceptual approach

Brand awareness

According to Aaker (1991), brand awareness is the first step towards the creation of brand equity and is defined as the potential ability of a consumer to recognize and/or remember the brand name. This variable is related to the strength of the brand in consumer's mind and is reflected

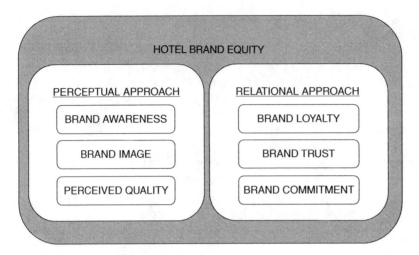

Figure 19.1   Perceptal and relational approach to hotel brand equity

in the consumer's ability to identify the brand under different conditions (Aaker 1991; Keller 1993) through recall or recognition (Keller 2003). As brand awareness increases, consumers tend to feel familiar with the brand and consider it when they purchase a product or service. In addition, they tend to trust a high-awareness brand's products or services more than those of low-awareness brands (Keller 1993), thus enhancing brand equity.

When examining the brand awareness concept in the hotel context, Kim and Kim (2005) measured it through the following three steps: a) top-of-mind-brand, i.e., the name of a hotel that first comes to the consumer's mind; b) unaided brand recall, i.e., three other names of hotels that come to consumer's mind; and c) brand recognition, consisting of selecting brand names of which consumers are aware from a list of selected hotels. Although this brand awareness operationalization has been frequently adopted in the hospitality literature, the latest research on brand awareness in hotels (e.g. Kim et al. 2008; So and King 2010; Hsu et al. 2012; Šerić et al. 2016) has started to consider the concept as per the framework suggested by Yoo and Donthu (2001). According to this proposal, brand awareness and brand associations are combined into one dimension. In this regard, along with the awareness of the hotel brand and the ability to recognize it among other competitive hotel brands, the consumer's ability to recall some features of the hotel brand are also considered.

Brand image

Brand image is defined as "consumer perceptions of and preferences for a brand, as reflected by the various types of brand associations held in consumers' memory" (Keller 2009, p. 143). According to Biel (1992), brand image is the combined effect of its associations. Positive associations influence the creation of a positive image of the brand, thus enhancing its value (Aaker 1991). If these associations are connected together, they form perceptions in the consumer's mind that serve to consolidate brand image and indirectly increase brand awareness (Yoo et al. 2000). Brand image can also provide knowledge about the brand and has associations with different tangible and intangible attributes, thus enhancing differentiation and brand extension. It can contribute to the process of obtaining information and can help customers during their decision-making process. Owing to the fact that brand image can create positive feelings and attitudes towards the brand, it provides customers with a reason to buy (Aaker 1991).

In hospitality, brand image is considered as another key concept of customer-based brand equity due to its important role in determining the differential responses involved in brand equity (Kim and Kim 2004). In the hospitality literature on brand equity, this variable has been mainly considered as a unidimensional concept and was found to be positively related to other elements that contribute to brand equity enhancement. Thus, Nam et al. (2011) have examined the concept of self-congruence, i.e., the extent to which a consumer's ideal self-concept coincides with brand images of famous hotel and restaurant brands. Dioko and So (2012) have evaluated the social image of hotels in Macao, while Hsu et al. (2012) measured the brand image of Chinese hotels in terms of prestige, the "special feeling" offered by the hotel and the sophistication of their guests. Meanwhile, Tasci and Denizci Guillet (2011) used only one indicator to measure positive brand image in their experiment that sought to examine the effects of co-branding between a hotel and a restaurant. On the other hand, Lee and Kim's scale (2009) estimated brand image through two dimensions: organizational and symbolic.

However, the brand image scale proposed by Kim et al. (2003) and Kim and Kim (2005) is the most employed in the hospitality literature on brand equity (e.g. Kayaman and Arasli 2007; Hyun and Kim 2011; Šerić and Gil-Saura 2012; Šerić et al. 2016). These authors have developed a brand image scale in order to assess brand equity in luxury hotels and restaurant chains in South Korea. Thus, on the basis of the proposals of Aaker (1991) and Keller (1993) on one hand, and Low and Lamb Jr. (2000) on the other, they evaluated the brand image of luxury hotels using 14 indicators (comfortable, high level of service, clean image, luxury, expensive, high class, giving guests the feeling of being special, kind staff, large and spacious, quiet and relaxing, excessive service, long history, differentiated image and brand familiarity). Nevertheless, there is still no universally accepted valid and reliable scale that can be applied in measuring the image of hotel companies. This creates great confusion and ambiguity with the term, which makes its further development in the hospitality literature rather difficult.

Perceived quality

According to Aldridge and Rowley (1998), the concept of quality is considered as perceived quality in the services literature and is understood as the consumer's overall assessment of the service experience. Quality does not equal satisfaction, since it is a general attitude, while satisfaction is related to specific transactions. For Zeithaml (1988, p. 3), perceived quality is "the evaluation that a consumer makes about the excellence or superiority of a product." Zeithaml (1988) argued that consumer perceptions about quality change over time as a result of the increased availability of information, increased competition, and changes in expectations. Thereby, owing to customers' subjective assessment of quality, each customer's perception of the quality of the same product or service may differ (Hyun and Kim 2011). If a brand is perceived to be of high quality, this results in increased expected utility, which motivates consumers to purchase the same brand repeatedly (Erdem and Swait 1998). It can generate brand equity as it is strongly associated with price premiums, price elasticity, brand usage, and stock return (Aaker 1991).

There are two main approaches to the conceptualization of this variable in services in general and in hospitality in particular: one that understands service quality as a mismatch between consumers' expectations and perceptions of the service – SERVQUAL (Parasuraman et al. 1985), and another that focuses exclusively on consumer perceptions – SERVPERF (Cronin and Taylor 1992). Both scales evaluate the same quality dimensions (i.e. tangibles, reliability, responsiveness, assurance, empathy) with the difference that the second one supports only the perception-based aspect of the measure. However, the suitability of measuring the difference between expectations and perceptions in SERVQUAL was criticized due to the problems arising from such expectations, which may vary in different situations (Carman 1990). In addition, respondents had to evaluate the same set of items twice, which might cause boredom and confusion (Buttle 1996) and jeopardize the reliability of the results. Finally, conceiving service quality as the difference between expectations and perceptions creates ambiguity, as it can be confused with classic definitions of satisfaction (Cronin and Taylor 1992); this is why Cronin and Taylor (1992) proposed an alternative, SERVPERF model.

However, the discussion on the measurement of service quality as the difference between expectations and perceptions, or only in terms of perceptions, still exists. In their comparative study of the two models, Carrillat et al. (2007) carried out a meta-analysis of 17 empirical studies conducted in five continents, and concluded that the two scales are equally valid to predict service quality. On the basis of a thorough review of the literature on service quality, Seth et al. (2005) found that there is still no generally accepted conceptual definition nor a universal model of measuring perceived quality.

Relational approach

Brand loyalty

Loyalty is considered as a main driver of brand equity, owing to the fact that a loyal customer base represents a barrier to the entry of competitors, a basis for price premiums, and time to respond to competitor actions (Aaker 1991). Loyalty can be considered as a multidimensional construct, conceptualized from three main perspectives: a) behavioral; b) attitudinal; and c) composite (Bowen and Chen 2001). Oliver (1999, p. 34) approached loyalty from the behavioral perspective and defined it as:

> *a deeply held commitment to rebuy or repatronize a preferred product/service consistently in the future, thereby causing repetitive same-brand or same brand-set purchasing despite situational influences and marketing efforts having the potential to cause switching behaviour.*

This definition was criticized as it does not differentiate loyal customers from those who usually buy a product or service, as the simple repeat purchase might be provoked by inertia, indifference, or changed costs (Reichheld 2003). In this regard, Chahal and Kumari (2011) stressed the importance of the attitudinal approach and stated that loyalty indicates the degree to which a consumer's disposition toward a service is favorably inclined. This is connected with the consumer's willingness to recommend a service. In this way, loyal customers can also attract new ones through positive word-of-mouth communication (Mattila 2006). Finally, composite loyalty embraces both behavioral and attitudinal measures and considers frequency and recency of purchase, customer preferences, and propensity of brand switching (Bowen and Chen 2001). From the composite perspective, attitudinal loyalty and behavioral loyalty are closely related, since a consumer who has a positive attitude toward a company interacts with it through certain buying behavior (Kumar and Shah 2004). In general, literature suggests that attitudinal loyalty predicts behavioral loyalty (Choi et al. 2011).

From the review of various studies that have examined loyalty in the hotel environment, we note that the construct has been evaluated from the three identified perspectives, although attitudinal loyalty seems to receive the greatest interest (e.g. Barsky and Nash 2002; Kandampully and Suhartanto 2003; Ladhari 2012).

Brand trust

Morgan and Hunt (1994) define trust as the willingness of a party to rely on the other party in an exchange process. For Gulati (1995), trust is a company's belief that the other party will act positively and will not perform unexpected actions that have negative consequences for the company. This variable is presented as an essential element for successful relationships and a key factor in their quality, since it determines their duration and acts to reduce conflicts between the parties (Anderson and Narus 1990). Trust also defines the degree of cooperation (Morgan and Hunt 1994) and communication between the parties (Anderson and Weitz, 1992), and the level of involvement of the partners (Moorman et al. 1992).

Some studies have considered the role of trust in hotel brand equity formation (e.g. Kimpakorn and Tocquer 2010; Dioko and So 2012; Hsu et al. 2012, Šerić et al. 2016). Thus, Kimpakorn and Tocquer (2010) have evaluated brand trust in terms of confidence in the hotel brand, guests' previous experience, hotel brand reputation, honesty, keeping promises, and willingness to help and satisfy their guests. Their results revealed that brand trust predicts brand relationships in luxury hotels. On the other hand, Dioko and So (2012) developed a hotel brand equity measure and considered trust in the hotel staff as one of its dimensions. In particular, they examined trustworthiness, concern for the interests of the guests, and the guarantee that hotel staff do not take advantage of visitors. Finally, in their customer-based brand equity model for upscale hotels, Hsu et al. (2012) identified management trust as a significant component of hotel brand equity and stressed the importance of considering this variable in future operationalization of the concept. Šerić et al. (2016) employed this concept and found that brand trust is a significant driver of hotel brand equity.

Brand commitment

Commitment is described as an intention to build and maintain a long-term relationship (e.g. Anderson and Weitz 1992). According to Zins (2001), the commitment can be conceptualized from two perspectives: affective and calculated. While affective commitment is the sense of belonging and involvement of customers with the service provider, calculated commitment refers to the obligation felt by the client to continue the relationship with the supplier as a result of social or economic costs (Fullerton 2005). Overall, both dimensions of commitment positively influence repeat purchases, although the affective dimension has a stronger impact. In this sense, there is general consensus in the literature about the idea that affective commitment exerts the greatest effect on consumer loyalty (Bergman 2006).

Among the studies that have examined brand equity in the hotel industry, only a few have considered the dimension of commitment in their research (e.g. Kimpakorn and Tocquer 2010; Dioko and So 2012; Šerić et al. 2016). Kimpakorn and Tocquer (2010) have examined the relationship between employees' commitment and hotel brand equity and found that hotels with high brand equity have employees with greater brand commitment than hotels with low brand equity. The authors measured commitment through eight indicators reflecting the following five dimensions: affect, identification, willingness to stay, emotional attachment, and effort. On the other hand, Dioko and So (2012) and Šerić et al. (2016) approached the affective commitment of hotel guests, measured in terms of attachment, feelings, and affection towards the hotel brand. Both studies found a positive relationship between affective commitment and hotel brand equity.

Criticism and emerging issues regarding hotel brand equity

In the previous section we identified and discussed the variables that are considered in the literature as the most representative components of brand equity, as proposed by Aaker (1991) and Keller (1993). In addition, we examined brand trust and commitment owing to the strong relationship of these variables with brand loyalty.

However, although Aaker's (1991) and Keller's (1993) conceptualizations of brand equity continue to be the main benchmarks for the understanding of the concept, a number of studies have debated these two proposals. Thus, in their study on hotel customer-based brand equity, So and King (2010) argued that Aaker's (1991) assessment of brand equity does not involve marketing communication activities, while Keller's (1993) conceptualization of brand equity seems to be appropriate for manufactured goods. This is due to the high relevance of elements such as packaging, distribution channels and country of origin in Keller's (1993) proposal, which are not as important in the context of services. Therefore, it still seems to be unclear which dimensions actually drive brand equity and what is the role of marketing communications in its development.

Further, a number of other researchers have debated the proposals of Aaker (1991) and Keller (1993) and have questioned the real contribution of some of the proposed dimensions to brand equity building. Thus, brand awareness was found to be an insignificant dimension of customer-based brand equity in both marketing (e.g. Atilgan et al. 2005; Round and Roper 2012) and hospitality literature (e.g. Kim et al. 2003; Kim and Kim 2004, 2005; Bailey and Ball 2006; Kayaman and Arasli 2007; So and King 2010; Šerić et al. 2016), owing to the fact that brand awareness is focused on a company's actions rather than consumer perceptions (Round and Roper 2012). Another possible explanation of this finding might be the fact that perceptions based on experience are more likely to influence consumer decisions than brand awareness (So and King 2010). Besides, a number of hotels with high brand awareness do not always offer suitable service quality, meaning that there are other elements that are more important in brand equity building (Bailey and Ball 2006).

In addition, some studies concluded that brand image (e.g. Atilgan et al. 2005) and perceived quality (e.g. Atilgan et al. 2005; Wang et al. 2006) do not contribute significantly to brand equity development, due to the cognitive and attitudinal nature of these variables. This is why they do not have such a strong and significant effect on brand equity as loyalty does, a variable which also involves a behavioral component (Atilgan et al. 2005).

Further, a number of studies conducted in the field of hospitality (e.g. So and King 2010; Nam et al. 2011; Hsu et al. 2012; Šerić et al. 2016) argued that, rather than a brand equity dimension, brand loyalty is best understood as an outcome of brand equity. This is because brand equity is conceptually broader as it embraces brand familiarity, brand image, and perceived quality, while brand loyalty has been traditionally related to behavioral intentions, which is one of the effects of brand equity rather than a component of it (Brady et al. 2002).

Other difficulties might arise from including trust and commitment in brand equity operationalization due to the fact that the hospitality literature often considers these variables as components of other variables rather than independent constructs. Thus, for example, brand trust has been assessed as a dimension of service quality (e.g. Ladhari 2012), loyalty (e.g. Tideswell and Fredline 2004), or relationship quality (e.g. Kim et al. 2001), while commitment has been considered as a component of attitudinal loyalty (e.g. Tideswell and Fredline 2004; Choi et al. 2011) or even trust (e.g. Chathoth et al. 2011).

Finally, the most recent emerging issue on hotel brand equity seems to be whether to consider the variables that can contribute to brand equity formation as its dimensions or antecedents. Šerić et al. (2016) have discussed this issue in their recent work on drivers and consequences of hotel brand equity and concluded that, as well as other marketing concepts, hotel brand equity was first examined in terms of its dimensions (e.g. Kim and Kim 2004, 2005; Kimpakorn and Tocquer 2010; Hyun and Kim 2011; Šerić and Gil-Saura 2012). This means that variables such as brand awareness, brand image, perceived quality, and brand loyalty were considered as components of the concept. Subsequently, these variables have started to be considered as hotel brand equity antecedents and their impact on brand equity has been analyzed. Thus, So and King (2010) considered brand awareness and brand meaning as two direct antecedents of hotel brand equity, while Šerić et al. (2016) tested the impact of awareness, image, perceived quality, trust, and commitment on the overall brand equity of hotel firms.

Conclusion

The contribution of this chapter lies in identifying and discussing variables that are critical to brand equity creation in the hotel context. The findings suggest that hotel brand equity is still far from being a well-established concept. Six variables were examined in this study, three related to perceptions of the customer, i.e. awareness, image, and perceived quality, and the other three characterized by the relational component, i.e., loyalty, trust, and commitment. Having discussed some contradictory findings regarding the contribution of these variables to hotel brand equity creation, one of the challenges for future work is to determine which among them are highly significant for the development of hotel brand equity and which are not. In addition, future contributions need to establish whether perceptual variables play a more important role in creation of hotel brand equity than relational ones or *vice versa*. In order to do so, the definition and operationalization boundaries of these variables need to be well-established, as previous findings have revealed that differences among some of them still remain unclear.

Furthermore, the contribution of some other variables to hotel brand equity building could be considered, e.g. satisfaction. In fact, the reason why Aaker (1991) included brand loyalty in brand equity evaluation is the essential role of satisfaction in the brand equity building process. Although some researchers have included satisfaction in their studies on hotel brand equity, they have considered it as a loyalty item (e.g. Kim and Kim 2004, 2005; Kayaman and Arasli 2007; Hyun and Kim 2011; Šerić and Gil-Saura 2012). Future research should consider satisfaction as a separate construct, and satisfied customers are not necessarily loyal. In addition, the role of marketing communications in hotel brand equity creation needs to be considered (So and King, 2010). In particular, integrated marketing communications can influence some aspects of hotel brand equity (Šerić and Gil-Saura 2012), owing to the fact that they represent the "voice" of the brand through dialogue and creation of relationships with consumers (Keller 2009). However, their real potential still needs to be explored, especially regarding the way in which consumer perceptions of integrated marketing communications can influence the extra added value in consumers' minds.

Finally, as suggested by Šerić et al. (2016), more studies are necessary to establish the relationship between brand equity and loyalty. Competitive models that consider loyalty as a dimension and consequence of brand equity should be proposed and empirically tested. In addition, components of brand equity could begin to be considered as its antecedents in order to provide a better understanding of the concept.

Acknowledgments

The authors are thankful for the support of the projects ECO2016-76553-R and ECO2013-43353-R of the Spanish Ministry of Economy and Competitiveness.

References

Aaker, D.A., 1991. *Managing brand equity*. Free Press, New York.
Aldridge, S., and Rowley, J., 1998. Measuring customer satisfaction in higher education. *Quality Assurance in Education*, 6 (4), 197–204.

Anderson, E. and Weitz, B., 1992. The use of pledges to build and sustain commitment in distribution channels. *Journal of Marketing Research*, 29 (1), 18–34.

Anderson, J.C. and Narus, J.A., 1990. A model of distributor firm and manufacturer firm working partnerships. *Journal of Marketing*, 54 (1), 42–58.

Atilgan, E., Aksoy, S., and Akinci, S. 2005. Determinants of the brand equity: A verification approach in the beverage industry in Turkey. *Marketing Intelligence & Planning*, 23 (3), 237–248.

Bailey, R. and Ball, S., 2006. An exploration of the meanings of hotel brand equity. *The Service Industries Journal*, 26 (1), 15–38.

Barsky, J. and Nash, L. 2002. Evoking emotion: Affective keys to hotel loyalty. *Cornell Hotel and Restaurant Administration Quarterly*, 43 (1), 39–46.

Bergman, M.E., 2006. The relationship between affective and normative commitment: Review and research agenda. *Journal of Organizational Behaviour*, 27 (5), 635–667.

Biel, A.L., 1992. How brand image drives brand equity. *Journal of Advertising Research*, 32 (6), 6–12.

Bowen, J.T. and Chen, S.L., 2001. The relationship between customer loyalty and customer satisfaction. *International Journal of Contemporary Hospitality Management*, 13 (5), 213–217.

Brady, M.K., Cronin, J.J. Jr. and Brand, R.R., 2002. Performance-only measurement of service quality: A replication and extension. *Journal of Business Research*, 55 (1), 17–31.

Buttle, F., 1996. SERVQUAL: Review, critique, research agenda. *European Journal of Marketing*, 30 (1), 8–32.

Carman, J.M., 1990. Consumer perceptions of service quality: An assessment of the SERVQUAL dimensions. *Journal of Retailing*, 66 (1), 33–55.

Carrillat, F.A., Jaramillo, F., and Mulki, J.P., 2007. The validity of the SERVQUAL and SERVPERF scales: A meta-analytic view of 17 years of research across five continents. *International Journal of Service Industry Management*, 18 (5), 472–490.

Chahal, H. and Kumari, N., 2011. Consumer perceived value and consumer loyalty in the healthcare sector. *Journal of Relationship Marketing*, 10 (2), 88–112.

Chathoth, P.K., Mak, B., Sim, J., Jauhari, V. and Manaktola, K. (2011). Assessing dimensions of organizational trust across cultures: A comparative analysis of U.S. and Indian full service hotels. *International Journal of Hospitality Management*, 30 (2), 233–242.

Choi, H.Y., Lehto, X., and Brey, E.T., 2011. Investigating resort loyalty: Impacts of the family life cycle. *Journal of Hospitality Marketing & Management*, 20 (1), 121–141.

Cronin, J.J. Jr. and Taylor, S.A., 1992. Measuring service quality: A reexamination and extension. *Journal of Marketing*, 56 (3), 55–68.

Dioko, L. and So, S.I.A., 2012. Branding destinations versus branding hotels in a gaming destination: Examining the nature and significance of co-branding effects in the case study of Macao. *International Journal of Hospitality Management*, 31 (2), 554–563.

Erdem, T. and Swait, J., 1998. Brand equity as a signalling phenomenon. *Journal of Consumer Psychology*, 7 (2), 131–157.

Fullerton, G., 2005. How commitment both enables and undermines marketing relationships. *European Journal of Marketing*, 39 (11/12), 1372–1388.

Gulati, R., 1995. Does familiarity breed trust? The implications of repeated ties for contractual choice in alliances. *Academy of Management Journal*, 38 (1), 85–112.

Hsu, C.H.C., Oh, H., and Assaf, A.G., 2012. A customer-based brand equity model for upscale hotels. *Journal of Travel Research*, 51 (1), 81–93.

Hyun, S.S. and Kim, W., 2011. Dimensions of brand equity in the chain restaurant industry. *Cornell Hospitality Quarterly*, 52 (4), 429–437.

Kandampully, J. and Suhartanto, D., 2003. The role of customer satisfaction and image in gaining customer loyalty in the hotel industry. *Journal of Hospitality Marketing & Management*, 10 (1/2), 3–25.

Kayaman, R. and Arasli, H., 2007. Customer based brand equity: Evidence from the hotel industry. *Managing Service Quality*, 17 (1), 92–109.

Keller, K.L., 1993. Conceptualizing, measuring, and managing customer-based brand equity. *Journal of Marketing*, 57 (1), 1–22.

Keller, K.L., 2003. *Strategic brand management: Building, measuring, and managing brand equity.* 2nd ed. Prentice Hall, Upper Saddle River.

Keller, K.L., 2009. Building strong brands in a modern marketing communications environment. *Journal of Marketing Communications*, 15 (2/3), 139–155.

Kim, H.B. and Kim, W.G., 2005. The relationship between brand equity and firms' performance in luxury hotels and restaurants. *Tourism Management*, 26 (4), 549–560.

Kim, H.B., Kim, W.G., and An, J.A., 2003. The effect of customer-based brand equity on firms' financial performance. *Journal of Customer Marketing*, 20 (4), 335–351.

Kim, W.G., Han, J.S., and Lee, E., 2001. Effects of relationship marketing on repeat purchase and word of mouth. *Journal of Hospitality & Tourism Research*, 25 (3), 272–288.

Kim, W.G., Jin-Sun, B. and Kim, H.J., 2008. Multidimensional customer-based brand equity and its consequences in midpriced hotels. *Journal of Hospitality & Tourism Research*, 32 (2), 235–254.

Kim, W.G. and Kim, H.B., 2004. Measuring customer-based restaurant brand equity: Investigating the relationship between brand equity and firms' performance. *Cornell Hotel and Restaurant Administration Quarterly*, 45 (2), 115–131.

Kimpakorn, N. and Tocquer, G., 2010. Service brand equity and employee brand commitment. *Journal of Services Marketing*, 24 (5), 378–388.

Kumar, V. and Shah, D., 2004. Building and sustaining profitable customer loyalty for the 21st century. *Journal of Retailing*, 80 (4), 317–330.

Ladhari, R., 2012. The lodging quality index: An independent assessment of validity and dimensions. *International Journal of Contemporary Hospitality Management*, 24 (4), 628–652.

Lee, J.W. and Kim, H.B., 2009. Impacts of perception to alliance companies on hotel's brand equity according to the types of vertical integration. *International Journal of Tourism Sciences*, 9 (2), 1–21.

Lee, H.M., Lee, C.C., and Wu, C.C., 2011. Brand image strategy affects brand equity after M&A. *European Journal of Marketing*, 45 (7/8), 1091–1111.

Leeman, D. and Reynolds, D., 2012. Trust and outsourcing: Do perceptions of trust influence the retention of outsourcing providers in the hospitality industry? *International Journal of Hospitality Management*, 31 (2), 601–608.

Lemmink, J., Schuijf, A., and Streukens, S., 2003. The role of corporate image and company employment image in explaining application intentions. *Journal of Economic Psychology*, 24, 1–15.

Low, G.S. and Lamb Jr., C.W., 2000. The measurement and dimensionality of brand associations. *Journal of Product and Brand Management*, 9 (6), 350–368.

Mattila, A.S., 2006. How affective commitment boosts guest loyalty (and promotes frequent-guest programs). *Cornell Hospitality Quarterly*, 47 (2), 174–181.

Moorman, C., Zaltman, G., and Deshpandé, R., 1992. Relationship between providers and users of market research: The dynamics of trust within and between organizations. *Journal of Marketing Research*, 29 (3), 314–328.

Morgan, R.M. and Hunt, S.D., 1994. The commitment-trust theory of relationship marketing. *Journal of Marketing*, 58 (3), 20–38.

Nam, J., Ekinci, Y. and Whyatt, G., 2011. Brand equity, brand loyalty and consumer satisfaction. *Annals of Tourism Research*, 38 (3), 1009–1030.

Oliveira-Castro, J.M., Foxall, G.R., James, V.K., Pohl, R.H.B.F., Dias M.B., and Chang, S.W., 2008. Consumer-based brand equity and brand performance. *The Service Industries Journal*, 28 (4), 445–461.

Oliver, R.L., 1999. Whence consumer loyalty?. *Journal of Marketing*, 63 (special issue), 33–44.

Parasuraman, A., Zeithaml, V., and Berry, L., 1985. A conceptual model of service quality and its implications for further research. *Journal of Marketing*, 49 (4), 41–50.

Prasad, K. and Dev, C.S., 2000. Managing hotel brand equity: A customer-centric framework for assessing performance. *Cornell Hotel and Restaurant Administration Quarterly*, 41 (3), 22–31.

Reichheld, F.F., 2003. The one number you need to grow. *Harvard Business Review*, 81 (12), 46–54.

Round, D. and Roper, S., 2012. Exploring consumer brand name equity: Gaining insight through the investigation of response to name change. *European Journal of Marketing*, 46 (7/8), 938–951.

Šerić, M. and Gil-Saura, I., 2012. ICT, IMC, and brand equity in high-quality hotels of Dalmatia: An analysis from guest perceptions. *Journal of Hospitality Marketing & Management*, 21 (8), 821–851.

Šerić, M., Mikulić J. and Gil-Saura, I., 2016. Exploring relationships between customer-based brand equity and its drivers and consequences in the hotel context: An impact-asymmetry assessment, *Current Issues in Tourism*, doi:10.1080/13683500.2016.1209163

Seth, M., Deshmukh, S.G., and Vrat, P., 2005. Service quality models: A review. *International Journal of Quality & Reliability Management*, (22) 9, 913–949.

So, K.K.G. and King, C., 2010. When experience matters: Building and measuring hotel brand equity. The customers' perspective. *International Journal of Contemporary Hospitality Management*, 22 (5), 589–608.

Srivastava, R. and Shocker, A.D., 1991. Brand equity: A perspective on its meaning and measurement. *Marketing Science Institute Working Paper Series*, Marketing Science Institute Cambridge, 91–124.

Tasci, A.D.A. and Denizci Guillet, B., 2011. It affects, it affects not: A quasi-experiment on the transfer effect of co-branding on consumer-based brand equity of hospitality products. *International Journal of Hospitality Management*, 30 (4), 774–782.

Tideswell, C. and Fredline, E. 2004. Developing and rewarding loyalty to hotels: The guest's perspective. *Journal of Hospitality & Tourism Research*, 28 (2), 186–208.

Wang, Y., Kandampully, J.A., Lo, H.P. and Shi, G., 2006. The roles of brand equity and corporate reputation in CRM: A Chinese study. *Corporate Reputation Review*, 9 (3), 179–197

Yoo, B. and Donthu, N., 2001. Developing and validating a multidimensional consumer-based brand equity scale. *Journal of Business Research*, 52 (1), 1–14.

Yoo, B., Donthu, N., and Lee S., 2000. An examination of selected marketing mix elements and brand equity. *Journal of the Academy of Marketing Science*, 28 (2), 195–211.

Zeithaml, V.A., 1988. Consumer perceptions of price, quality and value: A means-end model and synthesis of evidence. *Journal of Marketing*, 52 (3), 2–22.

Zins, A.H., 2001. Relative attitudes and commitment in customer loyalty models. *International Journal of Service Industry Management*, 12 (3), 269–294.

Further reading

Aaker, D.A., 1996. Measuring brand equity across products and markets. *California Management Review*, 38 (3), 102–120.

Berry, L.L., 2000. Cultivating service brand equity. *Journal of the Academy of Marketing Science*, 28 (1), 128–137.

Cobb-Walgren, C.J., Ruble, C.A., and Donthu, N., 1995. Brand equity, brand preference and purchase intent. *Journal of Advertising*, 24 (3), 25–40.

Denizci, B. and Tasci, A.D.A., 2010. Modeling the commonly-assumed relationship between human capital and brand equity in tourism. *Journal of Hospitality Marketing & Management*, 19 (6), 610–628.

Hsu, T.H., Hung, L.C., and Tang, J.W., 2012. An analytical model for building brand equity in hospitality firms. *Annals for Operations Research*, 195 (1), 355–378.

Sun, L.B. and Ghiselli, R., 2010. Developing an empirical model of hotel brand equity based on Aaker's perspective. *Journal of Quality Assurance in Hospitality and Tourism*, 11 (3), 147–161.

Xu, J.B. and Chan, A., 2010. A conceptual framework of hotel experience and customer-based brand equity: Some research questions and implications. *International Journal of Contemporary Hospitality Management*, 22 (2), 174–193.

20

Sensory marketing in hotels

Understanding of sensory triggers for hotel operations

Bona Kim, Saerom Wang and Cindy Yoonjoung Heo

Introduction

Sensory marketing is regarded as a marketing strategy that engages consumers' senses and subsequently influences their perceptions, judgment and even behavior (Krishna 2012). It is based on appealing to one of, or a combination of, the five senses: sight, smell, sound, touch, and taste. In order to implement a sensory marketing strategy, companies can create intuitive triggers that appeal to the basic senses, and particular triggers lead to customers forming perceptions on abstract notions of products and services (Krishna 2012). Sensory marketing ultimately aims to provide consumers with memorable experiences in order to build a sustainable image and to elicit positive consumer behavior such as purchase intentions (Hultén, Broweus, & Van Dijk 2009; Pullman & Gross 2004). The existing literature has confirmed that stimulating consumers' senses increases their brand loyalty (Brakus, Schmitt, & Zarantonello 2009) as well as their willingness to pay more for the product (Lindstrom 2005). As such, sensory stimuli forge powerful connections between consumers and the brand. Such interaction allows sensory marketing to offer more individualized experiences than any other marketing strategy (Hultén et al. 2009).

A basic concept of sensation in sensory marketing was developed by Hultén et al. (2009). According to their work, sensation refers to how a company can express itself as sensory triggers are passed to the human brain through sense expressions. Sensations must be created and need to be strong enough for consumers to be stimulated by sensory expressions and to have a sensory experience.

In the process of sensory experience, sensation is created through five senses as a key element and is the initial stage that efficiently engages customers and generates their perceptions, judgment, and behavior. In addition, forming perceptions through sensation is a way of generating self-awareness or self-understanding of information about products or services. Subsequently, perceptions lead to certain customer behaviors (Brakus et al. 2009; Lindstrom 2005).

Hotels have adopted various sensory strategies in providing unique hotel stay experiences, and customers are aware that hotels are a provider of experiences through visible products and invisible services. Customers' perceptions are shaped when they coalesce sensory information formed from encounters with products and services (Carbone & Haeckel 1994). The encounters are created in the form of multisensory attributes and the sensory aspect is one of the dimensions of the customer experience (Knutson, Beck, Kim, & Cha 2009; Schmitt 1999; Titz 2008).

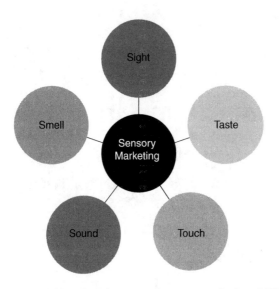

Figure 20.1   Five elements of sensory marketing: 3S2T
Source: Developed from Hultén et al. (2009).

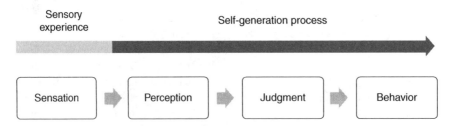

Figure 20.2   Process of sensory experience
Source: Modified from a framework of sensory marketing by Krishna (2012).

Sensory marketing is growing gradually as a research topic and sensory triggers are a key point that sheds light on customers' perceptions and their behavior (Krishna 2012). A few studies on consumer behavior have paid increasing attention to sensory marketing in the last decade (Krishna 2012). For example, Walls, Okumus, Wang, and Kwun (2011) identified several triggers for sensory attributes in the physical environment, such as color, odor, temperature, humidity, noise, music, and view. Kim and Perdue (2013) noted the significant effect of sensory attributes on hotel selection; however, sensory experience is only considered in two dimensions of room quality and overall atmosphere (e.g. cleanliness, comfortable bed, quietness, music, interior, and exterior). Focusing on the hotel lobby, Countryman and Jang (2006) pointed out four atmospheric elements (style, layout, colors, and lighting) and the effect of hotel lobbies on customer impressions. Their findings show that style, colors, and lighting have significant effects on customers' impression of a hotel lobby, whereas layout does not have such an effect. It was found that color is the most determinant attribute. However, little research has been conducted in the hotel context (Countryman & Jang 2006; Kim & Perdue 2013; Walls et al. 2011). There remains a lack of understanding about how hotels are managed from the sensory marketing point of view and which sensory triggers can aid hotel operations. This chapter will discuss how sensory marketing can be applied to hotel operations based on different types of sensory triggers.

Hotel sensory triggers

Sense of sight

Visual cues are one of the most widely applied sensory elements of marketing in practice, and positively affect a brand's identity and value (Underwood 2003). Companies can appeal to consumers visually through physical product and service landscapes such as shops and websites, as well as marketing activities such as advertising (Hultén et al. 2009). Visual sensory cues, such as package size and shape of containers, can be helpful in a company's marketing efforts as they can be informative (Hine 1995): for instance, package size signals how much food is contained in the product. Such visual cues therefore contribute to either increasing or lowering levels of consumption of the product (Wansink, Painter, & North 2005).

The hotel industry is composed of special visual cues that may be characterized by the nature of the service being provided. More specifically, service landscapes are where the most prevalent visual cues are utilized and hotels strive to provide visual cues to consumers across different departments. For instance, the oldest hotel in Hong Kong, The Peninsula Hong Kong, possesses its own unique Peninsula style and identity amongst the globe's most prestigious hotels (Bloomberg 2005). When guests arrive at the hotel, they are first greeted and welcomed at the entrance by an iconic Peninsula pageboy wearing a round-shaped white hat with a golden tassel. The pageboys are the personified example of hotel service as they connect with guests by recognizing guests and guests' names and are always ready to respond to their wants and needs. The traditional pageboy attire can generate a particular hotel image visualized at the entrance, and staff attitudes can be at the heart of the guest experience. Moreover, the tradition has been applied to retailing as a way to portray the image of the hotel. Hotel souvenirs such as the Peninsula bear as well as a snowman version of the pageboy are a way to represent the hotel staff, family, and even the hotel's heritage (The Peninsula 2013).

In an effort to visualize a hotel's check-in process, front desk staff demonstrate how guests can use the additional services by presenting them with a written service letter including information, a personalized greeting, service hours, food and beverage (F&B) offerings, and policies. However, the paperless check-in process enables guests to recognize eco-friendly policies in hotel management and also showcases visualization of the hotel's strategy. Meanwhile, a hotel's own specific branded folder with a pen represents the brand identity of the hotel.

At F&B facilities, a candle can be a tool for not only lighting but also creating ambience in the bar/lounge. It enables guests to read the menu (its physical function) and also emotionally provides a warm and relaxing ambiance. Lighting can be helpful in creating a mood that matches the product characteristics or in providing information, such as utilizing naked strip lights to showcase low prices (Stone, Bleibaum, & Thomas 2012). A neat, fresh, clean, and presentable table setting is identified as a basic element for visual stimuli, including table presentation, flatware, linens, napkins, plates, and vases. In addition, a preset menu on tables, signature food and beverage, a hotel's own cake, fresh and high quality food and beverages are examples of visual appeal. Overall cleanliness of the floor, walls, doors, ceiling, windows, furniture, equipment, and décor items are some of the significant visual cues through which the image of a hotel is developed and projected. For example, for public areas decorative features such as artwork, plants or fresh floral displays are other key visual triggers. Appropriate food presentation and table settings for guests are also identified as visual triggers. In some cases, food is required to be provided in a fresh and high quality form and with an appropriate portion size. Moreover, each beverage needs to be presented correctly: for example, each beverage needs to be served with a particular utensil package set or in appropriate glasses. In addition, cleanliness in the dining area is considered to be a basic but vital trigger in guests' visual perceptions. Taken together, these servicescapes exert great influence on the overall atmosphere of F&B facilities, which in turn positively influences customers' perceptions of the hotel as well as their behavioral intention.

In hotel rooms, amenities and promotional materials help hotels to communicate their strategic or marketing messages visually to customers. Linen re-use program notifications are presented in an effort to visualize hotels' eco-friendly marketing strategies (Goldstein, Griskevicius, & Cialdini 2007). Items available in closets with the hotel brand identity such as bathrobes with the hotel logo as well as hotel-branded notepads and pens are also important tools. Also, printed collateral stationery such as envelopes, memo pads, and brochures are used as other visual marketing materials to consistently remind guests of the hotel brand. A hotel communicates its commitment to safety through the installation of smoke detectors in each room and through door safety features.

Additionally, hotel management has attempted to advertise what hotels aim to promote in different ways. For example, hotel-related magazines and branded magazines are made available to guests in strategic places in the hotel. The television's guest directory is used as a direct advertisement to provide information about the hotel's amenities. Another effort made by hotels to visualize their offerings is in making tangible the service provided by staff. Concierge staff are required to offer guests information in a professional manner, e.g. when making a reservation for a guest, the reservation is noted on a printed confirmation card. For all hotel departments, staff uniforms and appearance are emphasized as basic visual triggers. Moreover, the overall attitude of staff members is also another key trigger in hotel operations.

Sense of smell

Smell is one of the most durable and powerful sensory stimulations, and is one that endures in individuals' memories up to months or years after exposure, while other sensory cues decay at a faster rate (Zucco 2003). Scent attracts consumers' attention toward a product or a brand in the short or long term and it grows into part of the brand's identity as well as its image (Bosmans 2006). Scent also allows consumers to remember and recall the brand more easily and contributes to the perceived quality of the product (Chebat & Michon 2003). Smell sensory cues are also capable of increasing consumers' browsing time in a store as well as the money spent (Morrin & Chebat 2005). Sense of smell is also closely related to emotional state and well-being such as pleasure (Goldkuhl & Styvén 2007). Smell is closely linked to consumers' emotions as the brain's olfactory system detects smells, fast-tracks signals to the limbic system, and links emotions with memories (Soars 2009). Lung and Prowant (2009) reported that guests at the Las Vegas Hilton spent 50 percent more time playing slot machines when the air around them was scented with a floral fragrance. In fact, memories triggered by smell tend to be more emotional than memories evoked by any other type of stimulus (Aggleton & Waskett 1999). When a positive emotional memory is formed, it increases consumers' brand loyalty (Grisaffe & Nguyen 2011).

Despite its importance, the sense of smell has been rarely identified as a sensory marketing tool in hotels. Recently, however, luxury hotels have launched their own scents, according to strict standards, for the hotel's common areas. In fact, companies generally try to link their brand image to specific scents, which are referred to as signature scents (Zemke & Shoemaker 2008). For example, Intercontinental Hotels Group uses the sense of smell to entice brand loyalty. Each

IHG brand caters to different target markets and therefore offers on-property scent options tailored to their specific guests' expectations and desires. Holiday Inn Hotels have a universal scent that is used at all properties worldwide to create a consistent and common experience. Such signature scents serve as a trademark that customers recall when they are reminded about the brand. In creating a signature scent, product congruency (i.e. the natural match between the smell and the product) helps to enhance customer satisfaction, amount of time spent in the store, and willingness to purchase the product in general (Lindstrom 2005). The effectiveness of product congruency is intensified when the consumers are in a good mood. When product congruency is high, in other words when the match between the product and smell is high, consumers are likely to have a positive brand experience, especially when they are in a good mood. This indicates that the use of a signature scent that is in line with the hotel's image should bring about positive responses from customers.

Sense of hearing

Sound is also capable of stimulating consumers' emotions and feelings, which eventually influences their behavioral intentions as well as brand perceptions (Krishna 2012). Sound has been widely utilized in marketing communications such as in TV commercials to intensify the message and strengthen brand awareness (Jackson 2003). Sound sensory stimuli such as music connect consumers and brands as memories are created, which eventually have a positive influence on consumer behavior such as their intention to purchase and the duration of time they spend in the store (Milliman 1982). Sound is especially effective in influencing consumer behavior when consumers are uncertain about a purchase (Herrington 1996). In some cases, sound itself has a more powerful influence on consumers' intention to purchase the product than the product itself (Morrison 2001).

In a hotel, ambient music is identified as an auditory trigger. Ambient music tends to be used in the lobby, while soft or lively background music tends to be used (without disrupting guests' conversations) during breakfast and dinner in hotel restaurants, and in the bar/lounge or club lounge. Use of music is an effective sound trigger as it embodies meaning and feelings (Stout & Leckenby 1988). In addition, music can affect customers' moods and actual time spent in a specific place and their perceptions of how they are spending their time (Krishna 2011). In fact, one of the most effective tools as a sensory marketing strategy is to create customized music. For example, W Hotels has invited global music directors and DJs to produce a sound platform and has defined the iconic identity of the W Hotel brand (W Hotels Worldwide 2016). The Plaza hotel in South Korea has worked with musicians to create a boutique sound compilation album (The Plaza Sound 2016). The sounds provide a changing boutique hotel ambience over time in different types of music genres. The signature sounds are used to represent a unique hotel brand and identity and to provide guests with a new audio experience.

Next, voice and language are other important auditory triggers in sensory marketing (Krishna 2012). Staff's tone of voice is controlled as a strategic trigger in order to influence guests' perceptions of a hotel brand. For example, at the reservation desk, a live voice, a hint of warmth in the receptionist's voice, and even a pleasant (but not monotonous) tone of voice is required in verbal communication between the customer and staff. In addition, the language used in conversation is another auditory strategy utilized. While hotel staff are required to speak to guests in local languages, in reality, using the guest's first language is likely to provide him or her with a stronger sense of belonging (Myers–Scotton 1998, 2002). That is, guests are likely to feel a stronger level of a sense of closeness and in-group association when using their first language. In fact, auditory communication between the employee and the guest is more effective than written communication. For instance, at check-in, an upselling strategy or CRM strategy could involve the receptionist appealing to guests' sense of hearing. In other words, employees' verbal communication with the guest instead of written communication is more effective for marketing strategies because it involves intimate interaction between the employee and the guest. Front desk staff verbally approach and ask for the guest's email address in order to develop the hotel guest e-folio, and mention the loyalty program of the hotel brand to promote its membership program. During the check-in process, most information is provided by hotel staff verbally through proactive conversations. The bellhop or concierge facilities and services available in the hotel property are described and most information about room features and complimentary services available during the guest's stay are verbally explained. These verbal communication strategies are required to be brief, helpful, and conversational. Lastly, guests are asked to report their satisfaction level in an effort to understand guests' perceptions of provided services at all stages.

At F&B facilities in hotels, staff members' personal recommendations and offering a second round of drinks as well as additional assistance are examples of auditory stimuli in a bar/lounge. At restaurants, special and house specialties, recommendations of menu items, staff members' verbal suggestions of signature menu recommendations are also effective upselling strategies compared with other forms of communication. In a similar manner, servers are required – after every course – to ask their customers if they are satisfied with their meal. Therefore, the verbal suggestions by staff at F&B facilities play a significant auditory role in the hotel's marketing strategy. As a result, across all departments, the use of appropriate verbiage, warm conversation, and personal recognition such as calling guests by their name and checking their satisfaction and dissatisfaction levels are required.

Sense of touch

A strategy addressing customers' sense of touch involves physical and psychological interaction between the consumer and the product (Hultén 2011). Sensory marketing utilizing the sense of touch, also referred to as tactile marketing, works as a conduit through which brands express their identity as well as their values (Moor 2003). When consumers are prompted to touch, squeeze, turn, and invert products, they are unconsciously engaged in an interaction with the product, which in turn increases the chances of impulsive purchase of the product (Hultén et al. 2009). As with other senses, a tactile strategy increases consumers' likelihood to purchase the product (Soars 2009). As consumers receive information about the product through tactile sensory stimulation, positive affect is aroused, which in turn influences consumers' attitudes towards the product (Peck & Wiggins 2006). In some cases, it is not necessary per se for every product to entail a tactile sensory experience. However, when objects in the surroundings of a hospitality space provide a pleasurable touch experience to consumers, this influences consumers' behavior. For instance, the tactile experience of the chair can be an important determinant in a consumer's overall evaluation of the dining experience depending on how comfortable it is. The texture of the food that consumers touch can also shape their experience, although appraisal of such a tactile experience can be subjective according to their preferences.

In hotels, items related to sleeping can include tactile stimuli (as part of a marketing strategy) since a hotel's bedding is in direct contact with the guest's skin. For instance, Westin Hotels have developed a unique sleeping experience they call the "Heavenly Bed Experience" and promote it in the form of tactile marketing (The Heavenly Bed 2016). They attempt to offer a restful and relaxing night's sleep by providing a specially designed Heavenly Bed and bedding. The Heavenly bathrobe, towels, and even all bedlinen is specially designed to awaken guests' sense of touch.

Another factor through which touch is expressed is temperature. Room temperature is always controlled and checked to ensure that the room is at the right temperature. Warm and relaxing ambiance and a comfortable room temperature are also identified as important features for bars. At restaurants, getting the food temperature right and keeping the room at a comfortable temperature are important in stimulating the tactile sense of guests. In fact, ensuring the temperature matches the product is necessary to enhance consumers' overall experience; when ordering a hot cup of coffee, consumers would have a much more pleasant experience if they receive a hot cup rather than a warm or cold cup (Williams & Bargh 2008).

Management interaction (e.g. chef, manager, non-uniformed supervisor, or sommelier) with guests is also important for enhancing the sense of touch. A tactile strategy encompasses employees' interaction with the guest, for instance by the employee explaining the menu to the guest. While such direct interaction between the employees and the guests enhances their overall experience and satisfaction level, indirect interaction can also be a helpful tactile sensory strategy in supporting guests when employees are unavailable for direct interaction with guests. In this sense, reading material is provided to a single diner during a meal as an alternative to direct interaction between the guest and the employee. For breakfast, newspapers are provided as a personalized tactile strategy.

Sense of taste

Taste is considered to be a unique emotional sense, as it facilitates social exchanges among people and connects consumers with products and brands at a personal level (Hultén et al. 2009). Previous studies argued that taste has the capacity to lure consumers to stay in the shop longer, which results in a stronger likelihood to spend more (Krishna 2011). Taste sensory cues usually interact with other types of senses, in an example of symbiosis (Hultén et al. 2009). In general, it is often connected to other senses such as smell and sight in getting consumers engaged with the product. Taste is closely associated with smell, which plays an important role in individuals' taste perceptions. In fact, taste also maximizes the effectiveness of interplay between other types of senses and the consumer (Hultén et al. 2009).

Hotel properties possess various F&B-related facilities and several particular tastes have been indicated as taste triggers. Sense of taste is recognized particularly at F&B facilities and departments such as the bar/lounge and restaurants. Some of the hotels have their own strategy in how taste is utilized in their product presentation. At the bar/lounge, savory snacks should be made available for guests and should be served at the right temperature. Furthermore, guests' special preferences are provided for such as a gluten-free menu, healthy options, age-appropriate menus for children, items made with organic, hormone-free, and preservative-free ingredients. Moreover, providing welcome food or drinks to consumers in the lobby or in the guest's hotel room, as a lot of hotels do, is a good differentiation strategy in stimulating consumers' senses. For example, DoubleTree Hotels by Hilton have been welcoming guests with a warm, chocolate chip cookie at check-in for more than 25 years.

As outlined by Hultén et al. (2009), expressions such as name, presentation and knowledge play an important role in how consumers react to the taste sensory cues. The names of dishes on the menu at a restaurant can be influential in how consumers process the sensory cues; for instance, descriptive menu names were found to be effective in a restaurant, increasing sales of the descriptively named menu by nearly 30 percent. Another important determinant that shapes individuals' taste experience is the presentation, that is, the color of the food in a dish, and eventually can influence consumers' appetite (Klosse, Riga, Cramwinckel, & Saris 2004). Furthermore, the restaurant's setting influences the taste experience to a great extent, i.e. the quality of the consumer's experience is further enhanced when the quality of the dining setting is perceived to be high (Edwards, Meiselman, Edwards, & Lesher 2003).

Conclusion

A hotel is a unique property that includes internal resources of a physical/technical nature and human-related resources such as employees (Grönroos 1982). Within these resources, a hotel attempts to provide sensory stimuli and to implement a sensory marketing strategy in order to create irreplaceable experiences and turn one-time customers into loyal ones (Hultén et al. 2009; Pullman & Gross 2004). This study explored sensory triggers in real hotel operations from the sensory marketing perspective. The following interesting conclusions can be made.

First, particular staff-oriented triggers are commonly identified as visual and auditory cues across all departments. There are a variety of sensory triggers which hotels generally practice; however, in practice, appropriate verbiage, staff uniforms, and the appearance of personnel are vital and fundamental cues in sensory marketing strategies insofar as they support the assertion that the most important asset in hotel management is hotel staff (Kim, Kim, & Heo 2016).

Second, appropriate and visible products are placed in different parts of a hotel as per the hotel's sensory marketing strategy. Despite its importance, it is not clear how hotels are utilizing color as their visual marketing strategy. Color is one of the major elements of visual cues that connects brands and consumers emotionally. Furthermore, when a color that matches the brand's identity is used, it increases brand awareness as well as the brand image. Different colors have different characteristics and psychological effects (e.g. red attracts the eye and symbolizes seduction) (Hultén et al. 2009). While blue tones tend to calm individuals, yellow is the color that human eyes notice most readily. Therefore, depending on the characteristics of the brand, the right color must be used, and the intended psychological effects must be taken into account.

In conclusion, while single sensory cues can be utilized, more than one of the five human senses can also be employed in the product and service consumption experience, which is referred to as a *multi-sensory experience*. For instance, vision, hearing, touch, and smell could converge in the consumption process in order to develop brand experience and brand image (Thesen, Vibell, Calvert, & Österbauer 2004). In fact, a synergistic effect is achieved and consumers have a more positive brand experience when certain senses are stimulated together, such as when taste and smell are employed simultaneously (Krishna 2011). However, using too many sensory triggers could confuse consumers (Soars 2009). Therefore, multi-sensory marketing strategies need to be carefully planned to be effective, with hotel management applying the appropriate mix of sensory stimuli.

References

Aggleton, J. P. and Waskett, L. (1999) "The ability of odours to serve as state-dependent cues for real-world memories: Can Viking smells aid the recall of Viking experiences?," *British Journal of Psychology* 90(1), 1–7.

Bloomberg (2005) Picturing Peninsula Hotels by Adeline Chong. Retrieved from www.bloomberg.com/news/articles/2005-08-01/picturing-peninsula-hotels.

Bosmans, A. (2006) "Scents and sensibility: When do (in) congruent ambient scents influence product evaluations?" *Journal of Marketing* 70(3), 32–43.

Brakus, J. J., Schmitt, B. H. and Zarantonello, L. (2009) "Brand experience: What is it? How is it measured? Does it affect loyalty?" *Journal of Marketing* 73(3), 52–68.

Carbone, L. P. and Haeckel, S. H. (1994) "Engineering customer experiences," *Marketing Management* 3(3), 8–19.

Chebat, J. C. and Michon, R. (2003) "Impact of ambient odors on mall shoppers' emotions, cognition, and spending: A test of competitive causal theories," *Journal of Business Research* 56(7), 529–539.

Countryman, C. C. and Jang, S. (2006) "The effects of atmospheric elements on customer impression: The case of hotel lobbies," *International Journal of Contemporary Hospitality Management* 18(7), 534–545.

Edwards, J. S., Meiselman, H. L., Edwards, A. and Lesher, L. (2003) "The influence of eating location on the acceptability of identically prepared foods," *Food Quality and Preference* 14(8), 647–652.

Goldkuhl, L. and Styvén, M. (2007) "Sensing the scent of service success," *European Journal of Marketing* 41(11/12), 1297–1305.

Goldstein, N. J., Griskevicius, V. and Cialdini, R. B. (2007) "Invoking social norms: A social psychology perspective on improving hotels' linen-reuse programs," *Cornell Hotel and Restaurant Administration Quarterly* 48(2), 145–150.

Grisaffe, D. B. and Nguyen, H. P. (2011) "Antecedents of emotional attachment to brands," *Journal of Business Research* 64(10), 1052–1059.

Grönroos, C. (1982) "An applied service marketing theory," *European Journal of Marketing* 16(7), 30–41.

Herrington, J. (1996) "Effects of music in service environments: A field study," *Journal of Services Marketing* 10(2), 26–41.

Hine, T. (1995) *The total packaging: The secret history and hidden meanings of boxes, bottles, cans and other persuasive containers*. Back Bay Books.

Hultén, B. (2011) "Sensory marketing: The multi-sensory brand-experience concept," *European Business Review* 23(3), 256–273.

Hultén, B., Broweus, N. and Van Dijk, M. (2009) What is sensory marketing? In *Sensory marketing* (pp. 1–23). Hampshire, UK: Palgrave Macmillan.

Jackson, D. (2003) *Sonic branding: An essential guide to the art and science of sonic branding*. Springer.

Kim, B., Kim, S. and Heo, C.Y. (2016) "Analysis of satisfiers and dissatisfiers in online hotel reviews on social media," *International Journal of Contemporary Hospitality Management* 28(9), 1915–1936

Kim, D. and Perdue, R. R. (2013) "The effects of cognitive, affective, and sensory attributes on hotel choice," *International Journal of Hospitality Management* 35, 246–257.

Klosse, P. R., Riga, J., Cramwinckel, A. B. and Saris, W. H. (2004) "The formulation and evaluation of culinary success factors (CSFs) that determine the palatability of food," *Food Service Technology* 4(3), 107–115.

Knutson, B. J., Beck, J. A., Kim, S. and Cha, J. (2009) "Identifying the dimensions of the guest's hotel experience," *Cornell Hospitality Quarterly* 50(1), 44–55.

Krishna, A. (2011) *Sensory marketing: Research on the sensuality of products*. Routledge.

Krishna, A. (2012) "An integrative review of sensory marketing: Engaging the senses to affect perception, judgment and behavior," *Journal of Consumer Psychology* 22(3), 332–351.

Lindstrom, M. (2005) *Brand sense: Build powerful brands through touch, taste, Smell. sight and sound*. Boston, Massachusetts: Free Press.

Lung, H. and Prowant, C. (2009) *Mental dominance*. Citadel, 1st edition.

Milliman, R. E. (1982) "Using background music to affect the behavior of supermarket shoppers," *The Journal of Marketing* 46(3), 86–91.

Moor, E. (2003) "Branded spaces The scope of 'new marketing'," *Journal of Consumer Culture* 3(1), 39–60.

Morrin, M. and Chebat, J. C. (2005) "Person–place congruency: The interactive effects of shopper style and atmospherics on consumer expenditures," *Journal of Service Research* 8(2), 181–191.

Morrison, M. (2001) "The power of music and its influence on international retail brands and shopper behaviour: A multi case study approach." Paper presented at the *Australia and New Zealand Marketing Academy Conference 2001*.

Myers-Scotton, C. (1998). "A theoretical introduction to the markedness model." In C. Myers-Scotton (Ed.), *Codes and consequences: Choosing linguistic varieties* (pp. 18–40). Oxford University Press.

Myers-Scotton, C. (2002). Contact Linguistics: Bilingual Encounter and Grammatical Outcomes. Oxford University Press.

Peck, J. and Wiggins, J. (2006) "It just feels good: Customers' affective response to touch and its influence on persuasion," *Journal of Marketing* 70(4), 56–69.

Pullman, M. E. and Gross, M. A. (2004) "Ability of experience design elements to elicit emotions and loyalty behaviors," *Decision Sciences* 35(3), 551–578.

Schmitt, B. (1999) "Experiential marketing," *Journal of Marketing Management* 15(1–3), 53–67.

Soars, B. (2009) "Driving sales through shoppers' sense of sound, sight, smell and touch," *International Journal of Retail & Distribution Management* 37(3), 286–298.

Stone, H., Bleibaum, R. and Thomas, H.A. (2012) *Sensory evaluation practices*. Academic Press.

Stout, P.A. and Leckenby, J.D. (1988) "The nature of emotional response to advertising: A further examination," *Journal of Advertising* 17(4), 53–57.

The Heavenly Bed (2016). Westin store. Retrieved from www.westinstore.cn/en/the-heavenly-bed.

The Peninsula (2013) The Peninsula hotels – photos by Sian Griffiths. Retrieved from http://news.peninsula.com/en/news/story/886-the-peninsula-hotels-photos/.

The Plaza Sound (2016) The Sound. Retrieved from www.hoteltheplaza.com/eng/experience/sound.jsp#.

Thesen, T., Vibell, J. F., Calvert, G. A. and Österbauer, R. A. (2004) "Neuroimaging of multisensory processing in vision, audition, touch, and olfaction," *Cognitive Processing* 5(2), 84–93.

Titz, K. (2008) "Experiential consumption: Affect-emotions-hedonism." In A. Pizam and H. Oh (eds.), *Handbook of Hospitality Marketing Management* (pp. 324–352). Butterworth-Heinemann.

Underwood, R. L. (2003) "The communicative power of product packaging: Creating brand identity via lived and mediated experience," *Journal of Marketing Theory and Practice* 11(1), 62–76.

Walls, A., Okumus, F., Wang, Y. and Kwun, D.J.W. (2011) "Understanding the consumer experience: An exploratory study of luxury hotels," *Journal of Hospitality Marketing & Management* 20(2), 166–197.

Wansink, B., Painter, J. E. and North, J. (2005) "Bottomless bowls: Why visual cues of portion size may influence intake," *Obesity Research* 13(1), 93–100.

W Hotels Worldwide (2016) W Hotels Music. Retrieved from www.starwoodpromos.com/whotels-music/.

Williams, L. E. and Bargh, J. A. (2008) "Experiencing physical warmth promotes interpersonal warmth," *Science* 322(5901), 606–607.

Zemke, D. M. V. and Shoemaker, S. (2008) "A sociable atmosphere: Ambient scent's effect on social interaction," *Cornell Hospitality Quarterly* 49(3), 317–329.

Zucco, G. M. (2003) "Anomalies in cognition: olfactory memory," *European Psychologist* 8(2), 77–86.

21

The silver segment

A case study on how to adapt marketing strategies to segmentation opportunities in the hospitality industry

Adela Balderas-Cejudo and Olga Rivera-Hernáez

Senior travellers as a growing market segment for the hospitality industry

Population ageing – the increasing share of older persons in the population – is poised to become one of the most significant social transformations of the twenty-first century, with implications for nearly all sectors of society (United Nations 2015). In future years, most countries in the world will experience the phenomenon of an ageing society, or, in other words, no country in the world can hide from the (inevitable) greying of its population (Leeson 2002). And as people age, patterns of consumption, decision criteria and travellers' behaviour will change considerably (Cetin and Walls 2016). Travel and leisure activities are now the biggest discretionary expenditure item for older consumers, particularly in developed and affluent countries across the globe (Wong 2007).

Thus, these population projections and changes in demand and travellers' behaviour make understanding senior tourism behaviour a necessary challenge to address so as to be able to cater for the diversity of needs of this market segment and to tailor services adapted to their requirements and expectations. In an era of fast-changing consumer profiles and behaviours, the hospitality industry must strive to obtain a thorough understanding of what guests want, and are willing to pay for. The importance of understanding new patterns of consumption and having a better knowledge of travellers in general, and seniors in particular, seems to be of great relevance and has provided a new challenge to the tourism industry.

Features

According to data from *World Population Prospects: The 2015 Revision* (United Nations 2015), the number of older persons—those aged 60 years or over—has increased substantially in recent years in most countries and regions, and that growth is projected to accelerate in the coming decades. Between 2015 and 2030, the number of people in the world aged 60 years or over is projected to grow by 56 per cent, from 901 million to 1.4 billion, and by 2050, the global population of older persons is projected to more than double its size from that of 2015, reaching nearly 2.1 billion (United Nations 2015).

However, becoming old does not necessarily restrict people's desire to travel; in fact, the opposite is occurring and this will have a great impact on the tourism industry (Balderas-Cejudo, Rivera-Hernáez and Patterson 2016; Chen and Wu 2009; Esichaikul 2012; Möller et al. 2007; Nimrod 2008; Patterson and Pegg 2009; Reece 2004). The increase in life expectancy and population ageing will allow seniors to travel more, travel later in life and travel differently. A significant number of studies and researchers have confirmed that this market segment will be one of the largest in history and will have a great impact on the tourism industry. The older adult segment is interesting not only because of its current size and purchasing power, but also as a result of demographic and social forecasts (Lohmann and Danielsson 2001; Nimrod 2008). Greater discretionary income, the changing age patterns of consumers and more free time are seen as essential factors for an increase in the travel demand of this segment. Senior tourists are healthier and wealthier, more educated and more independent than their counterparts in the past, and want to enhance their wellbeing and their retirement stage. They have more experience as travellers and have less family responsibilities. They also travel in off-peak season and are more frequently involved in package tours (Blazey 1992; Nimrod 2008). Accordingly, this interesting and challenging market segment is changing and evolving tremendously; the hospitality industry should be able to adapt and be ready for these changing individuals and circumstances.

Future evolution and threats

Demographic changes will undergo substantial shifts, challenges and threats over time. Global ageing represents a triumph of medical, social and economic advances, and also presents tremendous challenges for many regions of the world (Powell and Khan 2014).

Regarding present and future silver travellers, they will be better educated, wealthier and healthier. Senior tourists will be more active, more technological, will enjoy their leisure time and activities, will have flexible schedules and will have more experience as travellers to other regions and countries, so a more sophisticated traveller will emerge, willing to travel and experience.

Nevertheless, it is essential to bear in mind that along with these changes, several challenges appear that may have an influence on seniors' leisure travel behaviour. Thus, concurring with Harper (2014), the shift from predominantly young to predominantly older populations raises several concerns:

- The ability of nations to finance social security, long-term health and social care.
- The ability to reconfigure health and long-term care provision.
- The reconfiguration of social institutions to address issues of intergenerational fairness, dealing with access to economic, health and social resources.

Concerns about their welfare and external threats such as a stagnant economy or terrorism attacks may have a direct effect on the way seniors may travel. Also, seniors will be more independent and will not have responsibilities regarding their children. Nevertheless, they will have caring responsibilities for their parents, as there will be longer periods of living with disability toward the end of one's life (Harper 2014).

This ageing population will require increased support of various types, including income security and greater access to health care. An improved understanding of seniors by identifying sustainable and effective policy adjustments is key. Besides, it is essential that vital steps are taken to develop appropiate and innovative frameworks to address these changes and transform threats into opportunities.

Preliminary conclusions for the hospitality industry

Retiring from work is one of the major transitions in later life. For some people it may be fraught with feelings of loss of meaning and purpose, but for others it signifies an opportunity for a new beginning (Gee 1999). Being able to travel can seem almost the "essence of retirement" (Weiss 2005: 135) as there are no longer any limitations on the timing of travel and the duration of stay. Thus, leisure travelling does not only preserve old interests but provides a sense of continuity (Nimrod 2008).

Becoming aware of the potential of senior travellers and their needs is the first step to adapt to this changing market segment. Thus, as a result of emerging trends in senior tourism consumption, the hotel and resort industry must also be able to quickly respond to the changing needs of seniors in order to cater for their needs and achieve competitive advantage. In an attempt to attract seniors from different countries, hotels should firstly gain insights into this market segment and, secondly, be able to communicate their benefits and strengths. A more experienced, demanding, connected and sophisticated traveller seeks more than a place to sleep. From architecture to interior design, food, activities and staff, everything must provide the guest with a memorable experience (Patterson, Balderas-Cejudo and Rivera-Hernáez 2016). They want to feel that they are getting value for their money and they also want to experience the destination. The hospitality industry should keep up to date with the latest technology, which could be highly beneficial for improving the guest experience.

Senior traveller segment: Its heterogeneity causes and sub-segments

Many authors have pointed out the pronounced heterogeneity of the senior segment, without specifically studying the variables that could help explain that heterogeneity. Thus, a better understanding of the silver segment and of the sources of its heterogeneity will help in not only identifying variables that may affect this market segment but also will provide better decision guidelines for different stakeholders to follow when they establish their marketing strategies.

Toward a conceptual understanding of the causes of heterogeneity

A theoretical model (Figure 21.1) has been developed to obtain the main groups of variables that can explain the differences in the senior decision process and touristic behaviour.

This conceptual model illustrates how diverse personal or external determinants lead to diverse tourism motivation that in turn determine diverse consumer decision processes and different tourism behaviours in the senior market segment.

The tourism silver segment can show heterogeneity in the five major components shown in this graphic, components that are connected in a conceptual cause-effect relationship. Following the model, potential heterogeneity factors can emerge from:

- Personal determinants, such as age, education, socio-economic level, familial situation.
- External determinants such as climate, economic development, communication available due to geographic situation etc.

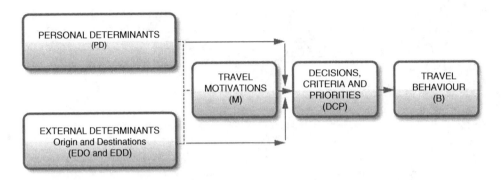

Figure 21.1 Conceptual model

- Motivations for travelling that are in part determined by the two above groups of variables, but also by the intrinsic priorities of individuals.

These three groups could of course be used for sub-segmentation purposes. It is clear that we could explain the emergence of very different situations through taking the following final two groups into consideration:

- Tourism decision process, including the way tourists develop their specific travel priorities and preferences about destinations, possible activities and selection of host destination.
- Touristic behaviour, considering the place, mode of transport, destination, company, length, expenses, activities.

This model has shown a powerful capability to order in a comprehensive way the research literature on senior tourism from 1980 to 2016. All of the research papers, in which determinants, motivations, decision criteria and behaviour in senior tourism were identified, have been analysed in order to classify key variables that emerge as relevant.

The model – accomplished through the meta-analysis of the literature – was also a key instrument to strengthen our research method since it was used in order to systematically sort the different variables that emerged from each paper studied.

Seventy-eight variables were identified, reviewed and analysed, and then listed, numbered and prioritised, to understand to what extent and why seniors consume tourism and make travel decisions in a very heterogeneous way.

The main conclusions in each group of variables can be summarized as follows:

Personal determinants

Twenty personal determinants have been identified as factors of heterogeneity, and can be classified into six different sub-categories. The order in which we mention them is linked to their relative frequency in the literature review: (1) state of physical and mental health; (2) socioeconomic status; (3) age; (4) professional status; (5) emotional, personal, familial and social status; and (6) previous experiences.

External determinants

It is very interesting to note that the external determinants related to the country of origin are very under-represented in the state-of-the-art analysis presented in research studies, due to the almost exclusive research focus on a single country. Therefore, we identified mostly external determinants of the destination that are considered by seniors when making travel plans. Twenty new variables emerged that can be classified into three different groups, which by relative importance are as follows: (1) regional environment; (2) travel determinants; (3) hotel determinants.

Motivations

Twenty-three different motivations have been identified and clustered in nine groups of motivators. The most relevant are: (1) socializing; (2) feel and look better; (3) treasure new experiences; (4) acquire education and skills. In a second level of relevance we have found: (5) be in contact with family and friends; and (6) revive previous experiences; and (7) having fun, enjoyment, pleasure entertainment; with a minor occurrence of variables appear related to (8) reward and (9) membership.

Decision process and criteria

Not many papers have analysed the decision process and criteria that seniors follow when deciding to go on their trips. Thus, only eight variables have emerged concerning the part of the conceptual model related to decisions, criteria and setting priorities. Most of the variables have mainly focused on the marketing variables related to the trip such as package tours, promotions and communication with seniors, all of which are strongly connected with marketing strategies in the hospitality industry.

Senior tourism travel behaviour

In this category, seven variables can be highlighted: (1) travel in the off-peak season; (2) more frequent travel; (3) spend more money on tourism, trips, entertainment and meals; (4) length of the trip (stay longer); (5) number of vacation days that change with the age cycle; (6) travel greater or longer distances; and (7) less sensitive to price at restaurants. Most of these variables are assumed to be a common behavioural rule of the senior travellers, and we would support this proposition if we compare seniors with other demographic segments that are still working or studying as a main activity. But we prefer to understand those variables as related to the previous groups of variables, and as motivating different behaviours in seniors depending on their motivations or determinants.

Table 21.1 Senior tourism travel behaviour

Subclassification	Type	Relative importance index (Average RII)	Variables
Seniors' behaviour	B	30.36%	Travel in off-peak season
	B	19.64%	Travel more frequently
	B	19.64%	Spend more money on tourism, trips, entertainment and meals
	B	19.64	Length of the trip/stay longer
	B	16.07%	Number of vacation days changes with age cycle
	B	14.29%	Travel greater/longer distances
	B	1.79%	Less sensitive to price at restaurants

Heterogeneity and sub-segments

Many authors have pointed out the heterogeneity of this market segment (Balderas-Cejudo et al. 2016; Bone 1991; Jang and Ham 2009; Moschis and Ünal 2008; Nimrod, 2008). Furthermore, several authors have agreed on the increasing importance of analysing and providing an in-depth understanding of this heterogeneous travel market. Their heterogeneity is so extensive that there is not even any consensus on how to describe them in the marketing and management literature. Additionally, the travel industry has been criticized for failing to recognize the diversity of travel preferences within the senior travel market (Javalgi, Thomas and Rao 1992), and part of the problem underlying this perception of the travel industry stems from an inaccurate and stereotyped view of senior travellers

Shoemaker (2000) researched the senior travel market in the state of Pennsylvania in an attempt to segment that market into smaller homogeneous groups in terms of their reasons and/or motivations for pleasure travel. Thus, three cluster groups emerged: (1) family travellers whose primary reason to engage in pleasure travel is to spend time with their immediate family; (2) active resters, who engage in pleasure travel to seek spiritual and intellectual enrichment; and (3) the older set. Members of the latter group are older than members of clusters (1) and (2) and like to stay in resorts where everything is included.

These findings suggest that members of the senior market can be segmented into smaller homogeneous groups based on their reasons (motivations) for pleasure travel, although the study is limited to Pennsylvania. It also indicates that the senior market is a collection of sub-markets, each with its own reasons for travel.

Entirely consistent with Cleaver, Green and Muller (2000), the tourism and hospitality marketer will need to tailor offerings to each senior cohort group because they all have different psychological needs, values and concerns, and these will drive consumer behaviour in the tourism marketplace. In an attempt to make the evidence clearer, the following case study sheds light on heterogeneity and segmentation criteria in the silver market segment, addressing other countries and age cohorts.

Case study 1: Segmentation criteria in the silver tourism market from the Basque Country and Oxfordshire

This case study shows the main conclusions of an empirical analysis based on in-depth and semi-structured interviews conducted during the second semester of 2015 on a convenience sample of 42 seniors from the Basque Country in Spain and the county of Oxfordshire in the UK. The interviews were inspired by the conceptual model presented in this chapter, designed to classify the main drivers of possible heterogeneity within the senior tourism segment. These interviews underwent a rigorous codification process, enabling the implementation of multivariate analysis. As a result, five principal components were identified that account for more than 50% of the data variability. These components are the following:

1. Need to vary destination

This first principal component accounts for 14.6% of the total variability, and reflects travel as a form of pleasure consumption, with individuals being separated into two groups according to their different attitudes towards the destination:

- individuals that travel looking for new destinations
- those that prefer well-known destinations, familiar to them, and repeat their trips frequently with small variations

2. Need for professional support in the travel planning process

The second principal component accounts for 12.59% of the total variability. It separates individuals into two groups regarding the way they organize and plan their trips:

- individuals who organize their trips through a travel agency, preferring very programmed trips
- those who prefer to organize their trips by themselves, through the internet

3. Need for novelty and discovery experiences

The third principal component accounts for 9.9% of the total variability. It separates individuals into two categories:

- individuals that conceive travelling as a completely new experience that will connect them with current and new friends
- those that conceive travelling as a family and familiar experience

4. Length, companionship and motivation

The fourth principal component accounts for 9.2% of the total variability. This principal component differentiates two types of travel:

- long trips to fulfil intrinsic motivations to travel and that emerge in a very individualistic way
- trips motivated by an immediate impulsion and that emerge in a spontaneous way, usually being realized as a short stay in couples

5. Preparation and reflection

Finally the fifth main component accounts for 7.7% of the total variability of the data set and defines two groups:

- those that prepare their trips and see this preparation time as part of the travel itself
- those that prefer improvization to devoting time to think about the trip, and who make the travel decision in a more impulsive manner

Emergent segments and strategic marketing consequences

Thirty-six possible market segments can be defined inside the senior tourism market segment combining the five dimensions. We could also produce an interesting segmentation using the principal components (PCs) in pairs. We will take the two dimensions related to the innovation and variation needed in senior travel (PC1 and PC3) and examine the four segments that can be conceptualized and the different marketing strategic approaches they require:

1. Hyper-conservatives (32.98% of our sample)

They see no need to change destination, and see the leisure trip as a familiar experience. Consequently, they are happy to keep going to the same destination and having the same experiences.

Hyper-conservatives should be addressed in a very classic way to maintain their interest. They prefer travel to established destinations offering recognized experiences marketed in a traditional manner. This segment is not interested in new destinations or new experience creators; by contrast, it is a "must" for destinations and experiences to have achieved a high level of excellence. They are also very important to the hospitality industry because of their loyalty.

2. Conservatives (26.18% of our sample)

They love a diversity of destinations; they visit their relatives at their travel destination and search for social interaction, comfort and relaxation. They change destinations but consider leisure travel to be a familiar experience.

Conservatives are less loyal to their destinations: they change among destinations that offer similar experiences, based on reputed and well-known services. They are the priority segment for chain hotels that can offer similar experiences all over the world.

3. Stable innovators (17.03% of our sample)

They prefer not to change destinations but enjoy novelty and new experiences on their leisure trips.

Stable innovators represent a very demanding segment for destinations because they need new experiences and offers: if they are an important market segment in a region or country, they create an important drive for innovation in experiences and offers that can be translated to other countries or regions, achieving an interesting competitive advantage in the hospitality industry.

4. Restless innovators (23.80% of our sample)

These individuals seek new comfortable destinations, looking for novelty and new experiences. Restless innovators are the dream segment for new destinations that aspire to achieve a market share in senior tourism as this market segment is eager to try new experiences.

Case study 2: Is the silver tourism market global or should it be segmented by nationalities? The Basque Country/Oxfordshire contrast.

In the literature on senior tourism, the global/multidomestic debate is not explicit. Many authors assume that seniors constitute a global market due to their demographic features, even if differences in economic development, education, culture or social welfare create enormous differences among the tourism behaviour and consumption patterns of seniors from different countries.

The practical considerations on this issue are very important for the tourism and hospitality industry, because they condition whether strategic positioning and marketing strategies can be mostly globally defined for all countries with minor adaptations, or whether these strategies should be adapted to the specific features of the seniors of each country.

We have tried to find evidence about this debate, analysing how differently or similarly senior tourists act from two countries/regions that do not differ much in some country-dependent variables such as economic development, social welfare or educational level. The same sample used to identify segments, explained in Case Study 1, was used to investigate whether the variable of country of origin impacts them in some way.

Global/local approach

The country of origin appears as a relevant variable in three of the five principal components (PC) that explain 54.05% of the data set inertia, having an impact on more than 30% of the total variation.

This result shows that the variable of country of origin in our sample is associated with important differences in the modes of travel, criteria, motivations and sources of differential decisions, showing the need to adapt offers to seniors from different countries; but also that in the two other components (accounting for 24.04% of the variation), the variable of country is not a relevant source of difference.

This allows the proportion of global and local approaches to travel in our sample to be established: **30% local, 24% global**, which is a quiet balanced score resulting from the comparison of two European, developed and educated regions. This could be understood as showing a high rate of "country of origin adaptation need" in the senior market, a percentage that probably will increase when considering other more diverse countries. So, looking to the practical implications, we would say that **country of origin is a very strategic criterion for segmentation**.

Relative weight of senior tourism segments in each country

A different perspective on the case study question would be to measure if we can also comprehend the different relative weight (RW) of each senior tourism segment in each country's senior tourism market.

We have calculated the RW for each of the segments that can be identified by crossing PC1 and 3 (see Case Study 1) and also for the segments that emerge by crossing PC3 and PC5:

- **Impulsive Classical.** Individuals who do not need any special preparation when organizing their trips as they prefer to travel to already known places with their family and to organize their journey by themselves in a more impulsive mode.
- **Spontaneous Adventurous.** They prefer impulsive trips to new and discovery experiences.
- **Reflexive Adventurous.** Travel preparation is important for them; they seek discovery and different experiences, preparing them carefully and with an important preparation time.
- **Reflexive Classical.** They are thoughtful, enjoy organizing their trip, and prepare every detail well, even when they do not change destination.

Results of this calculation can be appreciated in Figure 21.2.

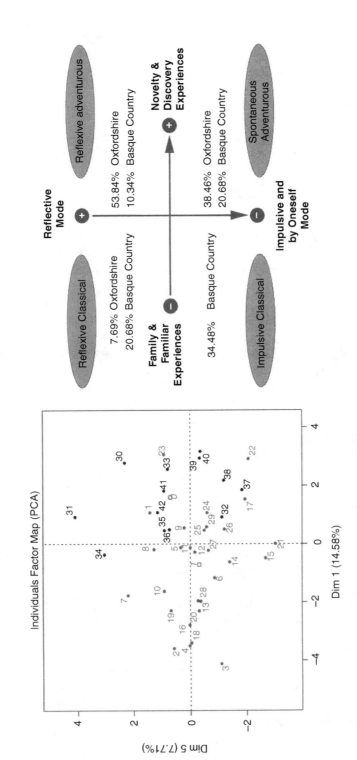

Figure 21.2 Relative weight of segments in each country/region

The preliminary conclusions and practical implications for the tourism and hospitality industry can be summarized as follows:

- There is one segment which has no presence in either country, even if – in our view – this could be a consequence of the small size of our sample; it probably exists in the senior population but with a low RW. This makes it possible to state that some segments will only have a local presence in some countries; this should be analysed in further research.
- All of the other segments have a presence in both countries, even if there are bigger differences in the RW and the majority segment in Oxfordshire does not coincide with the Basque Country one. This means that some segments are global ones, and will allow fast-growing global strategies if the companies decide to specialize in them with a global approach.
- There are countries with greater homogeneity as Oxfordshire has one segment that accounts for more than 50% of the sample analysed. Those countries – especially those with larger populations – would also allow a specialization strategy, focusing on their national features.

Preliminary conclusions

The conceptual model showed a cause and effect relationship between tourism motivations and consumption for the senior market segment. Furthermore, it was flexible enough to include and validate further research, as previously stated. Thus, in order to understand the decision-making process of seniors regarding the selection criteria involved in leisure trips, it is important to understand that it is a process. Personal determinants (which can be both enhancers or constraints), external determinants or motivations will influence the decision-making process. Within the senior segment, each individual will display different tourist behaviour depending on the different determinants that may influence the motivations as either enhancers or inhibitors. Consequently, it is essential to highlight the variability of the senior market segment, which makes it difficult to define variables that determine heterogeneous behaviour. Motivations, personal determinants and external determinants influence behaviour and criteria, despite the different life events that seniors are going through.

Regarding the global/local approach and the importance of the country of origin, obtaining a deeper understanding of the senior tourism market through an exploration of the global/local dimension of international strategies will assist firms and destinations to implement change to respond to this growing demand segment of senior travellers. This market trend is a global one, with an increasing presence in all continents and countries, from the most advanced to developing countries. Nevertheless, it does not mean that the answer will always be a global strategy, meaning providing the same touristic product to all seniors in every country. To determine an international strategy, it is important to know whether the tourism behaviour of seniors, and their motivations and determinants, are common internationally; or are their substantial differences that require strategic adaptation, depending on the country of origin.

Adaptations and opportunities in the hospitality industry regarding the silver market segment

Senior travellers will be experienced, with clear ideas of what they want, making it more difficult to surprise them, and they will demand "personalised" offerings to meet their travel needs.

All stakeholders will need to cater for seniors' travel motivations, and the need for social interaction, special events, memorable experiences, cultural amenities, educational offerings and a desire for self-fulfilment. These will be important aspects to take into account in order to offer products and services that seniors seek and value. A more experiential senior traveller will seek authenticity, self-improvement and the discovery of new experiences.

There are a number of practical suggestions for hotels to implement under the following five headings that will be briefly discussed in turn.

The weight of the external determinants of destination

External determinants are not only important for hotels, but also need to be considered by tour operators and travel agencies. The key external determinants that need to be developed and explored by the hospitality industry include synergies, cooperation and the development of clusters with other stakeholders which may increase business efficiency and enhance the possibilities of competitive advantage. Thus, as a cluster strategy or at a cooperative level, they can influence destination managers through their ability to attract tour operators by offering them destinations with more accessibility.

The importance of a global strategy to attract seniors from different countries

In an attempt to attract senior tourists from different countries, hotels need to firstly understand the insights about this market segment and, secondly, be able to communicate to them the benefits and strengths of the destination. The key aspects that need to be implemented are a friendly internet site, together with cooperation with other key internet providers, opinions from actual travellers and consistent communication with potential clients.

The importance of a multi-domestic strategy that can be adopted by each country

Understanding the needs of senior travellers from other countries is not just a suggestion but is essential for hotel management. Therefore, gastronomy, cultural understandings, speaking different languages and service skills will make a difference to service quality. Customers will remember these emotional experiences and therefore staff at a specific hotel need to be aware that they will play a key role in providing a memorable experience that may be shared through social media and provide important positioning for the hotel. In this sense, the strategy should include not only good design features, comfortable rooms and facilities, but also friendly and committed staff.

The practical importance of different market segments

The identified segments provided clear examples of the heterogeneity and the importance of customer orientation for older travellers. Travellers want to feel comfortable at their hotel and at specific destinations. From interesting architecture to interior design, excellent food, a wide range of lesiure activities and well-trained staff, everything must be provided to the guest so that they have a memorable experience. Patterson, Balderas-Cejudo and Rivera-Hernáez (2016) stated that a hotel brand needs to create a framework that permits guests to achieve the experience that they are seeking, and for many, the hotel design needs to be inextricably linked to the place that they are visiting.

The importance of changing trends for future pre-seniors

Becoming aware of the potential of this market segment and their needs is the first step that needs to be taken to adapt to the changing trends regarding pre-seniors. That is, they are generally more experienced, demanding, connected and sophisticated travellers that seek more than merely a place to sleep. They want to receive value for their money and also to experience the destination through its gastronomy, authenticity and excellent staff. Social interaction is also an important motivator so hotels must be able to offer a social connection through activities, and a welcoming atmosphere. Furthermore, the hospitality industry should be regularly updated with the latest technology, which generally helps in receiving positive feedback on the guest experience.

Thus, as a result of these emerging trends in the consumption of senior tourism, the hotel industry must respond quickly to the changing and sophisticated needs and expectations of seniors, and tailor to the needs of this market segment, which will also help to achieve competitive advantage. When considering how to make strategic decisions in the hospitality industry, the marketing mix needs to play a crucial role in communicating the benefits of staying at a particular hotel so as to attract the attention of the senior tourist. A friendly internet site, attractive photos with a key message, welcoming staff and a commitment to quality service will be key aspects that need to be developed.

Further research

The results of this study suggest further avenues for research into senior tourism segmentation criteria. In addition, the limitations of this research highlight a number of key recommendations to be addressed in the future.

Thus, besides advocating the importance of expanding research beyond the geographical areas of this study, it is also recommended that there is a need to incorporate a larger sample size of respondents. Further research should also include more variables, including the results that emerged from the historical findings relating to senior travellers.

The recommendations for further research strongly suggest that there is much to be gained from conducting in-depth and semi-structured interviews when comparing different regions and countries, as well as between pre-senior and senior cohort groups.

References

Balderas-Cejudo, A., Rivera-Hernáez, O., and Patterson, I. (2016). "The strategic impact of country of origin on senior tourism demand: The need to balance global and local strategies". *Journal of Population Ageing*, 9(4): 345–73.

Blazey, M. A. (1992). "Travel and retirement status". *Annals of Tourism Reseach*, 19(4): 771–783.

Bone, P. F. (1991) "Identifying mature segments". *Journal of Services Marketing*, 5(1): 47–60.

Cetin, G., and Walls, A. (2016) "Understanding the customer experiences from the perspective of guests and hotel managers: Empirical findings from luxury hotels in Istanbul, Turkey". *Journal of Hospitality Marketing & Management*, 25(4): 395–424.

Chen, C. F., and Wu, C. C. (2009). "How motivations, constraints, and demographic factors predict seniors' overseas travel propensity". *Asia Pacific Management Review*, 14(3): 301–312.

Cleaver, M., Green, B. C., and Muller, T. E. (2000). "Using consumer behavior research to understand the baby boomer tourist". *Journal of Hospitality & Tourism Research*, 24(2): 274–287.

Esichaikul, R. (2012). "Travel motivations, behaviour and requirements of European senior tourists to Thailand". PASOS. *Revista de Turismo y Patrimonio Cultural*, 10(2): 47–58

Gee, S. (1999). "Happily ever after? An exploration of retirement expectations". *Educational Gerontology*, 25(2): 109–128.

Harper, S. (2014). "Economic and social implications of aging societies". *Science*, 346(6209): 587–591.

Harper, S., and Leeson, G. (2008). "Introducing the Journal of Population Ageing". *Journal of Population Ageing*, 1(1): 1–5.

Jang, S. S., and Ham, S. (2009). "A double-hurdle analysis of travel expenditure: Baby boomer seniors versus older seniors". *Tourism Management*, 30(3), 372–380.

Javalgi, R. G., Thomas, E. G., and Rao, S. R. (1992). "Consumer behavior in the US pleasure travel market-place: An analysis of senior and nonsenior travellers". *Journal of Travel Research*, 31(2): 14–19.

Leeson, G. W. (2002). *The Changing Face of the Population of Europe: Geographical Distribution, Urbanization, Depopulation, and International Migration*. Stockholm: Nordregio.

Lohmann, M., and Danielsson, D. (2001). "Predicting travel patterns of senior citizens: How the past may provide a key to the future". *Journal of Vacation Marketing*, 7(4): 357–366.

Möller, C., Weiermair, K., and Wintersberger, E. (2007). "The changing travel behaviour of Austria's ageing population and its impact on tourism". *Tourism Review*, 62(3/4): 15–20.

Moschis, G. P., and Ünal, B. (2008). "Travel and leisure services preferences and patronage motives of older consumers". *Journal of Travel & Tourism Marketing*, 24(4): 259–269.

Nimrod, G. (2008). "Retirement and tourism themes in retirees' narratives". *Annals of Tourism Research*, 35(4): 859–878.

Patterson, I., and Pegg, S. (2009). "Marketing the leisure experience to baby boomers and older tourists". *Journal of Hospitality Marketing & Management*, 18(2–3): 254–272.

Patterson, I., Balderas-Cejudo, A., and Rivera-Hernáez, O. (2016). "Baby boomer tourist market: Hotel memorable experiences". *Journal of Hospitality Marketing & Management* (accepted for publication).

Powell, J. L., and Khan, T. A. (2014). "Ageing in post-industrial society: Trends and trajectories". *Journal of Globalization Studies*, 5(2), 143–151.

Reece, W. S. (2004). "Are senior leisure travelers different?" *Journal of Travel Research*, 43(1): 11–18.

Shoemaker, S. (2000). "Segmenting the mature market: 10 years later". *Journal of Travel Research*, 39(1): 11–26.

United Nations, Department of Economic and Social Affairs, Population Division (2015). *World Population Prospects* (ST/ESA/SER.A/390).

Wang, K. C., Chen, J. S., and Chou, S. H. (2007). "Senior tourists' purchasing decisions in group package tour". *Anatolia*, 18(1): 23–42.

Weiss, R. (2005). *The Experience of Retirement*. Ithaca, NY: Cornell University Press.

Wong, Y. (2007). *The Glittering Silver Market: The Rise of the Elderly Consumers in Asia*. Singapore; Chichester, England: John Wiley & Sons (Asia).

Further reading

Chen, S. C., and Shoemaker, S. (2014). "Age and cohort effects: The American senior tourism market". *Annals of Tourism Research*, 48: 58–75. (Time series data and three generations compared.)

Dolnicar, S. (2008). "Market segmentation in tourism", in Woodside, A. G. and Martin, D. (eds.), *Tourism Management: Analysis, Behaviour and Strategy*. Cambridge: CAB International, 129–150.

Harper, S., and Hamblin, K. (eds.). (2014). *International Handbook on Ageing and Public Policy*. Cheltenham, UK: Edward Elgar Publishing. (An international exploration of challenges from the ageing of population.)

Sellick, M. C. (2004). "Discovery, connection, nostalgia: Key travel motives within the senior market". *Journal of Travel & Tourism Marketing*, 17(1), 55–71. (A focus on several characteristics/motives of travelling for leisure.)

Part IV
Hospitality consumer behavior

22

Hospitality consumers' decision-making

Haywantee Ramkissoon

Introduction

The rapidly growing competitive market and fundamental paradigm change in hospitality consumers' behavior has encouraged hospitality providers to incorporate best practices to provide an improved customer experience. Constant demand for environmentally friendly products requires hospitality providers to have a more profound understanding of consumer decision-making, in order to satisfy their customers (Tang, 2016). Many hotels are devoting considerable effort to this aspect, incorporating the concept of sustainability defined as "the ability of the present generation to meet the needs of the present without compromising the ability of future generations to meet their own needs" (Brundtland, 1987, p. 16), to improve or develop new facilities and services to address the new demands and migratory behavior of sustainable hospitality consumers.

There is a plethora of studies in the literature on green consumerism. Lodging and restaurant operators are developing guidelines and programs as part of their core business strategies (Ramkissoon & Mavondo, 2016), focusing on green practices to improve their image and consumer ratings (Namkung & Jang, 2013; Peiró-Signes et al., 2014; Pizam, 2009) and business performance (Singal, 2014). This chapter aims to provide a detailed explanation of models of consumer decision-making, followed by a conceptualization of the relationships among the constructs of information processing, personal efficacy, innovation, and image proposed as antecedents of hospitality consumers' decisions when choosing sustainable hospitality products and services. An investigation of the relationships between the above-mentioned constructs will fill the gaps in the literature.

Models of consumer decision-making

A range of studies have examined the decision-making processes of travelers and hospitality consumers. Behavioral models that are most relevant to choice of hospitality products and services are reviewed in this section. Van Raaij and Francken's (1984) consumer decision-making model places great emphasis on the influence of family members in the decision process, arguing that the buying process for tourism and hospitality-related products and services is influenced not only by personal/individual factors (i.e. attitudes and aspirations), but also by household-related factors (i.e. power structure, role, decision-making styles and lifestyles). The interaction of all these factors results in the decision-making process. The role of family members differs with the type of decision activity. While husbands decide on monetary factors and timing of vacations, children influence the types of activities and duration of vacation. Spouses differ in their involvement with different trip-related tasks (Zalatan, 1998), with husbands being more influential in financial matters, and wives in other related aspects of the trip.

Based on a review of social science disciplines, Woodside and Lysonski's (1989) decision model postulates that the consumer's decision process is a categorization process of products from which final decisions are made. Individuals have mental sets where they place all destinations/hospitality products and services that they are familiar with, and marketing and personal variables influence the process. The image of the destination, positive or negative, influences the final preference in the mental set. The final choice is influenced by the intention to visit the destination, a process which is affected by situational variables. Hong et al. (2006) investigate the role of categorization, affective image and constraints on the consumer's decision-making process. They argue that consumers use a simplifying strategy which narrows down the number of alternatives by grouping those perceived as similar in order to reduce their cognitive effort.

The Means-End Chain theory developed in marketing has also been found to be useful in the study of the decision-making process in purchasing hospitality products (McIntosh & Thyne, 2005). The theory postulates that consumers select those products and services whose attributes produce desired consequences or benefits, while at the same time minimizing unwanted consequences (Klenosky et al., 1993). The model is based on theories of "consumers' cognitive structures, depicting the way in which concrete product characteristics are linked to valued end states desired by consumers" (McIntosh & Thyne, 2005, pp. 259–260). Research using the Means-End theory has been used to analyze relationships between personal values and product attributes. Product attributes are defined as 'means' which are linked to consequences or benefits, which ultimately lead to consumers' personal values or motives, defined as 'ends' (e.g., Nunkoo & Ramkissoon, 2009).

The theory is useful for understanding personal values as the basis of travelers' motivations. Several researchers argue that personal values are important predictors of tourist behavior (Gnoth, 1999). Means-End Chain theory has been applied to obtain an understanding of consumer behavior, focusing on the areas of accommodation choice (Mattila, 1999; Thyne and Lawson, 2001), destination choice (Klenosky, 2002; Klenosky et al., 1993), museum and heritage visiting (Crotts & Van Rekom, 1998; McIntosh & Prentice, 1999; Thyne, 2001), and nature-based experiences (Klenosky et al., 1993; Frauman & Cunningham, 2001). The Means-End Chain theory provides a sound conceptual model for understanding the meanings that hospitality consumers associate with purchasing, experiencing and consuming products and services, and with the personal values associated with them (McIntosh & Thyne, 2005).

The above discussion on the application of the Means-End theory emphasizes the importance of values. Different approaches have been used to measure this concept in tourism and hospitality research. Such approaches include the Rokeach Value Survey (RVS) (Rokeach, 1968), the List of Value (LOV) scale (Kahle & Kennedy, 1988), the Value and Lifestyle (VAL) tool (Mitchell, 1983) and laddering techniques (Gutman and Reynolds, 1979) to achieve an empirical measurement of personal values. The RVS details two sets of values: 18 instrumental and 18 terminal, each of which are ranked by respondents in order of the value's importance. The LOV scale was developed because the RVS was criticized as being too general. The former method is considered to be more related to values of major roles in life such as marriage, parenting, work and leisure (Thyne, 2001). VAL, on the other hand, was developed out of a combination of values and lifestyle information combined with demographic data. The laddering method involves semi-structured, one-to-one interviews to be conducted where, in the first place, prob-ing questions are asked (commonly associated with the Means-End technique) to analyze why a particular factor is important to the respondent. The responses are then used to formulate the next question, which is based around 'why is that important to you?' This approach, rather than forcing respondents to select from pre-determined value categories, enables them to define and express their personal values and attitudes in their own words. Laddering thus guides the respondents up or down the ladder of abstraction, facilitating an inductive perspective in under-standing the relationship between personal values and attitudes.

The Purchase Consumption System (PCS) is an alternative model, proposed by Woodside and King (2001). The model has been found useful for mapping the choice decisions of consum-ers before and during a trip and also for evaluating the actual experiences which might have an influence on future decisions (Sirakaya & Woodside, 2005). The model is concerned with the sequential process of mental and observable steps a consumer goes through while purchasing a product. The model further explains the impacts of services that might explain future purchases. Studies such as those by Bansal and Eiselt (2004) and Lue et al. (1996) support the PCS model. In their study on tourist decision-making, Bansal and Eiselt (2004) provided a two-phase frame-work consisting of the planning phase and the modification phase. According to these research-ers, prior to a vacation, decisions about the basic parameters of the trip are taken at home much earlier than the actual trip is made; however, these decisions might not be finalized – they can be modified or even completely changed. This is referred to as the planning phase whereas the modification phase is attributed to the changes made during the trip, e.g. travelers deciding on impulse to stay at a hotel whose services are announced on a billboard or tourists modifying their choices of sites to visit (Bansal & Eiselt, 2004). This framework conforms to the PCS model in determining tourists' decision-making before and during a trip.

While the above-discussed models do provide conceptual bases for understanding consumer behavior in tourism and hospitality, they assume that the individual is a rational consumer who exhibits rationalistic behavior (Sirakaya & Woodside, 2005) and that during the information acquisition phase, memory and external sources of information are used for retrieval of informa-tion (Mullen & Johnson, 1990; Wicks & Schuett, 1991). The models postulate that the consumer chooses products which offer the greatest utility within the boundaries of social and individual constraints (Sirakaya & Woodside, 2005). However, consumers are not always rational in their decision-making as a number of factors may influence their rational behavior sometimes, leading to irrational behavior (Bettman et al., 1998).

The theory of planned behavior, proposed by Fishbein and Ajzen in 1975, has been offered as a comprehensive framework for understanding consumer decision-making in tourism and hos-pitality research. A number of studies have sought to explore and test this theory (e.g. Lam and Hsu, 2006; Nunkoo & Ramkissoon, 2010; Ramkissoon et al., 2013; Sparks, 2007). It is argued to be a reliable behavioral model in explaining consumer decision-making (Sirakaya & Woodside, 2005), and is considered to be one of the most influential models developed to explain human behavior (White, 2005). As an extension of the theory of reasoned action introduced by Fishbein (1967), it was refined by Fishbein and Ajzen (1975) into the theory of planned behavior.

Ajzen and Fishbein (1980) clearly demonstrate that an individual usually thinks rationally and behaves in a sensible manner. He/she uses the information available to him or her in a systematic way. As Ajzen (1985) explains further, the individual considers the implications of his or her actions. The likely consequences of his or her behavior are called 'behavioral beliefs' (Ajzen & Fishbein, 1980; Fishbein & Ajzen, 1975). According to the theory of rea-soned action, these beliefs are determined by two basic elements, the first being personal in nature and the second reflecting social influence. Ajzen and Fishbein (1980) made a clear distinction between these two dimensions. The 'personal' factor relates to the individual's behavior towards an action, which in turn determines attitudes towards the behavior. This demonstrates that attitudes are a function of beliefs. As an example, an individual believing that his or her behavior will give rise to positive outcomes will have positive attitudes towards performing that behavior. The second factor, termed as 'subjective norm,' relates to perceived social pressure. These beliefs are termed as 'normative beliefs.' In the case where an individual believing that most referents with whom he/she is motivated to comply thinks he/she should behave in a particular way (subjective norm), this will thereby exert pressure on him/her to behave accordingly. Ajzen and Fishbein (2005) further argue that, if, however, normative beliefs are antagonistic, the perceived social norm will exert pressure on the individual not to perform the behavior. According to Ajzen (1985), people tend to perform a particular behavior when they perceive it positively and when they feel that important others believe they should perform it. Fishbein and Manfredo (1992, p. 33) argue that "considerable research demonstrates that, when properly measured, correspondent intentions are very accurate predictors of most social behaviors."

The theory of planned behavior, developed following Ajzen and Fishbein (1980), argues that behaviors that are not fully volitional are also influenced by the individual's perception of his or her ability to perform the behavior. This idea was therefore incorporated and extended to the theory of planned behavior. It is a modified version of the theory of reasoned action, and as argued by Ajzen (1985), considers not only perceived but also actual behaviors of individuals. Ajzen (1991) argues that this extended theory advocates a joint function of intentions and perceived behavioral control whereby both factors must be assessed in relation to the particular behavior of interest, and the specified context must be the same as that in which the behavior is to occur. This theory is especially applicable to behaviors that are not entirely under volitional control (Corby et al., 1996).

Ajzen and Driver (1991) explain the theory of planned behavior as having three conceptually independent determinants of behavior: attitude towards the behavior, subjective norm, and lastly the degree of perceived behavioral control. The latter includes an individual's available resources (Liska, 1984), facilitating factors (Triandis, 1977), and opportunity. Sirakaya and Woodside (2005) share a similar view to that of Ajzen and Driver (1991) in asserting that these three constructs interact with each other and influence intention formation. Most importantly, they argue that these constructs summarize many essential elements found in most tourism and hospitality consumer decision models, such as travelers' attitudes, family and friend influences which are termed as 'subjective norms' and the role of past experiences and constraints, referred to as 'perceived behavioral control.' Congruent with this, several studies (e.g. Sparks, 2007) explain how these three constructs drive behavior and further explain 'attitude' as being the overall evaluation of the behavior, 'subjective norm' being the influence of others on whether to engage in the behavior and 'perceived behavioral control' as the perceived ability to engage in the behavior.

Lam and Hsu (2006) define 'perceived behavioral control' as how easy or difficult an individual thinks it is to perform a behavior. They argue that the higher the perceived behavioral control, the more likely it is that the individual will perform the act. The theory of planned behavior has been well researched from several discourses and applied in a variety of fields; its application in hospitality research continues to proliferate. The theory of planned behavior adopts an attitudinal approach to understand goal-directed behavior. More studies are needed in its application to hospitality consumers' decision-making, which is influenced by both social (subjective norms) and psychological factors (attitudes). Patterns often reflect the complex decision-making processes of hospitality consumers, who form part of the social structure reflecting typical norms, traditions, culture and beliefs.

Sparks (2007) predicts potential wine tourists' intentions to take a wine-based travel vacation using a model based on the theory of planned behavior. Interestingly, congruent with the findings of Lam and Hsu (2006), Sparks (2007) demonstrates that there is no relationship between emotional attitudes and intentions. He further defines perceived behavioral control as the beliefs of wine tourists as to whether they have the required resources (e.g., money and time) to take the holiday. He measured this construct using a three-item Likert scale from 1 'strongly disagree' to 7 'strongly agree' with items such as 'I feel I have enough money to take a wine holiday in the next 12 months' or 'I feel I have enough time to take a wine holiday in the next 12 months.' Sparks (2007) argues that perceived behavioral control is the major predictor of tourists' intentions to take a wine holiday. His findings are congruent with Lam and Hsu (2004, 2006), concluding that perceived behavioral control is indeed an important construct in predicting tourism and hospitality consumers' behavior. It provides information about how an individual perceives the potential constraints on the action to be performed.

Recent approaches to tourism discourse has often described the tourist's decision-making process as sequential in nature and comprised of sets (Sirakaya & Woodside, 2005). Prentice (2006, p. 1154) argues that this approach is known as the choice sets modeling, which according to Sirakaya and Woodside (2005) has received remarkable attention in consumer decision-making research because of its practicability. The pioneer of the choice set model was Howard (1963). The model was further developed by Howard and Sheth (1969), Narayana and Markin (1975), Brisoux and Laroche (1981) and Spiggle and Sewall (1987). The importance of the choice set in the information search process has also been recognized by Ankomah et al. (1996). Individuals have choice sets (reject, inert, late, inaction and action) which determine their confidence with or belief in a given choice (Um & Crompton, 1990).

Choice set models, which seek to bring more applicable results to the study of destination choice behavior (Sirakaya & Woodside, 2005), have been applied in several studies. Choice set models possess many advantages over behavioral models, which have often been criticized as being too complex and difficult to test empirically (Sirakaya & Woodside, 2005). Prentice (2006) argues that choice set models assume rationality on the part of the consumers, and based on this assumption he argues that "assuming choices are made rationally, decision sets models also offer us the potential of charting the fortunes of destinations through an appraisal process. They are managerially attractive in the stimulation of remedies to rejection." Sirakaya and Woodside (2005, p. 824) argue that "a potential traveler generates a series of choice sets with an ever-decreasing number of remaining alternatives in a funnel-like process over time until a final decision is made." They further argue that choice sets models are useful in analyzing the role of attitudes in the decision process. Um and Crompton (1990) in their study of destination choice used a three-stage process involving firstly the composition of awareness set; secondly, the evoked set and lastly, the final destination selection, which is a condensed form of the former. The latter arises when the traveler gathers passive information from the external environment. The evoked set is formed when the tourist actively searches for information from external sources such as friends and relatives etc. The motives, attitudes and values, also known as the socio-psychological set of the traveler, influence his/her awareness set and once it is developed, the active choice process begins. This framework has been used by Um and Crompton (1990) to measure the effectiveness of attitudes in an active choice situation, showing that attitude is an important determinant of whether a potential traveler will choose a particular destination from the awareness set or not. Sirakaya and Woodside (2005) further argue that choice set models enable tourism and hospitality marketers to identify marketing potential.

Prentice (2006) emphasizes the integrated choice set model, which focuses on sequential conceptualizations with constructs of familiarity and imagery. Its core is made up of three stages: consumer filters (socio–demographics and income, preferences and credibility), the evoked set (knowledge, imagery and familiarity) and the action set (propensity). The integrated choice set possesses an advantage over the traditional choice set model as it focuses on the actual choice process. Attention is here focused on tourism and hospitality products which remain in the system of choice instead of having a system of reject boxes as in the traditional choice set model.

Choice set models are however not left without limitations. One barrier to the practical implementation of choice set models is the measurement question of how to estimate which alternatives are in the consideration set for each individual for a given choice decision (Gensch & Soofi, 1995). The traditional choice set models assume rationality in decision-making, which may be far from universal. For instance, they underplay the concept of familiarity and imagery in the decision process, dimensions which can affect the hospitality consumer's decisions. The theory of planned behavior includes a similar assumption.

Hospitality consumers' decision-making

Information processing and personal efficacy

It comes as no surprise that today's more environmentally conscious consumers favor sustainable hospitality businesses, which are well committed to environmental practices (Han et al., 2009). Often the environmentally conscious hospitality consumers engage in behaviors which make them feel they have contributed to the environment, e.g., consumers show greater willingness to pay for green products (Kim et al., 2015; Susskind, 2014).

Green practices in hospitality businesses are seen to have a major influence on consumers' decision-making process (Xu & Gursoy, 2015). If they are not well marketed, however, hospitality customers' awareness of sustainable products and programs may also be low, impacting negatively on their choices (Parsa et al., 2015). High levels of information provision on eco-friendly hospitality products are shown to predict higher degrees of personal efficacy (Kellstedt et al., 2008; Ockwell et al., 2009). Personal efficacy is defined as an individual's judgement of his/her capability to execute a particular behavior (Chen et al., 2012; Ramkisoon & Smith, 2014). People feel concerned to solve environmental issues they are informed of (Milfont, 2012). They experience personal efficacy, which encourages intrinsic motivation to act out of concern (Ramkissoon & Smith, 2014), and are often willing to make more effort when they perceive that their contribution can help alleviate the crisis (Van Vugt, 2009). This is well aligned with the knowledge-deficit approach.

Drawing on the information processing theory (Petty and Cacioppo, 1986), it can be said that hospitality consumers process information systematically and heuristically (Xie et al., 2011). In the decision-making process, hospitality consumers are motivated to deeply analyze and systematically process the information before arriving at a conclusion (Petty & Cacioppo, 1986) on their choice of hospitality products and services. Consumers are also inclined to heuristic processing and to conserve their cognitive resources, when evaluating likely outcomes (Hanks, Line, & Kim, 2017). Relevant information on hospitality products and services may be disseminated with the expectation that it will lead to increased awareness, in turn leading to sustainable choices and minimizing environmental impacts (Owens, 2000; Ramkissoon & Smith, 2014). Remarkably, information processing can encourage people to take personal responsibility for their actions, opting for more sustainable hospitality products and services. It is proposed that consumers' information processing positively influences their choice of sustainable hospitality products, services and facilities, and consumers' personal efficacy positively influences their choice of sustainable hospitality products, services and facilities.

Innovation in hospitality

As consumers are becoming increasingly aware of serious environmental degradation, there is a widespread transition to sustainability-oriented values (Axsen & Kurani, 2013), with customers engaging in more pro-environmental behaviors (Ramkissoon & Mavondo, 2016; van Riper & Kyle, 2014) to support sustainability goals. Such shifts in behaviors have called for hospitality providers to place a critical focus on product innovation (Chen et al., 2014) in order to be equipped with tools to design new products and services required by sustainable hospitality consumers. Informed customers look for creativity and increased service efficiency from hospitality providers.

Service innovativeness, defined as the capacity to develop new services, and to continually improve existing services (Tang, 2016), is important to create lasting and memorable experiences, which have benefits both for hotel management and its customers (Subramaniam & Youndt, 2005). Responding to the market's demands, proactive bed and breakfast (B&B) owners improved existing services and developed new services, optimizing on quality, and yet at a lower operating cost, with increased profits (Tang, 2015).

A focus on service innovation brings a competitive advantage to hospitality providers. Hospitality providers need to constantly study the market, and embrace new challenges and opportunities (Haase & Franco, 2011; Okumus, 2004) to equip their staff with transformational leadership to ensure more innovative sustainable hospitality facilities and service (Chen et al., 2014). Theoharakis and Hooley (2008) suggest that this may retain customers, and may be regarded as a long-term investment by hospitality providers (Han et al., 1998). From a review of the existing literature, it is proposed that product and service innovation have positive influences on consumers' choice of sustainable hospitality services and facilities. The implications form this finding can guide hospitality providers to emphasize product and service innovation, and to achieve their profit objectives.

Image

Researchers have provided a wealth of studies on the role of image in promoting hospitality products and services. Regarded as a multidimensional construct (e.g., Hosany et al., 2006; Jiang et al., 2016), image remains complex in nature. It a composite concept comprising interrelated cognitive and affective evaluations woven into overall impressions (Assael, 1984; Gartner, 1993; MacKay and Fesenmaier, 1997), the latter being interpreted as the affective quality of feelings towards the product attributes and surrounding environment and the former as a set of beliefs about the physical attributes of the destination (Baloglu & McCleary, 1999). Crompton (1979) defines destination image as an attitudinal concept consisting of the sum of beliefs, ideas and impressions that a tourist holds of a destination.

The analysis of image, with its cognitive and affective elements (e.g. Pike and Ryan, 2004; White, 2004), is an integral and influential component of the consumer's decision-making process and behaviors (Baloglu and Brinberg, 1997; Gallarza et al., 2002). It has to date received great interest in tourism marketing due to its intrinsic multidimensionality (Hunter, 2008), and remains a pivotal marketing concept (Kim & Richardson, 2003). A number of empirical studies suggest a strong and direct association between travelers' perceived image of the destination and their destination choices (e.g., Lee et al., 2002; Milman & Pizam, 1995). Visitors are conditioned by the image they have of the destination, with more positive and favorable images influencing their choice of destination (Chi & Qu, 2008). Several authors similarly posit that destinations with stronger positive images have a higher probability of inducing the potential visitor to choose the destination, resulting in an increase in the already intense competition among destinations (Baloglu & Mangaloglu, 2001; Buhalis, 2000). Ramkissoon and Uysal (2014) further note that some places may be required to increase their supply resources to match consumer demand, thus providing an enhanced image of the destination. As argued by Chaudhary (2000) and Fakeye and Crompton (1991), effective destination positioning strategies are often used to appeal to potential visitors. One such example is the development of a competitive image and positioning strategy for the city of Macau (Choi et al., 2007). Tourists' intentions to revisit destinations in the future largely depend on their positive perceptions of the destination (Chi & Qu, 2008). Their individual subjective perceptions determine their subsequent behavior and destination choice (Chon, 1990, 1992; Etchner & Ritchie, 1991).

Hospitality providers provide experiential products where the consumption is an end in itself (Govers et al., 2007), but whereby the decision-making process can be an enjoyable process where emotions play an important role. This is often referred to as a hedonic consumption experience (Vogt & Fesenmaier, 1998). Numerous empirical studies in the hospitality setting have revealed that a firm's overall image has a critical role in influencing sustainable choices of hospitality products and services. The eco-friendly image of hospitality businesses could be reinforced with provision of green choices such as the use of organic ingredients (Kwok et al., 2016), perceived as more healthy by customers who prioritize their health. As such, this may influence the customers' decisions (e.g., Han et al., 2009; Hu et al., 2010; Jang et al., 2011). Todd (2001) investigated the affective construct of destination image by using one's perception of oneself or the self-concept to understand consumers' reasons for selecting certain hospitality products. She notes that people strive to achieve congruity, or a match between how they perceive themselves and the images of the products that they consume, thus deriving both economic and psychological benefits from their product choices. Researchers argue that image is a crucial aspect of destination marketing strategy (Gallarza et al., 2002; Ramkissoon & Nunkoo, 2008; Ramkissoon et al., 2009), involving many aspects intended to convey the overall idea or experience that the hospitality consumer can expect (e.g., Blain et al., 2005). This study proposes that the organization's image has a positive influence on consumers' choice of sustainable hospitality services and facilities. With the growing shift in hospitality consumers' sustainability values, establishing the relationship between the two constructs will have important implications for practitioners.

Conclusion

The goal of this chapter was to review customer decision-making in the hospitality sector, and to discuss the interplay of relationships between hospitality consumers' information processing and personal efficacy, innovation, and image in the hospitality industry. Future researchers can build on this review and test the proposed relationships, and contribute to the body of existing studies in the hospitality marketing literature. Empirical findings may enable hospitality providers to take a step forward in designing, communicating and disseminating information through distribution channels for their target audience. With the increase in hospitality consumers focusing closely on sustainability practices of organizations, offering sustainability products that really add value is an important initiative for hospitality providers to emphasize. The image of hospitality organizations remains an important factor influencing the decision-making of the more ecologically conscious consumer. With innovative products and services, hospitality businesses could enhance their companies' image and reputation, and attract new customers while retaining existing ones. Testing the interplay of the proposed relationships between the constructs will contribute to the theoretical body of knowledge and assist practitioners in predicting hospitality consumers' choice of sustainable products and services.

References

Ajzen, I. (1985). From intentions to actions: a theory of planned behavior. *In* J. Kuhl and J. Beckman (Eds.), *Action-control: from cognition to behavior* (pp. 11–39). Heidelberg, Germany: Springer.

Ajzen, I. (1991). The theory of planned behavior. *Organisational Behavior and Human Decision Processes*, 50, 179–211.

Ajzen, I., & Driver, B. (1991). Prediction of leisure participation from behavioral, normative, and control beliefs: an application of the theory of planned behavior. *Leisure Sciences*, 13, 185–204.

Ajzen, I., & Fishbein, M. (1980). *Understanding attitudes and predicting social behavior*. Englewood-Cliffs, NJ: Prentice- Hall.

Ajzen, I., & Fishbein, M. (2005). The influence of attitudes on behavior. *In* D. Albarracin, B. T. Johnson and M. P. Zanna (Eds.), *Handbook of attitudes and attitude change: basic principles* (pp. 173–221). Mahwah, NJ: Lawrence Erlbaum Associates.

Ankomah, P., Crompton, J., & Baker, D. (1996). Influence of cognitive distance in vacation choice. *Annals of Tourism Research*, 23, 138–150.

Assael, H. (1984). *Consumer behavior and marketing action*. Boston, MA: Kent Pub. Co.

Axsen, J., & Kurani, K. S. (2013). Hybrid, plug-in hybrid, or electric—What do car buyers want?. *Energy Policy*, 61, 532–543.

Baloglu, S., & Brinberg, D. (1997). Affective images of tourism destinations. *Journal of Travel Research*, 35(4), 11–15.

Baloglu, S., & Mangaloglu, M. (2001). Tourism destination images of Turkey, Greece and Italy as perceived by US-based tour operators and travel agents. *Tourism Management*, 22, 1–9.

Baloglu, S., & McCleary, K (1999). U.S. international pleasure travelers' images of four Mediterranean destinations: a comparison of visitors and nonvisitors. *Journal of Travel Research*, 38, 144–152.

Bansal, H., & Eiselt, H. A. (2004). Exploratory research of tourism motivations and planning. *Tourism Management* 25(3), 387–396.

Bettman, J. R., Luce, M. F., & Payne, J. W. (1998). Constructive consumer choice process. *Journal of Consumer Research* 25(3), 187–217.

Blain, C., Levy, S. E., & Ritchie, J. R. B. (2005). Destination branding: insights and practices from destination management organizations. *Journal of Travel Research*, 43, 328–338.

Brisoux, J., & Laroche, M. (1981). Evoked set formation and composition: an empirical investigation under a routinised response behaviour situation. *Advances in Consumer Research*, 8(1), 357–361.

Brundtland, G. H. (1987). *Report of the World Commission on Environment and Development: our common future*. Oslo: United Nations.

Buhalis, D. (2000). Marketing the competitive destination of the future. *Tourism Management*, 21, 97–116.

Chaudhary, M. (2000). India's image as a tourist destination: a perspective of foreign tourists. *Tourism Management*, 21(3), 293–297.

Chen, S. S., Chuang, Y. W., & Chen, P. Y. (2012). Behavioral intention formation in knowledge sharing: examining the roles of KMS quality, KMS self-efficacy, and organizational climate. *Knowledge-Based Systems*, 31, 106–118.

Chen, Y., Tang, G., Jin, J., Xie, Q., & Li, J. (2014). CEOs' transformational leadership and product innovation performance: the roles of corporate entrepreneurship and technology orientation. *Journal of Product Innovation Management*, 31(S1), 2–17.

Chi, C., & Qu, H. (2008). Examining the structural relationships of destination image, tourist satisfaction and destination loyalty: an integrated approach. *Tourism Management*, 29, 624–636.

Choi, S., Lehto, X., & Morrison, A. (2007). Destination image representation on the web: content analysis of Macau travel related websites. *Tourism Management*, 28, 118–129.

Chon, K. S. (1990). The role of destination image in tourism: a review and discussion. *Tourism Review*, 45, 12–19.

Chon, K. S. (1992). The role of destination image in tourism: an extension. *Tourism Review*, 47(1), 2–8.

Chuang, S. C., Cheng, Y. H., Chang, C. J., & Yang, S. W. (2012). The effect of service failure types and service recovery on customer satisfaction: a mental accounting perspective. *The Service Industries Journal*, 32(2), 257–271.

Corby, N. H., Jamner, M. S., & Wolitski, R. J. (1996). Using the theory of planned behavior to predict intention to use condoms among male and female injecting drug users. *Journal of Applied Social Psychology*, 26(1), 52–75.

Crompton, J. (1979). An assessment of the image of Mexico as a vacation destination and the influence of geographical location upon that image. *Journal of Travel Research*, 17, 18–23.

Crotts, J., & Van Rekom, J. (1998). Exploring and enhancing the psychological value of a fine arts museum. *Tourism Recreation Research*, 23(1), 31–38.

Etchner, C., & Ritchie, J. (1991). The meaning and measurement of destination image. *The Journal of Tourism Studies*, 2(2), 2–12.

Fakeye, P., & Crompton, J. (1991). Image differences between prospective, first time and repeat visitors to the Lower Rio Grande Valley. *Journal of Travel Research*, 30(2), 10–16.

Fishbein, M. (1967). Attitude and prediction of behavior. *In* M. Fishbein (Ed.), *Readings in attitude theory and measurement* (pp. 477–492 New York: John Wiley.

Fishbein, M., & Ajzen, I. (1975). *Belief, attitude, intention and behavior: an introduction to theory and research*. Boston: Addison-Wesley.

Fishbein, M., & Manfredo, M. J. (1992). A theory of behavior change. *In* M. J. Manfredo (Ed.), *Influencing human behavior: theory and applications in recreation, tourism and natural resources management* (pp. 29–50). Champaign, IL: Sagamore.

Frauman, E., & Cunningham, P. (2001). Using a Means-End approach to understand the factors that influence greenway use. *Journal of Park and Recreation Administration*, 19, 93–113.

Gallarza, M. G., Saura, I. G., & Garcia, H. C. (2002). Destination image: toward a conceptual framework. *Annals of Tourism Research*, 29(1), 56–78.

Gartner, W. C. (1993). Image formation process. *Journal of Travel and Tourism Marketing*, 2(2/3), 191–216.

Gensch, D., & Soofi, E. (1995). Information-theoretic estimation of individual consideration set. *International Journal of Research in Marketing*, 12, 25–38.

Gnoth, J. (1999). Tourism expectations formation: the case of camper-van tourists in New Zealand. *In* A. Pizam and Y. Mansfeld (Eds.), *Consumer behavior in travel and tourism* (pp. 245–265). New York: The Haworth Hospitality Press.

Govers, R., Go, F., & Kumar, K. (2007). Promoting tourism destination image. *Journal of Travel Research*, 46(1), 14–23.

Gutman, J., & Reynolds, T. J. (1979). An investigation of the levels of cognitive abstraction utilized by consumers in product differentiation. *In* J. Eighmey (Ed.), *Attitude research under the sun* (pp. 128–150). Chicago: American Marketing Association.

Haase, H., & Franco, M. (2011). Information sources for environmental scanning: do industry and firm size matter? *Management Decision*, 49(10), 1642–1657.

Han, H., Hsu, L. T. J., & Lee, J. S. (2009). Empirical investigation of the roles of attitudes toward green behaviors, overall image, gender, and age in hotel customers' eco-friendly decision-making process. *International Journal of Hospitality Management*, 28(4), 519–528.

Han, J., Kim, N., & Srivastava, R. (1998). Market orientation and organizational performance: is innovation a missing link? *The Journal of Marketing*, 62(4), 30–45.

Hanks, L., Line, N., & Kim, W. G. W. (2017). The impact of the social servicescape, density, and restaurant type on perceptions of interpersonal service quality. *International Journal of Hospitality Management*, 61, 35–44.

Hong, S. K., Kim, J. H., Jang, H., & Lee, S. (2006). The roles of categorization, affective image and constraints on destination choice: an application of the NMNL model. *Tourism Management*, 27(5), 750–761.

Hosany, S., Ekinci, Y., & Uysal, M. (2006). Destination image and destination personality: an application of branding theories to tourism places. *Journal of Business Research*, 59(5), 638–642.

Howard, J. A. (1963). *Marketing management* (2nd Ed.). Homewood, IL: Irwin Publishing.

Howard, J. A., & Sheth, J. N. (1969). *The theory of buyer behaviour*. New York: John Wiley.

Hu, J. L., Chiu, C. N., Shieh, H. S., & Huang, C. H. (2010). A stochastic cost efficiency analysis of international tourist hotels in Taiwan. *International Journal of Hospitality Management*, 29(1), 99–107.

Hunter, W. (2008). A typology of photographic representations for tourism: depictions of groomed spaces. *Tourism Management*, 29(2), 354–365.

Jang, Y. J., Kim, W. G., & Bonn, M. A. (2011). Generation Y consumers' selection attributes and behavioral intentions concerning green restaurants. *International Journal of Hospitality Management*, 30(4), 803–811.

Jiang, Y., Ramkissoon, H., Mavondo, F. T., & Feng, S. (2016). Authenticity: the link between destination image and place attachment. *Journal of Hospitality Marketing & Management* (accepted for publication).

Kahle, L., & Kennedy, P. (1988). Using the list of values (LOV) to understand consumers. *The Journal of Services Marketing*, 2(4), 49–56.

Kellstedt, P. M., Zahran, S., & Vedlitz, A. (2008). Personal efficacy, the information environment, and attitudes toward global warming and climate change in the United States. *Risk Analysis*, 28(1), 113–126.

Kim, H., & Richardson, S. L. (2003). Motion pictures impacts on destination images. *Annals of Tourism Research*, 30(1), 216–237.

Kim, M., Vogt, C. A., & Knutson, B. J. (2015). Relationships among customer satisfaction, delight, and loyalty in the hospitality industry. *Journal of Hospitality & Tourism Research*, 39(2), 170–197.

Klenosky, D. (2002). The "pull" of tourism destinations: a means-end investigation. *Journal of Travel Research*, 40, 385–396.

Klenosky, D., Gengler, C., & Mulvey, M. (1993). Understanding the factors influencing ski destination choice: a Means-End analytic approach. *Journal of Leisure Research*, 25, 362–379.

Kwok, L., Huang, Y., & Hu, L. (2016). Green attributes of restaurants: what really matters to consumers. *International Journal of Hospitality Management*, 55, 107–117.

Lam, T., & Hsu, C. H. C. (2004). Theory of planned behavior: potential travelers from China. *Journal of Hospitality and Tourism Research*, 28(4), 463–482.

Lam, T., & Hsu, C. H. (2006). Predicting behavioral intention of choosing a travel destination. *Tourism Management*, 27(4), 589–599.

Lee, G., O'Leary, J., & Hong, G. (2002). Visiting propensity predicted by destination image: German long-haul pleasure travelers to the US. *International Journal of Hospitality and Tourism Administration*, 3(2), 63–92.

Liska, A. E. (1984). A critical examination of the causal structure of the Fishbein/Ajzen attitude-behaviour model. *Social Psychology Quarterly*, 47, 61–74.

Lue, C., Crompton, J., & Stewart, W. (1996). Evidence of cumulative attraction in multidimensional recreational trip decisions. *Journal of Travel Research*, 34(1), 41–49.

MacKay, K., & Fesenmaier, D. (1997). Pictorial elements of destination in image formation. *Annals of Tourism Research*, 24(3), 537–565.

McIntosh, A., & Prentice, R. (1999). Affirming authenticity: consuming cultural heritage. *Annals of Tourism Research*, 26, 589–612.

McIntosh, A., & Thyne, M. (2005). Understanding tourist behavior using means-end chain theory. *Annals of Tourism Research*, 32(1), 259–262.

Mattila, A. (1999). An analysis of means-end hierarchies in cross-cultural context: what motivates Asian and Western business travelers to stay at luxury hotels? *Journal of Hospitality and Leisure Marketing*, 6(2), 19–28.

Milfont, T. (2012). The interplay between knowledge, perceived efficacy, and concern about global warming and climate change: a one-year longitudinal study. *Risk Analysis*, 32(6), 1003–1020.

Milman, A., & Pizam, A. (1995). The role of awareness and familiarity with a destination: the Central Florida case. *Journal of Travel Research*, 33, 21–27.

Mitchell, A. (1983). *The nine American lifestyles*. New York: Warner.

Mullen, B., & Johnson, C. (1990). *The psychology of consumer behavior*. Hillsdale, MI: Lawrence Erlbaum Associates.

Namkung, Y., & Jang, S. S. (2013). Effects of restaurant green practices on brand equity formation: do green practices really matter? *International Journal of Hospitality Management*, 33, 85–95.

Narayana, C., & Markin, R. (1975). Consumer behaviour and product performance: an alternative conceptualisation. *Journal of Marketing*, 39(4), 1–6.

Nunkoo, R., & Ramkissoon, H. (2009) The potential of using the means-end chain theory and the laddering technique to the study of host attitudes to tourism. *Journal of Sustainable Tourism*, 17(3), 337–355

Nunkoo, R., & Ramkissoon, H. (2010). Gendered theory of planned behavior and resident support for tourism. *Current Issues in Tourism*, 13(6), 525–540.

Ockwell, D., Whitmarsh, L., & O'Neill, S. (2009). Reorienting climate change communication for effective mitigation: forcing people to be green or fostering grass-roots engagement? *Science Communication*, 30(3), 305–327

Okumus, F. (2004). Implementation of yield management practices in service organisations: empirical findings from a major hotel group. *The Service Industries Journal*, 24(6), 65–89.

Owens, S. (2000). 'Engaging the public': information and deliberation in environmental policy. *Environment and Planning A*, 32(7), 1141–1148.

Parsa, H. G., Lord, K. R., Putrevu, S., & Kreeger, J. (2015). Corporate social and environmental responsibility in services: will consumers pay for it? *Journal of Retailing and Consumer Services*, 22, 250–260.

Peiró-Signes, A., Verma, R., Mondéjar-Jiménez, J., & Vargas-Vargas, M. (2014). The impact of environmental certification on hotel guest ratings. *Cornell Hospitality Quarterly*, 55(1), 40–51.

Petty, R. E., & Cacioppo, J. T. (1986). The elaboration likelihood model of persuasion. In *Communication and persuasion* (pp. 1–24). Springer: New York.

Pike, S., & Ryan, C. (2004). Destination positioning analysis through a comparison of cognitive, affective and conative perceptions. *Journal of Travel Research*, 42(4), 333–342.

Pizam, A. (2009). Green hotels: a fad, ploy or fact of life? *International Journal of Hospitality Management*, 28(1), 1.

Prentice, R. (2006). Evocation and experiential seduction: updating choice-sets modelling. *Tourism Management*, 27, 1153–1170.

Ramkissoon. H., & Mavondo, F. (2016). Managing customer relationships in hotel chains: a comparison between guest and manager perceptions. In: V. Magnini, M. Ivanova and S. Ivanov (Eds.), *The Routledge handbook of hotel chain management* (pp. 295–304). Abingdon, Oxon: Routledge.

Ramkissoon, H., & Mavondo, F. (in press). Pro-environmental behaviour: critical link between satisfaction and place attachment in Australia and Canada. *Tourism Analysis*.

Ramkissoon, H., & Nunkoo, R. (2008). Information search behavior of European tourists visiting Mauritius. *Tourism: An International Interdisciplinary Journal*, 56(1), 7–21.

Ramkissoon, H., Nunkoo, R., & Gursoy, D. (2009). How consumption values affect destination image formation. In: A. G. Woodside, C. M. Megehee and A. Ogle (Eds.), *Advances in culture, tourism and hospitality research* (pp. 143–168). Emerald Group Publishing Limited.

Ramkissoon, H., & Smith, L. (2014). The relationship between environmental worldviews, emotions and personal efficacy in climate change. *International Journal of Arts & Sciences*, 7(1), 93.

Ramkissoon, H., Smith, L., & Weiler, B. (2013). Testing the dimensionality of place attachment and its relationships with place satisfaction and pro-environmental behaviours: a structural equation modelling approach. *Tourism Management*, 36, 552–566.

Ramkissoon, H., & Uysal, M. S. (2014). Authenticity as a value co-creator of tourism experiences. In: N. K. Prebensen, J. S. Chen and M. Uysal (Eds.), *Creating experience value in tourism* (pp. 113–124). Wallingford, UK: CABI.

Rokeach, M. (1968). *Beliefs, attitudes and values*. San Francisco: Jossey Bass.

Singal, M. (2014). Corporate social responsibility in the hospitality and tourism industry: Do family control and financial condition matter? *International Journal of Hospitality Management*, 36, 81–89.

Sirakaya, E., & Woodside, A. G. (2005). Building and testing theories of decision making by travelers. *Tourism Management*, 26, 815–832.

Sparks, B. (2007). Planning a wine tourism vacation? Factors that help to predict tourists' behavioral intentions. *Tourism Management*, 28(5), 1180–1192.

Spiggle, S., & Sewall, M. (1987). A choice set model of retail selection. *Journal of Marketing*, 51(2), 97–111.

Subramaniam, M., & Youndt, M. A. (2005). The influence of intellectual capital on the types of innovative capabilities. *Academy of Management Journal*, 48(3), 450–463.

Susskind, A. M. (2014). Guests' reactions to in-room sustainability initiatives: an experimental look at product performance and guest satisfaction. *Cornell Hospitality Quarterly*. doi: 1938965514533744.

Tang, T. (2015). Competing through customer social capital: the proactive personality of bed and breakfast operators. *Asia Pacific Journal of Tourism Research*, 20(2), 133–151.

Tang, T. (2016). Making innovation happen through building social capital and scanning environment. *International Journal of Hospitality Management*, 56, 56–65.

Theoharakis, V., & Hooley, G. (2008). Customer orientation and innovativeness: differing roles in New and Old Europe. *International Journal of Research in Marketing*, 25(1), 69–79.

Thyne, M. (2001). The importance of values research for nonprofit organizations: the motivation-based values of museum visitors. *International Journal of Nonprofit and Voluntary Sector Marketing*, 6(2), 116–130.

Thyne, M., & Lawson, R. (2001). Values as a basis for understanding motivations towards accommodation and activity choices. In: M. Robinson, P. Long, N. Evans, R. Sharpley and J. Swarbrooke (Eds.), *Reflections on international tourism: motivations, behaviour and tourist types*. Sheffield: Centre for Travel and Tourism.

Todd, S. (2001). Self-concept: a tourism application. *Journal of Consumer Behavior*, 1(2), 184–196.

Triandis, H. C. (1977). *Interpersonal behaviour*. Monterey, CA: Brooks/Cole.

Um, S., & Crompton, J. (1990). Attitudes determinants in tourism destination choice. *Annals of Tourism Research*, 17, 432–448.

Van Raaij, W. F., & Francken, D. A. (1984). Vacation decisions, activities, and satisfactions. *Annals of Tourism Research*, 11(1), 101–112.

van Riper, C. J., & Kyle, G. T. (2014). Understanding the internal processes of behavioral engagement in a national park: a latent variable path analysis of the value-belief-norm theory. *Journal of Environmental Psychology*, 38, 288–297.

Van Vugt, M. (2009). Averting the tragedy of the commons: using social psychological science to protect the environment. *Current Directions in Psychological Science*, 18(3), 169–173.

Vogt, C., & Fesenmaier, D. (1998). Expanding the functional information search. *Annals of Tourism Research*, 25(3), 551–578.

White, C. (2004). Destination image: to see or not to see? *International Journal of Contemporary Hospitality Management*, 16(5), 309–314.

White, C. (2005). Culture, emotions and behavioral intentions: implications for tourism research and practice. *Current Issues in Tourism*, 8(6), 510–531.

Wicks, B., & Schuett, M. (1991). Examining the role of tourism promotion through the use of brochures. *Tourism Management*, 11, 301–312.

Woodside, A., & King, R. (2001). An updated model of travel and tourism purchase-consumption systems. *Journal of Travel and Tourism Marketing*, 10(1), 3–27.

Woodside, A., & Lysonski, S. (1989). A general model of traveler destination choice. *Journal of Travel Research*, 27(1), 8–14.

Xie, H. J., Miao, L., Kuo, P. J., & Lee, B. Y. (2011). Consumers' responses to ambivalent online hotel reviews: the role of perceived source credibility and pre-decisional disposition. *International Journal of Hospitality Management*, 30(1), 178–183.

Xu, X., & Gursoy, D. (2015). A conceptual framework of sustainable hospitality supply chain management. *Journal of Hospitality Marketing & Management*, 24(3), 229–259.

Zalatan, A. (1998). Wives' involvement in tourism decision process. *Annals of Tourism Research*, 25(4), 890–903.

23

Hospitality consumers' information search behavior

Reinforcement and displacement of traditional media

Haywantee Ramkissoon

Introduction

Advancement in technology is clearly changing the way people consume hospitality products and services. Consumers are now exposed to an excessive amount of readily available information, and have different information needs. Hospitality consumers' information search behavior is not a homogenous process, but rather is heterogeneous in nature (Ramkissoon & Nunkoo, 2008), prompting researchers and hospitality providers to focus in greater detail on how hospitality consumers access the flow of information across several communication channels. This is vital to assist in developing appropriate strategies and ensuring good service delivery, and in reinforcing customer loyalty. The prevalence of social media has become ubiquitous (Dréze & Hussherr, 2003; Jenkins & Deuze, 2008; Månsson, 2011; Nusair et al., 2011; Okazaki & Hirose, 2009; Xiang & Gretzel, 2010), which is a testament to the new era of media convergence.

Media convergence, also known as the digitization and reestablishment of established media into various new and interactive formats (Jenkins, 2006, 2012; Jenkins & Deuze, 2008), strongly affects the circulation of information. This is evidenced by the plethora of research on the use and effects of social media in hospitality and tourism (Ho et al., 2012; Månsson, 2011; Pan, 2015; Okazaki & Hirose, 2009; Xiang & Gretzel, 2010). Social media instils a participatory culture in society, whereby individuals actively engage in creating, sharing and communicating information through new media platforms (Jenkins, 2006, 2012). This is reflected in the role of social media in the circulation of travel-related information and in the pervasiveness of travel-related search engines. In Europe, 72 percent of air ticket sales and 70 percent of accommodation sales were booked via online channels, either directly from vendors' websites or through online travel agents (Grønflaten, 2009).

While some studies have investigated the role of online media referred to as the "new media" on hospitality consumers' information search behavior, this important domain continues to attract significant interest from scholars and hospitality businesses. An important gap to address is how the "new media" reinforces or displaces traditional media for hospitality consumers, at this moment of media transition which has seen an intense shift in our communication infrastructure. Hospitality users now have access to different channels of information, which also seem to allow participation, and co-creation, with other users (Ramkissoon & Uysal, 2014), often providing them with increasing control over the information flow (Krishnan & Jones, 2005).

Jenkins (2004, p. 37) refers to this trend as a convergence culture, which is defined as:

> both a top-down corporate-driven process and a bottom-up consumer-driven process. Media companies are learning how to accelerate the flow of media content across delivery channels to expand revenue opportunities, broaden markets and reinforce viewer commitments. Consumers are learning how to use these different media technologies to bring the flow of media more fully under their control and to interact with others.

Analyzing consumption of hospitality products and services, with a focus on how people receive and give meanings to information, will have important implications for hospitality providers. This chapter contributes to the theoretical advancement of knowledge by examining the significance of current trends in hospitality consumers' information search behavior through the lens of convergence culture. The "new media," displacement, and reinforcement are discussed in the context of the pervasiveness of travel search engines and the role of social media in hospitality.

Hospitality consumers' information search behavior

Extant research indicates that the ways in which hospitality consumers search for and acquire information before making purchase decisions are of crucial importance in understanding their behavior (Li et al., 2009; Pan & Fesenmaier, 2006) and are important for marketing management decisions (Ramkissoon & Uysal, 2011; Srinivasan, 1990). Gursoy and Umbreit (2004) argue that the first step of destination decision-making is the search for information, defined as the "motivated activation of knowledge stored in memory or acquisition of information from the environment" (Engel et al., 1995, p. 182). The search initially takes place internally, where past experiences are used to make decisions, and extends to external sources if the individual's memory is not sufficient to make decisions (Fodness & Murray, 1997). The process of information search may be conceptualized as starting when an individual recognizes a need (Kerstetter & Cho, 2004) and is likely to take place when the hospitality consumer has to make a decision on the purchase of hospitality products and services.

Most studies on information search behavior are guided by two main models: the strategic model and the contingency model (Fodness & Murray, 1997). The strategic model, proposed by Snepenger et al. (1990) has as its main focus the number and combination of information sources utilized by consumers. However, many studies which have used this source-based approach have considered only one type of information source used by consumers of facilities and services (Fodness & Murray, 1997). Snepenger et al. (1990, p. 22) define a search strategy as "the combination of information sources used by a travel party to plan a trip." Other studies evidence that travelers tend to use different information sources such as travel consultants, family and friends, destination-specific literature, and the media when planning a vacation (Ramkissoon & Nunkoo, 2008, 2012; Xiang et al., 2017) and do not depend only on one information source to choose the product.

One of the most important developments in communication technology is the expansion of the internet (Morgan et al., 2001), which has changed the ways people search for information (Kim et al., 2007; Ozturan & Roney, 2004). This has indeed made traditional marketing practices potentially obsolete (Buhalis, 1998). The internet has been found to be a useful source of information (Gursoy & Umbreit, 2004; Money & Crotts, 2003; Pan & Fesenmaier, 2006), making it easier for travelers to collect information before finalizing their purchase of tourism and hospitality products (Jun et al., 2007).

There is a plethora of studies on internet use and information search behavior (e.g. Beldona, 2005; Jun et al., 2007; Pan and Fesenmaier, 2006). The more one spends time online, the more searching skills one acquires and the more comfortable one becomes searching for information online (Hargittai, 2002). Online satisfaction has been found to have a positive impact on purchase intentions (Bai et al., 2008; Jeong et al., 2003). The development of medical tourism in Asian countries such as Thailand and India, with medical tourists consuming a range of hospitality products and services, has been attributed to the increased dominance of internet marketing (Connell, 2006).

The strategic model also deals with the influence of socio-demographic characteristics on the use of external information sources (Snepenger et al., 1990). One of the advantages of the strategic model is that it attempts to look into the different sources of information likely to be utilized by hospitality consumers. Its weakness is that it does not help us to understand the reasons why hospitality consumers utilize certain types of external information sources and reject others. Also, it does not attempt to analyze factors (other than consumers' demographic characteristics) that may affect consumers' use of external sources of information available.

The contingency model was first proposed by Schul and Crompton (1983); it uses consumer characteristics such as travel-specific lifestyles, previous trip experience, number of sources, product characteristics, and situational influences to define information search (Fodness & Murray, 1997; Schul and Crompton, 1983). Schul and Crompton (1983) argue that travel-specific lifestyles and individual differences are better determinants of travel and hospitality consumers' information search behavior than socio-demographic variables. Fodness and Murray (1997) further developed the contingency model to include other elements such as the nature of decision-making: routine, limited, or extended; composition of travel party (situational factors); product characteristics; consumer characteristics (family life cycle and socio-economic status); and search outcomes (e.g. length of stay, number of attractions visited, travel-related expenditure) which are also likely to affect the external information search behavior of hospitality consumers.

Although both the strategic and the contingency models consider the influence of the composition of the travel party, prior product knowledge, and the degree of familiarity associated with the hospitality products and services on the type of external information sources selected, the contingency model is considered superior to the strategic model since it examines several other factors that are likely to influence consumers' search behavior. Nevertheless, although it is considered to be superior to the strategic model, the contingency model ignores motivational and psychological factors that may affect information search behaviour. However, as argued by some scholars, consumers gather information to protect themselves and optimize their experiences (Bettman, 1979, Murray, 1991; Urbany et al., 1989), which implies that their motivations are likely to influence their information search behavior.

The contingency model postulates that those familiar with and/or experts of the hospitality products are not likely to search for additional information to make their decision. In other words, they will reach their decision through a routine or limited problem-solving process. Consumer behavior literature also suggests that knowledgeable consumers can better understand the meaning of product information compared to novices, and thus are more likely to search for new information prior to making their decision (Alba & Hutchinson, 1987; Duncan & Olshavsky, 1982; Johnson & Russo, 1984). Novices are more likely to refer to the opinions of others (Brucks, 1985) as they have a limited ability to process the product-related information compared to knowledgeable consumers who are likely to focus on particular product attributes as they are already aware of their existence.

Media displacement and reinforcement

The World Wide Web was initially created as an effective and convenient means of sharing information (Leiner et al., 2009). With advancements in technology, it is no secret that the internet has made it possible for individuals to seek information in real time and with no significant effort (Xiang & Gretzel, 2010). This accessibility has in turn increased the level of competition in the market, thus creating intense competition between market players (Okazaki & Hirose, 2009). Consequently, hospitality and tourism businesses have used gratifications presented in various forms to gain a competitive advantage over their online and offline competitors (Okazaki & Hirose, 2009). Drawing on the concept of media displacement and reinforcement, the use of gratifications in new media will either reinforce or completely displace traditional media.

The argument of media displacement and reinforcement has created a discourse, with some believing that new media reinforces traditional media (Grønflaten, 2009; Hernández-Méndez & Muñoz-Leiva, 2015; Ho et al., 2012; Okazaki & Hirose, 2009; Tsao & Sibley, 2004) and others believing that new media displaces traditional media (Lyu & Hwang, 2015; Månsson, 2011). To better illustrate the above discussion on media displacement, in November 2015, Qantas launched a TV campaign titled "feels like home" (Qantas, 2015). The advertisement did not contain information regarding specific flight details or the services it entails. Instead, it promoted the hashtag #feelslikehome, which consumers could use on social media to share and obtain information regarding Qantas services. As the television commercial was used as a means to encourage online user-generated content regarding Qantas (i.e. on social media such as Facebook, YouTube, and Twitter), this was an example of using new media as a reinforcement of traditional media.

With the ever-increasing accessibility of online information, Ironside (2016) reported that Australian consumers prefer researching travel information through new media due to convenience. Furthermore, travel search engines are the number one source of travel information for consumers (Ironside, 2016). In addition, consumers also seek travel-related information from social networking sites such as Facebook, Twitter, and blogs, as they contain user-oriented and/or generated content (Månsson, 2011). Perhaps a consumer-to-consumer point of view makes the information appear to be more trustworthy and reliable, and is considered by some as a true representation of the service.

Despite the convenience of online information research, previous studies have found that consumers who prefer traditional media are unlikely to change their information search behavior from traditional means to new media (Okazaki & Hirose, 2009). Tsao and Sibley (2004) also found that although internet advertising carries many benefits, it has not displaced traditional media. Hence, new media is considered as a reinforcement of traditional media, rather than a replacement as such. Some studies show that those familiar with traditional media (i.e. brochures, and television and print adverts) will continue to seek information through offline advertisements and travel agents, whereas those who prefer online new media will seek information through travel search engines and will base their decision on the best deal that satisfies them (Okazaki & Hirose, 2009). Despite the significance of new media in hospitality and tourism, consumers have other options for obtaining information (Ho et al., 2012). These options include traditional means such as travel agents, brochures, and other offline media. Consumers merely search for information online as a form of enjoyment and as a means to interact with other travelers (Grønflaten, 2009), making it unlikely for online information to be the sole source of consumers' search for hospitality services.

Drawing from Jenkins' (2006) concept of media convergence, the circulation of information will eventually shift into fully embracing new media as its platform. Some scholars argue that with further advancements in technology, online media will gradually become the sole source of information for hospitality consumers, eventually displacing traditional media information sources (e.g. Lyu & Hwang, 2015; Månsson, 2011). In their recent study using the technology acceptance model (TAM), Lyu and Hwang (2015) report a negative correlation in the relationship between those who obtain travel information online and their attitudes toward and intention to visit tourism information centers. They argue that it is more likely for traditional sources of information to be discontinued in the future owing to further developments in technology.

Generation X and Y

Despite the arguments on whether new media displaces or reinforces traditional media, consumers often search for information through methods they are familiar with and are confident in using (Grønflaten, 2009; Månsson, 2011; Nusair, et al., 2013; Okazaki & Hirose, 2009). Information search behavior differs among individuals with different socio-demographic characteristics such as age, gender, or income level (Ramkissoon & Nunkoo, 2008; Ramkissoon & Uysal, 2011). Purpose of trip has a great influence on consumers' information search behavior (Moutinho, 1987). A study conducted by Fodness and Murray (1997) revealed that vacationers were the most active information gatherers as compared to those visiting their friends and relatives, who are in turn more likely to be associated with passive information search or possession of information from their past experiences. These studies postulate the use of contingency models. A similar view is shared by Etzel and Wahlers (1985) and Snepenger and Snepenger (1993), who conclude that tourists visiting families and friends or making repeat visits may not gather additional information but instead use information acquired from their past experiences.

Importantly, the existing literature shows age to be a determining factor in consumers' readiness to accept and use "new media" in their search for information (e.g. Khare, et al., 2012; Lissitsa & Kol, 2016). Generation Y is defined as consumers born between 1980 and 1999, Generation X as consumers born between 1961 and 1979, and older generations before 1961 (Lissitsa & Kol, 2016). A study conducted by Destination NSW, in Australia, found that the most effective way to engage with tourists within a young-to-young adult age group is through online media such as online travel agents, online marketing, and social media (Destination NSW, 2013). Young adults are known to be technologically savvy, thus having a stronger tendency to embrace new media (Lester et al., 2005; Nusair et al., 2013; Sun et al., 2015). Those born between 1978 and 1994 were not only found to be fond of online travel planning, but are also committed to searching for information and deciding to purchase travel services online (Nusair et al., 2011).

The most prominent antecedent of young adults' online search behavior is the convenience of being able to obtain a comprehensive understanding regarding the travel services offered (Grønflaten, 2009; Sun et al., 2015). Consumers within this age group argue that conducting information research through online media allows them to easily assess the most beneficial deal that would satisfy their needs (Gursoy & Chen, 2000; Parra-Lopéz, et al., 2011; Sun et al., 2015).

Similar to those within the young adult age group, those considered as Generation X are also known to have a high adoption rate of new technology (Lissitsa & Kol, 2016). In relation to consumers within this age group, Lissitsa and Kol (2016) cited a study conducted by MasterCard (2012), where 36 percent of its Generation X consumers used online services to book travel itineraries, including flights and accommodation. Generation X independent travelers prefer to search for hospitality and tourism information through online media with no face-to-face or traditional encounters (Grønflaten, 2009). However, the study also found that those between 40 and 49 years of age prefer to seek information through a combination of face-to-face interaction (traditional information research) and new media (Grønflaten, 2009).

Consumers from an older generation are considered to have a high purchasing power (Alén et al., 2016). Some studies suggest that senior tourists and hospitality consumers (above the age of 59) are likely to search for information traditionally, both face to face and through travel agents, and the internet is used mainly for social interactions (e.g. Grønflaten, 2009; Vojvodic, 2015). They are also likely to search for new information within their circle of family and friends. There is a need for further research on Generation X's attitudes to "new media" and their information search behavior in the hospitality industry.

Experience of use of "new media"

Information search behavior has also been used as a segmentation criterion (Moutinho, 1987). The digital divide, or the segregation between those who are technologically savvy or slow, is still present (Pick & Azari, 2007). A number of studies suggest that consumers who are technologically savvy tend to search for information through new media (Khare et al., 2012; Lissitsa & Kol, 2016; Munar & Jacobsen, 2014). As evidenced by the literature, consumers who fall under Generation Y and Generation X are more likely to use new media as their information search platforms (Lester et al., 2005; Lissitsa & Kol, 2016; Nusair et al., 2013; Sun et al., 2015). This is because younger generations, specifically Generation Y, are known to be more technologically savvy compared to older ones (Lester et al., 2005). However, the segregation of the digital divide has significantly diminished.

Only a few studies have looked at senior consumers' use of "new media" in their consumption of hospitality services. Interestingly, there has been a significant rise in the number of senior consumers using social media platforms (Jung & Sundar, 2016). Consequently, consumers' level of technology and media savviness has generally increased. Based on the above discussion, Generation Y hospitality consumers can be considered as technologically savvy, Generation X hospitality consumers as moderately savvy and older generation hospitality consumers to be in the early stages of technology savviness.

Technologically savvy consumers tend to spend less time searching for information on new media than those who are regarded as less savvy (Hernández-Méndez & Muñoz-Leiva, 2015). For example, technologically savvy consumers are more inclined to look to book hotels and use other services through community and social media such as TripAdvisor, Instagram, Facebook, and Twitter (Grønflaten, 2009; Hernández-Méndez & Muñoz-Leiva, 2015; Okazaki & Hirose, 2009; Tsao & Sibley, 2004).

Previous studies have found that to ensure that the targeted group of consumers obtain the necessary information during their research and planning period, online advertisements in the form of banners are effective in targeting consumers within the older demographic or those who are less technologically savvy (Danaher & Mullarkey, 2003; Hernández-Méndez & Muñoz-Leiva, 2015). This is because, although they visit the same pages as younger consumers, they spend considerably more time examining all of the given information upon visiting a website than younger consumers do (Dréze & Hussherr, 2003; Hernández-Méndez & Muñoz-Leiva, 2015).

On the contrary, the use of user-generated and oriented content was found to be effective in engaging with a younger group of consumers or those who are considered to be technologically savvy (Nusair et al., 2011, 2013). Studies evidence that this group of consumers is familiar with social media and travel-specific websites, specifically community-centered websites containing travel discussions such as TripAdvisor, Yelp, Yahoo Travel, Kayak.com.au, and Expedia (Ayeh et al., 2013; Nusair et al., 2011; Nusair et al., 2013; Parra-Lopéz et al., 2011; Sun et al., 2015; Xiang & Gretzel, 2010; Yoo & Gretzel, 2011). Based on the above discussion, consumers' level of experience of use with "new media" plays an important role in understanding hospitality consumers' information search behavior, and warrants further investigation.

Conclusion

This chapter has addressed the importance of hospitality consumers' information search behavior in the context of a convergence culture, represented by the prevalence of new media. It has presented the discourse of arguments on how new media could act as a reinforcement to traditional media or could displace traditional media. Previous studies have found that consumers visit travel community websites during their travel decision-making process (e.g. Ramkissoon & Nunkoo, 2012; Ramkissoon & Uysal, 2011). This informs their decisions on the hospitality products to be purchased for their trip. The existing literature suggests that consumers' successful online information searches may not only result in purchase behavior, but also in the displacement of traditional media for consumers of hospitality services.

Studies show how it is plausible that both Generation X and Y consumers may have positive attitudes towards "new media" regarding searching for hospitality products and services, while the older generation consumers may have negative attitudes towards new media, with a preference for traditional sources of information. Hospitality consumers can be categorized as technologically savvy and less technologically savvy, based on their age group, and this determines their information search behavior for hospitality products. From such a perspective, their level of experience of use of new media might prompt different information search behavior. Hospitality consumers who are more familiar with new media such as online travel community websites may have a stronger tendency to use online information search engines, and to eventually reconsider the need for traditional media altogether. Future studies could build on this line of research and keep track of the role of new media on the information search behavior of consumers of hospitality products and services. Empirical findings would be useful and timely for hospitality providers, and may have the potential to identify and fulfil the different needs of hospitality consumers at an early stage of product development.

References

Alba, J., & Hutchinson, J. (1987). Dimensions of consumer expertise. *Journal of Consumer Research*, 13, 411–453.

Alén, E., Losada, N., & Domíniguez, T. (2016). The impact of ageing on the tourism industry: An approach to the senior tourist profile. *Social Indicators Research*, 127(1), 303–322.

Ayeh, J. K., Au, N., & Law, R. (2013). Predicting the intention to use consumer-generated media for travel planning. *Tourism Management*, 35, 132–143.

Bai, B., Law, R., & Wen, I. (2008). The impact of website quality on customer satisfaction and purchase intentions: Evidence from Chinese online visitors. *International Journal of Hospitality Management*, 27, 391–402.

Beldona, S. (2005). Cohort analysis of online travel information search behavior: 1995–2000. *Journal of Travel Research*, 44, 135–142.

Bettman, J. (1979). *An information processing theory of consumer behaviour*. Reading: Addison-Wesley.

Brucks, M. (1985). The effects of product class knowledge on information search behaviour. *Journal of Consumer Research*, 12, 1–16.

Buhalis, D. (1998). Strategic use of information technologies in the tourism industry. *Tourism Management*, 19(5), 409–421.

Connell, J. (2006). Medical tourism: Sea, sun, sand and … surgery. *Tourism Management*, 27, 1093–1100.

Danaher, P. J., & Mullarkey, G. W. (2003). Factors affecting online advertising recall: A study of students. *Journal of Advertising Research*, 43(3), 182–194.

Destination NSW. (2013). *International Youth Leisure Market*. Retrieved from Destination NSW: www.destinationnsw.com.au/wp-content/uploads/2013/10/Youth-Fact-Sheet.pdf

Dréze, X., & Hussherr, F.-X. (2003). Internet advertising: Is anybody watching? *Journal of Interactive Marketing*, 17(4), 8–23.

Duncan, C., & Olshavsky, R. (1982). External search: The role of consumer beliefs. *Journal of Marketing Research*, 19, 32–43.

Engel, J., Blackwell, R., & Miniard, P. (1995). *Consumer behaviour* (8th Ed.). Fort Worth, TX: The Dryden Press.

Etzel, M. & Wahlers, R. (1985). The use of requested promotional material by pleasure travelers. *Journal of Travel Research*, 23(4), 2–6.

Fodness, D., & Murray, B. (1997). Tourist information search. *Annals of Tourism Research*, 24(3), 503–523.

Grønflaten, Ø. (2009). Predicting travelers' choice of information sources and information channels. *Journal of Travel Research*, 48(2), 230–244.

Gursoy, D., & Chen, J. S. (2000). Competitive analysis of cross cultural information search behavior. *Tourism Management*, 21(6), 583–590.

Gursoy, D., & Umbreit, W. T. (2004). Tourist information search behaviour: Cross-cultural comparison of European Union member states. *Hospitality Management*, 23, 55–70.

Hargittai, E. (2002). Second-level digital divide: Differences in people's online skills. *First Monday*, 7(4). Retrieved from www.firstmonday.dk/issues/issue7_4/hargittai/

Hernández-Méndez, J., & Muñoz-Leiva, F. (2015). What type of online advertising is more effective for eTourism 2.0: An eye tracking study based on the characteristics of tourists. *Computers in Human Behavior*, 50, 618–625.

Ho, C.-I., Lin, M.-H., & Chen, H.-M. (2012). Web users' behavioural patterns of tourism information search: From online to offline. *Tourism Management*, 33(6), 1468–1482.

Ironside, R. (2016). *Aussies Seeing the World in Just Three Days*. Retrieved July 1, 2016, from www.couriermail.com.au/travel/holiday-ideas/short-breaks/aussies-seeing-the-world-in-just-threedays/news-story/882cd93978307eda0bb2cd40860960bd

Jeong, M., Oh, H., & Gregoire, M. (2003). Conceptualizing website quality and its consequences in the lodging industry. *International Journal of Hospitality Management*, 22(2), 161–175.

Jenkins, H. (2004). The cultural logic of media convergence. *International Journal of Cultural Studies*, 7(1), 33–43

Jenkins, H. (2006). *Fans, bloggers and gamers: Exploring participatory culture*. New York: New York University Press.

Jenkins, H. (2012). *Textual poachers: Television fans and participatory culture*. New York: Routledge.

Jenkins, H., & Deuze, M. (2008). Editorial: Convergence culture. *The International Journal of Research into New Media Technologies*, 14(1), 5–12.

Johnson, E., & Russo, J. (1984). Product familiarity and learning new information. *Journal of Consumer Research*, 11, 542–550.

Jun, S. H., Vogt, C., & MacKay, K. J. (2007). Relationships between travel information search and travel product purchase in pre-trip context. *Journal of Travel Research*, 45, 266–274.

Jung, E. H., & Sundar, S. S. (2016). Senior citizens on Facebook: How do they interact and why? *Computers and Human Behavior*, 61, 27–35.

Kim, D. Y., Lehto, X., & Morrison, A. (2007). Gender differences in online travel information search: Implications for marketing communications on the internet. *Tourism Management*, 28, 423–433.

Kerstetter, D., & Cho, M. (2004). Prior knowledge, credibility and information search. *Annals of Tourism Research*, 31(4), 961–985.

Krishnan, A., & Jones, S. (2005). TimeSpace: Activity-based temporal visualization of personal information spaces. *Personal Ubiquitous Computing*, 9, 46–65.

Khare, A., Khare, A., & Singh, S. (2012). Attracting shoppers to shop online: Challenges and opportunities for the Indian retail sector. *Journal of Internet Commerce*, 11(2), 161–185.

Leiner, B. M., Kahn, R. E., Postel, J., Cerf, V. G., Kleinrock, L., Roberts, L. G., et al. (2009). A brief history of the internet. *ACM Computer Communication Review*, 39(5), 22–31.

Lester, D. H., Forman, A. M., & Loyd, D. (2005). Internet shopping and buying behavior of college students. *Services Marketing Quarterly*, 27(2), 123–138.

Li, X. R., Pan, B., Zhang, L., & Smith, W. (2009). The effect of online information search on image development: Insights from a mixed-methods study. *Journal of Travel Research*, 48(1), 45–57.

Lissitsa, S., & Kol, O. (2016). Generation X vs Generation Y – A decade of online shopping. *Journal of Retailing and Consumer Services*, 31, 304–312.

Lyu, S. O., & Hwang, J. (2015). Are the days of tourist information centers gone? Effects of the ubiquitous information environment. *Tourism Management*, 48, 54–63.

Månsson, M. (2011). Mediatized tourism. *Annals of Tourism Research*, 38(4), 1634–1652.

MasterCard. (2012). *Index MasterCard – Online Consumer Survey*. Retrieved from www.isoc.org.il/sts-data/10710

Money, R. B., & Crotts, J. C. (2003). The effect of uncertainty avoidance on information search, planning and purchases of international travel vacations. *Tourism Management*, 24, 191–202.

Morgan, N. J., Pritchard, A., & Abbott, S. (2001). Consumers, travel and technology: A bright future for the Web or television shopping. *Journal of Vacation Marketing*, 7, 110–124.

Moutinho, L. (1987). Consumer behaviour in tourism. *European Journal of Marketing*, 21, 5–44.

Munar, A. M., & Jacobsen, J. K. (2014). Motivations for sharing tourism experiences through social media. *Tourism Management*, 43, 46–54.

Murray, K. B. (1991). A test of services marketing theory: Consumer information acquisition activities. *Journal of Marketing*, 55, 10–23.

Nusair, K., Bilgihan, A., Okumus, F., & Cobanoglu, C. (2013). Generation Y travelers' commitment to online social network websites. *Tourism Management*, 35, 13–22.

Nusair, K., Parsa, H. G., & Cobanoglu, C. (2011). Building a model of commitment for Generation Y: An empirical study on e-travel retailers. *Tourism Management*, 32, 833–843.

Okazaki, S., & Hirose, M. (2009). Does gender affect media choice in travel information search? On the use of mobile internet. *Tourism Management*, 30(6), 794–804.

Ozturan, M., & Roney, S. A. (2004). Internet use among travel agencies in Turkey: An exploratory study. *Tourism Management*, 25, 259–266.

Pan, B. (2015). The power of search engine ranking for tourist destinations. *Tourism Management*, 47, 79–87.

Pan, B., & Fesenmaier, D. (2006). Online information search: Vacation planning process. *Annals of Tourism Research*, 33(3), 809–832.

Parra-López, E., Bulchand-Gidumal, J., Gutiérrez-Taño, D., & Díaz-Armas, R. (2011). Intentions to use social media in organizing and taking vacation trips. *Computers in Human Behavior*, 27, 640–654.

Pick, J. B., & Azari, R. (2007). *Worldwide digital divide: Influences of education, workforce, economic, and policy factors on information technology*. New York: SIGMIS CPR Conference.

Ramkissoon, H., & Nunkoo, R. (2008) Information search behaviour of European tourists visiting Mauritius. *Tourism*, 56(1), 7–21.

Ramkissoon, H., & Nunkoo. R. (2012). More than just biological sex: Examining the structural relationship between gender identity and information search behavior. *Journal of Hospitality and Tourism Research*, 36(2), 191–215.

Ramkissoon, H., & Uysal, M. (2011). The effects of perceived authenticity, information search behavior, motivation and destination imagery on cultural behavioral intentions of tourists. *Current Issues in Tourism*, 14(6), 537–562.

Ramkissoon, H., & Uysal, M. (2014). Authenticity as a value co-creator of tourism experiences, in N. K. Prebensen, J. S. Chen & M. Uysal (Eds.), *Creating experience value in tourism*. Wallingford, UK: CABI, pp. 113–124.

Qantas. (2015). *Feels Like Home Qantas*. Retrieved June 29, 2016, from YouTube: www.youtube.com/watch?v=XbAXMjcwCc4

Schul, P., & Crompton, J. L. (1983). Search behavior of international vacationers: Travel-specific lifestyle and sociodemographic variables. *Journal of Travel Research*, 22(3), 25–31.

Snepenger, D., & Snepenger, M. (1993). Information search by pleasure travelers, in M. A. Kahn & M. D. Olsen (Eds.), *Encyclopedia of hospitality and tourism*. New York: Van Nostrand Reinhold, pp. 830–835.

Snepenger, D. J., Meged, K., Snelling, M., & Worrall, K. (1990). Information search strategies by destination-naïve tourists. *Journal of Travel Research*, 29(2), 13–16.

Srinivasan, N. (1990). Pre-purchase external information search for information, in V. E. Zeithaml (Ed.), *Review of marketing*. Chicago, IL: American Marketing Association, pp. 153–189

Sun, S., Fong, L. H., Law, R., & Luk, C. (2015). An investigation of Gen-Y's online hotel information search: The case of Hong Kong. *Asia Pacific Journal of Tourism Research*, 21(4), 443–456.

Tsao, J. C., & Sibley, S. D. (2004). Displacement and reinforcement effects of the internet and other media as sources of advertising information. *Journal of Advertising Research*, 44(1), 126–142.

Urbany, J., Dickson, P., & Wilkie, W. (1989). Buyer uncertainty and information search. *Journal of Consumer Research*, 16, 208–215.

Vojvodic, K. (2015). Understanding the senior travel market: A review. *Tourism in South Eastern Europe*, 3, 479–488.

Xiang, Z., Du, Q., Ma, Y., & Fan, W. (2017). A comparative analysis of major online review platforms: Implications for social media analytics in hospitality and tourism. *Tourism Management*, 58, 51–65.

Xiang, Z., & Gretzel, U. (2010). Role of social media in online travel information search. *Tourism Management*, 31(2), 179–188.

Yoo, K.-H., & Gretzel, U. (2011). Influence of personality on travel-related consumer-generated media creation. *Computers in Human Behavior*, 27, 609–621.

24

Customer motivation, attitude and beliefs

Girish Prayag

Introduction

This chapter critically evaluates the current state of research on customer motivation, attitudes and beliefs in the field of hospitality marketing. From the outset, it is clear that much of what has been written on the three concepts is drawn primarily from the psychology and consumer behavior (CB) literature. A recent review of research on hospitality marketing over a period of 25 years by Morosan, Bowen and Atwood (2014) in one of the leading hospitality journals found that CB topics remain very popular in the discipline. However, this review fails to identify which specific topics within the CB literature have dominated research in hospitality marketing. This is perhaps where an earlier review by Line and Runyan (2012) is of value, which reviews the hospitality marketing literature published in the four top hospitality journals from 2008 to 2010. These authors found that out of the 101 studies they reviewed, motivation and attitudes were explicitly covered by only six and five studies, respectively. Surprisingly, the beliefs and values of consumers do not appear in their list of topics researched in the literature. Consumer attitudes are informed by many factors, including motivation and beliefs (Horner and Swarbrooke, 2016). However, the 'common-sense' understanding of these terms has often hampered conceptualization, and eventual operationalization, of these terms (Sherif and Cantril, 1945). Accordingly, the chapter is organized with a particular focus on the conceptual and measurement issues surrounding the three concepts (motivation, attitudes and beliefs), highlighting their importance for both academic research and managerial practice. The chapter begins with a definition of motivation, and the leading theories that have been applied in hospitality marketing to understand motivation. Thereafter, a similar approach is used to review the concepts of consumer attitudes and beliefs. The chapter concludes by highlighting some important gaps in the conceptualization and operationalization of these terms in the hospitality marketing literature.

Customer motivation: Conceptualization and measurement

Motivation can be described as the "psychological/biological needs and wants, including integral forces that arouse, direct and integrate a person's behavior and activity" (Yoon and Uysal, 2005, p. 46). Gnoth (1997) distinguishes between motives and motivations, arguing that the former is the visitor's lasting disposition, recurring with cyclical regularity (behaviorist approach), while the latter indicates object-specific preferences (cognitivist approach). To the contrary, McCabe (2000) argues that motivation is neither characterized by a behaviorist nor cognitivist approach but rather by a combination of both. It is therefore not surprising that a theoretically robust conceptualization of motivation remains elusive in the tourism and hospitality fields (White and Thompson, 2009). To complicate matters further, distinctions are made between expressed and real motivators (Horner and Swarbrooke, 2016), intrinsic and extrinsic motivation (Ryan and Deci, 2000a), normative and hedonic motives (Lindenberg and Steg, 2007), and primary and selective motives (Kollmuss and Agyeman, 2002). These different types of motives are often associated with the specific objects, subjects and behaviors being investigated.

Expressed motivators, for example, refer to what consumers express as their motives for booking a hotel online while real motivators could be the subconscious or unconscious motives guiding their behavior (Horner and Swarbrooke, 2016). The distinction between normative and hedonic motives as well as that between primary and selective motives tends to be made in relation to consumers' environmental behaviors. Researchers (e.g., Miao and Wei, 2013) suggest that normative motives refer to the motivation to act appropriately in relation to self and others, whereby consumers may feel obligated to display, for example, pro-environmental behaviors (Lindenberg and Steg, 2007). Hedonic motives, on the other hand, are associated with the need to feel better 'right now' through seeking pleasure, personal comfort and excitement (Lindenberg and Steg, 2007). While multiple motives may co-exist in a given situation, a particular motive may be dominant while other motives may only serve as a background to reinforce the main motive (Miao and Wei, 2013). In this context, researchers distinguish between primary and selective motives, whereby the former are those motives that lead an individual to engage in pro-environmental behaviors, for example, while the latter refers to situational non-environmental motives that are intense enough to influence the specific situation (Kollmuss and Agyeman, 2002).

Within the hospitality literature, research on the motivation of employees (Chiang and Jang, 2008; Lee-Ross, 1998) is less common in comparison to the motivation of customers, clearly highlighting a bias towards demand-oriented factors. Within the literature on consumer motivation, topics such as motives guiding accommodation choice (Chan and Baum, 2007; Chen et al., 2013), motives towards green behavior in hotels (Miao and Wei, 2013), motivation of different segments such as older customers (Sun and Morrison, 2007) and golfers (Han and Hwang, 2014), and motivation towards food consumption by tourists (Mak et al., 2013) have been researched. More recently, researchers have given attention to the motivation of customers to take part in online word-of-mouth (Yen and Tang, 2015). The latter is more commonly known as e-WOM motivation and is thought to impact hotel performance (Yen and Tang, 2015). For example, factors such as self-enhancement, extraversion, altruism, economic incentives and social benefits (Hennig-Thurau et al., 2004; Yen and Tang, 2015) are thought to be the underlying motives that influence consumers to post their hotel experiences online.

Leading motivation theories in hospitality marketing

The central concept that underlies motivation is unmet needs, which has remained unchanged in the various theories that have been proposed to understand motivation (Pincus, 2004). Need theories, including Maslow's (1943) hierarchy of needs and McClelland's need theory (1965), were at the forefront of research on motivation in the early days. Need theories at their core attempt to identify internal factors that energize behavior, and unmet needs are seen as psychological states that drive the individual towards a goal (Pincus, 2004). As a need theory, Deci's (1975) motivation theory is often used to underpin studies on consumer motivation in the hospitality field (e.g., Ayeh et al., 2016). Motivation theory postulates that people engage their efforts as a result of intrinsic and extrinsic motivation. An extension of this theory is self-determination theory, which distinguishes between different types of motivation based on the different goals that encourage people to adopt a specific behavior (Ryan and Deci, 2000a). The most basic distinction between intrinsic and extrinsic motivation is that the former refers to doing something because it is inherently interesting or enjoyable, while the latter refers to doing something because it leads to a separable outcome (Ryan and Deci, 2000b). The theory also discusses "amotivation," which is when an individual has very low levels of motivation towards any task.

Researchers have also adopted the push–pull approach (Crompton, 1979), which remains the most widely applied theory for explaining motivation. According to this need theory, tourists are pushed by their emotional needs to travel and pulled by destination attributes (Yoon and Uysal, 2005). For example, Ahmad, Jabeen and Khan (2014) use this approach to understand entrepreneurs' motivation for choosing home-stay accommodation businesses in Malaysia. Chang, Ryan, Tsai and Wen (2012) suggest that customers at Taiwanese love motels were pushed by the need for escape and pulled by the comfort and privacy offered by such hotels. The push–pull approach remains widely adopted given its simplicity and intuitive approach (Klenosky, 2002).

One significant lacuna in existing research in the field of hospitality marketing is the use of instinct theories that rely on Darwin's insights on species survival to explain motivation. Instinct theories (Pincus, 2004), or what is most commonly referred to as evolutionary approaches, have been shown to effectively explain CB (Saad, 2006; Saad and Gill, 2000). In the field of tourism, Crouch (2013) argues that factors such as motivation and attitude formation and change are the enablers of tourism consumption, underpinned by Darwinian drivers such as the search for improved resources, display of health, status and capability, and fleeing danger. The need for escape as a tourist motive is a classic example of the 'fleeing danger' etiology. The hospitality marketing literature has yet to explain hotel and food choices by tourists using evolutionary approaches.

Measuring motivation

The leisure-motivation scale (Beard and Ragheb, 1983) has been widely applied in leisure and recreation settings to understand the relationship between motives, behavior, and satisfaction. The scale has been adapted in the tourism literature to understand visitor motivation (Fodness, 1994; Ryan and Glendon, 1998) at the destination or product level rather than specifically measuring the motivation for a hotel choice. The leisure-motivation scale is derived from the work of Maslow and suggests that four motives determine satisfaction derived from leisure pursuits. The first, an intellectual motive, is related to the extent to which individuals are motivated to engage in leisure activities that involve mental activities such as learning, exploring, discovering, thought, or imagining. Second, there is a social motive, which refers to the extent to which individuals engage in leisure activities for social reasons such as need for friendship and interpersonal relationships or the need to obtain self-esteem from interactions with others. The third motive refers to individuals seeking to achieve, master, challenge, and compete in a leisure pursuit. Fourth, there is a stimulus-avoidance motive, which assesses the drive to escape and get away from routine. It is related to the need for individuals to avoid social contact, to seek solitude and calm conditions, while others tend to seek to rest and unwind (Beard and Ragheb, 1983). Much of the literature around the push and pull approach of measuring motivation draws on these four motives to measure the push factors (Prayag and Ryan, 2011). Others (e.g., Kim et al., 2011) combine different scales from other fields, for example, to measure consumers' motivation to read online reviews. As such, there are no tourism or hospitality-specific scales to measure motivation with respect to hospitality decision-making and choices.

Consumer attitude: Conceptualization and measurement

The concept of attitude is probably the most distinctive and indispensable concept in the marketing literature. A wide variety of meanings has been ascribed to the term and much of the existing research on attitudes in the hospitality field has nothing to do with attitude theory. Attitude is used more as a common-sense explanation, rather than for the establishment of a genuine causal relationship between objects (e.g., hotel attributes) and subjects (e.g., customers, employees, and suppliers etc.). Attitude can be defined as a learned predisposition with respect to a given object (Ajzen and Fishbein, 1975) and expresses an important aspect of one's personality (Eagly and Chaiken, 1993). Attitudes have three components (cognitive, affective, and behavioral). The cognitive component refers to what consumers know about an object while the affective component refers to how they feel towards the object. According to Ajzen and Fishbein (1975), the three components are not always distinguishable. In tourism research in particular, the cognitive component is thought to be an antecedent of the affective component (Vogt and Andereck, 2003). The behavioral component is based on overt actions that consumers exhibit in relation to the attitude object (Eagly and Chaiken, 1993). While it has been argued that it is conceptually important to distinguish between attitude-toward-object and attitude-toward-situation (Rokeach and Kliejunas, 1972), this distinction is rarely made in the hospitality literature. For example, a hotel guest may have a positive attitude towards children in general but not in the context of a honeymoon.

There is an underlying motivational appeal in the formation of attitudes as these attitudes are often formed in relation to objects (e.g., hotel décor), persons (e.g., hotel employee), groups of people (e.g., other customers at the hotel), and institutions (e.g., hospitality schools). However, attitudes can also exist without a motivational basis (Sherif and Cantril, 1945). Attitudes are also derived from past behavior formed by direct and indirect experiences. Yet, studies in the psychology and marketing fields have generally found a lack of correspondence between verbally expressed attitudes and overt behavior (Rokeach and Kliejunas, 1972). The dominant view in explaining what an attitude is remains the dichotomy between positive and negative affective reactions. It has been argued that consumers who have positive affective reactions to an experience with a hotel, for example, are more likely to evaluate an attitude object (e.g., food and beverage at the hotel) more favorably compared to consumers who develop negative affect reactions from the experience (Eagly and Chaiken, 1993). Attitudes categorized as strong have a greater impact on cognitive processes than attitudes categorized as weak (Krosnick and Petty, 1995).

Leading theories to understand attitude and behavior

Researchers have mainly used the theory of reasoned action (TRA) (Ajzen and Fishbein, 1980) and the theory of planned behavior (TPB) (Ajzen, 1991), which suggests that attitudes impact behavioral intentions, which in turn influence behavior. TRA assumes that an intention to perform a behavior is related to the attitude toward performing the behavior and the subjective norm for performing the behavior (Ajzen and Fishbein, 1975). Attitude and subjective norm are defined as beliefs about the outcomes of performing the behavior. According to TRA, attitude can be viewed as the degree to which the outcomes are evaluated as either positive or negative, while beliefs are considered as the degree to which important others approve or disapprove of the performance of the behavior. TRA models the decision-making processes of consumers as having a high degree of volitional control and that consumers are capable of making reasoned choices among alternatives. For example, Buttle and Bok (1996) used TRA to understand beliefs towards a hotel, subjective norms with respect to staying at the hotel again, and intention to perform the behavior. Xu and Gursoy (2015), for example, measured customers' attitudes toward hospitality supply chain members' sustainability actions related to environmental, social, and economic dimensions of sustainable management.

One question largely ignored by TRA is how an intention translates into actual behavior. To this end, TPB is usually considered to be a much stronger theory as it includes behavioral control as a measure of a consumer's confidence in his or her ability to perform a particular behavior (Ajzen, 1988). Hence, a major contribution of TPB is the notion that intention mediates the relationship between attitude and behavior, and that intention predicts behavior more accurately than attitude. A further improvement on TPB is the Model of Goal-directed Behavior (MGB), which is an extension of TPB (Perugini and Bagozzi, 2001). Unlike TRA and TPB, which are solely dependent on the volitional and non-volitional aspects of a consumer's behavior, MGB incorporates both a motivational and affective dimension, enabling a more accurate prediction of a specific behavior (Perugini and Bagozzi, 2001). MGB has been rarely applied in the hospitality literature, with a few exceptions. For example, Han and Hwang (2014) utilize MGB to understand golfers' decision-making processes.

The hospitality marketing literature remains thin in terms of explaining the effects of motivation and ability on the attitude-behavior process. In the psychology literature, several models attempt to understand these relationships. For example, models such as the Elaboration Likelihood Model of Persuasion (ELM) (Petty and Cacioppo, 1986) and the Heuristic-Systematic Model (HSM) (Eagly and Chaiken, 1984) have been developed. In the hospitality marketing literature, ELM has been used to understand consumers' online tourism information confusion (Lu and Gursoy, 2015). In a review of the application of social psychology theories and concepts in hospitality and tourism studies, Tang (2014) found only seven studies using ELM but no study has used HSM to date as the conceptual framework.

Measurement of attitude

In the context of traditional attitude research, researchers have used scales anchored along a positive/negative continuum to measure the concept (Eagly and Chaiken, 1993). Recent theorizing in psychology suggests that beyond measuring the components of attitude, attitude strength which has underlying properties of importance, accessibility, extremity, certainty, intensity, and personal relevance amongst others must also be assessed (Bassili, 1996). However, hospitality marketing studies have generally not gone beyond the measurement of "overall attitude" using the positive–negative continuum. For example, previous research (Han and Hwang, 2014) utilizes a combination of cognitive (e.g., disadvantageous vs. advantageous, foolish vs. wise) and affective items (e.g., unpleasant vs. pleasant, joyless vs. joyful) to measure consumers' overall attitude. Attitudes at the global level have also been measured using scales such as Useless-Useful, Foolish-Wise, and Harmful-Beneficial in relation to instrumental attitude towards an act (e.g., playing video games) (Magnini et al., 2013). Others equate overall attitude with image characteristics. For example, Ekinci, Dawes and Massey (2008) describe consumers' overall attitude to a service firm as the global image of that firm which can be developed before or after purchasing, and measure the concept using Likert scales anchored on Like/Dislike, Positive/Negative and Worthless/Valuable.

Rather than focusing on the individual's response to a particular object, it is high time for hospitality researchers to be concerned with the interactive and dynamic relationships embodied within the concept of attitude. For example, rather than measuring attitude towards the hotel environment alone, researchers should be measuring social representations within the hotel environment. Howarth (2006) argues that the starting point for attitude is the individual while the starting point of social representation is social knowledge. Social representations exist both outside the individual as well as within the individual's mind.

Consumer beliefs: Conceptualization and measurement

Beliefs often guide, motivate, and influence attitudes and behaviors (Engel et al., 1995). Beliefs are defined as the general opinions that are formed by consumers from experience and used to reduce complex judgments to simpler cognitive operations (Duncan, 1990). Unlike knowledge, beliefs need not be objectively "true" or "correct." Beliefs are acquired either through personal experience or through other socialization processes. Hence, beliefs and knowledge are the net results of experience (Duncan and Olshavsky, 1982). It has been argued that changing consumer attitudes is all about changing the beliefs of consumers (Horner and Swarbrooke, 2016). Beliefs tend to simplify consumer decision-making by directing search and evaluation activities and may range from broad overall impressions to very detailed opinions (Duncan, 1990). In the marketing literature, beliefs typically have been conceptualized in narrow, object-attribute terms. This means that beliefs are basically linkages between a particular brand and specific brand attributes (Duncan, 1990). For example, Ritz-Carlton hotels are associated with attributes such as luxury, high quality, professional staff, and attentiveness to customer service, amongst others. However, as Duncan and Olshavsky (1982) point out, not all consumer beliefs are of this kind. Beliefs may also express more generalized associations—between classes of objects (e.g., buyers, products, vendors), between product attributes (e.g., price, quality), and as notions of how the marketplace operates over time (e.g., competition, change).

According to the principle of cognitive consistency, as soon as a belief is changed, it has a ripple effect on affect and behavior. Generally, marketing strategies used to change attitudes towards a product or behavior are all based around changing beliefs. For example, the cognitive structure of an attitude can be changed by changing beliefs about the attributes of the product, changing the relative importance of existing beliefs, adding new beliefs, and changing beliefs about the attributes of competitors' products (Quester et al., 2014). In the hospitality literature, researchers tend to conceptualize beliefs in relation to ideas such as "ethics" (Yiu-cho Yeung et al., 2002), "trust" (Lee and Hyun, 2016), but also beliefs towards hospitality-specific activities such as tipping (Lynn and Williams, 2012).

Leading theories for understanding consumer beliefs

Consumer beliefs are more central to models such as theories of reasoned action (TRA) and planned behavior (TPB), as discussed previously. Several theories (e.g., TRA and TPB) imply that people distinguish between beliefs about the consequences of performing a behavior and beliefs about the opinions of important others toward performing that behavior. A distinction is therefore made between three kinds of salient beliefs: normative, behavioral, and control beliefs. Behavioral beliefs are assumed to influence attitudes toward the behavior, normative beliefs constitute the underlying determinants of subjective norms, and control beliefs provide the basis for perceptions of behavioral control (Ajzen, 1991). Normative beliefs are viewed as the extent to which other people would want the person to perform the behavior, weighted by his or her motivation to comply with each of these referents (motivation to comply). Behavioral beliefs are the outcomes associated with the behavior that will occur, weighted by evaluations of each of the outcomes (i.e., how good or bad they are; outcome evaluations). Control beliefs are concerned about whether resources and opportunities are available to perform the behavior, weighted by the expected impact these factors would have if they were to occur/be present (perceived power) (Ajzen, 1991).

Beyond TRA and TPB, the Value-Belief-Norm (VBN) theory has been used to investigate consumers' intention to visit a green hotel (Choi et al., 2015). It examines green behavior by considering several elements such as environmental values and ecological worldview (Stern, 2000). VBN, for example, brings together motivation and beliefs in the sense that VBN considers the pro-social motives of individuals as influencing their beliefs and green behavioral intentions (De Groot and Steg, 2009).

Measurement of beliefs

Consumer beliefs have received considerable attention in the marketing literature in the context of multi-attribute attitude models of preference formation (Duncan and Olshavsky, 1982). Researchers have measured beliefs about products, brands, and behaviors. In the context of multi-attribute attitude models, beliefs are defined strictly in terms of the likelihood that a specific brand has a specific attribute (Duncan and Olshavsky, 1982). There are different techniques for gauging consumers' beliefs about attributes. Among the most popular are the "free choice," "scaling," and "ranking" techniques. For example, one distinction that can be made when measuring beliefs is whether respondents have free choice versus forced choice. Another is whether respondents are asked for an all-or-none response in associating a brand with an attribute or to indicate degrees of belief for finer discrimination. Absolute measures ask about one brand/attribute combination in isolation, whereas comparative techniques ask about it in relation to other brands or attributes. Finally, the respondent may be asked belief questions attribute by attribute (covering all brands for each attribute in turn) or brand by brand (covering all attributes for each brand in the choice set) (Barnard and Ehrenberg, 1990). It is not surprising that the hospitality literature is replete of studies examining the relationship between beliefs about the attributes of a product and the subsequent intentions or behavior (e.g., Chen, 2015; Cho et al., 2014; Stumpf et al., 2014). TRA (Untaru et al., 2016) and TPB (Chen and Tung, 2014; Jun and Arendt, 2016; Lee and Gould, 2012) have been applied extensively to measure attitudes toward food consumption, green hotels, and other environmental issues. However, there is no single study that evaluates the psychological aspects of beliefs such as composition of beliefs and belief structures, and the conditions under which beliefs influence attitudes and behaviors.

Conclusion

This chapter sought to examine the hospitality marketing literature in terms of the conceptualization and measurement of three psychological concepts: motivation, attitude, and beliefs. Researchers continue to make calls for integrating the various motivation theories (Steel and König, 2006) but the hospitality marketing literature has been slow at addressing such calls. To this end, it would be also worthwhile for researchers to use evolutionary approaches that can explain hospitality-related choices and behaviors. Individual attitudes have been prioritized in the literature at the expense of social attitudes. While the theory of reasoned action and the theory of planned behavior are widely applied by researchers to understand the relationship between attitude, beliefs, and behavior, the lack of studies integrating social aspects of consumption and their impacts on beliefs and attitudes is omnipresent. Past research suggests that market beliefs, as part of the consumer's knowledge structure, do exert an influence on information processing and final choice behavior (Duncan, 1990). To date, the hospitality marketing literature has not addressed the effects of market beliefs on attitudes and behavior. From this review of the literature on the three concepts outlined previously, it is clear that there are several knowledge gaps and plenty of opportunities exist to examine the three concepts in isolation or as part of models used to predict attitudes and behavior.

References

Ahmad, S. Z., Jabeen, F., & Khan, M. (2014). Entrepreneurs choice in business venture: Motivations for choosing home-stay accommodation businesses in Peninsular Malaysia. *International Journal of Hospitality Management*, 36, 31–40.

Ajzen, I. (1988). *Attitudes, Personality & Behavior*. Chicago, IL: Dorsey Press.

Ajzen, I. (1991). The theory of planned behavior. *Organizational Behavior and Human Decision Processes*, 50(2), 179–211.

Ajzen, I., & Fishbein, M. (1975). *Belief, Attitude, Intention and Behavior: An Introduction to Theory and Research*. Reading, MA: Addison-Wesley.

Ajzen, I., & Fishbein, M. (1980). *Understanding Attitudes and Predicting Social Behaviour*. Englewood Cliffs, NJ: Prentice Hall.

Ayeh, J. K., Au, N., & Law, R. (2016). Investigating cross-national heterogeneity in the adoption of online hotel reviews. *International Journal of Hospitality Management*, 55, 142–153.

Barnard, N. R., & Ehrenberg, A. S. (1990). Robust measures of consumer brand beliefs. *Journal of Marketing Research*, 27(4), 477–484.

Bassili, J. N. (1996). Meta-judgmental versus operative indexes of psychological attributes: The case of measures of attitude strength. *Journal of Personality and Social Psychology*, 71(4), 637–653.

Beard, J. G., & Ragheb, M. G. (1983). Measuring leisure motivation. *Journal of Leisure Research*, 15(3), 219–228.

Buttle, F., & Bok, B. (1996). Hotel marketing strategy and the theory of reasoned action. *International Journal of Contemporary Hospitality Management*, 8(3), 5–10.

Chan, K-L. J., & Baum, T. (2007). Motivation factors of ecotourists in ecolodge accommodation: The push and pull factors. *Asia Pacific Journal of Tourism Research*, 12(4), 349–364.

Chang, J., Ryan, C., Tsai, C. T. S., & Wen, H.Y. S. (2012). The Taiwanese love motel – An escape from leisure constraints?. *International Journal of Hospitality Management*, 31(1), 169–179.

Chen, L. C., Lin, S. P., & Kuo, C. M. (2013). Rural tourism: Marketing strategies for the bed and breakfast industry in Taiwan. *International Journal of Hospitality Management*, 32, 278–286.

Chen, L. F. (2015). Exploring asymmetric effects of attribute performance on customer satisfaction using association rule method. *International Journal of Hospitality Management*, 47, 54–64.

Chen, M. F., & Tung, P. J. (2014). Developing an extended Theory of Planned Behavior model to predict consumers' intention to visit green hotels. *International Journal of Hospitality Management*, 36, 221–230.

Chiang, C. F., & Jang, S. S. (2008). An expectancy theory model for hotel employee motivation. *International Journal of Hospitality Management*, 27(2), 313–322.

Cho, M., Bonn, M. A., & Kang, S. (2014). Wine attributes, perceived risk and online wine repurchase intention: The cross-level interaction effects of website quality. *International Journal of Hospitality Management*, 43, 108–120.

Choi, H., Jang, J., & Kandampully, J. (2015). Application of the extended VBN theory to understand consumers' decisions about green hotels. *International Journal of Hospitality Management*, 51, 87–95.

Crompton, J. L. (1979). Motivations for pleasure vacation. *Annals of Tourism Research*, 6(4), 408–424.

Crouch, G. I. (2013). Homo sapiens on vacation: What can we learn from Darwin? *Journal of Travel Research*, 52(5), 575–590.

Deci, E. L. (1975). *Intrinsic Motivation*. New York: Plennum Press.

De Groot, J. I., & Steg, L. (2009). Morality and prosocial behavior: The role of awareness, responsibility, and norms in the norm activation model. *The Journal of Social Psychology*, 149(4), 425–449.

Duncan, C. P. (1990). Consumer market beliefs: A review of the literature and an agenda for future research. In M. E. Goldberg, G. Gorn, and R. W. Pollay (Eds.), *Advances in Consumer Research*, 17, Provo, UT: Association for Consumer Research (pp. 729–736).

Duncan, C. P., & Olshavsky, R. W. (1982). External search: The role of consumer beliefs. *Journal of Marketing Research*, 19(1), 32–43.

Eagly, A. H., & Chaiken, S. (1984). Cognitive theories of persuasion. In L. Berkowitz (Ed.), *Advances in Experimental Social Psychology*, 17 (pp. 267–359). New York: Academic Press.

Eagly, A. H., & Chaiken, S. (1993). *The Psychology of Attitudes*. Fort Worth, TX: Harcourt Brace Jovanovich College Publishers.

Ekinci, Y., Dawes, P. L., & Massey, G. R. (2008). An extended model of the antecedents and consequences of consumer satisfaction for hospitality services. *European Journal of Marketing*, 42(1/2), 35–68.

Engel, J. F., Blackwell, R. D., & Miniard, P. W. (1995). *Consumer Behavior* (8th Ed.). New York: Dryder.

Fodness, D. (1994). Measuring tourist motivation. *Annals of Tourism Research*, 21(3), 555–581.

Gnoth, J. (1997). Tourism motivation and expectation formation. *Annals of Tourism Research*, 24(2), 283–304.

Han, H., & Hwang, J. (2014). Investigation of the volitional, non-volitional, emotional, motivational and automatic processes in determining golfers' intention: Impact of screen golf. *International Journal of Contemporary Hospitality Management*, 26(7), 1118–1135.

Hennig-Thurau, T., Gwinner, K. P., Walsh, G., & Gremler, D. D. (2004). Electronic word-of-mouth via consumer-opinion platforms: What motivates consumers to articulate themselves on the Internet? *Journal of Interactive Marketing*, 18(1), 38–52.

Horner, S., & Swarbrooke, J. (2016). *Consumer Behaviour in Tourism*. London: Routledge.

Howarth, C. (2006). How social representations of attitudes have informed attitude theories: The consensual and the reified. *Theory & Psychology*, 16(5), 691–714.

Jun, J., & Arendt, S. W. (2016). Understanding healthy eating behaviors at casual dining restaurants using the extended theory of planned behavior. *International Journal of Hospitality Management*, 53, 106–115.

Klenosky, D. B. (2002). The 'pull' of tourism destinations: A means-end investigation. *Journal of Travel Research*, 40(May), 385–395.

Kim, E. E. K., Mattila, A. S., & Baloglu, S. (2011). Effects of gender and expertise on consumers' motivation to read online hotel reviews. *Cornell Hospitality Quarterly*, 52(4), 399–406.

Kollmuss, A., & Agyeman, J. (2002). Mind the gap: Why do people act environmentally and what are the barriers to pro-environmental behavior? *Environmental Education Research*, 8(3), 239–260.

Krosnick, J. A., & Petty, R. E. (1995). Attitude strength: An overview. In R.E. Petty & J. A. Krosnick (Eds.), *Attitude Strength: Antecedents and Consequences* (pp. 1–24). Mahwah, NJ: Lawrence Erlbaum Associates.

Lee, K. H., & Hyun, S. S. (2016). A model of value-creating practices, trusting beliefs, and online tourist community behaviors: Risk aversion as a moderating variable. *International Journal of Contemporary Hospitality Management*, 28(9), 1868–1894.

Lee, K. I., & Gould, R. (2012). Predicting congregate meal program participation: Applying the extended theory of planned behavior. *International Journal of Hospitality Management*, 31(3), 828–836.

Lee-Ross, D. (1998). A practical theory of motivation applied to hotels. *International Journal of Contemporary Hospitality Management*, 10(2), 68–74.

Lindenberg, S., & Steg, L. (2007). Normative, gain and hedonic goal frames guiding environmental behavior. *Journal of Social Issues*, 63(1), 117–137.

Line, N. D., & Runyan, R. C. (2012). Hospitality marketing research: Recent trends and future directions. *International Journal of Hospitality Management*, 31(2), 477–488.

Lu, A. C. C., & Gursoy, D. (2015). A conceptual model of consumers' online tourism confusion. *International Journal of Contemporary Hospitality Management*, 27(6), 1320–1342.

Lynn, M., & Williams, J. (2012). Black–white differences in beliefs about the US restaurant tipping norm: Moderated by socio-economic status? *International Journal of Hospitality Management*, 31(3), 1033–1035.

Magnini, V. P., Karande, K., Singal, M., & Kim, D. (2013). The effect of brand popularity statements on consumers' purchase intentions: The role of instrumental attitudes toward the act. *International Journal of Hospitality Management*, 34, 160–168.

Mak, A. H., Lumbers, M., Eves, A., & Chang, R. C. (2013). An application of the repertory grid method and generalised Procrustes analysis to investigate the motivational factors of tourist food consumption. *International Journal of Hospitality Management*, 35, 327–338.

Maslow, A. H. (1943). A theory of human motivation. *Psychological Review*, 50(4), 370–396.

McCabe, S. (2000). Tourism motivation process. *Annals of Tourism Research*, 27(4), 1049–1052.

McClelland, D. C. (1965). Toward a theory of motive acquisition. *American Psychologist*, 20(5), 321–333.

Miao, L., & Wei, W. (2013). Consumers' pro-environmental behavior and the underlying motivations: A comparison between household and hotel settings. *International Journal of Hospitality Management*, 32, 102–112.

Morosan, C., Bowen, J. T, & Atwood, M. (2014). The evolution of marketing research. *International Journal of Contemporary Hospitality Management*, 26(5), 706–726.

Perugini, M., & Bagozzi, R. P. (2001). The role of desires and anticipated emotions in goal-directed behaviours: Broadening and deepening the theory of planned behaviour. *British Journal of Social Psychology*, 40(1), 79–98.

Petty, R. E., & Cacioppo, J. T. (1986). The elaboration likelihood model of persuasion. In R. E. Petty & J. T. Cacioppo (Eds.), *Communication and Persuasion* (pp. 1–24). New York: Springer.

Pincus, J. (2004). The consequences of unmet needs: The evolving role of motivation in consumer research. *Journal of Consumer Behaviour*, 3(4), 375–387.

Prayag, G., & Ryan, C. (2011). The relationship between the 'push'and 'pull' factors of a tourist destination: The role of nationality – an analytical qualitative research approach. *Current Issues in Tourism*, 14(2), 121–143.

Quester, P., Pettigrew, S., Kopanidis, F., Hill, S. R., & Hawkins, D. I. (2014). *Consumer Behaviour: Implications for Marketing Strategy* (7th Ed.). Sydney: McGraw-Hill.

Rokeach, M., & Kliejunas, P. (1972). Behavior as a function of attitude-toward-object and attitude-toward-situation. *Journal of Personality and Social Psychology*, 22(2), 194–201.

Ryan, C., & Glendon, I. (1998). Application of leisure motivation scale to tourism. *Annals of Tourism Research*, 25(1), 169–184.

Ryan, R. M., & Deci, E. L. (2000a). Self-determination theory and the facilitation of intrinsic motivation, social development, and well-being. *American Psychologist*, 55(1), 68–78.

Ryan, R. M., & Deci, E. L. (2000b). Intrinsic and extrinsic motivations: Classic definitions and new directions. *Contemporary Educational Psychology*, 25(1), 54–67.

Saad, G. (2006). Applying evolutionary psychology in understanding the Darwinian roots of consumption phenomena. *Managerial and Decision Economics*, 27(2–3), 189–201.

Saad, G., & Gill, T. (2000). Applications of evolutionary psychology in marketing. *Psychology & Marketing*, 17(12), 1005–1034.

Sherif, M., & Cantril, H. (1945). The psychology of attitudes – Part 1. *The Psychological Review*, 52(6), 295–319.

Steel, P., & König, C. J. (2006). Integrating theories of motivation. *Academy of Management Review*, 31(4), 889–913.

Stern, P. C. (2000). New environmental theories: Toward a coherent theory of environmentally significant behavior. *Journal of Social Issues*, 56(3), 407–424.

Stumpf, T. S., Park, J., & Kim, H. J. (2014). Appreciative and consumptive lodging attributes: Conceptualization and measurement. *International Journal of Hospitality Management*, 40, 71–80.

Sun, Y. H. C., & Morrison, A. M. (2007). Senior citizens and their dining-out traits: Implications for restaurants. *International Journal of Hospitality Management*, 26(2), 376–394.

Tang, L. R. (2014). The application of social psychology theories and concepts in hospitality and tourism studies: A review and research agenda. *International Journal of Hospitality Management*, 36, 188–196.

Untaru, E. N., Ispas, A., Candrea, A. N., Luca, M., & Epuran, G. (2016). Predictors of individuals' intention to conserve water in a lodging context: The application of an extended Theory of Reasoned Action. *International Journal of Hospitality Management*, 59, 50–59.

Vogt, C. A., & Andereck, K. L. (2003). Destination perceptions across a vacation. *Journal of Travel Research*, 41(4), 348–354.

White, C. J., & Thompson, M. (2009). Self-determination theory and the wine club attribute formation process. *Annals of Tourism Research*, 36(4), 561–586.

Xu, X., & Gursoy, D. (2015). Influence of sustainable hospitality supply chain management on customers' attitudes and behaviors. *International Journal of Hospitality Management*, 49, 105–116.

Yen, C. L. A., & Tang, C. H. H. (2015). Hotel attribute performance, eWOM motivations, and media choice. *International Journal of Hospitality Management*, 46, 79–88.

Yiu-cho Yeung, S., Chak-keung Wong, S., & Man-leong Chan, B. (2002). Ethical beliefs of hospitality and tourism students towards their school life. *International Journal of Contemporary Hospitality Management*, 14(4), 183–192.

Yoon, Y., & Uysal, M. (2005). An examination of the effects of motivation and satisfaction on destination loyalty: A structural model. *Tourism Management*, 26, 45–56.

25

Relationship marketing management and loyalty in hospitality firms

Roya Rahimi, Fevzi Okumus and Mehmet Ali Köseoglu

Evolution of relationship marketing

Marketing theories started to emerge around 1960. New theories in the marketing literature have been constructed by considering various perspectives to (re)define marketing concepts in the last decades. "Marketing mix", called the 4Ps (standing for price, product, place, and promotion) has a strong focus on how companies gain customers. This transactional approach of marketing is product-oriented with a very short-term focus. Since the core product is the only thing that companies can offer, the customers do not feel attached to the seller and cannot be retained. This makes the price the determining factor when there is a rise in competition (Grönroos 1994).

Relationship marketing is defined by Grönroos (1994) as identifying and establishing, maintaining and enhancing, and when necessary, also terminating relationships with customers and other stakeholders, at a profit, so that the objectives of all parties are met, and this is done by a mutual exchange and fulfilment of promises. Relationship marketing is one of the new concepts and strategies in the marketing literature. This new approach has drawn the attention of scholars and practitioners and can be considered as one of the key developmental areas of modern marketing. Relationship marketing was embraced in the early 1990s, to help marketing departments to know their customers' preferences more intimately and to increase the chances of retaining them. Relationship marketing focuses on customer loyalty and long-term customer engagement. This approach is an attempt to replace earlier notions of transactional marketing; the firm creates more value for its customers. Gaining customers is much more expensive than keeping them; hence, in the relationship marketing approach, companies focus on how the relationship between customers and companies should be managed. In this circumstance, customers become more loyal and less sensitive to the price attraction of competitors. This generates more profit for the organisation.

Relationship marketing focuses on how companies create and manage unique relationships between customers and the company. In this approach, customers have a crucial role in developing and/or improving services and/or processes, thus companies place customers at the centre of the process or services to gain and keep them. Relationship marketing creates databases of consumers' buying behaviours/preferences that allow firms to tailor their marketing strategies and create additional values (Rahimi and Kozak 2016). Relationship marketing consists of three phases: i) gathering customers' personal data, ii) analysing the data to formulate and implement strategies to improve quality and create customer retention, and offering loyalty incentive schemes, iii) providing customised services and/or products.

Creating an ongoing relationship with customers offers them feelings of security, control and trust, which minimises their purchasing risk and hence reduces the costs of being a customer of the organization (Grönroos 2004). In a highly competitive environment, quality relationships are key elements of business differentiation. Economic benefits are one of the main advantages of implementing relationship marketing for hospitality companies. This is based on two notions: i) acquiring customers is much more expensive than keeping them, and ii) the longer the relationship is maintained between the organisation and customer, the more profitable the relationship is to the firm (Gilbert and Tsao 2000; Buttle 1996). This one-to-one approach of relationship marketing, which was introduced for the first time by Berry (1983), was very popular throughout the 1990s. It was later replaced by a new approach known as Customer Relationship Management (CRM). Since relationship marketing is a facet of CRM, these two terms are used interchangeably. Relationship marketing constructs trust between customers and companies to maximise benefits. However, CRM using information technology helps companies to quickly and consistently deliver what customers are looking for within each and every interaction.

Customer satisfaction and loyalty in relationship marketing management

From the customer perspective, relationship marketing builds confidence by creating faith in the product or service provider and a feeling of trustworthiness of the provider. It also has some social benefits such as personal recognition and being familiar with employees, and the development of friendship. Relationship marketing offers special treatment to customers such as extra services, special prices and higher priority than other customers, which increase customer satisfaction (Gwinner et al. 1998). On the firm side, relationship marketing increases customer satisfaction and loyalty. Customer satisfaction is related to how customers' expectations are met. However, customer loyalty is related to the willingness of customers to return to the company and/or help the company promote products and services. Both customer satisfaction and customer loyalty play vital roles in the profitability of hospitality firms. Reichheld and Sasser (1990) found that when an organisation turns 5 per cent of its customers into loyal customers, its profits can increase by 25 per cent to 125 per cent.

Loyal customers effectively use word-of-mouth to promote companies' products/services. They are excellent marketing forces as they provide recommendations and this is the best available advertising an organisation can obtain (Litvin et al. 2008). For example, in hotels loyal guests tell other guests about hotel facilities such as restaurants, spa facilities or the golf club. In casinos, loyal customers mention the atmosphere or ambience of the casino. On flights, passengers tell other passengers about the behaviour of flight attendants, food quality, or the variety of drinks. Therefore, loyal customers are one of the most important components of marketing practices as they serve as an information source for other customers. Loyal guests are less likely to switch to other competitors because of the price. They purchase a wider variety of the hotel's products and make more frequent purchases than similar non-loyal customers (Reichheld and Sasser 1990). In order to increase customer satisfaction and loyalty, companies must follow key steps. Firstly, they need to know how their customers define their values. They should then meet these values and try to maintain customer relationships and work toward ensuring retention and loyalty (Yang and Peterson, 2004).

In the high-involvement service settings, strong relationships between satisfaction and loyalty have been proven (Bowen and Chen 2001). For example, in hotels the increased profit from loyal guests comes from reduced marketing costs, increased sales and reduced operational costs. Hospitality companies face a challenge in identifying the components of customer loyalty; identifying the attributes that will increase customer loyalty is one of the biggest challenges they face. Customer loyalty happens when a customer is strongly loyal to a specific brand and he/she buys this brand repeatedly and shows a positive attitude toward it. The key terms here are repeated behaviour and positive attitude. These are the outcomes of customer satisfaction and contribute to higher levels of profitability in the firm.

Customers may be satisfied with the products or services offered. However, this does not mean that they are loyal customers. Loyalty is strongly dependent on the level of satisfaction, whether it is a high degree of satisfaction, complete satisfaction or delight (Little and Marandi 2003). This satisfaction level creates trust and commitment, and it enables loyalty to emerge. There are situations where dissatisfied customers continue to stay loyal simply because there are no better service providers. An excellent example of this situation is Turkish Airlines. Turkey is a popular destination for Iranian tourists: 1,700,385 Iranian tourists visited Turkey in 2015 for leisure and business purposes. After Tehran, Isfahan is the second largest city in Iran, from which a high volume of tourists visit Istanbul. Turkish Airlines is the only airline that offers direct flights from Isfahan to Istanbul. The price of flights is extremely high with a medium to low level of service. In this situation, dissatisfied passengers continue to stay loyal simply because there are no other service providers. This could be regarded as apathetic loyalty and these types of customers could be considered as hostage. These customers are looking for the first real opportunity to exit. In intense competition markets where alternatives are easily available, suppliers must ensure that they achieve the highest level of satisfaction among their customers to keep them loyal (Little and Marandi 2003).

To gain sustainable competitive advantage, companies need to measure customer satisfaction, loyalty and customer experience with performance indicators (Fornell 1992). Customer loyalty can be measured via three distinctive measurement approaches (Bowen and Chen 2001): behavioural, attitudinal and composite measurements. The behavioural measurement approach considers consistent repetitious purchase behaviour as an indicator of loyalty. The main problem with this type of measurement is that repeat purchase is not always a sign of psychological commitment toward a brand. For example, a business traveller maybe selects a specific hotel because of its central location but if another hotel opened in the same area offering better value for money, he or she could switch. Attitudinal measurements use attitudinal data to predict emotional and psychological attachment. Attitudinal measurements can be used when a customer holds a positive attitude toward a hotel and recommends the hotel to others but, for example, do not have the purchasing power to stay at the hotel. Composite measurements combine behavioural and attitudinal measurements and measure loyalty through customers' product preferences, propensity of brand-switching, frequency of purchase, and total amount of purchase.

Loyalty programmes

Loyalty programmes are one of the main tools of relationship marketing. They are rewards programmes offered by hospitality firms to their customers who are frequent buyers. Hospitality firms have already applied a "points" currency approach to build relationships with customers and keep them in the loop. As part of loyalty programmes, customers have cards called loyalty cards (McCall and Voorhees 2010). They are called rewards cards in the United Kingdom, points cards in Canada, or discount cards, club cards or rewards cards in the United States. Customers can earn points and redeem them for different services and benefits. These can be hard benefits such as currency or soft benefits like exclusive offers. The ability for customers to earn points and easily redeem them for different hard or soft offers (such as the Hilton Honors program, Hyatt Gold Passport or Jurys Inn reward card) is highly satisfying and it is a competitive differentiator among loyalty programmes.

Creating and harnessing customers' data can help companies to tailor their products based on the customers' purchasing patterns. This provides customers with a more customisable experience based on individual customers' needs (Rahimi 2017a). In the hotel industry, now more than ever, travellers choose their hotels through social channel chatter, customer reviews and rewards. This has forced hoteliers to adopt loyalty programmes and offer incredible bonuses to their most loyal customers. Most hotel loyalty programmes are centred on earning points that can be redeemed for a free night. Some hotels offer perks such as personalised room services, rewards (free box of chocolates and favourite wine), coupons for the restaurant or spa, free Internet access, guaranteed room or late check-out times.

In the hotel industry, the relationship between customer satisfaction and loyalty programmes depends on how you earn or redeem points and what brands are in the loyalty programme network. Hence companies have to differentiate their loyalty programmes to maximise customer satisfaction (McCall and Voorhees 2010). For example, the Jurys Inn reward card generates a high level of satisfaction since customers can earn points easily and redeem them to meet more worthy wants and needs. Jurys Inn is is a budget chain hotel. They are located in the UK, Ireland and the Czech Republic. The chain believes that loyalty deserves a reward, hence they give treats to their loyal customers through their Jurys Rewards scheme. The programme allows guests to earn points each time they stay at the hotel. As they build up those points, they can then redeem them against a stay in any Jurys Inn hotel throughout the UK, Ireland and the Czech Republic or against a range of high street gift vouchers. The Rewards card is credited with ten points for every £1 or €1 guests spend. Jurys Inn also offer one lucky Jurys Rewards member the chance to win 100,000 points instantly by simply booking a stay online at jurysinns.com and showing their Jurys Rewards card on check-in. Ten thousand points could get the lucky guest between a five- and fifteen-night stay at Jurys Inns or over £550/€550 worth of vouchers for Love2Shop. Love2Shop vouchers can be redeemed in over 20,000 shops throughout the UK and at over 500 stores in Ireland. Customers can also mix and match and combine a couple of nights' stay with shopping (Jurys Inn 2016). In this respect, customers' experience in loyalty programmes impacts the levels of retention.

Despite the popularity of loyalty card programmes among hospitality firms, it must be noted that the customer experience is the most important loyalty-building tool. Although loyalty programmes are beneficial and are tools for encouraging customers to return, they are not the main loyalty-building factor (Uncles et al. 2003). Another key thing to remember is that in the coming years, a significant change will occur in the way loyalty programmes operate (Harrison 2015). With technology offering more opportunities, it will not be necessary to carry around a wallet full of cards to be recognised as a customer. Instead, apps on phones will end the card approach and allow customers more control over how they interact with suppliers (Hassan and Rahimi 2016).

The constructs of relationship marketing

The importance of customer loyalty is explained earlier. The main question here is how hospitality firms can implement relationship marketing to increase their customer loyalty and retention. With increased competition, the key to survival is the ability to adapt the services and products provided based on the changing preferences and lifestyles of ever-more demanding customers. Relationship marketing implementation has three main components, namely, technology, process and people (Rahimi and Gunlu 2016; Chen and Popovich 2003; Fui-Hoon Nah et al. 2001). The *technology* component plays a key role in the success of relationship marketing strategies. In the late nineteenth and early twentieth centuries, hospitality firms did not always intend to take the lead in implementing and using information technology for running their operations. However, nowadays firms of almost all sizes realise that technology helps them to develop a detailed profile of their customers and to target their valued customers for special treatment. Information technology helps hospitality businesses to create a customer database, analyse it and create relationship-oriented integrated marketing communications. Data mining and profiling of customers is the most important basis for relationship marketing and subsequent development of a customer retention strategy. This helps companies to understand who their customers are, what they buy, and how to provide for them over the long term. In other words, they segment their customers and hence segment their strategies. For example in hotels there are three types of information that could be collected for profiling guests: a) front-line data (guest profile information), b) spontaneous data (information provided by the guests), and c) behavioural data (guest transaction data or preference information input by staff into the computer system).

Information technology helps businesses to discover the hidden knowledge and unexpected patterns of their customers' behaviours. For example, for formulation of a successful relationship marketing strategy in hotels, managers have to know and understand customer's wants and needs based on their demographic characteristics. For instance, customers' nationality is a significant indicator of travel purpose.

The Internet helps companies to build relationships with their customers (Bauer et al. 2002). It makes it easy for them to store, analyse and use customers' information to segment their customers and develop tailored relationship marketing strategies. Social media platforms are also critical sources of information for hospitality businesses. Websites and blogs, Facebook, Instagram, Twitter, LinkedIn, YouTube, Flickr and Google+ have empowered users to connect, share and collaborate, and provide valuable sources of data for managers that allow businesses to engage with their customers in an informal and ongoing manner (Szmigin et al. 2005). Customers are no longer passive participants and can participate in the value-adding and marketing mix decisions of companies with relatively low costs and higher levels of efficiency than traditional communication methods. Social media platforms allow companies to monitor and respond to customer issues, which in turn help to maintain a better brand image. Social media platforms are also a great way to turn fans ("likes"), friends, followers and networks into paying guests. Hence, a social media marketing approach needs to be developed as part of the relationship marketing strategy.

The relationship marketing strategy involves the improvement of the operations of firms; hence, reengineering all existing *processes* is required. It involves revising major aspects of the way an organisation conducts its business in order to become more customer centric. Firms need to understand the aspect of customer value and value-generating processes (customer value chain). Better two-way internal and external communications with both customers and staff need to be built, maintained and enhanced (Rahimi 2017b). The success of relationship marketing strategies requires motivated and involved employees. Even in the most technologically oriented hotels, relationship marketing practices can be sustainable only with capable and passionate employees with strong enthusiasm for their job (Rahimi and Gunlu 2016). Hence, it is important to get *People* involved with the relationship marketing strategy and motivate them to reach the objectives, especially in hospitality firms due to their human-based nature where services cannot be delivered without their participation. Human resistance is one of the most important failure factors of relationship marketing strategies. Hence, staff training and staff development programmes are essential. Once a relationship marketing strategy is implemented, there needs to be a set of metrics that can be used to measure the level of success (Mendoza et al. 2007).

Critical success factors for relationship marketing

It is often assumed that implementing a relationship marketing strategy goes hand in hand with stimulating growth and achieving success. However, most hospitality firms are not taking full advantage of relationship marketing strategies and struggle to succeed (Rahimi and Kozak, 2016). Previous studies have referred to different critical factors for the success of the relationship marketing strategy in hospitality firms (Rahimi 2017b; Rahimi and Gunlu 2016; Mendoza et al. 2007; Croteau and Li 2003). These studies found that organisational readiness is one of the critical factors for successfully implementing a relationship marketing strategy. This refers to the organisational variables that affect relationship marketing, including organisational commitment and top management support for changing processes, training employees so that they are ready for the changes, employee empowerment and organisational culture. Among these factors organisational culture is playing a key role (Rahimi and Gunlu 2016; Iriana and Buttle 2007). This refers to both the culture of the organisation and the culture of the external environment (macro level). In international markets with an intercultural environment, the cultural variable should not be ignored. The concept of relationship is interpreted and valued differently by different cultures and this influences the process, quality and sustainability of relationship building. For example, the cultures of Taiwan, China, Hong Kong, Macau and Singapore are relationally oriented in comparison to Western cultures. This links to Hofstede's (1984) study emphasising the way in which national cultural differences have an impact on the way businesses work and operate.

Times changed and the new generation of relationship marketing is heavily reliant on information technology. Especially in hospitality firms with a large amount of information to manage, successful relationship marketing implementation requires significant investments in technologies that allow customer information to be collected and analysed and used to develop highly personalised offers. Rahimi and Gunlu (2016) modified the critical success factors from Mendoza et al. (2007) that can be used for implementing relationship marketing strategies in hotel firms. These factors are summarised as follows:

- A customer satisfaction programme needs to be present in the hotel's strategic plan.
- Hotel managers need to participate in implementing a relationship marketing strategy.
- Hotel managers' daily roles need to be related to compliance of relationship marketing plans.
- Managers of each part of the hotel should be responsible for implementing the relationship marketing strategy.
- There needs to be a designated budget and resources for all initiatives related to the relationship marketing strategy.
- There need to be frequent follow-up meetings and personnel should have a favourable disposition to share information.
- There need to be public documents related to the relationship marketing strategy for staff to consult.
- There need to be integrated and multifunctional teams for implementation and follow up of the relationship marketing strategy.
- Staff should be motivated, trained and be aware of the significance of the implementation of the relationship marketing strategy.

- The outcomes/benefits of implementing the relationship marketing strategy should be shared with staff (using internal posters, bulletins, publications and newsletters).
- There needs to be investment in IT and data mining.
- Customers' satisfaction needs to be measured every month and there should be a target of less than 1 per cent complaints related to sold services.
- Relationship marketing needs to be imbedded in all three stages of the guest cycle (pre-stay, during stay and post-stay) and there needs to be a guest segmentation strategy.
- There need to be internal support units for implementing the relationship marketing strategy.

From a more generic approach, Rashid (2003) mentioned that food businesses such as restaurants need to consider nine dimensions for successfully implementing relationship marketing strategies. The first is building the relationship based on mutual *Trust*. A high level of trust increases positive attitudes, which can result in a higher level of customer orientation and loyalty. A successful relationship also depends on *Commitment*. The level of commitment customers feels toward the organisation is of great importance in developing and maintaining the relationship. Trust and commitment are paired in the relationship marketing literature and are invariably associated. *Social Bonding* forms a feeling of affection, a sense of belonging to the relationship, and indirectly results in a sense of belonging to the organisation. In a high level of social bonding, both the customers and organisation are strongly committed to maintaining the relationship. Creating *Empathy* and seeing customers' point of view is increasingly important. Building a *Good Experience* is another factor in the successful implementation of relationship marketing. Negative experiences may lead to customer defection and building relationships with competitors. The more satisfied the customer is, the stronger the relationship. *Fulfilment of Promise* is the core concept in the relationship marketing strategy. It can determine whether the relationship is to continue or terminate. Failing to fulfil promise not only causes customer dissatisfaction and damages the image of the organisation but also dissatisfies personnel who are in contact with the customers, as they experience more frustration than satisfaction in the workplace, resulting in high staff turnover. *Customer Satisfaction* should be the main goal of the organisation. *Internal Relationship Marketing* needs to be created for internal customers by empowerment, internal relationship management and internal communication. Last but not least, *Communication* is a vital component in the establishment of relationships; it is not only an important element in its own right, but also has the propensity to influence levels of trust between customers and the organisation.

Conclusion

This chapter reviewed the notion of relationship marketing and its evolution within the hospitality field during the last 20 years. Building strong one-to-one customer relationships is vital for the success of hospitality firms as it focuses on maximizing the revenue from each guest over time. In this chapter, the concept of relationship marketing strategy has been discussed. The main benefit of implementing a relationship marketing strategy in hospitality firms is an increased level of customer satisfaction, which will result in more loyalty and retention. This has a direct impact of the profitability of the business. For implementing relationship marketing, the three main components of people, process and technology need to be addressed. For successful relationship marketing outcomes, companies need to focus on a set of critical success factors, which have been discussed together with their different implementation approaches in this chapter.

References

Bauer, H. H., Grether, M., & Leach, M. (2002). Building customer relations over the Internet. *Industrial Marketing Management*, 31(2), 155–163.

Berry, L.L. (1983). Relationship marketing. In Berry, L. L., Shostack, G. L. and Upah, G. D. (Eds), *Emerging Perspectives on Services Marketing*, Proceedings Series. Chicago, IL: American Marketing Association, pp. 25–28.

Bowen, J. T., & Chen, S. L. (2001). The relationship between customer loyalty and customer satisfaction. *International Journal of Contemporary Hospitality Management*, 13(5), 213–217.

Buttle, F. (1996). *Relationship Marketing: Theory and Practice*. London: Paul Chapman.

Chen, I. J., & Popovich, K. (2003). Understanding customer relationship management (CRM) People, process and technology. *Business Process Management Journal*, 9(5), 672–688.

Croteau, A. M., & Li, P. (2003). Critical success factors of CRM technological initiatives. *Canadian Journal of Administrative Sciences/Revue Canadienne des Sciences de l'Administration*, 20(1), 21–34.

Fornell, C. (1992). A national customer satisfaction barometer: The Swedish experience. *Journal of Marketing*, 56, 6–21.

Fui-Hoon Nah, F., Lee-Shang Lau, J., & Kuang, J. (2001). Critical factors for successful implementation of enterprise systems. *Business Process Management Journal*, 7(3), 285–296.

Gilbert, D., & Tsao, J. (2000). Exploring Chinese cultural influences and hospitality marketing relationships. *International Journal of Contemporary Hospitality Management*, 12(1), 45–54.

Grönroos, C. (1994). From marketing mix to relationship marketing: Towards a paradigm shift in marketing. *Management Decision*, 32(2), 4–20.

Grönroos, C. (2004). The relationship marketing process: Communication, interaction, dialogue, value. *Journal of Business & Industrial Marketing*, 19(2), 99–113.

Gwinner, K. P., Gremler, D. D., & Bitner, M. J. (1998). Relational benefits in services industries: The customer's perspectives. *Journal of the Academy of Marketing Science*, 26(2), 101–114.

Harrison, O. (2015). The future of loyalty programmes. [online] Available at: www.dunnhumby.com/future-loyalty-programmes [Accessed 14 Nov. 2016].

Hassan, A. & Rahimi, R. (2016). Consuming "innovation": Augmented reality as an innovation tool in digital tourism marketing. In P. Nikolaos and I. Bregoli (Eds.), *Global Dynamics in Travel, Tourism, and Hospitality*. Hershey, PA: IGI Global, pp. 130–147.

Hofstede, G. (1984). Cultural dimensions in management and planning. *Asia Pacific Journal of Management*, 1(2), 81–99.

Iriana, R., & Buttle, F. (2007). Strategic, operational, and analytical customer relationship management: Attributes and measures. *Journal of Relationship Marketing*, 5(4), 23–42.

Jurys Inn. (2016). What would you do with 100,000 Jurys Reward Points? [online] Available at: www.jurysinns.com/jurysinnformation/100K-jurys-rewards-points [Accessed 14 Nov. 2016].

Little, E., & Marandi, E. (2003). *Relationship Marketing Management*. Singapore: Thomson Learning.

Litvin, S. W., Goldsmith, R. E., & Pan, B. (2008). Electronic word-of-mouth in hospitality and tourism management. *Tourism Management*, 29(3), 458–468.

McCall, M., & Voorhees, C. (2010). The drivers of loyalty program success: An organizing framework and research agenda. *Cornell Hospitality Quarterly*, 51(1), 35–52.

Mendoza, L. E., Marius, A., Pérez, M., & Grimán, A. C. (2007). Critical success factors for a customer relationship management strategy. *Information and Software Technology*, 49(8), 913–945.

Rahimi, R. (2017a). Organizational culture and customer relationship management: A simple linear regression analysis. *Journal of Hospitality Marketing & Management*.

Rahimi, R. (2017b). Customer relationship management (people, process and technology) and organisational culture in hotels: Which traits matter? *International Journal of Contemporary Hospitality Management*, 29(5). doi: 10.1108/IJCHM-10-2015-0617.

Rahimi, R., & Gunlu, E. (2016). Implementing customer relationship management (CRM) in hotel industry from organizational culture perspective: Case of a chain hotel in the UK. *International Journal of Contemporary Hospitality Management*, 28(1), 89–112.

Rahimi, R., & Kozak, M. (2016). Impact of customer relationship management on customer satisfaction: The case of a budget hotel chain. *Journal of Travel & Tourism Marketing*, 1–12.

Rashid, T. (2003). Relationship marketing: Case studies of personal experiences of eating out. *British Food Journal*, 105(10), 742–750.

Roya Rahimi et al.

Reichheld, F., & Sasser, W. E. (1990). Zero defections: Quality comes to services. *Harvard Business Review*, 68(September/ October), 105–111.

Szmigin, I., Canning, L., & Reppel, A. E. (2005). Online community: Enhancing the relationship marketing concept through customer bonding. *International Journal of Service Industry Management*, 16(5), 480–496.

Uncles, M. D., Dowling, G. R., & Hammond, K. (2003). Customer loyalty and customer loyalty programs. *Journal of Consumer Marketing*, 20(4), 294–316.

Yang, Z., & Peterson, R. T. (2004). Customer perceived value, satisfaction, and loyalty: The role of switching costs. *Psychology & Marketing*, 21(10), 799–822.

Further reading

Buttle, F. (Ed.). (1996). *Relationship marketing: theory and practice*. Sage.

Buttle, F. (2009). *Customer relationship management: concepts and technologies*. Routledge.

Christopher, M., Payne, A., & Ballantyne, D. (2013). *Relationship marketing*. Taylor & Francis.

Hofstede, G. (1984). Cultural dimensions in management and planning. *Asia Pacific Journal of Management*, 1(2), 81–99.

Little, E., & Marandi, E. (2003). *Relationship marketing management*. Thomson Learning.

26

Customer delight

A new marketing strategy to build up trust

Soma Sinha Roy

Introduction

With the advent of media and the active role that it played in educating the general public, customers learnt what they should ideally expect from a product. Moreover, smart marketers went a step further to teach the customer what they could expect from an offering. This gave birth to Customer Experience Management. Customer delight falls under the scope of Customer Experience Management, whereby marketers teach customers what to expect. Marketers are therefore in a position to anticipate customer requirements and exceed customer expectations.

Customer delight is defined as offering a product or service with some benefits in addition to the functional benefits derived from a brand so that the customers' expectations of an offering are exceeded.

Consistent delivery of delight creates involvement or a sense of belonging with the marketer and this gradually helps in building up trust. Trust enhances the extent of reliability enjoyed by an organization. If trust can be built up firmly, the organization gains customer loyalty. Research indicates that loyalty increases profitability.

Trust is defined as the level of confidence that the parties to the exchange process have upon each other.

This chapter aims to explore the perspective of delight and the building up of trust as a result of delight, which eventually leads to the enhancement of customer loyalty.

Impact of delight on trust

The practice of marketing started with mass marketing, in an era that was marked by the mass production of goods. Organizations generally believed that the higher the magnitude of production, the higher the sales would be as a result. Irrespective of the quality of the goods produced, the quantity produced was of primary concern. The mass market was content with whatever was served to them. They had limited choices and were mostly unaware of what they could expect from a product. However, with the proliferation of media in the lives of the general public, public awareness was enhanced. People were exposed to a wider market, where they could select from a wide array of products. With this kind of expansion of the horizon, people started gauging the various attributes that were present in the products. This gradually evoked a subtle comparison of similar products manufactured by different producers. This was the birth of market competition. With the passage of time, more and more producers entered the market and thus the types of market, and the types of products available in the market started multiplying. With time, competition grew and intensified, making product differentiation indispensable. Producers or marketers started differentiating their offerings on the basis of product features, distribution channels, organizational personnel and image. Such distinctions formed the Points of Differences (PODs) among similar products, which together with the Points of Parity (POPs) form the Unique Selling Proposition (USP) for each product. With similar types of POPs and PODs, marketers felt it necessary to attach a unique identity to the products manufactured by them through the usage of specific names, terms, symbols or logos; thereby giving rise to the concept of branding. Each brand was thereafter backed by a distinct USP and was therefore positioned in the market.

The positioning of each product or brand in the market created a picture of the product or brand in the minds of customers. This picture enabled and aided customers to carefully choose the products or brands which they felt would meet their expectations and serve their purposes through various functional attributes. Gradually, customers' expectations started growing. They started looking for certain specific attributes in the products or brands which would be translated into functional benefits. Minor deviations from expectations resulted in brand switching within a specific price band. To prevent such brand switching, meeting customer expectations became inevitable on the part of marketers, so that they could offer products that would meet the expectations of customers. Customer satisfaction was thus conceptualized as an important aspect of marketing (Yang and Hanks, 2016).

With the markets maturing further, customer satisfaction as a concept became saturated and started heading towards obsolescence. USP as a concept also started fading and was gradually replaced by Emotional Value Proposition (EVP). While USP laid emphasis on the product features and thereby end-user benefits, EVP emphasized the emotional value of the products or brands. Products or brands were no longer considered to be confined within the boundaries of their functional value but to move beyond this and provide emotional benefits to the users. Rational purchases were complemented by emotional backup. It was realized that the rationale behind all product or brand usage and purchase had to be supported by the emotional utility of the products or brands and thereby contribute to the feel-good factor of usage. It was presumed that products or brands that contribute to an overall pleasant usage experience rate high on recall and enhance emotional buying. Customer satisfaction slowly started to recede into the background. Customer Experience Management evolved and became popularized. Marketers started anticipating customer expectations and delivering them. In the wake of such a process, marketers actually started educating customers as to what they should expect from the products or brands. In this scenario, customer delight emerged and gradually replaced customer satisfaction. Customer delight was defined as exceeding customer expectations. As competition stiffened, anticipating customer requirements became imperative and thereafter came the task of delighting them.

Berman (2005) has identified the following positive consequences of customer delight:

a) Delighted customers are more likely to tell others about their experiences due to the surprise and joy elements associated with the transaction and the product/service.
b) Positive word-of-mouth and a high proportion of repeat customers can lower promotional costs.
c) Lower promotional expenses and higher brand and store loyalty may lower customer acquisition costs. Customer acquisition costs can also be reduced through fewer customer defections.

d) Delighted customers may increase the degree of brand or store loyalty. Increase in customer loyalty can have a major impact on company profitability since satisfied customers may buy a firm's products more often and in greater quantity.

e) The elements that cause delight can be a competitive advantage or a barrier to entry if not equally accessible to current and potential competitors.

Keiningham and Vavra (2001) laid down the following principles of customer delight:

a) Customers rate performance attributes in terms of two parameters – satisfaction-maintaining attributes and delight-creating attributes.

b) To maximize satisfaction with satisfaction-maintaining attributes, one must first insure against negative performance.

c) To enhance the effect of delight-creating attributes, it is imperative to identify the performance level at which the improvement is significant.

d) Improved retention rates are the primary conduit between increased performance, which creates heightened satisfaction, and profitability.

e) Segments of customers within a firm's customer base and the aggressiveness of competitors increase customer expectations of improvement in performance.

f) Firms should assess the lifetime value of customers for effective delight progression.

In the year 1984, Kano introduced the model of customer delight. According to this model, any product or service attribute can categorized as a One-dimensional, Must-be and/or Attractive attribute. One-dimensional attributes are basically satisfiers. The higher the presence of these attributes, the higher is the proportion of satisfaction. These attributes are explicitly demanded by customers. Must-be attributes, as the name suggests, are the basic criteria of a product. If these requirements are not fulfilled, the customers are extremely dissatisfied. The presence of these attributes does not satisfy or delight them. These attributes are prerequisites and are taken for granted. They are not explicitly expressed or demanded by customers. If the Must-be attributes are not present, customers are not interested in the product. Attractive attributes are those attributes that generate customer delight. Attractive attributes are neither explicitly demanded nor expected by the customers. Fulfilling these requirements leads to delight; however, their absence does not result in dissatisfaction or outrage.

With the market being flooded with innumerable players manufacturing and marketing similar products, identifying and incorporating the attractive attributes makes it easier for marketers to fulfill the requirements of the target audience. Different product or service attributes get translated into different functional benefits which thereby give rational support to the purchase decision. Once the purchase decisions are justified, it is the feeling of self-gratification (upon need fulfilment or problem solving) that appeals to the emotions of the users.

As depicted by the Elaboration Likelihood Model, every purchase is rationalized by a logical interpretation and is then complemented by the emotions of the customers. The left side of the brain, being the emotional interpreter, takes cues from the environment and gives an emotional bent to product purchase decisions. On the other hand, the right side of the brain is involved in judging the quality of the product or brand based upon its performance. The product or brand performance determines its image and the judgments about the product determine how customers feel about it. If all four parameters are positive, then the brand resonates with customers, in which case they feel that they are 'in sync' with the brand. Resonance is generally characterized in terms of the depth of psychological bonding that is established with customers.

This psychological bonding creates an emotional appeal by rendering joy to the user of the product or brand. The joy of need-fulfillment evokes delight. Thus, this psychological bonding gradually engenders loyalty by co-creating delight.

Loyalty can be conceptualized broadly in terms of three dimensions: cognitive, conative and behavioral. Cognitive loyalty is the weakest type of loyalty since it is mainly confined to the price (costs) and benefits and not the brand name or associations. Cognitive loyalty is largely based on customers' evaluations regarding the value of the product (cost–benefit ratio). Therefore, customers are likely to switch over to products that will offer them the strongest benefit. Affective loyalty pertains to favorable attitudes towards the brand. This is also subject to deterioration, due to the attractiveness of competitors' offerings. Upon finding a competitor's brand attractive, there is a high probability that customers will develop a favorable attitude towards it and will gradually shift towards it. Conative loyalty implies that attitudinal loyalty must be accompanied by a desired action. Consumers are more likely to try alternative product or service offerings if they regularly face any kind of failure.

Based upon attitudes and behavior, there are four loyalty levels: true loyalty, latent loyalty, spurious loyalty and no loyalty. Customers with true loyalty are strongly attached to the brand or organization. They are less vulnerable to competitor offerings and are ready to pay a price premium. They are even willing to possess the item if it involves a high acquisition cost. Customers with latent loyalty generally exhibit low patronage, although they bear a strong attitudinal commitment towards the organization. Their patronage may be measured as low because of inadequate resources to enhance their patronage, or because the company's price, distribution system, etc. are not in sync with the requirements of the target audience. Customers with spurious loyalty make frequent purchases but they exhibit a low emotional attachment to the brand. Their repeat purchasing may occur because of two reasons: there is no substitute brand in the market or there may not be a better alternative; the customers may be habituated to buy the product or the brand.

The study of loyalty in terms of both attitudinal and behavioral dimensions has its own significance. It gives a complete picture of of customers' purchase behavior or loyalty. This enables marketers to decide upon appropriate strategies to increase their market share over time. Marketers must patronize true loyal customers so that they advocate the product or the brand and enhance positive word-of-mouth. Of late, marketers prefer to introduce and run loyalty programs so that they deliver more value to the truly loyal customers. Marketers must try to explore the reasons behind customers' switching or shifting status in spite of their favorable attitudes towards an organization. Customers with spurious loyalty can be brought under a loyalty program so as to establish a symbiotic relationship in which there is value creation and delivery by the marketers and the customers gradually move towards truly patronizing the brand. The problem lies with the 'not loyal' category of customers. Being prone to low-price purchases, marketers may reduce their prices to a logical extent to attract these customers. However, such attraction will only be temporary and will last until this category of customers find a cheaper alternative. Constant reduction of price may trigger a price war which in the long run will dampen the brand image. A better alternative would be to introduce a scaled-down version of the product at a cheaper price. This would entail offering a standard quality product at a reasonable price, which would appeal to the price-sensitive group of people.

Increased loyalty has been found to be a profit-generating phenomenon. This is largely due to the fact that loyalty decreases costs in at least six areas:

a) reduced marketing costs (customer acquisition costs are always high)
b) lower transaction costs such as contract negotiation and order processing

c) reduced customer turnover expenses
d) increased cross-selling success leading to a larger share of customers
e) more positive word-of-mouth
f) reduced failure costs

The impact of loyalty on the above six areas is primarily due to the trust built up as a result of cultivating the customer relationship. A healthy relationship goes a long way in nurturing trust between marketers and customers. Trust basically emanates from commitment towards the brand. With the cultivation of a healthy relationship, the customer development process begins. The suspects (those who are suspected of using the product) are gradually converted into prospects (potential buyers). Organizations carry out various promotional activities so as to induce prospects trialling products to convert them from first-time users to repeat buyers. With the passage of time, the repeat buyers gain adequate product knowledge and they can be the voice of the organization to spread positive word-of-mouth, thereby converting the repeat buyers to clients. In the wake of spreading positive word-of-mouth, the clients gain the status of advocates. Finally, the advocates become partners whereby they start investing in the organization. As the customer development process continues, the magnitude of commitment towards the organization is enhanced. Commitment with a product or brand is of two types:

a) Calculative commitment – the commitment based on switching cost and uncertainty of the product quality of the available alternatives.
b) Affective commitment – indicates emotional attachment to the organization.

The higher the switching cost and the degree of uncertainty of an alternative, the higher is the calculative commitment. Emotional attachment with a brand will occur if the brand is successful in delighting its customers. Stronger commitment will lead to stronger product or brand attachment. Brand attachment generally stems from the ability of a brand to create and maintain customer identity. Bonding with the brand will be stronger if brand associations are successfully translated to brand identity –which will help customers to enhance their self-image. When a brand has positive emotional associations, the feelings towards the brand are extended towards the product category, as a result of which customer-based brand equity is improved. This in turn increases the attachment to the product or brand, because this strong feeling actually highers the barrier against brand switching, which in turn increases the commitment towards the brand. Committed customers are more likely to show a high degree of resistance to brand switching. As a result of their commitment, the customers' degree of involvement with the product or brand also increases. Customer involvement is a crucial factor in influencing buying decisions. However, it should be borne in mind that the degree of involvement with a product is also dependent upon the degree of relevance of the brand or product in their lives. Kapferer and Laurent (1993) conceptualized customer involvement as a multidimensional construct consisting of five determinants:

a) Personal meaning and reference
b) Ability to provide pleasure
c) Ability to express the person's self
d) Perceived importance of negative consequences
e) Perceived probability of perceived risk

A high degree of involvement with a brand or product invokes trust in it. Morgan and Hunt (1994) defined trust as the level of confidence in an exchange partner's reliability and integrity. The trust built in a brand or product is indicative of the value it delivers and its ability to deliver an enjoyable usage experience.

Like commitment, trust has two components: cognitive and affective. The cognitive component of trust refers to its credibility. This develops from the rational evaluation of a brand or product regarding its functional attributes vis-à-vis its performance and ability to fulfill users' needs. The affective component of trust is integrity. It is the evaluative aspect of a brand's motivational ability. A product or brand that appeals to the cognitive and affective components simultaneously is more successful in gaining the trust of customers. The emotional well-being to be obtained upon using the brand is firmly supported by rationale. The customers not only enjoy using the product but also have their post-purchase cognitive dissonance minimized. This further enhances their post-purchase positive behavior and also builds up brand trust.

However, managing stakeholders' trust is a difficult task, because there are many stakeholder groups, each with their own separate needs and perspectives. Managing customer trust is equally difficult because different groups of customers have different perspectives on trust. For a particular group of customers, the technical know-how of employees may contribute to a build up of trust; for others, trust may be the aftermath of good after-sales service. Delivering a good quality product in a consistent manner can also build up trust. A favorable corporate image can also affect trust. No matter what may contribute to trust building, research has highlighted that the following factors have contributed to the building up of trust:

a) Transparency
b) Integrity
c) Competence
d) Value

Transparency is supposed to play a very powerful role in building up trust. Increasing transparency makes it difficult to engage in illicit activities, thereby making the organization less culpable. With an open and clear system, an organization is less vulnerable to any malefactor activities. However, research has unfolded a different perspective. Transparency has been found to have little relevance to the building up of trust. This may be due to several reasons. Forced disclosure may hamper the quality of information that is disclosed. There may be some sensitive information which cannot be disclosed wholeheartedly. Such situations entail giving the bare minimum of information or inaccurate information. This may result in a situation where transparency will backfire. Further, some research suggests that disclosure may aggravate the problem. Disclosure of information may be followed by a chain of events which will reveal further information and may trigger conflict.

Honesty and integrity have always been considered as a strong premise for building trust. However, for customers, an organization's honesty and integrity may be difficult to gauge. It generally depends upon company identity, which gradually transforms into image. At times, honesty and integrity are not enough. Broadly speaking, a favorable image in terms of honesty and integrity is actually a matter of perception. A company that calls for the withdrawal of a damaged set of products proactively rather than waiting for market upheaval will definitely rate high on integrity and will be considered trustworthy. However, if the same organization has accidentally caused some irrevocable damage to its customers, it will no longer be trusted.

Incompetency erodes stakeholders' trust. Incompetency encompasses managerial incompetencce and technological incompetence. Investors and employees are more concerned with managerial (in)competence; on the other hand, customers and suppliers are more concerned with technological (in)competence: the organization's ability to deliver high-quality offerings. There has to be a balance in maintaining competence in all areas and aspects. Managerial competence aids the smooth running of the organization whereas technological competence ensures good quality of manufactured product. An environment that is conducive to support innovation reflects both managerial and technological competence. Such an environment portrays the organization's concern for the requirements of its customers. It nurtures in them a feeling of care, i.e. customers feel that their needs and problems are being duly taken care of and addressed. This nurtures a sense of commitment towards the organization and therefore builds up trust.

The values of an organization, which are reflected in the organizational culture, are also one of the major determinants of trust. Value congruence strengthens the customer relationship and builds up trust. Customers develop strong bonds with those organizations whose values are in congruence with their personal values. This nurtures a sense of belonging with the organizations. Customers find it easy to identify themselves with organizations with which they share a similar value system. Such commonality in value systems fosters trust. However, considering the value systems of customers, preferences will vary from one group of customers to another. It is rather a very difficult task to align the value system of an organization with that of its target audience.

The concept of trust has to be approached very carefully. What may be considered to be trustworthy by one group of customers may not be of equal importance to another group. However, all organizations must realize that trust is inevitable. Trust can be the core asset of an organization. If trust can be built up successfully, the organization will be successful in cultivating a good image. Its organizational image will be transferred to its offerings. A favorable image aids brand evangelism.

For successful marketing endeavors, marketers must design their offerings in a manner that will proactively address the needs and wants of customers. Proactive marketing has to be followed by reactive marketing to ensure that the organization is successfully implementing whatever it had intended to deliver and that the offerings are in line with customers' requirements. Organizations can carry out surveys prior to the designing of the offerings to find out what customers are looking for. Upon introducing the products or services, organizations can carry out intermittent surveys to determine the success of the products in terms of the fulfillment of its functional and psychological benefits, and whether any changes are desired in the offerings. There might be a brief comparison of competitors' products regarding their functional performance. Considering the total concept of marketing further strengthens the practice of a well-thought-out course of action that takes care to deliver quality products consistently so that customers feel pampered by the organization. This sense of belonging will culminate in customer involvement. Involvement will render organizational commitment. Persistent commitment will lead to trust and that will finally pave the way towards attaining a loyal customer base.

Thus, trust plays a pivotal role in today's marketing scenario. It is a powerful tactic to prevent customer attrition. Marketers need to be extra cautious these days. Customers are not only educated; their level of awareness is also very high. By virtue of exposure to the world, they are highly conversant in the market and know what to demand. Customers are constantly bombarded with messages from different marketers. Each marketer claims a host of attributes regarding their offerings. This enhances customers' chance of being exposed to the width and depth of the market, and customers can claim/demand certain attributes. Since the market is flooded with substitute products (alternatives), switching costs are very insignificant. This enables customers to be very meticulous about how and why they choose a particular product.

Once trust is built, the emotional attachment to a product or brand is strengthened, which will ensure that customers are hardcore loyal. Customer trust results in a symbiotic relationship with the organization – the customers are ensured a consistently good-quality product or service; the organization will benefit from the unconditional support of its customers during any crises. This will make brand acceptance and/or revitalization much easier. But the feeling of trust is highly vulnerable. Consistency in delivery has to be maintained. Besides, if the organization undergoes any change, it has to be communicated candidly so that the customers get first-hand information from the organization. If there is a failure to communicate on time, chances are that the delay may be perceived as an intentional move to conceal facts.

Brand trust can be built up by conforming to product standards and delivering this consistently. Corporate trust can be built through public relations activities. Proper PR can help in building up a relationship with stakeholders and if this is nurtured in the right manner, it builds up trust in the organization. This organizational trust ultimately trickles down to the offerings. Trust is ultimately reflected by loyalty.

Trust and loyalty programs both have the ability to induce loyalty. However, trust has an edge over loyalty programs. Trust is innate and once created it can never be broken unless there is a significant failure by the organization. On the other hand, loyalty programs are designed by organizations and therefore these are externally influenced. The loyalty programs involve costs in order to implement them, and the loyalty programs must be designed according to the preferential pattern of the target audience. Building trust, on the other hand, does not involve cost; it just involves a good consistent delivery of promises. The feeling of security that revolves around trust cannot be generated through loyalty programs. This feeling is enduring and multiplies with time. Loyalty programs need to be revised from time to time. They can be emulated by other organizations in the same industry; loyalty programs therefore call for innovation. Since there is a universally accepted loyalty program, marketers need to review their strategies from time to time. Besides, these loyalty program initiatives must vary across different groups of customers.

In deciding upon the loyalty program to be implemented, the basic question that needs to be addressed is how much should the organization invest in building loyalty. The magnitude of investment is dependant upon the category of customers who are addressed through the loyalty program vis-à-vis the marketing strategies undertaken. It is always desirable to build up trust amongst stakeholders to minimize costs and maximize the aftermath of strong bonding. Organizations should adopt a customer delight approach in building up trust so that customers become hardcore loyal and to maximize profitability and retention.

An insight: Importance of building trust in restaurants

Developing trust is crucial in the service sector, more so than the products sector. Products, being tangible, have a shelf life. The nature of services inhibits similar behavior. Services, being intangible in nature, lack any specific description. Besides, services are perishable and are produced and consumed simultaneously. This prevents them from being stored for future reference and consumption. As a result, service providers do not get a second chance to rectify their offers in case of service failure. On the incidence of service failure, brand trust can be adversely affected by negative word-of-mouth. But in the case of a trusted name, often the consumers can excuse the failure. A survey of restaurant guests in the city of Kolkata revealed that when it comes to service organizations, consumers place a greater emphasis on the credence attributes of the organizations. Credence attributes are generally communicated through word-of-mouth.

The hospitality sector falls under a hybrid category in the product-service continuum. The hospitality sector includes both hotels and restaurants. The hybrid category demands equal importance to be meted out to both the service as well as the product aspect of the entire offerings. For such a category, cleanliness, hygiene, food, furniture, layout and other ambient factors are as important as reliability, responsiveness and empathy of the support staff.

A discussion with various restauranteurs further established the theory that they place equal emphasis on the tangible items that make up the service area and staff training. According to the restaurateurs, whenever a guest walks in the premises, both the cognitive and affective component of their attitude become active. A pleasing environment triggers a certain degree of expectation and this is further reinforced by a supportive front-line employee. Marketers, therefore, find it absolutely essential to deliver both with a high degree of caution. According to them, at every juncture of the service encounter, the consumers are highly judgmental and together the entire experience contributes toward creating a favorable or unfavorable attitude towards the restaurant. This will eventually result in generating favorable or unfavorable word-of-mouth. Positive word-of-mouth results in building up trust that instils consumer commitment towards the brand. The restaurateurs have emphasized staff retention. They feel that if guests come and meet the same waiters, they feel comfortable. This comfort that is developed enables them to explain their requirement to the service providers. Hence, guest participation in the overall encounter is enhanced. On the other hand, repeated service delivery to the same guests enables waiters to offer a better service by paying individual attention to the guests – taking care of their intricate likes and dislikes.

Eighty percent of the restaurateurs expressed that they prefer service transparency. They stated that failures should be confessed and addressed promptly. This minimizes or even eradicates any suspicion that may develop. Maintaining transparency with employees has its own advantages as well. In case of any failure, the employees may take the onus for the failure and come up with an appropriate solution. The front-line employees are well versed with the policies of the restaurants so that these are translated into services of the desired standard. Most restaurateurs mentioned that they do not "let down" their guests and employees. The marketing programs are framed in a manner that will not overpromise nor underpromise. All of the service providers gave assurance that they do not make false promises, as it will result in a breach of trust.

On the other hand, the consumers openly discussed their criterion of choosing restaurants primarily for the service quality – most emphasis has been laid on food quality and hygiene factors. The most reliable source of information has been found to be friends and peer groups. Besides, a large proportion (60 percent) of guests interviewed have also referred to social networks for online reviews. Price and location occupy less important positions. Guests have also enquired about food-related outbreaks to their friends or peers. Such incidents have been found to be consequences of unhygienic kitchens. Many guests emphasized restroom cleanliness, associating it with staff hygiene. According to the results of the survey, advertisements supply only limited information and play a role only in name identification. Direct feedback actually results in accumulation/generation of expectations. Upon service, the trust might develop or perish depending upon the extent to which the expectations can be fulfilled or left unaddressed. If a brand successfully gains trust, the extent of commitment is automatically generated. This is primarily due to the fact that a trusted name will minimize the risk of consumption. Moreover, trust indicates good or exceptionally good service quality. Commitment will lead to a delightful consumption experience through positive bonding. Eventually delight will lead to loyalty.

Conclusion

It should be borne in mind that customer delight should not be generated if the cost of delivering such values requires the organization to bear extra costs. Under such a circumstance the delight will actually be converted to disgust. Customers are always willing to pay extra if trust can be built up. But beyond a certain limit, no matter how hard the marketers try to deliver quality offerings, it will not be viewed favorably. Customers will start searching for better alternatives in terms of value and will be skeptical regarding any effort undertaken by the marketers. In the wake of such a process, trust will break instead of building up. Loyalty will thus be disrupted. The negative reputation that will spread will erode any positive inclination towards the company. When considering incorporating attractive attributes into any product or service, there has to be a proper cost-benefit analysis prior to incorporating them. If a particular attribute is found to be worthwhile, only then can the organization consider including the attribute. It has to be remembered that if the cost is high, it will ultimately percolate down to the customers. Beyond a certain limit, they will refuse to pay extra.

References

Berman, B. (2005). "How to Delight Your Customers". *California Management Review*, 48(1), 129–151.

Kapferer, J.N. and Laurent, G. (1993). "Further Evidence on Consumer Involvement Profile: Five Antecedents of Involvement". *Psychology and Marketing*, 10(4), 347–357.

Keiningham, T. and Vavra, G. (2001). *The Customer Delight Principle*, McGraw-Hill.

Morgan, R.M. and Hunt, S.D. (1994). "The Commitment Trust Theory of Relationship Marketing". *Journal of Marketing*, 58, 20–38.

Yang, W. and Hanks, L. (2016). "Preconsumption Mood, Causal Explanations, and Postrecovery Reactions". *Journal of Hospitality Marketing & Management*, 25(1), 69–90.

27

Generation Y perspective of hotel disintermediation and user-generated content

The case of Taiwan

Giacomo Del Chiappa and Anestis Fotiadis

Introduction

In the last decades, the Internet has experienced significant growth worldwide. According to Internet World Stats (2016a), more than 3.6 billion people worldwide are active Internet users, with an increase of 10 percent since 2015. More specifically, Internet penetration varies considerably among countries, but an average of 46 percent has been observed worldwide (Internet World Stats 2016a). By mid-2016, in Taiwan there were 19,666,364 Internet users over a total population of 23,464,787 inhabitants, thus representing a penetration rate of 83.81 percent (Internet World Stats 2016b). Tourism has become the foremost industry in terms of online market share, and travel planning and booking are two of the most popular online activities (e.g., Guo et al. 2013), with the development of the Internet, information and communication technologies and social media significantly changing the bridging role of traditional tourism intermediaries (Bennett and Lai 2005; Tsai et al. 2005).

The Internet and social media are among the most important information sources consulted during pre-purchase information searches (Labrecque et al. 2013), with online information sources playing a much more crucial role than traditional mediums (Jin et al. 2014). In this context, Generation Y has been considered as a new sizeable market (Sullivan and Heitmeyer 2008) that is changing and will change even more in the near future, due to the fast-changing landscape of the Internet. A recent study has shown that 62 percent of millennial shoppers' shopping behavior is influenced by a prior online search (Bazaarvoice 2014) and that consumers from Generation Y spend a considerable amount of time contributing, sharing, searching for and consuming content on social media platforms (e.g., Pempek et al. 2009; Bolton et al. 2013).

In the US alone, Generation Y consists of 82 million people, spending nearly US$200 billion annually (e.g., Djamasbi et al. 2010). In 2012, as reported by the UNWTO, youth travel generated US$182 billion, and the total number of international trips by this generation is estimated to increase to 300 million trips a year by 2020 (IPK International 2013). Based on these figures, it is easy to explain why Generation Y is widely recognized as the future market of the travel and tourism industry (Benckendorff et al. 2010).

That said, it is clear that it is crucial to have a deep understanding of the needs and demands of travelers from Generation Y and of how to capture their attention; in fact, with this knowledge, destination marketers and hospitality managers are provided with relevant information that can be used to predict the future information-search behavior of tourists from Generation Y (Sun et al. 2016). In Taiwan, the debate on disintermediation and re-intermediation is rather common and has nowadays become a hot issue for scholars and practitioners alike. Existing studies (e.g., Law 2009; Del Chiappa 2013), focused on specific geographical areas, such as Hong Kong and Italy, rarely consider the relative power that User-Generated Content (UGC) exerts on tourists' choices compared to information delivered by travel agencies (e.g., Del Chiappa et al. 2016), and very few pay attention to Generation Y (e.g., Prayag and Del Chiappa 2014).

Some existing studies are focused on investigating the impact of the Internet and e-commerce technologies on traditional tourism intermediaries (e.g., Bennett and Lai 2005; Tsai et al. 2005). However, online behavior with respect to accommodation purchase is comparatively under-researched in Taiwan. Hence, the main purpose of this chapter is to provide a case study that deepens the knowledge of the extent to which young Taiwan travelers are in favor of or against the disintermediation of hotel reservations, and the extent to which they trust and use UGC when making hotel reservations.

Background information

According to Jin et al. (2014: 618), "the term generation refers to people who are born in the same general time span and experience the same key historical or social life events." Similarly, Noble and Schewe (2003: 979) state that generations or generational cohorts can be defined as "proposed groups of individuals who are born during the same time period and who experienced similar external events during their formative or coming-of-age years." Based on Moscardo et al. (2011), the reason why it is important to consider these formative experiences is that they significantly influence the preferences, beliefs and psychographic tendencies of individuals belonging to a certain generation.

Currently, there is still little consensus about the age ranges used to define the young tourist (Seekings 1998). Youth tourism covers the age bracket of 16–24 in some cases, 16–29 in other cases, and 16–35 in still other studies (Carr 1999). In this chapter, we consider Generation Y as people aged 18–35 (Sheahan 2009; Prayag and Del Chiappa 2014).

Generation Y has received increasing attention from scholars (e.g., Howe and Strauss 2000; McCrindle 2003; Eisner 2005; Donnison 2007; Benckendorff et al. 2010), and there are several reasons to explain this. First, it is noteworthy that in 2012, as reported by UNWTO, youth travel generated US$182 billion (the average cost by trip was US$910) and represented more than 20 percent of the more-than-one-billion international arrivals; the total number of international trips by Generation Y is estimated to rise 3,000 million trips a year by 2020 (IPK International 2013). Second, in the last few years, youth and student travel has been experiencing significant growth, as the international student population is increasing (Richards and Wilson 2003). Further, Generation Y will become dominant players in the prime age workforce; thus, their prospective purchasing power cannot be ignored. Generation Y is expected to be the next-largest cohort, after the baby boomers, that will generate significant influence and impacts on the tourism sector, especially given the fact that they seem to be characterized by a higher frequency of travel and greater willingness to spend more on international travel (Pendergast 2010; Hritz et al. 2014). Youth travelers tend to travel more frequently and for longer periods (Richards and Wilson 2003), are more digitally savvy and are more involved in travel planning (Xiang et al. 2015). Finally, a substantial and growing number of international students are traveling abroad to undertake study programs, thus hugely benefiting the economy of the host countries (ICEF Monitor 2015).

In the last decade, members of Generation Y have significantly increased the usage of the Internet to search for information and to buy tourism products (Nusair et al. 2013; Xiang et al. 2015). Further, they have been becoming intensive users of social media, both for searching information about travel services and to share their experiences during and after consumption (Moscardo et al. 2011), posting comments, reviews, photos and videos that affect the online reputation of service providers and influence the choices of their peers (Jin et al. 2014). The Taiwanese seem not to pay great attention to privacy issues when using the Internet to plan and purchase travel products but seem to be concerned about online security; for them, online travel communities are perceived as an effective tool to reduce the perceived risk of online travel purchasing (Ling et al. 2009). Prior studies have shown that the cultural environment, e.g., individualistic versus collectivistic (Hofstede 1980), can affect the nature and intensity of social media usage (Ribière et al. 2010; Bolton et al. 2013). Specifically, members of collectivistic countries (e.g., Taiwan) have significantly more online social ties with people they have never met in person, thus somehow suggesting that they tend to like/trust social media more than those belonging to individualistic countries (Cardon et al. 2009).

The extent to which the Internet allows consumers to seek information and to make their hotel reservations online, including the possibility to change the accommodation suggested by a travel agency based upon UGC (Del Chiappa 2013; Del Chiappa et al. 2015), raises questions about the future of travel agents. The disintermediation hypothesis, which is the idea that the role of the middleman will be eliminated (Buhalis 1998), has also captured the attention of both researchers and practitioners in the context of Generation Y.

Prominent arguments exist in the literature for and against disintermediation of the tourism distribution channel (Buhalis 1998; Law 2009). Based on a demand-side perspective, the Internet and information and communication technologies allow consumers to search for information, saving time and costs, to generate electronic word of mouth (e-WOM), to tailor the products they buy and to access a wider selection of travel service providers without any constraints in time and space (e.g., Anckar 2003). Despite this, there are several reasons for favoring traditional travel agencies. For example, consumers might prefer to rely on a traditional travel agent to cope with the huge amount of information available online. Further, consumers might prefer to use a street travel agency to avoid any concerns related to the safety and security of online booking (e.g., Chen 2001) and to receive tailored advice, experiencing a personal touch (Palmer and McCole 1999).

However, it should be noted that consumers tend to rely on the Internet or on a travel agent based on product characteristics and their socio-demographic characteristics. Previous studies have shown that consumers generally purchase low-involvement products and services online (such as short trips), whereas they rely on the traditional intermediaries for the purchase of more complex or high involvement products, such as honeymoons or intercontinental travel (e.g., Prayag and Del Chiappa 2014). Considering the existing studies on the influence that socio-demographic (e.g., age, gender, etc.) and tripographic (e.g., frequency of traveling, etc.) characteristics exert on online behaviors, some contradictory findings seem to exist. Gender generally has no influence on online behaviors (Kim and Kim 2004; Ip et al. 2012), except in the study by Del Chiappa (2013). Education level influences online behaviors in some studies (Weber and Roehl 1999; Morrison et al. 2001; Ip et al. 2012) but not in others (Kim and Kim 2004). Likewise, income level has no influence on online behavior in some studies (Kim and Kim 2004) but does have an influence in others (Ip et al. 2012; Del Chiappa 2013). In the specific context of youth travelers, gender and age had a significant influence on the views concerning the topic of hotel disintermediation (e.g., Prayag and Del Chiappa 2014).

Somewhat contradictory findings emerge when analyzing the extent to which travelers trust UGC and rely on it when making their choices. For example, prior studies have found that female (Gretzel and Yoo 2008) and frequent travelers (Gretzel et al. 2007) gain more benefits from reading reviews compared to their counterparts. That said, it could be expected that frequent travelers trust UGC more than others. Despite this, Prayag and Del Chiappa (2014), in their study on the French Generation Y, did not find any significant difference among occasional, moderate and frequent buyers, based on the extent to which their choices are finally influenced by UGC rather than on information delivered by traditional agencies, thus providing some contradictory insights.

Tourists, based on how they make their choices, can be divided into those who only wish to acquire information (lookers) and those who also use it to buy tourism services and products (bookers) (e.g., Morrison et al. 2001). In 2008, 65 percent of the members of Generation Y made travel arrangements online (Jones and Fox 2009). However, other studies have shown that Generation Y travelers mostly tend to use the Internet when planning their trips and use travel agents when booking (Beldona et al. 2009), thus acting mostly as lookers. Prior research on a sample of 1,429 students at 11 universities located in 11 different countries (Pizam et al. 2004) showed that 46.5 percent of the respondents booked and purchased their trips using a travel agent, especially those characterized by low risk-taking and sensation-seeking attitudes.

All that said, it could be argued that the literature devoted to analyzing the views of Generation Y travelers toward the Internet and UGC is still relatively poor, concentrated in a few countries (mainly focusing on the USA and/or Europe) and characterized by somewhat contradictory findings. This renders any effort to further deepen the scientific debate around this research area particularly relevant, especially when the Asian countries are considered.

Methodology

For the purpose of this case study, we adopted a survey instrument used in previous studies (Del Chiappa 2013; Prayag and Del Chiappa 2014). A qualifying question about whether respondents had any previous experience of booking hotel rooms online was included at the beginning of the survey. Only people who answered positively were allowed to complete the questionnaire. Respondents were then asked to express their level of agreement with a list of statements used to investigate their views concerning the use of online booking and the use of traditional travel agencies when making hotel reservations; the respondents gave their answers using a 5-point Likert scale (1 = I completely disagree, 5 = I completely agree). The third section included several questions related to the use of the Internet for different types of holidays at different geographical scales (national, European-based and non-European-based, and the length of the trip – short vs. medium/long). Respondents were also asked to tell us if they have ever changed the hotel accommodation suggested by a traditional travel agency based on UGC (Yes/No). Finally, several socio-demographics, such as age, gender, education level and average monthly income, were also measured.

The questionnaire was originally designed in English and then translated into Taiwanese. The method of back-translation was used to ascertain the content of the translated version and was pre-tested on 20 Taiwanese from the target population. The questionnaire was administered using a self-completion method to Taiwanese student travelers between the ages of 18 and 35 at one of the largest private universities in Taiwan (I-Shou University). A total of 700 questionnaires were distributed, of which 514 were returned; 466 were complete and usable for data analysis (response rate: 90.67%).

Results and discussion

Most of the respondents were female (57.1%), belonging to the 18–25 age bracket (94.6%), with a university degree (90.7%) or high school diploma (5.1%); 10.5 percent of respondents described their average monthly income as less than 1,000 NTD.

To better examine the dimensions underlying the young travelers' perceptions of disintermediation, a principal component factor analysis with varimax rotation was undertaken. Prior to that, the KMO measure of sampling adequacy (0.892) and the significant Bartlett's test of sphericity ($\chi2=2507.48, p<0.001$) confirmed the suitability of the data for factorization. The 16 factor items yielded four factors with eigenvalues greater than one (Table 27.1).

The four factors explained 61 percent of the variance and were labeled: F1 – Benefits of Online Reservation; F2 – Benefits of Travel Agency; F3 – Transaction Costs of Travel Agency; and F4 – Online Trust & Search Behavior. In order to investigate whether significant differences do exist based on the socio-demographic characteristics on the four factors, T-Test and Anova tests were applied. The results did not reveal any significant influence on the investigated factors. In order to go deeper with our analysis, T-Test and Anova tests were also applied to the list of the 16 items. The results revealed that all the socio-demographic characteristics significantly influence 10 out of 16 items used to assess the respondents' views for and against the topic of disintermediation (Table 27.2). For example, significant differences based on gender exist in how respondents search for information through the Internet and how they check reviews, comments, photos and videos uploaded online ($t=-2.418, p<0.05$), with females ($M=4.13, SD=0.963$) expressing a more positive view than males ($M=3.90, SD=1.019$). This seems to confirm the idea that young women have a likely tendency to be browsers and sharers in the Travel 2.0 domain (Rong et al. 2012). Further, significant differences based on gender exist in relation to respondents' views toward the idea that travel agencies are able to offer a human touch and interface with the hotel industry ($T=-2.512, p= 0.012$), with females ($M=3.58, SD=0.867$) supporting this comment more than males ($M=3.37, SD=0.911$). Significant differences based on age do exist in the way that youth travelers think travel agencies are able to personalize the products/services ($t=2.804, p<0.01$), with travelers aged less than 25 years old ($M=3.47, SD=0.758$) supporting this view more than travelers 26–35 years old ($M=3.00, SD=1.024$). Significant differences also exist based on education, such as, for example, in the way respondents think the Internet provides tourist information in such a way that it is easy to choose hotels and spend free time online ($F=4.442, p<0.01$).

Specifically, young travelers with university degrees have lower mean scores ($M=3.46, S.D=0.820$) than secondary graduates ($M=4.00, SD=0.853$).

The respondents were also asked about the most common purpose and duration of their travel (Table 27.3).

In previous studies (e.g., Law et al. 2004), the propensity to purchase travel products online was found to be influenced by the travel purpose and the duration of travel (short haul vs. long haul). Our findings reveal that the respondents used the Internet mostly to book accommodation related to national travel (78.85%) more than for European-based (47.30%) and

Table 27.1 Results of factor analysis

Items	M.	S.D.	F1	F2	F3	F4
A. Technology, particularly the Internet, allows consumers to perform most hotel searching and purchasing conveniently.	3.49	0.891	**0.766**	0.165	0.140	0.101
B. When choosing hotels, I search for information through the Internet, and I check reviews, comments, photos and videos uploaded online by tourists.	4.23	0.957	**0.733**	0.147	0.277	0.025
C. Websites (e.g., electronic intermediaries, such as booking.com) are more flexible and can offer many more choices than travel agencies for hotel rooms.	3.44	0.886	**0.716**	0.190	0.142	0.092
D. I trust the tourism information available online through reviews and comments posted online in blogs, social networks and online travel agencies.	3.17	0.975	**0.686**	0.215	0.090	0.198
E. The Internet allows people to use their time in a very productive way, as they can search for information and make reservations whenever they want.	3.55	0.897	**0.671**	0.118	0.514	0.068
F. Travel agencies are able to understand the need and desires of their customers and recommend the most suitable hotel accommodation.	3.48	0.886	0.052	**0.745**	0.336	0.030
G. It is more convenient to seek advice from travel agencies on hotel reservations than from using online technology only.	3.78	0.902	0.080	**0.729**	-0.002	0.174
H. Travel agencies are professional counselors for hotel rooms and offer valuable service and advice.	3.33	0.929	0.254	**0.711**	-0.002	-0.010
I. Travel agencies are able to personalize the products/services they provide to their customers.	4.04	0.992	0.209	**0.697**	0.244	0.151
L. Travel agencies offer a human touch and interface with the hotel industry.	3.72	0.940	0.447	**0.482**	0.060	0.021
M. The Internet allows saving money when making hotel reservations.	3.45	0.779	0.265	0.048	**0.801**	0.086
N. The Internet provides tourist information in such a way that it is easy to choose hotels and spend free time online.	3.37	0.822	0.068	0.276	**0.627**	0.294
O. The Internet allows people to save a lot of time in making hotel room reservations compared to the use of traditional travel agencies.	3.83	0.968	0.485	0.119	**0.592**	-0.070
P. Consumers ultimately have to bear the cost of commissions for travel agencies for their hotel rooms.	4.00	0.945	-0.055	0.219	0.131	**0.783**
Q. Travel agencies are usually in favor of companies who offer more attractive commissions or partners and thus make biased recommendations for hotels.	3.51	0.921	0.469	-0.135	0.118	**0.656**
R. Travel agencies can reduce booking insecurity, as they are responsible for all arrangements.	3.51	0.848	0.378	0.385	0.023	**0.458**
Eigenvalues			5.828	1.748	1.129	1.057
% of explained variance			22.193	17.257	12.379	9.188
Cronbach's alpha			0.814	0.772	0.557	0.697

Table 27.2 ANOVA and independent *T*-Tests

Items	M.	S.D	Gender T	Age T	Education F	Income F
Factor 1	3.64	0.711	−1.916	0.496	0.225	1.584
A.	3.49	0.891	−0.678	−0.618	0.615	1.748
B.	4.23	0.957	**−2.418***	0.611	0.852	1.724
C.	3.44	0.886	−0.841	0.201	0.390	0.779
D.	3.17	0.975	−1.309	−0.998	1.030	**2.005***
E.	3.55	0.897	−1.041	1.846	0.427	0.952
Factor 2	3.38	0.657	−1.431	1.040	1.089	1.401
F.	3.48	0.886	−1.257	1.410	0.345	0.625
G.	3.78	0.902	0.009	0.772	**2.968***	1.789
H.	3.33	0.929	−0.1073	−0.569	1.870	0.646
I.	4.04	0.992	−0.765	**2.804****	0.567	0.852
L.	3.72	0.940	**−2.512***	−0.508	0.889	1.301
Factor 3	3.40	0.612	−0.314	−0.592	0.638	1.329
M.	3.45	0.779	0.413	−1.674	1.063	1.090
N.	3.37	0.822	−0.548	−1.318	**4.442****	**1.986***
O	3.83	0.968	−1.034	−0.023	0.657	**2.143***
Factor 4	3.87	0.729	−0.713	−1.069	1.202	1.777
P.	4.00	0.945	−1.712	0.238	1.377	**1.606***
Q.	3.51	0.921	1.596	**−2.008***	1.197	2.125
R.	3.51	0.848	−0.169	0.229	**3.622***	0.757

* Significant at 0.05% level, ** Significant at 0.01% level

Table 27.3 Types of travel and online booking of hotels

	National	European-based	Non-European-based	Short-term journeys	Medium-term journeys
				(≤4 days)	(≥5 days)
Leisure/Holidays	78.85%	47.30%	64.20%	74.70%	77.00%

non-European-based travel (64.20%). Our findings seem to contradict those of Prayag and Del Chiappa (2014), who found that French students from Generation Y book accommodation online for traveling in other European countries (81.3%) more than for traveling domestically (79.8%) and outside Europe (64.3%). On the whole, this seems to suggest that cultural differences still exist in the way in which tourists use the Internet for searching for and booking hotel rooms. Moreover, Generation Y travelers were found to book online slightly more often for medium- to long-term journeys (77%) than for short-term journeys (74.70%), thus partially disconfirming the idea that the longer the duration of the stay, the greater the number of travelers using travel agencies (e.g., Del Chiappa 2013; Prayag and Del Chiappa 2014).

According to previous research (e.g., Law 2009; Del Chiappa 2013), we grouped online buyers into occasional buyers (those who have used the Internet to make bookings one or two times), moderate buyers (three to four times) and frequent buyers (more than four times).

Hence, a series of chi-square tests was used to investigate whether occasional, moderate and frequent buyers were more or less likely to change the accommodation suggested by a travel

Table 27.4 Perceptions of trust about UGC

Have you ever changed the accommodation suggested by a travel agency based on UGC?	Occasional buyers	Moderate buyers	Frequent buyers	Total
Yes	68.1%	75.0%	60.9%	68.0%
No	31.9%	25.0%	39.1%	32.0%
Total	100%	100%	100%	100%

agency based on UCG (Table 27.4). Findings suggest that no significant differences exist among the groups.

Conclusion, managerial implications and limitations

Findings revealed that young Taiwanese travelers express, even if slightly, positive feelings toward the role of travel agencies. However, their attitudes toward the Internet and UGC as a tool to make reservations are stronger, thus confirming the relevant role of the Internet as a holiday planning tool for Generation Y (e.g., Nusair et al. 2013). Further, the case study found four underlying dimensions of perceptions of disintermediation, namely: "Benefits of Online Reservation," "Benefits of Travel Agency," "Online Trust & Search Behavior" and "Transaction Costs of Travel Agency." Socio-demographic characteristics were found not to exert any significant influence on the aforementioned dimensions. In contrast, significant differences were found when the analysis was carried out on each item; specifically, they were found for 10 out of the 16 considered items. In some way, these findings disconfirm previous studies (e.g., Prayag and Del Chiappa 2014), where age was found to exert a significant influence. This suggests that, despite the widely accepted increasing use of the Internet for information searches and for making hotel purchases, country-based differences may still exist and merit further investigation. Findings of this study add to the current body of knowledge, providing further insights into the scientific debate on disintermediation and the perceived trustworthiness of UGC for travelers from Generation Y, thus expanding the geographical understanding of the hotel disintermediation phenomenon to Taiwan, where no up-to-date and published paper devoted to this research area currently exists.

Our findings provide interesting managerial implications. Given that the benefits of the Internet for hotel booking outweighed the benefits offered by travel agencies, our results first suggest that hotel marketers could find it profitable to redistribute the hotel room quota, placing more hotel rooms on the Internet to increase their revenue. Further, given that the study reported a considerable proportion of occasional, moderate and frequent youth travelers having changed the accommodation suggested by their travel agent based on UGC, findings strongly suggest that hotel marketers should monitor their online reputation, even when they specifically aim to distribute their rooms via street travel agencies. Finally, with the aim of incentivizing consumers to book using hotel websites instead of travel agencies, hotel marketers should offer bonus loyalty points to those consumers returning to their websites to book another stay in their accommodation. Assuming that most of the booking services traditionally provided by travel agents can now be carried out over the Internet, our results suggest that travel agents should create and maintain a presence in the electronic marketplace, also relying on the use of social media (e.g., Huang 2012); they should behave more as professional counselors and should improve their customer service and ability to satisfy the needs and expectations of Generation Y (Anckar 2003). When doing this, travel agencies should suggest tailored solutions to their guests by complementing the information found in the catalogs offered by tour operators with UGC that travelers upload online; by doing this, travel agents could show customers that the offer is the most suitable for their needs, based on both offline (business-to-consumer) and online (peer-to-peer) content. Finally, travel agencies should use marketing tactics to create and develop Internet-based interaction with travelers from Generation Y (e.g., creating an avatar on their official website) and to incentivize them to share UGC and to become advocates of their online services.

Although this study helps to fill a gap in the existing knowledge in the literature and proposes some implications for practitioners, several limitations still remain. First, the fact of having used a convenience sample of college students, who are obviously a sub-segment of Generation Y, renders our findings hardly generalizable to the overall Taiwanese Generation Y (Nusair et al. 2013). Further, our study is site-specific (i.e., a single country was investigated) and did not explicitly consider the moderating effect that perceived risk and security exert on online tourist behavior; future case studies and empirical investigations could be devoted to analyzing this latter aspect and also making a cross-cultural comparison.

References

Anckar, B. (2003) "Consumer intentions in terms of electronic travel distribution: Implications for future market structures," *E-Service Journal*, 2, 68–86.

Bazaarvoice (2014). "Social trends report", retrieved from www.bazaarvoice.com/research-and-insight/social-commerce-statistics/ (last accessed February 2015).

Beldona, S., Nusair, K. and Demicco, F. (2009). "Online travel purchase behavior of generational cohorts: A longitudinal study," *Journal of Hospitality Marketing & Management*, 18, 406–420.

Benckendorff, P., Moscardo, G. and Pendergast, D. (ed.) (2010). *Tourism and Generation Y*. Oxford: CABI.

Bennett, M. M. and Lai, C. W. K. (2005). "The impact of the internet on travel agencies in Taiwan," *Tourism and Hospitality Research*, 6(1), 8–23.

Bolton, R. N., Parasuraman, A., Hoefnagels, A., Migchels, N., Kabadayi, S., Gruber, T., … and Solnet, D. (2013). "Understanding Generation Y and their use of social media: A review and research agenda," *Journal of Service Management*, 24(3), 245–267.

Buhalis, D. (1998). "Strategic use of information technologies in the tourism industry," *Tourism Management*, 19(5), 409–421.

Cardon, P. W., Marshall, B., Choi, J., El-Shinnaway, M. M., North, M., Svensson, L., … and Valenzuala, J. B. (2009). "Online and offline social ties of social network website users: An exploratory study in eleven societies," *Journal of Computer Information System*, Fall, 54–64.

Carr, N. (1999). "A study of gender differences: Young tourist behaviour in a UK coastal resort," *Tourism Management*, 20, 223–228.

Chen, S. L. (2001). "Effects of value, affect, security, and web content on informational and transactions usage of the Internet," *Asia Pacific Journal of Tourism Research*, 6(1), 63–72.

Del Chiappa, G. (2013). "Internet versus travel agencies: The perception of different groups of Italian online buyers," *Journal of Vacation Marketing*, 19(1), 1–12.

Del Chiappa G, Alarcón-del-Amo, M. and Lorenzo-Romero, C. (2016) "Internet and user-generated content versus high-street travel agencies: A latent gold segmentation in the context of Italy," *Journal of Hospitality Marketing and Managament*, 25(2), 197–217.

Del Chiappa, G., Lorenzo-Romero, C. and Gallarza, M. (2015). "Attitude toward disintermediation in hotel reservations: Spanish travellers profile," *European Journal of Tourism Research*, 9, 129–143.

Djamasbi, S., Siegel, M. and Tullis, T. (2010). "Generation Y, web design, and eye tracking," *International Journal of Human Computer Sciences*, 68(59), 307–323.

Donnison, S. (2007). "Unpacking the millennials: A cautionary tale for teacher education," *Australia Journal of Teacher Education*, 32(3), 1–13.

Eisner, S. P. (2005) "Managing Generation Y," *SAM Advanced Management Journal*, 70(49), 4–15.

Gretzel, U. and Yoo, K. H. (2008). "Use and impact of online travel reviews." In *Proceeedings of the International Conference on Information and Communication Technologies in Tourism* (pp. 35–46). Innsbruck, Austria: Springer.

Gretzel, U., Yoo, K. H. and Purifoy, M (2007). *Online travel review study: The role and impact of online travel reviews.* College Station, TX: Laboratory for Intelligent Systems in Tourism.

Guo, X., Ling, L., Dong, Y. and Liang, L. (2013). "Optimal pricing strategy based on market segmentation for service products using online reservation systems: An application to hotel rooms," *International Journal of Hospitality Management,* 35, 274–281.

Hofstede, G. (1980). *Culture's consequences.* Beverly Hills, CA: Sage Publications.

Howe, N. and Strauss, W. (2000). *Millennials rising: The next great generation.* New York, NY: Vintage Books.

Hritz, N., Sidman, C. L. and D'Abundo, M. (2014). "Segmenting the college educated Generation Y health and wellness traveler," *Journal of Travel & Tourism Marketing,* 31, 132–145.

Huang, L. (2012). "Social media as a new play in a marketing channel strategy: Evidence from Taiwan travel agencies' blogs," *Asia Pacific Journal of Tourism Research,* 17(6), 615–634.

ICEF Monitor (2015). "The state of international student mobility in 2015." Retrieved from http://monitor.icef.com/2015/11/the-state-of-international-student-mobility-in-2015/ (last accessed 29 September 2016).

Internet World Stats (2016a). "Internet usage statistics. The Internet big picture world internet users and 2016 population stats." Retrieved from: www.internetworldstats.com/stats.htm (last accessed 28 September 2016).

Internet World Stats (2016b). "Asia Internet use, population data and Facebook Statistics – June 2016." Retrieved from www.internetworldstats.com/stats3.htm (last accessed 28 September 2016).

Ip, C., Lee, H. A. and Law, R. (2012). "Profiling the users of travel websites for planning and online experience sharing," *Journal of Hospitality & Tourism Research,* 36, 418–426.

IPK International (2013). *ITB world travel trends report.* Berlin, Germany: Messe Berlin GmbH.

Jin, T., Lin, V. S. and Hung, K. (2014). "China's Generation Y's expectation on outbound group package tour," *Asia Pacific Journal of Tourism Research,* 19(6), 617–644.

Jones, A. and Fox, S. (2009). *Generations online 2009.* Washington, DC: Pew Internet & American Life Project.

Kim, W. G. and Kim, D. J. (2004). "Factors affecting online hotel reservation intention between online and non-online customers," *Hospitality Management,* 23(4), 381–395.

Labrecque, L., Mathwisk, C., Novak, T. P. and Hofacker, C. (2013) "Consumer power: evolution in the digital age," *Journal of Interactive Marketing,* 27(4), 257–269.

Law, R. (2009). "Disintermediation of hotel reservations: The perception of different groups of online buyers in Hong Kong," *International Journal of Contemporary Hospitality Management,* 21(6), 766–772.

Law, R., Leung, K. and Wong, J. (2004). "The impact of the Internet on travel agencies," *International Journal of Contemporary Hospitality Management,* 16, 100–107.

Ling, P. J., Jones, E. and Westwood, S. (2009). "Perceived risk and risk-relievers in online travel purchase intentions," *Journal of Hospitality Marketing & Management,* 18(8), 782–810.

McCrindle, M. (2003). *Understanding Generation Y.* North Parramatta: The Australian Leadership Foundation.

Morrison, A., Jing, A., O'Leary, J. and Cai, L. (2001). "Predicting usage of the Internet for travel bookings: An exploratory study," *Information Technology and Tourism,* 4(1), 15–30.

Moscardo, G., Murphy, L. and Benckendorff, P. (2011). "Generation Y and travel futures," in I. Yeoman, C. H. Hsu, K. Smith, and S. Watson (Eds.), *Tourism and demography* (pp. 87–100). Oxford: Goodfellow Publishers.

Noble, S. M., and Schewe, C. D. (2003). "Cohort segmentation: An exploration of its validity," *Journal of Business Research,* 56(12), 979–987.

Nusair, K. K., Bilgihan, A. and Okumus, F. (2013). "The role of online social network travel websites in creating social interaction for Generation Y travellers," *International Journal of Tourism Research,* 15(5), 458–472.

Palmer, A. and McCole, P. (1999). "The virtual re-intermediation of travel services: A conceptual framework and empirical investigation," *Journal of Vacation Marketing,* 6(1), 33–47.

Pempek, T. A., Yermolayeva, Y. A. and Calvert, S. L. (2009). "College students' social networking experiences on Facebook," *Journal of Applied Developmental Psychology,* 30(3), 227–238.

Pendergast, D. (2010). "Getting to know the Y Generation," in P. Benckendorff, G. Moscardo, and D. Pendergast (Eds.), *Tourism and Generation Y* (pp. 1–15). Cambridge, MA: CAB International.

Pizam, A., Jeong, G. H., Reichel, A., Van Boemmel, H., Lusson, J. M., Steynberg, L., … Montmany, N. (2004). "The relationship between risk-taking, sensation-seeking, and the tourist behavior of young adults: A cross-cultural study," *Journal of Travel Research,* 42, 151–260.

Prayag, G. and Del Chiappa, G. (2014). "French young travelers' perceptions of hotel disintermediation," *Anatolia: An International Journal of Tourism and Hospitality Research,* 25(3), 417–430.

Ribière,V. M., Haddad, M. and Vande Wiele, P. (2010). "The impact of national culture traits on the usage of Web 2.0 technologies," *VINE*, 40(3/4), 334–361.

Richards, G. and Wilson, J. (2003). *New horizons in independent youth and student travel*. A report for the International Student Travel Confederation (ISTC) and the Association of Tourism and Leisure Education (ATLAS). International Student Travel Confederation (ISTC, Amsterdam. Retrieved from www.atlas-euro.org/pages/pdf/FINAL_Full_Report.pdf) (last accessed: 20 September 2014).

Rong, J.,Vu, H. Q., Law, R. and Li, G. (2012). "A behavioral analysis of web sharers and browsers in Hong Kong using targeted association rule mining," *Tourism Management*, 33, 731–740.

Seekings, J. (1998). "The youth travel market," *Travel and Tourism Analyst*, 5, 37–55.

Sheahan, P. (2009). *Gen Y: Thriving and surviving with Gen Y at work*. New York: Hardie Grant Books.

Sullivan, P. and Heitmeyer, J. (2008) "Looking at Gen Y shopping preferences and intentions: Exploring the role of experience and apparel involvement," *International Journal of Consumer Studies*, 32, 285–295.

Sun, S., Fong, L. H. N., Law, R. and Luk, C. (2016). "An investigation of Gen-Y's online hotel information search: The case of Hong Kong," *Asia Pacific Journal of Tourism Research*, 21(4), 443–456.

Tsai, H. T., Huang, L. and Lin, C. G. (2005). "Emerging e-commerce development model for Taiwanese travel agencies," *Tourism Management*, 26, 787–796.

Weber, K. and Roehl, W. S. (1999). "Profiling people searching for and purchasing travel products on the World Wide Web," *Journal of Travel Research*, 37, 291–298.

Xiang, Z., Magnini,V. P. and Fesenmaier, D. R. (2015). "Information technology and consumer behavior in travel and tourism: Insights from travel planning using the Internet," *Journal of Retailing and Consumer Services*, 22, 244–249.

Further reading

Frost, F. A. and Shanka, T. (1999). "Asian Australian student travel preferences: An empirical study," *Asia Pacific Journal of Tourism Research*, 4(2), 19–26. (How Asian Australian students plan their trips.)

Heung,V. C. and Leong, J. S. (2006). "Travel demand and behavior of university students in Hong Kong," *Asia Pacific Journal of Tourism Research*, 11(1), 81–96. (Travel behavior and travel patterns of Hong Kong university students.)

Jani, D., Jang, J. H. and Hwang,Y. H. (2014). "Big five factors of personality and tourists' internet search behavior," *Asia Pacific Journal of Tourism Research*, 19(5), 600–615. (Personality items that better predict tourists' Internet search behaviours.)

Lee, C. F. and King, B. (2016). "International students in Asia: Travel behaviors and destination perceptions." *Asia Pacific Journal of Tourism Research*, 21(4), 457–476. (Incidence of international student travel in Taiwan.)

Lu, Q. S.,Yang,Y. and Yuksel, U. (2015). "The impact of a new online channel: An empirical study," *Annals of Tourism Research*, 54, 136–155. (The impact of adding a direct online channel.)

Part V

Impact of culture on hospitality marketing

28

Impact of culture on production and delivery of hospitality products/services

Shangzhi (Charles) Qiu, Dan Jin and Saerom Wang

Introduction

The prominence of cultural impact on hospitality service management received academic attention as early as the 1980s, under the wave of economic globalization (Shames and Glover 1988). Service consumption experience is strongly influenced by the cultural backgrounds of both customers and service employees (Patterson et al. 2006, Tsang 2011). Although various definitions of culture exist to date, it is generally referred to as the shared values, beliefs, norms and patterns of behavior or collective programming of the mind that distinguishe one group from the other (Li 2012). Culture can be categorized into various levels of society. This chapter focuses on the national level of culture, which is the most widely studied in hospitality marketing (Chen et al. 2012).

One of the most commonly used cultural analysis frameworks in hospitality marketing is Hofstede's (1980) framework of cultural dimensions. According to Hofstede (1980), national culture can be measured in five dimensions: *individualism versus collectiveness*, *power distance*, *avoidance of uncertainty*, *masculinity versus femininity*, and *long-term orientation* (Hofstede 1980). In the service literature, the first three are the mostly discussed (Patterson et al. 2006). *Individualism versus collectiveness* refers to the degree to which individuals are integrated into groups. In a collectivist country, the benefits of the group are valued more highly than the benefits of the individual. *Power distance* is the extent to which the powerful individuals in a society are more respected (Hofstede 1980). *Uncertainty avoidance* is "the extent to which people feel threatened by uncertain or unknown situations" (Hofstede 1991, p. 113).

Cross-cultural comparison vs. influence of cultural values

Studies exploring cultural influence on hospitality service delivery have covered the topics of customer satisfaction and loyalty (Jin Hoare and Butcher 2008), service evaluation (Hartman et al. 2009), response to service failure (Li et al. 2016), joint production (Chathoth et al. 2016), service interaction (Alshaibani and Bakir 2016), and employee training (Bharwani and Jauhari 2013). Mainstream research in this field tends to focus on intercultural service encounters in which the cultural differences between employees, organizations and customers interactively affect the service outcome (Alshaibani and Bakir 2016).

One popular stream of research in the area features cross-cultural studies, where consumers and employees from different cultural backgrounds have been contrasted. The majority of cross-cultural studies have explored the differences between Western and Eastern individuals or used Hofstede's (1980) cultural framework to classify consumers (Li 2012). Previous research indicated that cultural differences also exist within the boundaries of Eastern and Western countries (Baek et al. 2006). For example, consumers from different Asian countries exhibit cross-national differences in their service expectations. In addition to cross-cultural study, attention to specific national values has gained popularity in recent literature (Li 2012, Bu et al. 2013). One of the most discussed values is "face," a universal concept originated from the Chinese culture (Li et al. 2016). People concerned with face believe that their aggressive behavior in the public could result in face loss. Thus, researchers traditionally tend to believe that they are less likely to engage in complaining behavior, regardless of how unsatisfied they were with the product or service purchased (Lee and Sparks 2007).

The synthesized findings on the impact of culture on customer response toward hospitality service and how service providers deal with the multicultural environment and intercultural encounters will contribute to our understanding of the cultural influence on hospitality service/product delivery and production. Accordingly, this chapter is structured as follows: (1) impact of culture on how customers interpret the hospitality service/product; (2) how companies produce and deliver the hospitality service/product in a multicultural environment; and (3) conclusion and implications.

Customer culture and hospitality service perception

Hospitality could be defined differently among cultures (Mattila 2000). In many Asian countries such as Japan, Korea and Thailand, the key ingredient of good service seems to be personal attention or customization rather than the efficiency which may be highly valued in the West (Schmitt and Pan 1994). The Islamic community also has its unique understanding of hospitality, which traditionally encompasses congeniality and reverence as the two fundamental elements (Stephenson 2014). The institutionalized service concepts are a critical element of overall quality to the customers raised in such cultural environments (Mattila 2000). The following section reviews the studies that have discussed how culture influences customers' service evaluation and perceptions of service failure and how service could be delivered to meet diverse multicultural expectations.

Cultural differences in hospitality service evaluation

Evaluation of service quality depends on whether the service performance meets the culturally determined service expectations of customers (Kim et al. 2016). Service expectations can be defined as a customer's beliefs about service delivery that serve as standards against which the quality of a service is judged (Zeithaml et al. 2006). Many studies have been conducted on how hospitality service expectations differ across cultures, mainly through comparison between different nations (Zhao and Lin 2014) based on Hofstede's (1980) cultural dimensions. Traditionally, countries from North America, Western Europe, and East Asia have often been chosen as the samples in cross-cultural studies (Li 2012). Many researchers have agreed that compared with Asian customers, Western customers pay more attention on tangibles, hedonic features, assurance, and efficiency whereas Asian customers have higher expectations with regard to empathy, reliability, and responsiveness (Mattila 1999, Tsaur et al. 2005, Hsieh and Tsai 2009). Moreover, Asian customers tend to give more importance to the service process (i.e. interaction quality) while Western customers focus more on the service outcome (Mattila 2000, Chan and Wan 2008, Wan 2013).

The differences discussed above have been widely attributed to cultural dimensions such as individualism/collectivism and power distance (Tsaur et al. 2005, Chan and Wan 2008, Kim et al. 2016) and should be applicable to countries with corresponding cultural characteristics. Specifically, individualism is often associated with the efficiency and hedonism of the outcome while collectivists place an emphasis on responsiveness and empathy in the process (Sabiote-Ortiz et al. 2016). Higher power distance cultures encourage customers to expect manifestation of status difference through responsive service, reliability of servers and empathy in interaction (Hsieh and Tsai 2009).

Previous research has concluded that cultural values are strong predictors of customer service quality evaluation (Tsaur et al. 2005, Hartman et al. 2009). Meanwhile, this relationship is mediated by service expectation (Wang et al. 2008, Karami et al. 2016). In the hospitality literature, measurement of service quality conventionally follows the framework of Parasuraman et al.'s (1988) SERVQUAL scale, which defines service quality as the gap between customer expectations and perceived service performance (Parasuraman et al. 1988). This framework posits that service quality should be evaluated in terms of five dimensions: tangibles, reliability, responsiveness, assurance, and empathy. For instance, adopting the SERVQUAL scale, Tsaur et al. (2005) found that tourists from English heritage cultures tend to perceive better service quality than Asian and European groups in terms of tangibles, reliability, and empathy of hotel services in Taiwan (Tsaur et al. 2005).

However, a growing number of researchers have identified that consumers in different cultures have dissimilar interpretations of SERVQUAL dimensions, resulting in inaccurate evaluations (Zhang et al. 2008, Karami et al. 2016). Many researchers adjusted the scale to accommodate specific cultural contexts. For example, Wang et al. (2008) adjusted the SERVQUAL scale according to Chinese cultural values and found that UK hotels were not able to meet the high expectations of Chinese tourists regarding ritualistic greetings, considerate waiters, culinary experience and hardworking employees, resulting in negative perceptions of service quality. In addition to investigating the cultural impact on service quality evaluation, many researchers have been exploring cross-cultural customer responses to service delivery, including satisfaction level and perceptions of service failure (Chan et al. 2007, Sabiote-Ortiz et al. 2016).

Cross-cultural responses to service failure and recovery

Service failures occur when customer expectations are not met in intercultural service encounters and often result in disappointment, fear, loneliness and even cultural conflict (Weiermair 2000). Although hospitality businesses are trying their best to deliver superior customer service, service failure is inevitable (Zeithaml et al. 1990). Therefore, customers' perceptions and behavioral responses to hospitality service failure has received significant attention, with cultural values identified as important explanatory variables (Baloglu et al. 2010). Most of the studies in this field have focused on the cross-cultural differences in responses while research that focuses on specific local values has begun to emerge in recent literature (Lee et al. 2013, Li et al. 2016).

Individualism vs. collectivism has been commonly applied to explain the cross-cultural differences in service failure perceptions, as well as service recovery efforts (Mattila and Patterson 2004, Wan 2013). Many researchers have argued that collectivistic Asian customers tend to be more dissatisfied with service failure that threatens social resources (Chan et al. 2007) but are more likely to refrain from confrontational responses (e.g., direct voice complaints) and prefer methods such as switching and word-of-mouth (Wan 2013). In contrast, individualistic Westerners focus on personal welfare and freedom and are more inclined to complain about failures that cause economic loss (Chan and Wan 2008).

However, the conventional view that collectivists prefer non-confrontational responses has been challenged in recent research. A growing number of research studies have attested that failure perception and response are the product of interaction between culture and other factors such as price level (Kim et al. 2014), face concern (Lee et al. 2013) and presence of others (Fan et al. 2015). For example, highly face-concerned customers are less likely to voice their frustration in public in order to save face and keep harmony but will be motivated to do so when service failure threatens their face (Li et al. 2016). In addition, the degree of perceived face loss is dependent on the relationship with other customers (Fan et al. 2015). Moreover, research attention has gone beyond cultural origin to consider the acculturation of ethnic segments that possess multiple cultural characters. Weber et al. (2016) found that Chinese Americans and Mainland Chinese could adopt different responses to service failure due to different acculturation (Weber et al. 2016).

Previous research has highlighted the opportunity to regain customers' trust and loyalty through service recovery effort in the event of service failure by engaging customers in order to regain their satisfaction or delight (Kuo et al. 2013). Recovery methods widely discussed in the literature include compensation (i.e., using tangible benefits to address complaints), apology (i.e., psychological compensation to address loss of social resources such as self-esteem and face), and explanation (Baloglu et al. 2010, Gelbrich and Roschk 2010). Collectivists are more sensitive to proper explanations and apologies whereas individualists prefer tangible compensation, such as cash refund and replacement (Mattila and Patterson 2004). However, tangible compensation is also effective in collectivistic cultures concerned with face when it is perceived as a symbol of serious apology or attention to the problem (Magnini and Ford 2004). The perceived justice of recovery effort is another factor that has been receiving much attention. Previous research has shown that expectations of procedural justice, distributive justice and interpersonal justice in the recovery effort differ across cultures (Gi Park et al. 2014) and determine customer satisfaction with the recovery effort (Ha and Jang 2009).

Meeting customer expectations in multicultural environments

In the global hospitality industry, businesses need to meet customer expectations with a service portfolio that accommodates a variety of culturally determined service expectations in order to create delightful experiences and build customer loyalty (Torres et al. 2014). Factors that lead to customer satisfaction, customer delight and customer loyalty vary across cultures (Crotts and Erdmann 2000, Jin Hoare and Butcher 2008, Pantouvakis 2013, Torres et al. 2014), requiring global hospitality businesses to acquire sufficient knowledge on local cultures before entering a foreign market. For instance, service interaction quality is the baseline of customer satisfaction in high power distance societies, even in the context of consumption of low-cost services (Schmitt and Pan 1994, Mattila 1999).

There are also cross-national differences which are difficult to explain with Hofstede's taxonomy. For example, the interactive element is critical to US hotel guests' satisfaction in contrast to that of Australians, although both countries are highly individualistic and have low power distance (Pantouvakis 2013). Some studies explored beyond Hofstede's framework and found that satisfaction with service interaction also depends on the communication style rooted in customers' cultural values (Hopkins et al. 2005, Al-Refaie 2015). According to Hall's (1976) high/low-context culture framework, customers from high-context cultures depend heavily on nonverbal cues in communication, whereas those from low-context cultures are more used to explicit verbal communication (Hall 1976). Communication between the two cultures tends to cause misunderstanding and service dissatisfaction.

Understanding customer expectations and the cultural factors that underlie customer satisfaction is the key to marketing success in multicultural environments. However, some researchers have pointed out that avoiding service failure and ensuring satisfaction is no longer sufficient for building a competitive edge and increasing customer loyalty (Wang 2011). Customer delight, which goes beyond satisfaction and involves a pleasurable experience, has become a new goal for many hospitality businesses since it is more powerful than satisfaction in predicting customer loyalty. However, what delights a guest from one culture might not delight all the other guests. For instance, to delight US guests, hotels need to provide flexible services, fulfill their need for esteem, and demonstrate professionalism. In Northern European countries, friendliness and problem solution are the most important drivers of customer delight (Torres et al. 2014).

Cross-cultural service production and delivery

Understanding cultural differences in service perceptions helps to assess the service provider's performance and to design an effective cross-cultural service production and delivery strategy. Awareness of the 'other' culture enables service providers to communicate more effectively and sensitively (Wang et al. 2015). The following section is a review of studies that have discussed how hospitality companies should produce and deliver services in today's multicultural marketplace.

Culture and value co-creation in hospitality service

Service production can be categorized into three types based on the degree of customer participation: firm production, joint production, and customer production (Kuo and Cranage 2010). In the hospitality literature, attention to joint production that involves both customer and servers and the value co-creation process is increasing (Kuo and Cranage 2010, Chathoth et al. 2013, Kuo et al. 2013). The concept of value co-creation derives from the service-dominant (S-D) marketing logic (Vargo and Lusch 2004), which proposed that value realization depends on the customer's participation in the exchange and consumption process. An increasing number of researchers have argued that service production should no longer be viewed as a firm-dominant activity. It needs to involve customers in every step of the value creation process (Bharwani and Jauhari 2013, Chathoth et al. 2013).

The value co-creation process is also culturally mediated (Akaka et al. 2013). According to the value-in-cultural-context framework developed by Akaka et al. (2013), "value is co-created in cultural context through the enactment of practices and integration of resources, which are guided by norms and collective meanings" (p. 276). The view of the culturally mediated value co-creation process has been demonstrated in the hospitality services literature (Kuo and Cranage 2010, Shaw et al. 2011, Bharwani and Jauhari 2013, Chathoth et al. 2016). Effective value co-creation in hospitality service requires a high level of customer participation (Chathoth et al. 2016). Shaw et al. (2011) proposed that customer participation in hotel service co-creation requires exploiting cultural capital, which refers to the education and knowledge acquired over a period of time that provide customers with social relation foundations during the exchange mechanism. Chathoth et al. (2016) argued that co-creation experiences have not yet extensively existed, even in reputable high-end hotels. Cultural and contextual barriers are important factors that have enhanced the desire for more differentiated features.

National cultures also affect customers' participation. For example, customization is a popular co-creation practice in food service (Chathoth et al. 2016). Customers participate through designing their own dishes or even cooking the food. Customization often requires customers to commit their knowledge and physical effort (Ford and Bowen 2004). Kuo and Cranage (2010) proposed that consumers from individualistic cultures should have more positive responses to customization than consumers from collectivistic cultures because it enables them to express their individual personality or unique characters (Kuo and Cranage 2010). However, collectivists are more satisfied with a high level of participation (i.e., cooking their own food) because it is a way to interact with other customers and gain public recognition.

Customers' adoption of self-service technology to improve efficiency and convenience also differs across cultures (Lee 2016). For instance, due to the concern of saving face, hotel guests from high power distance cultures or with higher uncertainty avoidance are less predisposed to accept self-service technology in order to prevent the plight of engaging in service failure (Fisher and Beatson 2002). Lee (2016) adjusted the Western culture-based technology adoption model (Davis 1989) to accommodate to Asian hospitality customers and found that word-of-mouth and customization are two important factors for web-based self-service technology adoption in collectivistic cultures.

Culture of employees and service delivery

Employee behavior is a function of the culture in which they are born and raised. Although the impact of customers' cultural orientation has been widely recognized, how service employees' national cultures affect service quality outcomes is largely overlooked in the literature (Yayla-Küllü et al. 2015). Employees' national cultures could determine their service predisposition (e.g., service style, attitude, work pattern) that affects the service outcome (Lorenzoni and Lewis 2004, Johns et al. 2007, Metters et al. 2010). For instance, Lorenzoni and Lewis (2004) reported that service recovery behavior differed between British and Italian airline personnel. In addition, the difference in airplane loss rate between U.S. carriers and Korean Air was attributed to cultural difference in that subordinates in Korean Air would not contradict the Captain even though the Captain's actions were dangerous (Metters et al. 2010). Yayla-Küllü et al. (2015) proposed a comprehensive conceptual framework that connects employee cultural values with service delivery quality. This framework includes Hofstede's five cultural dimensions plus gender egalitarianism, assertiveness, performance orientation and humane orientation as explanatory variables. Many of the propositions in this study deserve investigation in the area of hospitality.

As a supplement to Hofstede's framework which was criticized as biased toward the Western culture, Chinese Culture Connection (1984) developed four cultural dimensions of "integration," "moral discipline," "human heartedness" and "Confucian work dynamism" based on traditional East Asian values (Hofstede 1984). With a sample of multiple nations, Johns et al. (2007) found that hospitality employees' service predisposition was significantly associated with these dimensions and the explanatory power of these dimensions on service predisposition components was even stronger than Hofstede's dimensions (Johns et al. 2007).

In some societies, local values strongly influence employees' service behavior. Tsang (2011) identified that Chinese cultural values of integration (towards work and people), moral discipline, status and relationships, and moderation directly affect Chinese employees' attitudes towards service provision. It is suggested that Western management practices should be adopted critically in the organizations of such societies. For instance, while empowerment is such a good motivator in individualistic Western companies, Chinese organizations have encountered the problem of risk avoidance when starting their empowerment programs (Tsang 2011).

Delivering services in the multicultural marketplace

Interactions between employees and customers involve dialogue between cultures. There may be a gap in the cultural exposure of the locally recruited employees and that of the organization or guests. The degree of cultural empathy and cultural proximity influences the ability of frontline employees to deliver on the guest experience (Bharwani and Jauhari 2013). Cultural intelligence, which refers to the capabilities of service providers to intelligently deal with situations marked by cultural diversity (Earley and Ang 2003), was regarded as a critical competence required to co-create memorable experiences. Alshaibani and Bakir (2016) conducted a thorough review of the literature on the role of employees' attitudes and behavior in cross-cultural service interaction. Employees' cultural intelligence was particularly examined as an important factor that affects performance and service quality. As a result, the development of cultural intelligence was suggested as a prominent objective for service employee training (Alshaibani and Bakir 2016).

The cultural distance between customers and service providers can influence the interaction comfort. Customers may feel more anxious, insecure or worried in a service encounter if cultural distance is higher. Employees could also experience negative effects from cultural distance (Sharma et al. 2015). Therefore, some scholars have suggested that it might be a good strategy to minimize the cultural distance between employees and target customers (Hsieh and Tsai 2009, Bharwani and Jauhari 2013). For instance, appropriate customer education and employee training would be helpful in facilitating mutual understanding, improving employee attitudes and increasing awareness of the advantages of cultural diversity (Sharma et al. 2015). Another service delivery strategy that has received significant academic attention is intercultural communication accommodation (e.g., a culturally congruent service provider and/or the use of the native language) (Wang et al. 2015). For example, adapting a hotel's menus and directories to foreign customers' native language can make the difference in creating a satisfied guest (Heo et al. 2004). Wang et al. (2015) identified that a culturally incongruent service provider using a customer's native language to serve the customer is effective in increasing customer satisfaction.

Cross-cultural marketing communication also plays a critical role in facilitating service production and delivery. Such marketing communication is important as it shapes the initial perceptions of the service and product. When targeting a specific market, the effectiveness of an advertisement tends to be high when the cultural values embedded in the message are congruent with that of the message recipients (Laroche et al. 2014). For instance, marketing messages that focus on group benefit and harmony are more effective for individuals from a collectivist country whereas expressing personal benefits tends to be more effective for individualists.

Conclusion: Managing intercultural service encounters

Delivering a consistent yet adaptive service to diverse customers has long been a major challenge for many hospitality managers. This challenge has become more significant in today's multicultural environment. Culture determines what the service providers and customers perceive as needs and the patterns of their reactions. Both providers and customers enter the service encounter with a predisposition based on their national or ethnic culture. Managing a service organization includes managing people and their cultures. A culturally intelligent service team can recognize the cultural impact on the workplace, clientele, operation, and bottom line.

343

Studies reviewed in this chapter indicate that in building a culturally intelligent service team, hospitality service organizations need to conduct thorough research on the cultural values of the target customers and understand how they influence the service expectation, service quality evaluation, satisfaction, loyalty, response to service failure, and perception of different service recovery methods. Only by acquiring this knowledge can organizations produce and deliver the hospitality services that optimize the value co-creation process in order to maximize customer enjoyment, positive word-of-mouth, and loyalty. Employees' cultural values should be considered in selecting the most suitable team members to serve certain customer segments. Managers should pay attention to such factors as cultural distance, work attitude related cultural values, cultural service predispositions, and value conflicts in team building.

In investigating cultural impact, academics should spend more effort on localizing their research methods. Investigation beyond Hofstede's culture analysis framework is needed to discover the associations between local values and service perceptions or to explain various cross-national differences. In achieving this goal, instruments need to be designed based on target cultures to minimize response bias. As suggested by Zhang et al. (2008), even the cultural dimensions of Hofstede (1980) and Hall (1976) are not reliable for service evaluation without appraisal in terms of the depth and type of language used.

References

Akaka, M. A., Schau, H. J. & Vargo, S. L. (2013) "The co-creation of value-in-cultural-context," *Research in Consumer Behavior* 15, pp. 265–284.

Al-Refaie, A. (2015) "Effects of human resource management on hotel performance using structural equation modeling," *Computers in Human Behavior* 43, pp. 293–303.

Alshaibani, E. & Bakir, A. (2016) "A reading in cross-cultural service encounter: Exploring the relationship between cultural intelligence, employee performance and service quality," *Tourism and Hospitality Research*, doi: 1467358416651474.

Baek, S.-H., Ham, S. & Yang, I.-S. (2006) "A cross-cultural comparison of fast food restaurant selection criteria between Korean and Filipino college students," *International Journal of Hospitality Management* 25(4), pp. 683–698.

Baloglu, S., Erdem, M., Brewer, P., Mayer, K., Gyung Kim, M., Wang, C. & Mattila, A. S. (2010) "The relationship between consumer complaining behavior and service recovery: An integrative review," *International Journal of Contemporary Hospitality Management* 22(7), pp. 975–991.

Bharwani, S. & Jauhari, V. (2013) "An exploratory study of competencies required to co-create memorable customer experiences in the hospitality industry," *International Journal of Contemporary Hospitality Management* 25(6), pp. 823–843.

Bu, K., Kim, D. & Son, J. (2013) "Is the culture–emotion fit always important? Self-regulatory emotions in ethnic food consumption," *Journal of Business Research* 66(8), pp. 983–988.

Chan, H. & Wan, L. C. (2008) "Consumer responses to service failures: A resource preference model of cultural influences," *Journal of International Marketing* 16(1), pp. 72–97.

Chan, H., Wan, L. C. & Sin, L. Y. (2007) "Hospitality service failures: Who will be more dissatisfied?," *International Journal of Hospitality Management* 26(3), pp. 531–545.

Chathoth, P., Altinay, L., Harrington, R. J., Okumus, F. & Chan, E. S. (2013) "Co-production versus co-creation: A process based continuum in the hotel service context," *International Journal of Hospitality Management* 32, pp. 11–20.

Chathoth, P. K., Ungson, G. R., Harrington, R. J. & Chan, E. S. (2016) "Co-creation and higher order customer engagement in hospitality and tourism services: A critical review," *International Journal of Contemporary Hospitality Management* 28(2), pp. 222–245.

Chen, X.-P., Liu, D. & Portnoy, R. (2012) "A multilevel investigation of motivational cultural intelligence, organizational diversity climate, and cultural sales: Evidence from US real estate firms," *Journal of Applied Psychology* 97(1), p. 93.

Crotts, J. C. & Erdmann, R. (2000) "Does national culture influence consumers' evaluation of travel services? A test of Hofstede's model of cross-cultural differences," *Managing Service Quality: An International Journal* 10(6), pp. 410–419.

Davis, F. D. (1989) "Perceived usefulness, perceived ease of use, and user acceptance of information technology," *MIS Quarterly*, 13(3), pp. 319–340.

Earley, P. C. & Ang, S. (2003) *Cultural intelligence: Individual interactions across cultures.* Palo Alto, CA: Stanford University Press.

Fan, A., Mattila, A. S. & Zhao, X. (2015) "How does social distance impact customers' complaint intentions? A cross-cultural examination," *International Journal of Hospitality Management* 47, pp. 35–42.

Fisher, G. & Beatson, A. (2002) "The impact of culture on self-service on technology adoption in the hotel industry," *International Journal of Hospitality & Tourism Administration* 3(3), pp. 59–77.

Ford, R. C. & Bowen, J. T. (2004) "Getting guests to work for you," *Journal of Foodservice Business Research* 6(3), pp. 37–53.

Gelbrich, K. & Roschk, H. (2010) "A meta-analysis of organizational complaint handling and customer responses," *Journal of Service Research*, doi: 1094670510387914.

Gi Park, S., Kim, K. & O'Neill, M. (2014) "Complaint behavior intentions and expectation of service recovery in individualistic and collectivistic cultures," *International Journal of Culture, Tourism and Hospitality Research* 8(3), pp. 255–271.

Ha, J. & Jang, S. S. (2009) "Perceived justice in service recovery and behavioral intentions: The role of relationship quality," *International Journal of Hospitality Management* 28(3), pp. 319–327.

Hall, E. T. (1976) *Beyond culture.* Garden City, NY: Anchor.

Hartman, K. B., Meyer, T. & Scribner, L. L. (2009) "Retail and service encounters: The inter-cultural tourist experience," *Journal of Hospitality Marketing & Management* 18(2–3), pp. 197–215.

Heo, J. K., Jogaratnam, G. & Buchanan, P. (2004) "Customer-focused adaptation in New York City hotels: Exploring the perceptions of Japanese and Korean travelers," *International Journal of Hospitality Management* 23(1), pp. 39–53.

Hofstede, G. (1980) "Motivation, leadership, and organization: Do American theories apply abroad?," *Organizational Dynamics* 9(1), pp. 42–63.

———— (1984) *Culture's consequences: International differences in work-related values.* Beverley Hills, CA: Sage.

———— (1991) *Cultures and organizations: Software of the mind.* London: McGraw Hill.

Hopkins, S. A., Hopkins, W. E. & Hoffman, K. D. (2005) "Domestic inter-cultural service encounters: An integrated model," *Managing Service Quality: An International Journal* 15(4), pp. 329–343.

Hsieh, A.-T. & Tsai, C.-W. (2009) "Does national culture really matter? Hotel service perceptions by Taiwan and American tourists," *International Journal of Culture, Tourism and Hospitality Research* 3(1), pp. 54–69.

Jin Hoare, R. & Butcher, K. (2008) "Do Chinese cultural values affect customer satisfaction/loyalty?," *International Journal of Contemporary Hospitality Management* 20(2), pp. 156–171.

Johns, N., Teare, R., Johns, N., Henwood, J. & Seaman, C. (2007) "Culture and service predisposition among hospitality students in Switzerland and Scotland," *International Journal of Contemporary Hospitality Management* 19(2), pp. 146–158.

Karami, M., Maleki, M. M. & Dubinsky, A. J. (2016) "Cultural values and consumers' expectations and perceptions of service encounter quality," *International Journal of Pharmaceutical and Healthcare Marketing* 10(1), pp. 2–26.

Kim, M. G., Lee, C. H. & Mattila, A. S. (2014) "Determinants of customer complaint behavior in a restaurant context: The role of culture, price level, and customer loyalty," *Journal of Hospitality Marketing & Management* 23(8), pp. 885–906.

Kim, S., Chung, J.-E., Suh, Y., Okumus, F. & Okumus, F. (2016) "Multiple reference effects on restaurant evaluations: A cross-cultural study," *International Journal of Contemporary Hospitality Management* 28(7), pp. 1441–1466.

Kuo, N.-T., Chang, K.-C., Cheng, Y.-S. & Lai, C.-H. (2013) "How service quality affects customer loyalty in the travel agency: The effects of customer satisfaction, service recovery, and perceived value," *Asia Pacific Journal of Tourism Research* 18(7), pp. 803–822.

Kuo, P.-J. & Cranage, D. A. (2010) "Consumers' responses to participation and customization in food services: A cultural perspective," *Journal of Hospitality Marketing & Management* 20(1), pp. 24–39.

Laroche, M., Vinhal Nepomuceno, M. & Richard, M.-O. (2014) "Congruency of humour and cultural values in print ads: Cross-cultural differences among the US, France and China," *International Journal of Advertising* 33(4), pp. 681–705.

Lee, L. Y.-S. (2016) "Hospitality industry web-based self-service technology adoption model: A cross-cultural perspective," *Journal of Hospitality & Tourism Research* 40(2), pp. 162–197.

Lee, S.-H. & Sparks, B. (2007) "Cultural influences on travel lifestyle: A comparison of Korean Australians and Koreans in Korea," *Tourism Management* 28(2), pp. 505–518.

Lee, Y. L., Sparks, B. & Butcher, K. (2013) "Service encounters and face loss: Issues of failures, fairness, and context," *International Journal of Hospitality Management* 34, pp. 384–393.

Li, M. (2012) "Cross-cultural tourist research: A meta-analysis," *Journal of Hospitality & Tourism Research* 38(1), doi: 1096348012442542.

Li, M., Qiu, S. C. & Liu, Z. (2016) "The Chinese way of response to hospitality service failure: The effects of face and guanxi," *International Journal of Hospitality Management* 57, pp. 18–29.

Lorenzoni, N. & Lewis, B. R. (2004) "Service recovery in the airline industry: A cross-cultural comparison of the attitudes and behaviours of British and Italian front-line personnel," *Managing Service Quality: An International Journal* 14(1), pp. 11–25.

Magnini, V. P. & Ford, J. B. (2004) "Service failure recovery in China," *International Journal of Contemporary Hospitality Management* 16(5), pp. 279–286.

Mattila, A. S. (1999) "The role of culture in the service evaluation process," *Journal of Service Research* 1(3), pp. 250–261.

———— (2000) "The impact of culture and gender on customer evaluations of service encounters," *Journal of Hospitality & Tourism Research* 24(2), pp. 263–273.

Mattila, A. S. & Patterson, P. G. (2004) "Service recovery and fairness perceptions in collectivist and individualist contexts," *Journal of Service Research* 6(4), pp. 336–346.

Metters, R., Zhao, X., Bendoly, E., Jiang, B. & Young, S. (2010) "'The way that can be told of is not an unvarying way': Cultural impacts on operations management in Asia," *Journal of Operations Management* 28(3), pp. 177–185.

Pantouvakis, A. (2013) "The moderating role of nationality on the satisfaction loyalty link: Evidence from the tourism industry," *Total Quality Management & Business Excellence* 24(9–10), pp. 1174–1187.

Parasuraman, A., Zeithaml, V. A. & Berry, L. L. (1988) "Servqual," *Journal of Retailing* 64(1), pp. 12–40.

Patterson, P. G., Cowley, E. & Prasongsukarn, K. (2006) "Service failure recovery: The moderating impact of individual-level cultural value orientation on perceptions of justice," *International Journal of Research in Marketing* 23(3), pp. 263–277.

Sabiote-Ortiz, C. M., Frías-Jamilena, D. M. & Castañeda-García, J. A. (2016) "Overall perceived value of a tourism service delivered via different media: A cross-cultural perspective," *Journal of Travel Research* 55(1), pp. 34–51.

Schmitt, B. H. & Pan, Y. (1994) "Managing corporate and brand identities in the Asia-Pacific region," *California Management Review* 36(4), pp. 32–48.

Shames, G. & Glover, G. (1988) "Service management as if culture exists," *International Journal of Hospitality Management* 7(1), pp. 5–7.

Sharma, P., Tam, J. L. & Kim, N. (2015) "Service role and outcome as moderators in intercultural service encounters," *Journal of Service Management* 26(1), pp. 137–155.

Shaw, G., Bailey, A. & Williams, A. (2011) "Aspects of service-dominant logic and its implications for tourism management: Examples from the hotel industry," *Tourism Management* 32(2), pp. 207–214.

Stephenson, M. L. (2014) "Deciphering 'Islamic hospitality': Developments, challenges and opportunities," *Tourism Management* 40, pp. 155–164.

Torres, E. N., Fu, X. & Lehto, X. (2014) "Examining key drivers of customer delight in a hotel experience: A cross-cultural perspective," *International Journal of Hospitality Management* 36, pp. 255–262.

Tsang, N. K. (2011) "Dimensions of Chinese culture values in relation to service provision in hospitality and tourism industry," *International Journal of Hospitality Management* 30(3), pp. 670–679.

Tsaur, S.-H., Lin, C.-T. & Wu, C.-S. (2005) "Cultural differences of service quality and behavioral intention in tourist hotels," *Journal of Hospitality & Leisure Marketing* 13(1), pp. 41–63.

Vargo, S. L. & Lusch, R. F. (2004) "Evolving to a new dominant logic for marketing," *Journal of Marketing* 68(1), pp. 1–17.

Wan, L. C. (2013) "Culture's impact on consumer complaining responses to embarrassing service failure," *Journal of Business Research* 66(3), pp. 298–305.

Wang, C.-Y., Miao, L. & Mattila, A. S. (2015) "Customer responses to intercultural communication accommodation strategies in hospitality service encounters," *International Journal of Hospitality Management* 51, pp. 96–104.

Wang, X. (2011) "The effect of unrelated supporting service quality on consumer delight, satisfaction, and repurchase intentions," *Journal of Service Research* 14(2), pp. 149–163.

Wang, Y., Royo Vela, M. & Tyler, K. (2008) "Cultural perspectives: Chinese perceptions of UK hotel service quality," *International Journal of Culture, Tourism and Hospitality Research* 2(4), pp. 312–329.

Weber, K., Hsu, C. & Sparks, B. (2016) "Same but different: Chinese-American and Mainland Chinese consumers' perceptions of and behavior in a service failure situation," *Journal of Travel & Tourism Marketing* 33(4), pp. 471–496.

Weiermair, K. (2000) "Tourists' perceptions towards and satisfaction with service quality in the cross-cultural service encounter: Implications for hospitality and tourism management," *Managing Service Quality: An International Journal* 10(6), pp. 397–409.

Yayla-Küllü, H. M., Tansitpong, P., Gnanlet, A., Mcdermott, C. M. & Durgee, J. F. (2015) "Employees' national culture and service quality: An integrative review," *Service Science* 7(1), pp. 11–28.

Zeithaml, V. A., Bitner, M. J. & Gremier, D. D. (2006) *Services marketing: Integrating customer focus across the firm.* Columbus, OH: McGraw-Hill.

Zeithaml, V. A., Parasuraman, A. & Berry, L. L. (1990) *Delivering quality service: Balancing customer perceptions and expectations.* New York: Free Press.

Zhang, J., Beatty, S. E. & Walsh, G. (2008) "Review and future directions of cross-cultural consumer services research," *Journal of Business Research* 61(3), pp. 211–224.

Zhao, D. & Y. Lin, I. (2014) "Understanding tourists' perception and evaluation of inter-cultural service encounters: A holistic mental model process," *International Journal of Culture, Tourism and Hospitality Research* 8(3), pp. 290–309.

Further reading

Hofstede, G. (1984) *Culture's consequences: International differences in work-related values* (Vol. 5). Beverly Hills, CA: Sage.

Hofstede, G. H. & Hofstede, G. (2001) *Culture's consequences: Comparing values, behaviors, institutions and organizations across nations.* Thousand Oaks, CA: Sage.

Mok, C., Sparks, B., & Kadampully, J. (2013) *Service quality management in hospitality, tourism, and leisure.* London: Routledge.

Rugimbana, R. & Keating, B. (2003) "Cross-cultural marketing channels," *Cross-cultural marketing.* London: Thomson, pp. 129–140.

29

Impact of culture on hospitality customers' decision-making process

Eun-Kyong (Cindy) Choi, Inna Soifer and Hyun-Woo Joung

Culture and its characteristics

Globally, the tourism and hospitality industry has experienced tremendous growth with an increasing number of international tourists over the last decades. Compared to the 25 million international tourist arrivals in 1950, nearly 980 million tourists travelled internationally in 2011. With an increased number of tourists coming from developing countries (e.g. China), the number of international tourists is expected to reach 1.8 billion by 2030 (UNWTO 2011). In order to meet the increasing number of international tourists' needs and wants, and to make them feel satisfied, it is more important than ever for managers and employees in the tourism and hospitality industry to understand cultural differences and their role in customers' decision-making process.

Culture is one of the most influential factors affecting the decision-making of customers, but there is no universally accepted definition of culture because culture can be applied to any group (e.g. based on gender, generation, social class, or nation). For example, the definition of culture is focused on tribes or ethnic groups in anthropology whereas it is limited to nations in political science. In the sociology and management disciplines, culture is used for either nations or organizations. However, several researchers (e.g., Correia, Kozak, and Ferradeira 2011; Schwartz and Ros 1995) have widely studied national culture and its impact on behavior because national cultural differences are more distinguishable compared to other subcultures within a nation. Therefore, this chapter focuses on national culture.

In the cross-cultural literature, researchers have implemented both emic and etic perspectives to determine culture (Li 2012). Morris et al. (1999) identified the etic approach as an outside perspective following the tradition of psychology, where a culture is examined from an observer's point of view. On the other hand, the emic approach systemizes culture from a subject's point of view following the tradition of behaviorist psychology (Morris et al. 1999).

The emic approach views culture from the perspective of participants themselves as part of an interconnected whole (Pearce 2011). For instance, Yang, Ryan and Zhang (2013) analyzed the data obtained from a 12-month field project in the ethnic community of Xinjiang in China for their study of social conflicts in communities impacted by tourism. This study followed the tradition of the emic approach in which a researcher immerses him or herself in a cultural group, developing relationships with the locals and conducting ethnographic observation.

Several studies conducted by Greet Hofstede, the most well-known researcher in cross-cultural studies, embraced the etic approach and argued that human behavior is partially predetermined by the mental and emotional patterns acquired in early childhood within an individual's family and different social groups (Hofstede 1980, 1986, 1998; Hofstede and Hofstede 2003). Cultural differences manifest themselves through symbols, heroes, rituals, and values. Values refer to "broad tendencies to favor a certain state of affairs over others" (Hofstede 1984: 18). They are considered as the core of culture and serve as the basis of rituals that include collective activities, heroes that serve as models for behavior, and symbols that represent a particular implication that is recognized in the same way only by individuals who share the same culture (Hofstede, Hofstede and Minkov 2010).

Despite the variations in the definition of culture, culture possesses three common characteristics, which are as follows:

a. Culture is developed through the socialization process

Unlike individual personalities which are inherited and learned, culture is learned from an individual's social environment (Spencer-Oatey 2012). Kotler and Keller (2009) defined culture as the fundamental determinant of an individual's wants and behaviors developed through a socialization process with other members in their group. Similarly, Crotts and Litvin (2003) argued that culture is learned early in life and that is why country of residence explained respondents' culture better than their country of birth or citizenship. Family members and teachers educate individuals how to behave in order to be accepted by others and culture influences the moral and shared values which serve as guiding principles for their behaviors. For example, women are equally treated with men in some countries, while Muslim countries consider women as having a subordinate position.

b. Culture distinguishes individuals of one group from individuals of other groups

Members of a nation tend to possess similar characteristics of language, history, and religion driven by culture, a combination of shared meanings and traditions, and the shared characteristics that help to identify one culture from others (Woodside, Hus, and Marshall 2011). Several researchers in cross-cultural studies (e.g. Fan 2000; Moura, Gnoth, and Deans 2014) have underlined the characteristic that culture differentiates one group from others. For instance, Moura, Gnoth, and Deans (2014: 529) referred to culture as "specific collective ways of thinking, behaving and feeling, which characterize individuals of one group and distinguish them from individuals of other groups." Because of this characteristic, a specific behavior that is totally accepted in one culture might not be accepted by other cultures. Japanese consider people laughing with their mouth wide open as rude, but it is acceptable in the United States.

c. Culture affects individuals' behavior

Culture includes several elements such as language, religion, social structures, economic, political, and educational systems (Triandis 1989). Another definition of culture by Solomon (1996) also supports the notion that culture is a combination of shared meaning, rituals, norms, and traditions among members of a group. The accumulated aspects of culture heavily influence individuals' behavior by shaping their perceptions, beliefs, and norms (Triandis, 1989). For example, in

Western culture, people try to avoid the number 13 because the number is considered unlucky, whereas the number 4 is an unlucky number in some East Asian cultures.

Theories of culture

Hofstede (1984) published his original cultural value dimensions in a book entitled, *Culture's Consequences: International Differences in Work-Related Values*. In the book, based on the values of IBM employees from 40 countries, Hofstede divided the cultural values that differentiate one country from another into four groups: *power distance, individualism versus collectivism, femininity versus masculinity*, and *uncertainty avoidance*. Later in 2010, Hofstede, Hofstede and Minkov expanded Hofstede's original theory of four dimensions to six dimensions by adding *long-term orientation versus short-term orientation* and *indulgence versus restraint*.

The *Power Distance Index (PDI)* is one of the dimensions of national culture and represents the way that societies deal with inequalities among people. Countries with high PDI scores such as Malaysia, Russia, and Mexico accept a strict hierarchy and a gap between the less powerful and the more powerful members of society. Countries that score low on this dimension, for example, Sweden, Latvia, the United States, Great Britain, Australia, and Canada, are proud of their values: independence, equal rights, and decentralized power (Hofstede, Hofstede and Minkov 2010: 53–88).

Individualism versus Collectivism (IDV) indicates whether a society defines itself in terms of "I" or "we." Countries with the highest IDV scores, such as the United States and Australia, emphasize the importance of freedom and have formed loosely knit societies in which one is expected to only take care of his or her immediate family. On the contrary, countries with low IDV score, for example, Pakistan and Indonesia, value the power of the group that protects a person throughout one's life in exchange for loyalty (Hofstede, Hofstede and Minkov 2010: 89–134).

Masculinity versus Femininity (MAS) represents a society's preference for personal achievement, opportunities for one's advancement, and material possessions versus quality of life, cooperation, and positive relationships at work. Examples of the most feminine-scoring countries include Sweden, Norway, and Latvia. On the opposite end of the scale are Slovakia and Japan (Hofstede, Hofstede and Minkov 2010: 135–86).

The *Uncertainty Avoidance Index (UAI)* expresses the degree to which societies accept unpredictable situations and ambiguity. High UAI occurs in countries such as Greece, Japan, and South Korea. Countries with a low UAI score, such as Singapore and Jamaica, are least threatened by unknown situations (Hofstede, Hofstede and Minkov 2010: 187–234).

Long-Term Orientation versus Short Term Normative Orientation (LTO) demonstrates whether a society is focused on future rewards or the past and present. China and Hong Kong are examples of long-term oriented societies. Ghana, Egypt, and Nigeria are considered short-term oriented societies (Hofstede, Hofstede and Minkov 2010: 235–276).

Indulgence versus Restraint (IND) displays a tendency in a society to accept basic human needs and the enjoyment of life or to suppress such desires and to regulate them by strict norms. Countries that score high on this dimension are Venezuela and Mexico. Pakistan and Egypt have the lowest IND Index (Hofstede, Hofstede and Minkov 2010: 280–296).

A large number of studies have implemented Hofstede's cultural dimensions in order to analyze cultural differences in tourism and hospitality consumer behavior. For instance, Kang and Mastin (2008) employed Hofstede's cultural dimensions as a framework in order to explain the differences in countries' official tourism websites and found different features on different countries' tourism websites. Specifically, countries with low PDI provided special menus for lesbian and gay populations on their websites. Countries with low UAI, such as India, China, and Ireland, preferred simple designs while high UAO countries including Panama, Portugal, Chile, and Spain featured creative website designs. Countries with high IDV featured photographs of individuals and couples, while group photographs were the norm on the websites of the countries that scored low on IDV. However, Hofstede's cultural dimensions have some limitations. Specifically, several researchers have proposed several critiques of the cultural dimensions such as the validity of the dimensions (Schmitz and Weber 2014).

Another of the well-known applications of the cultural dimensions theory is Schwartz's theory of basic values, which was introduced in 1994. Schwartz (2012) identified ten motivational types of values and classified them into four dimensions: *openness to change, conservation, self-enhancement,* and *self-transcendence.* The *Openness to Change* dimension includes such values as hedonism, stimulation, and self-direction. Opposing this is the *Conservation* dimension with such values as security, conformity, and tradition. The *Self-enhancement* dimension (achievement and power) is contrasted with the *Self-transcendence* dimension (universalism and benevolence) (Schwartz 2012).

One of the latest cross-cultural models developed as a result of Hofstede's work is the Lewis Model. Lewis (2005) proposed three dimensions based on human behavior: *Linear-active, Multi-active* and *Reactive.* They are placed as the points of a triangle. *Linear-active* groups (e.g. North America, Britain, Australia, New Zealand, and Northern Europe) are described as "task-oriented, highly organized planners" (Lewis 2005: 40). Reactive groups, located in all major Asian countries, are "introverted, respect-oriented listeners" (Lewis 2005: 40). Finally, *Multi-active* groups, which are more scattered and represent such areas as South America, Mediterranean countries, and the Arab world, are "people-oriented, loquacious interrelators" (Lewis 2005: 40). Based on the LMR (linear/multi/reactive) Personal Cultural Profile, Lewis (2005) placed cultural groups along the sides of a triangle to illustrate the degree of manifestation on each of the three dimensions. The Lewis Model can be applied to the impact of culture on tourism and hospitality consumer decision-making processes. For example, Lewis (2005) points out that linear-active people, for example Americans and Germans, often fail to recognize the importance of building trust and developing personal relationships. Lewis notes that people from multi-linear and reactive cultures "buy from people they like, not necessarily from those who offer the best product at the best price" (Lewis 2005: 143).

A broad variety of cultural theories have contributed to the foundations of cultural studies. Following Reisinger's argument (2009) that Hofstede's cultural dimensions theory serves as an international guide to explain national cultural differences, this chapter adopts Hofstede's cultural dimensions as a theoretical basis.

The impact of culture on hospitality customers' decision-making process

Various factors (e.g. income, a reason or purchase, social class, and family) affect individuals' decision-making processes and these factors can be categorized into situational, psychological, and social factors (Pride and Ferrell 2010). As a social factor, culture has been identified as one of the most influential factors. The following sections explain how culture influences each stage of the decision-making process; the discussion will be based on a combination of Hofstede's cultural dimensions theory and the traditional five steps of customers' decision-making process for buying: need recognition, information search, alternative evaluation, purchase decision, and post-purchase evaluation proposed by Engel, Blackwell, and Kollat (1978).

Need recognition

As the first stage of the decision-making process, a customer identifies what his or her needs are in order to determine which product would be able to meet these needs. Needs which generate motivations are important antecedents of behaviors. While some researchers use needs and motivations (or motives) interchangeably, customer behavior researchers often stress employee motivations over needs (Kozak 2002).

National culture affects this stage because individuals in a nation share the same values that trigger their motivation to buy certain products (Reisinger 2009). Even though it is impossible for individuals to possess the exact same needs and motivations across a country, comparing national motivations benefits marketers by providing a general idea of people in a country.

In the hospitality and tourism industry, the area of tourist motivation has been widely examined. In particular, researchers have investigated cultural differences in tourist motivations and have revealed that tourist motivations are influenced by their culture along with their background and previous experience. Tourist motivation is a combination of push factors, internal driving needs in order to escape from an ordinary life, and pull factors, the external factors that determine "where to go" (Meng, Tepanon and Uysal 2008). You et al. (2000) confirmed the cultural differences in tourist motivations by identifying the different push factors of tourists from the United Kingdom and Japan. Specifically, out of seventeen tourist motivation variables, the two groups showed differences in thirteen items. For instance, the UK tourists ranked exploring new places as the top travel motivation, but Japanese tourists were motivated by having fun and being entertained.

Information search

The impact of cross-cultural differences on travel information search behavior has been one of the most popular research topics in the hospitality and tourism industry due to its effects and the various search options that travelers can choose from. The ultimate goal of information search is selecting the best choice in the purchase decision by effectively utilizing available information that is collected. Marketers can actively participate in this stage of the decision-making process compared to other stages through effective communication strategies (Gursoy and McCleary 2004).

Information can be collected internally as well as externally. As early as 1979, Bettman identified two types of information search behavior: internal information search and external information search. Internal information search refers to retrieving information from memory which was gathered from past experience and previous information searches (Money and Crotts 2003; Lee and Cranage 2010). When confronted with a choice, tourism and hospitality customers first evaluate the quality of existing knowledge and information, and their appropriateness, in order to examine whether an additional information search is needed. If internal information is not sufficient, hospitality and tourism customers will seek additional information from external sources in order to reduce perceived risk (Gursoy and McCleary 2004; Lee and Cranage 2010).

External information search refers to the activity of information acquisition from the environment (Fodness and Murray 1999). Examples of external information sources include non-market dominated sources of information such as personal advice from family and friends and direct observation as well as market-dominated sources of information such as media (Lee and Cranage 2010; Litvin, Crotts and Hefner 2004). Gursoy and Umbreit (2004) identified cross-cultural differences in external information search behavior from European Union member states. Likewise, Osti, Turner, and King (2009) confirmed the cultural differences in information search among Japanese, Korean, Chinese, and North American tourists by examining travel guidebooks.

External information search encompasses pre-purchase search and on-going search. On-going search consists of activities aiming to update product knowledge, while pre-purchase information search is strongly related to the actual purchase and purchase decision. Even though both pre-purchase search and on-going search assist customers with their purchase decisions, pre-purchase search is more likely to occur when customers seek to reduce uncertainty for specific purchases (Lee and Cranage 2010). Therefore, the pre-purchase information search has been identified as one of the key components of the decision-making process and this is why it has been widely studied.

Information search is characterized by the degree of search, direction of search, and sequence of search (Lee and Cranage 2010). The degree of search represents the amount of search activity, while the direction of search is related to which brands or products customers consider and the contexts that customers evaluate (Chaturvedi and Chaturvedi 2013). Finally, the sequence of search refers to the order of search activities (Kumar 2009). These characteristics of information search differ depending on the types of customers. For example, first-time visitors will spend more time searching for information about the destination than repeat visitors.

This stage of the decision-making process is associated with costs which can be divided into monetary costs and cognitive search costs. Monetary costs cover the additional energy, time, and money effort, and cognitive search costs refer to the amount of cognitive effort (e.g. the evaluation of information collected) needed to undertake information search and other psychological costs (Gursoy and McCleary 2004; Lee and Cranage 2010). The benefits gained from collected information should exceed the costs of searching for information in order to make this process meaningful. In addition, the benefits gained accommodate psychological gains such as customer satisfaction with their decisions (Lee and Cranage 2010).

Following the emergence of technologies (e.g. Internet and smartphones) and the popularity of social networking platforms such as Facebook, online information search—collecting information through the Internet—has become popular over the last decades (Xiang, Magnini, and Fesenmaier 2015). The Internet enables tourism and hospitality customers to find vast product information such as product attributes, availability, and alternatives in a convenient and inexpensive way (Lee and Cranage 2010). In addition, customers can easily compare a wide range of product choices and prices and customize their search (Dholakia and Bagozzi 2001; Lee and Cranage 2010). This cost-effective source also enables customers to obtain peer reviews about products, which is considered as an even more reliable source than the traditional promotional materials prepared by marketers (e.g. radio advertisement), through customer reviews in the form of ratings and comments (Choi, Fowler, Goh and Yuan 2015). However, the perception of online information might be different depending on customers' cultures. For example, the effects of online information differ among German, Japanese, and Americans (Vishwanath 2003). An important point that should be addressed related to online information search is that the information available on the Internet can be easily manipulated by marketers and other users (Pan and Chiou, 2011), and that is why the next stage of evaluating alternatives is so important.

Evaluating alternatives

The evaluating alternatives stage, along with the information search stage, is driven by the need to reduce perceived risk. Perceived risk arises when the level of uncertainty increases. Therefore, among Hofstede's cultural dimensions, the UAI serves as a strong determinant for cultural differences in risk-taking (Money and Crotts 2003; Kozak, Crotts and Law 2007). For instance, tourists from countries with a high UAI score (e.g. Greece) prefer travelling to places that are popularly visited by other tourists among several options, while tourists from low uncertainty avoidance countries (e.g. Hong Kong) enjoy a sense of adventure by exploring countries that have been less discovered by others. Similarly, tourists who live in countries that have a high UAI culture tend to join travel packages or travel in larger numbers in order to reduce travel-related risks, whereas tourists who live in countries that possess a low UAI culture often travel alone.

Perceived risk, as well as the level of uncertainty, will likely be reduced when a customer trusts the information provided. However, with the massive amount of information available on the Internet in today's marketplace, it has become difficult for customers to evaluate the trustworthiness of information found online and the credibility of the websites they find information from (Pan and Chiou 2011). In addition, hospitality customers value information differently depending on the information source. For example, tourists perceive information from a website with user-generated content and a city's tourism organization website to be more reliable and sincere than information from a marketing service provider's website (Dickinger 2011).

National culture also influences the evaluation criteria for tourism-related options such as hotels and restaurants. Collectivist cultures such as Russia are more likely to decide based on brand, prices, and the number of alternatives, whereas individualist cultures such as the United States tend to utilize their own criteria (Correia, Kozak and Ferradeira 2011).

Purchase decision

The purchase decision stage is one of the most complex aspects of the decision-making process because of the wide variety of criteria that individuals adopt (Nayeem 2012). When a tourist reaches the final decision-making stage regarding his or her trip, he or she needs to decide not only whether they will take a trip or not but also important details relating to the trip including his or her travel companion, the length of the trip, and number of destinations that will be visited (Money and Crotts 2003). Tourists from UAI cultures, such as Japan, will purchase pre-planned packages and travel in larger groups than tourists from high UAI cultures (Money and Crotts 2003).

National culture also influences purchase decisions for gifts and souvenirs because, in collectivist countries, tourists are almost expected to bring gifts and souvenirs when they return from their trip. In the case of Japan, tourists spend about $800 on gifts and souvenirs during their international trips (Rosenbaum and Spears 2005).

Post-purchase evaluations

In this stage, hospitality customers determine their satisfaction with the products or services received and determine behavioral intentions such as repurchase intention (Williams and Soutar 2009).

Customer satisfaction refers to the affective response to the product or service received (Oliver 1980), and customer expectations are one of the strong determinants of customer satisfaction. The impact of national culture on customer satisfaction is significant because national culture is associated with social norms which affect customers' expectations. For instance, countries with a high masculine culture tend to have less positive evaluations compared to countries with moderate and low masculinity (Crotts and Erdmann 2000).

When customers are not satisfied, they express their dissatisfaction. However, the willingness to report their dissatisfaction and the service recovery process differ depending on many factors, including national culture. Customers from high masculine societies (e.g. Germany) tend to express their dissatisfaction while customers from low masculine societies (e.g. Sweden) are not willing to address their dissatisfaction (Crotts and Erdmann, 2000). In addition, customers from low PDI cultures (e.g. Australia) and customers from high PDI cultures (e.g. Thailand) differ in their expectations and perceptions of a hospitality company's service recovery system. For example, Thai customers are more sensitive to the status of the employee delivering an apology than is the case with Australian customers (Patterson, Cowley and Prasongsukarn 2006). As a consequence, it is recommended that a manager should be involved in the service recovery process when offering an apology to guests from high PDA cultures.

Conclusion and implications

National culture plays an important role by shaping how individuals in a nation think, react, and behave. Understanding cultural differences and their impact on the purchase decision-making process is especially important in the tourism and hospitality industry with the increasing number of tourists travelling globally. From planning a trip by identifying needs and motivations for travelling, to satisfaction and revisit intention in the form of post-purchase evaluations, national culture serves as a strong force in making certain decisions in hospitality and tourism-related behaviors.

The impacts of cultural differences on the tourist decision-making process can serve as an important foundation for marketers to tailor their offerings and marketing strategies to appeal to their target market in different countries. Employees at tourism and hospitality-related companies and organizations should also understand cultural effects and be ready to accommodate the needs and wants of customers from different nations in order to satisfy them. Satisfied tourists will come back and spread positive word-of-mouth reviews regardless of their national culture, which is the ultimate goal of managers.

References

Chaturvedi, P. and Chaturvedi, M. (2013) *Business Communication: Skills, Concepts, and Applications* (3rd Ed.), New Delhi, India: Dorling Kindersley.

Choi, E., Fowler, D., Goh, B., and Yuan, J. (2015) "Social Media Marketing: Applying the Uses and Gratifications Theory in the Hotel Industry," *Journal of Hospitality Marketing & Management*, 25(7), 1–26.

Correia, A., Kozak, M., and Ferradeira, J. (2011) "Impact of Culture on Tourist Decision-Making Styles," *International Journal of Tourism Research* 13, 433–46.

Crotts, J. and Erdmann, R. (2000) "Does National Culture Influence Consumers' Evaluation of Travel Services? A Test of Hofstede's Model of Cross-Cultural Differences," *Managing Service Quality: An International Journal* 10, 410–19.

Crotts, J. and Litvin, S. (2003) "Cross-Cultural Research: Are Researchers Better Served by Knowing Respondents' Country of Birth, Residence, or Citizenship?" *Journal of Travel Research* 42, 186–90.

Dholakia, U. and Bagozzi, R. (2001) "Consumer Behavior in Digital Environments," *Digital Marketing*, 163–200.

Dickinger, A. (2011) "The Trustworthiness of Online Channels for Experience- and Goal-Directed Search Tasks," *Journal of Travel Research* 50, 378–91.

Engel, J., Blackwell, R., and Kollat, D. (1978) *Consumer Behavior* (3rd Ed.), Chicago: The Dryden Press.

Fan, Y. (2000) "A Classification of Chinese Culture," *Cross Cultural Management: An International Journal* 7, 3–10.

Fodness, D. and Murray, B. (1999) "A Model of Tourist Information Search Behavior," *Journal of Travel Research* 37, 220–30.

Gursoy, D. and McCleary, K. (2004) "An Integrative Model of Tourists' Information Search Behavior," *Annals of Tourism Research* 31, 353–73.

Gursoy, D. and Umbreit, W. (2004) "Tourist Information Search Behavior: Cross–Cultural Comparison of European Union Member States," *International Journal of Hospitality Management* 23, 55–70.

Hofstede, G. (1980) "Culture and Organizations," *International Studies of Management & Organization* 10, 15–41.

——— (1984) *Culture's Consequences: International Differences in Work-Related Values*, Beverly Hills, CA: Sage.

——— (1986) "Editorial: The Usefulness of the 'Organizational Culture' Concept," *Journal of Management Studies* 23, 253–7.

——— (1998) "Attitudes, Values and Organizational Culture: Disentangling the Concepts," *Organization Studies* 19, 477–93.

Hofstede, G. and Hofstede, G. (2003) *Culture's Consequences: Comparing Values, Behaviors, Institutions and Organizations Across Nations*, Thousand Oaks, CA: Sage.

Hofstede, G., Hofstede, G., and Minkov, M. (2010) *Cultures and Organizations: Software of the Mind: Intercultural Cooperation and its Importance for Survival*, Maidenhead: Mcgraw-Hill.

Kang, D. and Mastin, T. (2008) "How Cultural Difference Affects International Tourism Public Relations Websites: A Comparative Analysis Using Hofstede's Cultural Dimensions," *Public Relations Review* 34, 54–6.

Kotler, P. and Keller, K. (2009) *Marketing Management*, Upper Saddle River, NJ: Pearson Prentice Hall.

Kozak, M. (2002) "Comparative Analysis of Tourist Motivations by Nationality and Destinations," *Tourism Management* 23, 221–32.

Kozak, M., Crotts, J., and Law, R. (2007) "The Impact of the Perception of Risk on International Travelers," *International Journal of Tourism Research* 9, 233–42.

Kumar, S. (2009) *Consumer Behaviour and Branding: Concepts, Readings and Cases – The Indian Context*, New Delhi, India: Dorling Kindersley

Lee, C. and Cranage, D. (2010) "Customer Uncertainty Dimensions and Online Information Search in the Context of Hotel Booking Channel," *Journal of Hospitality Marketing & Management* 19, 397–420.

Lewis, R. (2005) *When Cultures Collide* [Kindle E-Book], London: Nicholas Brealey Publishing.

Li, M. (2012) "Cross-Cultural Tourist Research: A Meta-Analysis," *Journal of Hospitality & Tourism Research* 38(1). doi: 1096348012442542.

Litvin, S., Crotts, J., and Hefner, F. (2004) "Cross-Cultural Tourist Behaviour: A Replication and Extension Involving Hofstede's Uncertainty Avoidance Dimension," *International Journal of Tourism Research* 6, 29–37.

Meng, F., Tepanon, Y., and Uysal, M. (2008) "Measuring Tourist Satisfaction by Attribute and Motivation: The Case of a Nature-Based Resort," *Journal of Vacation Marketing* 14, 41–56.

Money, R. and Crotts, J. (2003) "The Effect of Uncertainty Avoidance on Information Search, Planning, and Purchases of International Travel Vacations," *Tourism Management* 24, 191–202.

Morris, M., Leung, K., Ames, D., and Lickel, B. (1999) "Views from the Inside and Outside: Integrating Emic and Etic Insights about Culture and Justice Judgment," *Academy of Management Review* 24, 781–96.

Moura, F., Gnoth, J., and Deans, K. (2014) "Localizing Cultural Values on Tourism Destination Websites: The Effects on Users' Willingness to Travel and Destination Image," *Journal of Travel Research*, doi: 0047287514522873.

Nayeem, T. (2012) "Cultural Influences on Consumer Behaviour," *International Journal of Business And Management* 7, 78–91.

Oliver, R. (1980) "A Cognitive Model of the Antecedents and Consequences of Satisfaction Decisions," *Journal of Marketing Research* 17(4), 460–9.

Osti, L., Turner, L., and King, B. (2009) "Cultural Differences in Travel Guidebooks Information Search," *Journal of Vacation Marketing* 15, 63–78.

Pan, L. and Chiou, J. (2011) "How Much Can You Trust Online Information? Cues for Perceived Trustworthiness of Consumer-Generated Online Information," *Journal of Interactive Marketing* 25, 67–74.

Patterson, P., Cowley, E., and Prasongsukarn, K. (2006) "Service Failure Recovery: The Moderating Impact of Individual-Level Cultural Value Orientation on Perceptions of Justice," *International Journal of Research In Marketing* 23, 263–77.

Pearce, P. (2011) *Tourist Behaviour and the Contemporary World (Aspects of Tourism)*, Bristol: Channel View Publications.

Pride, W. and Ferrell. C. (2010) *Marketing Express*, Mason, TN: Nelson Education.

Reisinger, Y. (2009) *International Tourism: Culture and Behavior*, Burlington, MA: Elsevier.

Rosenbaum, M. and Spears, D. (2005) "Who Buys That? Who Does What? Analysis of Cross-Cultural Consumption Behaviours among Tourists in Hawaii," *Journal of Vacation Marketing* 11, 235–47.

Schmitz, L. and Weber, W. (2014) "Are Hofstede's Dimensions Valid? A Test for Measurement Invariance of Uncertainty Avoidance," *Interculture Journal: Online-Zeitschrift Für Interkulturelle Studien* 13, 11–26.

Schwartz, S. (1994) "Are There Universal Aspects in the Structure and Contents of Human Values?," *Journal of Social Issues* 50, 19–45.

Schwartz, S. (2012) "An Overview of the Schwartz Theory of Basic Values," *Online Readings in Psychology and Culture* 2(1).

Schwartz, S. and Ros, M. (1995) "Values in the West: A Theoretical and Empirical Challenge to the Individualism-Collectivism Cultural Dimension," *World Psychology* 1, 99–122.

Soloman, J. (1996) "School Science and the Future of Scientific Culture," *Public Understanding of Science* 5, 157–66.

Spencer-Oatey, H. (2012) *What Is Culture? A Compilation of Quotations.* Globalpad Core Concepts. Available at: www2.Warwick.Ac.Uk/Fac/Soc/Al/Globalpad/Interculturalskills/ [Accessed 1 Oct. 2016].

Triandis, H. (1989) "The Self and Social Behavior in Differing Cultural Contexts," *Psychological Review* 96, 506–20.

United Nations World Tourism Organization (UNWTO). (2011) *Market Trend.* Available at: http://cf.cdn.unwto.org/sites/all/files/pdf/annual_report_2011.pdf [Accessed 14 Sept. 2016].

Vishwanath, A. (2003) "Comparing Online Information Effects: A Cross-Cultural Comparison of Online Information and Uncertainty Avoidance," *Communication Research* 30, 579–98.

Williams, P. and Soutar, G. (2009) "Value, Satisfaction and Behavioral Intentions in an Adventure Tourism Context," *Annals of Tourism Research* 36, 413–38.

Woodside, A., Hsu, S., and Marshall, R. (2011) "General Theory of Cultures' Consequences on International Tourism Behavior," *Journal of Business Research* 64, 785–99.

Xiang, Z., Magnini, V., and Fesenmaier, D. (2015) "Information Technology and Consumer Behavior in Travel and Tourism: Insights from Travel Planning Using the Internet," *Journal of Retailing and Consumer Services* 22, 244–9.

Yang, J., Ryan, C., and Zhang, L. (2013) "Social Conflict in Communities Impacted by Tourism," *Tourism Management* 35, 82–93.

You, X., O'Leary, J., Morrison, A., and Hong, G.S. (2000) "A Cross-Cultural Comparison of Travel Push and Pull Factors: United Kingdom Vs. Japan," *International Journal of Hospitality & Tourism Administration* 1, 1–26.

Further reading

House, R., Hanges, P., Javidan, M., and Gupta, V. (2004) *Culture, Leadership, and Organizations: The GLOBE Study of 62 Societies,* Thousand Oaks, CA: Sage Publishers. (Results of the Global Leadership and Organizational Behavior Effectiveness (GLOBE) research program.)

Hsu, C. and Huang, S. (2016) "Reconfiguring Chinese cultural values and their tourism implications," *Tourism Management* 54, 230–242. (Contemporary Chinese cultural values and discussion of the relevance of traditional cultural theories to modern China.)

Madera, J.M. (2013) "Best practices in diversity management in customer service organizations: An investigation of top companies cited by Diversity Inc," *Cornell Hospitality Quarterly* 54(2), 124–135. (An analysis of diversity management practices used by fourteen customer service organizations.)

Part VI

Sustainability and the environment

30

Hospitality sustainability practices, consumer behavior and marketing

C. Michael Hall

Introduction

Hospitality is becoming a significant focus for research on sustainability. After aviation and car transport, the accommodation sector is estimated to contribute approximately 21 percent of tourism's global greenhouse gas (GHG) emissions (UNWTO & UNEP 2008), about 1 percent of all GHG emissions. The World Economic Forum (WEF 2009) estimated that emissions for what they described as the accommodation cluster (hotels and similar establishments, such as lodges and motels; and all other types of accommodation) were 284 $MtCO_2$ in 2005, less than 5 percent of global building emissions. However, this figure was only based on direct emissions based on energy use and was likely an underestimate, and did not include any emissions from the transportation and production of hotel consumables, such as food and drink, which may be substantial (Gössling & Hall 2013). The sector is also a major user of land and water resources as well as a contributor to water, food and other waste (Tortella & Tirado 2011; Gössling & Hall 2013; Hall & Gössling, 2013; Kasim et al. 2014; Gössling et al. 2015; Rutty et al. 2015), while social dimensions are often incorporated into Fair Trade and local food purchasing (Tzschentke et al. 2008; Hall 2010a; Hall & Gössling 2013; Roy et al. 2016; Gössling & Hall 2016) as well as specific programmes for local and/or refugee employment and training.

Attempts to encourage more sustainable consumption practices in hospitality tend to focus on encouraging greater efficiencies in resource use on a per room, property or customer basis via improvements in design and/or technology (Ayuso 2007; Kasim 2007; Ali et al. 2014; Zografakis et al. 2011; Coles et al. 2014; Gössling et al. 2015), or behavioral interventions focused on staff and/or consumers (Hall et al. 2016). Both approaches directly or indirectly influence consumer behavior but the technological efficiency approach dominates. For example, the World Economic Forum (2009: 7) suggest that, for what they described as the accommodation cluster (hotels and similar establishments, such as lodges and motels; and all other types of accommodation, such as vacation homes, staying with friends and relatives and in camps), reductions in carbon emissions will primarily be driven by 'the use of existing mature technologies in lighting, heating and cooling that can significantly improve hotel energy efficiency.' However, ideally both approaches need to be implemented together as part of a more strategic approach to encouraging sustainable consumption practices (Hall 2010b, 2015).

Greater efficiencies are an important component of sustainable hospitality operations. However, concerns also exist about the extent to which they contribute to undesirable economic and behavioral rebound effects unless there is also simultaneous attention to consumption behavior and the adoption of system-wide technological, behavioral and policy innovations (Hall 2010b; Aall et al. 2016; Scott et al. 2016a, 2016b, 2016c). Concerns over consumption behavior and practices have therefore become incorporated into longer-standing interests in the attitudinal and behavioral dimensions of sustainable hospitality, especially with respect to accommodation and lodging, as well as the persistent gap between consumers' typically positive explicit attitudes towards sustainability and their behaviors (Luchs et al. 2010; Gössling et al. 2012; Hall 2013; Cohen et al. 2014; Hall et al. 2016).

Research on sustainable hospitality attitudes, behaviors and practices examines both producers and consumers (Hall et al. 2016). Producer research tends to focus on the attitudes of managers, owners and employees toward sustainability and environmental policies and practices. Consumer research examines the perceptions and behaviors of tourists toward environmental practices, consumer practices, support for green-branded hospitality products, and the impacts of regulation, technology and/or behavioral interventions on behavior. Surprisingly, there is relatively little research that simultaneously examines the attitudes, behaviors and practices of the consumers and producers of the hospitality experience (Firth & Hing 1999; Lee et al. 2010; do Paço et al. 2012; Chan 2013). Much of the research on producer perspectives is focused on surveys of managers and owners rather than the general staff who implement many sustainability measures and who are involved in face-to-face interaction with customers (Chan & Hawkins 2010; do Paço et al. 2012; Chou 2014; Teng et al. 2014). This situation therefore means that there are significant gaps in our understanding of sustainability practices within the hospitality industry (Hall et al. 2016). Nevertheless, there are a number of major themes that can be identified with respect to sustainability practices, as discussed below

Business adoption of sustainable practices and social license

Demand for environmentally friendly products (D'Souza et al. 2015) and the substantial contribution of tourism and hospitality to environmental change (Rutty et al. 2015) creates significant pressure on businesses to strategically respond to sustainability concerns (Aragon-Correa et al. 2015). Although customer communication strategies often emphasize the environmental benefits, the main driver for the adoption of green hospitality practices is the cost–benefit relationship and contribution to profitability (Bohdanowicz 2005; Dodds & Holmes 2011; Manganari et al. 2016). Concern over cost is regarded as the main obstacle to improving sustainability practices in hotel operations (Fotiadis et al. 2013), although much depends on the time scale used for return on investment in new technologies, such as water-saving devices (Gössling et al. 2015). Incremental adoption and change is more likely in the absence of mandatory standards or specific regulated requirements, with hotels tending to implement smaller-scale activities, such as efficient waste management, in order to acquire immediate cost savings (Tarí et al. 2010).

Despite knowledge of their actual or potential contribution to environmental damage, many companies are unwilling to adopt recommended pro-environmental behaviors (Su et al. 2013). A major obstacle to behavioral change is the perceived lack of direct benefits accrued through adoption of sustainable practices (Searcy 2012). Therefore, legislative policies and government initiatives are often needed to encourage change (Bramwell & Lane 2011; Hall 2011a), whether through creating a level playing field in terms of costs or providing 'carrots,' i.e. tax benefits, or 'sticks,' i.e. making certain practices mandatory, in policy and regulatory terms. Deregulated market-oriented governance approaches that encourage industry self-governance and responsibility in light of market pressures and limited specific government regulation is inadequate for achieving sustainable business behaviors (Hall 2013, 2014). Although formal guidelines for sustainable practice may be promoted (Hsieh 2012), i.e. recommendations to adopt ISO standards for environmental management, in the absence of regulation or other cost incentives to adopt such practices their use often appears limited to higher profile international brands and 'niche' 'green' hotels.

Unlike other industries, the hospitality sector has not usually seen itself as requiring a Social License to Operate (SLO) (Parsons & Moffat 2014), even though there is widespread recognition of the need for hospitality businesses to engage with stakeholders, including the community, in the context of environmental protection. Gunningham et al. (2004: 308) defined SLO as "the demands on and expectations for a business enterprise that emerge from neighborhoods, environmental groups, community members, and other elements of the surrounding civil society," while Weldegiorgis and Franks (2014: 282) have interpreted SLO with respect to the "intangible and unwritten, tacit, contract with society, or a social group" by a business or organization. Although it has its origins in extractive industries, SLO has been adopted within a wider business context; for example, New Zealand's Sustainable Business Council (SBC) (2013), which includes several tourism and hospitality-oriented corporations, described SLO as:

> the ability of an organisation to carry on its business because of the confidence society has that it will behave in a legitimate, accountable and socially and environmentally acceptable way. It does not just derive from a need for legal or regulatory compliance but takes into account the inputs from a wider group of stakeholders and a sense of transparency and accountability in its external reporting. It is the foundation for acquiring operational certainty, realising future opportunities and lowering risk for the business
>
> *(SBC 2013: 2).*

The notion of an SLO is significant because it raises questions about why a business seeks to implement sustainability practices beyond that required by the law and how businesses frame their behavior. From a consumer behavior perspective, this also connects with the need to understand marketing and communication practices in the hospitality sector, consumer demands for sustainable services, and the brand values that accrue from sustainability. All of these provide significant commercial reasons for adopting sustainable practices and favorably influencing consumer behavior.

Sustainability marketing and communication

Sustainable marketing consists of the marketing practices, policies and procedures that explicitly account for concerns about conservation of natural capital, the quality of the social environment, and economic equity in society in pursuing the goal of creating revenue and providing outcomes that satisfy organizational and individual objectives for a product or an organization. Sustainable marketing programs are therefore those designed to accomplish a firm's strategic and financial goals in ways that positively contribute to sustainability. The notion of 'green' marketing is more narrowly defined and reflects the preceding goals but with respect to the natural environment (Leonidou et al. 2013a, 2013b). Similarly, the term 'green hotel' is often used in the literature to refer to hotels and firms that take measures to prevent causing harm to the natural environment through efficient use of energy, water and other materials (Tilikidou et al. 2013).

Despite positive public attitudes towards sustainable practices, it has proven difficult to leverage significant widespread and long-term behavioral change (Hall 2014). Hospitality providers are generally ineffective in encouraging pro-environmental behavior among consumers who are either not interested or lack knowledge about environmental issues (Nicholls & Kang 2012; Mair & Laing 2013). Such negative responses may be attributed to the perceived effort and utility that some consumers associate with behaving sustainably and make it difficult to implement a strategy to encourage such behaviors (McDonald & Oates 2006).

Consumers' eco-friendly attitudes are strongly associated with the level of perceived importance of the environment (Chen 2015). If they are environmentally aware, and feel that these issues are important and need to be solved, then their attitudes and behavioral intentions towards green hotels are likely to be favorable (Lee et al. 2010). Consumers who are better educated express higher levels of intention to stay at a green hotel (Chen & Peng 2012; Tilikidou et al. 2013), and this is a major determinant of customer engagement in eco-friendly behaviors (Han & Yoon 2015).

The theory of planned behavior, which suggests that attitudes, social norms and perceived control affect people's behavioral intentions, and that these intentions lead to their actual behavior, is a common theoretical reference point for hospitality studies (e.g. Han & Kim 2010; Han et al. 2010; Chen & Tung 2014). However, the approach has been criticized due to the fact that behavioral intentions do not necessarily translate into actual behavior and that the link between the two concepts is quite weak, resulting in a distinct attitude–behavior gap in consumption behavior (Juvan & Dolcinar 2014), which can mean that consumer *intention* to stay at an environmentally friendly property is much higher than any actions toward *actually* staying (Tilikidou et al. 2013). Several possible reasons for the attitude–behavior gap include issues other than the environment being of greater importance in purchasing decisions; the notion of a 'vacation' or hotel stay being an 'escape' from environmental responsibilities; insufficient information; or consumers being too busy to change their behavior (Wearing et al. 2002; Juvan & Dolcinar, 2014).

Several factors have been identified as barriers to purchasing stays at green hotels. These include the perception that green hotel products may be lower in quality, have reduced performance, or be less indulgent, and that they cost more (Luchs et al. 2010; Han et al. 2011; Susskind & Verma 2011). Some consumers also believe they should be rewarded for their green behavior via hotel reward points and/or discounts (Tzschentke et al. 2004). This insight is significant as it suggests that, for some consumers, the satisfaction of undertaking behavior solely for the sake of the environment is not always enough.

One strategy that has been used to try to close the attitude–behavior gap and change customer behavior is the promotion of ecolabels and 'green' certification (Millar & Baloglu 2011). However, the framing of promotion and messaging is extremely important. Wehrli et al. (2014) reported that consumers are more persuaded by sustainability messages when they are presented in an emotional tone, using text that directly addresses customers and with accompanying visual elements. Rational justifications for the adoption of sustainable behaviors were found to not be persuasive and consumers ignored such messages. One reason for this outcome could be because consumers tend to book hospitality products based on emotional factors, rather than just rational ones. However, such responses to environmental-based messaging are not consistent over time or across cultures (Cummins et al. 2014).

The effectiveness of behavioral initiatives

Although environmental initiatives appear to be becoming more common across the hospitality sector, especially for international chains, consumer participation is relatively passive (Miao &

Wei 2013). Nevertheless, service-dominant providers have sought ways for consumers to participate (Theotokis & Manganari 2015). One of the most obvious areas where this has occurred is
with hotels using message-based appeals to urge guests to reuse their towels in water and energy
conservation efforts (Goldstein et al. 2007, 2008; Shang et al. 2010; Dimara et al. 2017). Some
of the ways in which hotels have effectively encouraged guest participation are discussed below.

Consumer motivations and social marketing

Hotel reuse programs that urge consumers to take voluntary action to contribute to environmental protection efforts are often regarded as a form of social marketing. Social marketing is the
use of commercial marketing concepts and tools to create voluntary behavioral change for the
benefit of individuals, society or the environment (Hall 2014). Although some hotels and firms
may exhibit altruistic motives for encouraging behavioral change as part of their social license
to operate, potential cost benefits (e.g. reducing laundry costs, improving brand relationships) are
often key drivers. The transparency of such actions may be important to customers. Shang et al.
(2010) found that reuse programs elicit a more positive behavioral intention from guests when
the subsequent cost savings resulting from reuse compliance are donated to charity. However,
Shang et al. (2010) also found that the social influence of stating the percentage of guests that
reused their towels and linen also had a positive effect on compliance, even in the absence of
hotels making charitable donations, while they also suggested that identifying the hotel as the
message source indicated to guests a more genuine commitment.

Settings also influence environmental behaviors. Although normative motives are the strongest predictor of pro-environmental behavior in a household setting, hedonic motives are the
dominant determinant in hotels (Miao & Wei 2013). Given the situational nature of environmental behavior and the underlying motivations, it is therefore important to adopt a tailored
approach to appeal to consumers in a hospitality setting. Miao and Wei (2013) therefore suggest
that hotels need to better align the benefits of green initiatives with consumers' hedonic motives
(i.e. direct pleasure, enjoyment and personal comfort).

Social norms: normative and injunctive messages

Appropriate message-based appeals can be effective in encouraging behavioral change. Several studies
(Cialdini & Goldstein 2002; Goldstein et al. 2007; Schultz et al. 2008; Reese et al. 2014; Dimara et al.
2017) show that green messages referring to social norms effectively encourage pro-environmental
compliance with towel reuse programs. Goldstein et al. (2007) found that message-based appeals
containing descriptive norms, to imply that guests often reuse their towels, are more effective than
injunctive norms (correct behavior), since people tend to take action under what is socially approved.
Several studies (e.g. Goldstein et al. 2008; Reese et al. 2014) also provide evidence that normative
appeals are most effective in eliciting pro-environmental behavior when supplemented by provincial
norms (i.e. when norms are related to the immediate situation) (Hall et al. 2016).

Morgan and Chompreeda (2015) evaluated the effectiveness of message-based appeals in
eliciting guest participation in the towel reuse program at a Thai resort. Approximately two-
thirds of guests reused their towels after exposure to one of four water conservation messages in
their room, while 25.5 percent complied without being prompted, which suggests that guests
with prior exposure to towel reuse messages have adopted this practice (Morgan & Chompreeda
2015). However, the study also found that injunctive messages were the most effective at encouraging participation in the towel reuse program with an 84.5 percent compliance rate, followed
by combined descriptive and injunctive messages (65.5%). The results of the relative impact
of social, injunctive and provincial norms on environmental behaviors suggest that greater

understanding is required of the context within which hospitality providers are situated and the nature of their market, especially with respect to the cultural context of norm-related behavior

Choice architecture and nudging

The notion of 'choice architecture' and 'nudging' assumes that the environment can be designed to influence consumer decisions (Thaler & Sunstein 2008), and has become increasingly influential in public and private behavioral interventions in tourism and hospitality (Hall 2013, 2014, 2016). Theotokis and Manganari (2015) studied the effectiveness of default policies, "the alternative the consumer receives if he/she does not explicitly request otherwise" (Brown & Krishna 2004: 530), in nudging guests to participate in a towel reuse program and found that an opt-out policy elicited higher compliance rates than an opt-in policy, though they also noted that anticipated guilt was the main explanatory variable for the policy's effectiveness. The role of guilt as a motivator for environmental protection in some countries and cultures is significant, given that environmental protection is a widely held moral standard (Peloza et al. 2013). However, critical to such guilt, and its value as a long-term tactic of behavioral change, is the notion that the effects of non-action are believable (Razzaq et al. 2016). Theotokis and Manganari (2015) also suggest that a forced choice policy, whereby consumers actively choose between alternatives with no default option provided (Keller et al. 2011), invokes a similarly high participation rate to the opt-out default policy. Default policies may be strengthened when properties are perceived to unconditionally support a cause where a reciprocal-based cooperation strategy, comprising an unconditional exchange where the company offers resources or performs certain behaviors (such as donating to a cause or protecting the environment), is undertaken (Theotokis & Manganari 2015). For example, Goldstein et al. (2011) found that an already made donation on behalf of guests encouraged consumer participation in green initiatives, through harnessing consumers' sense of social obligation under norms of reciprocity.

While choice architecture and nudging is useful to encourage behavioral change, it has been criticized as failing to recognise the embeddedness of consumption practices in socio-technical regimes (Hall 2013). Regimes are the recursively reproduced rules, institutions and structures which are used and changed by policy actors (Giddens 1984). The nature of regimes means that despite the best of intentions, consumers and producers are 'locked-in' to particular social practices of behaving, consuming and producing/supplying that are unsustainable (Unruh 2000). These issues are extremely significant for hospitality as they connect back to questions of exactly how sustainability in hospitality can actually be achieved, whether by focusing on efficiency or sustainable consumption strategies (Hall 2011b). Focusing on improving efficiency in isolation means not being aware of, for example, the nature of the energy source being used, i.e. a property may be reducing its energy consumption but if the energy is derived from coal-fired power stations how helpful is it? Furthermore, even if energy savings have been made, what are the associated energy and monetary savings being used for? If they are being used for further consumption, then real energy savings may actually be negligible. Therefore, becoming more sustainable in hospitality requires a deeper understanding of consumer behavior and the socio-technical system within which properties and firms are located.

Conclusions

This chapter has examined how sustainability practices in hospitality are connected to consumer behaviors and attitudes as well as the wider system within which they are located. The chapter commenced with an outline of some of the environmental issues facing the hospitality sector. These issues are magnified because in most jurisdictions and clearly at the global scale, accommodation and restaurant supply continues to grow. However, this growth poses a major challenge because the rate of growth is greater than any efficiency gains; hence, the absolute amount of resources the sector uses and the emissions it produces continues to grow. Therefore, in order to try to achieve more sustainable operations greater emphasis is being placed on understanding consumer behavior and practices.

The chapter has outlined some of the main emphases in sustainable behavior in the hospitality sector. Interest in marketing and communication has highlighted the significance of attitude–behavior gaps (Chan 2013; Juvan & Dolcinar 2014). Several possible reasons for the attitude–behavior gap were identified as well as barriers to purchasing stays at green hotels. Social marketing was noted as one potential path for influencing consumer behavior, while there has been considerable interest in the role of norms in influencing consumption and environmental behavior. Nevertheless, numerous gaps remain (Hall et al. 2016). First, there are clearly differences between markets and cultures with respect to the effectiveness of norm-based messaging. Second, research on hospitality sustainability is concentrated in certain countries as well as on particular accommodation types. Much more is known about high quality properties than lower quality ones. Given the role of international chains in higher quality properties and brands and the potential for innovation-diffusion, this may distort the realities of the sector's adoption of environment practices. A critical issue here is the lack of information on self-contained rental accommodation; given the rise of Airbnb and similar providers, the potential environmental impacts of such a private accommodation market is huge, Third, and ironically given the subject matter, the sustainability of pro-environmental behaviors over the longer term is unknown. Although there some suggestions can be made, we do not know if on-site behavioral change leads to fundamental sustained changes in practices – and why. Fourth, knowledge of hospitality sustainability practices outside of environmental behaviors, the significance of social justice, economic equity and gender, for example, is virtually unknown. Finally, much research on sustainability and the environment in hospitality is extremely narrowly focused and fails to address the socio-technical system within which hospitality and consumption practices are embedded. This is arguably the biggest challenge, as while many hospitality consumers and operators are environmentally aware they have not shown themselves to be capable of sustainable pro-environmental change.

Acknowledgments

The contributions of Natasha Dayal, Dea Majstorović, Hamish Mills, Leroy Paul-Andrews, Helena Power and Chloe Wallace to the literature analyses on which this review is partly based and their associated comments are gratefully noted.

References

Aall, C., Hall, C.M. and Groven, K. (2016) "Tourism: Applying rebound theories and mechanisms to climate change mitigation and adaptation," in T. Santarius, H.J. Walnum and C. Aall (eds) *Rethinking Climate and Energy Policies: New Perspectives on the Rebound Phenomenon*, Cham, Switzerland: Springer International Publishing, 209–26.

Ali, Y., Mashal, K., Mohsen, M. and Mustafa, M. (2014) "Energy and environmental performance: Exploratory indicators in the accommodation sector in Jordan," *International Journal of Applied Engineering Research* 9, 4467–80.

Aragon-Correa, J.A., Martin-Tapia, I. and de la Torre-Ruiz, J. (2015) "Sustainability issues and hospitality and tourism firms' strategies: Analytical review and future directions," *International Journal of Contemporary Hospitality Management* 27, 498–522.

Ayuso, S. (2007) "Comparing voluntary policy instruments for sustainable tourism: The experience of the Spanish hotel sector," *Journal of Sustainable Tourism* 15, 144–59.

Bohdanowicz, P. (2005) "European hoteliers' environmental attitudes: Greening the business," *Cornell Hotel and Restaurant Administration Quarterly* 46, 188–204.

Bramwell, B. and Lane, B. (2011) "Critical research on the governance of tourism and sustainability," *Journal of Sustainable Tourism* 19, 411–21.

Brown, C.L. and Krishna, A. (2004) "The skeptical shopper: A metacognitive account for the effects of default options on choice," *Journal of Consumer Research* 31, 529–39.

Chan, E. (2013) "Gap analysis of green hotel marketing," *International Journal of Contemporary Hospitality Management*, 25, 1017–48.

Chan, E.S. and Hawkins, R. (2010) "Attitude towards EMSs in an international hotel: An exploratory case study," *International Journal of Hospitality Management* 29, 641–51.

Chen, A. and Peng, N. (2012) "Green hotel knowledge and tourists' staying behavior," *Annals of Tourism Research* 39, 2211–6.

Chen, M. and Tung, P. (2014) "Developing an extended Theory of Planned Behaviour model to predict consumers' intention to visit green hotels," *International Journal of Hospitality Management* 36, 221–30.

Chen, R. (2015) "From sustainability to customer loyalty: A case of full service hotels' guests," *Journal of Retailing and Consumer Services* 22, 261–5.

Chou, C. (2014) "Hotels' environmental policies and employee personal environmental beliefs: Interactions and outcomes," *Tourism Management* 40, 436–46.

Cialdini, R.B. and Goldstein, N.J. (2002) "The science and practice of persuasion," *Cornell Hospitality Quarterly* 43(2), 40–50.

Cohen, S.A., Higham, J., Gössling, S. and Peeters, P. (eds) (2014) *Understanding and Governing Sustainable Tourism Mobility: Psychological and Behavioural Approaches.* Abingdon: Routledge.

Coles, T., Zchiegner, A. and Dinan, C. (2014) "A cluster analysis of climate change mitigation behaviours among SMTEs," *Tourism Geographies* 16, 382–99.

Cummins, S., Reilly, T.M., Carlson, L., Grove, S.J. and Dorsch, M.J. (2014) "Investigating the portrayal and influence of sustainability claims in an environmental advertising context," *Journal of Macromarketing* 34, 332–48.

Dimara, E., Manganari, E. and Skuras, D. (2017) "Don't change my towels please: Factors influencing participation in towel reuse programs," *Tourism Management* 59, 425–37.

do Paço, A., Alves, H. and Nunes, C. (2012) "Ecotourism from both hotels and tourists' perspective," *Economics and Sociology* 5, 132–42.

Dodds, R. and Holmes, M.R. (2011) "Sustainability in Canadian B&Bs: Comparing the east versus west," *International Journal of Tourism Research* 13, 482–95.

D'Souza, C., Taghian, M., Sullivan-Mort, G. and Gilmore, A. (2015) "An evaluation of the role of green marketing and a firm's internal practices for environmental sustainability," *Journal of Strategic Marketing* 23, 600–15.

Firth, T. and Hing, N. (1999) "Backpacker hostels and their guests: Attitudes and behaviours relating to sustainable tourism," *Tourism Management* 20, 251–54.

Fotiadis, A.K., Vassiliadis, C.A. and Rekleitis, P.D. (2013) "Constraints and benefits of sustainable development: A case study based on the perceptions of small-hotel entrepreneurs in Greece," *Anatolia* 24, 144–61.

Giddens, A. (1984) *The Constitution of Society: Outline of the Theory of Structuration,* Berkeley: University of California Press.

Goldstein, N., Cialdini, R. and Griskevicius, V. (2008) "A room with a viewpoint: Using social norms to motivate environmental conservation in hotels," *Journal of Consumer Research* 35, 472–82.

Goldstein, N.J., Griskevicius, V. and Cialdini, R.B. (2007) "Invoking social norms: A social psychology perspective on improving hotels' linen-reuse programs," *Cornell Hotel and Restaurant Administration Quarterly* 48(2), 145–50.

Goldstein, N.J., Griskevicius, V. and Cialdini, R.B. (2011) "Reciprocity by proxy: A novel influence strategy for stimulating cooperation," *Administrative Science Quarterly* 56, 441–73.

Gössling, S. and Hall, C.M. (2013) "Sustainable culinary systems: An introduction," in C.M. Hall and S. Gössling (eds) *Sustainable Culinary Systems: Local Foods, Innovation, and Tourism & Hospitality,* Abingdon: Routledge, 3–44.

Gössling, S. and Hall, C.M. (2016) "Developing regional food systems: A case study of restaurant–customer relationships in Sweden," in C.M. Hall and S. Gössling (eds) *Food Tourism and Regional Development: Networks, Products and Trajectories*, Abingdon: Routledge, 76–89.

Gössling, S., Hall, C.M. and Scott, D. (2015) *Tourism and Water*, Bristol: Channel View.

Gössling, S., Scott, D., Hall, C.M., Ceron, J-P. and Dubois, G. (2012) "Consumer behaviour and demand response of tourists to climate change," *Annals of Tourism Research* 39, 36–58.

Gunningham, N., Kagan, R.A. and Thornton, D. (2004) "Social license and environmental protection: Why businesses go beyond compliance," *Law & Social Inquiry* 29, 307–41.

Hall, C.M. (2010a) "Blending coffee and Fair Trade hospitality," in L. Joliffe (ed) *Coffee Culture, Destinations and Tourism*, Bristol: Channel View, 159–71.

Hall, C.M. (2010b) "Changing paradigms and global change: From sustainable to steady-state tourism," *Tourism Recreation Research* 35, 131–45.

Hall, C.M. (2011a) "A typology of governance and its implications for tourism policy analysis," *Journal of Sustainable Tourism* 19, 437–57.

Hall, C.M. (2011b) "Policy learning and policy failure in sustainable tourism governance: From first and second to third order change?," *Journal of Sustainable Tourism* 19, 649–71.

Hall, C.M. (2013) "Framing behavioural approaches to understanding and governing sustainable tourism consumption: Beyond neoliberalism, 'nudging' and 'green growth'?," *Journal of Sustainable Tourism* 21, 1091–109.

Hall, C.M. (2014) *Tourism and Social Marketing*, Abingdon: Routledge.

Hall, C.M. (2015) "Economic greenwash: On the absurdity of tourism and green growth," in V. Reddy and K. Wilkes (eds) *Tourism in the Green Economy*, London: Earthscan, 339–58.

Hall, C.M. (2016) "Intervening in academic interventions: Framing social marketing's potential for successful sustainable tourism behavioural change," *Journal of Sustainable Tourism* 24, 350–75.

Hall, C.M. and Gössling, S. (eds) (2013) *Sustainable Culinary Systems: Local Foods, Innovation, and Tourism & Hospitality*, Abingdon: Routledge.

Hall, C.M., Dayal, N., Majstorović, D., Mills, H., Paul-Andrews, L., Wallace, C. and Truong, V.D. (2016) "Accommodation consumers and providers' attitudes, behaviours and practices for sustainability: A systematic review," *Sustainability* 8, 625

Han, H. and Kim, Y. (2010) "An investigation of green hotel customers' decision formation: Developing an extended model of the theory of planned behavior," *International Journal of Hospitality Management* 29, 659–68.

Han, H. and Yoon, H. (2015) "Hotel customers' environmentally responsible behavioural intention: Impact of key constructs on decisions in green consumerism," *International Journal of Hospitality Management* 45, 22–33.

Han, H., Hsu, L.T.J. and Sheu, C. (2010) "Application of the theory of planned behavior to green hotel choice: Testing the effect of environmental friendly activities," *Tourism Management* 31, 325–34.

Han, H., Hsu, L.T.J., Lee, J.S. and Sheu, C. (2011) "Are lodging customers ready to go green? An examination of attitudes, demographics, and eco-friendly intentions," *International Journal of Hospitality Management* 30, 345–55.

Hsieh, Y.C. (2012) "Hotel companies' environmental policies and practices: A content analysis of their web pages," *International Journal of Contemporary Hospitality Management* 24, 97–121.

Juvan, E. and Dolcinar, S. (2014) "The attitude-behaviour gap in sustainable tourism," *Annals of Tourism Research* 48, 76–95.

Kasim, A. (2007) "Corporate environmentalism in the hotel sector: Evidence of drivers and barriers in Penang, Malaysia," *Journal of Sustainable Tourism* 15, 680–99.

Kasim, A., Gursoy, D., Okumus, F. and Wong, A. (2014) "The importance of water management in hotels: A framework for sustainability through innovation," *Journal of Sustainable Tourism* 22, 1090–107.

Keller, P.A., Harlam, B., Loewenstein, G. and Volpp, K.G. (2011) "Enhanced active choice: A new method to motivate behavior change," *Journal of Consumer Psychology*, 21, 376–83.

Lee, J., Hsu, L., Han, H. and Kim, Y. (2010) "Understanding how consumers view green hotels: How a hotel's green image can influence behavioural intentions," *Journal of Sustainable Tourism* 18, 901–14.

Leonidou, C.N., Katsikeas, C.S. and Morgan, N.A. (2013a) "'Greening' the marketing mix: Do firms do it and does it pay off?," *Journal of the Academy of Marketing Science* 41, 151–70.

Leonidou, L.C., Leonidou, C.N., Fotiadis, T.A. and Zeriti, A. (2013b) "Resources and capabilities as drivers of hotel environmental marketing strategy: Implications for competitive advantage and performance," *Tourism Management* 35, 94–110.

Luchs, M.G., Naylor, R.W., Irwin, J.R. and Raghunathan, R. (2010) "The sustainability liability: Potential negative effects of ethicality on product preference," *Journal of Marketing* 74(5), 18–31.

Mair, J. and Laing, J.H. (2013) "Encouraging pro-environmental behaviour: The role of sustainability-focused events," *Journal of Sustainable Tourism* 21, 1113–28.

Manganari, E.E., Dimara, E. and Theotokis, A. (2016) "Greening the lodging industry: Current status, trends and perspectives for green value," *Current Issues in Tourism*, 19, 223–42.

McDonald, S. and Oates, C.J. (2006) "Sustainability: Consumer perceptions and marketing strategies," *Business Strategy and the Environment* 15(3), 157–70.

Miao, L. and Wei, W. (2013) "Consumers' pro-environmental behaviour and the underlying motivations: A comparison between household and hotel settings," *International Journal of Hospitality Management* 32, 102–12.

Millar, M. and Baloglu, S. (2011) "Hotel guests' preferences for green guest room attributes," *Cornell Hospitality Quarterly* 52, 302–11.

Morgan, M. and Chompreeda, K. (2015) "The relative effect of message-based appeals to promote water conservation at a tourist resort in the Gulf of Thailand," *Environmental Communication* 9, 20–36.

New Zealand Sustainable Business Council (SBC) (2013) *What is a Social Licence to Operate?* Auckland: New Zealand Sustainable Business Council.

Nicholls, S. and Kang, S. (2012) "Going green: The adoption of environmental initiatives in Michigan's lodging sector," *Journal of Sustainable Tourism* 20, 953–74.

Parsons, R. and Moffat, K. (2014) "Constructing the meaning of social licence," *Social Epistemology*, 28, 340–63.

Peloza, J., White, K. and Shang, J. (2013) "Good and guilt-free: The role of self-accountability in influencing preferences for products with ethical attributes," *Journal of Marketing* 77, 104–19.

Razzaq, S., Hall, C.M. and Prayag, G. (2016) "The capacity of New Zealand to accommodate the halal tourism market—or not," *Tourism Management Perspectives* 18, 92–97.

Reese, G., Loew, K. and Steffgen, G. (2014) "A towel less: Social norms enhance pro-environmental behavior in hotels," *Journal of Social Psychology* 154, 97–100.

Roy, H., Hall, C.M. and Ballantine, P. (2016) "Barriers and constraints in the use of local foods in the hospitality sector," in C.M. Hall and S. Gössling (eds) *Food Tourism and Regional Development: Networks, Products and Trajectories*, Abingdon: Routledge, 255–73.

Rutty, M., Gössling, S., Scott, D. and Hall, C.M. (2015) "The global effects and impacts of tourism: An overview," in C.M. Hall, S. Gössling and D. Scott (eds) *The Routledge Handbook of Tourism and Sustainability*, Abingdon: Routledge, 36–63.

Schultz, P.W., Khazian, A.M. and Zaleski, A.C. (2008) "Using normative social influence to promote conservation among hotel guests," *Social Influence* 3, 4–23.

Scott, D., Hall, C.M. and Gössling, S. (2016a) "A review of the IPCC 5th Assessment and implications for tourism sector climate resilience and decarbonization," *Journal of Sustainable Tourism*, 24, 8–30.

Scott, D., Hall, C.M. and Gössling, S. (2016b) "The Paris Climate Change Agreement and its implications for tourism: Why we will always have Paris," *Journal of Sustainable Tourism*, 24, 933–48.

Scott, D., Gössling, S., Hall, C.M. and Peeters, P. (2016c) "Can tourism be part of the decarbonized global economy?: The costs and risks of carbon reduction pathways," *Journal of Sustainable Tourism* 24, 52–72.

Searcy, C. (2012) "Corporate sustainability performance measurement systems: A review and research agenda," *Journal of Business Ethics* 107, 239–53.

Shang, J., Basil, D.Z. and Wymer, W. (2010) "Using social marketing to enhance hotel reuse programs," *Journal of Business Research* 63(2), 166–72.

Su, Y.P., Hall, C.M. and Ozanne, L. (2013) "Hospitality industry responses to climate change: A benchmark study of Taiwanese tourist hotels," *Asia Pacific Journal of Tourism Research* 18, 92–107.

Susskind, A. and Verma, R. (2011) "Hotel guests' reactions to guest room sustainability initiatives," *Cornell Hospitality Report* 11(6), 4–13.

Tarí, J.J., Claver-Cortés, E., Pereira-Moliner, J. and Molina-Azorín, J.F. (2010) "Levels of quality and environmental management in the hotel industry: Their joint influence on firm performance," *International Journal of Hospitality Management* 29, 500–10.

Teng, C.C., Horng, J.S., Hu, M.L.M. and Chen, P.C. (2014) "Exploring the energy and carbon literacy structure for hospitality and tourism practitioners: Evidence from hotel employees in Taiwan," *Asia Pacific Journal of Tourism Research* 19, 451–68.

Thaler, H.R. and Sunstein, C.R. (2008) *Nudge: Improving Decisions About Health, Wealth, and Happiness*, New Haven: Yale University Press.

Theotokis, A. and Manganari, E. (2015) "The impact of choice architecture on sustainable consumer behavior: The role of guilt," *Journal of Business Ethics* 131, 423–37.

Tilikidou, I., Delistavrou, A. and Sapountzis, N. (2013) "Customers' ethical behaviour towards hotels," *Procedia Econoomics and Finance* 9, 425–32.

Tortella, B.D. and Tirado, D. (2011) "Hotel water consumption at a seasonal mass tourist destination: The case of the island of Mallorca," *Journal of Environmental Management* 92, 2568–79.

Tzschentke, N., Kirk, D. and Lynch, P. (2004) "Reasons for going green in serviced accomodation establishments," *International Journal of Contemporary Hospitality Management* 16, 116–24.

Tzschentke, N., Kirk, D. and Lynch, P. (2008) "Going green: Decisional factors in small hospitality operations," *International Journal of Hospitality Management*, 27, 126–33.

United Nations World Tourism Organization and United Nations Environment Programme (UNWTO & UNEP) (2008) *Climate Change and Tourism: Responding to Global Challenges*, Madrid: UNWTO & UNEP.

Unruh, G.C. (2000) "Understanding carbon lock-in," *Energy Policy* 28, 817–30.

Wearing, S., Cynn, J., Ponting, J. and McDonald, M. (2002) "Converting environmental concern into ecotourism purchases: A qualitative evaluation of international backpackers in Australia," *Journal of Ecotourism* 1, 133–48.

Wehrli, R., Priskin, J., Demarmels, S., Schaffner, D., Schwarz, J., Truniger, F. and Stettler, J. (2014). "How to communicate sustainable tourism products to customers: Results from a choice experiment," *Current Issues in Tourism*, doi:10.1080/13683500.2014.987732.

Weldegiorgis, F.S. and Franks, D.M. (2014) "Social dimensions of energy supply alternatives in steelmaking: Comparison of biomass and coal production scenarios in Australia," *Journal of Cleaner Production* 84, 281–88.

World Economic Forum (WEF) (2009) *Towards a Low Carbon Travel & Tourism Sector*, Gland, Switzerland: WEF.

Zografakis, N., Gillas, K., Pollaki, A., Profylienou, M., Bounialetou, F. and Tsagarakis, K.P. (2011) "Assessment of practices and technologies of energy saving and renewable energy sources in hotels in Crete," *Renewable Energy* 36, 1323–28.

Further reading

Dimara, E., Manganari, E. and Skuras, D. (2017) "Don't change my towels please: Factors influencing participation in towel reuse programs," *Tourism Management* 59, 425–37. (Meta-analysis of towel resuse programs.)

Gössling, S. and Hall, C.M. (2013) "Sustainable culinary systems: An introduction," in C.M. Hall and S. Gössling (eds) *Sustainable Culinary Systems: Local Foods, Innovation, and Tourism & Hospitality*, Abingdon: Routledge, 3–44. (Details the environmental impacts of culinary systems.)

Hall, C.M. (2014) *Tourism and Social Marketing*, Abingdon: Routledge. (Outlines behavioural interventions from a social marketing perspective.)

Hall, C.M., Dayal, N., Majstorović, D., Mills, H., Paul-Andrews, L., Wallace, C. and Truong, V.D. (2016) "Accommodation consumers and providers' attitudes, behaviours and practices for sustainability: A systematic review," *Sustainability* 8, 625 (Systematic review of journal literature.)

Manganari, E.E., Dimara, E. and Theotokis, A. (2016) "Greening the lodging industry: Current status, trends and perspectives for green value," *Current Issues in Tourism*, 19, 223–42. (Review of green lodging.)

Rutty, M., Gössling, S., Scott, D. and Hall, C.M. (2015) "The global effects and impacts of tourism: An overview," in C.M. Hall, S. Gössling and D. Scott (eds) *The Routledge Handbook of Tourism and Sustainability*, Abingdon: Routledge, 36–63. (Comprehensive assessment of impacts; other chapters in the book discuss various facets of sustainability in tourism and hospitality.)

31

Promoting sustainability initiatives in the hospitality industry

Bidisha Burman and Pia A. Albinsson

Introduction

The idea of sustainability is growing by leaps and bounds in corporations across various industries. It is indicative of the growing awareness of mankind towards the environmental, economic, and social consequences of human and business activities (Grosbois 2012). Companies are facing increased public expectations and demand for implementation of sustainability efforts in their business operations. Initially, the hospitality industry (e.g., hotels, airlines, casinos, restaurants, and cruise lines among others) faced less attention compared to other more evidently polluting business sectors such as mining and manufacturing. However, there is growing concern about the negative impact of the tourism industry. The hotel industry is one of the most energy- and water-intensive industries since its goal is to maximize customer comfort (Han et al. 2010). It is believed that hotels have caused enormous harm to the environment by generating tremendous amounts of waste, emitting pollutants in the air, water, and soil; consuming huge amounts of energy and water; and using vast quantities of non-recyclable products, among others (Bohdanowicz 2005, Chan 2005, Kim & Han 2010). The hospitality industry is one of the world's fastest growing industries and with growing concern from the public and consumers, an increasing number of hospitality companies are engaging in sustainability-related efforts (Grosbois 2012). Further, Grosbois (2012) notes an increased effort on the part of hotels to communicate their sustainability-related activities to the public.

Recent research suggests that sustainability practices are becoming increasingly vital and almost a necessity to a hotel's competitiveness (Berezan et al. 2013, Kim & Han 2010, Tierney et al. 2011) due to an increase in guest expectations of environmental attributes of hotels (Robinot & Giannelloni 2010). Interestingly, some sustainability practices are now considered basic in some countries and are no longer considered innovative (Berezan et al. 2013). Tourists are becoming more aware of significant sustainability practices and are increasingly becoming interested in learning about company efforts to reduce their environmental impact (Grosbois 2012). Some customers are even making green practices a criterion when choosing resorts (Tierney et al. 2011). Their demands for green establishments have been increasing and customers are looking for more eco-friendly practices in hotels

(Foster et al. 2000, Han et al. 2010, Manaktola & Jouhari 2007). However, even though there are increased efforts to communicate sustainability efforts to customers, not enough is being done. As the two short case studies in this chapter will illustrate, not all environmental practices are promoted or communicated clearly to the end-user. The chapter also illustrates that third-party booking sites such as istaygreen.com can be useful as they assist environmentally conscious consumers in their selection of green hotels by offering various "green ratings" of hotels.

Corporate social responsibility and sustainability

Based on the corporate social responsibility (CSR) literature, there are two ways to go about sustainable activities – to enhance positive sustainability activities or to reduce negative sustainability activities (Kang et al. 2010). While CSR broadly refers to companies' contribution to social welfare beyond self-interest as well as economic, legal, and ethical aspects of company operations (Kang et al. 2010, Schwartz & Carroll 2003), sustainability refers to going above and beyond. The idea of sustainability has three pillars – economic, environmental, and social action (Grosbois 2012). Some authors have labeled sustainability primarily as "green" and "eco-friendly" actions that reduce harm done to the planet (e.g. recycling) (Kim & Han 2010, Wolfe & Shanklin 2001). Green hotels can be described as environmentally responsible hotels that follow eco-friendly guidelines, practice environmental management, and implement green programs and practices. Some strive to improve their efforts by acquiring various certifications and displaying eco-labels such as Department of Environmental Protection, Green Hotels Association (GHA), International Hotels Environmental Initiative/International Tourism Partnership, and Leadership in Energy and Environmental Design (Kim & Han 2010, Berezan et al. 2013). Today, we see the terms CSR/Sustainability/Green used almost interchangeably. For example, the Hilton Worldwide webpage has a dedicated section named "corporate responsibility/sustainability" (Hilton Worldwide 2016).

Importance of sustainability in hospitality

Although it may seem that CSR and/or sustainability activities may bring any industry financial benefits, research has shown mixed results in the hospitality industry. Johnson (2003) found that while socially irresponsible activities hurt financial performance, positive CSR did not bring financial advantage. Lee and Park (2009) found a positive relationship between CSR and hotels but none for casinos. Kang et al. (2010) found that CSR helps in increasing firm value for hotels and restaurants by increasing socially responsible activities and increased firm value for airlines by reducing irresponsible activities. They found no such relationship for casinos.

Further, CSR activities enhance the brand image of hotels, which in turn leads to better financial performance, and the opposite may occur if a hotel practices environmentally unsound activities (Kang et al. 2010). Therefore, CSR/sustainability activities contribute to improved stakeholder relationships. Green practices also favorably impact intention to revisit (Lee et al. 2013, Berezan et al. 2013). They affect the overall hotel image, improving visit intention, word-of-mouth, and willingness to pay more (Han et al. 2010, Lita et al. 2014).

Being green directly affects the bottom line – resulting in the higher long-term value of property, repeat customers, lower energy bills, lower water bills, reduction in waste hauling (vendors are asked to reduce packaging materials and to pick up packaging materials the next day), positive media and public attention, and most of all, happier, healthier guests, staff, and management (Green Hotels Association 2016).

Bidisha Burman and Pia A. Albinsson

Challenges and the role of the green consumer

Increased customer awareness is making sustainability practices a criterion for hotel choices (Kim & Han 2010, Tzschentkea et al. 2008). Customers increasingly feel the need to contribute to environmentally friendly activities by choosing green practices over non-green alternatives. Offering them green choices and encouraging environmentally conscious behaviour is likely to lead to customer loyalty. Evanschitzky et al. (2006) suggest that emotional bonds with customers lead to stronger customer loyalty as compared to economic incentives. Chan and Han (2014), found that hotel advertisements with perceived high impact environmental practices (e.g. global environmental concern rather than a local one) triggered a more favorable effect, especially from consumers with stronger concern for the environment.

However, sustainability practices in the hospitality industry are not easy to achieve. Unlike manufacturing industries, it is not an industry that is at the forefront of causing harm but is at the forefront of reducing harm through measures such as reducing unnecessary material and energy consumption and reducing pollution. Since hospitality organizations focus on providing the best consumer experience, abundance of supply is difficult to avoid – for example, food, towels, water supply (high-pressure shower heads, swimming pool, saunas and hot tubs etc.). Restricting these may hurt the perceived quality of service (Rahman et al. 2012).

Inconveniences to hotel customers choosing a green hotel may include "towel reuse, limited use of disposal products, use of recycled products/furniture, recycling bins, buffet-style foods without garnishes, meeting tables without tablecloths, minimized decor, non-smoking areas, dispensers for soap/shampoo, etc." (Kim & Han 2010: 1012). While customers are willing to accept minor inconveniences due to green initiatives, Berezan et al. (2013) found green practices such as low-flow shower heads, inconvenient recycling may have a negative impact even on those who are willing to stay in green hotels, and therefore suggest that such decisions for a hotel should be informed decisions based on what customers want.

On the bright side, more people are becoming aware of environmental issues, and are engaging in environmentally friendly activities by recycling and making environmentally conscious purchase decisions. In the process, they are aware that by embracing sustainability efforts, there are personal inconveniences in everyday life, such as accepting lower performance in eco-friendly products, and even paying extra to buy green products (Han et al. 2010, Manaktola & Jauhari 2007).

However, customer willingness to pay more despite environmental consciousness varies across countries, demographic characteristics, hotel types, and so on. (Lita et al. 2014). Dodds et al. (2010) found that a willingness to pay more for environmental reasons came from younger tourists, those with higher levels of income, and those from English-speaking countries. Not only does the willingness depend on the individual's perception of the effectiveness of the initiatives in reducing environmental impact, it also depends on whether the customer performs environmentally friendly activities in his or her day-to-day life such as recycling, saving energy, and reducing waste. (Kim & Han 2010).

Green consumers make green decisions if they are aware of the favorable outcomes and the benefits of their green behavior. Kim and Han (2010) strongly suggest that hotel marketers should actively inform past and future customers of the positive outcomes of green actions such as eating healthily, living in a clean environment, and implementing social responsibility in day-to-day life. Based on the findings of their study, they state that one of the foremost promotional tasks for green hotel marketers is to continuously inform their current and potential customers about overutilization of limited resources and pollution, and to constantly show the positive changes resulting from individuals' green actions through persuasive communication

374

channels, emphasizing the ability of the individual customer to reduce environmental degradation. Overall, we find that not just undertaking green initiatives, but promoting these initiatives to current and potential customers is a vital part of the marketing strategy of sustainable hotels.

Transparency and communication

Consumer support for green initiatives will further grow with transparency, better information, and more trustworthy information from providers (Tierney et al. 2011). A study showed that out of 267 respondents, 37.6 percent agreed that they specifically sought green service providers when they made their travel plans. Conversely, 45.6 percent of the respondents agreed that lack of knowledge about which travel/tourism companies have eco-friendly practices is a major factor holding them back from supporting these companies. Further, 33.7 percent were not familiar with green practices in the travel industry (Tierney et al. 2011).

The above findings are strong indicators of the need for better strategies in informing the public about green practices in the hospitality industry. Companies should strengthen their communications strategies, with a greater focus on increasing awareness about the importance of sustainable practices, the efforts undertaken thereof, and also, the impact and outcomes of such efforts. Accomplishing sustainability is not possible by one company alone; it needs its customers' support all the way. Additionally, it is also important that a company makes sure that its sustainability efforts are viewed as credible. Skepticism and lack of trust can significantly hinder consumers from supporting eco-friendly travel companies and their sustainability efforts. Tierney et al. (2011) found that nearly one-third of their respondents (29.6 percent) believe that most green practices are just for the purpose of public relations and have no real substance. In reality, it is very difficult for consumers to verify the authenticity of hotels' green claims. Often hotels make such claims without legitimate qualification. This again calls for better promotion tactics involving an assurance of meeting some national/international standards and approved by credible third-party organizations that offer a valid green label to signal the authenticity of green claims. Organizations such as GHA and LEED provide certifications which lend legitimacy to green claims made by hotels (Rahman et al. 2012).

Some hotels have adopted self-regulatory initiatives such as environmental management systems (EMS) to develop a systematic approach to improve environmental performance. Some of the claimed benefits of EMS are cost savings, improvement of corporate image, and operational efficiency. (Chan 2008, Peattie and Peattie 1995, Taylor 1992, Welford 1998). Others have established green performance systems that provide transparency on the real positive outcomes of their sustainability efforts. However, it is sufficient and effective communication of such vital information regarding hotels' sustainable practices that may bring about more consumer awareness, acceptance, and participation in such efforts in the hospitality industry.

Han et al. (2010) emphasize that eco-friendly practices should be communicated to current and potential customers through advertising, videos, and green labeling, so that consumers make better and more informed decisions. They suggest that marketers of green hotels should promote green campaigns and work on building favorable attitudes towards green consumption in the long run. The authors further suggest that hotels must educate customers about green hotels being a healthier choice as a result of natural, organic, and non-chemical base amenities, as a customer attraction strategy (Han et al. 2010). Further, hotel marketers should realize that environmental advertising alone is not sufficient; instead, a comprehensive marketing communications program is required to effectively communicate environmental initiatives and to build a distinctive brand image (Chan & Han 2014).

The Green Hotels Association (GHA), a US-based organization with worldwide membership, mentions that one of their goals is to keep clients informed through webpages on what the hotel has to offer regarding greening; therefore, in the cases of weddings, conventions, and business meetings, guests can implement these green activities pre and post event. GHA exists with the purpose of bringing together hotels interested in environmental issues. The idea is to save energy, save water, "to help protect our one and only earth," and at the same time save money (Green Hotels Association 2016). Being a member of this association has numerous benefits, including not only receiving ideas and guidelines to reduce impact on the destination, but also heavy media attention which is undoubtedly important to spread information to the public. In addition, hotels earn visibility via the GHA website as well as open identification as a green hotel via front desk and outdoor flags. GHA sends out press releases and specifically emphasizes promoting green hotels through media attention.

"Media attention has always been almost ecstatic, which brings special attention to all of our members" (Green Hotels Association 2016). GHA suggests developing an environmental webpage to let clients know about green activities and green offers at the hotel, with additional environmental sections addressing separate client segments (weddings, reunions, business meetings, conventions, etc.), and at least one press release to be distributed each year to all media contacts within 300 miles of the property regarding members' green achievements and plans (Green Hotels Association 2016).

As some of today's consumers expect hotels to be green, failure to communicate efforts effectively may result in losing potential customers (Butler 2008, Rahman et al. 2012). Such initiatives come to public view via the voluntary corporate communication of CSR. There are no globally accepted international standards and/or regulations on CSR disclosure and most of the corporate social reporting in the United States and EU have been voluntary (Grosbois 2012). In the last ten years, CSR communication activities have grown considerably due to the realization of the benefits of CSR reporting (better image, customer satisfaction) but beyond sustainability or CSR reporting, prior research shows that companies also include advertising campaigns on television, press releases, and the Internet (Grosbois 2012).

Grosbois (2012) examined not only different methods of informing the public (CSR reports, press releases, newsletters/magazines/blogs) but also the amount of information and the different sections of the webpage itself used to provide CSR information (webpage devoted to CSR, 'about us' section, career section, press room etc.). The author examined 150 global hotels and found that 31 percent had no CSR-related information, 26 percent used one communication method, and only 2 percent used all of the above methods. The author agrees that it is difficult to distinguish between companies with a genuine sustainability commitment and those that exaggerate their commitment for competitive reasons. In addition to third-party verification, the author also suggests the implementation of common reporting standards of CSR performance in the hospitality industry to allow comparisons to be made between hotels.

According to Dinan and Sargeant (2000), social marketing is appropriate for communicating corporate sustainable practices to directly influence target audience behaviour, since in the past, social marketing has impacted broader social issues including health, drunk driving, and alcohol. On the other hand, there are creative ways to build consumer awareness with little things that may have the simplest solutions, but with a big impact. For example, thousands of slightly used soap bars are discarded every day. The simplest solution that had been overlooked was suggested by GHA, which was to encourage guests to take them home with the words "Take Me Home and Use Me" printed on the wrapper and imprinted on the soap. These are examples of not only devotion to the cause but also a good way of generating positive word of mouth as well as educating the public.

Overall, there is very large support for sustainability efforts but many more will patronize such providers that give better and more trustworthy information of what are and who undertakes green practices (Tierney et al. 2011). Previous literature has shown an attempt to classify sustainability initiatives and to provide effective communication method recommendations (Table 31.1). However, recommendations also focus on standardization of methodologies and the production of an agreed-upon set of measures to enable greater clarity of sustainability reporting (Grosbois 2012).

Table 31.1 Communicating sustainability efforts

Hotels' green initiatives classified/category	Communication recommendations
Environment Employment quality Diversity and accessibility Society/community wellbeing Economic prosperity (Grosbois 2012)	Annual CSR report Website sections on CSR, About Us Career section on website Press releases Newsletters/magazines/blogs for employees and customers Social Marketing *Note:* Report environmental awards
Reduce hotel's impact on destination Save money (Green Hotels Association 2016)	Media Webpage Green newsletter Press release Public identification as a green hotel (pole, front desk flags)
Reducing environmental damages (emission) Reducing wasting/harming of environmental resources (excessive consumption) Donation (Han et al. 2010)	Use of various media Advertise Eco/green labeling Use of videos
Recycling/re-use/reduce Purchasing local produce Implementing rigorous LEED certification Standards (Berezan et al. 2013)	Educating guests, emphasizing green policies Word of mouth
Satisfying eco-friendly customers' green needs Fulfils the requirements of government regulations Substantially decreases costs through waste reduction Water/ energy conservation Recycling (Kim & Han 2010)	Use of persuasive communication channels
Local society Local resources Local economy (Dinan & Sargeant, 2000)	Social marketing
Energy saving Absence of single-use consumables (Chan et al. 2014)	A comprehensive marketing communications program

Note: Emphasize high-impact practices such as global environmental issues more than local environmental issues.

Green performance measurability

The sustainability concept in the hospitality industry can be a tricky one to implement since hotels may be highly involved with green efforts but at the same time may be encouraging conspicuous consumption, or focusing on continuing growth with heavy demands on natural resources (Jones et al. 2016). There are numerous ways to be green and to claim that the corporation is environmentally friendly and socially responsible. The focus, therefore, should be on the measurability of green performance. In our research, we found that hotels are indeed taking some steps to show their sustainability commitment by adopting measurement platforms and making such information available to the public via their corporate websites. For example, Hilton Worldwide has received the Environment Leader's 2016 Product of the Year Award for its state-of-the-art proprietary corporate responsibility performance measurement platform, LightStay. LightStay allows each of Hilton's 4,660 hotels in over 104 countries to track and measure their environmental and social impact and encourages continued positive change (Hilton Worldwide 2016). Intercontinental Hotel Group has designed the IHG Green Engage System, which is a measurement platform for their environmental impact. All IHG hotels use the IHG Green Engage system, which is an online environmental sustainability system that allow hotels to measure and manage their impact on the environment. The hotels can choose from over 200 'Green Solutions' that are designed to help reduce energy, water, waste, and decrease negative environmental impact (Intercontinental Hotel Group 2016). Wyndham Worldwide has developed the Wyndham Green Toolbox, which is a system that allows both owned and managed properties, as well as independently owned and operated franchises, to track, measure, and report on global assets in which Wyndham Worldwide has direct operational control (Wyndham Worldwide 2016). Marriott's annual environmental performance report is disclosed on their website and clearly states their goals and global performance (Marriott 2016). Their reporting is through the Green Hotels Global tool, about which not much information is available unless one is a member hotel or hotel group/convention booker (Green Hotels Global 2016).

Next we present two case studies of two hotels that handle the promotion of their environmental and sustainability initiatives very differently: the Orchard Garden Hotel in San Francisco, United States, and Hilton Stockholm Slussen in Stockholm, Sweden.

Case studies

Case study 1: Promoting a San Francisco hotelier's green efforts

"Our company's future and the future of our environment are interconnected."

This quote by Stefan Muhle, General Manager and Regional Director at Portfolio Hotels & Resorts, sums up the dedication and mindset of the Orchard Garden Hotel in San Francisco, a hotel that has received the official GS 33 (Silver) certification by Green Seal, a nonprofit, independent sustainability organization, and has been certified as a San Francisco Green Business by the City of San Francisco (I Stay Green 2016).

According to istaygreen, a hotel booking site that promotes green hotels, the Orchard Garden Hotel has completed an istaygreen audit of over 70 eco-initiatives (I Stay Green 2016). The hotel, which is a member of the Green Hotels Association, has confirmed over 48 eco-initiatives in its audit, and has therefore received the 5 Green Eco-leaf rating from this third-party booking site (I Stay Green 2016). Currently, although there are about 40 "green" hotels listed in the San Francisco area, only 17 have completed the eco-audit with istaygreen.org.

The Orchard Garden Hotel is a boutique hotel that was built in 2006. It was the second hotel in California to be LEED certified (the fourth in the United States) by the US Green Building Council. The hotel encourages its guests to recycle, reduce their energy use with its key card energy management system, and to use alternative transportation by providing commuter checks to employees and bike racks for everyone. In their restaurant, they source local and organic foods and they convert their frying oil into bio-fuel. They also compost all food scraps. Their housekeeping uses citrus-based cleaning agents that are safe for both people and the environment. Rooms offer environmentally friendly bath products in dispensers for their guests. Potential guests are introduced to the Orchard Garden Hotel's environmental efforts in the short introduction to the hotel on their webpage. Certifications and eco-labels are clearly visible on the lower right-hand corner of the webpage under "Green Initiatives." Under the green initiatives tab, which is listed both in a navigation table at the top left, and the lower right-hand corner on the webpage, current and potential guests can read about further actions and efforts by the hotel. (The Orchard Garden Hotel 2016). The hotel provides information and resources at the front desk to inform guests of its efforts. The hotel trains its staff and encourages feedback and questions from its guests. To promote customer feedback, both positive and negative, it plants a tree for every customer review on TripAdvisor through The Nature Conservancy's Plant a Billion Trees project (The Orchard Garden Hotel 2016).

Case study 2: Buzzing bees at Hilton Stockholm Slussen

The second author was introduced to Hilton Stockholm Slussen's green efforts when she stayed there as a guest in 2014. She was impressed with their sustainability initiatives when she read their environmental statement, which was placed on the desk in her room. However, she found out that it was much more difficult to find out about their environmental efforts online. The only information that is available on the Hilton Stockholm website is an eco-label, the Nordic ecolabel, consisting of a green and white swan (Hilton Stockholm Slussen 2016). She also found an older edition of their Environmental Statement online but not the current 2014 edition (it is updated every two years). The lack of promotional communication about their efforts led to an interview with Mr. Emil Gammeltoft, their Purchasing & Procurement and Environmental specialist in September 2016. He confirmed that due to branding guidelines, all Hilton Hotel home pages had to conform to certain standards and that is why only the Nordic ecolabel was present and no other information was available. When asked how guests found out about their efforts, he said, "through their environmental statement available in the rooms and their environmental reporting corner in the lobby" (Mr. Emil Gammeltoft, 2016, pers. comm, 27 September). The environmental corner in the main lobby consists of three wall boards with the titles "Environmental board," "Did you know that…," and "Our Environmental Objective." These list some of the hotel's major accomplishments and current efforts in their quest to be the most environmentally friendly hotel in Europe and beyond.

Hilton Stockholm Slussen started their environmental efforts in 1994 and they aim to be the most environmentally adapted Hilton in Europe according to Peter Eriksson, General Manager (Environmental statement, 2014, p. 3). The following information is from their environmental statement:

Hilton Stockholm Slussen is home to 60,000 bees who make the honey that is served on their eco-labeled (KRAV) breakfast buffet. In addition to the Nordic Swan eco label certification, which they have had for over 15 years, and KRAV certification (since 1991), they are also ISO 14001 certified. Emil Gammeltoft has trained over 1,000 Hilton personnel on their environmental standards and efforts and through external education programs, he has reached over 900 other people.

Hilton Stockholm Slussen's energy consumption has been reduced from 58.69 kWh/ guest in 2003 to 50.57 KWh/ guest in 2013. Since 2010, they only purchase "Good Environmental Choice" certified electricity generated from wind and water. In terms of water, they have reduced consumption per guest from 442.80 liters/guest in 2003 to 291.00 liters/guest in 2013. Waste has remained the same since mid-1997 at about 300–350 grams/guest, which is a 76 percent reduction from 1996. In total waste, that is a reduction from 12.5 tons/month to 3 tons/month. The hotel sorts 23 types of waste for recycling/reuse/safe storage including items such as candle stumps, hard plastics, coat-hangers, paint spills, solvents, and metal packaging. The candle stumps are given to a local church that melts them down and produces new candles sold to support volunteer work in the Philippines giving vaccinations to children.

Hilton Stockholm uses only one cleaning agent in the rooms, compared to five previously. It has eco-labeled soap and shampoo in all rooms in dispensers instead of individual bottles.

It limits transportation of purchased goods to once a month and if possible, they use cycle couriers for lightweight transportation within Stockholm.

In terms of environmentally friendly entertainment at Hilton Stockholm, it provides "Hilton Unplugged" events where bands play live acoustic music in their Eken Bar. Other popular events include "Stand Up Comedy in the Dark."

According to Mr. Emil Gammeltoft, very few new guests will know about the hotel's environmental efforts prior to check-in; despite this, it remains hugely competitive in the group bookings and conferences sector. Corporations and groups have shown increased interest in reducing their environmental impact and this is where Hilton Stockholm Slussen is the benchmark hotel in the Stockholm area (Mr. Emil Gammeltoft, 2016, pers. comm, 27 September).

Conclusion

There are major differences in how the two hotels in the above case studies promote their green initiatives. The Orchard Garden Hotel seems to take every opportunity to showcase its initiatives and on-going work to reduce its environmental impact in its everyday operations. As a LEED certified hotel, its environmental efforts are not an afterthought but are ingrained in the hotel's conception, supported by the owner, Mr. S. C. Huang. The hotel openly lists many of its eco-initiatives on its home page under "Green Initiatives" and has collaborated with third-party sites such as istaygreen by completing an eco-audit.

Although Hilton Stockholm Slussen began its environmental efforts in 1994, 12 years prior to the Orchard Garden Hotel being built, and has continued ever since, this is not heavily promoted. As Sweden is a country that is known for its sustainability efforts at many levels in society and has been ranked as the most sustainable country in the world (Korosec 2013), it may not be surprising that hotels engage in sustainability efforts. However, it seems that Hilton Stockholm Slussen is missing out on targeting the conscious traveler segment by not promoting its efforts more openly.

In conclusion, focus on sustainability is rewarding for the hospitality industry. However, to increase their competitiveness, hotel marketers should have an effective communications plan in place to disseminate their sustainability efforts and the positive outcome thereof. Consumers fail to patronize and support companies with a genuine commitment to sustainability due to companies' failure to inform consumers of the extent of their environmental initiatives and the resulting positive impact.

References

Berezan, O., Raab, C., Yoo, M., Love, C. (2013) "Sustainable Hotel Practices and Nationality: The Impact on Guest Satisfaction and Guest Intention to Return," *International Journal of Hospitality Management* 34, 227–233.

Bohdanowicz, P. (2005) "Environmental Awareness and Initiatives in the Swedish and Polish Hotel Industries – Survey Results," *Hospitality Management* 25, 662–682.

Butler, J. (2008) "The Compelling 'Hard Case' for 'Green' Hotel Development," *Cornell Hospitality Quarterly* 49, 234–244.

Chan, E. (2008) "Barriers to EMS in the Hotel Industry," *International Journal of Hospitality Management* 27, 187–196.

Chan, K., Han, X. (2014) "Effectiveness of Environmental Advertising for Hotels," *Services Marketing Quarterly* 35, 4, 289–303.

Chan, W.W. (2005). Predicting and Saving the Consumption of Electricity in Sub-Tropical Hotels. *International Journal of Contemporary Hospitality Management* 17, 228–237.

Dinan, C., Sargeant, A. (2000) "Social Marketing and Sustainable Tourism – Is There a Match?" *International Journal of Tourism Research* 2, 1–14.

Dodds, R., Graci, S.R., Holmes, M. (2010) "Does the Tourist Care? A Comparison of Tourists in Koh Phi Phi, Thailand and Gili Trawangan, Indonesia," *Journal of Sustainable Tourism* 18, 207–222.

Environmental statement. (2014) *Hilton Stockholm Slussen.* Older version available online from: www.esomar.org/uploads/public/events-and-awards/events/2014/digital-dimensions/documents/Hilton-Stockholm-Slussen-ENVIRONMENTAL-STATEMENT.pdf

Evanschitzky, H, Iyer, G.R., Plassmann, H., Niessing, J., Meffert, H. (2006) "The Relative Strength of Affective Commitment in Securing Loyalty in Service Relationships," *Journal of Business Research* 59, 1207–1213.

Foster, S., Sampson, S., Dunn, S. (2000) "The Impact of Customer Contact on Environmental Initiatives for Service Firms," *International Journal of Operations & Production Management* 20, 187–203.

Green Hotels Association (2016) *Green Hotels Association Home Page. GHA's Goals.* July 13, 2016. Available from: www.greenhotels.com

Green Hotels Global (2016). *Green Hotels Global Home Page.* October 21, 2016. Available from: https://green-hotelsglobal.wordpress.com/2012/09/06/more-on-marriotts-recently-released-sustainability-report/

Grosbois, D. (2012) "Corporate Social Responsibility Reporting by the Global Hotel Industry: Commitment, Initiatives and Performance," *International Journal of Hospitality Management* 31, 896–905.

Han, H., Hsu, L.T., Sheu, C. (2010) "Application of the Theory of Planned Behavior to Green Hotel Choice: Testing the Effect of Environmental Friendly Activities," *Tourism Management* 31, 325–334.

Han, H., Kim, Y. (2010) "An Investigation of Green Hotel Customers' Decision Formation: Developing an Extended Model of the Theory of Planned Behavior," *International Journal of Hospitality Management* 29, 659–668.

Hilton Stockholm Slussen (2016). *Hilton Stockholm Slussen Home Page.* July 13, 2016. Available from: www3.hilton.com/en/hotels/sweden/hilton-stockholm-slussen-STOSLHI/index.html?WT.mc_id=zELWAKN0EMEA1HI2DMH3LocalSearch4DGGenericx6STOSLHI

Hilton Worldwide (2016). *Hilton World Wide News.* August 10, 2016. Available from: http://news.hilton-worldwide.com/index.cfm/newsroom/detail/30697.

Intercontinental Hotel Group (2016). *Intercontinental Hotel Group Home Page.* July 5, 2016. Available from: www.ihg.com/hotels/us/en/global/support/green_engage).

Bidisha Burman and Pia A. Albinsson

I Stay Green (2016) I Stay Green Home Page. 28 September, 2016. Available from: www.istaygreen.org/ecoaudit.cfm/hid/11345299

Johnson, H. (2003) "Does It Pay to Be Good? Social Responsibility and Financial Performance," *Business Horizons* 46, 34–40.

Jones, P., Hillier, D., Comfort, D. (2016) "Sustainability in the Hospitality Industry: Some Personal Reflections on Corporate Challenges and Research Agendas," *International Journal of Contemporary Hospitality Management* 28, 36–67.

Kang, K., Seoki, L., Huh, C. (2010) "Impacts of Positive and Negative Corporate Social Responsibility Activities on Company Performance in the Hospitality Industry," *International Journal of Hospitality Management* 29, 72–82.

Kim, Y., Han, H. (2010). "Intention to Pay Conventional-Hotel Prices at a Green Hotel – A Modification of the Theory of Planned Behavior," *Journal of Sustainable Tourism* 18, 997–1014.

Korosec, K. (2013) "Sweden 'Most Sustainable Country in the World," *Environmental Leader*, August 19. Available from: www.environmentalleader.com/2013/08/19/sweden-most-sustainable-country-in-the-world/

Lee, C., Song, H., Lee, H., Lee, S., Bernhard, B. (2013) "The Impact of CSR on Casino Employees' Organizational Trust, Job Satisfaction, and Customer Orientation: An Empirical Examination of Responsible Gambling Strategies," *International Journal of Hospitality Management* 33, 406–415.

Lee, S., Park, S.Y. (2009) "Do Socially Responsible Activities Help Hotels and Casinos Achieve their Financial Goals?" *International Journal of Hospitality Management* 28, 105–112.

Lita, R.P., Surya, S., Ma'ruf, M., Syahrul, L. (2014) "Green Attitude and Behavior of Local Tourists towards Hotels and Restaurants in West Sumatra, Indonesia," *Procedia Environmental Sciences* 20, 261–270.

Manaktola, K., Jauhari, V. (2007) "Exploring Consumer Attitude and Behavior towards Green Practices in the Lodging Industry in India," *International Journal of Contemporary Hospitality Management* 19, 364–377.

Marriott (2016) *Marriott Home Page.* October 21, 2016. Available from: www.marriott.com/corporate-social-responsibility/corporate-responsibility.mi

Peattie, K., Peattie, S. (1995) "Sales Promotion – a Missed Opportunity for Services Marketers?" *International Journal of Service Industry Management* 6, 22–39.

Rahman, I., Reynolds, D., Svaren, S. (2012) "How "Green" are North American Hotels? An Exploration of Low-Cost Adoption Practices," *International Journal of Hospitality Management* 31, 720–727.

Robinot, E., Giannelloni, J.L. (2010) "Do Hotels' "Green" Attributes Contribute to Customer Satisfaction?" *Journal of Services Marketing* 24, 157–169.

Schwartz, M.S., Carroll, A.B. (2003) "Corporate Social Responsibility: A Three-Domain Approach," *Business Ethics Quarterly* 13, 503–530.

Taylor, S. (1992) "Green Management: The Next Competitive Weapon," *Futures* 24, 669–680.

The Orchard Garden Hotel (2016) The Orchard Garden Hotel Home Page. August 23, 2016. Available from: www.theorchardgardenhotel.com/green-initiatives-en.html

Tierney, P., Hunt, M., Latkova, P. (2011) "Do Travelers Support Green Practices and Sustainable Development?" *Journal of Tourism Insights* 2.

Tzschentke, N., Kirk, D., Lynch, P.A. (2008) "Going Green: Decisional Factors in Small Hospitality Operations," *International Journal of Hospitality Management* 27, 126–133.

Welford, R.J. (1998) "Editorial: Corporate Environmental Management, Technology and Sustainable Development: Postmodern Perspectives and the Need for a Critical Research Agenda," *Business Strategy and the Environment* 7, 1–12.

Wolfe, K., Shanklin, C. (2001) "Environmental Practices and Management Concerns of Conference Center Administrators," *Journal of Hospitality & Tourism Research* 25, 209–216.

Wyndham Worldwide (2016) Wyndham Worldwide Home Page. July 5, 2016. Available from: www.wyndhamworldwide.com/category/green-toolbox

Further reading

Chang, C. (2011) "Feeling Ambivalent about Going Green: Implications for Green Advertising Processing," *Journal of Advertising* 40, 4, 19–32. (An examination of consumer processing of green claims in marketing communications.)

Holcomb, J.L., Upchurch, R.S., Okumus, F. (2007) "Corporate Social Responsibility: What Are Top Hotel Companies Reporting?" *International Journal of Contemporary Hospitality Management* 19, 6, 461–475. (An exposé of limited sustainability focus and reporting.)

Horng, J., Wang, C., Liau, C., Chou, S, Tsai, C. (2016), "The Role of Sustainability Service Innovation in Crafting the Vision of the Hospitality Industry," *Sustainability* 8, 3, 223. (Analysis of sustainable service innovation characteristics.)

Milne, M.J., Gray, R. (2013) "W(h)ither Ecology? The Triple Bottom Line, the Global Reporting Initiative, and Corporate Sustainability Reporting," *Journal of Business Ethics* 188 1, 13–29. (A critique of sustainability reporting.)

Myung, E., McClaren, A., Li, L. (2012) "Environmentally Related Research in Scholarly Hospitality Journals: Current Status and Future Opportunities," *International Journal of Hospitality Management* 31, 1264–1275. (A review of recent developments in environmental research in the hospitality field.)

Sloan, P., Legrand W., Silken J. (2013), *Sustainability in the Hospitality Industry: Principles of Sustainable Operations*. New York: Routledge. (An extended account of best practices of sustainability efforts in the hospitality industry.)

32

Impact of sustainability practices on hospitality consumers' behaviors and attitudes

The case of LUX* Resorts & Hotels

Vishnee Sowamber, Haywantee Ramkissoon and Felix Mavondo

Introduction

In recent years, both practitioners and academics have shown growing interest in sustainability issues in the hospitality industry (Berezan, Raab, Yoo, and Love, 2013). In the past decade, there has been a dramatic shift in corporate uptake of mainstream Triple Bottom Line Sustainability. This includes Corporate Social Responsibility (CSR) and environmental initiatives (Segarra-Õna, Peiró-Signes, Verma, and Miret-Pastor, 2012). Travelers pay close attention to sustainable competitive strategies implemented by companies (Ramkissoon and Mavondo, 2016). They have positive attitudes towards companies which are implementing sustainability initiatives (Xu and Gursoy, 2015). The impact of sustainability practices have been shown to have an influence on hospitality consumers' attitudes and behaviors. Studies show that CSR performance positively influences consumers' purchase intentions (Tian, Wang, and Yang, 2011) and contributes to customer satisfaction (Luo and Bhattacharya, 2006).

Detrimental environmental impacts in the tourism and hospitality industry have attracted significant interest from both researchers and practitioners, who have called for more research on the implementation of branded sustainability programs (Cainelli, Mazzanti, and Zoboli, 2011; Erdogan and Tosun, 2009; McNamaraa and Gibson, 2008; Segarra-Õna et al., 2012; Tzschentke, Kirk, and Lynch, 2008). This often includes socially focused initiatives encompassing consumer choice, perception and support (Dhaoui, 2014).

A number of tour operating businesses have conservation and community benefit programs. There is a growing trend to include stakeholder management in strategic performance models (Kolodinsky, Madden, Zisk, and Henkel, 2010). The amount of resource consumption in terms of energy and water needed in order to produce the services required by resorts has resulted in a growing interest in sustainable practices. Other push factors include environmental degradation, which may be caused through unmanaged growth and development. With severe threats of environmental degradation faced by the hospitality sector, adopting sustainable environmental practices have become a necessary step in assisting hospitality managers to contribute to sustainable development goals.

Drivers of loyalty in hospitality businesses have attracted much attention from scholars (Mattila, 2006; So, King, Sparks, and Wang, 2013; Tanford, Carola, and Kinb, 2012). Successful environmental CSR performance can enhance a service provider's reputation (Marin and Ruiz, 2007). Environmental CSR is now increasingly understood by consumers and the media (Rahbar and Abdul Wahid, 2011). This is evidenced by the growing number of customers willing to seek and stay in green hotels (Deloitte, 2008). This further implies that CSR can be a factor which influences brand building (Chomvilailuk and Butcher, 2010; Hoeffler and Keller, 2002).

Bohdanowicz (2005, p. 188) states that "the development and well-being of the hotel industry in tourism destinations depends on a constant availability of natural resources." Almost all WTTC (World Travel & Tourism Council) hotel members have towel reuse and linen programs. Some programs, such as Accor's "Plant for the Planet" and Starwood's "Make a Green Choice" programs, are driving consumers' decision-making. On the other hand, Starwood Hotels & Resorts has rolled out the hotel brand Element, which sells itself as an environmentally friendly chain with sustainability at the core of its operations. Marriott International and Hilton Hotels and Resorts have pledged to cut water and energy consumption rates in addition to having their buildings LEED-certified (Leadership in Energy and Environmental Design).

In collaboration with 11 international hotel groups, comprising 8,880 hotels across the world, Cornell University's Center for Hospitality Research has released the latest set of benchmarks. These benchmarks have the objective to enable hotel owners and operators to measure the water and electricity usage and carbon emissions levels at their properties (Ricaurte, 2016). To date, companies representing over 21,000 hotels are using HCMI (Hotel Carbon Measurement Initiative) to assess their carbon footprint and hence to be in a position to offset it. Consumers can differentiate between "greenwashing" and genuine commitments communicated by the hotel chain (Chen and Chang, 2013; Horiuehi and Schuchard, 2009; Pomering and Johnson, 2009).

CSR is increasingly seen as an important business strategy aspect. The key issue is that it relates to how the organization is seen by various important stakeholders, i.e. government, financial markets, customers, employees and a host of environmental enthusiasts in the local community. While financial benefits and increased competitiveness are at the heart of CSR (Kang, Lee, and Huh, 2010; Kim and Han, 2010; Segarra-Õna et al., 2012; Tarí, Claver-Cortés, Pereira-Moline, and Molina-Azorin, 2010), this must be achieved without sacrificing the environment, employees and the local community. CSR has benefits for corporate reputation and hotel branding, both of which could be sources of competitive advantage. These marketing implications have major implications in a competitive environment. CSR generates goodwill among key stakeholders and shields the organization from criticism of a sole focus on profit. Fortunately, in the medium term there is no trade-off between CSR and profitability, especially if the starting point in its implementation are managers and front-line employees. This demands a change in attitude, constantly reinforced by senior management and made visible to customers and other key stakeholders.

Recent research has shown that the enhancement of employees' health and safety, and training and development opportunities would not only increase employees' job satisfaction but also enhance the level of customer satisfaction (de Leaniz and Rodriguez, 2015). In response to the need for responsible business, hotels could implement policies in order to enhance investor relations, employees commitment and job satisfaction (Rahman, Reynolds, and Svaren, 2012). The investment need not be too onerous as long as effective communication is implemented. The process can be built over time, starting with key priority areas that are of interest to key stakeholders. This chapter uses LUX★ Resorts & Hotels as a case study to illustrate a successful implementation of CSR and environmental sustainability across the LUX★ properties.

Literature review

Triple Bottom Line Sustainability (3Ps)

Triple Bottom Line Sustainability (also known as 3Ps – People, Planet, Profit) helps to guide an organization to take into account the environmental, economic, and socio-cultural sustainability of its business practices as opposed to only focusing on economic performance (Elkington, 1997; Faux, 2005; Tyrrell and Johnston, 2012). A further expansion of the concept includes accountability towards key stakeholders such as individuals and society (Cavagnaro and Curiel, 2012). Sustainability is essential to the success of hospitality businesses (Hawkins and Cunningham, 1996; Myung, McClaren, and Li, 2012). The guiding principles of sustainability help to mitigate negative impacts on the 3Ps and increase the positive impacts (Faux, 2005; Stoddard, Pollard, and Evans, 2012; Tyrrell, Paris, and Biaett, 2013; Weaver, 2006, 2010). Dwyer (2005) and Stoddard et al. (2012) linked economic benefits to sustainability practices in the hospitality sector. Research on environmental sustainability also evidences water and energy optimization and provides significant potential for cost savings to be achieved through sustainability initiatives (Bohdanowicz, 2005). Further, a sustainable core business strategy helps in organizational performance (Sloan, Legrand, and Chen, 2012). Having sustainability at the core of business strategy implies the optimization of resources through cost savings, and also leads to better stakeholder relationships, competitiveness and improved strategic decision-making (Tyrrell et al., 2013).

Corporate Social Responsibility (CSR)

Carroll (1991) introduced the CSR pyramid, which has four layers representing corporate responsibilities. The four different responsibilities include economic, legal, ethical and philanthropic. Carroll (2004) reproduced the pyramid in an attempt to incorporate the notion of stakeholders. He stated that the economic responsibility is that which is required by the global stakeholders while legal and ethical responsibilities are those which are expected by global stakeholders. Philanthropic responsibility is rather that which is desired by global stakeholders. In the hospitality sector, there has been a lot of focus on environmental commitments which are referred to as sustainability practices (Epler and Leray, 2005). CSR has been a contested and yet dynamic concept (Crane, Matten, and Spence, 2008). Nevertheless, the definition has been fairly accepted (Mandhachitara and Poolthong, 2011). The corporate responsibilities are clear and include economic, environmental and social responsibilities. The four types of responsibilities documented in the literature include economic, legal, ethical and philanthropic responsibilities (Matten and Crane, 2005). CSR activities have the potential to strengthen the relationship between organizations and their stakeholders (Peloza and Shang, 2011). As such, social responsibility is defined as the degree to which firms assume economic, legal, ethical and discretionary responsibilities toward their stakeholders (Maignan, Ferrell, and Hult, 1999). The economic responsibility is more about the firm's ability to sustain, in terms of growth in profitability and revenue, while environmental responsibility is mostly about environmental management (Rahman, Reynolds, and Svaren, 2012).

Turker (2009) states that CSR includes a company's responsibility to operate in ways that affect stakeholders positively, enabling the firm to progress beyond its economic interests. Governmental legislative policies are also dominant drivers for environmental CSR activity. This has been due to a push factor by business leaders who wish to see national governments take leading roles to encourage and enforce environmental responsibility (Dummett, 2006).

Resorts are implementing CSR practices through the concept of stakeholder inclusiveness. They are working on promoting their environmental and social commitments to the stakeholders involved, who include their guests, employees, the local community as well as other key players in the value creation process. Turker (2009) states that with respect to society, CSR refers to activity that contributes to the well-being of the local community. CSR has a significantly strong and positive association with attitudinal loyalty (Mandhachitara and Poolthong, 2011).

CSR activities can take many forms, such as the use of green materials, donations of money to charitable causes, diversity initiatives, program support of community events and recycling. Singh, Sanchez, and del Bosque (2008) argue that engaging in CSR initiatives is prevalent across different types of businesses in various industries and countries. Companies have the ability to differentiate their products and services by creating a more positive brand image through CSR commitments that enhance the firm's reputation (Hsu, 2012).

It has also been demonstrated that CSR shields firms from negative information about CSR practices (Eisingerich, Rubera, Seifert, and Bhardwaj, 2011). CSR can provide firms with an insurance-like protection and lower risks with regard to their reputation (Luo and Bhattacharya, 2009). The recognition by consumers, workers and government that a business does not only exist in order to make profit, but also to create value for stakeholders involved in the value creation chain has triggered businesses to incorporate CSR in their business strategy. CSR is becoming an essential element of successful business competition. Factors such as ethical tendencies, values correlation and social trends are essential to determine the success of CSR (Mirabi, 2014).

The different forms of CSR initiatives programs are targeted to improve conditions in the local community, fair trade relationships with suppliers, safe workplace conditions and responsibility towards broader stakeholders (Marin and Ruiz, 2007; Peloza and Shang, 2011; Vermeir and Verbeke, 2006). These can also extend to environmental protection programs, such as reducing the level of pollution (Peloza and Shang, 2011). Larger firms and global corporations integrate CSR programs into business planning and operations, engaging in activities such as social service, environmental conservation and contribution of funds to humanitarian projects and causes (Rangan, Chase, and Karim, 2012).

Customers' behaviors and attitudes

Corporate reputation and brand preference

Hillenbrand and Money (2007) argue that there is a positive relationship between the concepts of Corporate Social Responsibility (CSR) and corporate reputation. The value of a brand name is defined as its brand equity. To generate branding benefits, there needs to be positive brand associations, perceived quality and brand loyalty in all strategic efforts (Yoo, Donthu, and Lee, 2000). CSR has a positive influence on brand image (Singh et al., 2008).

Corte, Piras, and Zamparelli (2010) show that brand preference is often applied as a symbolic predictor to consumers' purchase. In building the brand equity, it has become essential to integrate CSR programs as an integral part of the business strategy. Sustainability practices of firms have an impact on customers' behaviors and attitudes towards the brand (Torres, Bijmolt, Tribo, and Verhoef, 2012). In a study involving 57 global brands from ten countries, Torres et al. (2012) show that CSR has a positive effect on global brand equity. The study further demonstrates a positive effect of CSR on brand equity when global brands respect local communities' social responsibility.

The hospitality sector is one of the world's fastest growing industries. It plays an essential role in the tourism economy, as tourists are undertaking travel to distant places and locations, in increasing numbers (De Grosbois, 2012). Positive impacts include job creation, understanding of different cultures and sensitization of environment among others (Bohdanowicz and Zientara, 2009). The increasing pressure on the resources, however, causes deleterious impacts such as waste generation, non-compliance with fundamental labor standards, biodiversity loss, prostitution, and air and noise pollution. Hence, integrating CSR in the strategy helps to mitigate the various negative socio-cultural and environmental impacts (Chan, 2009).

CSR behaviors intended to enhance social interests are positively related to brand image (Singh et al., 2008). CSR has a very strong and positive association with attitudinal loyalty (Mandhachitara and Poolthong, 2011). A firm's brand image and customer behaviors can be enhanced significantly through sincere and generous initiatives for the stakeholders involved (Henderson, 2007). Studies show that status-seeking consumers exhibit higher levels of pro-social behaviors and higher empathy towards larger national causes, for example, as an activity promoting peace (Mattila and Hanks, 2012). There is a positive relationship between CSR and customers' brand preference (Torres et al., 2012; Turker, 2009). This is often referred as stakeholder inclusiveness, including government, final customers, employees, suppliers and shareholders as main stakeholders (Torres et al., 2012).

The CSR–brand performance link is partially mediated by corporate reputation (Lai, Cheng, and Tang, 2010). He and Li (2011) found a mediating effect of brand identification between CSR activities and service quality. Alamro and Rowley (2011) report that perceived positive corporate reputation has a positive impact on brand preference. Consumers' positive attitudes toward corporate social activity could influence their perceptions and behaviors regarding brand preference (Kolodinsky et al., 2010). Brand preference is regularly applied as a symbolic predictor of consumers' purchase (Corte et al., 2010).

Corporate images can be further improved through investment in environmental initiatives, thereby enhancing the competitive advantages and gaining new markets (Chen, 2010). There is a positive relationship between customers' purchasing behavior and their perception of an eco-friendly brand (Rahbar and Abdul Wahid, 2011). The influence of CSR on consumer behavior such as purchase intention, buying behavior and repurchase intention has shown to be impactful (Jose, Rugimbana, and Gatfield, 2012; Sen, Bhattacharya and Korschun, 2006). Yusof, Musa, and Rahman (2011) found that store loyalty was affected by the green image of retailers. The perceived environmental degradation has led to increasing calls for more socially and environmentally responsible behaviors.

There is a direct association between customer attraction and a firm's reputation regarding how much it cares about CSR and environmental protection (Marin and Ruiz, 2007). This is in line with Chen's (2010) finding that consumers' satisfaction is positively associated with brand image. Chen (2010) tried to identify the relationship between CSR and customer satisfaction. Luo and Bhattacharya (2006) found that CSR contributes to customer satisfaction and financial success. Tian, Wang, and Yang (2011), supporting this claim, report that CSR positively influences consumers' purchase intentions. Alamro and Rowley (2011) argue that both customer satisfaction and recognition of the service provider as a responsible firm have a positive impact on brand preference.

Loyalty

Given that customers perceive a greater risk in the choice of services, companies see customer loyalty as key in the service sector (Polo, Frías, and Rodríguez, 2013). Studies show that it is unlikely for loyal customers to consider competitor hotel brands in their purchase decisions solely for financial reasons (Yoo and Bai, 2013). A sustainable firm has increased attractiveness in the eyes of customers (Becker, 2009; Lee, 2011). According to Berezan et al. (2013), customers' perceptions and their decision-making process are both influenced by the firm's sustainability practices. Mandhachitara and Poolthong (2011) confirm that there is a direct positive relationship between customer loyalty and CSR. A firm's reputation can be improved through green management of hospitality businesses and supply chains. This has a positive impact on customers' loyalty and enhances visit intentions (Han, Hsu, Lee, and Sheu, 2011).

Teng, Horng, Hu, Chien, and Shen, (2012) argue that customer loyalty and willingness to pay a premium can be greatly enhanced by the sustainability practices of hospitality companies. These practices include environmental management (Rahman et al., 2012) and CSR (Paek, Xiao, Lee, and Song, 2013). The growing issues of climate change such as environmental degradation, global warming, air and water pollution and habitat destruction are pushing customers to consider eco-friendly options during their purchase decision-making (Hsieh, 2012; Jones, Hillier, and Comfort, 2014).

Customer satisfaction is an antecedent of loyalty. Some scholars argue that the positive link between customer satisfaction with hotels and their loyalty has been solid and strong in the last several decades (Chen and Chang, 2013; Xu and Gursoy, 2015; Kim and Han, 2010). In their studies, Mathies and Gudergan (2012) found that loyal customers are willing to pay more for their preferred brand; they are hence unaffected by an increase in price when making a purchase decision. Loyal customers are also willing to recommend the hotel (Gursoy et al., 2014). There is an increase in customers' visit intentions when hospitality businesses show green management (Han, Hsu, Lee, and Sheu, 2011). This may be explained by the fact that such initiatives improve the firm's reputation and enhance its competitive advantage as a brand. Nikolaeva and Bicho (2011) confirm that stronger customer loyalty is achieved when the company has a reputation of being socially responsible.

Customer satisfaction

Berezan et al. (2013) suggest that positive influences on customer satisfaction are likely to occur through the environmental dimension of sustainable hospitality supply chain management. Lee and Heo (2009) found that the social dimension actions of sustainable hospitality supply chain management increase customer satisfaction. Customers see eco-friendly actions as an integral part of a service offered by a firm, which positively influences their overall satisfaction (Berezan et al., 2013). Hence, organizations tend to take their environmental responsibility seriously (Chan, 2013). It is recommended that new corporate strategies such as green marketing should be developed by companies to respond to these environmental demands (Chen, 2010; Kang and Hur, 2012).

Other studies found that an increase in customer satisfaction regarding a hotel's corporate reputation affects customer loyalty (Loureiro and Kastenholz, 2011). Customer satisfaction and customer trust is crucial in order to develop lasting relationships with consumers (Delgado and Munuera, 2005; Lee and Heo, 2009). Researchers also found that there is a positive effect of CSR on customer identification (Lichtenstein, Drumwright, and Braig, 2004; Marin, Ruiz, and Rubio, 2009) and customer satisfaction (He and Li, 2011; Luo and Bhattacharya, 2006). Luo and Bhattacharya (2006) argue that customer identification mediates the relationship between CSR and customer satisfaction. The mitigation of negative effects of internal causes of attribution on customer identification can be achieved through socially responsible actions. This can help improve the post-recovery satisfaction (Siu, Zhang, and Kwan, 2014).

Certification requirements by customers

Customers have a good level of awareness and are becoming more knowledgeable; they can often distinguish between greenwashing and real commitment (Pomering and Johnson, 2009). Sustainability is becoming so essential to stakeholders that there is a growing interest in external assurance. An element which is being requested from resorts and hotels is certification for implemented initiatives. Certification has become an important part of the marketing strategy. These certifications are expected to be from an independent and accredited organization such as Green Globe, Earthcheck, EU Ecolabel and Travelife. Very often, this initiative is undertaken by committed managers (Park, Kim, McCleary, 2014). It also depends on the place where the resort is located (Bohdanowicz, 2006) or whether the resort is part of a resort chain affiliation where such practices are already in place (Bohdanowicz, 2005).

Consumers often ask questions about the information being presented to them (Chen and Chang, 2013; Horiuchi and Schuchard, 2009; Pomering and Johnson, 2009). Companies try to build positive corporate images by communicating only positive information (Lyon and Maxwell, 2011). Hence, it is essential to obtain third-party certifications to ensure the integrity of information being communicated with regard to sustainability commitments.

These certifications can result in cost savings, lead to a competitive advantage and hence improve the image of a hotel (Bernardo, Casadesus, Karapetrovic and Heras, 2009; Chan, 2009; Segarra-Õna et al., 2012). For example, it was found that hotels with an ISO 14001 certification perform better financially (Segarra-Õna et al., 2012). The claims of 'greenwash' can be reduced when using the name and logo of a third-party certification (Parguel, Benoît-Moreau, and Larceneux, 2011).

Relevance of sustainable development and CSR to LUX* Resorts & Hotels

This section critically assesses the role of sustainable development and CSR at LUX* Resorts & Hotels, a Mauritian hotel group. Mauritius, a small island located on the east coast of Africa, is a developing state, where tourism and hospitality play an important role in sustaining its economy (Nunkoo and Ramkissoon, 2011, 2016; Ramkissoon and Uysal, 2010; 2011). The main objective of this section is to provide preliminary insights on the importance of sustainability initiatives for the brand's reputation.

Company profile

Founded in 1987, LUX* Resorts & Hotels is a Mauritian hotel group with properties in the Indian Ocean islands, Mauritius, the Maldives, La Reunion, China and Turkey. LUX* is an affiliate member of IBL Ltd (Ireland Blyth Ltd), a major economic player in the Indian Ocean, and is the leader of the "Top 100" Mauritian companies. Listed on the Stock Exchange of Mauritius (SEM) and mainly Mauritian owned, LUX* has more than 2,810 shareholders and around 3,000 Team Members. LUX* is a collection of premium hotels offering guests the opportunity to celebrate life and enjoy light living. The resorts in the LUX* portfolio are LUX* Belle Mare Mauritius (5*), LUX* Le Morne, Mauritius (5*), LUX* Grand Gaube, Mauritius (5*), LUX* South Ari Atol Maldives (5*), LUX* St Gilles Ile de la Réunion (5*), LUX* Tea Horse Road Benzilan (5*), LUX* Tea Horse Road Lijiang (5*) and LUX* Bodrum, Turkey. The other properties (Tamassa and Merville Beach in Mauritius and Hotel Le Recif in Reunion) are part of the Produced by LUX* portfolio. LUX* also operates a private paradise islet in Mauritius, the Ile des Deux Cocos. The company also has new openings scheduled in the next few years in the UAE, the Maldives, China and Vietnam.

Sustainability initiatives and corporate reputation

Paul Jones, CEO of LUX*, states, "By showing its commitment in leading participation in Stock Exchange of Mauritius Sustainability Index, LUX* has been able to achieve a positive image for the company, and hence creates brand preference among stakeholders." This corroborates with Marin and Ruiz (2007), who mention that successful CSR performance can enhance reputation. They also imply that there is a direct association between customers' attraction and the company's reputation regarding how much it cares about CSR and environmental protection.

LUX* intends to be the number one employer in the hospitality sector by providing a healthy working environment. Through team member engagement, LUX* provides growth and development opportunities for its human resources. Training and development is key to ensuring a culture of continuous learning and growth. In 2016, an amount of 719,659 USD was invested in training as compared to 648,628 USD the previous year. Diversity and equal opportunity are essential, and hence LUX* ensures equal treatment at all levels. "To empower our Team Members we are providing trainings on Human Rights. This also enhances high service quality for our guests. It has a positive impact on brand preference," notes Paul Jones, CEO. This is consistent with literature by Torres et al. (2012), who state that there is a positive relationship between CSR and customers' brand preference. The present situation shows stakeholder inclusiveness, where the wellbeing of team members is being taken care of.

Recognising the impacts of climate change due to greenhouse gas emissions, LUX* has introduced a new environmental initiative, "Tread Lightly, Carbon Neutral Holidays," to offset its carbon footprint. The offset amounted to 16,692.2 tCO_2 during the financial year 2014–2015 and 25,304 tCO_2 during the financial year 2015–2016. Such initiatives enhance the corporate image. This is in line with Chen (2010) and Segarra-Õna et al. (2012), who argue that consumers' satisfaction is positively associated with brand image and that these initiatives can result in cost savings, lead to a competitive advantage and better financial performance. These actions help to mitigate the environmental impacts (Chan, 2011) and enhance customers' brand preference (Turker, 2009; Torres et al., 2012).

"From a social perspective, the Ray of Light project has been introduced to provide a platform to enhance integration, involvement and participation of different stakeholders for the enhancement of the community," notes Paul Jones, CEO of LUX*. Sincere and generous stakeholder initiatives enhance the brand image and customer behaviors (Henderson, 2007). The brand identity is also associated with corporate philanthropic activities (Ricks, 2005).

"The challenges faced are that sustainability and CSR are not as straightforward concepts as finance and marketing. It takes time to have it embedded in the culture. Policies, trainings and constant communication are being implemented to further enhance collaboration," notes Paul Jones.

The initial assessment of outcomes is that LUX* has a competitive advantage in terms of attracting investors, owners, tour operators and clients to engage in new projects and agreements. CSR is a factor which influences brand building (Chomvilailuk and Butcher, 2010). Tour operators and sophisticated customers can differentiate between "greenwashing" and genuine commitments (Chen and Chang, 2013; Pomering and Johnson, 2009). LUX* is in the process of implementing Renewable Energy Projects such as the Solar Renewable Energy Project. The group will continue to find innovative projects to align with its sustainable development strategy. It also ensures high customer satisfaction through innovation and constant training and development of its team members. Another interesting outcome is that competitors are following this strategy. This has great benefits for the society and environment as more innovative projects are being introduced for a sustainable future.

Implications

The chapter gives insights into the link between sustainability and CSR practices and brand reputation. Taking into account this relationship can help a company leverage its brand in the eyes of customers and gain a competitive advantage. The activities of a business have an impact on the brand reputation. Positive CSR performance has a positive influence on the brand image. There is a shift happening where customers are paying close attention to the sustainability actions of a company and are seeking responsible behaviors. To align with this shift in demand, CSR can be a factor which influences brand building. This must be achieved without sacrificing the environment, employees or the local community (Segarra-Õa et al., 2012). Companies can differentiate their products and services by creating a more positive brand image and corporate reputation (Hsu, 2012). Sustainability initiatives can improve a firm's reputation and enhance its competitive advantage as a brand (Hsu, 2012). Companies can hence improve their reputation.

There is a direct positive relationship between customer loyalty and CSR. Mandhachitara and Poolthong (2011) indicate that CSR has a significantly strong and positive association with attitudinal loyalty. Customer loyalty and their willingness to pay a premium can be greatly enhanced by sustainability practices. Hotels' green actions have a positive impact on brand identity and customer loyalty (Mandhachitara and Poolthong, 2011). Through improvement of reputation in terms of sustainability initiatives, customer loyalty can be cultivated. Stronger customer loyalty is achieved when the company has a reputation of being socially and environmentally responsible (Yusof et al., 2011). Businesses can optimize this relationship to enhance customer loyalty. Consumers' positive attitudes toward corporate social activity affect their perceptions and behaviors. An increase in loyalty implies a reduction in marketing costs and increased revenue.

Guests and tour operators care about how resorts are managing their social and natural capital. Investors and authorities are also monitoring how well policies are being implemented, while customers are expecting businesses to behave responsibly. For both tour operators and customers, there is an increasing need for resorts to have sustainability certifications. CSR performance positively influences consumers' purchase intentions (Tian et al., 2011), and it also contributes to customer satisfaction (Luo and Bhattacharya, 2006). This is an opportunity for businesses to optimize on customer satisfaction and future purchase intentions. At the same time, CSR can provide firms with an insurance-like protection and reduce idiosyncratic risk (Luo and Bhattacharya, 2009). By taking into consideration the benefits of sustainability and CSR, firms have the opportunity to leverage their brand reputation.

This chapter provides some insights to help hotel practitioners align their strategies with CSR to optimize on best outcomes. It highlights the relationship between sustainability initiatives and brand reputation. It is hoped that it will fuel further research linking brand, sustainability and CSR practices.

References

Alamro, A. and Rowley, J., 2011. "Antecedents of brand preference for mobile telecommunications services", *Journal of Product & Brand Management* 20 (6), 475–486.

Becker E. J., 2009. *The Proximity Hotel: A Case Study on Guest Satisfaction of Sustainable Luxury Environments.* Master's Thesis. Greensboro, NC: The University of North Carolina at Greensboro.

Berezan, O., Raab, C., Yoo, M., and Love, C., 2013. Sustainable hotel practices and nationality: the impact on guest satisfaction and guest intention to return. *International Journal of Hospitality Management* 34, 227–233.

Bernardo, M., Casadesus, M., Karapetrovic, S., and Heras, I., 2009. How integrated are environmental, quality and other standardised management systems? An empirical study. *Journal of Cleaner Production* 17(8), 742–750.

Bohdanowicz, P., 2005. European hoteliers' environmental attitudes: greening the business. *Cornell Hotel and Restaurant Administration Quarterly* 46(2),188–204.

Bohdanowicz, P., 2006. Environmental awareness and initiatives in the Swedish and Polish hotel industries – survey results. *International Journal of Hospitality Management* 25(4), 662–682.

Bohdanowicz, P. and Zientara, P., 2009. Hotel companies' contribution to improving the quality of life of local communities and the well-being of their employees. *Tourism and Hospitality Research* 9(2), 147–158.

Cainelli, G., Mazzanti, M., and Zoboli, R., 2011. Environmentally oriented innovative strategies and firm performance in services: micro-evidence from Italy. *International Review of Applied Economics* 25(1), 61–85.

Carroll, A. B., 1991. The pyramid of corporate social responsibility: toward the moral management of organizational stakeholders. *Business Horizons* 34, 39–48.

Cavagnaro E. and Curiel G. H., 2012. *The Three Levels of Sustainability*. Sheffield: Greenleaf.

Chan, C. K. C., 2013. Promoting freedom of association in China? Putting transnational corporate social responsibility into a national context. *Journal of Comparative Asian Development*, 12(1), 6–34.

Chan, E. S. W., 2011. Implementing environmental management systems in small and medium-sized hotels: obstacles. *Journal of Hospitality and Tourism Research*, 35(1), 3–23.

Chan, W.W., 2009. Environmental measures for hotels' environmental management systems: ISO 14001. *International Journal of Contemporary Hospitality Management* 21(5), 542–560.

Chen, Y., 2010. The drivers of green brand equity: green brand image, green satisfaction, and green trust. *Journal of Business Ethics*, 93(2), 307–319.

Chen, Y. S. and Chang, C. H., 2013. Greenwash and green trust: the mediation effect of green consumer confusion and green perceived risk. *Journal of Business Ethics* 114(3), 489–500.

Chomvilailuk, R. and Butcher, K., 2010. Enhancing brand preference through corporate social responsibility initiatives in the Thai banking sector. *Asia Pacific Journal of Marketing and Logistics*, 22(3), 397–418.

Corte, V. D., Piras, A., and Zamparelli, G., 2010. Brand and image: the strategic factors in destination marketing. *International Journal of Leisure and Tourism Marketing*, 1 (4), 358–377.

Crane, A., Matten, D., and Spence, L.J., 2008. *Corporate Social Responsibility: Readings and Cases in a Global Context*. Abingdon, Oxon: Routledge.

De Grosbois, D., 2012. Corporate social responsibility reporting by the global hotel industry: commitment, initiatives and performance. *International Journal of Hospitality Management* 313, 896–905.

de Leaniz, P. M. G. and Rodriguez, I. R. D. B., 2015. Exploring the antecedents of hotel customer loyalty: a social identity perspective. *Journal of Hospitality Marketing & Management*, 24(1), 1–23.

Delgado, E. and Munuera, J. L., 2005. Does brand trust matter to brand equity?, *The Journal of Product and Brand Management*, 14(3), 187–196.

Deloitte Consumer Survey, 2008, June 5. Business travelers are starting to demand green lodging.

Dhaoui, C., 2014. An empirical study of luxury brand marketing effectiveness and its impact on consumer engagement on Facebook. *Journal of Global Fashion Marketing*, 5, 209–222.

Dummett, K., 2006. Drivers for corporate environmental responsibility (CER), *Environment, Development and Sustainability*, 8(3), 375–389.

Dwyer, L., 2005. Relevance of triple bottom line reporting to achievement of sustainable tourism: a scoping study. *Tourism Review International*, 9(1), 79–93.

Eisingerich, A. B., Rubera, G., Seifert, M., and Bhardwaj, G., 2011. Doing good and doing better despite negative information? The role of corporate social responsibility in consumer resistance to negative information/ *Journal of Service Research*, 14(1), 60–75.

Elkington, J., 1997. *Cannibals with Forks: The Triple Bottom Line of 21st Century Business*. Oxford, UK: Capstone Publishing.

Epler Wood, M., Leray, T., 2005. *Corporate Responsibility and the Tourism Sector in Cambodia*. Washington, DC: World Bank Group.

Erdogan, N. and Tosun, C., 2009. Environmental performance of tourism accommodations in the protected areas: case of Goreme Historical National Park. *International Journal of Hospitality Management* 28(3), 406–414.

Faux, J., 2005. Theoretical and practical contexts of triple bottom line performance and reporting: implications for the tourism sector. *Tourism Review International* 9(1), 95–105.

Gursoy, D., Chen, J. S., and Chi, C. G., 2014. Theoretical examination of destination loyalty formation. *International Journal of Contemporary Hospitality Management*, 26(5), 809–827.

Han, H., Hsu, L. J., Lee, J. S., and Sheu, C., 2011. Are lodging customers ready to go green? An examination of attitudes, demographics, and eco-friendly intentions. *International Journal of Hospitality Management*, 30, 345–355.

Hawkins D. and Cunningham J., 1996. It is "never-never land" when interest groups prevail. In: Harrison L. C. and Husbands, W. (eds), *Practicing Responsible Tourism*. New York, NY: John Wiley & Son Inc., pp. 350–365.

He, H. and Li, Y., 2011. CSR and service brand: the mediating effect of brand identification and moderating effect of service quality. *Journal of Business Ethics* 100, 673–688.

Henderson, J., 2007. Corporate social responsibility and tourism: hotel companies in Phuket, Thailand, after the Indian Ocean tsunami. *International Journal of Hospitality Management*, 26(1), 228–239.

Hillenbrand, C. and Money, K., 2007. Corporate responsibility and corporate reputation: two separate concepts or two sides of the same coin? *Corporate Reputation Review*, 10(4), 261–277.

Hoeffler, S. and Keller, K. L., 2002. Building brand equity through corporate societal marketing. *Journal of Public Policy and Marketing*, 21(1), 78–89.

Horiuchi, R. and Schuchard, R., 2009. *Understanding and Preventing Greenwash: A Business Guide*. London: Futerra Sustainability Communications.

Hsieh, Y. C., 2012. Hotel companies' environmental policies and practices: a content analysis of their web pages. *International Journal of Contemporary Hospitality Management*, 24(1), 97–121.

Hsu, K., 2012. The advertising effects of corporate social responsibility on corporate reputation and brand equity: evidence from the life insurance industry in Taiwan. *Journal of Business Ethics*, 109(2), 189–201.

Jones, P., Hillier, D., and Comfort, D., 2014. Assurance of the leading UK food retailers' corporate social responsibility/sustainability reports. *Corporate Governance*, 14(1), 130–138.

Jose, S., Rugimbana, R., and Gatfield, T., 2012. Consumer responses to CSR driven microfinance strategy of bank – An empirical investigation based on India. *International Journal of Business and Management*, 7(21), 1–14.

Kang, K. H., Lee, S., and Huh, C., 2010. Impacts of positive and negative corporate social responsibility activities on company performance in the hospitality industry. *International Journal of Hospitality Management*, 29(1), 72–82.

Kang, S. and Hur, W. M., 2012. Investigating the antecedents of green brand equity: a sustainable development perspective. *Corporate Social Responsibility and Environmental Management*, 19(5), 306–316.

Kim, Y. and Han, H., 2010. Intention to pay conventional-hotel prices at a green hotel – A modification of the theory of planned behavior. *Journal of Sustainable Tourism*, 18, 997–1014. doi:10.1080/09669582.2010.490300

Kolodinsky, R., Madden, T., Zisk, D., and Henkel, E., 2010. Attitudes about corporate social responsibility: business student predictors. *Journal of Business Ethics*, 91 (2), 67–81.

Lai, K. H., Cheng, T. C. E., and Tang, A. K. Y., 2010. Green retailing: factors for success. *California Management Review*, 52(2), 6–31.

Lee, S. and Heo, C. Y., 2009. Corporate social responsibility and customer satisfaction among US publicly traded hotels and restaurants. *International Journal of Hospitality Management*, 28, 635–637.

Lee, T. J., 2011. Role of hotel design in enhancing destination branding. *Annals of Tourism Research*, 38(2), 708–711.

Lichtenstein, D. R., Drumwright, M. E., and Braig, B.M., 2004. The effect of corporate social responsibility on customer donations to corporate-supported nonprofits. *Journal of Marketing*, 68, 16–32.

Loureiro, S. M. C. and Kastenholz, E., 2011. Corporate reputation, satisfaction, delight, and loyalty towards rural lodging units in Portugal. *International Journal of Hospitality Management*, 30, 575–583.

Luo, X. and Bhattacharya, C. B., 2006. Corporate social responsibility, customer satisfaction, and market value. *Journal of Marketing*, 70(4), 1–18.

Luo, X. and Bhattacharya, C. B., 2009. The debate overdoing good: corporate social performance, strategic marketing levers, and firm-idiosyncratic risk. *Journal of Marketing*, 73(6), 198–213.

Lyon, T. P. and Maxwell, J. W., 2011. Greenwash: corporate environmental disclosure under threat of audit. *Journal of Economics and Management Strategy*, 20(1), 3–41.

Maignan, I., Ferrell, O. C. and Hult, G. T. M., 1999. Corporate citizenship: cultural antecedents and business benefits. *Academy of Marketing Science Journal*, 27(4), 455–469.

Mandhachitara, R. and Poolthong, Y., 2011. A model of customer loyalty and corporate social responsibility. *Journal of Services Marketing*, 25(2), 122–133.

Marin, L. and Ruiz, S., 2007. "I need you too!" Corporate identity attractiveness for consumers and the role of social responsibility. *Journal of Business Ethics*, 71(3), 245–260.

Marin, L., Ruiz, S., and Rubio, A., 2009. The role of identity salience in the effects of corporate social responsibility on consumer behavior. *Journal of Business Ethics*, 84(1), 65–78.

Mathies, C. and Gudergan, S., 2012. Do status levels in loyalty programs change customers' willingness to pay? *Journal of Revenue Pricing Management*, 11(3), 274–288.

Matten, D. and Crane, A., 2005. Corporate citizenship: toward an expected theoretical conceptualization. *Academy of Management Review*, 30(1), 166–179.

Mattila, A. S., 2006. How affective commitment boosts guest loyalty (and promotes frequent-guest programs). *Cornell Hotel and Restaurant Administration Quarterly*, 47(2), 174–181.

Mattila, A. S. and Hanks, L., 2012. Antecedents to participation in corporate social responsibility programs. *Journal of Service Management*, 23(5), 664–676.

Mirabi, V. R., Asgari. A., Tehrani, A. G., and Moghaddam, B. H., 2014. The impact of corporate social responsibility (CSR) on the bank preference in banking industry: The case study: Bans of Mellat and Refah in Iran. *Kuwait Chapter of Arabian Journal of Business and Management Review*, 3(7), 476–487.

McNamaraa, E. K., and Gibson, C., 2008. Environmental sustainability in practice? A macro-scale profile of tourist accommodation facilities in Australia's coastal zone. *Journal of Sustainable Tourism*, 16(1), 85–100.

Myung E., McClaren A. and Li, L., 2012. Environmentally related research in scholarly hospitality journals: current status and future opportunities. *International Journal of Hospitality Management*, 31(4), 1264–1275.

Nikolaeva, R. and Bicho, M., 2011. The role of institutional and reputational factors in the voluntary adoption of corporate social responsibility standards. *Journal of Academic Marketing Science*, 39(1), 136–157.

Nunkoo, R. and Ramkissoon, H., 2011. Developing a community support model for tourism. *Annals of Tourism Research*, 38(3), 964–988.

Nunkoo, R. and Ramkissoon, H., 2016. Stakeholders' views of enclave tourism: a Grounded theory approach. *Journal of Hospitality & Tourism Research*. doi: 10.1177

Park, J., Kim, H. J., and McCleary, K. W., 2014. The impact of top management's environmental attitudes on hotel companies' environmental management. *Journal of Hospitality and Tourism Research*, 38(1), 95–115.

Paek, S., Xiao, Q., Lee, S., and Song, H., 2013. Does managerial ownership affect different corporate social responsibility dimensions? An empirical examination of U.S. publicly traded hospitality firms. *International Journal of Hospitality Management*, 34, 423–433.

Parguel, B., Benoît-Moreau, F., and Larceneux, F., 2011. How sustainability ratings might deter 'greenwashing': a closer look at ethical corporate communication. *Journal of Business Ethics*, 102(1), 15–28.

Peloza, J. and Shang, J., 2011. How can corporate social responsibility activities create value for stakeholders? A systematic review. *Journal of the Academy Marketing Science*, 39(1), 117–135.

Polo, A. I., Frías, D. M., and Rodríguez, M. A., 2013. Antecedents of loyalty toward rural hospitality enterprises: the moderating effect of the customers' previous experience. *International Journal of Hospitality Management*, 34(1), 127–137.

Pomering, A. and Johnson, L. W., 2009. Advertising corporate social responsibility initiatives to communicate corporate image: inhibiting scepticism to enhance persuasion. *Corporate Communications: An International Journal*, 14(4), 420–439.

Rahbar, E. and Abdul Wahid, N., 2011. Investigation of green marketing tools' effect on consumers' purchase behavior. *Business Strategy Series*, 12(2), 73–83.

Rahman, I., Reynolds, D., and Svaren, S., 2012. How green are North American hotels? An exploration of low-cost adoption. *International Journal of Hospitality Management*, 31, 720–727.

Ramkissoon, H. and Mavondo, F., 2016. Managing customer relationships in hotel chains: a comparison between guest and manager perceptions. In M. Ivanova, S. Ivanov, and V. Magnini (eds.), *The Routledge Handbook of Hotel Chain Management*. Abingdon, UK: Routledge, p. 295.

Ramkissoon, H. and Uysal, M., 2010. Testing the role of authenticity in cultural tourism consumption: a case of mauritius. *Tourism Analysis*, 15, 571–583.

Ramkissoon, H. and Uysal, M., 2011. The effects of perceived authenticity, information search behavior, motivation and destination imagery on cultural behavioral intentions of tourists. *Current Issues in Tourism*, 14(6), 537–562.

Rangan, K., Chase, L., and Karim, S., 2012. Why every company needs a csr strategy and how to build it. Working Paper No. 12–088, *Harvard Business School,* Boston, MA.

Ricaurte, E., 2016. Hotel sustainability benchmarking index 2016: Energy, water, and carbon. *Cornell Hospitality Report*, 16(16), 3–13.

Ricks, J. M., 2005. An assessment of strategic corporate philanthropy on perceptions of brand equity variables. *Journal of Consumer Marketing*, 22(3), 121–134.

Segarra-Õna, M., Peiró-Signes,Á.,Verma, R., and Miret-Pastor, L., 2012. Does environ-mental certification help the economic performance of hotels? Evidence from the Spanish hotel industry. *Cornell Hospitality Quarterly*, 53(3), 242–256.

Sen, S., Bhattacharya, C. B., and Korschun, D., 2006.The role of corporate social responsibility in strengthening multiple stakeholder relationships: a field experiment. *Academy of Marketing Science*, 34(2), 158–166.

Singh, J., Sanchez, M., and del Bosque, I., 2008. Understanding corporate social responsibility and product perceptions in consumer market: a cross-culture evolution. *Journal of Business Ethics*, 80(3), 597–611.

Siu, N.Y., Zhang,T.J., and Kwan, H., 2014. Effect of corporate social responsibility, customer attribution and prior expectation on post-recovery satisfaction. *International Journal of Hospitality Management*. 43, 87–97.

Sloan, P., Legrand,W., and Chen, J. S., 2012. *Sustainability in the Hospitality Industry: Principles of Sustainable Operations*, 2nd ed. London: Routledge.

So, K. K. F., King, C., Sparks, B., and Wang,Y., 2013.The influence of customer brand identification on hotel brand evaluation and loyalty development. *International Journal of Hospitality Management*, 34(1), 31–41.

Stoddard, J. E., Pollard, C. E., and Evans, M. R., 2012. The triple bottom line: a framework for sustainable tourism development. *International Journal of Hospitality & Tourism Administration*, 13(3), 233–258.

Tanford, S., Carola, R., and Kimb,Y. S., 2012. Determinants of customer loyalty and purchasing behavior for full-service and limited-service hotels. *International Journal of Hospitality Management*, 31(2), 319–328.

Tarí, J. J., Claver-Cortés, E., Pereira-Moline, J., and Molina-Azorin, J. F., 2010. Levels of quality and environmental management in the hotel industry: their joint influence on firm performance. *International Journal of Hospitality Management*, 29(3), 500–510.

Teng, C. C., Horng, J. S., Hu, M. L., Chien, L. H., and Shen,Y. C., 2012. Developing energy conservation and carbon reduction indicators for the hotel industry in Taiwan. *International Journal of Hospitality Management*, 31, 199–208.

Tian, Z.,Wang, R., and Yang, W., 2011. Consumer responses to corporate social responsibility (CSR) in China. *Journal of Business Ethics*, 101(2), 197–212.

Torres, A., Bijmolt, T., Tribo, J., and Verhoef, P., 2012. Generating global brand equity through corporate social responsibility to key stakeholders. *International Journal of Research in Marketing*, 29(1), 13–24.

Turker, D., 2009. Measuring corporate social responsibility: a scale development study. *Journal of Business Ethics*, 85(4), 411–427.

Tyrrell, T. and Johnston J.R., 2012. The role of tourism in sustainable communities. In: M. Uysal, R. Perdue, and M. J. Sirgy (eds.), *Handbook of Tourism and Quality of Life Research*.Vol. 1. Dordrecht, The Netherlands: Springer, pp. 565–582.

Tyrrell,T., Paris, C. M., and Biaett,V., 2013. A quantified triple bottom line for tourism: experimental results. *Journal of Travel Research*, 52(3), 279–293.

Tzschentke, N. A., Kirk, D., and Lynch, P. A., 2008. Going green: decisional factors in small hospitality operations. *International Journal of Hospitality Management*, 27, 126–133. doi:10.1016/j.ijhm.2007.07.010

U.S. Travel Association, 2009. American travelers more familiar with 'green travel' but unwilling to pay more to support it. Retrieved from www. ustravel.org/news/press-releases/american-travelers-more-familiar-%E2%80%98green-travel%E2%80%99

Vermeir, I. and Verbeke, W., 2006. Sustainable food consumption: exploring the consumer attitude-behavioral intention. *Journal of Agricultural & Environmental Ethics*, 19(2), 169–194.

Weaver, D., 2006. *Sustainable Tourism: Theory and Practice*. London: Elsevier.

Weaver, D., 2010. Geopolitical dimensions of sustainable tourism. *Tourism Recreation Research*, 35(1), 45–51.

Yoo, B., Donthu, N., and Lee, S., 2000. An examination of selected marketing mix elements and brand equity, *Journal of the Academy of Marketing Science*, 28(2), 195–211.

Yoo, M. and Bai, B., 2013. Customer loyalty marketing research: A comparative approach between hospitality and business journals. *International Journal of Hospitality Management*, 33, 166–177.

Yusof, J. M., Musa, R., and Rahman, S. A., 2011. Functional store image and corporate social responsibility image: a congruity analysis on store loyalty. *World Academy of Science, Engineering and Technology*, 77(7), 1233–1240.

Xu, X. and Gursoy, D., 2015. A conceptual framework of sustainable hospitality supply chain management. *Journal of Hospitality Marketing & Management*, 24, 229–259.

33

Sustainable practices in Spanish and Hungarian hotels

A Triple Bottom Line approach[1]

Irene Gil-Saura and María-Eugenia Ruiz-Molina

Introduction

As tourism grows as an economic activity, an important challenge should be to conciliate sustainability and development with the quality of life of all stakeholders (Uysal et al. 2016). In highly developed tourism destinations, such as Spain, locals have generally informed positive attitudes in terms of improved economic quality of life (Teye et al. 2002). Notwithstanding, many tourism destinations develop to meet tourists' needs and wants without caring about the environmental impact of tourism activities (Andereck et al. 2005). In view of all this, the challenge for tourism destinations is to minimize the negative impacts of tourism while maintaining the quality of life of residents, and to maximize the positive impacts of tourism through "sustaining resources that provide quality experience and services for both tourists and locals" (Uysal et al. 2012, p. 433).

Several studies have examined the sustainable practices of hospitality companies (Teng et al. 2012), but most of them have only focused on environmental sustainability (e.g., Kim et al. 2012; Rahman et al. 2012; Chen 2015), or social practices such as corporate social responsibility (e.g., Bohdanowicz and Zientara 2009; Paek et al. 2013; Park and Levy 2014). In the present chapter, we address the study of sustainability in hotels assuming a Triple Bottom Line (TBL) approach, used as a tool to analyze organizational performance in terms of economic, social and environmental issues (Elkington 1994).

This chapter has three objectives: first, it aims to review the main sustainable practices in hospitality via a discussion of the three TBL pillars. Second, it provides evidence of the importance of these practices in the main hotel chains, with 4- and 5-star hotels in two countries representing highly visited tourism destinations (Spain) and emergent tourism destinations (Hungary). Last, we critically discuss some issues to be taken into consideration by hotel groups for the design and implementation of sustainable practices in increasingly globalized markets, and suggest some avenues for further research.

Sustainable practices in hospitality

In the tourism marketing literature, it has been argued that, as a business goal, sustainability should be viewed as a TBL responsibility, with the expectation that business results should be based not only on economic prosperity, but should also take into account the criteria of environmental integrity and social equity (Mihalic et al. 2012; Stylos and Vassiliadis 2015), as well as their interrelationships (Farsari 2012). Economic, social and environmental sustainability have been highlighted as sources of benefits for hotels, local communities and the natural environment (Cvelbar and Dwyer 2013; Ryan 2003), allowing the achievement of firm financial goals and competitiveness (Bryson and Lombardi 2009; Zink and Fischer 2013). In a survey conducted on U.S. consumers who frequently stay at hotels from a TBL approach, Xu and Gursoy (2015) conclude that all sustainability actions of a supply chain can increase customers' satisfaction, which in turn can lead to higher customer loyalty, and ultimately increase customers' willingness to pay a premium. However, many tourism companies still follow a short-term approach, focusing on economic benefits while neglecting social and environmental sustainability (Bach et al. 2014).

In view of the importance of sustainability, a number of frameworks and guidelines for reporting sustainability initiatives are available to organizations, e.g. the European Union's Eco-Management and Audit Scheme (EMAS), the Global Reporting Initiative (GRI), and the International Organization for Standardization (ISO) IS 14603:2012 and IS 26000:2010 standards. Possibly the most important standards in TBL reporting is GRI's Sustainability Reporting Framework G4 release, since they give the possibility for a company – regardless of its industry – to report on a broad spectrum of economic, social and environmental sustainability activities and allow for comparability (Legrand et al. 2014). Next, the three pillars of TBL are further discussed.

Economic pillar

Economic or financial sustainability refers to a business's ability to make a profit to survive and to benefit the economic systems at the local and international level (Roberts and Tribe 2008). The Global Reporting Initiative (GRI 2013) states that the economic dimension of sustainability concerns the impacts of an organization on the economic conditions of its stakeholders and on economic systems at local, national and global levels, and points out that it does not focus on the financial condition of the organization.

According to GRI (2013), organizations can provide evidence of their economic sustainable practices by reporting their economic performance in terms of direct and indirect economic value generated and distributed, market presence, indirect economic impacts of their activities in terms of development and impact of infrastructure investments and services supported, and procurement practices (e.g. proportion of spending on local suppliers at significant locations of operation).

In the hospitality industry, Assaf et al. (2012) consider several financial indicators (e.g. profit growth, return on assets, profitability of capital, solvency ratio and cash flow). Moreover, in a survey conducted on Greek hotel managers regarding their perceptions of TBL sustainability policies, Stylos and Vassiliadis (2015) list several business ratios and formulas, as well as marketing metrics related to economic tools and practices, covering marketing, human resources management, financial management, strategy, business administration and innovation.

Marketing metrics include market share, brand penetration, customer satisfaction and loyalty evaluation, and profit margins and promotional costs calculations, among others. Human resources management includes calculation of personnel workload and estimations of sales force effectiveness. Financial management gathers debt to equity and return on investment (ROI) ratios as well as internal rate of return (IRR), among others. Strategy items refer to the use of models for planning, implementation, and control of investments and relevant budgets, perceptual analysis for depicting the position of the hotel in relation to competitors in customers' minds and the hotel's strategies in comparison to those of competitors. Regarding business administration, the authors point out the use of standardized procedures for human resources planning and for recruiting, training, evaluating and rewarding personnel, and the use of a robust management system (e.g., ERP) to manage supplies and logistics. Last, innovation items assess the efforts of a hotel to support, analyze, record, and assess proposed and innovative ideas, processes, and services on behalf of personnel, and the hotel's degree of innovation.

Social pillar

The social dimension of sustainability includes the actions taken toward enhancing the welfare of internal and external stakeholders (Assaf et al. 2012), mainly focused on employees, communities, suppliers and governments. Social sustainability is difficult to define, as it includes definitions of society, culture, and community, being concerned with the social interaction relations, behavioral patterns and values between people (Roberts and Tribe 2008). The term corporate social responsibility (CSR) is used to describe the organization's social activities, such as those labelled as "strategic philanthropy" or "corporate citizenship" (Hubbard 2009).

Following the GRI G4 structure (GRI 2013), social sustainability refers to labor practices and decent work[2] (e.g. employee turnover, benefits provided to employees, occupational health and safety, staff training and education, diversity and equal opportunity, equal remuneration for women and men, supplier assessment for labor practices), human rights (e.g. freedom of association and collective bargaining, child labor, forced or compulsory labor, indigenous rights, supplier human rights assessment), societal responsibility (e.g. actions on behalf of local communities, anticorruption, public policy) and product responsibility (e.g. customer health and safety, ethics in marketing communications, customer privacy).

In the hospitality industry, Assaf et al. (2012) mention cooperation with local residents, measuring customers' satisfaction level, cooperation with nongovernmental environmental organizations, higher employee salaries in comparison with other hotels, and satisfaction of local residents with the development of the hotel as examples of social sustainability practices. Also for hotels, Stylos and Vassiliadis (2015) identify several items used to assess a firm's social sustainability, classified under the categories of personnel policies, human rights, and local community impact and activities.

Notwithstanding, labor market regulations and work conditions may differ considerably from country to country (Serafini and Szamosi 2015). In this sense, international hotel groups should consider the suitability of implementing uniform sustainability practices in terms of human resources in their different subsidiaries.

Environmental pillar

Tourism is an industry that very much depends on the natural environment (Weaver 2012). Research has widely emphasized the importance of the environment for tourism activity and development (Butler 2008). Likewise, there is also a big concern about the impacts that tourism has on natural resources (Green et al. 1990; Claver-Cortés et al. 2007). The hotel industry generates much more negative environmental impacts that is perceived by public opinion, consuming a vast amount of local and imported nondurable goods, energy and water, as well as emitting a large amount of carbon dioxide (Bohdanowicz 2006). This fact explains why, since the early 1990s, tourism companies, mostly hotels, have undertaken different initiatives to mitigate the environmental impact of their activity as well as to provide evidence of their commitment to sustainable tourism.

According to GRI (2013), the environmental dimension of sustainability concerns an organization's impact on living and non-living natural systems, including land, air, water and ecosystems. This category covers impacts related to inputs (such as energy and water) and outputs (such as emissions, effluents and waste), biodiversity, transport, and product and service-related impacts, as well as environmental compliance and expenditures.

Among the tools and mechanisms applied by the hotel industry in terms of environmental sustainability, the most common ones are codes of conduct, best environmental practices, eco-labels, environmental management systems (EMS) and environmental performance indicators.

As indicators of hotel Environmental Management Standards (EMS), items included in the ISO14000 standards are considered. Some representative foreign green hotel assessment systems are also commonly considered as a reference in this industry, e.g. the Green Hotels Association, the State Economic and Trade Commission, the Caribbean Hotel Association, Grecotels, the Coalition for Environmental Responsible Economies (CERES), the South Pacific Tourism Organization (SPTO), the Global Stewards and the benchmarkhotel.com website. These systems frequently undertake hotel and tourism environmental cooperation programs and activities. They are committed to promoting the effective management of natural resources and to achieving sustainable tourism. These indicators consider the impact on the environment of both the internal management (services, operations, personnel, administration, marketing, and finance) and to the external environment (economics, technology, social trends, ecological environment, customers, competitors, and suppliers).

When implementing an environmental policy, hotels mainly focus on technical efficiency (Hathroubi et al. 2014) and cost efficiency (Shieh 2012). In this sense, there is evidence in the hospitality industry of the importance of the savings arising from efficient water management (e.g. Kasim et al., 2014), measuring and implementing practices to reduce energy consumption (e.g. Sheivachman 2011; Day and Cai 2012; Abdi et al. 2013; Araki et al. 2013), and the benefits of recycling solid waste (Singh et al. 2014). Examples of sustainable practices related to the creation of a healthy and safe indoor environment in hotels are also provided in the literature, e.g. hotel management of construction (Cui and Hui 2011), LEED certification for buildings (De Lima et al. 2012), design (Brody 2014) and green renovation schedule requirements (Dienes and Wang 2010).

In Assaf et al. (2012), hotel environmental sustainability indicators include quantity of solid waste, quantity of water consumption, CO_2 emissions, the number of ecological quality labels and quantity of recycling waste. Furthermore, Stylos and Vassiliadis (2015) detail several indicators of hotel power-saving practices, energy and environmental impact mitigation, use of resources and water, and reuse and recycle measures, such as reuse of towels/linen and communication materials, and donation of used clothes and leftover food, among others.

Sustainable practices in mature and emergent destinations: Two case studies

The second objective of this chapter is to provide an overview about the level of implementation of several sustainability practices in highly visited and emergent tourism destinations. The main hotel chains with 4- and 5-star hotels in Spain and Hungary are considered as an example. Hotel chains are prone to standardize their procedures and manuals (Kasim 2007), while upscale hotels are a reference point in this industry (Stylos and Vassiliadis 2015).

A survey was conducted based on a questionnaire distributed to hotel managers. Following the TBL approach suggested by Elkington (1994), we included items on the questionnaire for measuring the level of development or implementation of practices for the economic, social and environmental sustainability of each hotel. The items were adapted from Stylos and Vassiliadis (2015).

In particular, the importance of economic sustainability for each hotel was measured through the relevance of economic feasibility (13 items) and innovation (4 items), according to the hotel managers. Social sustainability was assessed through personnel policies (8 items), human rights

(3 items), and local community impact and activities (4 items). Last, environmental sustainability was measured through the hotel manager's assessment of the importance of the hotel's environmental policy (4 items), water management (8 items), energy (7 items), solid waste (7 items), indoor environment (health and safety, 8 items), and green purchasing (5 items). All items were measured using a 5-point Likert scale (1 = not at all important; 5 = totally important).

The questionnaire was written in English, and was translated into Spanish and Hungarian or Magyar by native translators in these languages, and subsequently subjected to back translation to ensure equivalence between versions in different languages.

Regarding the data collection, hotel managers of 39 hotel chains with 4- and 5-star hotels on the Mediterranean coast of Spain were telephoned and invited to participate in the survey; they were then sent the link to the questionnaire by e-mail. Fifteen valid questionnaires were received, representing a response rate of 38.46 percent. In Hungary, following the same procedure, hotel managers of 48 hotel chains with 4- and 5-star hotels in Budapest and the surrounding region were contacted, with 36 valid questionnaires received (response rate: 75%).

Descriptive analyses were conducted to provide an overview regarding the importance of economic, social and environmental sustainable practices from the point of view of the hotel chain.

Case study: Sustainable practices in Spanish hotels

Spain is the third most popular tourism destination in the world in terms of tourist arrivals (UNWTO 2016), with more than 60 million tourists visiting each year. Accommodating these visitors resulted in a 5 percent retail value growth in 2015 to reach a total of €20.3 billion, with a revenue of €16.5 billion being generated by hotels (Euromonitor International 2016b), and has boosted the creation and development of hotel groups with important presence both in Spain and internationally, such as Meliá Hotels, the market leader in Spain and the third biggest hotel group in Europe (HOTELS 2016). The Spanish hospitality industry excels also in terms of quality, since Spain has the seventh highest number of 5-star hotels in the world. Table 33.1 shows the top-ten ranking of hotel groups operating in Spain, where all hotel groups except for Accor have a Spanish origin. Moreover, this industry is highly atomized, since the first ten hotel groups only comprise 17.2 percent of the market quota, in terms of retail value at retail selling price.

Table 33.1 Hotels national brand owner company shares (% retail value rsp), Spain

	% Value 2015
1. Meliá Hotels International SA	3.5
2. AC Hotels by Marriott – ACHM Spain Management	2.3
3. NH Hotel Group SA	2.1
4. Barceló, Grupo	1.7
5. Iberostar SA, Grupo	1.5
6. Paradores de Turismo de España SA	1.4
7. H10 Hotels, Group	1.4
8. Accor Hoteles España SA	1.3
9. Riu Hoteles SA	1.1
10. Nacional Hotelera SL	0.9

Source: Euromonitor International (2006b).

In view of these figures, it may be argued that a trade-off exists between the contribution of tourism to GDP and job creation, and the economic, social and environmental impact of this activity on Spain. Sustainable practices may allow economic benefits to be harnessed together with the mitigation of the negative impact on the quality of life of residents and visitors. In order to assess the level of development or implementation of practices for economic, social and environmental sustainability by upscale hotels in Spain, a survey of hotel managers was conducted. Mean values and standard deviations for the items in each relevant area of economic, social and environmental sustainability are shown in Table 33.2.

Table 33.2 Implementation of sustainable practices in 4- and 5-star hotels in Spain

	Mean	*St. dev.*
Economic sustainability	**4.29**	**0.25**
Hotel economic feasibility	4.46	0.30
Innovation	4.11	0.29
Social sustainability	**3.38**	**0.36**
Personnel policies	3.79	0.68
Human rights	3.25	0.18
Local community impact and activities	3.11	0.16
Environmental sustainability	**4.05**	**0.18**
Hotel environmental policy	3.86	0.18
Water resource	4.16	0.20
Energy	4.24	0.18
Solid waste	3.98	0.57
Indoor environment (health and safety)	4.23	0.20
Green purchasing	3.84	0.18

Although the Spanish hotel managers of upscale hotels interviewed declared that they considered most of the items used to assess economic, social and environmental sustainability to be very important or totally important, the TBL pillar related to economic viability has the highest scores, in line with previous studies (e.g. Bianchi 2004; Harrison et al. 2003). This evidence is also consistent with the strong rivalry between hotel groups in Spain, a mature tourism destination where there are many players and where the market leader only holds 3.5 percent of the market quota.

Environmentally sustainable practices are also prioritized by hotel chains, especially those that are increasing efficiency and reducing costs in the use of water and energy resources. In contrast, there is high variability in the implementation of practices related to solid waste management.

In comparison to practices oriented towards economic and environmental sustainability, social sustainability issues are not considered as important. Many researchers have underlined the importance of social sustainability for the hotel industry (Kang et al. 2010; Xu and Gursoy 2015). Moreover, high variability in responses is observed for "personnel policies," evidencing the mixed level of development of such practices by the main hotel chains in Spain.

Concerning stakeholders, more attention is paid to practices related to sustainability for internal groups of interest (i.e. corporate management and staff education) in comparison to external stakeholders (e.g. local community). Therefore, there is a need for hotels to consider all stakeholders in order to bring a holistic sustainable strategy into the hospitality industry.

Case study: Sustainable practices in Hungarian hotels

Hungary is the European Union (EU) country of Central and Eastern Europe that has experienced the biggest increase in the number of visitors in recent years. Forecasts by the World Tourism Organization (UNWTO 2016) predict an 83.33 percent growth in visitors from 2010 to 2030, the biggest increase in Europe.

Growth is mainly explained by the increased disposable incomes allocated from household budgets to domestic travel and the increase in the number of inbound trips due to the popularity of Budapest as a low-cost airlines destination.

Hungarian hotels consistently reported a record year in 2015, as they improved on all major parameters, such as value sales and room occupancy rates. Most of the luxury-positioned outlets cover Budapest and spa/lakeside locations with high tourist traffic across the whole year. Seven new luxury hotels and 25 non-rated hotels which opened during 2015 also contributed to the 9 percent current value growth in hotels in that year (Euromonitor International 2016a).

A local hotel group, Danubius Hotels, runs the largest network of premium-positioned hotels in Hungary (Table 33.3). There is also an important presence of foreign hotel groups (e.g. Accor, Marriott, Boscolo) and hotel brands (e.g. Best Western Radisson Blue and Hilton hotels in Hungary managed by Danubius Hotels Zrt; Holiday Inn hotels, managed by Alliance Hotel Budapest Kft; InterContinental hotels, managed by Mansion Danube Hungary Kft). The top ten hotel groups in Hungary account for 37.7 percent of the market quota.

Table 33.3 Hotels national brand owner company shares (% retail value rsp), Hungary

	% Value 2015
1. Danubius Hotels Zrt	11.7
2. Accor-Pannonia Hotels ZRt	10.7
3. Hunguest Hotels ZRt	3.8
4. Marriott International Inc	3.7
5. Mansion Danube Hungary Kft	2.6
6. Boscolo Hotels Hungary Kft	2.3
7. Mellow Mood Ltd	1.2
8. West End Szállodaüzemelteto Kft	1.1
9. Alliance Hotel Budapest Kft	0.3
10. Mad-Hotel és Iroda Kft	0.3

Source: Euromonitor International (2016a).

Regarding the importance of sustainability measures for Hungarian upscale hotels, mean values and standard deviations for responses from the hotel manager assessment are shown in Table 33.4.

For hotels in Hungary, average scores for sustainable practices are high, with scores of around 4 in the 5-point Likert scale (i.e. important). The low variability of responses (as reflected in standard deviations) may be explained by the wide consensus regarding the high level of implementation of sustainable practices by hotels in Hungary.

Table 33.4 Implementation of sustainable practices in 4- and 5-star hotels in Hungary

	Mean	St. dev.
Economic sustainability	**3.98**	**0.01**
Hotel economic feasibility	3.98	0.13
Innovation	3.97	0.14
Social sustainability	**4.01**	**0.04**
Personnel policies	4.04	0.15
Human rights	4.01	0.07
Local community impact and activities	3.97	0.15
Environmental sustainability	**3.98**	**0.02**
Hotel environmental policy	3.95	0.16
Water resource	4.00	0.08
Energy	3.96	0.10
Solid waste	4.02	0.14
Indoor environment (health and safety)	3.99	0.13
Green purchasing	3.97	0.16

Personnel policies emerge as the most relevant topic for Hungarian upscale hotels. Among these practices, the highest scores are for "The hotel tries to avoid high staff turnover" (4.28) and "Salaries and working conditions are above average within the local market" (4.22).

Moreover, in comparison to Spanish hotels, hotel chains established in Hungary show a greater appreciation of the importance of relations with the local community. This could be explained by the fact that, while the hotel groups involved in the quantitative study for Spain are mainly Spanish, most of the hotel chains established in Hungary are foreign companies, which can lead them to engage in activities that contribute to closer relations with the local community as a way to improve the perception of residents towards the companies.

Since 2007, Hungary has implemented a National Strategy for Sustainable Tourism Development in line with the guidelines of the EU and the World Tourism Organization (Vargáné Csobán and Bauerné Gáthy 2009), and more than a hundred hotels are already certified with a seal of environmental sustainability (Juhász-Dóra et al. 2015).

Managerial implications and avenues for further research

In this last section, we critically discuss some issues to be taken into consideration by hotel groups for the design and implementation of sustainable practices in increasingly globalized markets, and suggest some avenues for further research.

This chapter has provided an overview of sustainable practices from a TBL approach, paying special attention to hotel groups in an established tourist destination (i.e. Spain) and an emerging tourist destination (i.e. Hungary). Based on previous research and the evidence provided in the two case studies, some issues to be taken into consideration by hotel groups for the design and implementation of sustainable policies are discussed next.

First, recent research has provided evidence of the positive impact of sustainable policies of all TBL pillars – economic, social and environmental sustainability – on customer loyalty (e.g. Xu and Gursoy 2015). The impact of these hotel practices is amplified if they are integrated into the whole supply chain, thus generating significantly more positive effects compared with the effects obtained from sustainability actions implemented by only an individual hotel business (Ashby et al. 2012), such as an individual hotel (Xu and Gursoy 2015).

Second, regarding the level of implementation of sustainable practices in the hospitality industry in emergent destinations in comparison to hotels in well-established tourism destinations, from the strong implementation of these practices in the Hungarian case it may be inferred that international hotel groups are transferring their experience and capabilities to hotels in these destinations, whereas local hotel chains are making an effort to adopt the best practices. In this vein, hotel groups have to cope with global competition of tourism destinations where they are not present, and competition of other hotels and lodging facilities in the cities and regions where they are established. Moreover, increasingly demanding customers, often facing a trade-off between their desire for lower-priced products and their moral desire to contribute to companies' socially responsible actions (Hess et al. 2002), make sustainability issues a priority for hotels. However, even though sustainability actions are likely to generate significant benefits for hospitality companies, many of these actions are implemented because of regulatory enforcement instead of voluntary actions (Buckley 2012). Sustainability actions are therefore developed in many cases as a way to adapt to the competitive environment of the country or region where the hotel is located. In this sense, from the literature it has been noted that hotel location is a determining factor in the implementation of sustainable practices (e.g. Erdogan and Baris 2007; Le et al. 2006; Ruiz-Molina et al. 2010). The importance of sustainable practices may also differ depending on the hotel category or the characteristics of the hotel chain (Han et al. 2011; Ruiz-Molina et al. 2012).

To conciliate the trade-off between the need for standardization and adaptation, a "glocal" sustainability strategy may assist international hotel groups in achieving competitive advantages over rivals at a national and international level. This approach involves maintaining some core policies to guarantee brand consistency across outlets of the hotel group (e.g. Planet 21 environmental program in Accor Hotels) while taking into account the unique needs and limitations of each destination, geographical characteristics, environmental characteristics, and the socio-cultural characteristics of the different hotel locations.

Even if the present research is not free from limitations, mainly due to the reduced sample size, the two case studies allow us to suggest some further lines of research. First, the literature highlights the need to address economic, social and environmental aspects of sustainable business practices simultaneously, which has seldom been seen and tested in previous studies (Høgevold et al. 2015).

Moreover, further research should address the study of other hotel categories and lodging facilities, such as hostels, apartments and campsites, for instance. It may also allow for comparisons to be conducted to test if hotel location is a determinant of the implementation of sustainable practices, as some researchers suggest (e.g. Erdogan and Baris 2007; Le et al. 2006).

Furthermore, in our survey, only one respondent, i.e. the hotel manager, was interviewed in each organization. Additional responses of other members of the hotel staff, and other hotels in the same hotel chain may provide a more objective overview of the perceived importance of the sustainable practices of each organization. In this sense, it would be interesting to analyze whether the importance of sustainable practices differs across hotel category or hotel chain characteristics. Qualitative research could be employed in order to gain insight into the reasons for prioritizing a certain dimension of sustainability in comparison to others. Moreover, the customer point of view should be also taken into consideration, since triangulation may shed additional light on the prioritization of certain sustainable practices and the inherent investment in their implementation by the hotel.

In addition, from a methodological point of view, sustainability, hereby defined as a multidimensional construct, requires the development and validation of a scale for its measurement, and an assessment of the structural properties between the TBL-dimensions, which are still mostly unexplored. As suggested by Høgevold et al. (2015), further research should explore causal relationships between economic, social and environmental efforts of sustainable business practices, as well as their impact on guest trust and commitment, in to build long-lasting relations.

Notes

1   The authors are very grateful for the support of the projects ECO2013-43353-R and ECO2016-76553-R of the Spanish Ministry of Education and Science, as well as the "Pioneers into Practice 2015" Program financed by EIT-Climate KIC and the professionals collaborating in this research, Pablo Pintado and Katalin Juhász-Dóra.
2   According to the International Labour Organization, "Decent work involves opportunities for work that is productive and delivers a fair income, security in the workplace and social protection for families, better prospects for personal development and social integration, freedom for people to express their concerns, organize and participate in the decisions that affect their lives and equality of opportunity and treatment for all women and men" (www.ilo.org/global/topics/decent-work/lang--en/index.html).

References

Abdi, H., Creighton, D. and Nahavandi, S. (2013) "A sustainable energy saving method for hotels by green hotel deals", Chapter 62, in A. Håkansson, M. Höjer, R.J. Howlett, and L.C. Jain (eds.) *Sustainability in Energy and Buildings, Smart Innovation, Systems and Technologies* 22, Berlin Heidelberg: Springer-Verlag, 669–677.

Andereck, K.L., Valentine, K.M., Knopf, R.C. and Vogt, C.A. (2005) "Residents' perceptions of community tourism impacts", *Annals of Tourism Research* 32(4), 1056–1076.

Araki, H., Fujiwara, S., Jishi, T., Fujii, M., Yokota, T. and Nishida, T. (2013) "Winter production of green asparagus by using surplus heat from machinery room and used hot water from hotel's spa", in *International Symposium on New Technologies for Environment Control, Energy-Saving and Crop Production in Greenhouse and Plant Proceedings*, pp. 155–161. Available at www.actahort.org/books/1037/1037_15.htm [Accessed 10 August 2016].

Ashby, A., Leat, M. and Smith, M.H. (2012) "Making connections: A review of supply chain management and sustainability literature", *Supply Chain Management* 17(5), 497–516.

Assaf, A.G., Josiassen, A. and Cvelbar, L.K. (2012) "Does triple bottom line reporting improve hotel performance?", *International Journal of Hospitality Management* 31, 596–600.

Bach, M.P., Zoroja, J. and Merkac-Skok, M. (2014) "Social responsibility in tourism: System archetypes approach", *Kybernetes* 43(3/4), 587–600.

Bianchi, R.V. (2004) "Tourism restructuring and the politics of sustainability: A critical view from the European periphery (The Canary Islands)", *Journal of Sustainable Tourism* 12(6), 495–529.

Bohdanowicz, P. (2006) "Environmental awareness and initiatives in the Swedish and Polish hotel industries—survey results", *International Journal of Hospitality Management* 25(4), 662–682.

Bohdanowicz, P. and Zientara, P. (2009) "Hotel companies' contribution to improving the quality of life of local communities and the well-being of their employees", *Tourism and Hospitality Research* 9(2), 147–158.

Brody, D. (2014) "Go green: Hotels, design, and the sustainability paradox", *Design Issues* 30(3), 5–15.

Bryson, J.R. and Lombardi, R. (2009) "Balancing product and process sustainability against business property development process", *Business Strategy and the Environment* 18(2), 97–107.

Buckley, R. (2012) "Sustainable tourism: research and reality", *Annals of Tourism Research* 39(2), 528–546.

Butler, J. (2008) "The compelling 'hard case' for 'green' hotel development", *Cornell Hospitality Quarterly* 49(3), 234–244.

Chen, R.J.C. (2015) "From sustainability to customer loyalty: A case of full service hotels' guests", *Journal of Retailing and Consumer Services* 22, 261–265.

Claver-Cortés, E., Molina-Azorín, J.F., Pereira-Moliner, J. and López-Gamero, M.D. (2007) "Environmental strategies and their impact on hotel performance", *Journal of Sustainable Tourism* 15(6), 663–679.

Cui, B. and Hui, Z. (2011) "Research on the green hotel management of construction", ICEIS 2011 Proceedings of the 13th International Conference on Enterprise Information Systems, 1 DISI, pp. 453–456.

Cvelbar, L.K. and Dwyer, L. (2013) "An importance–performance analysis of sustainability factors for long-term strategy planning in Slovenian hotels", *Journal of Sustainable Tourism* 21(3), 487–504.

Day, J. and Cai, L. (2012) "Environmental and energy-related challenges to sustainable tourism in the United States and China", *International Journal of Sustainable Development and World Ecology* 19(5), 379–388.

De Lima Medeiros, M., Machado, D.F.C., Passador, J.L. and Passador, C.S. (2012) "Adopting LEED certification in lodging facilities: Greening the hospitality industry", *RAE Revista de Administracao de Empresas* 52(2), 179–192.

Dienes, C.J. and Wang, L. (2010) "Using a capacity control model to define optimal green hotel renovation schedule requirements", *International Journal of Operations and Quantitative Management* 16(3), 255–283.

Elkington, J. (1994) "Towards the sustainable corporation: Win-win-win business strategies for sustainable development", *California Management Review* 36(2), 90–100.

Erdogan, N., and Baris, E. (2007) "Environmental protection programs and conservation practices of hotels in Ankara, Turkey", *Tourism Management* 28(2), 604–614.

Euromonitor International (2016a). *Lodging in Hungary*. Category Briefing, 3 August.

Euromonitor International (2016b). *Lodging in Spain*. Category Briefing, 3 August.

Farsari, I. (2012) "The development of a conceptual model to support sustainable tourism policy in North Mediterranean destinations", *Journal of Hospitality Marketing & Management* 21(7), 710–738.

Green, H., Hunter, C. and Moore, B. (1990) "Assessing the environmental impact of tourism development: Use of the Delphi Technique", *Tourism Management* 11(2), 111–120.

GRI (2013) "G4 Sustainability reporting guidelines". Available at www.globalreporting.org/standards/g4/Pages/default.aspx [Accessed 10 August, 2016].

Han, H., Hsu, L.J., Lee, J.S. and Sheu, C. (2011) "Are lodging customers ready to go green? An examination of attitudes, demographics, and eco-friendly intentions", *International Journal of Hospitality Management* 30, 345–355.

Harrison, L.C., Jayawardena, C. and Clayton, A. (2003) "Sustainable tourism development in the Caribbean: Practical challenges", *International Journal of Contemporary Hospitality Management* 15(5), 294–298.

Hathroubi, S., Peypoch, N. and Robinot, E. (2014) "Technical efficiency and environmental management: The Tunisian case", *Journal of Hospitality and Tourism Management* 21, 27–33.

Hess, D., Rogovsky, N. and Dunfee, T.W. (2002) "The next wave of corporate community involvement: Corporate social initiatives", *California Management Review* 44(2), 110–125.

Høgevold, N.M., Svensson, G., Klopper, H.B., Wagner, B., Valera, J.C.S., Padin, C., Ferro, C. and Petzer, D. (2015) "A triple bottom line construct and reasons for implementing sustainable business practices in companies and their business networks", *Corporate Governance* 15(4), 427–443.

HOTELS (2016) "325 Hotels". Available at www.hotelsmag.com/Search/Results/?SearchTerm=hotels%20ranking&SectionIDs[0]=2&SectionIDs[1]=12&SectionIDs[2]=7 [Accessed 10 August 2016].

Hubbard, G. (2009) "Measuring organizational performance: Beyond the triple bottom line", *Business Strategy and the Environment* 19(1), 171–191.

Juhász-Dóra, K., Ásványi, K., Michalkó, G. and Jászberényi, M. (2015) "The role of renewable energy in the hotel competitiveness", EUGEO Conference Proceedings. Available at www.gi.sanu.ac.rs/site/media/com_form2content/documents/c14/a194/f313/programme_and_abstracts_eugeo2015.pdf [Accessed 10 August 2016].

Kang, K.H., Lee, S. and Huh, C. (2010) "Impacts of positive and negative corporate social responsibility activities on company performance in the hospitality industry", *International Journal of Hospitality Management* 29(1), 72–82.

Kasim, A. (2007) "Towards a wider adoption of environmental responsibility in the hotel sector", *International Journal of Hospitality & Tourism Administration*, 8(2), 25–49.

Kasim, A., Gursoy, D., Okumus, F. and Wong, A. (2014) "The importance of water management in hotels: A framework for sustainability through innovation", *Journal of Sustainable Tourism* 22(7), 1090–1107.

Kim, Y.J., Palakurthi, R. and Hancer, M. (2012) "The environmentally friendly programs in hotels and customers' intention to stay: An online survey approach", *International Journal of Hospitality and Tourism Administration* 13(3), 195–214.

Le, Y., Hollenhorst, S., Harris, C., McLaughlin, W. and Shook, S. (2006) "Environmental management: A study of Vietnamese hotels", *Annals of Tourism Research* 33(2), 545–567.

Legrand, W., Huegel, E.B. and Sloan, P. (2014) "Learning from best practices: Sustainability reporting in international hotel chains," in Chen, J.S. (ed.) *Advances in Hospitality and Leisure*, Emerald Group Publishing Limited, 119–134.

Mihalic, T., Žabkar, V. and Cvelbar, L.K. (2012) "A hotel sustainability business model: Evidence from Slovenia", *Journal of Sustainable Tourism* 20(5), 701–719.

Paek, S., Xiao, Q., Lee, S. and Song, H. (2013) "Does managerial ownership affect different corporate social responsibility dimensions? An empirical examination of U.S. publicly traded hospitality firms", *International Journal of Hospitality Management* 34, 423–433.

Park, S.Y. and Levy, S.E. (2014) "Corporate social responsibility: Perspectives of hotel frontline employees", *International Journal of Contemporary Hospitality Management* 26(3), 332–348.

Rahman, I., Reynolds, D. and Svaren, S. (2012) "How green are North American hotels? An exploration of low-cost adoption", *International Journal of Hospitality Management* 31, 720–727.

Roberts, S. and Tribe, J. (2008) "Sustainable indicators for small medium tourism enterprises – and exploratory perspective", *Journal of Sustainable Tourism* 16(5), 585–594.

Ruiz-Molina, M.E., Gil-Saura, I. and Moliner-Velázquez, B. (2010) "Information and communication technologies in rural hotels", *International Journal of Sustainable Economy* 2(1), 1–15.

Ruiz-Molina, M.E., Gil-Saura, I. and Moliner-Velázquez, B. (2012) "Environmental sustainability in hotels: A matter of category?", *International Journal of Environmental and Sustainable Development* 11(2), 148–163.

Ryan, P. (2003) "Sustainability partnerships: Eco-strategy theory in practice?" *Management of Environmental Quality: An International Journal* 14(2), 256–278.

Serafini, G.O. and Szamosi, L.T. (2015) "Five star hotels of a Multinational Enterprise in countries of the transitional periphery: A case study in human resources management", *International Business Review* 24(6), 972–983.

Sheivachman, A. (2011) "Efficiency leads to savings: Mobility", *Hotel Management*, 96.

Shieh, H.S. (2012) "The greener, the more cost efficient? An empirical study of international tourist hotels in Taiwan", *International Journal of Sustainable Development and World Ecology* 19(6), 536–545.

Singh, N., Cranage, D. and Lee, S. (2014) "Green strategies for hotels: Estimation of recycling benefits", *International Journal of Hospitality Management* 43, 13–22.

Stylos, N. and Vassiliadis, C. (2015) "Differences in sustainable management between four- and five-star hotels regarding the perceptions of three-pillar sustainability", *Journal of Hospitality Marketing and Management* 24(8), 791–825.

Teng, C.C., Horng, J.S., Hu, M.L., Chien, L.H. and Shen, Y.C. (2012) "Developing energy conservation and carbon reduction indicators for the hotel industry in Taiwan", *International Journal of Hospitality Management* 31, 199–208.

Teye, V., Sirakaya, E. and Sönmez, S.F. (2002) "Residents' attitudes toward tourism development", *Annals of Tourism Research* 29(3), 668–688.

UNWTO (2016) "UNWTO Tourism Highlights, 2015 Edition". Available at: http://mkt.unwto.org/es/node/36698/ [Accessed 10 August 2016].

Uysal, M., Sirgy, M.J., Woo, E. and Kim, H.L. (2016) "Quality of life (QOL) and well-being research in tourism", *Tourism Management* 53, 244–261.

Uysal, M., Woo, E. and Singal, M. (2012) "The Tourist Area Life Cycle (TALC) and its effect on the Quality of Life (QOL) of destination community", in Uysal, M., Perdue, R. and Sirgy, M.J. (eds.) *Handbook of Tourism and Quality-of-life Research: Enhancing the Lives of Tourists and Residents of Host Communities*. Dordrecht: Springer Science & Business Media, 423–444.

Várgáné Csobán, K. and Bauerné Gáthy, A. (2009) "Long-term government responses to sustainable tourism development: Principles and strategies", *Applied Studies in Agribusiness and Commerce* 3, 89–92.

Weaver, D.B. (2012) "Organic, incremental and induced paths to sustainable mass tourism convergence", *Tourism Management* 33(5), 1030–1037.

Xu, X. and Gursoy, D. (2015) "Influence of sustainable hospitality supply chain management on customers' attitudes and behaviors", *International Journal of Hospitality Management* 49, 105–116.

Zink, K.J. and Fischer, K. (2013) "Do we need sustainability as a new approach in human factors and ergonomics?", *Ergonomics* 56(3), 348–356.

Further reading

Bansal, P. (2005) "Evolving sustainability: A longitudinal study of corporate sustainable development", *Strategic Management Journal* 26(3), 197–218. (Identification of organizational determinants of corporate sustainable development.)

Boley, B.B. and Uysal, M. (2013) "Competitive synergy through practicing triple bottom line sustainability: Evidence from three hospitality case studies", *Tourism and Hospitality Research* 13(4), 226–238. (Description of benefits discovered by hotels from implementing sustainable initiatives.)

Chabowski, B.R., Mena, J.A. and Gonzalez-Padron, T.L. (2011) "The structure of sustainability research in marketing, 1958–2008: A basis for future research opportunities", *Journal of the Academy of Marketing Science* 39(1), 55–70. (Extensive literature review on sustainability research in marketing.)

Crittenden, V.L., Crittenden, W.F., Ferrell, L.K., Ferrell, O.C. and Pinney, C.C. (2011) "Market-oriented sustainability: A conceptual framework and propositions", *Journal of the Academy of Marketing Science* 39(1), 71–85. (Directions for sustainability theory, research, and practice.)

Dwyer, L. (2005) "Relevance of triple bottom line reporting to achievement of sustainable tourism: A scoping study", *Tourism Review International* 9(1), 79–93. (Identification of potential benefits of the TBL approach to tourism organizations and conditions necessary for integrating TBL into organization activities.)

Hassini, E., Surti, C. and Searcy, C. (2012) "A literature review and a case study of sustainable supply chains with a focus on metrics", *International Journal of Production Economics* 140(1), 69–82. (Literature review on sustainable supply chains between 2000 and 2010.)

Ricaurte, E. (2011) "Developing a sustainability measurement framework for hotels: Toward an industry-wide reporting structure", *Cornell Hospitality Report* 11(13), 6–30. (Analysis of sustainability reports of major hotel companies.)

Xu, X. and Gursoy, D. (2015) "A conceptual framework of sustainable hospitality supply chain management", *Journal of Hospitality Marketing and Management* 24, 229–259. (A proposal of a conceptual hospitality supply chain framework based on a comprehensive review of sustainability literature in hospitality.)

Part VII

Innovation in hospitality marketing

34

A critical review of innovation in hospitality marketing

Eojina Kim, Liang (Rebecca) Tang and Robert Bosselman

Introduction

The most prominent issue emerging in contemporary business marketing is innovation, which is vital for any commercial entity to create and maximize value. The role of marketing leads to customer satisfaction and loyalty, which are essential benchmarks for positive business performance. Innovation is widely accepted as a key component for successfully navigating competitive business environments (Organisation for Economic Co-operation and Development [OECD] 2012), internally and externally. Capability for innovation provides a business with the foundation to attain a competitive advantage in the marketplace (Barney 1991; Day 1994). However, previous studies predominantly investigated high-technology and manufacturing industries rather than service industries despite the acknowledged significance of innovation for all types of businesses (Ettlie and Rosenthal 2011; Hogan, Soutar, McColl-Kennedy and Sweeney 2011). Hipp and Grupp (2005) further suggested that simple transposition of the well-established notion of innovation in the manufacturing sector into the service sector was inappropriate. Over the past few years, although practitioners in the hospitality industry increasingly attend to and allocate more resources to innovation, relevant scientific research in academia has advanced slowly (e.g., Ariffin and Aziz 2012; Nasution and Mavondo 2008).

In order to highlight the importance of innovation as a policy, this chapter first reviews the underlying concepts and presents an organizing framework for innovation research in the general business and hospitality literature. The following section highlights key issues and managerial challenges as well as opportunities associated with innovation in hospitality marketing.

Review of innovation research

Innovation and innovativeness

Innovation is the basic behavior in the diffusion process (Rogers 1995). Innovation focuses on the outcomes of new elements or a new combination of traditional elements in a firm's activities (Schumpeter 1934), while innovativeness refers to a broader outcome of activities and denotes the capability of a firm to be amenable to new ideas, services and promotions (Crawford and Di

Benedetto 2008; Kunz, Schmitt and Meyer 2011). In the marketing and management literature, innovativeness represents "the notion of openess to new ideas as an aspect of a firm's culture" (Hurley and Hult 1998: 44). The terms "innovation" and "innovativeness" are frequently used interchangeably in the general business and hospitality literature. Therefore, we use the term innovation consistently throughout the chapter.

Innovation is necessary for a firm's survival and growth; dynamic markets constantly winnow organizations that lack the capability to explore new market opportunities (Luo and Bhattacharya 2006; Schumpeter 1934). The key issue for innovation from a managerial perspective is its impact on customer retention. Diffusion of innovation, which has a long history in sociology, focuses on diffusing innovation throughout society (Mahajan, Muller and Bass 1990; Rogers 1962). Early researchers only investigated innovation as a general concept (e.g. Gatignon and Robertson 1985) rather than in a systematic approach. Rogers (1962) proposed diffusing innovation theory, which provides a precise definition of innovation, procedure, and system, perceived to be unique by whomever adopts it. The theory also suggests the characteristics of innovation, including relative advantage, compatibility, complexity, trialability, observability, and diffusion/adoption (Rogers 1962).

Directions of innovation research

Aspects of innovation: Comprehensive view vs. myopic view

For an extended period, research on innovation has been myopic by focusing on specific technologies or new products while neglecting the business concept of innovation (Sawhney, Wolcott and Arroniz 2006; Vilà and MacGregor 2007). As the nature of innovation has changed, its scope has broadened and stretched beyond technological innovation. Business innovation is "the successful implementation of creative ideas within an organization" (Amabile, Conti, Coon, Lazenby and Herron 1996: 1155). More recently, Sawhney et al. (2006: 29) defined innovativeness from a business perspective as "the creation of substantial new value for customers and the firm by creatively changing one or more dimensions of the business system," and suggested four "business anchors": offerings, customers, processes, and presence.

In the marketing literature, to date, research has focused on analyzing a single concept of innovativeness: the subjective perceptions of outcomes (Atuahene-Gima 1996). However, the concept of newness manifests itself not only in attributes of products or technologies, but also in other aspects, including design, process, and marketing (Kunz et al. 2011). In the past decade, investigations of the conceptualization and measurement of the innovativeness of firms or brands have focused on various perspectives, including product innovativeness (e.g., Shams, Alpert and Brown 2015), service innovativeness (e.g., Victorino, Verma, Plaschka and Dev 2005), experience innovativeness (e.g., Ottenbacher and Harrington 2010), and promotional innovativeness (Lin, Marshall and Dawson 2013). While these studies empirically tested different components of innovativeness, gaps in research remain despite the quest to validate a holistic concept of innovation.

Research of innovation in hospitality has rapidly extended to new areas (see Andrea 2012). However, while most studies contained innovation in their titles they did not consider innovation in the text or only mentioned the concept cursorily without deep exploration. To the best current knowledge, few previous studies examined the key aspects of innovation from theoretical and empirical perspectives or methods for categorizing or measuring innovation. Moreover, as Andrea (2012) suggested, studies of hospitality during the past decade investigated innovation myopically or from the narrow aspect of innovation as applied to technology. For example, several studies (Kumar, Kumar and de Grosbois 2008; Orfila-Sintes, Crespí-Cladera and Martínez-Ros 2005; Wang and Qualls 2007) focused on innovation by analyzing adoption of technology or capability of innovation in hospitality businesses while a study by López-Fernández, Serrano-Bedia and Gómez-López (2011) examined technological innovation in Spanish hospitality firms. A study by Ariffin and Aziz (2012) considered physical environment innovation; whereas Hu, Horng and Sun (2009) assessed service innovation for hotel businesses, and Ottenbacher and Harrington (2009) investigated product innovation among restaurant chains. Sandvik, Duhan and Sandvik (2014) analyzed a hotel's efforts at continuously improving innovation. Few studies focused on holistic concepts of innovation. For example, Kim (2016) conceptualized innovation through a comprehensive assessment of products, service-related technologies, experiences, and promotions.

Perspectives of innovation: Firm centric vs. customer centric

Scholars in disciplines involving businesses, in general, reached agreement that managers and consumers may view innovation differently (e.g., Danneels and Kleinschmidt 2001; Kunz et al. 2011). Accordingly, a firm-centric view of innovation focuses solely on technical and functional aspects, while a customer-centric view adopts profound interest in a customer's subjective perception of a firm's capability to provide novel and creative performance (Danneels and Kleinschmidt 2001). Purely manager-based perspectives can fail to provide solutions to satisfy actual needs of customers. Consequently, Kunz et al. (2011) put forward an essential, customer-centric perspective, since customers ultimately determine the success of innovation while a firm's capability to provide novel and innovative characteristics and performance is observed and experienced by the customer.

Most research on innovation in general marketing investigated the perspectives of managers or firms (e.g., Chandy and Tellis 2000; Hogan et al. 2011; Zhou, Yim and Tse 2005; Zolfagharian and Paswan 2008), while only a few studies dealt with concepts of innovation from a customer-centric perspective (e.g., Grewal, Ailawadi, Gauri, Hall, Kopalle and Robertson 2011; Hoeffler 2003; Kunz et al. 2011; Lin et al. 2013). In a similar vein, the majority of recent theoretical studies on innovation in hospitality marketing investigated the innovation of hospitality firms from the manager's perspective by examining managers' evaluations. For example, Binder, Kessler, Mair and Stummer (2016) identified four components of innovation in hotels: systematic renewal, systematic improvement, adaptation, and startups. Chang, Gong and Shum (2011), Chen (2011), Tajeddini and Trueman (2014) and Sandvik et al. (2014) investigated employees' perceptions of innovation in hotels located in China, Taiwan, Iran and Norway, respectively.

Among the studies that take a customer-centric perspective in various industries, few have investigated innovation in service industries (e.g. Anselmsson and Johansson 2009; Lin 2015; Zhang and Wedel 2009), and research for the hospitality industry has been even less common (e.g. Ariffin and Aziz 2012; Kim 2016).

Effects of innovation

Besides the innovation studies discussed above, other scholars in the hospitality literature focused on the influences of innovation or innovativeness on firms' performance or the adverse effects of management practices on innovation. Examples of previous studies on the impact of innovation on business performance in hospitality marketing are Sandvik et al. (2014), Ottenbacher, Shaw and Lockwood (2006), Tajeddini (2010), Tajeddini and Trueman (2012), and Tseng, Kuo and Chou (2008). Specifically, Nicolau and Santa-María (2013) analyzed the effect of innovations on hotel value and sales by distinguishing the potentially different impacts of distinct innovation types: product, process, organization and marketing. Grissemann, Plank and Brunner-Sperdin (2013) found that employees' perceptions of innovation relate to the financial performance of the hotel.

Another approach was to investigate the influence of business practices on innovation. For example, Ottenbacher and Gnoth (2005) identified nine factors that promote successful service innovations in German hotels. Chang et al. (2011) investigated hospitality businesses' promotion of innovation through human resource management, while Nasution, Mavondo, Matanda, and Ndubisi (2011) studied the impact of human resource practices and customer value on innovation in Indonesian hotels. Ordanini, Miceli, Pizzetti and Parasuraman (2011) investigated the effects of customers' collaboration, business partners' collaboration, customers' orientation, innovation orientation, employees' collaboration, and knowledge of integrated mechanisms on innovation outcomes in Italian hotels. Martínez-Ros and Orfila-Sintes (2012) found that plans for training employees affect innovation-related decisions.

Dimensions of innovation

This section discusses the primary aspects of innovation in the hospitality industry and the drivers which shape this aspect in hospitality marketing. An overview of innovation in hospitality marketing is presented in Table 34.1. Based on the literature review, the dimensions of innovation in hospitality marketing, including product innovation, service-related technology innovation,

Table 34.1 Innovation in hospitality marketing

	Product Innovation	Service-related Technology Innovation	Experiential Innovation	Promotional Innovation
Basis of Value	Co-Value Creation			
Definition	Firm's capability to provide the newness and uniqueness of a product to customers	Firm's capability to generate an idea for a performance enhancement that customers perceive to offer a new benefit	Firm's capability to create an environment that is a personalized and lifestyle-based experience	Firm's capability to offer multiple opportunities to effectively target customers
Examples	Airbnb's product innovation City Grit's menu innovation	Starwood Hotels and Resorts Worldwide: wearable technology using Apple Watch app	Starbucks: Round table	Priceline: Name your own price
Key Functions	Shared economics	Robust data to use in understanding customers' behavior and desires	Eliminate customers' feelings of isolation	Minimize unused perishable products
Benefits to a Firm	Operational effectiveness	Operational effectiveness	Added value for customers; Customers' experiences	Volume-based discounts
Benefits to a Customer	Financial opportunity Customization	Customer convenience	Emotional involvement	Financial benefits Added value for customers

experiential innovation, and promotional innovation, constitute a comprehensive categorization of the concept.

Product innovation

Product innovation is the customer's recognition of the newness and uniqueness of a product (Ali, Krapfel and LaBahn 1995). This notion allows assessment of the differentiation between new offerings and previous ones (Garcia and Calantone 2002) and which, if any, new offerings are perceived as valuable, useful, and meaningful to consumers (Rubera, Ordanini and Griffith 2011). The majority of previous research on product innovation (e.g., Calantone, Chan and Cui 2006; Danneels and Kleinschmidt 2001) described this concept based on a firm's perception of innovation, depending upon the combination between marketing and technical functions of the organization (Calantone et al. 2006), while acknowledging the necessity of considering a consumer's perspective. Shams et al. (2015) subsequently emphasized the role of consumers' perceptions of product innovation. The conceptualization and operationalization of consumer-perceived innovation at the product level has typically focused on technological innovation characteristic of a product's features or functionality (Atuahene-Gima 1995; Danneels and Kleinschmidt 2001; Lee and Colarelli O'Connor 2003; McNally, Cavusgil and Calantone 2010).

The hospitality industry has abundant options for adding innovations when delivering services since customized and personalized offerings to customers have emerged as a major practice toward innovation. Airbnb may be a good example of an innovation that introduces new offerings differing from traditional ones in the hospitality industry. Airbnb (2008) has grown in popularity by building an online short-term rental platform while delivering an innovative experience by enabling travelers to reside, temporarily, in the homes of residents. This new idea did not change the concept of providing accommodation: it completely revised hotels offering a product, the space, for customers' needs.

Service-related technology innovation

Service innovation is "an idea for a performance enhancement that customers perceive the offering to be a new benefit of sufficient appeal that it dramatically influences behavior, as well as the behavior of competing companies" (Berry, Shankar, Parish, Cadwallader and Dotzel 2006: 56). Driven by a service-dominant logic (Vargo and Lusch 2004), the notion of service innovation has become an essential construct in the marketing literature, used to generate benefits for new markets (Berry et al. 2006; Kim and Mauborgne 1999; Kleijnen, de Ruyter and Andreassen 2005; Meuter, Bitner, Ostrom and Brown 2005). Service innovation can explain the approaches a firm uses to offer intangible services and to create an advantage for the consumer through new service-delivery processes. Therefore, knowledge of customers' needs and desires regarding service innovation from a customer-centric perspective is critical. The use of information technology represents an example of service innovation (Reid and Sandler 1992). As technology enables customers to increasingly engage in services, service innovation has gained increased investigative interest from a technology-based perspective. The dimension of technology related to service innovation shows that hospitality businesses can offer technologically innovative service and create a seamless experience for customers through the delivery process.

Leading hospitality businesses have offered new mobile interfaces and applications (apps) or online ordering tools, to deliver cutting-edge services. A good example is wearable technology. Starwood Hotels and Resorts Worldwide (2015) launched the Apple Watch app, which enables customers to be free of room keys, credit cards or services from the reception desk. In addition, the firm can access robust data to analyze customers' expectations and behavior. To gain an in-depth understanding of the usage and effectiveness of technological tools, hospitality businesses need to consider the actuality of the effects of technology on customers' experiences and the creation of value, rather than just which functions and features to provide.

Experiential innovation

Experiential innovation is innovation of an experience in an environment that uses the firm's capability to create personalized and lifestyle-based experiences for individual consumers (Prahalad and Ramaswamy 2003). Firms search for new ways to distinguish themselves and attract customers' attention (Binkhorst and Den Dekker 2009). The unique characteristics of hospitality marketing promote the relationships between customers and providers, and become the focal point of engagement platforms (Sashi 2012). Hence, experiential innovation may require utilizing employees who influence consumers' satisfaction as the ultimate moderators for differentiating services (Ottenbacher and Harrington 2010; Zeithaml, Bitner and Gremler, 2006). Experiential innovation in hospitality marketing emphasizes the creation of an environment in which customers interact with employees in innovative ways, and thus build long-term relationships.

Hospitality businesses can generate positive returns by delivering unique and unexpected signature moments as customers respond favorably to innovation atmospherics and design. For example, Starbucks has succeeded in experiential innovation by offering customers options and choices, which gives customers ownership of customized products ordered. Moreover, Starbucks creates an environment which makes customers feel welcome and socially engaged by offering rounded tables or comfortable chairs (Berry et al. 2006). City Grit (2015) in New York City also creates a unique experience by providing communal tables that encourage an interactive atmosphere. Experiential innovation generally adds greater opportunity to customers than advancing core products such as food or rooms in hospitality settings.

Promotional innovation

Promotion is an important tool for a firm to deliver messages to target customers (Grewal et al. 2011). Even though promotional techniques and established products are not new, promotional innovation such as a new product mix for discounts or new designs for gifts gives customers a fresh perspective on a firm (Lin et al. 2013). Therefore, promotional innovation offers multiple opportunities to effectively target the firm's customers (Grewal et al. 2011), and the ability to generate promotional innovation is likely to attract customers' attention and increase purchasing (Lin 2015).

For example, Priceline's (2015) "name your own price" is a great example of promotional innovation, which allows the firm to minimize unused, perishable products and customers to gain financial benefits from the unique promotional approach (Sorescu, Frambach, Singh, Rangaswamy and Bridges 2011). Moreover, promotional innovation encompasses innovative rewards (membership) programs, deals, and marketing programs through using multiple channels to attract customers' attention and communicate with them.

Challenges and opportunities

Creating innovation among firms and customers has been critical to the success of hospitality marketing. Although research on hospitality innovation has grown recently, less attention has been given to innovation in the hospitality literature than in the general business or service marketing literature. When reflecting on the nature of customers and businesses in hospitality marketing, identifying hospitality's unique market phenomena for customers' behavior is a critical issue in both academia and industry. Recently, significant environmental, economic, technological, and generational changes have been shaping innovation in hospitality marketing. This has encouraged academia and industry to focus on both customer- and industry-based challenges.

The most significant challenge related to customers in innovation involves generational influences on business marketing, especially understating and adjusting to the latest group of new customers entering markets. Different behaviors between generations are driving profound adjustments in hospitality marketing as well as marketing in general. Recently, aging Baby Boomers are retiring, Generation Y has entered and Generation Z is entering the economic marketplace (U.S. Census Bureau 2014) with independent purchasing power. Generation Z's consumption will become a dominant driver of economies. Generation Z, exposed to digital technology early, is more likely to seek innovation, which suggests a potential topic for hospitality research whereas hospitality research has already focused on Generation Y's behavior. Different marketing strategies, changing among generations, could motivate exploration of product innovation though personalization or customization, service-related technological innovation using information technology, promotional innovation via social media, and experiential innovation through diversity of services and sustainability of products.

Industry-based challenges in innovation involve competition and rapidly evolving technology and consumer tastes. Competition between hospitality firms tends to be relatively intense; thus, a firm's opportunities for innovation in hospitality marketing are mainly dependent on its capability to create new ideas and innovative strategies that, accordingly, respond to changes in competitive market conditions. Of increasing importance is understanding key strategies for introducing the best new experiences in the rapidly changing circumstances.

While the role of the customer and the firm in creating innovation has become a key concept in hospitality marketing, questions remain regarding the mechanisms to guide a firm's innovation that impact customers' behavior. Recent studies on hospitality innovation heavily focused on the influences of business practices on the outcomes of innovation or the effects of innovation on business finance and non-financial performance. On the other hand, research on innovation seems deficient in exploration of customer-based perceptions. Hence, the development of new knowledge or frameworks through customer-centric research is essential in hospitality marketing.

Undoubtedly, innovation creates values, but business practitioners have to accept increasing pressure from value creation and differentiation through innovation in competitive markets. As the hospitality industry attempts to become more innovative, questions arise as to whether or not customers truly recognize innovative services, and if so, the nature of the exact perceptions. Such efforts are in vain if customers' awareness is absent. To this end, future studies need to focus on the nature of the effects of innovation on customers' behavior. Hospitality businesses cannot fully understand customers' needs and desires without customers' collaboration and their willingness to share comprehensive information in order to create customized services and provide sufficient responses to their needs. Contrarily, customers cannot benefit from the resources and marketing efforts of hospitality businesses unless hospitality businesses devote attention to customers' needs.

Consequently, understanding the mechanisms for experiencing innovation from the customers' perspective has become important to hospitality marketing.

Research on ensuring the implementation of innovations that enhance the uniqueness of customers' experiences may also hold the key to maintaining competitive advantage derived from innovation in hospitality marketing. Customers' behavior such as their experiences or levels of acceptance of innovation and customers' characteristics such as demographics or psychological effects of the drivers of innovation can operate as moderators. Innovations affect customers' innovation behavior, which in turn reshape firms' innovations. Therefore, the relationship between the firm's innovation practices and customers' behavior is bidirectional. Thus, an exploration of the role of innovation in delivering services within hospitality marketing, the conceptualization of the innovation construct, and the approach to decipher innovation phenomena, systematically, are essential for agendas of future research.

Last, despite the present chapter addressing a customer-centric view of innovativeness, the firm-centric view of innovation cannot be ignored. Perspectives of firms can result in inspiring ideas being raised and vigorous debate that could confirm the innovation phenomena and contribute to its evolution. The two directions of innovation should co-exist and maintain a balance in research. Investigation of different perspectives of the concepts of innovation could facilitate the progress of evolution and creation of new ideas for future research.

References

Airbnb (2008) Available at: www.airbnb.com [Accessed 16 Oct. 2016].

Ali, A., Krapfel, R. and LaBahn, D. (1995) "Product innovativeness and entry strategy: Impact on cycle time and break-even time," *Journal of Product Innovation Management* 12(1), 54–69.

Amabile, T. M., Conti, R., Coon, H., Lazenby, J. and Herron, M. (1996) "Assessing the work environment for creativity," *Academy of Management Journal* 39(5), 1154–1184.

Andrea, N.A.G.Y. (2012) "A review of tourism and hospitality innovation research," *Annals of Faculty of Economics* 1(2), 364–370.

Anselmsson, J. and Johansson, U. (2009) "Retailer brands and the impact on innovativeness in the grocery market," *Journal of Marketing Management* 25(1–2), 75–95.

Ariffin, A. A. M. and Aziz, N. A. (2012) "The effect of physical environment's innovativeness on the relationship between hosting quality and satisfaction in hotel services," *International Journal of Trade, Economics and Finance* 3(5), 337–342.

Atuahene-Gima, K. (1995) "An exploratory analysis of the impact of market orientation on new product performance," *Journal of Product Innovation Management* 12(4), 275–293.

Atuahene-Gima, K. (1996) "Market orientation and innovation," *Journal of Business Research* 35(2), 93–103.

Barney, J. (1991) "Firm resources and sustained competitive advantage," *Journal of Management* 17(1), 99–120.

Berry, L. L., Shankar, V., Parish, J. T., Cadwallader, S. and Dotzel, T. (2006) "Creating new markets through service innovation," *MIT Sloan Management Review* 47(2), 56–63.

Binder, P., Kessler, A., Mair, M. and Stummer, K. (2016) "Organizational innovativeness and its results: A qualitative analysis of SME hotels in Vienna," *Journal of Hospitality & Tourism Research* 40(3), 339–363.

Binkhorst, E. and Den Dekker, T. (2009) "Agenda for co-creation tourism experience research," *Journal of Hospitality Marketing & Management* 18(2–3), 311–327.

Calantone, R. J., Chan, K. and Cui, A. S. (2006) "Decomposing product innovativeness and its effects on new product success," *Journal of Product Innovation Management* 23(5), 408–421.

Chandy, R. K. and Tellis, G. J. (2000) "The incumbent's curse? Incumbency, size, and radical product innovation," *The Journal of Marketing* 64(3), 1–17.

Chang, S., Gong, Y. and Shum, C. (2011) "Promoting innovation in hospitality companies through human resource management practices," *International Journal of Hospitality Management* 30(4), 812–818.

Chen, W. J. (2011) "Innovation in hotel services: Culture and personality," *International Journal of Hospitality Management* 30(1), 64–72.

City Grit (2015) Available at: http://citygritnyc.com [Accessed 16 Oct. 2016].

Crawford, C. M. and Di Benedetto, C. A. (2008) *New products management,* New York: Tata McGraw-Hill Education.

Danneels, E. and Kleinschmidt, E. J. (2001) "Product innovativeness from the firm's perspective: Its dimensions and their relation with project selection and performance," *Journal of Product Innovation Management* 18(6), 357–373.

Day, G. S. (1994) "The capabilities of market-driven organizations," *The Journal of Marketing* 58(4), 37–52.

Ettlie, J. E. and Rosenthal, S. R. (2011) "Service versus manufacturing innovation," *Journal of Product Innovation Management* 28(2), 285–299.

Garcia, R. and Calantone, R. (2002) "A critical look at technological innovation typology and innovativeness terminology: A literature review," *Journal of Product Innovation Management* 19(2), 110–132.

Gatignon, H. and Robertson, T. S. (1985) "A propositional inventory for new diffusion research," *Journal of Consumer Research*, 11, 849–867.

Grewal, D., Ailawadi, K., Gauri, D., Hall, K., Kopalle, P. and Robertson, J. (2011) "Innovation in pricing and promotion strategies," *Journal of Retailing*, 87(1), S43–53.

Grissemann, U., Plank, A. and Brunner-Sperdin, A. (2013) "Enhancing business performance of hotels: The role of innovation and customer orientation," *International Journal of Hospitality Management* 33, 347–356.

Hipp, C. and Grupp, H. (2005) "Innovation in the service sector: The demand for service-specific innovation measurement concepts and typologies," *Research Policy* 34(4), 517–535.

Hoeffler, S. (2003) "Measuring preferences for really new products," *The Journal of Marketing Research* 40(4), 406–420.

Hogan, S. J., Soutar, G. N., McColl-Kennedy, J. R. and Sweeney, J. C. (2011) "Reconceptualizing professional service firm innovation capability: Scale development," *Industrial Marketing Management* 40(8), 1264–1273.

Hu, M. L. M., Horng, J. S. and Sun, Y. H. C. (2009) "Hospitality teams: Knowledge sharing and service innovation performance," *Tourism Management* 30(1), 41–50.

Hurley, R. F. and Hult, G. T. M. (1998) "Innovation, market orientation, and organizational learning: An integration and empirical examination," *The Journal of Marketing*, 42–54.

Kim, E. (2016) *Understanding customer perception of restaurant innovativeness and customer value co-creation behavior.* Ph.D thesis. Iowa State University.

Kim, W. C. and Mauborgne, R. (1999) "Strategy, value innovation, and the knowledge economy," *MIT Sloan Management Review* 40(3), 41–54.

Kleijnen, M., De Ruyter, K. and Andreassen, T. W. (2005) "Image congruence and the adoption of service innovations," *Journal of Service Research* 7(4), 343–359.

Kumar, U., Kumar, V. and de Grosbois, D. (2008) "Development of technological capability by Cuban hospitality organizations," *International Journal of Hospitality Management* 27(1), 12–22.

Kunz, W., Schmitt, B. and Meyer, A. (2011) "How does perceived firm innovativeness affect the consumer?," *Journal of Business Research* 64(8), 816–822.

Lee, Y. and Colarelli O'Connor, G. (2003) "The impact of communication strategy on launching new products: The moderating role of product innovativeness," *Journal of Product Innovation Management* 20(1), 4–21.

Lin, C. Y. (2015) "Conceptualizing and measuring consumer perceptions of retailer innovativeness in Taiwan," *Journal of Retailing and Consumer Services* 24, 33–41.

Lin, C. Y., Marshall, D. and Dawson, J. (2013) "How does perceived convenience retailer innovativeness create value for the customer?," *International Journal of Business and Economics* 12(2), 171–179.

López-Fernández, M. C., Serrano-Bedia, A. M. and Gómez-López, R. (2011) "Factors encouraging innovation in Spanish hospitality firms," *Cornell Hospitality Quarterly* 52(2), 144–152.

Luo, X. and Bhattacharya, C. B. (2006) "Corporate social responsibility, customer satisfaction, and market value," *The Journal of Marketing* 70(4), 1–18.

Mahajan, V., Muller, E. and Bass, F. M. (1990) "New product diffusion models in marketing: A review and directions for research," *The Journal of Marketing* 54(1), 1–26.

Martínez-Ros, E. and Orfila-Sintes, F. (2012) "Training plans, manager's characteristics and innovation in the accommodation industry," *International Journal of Hospitality Management* 31(3), 686–694.

McNally, R. C., Cavusgil, E. and Calantone, R. J. (2010) "Product innovativeness dimensions and their relationships with product advantage, product financial performance, and project protocol," *Journal of Product Innovation Management* 27(7), 991–1006.

Meuter, M. L., Bitner, M. J., Ostrom, A. L. and Brown, S. W. (2005) "Choosing among alternative service delivery modes: An investigation of customer trial of self-service technologies," *The Journal of Marketing* 69(2), 61–83.

Nasution, H. N. and Mavondo, F. T. (2008) "Customer value in the hotel industry: What managers believe they deliver and what customer experience," *International Journal of Hospitality Management* 27(2), 204–213.

Nasution, H. N., Mavondo, F. T., Matanda, M. J. and Ndubisi, N. O. (2011) "Entrepreneurship: Its relationship with market orientation and learning orientation and as antecedents to innovation and customer value," *Industrial Marketing Management* 40(3), 336–345.

Nicolau, J. L. and Santa-María, M. J. (2013) "The effect of innovation on hotel market value," *International Journal of Hospitality Management* 32, 71–79.

OECD (Organisation for Economic Co-operation and Development) (2012, May) *Innovation for development.* Paris: Organisation for Economic and Co-operative Development.

Ordanini, A., Miceli, L., Pizzetti, M. and Parasuraman, A. (2011) "Crowd-funding: Transforming customers into investors through innovative service platforms," *Journal of Service management* 22(4), 443–470.

Orfila-Sintes, F., Crespí-Cladera, R. and Martínez-Ros, E. (2005) "Innovation activity in the hotel industry: Evidence from Balearic Islands," *Tourism Management* 26(6), 851–865.

Ottenbacher, M. and Gnoth, J. (2005) "How to develop successful hospitality innovation," *Cornell Hotel and Restaurant Administration Quarterly* 46(2), 205–222.

Ottenbacher, M. C. and Harrington, R. J. (2009) "The product innovation process of quick-service restaurant chains," *International Journal of Contemporary Hospitality Management* 21(5), 523–541.

Ottenbacher, M. C. and Harrington, R. J. (2010) "Strategies for achieving success for innovative versus incremental new services," *Journal of Services Marketing* 24(1), 3–15.

Ottenbacher, M., Shaw, V. and Lockwood, A. (2006) "An investigation of the factors affecting innovation performance in chain and independent hotels," *Journal of Quality Assurance in Hospitality & Tourism* 6(3–4), 113–128.

Prahalad, C. K. and Ramaswamy, V. (2003) "The new frontier of experience innovation," *MIT Sloan Management Review* 44(4), 12–18.

Priceline (2015) Available at: www.priceline.com [Accessed 16 Oct. 2016].

Reid, R. D. and Sandler, M. (1992) "The use of technology to improve service quality," *The Cornell Hotel and Restaurant Administration Quarterly* 33(3), 68–73.

Rogers, E. M. (1962) *Diffusion of innovations,* 1st ed. New York: Simon and Schuster.

Rogers, E. M. (1995) "Diffusion of innovations: Modifications of a model for telecommunications," *Die Diffusion von Innovationen in der Telekommunikation,* 25–38. Berlin, Heidelberg: Springer.

Rubera, G., Ordanini, A. and Griffith, D. A. (2011) "Incorporating cultural values for understanding the influence of perceived product creativity on intention to buy: An examination in Italy and the US," *Journal of International Business Studies* 42(4), 459–476.

Sandvik, I. L., Duhan, D. F. and Sandvik, K. (2014) "Innovativeness and profitability: An empirical investigation in the Norwegian hotel industry," *Cornell Hospitality Quarterly* 55(2), 165–185.

Sashi, C. M. (2012) "Customer engagement, buyer-seller relationships, and social media," *Management Decision,* 50(2), 253–272.

Sawhney, M., Wolcott, R. C. and Arroniz, I. (2006) "The 12 different ways for companies to innovate," *MIT Sloan Management Review* 47(3), 74–81.

Schumpeter, J. A. (1934) *The theory of economic development: An inquiry into profits, capital, credit, interest, and the business cycle* (Vol. 55). Transaction Publishers.

Shams, R., Alpert, F. and Brown, M. (2015) "Consumer perceived brand innovativeness: Conceptualization and operationalization," *European Journal of Marketing* 49(9/10), 1589–1615.

Sorescu, A., Frambach, R. T., Singh, J., Rangaswamy, A. and Bridges, C. (2011) "Innovations in retail business models," *Journal of Retailing,* 87, S3–S16.

Starwood Hotels and Resorts Worldwide (2015) Available at: www.spgpromos.com [Accessed 16 Oct. 2016].

Tajeddini, K. (2010) "Effect of customer orientation and entrepreneurial orientation on innovativeness: Evidence from the hotel industry in Switzerland," *Tourism Management* 31(2), 221–231.

Tajeddini, K. and Trueman, M. (2012) "Managing Swiss hospitality: How cultural antecedents of innovation and customer-oriented value systems can influence performance in the hotel industry," *International Journal of Hospitality Management* 31(4), 1119–1129.

Tajeddini, K. and Trueman, M. (2014) "Perceptions of innovativeness among Iranian hotel managers," *Journal of Hospitality and Tourism Technology,* 5(1), 62–77.

Tseng, C. Y., Kuo, H. Y. and Chou, S. S. (2008) "Configuration of innovation and performance in the service industry: Evidence from the Taiwanese hotel industry," *The Service Industries Journal* 28(7), 1015–1028.

U.S. Census Bureau (2014) *The baby boom cohort in the United States: 2012 to 2060*. U.S. Department of Commerce.

Vargo, S. L. and Lusch, R. F. (2004) "Evolving to a new dominant logic for marketing," *The Journal of Marketing* 68(1), 1–17.

Victorino, L., Verma, R., Plaschka, G. and Dev, C. (2005) "Service innovation and customer choices in the hospitality industry," *Managing Service Quality: An International Journal* 15(6), 555–576.

Vilà, J. and MacGregor, S. P. (2007) "Business innovation: What it brings, what it takes," *IESE Alumni Magazine* 8, 24–36.

Wang, Y. and Qualls, W. (2007) "Towards a theoretical model of technology adoption in hospitality organizations," *International Journal of Hospitality Management* 26(3), 560–573.

Zeithaml, V. A., Bitner, M. J. and Gremler, D. D. (2006) *Services marketing: Integrating customer focus across the firm*, 4th ed. New York: McGraw Hill.

Zhang, J. and Wedel, M. (2009) "The effectiveness of customized promotions in online and offline stores," *Journal of Marketing Research* 46(2), 190–206.

Zhou, K. Z., Yim, C. K. and Tse, D. K. (2005) "The effects of strategic orientations on technology-and market-based breakthrough innovations," *The Journal of Marketing* 69(2), 42–60.

Zolfagharian, M. and Paswan, A. (2008) "Do consumers discern innovations in service elements?," *Journal of Services Marketing* 22(5), 338–352.

35

Innovation in product/service development and delivery

Adina Letiţia Negruşa, Valentin Toader and Veronica Rozalia Rus

Introduction

Hospitality enterprises are among the first adopters of innovation. According to Camisón and Monfort-Mir (2012), the tourism industry has always been receptive to the adoption of technological innovations for improving back-office and front-office operations. The use of Customer-Relationship Management (CRM), Yield Management applications and web-based tools are some examples of innovations implemented by hospitality enterprises. However, the diffusion of innovation among tourism enterprises, especially in the case of small enterprises, is nonetheless characterized by a low propensity for the development of new products and processes (Camisón & Monfort-Mir, 2012).

Types of innovation (introducing the concepts of product and process innovation)

There are many definitions of innovation but for the purposes of this chapter we will use the definition provided by the OECD in the OSLO Manual: "An innovation is the implementation of a new or significantly improved product (good or service), or process, a new marketing method, or a new organizational method in business practices, workplace organization or external relations" (OECD, 2005, p. 46). Four types of innovation can be distinguished (OECD, 2005):

- product innovation: the introduction of a new or significantly improved good or service;
- process innovation: implementation of a new or significantly improved production or delivery method;
- marketing innovation: implementation of a new marketing method involving significant changes in product design or packaging, product placement, product promotion or pricing;
- organizational innovation: implementation of a new organizational method in the firm's business practices, workplace organization or external relations.

The criteria that can help in recognizing innovation are: to have a degree of novelty, to generate a significant improvement, and to diffuse on the market. An innovation can be new to an organization, new to the market, or new to the world. The minimum requirement for an innovation is that it must be new (or significantly improved) to the firm (OECD, 2005). The implementation of the innovation is also important. A new product is implemented when it is introduced on the market.

In services, product innovation can consist of the introduction of entirely new services or in significant improvements in the way they are provided to clients, or the addition of new functions or characteristics to the existing services offered to customers (OECD, 2005). Examples of product innovations are: the introduction of significant improvements to the online booking engine, or the addition of significantly improved functions and improvements in the user interface. Significant changes in techniques, equipment and/or software are considered as process innovation.

Process innovation includes new or significantly improved methods, equipment and/or skills for the creation and provision of services. Examples of process innovation are: the introduction of GPS tracking devices for transport services, the implementation of a new reservation system in a travel agency (OECD, 2005), the introduction of automated hotel self-check-ins to improve guests' check-in experience and reduce the time necessary to check-in, the introduction of robots to automate the delivery of items in hotels/restaurants in order to increase productivity (e.g. the Relay robot created by Savioke), or the introduction of a new method to manage hotel laundry using RFID technologies.

In the case of services, it is difficult to distinguish between product and process innovations, because the production, delivery and consumption of many services can occur at the same time. Very often these two types of innovation are intercalated and it is very hard to distinguish between them. For example, if a travel agency introduces a new touristic package, this can be seen as a change in product or process.

Innovation can be common to a specific sector or it can be common to the world. Depending on the degree of novelty involved, innovation can be minor, incremental or radical (Tidd et al., 2005). Most of the innovation in hospitality is incremental and it is based on previous innovation. If for a small hospitality enterprise the implementation of a new Property Management System (PMS) can constitute a significant change, for a big hotel that has already used this type of software for many years this is not considered an important change.

Factors of innovation in hospitality

Alongside the explosive growth of the hospitality and tourism sectors, the concept of innovation has been used increasingly over the past decade, for many purposes (from better serving customers, to marketing or to product development). A wide range of challenging characteristics make companies determined to look forward and become able to work in an innovative environment; such features include: the level of competition and the maturity of the marketplace, technological and communication developments, consumer behaviors and expectations, the involvement of public institutions and changes in the legal framework, governmental constraints, and globalization (Ottenbacher, 2008).

Competition

Competition is one of the major driving factors of tourism and hospitality. Once travel constraints reduced, the competition among multinational players in tourism and hospitality, and local units intensified; the increased competitiveness eventually pushed all of them to make inward investments and to operate innovatively (Hall & Williams, 2008). The newly established brands or the new players who entered these markets were forced to offer an unforgettable experience, in order to attract and increase clients' loyalty. On the other hand, the already established and traditional companies have to review and/or to innovate their operations and facilities so that they meet the expanding needs of their changing customers or to control operations better and more efficiently.

Besides the traditional competitors, in the accommodation, food services and travel markets, new elements emerged and changed the entire business landscape, such as: peer-to-peer networks (Airbnb), multi-sided platforms (Ticketmaster) or free business models (Couchsurfing). These platforms and networks, which have become more professional and have gained increasing popularity, lead to a new type of competitor and support small units to compete better on the market.

Customer behavior

Due to the fact that the standard of living has increased, tourist and customer expectations have also changed. Travelers have become more demanding, expecting access to more luxury/luxurious products/services. Thus, in order to fulfill these needs, lodging players have invested in product innovation. As a result, services and products that were previously considered luxurious in hotel rooms (such as: Jacuzzi baths, Internet or Wi-Fi services, LCD TVs, in-room computers) are now considered standard offerings of quality rooms. On the other hand, today's more experienced, educated and sophisticated customers emphasize their preference for unique and authentic experiences provided by the destination or unit they visit. To differentiate themselves, hotels and lodging players create innovative services and products. Because customers strive to obtain more added value and are willing to pay more with a trade-off, such as saving time, extreme segmentation helps not only for differentiation strategies but also for a quicker buying decision.

This trend is intensified by an important change in the customer segment for hospitality and tourism products, namely the growing number of millennial consumers. This demographic group is expected to represent 50 percent of all travelers by 2025 (EY, 2016); because technology is an essential feature for this demographic group, hotels and other service players in the hospitality industry have to rethink some of their services and to implement new applications for meeting their customers' needs.

Technology development

New advances in science and technology play a critical role in the innovation activities of hospitality and tourism businesses (Coombs et al., 1987). The increased usage of powerful and sophisticated smartphones marked the beginning of the digital era. The development of ICT has changed the way in which people communicate and access information, and also their habits and expectations as consumers (San Martin et al., 2010). The distribution channels used for services were innovated by taking advantage of the opportunities provided by online booking systems (Sangster, 2001). GPS and various gadgets and digital devices offered innovative solutions for museums and other heritage attractions, facilitating communication with the public and the improvement of their guests' experiences, permitting higher visual and technical quality, at lower costs (Camarero & Garrido, 2011). Additionally, the development of hotel and restaurant information systems provides them with the ability to adopt new concepts for their products, to target better locations or to locate new labor markets, to attract new market segments and to track customer satisfaction (Jin-Zhao & Jing, 2009; Siguaw & Enz, 1999).

It can be concluded that the entire concept of ICT determined a dynamic innovation impact upon different fields in tourism and hospitality, and provided them with the opportunity to redefine their products, operations and strategies.

The food sector was influenced to a significant extent by technical progress, such as: automatic kitchen equipment, robot or sensor controlled cooking and flavoring methods, and/or devices developed in order to reduce waste and energy consumption and to bring about greater efficiency and flexibility (Rogers, 2007).

The impact of the implementation of new technologies has also been described in the literature with regard to its strong potential for incremental innovation process(es) (Hjalager, 2010); in the first stage, the use of equipment and devices in different operations ensures the benefits of process innovation, followed by changes at the organizational level, which determine organizational innovation. In the end, when technology is well known, the company starts to explore it and new products or services are/can be generated; thus, product innovation may occur.

Governmental implication

The direct influence of state and governmental authorities in hospitality and tourism development was described by Hall and Williams (2008) in terms of the aspects of coordination, planning, legislation and regulation, entrepreneurship encouragement, promotion and interest protection. Based on these elements, this influence can also converge with innovation.

The increasing competition between destinations all over the world puts major pressure on regional and local authorities to develop appropriate tourism strategies and policies coordinated by destination management or marketing organizations (DMOs). Because of their vital role in ensuring that the expectations of stakeholders (both internal and external) are satisfied at the highest level possible, DMOs play a significant role in tourism innovation. This role becomes more critical in less-developed economies where the risks associated with innovation represent an important constraint.

Being part of the national/regional/local administrative power, DMOs also provide financial means for innovation, commonly through regional economic development programs. Thus, national governments get more involved in public–private partnerships with respect to developing new tourism initiatives and infrastructure. The decisions of DMOs related to defining and promoting the destination's competitive attributes and purpose have a substantial influence in developing a destination's necessary innovation skills and in establishing what, how and whom to finance in this respect. Thus, the state has an indirect influence upon the innovation capabilities of private companies and upon their long-term strategies. On the other hand, the tendency toward sustainable tourism development has required governments and local authorities to provide specific policies and regulations, which encourage innovation.

Sources of product and process innovation in hospitality

Nowadays, tourists increasingly search for unforgettable experiences, an aspect which stimulates and obliges entrepreneurs to provide them with more than singular tourism products. According to Weiermair (2004), innovation and product development represent one answer to this challenge. By adding customer value and at the same time adding to the firm's knowledge store (Sullivan & Dooley, 2008), innovation should be a "dynamic capability" (Perdomo-Ortiz et al., 2006) resulting from people's interaction and/or the interaction between them and the firm. Thus, innovation is the result of a cumulative learning process based on the capacity of stakeholders to learn and implement the appropriate measures to increase the firm's performance.

The sources of innovation can be:

- **internal** (from employees, entrepreneurs) and
- **external**: market sources, institutional sources and other sources (Camisón & Monfort-Mir, 2012).

Internal sources

Employees' suggestions and *entrepreneurs' experience and concerns* represent the main sources of internal innovation.

a) Front-line employees can be a major source of innovation (Chang et al., 2011), especially in tourism and hospitality where the interaction between customers and employees has a significant impact upon customer satisfaction. Therefore, human resource strategies are essential in facilitating innovation (Davila et al., 2006), at least from the following points of view:
   - the employees' level of innovativeness is the result of their "tacit knowledge" (Hall & Williams, 2008) and the environment of the firm, while
   - one of the main challenges for firms is to create a mechanism which will guarantee the transmission of innovative ideas from employees to managers (Chang et al., 2011).
b) Migrant workers represent another category of employees, specific to the tourism and hospitality industry, with a potential impact on innovation. The seasonality of tourist flows generates fluctuations in labor demand at both national and international levels, and, due to the dynamics of the industry, there is an increasing number of migrant workers in hospitality and tourism all over the world. Their international mobility, together with their cultural characteristics, contribute to the development of their "tacit knowledge," facilitating knowledge transfer (Williams & Shaw, 2010). This aspect is recognized in an ILO study, where the migrants are described as "a vital source of skills and labor for the hotel industry" (Baum, 2012, p. 39).
c) Hiring some persons just because of their lack of knowledge about the industry could represent a strategy with strong potential for innovation. "The wrong employees" do not have the same way of thinking as the traditional ones, an aspect which allows them to harness the firm's resources and the market opportunities in a different and more creative way (Davila et al., 2006).
d) The suggestions and concerns of entrepreneurs may have a significant innovative impact, especially because they are coming from the people with the power to decide the shape of the firm's expansion path. Innovation is critical in tourism and hospitality, which is why innovativeness is recognized as a characteristic of successful entrepreneurs (Lumpkin & Dess, 2001). In their case, product and process innovation may result from (Negruşa et al., 2015):
   - entrepreneurs' passion for what they are doing;
   - their ability to harness the endogenous resources of the region in a sustainable manner;
   - their capacity to implement ICT tools in their business;
   - entrepreneurs' multicultural and learning skills;
   - their aptitude to attract valuable employees and trusted business partners.

External sources

Many of the innovation sources in tourism and hospitality are external, most of these being related to the market sources: tourists, competitors, suppliers, both for raw materials and technology, and commercial laboratories or R&D institutes (Hall & Williams, 2008; Williams & Shaw, 2010). To these, one may add the institutional sources (public institutions, universities) and other sources, such as professional associations and NGOs, tourism fairs and exhibitions, and scientific publications (Camisón & Monfort-Mir, 2012).

a) Starting from their *tourists*, firms may identify at least three sources of innovation: the tourists' needs and desires, their tourism experience and their knowledge about tourism products. Due to a permanent expansion of the previous aspects, tourism firms may look at the tourist as a source of ideas to develop new products, to improve the existing ones or to customize their products. They are "a source of knowledge" (Williams & Shaw, 2010), challenging firms to adapt their products and processes to the identified market trends. The result is an increase in the use of experiential learning or "learning by doing, using and interacting" as an innovation source in the tourism sector. For example, there are many product or process innovations based on firms integrating technology developments into their activity in order to be closer to their clients. Moreover, over recent years, due to the expansion of ITC, more and more tourists have started to plan holidays on their own, becoming "miniscule-scale tour operators" (Hall & Williams, 2008), providing in this way valuable information about their needs and behavior.

b) Analyzing their *competitors*, tourism firms have the possibility to identify their weaknesses and what they should do in order to overcome them (for example, improve their supply, increase tourists' satisfaction or identify other market opportunities). One way to find out the latest trends promoted by destinations, the structure of tourism products, special services provided, technological evolutions on tourism equipment, and many other aspects, is to attend *tourism fairs and professional exhibitions*. Such events represent a good opportunity to exchange ideas and share information with competitors and, sometimes, such information may evolve into formal agreements with an impact upon product or process changes. The process is called "coopetition" instead of competition and it leads to the formation of tourism networks and clusters (Decelle, 2004). Similar results can be obtained through membership of professional *associations* or partnerships with *NGOs* providing tourism or complementary tourism services/products.

c) Good partnerships with *suppliers* (both for raw materials and technology) and *distributors* may represent an important source of innovation. Distributors working with tourists have the possibility to provide valuable information concerning their needs, which can be used in order to customize or develop the tourism products or to improve the tourism processes. On the other side, suppliers may come up with new or improved knowledge, technologies or materials which can be used to innovate tourism products or processes. For example, nowadays, due to the emergence of Internet and mobile technologies, many tourists use an online or offline smartphone app to navigate through cities, to find a restaurant, to book accommodation, to check-in at the airport or to evaluate the services consumed. All of these technological developments have changed tourists' behavior and represent an incentive for the tourism firm to adapt their products and processes.

d) In tourism, cooperation with *public or commercial laboratories and R&D institutes* is not so common because in this sector patenting is rare; any innovation purchased from these institutions is easy to imitate by competitors (Hall & Williams, 2008). As a result, there is no incentive for tourism firms to devote resources to this source of innovation.

e) The role of *government and other public institutions* related to innovation in tourism is primarily to coordinate and plan different actions of communication and collaboration, which will lead directly to different forms of organizational innovation (Hall & Williams, 2008; Mei et al.,

2013). Furthermore, these new forms of cooperation between public and private stakeholders may represent a source of product and process innovation.

Through the means of regulation, the government may stimulate and sometimes even oblige tourism firms to improve the products or services they provide. For example, the legislation may require new aspects related to tourists' security, special facilities for disabled travelers or protection of tourism resources. Also, governments may stimulate R&D activities, the penetration of technology or infrastructure developments in tourism through subsidies, public investments or other forms of funding. An adequate example in this sense is the European Commission, which implements a series of actions to help SMEs in the tourism industry to use smart technologies: there is a digital tourism network, a tourism business portal and a series of webinars – all of these actions being implemented in order to boost the ICT-driven innovation potential of tourism SMEs (European Commission, n.d.).

The effects of product and delivery innovation

According to the previous definitions, product innovations imply a new good or service or a significantly improved one, incorporating new technical specifications, other fundamental characteristics, immaterial components or a different usage. Process innovations are all the improvements in the production technology and methods of delivering services. Product and process innovations are the most common types of innovation in the hospitality industry because entrepreneurs and hotel developers expect significant outcomes. Still, innovations are not all equal; each type may have different implications and types of results (Hjalager, 2010). So far, each type of innovation has had a differentiated effect on the performance of a business, because some innovations have an indirect or hidden impact. On the other hand, most units introduce more than one type of innovation and it becomes difficult to isolate the origins of the effects. In this regard, the results of different studies revealed that:

- process innovations are more influential than product innovations (Hjalager, 2002);
- new technological systems of delivery provide cost reduction opportunities (Chan et al., 1998);
- the strategic importance of product innovation and service quality affect brand equity (Hanaysha & Hilman, 2015).

a) The main purpose of hospitality and tourism firms to invest in product and process innovation is to *ameliorate their competitiveness* (Klomp & Van Leeuwen, 2001; Victorino et al., 2005). According to Porter's theory regarding competitive advantage, there are three generic strategies for hospitality units:
- differentiation;
- cost-leadership; and
- focus.

Increased competition in the tourism and hospitality markets has forced the players to extremely differentiate themselves. It was revealed that travelers decide to book accommodation based on its price, service quality and image of the establishment (Baum & Haveman, 1997). Because of that, an accommodation unit tries to differentiate its services or the delivery process from those of its close competitors. In their attempt to construct the unique characteristics of their products and services, such as design and brand image, quality, and customer service, hospitality players concentrate on product development.

b) When hospitality and tourism firms provide innovative products and services, they obtain an improved image, which has an important influence upon brand awareness and a significant impact on clients' perceptions towards the innovativeness and added value of their products. Thus, another outcome determined by product innovation is *building brand equity or reinforcing it* (Beverland, 2005).

A good example of product and process innovation used for reshaping the service provided and for creating some unique characteristics is "4food restaurant," a unit which proposed a "de-junking food" concept for burgers. The idea of healthy burgers, was innovative for a quick service restaurant. In order to attract more customers, even those who are undecided regarding the consumption of healthier food, and to build brand awareness, the entrepreneur considers social interaction to be part of the business concept. Thus, the quick service restaurant provided a web-based application allowing clients to create their own type of burgers, name their own creations and market them via social media. This system was integrated in the delivery process, functioning as an order before customers arrive at the restaurant. Besides the advantage of improving the production flow, the innovative idea of the application is that clients could learn more about each ingredient, enabling customers to choose healthier options to eat. The company used a suite of web-based technologies, which offer the possibility to build the customer profiles, to match menu items to a particular profile feature and to generate incentives. Also, this method transforms customers into supporters of different causes associated with the main purpose of the business unit, namely healthier food consumption, by donating a part of the price to such actions. These types of innovation are an excellent way of not only applying a differentiated strategy based on unique products but also help to strengthen brands' image as customer-friendly, socially minded and community-involved (Negruşa et al., 2015).

c) Property renovation is considered an essential, if not the most important, tool for product innovation in the hotel sector (Hassanien & Baum, 2002). If this process is well planned and implemented, it leads to *enhanced profitability, to guest's satisfaction and to market leadership*. Thus, it was observed that nowadays existing properties are being renovated and converted into new concepts, emphasizing local and authentic experiences. Therefore, a hotel's design has became a strategic element used for differentiation, with potential influences (Negrusa & Ionescu, 2005):
   - a well-designed property with a captivating customer experience thereby creates a positive impression and strong brand awareness, with direct impact on occupancy rates;
   - when the back-of-house is well laid out, it can produce greater operating efficiencies, thereby reducing staff costs, which in general account for over 50 percent of a hotel's operating expenses;
   - well-designed environments that are pleasant to work in can increase morale and productivity.
d) Innovations related to accommodation units in room facilities, in the reservation process and distribution channels are related to *service quality improvement* (Blake et al., 2006; Hall & Williams, 2008). A better serving process leads to a higher number of loyal customers. The *increase in clients' loyalty* determines an increase in overnight stays or service consumption, an improvement in cash flow and a rise in the companies' brand notoriety (Lee et al., 2014; Nunes & Drèze, 2006). The increase in the length of stay at the same location also has an important environmental effect, reducing the amount of consumed resources such as water, energy and working time, and it leads, eventually, to stronger socio–cultural interaction between tourists and residents.

As a differentiation strategy is aimed at a broad market, which is associated with cost vulnerabilities, small independent accommodation units embrace a focus strategy. The initiation and development of the boutique hotel concept is considered a direct output of this trend. Their innovative idea is to ensure a customer experience differentiation based on personalized services. In this regard, the boutique hotel concept uses the following driving factors:

- small-scale establishments;
- individual design features;
- unique architecture characteristics;
- one-of-a-kind experience;
- home-comfort notion;
- location.

If the boutique hotel concept stresses its wide scale of services, quality and pricing, a new concept is developed. A hostel/hotel combination concentrates on affordability, convenient location and social experience. Common areas, such as lounges and bars, very often blended with the lobby, represent the central point of the concept where guests are invited to spend more time. Their concepts and design are intended to also be attractive to local demand. Thus, innovation in facilities (room equipment and design) becomes crucial for an independent hotel to be competitive against international hotel chains. New technologies alongside process innovations are used to ensure the comfort of limited services: cozy small rooms, grab-and-go- food and beverage outlets, free Wi-Fi and iPad usage and pay-as-you-go amenities. Also, alternative lodging concepts, with smaller rooms, using nontraditional spaces, have penetrated successfully into metropolitan cities, as a reaction in response to the urbanization tendency, with its challenge of limited development space (EY, 2016).

A firm's competitiveness can also be achieved through cost reductions; therefore, new technologies introduced to service delivery have contributed to this (Chan et al., 1998). For example when accommodation units introduced call centers to deal with customers' queries, as a process innovation, results were not limited to enabling the cutting of costs for this operation, but also functioned to improve their customer relationship, due to the fact that it allows employees to have more time to engage with the core competencies of the unit (Lin & Hwan-Yann, 2007).

Nowadays, it is considered vital to manage a hospitality or tourism firm according to three dimensions: economic, social and environmental. The rising interest of local residents, customers and authorities in sustainability brings an innovative edge to tourism products (Hjalager, 2002). Studies comparing resource consumption (water, energy, food, gas, etc.) during holidays to everyday life emphasize an accentuated level of consumption and waste during holidays (Bin & Hadi, 2005; Schipper et al., 1989; Tribe, 2012). Therefore, some product or process innovations are targeted at raising awareness about sustainable consumption during holidays or at creating tools for changing tourists' consumption behavior. Some hotels have developed in the area of eco-tourism, dealing with the challenges of conserving the natural environment and the well-being of local people, and have engaged with novelty through responsible travel. An important quota of the lodging sector has focused on reducing energy intensity based on an engineering approach known as commissioning. In this regard, recent advances in renewable sources of energy have opened the possibility to also improve units' efficiency from an economic point of view. For example, several benefits have been identified with the new eco-hotel concept:

- reduction of costs associated with their activity;
- maintaining a clean environment and reducing the intrinsic risks of the hospitality units' activity;

- increasing the level of satisfaction of more sophisticated and ecologically conscious guests;
- consolidating their corporate image;
- helping them to differentiate from their competitors.

Even if it has been mentioned in many situations that companies use innovations to build a green/eco profile just for improving their brand image awareness rather than for showing sustainable behavior, these benefits represent significant driving factors towards its implementation.

As has already been argued, hospitality businesses which have implemented process innovations and differentiated their products or services are more competitive than those which do not apply them (Walsh et al., 2008). But the innovation process generates a snowball effect and another important result is enhancement of human capital development (Orfila-Sintes & Mattsson, 2009).

Employees' and managers' skills, abilities, creativity and motivation have been influenced by the adoption of ICT. For example the involvement of gamification applications in recruiting, training and motivation creates a learning environment which activates employees' intrinsic motivation to learn and to progress.

Finally, the effects of product and process innovations on business activity are mostly economic. Two other aspects have been identified, namely social and environmental aspects, which transform the innovation process into an aggregate framework for sustainable development. The idea that the innovation process is not episodic, but rather continuous and never-ending can be added to this approach.

Barriers to product and delivery innovation

Similar to innovation sources, the barriers to innovation may be internal or external; in general, the barriers to innovation are related to internal factors. Previously, employees' suggestions and entrepreneurs' experience and concerns were identified as internal sources of innovation, and therefore is the reason why any factor affecting their propensity to innovate could be considered an innovation barrier. As a result, their lack of skills and know-how, their risk aversion and resistance to change, their incapacity to attract financial resources or to implement technological developments in the business process, or an organizational structure (top-down) which does not stimulate the development of an innovation culture are noted as the main innovation threats in tourism product and process innovation (Blake et al., 2006; Decelle, 2004; Hall & Williams, 2008). Regarding the external barriers, some of the industry features, such as the bureaucracy and politics, could represent possible obstacles that could endanger the planned innovation activities.

Internal barriers

Entrepreneurs' lack of concern about innovation can be considered the most important barrier. In order to innovate, entrepreneurs have to explore their business, identify the potential sources of improvement and encourage idea formation and experimentation. They have to accept that innovation presumes resources consumption and the risk of a potential failure. As a result, if the entrepreneurs consider innovation too costly or too risky there will be no incentive to promote innovation. Moreover, the chances of having such an attitude towards innovation will be even higher if the business was functioning in the past in the same way and the results were satisfactory for the entrepreneur.

Another factor reducing the incentive to innovate is *the ease in which competitors can imitate the innovation* (Hall & Williams, 2008). This is a characteristic of the sector which reduces the efficiency of the innovation (the economic advantage obtained is too short-term to generate a satisfactory return) and means that managers are not only reluctant to innovate, but also encourages them to act as free-riders: instead of focusing on their own business and identifying innovation opportunities, they will focus on competitors' innovation processes to see what could be easily copied.

The size of the business also affects entrepreneurs' propensity to innovate. According to the literature, smaller tourism firms have the capacity to generate more product or process innovations than bigger ones, but the value and efficiency of innovations are higher in the case of bigger firms due to the economies of scale (Camisón & Monfort-Mir, 2012; Hall & Williams, 2008). As a result, small tourism firms facing the problem of limited financial resources and of reduced capacity to attract external funds have limited access to technology, ICT tools and skills in order to use them in their daily activity (Najda-Janoszka & Kopera, 2013). Similar results were obtained in a study conducted on rural-area tourism units (all of the units being micro and small tourism firms) from Cluj County, Romania, where the most significant internal barriers to innovation were identified as a lack of financial resources, a limited capacity to attract European funds and the perception that the cost of innovation is too high (Gică & Toader, 2014).

The fact that migrant workers are an important source of innovation represents only half of the whole picture. The receiving destinations and units benefit from their skills, while the outbound regions and their tourism firms have real problems in *finding skilled workers who are able to innovate*. This situation generates fluctuations in the labor force and a negative selection of specialized workers, with educated and skilled employees being tempted to migrate to other countries/regions where they can earn enough money in the peak season (Sofica & Toader, 2013). The result is a reduced incentive to learn and acquire the knowledge and skills necessary to progress and to enlarge their pool of tacit knowledge (Najda-Janoszka & Kopera, 2013). Therefore, it cannot be expected for too many suggestions to improve the tourism products or the delivery processes to come from this category of employees.

External barriers

Seasonality of tourism demand represents an important external barrier to innovation, especially in the case of tourism, where most of the firms are micro, small and medium units. The tourism entrepreneurs managing their businesses in destinations where the peak season is only in the summer and winter consider that it is not worth investing in making radical changes or improvements to their products or facilities as the flow of tourists is fluctuating across the year (Gică & Toader, 2014).

Government regulations can create barriers to the development of new or improved products and production processes: some regulations reduce or forbid tourists' access in time and space in specific locations, limit the choices of tourism companies in using specific technologies or in developing different activities, and so on. In fact, most of these rules result in an increase in operational costs, which may mean that the entrepreneurs give up on the idea of improving their products or processes. Moreover, as was mentioned above, the legislation regarding the legal protection of innovations in tourism is scarce, an aspect which reduces entrepreneurs' propensity to innovate.

In order to eliminate the barriers to innovation, first of all it has to be determined where specific barriers are located and then plans need to be developed and actions taken to overcome these innovation barriers, using ideas and creativity to identify the best ways to harness the firm's resources through innovation.

References

Baum, J. A. C. & Haveman,. H. A., 1997. Love the neighbour? Differentiation and agglomeration in the Manhattan hotel industry. *Administrative Science Quarterly*, 42(2), pp. 304–338.

Baum, T., 2012. *International Labour Office – Migrant workers in the international hotel industry*. [Online] Available at: www.ilo.org/wcmsp5/groups/public/---ed_dialogue/---sector/documents/publication/wcms_180596.pdf [Accessed 1 September 2016].

Beverland, M. B., 2005. Managing the design innovation-brand marketing interface: Resolving the tension between artistic creation and commercial imperatives.. *Journal of Product Innovation Management*, 22(2), pp. 193–207.

Bin, S. & Hadi, D., 2005. Consumer lifestyle approach to US energy use and the related CO2 emissions. *Energy Policy*, 33, pp. 197–208.

Blake, A., Sinclair, M. & Soria, J., 2006. Tourism productivity: Evidence from the United Kingdom. *Annals of Tourism Research*, 33, pp. 1099–1120.

Camarero, C. & Garrido, E., 2011. Fostering innovation in cultural contexts: Market orientation, service orientation, and innovations in museums. *Journal of Service Research*, 15(1), pp. 39–58.

Camisón, C. & Monfort-Mir, V. M., 2012. Measuring innovation in tourism from the Schumpeterian and the dynamic-capabilities perspectives. *Tourism Management*, 33(4), pp. 776–789.

Chan, A., Go, F. M. & Pine, R., 1998. Service innovation in Hong Kong: Attitudes and practice. *The Service Industries Journal*, 18(2), pp. 112–124.

Chang, S., Gong, Y. & Shum, C., 2011. Promoting innovation in hospitality companies through human resource management practices. *International Journal of Hospitality Management*, 30, pp. 812–818.

Coombs, R., Saviotti, P. & Walsh, V., 1987. Economics and technological-change. *Manchester School of Economic and Social Studies*, 55(4), pp. 426–427.

Davila, T., Epstein, M. J. & Shelton, R. D., 2006. *Making Innovation Work: How to Manage It, Measure It, and Profit From It*. Upper Saddle River, NJ: Pearson Education, Inc.

Decelle, X., 2004. *OECD – A Conceptual and Dynamic Approach to Innovation in Tourism*. [Online] Available at: www.oecd.org/cfe/tourism/34267921.pdf [Accessed 5 September 2016].

European Commission, n.d. *Digital Tourism*. [Online] Available at: https://ec.europa.eu/growth/sectors/tourism/support-business/digital_en [Accessed 7 September 2016].

EY, 2016. *Global Hospitality Insights*. [Online] Available at: www.ey.com/Publication/vwLUAssets/EY-global-hospitality-insights/$FILE/EY-global-hospitality-insights-2016.pdf [Accessed 18 September 2016].

Gică, O. A. & Toader, V., 2014. Innovation in rural tourism: Evidence from Cluj County. *Studia Universitatis Babes Bolyai-Negotia*, pp. 57–73.

Hall, M. & Williams, A. M., 2008. *Tourism and Innovation*. New York: Routledge.

Hanaysha, J. & Hilman, H., 2015. Product innovation as a key success factor to build sustainable brand equity. *Management Science Letters*, 5(6), pp. 567–576.

Hassanien, A. & Baum, T., 2002. Hotel innovation through property renovation. *International Journal of Hospitality & Tourism Administration*, 3(4), pp. 5–24.

Hjalager, A. M., 2002. Repairing innovation defectiveness in tourism. *Tourism Management*, 23(5), pp. 465–474.

Hjalager, A.-M., 2010. A review of innovation research in tourism. *Tourism Management*, 31(1), pp. 1–12.

Jin-Zhao, W. & Jing, W., 2009. Issues, challenges, and trends, that facing hospitality industry. *Management Science and Engineering*, 3(4), pp. 53–58.

Klomp,. L. & Van Leeuwen, G., 2001. Linking innovation and firm performance: A new approach. *International Journal of the Economics of Business*, 8(3), pp. 343–364.

Lee, J. J., Capella, M. L., Taylor, C. & Gabler, C., 2014. The financial impact of loyalty programs in the hotel industry: A social exchange theory perspective. *Journal of Business Research*, 67, pp. 2139–2146.

Lin, Y. & Hwan-Yann, S., 2007. Strategic analysis of customer relationship management. *Total Quality Management and Business Excellence*, 14(6), pp. 715–731.

Lumpkin, G. T. & Dess, G. G., 2001. Linking two dimensions of entrepreneurial orientation to firm performance: The moderating role of environment and industry life cycle. *Journal of Business Venturing*, 16(5), pp. 429–451.

Mei, X.Y., Arcodia, C. & Ruhanen, L., 2013. Innovation and collaboration: The role of the national govern-ment in Norway. *Tourism Analysis*, 18, pp. 519–531.

Najda-Janoszka, M. & Kopera, S., 2013. Exploring barriers to innovation in tourism industry – the case of southern region of Poland, 110, pp. 190–201.

Negrusa, A. L. & Ionescu, C. E., 2005. Design implications in creating a competitive advantage for hospital-ity small business. *Studia Universitatis Babes Bolyai-Negotia*, 1, pp. 99–108.

Negruşa, A. L., Toader, V., Rus, R. V. & Sofică, A., 2015. *Characteristics of Innovative Entrepreneurs in Rural Tourism*. s.l., "Science in Technology" SCinTE 2015 international conference.

Negruşa, A. L. et al., 2015. Exploring gamification techniques and applications for sustainable tourism. *Sustainability*, 7(8), pp. 11160–11189.

Nunes, J. & Drèze, X., 2006. Your loyalty program is betraying you.. *Harvard Business Review*, 84, pp. 124–131.

OECD, 2005. *Oslo Manual: Guidelines for Collecting and Interpreting Innovation Data*. s.l.: OECD Publishing.

Orfila-Sintes, F. & Mattsson, J., 2009. Innovation behaviour in the hotel industry. *OMEGA: The Internatioinal Journal of Management Science*, 37(2), pp. 380–394.

Ottenbacher, M., 2008. Innovation management. In: P. Jones, ed., *Handbook of Hospitality Operations and IT*. Oxford: Elsevier Ltd., pp. 340–366.

Perdomo-Ortiz, J., Gonzalez-Benito, J. & Galende, J., 2006. Total quality management as a forerunner of business innovation capability. *Technovation*, 26, pp. 1170–1185.

Rogers, S., 2007. Innovation in food service technology and its strategic role. *International Journal of Hospitality Management*, 26(4), pp. 899–912.

San Martin, G. S., Camarero, I. C. & San José, C. R., 2010. Product and channel-related risk and involvement in online contexts. *Electronic Commerce Research and Applications*, 9, pp. 263–273.

Sangster, A., 2001. The importance of technology in the hotel industry. *Travel and Tourism Analyst*, 3, pp. 43–56.

Schipper, L., Bartlett, S., Hawk, D. & Vine, E., 1989. Linking life-styles and energy use: A matter of time? *Annual Review of Energy*, 14, pp. 273–320.

Siguaw, J. A. & Enz, C. A., 1999. Best practices in information technology. *Cornell Hotel and Restaurant Administration Quarterly*, 40(5), pp. 58–71.

Sofica, A. & Toader, V., 2013. Human resource recruiting techniques in rural tourism – Cluj County, Romania. *Studia Universitas Babes-Bolyai Negotia*, pp. 61–72.

Sullivan, D. & Dooley, L., 2008. *Applying Innovation*. s.l.: Sage Publications.

Tidd, J., Bessant, J. & Pavitt, K., 2005. *Managing Innovation: Integrating Technological, Market and Organizational Change*. Third Edition. s.l.: John Wiley & Sons.

Tribe, J., 2012. *The Economics of Recreation, Leisure and Tourism*. London: Routledge.

Victorino, L., Verma, R., Plaschka, F. & Dev, C., 2005. Service innovation and customer choices in the hos-pitality industry.. *Managing Service Quality*, 15(6), pp. 555–576.

Walsh, K., Enz, C. A. & Canina, L., 2008. The impact of strategic orientation on intellectual capital invest-ments in customer service firms. *Journal of Service Research*, 10(4), pp. 300–317.

Weiermair, K., 2004. *OECD*. [Online] Available at: www.oecd.org/cfe/tourism/34267947.pdf [Accessed 29 August 2016].

Williams, A. M. & Shaw, G., 2010. Internationalization and innovation in tourism. *Annals of Tourism Research*, 38(1), pp. 27–51.

36

Innovation in hospitality service experience creation and delivery

James Brian Aday, Steve Lui and Andrew R. Walls

Introduction

Traditional hospitality companies are embracing the use of modern technologies to enhance the services they offer and to gain high levels of guest satisfaction and customer loyalty. In the hyper-competitive environment of hospitality, it has become critical for companies to find innovative means to enhance and differentiate their product and service offerings (Neuhofer, Buhalis, & Ladkin, 2012) and, subsequently, lead to customer loyalty (Lee, Barker, & Kandampully, 2003). Electronic-commerce (e-commerce) is a term which encompasses a wide range of technologies utilized to facilitate online communications to guests and potential customers.

The hotel industry is only one segment in which mobile application technology is being employed to enhance customer satisfaction and brand loyalty. With mobile technology, guests will be able to have more control over their stay in the palms of their hands and will be able to do things such as request towels, order room service, or request a car from valet parking. Guests may also be able to use their own smartphone device as a remote control for their hotel room TV, lighting settings, and a variety of other in-room functions. These digital techniques can be an important piece of the corporation's customer relationship management (CRM) strategy. None of this, however, would be possible without the advent of electronic commerce (e-commerce) and the marketing options made possible through technology.

Brief history of technology in marketing

Electronic marketing (e-marketing) is defined as delivering advertisements and offers, as well as building relationships between a firm and potential customers, via the Internet (Shaltoni & West, 2010; Verma, Sharma, & Sheth, 2016). E-marketing was first introduced two decades ago when the Internet became readily available in everyday households (Taylor & Strutton, 2010). Around the same time, e-marketing research emerged. In the last 15 years, journals such as the *Journal of Interactive Marketing*, *International Journal of Electronic Commerce*, and *Electronic Commerce Research* have emerged as publications dedicated to the study of online consumer and business activities (Taylor & Strutton, 2010).

E-marketing was first developed in the early 1990s as the expansion of the Internet to the public sector was followed by the creation of online businesses such as Amazon.com and eBay.com (Mowery & Simcoe, 2002). The first form of online advertising was a banner advertisement which appeared on the Hotwired website, an online version of the print magazine *Wired*, in 1994 (Hollis, 2005). In 1994, search engines such as Yahoo! began to surface and relied upon funding from advertisers in the form of cost-per-click ads (Evans, 2009). Soon after, Hotwired, an industry leader in e-marketing, partnered with the world-renowned research firm Millward Brown International, and produced one of the first studies measuring the effectiveness and influence of online advertising (Hollis, 2005). Between 1996 and 2001, online marketing expanded each year, with revenue generated from the sale of Internet ads producing over $7 billion in 2001 (Evans, 2008). The "dot-com bust" (Evans, 2008) of the early 2000s reduced the demand for online advertising; however, between 2004 and 2007 online advertising sales rebounded with estimated revenues of over $21 billion in 2007. Social media sites such as Facebook, MySpace, Twitter, YouTube, and blogs gained prominence in the multimedia realm beginning in 2005 (Weinberg & Berger, 2011). Advertisements in these social forums might incorporate computer matching, based on user preferences from their profiles, or mass-generated propaganda (Wright, Khanfar, Harrington, & Kizer, 2010). The social format also allows for personal opinions, *likes*, affirmations, and sharing of advertisements from user to user (Weinberg & Berger, 2011). Over the past ten years, the web-based advertising market has become one of the fastest growing media segments, with a global revenue of over $66 billion anticipated for 2016 (Tadena, 2015). Furthermore, spending on digital advertisements is anticipated to surpass spending on traditional TV advertisements for the first time in 2016 as well (Tadena, 2015).

Growth of digital marketing

The heightened use of search engines has extended the viability of online marketing; findings from the Pew Research Center's Internet and American Life Project (Pew, 2012) established that 73 percent of all Americans have utilized a search engine. Search engine sites rely upon advertising dollars for financial sustainability, displaying ads every time a user conducts a search (Ghose & Yang, 2009). Based on data available from the U.S. Census Bureau (2016a), there were over 323 million Americans as of July 2016. The findings of the Pew (2012) study, coupled with U.S. Census Bureau (2016b) data, equates to 232 million Americans being exposed to e-marketing through search engine usage. In 2015, search engine usage on mobile devices, smartphones and tablets surpassed the number of searches performed on traditional computers (Thomas, 2015).

The growth of the Internet over the past decade has created the modern availability of and demand for online retailing and websites which supplement traditional brick and mortar stores and in-person interactions (Yani-de-Soriano & Slater, 2009). The ability to order goods and services from the Internet has resulted in higher control of consumer choice and empowered consumers like never before (Yani-de-Soriano & Slater, 2009). As such, consumers have developed heightened opinions regarding the appropriateness of digital advertising. For example, pop-up advertisements are designed to capture the user's attention and prevent them from proceeding to the actual website until the advertisement has been closed (Edwards, Li, & Lee, 2002). Numerous academic-based studies have identified consumers' distaste for pop-ups, with respondents repeatedly protesting the intrusive nature of these ads (McCoy, Everard, & Loiacono, 2009) and insisting that the appearance of a company in such an ad can lead to negative feelings of the consumer towards the brand (Madhavaram & Appan, 2010).

Types of electronic advertising medium

Electronic commerce provides a unique medium for delivering content-specific and mass distribution advertisements to a wide assortment of consumers (Huang, Chen, & Wu, 2009). Electronic advertisements are delivered through a multitude of mediums (Kim & McMillan, 2008), including mobile platforms (Gao, Sultan, & Rohm, 2010), direct e-marketing (Wright & Cawston, 2012), email and listserv (Illum, Ivanov, & Liang, 2010), and databases (Pels, Coviello, & Brodie, 2000). While these e-marketing platforms are not a complete list, they are identified in the literature as the most widely used forms of web-based advertising.

Email and listserv

Listserv was created in the late 1980s and is a program that manages email distribution lists for mass e-mailings (Grier & Campbell, 2000). Email marketing is a direct, inexpensive, and asynchronous channel to target end-users in a non-obtrusive manner (Murphy & Gomes, 2003). This type of marketing is continuous and provides interactive feedback to the firm, allowing them to garner responses related to effectiveness in a timely manner (Miller, 2010). The expanded reach of email as a marketing medium has resulted in a majority of firms investing in this tool, as over 85 percent of online consumers use email at least once per month (VanBoskirk, 2007).

Databases

Database marketing has transformed how firms collect and manage customer information (Zwick & Dholakia, 2004). Utilizing software such as cookies and click-through monitoring, businesses are able to record every detail of a user's visit to their site (Miyazaki, 2008). This type of data collection, or customer database, allows the firm to analyze the results of site visitation through specially designed software which identifies trends, purchase behavior, and creates a digital identity for each customer (Zwick & Dholakia, 2004). The employment of database marketing in the online context allows the firm to present customers with specialized products, based on previous visits, and aids in establishing a relationship marketing experience (Schoenbachler & Gordon, 2002). Database marketing has been incorporated into the CRM policies of firms, as they strive to establish a bond between the business and customer that will potentially garner future sales (O'Leary, Rao, & Perry, 2004). Numerous studies have examined the key inputs associated with effective CRM or relationship marketing strategies, and the common denominator in the research findings revolves around the trust the consumer has in the firm (Zwick & Dholakia, 2004).

Direct e-marketing

Direct marketing was established as a means of communicating personalized messages to consumers and overcoming the high costs associated with the traditional forms of marketing (Palmer & Koenig-Lewis, 2009). The global recession of 2008 forced marketing managers to slash their budgets and identify new, cost-effective measures to reach potential target audiences (Palmer & Koenig-Lewis, 2009). Direct e-marketing involves sending or displaying advertisements which are highly specified to consumers' preferences based on previous purchase behavior or identified information from websites, including social media, and mobile applications (Ström, Vendel, & Bredican, 2014; Wang, Malthouse, & Krishnamurthi, 2015).

Direct marketing relies upon the firm consistently adjusting their advertising strategy until sales are achieved (Bose & Chen, 2009). For example, a firm may email or display an advertisement for a potential customer which is highly customized, and depending on whether or not the ad generates a sale, the firm may be required to go back and change the direct marketing message to more effectively influence the customer (Bose & Chen, 2009). Research studies have identified that consumers who are influenced by direct marketing are likely to pass company information along to their social circles (Phelps, Lewis, Mobilio, Perry, & Raman, 2004). Direct marketing can be incorporated into a firm's CRM strategy, creating positive relationships and potentially higher profit margins (Morgan, Slotegraaf, & Vorhies, 2009).

Mobile platforms

Mobile-based marketing is a relatively new concept in the realm of e-marketing and only became a focus of research in the latter half of the 2000s (Okazaki, 2009). Scholarly based research publications on mobile advertising have primarily focused on content delivery and ease of use (Okazaki, 2009). The unique portability of mobile devices gives firms the capability to communicate with consumers on the go.

Recent data implies that mobile penetration, or the number of individuals within a given population who have access to a mobile device, is nearing 100 percent in most Western countries (Leek & Christodoulides, 2009). Businesses are recognizing the limitless potential of this as they have the ability to capture the attention of a large target market via mobile media (Friedrich, Grone, Holbling, & Peterson, 2009). Other firms are relying upon location or spot-specific advertising, sending messages to a mobile device via Bluetooth technology with personalized ads whenever a consumer is in proximity to a particular business (Leek & Christodoulides, 2009). A recent phenomenon is the availability of apps from businesses which are downloaded by consumers and allow instant access to the firm. Recent data indicates that the Apple App Store maintains over 1.2 million apps (Perez, 2014), while Google's Play Store offers approximately 1.4 million apps (Smith, 2014).

Product and brand-driven consumers

Brand loyalty

Loyalty to a particular brand is generated when companies are viewed as credible by consumers and previous purchases have proven to exceed expectations (Dick & Basu, 1994). Marketing mediums and elements of the marketing mix (price, place, product, and promotion) are influential in establishing brand loyalty, and might serve as the primary step in establishing loyalty to firms with which consumers are unfamiliar (Olsen, 2002; Yoo, Donthu, & Lee, 2000). Users of mobile applications might encounter a featured business for the first time through this medium, and this advertisement and subsequent features will determine the likelihood of purchase by the consumer. Well-established brands with a loyal customer following might further benefit from mobile application offerings as they already have an established customer base.

Brand preference

Buyers are influenced by brands with which they have previous experience. Prior interactions, if positive, can establish purchasers who develop a preference for a particular firm's products or services (Chang & Liu, 2009). The image a brand conveys to the consumer, relies upon the established equity of the brand (Chang & Liu, 2009; Faircloth, Capella, & Alford, 2001). However, recent literature has identified that consumers who have developed a brand preference but not loyalty towards the firm are willing to switch brands to experience new and innovative products (Lam, Ahearne, Hu, & Schillweaert, 2010); they are also willing to switch brands if the relationship between the firm and the consumer has relied solely upon previous purchase experiences and a personal relationship between the two parties is weak or non-existent (Lam et al., 2010).

Customer satisfaction is the leading principle for determining the level of quality that is delivered to customers through the service/product (Vavra, 1997). This psychological concept involves the feeling of well-being and pleasure that results from obtaining what one hopes for and expects from an appealing product and/or service (Pizam & Ellis, 1999). Klaus (1985, p. 21) defines satisfaction as "the customer's subjective evaluation of a consumption experience, based on some relationship between the customer's perceptions and objective attributes of the product." Satisfaction has been broadly defined as the psychological state that results when unmet expectations are compared to the consumer's feeling prior to the consumption experience (Oliver, 1981). Customer satisfaction influences both brand loyalty and brand preference.

The mobile revolution of hotel marketing

Technology applications in the hospitality industry have traditionally focused on the reservation and pre-arrival phase of the guest experience. The industry has seen a tremendous shift toward online bookings through internet-based Online Travel Agent (OTA) booking sites and brand booking sites. These digital travel bookings are now evolving to mobile device bookings. Based on a late 2015 study by Emarketer.com, mobile travel bookings have increased from 38.3% in 2014 to 43.8% in 2015 to an estimated 51.8% in 2016, representing more than half of all digital bookings (eMarketer.com, 2015). Out of the 48.5 million US adults who booked travel using mobile devices in 2015, 78.6% of them will use smartphones (eMarketer.com, 2015). As mobile travel booking has become more advanced, potential guests have more options during the room type selection process, allowing them to preview room accommodation, pre-order amenities and book other services. Most of the full service major hotel companies also offer the guest digital check-in (mobile or online) prior to arrival to minimize some of the onsite check-in time and hassle.

As hotels fight to retain and grow brand loyalty from OTAs and other brands, some companies are embedding new technology throughout the customer experience. The hope is to provide enhanced and unique service offerings to the guest, which can be viewed as a brand differentiator. The savvy digital traveler has come to expect a high level of sophistication and innovation in digital apps as they are accustomed to mobile-specific apps such as Uber and Lyft. Hotel companies are now trying to develop more cutting-edge technology enhancements to their own brand smartphone apps to entice guests to not only download the app, but to join the brand loyalty program so they can use the app to its fullest potential. This is a creative, indirect way of building brand loyalty by driving value proposition through providing "must have" features otherwise unavailable to a non-loyalty member.

Online mobile check-in

Some of the major hotel companies such as Marriott, Starwood, and Hilton allow a guest with a future reservation to check-in to their guest room prior to arrival at the hotel through the brand mobile app or the company website. Online check-in does not allow a guest to completely bypass the front desk and avoid frustrating long lines. Guests still need to stop by the registration desk to obtain their room key. Most hotel systems that offer online digital check-in will automatically select the room for the guest based on the rate plan and room preference of the guest.

Hilton Hotels is taking this a step further and is currently the only company to give guests the opportunity to choose their exact room during the digital check-in process. This requires a room floor map to be uploaded for every hotel in the system with accurate room numbers. Guests are able to browse the floor plan and choose an available room not only based on room preference, but also on a floor location preference. Hilton recently enhanced their digital check-in feature by integrating Google Maps into the room selection process so that guests could also view geographical information on the surroundings of the building. This feature provides guests with a higher level of personalization, allowing them to not only choose a room, but also to visualize where rooms are in relation to landmarks around the building. Hilton is the only full service global company that has introduced this level of detail into the online and mobile smartphone check-in process. They have seen strong usage of the digital check-in feature with over 13 million guest digital check-in transactions (Hilton Worldwide, 2016).

Smartphone-based keys (virtual key)

Smartphone-based key or virtual key entry is a true differentiator because it is the missing ingredient to allow a guest to bypass the front desk completely. It is the first feature that is only available on the mobile app and must be used on the actual smartphone device while at the destination. It is both a mobile software feature and a physical feature. The implementation of digital key technology requires a few pre-requisites. The guest must have a smartphone and be a member of the brand loyalty program since the key is driven directly through the brand app. They also need to be checked in via mobile or online check-in so they can be presented with a key through the app prior to arrival. Once the guest is checked into a guest room, a unique "key" can be pushed through the smart phone app to the guest who no longer needs a physical plastic key card to access the room.

The most recent and advanced deployments of smartphone-based virtual key systems use a low-powered Bluetooth technology also referred to as Bluetooth LE (low energy), Bluetooth 4.0+ or Bluetooth Smart (Bluetooth.com, 2016). Bluetooth LE technology is really designed for the Internet of Things (IoT), which allows everyday devices such as watches, appliances and music devices to communicate via Bluetooth to smartphones using a minimal amount of power (Bluetooth.com, 2016). Bluetooth LE devices know how to manage power extremely well and go into idle power modes when needed so they are not consuming a large amount of power when not in use, which maximizes battery life (Donovan, 2011). Hotels looking to implement smartphone virtual keys usually have to go through some kind of retrofit on the existing physical door lock to add the Bluetooth LE chip device inside the lock. It is important to note that whatever door lock is used, it must continue to also accept the traditional key card for guests that do not possess smartphones and also for additional occupants of the room. Most of the major brands are in the planning or deployment phase for smartphone-based keys.

Two companies in particular have taken a leadership role in this arena – Starwood and Hilton. Starwood's smartphone-based key system is branded "SPG Keyless," and is built around the Starwood Preferred Guest (SPG) guest loyalty program. The system requires the guest to be a member of the SPG program and to have the smartphone app downloaded on their device. The guest is also required to register their device through the app prior to using the key. The day prior to arrival, the SPG app pushes a notification to the smartphone of the arriving guest who can then opt-in for the digital key. The guest is asked to confirm trip details such as arrival and departure times. Platinum members of the SPG program are presented with their choice of amenity such as bonus points or continental breakfast. The SPG app also takes the opportunity to ask the guest if they would like to decline housekeeping services as part of Starwood's "green initiative," which will earn the guest an additional 500 bonus points. On the day of arrival, the guest will be checked-in to a room automatically and will receive another push notification that the SPG Keyless feature is "active." Bluetooth must be active on the guest's smartphone and they can go straight to their room and unlock the door by holding the phone in Bluetooth range of the door lock to access the room. Starwood has 176 SPG Keyless enabled hotels across multiple countries and regions and currently has an Apple App Store rating of 4.5 stars.

The Hilton smartphone-based key system is branded "Hilton Digital Key" and is integrated into the Hilton Honors App available for Android smartphone devices (4.3 OS or higher) and iPhone devices (iOS 8 or higher). The guest must be a registered member of the Hilton Honors Loyalty Program to take advantage of Hilton Digital Key. The system works in a similar way to the Starwood SPG app with the exception of the additional benefit of allowing the guest to choose their specific room. When the specific room is ready, the guest will receive an email and the app will indicate that the digital key is active and ready to use. When the guest approaches the guest room, he or she taps the Hilton Digital Key icon for the current reservation, and the key is presented on the smartphone. Hilton currently leads the industry with 345 hotels deployed with Digital Key and has the goal of installing Digital Key in over 4,000 hotels globally.

Mobile app guest services features

As more guests utilize brand mobile apps for cutting-edge services, it paves the way for hotel companies to bring more and more services to the mobile app as adoption and acceptance of mobile services grow. Once the guest's attention is "captured" with features like SPG Keyless or Hilton Digital Key, it becomes much easier to push other features and services to this captive audience that is now accustomed to using the smartphone app. Useful and relevant bring your own device (BYOD) hotel service offerings can drive even more new customers to the brand hotel app and in turn, drive new guests to register for the loyalty program. Mobile features such as these are intended to provide a simple, streamlined set of services available through a single hotel app. Most of the major brands are exploring adding more guest service features to their mobile applications.

Location-based technology using beacons

Location-based services (LBS) can be defined as the "use of real-time geo-data from a mobile device or smartphone to provide information, entertainment or security" (Goodrich, 2013). The hospitality industry wants to take this further by not only providing guests with information and services based on their geo-location and proximity to services, but to also better understand guest behavior, patterns and preferences while on-site. The intent is to have a deeper knowledge of the overall movements of a guest so that contextual, localized information, marketing materials and promotions can be proactively "pushed" to the guest.

One of the more popular methods of tracking guests based on location is with the use of Bluetooth beacons placed strategically around the property. The beacons are equipped with Bluetooth Low Energy chipsets that send out beacon requests to guests' smartphone apps that "listen" for the beacons. For beacon location-based technology to work, it requires the guest to have a smartphone that supports Bluetooth LE and an app that is able to listen for the beacons. Again, the most logical app for the hotel industry is the brand app that a guest might have already used to check-in to their hotel, unlock their room door and order hotel services. It is just another value-added feature that hotels are looking to offer guests.

Beacon location-based technology is not to be confused with other macro location-based services such as FourSquare and Yelp which rely on GPS technology for location tracking using cell tower triangulation. WiFi positioning can also be used for location-based services, but it requires software that tracks Wireless Access Points that have been registered in mostly hot-spot environments. Beacon technology is much more of a micro-level technology, usually contained within a physical building or group of buildings. The locations of the beacons have to be planned out to best capture guest foot traffic. For example, a large resort might place multiple beacons in strategic areas of the resort to understand the flow of the guests and to provide promotional items to their smartphones depending on where they are in the resort. These items can be offered on the spot and are relevant to where the guest is located, such as coupons for retail shops in a resort when the guest enters that space.

Hospitality companies that implement beacon location-based technology can also gather pertinent guest information to build a guest profile that is based on past behaviors and preferences, which allows future marketing to the guests to be targeted specifically at them. If a guest has a history of visiting specific restaurants or spa services, promotional offers and marketing information can be sent to that guest. It is important to note that a guest must "opt-in" and agree to participate before they start using the location-based features built into the app. This addresses concerns guests might have regarding unapproved tracking and monitoring.

Service quality and guest satisfaction

Hospitality suppliers, in an effort to maximize profitability, competitiveness and efficiencies, have embraced the latest developments and changes, particularly in technology-related arenas, in an effort to empower their guests to co-create their own experiences (Prahalad & Ramaswamy, 2004). Traditional roles, structures and processes of hospitality companies are changing with the dynamic improvements in technologies (Neuhofer et al., 2012). This shift has shown the transformational role that technology has had on the traditional path that hospitality has followed as well as how guests' experiences are initiated.

Service quality, broadly defined, is the manner in which a service is provided as it influences the degree of satisfaction with a good or service (Zeithaml, 1988). By extension, "perceived quality can be defined as the consumer's judgment about an entity's overall excellence or superiority" (Zeithaml, 1988, p. 3). These perceived quality standards are the basis upon which customer satisfaction is determined. The implementation of innovative smartphone apps by corporations such as Starwood and Hilton is personalizing the customer experience in a way which differentiates them from the crowd of other market competitors. These cutting-edge digital techniques are focused on anticipating a guest's needs even before the guest realizes what that need is.

The concept of customer satisfaction is critical for businesses to understand because of its impact on future behavioral intention and word-of-mouth recommendations (Assal, 1987). Given the nature of the service industry (Parasuraman, Zeithaml, & Berry, 1988), it is likely that customers will receive differing levels of satisfaction from the same hospitality experience. For example, two individuals checking in to a hotel at the front desk may have very different service experiences and, consequently, differing satisfaction levels. This is where the options provided by technology come into play. Providing a tech-savvy customer with the opportunity to have a meaningful check-in experience through a digital framework while also allowing the more traditional customer to choose a face-to-face check-in process means that a hotel can meet satisfaction levels for a variety of customer types.

Consumption encounters involve more than mere delivery of products and services; rather, researches have argued that businesses should emphasize high-quality products and services and "staged" experiences that create memorable and lasting guest experiences (Gilmore & Pine, 2002; Titz, 2008). According to Walls (2012), a consumer experience is a blend of many individual elements that come together and may involve the consumer emotionally, physically, and intellectually. People's interactions with products, services, and businesses form a multidimensional takeaway that in turn defines positive emotional or cognitive encounters. This concept has been expanded to emphasize that consumers are not inert purchasers but rather co-producers who actively build their own consumption experiences though interaction with the environment, sellers and other consumers (Prahalad & Ramaswamy, 2004; Walls, Okumus, Wang, & Kwun, 2010). The digital solutions appearing in the hospitality industry are designed for a world adept at multi-modal communication and used to the concept of playing an active role in the consumer experience. No longer are consumers passively waiting for a single person to provide them with needed information; rather, they are actively incorporating digital and web-based devices and expecting service providers to do the same.

References

Assal, H. (1987) *Consumer Behavior and Marketing Action* (3rd ed.), Boston: PSW-Kent.
Bluetooth.com (2016) "Low energy," *Bluetooth.com.* Available from www.bluetooth.com/what-is-bluetooth-technology/bluetooth-technology-basics/low-energy (30 September 2016).
Bose I. & Chen, X. (2009) "Quantitative models for direct marketing: A review from systems perspective," *European Journal of Operational Research* 195, 1–16.
Chang, H.H. & Liu, Y.M. (2009) "The impact of brand equity and brand preference and purchase intentions in the service industries," *The Service Industries Journal* 29, 1687–1706.
Dick, A.S. & Basu, K. (1994) "Customer loyalty: Toward an integrated conceptual framework," *Journal of the Academy of Marketing Science* 22, 99–113.
Donovan, J. (2011) "Bluetooth goes ultra-low-power," Digi-Key Electronics, 1 December. Available from www.digikey.com/en/articles/techzone/2011/dec/bluetooth-goes-ultra-low-power (2 October 2016).
Edwards, S.M., Li, H. & Lee, J.H. (2002) "Forced exposure and psychological reactance: Antecedents and consequences of the perceived intrusiveness of pop-up ads," *Journal of Advertising* 31, 83–95.
eMarketer.com. (2015) "By 2016, most digital travel bookers will use mobile devices," *eMarketer.com*, 19 November. Available from www.emarketer.com/Article/By-2016-Most-Digital-Travel-Bookers-Will-Use-Mobile-Devices/1013248 (2 October 2016).
Evans, D.S. (2008) "The economics of the online advertising industry," *Review of Network Economics* 7, 359–391.
Evans, D.S. (2009) "The online advertising industry: Economics, evolution, and privacy," *Journal of Economic Perspectives* 23, 37–60.
Faircloth, J.B., Capella, L.M. & Alford, B.L. (2001) "The effect of brand attitude and brand image on brand equity," *Journal of Marketing Theory and Practice* 9, 61–75.
Friedrich, R., Grone, F., Holbling, K. & Peterson, M. (2009) "The march of mobile marketing: New chances for consumer companies, new opportunities for mobile operators," *Journal of Advertising Research* 49, 54–61.
Gao, T., Sultan, F. & Rohm, A.J. (2010) "Factors influencing Chinese youth consumers' acceptance of mobile marketing," *Journal of Consumer Marketing* 27, 574–583.
Ghose, A. & Yang, S. (2009) "An empirical analysis of search engine advertising: Sponsored search in electronic markets," *Management Science* 55, 1605–1622.

Gilmore, J.H. & Pine, J. (2002) "Differentiating hospitality operations via experiences: Why selling services is not enough," *Cornell Hotel and Restaurant Administration Quarterly* 43, 87–96.

Goodrich, R. (2013) "Location-based services: definition & examples," *Business News Daily*, 30 October. Available from www.businessnewsdaily.com/5386-location-based-services.html (2 October 2016).

Grier, D.A. & Campbell, M. (2000) "A social history of Bitnet and Listserv, 1985–1991," *Annals of the History of Computing* 22, 32–41.

Hilton Worldwide (2016) "Responding to popular demand, Hilton taps Google Maps to help HHonors members see more when choosing their room," *Hilton Worldwide: News*, 11 May. Available from http://news.hiltonworldwide.com/index.cfm/news/responding-to-popular-demand-hilton-taps-google-maps-to-help-hhonors-members-see-more-when-choosing-their-room (2 October 2016).

Hollis, N. (2005) "Ten years of learning on how online advertising builds brands," *Journal of Advertising Research* 45, 255–268.

Huang, L., Chen, K.H. & Wu, Y.W. (2009) "What kind of marketing distribution mix can maximize the wholesaler travel agencies' perspective?," *Tourism Management* 30, 733–739.

Illum, S.F., Ivanov, S.H. & Liang, Y. (2010) "Using virtual communities in tourism research," *Tourism Management* 31, 335–340.

Kim, J. & McMillan, S.J. (2008) "Evaluation of Internet advertising research: A bibliometric analysis of citations from key sources," *Journal of Advertising* 37, 99–112.

Klaus, P.G. (1985) "Quality epiphenomenon: The conceptual understanding of quality in face-to-face service encounters," in C. Surprenant & M. Solomon, (eds), *The service encounter: Managing employee/customer interaction in service business*, pp. 17–33, Lexington, MA: Lexington Books.

Lam, S.K., Ahearne, M., Hu, Y. & Schillewaert, N. (2010) "Resistance to brand switching when a radically new brand is introduced: A social identity theory perspective," *Journal of Marketing* 74, 128–146.

Lee, S.C., Barker, S. & Kandampully, J. (2003) "Technology, service quality, and customer loyalty in hotels: Australian managerial perspectives," *Managing Service Quality: An International Journal* 13, 423–432.

Leek, S. & Christodoulides, G., (2009) "Next-generation mobile marketing: How young consumers react to Bluetooth-enabled advertising," *Journal of Advertising Research* 49, 44–53.

Madhavaram, S. & Appan, R. (2010) "The potential implications of web-based marketing communications for consumers' implicit and explicit brand attitudes: A call for research," *Psychology and Marketing* 27, 186–202.

McCoy, S., Everard, A. & Loiacono, E.T. (2009) "Online ads in familiar and unfamiliar sites: Effects on perceived website quality and intention to reuse," *Info Systems Journal* 19, 437–458.

Miller, R. (2010) "Online marketing," in J.M. Korman & H.J. Furnas (eds.), *The business of plastic surgery: Navigating a successful career*, pp. 149–168, Tuck Link, Singapore: World Scientific Publishing Co.

Miyazaki, A.D. (2008) "Online privacy and the disclosure of cookie use: Effects on consumer trust and anticipated patronage," *Journal of Public Policy & Marketing* 27, 19–33.

Morgan, N.A., Slotegraaf, R.J. & Vorhies, D.W. (2009) "Linking marketing capabilities with profit growth," *International Journal of Research in Marketing Research* 26, 284–293.

Mowery, D.C. & Simcoe, T. (2002) "Is the Internet a US invention? An economic and technological history of computer networking," *Research Policy* 31, 1369–1387.

Murphy J. & Gomes, L. (2003) "E-mail customer service by Australian educational institutions," *Australasian Marketing Journal* 11, 56–69.

Neuhofer, B., Buhalis, B. & Ladkin, A. (2012) "Conceptualising technology enhanced destination experiences," *Journal of Destination Marketing & Management* 1, 36–46.

Okazaki, S. (2009) "The tactical use of mobile marketing: How adolescents' social networking can best shape brand extensions," *Journal of Advertising Research* 49, 12–26.

O'Leary, C., Rao, S. & Perry, C. (2004) "Improving customer relationship management through database/Internet marketing: A theory-building action research project," *European Journal of Marketing* 38, 338–354.

Oliver, R.L. (1981) "Measurement and evaluation of satisfaction processes in retail settings," *Journal of Retailing* 57, 25–48.

Olsen, S.O. (2002) "Comparative evaluation and the relationship between quality, satisfaction, and repurchase loyalty," *Journal of the Academy of Marketing Science* 30, 240–249.

Palmer, A. & Koenig-Lewis, N. (2009) "An experiential, social network-based approach to direct marketing," *Direct Marketing: An International Journal* 3(3), 162–176.

Parasuraman, A., Zeithaml, V.A. & Berry, L. (1988) "SERVQUAL: A multiple-item scale for measuring consumer perceptions of service quality," *Journal of Retailing* 64, 12–40.

Pels, J., Coviello, N.E. & Brodie, R.J. (2000) "Integrating transactional and relational marketing exchange: A pluralistic perspective," *Journal of Marketing Theory and Practice* 8, 11–20.

Perez, S. (2014) "iTunes app store now has 1.2 million apps, has seen 75 billion downloads to date," *TechCrunch.com*, 2 June. Available from https://techcrunch.com/2014/06/02/itunes-app-store-now-has-1-2-million-apps-has-seen-75-billion-downloads-to-date/ (29 July 2016).

Pew. (2012) "Search engine use 2012," *Pew Internet & American Life Project: A Project of the PewResearchCenter*, 9 March. Available from http://pweinernet.org/Reports/2012/Search-Engine-Use-2012.aspx (29 June 2016).

Phelps, J.E., Lewis, R., Mobilio, L., Perry, D. & Raman, N. (2004) "Viral marketing or electronic word-of-mouth advertising: Examining consumer responses and motivations to pass along email," *Journal of Advertising Research* 44, 333–348.

Pizam, A. & Ellis, T. (1999) "Customer satisfaction and its measurement in hospitality enterprises," *International Journal of Contemporary Hospitality Management* 11, 326–339.

Prahalad, C.K. & Ramaswamy, V. (2004) "Co-creation experiences: The next practice in value creation," *Journal of Interactive Marketing* 18, 5–14.

Schoenbachler, D.D. & Gordon, G.L. (2002) "Trust and customer willingness to provide information in database-driven relationship marketing," *Journal of Interactive Marketing* 16, 2–16.

Shaltoni, A.M. & West, D.C. (2010) "The measurement of e-marketing orientation (EMO) in business-to-business markets," *Industrial Marketing Management* 39, 1097–1102.

Smith, D. (2014) "Apple's app store breaks records, but Google Play is catching up," *Readwrite.com*, 8 January. Available from http://readwrite.com/2014/01/08/app-store-sales-google-play-android/ (22 July 2016)

Ström, R., Vendel, M, & Bredican, J. (2014) "Mobile marketing: A literature review on its value for consumers and retailers," *Journal of Retailing and Consumer Sciences* 21, 1001–1012.

Tadena, N. (2015) "Digital ad spending in U.S. to surpass television spending in 2016," *The Wall Street Journal*, 15 October. Available from www.wsj.com/articles/digital-ad-spending-in-u-s-to-surpass-television-spending-in-2016-1444937398 (9 September 2016).

Taylor, D.G. & Strutton, D. (2010) "Has e-marketing come of age? Modeling historical influence on post-adoption era Internet consumer behaviors," *Journal of Business Research* 63, 950–956.

Thomas, P. (2015) "Google's search engine market fell to 64%," *Yahoo Finance*, 29 December. Available from http://finance.yahoo.com/news/google-search-engine-market-share-170640710.html (25 August 2016)

Titz, K. (2008) "Experiential consumption: Affect – emotions – hedonism" in A. Pizam & H. Oh (eds.), *Handbook of hospitality marketing management*, pp. 324–352. Oxford, UK: Butterworth-Heinemann.

U.S. Census Bureau (2016a) "State & county quickfacts," *U.S. Census Bureau*. Available from www.census.gov/quickfacts/ (13 August 2016).

U.S. Census Bureau. (2016b) "U.S. and World Population Clock," *U.S. Census Bureau*. Available from www.census.gov/popclock/ (18 August 2016).

VanBoskirk, S. (2007) "US interactive marketing forecast, 2007 to 2012," *Interactive Marketing Professionals*. Available from http://impaqt.com/downloads/WP_mediaMix_03-08.pdf (30 April 2016).

Vavra, T.G. (1997) *Improving your measurement of customer satisfaction: A guide to creating, conducting, analyzing, and reporting customer satisfaction measurement programs*, Milwaukee, WI: ASQC Quality Press.

Verma, V., Sharma, D. & Sheth, J. (2016) "Does relationship marketing matter in online retailing? A meta-analytic approach," *Journal of the Academy of Marketing Science* 44, 206–217.

Walls, A.R. (2012) "A cross-examination of hotel consumer experience and relative effects on consumer values," *International Journal Hospitality Management* 32, 179–192.

Walls, A.R., Okumus, F., Wang, Y. & Kwun, D. (2010) "An epistemological view of consumer experiences," *International Journal Hospitality Management* 30, 10–21.

Wang, R.J.H., Malthouse, E.C. & Krishnamurthi, L. (2015) "On the go: How mobile shopping affects customer purchase behavior," *Journal of Retailing* 91, 217–234.

Weinberg, B.D. & Berger, P.D. (2011) Connected customer lifetime value: The impact of social media," *Journal of Direct, Data and Digital Marketing Practice* 12, 328–344.

Wright, S. & Cawston, J.A. (2012) "The shifting sands of university funding: A values-driven approach to formulating employer liaison direct marketing activity," *International Journal of Marketing Principles and Practices* 2, 6–19.

Wright, E., Khanfar, N.M., Harrington, C. & Kizer, L.E. (2010) "The lasting effects of social media trends on advertising," *Journal of Business and Economics Research* 8, 73–80.

Yani-de-Soriano, M. & Slater, S. (2009) "Revisiting Drucker's theory: Has consumerism led to the overuse of marketing?," *Journal of Management History* 15, 452–466.

Yoo, B., Donthu, N. & Lee, S. (2000) "An examination of selected marketing mix elements and brand equity," *Journal of the Academy of Marketing Science* 28, 195–211.

Zeithaml, V.A. (1988) "Consumer perceptions of price, quality, and value: A means-end model and synthesis of evidence," *The Journal of Marketing* 52, 2–22.

Zwick, D. & Dholakia, N. (2004), "Whose identity is it anyway? Consumer representation in the age of database marketing," *Journal of Macromarketing* 24, 31–43.

37

Integrated marketing communications in the hospitality and tourism industry

Chuhan (Renee) Wang and Ercan Sirakaya-Turk

Opening vignette – McDonald's Integrated Marketing Communications (IMC) campaign in China

The first McDonald's restaurant in China opened in Shenzhen in 1990. Today, with over 2,000 restaurants across more than 80 cities in mainland China, McDonald's plays a critical role in the Chinese fast food industry (Horwitz, 2016). Such a rapid expansion within a relatively short period brought several challenges that McDonald's had to deal with. For example, McDonald's traditionally targeted families with children when it first stepped into the Chinese fast food industry. But the demographics of McDonald's potential customers in China had changed – people tend to marry at an older age and some couples prefer to have no children. Chinese customers also had concerns about McDonald's food safety and associated health issues, especially after the World Health Organization (WHO) announced that fried food causes cancer. In 2002, McDonald's stock price reached the lowest point and the company suffered huge economic loss due to the strategic failure in China (Zhang, 2002). After a careful analysis of the weaknesses and strengths of McDonald's in the Chinese market, the new CEO, Larry Light, designed a set of new IMCHT strategies that allowed the rebranding of McDonald's in China (Light, 2015).

Since 2003, McDonald's started a localization strategy by integrating local Chinese flavors into its menu. Popular Chinese dishes such as fried rice, meat porridge, and curry noodles were added but cooked in the McDonald's way, which was welcomed by the Chinese. McDonald's started to target younger people by emphasizing "cool," "freestyle," and "fashion" concepts in its in-store flyer design. TV commercials became an instant hit when McDonald's hired Ming Yao, a popular Chinese NBA basketball player among young people, as the spokesperson of McDonald's. This series of commercials deliver a healthy, active, and modern restaurant image to customers. As most Chinese, especially young people, use public transportation, McDonald's put a lot of ads on buses, subways, and taxis to reach its target audience effectively and broadly. The majority of the ads contain the latest discounts and promotions.

In addition, McDonald's distributes coupons in print media such as local newspapers and magazines. Meanwhile, McDonald's collaborates with a Chinese mobile carrier called M-Zone to promote an "unlimited meal and data combo" to appeal to the youth; the ads posted on M-Zone's company website receive a great number of reviews. In the digital age, McDonald's utilizes social media as an effective communication strategy, promoting its brand on the most widely used Chinese social media sites such as Weibo and WeChat. McDonald's IMC strategies seem to be very successful in China, as the sales and stock price have both increased after delivering the brand message via multiple media outlets toward its target audience.

Consider the following questions:

1. What does Integrated Marketing Communications in Hospitality and Tourism (IMCHT) mean? How does it work in the hospitality and tourism industry?
2. What specific IMCHT plans did McDonald's use?
3. Can you apply McDonald's IMC strategy in China to other countries such as the U.S.?

An overview of IMCHT

If a brand fails to occupy a spot in consumers' minds, the whole business will fail in the market. An effective way to deliver the value of a brand to prospective consumers is via IMC. Since the early 1990s, IMC has experienced an evolution in its conceptualization and application in many different disciplines, including tourism and hospitality. With the development of information and communication technology (ICT), IMC has begun to show its efficacy and superiority in effectively delivering important messages from hospitality firms to their existing and future customers.

Conceptualization of IMCHT

Since the time IMC first started appearing in professional and scientific journals in the early 1990s (Holm, 2006), for a long time researchers have been debating the scope of IMC and what it really means in the digital age (see Table 37.1 for definitions). The main idea of IMC is to link all business-related communication channels together and deliver "one integrated voice" to the customers (Porcu, del Barrio-García, & Kitchen, 2012). We liken this to a symphony that consists of a well-orchestrated piece performed by a variety of musicians to create a whole integrated piece, which sounds better than its individual parts. The competition in the hospitality industry has become fierce; more and more customers are seeking customized products and services, so it is important for hoteliers to optimize their limited resources and opportunities to win new customers and keep the old ones. IMCHT refers to a strategic plan that allows the coordination of all possible communication mediums in a concerted and integrated marketing campaign, in order to: a) establish a differentiated image of the firm, b) demonstrate the efficacy and competitive advantages of the products and services, and c) deliver the core values of the brand to its customers.

The basic premise of IMCHT is to provide a consistent message to enhance the firm's brand equity. In the hotel industry, large hotel chains and luxury hotels perform better when utilizing an effective IMC strategy as opposed to small to mid-scale and local hotels. For example, Radisson Hotels makes the best use of the communication mix, including advertising, personal selling, public relations, and direct marketing to promote its brand through a clear, consistent, and compelling message.

The IMCHT toolbox

There are different forms of IMCHT, which are classified as different communication tools under the traditional marketing 4Ps (product, price, place, and promotion) (McCarthy, 1964). Generally, the four major aspects of IMCHT are advertising, public relations, sales promotion, and personal selling (Blythe, 2000). For each aspect there is a variety of tools that help marketers

Table 37.1 Definitions of IMC

Author/Year	Definition
American Association of Advertising Agencies (1989)	A concept of marketing communications planning that recognizes the added value of a comprehensive plan that evaluates the strategic roles of a variety of communication disciplines – general advertising, direct response, sales promotion, and public relations – and combines these disciplines to provide clarity, consistency, and maximum communication impact.
Schultz (1992)	IMC is the process of managing all sources of information about a product/service to which a customer or prospect is exposed which behaviorally moves the consumer toward a sale and maintains customer loyalty.
Duncan & Everett (1993)	The strategic coordination of all messages and media used by an organization to collectively influence its perceived brand value.
Nowak & Phelps (1994)	Integrated marketing communications are "one voice," "integrated," and "coordinated" marketing communications.
Kotler, Armstrong, Saunders, & Wong (1997)	The concept under which a company carefully integrates and coordinates its many communications channels to deliver a clear, consistent, and compelling message about the organization and its products.
Naik & Raman (2003)	IMC emphasizes "the benefits of harnessing synergy across multiple media to build brand equity of products and services."
Kliatchko (2005)	IMC is the concept and process of strategically managing audience-focused, channel-centered, and results-driven brand communication programs over time.
Shimp (2008)	IMC is a communications process that entails the planning, creation, integration, and implementation of diverse forms of marcom (advertisements, sales promotions, publicity releases, events, etc.) that are delivered over time to a brand's targeted customers and prospects.

reach their customers, such as print media, broadcast media, digital marketing, trade shows, and so on. It is important for hotel marketers to choose the appropriate IMCHT tools based on the type, size, management structure, resources, and capabilities of the hotel property. Furthermore, the timeline, cost, content, and estimated results should be considered when choosing the right tools (Šerić & Gil-Saura, 2011). Compared to using a single media platform to communicate, a multimedia synergistic approach has attracted marketers' attention in order to yield more positive communication results to potential customers. Table 37.2 lists the commonly used IMCHT tools.

Hilton, for instance, implements its online IMCHT strategy by integrating online ads, banner ads, map ads, email ads, and the like to unify the brand image and improve customers' perceptions of Hilton as a premium hotel brand. Another example is Moxy Hotels, Marriott's newest brand targeting Millennials, which has adopted a variety of communication tools to attract the youth, particularly focusing on the usage of YouTube, Vimeo, and Instagram. CitizenM Hotels is a leader in adopting a multimedia strategy to engage students – their main target market. Although new tools are becoming more prevalent with the development of technology, public relations (PR) professionals are still regarded as important to the marketers of big hotel chains. Integrating PR professionals is seen as the most reliable way to design, facilitate, and execute the IMCHT strategy. W Hotels fully utilize the power of PR to promote its consistent and compelling brand image to customers.

Table 37.2 The tools of IMCHT

1. Media Advertising	5. Trade- and Consumer-Oriented	6. Event Marketing &
- TV	Promotions	Sponsorships
- Radio	- Trade deals & buying allowances	- Sponsorship of
- Magazines	- Display & advertising allowances	sporting events
- Newspapers	- Trade shows	- Sponsorship of arts,
2. Direct Response & Interactive	- Cooperative advertising	fairs, & festivals
Advertising	- Samples	- Sponsorship
- Direct mail	- Coupons	of causes
- Telephone solicitation	- Premiums	7. Marketing-Oriented
- Online advertising	- Refunds/rebates	Public Relations &
3. Place Advertising	- Contests/sweepstakes	Publicity
- Billboards & bulletins	- Promotional games	Personal Selling
- Posters	- Bonus packs	
- Transit ads	- Price-off deals	
- Cinema ads		
4. Store Signage & Point-of-		
Purchase Advertising		
- External store signs		
- In-store shelf signs		
- Shopping cart ads		
- In-store radio and TV		

Advertising Tools. Brand equity can be defined as "a set of processes including acquiring, developing, nurturing, and leveraging an effectiveness–enhancing, high–equity brand or portfolio of brands" (Madhavaram, Badrinarayanan, & McDonald, 2005, p. 69). The integrated marketing communications are essential components of a business's brand equity strategy. One of the very important forms of IMCHT is advertising. Therefore, effective advertising could further help establish the high brand equity of a company.

Advertising is a "paid, mediated form of marketing communication from an identifiable source designed to persuade the receiver to take some action, now or [in the] future" (Shimp, 2008, p. 180). Typically, firms pay newspapers, magazines, TV, radio, mailing companies, and the Internet to disseminate the message of the values of a brand. Advertising functions in identifying brands, informing the public of the brand, persuading consumers to purchase, previewing new trends of products, services, and ideas, and reinforcing the values of the brand to attain loyal customers. When implementing an advertising strategy, it is important for marketers to first identify the goal and the audience of the advertisement, choose the most appropriate media based on the budget, and measure the effectiveness of advertisements. Generally, effective advertising serves as the most crucial actionable item for a feasible IMCHT strategy. Moriarty et al. (2014) proposed a facet model to evaluate ads in terms of perception, cognition, emotion, association, persuasion, and behavior (see Figure 37.1).

Starbucks used to have low levels of advertising due to the popularity of its brand. However, people claim that Starbucks has saturated the coffee market and there are emerging competitors who provide quality products and services at a lower price such as Costa Coffee. According to the product lifecycle theory, it is possible for the Starbucks brand to experience a decline in sales and popularity after staying too long in the maturity stage. Acting on this assumption, from 2007, the executives of Starbucks decided that one way to maintain Starbucks' competitiveness and market share would be to increase the level of advertising efforts. The first national television advertising campaign was launched in November 2007

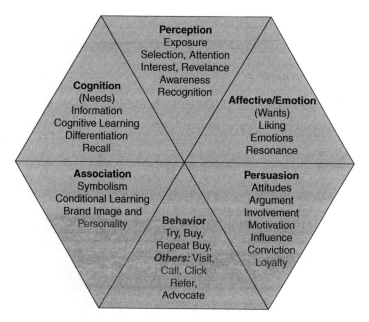

Figure 37.1 The facets model of effective advertising

and the move to national television commercials helped Starbucks to sustain store growth and reach out to a broader audience that had not previously experienced Starbucks. Since then, a series of 78 Starbucks TV commercials have appeared in consumers' daily lives.

In 2016, a list of the best hotel and lodging advertisements was provided by the Web Marketing Association's Internet Advertising Competition (IAC) (see Table 37.2). The judging criteria included the design, interactivity, use of technology, ease of use, copywriting, innovation, and content. Marriott won the Best Hotel and Lodging Email Message. At the same time, Marriott's Travel Brilliantly campaign was a big success in telling a story through rebranding a major hotel chain to attract digitally savvy generations. Double Tree by Hilton launched the Little Things Project campaign, which has been recognized as one of the best utilizations of social media. Kimpton Hotels ran a campaign called Yoga Mat in Every Room through viral videos that clearly communicate the message to customers. The form of advertising is abundant and flexible, and the ultimate goal is to effectively communicate the values of the brand to prospective customers, particularly for the hospitality industry, in which customer-oriented services dominate.

Media tools. The execution of effective IMCHT is completed through media tools. The primary types of media used in IMC include print media, broadcast media, and Internet media. With the development of Web 2.0, an interactive platform where end-users provide content, and the popularity of mobile technology, social media and corresponding mobile apps have become "mega trends" in hospitality communications. Hotels choose to use a combination of different media tools to enhance the effectiveness of their communications, which is another important feature of IMCHT multimedia channel.

Print media. Print media is the most traditional media tool that includes newspapers, magazines, newsletters, journals, books, flyers, and other printed materials. Although more and more people are exposed to digital media, and the use of print media has declined over the past decades, a substantial portion of the U.S. population, especially baby-boomers, still consider newspapers and magazines to be part of their lives. Therefore, hotel marketers cannot neglect the influence of print media today.

Table 37.3 2016 Hotel and Lodging ad winners

Name	Award	Winner
Marriott – Marriott Rewards Atlantis Resort email	Best Hotel and Lodging Email Message	Yes Lifecycle Marketing
Be Our Guest: Email and Newsletters for Kimpton Hotels & Restaurants	Best Hotel and Lodging Email Message Campaign	BKV
The Modern Honolulu Friends With Benefits Guest Loyalty Program	Best Hotel and Lodging Integrated Ad Campaign	The Modern Honolulu and Miles
Grand Hotel Amrath Kurhaus The Hague iHotelier Web 3.0 Booking Engine	Best Hotel and Lodging Interactive Application	TravelClick/Grand Hotel Amrath Kurhaus The Hague
The Broadmoor	Best Hotel and Lodging Online Ad	Cendyn/ONE
'Selfie in the City' Multichannel Campaign	Best Hotel and Lodging Online Campaign	HeBS Digital
Bukovina	Best Hotel and Lodging Website	Profitroom

Broadcast media. Broadcast media transmits information in a speedy way to a larger audience group. The most commonly used broadcast media are television and radio. With the development of collaboration between the film industry and the hospitality and tourism industry, film has also been considered a means of broadcast media. Broadcast media involves audio or visual motion, which makes the advertisements more vivid but at the same time the cost is higher and there is less control over output.

Internet media. Gradually, the traditional media are being replaced by social media sites. Internet media delivers message through online sources such as web portals, newsgroups, podcasts, blogs, and news feeds on social media. Social media marketing has become a serious business. A healthy mix of media is always necessary, depending on the business's goals and audiences. Within the social media context, Forrester's Sean Corcoran (2009) gave a more detailed overview of owned media, paid media and earned media, as shown in Table 37.4.

There are several ways of better utilizing social media as a tool for IMCHT campaigns. First, it is important to know who the audiences are and to connect with them by tapping into their passion points. Triumph Hotels launched a campaign called "Countdown to Your New York City Dream" by establishing a price point and emotive message to appeal to their target groups. Second, it is necessary to engage with the consumers as much as possible. Although it seems obvious, it is surprising how few firms bother to actively engage with their customers on social media – especially those in the hospitality industry. Interactive technology with appropriate visual aids on Facebook, Twitter, Pinterest, Instagram, and all possible outlets is critical nowadays to hotel marketers. Third, content needs to be relevant, original, and with social components. Original content that focuses on what people care about and enables more people to get involved makes a big difference to IMCHT campaigns.

Implementation of IMCHT

IMC has unique features such as being audience-focused, channel-centered, and results-oriented (Kliatchko, 2005), making the planning and implementation of IMCHT different from regular

Table 37.4 Three types of media

Media Type	Definition	Examples	The role	Benefits	Challenges
Owned Media	Channel and brand controls	Website Mobile site Blog Twitter	Build longer-term relationships with existing and potential customers and earn media	Control Cost efficiency Longevity Versatility Niche audiences	No guarantees Company communication not trusted Takes time to scale
Paid Media	Brand pays to leverage a channel	Display ads Paid search Sponsorships	Shift from foundation to a catalyst that feeds owned and creates earned media	In demand Immediacy Scale Control	Clutter Declining response rates Poor credibility
Earned Media	When customers become the channel	WOM Buzz "Viral"	Listen and respond –earned media is often the result of well-executed and well-coordinated owned and paid media	Most credible Key role in most sales Transparent and lives on	No control Can be negative Scale Hard to measure

marketing communication concepts. Although many hoteliers have embraced the IMC strategy, sometimes IMC can fail. An effective IMCHT strategy process usually consists of several comprehensive steps and it is the marketers' job to make sure that each step is successfully implemented. Based on Caemmerer (2009)'s study on the IMC implementation process, the following tactics and steps should be taken into consideration when designing and executing an IMC plan in the hospitality industry.

Tactics and steps in planning and implementing IMCHT

Consumer/Guest analysis. IMCHT differs from traditional marketing communications in that the consumers are at the heart of the strategy and the final performance relies on consumers' purchase behaviors. Therefore, it is necessary to establish an internal customer database that contains information about consumer values, lifestyles, psychological attitudes, and their historical buying behaviors if available. After obtaining the valuable information, it is important to analyze the consumer information and segment the markets based on it. According to Caemmerer (2009), there are mainly three kinds of consumers in the IMC process: those who are loyal to your brand, those who are loyal to other brands, and those in between. Understanding consumer preferences and their behavioral intentions is very important.

Communication objectives identification. This step ranges from generating awareness to countering the competition. After segmenting the market, there should be one or more particular markets to target, and the positioning of the brand determines what marketing communication opportunities are readily accessible. For example, an on-campus small–mid-scale hotel in the northeast of the United States distributed guest comment cards to over

10,000 customers over a one-year period. After a detailed analysis of all the primary data, the Marketing Director concluded that for most of the customers the available venue and cozy environment for alumni reunion and student activities are the driving factors of their consumption behaviors. Thus, the hotel started to emphasize its faculty-, student-, alumni-, and parent-oriented features in its advertising.

Content design. The content or theme of the whole strategy plays a critical role in the IMCHT process. The question of what information should be delivered to whom and when needs to be answered first before proceeding to the next stage. The content should be consistent with the measurable communication objectives and has implications for the agency and communication methods selection in the next step. Loews Hotels and Resorts recently launched a campaign that used real guests' Instagram photos rather than staged, professional shots in their marketing materials. They intended to convey an authentic, curated, and experiential message to their customers and the distinguished content design made the campaign a big success.

Communication media selection. In general, there are various marketing communications mix elements available to marketers, such as advertising, public relations, personnel selling, and sales promotion (Caemmerer, 2009, p 528; Pickton & Broderick, 2005), as discussed in the previous section. The criteria used to select communication methods and how to evaluate the appropriateness of the methods selected are very important to marketers. The communication mix serves as the basis for media selection. With that being said, the nature of the product, the geographic scope of the market, various price offerings, the funds available for promotion, and the product lifecycle stage should all be taken into consideration. What needs to be noted is that not only advertising, direct marketing, sales and promotion, and public relations are important to use as reliable and effective communication tactics; packaging, product exhibitions, and trade shows, as well as in-store discounts are also useful methods. The advantages and disadvantages of different media tools are summarized in Table 37.5. Hotels need to have a thorough review of these during this stage to make sure that the IMCHT campaign works as expected. Due to the prevalence

Table 37.5 A comparison of various media types

Medium	Advantages	Disadvantages
Print Newspaper	Flexibility; timeliness; good local market coverage; broad acceptability; believability	Short life; poor production quality
Print Magazine	High geographic and demographic selectivity; credibility and prestige; quality production; long life; good pass-along	High cost; no guarantee of position
TV	Good mass-market coverage; low cost per exposure; combines sight, sound, and motion; appealing to the senses	High absolute cost; high clutter; less audience selectivity
Radio	Good local acceptance; high geographic and demographic selectivity; low cost	Audio only; low attention; fragmented audiences
Outdoor	Flexibility; high repeat exposure; low cost; low message competition; good positional selectivity	Little audience selectivity; creative limitations
Online	High selectivity; low cost; immediacy; interactive capabilities	Small, demographically skewered audience; low impact; audience controls exposure

of social media, it is also important to identify which social media platforms fit the businesses' goals better.

Campaign evaluation and future plans. After the IMCHT plan is launched, the next step is to assess the effectiveness and efficiency of the communication effort. The most straightforward method to evaluate the plan is to examine direct sales. Another more commonly used and easier-to-conduct method is monitoring key performance indicators and metrics. For example, Facebook is collaborating with a data-tracking company called "Facebook Insight" to measure the effectiveness of IMCHT campaigns launched on Facebook. Research studies can also provide reliable and accurate results that could help to measure the effectiveness of the IMC plan. Based on the evaluation, marketers can determine whether a follow-up campaign is needed to maintain that specific spot in customers' minds and future plans should be proposed at this point. Realizing the benefits of the success from the online campaign in 2013 called "Go Fresh," the top management team of Hilton headquarters encouraged Hilton Sandestin Resort to launch another campaign called "Integrated Ad Campaign" in the same year. This is a good way to remind customers of the brand and to reinforce the successful image of the hotel brand.

Benefits and challenges of IMCHT

The application of IMCHT has both advantages and disadvantages (Gylling & Lindberg-Repo, 2006; Holm, 2006; Low & Mohr, 1999; McGoon, 1998; McGrath, 2005; Schultz & Kitchen, 2004). Based on the findings of previous studies, the advantages or benefits of hoteliers adopting an IMCHT strategy can be summarized as follows:

Brand reinforcement. At the brand performance level, IMCHT provides clarity and consistency to brand messages to create loyal customers. The core values of the hotel brand Marriott are emphasized through various media forms such as viral videos and magazines, and will take the "share of minds" of its customers.

Marketing campaign effectiveness. IMCHT is seen as the superior way to guarantee the success of a creative marketing campaign. The media synergy and communication mix make the marketing campaign innovative and ensure that it gets more exposure than would be possible with traditional marketing strategies. Media leaders launched a successful month-long campaign for the Palms Hotel to track their social media activities from every perspective.

Enhanced customer trust. Integrating the messages and keeping them consistent to make sure that customers receive "one voice" can help reduce customers' skeptical attitudes. The soup company Campbell's new portfolio advertising campaign addresses the fact that "We make real food for real people," by showing a collection of moments inspired by the lives of modern American families. Customers are more convinced when seeing the "real moments" and a trustworthy relationship has been built via this campaign.

Increased efficiency and competitive advantages. IMCHT helps to streamline the process of marketing campaigns or plans by providing consistent messages with less time and resources needed. The ability to reach a wider range of diversified audiences improves the competitive advantages from various aspects. For example, Disney used the same staff to manage different media channels and reduced the number of meetings in their advertising campaigns.

Reduced cost and increased ROI. At the hotel operation level, crafting a consistent message across all channels and eliminating the need for duplication reduce the average marketing costs to a large extent. A clearly defined IMCHT media plan provides a cost-effective combination of media to attain the company's media objectives. Effective IMCHT plans can help hoteliers achieve higher sales, sales growth, profitability, return on investment (ROI), and return on brand investment (ROBI) (Duncan & Mulhern, 2004).

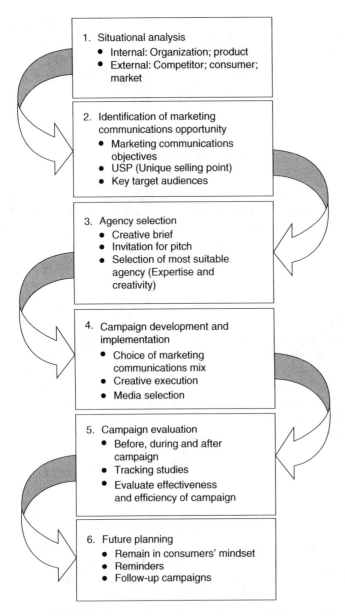

Figure 37.2   Stages in the planning and implementation of IMC

On the other hand, however, it is not always easy to plan and implement the IMCHT strategy. Many businesses comprehend the concept but fail in practice due to the barriers that come along with IMC (Duncan & Everett, 1993; Eagle & Kitchen, 2000; Hartley & Pickton, 1999; Gonring, 1994; Ratnatunga & Ewing, 2005; Swain, 2004). The primary concerns or challenges of planning and implementing an IMCHT strategy should be carefully considered by marketers.

Management support and resources. The organizational structure, culture, behavior, and communication determine how much support is given to a new IMCHT plan. It would be difficult to implement the IMCHT strategy if there is a lack of support from the management level or a lack of needed resources such as money, facilities, and human capital. In addition, managers' experience positively associates with IMCHT implementation.

Knowledge and skills. New skills and knowledge are needed in new marketing communication areas (Duncan & Everett, 1993). Some hotels hire part-time students or assign insufficient staff to be in charge of the entire IMCHT plan, which results in the low quality and reliability of the IMCHT strategy overall. The perceived lack of knowledge and skills on both the customer side and the company side has negatively influenced the effectiveness of IMCHT plans.

Multimedia creativity. Different people perceive creativity in different ways and sometimes there is a cognitive mismatch. How hoteliers make the marketing campaign more creative has been a critical issue to address in order to outperform competitors. Paid, earned, and owned campaign elements are needed in order to enhance the effectiveness of the IMCHT strategy. Creativity should start from the design, content, and methods to distinguish marketing efforts from those of competitors.

Technology and infrastructure. The availability and function of information technology and infrastructure can either enhance or prohibit the flow of IMC-relevant information, depending on the ability to track and analyze data (Gould, Lerman, & Grein, 1999). Technology is fundamental to the entire IMCHT implementation, indicating that hardware, software, and relevant knowledge are essential components in an IMCHT strategy. However, many small–mid-scale hotels lack appropriate technology or infrastructure to execute the IMCHT strategy, making it difficult to make the best use of the benefits of IMCHT.

IMCHT and technology in luxury hotels

The advancement of information and communication technology (ICT) is considered as one of the most significant driving forces of IMCHT (Caywood, 1997). Luxury hotels perform better at using IMCHT strategy in their marketing campaigns. Marriott has produced a variety of short films to appeal to their younger customers. These short films, such as the "Two Bellmen" and "French Kiss," were shot in Los Angeles and Paris respectively, getting over ten million views in total. Fairmont's ongoing Fairmont Moments Campaign emphasized guest experiences and unique Fairmont moments and the brand has even developed a separate mobile site to reach a wider range of audiences. Hotel Pennsylvania found that international travelers often take selfies near iconic landmarks as a badge of honor, so they developed a strategy to capitalize on this cultural phenomenon.

Mobile technology has become increasingly popular nowadays, so luxury hotels have started to invest money in mobile marketing. Consumers now spend over 85 percent of their time on smartphones using native applications (Perez, 2015). Hilton's mobile-first 360-Degree Video brings prospective guests to the chain's Barbados property. Luxury hotels and resorts in Macau create accounts on WeChat, the Chinese mobile chatting software, and promote real-time hotel information and events to their subscribers with an interactive page design. Users can send messages to the hotel's WeChat public account and get an immediate reply that is relevant to their questions or inquiries. The interactive mobile marketing strategy adopted by luxury hotels and resorts has been proved to be successful in China.

Summary

This chapter has introduced various definitions of IMC and extended the definition to the hospitality industry. IMCHT is defined as the strategic plan that is used to coordinate all possible communication channels in a marketing campaign to establish a distinguished image of the hotel, to demonstrate the competitive advantages of the products and services, and to deliver the core values of the brand to customers. The primary tools of IMCHT include advertising, public relations, sales promotion, and personal selling. Advertising and media strategies are more widely used in the hospitality industry, with social media the most popular tool for communication.

This chapter then streamlined the five major steps in planning and implementing IMCHT strategy: consumer analysis, communication objectives identification, content design, communication media selection, and campaign evaluation and future plans. The associated benefits of IMCHT include brand reinforcement, marketing campaign effectiveness, enhanced customer trust, increased efficiency and competitive advantages, and reduced cost and increased ROI. The challenges or concerns facing IMCHT strategy adopters are management support and resources, knowledge and skills, multimedia creativity, and technology and infrastructure. Lastly, the collaboration of technology, especially mobile technology, and IMCHT, has become a trend for hoteliers. Furthermore, the luxury hotel chains perform better in utilizing effective IMCHT strategy.

Discussion questions

1. What is the definition of IMCHT? What are the commonly used IMCHT tools? If you were a marketing director of a big hotel chain, what tools would you use to communicate your brand to your customers, and why?
2. Imagine you are working for a luxury beach resort to develop a marketing campaign for the summer vacation. How would you apply the IMCHT strategy in your campaign? What would the process be like?
3. How do you evaluate the benefits and challenges of the implementation of IMCHT strategy? What will be the future trend of IMCHT and relevant technology in the hospitality field?

Case study 1: Coca-Cola's IMC strategy

A statement from the executives of Coca-Cola is that "we are selling water, while customers are buying the advertisement." Imagine Coca-Cola has no effective marketing efforts: would there still be many people purchasing the product, of which 99.61 percent of it is carbonic acid, sugar, and water?

Coca-Cola's very first marketing communications strategy was advertising. Let's trace back to the year 1886, when the first Coca-Cola print advertisement appeared, which mainly focused on the medical function of Coca-Cola – it repels thirst away. Later in 1904, in order to position itself as a good beverage choice rather than a medical drink, Coca-Cola changed its print advertisement statement to "delicious and refreshing." In 1926, Coca-Cola first adopted radio as another form of advertising and in 1950 the first TV commercial was launched. Later in 1953, Coca-Cola worked with the advertising agency D'Arcy to shoot its first motion video. From year 1956, Coca-Cola started to target younger generations and has invited sports and entertainment celebrities to represent its brand. From 1978, Coca-Cola adopted the differentiation strategy in advertising and has embraced various types of digital media as advertising channels since the 2000s.

In addition to the traditional advertising methods, Coca-Cola also adopted a direct marketing strategy by launching various IMC campaigns in different fields. For example, Coca-Cola collaborated with video game companies and chat software companies to conduct online marketing. Coca-Cola has been serving as the sponsor for the Olympics Games since 1928 and ten times the sponsor fee amount is used by Coca-Cola to develop its marketing campaigns. In the third season of 1996 (September to November), the sales of Coca-Cola increased by 21 percent, while its biggest competitor, Pepsi, dropped 77 percent in sales. Not only partnering with the Olympics, Coca-Cola also sponsors worldwide events such as the FIFA World Cup, NBA, F1, and so on. Coca-Cola designs interactive websites and social networks to attract more young consumers and uses public relations in its communication strategy through various events. Coca-Cola works with Apple to provide downloadable codes to consumers with which they can get free songs from iTunes. Inviting singers to get involved in the advertisement and collaborating with Disney are all examples of Coca-Cola's IMC strategies. In addition, Coca-Cola makes a great contribution to a charity foundation in China, particularly donating to provide children and teenagers with financial support for school.

*Note: much of the information presented in this case study is adopted from www.doczj.com/doc/cc630c7601f69e3143329469-6.html

Questions

1. What methods does Coca-Cola use to implement its IMC strategy?
2. Why is Coca-Cola successful in implementing its IMC strategy?
3. How do you evaluate Coca-Cola's IMC strategy? What suggestions do you have to make Coca-Cola's IMC strategy even better?

Case study 2: HAVAS's PR accomplishments for Rhode Island Commerce Corporation

The PR company HAVAS has been committed to advertising Rhode Island by establishing a positive image in consumers' minds. During the nine months from October 2015 to July 2016, HAVAS delivered 13 PR campaigns and hosted 16 familiarization tours that engaged more than 50 press and more than 90 local businesses—securing more than 200 earned media placements and generating almost 2,600 social media mentions. HAVAS placed 15 op-eds or bylined cover letters. It developed four paid media plans and executed two of them, created 14 business attractions banners and billboard ads and developed three video programs and produced one of them. Figure 37.3 shows that from October 1 through July 31, these efforts resulted in 207 featured article mentions and 2,582 social media mentions, which generated more than 466 million impressions and represents an advertising equivalency value of $4.3 million.

A monthly snapshot of the last month, July 2016, shows that Havas PR's earned media, social media and native advertising efforts generated $1.189 million in advertising value equivalency

		Tourism	Business Attraction	Brand/MIY	Total
Traditional Media	Featured Mentions	86	20	101	207
	Impressions	241,243,740	50,448,662	98,727,562	390,419,964
	AVE	$2,231,504	$466,650	$913,229	$3,611,384
Social Media	Social Posts or Hashtag Mentions*	798	1,305	479	2,582
	Impressions	15,475,107	10,200,000	3,300,000	28,975,107
	AVE	$143,144	$88,800	$30,525	$262,469
Native Advertising	Impressions	23,544,471	23,127,256	N/A	46,671,727
	AVE	$217,786	$213,927	N/A	$431,713
Total	Impressions	280,263,318	83,775,918	102,027,562	466,066,798
	AVE	$2,592,434	$769,377	$943,754	$4,305,565

*Reconciled to address some duplicate counts

Figure 37.3   Overall results: October 2015 to July 2016

(AVE) and 129.03 million impressions, including 18 agency-placed feature articles and blogs. Specific activities in the tourism sector include the following:

- Secured 16 editorial placements, generating 97.3 million impressions and an AVE of $1.005 million in outlets.
- Worked with Backpacker, USA Today, People.com, Thrillist, Travel + Leisure, Bustle, AdWeek and Essence.
- Hosted Thrillist travel writer Matt Meltzer for in-state tour in partnership with Providence and Newport.
- Amplified tourism editorial placements through Outbrain native advertising and VisitRhodeIsland's social media channels.
- Assisted Commerce with the competitive review of photographers for building a digital image library and composite images for the Big E.

*Note: much of the information presented in this case study is adopted from HAVAS PR (2016).

Questions

1. What are the advantages of using a PR company such as HAVAS to promote a tourism destination?
2. What are the PR campaigns conducted by HAVAS to successfully advertise Rhode Island?
3. What is the role of PR in remedying a tourism destination's negative image? How do PR companies respond to criticism of their clients?

References

American Association of Advertising Agencies (1989). Integrated marketing communications. Retrieved from http://www.aaaa.org/.

Blythe, J. (2000). *Marketing Communications* (Vol. 5, No. 4, pp. 235–235). Upper Saddle River, NJ: Financial Times/Prentice Hall.

Caemmerer, B. (2009). The planning and implementation of integrated marketing communications, *Marketing Intelligence & Planning*, 27 (4), 524–538.

Caywood, C. L. (1997). *The Handbook of Strategic Public Relations and Integrated Communications*. New York: McGraw Hill Professional.

Duncan, T. & Everett, S. (1993). Client perceptions of integrated marketing communications. *Journal of Advertising Research*, 33 (3), 30–39.

Duncan, T. R. & Mulhern, F. (2004). *IMC: A White Paper on the Status, Scope and Future of IMC*, Northwestern University and University of Denver.

Eagle, L. & Kitchen, P. J. (2000). IMC, brand communications, and corporate cultures: Client/advertising agency co-ordination and cohesion. *European Journal of Marketing*, 34 (5/6), 667–686.

Forrester Research, Inc. (2009). *Defining Earned, Owned and Paid Media* [Table]. Retrieved from http://blogs.forrester.com/interactive_marketing/2009/12/defining-earned-owned-and-paid-media.html, 11 October 2016.

Gould, S. J., Lerman, D. B., & Grein, A. F. (1999). Agency perceptions and practices on Global IMC. *Journal of Advertising Research*, 39 (1), 7–20.

Gonring, M. P. (1994). Putting integrated marketing communications to work today. *Public Relations Quarterly*, 39 (3), 45–48.

Gylling, C. & Lindberg-Repo, K. (2006). Investigating the links between a corporate brand and a customer brand. *Brand Management*, 13 (4/5), 257–267.

Hartley, B. and Pickton, D. (1999). Integrated marketing communications requires a new way of thinking. *Journal of Marketing Communications*, 5 (2), 97–106.

HAVAS PR. (2016). *HAVAS PR Accomplishments for Rhode Island Commerce Corporation* [Graph].

Holm, O. (2006). Integrated marketing communication: From tactics to strategy. *Corporate Communications: An International Journal*, 11 (1), 23–33.

Horwitz, J. (2016). McDonald's plans to revive its brand in China by getting out of the restaurant business. Retrieved from http://qz.com/713411/mcdonalds-plans-to-revive-its-brand-in-china-by-getting-out-of-the-restaurant-business/.

Internet Advertising Competition (2016). *Best Hotel and Lodging Ad, 2016* [Table]. Retrieved from www.iacaward.org/iac/winners_detail.asp?yr=all&award_level=best&category=Hotel%20and%20Lodging, 14 October 2016.

Kliatchko, J. (2005). Towards a new definition of integrated marketing communications (IMC). *International Journal of Advertising*, 24 (1), 7–34.

Kotler, P., Armstrong, G., Saunders, J., & Wong, V. (1997). *Principes van marketing: De Europese editie*. Schoonhoven, Netherlands: Prentice-Hall Europe.

Light, L. (2015). How to revive McDonald's. Retrieved from www.wsj.com/articles/larry-light-how-to-revive-mcdonalds-1423613708

Low, G. S. & Mohr, J. J. (1999). Setting advertising and promotion budgets in multi-brand companies. *Journal of Advertising Research*, 39 (1), 67–78.

McCarthy, J. E. (1964). *Basic Marketing: A Managerial Approach*. Homewood, IL: Irwin.

McGoon, C. (1998/1999). Cutting-edge companies use integrated marketing communication. *Communication World*, 16 (1), 15–19.

McGrath, J. M. (2005). A pilot study testing aspects of the integrated marketing communications concept. *Journal of Marketing Communications*, 11 (3), 1–20.

Madhavaram, S., Badrinarayanan, V., & McDonald, R. E. (2005). Integrated marketing communication (IMC) and brand identity as critical components of brand equity strategy: A conceptual framework and research propositions. *Journal of Advertising*, 34 (4), 69–80.

Moriarty, S., Mitchell, N. D., Wells, W. D., Crawford, R., Brennan, L., & Spence-Stone, R. (2014). *Advertising: Principles and Practice*. Melbourne: Pearson Australia.

Naik, P. A., & Raman, K. (2003). Understanding the impact of synergy in multimedia communications. *Journal of Marketing Research*, 40 (4), 375–388.

Nowak, G. & Phelps, J. (1994). Conceptualizing the integrated marketing communications' phenomenon: An examination of its impact on advertising practices and its implications for advertising research. *Journal of Current Issues and Research in Advertising*, 16 (1), 49–66.

Perez, S. (2015). Consumers spend 85% of time on smartphones in apps, but only 5 apps see heavy use. Retrieved from https://techcrunch.com/2015/06/22/consumers-spend-85-of-time-on-smartphones-in-apps-but-only-5-apps-see-heavy-use/

Pickton, D. & Broderick, A. (2005). *Integrated Marketing Communication*, 2nd ed. London: Prentice Hall Inc.

Porcu, L., del Barrio-García, S., & Kitchen, P. J. (2012). How Integrated Marketing Communications (IMC) works? A theoretical review and an analysis of its main drivers and effects/¿ Cómo funciona la Comunicación Integrada de Marketing (CIM)? Una revisión teórica y un análisis de sus antecedentes y efectos. *Comunicación y sociedad*, 25 (1), 313–348.

Ratnatunga, J. & Ewing, M. T. (2005). The brand capability value of integrated marketing communication (IMC). *Journal of Advertising*, 34 (4), 25–40.

Schultz, D. E. (1992). Integrated marketing communications. *Journal of Promotion Management*, 1 (1), 99–104.

Schultz, D. E. & Kitchen, P. J. (2004). Managing the changes in corporate branding and communication: Closing and re-opening the corporate umbrella. *Corporate Reputation Review*, 8 (4), 347–366.

Šerić, M., & Gil-Saura, I. (2011). Integrated marketing communications and information and communication technology in the hotel sector: An analysis of their use and development in Dalmatian first-class and luxury hotels. *Journal of Retail & Leisure Property*, 9 (5), 401–414.

Shimp, T. A. (2008). *Integrated Marketing Communication in Advertising and Promotion*, 8th ed. International edition. Mason, OH: South-Western College.

Swain, W.N. (2004). Perceptions of IMC after a decade of development: Who's at the wheel, and how can we measure success? *Journal of Advertising Research*, 44 (1), 46–65.

Zhang, X. (2002). How to make the best use of IMC? Retrieved from http://big.hi138.com/guanlixue/shichangyingxiao/200212/284266.asp#.WCtDD-YrLcs

Part VIII
Internet and technology

38

A critical review of the impact of technology and the internet on hospitality marketing

Blake H. Bai, Chloe S. Kim, Peter B. Kim and Simon Milne

Background

The advance of Information and Communication Technologies (ICTs) and the internet in the last two decades have brought significant changes to hospitality and tourism marketing innovation (Berezina et al., 2016). This has caused the decline of traditional intermediaries such as travel agencies (Hjalager, 2010). The internet has provided both customers and service providers with easy access to wide-ranging offers, in turn helping to save on costs for both parties. Today, consumers have become more dependent on the internet for information searching, planning and purchasing. For hospitality managers, the information-intensive nature of the industry, together with increasingly diversified customer needs, encourages them to embrace ICTs in business operation and marketing strategies. Integrating high-tech services into business operations will ultimately lead the industry to be defined within a new paradigm, presenting both new opportunities as well as new threats (Law et al., 2013).

The main purposes of hospitality and tourism organizations in their application of ICTs are to improve performance, increase customer satisfaction and gain a competitive advantage. Successful implementation of ICTs especially benefits the business in cost reduction, revenue maximization, operational efficiency, and service refinement. Over the past decade, ICTs have become an indispensable tool for hospitality and tourism operators in their promotion, distribution and customer communication (Ham et al., 2005). It has become a norm for hospitality organizations to apply internet-based ICTs in business operations, which are gradually replacing the traditional marketing tools and practices. As a result, internet marketing or e-marketing has become a major theme in research and practice, particularly since the year 2000 (Leung et al., 2015b).

Review of technology and internet research in hospitality marketing

The hospitality and tourism literature has reflected the development of the internet and technology, and new research fields related to ICTs emerged continuously during the 1980s. Researchers have thus felt the need to produce review studies of the use and impact of the internet and technology in the hospitality and tourism context (e.g., Buhalis & Law, 2008; Standing et al., 2014). This section of the chapter provides an overview of the existing internet and technology-related research in the hospitality and tourism literature. Key research areas will be identified based on an analysis of 15 review-type articles published in leading hospitality and tourism journals as listed by the *Social Science Citation Index* (SSCI) (Gursoy & Sandstrom, 2014).

The developing use of technology and the internet by the hospitality industry

The hospitality and tourism ICT publications reviewed generally reflect the development of technology. Based on the number of publications, research on internet and ICT marketing in the hospitality and tourism context has gone through three stages over the past two decades: from introduction, to growth, to maturity (Leung et al., 2015b).

Early reviews were more likely to focus on the overall technology implementation in business operations, marketing and customer service and/or technology acceptance in consumers' information searching, decision-making, and post-purchase behavior. For example, Law et al. (2013) identified six research areas for ICT adoption, including: computer hardware; computer software; networking (the most researched area in their review); information management; user interface; intelligent application; and miscellaneous. In the late 1990s, studies on the internet and networks, such as web advertising and data collection, exceeded those in ICT research areas and were mainly from a business perspective. Website evaluation appeared to be a key research area from the year 2000, owing to the fast development of hotel websites and the prosperity of online travel agencies (OTAs) influencing both business strategies and consumer behavior (e.g., Ip et al., 2011; Law et al., 2013; Park & Gretzel, 2007).

With the advent of Web 2.0 and smartphone platforms, new internet and technology research has emerged. Topics such as social media, e-WOM, digital experience, e-loyalty and mobile applications have been the focus, providing perspectives from both customers and suppliers. More recent review papers have emphasized specific technologies; for example, social media (Leung et al., 2013), eWOM (Cantallops & Salvi, 2014) and smartphone applications (Kim & Law, 2015). At the same time, we have witnessed an overall shift in research from a business to a customer perspective. The shift in focus is an indication that industry practitioners need to understand the emerging technology innovations in consumer markets and pay attention to customer relationship management via these new platforms and media.

There is a lack of general consensus on the categorization of research areas in the internet and technology-related literature in hospitality; categorizations have been mostly subject to researchers' own interpretations. Table 38.1 presents 15 review-type articles related to the internet and technology, published in leading hospitality and tourism journals. Most of these review papers attempt to reveal the progress of technology adoption in the industry from customers' as well as business operators' perspectives.

Key research areas

The internet has provided equal opportunities for small hospitality and tourism enterprises to compete in the market place, through online search engines. Therefore, it is critical for hospitality organizations to consider and manage the presentation of their service products on multiple online channels such as websites, smartphone apps and social media platforms (Xiang et al., 2008). The following section draws upon the previous internet and technology marketing

Table 38.1 Reviews of internet and technology in hospitality and tourism

No.	Author (year)	Review area
1	O'Connor & Murphy (2004)	IT research in hospitality
2	Park & Gretzel (2007)	Destination website evaluation
3	Buhalis & Law (2008)	eTourism research
4	Law, Leung & Buhalis (2009)	IT research in hospitality and tourism
5	Law, Qi & Buhalis (2010)	Website evaluation in tourism
6	Ip, Law & Lee (2011)	Website evaluation in hospitality and tourism
7	Ip, Leung & Law (2011)	ICT research in hospitality
8	Law, Leung, Au & Lee (2013)	IT research in hospitality
9	Leung, Law, Van Hoof & Buhalis (2013)	Social media in hospitality and tourism
10	Amaro & Duarte (2013)	Online purchase behaviour in tourism
11	Law, Buhalis & Cobanoglu (2014)	ICT research in hospitality and tourism
12	Standing, Tang-Taye & Boyer (2014)	Internet research in tourism
13	Cantallops & Salvi (2014)	eWOM in hotel industry
14	Leung, Xue & Bai (2015)	Internet marketing in hospitality and tourism
15	Kim & Law (2015)	Smartphone research in tourism

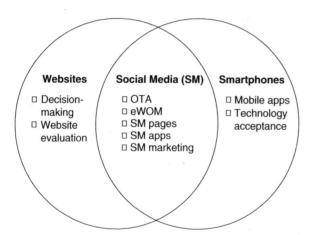

Figure 38.1   Key research areas of internet and technology marketing in hospitality and tourism

research to propose three critical areas of IT/ICT marketing. The latest trends and issues in these areas are also discussed.

Figure 38.1 identifies the three key areas that are critical to internet and technology marketing: websites, smartphones, and social media. Social media is presented as the intersection between websites and smartphones, as these information-sharing platforms rely on online channels such as websites and smartphone applications (mobile apps) to exist. Major topics underlying website research in hospitality have been customer decision-making and website evaluation. Within smartphone research, mobile apps and technology acceptance have been the most investigated topics (Morosan & DeFranco, 2016; Okumus et al., 2016). Online travel agencies (OTAs), social media platforms, electronic word of mouth (eWOM), and social media marketing are, in general, important topics within the realm of social media.

Blake H. Bai et al.

Hospitality websites

In the digital era, websites are among the most valuable promotion channels for information dissemination, and communication and transactions between consumers and suppliers, but are also valuable for networks within the hospitality and tourism industry. Both researchers and industry practitioners have advocated the importance of maintaining effective websites in customer relationship management and marketing, and are an important tool for product or experience development.

There are various kinds of hospitality websites, ranging from those used by hotels to restaurants, destination management organizations (DMOs), online travel agencies (OTAs), travel blogs, and so forth. A consistent and universal framework for evaluating the quality of hospitality websites is lacking in the literature. This reflects the fact that developing a unified and standard approach for measuring websites within all sectors of the industry is a challenging goal (Morrison et al., 2005). An evaluation model that is truly hospitality oriented, specific to the service sector and that targets market segments is encouraged for future website evaluation research.

The internet innovation, *Airbnb*, a website that allows consumers to become hosts for tourists who rent their own accommodation, has become a research focus in recent years. The novel business model of Airbnb embodies the rise of a sharing economy, featuring an informal peer-to-peer accommodation service (Fang et al., 2016; Zervas et al., 2016). Varma et al. (2016) suggested that Airbnb customers are significantly different from traditional hotel customers in adoption motivation. However, their interview with hospitality managers revealed that Airbnb has not yet become a competitor for the main players in the industry, even though it has intercepted business from small and medium-sized hotels. Future research related to the impacts of peer-to-peer business models on a destination's economy and dynamic stakeholders may be needed (Guttentag, 2015).

Social media

It is an understatement to say that the topic of social media has been widely discussed in recent years, which is also reflected within the field of hospitality research. The impact of social media has significantly changed travelers' decision-making patterns, tourism operations and management. For example, the emergence of social media has presented the hotel industry with a fundamentally different environment in which to conduct its marketing and distribution activities (Keenan & Shiri, 2009). Previous studies on social media have found that customers using social media platforms today are more knowledgeable, demanding, skeptical, and generally more in control than in previous times (Baird & Parasnis, 2011; Heinonen, 2011; O'Connor, 2008; Peters et al., 2013; Stewart & Pavlou, 2002). This shift has caused the internet to evolve from a business-to-customer to a customer-to-customer medium (Mangold & Faulds, 2009).

Social media has been adopted by travelers to search, organize, share, and annotate their travel stories and experiences through blogs, microblogs, online communities, media sharing sites, social bookmarking sites (e.g., *Delicious* and *Pinterest*), and social knowledge sharing sites (e.g., *Wikitravel*), to list a few. Such sharing activity produces user-generated content (UGC), which has been identified by scholars as providing a tool for promotion and marketing (Mangold & Faulds, 2009). According to Burmann (2010), academics had not fully examined the activity of UGC, introducing the term user-generated branding (UGB). Burmann's work defined user-generated content that was brand-related, as well as describing the strategic and operative management of UGB.

Social media has enabled hospitality firms to develop an interactive environment among their customers (Denizci Guillet et al., 2015). The strategic importance of social media in terms of tourism competitiveness has been made clear among studies, but research from a consumer perspective needs further examination to develop and clarify many issues. According to a *Skift* report (Oastes, 2015), Jeremy Jauncey, founder of *Beautiful Destinations*, the largest travel influencer on *Instagram* with over seven million followers (on four main accounts including *Beautiful Cuisines*), believes the opportunity still remains for travel brands to make better use of *Instagram*. Jauncey highlighted the fact that the travel industry has been the second slowest industry after financial services to adopt the medium. *Instagram* alone has over 80 million images shared between users in everyday life (second only to *Facebook*), whilst 353 million pieces of shared content on the networking service are travel-related (Oastes, 2015).

Although there have been several studies on the website effectiveness of businesses within the hospitality industry (Baloglu & Pekcan, 2006; Law & Cheung, 2005; Schmidt et al., 2008), scholars state there is still a gap to be filled in the hospitality literature on the topic of social media, as well as on strategies for manipulation and marketing effectiveness (Choi et al., 2016; Leung et al., 2013). Recent empirical studies have carried out comparisons between different social media platforms for hotel marketing, such as *Twitter* versus *Facebook* (Leung et al., 2015a). Researchers have found that information, convenience, and self-expression were the main antecedents of customer satisfaction in hotels' social media pages, rather than entertainment or social interaction factors. Future research focusing on providing a more valid and parsimonious model for measuring social media marketing effectiveness is needed.

Online travel agencies (OTAs)

Online travel agencies (OTAs), such as *TripAdvisor.com*, *Expedia.com*, and *Cheaptickets.com*, are tourism-related social media websites for travel booking and information sharing, featuring and offering dynamic pricing, transparent rates, special offers, and customer reviews for travelers all over the world (Leung et al., 2015b). Similarly, websites that serve as intermediaries and platforms for hotel booking and reviews (e.g., *Hotel.com*, *Agoda.com*, and *Trivago.com*) and restaurant booking and reviews (e.g., *Opentable.com*, *Yelp.com*, and *Urbanspoon.com*) are becoming increasingly popular among consumers. Although OTAs are a major cause of the disintermediation of traditional travel agencies, they play an unpretendingly important role as online distribution channels and the strategic business partners of hospitality organizations (Law et al., 2014).

OTAs can be divided into OTA websites or OTA mobile apps in terms of distribution channels. The two most frequently researched areas of OTAs are pricing strategy and online review management. Effective pricing strategy on OTAs contributes to an increase in direct transactions and the maintenance of customer relationships for hospitality operators. Managing user-generated-content or online reviews on these platforms is critical to the success of businesses, particularly in service recovery (Ip et al., 2011).

Electronic word-of-mouth (eWOM)

The engagement of social media has seen a shift in communication power to the side of consumers, and has further changed marketing strategies (Hjalager, 2010). Sharing experiences online has become an increasing phenomenon, owing to the prevalence of social media among consumers. Electronic word-of-mouth (eWOM) is defined as online interpersonal communication between consumers and brands regarding the use of their products or services – the digital form of word-of-mouth. eWOM is considered to be one of the most influential factors in the consumer purchase decision process and has become the most popular research topic in internet marketing (Cantallops & Salvi, 2014).

There are two main research foci under the topic of eWOM: eWOM generating factors and the impacts of eWOM. The first line of research refers to the reasons for sharing eWOM, which have been widely evaluated in the hospitality literature. Common online-review generating motivation includes service quality, failure and recovery, helping other tourists, and social identity; generally, however, customer satisfaction/dissatisfaction seems to be the most significant predictor of generating eWOM (Sun & Qu, 2011; Swanson & Hsu, 2009).

The second line of research focuses on the consequences of eWOM for business operations and consumer behavior. Online reviews are found to influence consumer attitudes and decision processes (e.g., booking intention, perceived trustworthiness, risk reduction, and loyalty) and, consequently, they impact on business performance, quality control, service recovery, online reputation, and other internet marketing strategies of hospitality organizations (Cantallops & Salvi, 2014).

Online reviews and other types of eWOM are particularly important for hospitality customers' decision-making because of the intangible nature of service products. Previous research has shown that dissatisfaction was more predictive of generating reviews than satisfaction, which means that dissatisfied customers are more likely to post a negative review online than satisfied customers are to post a positive review. Another challenge for hospitality marketers and academia lies in measuring and handling the masses of information embedded in eWOM.

In terms of the impact of online reviews, dimensions such as review valence (i.e., positive or negative), review time (i.e., early or recent), and review expertise (i.e., industry expert or customer) each have different effects on consumer attitudes and behavior. For instance, studies suggested that positive reviews had a stronger impact on customer behavior than negative reviews (Vermeulen & Seegers, 2009). Therefore, the effective management of eWOM is critical if hospitality companies are to employ it to gain competitive advantages through targeting new customers and maintaining current clients (Dickinger, 2010; Ye et al., 2009).

Smartphone and mobile applications

In the hospitality and tourism context, mobile commerce (m-commerce) has not only penetrated various stages of business but has also affected consumer behaviour (Morosan & DeFranco, 2016). Many major hotel organisations have launched their own mobile applications (for example, Starwood Hotels & Resorts SPG app) to help with advertising, sales promotion, customer data collection, and establishing electronic word-of-mouth (Kwon et al., 2013; Litvin et al., 2008; Wang et al., 2016). Meanwhile, mobile technology has significantly changed consumers' consumption behaviours due to the ubiquity and portability features of mobile phones. For instance, airline mobile apps have allowed clients to manage their travel plans by making bookings, selecting seats, receiving weather notifications, participating in rewards points programmes, and offering them mobile check-in and electronic boarding pass services. In more recent years we have seen that this technology has also provided a strong tool for customer relationship management, with the introduction of "hotel messaging." Whether it be via a hotel's native app or a third-party app such as *Facebook Messenger*, guests can now message the hotel with requests or questions, communicating with the hotel in the same way they would with friends or family (Ting, 2016). In short, mobile technology has advanced business operators' marketing efforts as well as facilitated customers' consumption experiences.

Smartphone-related research in hospitality and tourism has increased since 2000, and most studies have placed an emphasis on consumer perspectives. Mobile marketing mainly involves promotions and other communication between service providers and their customers, reflecting an interactive nature. Researchers believe that the advantages of mobile marketing are customization, interactivity, and the capability of reaching out to more potential customers with less temporal or spatial limitations (Kim & Law, 2015).

Mobile applications are the prevailing form of mobile technology, and can be defined as software programs on users' mobile devices that are designed to perform specific tasks (Kwon et al., 2013; Wang et al., 2016). Hospitality mobile apps are mobile programs that provide customers with hospitality-based electronic services, such as information searching, reviewing, directions, booking, reservation and so forth. These mobile apps can be downloaded from diverse online app stores to operate on mobile devices such as smartphones and tablets. Most OTAs have launched their own mobile apps in addition to web pages, which allow consumers to do all that they used to do on websites, but now on the move.

Research trends in relation to mobile apps include consumers' acceptance of new mobile apps, such as diet apps (Okumus et al., 2016) or mobile payment apps (Morosan & DeFranco, 2016). There is also a growth in research on the evolution of mobile apps and their use, applying various measurement models and performance matrices (Lu et al., 2015; Wang et al., 2016).

Future directions

The purpose of this chapter was to critically review the current debates and issues in hospitality internet and technology marketing. Fifteen review-type studies on the internet and technology published in leading hospitality and tourism journals were reviewed to provide a better understanding of the progress and main trends in ICT marketing research in this field. Three critical areas of internet marketing – namely, websites, social media, and smartphones – were identified based on the literature review. The most recent topics underlying these three key research areas have been discussed.

In sum, hospitality practitioners and researchers have shown great interest in the use of the internet and in technology development in the industry, and their enthusiasm continues to grow. We have seen how the orientation of ICT and internet research has shifted from new technology applications in functional areas to advanced applications (Law et al., 2013). Further internet and technology research covering more recent technologies such as cloud computing, data warehousing, business solutions and so forth will provide new contributions and insights to the industry, while critical features of internet marketing strategies, such as e-relationship management and e-loyalty, would be interesting avenues for future research.

In current internet and technology research, there is a gap in the application of sophisticated theoretical models. Future research within the hospitality and tourism disciplines should focus on developing theoretical frameworks which integrate technology, social psychology, and communication theories. In terms of research methods, future internet marketing enquiries might use qualitative or mixed methods more often, rather than focusing simply on quantitative research approaches (Leung et al., 2015b; Oh et al., 2004). In general, the focus of internet marketing research has shifted from a data collection era to a data analysis era. There is also a need to adopt novel research methods from multiple disciplines in order to investigate the wide range of internet-related issues facing hospitality and tourism.

From a practical perspective, this chapter has shown that ICT should be integrated into business strategies, with an emphasis on service quality. More investment in ICT training and learning for hospitality employers at all levels is encouraged to enhance operational efficiency and service quality (Ip et al., 2011). Implementation of new ICT technology and internet marketing strategies will improve the overall marketing efficiency and effectiveness of organizations.

For example, the proliferation of smartphone users and the development of mobile technology has enabled hospitality and tourism practitioners to reach out to customers in ways never seen before; in turn, enabling them to deliver tailored services though hospitality-oriented social media apps. In terms of smartphones, Kim and Law (2015) identified the need for more research from the marketer's perspective, especially relating to marketing strategies and practices, as the existing smartphone literature has been predominantly customer-focused. As for website marketing, Ip et al. (2011) suggested that hospitality marketers should not merely focus on providing information websites, emphasizing the importance of high exposure and easy access from search engines. Traversing this rapidly changing landscape of online technologies will continue to present challenges for practitioners; however, it is without doubt that these technologies will also bring new possibilities for businesses. We have seen opportunities for wider marketing exposure and stronger customer relationship management. Mastery of these opportunities will equip practitioners with the tools to potentially target greater numbers of customers with even deeper connections.

References

Amaro, S. & Duarte, P. (2013). "Online travel purchasing: A literature review," *Journal of Travel & Tourism Marketing* 30(8), 755–785.

Baird, C. H. & Parasnis, G. (2011). *From social media to Social CRM: What customers want*, New York: IBM Global Business Services.

Baloglu, S. & Pekcan, Y. A. (2006). "The website design and internet site marketing practices of upscale and luxury hotels in Turkey," *Tourism Management* 27(1), 171–176.

Berezina, K., Bilgihan, A., Cobanoglu, C. & Okumus, F. (2016). "Understanding satisfied and dissatisfied hotel customers: Text mining of online hotel reviews," *Journal of Hospitality Marketing & Management* 25(1), 1–24.

Buhalis, D. & Law, R. (2008). "Progress in information technology and tourism management: 20 years on and 10 years after the internet—The state of eTourism research," *Tourism Management* 29(4), 609–623.

Burmann, C. (2010). "A call for 'user-generated branding'," *Journal of Brand Management* 18(1), 1–4.

Cantallops, A. S. & Salvi, F. (2014). "New consumer behavior: A review of research on eWOM and hotels," *International Journal of Hospitality Management* 36, 41–51.

Choi, E.-K., Fowler, D., Goh, B. & Yuan, J. J. (2016). "Social media marketing: Applying the uses and gratifications theory in the hotel industry," *Journal of Hospitality Marketing & Management* 25(7), 771–796.

Denizci Guillet, B., Kucukusta, D. & Liu, L. (2015). "An examination of social media marketing in China: How do the top 133 hotel brands perform on the top four Chinese social media sites?," *Journal of Travel & Tourism Marketing* 1–23.

Dickinger, A. (2010). "The trustworthiness of online channels for experience- and goal-directed search tasks," *Journal of Travel Research* 50(4), 378–391.

Fang, B., Ye, Q. & Law, R. (2016). "Effect of sharing economy on tourism industry employment," *Annals of Tourism Research* 57, 264–267.

Gursoy, D. & Sandstrom, J. K. (2014). "An updated ranking of hospitality and tourism journals," *Journal of Hospitality & Tourism Research* [online]. doi:10.1177/1096348014538054

Guttentag, D. (2015). "Airbnb: Disruptive innovation and the rise of an informal tourism accommodation sector," *Current Issues in Tourism* 18(12), 1192–1217.

Ham, S., Kim, W. G. & Jeong, S. (2005). "Effect of information technology on performance in upscale hotels," *International Journal of Hospitality Management* 24(2), 281–294.

Heinonen, K. (2011). "Consumer activity in social media: Managerial approaches to consumers' social media behavior," *Journal of Consumer Behaviour* 10(6), 356–364.

Hjalager, A.-M. (2010). "A review of innovation research in tourism," *Tourism Management* 31(1), 1–12.

Ip, C., Law, R. & Lee, H. A. (2011). "A review of website evaluation studies in the tourism and hospitality fields from 1996 to 2009," *International Journal of Tourism Research* 13(3), 234–265.

Ip, C., Leung, R. & Law, R. (2011). "Progress and development of information and communication technologies in hospitality," *International Journal of Contemporary Hospitality Management* 23(4), 533–551.

Keenan, A. & Shiri, A. (2009). "Sociability and social interaction on social networking websites," *Library Review* 58(6), 438–450.

Kim, H. H. & Law, R. (2015). "Smartphones in tourism and hospitality marketing: A literature review," *Journal of Travel & Tourism Marketing* 32(6), 692–711.

Kwon, J. M., Bae, J.-I. & Blum, S. C. (2013). "Mobile applications in the hospitality industry," *Journal of Hospitality and Tourism Technology* 4(1), 81–92.

Law, R., Buhalis, D. & Cobanoglu, C. (2014). "Progress on information and communication technologies in hospitality and tourism," *International Journal of Contemporary Hospitality Management* 26(5), 727–750.

Law, R. & Cheung, C. (2005). "Weighing of hotel website dimensions and attributes," *Information and Communication Technologies in Tourism*. Vienna: Springer, 350–359.

Law, R., Leung, D., Au, N. & Lee, H. (2013). "Progress and development of information technology in the hospitality industry: Evidence from Cornell Hospitality Quarterly," *Cornell Hospitality Quarterly* 54(1), 10–24.

Law, R., Leung, R. & Buhalis, D. (2009). "Information technology applications in hospitality and tourism: A review of publications from 2005 to 2007," *Journal of Travel & Tourism Marketing* 26(5–6), 599–623.

Law, R., Qi, S. & Buhalis, D. (2010). "Progress in tourism management: A review of website evaluation in tourism research," *Tourism Management* 31(3), 297–313.

Leung, D., Law, R., Van Hoof, H. & Buhalis, D. (2013). "Social media in tourism and hospitality: A literature review," *Journal of Travel & Tourism Marketing* 30(1–2), 3–22.

Leung, X.Y., Bai, B. & Stahura, K.A. (2015a). "The marketing effectiveness of social media in the hotel industry: A comparison of Facebook and Twitter," *Journal of Hospitality & Tourism Research* 39(2), 147–169.

Leung, X. Y., Xue, L. & Bai, B. (2015b). "Internet marketing research in hospitality and tourism: A review and journal preferences," *International Journal of Contemporary Hospitality Management* 27(7), 1556–1572.

Litvin, S. W., Goldsmith, R. E. & Pan, B. (2008). "Electronic word-of-mouth in hospitality and tourism management," *Tourism Management* 29(3), 458–468.

Lu, J., Mao, Z., Wang, M. & Hu, L. (2015). "Goodbye maps, hello apps? Exploring the influential determinants of travel app adoption," *Current Issues in Tourism* 18(11), 1059–1079.

Mangold, W. G. & Faulds, D. J. (2009). "Social media: The new hybrid element of the promotion mix," *Business Horizons* 52(4), 357–365.

Morosan, C. & DeFranco, A. (2016). "It's about time: Revisiting UTAUT2 to examine consumers' intentions to use NFC mobile payments in hotels," *International Journal of Hospitality Management* 53, 17–29.

Morrison, A. M., Taylor, J. S. & Douglas, A. (2005). "Website evaluation in tourism and hospitality: The art is not yet stated," *Journal of Travel & Tourism Marketing* 17(2–3), 233–251.

Oastes, G., (2015). *Beautiful Destinations' Jeremy Jauncey on the new language of engagement at Skift Forum* [online]. Available from: https://skift.com/2015/10/14/beautiful-destinations-jeremy-jauncey-on-visuals-as-the-new-language-of-engagement-at-skift-forum/ [Accessed 05 Oct 2016].

O'Connor, P. (2008). "Distribution channels and e-commerce," *In:* Oh, H. and Pizam, A. eds. *Handbook of Hospitality Marketing Management*. Oxford, UK: Elsevier Ltd, 186–208.

O'Connor, P. & Murphy, J. (2004). "Research on information technology in the hospitality industry," *International Journal of Hospitality Management* 23(5), 473–484.

Oh, H., Kim, B.-Y. & Shin, J.-H. (2004). "Hospitality and tourism marketing: Recent developments in research and future directions," *International Journal of Hospitality Management* 23(5), 425–447.

Okumus, B., Bilgihan, A. & Ozturk, A. B. (2016). "Factors affecting the acceptance of smartphone diet applications," *Journal of Hospitality Marketing & Management* 25(6), 726–747.

Park, Y. A. & Gretzel, U. (2007). "Success factors for destination marketing web sites: A qualitative meta-analysis," *Journal of Travel Research* 46(1), 46–63.

Peters, K., Chen, Y., Kaplan, A. M., Ognibeni, B. & Pauwels, K. (2013). "Social media metrics: A framework and guidelines for managing social media," *Journal of Interactive Marketing* 27(4), 281–298.

Schmidt, S., Cantallops, A. S. & dos Santos, C. P. (2008). "The characteristics of hotel websites and their implications for website effectiveness," *International Journal of Hospitality Management* 27(4), 504–516.

Standing, C., Tang-Taye, J.-P. & Boyer, M. (2014). "The impact of the Internet in travel and tourism: A research review 2001–2010," *Journal of Travel & Tourism Marketing* 31(1), 82–113.

Stewart, D. W. & Pavlou, P. A. (2002). "From consumer response to active consumer: Measuring the effectiveness of interactive media," *Journal of the Academy of Marketing Science* 30(4), 376–396.

Sun, L. B. & Qu, H. (2011). "Is there any gender effect on the relationship between service quality and word-of-mouth?," *Journal of Travel & Tourism Marketing* 28(2), 210–224.

Swanson, S. R. & Hsu, M. K. (2009). "Critical incidents in tourism: Failure, recovery, customer switching, and word-of-mouth behaviors," *Journal of Travel & Tourism Marketing* 26(2), 180–194.

Ting, D. (2016). *How smart hotels use messaging to connect with guests* [online]. Available from: https://skift.com/2016/08/26/how-smart-hotels-use-messaging-to-connect-with-guests/ [Accessed 17 Oct 2016].

Varma, A., Jukic, N., Pestek, A., Shultz, C. J. & Nestorov, S. (2016). "Airbnb: Exciting innovation or passing fad?," *Tourism Management Perspectives* 20, 228–237.

Vermeulen, I. E. & Seegers, D. (2009). "Tried and tested: The impact of online hotel reviews on consumer consideration," *Tourism Management* 30(1), 123–127.

Wang, D., Xiang, Z., Law, R. & Ki, T. P. (2016). "Assessing hotel-related smartphone apps using online reviews," *Journal of Hospitality Marketing & Management* 25(3), 291–313.

Xiang, Z., Woeber, K. & Fesenmaier, D. R. (2008). "Representation of the online tourism domain in search engines," *Journal of Travel Research* 47(2), 137–150.

Ye, Q., Law, R. & Gu, B. (2009). "The impact of online user reviews on hotel room sales," *International Journal of Hospitality Management* 28(1), 180–182.

Zervas, G., Proserpio, D. & Byers, J. (2016). "The rise of the sharing economy: Estimating the impact of Airbnb on the hotel industry," *Boston University School of Management Research Paper* (2013–16).

Further reading

Buhalis, D. & Law, R. (2008). "Progress in information technology and tourism management: 20 years on and 10 years after the internet: The state of e-tourism research," *Tourism Management* 29(4), 609–623. (Review of 20 years of IT development in tourism and future trends.)

Cantallops, A. S. & Salvi, F. (2014). "New consumer behavior: A review of research on eWOM and hotels," *International Journal of Hospitality Management* 36, 41–51. (Review of eWOM motivations and impacts.)

Kim, H. H. & Law, R. (2015). "Smartphones in tourism and hospitality marketing: A literature review," *Journal of Travel & Tourism Marketing* 32(6), 692–711. (Review of smartphone marketing.)

Law, R., Leung, R. & Buhalis, D. (2009). "Information technology applications in hospitality and tourism: A review of publications from 2005 to 2007," *Journal of Travel & Tourism Marketing* 26(5–6), 599–623. (Review of IT application and management in hospitality and tourism.)

Law, R., Qi, S. & Buhalis, D. (2010). "Progress in tourism management: A review of website evaluation in tourism research," *Tourism Management* 31(3), 297–313. (Review of website evaluation research.)

Leung, D., Law, R., Van Hoof, H. & Buhalis, D. (2013). "Social media in tourism and hospitality: A literature review," *Journal of Travel & Tourism Marketing* 30(1–2), 3–22. (Review of social media from consumer and supplier perspectives.)

Leung, X. Y., Xue, L. & Bai, B. (2015). "Internet marketing research in hospitality and tourism: A review and journal preferences," *International Journal of Contemporary Hospitality Management* 27(7), 1556–1572. (Review of 331 internet marketing studies in eight leading journals.)

O'Connor, P. & Murphy, J. (2004). "Research on information technology in the hospitality industry," *International Journal of Hospitality Management* 23(5), 473–484. (Review of the use IT in distribution, pricing, and consumer interaction.)

Park, Y. A. & Gretzel, U. (2007). "Success factors for destination marketing web sites: A qualitative meta-analysis," *Journal of Travel Research* 46(1), 46–63. (A meta-analysis of destination website evaluation factors.)

Standing, C., Tang-Taye, J.-P. & Boyer, M. (2014). "The impact of the internet in travel and tourism: A research review 2001–2010," *Journal of Travel & Tourism Marketing* 31(1), 82–113. (Review of the impact of the internet on tourism.)

Wang, D., Xiang, Z., Law, R. & Ki, T. P. (2016). "Assessing hotel-related smartphone apps using online reviews," *Journal of Hospitality Marketing & Management* 25(3), 291–313.

39

Changes in the distribution of hospitality products and e-commerce

Marios Sotiriadis

Introduction

Information and communication technologies (ICTs) have affected the whole distribution apparatus in the tourism industry in general and the hospitality industry in particular (Buhalis & Licata 2002; Kracht & Wang 2010). Nowadays online distribution and sales are easier, faster and enhanced through online payment facilities and through improved website design, content and new applications for smartphones. With the advent of the internet, possibilities opened up for the consumer to gather information and make bookings (Benckendorff et al. 2014). At the turn of the millennium, booking a holiday typically entailed visiting the high-street travel agent; or for the more intrepid tourist, relying on word-of-mouth recommendations coupled with a hefty guidebook to set the travel itinerary. Today, thanks to technology breakthroughs, consumers have a much wider choice of electronic channels through which they can obtain information on travel and tourism; make bookings; search reviews on their phones of restaurants where they could possibly eat; and gather information on what to do while they are at a certain destination (Middleton et al. 2009; Morrison 2013).

The internet has provided a direct channel between buyers and sellers and, at the same time, increased the choice of channels through which tourism bookings can be made. Although direct bookings with suppliers have increased rapidly, so too have the number of new online intermediaries offering services similar to those of the traditional intermediaries (Buhalis & Licata 2002; Buhalis & Jun 2011).

Hotels have a variety of online distribution channels to help them sell rooms, including Online Tourism Intermediaries or Tourism eMediaries (TEMs), such as Expedia and Travelocity (Buhalis & Jun 2011; Middleton et al. 2009). The term "Tourism eMediaries" is often used interchangeably with other terms, including but not limited to, "online travel agents" (Kracht & Wang 2010), "third-party websites" (Toh et al. 2011) and "e-tourism intermediaries" (Buhalis & Licata 2002). The term "TEMs" is adopted for the purpose of this chapter. TEMs include a wide range of organizations, such as suppliers/principals (e.g. airlines and hotels) selling direct on the internet by allowing consumers to directly access their reservation systems; web-based travel agents or third-party websites; internet portals and auction sites (Buhalis & Licata 2002; Sotiriadis et al. 2015).

In the digital arena, the relationship between channel players is complex and requires a marketing management approach. When deciding which channels to use, hospitality organizations need to consider: (i) the consumption behavior of their target markets; (ii) the relative coverage of each channel; (iii) the comparative costs, revenue and net contribution of each channel; and (iv) the extent to which access is controlled by vertically integrated companies and the implications for businesses that are not directly connected (Middleton et al. 2009; Toh et al. 2011).

In this context, the chapter takes a hospitality business perspective and focuses on the supply/ provider side. The main aim is to analyze the changes brought about by the technological developments in the field of distribution of hospitality products and services, as well as in the function of e-commerce, by performing a review of the latest academic research. The chapter's specific objectives are: (i) to outline the online tourism market; (ii) to present the impact of digital tools on hospitality marketing; and (iii) to discuss the uses of social media (SM) and TEMs for distributing hospitality products and services. The chapter will conclude by highlighting the marketing implications and suggesting suitable strategies.

The online tourism market

Business reports and market intelligence show an impressive adoption and use of online bookings and purchase. A recent survey by Eurostat – the statistical office of the European Union (EU) – on ICT usage and e-commerce in enterprises highlights that ICTs have been a significant driver of changes to the way in which consumers book their trips and the workflow of enterprises in the tourism industry. On the one hand, tourists from the EU make extensive use of the internet for their trips. In 2014, more than two-thirds of air trips and more than half of train trips were booked online. Slightly more than two-thirds (67%) of flight trips made by EU tourists in 2014 were booked online. Rented tourist accommodation was booked online for the majority of the trips of EU residents in 2014 (55%). Accommodation was also booked online for more than half of the trips. On the other hand, enterprises working in the hospitality industry seem to be more advanced in using ICT than many other industries. While online ordering was offered by 17% of all enterprises in 2015, this share rose to 74% for the hospitality industry.

Websites are the starting point for e-business, and website functionalities are widely used by the hospitality industry. In 2015, 95% of all EU enterprises in the hospitality industry had a website, compared with 75% of enterprises of ten or more persons in the entire economy (Travel and Tour World, 2016).

The latest report by Phocuswright, 'Channel surfing: Where consumers shop for travel online', reveals that an increasing number of consumers are also booking online. By 2017, it is predicted that online will account for 37% of all bookings in Asia Pacific, 45% in the US, and 52% in Europe (Lulla, 2016). But the channels and devices consumers worldwide are using to research and book their trips differ, and are also affected by economic factors, cultural norms and the technology at their disposal. The Phocuswright report also highlights another significant trend: in each of the global marketplaces covered, the vast majority of consumers prefer booking with TEMs instead of provider websites (see Table 39.1).

In developed markets, 61–75% of customers used a TEM to book for hotels, but just 15–44% visited a hotel website. In emerging markets the gap is still greater. In China, for instance, 9 out of 10 online consumers used TEMs, but less than 4 out of 10 used hotel websites. While the reasons for this vary between regions, there are also key trends that specifically reveal why TEMs are gaining a bigger share.

Table 39.1 Hotel bookings: TEMs vs. hotel websites

Country	Distribution / Booking channel	
	TEMs	Hotel website
USA	72%	44%
UK	66%	28%
Australia	73%	21%
France	61%	15%
Germany	75%	17%
Russia	70%	12%
China	91%	39%
Brazil	75%	21%

Note: The question was "Which of the following travel websites or apps did you use to shop for hotels and accommodation? Please indicate if you used each website on your desktop computer, smartphone or tablet. Select all that apply."
Source: Retrieved from Phocuswright (2016).

Table 39.2 Reasons for online bookings through TEMs

Reason for choosing TEMs	Frequency (%)
The TEM's website is easy to use	47
I am used to booking travel via this channel	37
I trust the brand	34
TEMs typically have the best prices	30
It is easy to book all of the travel services in one place	29
TEM's website had the most selection	28
It is easier to change/cancel my booking	20
I like their mobile application	12
I could not find what I wanted to book anywhere else	10
I am a member of that TEM's loyalty/rewards program	8

Note: The question was: "Why did you book some or all of your travel via a TEM like Expedia or Last-minute? Please select all that apply."
Source: Retrieved from Phocuswright (2016).

What are the reasons of preference for TEMs? One of the reasons why TEMs are preferred boils down to content aggregation: they allow customers to compare a variety of products based on price, availability and guest reviews all in one place. When getting into specifics, the Phocuswright report identifies ten fundamental reasons why tourists book through TEMs over principal websites, as shown in Table 39.2.

The survey shows the top ten reasons why tourists use TEMs; and although perception of lower price is one of them, it is surprisingly not the top reason. TEMs have essentially achieved their business success by embracing and managing the inevitable digital trend and are thus very effectively serving consumers along with dealing with the needs of their partners, the principals in the tourism industry such as hotels, airlines, tour operators and car rental companies.

Documented statistics confirm that 65% of potential tourists start their trips while researching and seeking inspiration online; 78% of potential tourists use the internet for planning their itineraries; 60% use search engines while 48% use hotel and other principals' websites; 40% use TEMs for their travel planning (Storage Googleapis, 2014). At the same time, 67% of this activity is performed from mobile devices (e.g. smartphones and tablets). When it comes to idea gathering, research and inspiration, some 90% of potential tourists use the internet, while only 10% make use of a travel agent (Storage Googleapis, 2014). Today's potential tourist, the 'younger' growing market, does his or her own research and planning; decides what to book and then books and pays on the internet, using resources from Google, TEMs and meta engines, SM and review platforms (e.g. TripAdvisor).

Exploiting the full potential of digital tools: Web 2.0, SM and online consumer reviews

As information technology increasingly permeates all aspects of contemporary society, the hospitality industry has made huge investments to deploy e-commerce tools and develop appropriate strategies to attract and retain customers (Hua et al., 2015). It has become necessary for hoteliers to take advantage of the huge opportunities generated by internet technology by establishing their own websites for online promotion and e-commerce. It is believed that the crucial issue is how the hospitality industry could exploit the opportunities and face the challenges posed in the online arena efficiently.

Using all available tools efficiently

The present chapter argues that the hospitality industry should wisely and effectively use all digital tools in order to achieve better hotel sales management, and consequently achieve higher business performance. Literature suggests that the hospitality websites constitute promotional and selling tools; and remain the core of their digital strategy (e.g. Chan & Guillet 2011). However, the latest developments, such as the advent of Web 2.0 and SM and the establishment of online distribution channels, are now presenting new challenges and opportunities for hotels. It is believed that the efficient management of SM and online distribution channels is a pre-requisite for success (Inversini & Masiero 2014; Kim et al. 2015).

Therefore, the hospitality industry must (i) find ways to make the most effective possible use of available technology and distribution channels (Lee et al. 2013); (ii) manage online distribution channels (TEMs), their online presence and pricing strategy to increase revenues (Inversini & Masiero 2014; Toh et al. 2011); and (iii) invest and engage in SM to establish an interactive communication channel with tourists, leveraging on online reviews and feedback (Chan & Guillet 2011; Gretzel & Yoo 2013; Sotiriadis 2016). These are the megatrends in the online arena and hospitality businesses should seize the opportunities and deal with the challenges to remain competitive and sustainable (Filieri & McLeay 2014; Inversini & Masiero 2014). The academic research on issues regarding hospitality distribution is outlined in the following paragraphs.

Review of literature

Social media and online reviews

The major impacts of the digital revolution in the tourism field have come through websites, SM and mobile devices, as highlighted by scholars (Benckendorff et al. 2014; Law et al. 2014; Sigala et al. 2012). SM have become powerful social platforms for online communications, allowing consumers to interact and share their views; collaborate and contribute to developing, extending, rating and commenting on tourism experiences (Gretzel and Yoo 2013). When using SM, tourists become co-designers, co-producers, co-marketers and co-consumers of tourism experiences (Sigala et al. 2012).

These developments in Web 2.0 tools have a considerable impact on consumer behavior and present a host of new challenges as well as opportunities for tourism providers. One of the main functions of SM is to establish an interactive channel of communication, which is mutually beneficial to both parties involved: it offers a medium for tourists to express their desires and requirements; and gives tourism providers a tool to acquire customer feedback (Kim et al. 2015; Sotiriadis 2016). The Web 2.0 tools provide opportunities and challenges for hospitality businesses to better listen to and understand existing and potential customers.

The impressive adoption and extensive use of SM has revolutionized all tourism providers. More importantly, these developments have an influential impact on strategic and operational marketing and management in the tourism field (Law et al. 2014). Furthermore, they have been recognized as innovative knowledge sharing networks by enabling customers to connect, share with, and interact with others. For this reason, SM, as interactive platforms, are gaining attention in the tourism industry (Gretzel and Yoo 2013; Benckendorff et al. 2014).

Literature suggests that the Web 2.0 tools are excellent promotional tools (Inversini & Masiero 2014; Kim et al. 2015). Recent studies highlight the importance of SM as a marketing communications channel medium (Sotiriadis 2016). In addition, online consumer reviews are becoming an important focus of research into marketing hotel and other tourism services (Filieri & McLeay 2014). Online reviews in SM and e-complaint handling and management responses affect hotel sales; some studies have investigated the value of online consumer reviews and management responses to hotel performance (Xie & Zhang 2014; Kim et al. 2015; Zhao et al. 2015).

The incorporation of SM into hotel websites (embedded SM on hotel websites) was a major development for the hospitality industry because it enables managers to gain more insights into tourists' consumption behavior and the decision-making process (Aluri et al. 2015). However, the hospitality industry continues to struggle with the incorporation of online interaction tools into its communication strategy. The simple incorporation of SM onto the website seems to be inadequate because SM need a specific management approach (Inversini & Masiero 2014). SM should be seen simultaneously as a listening, interaction and promotion tool (Xie & Zhang 2014; Aluri et al. 2015; Kim et al. 2015). In addition, SM should be used as a source and channel for interactive communication and constructive dialogue to acquire customer feedback (Sotiriadis 2016).

Online distribution: TEMs

Simultaneously, online distribution has considerably expanded and has a significant impact on the hospitality industry. Online distribution has stimulated disintermediation followed by a re-intermediation with the consolidation and growth of TEMs, causing channel conflicts with the hotel industry (Kracht & Wang 2010; Lee et al. 2013; Myung et al. 2009).

TEMs, which emerged in the 1990s, play a crucial role in online distribution. They are third-party companies that have become increasingly more powerful than hotels when it comes to internet readiness and economic force, putting hotels in the disadvantaged position of selling a large portion of their inventory through third-party intermediaries at heavily discounted rates (Lee et al. 2013). TEMs have a tremendous advantage over hotels in that they offer multiple alternatives of hotels and room prices to tourists. The TEMs also have the advantage of bundling, based on economics of scope, which reduces overall costs (Kim et al. 2009). With product bundling, air travel, hotel accommodation, and rental cars are offered as a bundling package at attractive discounted prices. Even if the services are not bundled at a low price, one can buy an airline seat and hotel room on the same site, providing one-stop shopping: very convenient to tourists.

The scale and convenience of TEMs have created a challenge for hotel companies that want to lure tourists to their own websites (Lee et al. 2013). A study by Toh et al. (2011) examined how hotels can sell room inventory while maximizing net room revenues – principally by steering customers to their own sites. The following ways were proposed to strengthen sales on hotel websites: maintain a best-rate guarantee; optimize the website for search engines; mine data from customer profiles to provide custom offers; retain premium rooms for sale on the hotel website; offer discounts or other promotions to customers who book on the hotel website; offer incentives for returning guests who book on the hotel website; avoid giving loyalty points for TEM bookings; and enrich the hotel's website with information (Toh et al. 2011).

Other issues in the field of online distribution channels regarding the hospitality industry explored by previous studies are outlined below. First, the optimal pricing strategy of a hotel that establishes an online distribution channel through cooperation with a TEM was explored by Ling et al. (2014) and Guo et al. (2013), who attempted to provide useful suggestions to success-fully operate this cooperative relationship (Xiaolong et al. 2013). Guo et al. (2013) proposed the optimal dynamic pricing strategy, which ensures a high occupancy rate and generates more profit than fixed pricing in the online distribution channel. This strategy is based on market segmenta-tion for service products in the online distribution channel.

The second issue investigated is the performance of TEMs. A study by Berné et al. (2015) attempted to confirm a positive relationship (a cause–effect association) between the growing use of ICT by tourism intermediaries and their business performance. The main suggestion is that TEMs should intensify their relationships with those suppliers and tour operators whose strategies allow for improved effectiveness throughout the value chain.

Third, the websites of many hotels are incorporating SM as a marketing tool to provide direct contact with customers. A study by Wang et al. (2015) proposed that a trusting relationship with customers could be developed by conducting an investigation into hotel website development. It was found that hotel website quality is a strong predictor of online trust, which then also medi-ates the relationship between website quality and the online booking intentions of consumers.

Fourth, another challenging topic is the relationships with TEMs. Hotels are required to pay high commission fees when cooperating with TEMs to manage online channels. Thus, to maximize their revenues, hotels protect their income through their own distribution channels. Toh et al. (2011) stressed that it is expected that hotels and OTAs will make changes to the way in which they use internet technology to sell rooms; and the relationship between the OTAs and the hotel industry will continue to evolve. A study by Lee et al. (2013) analyzed the con-flicting relationship by reporting on a case study about the 2009 feud between Choice Hotels International and Expedia. The main suggestion was that hotels must find ways to make the most effective possible use of available technology and distribution channels, and perhaps even form consortia to share information about third-party distribution channels. In their study, Ling et al. (2015) proposed a method to manage room availability in the context of a hotel, by cooperating with a TEM on a room booking service.

Fifth, the effectiveness of e-commerce expenditures has been explored by Hua et al. (2015) who examined whether such expenditures affect performance in terms of revenue and gross operating profit. It was found that e-commerce expenses had a significant positive impact on hotel revenue. When subgroup analyses were performed by chain scale, it was found that e-commerce expenses significantly contributed to the gross operating profit for midscale and upscale hotels but not to the luxury, upper upscale, and the upper midscale categories.

Another issue is the influence of tourists' online reviews. Empirical findings of studies have shown such reviews have a significant impact on hotel booking intentions (Sparks & Browning

2011); influence the decision-making process of consumers (Ladhari & Michaud 2015) and also have an impact on online sales (Ye et al. 2011). This is the reason why SM must be efficiently managed as another tool within the context of distribution management (Sparks et al. 2016).

Using of SM and TEMs for distributing hospitality products and services

Lately, academic research has been interested in the combined effect of various digital platforms on hospitality distribution and sales. In this regard, a study by Inversini and Masiero (2014) constitutes a valuable contribution to understanding the major role played by TEMs and SM in the hospitality industry. The study focused on the use of SM and TEMs for online distribution by examining the reasons why hotel organizations choose to have a presence on TEM and SM websites for distribution purposes. It was found that there is a constant tension between visibility (through SM) and online sales (through TEMs) in the digital arena, as well as a clear distinction in SM and TEM website adoption between hospitality businesses, use of online management tools and employing personnel with specific skills. Hoteliers perceived a direct relationship between TEMs and SM, where the latter has a stronger impact on the importance of TEMs than TEMs have on the importance of SM. Therefore, the authors suggested that there is a need for the hospitality industry to maintain an effective presence on SM and OTAs in order to move towards creating a new form of social booking technology to increase their visibility and sales.

Kim et al.'s study (2015) examined the effectiveness of managing SM on hotel performance by exploring the effect of online reviews and other related information on hotel performance. The study's findings confirmed the positive relationship between online reviews and hotel firm performance. More specifically, the results indicated that response to negative online reviews is an important driver of hotel performance; the better the overall ratings and the higher the response rate to negative comments, the stronger the hotel performance. This is the reason why online reviews on SM, specifically overall rating and response to negative comments, should be managed as a crucial part of hotel marketing (Kim et al. 2015).

Xie and Zhang's study (2014) investigated and identified the business value of online consumer reviews and management responses to hotel performance. It constitutes a valuable contribution by proposing a rigorous quantification of the economic value of online reviews on hotel performance in the SM context where consumer reviews and management responses coexist. It was found that management responses have a positive impact on the relationship between location rating and hotel sales. It further suggested how management responses can be used to improve hotel business performance.

Along the same line of research, Zhao et al.'s study (2015) aimed at investigating the impact of online reviews on the online hotel booking intentions of tourists to offer suggestions for industry practitioners on how to better utilize online reviews as a marketing tool. This study identified (i) positive causal relationships between usefulness, reviewer expertise, timeliness, volume and comprehensiveness and the online booking intentions of respondents; and (ii) a significantly negative relation between negative online reviews and online booking intentions, whereas the impact of positive online reviews on booking intentions was not statistically significant.

Integrated marketing communications strategies

Let's summarize the strategies suggested by the related studies, and the actions that the hospitality industry should implement to tap into the full potential of SM and online consumer reviews. The main marketing task is to use all channels and media available in integrated marketing communications with potential and current customers by implementing the following strategies (Aluri et al. 2015; Bilgihan et al. 2016; Filieri & McLeay 2014; Kim et al. 2015; Sparks &

Browning 2011; Xie & Zhang 2014): create a virtual environment that builds a virtual community by engaging tourists to share their insights and knowledge; design SM communications in order to encourage tourists to share their experiences during and after their trips; make online consumer reviews a viable marketing channel; deal directly with consumer reviews to SM platforms; use travel-related SM as a communication tool with customers; use SM as a listening tool and as a way of interacting with customers; encourage engagement behavior/use social gratifications to enhance the participation and engagement of tourists on the hotel's own website; and place a stronger focus on the quality of the information provided in order to maintain high levels of trust. Additionally, hospitality organizations should take full advantage of online recovery encounters as a two-way communication tool to convert an unhappy customer into a loyal one through online responses. Therefore, they must develop an online review response plan and prepare operational manuals on how to respond to the negative online reviews of customers.

It is believed that the hospitality industry should seize the opportunities provided by various digital platforms and tools by using them as (i) a channel for interactive communication in engaging in conversation with consumers; and (ii) as a distribution channel. The combined effect of their suitable management uses and of appropriate communication strategies should (i) improve the effectiveness of distribution management; and (ii) enhance and boost online sales leading to more efficient sales management, ultimately achieving improved business performance.

Conclusion: Marketing implications and strategies

Innovations in ICTs drive the development of distribution channels in the tourism and hospitality industry. This chapter has explored the impact of ICTs on hospitality distribution systems and management. It has argued that ICTs have a considerable impact on hospitality distribution; this information technology and its advances have changed the distribution tools. However, the principles of distribution remain the same, regardless of the technology. The internet and Web 2.0 tools have also changed distribution channel relationships between some types of customer, hotels and intermediaries involving new management approaches. This process continues to evolve and there is a constant need for the hospitality industry to manage distribution more efficiently and drive down distribution costs.

This chapter can be concluded by suggesting marketing implications and strategies to achieve more efficient distribution management. The literature review points out the need to adopt and use all the available tools and media in the digital context efficiently in order to improve the effectiveness of hospitality distribution. It also highlights the need for the hospitality industry to have a comprehensive approach to distribution management and other functions of marketing communications on SM and TEMs; and to implement a multi-channel strategy. In doing so, the industry will improve the effectiveness and efficiency of digital marketing.

Hospitality distribution should be adequately managed in the function of sales management in order to increase business performance in the online market. A series of strategies and operational actions should be implemented, as suggested by related studies as outlined below.

First, regarding sales management (see, for instance, Blal & Sturman 2014; Inversini & Masiero 2014; Kim et al. 2015; Ladhari & Michaud 2015; Lee et al. 2013; Melián-González et al. 2013; Phillips et al. 2015; Toh et al. 2011; Xie & Zhang 2014; Zhao et al. 2015):

- Devote efforts to increasing the quantity of online reviews about the hospitality organization.
- Invest resources on hotels' own websites by enhancing trust in and value of online reviews.
- Focus on actions dealing with guest concerns and eventually increase the review scores without necessarily aiming for a high number of reviews.

- Collaborate with TEMs; develop a symbiotic relationship with close and long-term interactions with TEMs.
- Make more effective use of revenue management (RM) systems to allow effective inventory and pricing management. As distribution management is part of RM today, hotels should carefully examine TEMs and other online channels available to them (GDS and travel meta-search engines) to identify the channels that yield the most room sales at the best rates.
- Develop human resources with competencies needed to operate in TEMs and SM.
- Dedicate personnel to online sales management in order to be effectively active, both on SM and in TEMs.
- Use suitable performance measures (e.g. revenue per available room – RevPAR) to assess the impact of online reviews on hotel performance.

As far as hotel online distribution is concerned, it is believed that the following strategies are suitable (see, for instance, Inversini & Masiero 2014; Kim et al. 2015; Park & Allen 2013; Ye et al. 2011; Zhao et al. 2015):

- Create new distribution strategies for interplay between TEMs and SM.
- There is a need not only to select distribution channels carefully but also to extend their networks to encompass more TEM partners, thereby avoiding overreliance on one or just a few TEMs.
- Employ SM as an online distribution tool, a service recovery tool and a way to help develop relationships with customers and build brand loyalty.
- Use innovative forms of booking technology together with effective marketing to facilitate the link and interaction between TEMs and SM.
- Implement hotel-owned software to manage online distribution.
- Attend to proper online reviews in good time to increase the booking intentions of consumers.

It is believed that the hospitality industry will significantly improve the effectiveness of distribution management by exploiting the full potential of online platforms and Web 2.0 tools for interactivity and one-to-one communication.

References

Aluri, A., Slevitch, L. and Larzelere, R. (2015) "The Effectiveness of Embedded Social Media on Hotel Websites and the Importance of Social Interactions and Return on Engagement", *International Journal of Contemporary Hospitality Management* 27(4), 670–89.

Benckendorff, P., Sheldon, P.J. and Fesenmaier, D.R. (2014) *Tourism Information Technology* (2nd edn), London: CABI.

Berné, C., García-González, M., García-Uceda, M.E. and Múgica, J.M. (2015) "The Effect of ICT on Relationship Enhancement and Performance in Tourism Channels", *Tourism Management* 48, 188–98.

Bilgihan, A., Barreda, A., Okumus, F. and Nusair, K. (2016) "Consumer Perception of Knowledge-sharing in Travel-related Online Social Networks", *Tourism Management* 52(2), 287–96.

Blal, I. and Sturman, M.C. (2014) "The Differential Effects of the Quality and Quantity of Online Reviews on Hotel Room Sales", *Cornell Hospitality Quarterly* 55(4), 365–75.

Buhalis, D. and Jun, S.H. (2011) *E-Tourism*, Oxford: Goodfellow Publishers.

Buhalis, D. and Licata, M.C. (2002) "The Future eTourism Intermediaries", *Tourism Management* 23(3), 207–20.

Chan, N.L. and Guillet, B.D. (2011) "Investigation of Social Media Marketing: How Does the Hotel Industry in Hong Kong Perform in Marketing on Social Media Websites?", *Journal of Travel & Tourism Marketing* 28(4), 345–68.

Filieri, R. and McLeay, F. (2014) "E-WOM and Accommodation: An Analysis of the Factors that Influence Travelers' Adoption of Information from Online Reviews", *Journal of Travel Research* 53(1), 44–57.

Gretzel, U. and Yoo, K.-H. (2013) "Premises and Promises of Social Media Marketing in Tourism". In: McCabe, S. Ed., *The Routledge Handbook of Tourism Marketing*, 491–504. New York: Routledge.

Guo, X., Ling, L., Yang, C., Li, Z. and Liang, L. (2013) "Optimal Pricing Strategy Based on Market Segmentation for Service Products Using Online Reservation Systems: An Application to Hotel Rooms", *International Journal of Hospitality Management* 35, 274–81

Hua, N., Morosan, C. and DeFranco, A. (2015) "The Other Side of Technology Adoption: Examining the Relationships between E-commerce Expenses and Hotel Performance", *International Journal of Hospitality Management* 45, 109–20.

Inversini, A. and Masiero, L. (2014) "Selling Rooms Online: The Use of Social Media and Online Travel Agents", *International Journal of Contemporary Hospitality Management* 26(2), 272–92.

Kim, J., Bojanic, D.C. and Warnick, R.B. (2009) "Price Bundling and Travel Product Pricing Practices Used by Online Channels of Distribution", *Journal of Travel Research* 47(4), 403–12.

Kim, W.G., Lim, H. and Brymer, R.A. (2015) "The Effectiveness of Managing Social Media on Hotel Performance", *International Journal of Hospitality Management* 44(1), 165–71.

Kracht, J. and Wang, Y. (2010) "Examining the Tourism Distribution Channel: Evolution and Transformation", *International Journal of Contemporary Hospitality Management* 22(5), 736–57.

Ladhari, R. and Michaud, M. (2015) "eWOM Effects on Hotel Booking Intentions, Attitudes, Trust, and Website Perceptions", *International Journal of Hospitality Management* 46(1), 36–45.

Law, R., Buhalis, D. and Cobanoglu, C. (2014) "Progress on Information and Communication Technologies in Hospitality and Tourism", *International Journal of Contemporary Hospitality Management* 26(5), 727–50.

Lee, H.A., Guillet, B.D. and Law, R. (2013) "An Examination of the Relationship between Online Travel Agents and Hotels: A Case Study of Choice Hotels International and Expedia.com", *Cornell Hospitality Quarterly* 54(1), 95–107.

Ling, L., Dong, Y., Guo, X. and Liang, L. (2015) "Availability Management of Hotel Rooms under Cooperation with Online Travel Agencies", *International Journal of Hospitality Management* 50, 145–52.

Ling, L., Guo, X. and Yang, C. (2014) "Opening the Online Marketplace: An Examination of Hotel Pricing and Travel Agency On-line Distribution of Rooms", *Tourism Management* 45, 234–43.

Lulla, G. (2016) "Why do Travelers Prefer Booking with OTAs?" Available at: www.traveltripper.com/blog/ [Accessed 25 August 2016].

Melián-González, S., Bulchand-Gidumal, J. and López-Valcárcel, B.G. (2013) "Online Customer Reviews of Hotels: As Participation Increases, Better Evaluation is Obtained", *Cornell Hospitality Quarterly* 54(2), 274–83.

Middleton, V.T.C., Fyall, A., Morgan, M., with Ranchhod, A. (2009) *Marketing in Travel and Tourism* (4th edn), Oxford: Elsevier.

Morrison, A.M. (2013) *Marketing and Managing Tourism Destinations*, New York: Routledge.

Myung, E., Lan, L. and Bai, B. (2009) "Channel Relationships with E-wholesalers: Hotel Operators' Perspective", *Journal of Hospitality Marketing and Management* 18(8), 811–28.

Park, S.-Y. and Allen, J.P. (2013) "Responding to Online Reviews: Problem Solving and Engagement in Hotels", *Cornell Hospitality Quarterly* 54(1), 64–73.

Phillips, P., Zigan, K., Santos Silva, M.M. and Schegg, R. (2015) "The Interactive Effects of Online Reviews on the Determinants of Swiss Hotel Performance: A Neural Network Analysis", *Tourism Management* 50, 130–41.

Phocuswright (2016) "Phocuswright's Search, Shop, Buy: The New Digital Funnel". Available at www.phocuswright.com/Travel-Research/Consumer-Trends/Search-Shop-Buy-The-New-Digital-Funnel [Accessed 8 August 2016].

Sigala, M., Christou, E. and Gretzel, U. (Eds.) (2012) *Social Media in Travel, Tourism and Hospitality: Theory, Practice and Cases*, London: Ashgate.

Sotiriadis, M. (2016) "The Potential Contribution and Uses of Twitter by Tourism Businesses and Destinations", *International Journal of Online Marketing* 6(2), 62–77.

Sotiriadis, M., Loedolff, C. and Sarmaniotis, C. (2015) "Tourism E-mediaries: Business Models and Relationships with Providers of Tourism Services". In: Gursoy, D., Saayman, M. & Sotiriadis, M. Eds., *Collaboration in Tourism Businesses and Destinations: A Handbook*, 225–40. Bingley, UK: Emerald Publishing.

Sparks, A.B. and Browning, V. (2011) "The Impact of Online Reviews on Hotel Booking Intentions and Perception of Trust", *Tourism Management* 32(6), 1310–23.

Sparks, A.B., Fung So, K.K. and Bradley, L.G. (2016) "Responding to Negative Online Reviews: The Effects of Hotel Responses on Customer Inferences of Trust and Concern", *Tourism Management* 53(1), 74–85.

Storage Googleapis (2014) "Traveler's Road to Decision Research". Available at: https://storage.googleapis.com/think/docs/2014-travelers-road-to- decision_research_studies.pdf [Accessed 10 September 2016].

Toh, R.S., Raven, P. and DeKay, F. (2011) "Selling Rooms: Hotels vs. Third-party Websites", *Cornell Hospitality Quarterly* 52(2), 181–89.

Travel and Tour World (2016). "News". Available at: www.travelandtourworld.com/news/article/ec-reports-two-third-air-passengers-booked-tickets-online-in-2015/?utm_source [Accessed 19 May 2016].

Wang, L., Law, R., Guillet, B.D., Hung, K. and Chio Fong D.K. (2015) "Impact of Hotel Website Quality on Online Booking Intentions: eTrust as a Mediator", *International Journal of Hospitality Management* 47, 108–15.

Xiaolong Guo, X., Ling, L., Dong, Y. and Liang, L. (2013) "Cooperation Contract in Tourism Supply Chains: The Optimal Pricing Strategy of Hotels for Cooperative Third Party Strategic Websites", *Annals of Tourism Research* 41, 20–41.

Xie, L.K. and Zhang, Z. (2014) "The Business Value of Online Consumer Reviews and Management Response to Hotel Performance", *International Journal of Hospitality Management* 43(1), 1–12.

Ye, Q., Law, R., Gu, B. and Chen, W. (2011) "The Influence of User-Generated Content on Traveler Behavior: An Empirical Investigation on the Effects of e-Word-Of-Mouth to Hotel Online Bookings", *Computers in Human Behavior* 27(2), 634–39.

Zhao, X(R), Wang, L., Guo, X. and Law, R. (2015) "The Influence of Online Reviews to Online Hotel Booking Intentions", *International Journal of Contemporary Hospitality Management* 27(6), 1343–64.

Further reading

Aluri, A., Slevitch, L. and Larzelere, R. (2015) "The Effectiveness of Embedded Social Media on Hotel Websites and the Importance of Social Interactions and Return on Engagement", *International Journal of Contemporary Hospitality Management* 27(4), 670–89. (Role played by embedded SM channels, i.e. on hotel brand websites.)

Blal, I. and Sturman, M.C. (2014) "The Differential Effects of the Quality and Quantity of Online Reviews on Hotel Room Sales", *Cornell Hospitality Quarterly* 55(4), 365–75. (Analysis of the effects of eWOM on sales performance within hotel contextual factors/settings.)

Inversini, A. and Masiero, L. (2014) "Selling Rooms Online: The Use of Social Media and Online Travel Agents", *International Journal of Contemporary Hospitality Management* 26(2), 272–92. (Roles of TEMs and SM in hotel distribution.)

Kim, W.G., Lim, H. and Brymer, R.A. (2015) "The Effectiveness of Managing Social Media on Hotel Performance", *International Journal of Hospitality Management* 44(1), 165–71. (Effects of online reviews on hotel sales and business performance.)

Ling, L., Guo, X. and Yang, C. (2014) "Opening the Online Marketplace: An Examination of Hotel Pricing and Travel Agency On-line Distribution of Rooms", *Tourism Management* 45, 234–43. (Pricing strategy of a hotel for online distribution through cooperation with TEMs.)

Toh, R.S., Raven, P. and DeKay, F. (2011) "Selling Rooms: Hotels vs. Third-party Websites", *Cornell Hospitality Quarterly* 52(2), 181–89. (Suggestions on how hotels can sell rooms by steering customers to their own websites.)

Tranter, A.K, Stuart-Hill, T. and Parker, J. (2009). *An Introduction to Revenue Management for the Hospitality Industry: Principles and Practices for the Real World*, Upper Saddle River, NJ: Prentice Hall. (The key processes and stages of revenue management planning.)

Xie, L.K. and Zhang, Z. (2014) "The Business Value of Online Consumer Reviews and Management Response to Hotel Performance", *International Journal of Hospitality Management* 43(1), 1–12. (Quantifying the economic value of online reviews on hotel performance within the SM context.)

Zhao, X(R), Wang, L., Guo, X. and Law, R. (2015) "The Influence of Online Reviews to Online Hotel Booking Intentions", *International Journal of Contemporary Hospitality Management* 27(6), 1343–64. (Analysis of impacts of online reviews and source features on tourists' online hotel booking intentions.)

40

Impact of peer-to-peer review sites on hospitality consumer behaviors and product service/delivery

Myunghee Mindy Jeon

Introduction

Also known as social media, Web 2.0 applications have significantly affected the tourism and hospitality industry in recent times. Web 2.0 has become a prevailing channel for disseminating and obtaining information for both existing and prospective customers. Prospective customers tend to refer to word-of-mouth posted online before they make purchase decisions, especially for hospitality products/services. Online users tend to share experiences with others through posting reviews, comments, opinions, photos, or videos on social media (Buhalis and Law 2008). These social media or Web 2.0 platforms include a wide range of electronic interactive applications (e.g. social networks, peer-to-peer review sites, blogs, company interactive websites and photo- and video-sharing platforms) that enable online users to interact and collaborate in creating, exchanging, and using information (O'Connor 2008; Sigala et al. 2012). Web 2.0 provides users with an easy way of sharing information and helping strangers, as well as allowing users to actively contribute to online communications (Para-Lopez et al. 2011).

Given the growing influence of peer-to-peer review sites (P2Ps) on customer behavior and service delivery in the hospitality industry, it is a crucial and timely moment to contemplate the important function of P2Ps as a platform for fostering electronic word-of-mouth (eWOM) and to consider their impacts on customer behavior, which will be helpful practices when hospitality marketers implement their marketing strategies. Numerous studies (Bickart and Schindler 2001; Bronner and de Hoog 2011; and Hennig-Thurau et al. 2004) have been conducted in regard to the impact of word-of-mouth (WOM) or electronic word-of-mouth (eWOM) of social media on customer behavior. However, studies have been rare in the area of functions of P2Ps, as a platform of eWOM that has influenced customer behavior, as well as marketers' strategies in the delivery of their products and services in the context of the hospitality industry. Hence, this chapter provides readers with an insight into the current trends for sharing and searching information online, specifically P2Ps; the impact of P2Ps on customers' purchase decision-making processes; and the influence of P2Ps on service/product delivery of hospitality organizations. In addition, implications for hospitality management are suggested as well as ideas for future research.

Literature review

User-generated content (UGC) on peer-to-peer review sites (P2Ps)

Information created and shared by individuals through Web 2.0 in the form of user-generated content (UGC), consumer-generated content (CGC), or consumer-generated media (CGM) refers to any data or media contributed by individual website users. Using the Web 2.0 platform, Internet consumer opinion portals (COP) (Burton and Khammash 2010) have gained rapid popularity among users due to the provision of the function of peer-to-peer reviews and are considered as one of the fastest-growing communication channels among online users (Jeong and Jeon 2008). For example, TripAdvisor.com is the most-used P2P or customer-to-customer (C2C) (Gruen et al. 2006), providing exclusive customer reviews for hospitality organizations, including reviews on lodging, transportation, and dining (Buhalis and Law 2008). According to TripAdvisor, it is the largest travel site, operating in 48 markets worldwide, with 350 million visitors monthly, and has reached a total of 385 million reviews and opinions covering more than 6.6 million accommodations, restaurants, and attractions (TripAdvisor 2016) (see Figure 40.1). Although Tripadvisor.com has been criticized by the press for potential fraudulent posts (Morrison 2012), the growth in its users suggests that P2Ps will continue to play a pivotal role as the core of eWOM in consumers' purchasing decisions (Filieri and McLeay 2013). Similarly, Virtualtourist.com has 1.3 million members with information on 63,000 destinations (Virtualtourist.com 2016) and is connected to Tripadvisor.com so that users can also view Tripadvisor.com reviews on the same site.

Peer-to-peer review functions are also found on the online travel agency (OTA) sites, such as Expedia.com and Booking.com (Melián-González et al. 2013). There are reviews on Booking.com for more than 1 million properties and bookings are made by an average of 1.1 million travelers daily (Booking.com 2016) (see Figure 40.2). Expedia claims to offer reviews on more than 307,000 properties (Expedia.com 2016). Airbnb.com aims at a niche market of the bed and breakfast industry to provide its services in more than 34,000 cities and 191 countries to more

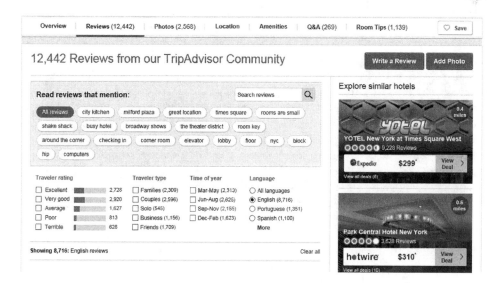

Figure 40.1   Rating details on TripAdvisor.com

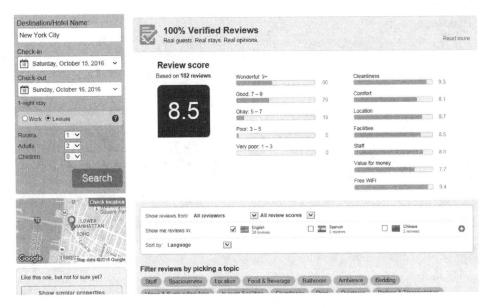

Figure 40.2 Rating details on Booking.com

than 60 million customers (Airbnb.com 2016). Yelp.com is a widely used P2P in the restaurant industry today. Users are encouraged to use a mobile app to write reviews. The site exceeded 108 million reviews and comments by the end of the second quarter of 2016 (Yelp.com 2016). It also provides users with statistics of a service provider by showing its rating patterns during the past several years (see Figure 40.3).

Today, a wide range of new technological applications of Web 2.0 or Travel 2.0, particularly in the tourism industry (Adam et al. 2007), are available to users, including media and content syndication, mash-ups (web application hybrids to make existing data more useful), AJAX (an important front-end web technology that makes websites more responsive and interactive), tagging, wikis, web forums and message boards, customer ratings and evaluation systems, virtual worlds (e.g., Second Life), podcasting, blogs, and online videos (or vlogs) (Schmallegger and Carson 2008; Xiang and Gretzel 2010). Owing to updated, advanced technologies, P2Ps encourage and better assist users to post and share their travel-related experiences, comments, opinions, and personal thoughts to help others (Pan et al. 2007; Xiang and Gretzel 2010). Specifically, frequently updated mobile phone applications for social network services have encouraged users to become actively involved in sharing information and be connected to not only friends or individuals in social groups, but also the general public. For instance, a social networking mobile community application that facilitates group communication functions as a P2P, where users share their experiences of products/services related to a travel destination; an example is "Band," which originates in South Korea and has now become popular and is available free of charge in 178 countries, including the U.S. (E27.co, 2015). Users can create separate spaces in Band, depending upon the purpose of a group, to exchange information in real time (EtNews.com 2014). Travel destination Bands typically have a large number of members and share very useful information regarding the destination, including accommodation, restaurants, transportation, shopping, entertainment, and activities.

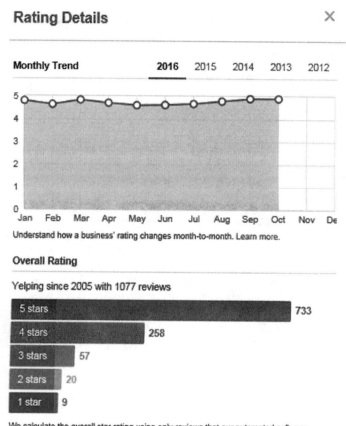

Rating Details   ✕

Monthly Trend   **2016**   2015   2014   2013   2012

Understand how a business' rating changes month-to-month. Learn more.

Overall Rating

Yelping since 2005 with 1077 reviews

5 stars 733
4 stars 258
3 stars ... 57
2 stars . 20
1 star . 9

We calculate the overall star rating using only reviews that our automated software

Figure 40.3   Rating details on Yelp.com

eWOM

Typically, word-of-mouth (WOM) spread on the web is referred to as electronic word-of-mouth (eWOM) (Bronner and de Hoog, 2011) and it is often fostered on peer-to-peer review sites (P2Ps). eWOM is defined as "all informal communications directed at customers through Internet-based technology related to the usage or characteristics of particular goods and services, or their sellers" (Litvin et al. 2008: 461) or as "any positive or negative statement made by potential, actual, or former customers about a product or company, which is made available to a multitude of people and institutions via the Internet" (Hennig-Thurau et al. 2004: 39). Research has shown that, similar to conventional WOM, eWOM may have higher credibility, empathy, and relevance to customers than marketer-created sources of information online (Bickart and Schindler 2001; Gretzel and Yoo 2008). Specifically, P2Ps have huge potential as eWOM sources, since they allow UGC where individuals post content about products and services that can be shared with the general public (Herrero et al. 2015).

The information posted by online users on P2Ps and companies' interactive websites may affect the behaviors of other individuals as a form of eWOM (Allsop et al. 2007; Litvin et al.

2008; Steffes and Burgee 2009). It is often considered that UGC provides users with frank opinions or experiences, whether they are satisfied or dissatisfied with certain products or services. Therefore, online reviews on P2Ps or other social media are considered as online word-of-mouth (Filieri and McLeay 2013), which has been gaining a powerful impact on prospective customers' decision-making processes. This is true, especially with hospitality and travel-related products and services, due to their major distinctive characteristics derived from intangibility, perishability, variability, and inseparability (Kotler et al. 2010). Due to their uncertainty of product quality and customer satisfaction, prospective customers often seek guidance before they make purchase decisions. Web 2.0 applications offering the function of peer-to-peer communication seem to also be actively utilized by marketers to create positive images and to nurture eWOM for tourist destinations and business organizations (Xiang and Gretzel 2010).

Motivation of creating UGC on peer-to-peer review sites (P2Ps)

To build a lasting relationship with customers, business organizations need to understand and satisfy the needs of their customers. Gaining insights into the motivations and decision-making process of customers will be helpful to understand customers' participatory behaviors on P2Ps (Kontu and Vecchi 2014). Numerous studies have focused on the motivations of participating in online communities, whether as a viewer or an online poster, such as personal, social benefit, social concern, function, quality assurance, and entertainment (Dholakia et al. 2004; Gretzel and Yoo 2008; Hennig-Thurau et al. 2004; Huang et al. 2007; Wang and Fesenmaier 2004). According to an empirical study measuring motivations of participants to post reviews, users participating in P2Ps rather than marketer-oriented review sites (e.g. Expedia.com or Hotels. com) or other sites were mainly discerned those with a low–medium level of self-directed (or self-oriented reason, such as rewards or retaliation) motivation; a high helping-others motivation; a high social-benefits motivation; a low customer-empowerment motivation; or a low help-ing-companies motivation (Bronner and de Hoog 2011). Based upon previous studies and the literature on user motivation to post reviews on P2Ps, user motivations for posting reviews on P2Ps can be categorized into two types:

- Self-construal value motivation
- Altruistic motivation

Self-construal value motivation

Often, P2Ps, such as Tripadvisor.com or Yelp.com, display users' login ID and the level of their contribution to the site by indicating the total number of reviews posted. These active partici-pants may be motivated by the numeric indicator of their level of contribution to post valuable reviews on the site. Indeed, these active participants will try to continue to maintain their con-tributions to the site because site visitors will acknowledge their contributions. Furthermore, it has become a norm for online users that posters will create content based upon truthful facts because they know it will result in responsible consequences. Such deep-rooted trust with P2Ps is not questioned (Gretzel 2006). A study of food service operators also shows that the self-construal value of customers was a salient driver of eWOM intentions rather than service quality value (Kim et al. 2015).

According to social facilitation theory, awareness of the social aspect—mere presence or absence of peers—will affect behaviors of other customers (Plantania and Moran 2001). In other words, an individual's behavior is often affected by the presence of others and the presence of others increases physiological arousal that, in turn, leads to increased performance when the task is easy or familiar (Zajonc 1965). This can be applied to online social spaces. Those who create UGC on social media post opinions derived from not only their self-construal value, but also from having an awareness of the presence of other online users, wanting their good deeds to be acknowledged by others. Ajzen (2002) also claims that having control of information in an information age strengthens self-efficacy or a sense of prestige, and such tendencies influence the participation behavior of users. People who share their knowledge and information on P2Ps do not know their audiences, but still consider making contributions to help others (Chen 2006). Anonymity does not dilute posters' self-efficacy motivated intentions to contribute to sharing information on P2Ps.

Altruistic motivation

Online users create, initiate, and circulate information on P2Ps with various sources to educate each other about products, brands, services, and other related issues (Blackshaw and Nazzaro 2006). Users feel they should repay the benefit previously received from information posted by others. It is a major motivation for them to collaboratively participate and contribute in the P2Ps (Wang and Fesenmaier 2004). Chae and Ko's (2016) study found that the motivation for participating in online communities, such as P2Ps, by posting reviews, is positively related to customer social participation, specifically using mobile devices which encourage users to set the notification function for information alert, enabling them to actively take part in social media (Chae and Ko 2016). Availability of real-time information exchange with other people using mobile devices appears to influence user behavior and participation activities online (Hennig-Thurau et al. 2002). Users write online reviews to share their own experiences with product/services and describe their levels of satisfaction to help other users (Yoo and Gretzel 2008). In general, social media users appear to possess high levels of self-efficacy and tend to feel elevated as well as obtaining altruistic pleasure from providing information that could help others (Chae and Ko 2016). Users seem to contribute to sharing information because it is enjoyable to some extent to help others and they do not seem to expect reciprocity from others (Wasko and Faraj 2005). As such, users use numerous methods of information dissemination and are most active on P2Ps. Consequently, users' altruistic intentions to help others, coupled with technology advancement, fosters their motivation to participate in online communities, where information is shared among participants.

Peer-to-peer review sites and consumer behavior

Information adoption from peer-to-peer review sites

It is believed that the credible information source of P2Ps influences consumer behavior. An empirical study found consumer behaviors to be influenced by the value of information, including the credibility of sources and degree of similarity between the readers and the posters of comments on P2Ps (Herrero et al. 2015). Another study on customers' use of eWOM found that written comments are mainly taken into consideration rather than the numeric ratings on Tripadvisor.com when making decisions to select their accommodation (Gretzel and Yoo 2008). The same study reported that three-quarters of travelers appear to consider online customer reviews as an information source when planning their trips. This confirms that information quality and credible content are influential for prospective customers when they seek online guidance from P2Ps. In the lodging sector, it has also been found that online opinions posted by other customers are one of the most important variables in prospective customers' accommodatin choice (Melián-González et al. 2013; Park et al. 2007; Ye et al. 2011). An experimental study also found that eWOM via P2Ps influences customers' product choices (Senecal and Nantel 2004).

It has been widely discussed that information on products/services posted on P2Ps gains greater credibility and is more likely to evoke empathy with customers than information distributed on marketer-designed websites (Bickart and Schindler 2001) because customers respond more sensitively to peers' evaluations and reviews than those of marketers (Yoo and Gretzel 2008). A study on customers' information adoption with regard to accommodation products found that customers tend to adopt information from P2Ps because they consider that information coming from real customers is an accurate evaluation of accommodation (Filieri and McLeay 2013). Findings from the same study revealed that some information quality dimensions are considered more important than others to predict prospective customers' adoption of information, such as information accuracy—a key element of UGC in P2Ps. Furthermore, customers perceive UGC on P2Ps and hotel interactive websites as more credible because it is generated by peers who may be similar to them in their needs and preferences (Herrero et al. 2015). It is believed that information adoption occurs when a prospective customer reviews postings on P2Ps, and the customer may choose to adopt the information received from the site in his/her decision-making process (Cheung et al. 2008; Sussman and Siegal 2003). Users of P2Ps understand that the exchange of information may develop an affective association with others who may be prospective customers, which may influence their loyalty intentions toward the online site and the product or the service involved in sharing on the site (Gruen et al. 2006).

E-subjective norms on peer-to-peer review sites

Subjective norms often influence an individual's normative beliefs and the evaluation of its consequences. Subject norm (SN) refers to the perceived expectations of specific referent individuals, such as family, relatives, friends, or social groups, and an individual's motivations to comply with their expectations (Fishbein and Ajzen 1975). Similarly, perceived expectations of online community members can motivate an individual's behavior to comply with these expectations in online environments. Social interactions taking place in online communities has nurtured *e-subjective norms* among users. In other words, not only the mere presence of customers' online sites, but also what others might have said or suggested is likely to influence the behaviors of existing and potential customers when making purchse decisions. It is not surprising to see results from a study revealing that customers' buying intentions appear to increase as the quality and the quantity of online reviews increase (Park et al. 2007). A study based on an experimental design using hotels found that negative eWOM generated negative customer attitudes toward hotels and concluded that repetition of negative eWOM can be highly damaging (Vermeulen and Seegers 2009). The range of referent for *e-subjective norm* is not limited to customers' close social groups, including family and friends, but is widely expanded to the general public on online sites. Consequently, it is strongly believed that customer behavior is influenced by the opinions and experiences of other people posting online (MacKay and Vogt 2012).

Peer-to-peer review sites and delivery of products or services

Positive eWOM as a source of advertisement for marketers

Information provided on peer-to-peer review sites (P2Ps) can also be a powerful source of advertisement for hospitality organizations. eWOM posted on P2Ps can help hospitality organizations when continuously monitored for both positive and negative content about their services and delivery. Although eWOM cannot be directly controlled by hospitality organizations in regard to their product, service, and delivery, they should try to follow the content and address it appropriately, in particular, when it is incorrectly or negatively posted on P2Ps (Herrero et al. 2015). Marketers in the hospitality and tourism industries have also recognized the importance of positive eWOM and include it on their company websites in the form of edited customer testimonials (Melián-González et al. 2013). From the management perspective, the Internet is a tool through which to directly interact with customers and has functions of information sharing among customers, which is far more effective than a unilateral method of online advertisement (Kim and Ko 2012).

Given the increased engagement of travelers in P2Ps and other social media (Litvin et al. 2008), marketers in the hospitality and tourism industries may perceive this phenomenon as a challenge (Xiang and Gretzel 2010). Gruen et al. (2006) discuss that positive eWOM on P2Ps significantly impacts the perceived overall value of the organization's offerings and has a direct relationship with loyalty intentions. Furthermore, hospitality organizations may utilize the P2Ps or other related social media as a recruiting opportunity for employees. As Ladkin and Buhalis (2016) suggest, eWOM of satisfactory service encounters with employees at a hospitality organization shared on P2Ps can create positive impressions about the organization, and it may provide the company with potential recruiting opportunities as an employees' choice.

Negative eWOM on P2Ps as an opportunity for marketers

Negative eWOM cases are also a valuable information source to help marketers improve their products and services (Melián-González et al. 2013). The motivation of users posting negative eWOM is mainly to warn others, and is a way to release negative emotions and practise their consumer rights (Bronner and de Hoog, 2011). Also, the anonymity afforded by the majority of P2Ps allows a greater degree of freedom and, in turn, a greater proposition of negative eWOM (Schindler and Bickart 2005). Unlike conventional WOM, which occurs some time after the event, eWOM is frequently initiated when the service is still taking place or shortly afterward and often there is little time for posters to have negative or unsatisfied feelings mitigated before they post (Melián-González et al. 2013). Melián-González et al. (2013) found that hotels with fewer online peer reviews seem to receive more negative reviews and typically the first reviews are worse than the later ones. Thus, by obtaining more reviews from customers, hotels will offset the damaging effects of negative eWOM and approach their real average score. For this reason, companies should encourage all customers to post reviews on P2Ps or companies' interactive websites to share their positive experiences with prospective customers in order to foster positive eWOM (Godes and Mayzlin 2009; Herrero et al. 2015).

A study of restaurants in London found that organizations can redirect negative situations through certain actions, such as keeping track of customers' feedback and reacting to unfavorable reviews with an apology or offering some type of compensation (Pantelidis 2010). It is believed that the most satisfied and most unsatisfied customers are more likely to generate reviews on P2Ps than those who are neutral (Bansal and Voyer 2000; Litvin et al. 2008), although most customers silently switch suppliers or share negative WOM or eWOM rather than make complaints to service providers (Melián-González et al. 2013). Therefore, hospitality organizations should find ways to remedy service shortcomings that negatively affect eWOM. Management should be committed to managing complaints, which is an important factor in meeting the demands of customers. Ekiz and Arasli (2007) argue that how negative eWOM is handled (and whether it is turned into opportunities to meet customer demand) depends on the commitment and interpersonal skills of management, and even job satisfaction within the company. By continually and diligently monitoring negative eWOM on P2Ps and other social media, marketers will be able to successfully communicate with unsatisfied customers and redress their damaged reputation in the delivery of products and services that they offer.

Managerial implications

Owing to the nature of customer participation on social media, P2Ps have become a challenge for marketers as well as a path to success for service industries (Chae and Ko 2016). Given the influence of P2P functions on customers' decision-making processes and behaviors (Ba and Pavlou 2002), hospitality marketers are expected to develop effective strategies to adequately manage eWOM about their products and services where they are actively present on P2Ps and other social media (Herrero et al. 2015). Most P2Ps offer various UGC about hospitality products or services using specific numerals or symbols (i.e. stars are used on TripAdvisor) and open-text comments. This function enables hospitality organizations to monitor P2Ps to analyze UGC and obtain information about customers' perceptions of their service, experiences, and reactions (Chen and Xie 2008; Pantelidis 2010). Furthermore, they can also examine user-generated evaluations about their competitors (Melián-González et al. 2013).

Increased UGC knowledge of influence on customers' decision-making processes will help hospitality and tourism marketers understand that different UGC information dimensions will differently impact customers' purchase decisions (Filieri and McLeay 2013). Management of hospitality and tourism organizations may consider customers' voices to become co-marketers (Sigala et al. 2012) because reviews posted on P2Ps influence other travelers' decisions more strongly than traditional marketing communications (Bickart and Schindler 2001). Unlike corporate interactive websites managed differently by administrators (Rowley 2001), P2Ps are consumer-centric platforms that function as open communities formed by millions of users. These platforms can be tourism-specific (e.g. TripAdvisor.com) or generic (e.g. Yellowbot.com). P2Ps may be useful to identify the strengths and weaknesses of an organization as perceived by users and opinion leaders in a non-biased environment. Therefore, marketers could use these media as a tool for market research, surveying the content to detect both negative and positive recurring comments (Herrero et al. 2015) and utilize these platforms as a communication tool by encouraging users to post content (Xiang and Gretzel, 2010). Ultimately, P2Ps are considered as an emerging form of a bottom-up evaluation system of the market because users are willing to trust their peers' opinions more than those of marketers (Filieri and McLeay 2013).

Conclusions

Summary

P2Ps as social media platforms, such as TripAdvisor.com or Yelp.com, provide customers with space to share their thoughts, comments, opinions, and reviews of products by facilitating active communication among individuals, and between business organizations and individuals (Kwok and Yu 2013; Xiang and Gretzel 2010). Often, those who post comments on P2Ps are motivated to share their product/service or providers' experiences, based upon their self-efficacy value and altruistic intentions. Meanwhile, customers reading reviews on P2Ps are motivated to adopt this information, based upon information quality and accuracy as well as influence of eWOM. Customers reading information posted on P2Ps seem to ascribe greater credibility to other customers' reviews than information distributed by marketers

(Bickart and Schindler 2001). They do not seem to question the truthfulness of information posted on P2Ps and are willing to act in line with recommendations as they are suggested by an anonymous majority online. Typically, P2Ps tend to function as a platform to foster eWOM. Positive eWOM serves as advertisements or promotional opportunities, while negative eWOM is also considered valuable to help marketers improve their products/services and delivery (Melián-González et al. 2013). Consequently, marketers may utilize P2Ps as a communication tool with their customers because P2Ps are an impactful channel of customer communication and a prevailing evaluation system today, due to their profound credibility in the eyes of customers within the hospitality and tourism industry. For instance, hospitality management may want to visit P2Ps, such as TripAdvisor.com or Booking.com for the hotel industry, and Yelp.com for the restaurant industry, on a regular basis to ensure that posted comments are addressed appropriately to mitigate potential damage caused by negative eWOM.

Suggestions for future study

Although customer reviews posted on P2Ps have grown in importance for tourism businesses, most studies have examined the effects of the content of reviews, named eWOM, and often negative reviews (Melián-González et al. 2013). Facilitating voluntary participation enhances convenience in the process of acquiring market information and reduces the costs involved in creating group intelligence, which is considered a new channel of marketing opportunities (Chae and Ko 2016). Studies shedding light on roles for P2Ps, as a platform in support of fostering eWOM in the delivery of products and services, are strongly encouraged and will be extremely beneficial for hospitality marketers to better understand customer behavior.

References

Adam, J., Cobos, X., and Liu, S. (2007). *Travel 2.0: Trends in Industry Awareness and Adoption*, New York: New York University and PhoCusWright Inc.

Airbnb.com (2016). *About us*. Retrieved from www.airbnb.com/about/about-us

Ajzen, I. (2002). "Perceived behavioral control, self-efficacy, locus of control, and the Theory of Planned Behavior," *Journal of Applied Social Psychology*, 32, 665–683.

Allsop, D.T., Bassett, B.R., and Hoskins, J.A. (2007). "Word-of-mouth research: Principles and applications," *Journal of Advertising Research*, 17(4), 398–411.

Ba, S., and Pavlou, P.A. (2002). "Evidence of the effect of trust building technology in electronic markets: Price, premiums and buyer behaviors," *MIS Quarterly*, 26 (3), 243–268.

Bansal, H.D., and Voyer, P.A. (2000). "Word of mouth processes within a services purchase decision context," *Journal of Service Research*, 3(2), 166–177.

Bickart, B., and Schindler, R.M. (2001). "Internet forums as influential sources of consumer information," *Journal of Interactive Marketing*, 15(3), 31–40.

Blackshaw, P., and Nazzaro, M. (2006). "Consumer-Generated Media (CGM) 101: Word-of-Mouth in the Age of the Web fortified Consumer (2nd Ed.)." *A Nielsen Buzz Metrics White Paper*. Retrieved on Aug. 26, 2016 from www.nielsen-online.com/downloads/us/buzz/nbzm_wp_CGM101.pdf

Booking.com (2016). *About booking.com*. Retrieved on Aug. 12, 2016 from www.booking.com/content/about. ko.html?label=gen173nr-1DCAEoggJCAlhYSDNiBW5vcmVmcgV1c19rc4gBAZgBF7gBBsgBDtgBA-gBAagCAw;sid=3832a0677d80f611cd07a1933042a351;dcid=1

Bronner, A.E., and de Hoog, R. (2011). "Vacationers and eWOM: Who posts, and why, where and what?" *Journal of Travel Research*, 50, 15–26.

Buhalis, D., and Law, R. (2008). "Progress in tourism management: Twenty years on and 10 years after the Internet: The state of eTourism research." *Tourism Management*, 29(4), 609–623.

Burton, J., and Khammash, M. (2010). "Why do people read reviews posted on customer-opinion portals?" *Journal of Marketing Management*, 26 (3–4), 230–255.

Chae, H., and Ko, E. (2016). "Customer social participation in the social networking services and its impact upon the customer equity of global fashion brands," *Journal of Business Research*, 69, 3804–3812.

Chen, C. (2006). "Identifying significant factors influencing consumer trust in an online travel site," *Information Technology & Tourism*, 8, 197–214.

Chen, Y., and Xie, J. (2008). "Online consumer review: Word-of-mouth as a new element of marketing communication mix," *Management Science*, 54(3), 477–491.

Cheung, C.K., Lee, M., and Rabjhon, N. (2008). "The impact of e-WOM: The adoption of online opinions in online customer communities," *Internet Research*, 18(3), 229–247.

Dholakia, U.M., Bagozzi, R.P., and Klein Pearo, L. (2004). "A social influence model of consumer participation in network and small-group-based virtual communities," *International Journal of Research in Marketing*, 21, 241–263.

Ekiz, E.H., and Arasli, H. (2007). "Measuring the impacts of organizational responses: Case of Northern Cyprus hotels," *Managing Global Transitions* 5(3), 271–287.

EtNews.com. (2014). *Local SNS regains the domestic market: Kakao Story and Band.* Retrieved on Aug. 24, 2016 from www.etnews.com/news/article.html?id=20140707000358

Expedia, Inc. (2016). *Overview.* Retrieved on Aug. 16, 2016 from www.expediainc.com/about/

E27.co. (2015, Oct.). *South Korean mobile app band hits 50 million downloads.* Retrieved on Aug. 23, 2016 from https://e27.co/south-korean-mobile-app-band-hits-50-million-downloads-20151001/

Filieri, R., and McLeay, F. (2013). "E-WOM and accommodation: An analysis of the factors that influence travelers' adoption of information from online reviews," *Journal of Travel Research*, 53(1), 44–57.

Fishbein, M., and Ajzen, I. (1975). *Belief, Attitude, Intention and Behavior: An Introduction to Theory and Research.* Reading, MA: Addison-Wesley.

Godes, D., and Mayzlin, D. (2009). "Firm-created word-of-mouth communication: Evidence from a field study," *Marketing Science*, 28(4), 721–739.

Gretzel, U. (2006). "Consumer generated content: Trends and implications for branding," *E-Review of Tourism Research*, 4(3), 9–11.

Gretzel, U., and Yoo, K. (2008). "Use and impact of online travel reviews," In P. O'Connor, W. Hopken & U. Gretzel (Eds.), *Information and Communication Technologies in Tourism 2008* (pp. 35–46). Vienna, Austria: Springer-Verlag Wien.

Gruen, T.W., Osmonbekow, T., and Czaplewski, A.J. (2006). "eWOM: The impact of customer-to-customer online know-how exchange on customer value and loyalty," *Journal of Business Research*, 59(4), 449–456.

Hennig-Thurau, T., Gwinner, K.P., and Gremler, D.D. (2002). "Understanding relationship marketing outcomes: An integration of relational benefits and relationship quality," *Journal of Services Research*, 4(3), 230–247.

Hennig-Thurau, T., Gwinner, K.P., Walsh, G., and Gremler, D.D. (2004), "Electronic word-of-mouth via consumer-opinion platforms: What motivates consumers to articulate themselves on the Internet?" *Journal of Interactive Marketing*, 18(1), 38–52.

Herrero, A., San Martin, H., and Hernandez, J. (2015) "How online search behavior is influenced by user-generated content on review websites and hotel interactive websites," *International Journal of Contemporary Hospitality Management*, 27(7), 1573–1597.

Huang, L.S., Chou, Y.J., and Lan, I.T. (2007). "Effects of perceived risk, message types, and reading motives on the acceptance and transmission of electronic word-of-mouth communication," *Contemporary Management Research*, 3(4), 299–312.

Jeong, M., and Jeon, M. (2008). "Customer reviews of hotel experiences through consumer generate media (CGM)," *Journal of Hospitality & Leisure Marketing*, 17(1–2), 121–138.

Kim, A., and Ko, E. (2012). "Do social media marketing activities enhance customer equity? An empirical study of luxury fashion brand," *Journal of Business Research*, 65(10), 1480–1486.

Kim, D., Jang, S.C., and Adler, H. (2015) "What drives café customers to spread eWOM?: Examining self-relevant value, quality value, and opinion leadership," *International Journal of Contemporary Hospitality Management*, 27(2), 261–282.

Kontu, H., and Vecchi, A. (2014). "Why all that noise: Assessing the strategic value of social media for fashion brands," *Journal of Global Fashion Marketing*, 5(3), 235–250.

Kotler, P., Bowen, J., and Makens, J. (2010). *Marketing for Hospitality and Tourism* (5th ed.), Upper Saddle River, NJ: Prentice Hall.

Kwok, L. and Yu, B. (2013). "Spreading social media messages on Facebook: An analysis of restaurant business-to-consumer communications," *Cornell Hospitality Quarterly*, 54(1), 84–94.

Ladkin, A., and Buhalis, D. (2016) "Online and social media recruitment: Hospitality employer and pro-spective employee considerations," *International Journal of Contemporary Hospitality Management*, 28(2), 327–345.

Litvin, S.W., Goldsmith, R.E., and Pan, B. (2008). "Electronic word-of-mouth in hospitality and tourism management," *Tourism Management*, 29(3), 458–468.

MacKay, K., and Vogt, C. (2012), "Information technology in everyday and vacation contexts," *Annals of Tourism Research*, 39(3), 1380–1401.

Melián-González, S., Bulchand-Gidumal, J., and López-Valcárcel, B. (2013) "Online customer reviews of hotels: As participation increases, better evaluation is obtained," *Cornell Hospitality Quarterly*, 54(3) 274–283.

Morrison, S. (2012, Jan. 31). "TripAdvisor under fire for 'real traveler' contribution claim." *The Guardian*. Retrieved on Aug. 29, 2015 from www.theguardian.com/media/2012/feb/01/tripadvisor-criticise-honest-contribution-claim

O'Connor, P. (2008). "User generated content and travel: A case study of TripAdvisor.com." In W. Höpken and U. Gretzel (eds.), *Information and Communication Technologies in Tourism 2008* (pp. 47–58). Wien, Austria: Springer.

Pan, B., MacLaurin, T., and Crotts, J.C. (2007). "Travel blogs and the implications for destination marketing," *Journal of Travel Research*, 46(1), 35–45.

Pantelidis, I.S. (2010) "Electronic meal experience: A content analysis of online restaurant comments," *Cornell Hospitality Quarterly*, 51(4), 483–491.

Para-Lopez, E., Bulchand-Gidumal, J., Gutierrez-Tano, D., and Diaz-Armas, R. (2011). "Intentions to use social media in organizing and taking vacation trips," *Computers in Human Behavior*, 27, 640–654.

Park, D.H., Lee, J., and Han, I. (2007). "The effect of online consumer reviews on consumer purchas-ing intention: The moderating role of involvement," *International Journal of Electronic Commerce*, 11(4), 125–148.

Plantania, J., and Moran, G.P. (2001). "Social facilitation as a function of the mere presence of others," *Journal of Social Psychology*, 141(2), 190–197.

Rowley, J. (2001). "Remodeling marketing communications in an Internet environment," *Internet Research*, 11(3), 203–212.

Schindler, R.M., and Bickart, B. (2005). "Published word of mouth: Referable, consumer-generated infor-mation on the internet," In C.P. Haugtvedt, K.A. Machleit, and R.F. Yalch (eds.), *Online Consumer Psychology: Understanding and Influencing Consumer Behavior in the Virtual World* (35–61). Hillsdale, MI: Lawrence Erlbaum Associates.

Schmallegger, D., and Carson, D. (2008). "Blogs in tourism: Changing approaches to information exchange, *Journal of Vacation Marketing*, 14, 99–110.

Senecal, S., and Nantel, J. (2004). "The influence of online product recommendations on consumers' onlince choices," *Journal of Retailing*, 80(2), 159–169.

Sigala, M., Christou, E., and Gretzel, U. (2012). *Social Media in Travel, Tourism and Hospitality: Theory, Practice and Cases*. Surrey, UK: Ashgate.

Steffes, E.M., and Burgee, L.E. (2009). "Social ties and online word of mouth," *Internet Research*, 19(1), 42–59.

Sussman, S.W., and Siegal, W.S. (2003). "Informational influence in organizations: An integrated approach to knowledge adoption," *Informational Systems Research*, 14(1), 47–65.

TripAdvisor (2016). *About TripAdvisor*. Retrieved on Aug. 12, 2016 from www.tripadvisor.com/PressCenter-c6-About_Us.html

Vermeulen, I.E., and Seegers, D. (2009). "Tried and tested: The impact of online hotel reviews on consumer consideration," *Tourism Management*, 30, 123–127.

Virtualtourist.com (2016). *Get travel advice from the people behind the places*. Retrieved on Sept. 2, 2016 from www.virtualtourist.com

Wang, Y., and Fesenmaier, D.R. (2004). "Modeling participation in an online travel community," *Journal of Travel Research*, 42, 261–270.

Wasko, M., and Faraj, S. (2005). "Why should I share? Examining social capital and knowledge contribution in electronic networks of practice," *MIS Quarterly*, 29(1), 35–57.

Xiang, Z., and Gretzel, U. (2010). "Role of social media in online travel information search," *Tourism Management*, 31, 179–88.

Ye, Q., Law, R., Gu, B., and Chen, W. (2011). "The influence of user generated content on traveler behav-ior: An empirical investigation on the effects of e-word-of-mouth to hotel online bookings," *Computers in Human Behavior*, 27(2), 634–639.

Yelp.com. (2016). *About us*. Retrieved on Sept. 28, 2016 from www.yelp.com/about

Yoo, K.H., and Gretzel, U. (2008). "The influence of perceived credibility on preferences for recommender systems as sources of advice," *Journal of Information Technology & Tourism*, 10(2), 133–146.

Zajonc, R.B. (1965). "Social facilitation," *Science*, 149, 269–274.

Further reading

Ajzen, I., and Fishbein, M. (1980). *Understanding Attitudes and Predicting Social Behavior*. Englewood Cliffs, NJ: Prentice Hall. (Explains the "Theory of Reasoned Action" model and applies the model to various cases.)

Cheng, S., Lam, T., and Hsu, C.H.C. (2006). "Negative word of mouth communication intention: An application of the Theory of Planned Behavior," *Journal of Hospitality & Tourism Research*, 30(1), 95–116. (Investigates the antecedents of negative WOM communication intention adopting the Theory of Planned Behavior.)

Murray, K.B. (1991). "A test of services marketing theory: Consumer information acquisition activities," *Journal of Marketing*, 55(1), 10–25. (Explores information needs of service consumers in the purchase decision-making process.)

Ye, Q., Law, R., and Gu, B. (2009). "The impact of online user reviews on hotel room sales," *International Journal of Hospitality Management*, 28, 180–182. (Empirically examines impacts of online consumer-generated reviews on hotel room sales.)

41

Social media and hospitality marketing

María Pilar Martínez-Ruiz, Isabel Llodrà-Riera and
Ana Isabel Jiménez-Zarco

Introduction

In recent years, researchers and companies have increasingly turned their attention to terms such as Web 2.0 and social media. Web 2.0 is the term used for describing those online platforms that put their users at the center of attention and facilitate the creation and dissemination of user-generated content. Applications rooted in Web 2.0 learn from their users, using a participatory architecture to not only improve the software interface, but also to extend the richness of the shared data (O'Reilly 2005). According to O'Reilly (2005), the principal features of Web 2.0 are: (1) services with cost-effective scalability; (2) control over unique, hard-to-recreate data sources that become richer as more people use them; (3) trusting users as co-developers; (4) harnessing collective intelligence; (5) leveraging the long tail through customer self-service; (6) software that transcends a single device; and (7) lightweight user interfaces, development models and business models.

Mangold and Faulds (2009) explain that the emergence of Internet-based social media has made it possible for one person to communicate with a lot of people about products and the companies that provide them. Thus, the impact of consumer-to-consumer communications has been greatly magnified in the marketplace. These authors argue that social media is a hybrid element of the promotional mix: in a traditional sense, it enables companies to talk to their customers, while in a nontraditional sense, it allows customers to talk directly to one another. Consumers can use a variety of Internet-based tools – "post," "tag," "digg," or "blog," and so forth – to create, circulate, and utilize numerous information sources, with the intent of educating each other about products, brands, services, and issues (Blackshaw and Nazzaro 2006).

The tourism and hospitality industry has changed significantly in the wake of Web 2.0 and social media. In this new, interactive environment, consumers can easily share and access information and feedback via eWOM (electronic word-of-mouth; Litvin et al. 2008). Indeed, online reviews, blogs, and other social media offer companies a way to enrich travel experiences at a relatively low cost, while also improving the comparison process and consumers' trust in firms' offers (Papathanassis and Buhalis 2007). Thus, hospitality and tourism marketers must understand that their guests are going online in increasing numbers and are being exposed to the many sites devoted to the selling or discussion of travel. For this reason, tourism marketers should take the lead in understanding and utilizing these emerging technologies, rather than being driven to simply adopt the strategies of their competitors (Litvin et al. 2008).

The proliferation of Web 2.0 has also engendered the development of social networking, which has emerged as a tool for the business workplace (Noti 2013), including the tourism industry (Buhalis and Law 2008). According to Boyd and Ellison (2007), social network sites (SNSs) are web-based services that enable individuals to construct a public or semi-public profile within a bounded system, construct a list of other users with whom they share a connection, and traverse lists of such connections within the system. SNSs represent a unique offering, allowing individuals to not only meet strangers, but also delineate and display their social networks. Such sites are structured as personal (or "egocentric") networks, with individuals at the center of their own community. According to Wellman (1988), this network concept more accurately mirrors unmediated social structures.

The introduction of SNS features has induced a new organizational framework for online communities (Boyd and Ellison 2007), which can extend from the general level (e.g., Web 2.0, social media, social network sites) to the concrete level (e.g., newsletters, chats, groups, blogs). Through these online platforms, customers can share and spread knowledge, experiences and opinions. As a consequence, users can easily and rapidly express their complaints about companies' offerings, which can significantly affect the image of said companies. For example, many consumers use eWOM to disseminate complaints about brands via the web, chats and forums (Gelb and Sundaram 2002), which other consumers then use to reduce perceived risks and uncertainty before making their purchases (Harrison-Walker 2001). However, tourists are also publishing their photos, trips and experiences, which serves to influence other travelers (WTTC 2011). In sum, social media plays a significant role in many aspects of tourism, especially in information search and decision-making behaviors, tourism promotion, and determining the best practices for interacting with consumers. Given these trends, it is not surprising that many countries acknowledge and rely on the great potential of social media to promote their tourism industries.

In light of these developments, the study of social media in the field of tourism and hospitality has gained increasing relevance. Thus, this chapter aims to help scholars by identifying the most prevalent lines of research in the existing literature and then highlighting valuable areas of future study. In the following section, we will explore the concept of social media as it applies to tourism and hospitality management, which is key to understanding the existing research in this area.

Social media conceptualization

Due to the rapid evolution of the Internet, it is difficult to maintain a consensus about the meaning and nature of social media. As Zeng and Gerritsen (2014) elucidate in their considerable discussion of social media, the term's definition is continually morphing as its uses change and expand.

The work of Cohen (2011) is pivotal in this respect. Having summarized thirty different definitions of social media, Cohen's (2011) efforts allowed Zeng and Gerritsen (2014) to identify some important and relatively stable characteristics of social media. In particular, these authors observed how social media: (a) depend on information technology since they are online tools, applications, platforms and media; (b) constitute peer-to-peer communication channels, which enables interactive web content creation, collaboration and exchange by participants and the public; and (3) link users across platforms to form a virtual community and thereby affect people's behaviors and real-life circumstances.

Building on these efforts, authors such as Carr and Hayes (2015) have striven to overcome the lack of a commonly accepted definition of social media, both functionally and theoretically. Specifically, these authors reviewed extant definitions of social media and their subcategories (e.g., social network sites) from various disciplines (e.g., public relations, information technology, management scholarship) and the popular press. On this basis, they developed a definition of social media that was precise enough to embody these technologies yet robust enough to remain applicable for future decades. Namely, Carr and Hayes (2015: 8) assert that:

> social media are Internet-based channels that allow users to opportunistically interact and selectively self-present, either in real-time or asynchronously, with both broad and narrow audiences who derive value from user-generated content and the perception of interaction with others.

These characteristics illuminate the particular dynamism and development enabled by social media in the hospitality industry. With Web 2.0, (e)WOM is increasingly able to influence our decision-making process, such that networking is currently transforming the relationships between supply and demand (Buonamano et al. 2013). In the hospitality industry, social media represent innumerable opportunities for companies to not only acquire information efficiently, but also to generate their own content and communicate with others (Drews and Schemer 2010). The following discussion of this domain's current research findings will serve to synthesize the main benefits and developments produced by social media in the hospitality industry.

Lines of research

In this section, we will present a review of the main lines of research on social media and hospitality marketing. In particular, we will describe three avenues of research that each contain a number of more specific research topics: assessing end consumers' behavior; user-generated content (UGC) and its implications for hospitality marketing; and industry operators' uses of social media.

Assessing end consumers' behavior

It is very important for operators in the hospitality industry to monitor tourists' behaviors as much as possible, as the success of any implemented strategies will depend on how accurately said strategies meet tourists' demands, requirements, needs and desires. Thus, a large amount of research in the field has been devoted to assessing tourists' behaviors.

Tourists demonstrate several relevant behaviors with respect to social media (Zeng and Gerritsen 2014). In general, tourists use social media to obtain information for planning their travels and/or publish information about their own travel experiences. On the former point, Sigala et al. (2012) suggested that a substantial number of travelers use social media for travel planning, particularly in terms of deciding where to go, how to go there, when to go, what to do, where to stay overnight, where to eat and where to shop. Similarly, Leung et al. (2013) outlined how consumers generally use social media during the research phase of their travel planning process. Furthermore, Huertas (2012) observed that, when the destination is known, users search for more information about leisure, cultural activities and restaurants, as well as recommendations from other users; when the destination is unknown, however, tourists tend to peruse official websites and seek general information about the place.

Sigala et al. (2012) identified several types of social media that are used in tourism—namely, travel reviews, tweets, photos, videos, blogs, blog comments, discussion forum postings and audio podcasts. However, not all social media are equally useful for travel planning. Some types of social media appeal to a broad group of travelers, while others are only employed by extensive social media users (Sigala et al. 2012). For example, many users turn to travel reviews to both generate ideas and make final decisions. Most readers perceive reviews as important for accommodation decisions; thus, hotels and online travel agencies typically send e-mails to travelers after their stay, asking them to provide a review. However, because social media makes reviews more accessible through mobile applications, there is an inceasing effort to reach users of mobile devices (Gretzel and Yoo 2008).

On this point, it is worth noting that social media has changed tourists' information search behaviors. Sigala et al. (2012) found that at least half of social media users spent more time planning, used more information sources and took more print-outs on the trip. Moreover, as highlighted by Zeng and Gerritsen (2014), social media can decrease users' uncertainty and increase the exchange utility. Lastly, the act of creating and sharing stories can facilitate a sense of belonging in virtual travel communities (Gretzel et al. 2006; Wang et al. 2002). These opinions and recommendations have tremendous value in terms of influencing the destination's perceived image, which is why researchers need to continue studying the effects exerted by travelers' cognitive and affective images of a tourist destination (Hidalgo et al. 2012). In short, academic research highlights how recommendations are an increasingly relevant source of tourist information (Dellarocas 2003; Hennig-Thurau et al. 2004).

In addition, social media technologies allow travelers to share their experiences (Pan et al. 2007); however, only a small portion of travelers actively create and disseminate content (Sigala et al. 2012). In general, a lot of tourist information is published by users in virtual travel communities (e.g., VirtualTourist, RealTravel) or on web platforms that specialize in user assessments of tourist services and products (e.g., TripAdvisor, Holidaycheck). These websites depend on the perception that the opinions of peer tourists hold greater credibility than traditional sources of tourist information (Schmallegger and Carson 2008). Trustworthiness is, in fact, a key antecedent in users' decision to use information found on social media (Leung et al. 2013).

Granted, not all users of social media play the same roles and exert the same influence on other potential tourists. For example, Zeng and Gerritsen (2014) outlined how those users who are regarded as travel opinion leaders or central travelers – despite being a small portion of the tourist population – have a more significant impact on the kinds of information seen by others (Vasiliki and Kostas 2010; Yoo et al. 2011). This is because they possess greater travel experience, show greater trust in official sources (Yoo et al. 2011), are more active in providing information, and are more accessible to a broad audience through a series of incoming links (Vasiliki and Kostas 2010).

UGC and its related implications for hospitality marketing

Following on from the previous line of research, several recent research studies have focused on user-generated content (UGC) and its potential implications for hospitality marketing. Scholars have found that social media can help tourism and hospitality companies engage potential guests, increase their online presence, and thereby generate greater online revenues (Leung et al. 2013). By allowing travelers to share photos, videos and comments with other readers via social media platforms and product search engines, UGC is changing how consumers decide on the characteristics of their trips (Zeng and Gerritsen 2014). Moreover, UGC is shaping the image of a tourist destination beyond the control of destination marketing organizations (DMO). Free from the influence of DMOs or suppliers, UGC via social media offers a source of information that rivals official channels, and thus influences people's motivations for visiting a place (Llodrà-Riera et al. 2015a, 2015b; MacKay and Vogt 2012). For instance, Simms (2012) found that a higher percentage of travelers turned to UGC when visiting a destination for the first time, as well as when visiting an international destination.

Given the widespread nature of UGC, researchers have turned to new tools such as sentiment analysis and opinion mining, which are outgrowths of the need to develop new technologies that can automate aspects of research. Sentiment analysis, for instance, has helped companies improve their social media management by identifying and analyzing opinions and emotions contained in residents' or tourists' reviews (Gao et al. 2015). Sentiment analysis and opinion mining involve detecting keywords and linking messages with a particular semantic field to find the key concepts of online comments. Applying this methodology to data from Booking. com and TripAdvisor, Gascón et al. (2016) concluded that semantic fields offer hotels a platform for observing their strengths and weaknesses, improving their services and, ultimately, refining their image.

As Xiang et al. (2015) explain, these tools represent a larger trend enabled by social media and UGC – namely, the development of so-called Big Data analytics to understand and solve real-life problems. These authors demonstrate the use of Big Data analytics for better under-standing important hospitality issues, such as the relationship between hotel guest experience and satisfaction. Specifically, their study applied a textual analysis to a large quantity of consumer reviews from Expedia.com, deconstructing hotel guests' experiences and examining their asso-ciation with satisfaction ratings. The findings revealed several dimensions of guest experience that carry varying weights and, more importantly, have novel, meaningful semantic compositions. The association between guest experience and satisfaction appears strong, suggesting that these two domains of consumer behavior are inherently connected. Thus, this study reveals that Big Data analytics can generate new insights into variables that have received extensive study in the hospitality literature.

It is important to note that not all UGC is authentic and legitimate: Sometimes there are people who publish harmful (or positive) information in order to destroy (or reinforce) a brand. For this reason, some researchers have begun to analyze the potential profiles of illegitimate reviewers. For instance, Choo et al. (2015) uncovered how to detect opinion spammer groups in review systems. They argue that most existing approaches typically build pure, content-based classifiers, using various features extracted from review content; however, spammers can superficially alter their review content to avoid detection. Their approach, by contrast, focused on identifying spammers through user relationships, applying sentiment analysis to user interactions in order to distinguish spam communities from non-spam ones. Through extensive experiments on a dataset collected from Amazon, they discovered that strongly positive communities are more likely to be opinion spammer groups. Thus, their work offers a method of reliably identifying spammer groups, even when spammers alter their content.

In light of the above, DMOs and suppliers should pay attention to the UGC shared through social media, observing whether their projected proposals and values align with the percep-tions transmitted by users. By recognizing when users encourage or discourage visiting a place or undertaking certain activities, DMOs and suppliers can alter or improve their offerings and communication strategies (Llodrà-Riera et al. 2015a, 2015b).

Operators' uses of social media

Several studies have focused on how operators in the hospitality industry differently employ social media. Leung et al. (2013), for instance, posited that industry operators use social media for five key purposes: promotion, product distribution, communication, management, and research. In addition, social media provide new means for tourism organizations – including destination marketing organizations (DMOs) – to reengineer their business models and operations, which might entail developing new services, marketing, networking and knowledge management. While not a cure-all, social media is an effective channel for integrating the communication and marketing of tourism services (Sotiriadis and van Zyl 2013), especially as these platforms facilitate an increasing mistrust toward traditional marketing tactics and a diminishing effect of traditional mass media (e.g., Fotis et al. 2010).

Additionally, there has been extensive research into operators' cocreation initiatives. As social media has evolved and allowed peers to share greater amounts of data, tourists and residents have begun to not only share opinions and experiences, but also have become producers and suppliers who add services to the tourist value chain. On this point, Gretzel et al. (2015) provide a schematic representation of a Smart Tourism Ecosystem, despite the difficulty of capturing its complexity. In a traditional tourist industry, consumers, producers and intermediaries can be clearly distinguished into a hierarchical value chain. In the Smart Tourism Ecosystem, by contrast, touristic consumers bring their own resources and use the digital ecosystem to organize among themselves or act like producers among the closely related residential consumers (a phenomenon often referred to as the sharing economy). These touristic and residential consumers produce data through social media activities or the use of location-based services, and consume data produced by other species or the physical environment, often made palatable through mobile apps. For these researchers, a Smart Tourism Ecosystem represents an extremely rich environment for identifying and studying new interaction paradigms and forms of value (co-)creation. In short, consumers, businesses and various collectives of different players are interacting with information and technologies in ways that have yet to be identified and understood.

On a similar note, Molz (2014) explains that the growing popularity of online hospitality exchange networks such as Couchsurfing and Airbnb points toward a new paradigm of sociality – a mobile and networked society where hospitable encounters among friends and strangers become entangled with social media and networking technologies. Inspired by Andreas Wittel's notion of 'network sociality,' Molz (2014) introduced the concept of 'network hospitality' to describe the kind of sociality that emerges around these new mobile, peer-to-peer, and online-to-offline social networks. Molz (2014) delineates five key features of network hospitality – namely, sharing with strangers; feeling like a guest; engineering randomness; pop-up assemblages; and guests without hosts – and illustrates how network hospitality reflects the way people now 'do togetherness,' whether that be online, offline, or somewhere in between.

With regard to communication, it is important to highlight how social media allows tourism practitioners to provide individual tourists with customized information that addresses their personal needs and preferences (Zeng and Gerritsen 2014). Indeed, many tourism organizations are already adopting social networks such as Facebook or Twitter for this very purpose (Munar 2011). Therefore, social media might serve as a new marketing strategy for industry operators – one aimed less at sales support and more at cultivating an interactive relationship with users and consumers in general (Zeng and Gerritsen 2014).

In this regard, operators could foster the use of social media in either international travel planning or international marketing by developing multi-language platforms or websites for tourists.

This would not only benefit suppliers, but would also generally increase demand (Zeng and Gerritsen 2014) by allowing non-English speaking countries to disseminate direct information to an English-dominated social media landscape (Hsu 2012). Of course, operators must be cautious: Such a new relationship between companies and users could generate sales by simplifying the value chain (Valls et al. 2013), but it could also harm the potential to build customers' loyalty (Senders et al. 2013). In any case, social media is challenging existing customer service, marketing and promotional processes throughout the tourism sector (Sigala et al. 2012).

DMOs and providers might also use social media as part of crisis communications. Although this research field is still in its infancy, scholars are increasingly assessing how social media can be used for crisis management. For example, it was observed how in some countries, among the drivers of social media use by DMO, the risk perceptions associated with diseases and health-related issues, crime, physical equipment failures, weather, political crises and cultural barriers were found (Zeng and Gerritsen 2014). Meanwhile, some researchers have begun analyzing the impact of social media on reputation management (Horster and Gottschalk 2012), brand management (Barreda et al. 2013; Barwise and Meehan 2010; Hede and Kellett 2012) and the reduction of risk associated with information search (Jacobsen and Munar 2012).

Lastly, it is worth noting that researchers in this field (e.g., Hardesty, 2011; Pesonen, 2011) distinguish between small to medium-sized enterprises and large companies when discussing the different uses of social media in hospitality marketing. This is partly due to the fact that smaller companies normally have fewer activities than larger companies. However, it remains unclear whether there exists some correlation between business scale and success in using social media, or between the number of tourist events and success in using social media. There is also a need for more discussion on the conflicting relationship between corporate and social media culture, as well as the challenges that traditional management structures face in the wake of innovative communication tools (Zeng and Gerritsen 2014).

Future lines of research

There are several future research directions that arise from the key issues identified by the above review. Two such directions, as indicated by previous research (e.g., Zeng and Gerritsen 2014), are the assessment of comprehensive marketing and the differentiation of destination management strategies.

On the first point, it would be interesting for future studies to focus on social media as one part of a comprehensive marketing strategy. It is common for operators in the hospitality industry to maintain their own social media websites and enable their customers to create UGC; nevertheless, operators do not often interact enough with customers through these platforms. This is a particularly relevant issue in light of growing phenomena such as the collaborative economy and the interchange of peer-to-peer services. At the same time, managing the overall travel cycle is becoming increasingly important, especially as the influence of eWOM influence spreads over the entire travel cycle and dictates the reputations of tourist destinations and their operators. Thus, operators could consider providing timely feedback to UGC, in terms of either building tourist trust and brand loyalty (for return visitation), or spreading more positive messages (attracting potential tourists). By customizing their social media marketing efforts, operators may be better able to approach specific market segments and thereby attract potential tourists to their websites and, ultimately, the target destinations.

It would also be interesting for future studies to assess whether the reviews and feedback posted on social media affect the salaries of hospitality employees. In addition, more studies are needed to verify whether firms consider a person's social media history when contracting new employees. Finally, researchers might look into devising methods of estimating future demand using social media commentary.

Conclusions

The growth of social media has outpaced its initial definitions. The rapid evolution of web tools has produced an array of new terms such as social media, social networks, user-generated content, sentiment analysis, opinion mining, and Big Data analytics. All of these terms are undoubtedly being applied to hospitality marketing, whether by tourists, operators, or both. For operators, monitoring the evolution of these trends is critical to the success of their marketing strategies.

New phenomena are appearing in tourism, which are transforming the way the hospitality industry traditionally operates. Residents and travelers are creating and sharing tourist content through reviews, assessments, blogs, comments, photos, videos, social networks and other online platforms. Furthermore, some consumers are stepping beyond the sharing of content into its production, creating tourist services within the new sharing economy. On the other side, operators in the hospitality industry are seeking to adopt social media as an information, communication and distribution channel, through which they can better know their customers and analyze their feelings, desires, experiences, recommendations and satisfaction.

In the wake of these developments, researchers are devoting more attention to analyzing users' behaviors, trust, credibility, opinions, influencers, spam efforts and brand associations, ultimately seeking to understand how all these impact the tourism industry and hospitality management. The amount of data generated by social media is so vast that researchers are developing new techniques and tools – such as those related to Big Data, sentiment analysis and opinion mining – to analyze tourist behavior. Relatedly, scholars are also exploring the potential benefits that social media pose for current and future operators in the industry.

Acknowledgments

This work was funded by Research Project ECO2014-59688-R, Planificacion e Implementacion de Estrategias de Gestion Optimas del Pdv Fisico, Online y Movil a Partir de las TIC y la Innovacion, Ministerio de Economía y Competitividad (Spain).

References

Barreda, A., Nusair, K., Bilgihan, A. & Okumus, F. (2013) "A brand structure pyramid model for travel-related online social networks", *Tourism Review*, 68(4), 49–70.

Barwise, P. & Meehan, S. (2010) "The one thing you must get right when building a brand", *Harvard Business Review*, 88(12), 80–84.

Blackshaw, P. & Nazzaro, M. (2006) *Consumer-generated media (CGM) 101: Word-of-mouth in the age of the web-fortified consumer*. New York: Nielsen BuzzMetrics.

Boyd, A. & Ellison, N. B. (2007) "Social network sites: Definition, history, and scholarship", *Journal of Computer-Mediated Communication* 13(1), 210–230.

Buhalis, D. & Law, R. (2008) "Progress in information technology and tourism management: 20 years on and 10 years after the Internet—The state of eTourism research", *Tourism Management* 29(4), 609–623.

Buonamano, O., Caurgno, M., D'Alessandro, S., Delfino, M. & Marcozzi, I. (2013) *Tourism and network-ing: The relational chain between tourism supply and demand on the web*. Pescara: Carsa Edizione.

Carr, C. T. & Hayes, R. A. (2015) "Social media: Defining, developing, and divining", *Atlantic Journal of Communication* 23(1), 1–43.

Choo, E., Yu, T. & Chi, M. (2015, July) "Detecting opinion spammer groups through community discovery and sentiment analysis." In *IFIP Annual Conference on Data and Applications Security and Privacy* (pp. 170–187). Cham, Switzerland: Springer International Publishing.

Cohen, H. (2011) 30 social media definitions. Posted by Heidi Cohen on May 9, 2011 on Actionable Marketing Social media 101 (Available from: http://heidicohen.com/social-media-definition).

Dellarocas, C. (2003) "The digitization of word-of-mouth: Promise and challenges of online feedback mechanisms", *Management Science* 49(10), 1407–1424.

Drews, W. & Schemer, C. (2010) "eTourism for all? Online travel planning of disabled people", in Drews, W. and Schemer, C. (eds.) *Information and Communication Technologies in Tourism*, Vienna: Springer, 507–518.

Fotis, J., Rossides, N. & Buhalis, D. (2010) "Social media impact on leisure travel: The case of the russian market and the challenges for the cyprus tourism industry". In 3rd Annual EuroMed Conference of the EuroMed Academy of Business-Conference Readings Book Proceedings-Business Developments across Countries and Cultures (pp. 1365–1367). Nicosia, Cyprus: EuroMed Press.

Gao, S., Hao, J. & Fu, Y. (2015) "The application and comparison of web services for sentiment analysis in tourism". In *2015 12th International Conference on Service Systems and Service Management (ICSSSM)* (pp. 1–6). Guangzhou, China: IEEE.

Gascón, J., Bernal, P., Román, E., González, M., Giménez, G., Aragón, Ó. & Crespo, J. (2016) "Sentiment analysis as a qualitative methodology to analyze social media: Study case of tourism", *CIAIQ*, 5, 22–31.

Gelb, B. D. & Sundaram, S. (2002) "Adapting to 'word of mouse'", *Business Horizons* 45(4), 21–25.

Gretzel, U., Fesenmaier, D. & O'Leary, J. (2006) "The transformation of consumer behavior". Tourism Business Frontiers: Consumers, Products and Industry, 9–18.

Gretzel, U., Werthner, H., Koo, C. & Lamsfus, C. (2015) "Conceptual foundations for understanding smart tourism ecosystems", *Computers in Human Behavior* 50, 558–563.

Gretzel, U. & Yoo, K. H. (2008) "Use and impact of online travel reviews", in O'Connor, P., Höpken, W. and Gretzel, U. (eds.) *Information and communication technologies in tourism*, Vienna: Springer, 35–46.

Hardesty, S. (2011) "Agritourism operators embrace social media for marketing", *California Agriculture* 65(2), 56.

Harrison-Walker, L. J. (2001) "The measurement of word-of-mouth communication and an investiga-tion of service quality and customer commitment as potential antecedents", *Journal of Service Research* 4(1), 60–75.

Hede, A. M. & Kellett, P. (2012) "Building online brand communities: Exploring the benefits, challenges and risks in the Australian event sector", *Journal of Vacation Marketing* 18(3), 239–250.

Hennig-Thurau, T., Gwinner, K., Walsh, G. & Gremler, D. (2004) "Electronic word-of-mouth via con-sumer-opinion platforms: What motivates consumers to articulate themselves on the Internet?", *Journal of Interactive Marketing* 18(1), 38–52.

Hidalgo, M. C., Sicilia, M. & Ruiz, S. (2012) "La imagen de destino y el contenido generado por otros usuarios: El caso del turismo rural", IX Congreso Turismo y Tecnologías de la Información y de la Comunicaciones (TURITEC 2012), Málaga, 365–379.

Horster, E. & Gottschalk, C. (2012) "Computer-assisted webnography: A new approach to online reputa-tion management in tourism", *Journal of Vacation Marketing* 18(3), 229–238.

Hsu, Y. L. (2012). "Facebook as international eMarketing strategy of Taiwan hotels", *International Journal of Hospitality Management* 31(3), 972–980.

Huertas, A. (2012) "¿Web sites o Social Media? ¿Dónde se busca la información turística de los destinos?" IX Congreso Turismo y Tecnologías de la Información y de la Comunicaciones (TURITEC 2012), Málaga, 75–93

Jacobsen, J. K. S. & Munar, A. M. (2012) "Tourist information search and destination choice in a digital age", *Tourism Management Perspectives*, 1, 39–47.

Leung, D., Law, R., Van Hoof, H. & Buhalis, D. (2013) "Social media in tourism and hospitality: A literature review", *Journal of Travel & Tourism Marketing* 30(1–2), 3–22.

Litvin, S. W., Goldsmith, R. E., & Pan, B. (2008) "Electronic word-of-mouth in hospitality and tourism management", *Tourism Management* 29(3), 458–468.

Llodrà-Riera, I., Martínez-Ruiz, M. P., Jiménez-Zarco, A. I. & Izquierdo-Yusta, A. (2015a) "A multidimensional analysis of the information sources construct and its relevance for destination image formation", *Tourism Management* 48, 319–328.

Llodrà-Riera, I., Martínez-Ruiz, M. P., Jiménez-Zarco, A. I. & Izquierdo-Yusta, A. (2015b) "Assessing the influence of social media on tourists' motivations and image formation of a destination", *International Journal of Quality and Service Sciences* 7(4), 458–482.

MacKay, K. & Vogt, C. (2012) "Information technology in everyday and vacation contexts", *Annals of Tourism Research* 39 (3), 1380–1401.

Mangold, W. G. & Faulds, D. J. (2009) "Social media: The new hybrid element of the promotion mix", *Business Horizons* 52(4), 357–365.

Molz, J. G. (2014) "Toward a network hospitality", *First Monday* 19(3).

Munar, A. M. (2011). "Tourist-created content: Rethinking destination branding", *International Journal of Culture, Tourism and Hospitality Research* 5(3), 291–305.

Noti, E. (2013)."Web 2.0 and its influence in the tourism sector", *European Scientific Journal* 9(20), 115–123.

O'Reilly, T. (2005) Web 2.0: compact definition. *Radar*, 137–158. Available online at http://radar.oreilly.com/2005/10/web-20-compact-definition.html.

Pan, B., MacLaurin, T. & Crotts, J. (2007) "Travel blogs and the implications for destination marketing", *Journal of Travel Research* 46(1), 35–45.

Papathanassis, A. & Buhalis, D. (2007) "Exploring the information and communication technologies revolution and visioning the future of tourism, travel and hospitality industries". Paper presented at the 6th e-Tourism Futures Forum: ICT Revolutionising Tourism, March 26–27, 2007, Guildford, United Kingdom.

Pesonen, J. (2011) "Tourism marketing in Facebook: Comparing rural tourism SME's and larger tourism companies in Finland". Paper presented at the International Conference on Information and Communication Technologies in Tourism, January 26–28, 2011, Innsbruck, Austria.

Schmallegger, D. & Carson, D. (2008) "Blogs in tourism: Changing approaches to information exchange", *Journal of Vacation Marketing* 14(2), 99–110.

Senders, A., Govers, R. & Neuts, B. (2013) "Social media affecting tour operators' customer loyalty", *Journal of Travel & Tourism Marketing* 30(1/2), 41–57.

Sigala, M., Christou, E. & Gretzel, U. (Eds.) (2012) *Social media in travel, tourism and hospitality: Theory, practice and cases.* Abingdon, Oxon, UK; New York: Ashgate Publishing, Ltd.

Simms, A. (2012). "Online user-generated content for travel planning – different for different kinds of trips?" e-*Review of Tourism Research* 10(3), 76–85.

Sotiriadis, M. D. & van Zyl, C. (2013) "Electronic word-of-mouth and online reviews in tourism services: The use of twitter by tourists", *Electronic Commerce Research* 13(1), 103–124.

Valls, J. F., Ouro, A., Freund, D. & Andrade, M. J. (2013) "Analysis of social media platforms and their potential value for the tourism industry". Working paper available at the University Ramon Llull. Available online at www.tsi.url.edu/img/user/content/file/3153__223.pdf.

Vasiliki, V. & Kostas, Z. (2010) "Locating central travelers' groups in travel blogs' social networks", *Journal of Enterprise Information Management* 23(5), 595–609.

Wang, Y., Yu, Q. & Fesenmaier, D. R. (2002) "Defining the virtual tourist community: Implications for tourism marketing", *Tourism Management* 23(4), 407–417.

Wellman, B. (1988). "Structural analysis: From method and metaphor to theory and substance". In B. Wellman & S. D. Berkowitz (Eds.), *Social Structures: A Network Approach* (pp. 19–61). Cambridge, UK: Cambridge University Press.

WTTC (2011). "Travel and tourism 2011", World Travel and Tourism Council 2011. Available online at www.wttc.org/site_media/uploads/downloads/traveltourism2011.pdf (Accessed May 22, 2013).

Xiang, Z., Schwartz, Z., Gerdes, J. H. & Uysal, M. (2015) "What can Big Data and text analytics tell us about hotel guest experience and satisfaction?", *International Journal of Hospitality Management* 44, 120–130.

Yoo, K., Gretzel, U. & Zach, F. (2011)."Travel opinion leaders and seekers". In R. Law, M. Fuchs & F. Ricci (Eds.), *Information and Communication Technologies in Tourism 2011: Proceedings of the International Conference* (pp. 525–535). New York: Springer.

Zeng, B. & Gerritsen, R. (2014) "What do we know about social media in tourism? A review", *Tourism Management Perspectives* 10, 27–36.

Further reading

Leung, X.Y., Bai, B. & Stahura, K. (2015) "The marketing effectiveness of social media in the hotel industry: A comparison of Facebook and Twitter", *Journal of Hospitality and Tourism Research* 39(2), 147–169. (A study of how hotel customers' social media experiences on Facebook and Twitter influence their attitudes toward social media sites and hotel brands, as well as their hotel booking intentions and intentions to spread eWOM.)

Minazzi, R. (2015). *Social media marketing in tourism and hospitality*. Cham, Switzerland: Springer International Publishing. (An interesting piece of work about future developments in social media regarding the tourism and hospitality industry.)

42

Mobile apps and hospitality marketing

Lu Zhang

Mobile apps can be defined as application software designed to provide utilitarian values (e.g., information) and hedonic values (e.g., entertainment) on mobile devices such as smartphones and tablets. These apps are either pre-installed on devices during manufacture, or downloaded by customers through software distribution platforms such as the App Store and Google Play (Ho and Syu, 2010). As of June 2016, Google's Google Play Store contained 2.2 million apps and Apple's App Store had 2 million available apps (Statista, 2016). The number of mobile app downloads worldwide has increased dramatically in the past few years. In 2009, worldwide mobile app downloads totaled approximately 2.52 billion and is expected to reach 268.69 billion in 2017 (Statista, 2016). The rapid growth of smartphones and mobile apps has changed the ways in which consumers interact with a brand (Kim, Wang, and Malthouse, 2015) and has provided marketers with another channel to reach out to their customers (Lin, Fang, and Hsu, 2014). More and more companies have welcomed mobile apps as a marketing tool that can be used to attract new customers and increase brand loyalty among existing ones (Wang, Kim, and Malthouse, 2016). As in all other services segments such as retailing, mobile apps have become very popular in the hospitality industry. Restaurants' branded apps allow customers to make reservations using the app, which tends to perform better than traditional call reservations in terms of hours, consistency, and record-keeping accuracy (Kimes, 2011). Hotel groups such as Marriott and Accor have been investing heavily in electronic assets to cement a digital presence that connects with customers in a meaningful way (Avery, Dev, and O'Connor, 2015). For example, Marriott Mobile, together with Marriott.com, are considered as two of their fastest growing booking channels (Marriott International, 2015). In 2015, the Marriott Mobile app alone exceeded $1 billion in gross bookings. They were the first hotel company to offer mobile check-in and checkout services, and the first global hospitality company to offer Apple Pay as another step that enables guests to engage more often with Marriott. Other major hotel companies such as IHG (InterContinental Hotel Group) and Hilton have their own mobile apps too. See Table 42.1 for a summary of the mobile apps and functions of six major hotel companies.

As shown in Table 42.1, most hospitality companies' mobile apps mainly focus on providing basic utilitarian benefits to customers (e.g., easy booking). Judging by the number of reviews and number of downloads, these apps have successfully reached a large group of consumers. However, research has shown that only about one-third of users continue to use an app one

Table 42.1 Hotel mobile apps

	Cost	Functions	Key figures	Customer ratings (1–5 stars)
Marriott	Free	• Booking • Easy access to rewards • Check-in and checkout • Chat with hotel associates • Make requests for amenities • Mobile key • Receive alert when room is ready	• Generated $1 billion in gross bookings in 2015 (Marriott International, 2015)	• 2.5 stars with 3498 ratings on App Store • 3.7 stars with 7907 ratings on Google Play
IHG	Free	• Booking • Access special offers and discounts • Check-in and checkout • Receive alert when room is ready	• 40% of digital visits on mobile devices • Over $1.2 billion annual mobile revenue in 2015, up from less than $50 million in 2010 • 27% downloads growth (IHG, 2015)	• 4.5 stars with 5325 ratings on App Store • 4.1 stars with 11198 ratings on Google Play
Hilton	Free	• Booking • Digital key • Check-in and checkout • Room selection • Request amenities • Access to special offers • Request Uber rides • Get recommendations about local hotspots	• Business generated from mobile app is up nearly 150% year-on-year • Downloads exceeding 70,000 a week, an increase of 200% from 2015 (Skift, 2016)	• 4.5 stars with 11785 ratings on App Store • 4.5 stars with 19616 ratings on Google Play
Choice	Free	• Booking • Explore local attractions • Earn rewards • Search for hotels • Access verified guests reviews	• 17% increase in revenue for the first quarter of 2016 compared to the same period last year because of direct mobile booking (Skift, 2016)	• 3.5 stars with 2334 ratings on App Store • 4.3 stars with 10274 ratings on Google Play
Accor	Free	• Booking • Access TripAdvisor reviews • Check-in • Request Uber rides • Wipolo: group all the details about flights, trains, hotels, etc. together • Easy access to rewards	• 40% of web visits are from mobile devices • 3 million app downloads (AccorHotels, 2015)	• 3.5 stars with 347 ratings on App Store • 4.1 stars with 18187 ratings on Google Play

month after first using it, and this number drops to just four percent after one year (Ding and Chai, 2015). With such a high dropout rate, it is important for hospitality companies to truly understand mobile apps and their impact on consumers. To help address this issue, this chapter will discuss (1) the platform (i.e. the characteristics of mobile devices); (2) the type of mobile apps and their basic functions; and (3) factors influencing consumers' adoption of mobile apps.

Mobile devices

Compared with other devices such as desktop computers, mobile devices have a few unique characteristics (Barnes, 2002; Gao, Rau, and Salvendy, 2009; Kannan, Chang, and Whinston, 2001), which will be discussed in the next sections.

Ubiquitous availability

Mobile devices are always "on" and connected. The fact that they are always available and users carry them every day and everywhere changes the way we interact with mobile devices. According to Weiser (1991), "The most profound technologies are those that disappear. They weave themselves into the fabric of everyday life until they are indistinguishable from it" (p. 94). Nowadays, people do not think of mobile devices as advanced technology. They are part of our daily routine and simply a feature of the world we take for granted (Fano and Gershman, 2002). An example of how mobile devices shape the way we act in the world is from the travel industry. People use mobile devices for all types of activities *before* (e.g., booking hotel rooms), *during* (e.g., taking photos), and *after* (e.g., posting pictures on social media) their trips. Nearly every touch point along the journey involves the usage of mobile devices.

Personal usage

While other traditional devices such as telephones and computers can usually be shared among different users (e.g., family members, officemates, etc.), mobile devices are more personal because they are usually carried and used by only one person and people tend to use them in a personal context (Gong and Tarasewich, 2004). Different users have various levels of skills, distinct usage habits, patterns, and preferences. Therefore, users are more likely to personalize their mobile device so that it carries his or her personal identity and reflects individual preferences. Additionally, due to the nature of personal usage, mobile ads are often perceived as more intrusive than traditional marketing techniques such as TV commercials and displayed ads on computers.

Interactivity

Interactivity has historically been defined as any form of communication that replicates face-to-face conversation (Rafaeli, 1988). Bucy (2004) suggested that interactivity consists of reciprocal communication exchanges that involve some form of media, or information, and communication technology. Interactivity as a media feature comes in the form of different modalities of information dissemination. While traditional mediums (e.g., newspapers) typically have two modalities, text and pictures, new digital media interfaces offer a wide variety of modalities that allow us to interact with several of our senses operating together, such as audio and video (Sundar, 2008). Moreover, with the development of tablet and mobile technology, users are often exposed to interactive modalities beyond just pointing and clicking, for example, dragging, sliding, and flipping. Several studies have found that interactivity produces positive outcomes. Basso et al. (2001) found that interactivity facilitates favorable judgments in online shopping experiences. In addition, Stout, Villegas, and Kim (2001) found that interactive tools can boost individuals' willingness to interact when searching for health-related information.

Context-aware ability

Context-aware computing refers to the ability to utilize contextual information such as location, display medium, and user profile in order to provide tailored functionality (Cheverst, Davies, Mitchell, Friday, and Efstratiou, 2000). Two types of contextual information are usually considered: *personal information* such as the consumer's personal interests, and *environmental information* such as the current location of the consumer. Given the context sensitivity of mobile apps, they can recommend restaurants for lunch either based on customers' previous visits (i.e., personal information) or suggest places within 300 feet of users (i.e., environmental information).

Types of mobile apps

Having established the characteristics of the platform for which mobile apps are developed, the discussion will now turn to the types of mobile apps currently on the market as well as the main values provided. Bellman and colleagues (2011) differentiate between two types of apps: informational and game-like apps. This chapter proposes a classification of four types of mobile apps based upon two studies (Gupta, 2013; Zhao and Balagué, 2015): *games and entertainment*; *utility*; *discovery*; and *social network*. Each type of mobile app provides a set of values that are unique to customers. The notion of "value" is central to services marketing (Larivière, Joosten, Malthouse, van Birgelen, Aksoy, Kunz, and Huang, 2013). It refers to the result of customers' assessments in weighing the bundle of benefits against the bundle of costs they expect to incur in evaluating, obtaining, and using the product or service (Kotler, 2000). Understanding what values customers intend to derive from mobile apps will help firms to create experiences that are engaging and meaningful (Lariviere et al., 2013).

Games and entertainment

Mobile apps are often used for satisfying individuals' entertainment needs. Consumers intentionally seek playfulness while using their mobile devices by engaging in activities such as playing games or watching YouTube videos. Popular game apps typically include casual games, which can be described as "easy-to-play, short-session games" (Bates, 2004, p. 10). They have an effortless learning curve compared to hardcore video games and require lower commitment in terms of time and resources (Speller, 2012). The growth of mobile devices/apps is one of the main contributors of the popularity of casual gaming.

Utility

The second type of mobile app focuses on providing functions that facilitate tasks that consumers are currently performing. For instance, Google Maps is a map utility that can be used for navigation purposes. Hotel mobile apps allow customers to enjoy their stay without directly interacting with front desk clerks. Also, by using airlines' mobile apps, consumers can purchase tickets, check their flight status, and select seats.

Table 42.2 Types of mobile app

Type of app	Examples	Value provided
Games and entertainment	Angry Birds, YouTube	Hedonic value – escape and relax
Utility	Google Maps, Calculator	Utilitarian value – facilitation
Discovery	Yelp, TripAdvisor	Utilitarian value – information search
Social network	Facebook, SnapChat	Both hedonic and utilitarian – communication

Discovery

This type of mobile app is usually used to find out about relevant events and conditions in the immediate surroundings, society, and the world (Lariviere et al., 2013). It offers customers the opportunity to search for information that is relevant in making purchasing decisions. For example, Yelp can be used to find restaurants and TripAdvisor can be used to search for hotel information. Customers can also use this type of mobile app to find out information about local hotspots as well as read other customers' evaluations of those places (i.e., online customer reviews).

Social network

From the user perspective, mobile apps for social networks are designed to allow users to stay connected and be able to communicate with their friends at all times. Due to the ubiquitous availability of mobile devices, apps such as Facebook and Twitter enable customers to share their thoughts and experiences with other people anytime and anywhere (Lariviere et al., 2013). Moreover, apps such as SnapChat and Vine take advantage of the built-in camera of mobile devices and offer customers greater flexibility in terms of the content (i.e., pictures and videos in addition to text) they can share with others. See Table 42.2 for a summary of the four types of mobile apps, examples, and values provided to users.

Consumers' adoption of mobile apps

Consumers' adoption and usage of a mobile app determines its success as a marketing tool (Carroll, 2007; Chen, Hsu, and Wu, 2012; Picoto, Palma-dos-Reis, and Bélanger, 2010), because adoption translates into bookings and revenue (Hu, 2011; Sangle and Awasthi, 2011). Consumers' intention to adopt and use mobile apps has been extensively examined by prior research and typically involves two theoretical frameworks: TAM (Technology Acceptance Model) and U&G (Uses and Gratifications). Next, these two models will be introduced, together with research related to mobile apps.

In 1989, Davis proposed the Technology Acceptance Model (TAM) to understand the psychological processes of information technology adoption and acceptance. Based on the theory of reasoned action (Fishbein and Ajzen, 1975) and the theory of planned behavior (Ajzen, 1991), TAM is one of the most widely accepted models in the area of technology adoption. The original TAM focuses on two theoretical constructs, perceived usefulness (PU) and perceived ease of use (PEOU), which are the fundamental determinants of system acceptance and use (Davis, 1989). According to Davis (1989), perceived usefulness is defined as the degree to which a person believes that using a particular system will enhance his or her job performance. Within an organizational context, users believe that an application high in perceived usefulness is more likely to produce a positive use-performance relationship. On the other hand, perceived ease of use refers to the degree to which a person believes that using a particular system would be free of effort. An application perceived to be easier to use is more likely to be accepted by users. Researchers further theorized that PU and PEOU will mediate the effect of external variables, such as interface design, on behavioral intentions (Venkatesh and Bala, 2008). In addition, TAM has gone through multiple waves of modifications. TAM2 was proposed by Venkatesh and Davis (2000) and it incorporated additional theoretical constructs spanning social influence processes (e.g., subjective norm) and cognitive instrumental processes (e.g., job relevance, output quality, and result demonstrability). Later, Venkatesh and Bala (2008) developed a more integrated model – TAM3 – to present a complete network of the determinants of individuals' IT adoption and use. Overall, TAM has been tested in different contexts, and has proven to be a robust theoretical model (Wang, Chung, Park, McLaughlin, and Fulk, 2012).

The examination of consumers' acceptance of mobile apps has been largely reliant on this framework. For example, Kim, Yoon, and Han (2014) used TAM to investigate the antecedents of mobile app usage among smartphone users. The results of their study indicated that four factors have a significant influence on consumers' attitudes towards app usage – perceived informative usefulness, perceived entertaining usefulness, perceived ease of use, and user review. Briz-Ponce and García-Peñalvo (2015) examined mobile apps and TAM in the context of medical education and included constructs such as PU, PEOU, social influence, facilitating conditions, self-efficacy, and anxiety.

The findings of these studies help marketers to have a better understanding of how and why people adopt mobile apps, given that advertising and app sales revenues are dependent upon adoption and usage (Gerlich, Drumheller, Babb, and De'Armond, 2015). However, researchers have argued that although TAM helps identify the antecedents of mobile app adoption, most of the drivers identified only describe the app itself or the sponsor of the app (i.e., the firm) and fail to explain how the app fits into the consumer's life (Alnawas and Aburub, 2016). Additionally, prior research that used TAM ignored the subsequent consumer behavior after adoption such as consumer satisfaction and purchase intentions.

Given these two factors, a stream of research has studied consumers' adoption of mobile apps using the "Uses and Gratifications" theory (U&G) (Katz, Blumler, and Gurevitch, 1974). U&G theory was developed to discuss the audience's motives for media usage. It focuses on the audience and their role in selecting a specific type of media, based on the assumption that media users are driven by individual needs and gratification-seeking motives (Blumler and Katz, 1974; Krcmar and Strizhakova, 2009). U&G theory has been applied to old media contexts such as radio and television, as well as new media such as social network sites (Wei, Lin, Lu, and Chuang, 2015) and mobile phones (Paragas, Clara, Main, and Rahman, 2011). Originally, Katz et al. (1974) proposed four types of benefits that an audience can derive from media usage: cognitive benefits, social integrative benefits, personal integrative benefits, and hedonic benefits. In terms of mobile applications, previous research studies identified a different set of motives for downloading/using mobile apps. For instance, Lewis, Brown, and Watkins (2014) explored the relationship between "gratifications sought" and consumers' attitudes and behavioral intention to download mobile apps. Gratifications identified in their research included personal productivity, entertainment/enjoyment, personal enjoyment, self-improvement, status, education, and communication/interaction with others.

Additionally, Alnawas and Aburub (2016) found four interaction-based benefits in the context of mobile apps: learning benefits (e.g., acquiring information to increase understanding/

knowledge of the environment), social integrative benefits (e.g., increase communication and make users feel more a part of their community and better citizens), personal integrative benefits (e.g., enhance the credibility, status, and confidence of the consumer), and hedonic benefits (e.g., enhance aesthetic or pleasurable experiences). Interestingly, only learning benefits and hedonic benefits are found to generate purchase intentions in relation to mobile apps. Lin et al. (2014) surveyed 441 mobile app users and found that social benefits, immediate access and mobility, entertainment, self-status seeking, pursuit of happiness, information seeking, and socializing were the primary factors driving app users' adopting behavior and addiction to apps. Moreover, previous research integrated the Theory of Planned Behavior, the Technology Acceptance Model, and the Uses and Gratification Theory to predict young American consumers' mobile app attitudes, intent, and usage (Yang, 2013). The results indicated that perceived enjoyment, usefulness, ease of use, perceived behavioral control, and subjective norms are significant predictors of users' attitudes and intent to use mobile apps.

In addition to TAM and U&G theory, theoretical frameworks such as personalization versus privacy (Morosan and DeFranco, 2016; Nyheim, Xu, Zhang, and Mattila, 2015), signaling theory and regulatory focus (Shen, 2015), and theory of consumption value (Peng, Chen, and Wen, 2014) have also been employed to study users' acceptance of mobile apps. For instance, Morosan and DeFranco (2016) examined hotel guests' intentions to use mobile apps via constructs such as personalization, privacy, personal innovativeness, and involvement. The results of their study provided evidence that consumers' personalization and privacy perceptions can be used to predict how consumers participate in m-commerce in hotels. Nyheim et al. (2015) recruited 159 Millennials and asked them to use Starbucks' apps for 30 days before completing a survey. Their findings suggested that (1) advertising irritation is positively related to ad avoidance, (2) perceived personalization has a negative impact on avoidance, and (3) privacy concern is not a significant predictor of avoidance. Table 42.3 provides a summary of research related to mobile apps, theories employed, and constructs/factors examined.

Table 42.3 Research on users' intention to adopt mobile apps

Author names	Purpose	Constructs	Theories
Alnawas and Aburub (2016)	To examine the effects of benefits generated from interaction with mobile apps on customer satisfaction and purchase intentions	• Learning benefits • Hedonic benefits • Personal integrative benefits • Social integrative benefits • Consumer satisfaction • Purchase intentions	U&G
Briz-Ponce and García-Peñalvo (2015)	To verify that TAM can be used to measure and explain the acceptance of mobile apps within medical education.	• Perceived usefulness • Perceived ease of use • Social influence • Facilitating conditions • Self-efficacy • Anxiety • Reliability • Recommendation • Attitude toward using technology • Behavioral intention to use the new technology	TAM

Table 42.3 (Cont.)

Author names	Purpose	Constructs	Theories
Ding and Chai (2015)	To understand the emotional experiences and their influences on continued usage of mobile apps.	• Disconfirmation • Experiential benefits • Instrumental benefits • Identity benefits • Social benefits • Negative emotions • Arousal • Positive emotions • Continuance intention	Expectancy disconfirmation theory (EDT)
Harris, Brookshire, and Chin (2016)	To explore factors influencing consumers' intention to install a mobile application.	• Perceived security • Application characteristics • Positive reputation • Familiarity • Desensitization • Consumer disposition to trust • Consumer disposition to risk • Perceived risk • Consumer trust • Perceived benefit • Intent to install	A trust-based consumer decision-making model
Ho and Syu (2010)	To understand users' motives for using mobile apps and degree of gratification after use.	• Entertainment • Instrumentality • Informativity • Sociability • Mentality • Trendiness • Learning	U&G
Kang (2014)	To predict use intention of mobile apps.	• Performance expectancy • Effort expectancy • Social influence • Entertainment motivation • Social utility motivation • Communication motivation • Intention	UTAUT (the Unified Theory of Acceptance and Use of Technology)
Kim, Yoon, and Han (2014)	To identify antecedents of mobile app usage among smartphone users.	• Perceived informative usefulness • Perceived entertaining usefulness • Perceived ease of use • User review • Attitude toward app usage • Behavioral intention to use mobile apps	TAM

(continued)

Table 42.3 (Cont.)

Author names	Purpose	Constructs	Theories
Kim, Wang, and Malthouse (2015)	To examine the effects of adopting and using a mobile app on subsequent purchases.	• Interactivity • Stickiness • Purchase behavior	N/A
Lewis, Brown, and Watkins (2014)	To explore needs that consumers expect to fulfill through apps and their influence on consumers' attitudes toward downloading apps.	• Personal productivity • Entertainment/enjoyment • Personal enjoyment • Self-improvement • Status • Education • Communication with others	U&G
Lin, Fang, and Hsu (2014)	To identify user motives to adopt and use a particular app.	• Social benefits • Immediate access and mobility • Entertainment • Self-status seeking • Pursuit of happiness • Information seeking • Socializing • Attitude toward apps • Addiction toward apps	U&G
Morosan and DeFranco (2016)	To examine the roles of personalization, privacy, and involvement on hotel guests' intentions to use mobile apps.	• General privacy concerns • App-related privacy concerns • Personal innovativeness • Perceived personalization • Involvement • Intentions	Personalization-privacy
Nyheim, Xu, Zhang, and Mattila (2015)	To investigate Millennials' perceptions of personalized smartphone app advertising avoidance.	• Privacy concern • Perceived personalization • Ad irritation • Ad avoidance • Perceived control	Personalization-privacy
Peng, Chen, and Wen (2014)	To understand factors influencing app adoption from the perspectives of brand relationship and consumption values.	• Brand attachment • Brand identification • Perceived value • Quality value • Acquisition value • Efficiency value • Emotion value • Intention to use branded apps	Theory of consumption value

Table 42.3 (Cont.)

Author names	Purpose	Constructs	Theories
Shen (2015)	To understand the effect of product type and message framing on users' adoption of mobile apps.	• App type • Perceived risk • Message framing • Mood • Reputation source • Product type • Perceived usefulness • Attitude toward apps • Intention to use	Signaling theory Regulatory focus theory
Wang and Wang (2010)	To examine the adoption of mobile hotel reservation services by considering both gain and loss elements influencing consumers' value perceptions.	• Information quality • System quality • Service quality • Technological effort • Perceived fee • Perceived risk • Perceived value • Behavioral intention	Theory of consumption value
Yang (2013)	To predict young American consumers' mobile app attitudes, intent and use.	• Perceived usefulness • Subjective norm • Perceived control • Ease of use • Perceived enjoyment • Perceived expressiveness • Attitude toward mobile apps • Intent to use mobile apps	TPB TAM U&G theory

References

AccorHotel, 2015. Powerful distribution and revenue management solutions. Available from: www.accorhotels-group.com/en/franchise-and-management/10-reasons-to-join-accorhotels/powerful-distribution-and-revenue-management.html. [15 October 2016].

Ajzen, I., 1991. The theory of planned behavior. *Organizational Behavior and Human Decision Processes*, 50(2), pp. 179–211.

Alnawas, I. and Aburub, F., 2016. The effect of benefits generated from interacting with branded mobile apps on consumer satisfaction and purchase intentions. *Journal of Retailing and Consumer Services*, 31, pp. 313–322.

Avery, J., Dev, C.S., and O'Connor, P., 2015. *Accor: Strengthening the brand with digital marketing*. Boston, MA: Harvard Business School Publishing.

Barnes, S.J., 2002. The mobile commerce value chain: Analysis and future developments. *International Journal of Information Management*, 22(2), pp. 91–108.

Basso, A., Goldberg, D., Greenspan, S. and Weimer, D., 2001. First impressions: Emotional and cognitive factors underlying judgments of trust e-commerce. In *Proceedings of the 3rd ACM Conference on Electronic Commerce* (pp. 137–143). New York: ACM.

Bates, B., 2004. *Game Design* (Second ed.). Boston, MA: Thomson.

Bellman, S., Potter, R.F., Treleaven-Hassard, S., Robinson, J.A. and Varan, D., 2011. The effectiveness of branded mobile phone apps. *Journal of Interactive Marketing*, 25(4), pp. 191–200.

Blumler, J.G. and Katz, E., 1974. *The uses of mass communications: Current perspectives on gratifications research. (Sage annual reviews of communication research, Volume III)*. Beverly Hills, CA: Sage.

Briz-Ponce, L. and García-Peñalvo, F.J., 2015. An empirical assessment of a technology acceptance model for apps in medical education. *Journal of Medical Systems*, 39(11), pp. 1–5.

Bucy, E.P., 2004. Interactivity in society: Locating an elusive concept. *The Information Society*, 20(5), pp. 373–383.

Carroll, J., 2007. July. Where to now? Generating visions for mBusiness from the drivers of use. In *International Conference on the Management of Mobile Business, 2007 (ICMB 2007)*. IEEE.

Chen, K.Y., Hsu, Y.L. and Wu, C.C., 2012. Mobile phone applications as innovative marketing tools for hotels. *International Journal of Organizational Innovation*, 5(2), p. 116. Online at http://search.proquest.com/openview/574071b81aafe117769a990a7180db83/1?pq-origsite=gscholar&cbl=55118

Cheverst, K., Davies, N., Mitchell, K., Friday, A. and Efstratiou, C., 2000, April. Developing a context-aware electronic tourist guide: Some issues and experiences. In *Proceedings of the SIGCHI Conference on Human Factors in Computing Systems* (pp. 17–24). ACM.

Davis, F.D., 1989. Perceived usefulness, perceived ease of use, and user acceptance of information technology. *MIS Quarterly*, 13(3), pp. 319–340.

Ding, Y. and Chai, K.H., 2015. Emotions and continued usage of mobile applications. *Industrial Management & Data Systems*, 115(5), pp. 833–852.

Fano, A. and Gershman, A., 2002. The future of business services in the age of ubiquitous computing. *Communications of the ACM*, 45(12), pp. 83–87.

Fishbein, M. and Ajzen, I., 1975. *Belief, attitude, intention and behavior: An introduction to theory and research.* Reading, MA: Addison-Wesley.

Gao, Q., Rau, P.L.P. and Salvendy, G., 2009. Perception of interactivity: Affects of four key variables in mobile advertising. *International Journal of Human-Computer Interaction*, 25(6), pp. 479–505.

Gerlich, R.N., Drumheller, K., Babb, J. and De'Armond, D., 2015. App consumption: An exploratory analysis of the uses & gratifications of mobile apps. *Academy of Marketing Studies Journal*, 19(1), pp. 69–79.

Gong, J. and Tarasewich, P., 2004, November. Guidelines for handheld mobile device interface design. In *Proceedings of DSI 2004 Annual Meeting* (pp. 3751–3756).

Gupta, S., 2013, For mobile devices, think apps, not ads. *Harvard Business Review*, 91, pp. 70–75.

Harris, M.A., Brookshire, R. and Chin, A.G., 2016. Identifying factors influencing consumers' intent to install mobile applications. *International Journal of Information Management*, 36(3), pp. 441–450.

Ho, H.Y. and Syu, L.Y., 2010, August. Uses and gratifications of mobile application users. In *International Conference on Electronics and Information Engineering (ICEIE), 2010* (Vol. 1, pp. V1-315–V1-318). IEEE.

Hu, Y., 2011. Linking perceived value, customer satisfaction, and purchase intention in e-commerce settings. In *Advances in Computer Science, Intelligent System and Environment* (pp. 623–628). Berlin, Heidelberg: Springer.

IHG, 2015. Annual report and form 20-F 2015. Available from: www.ihgplc.com/files/reports/ar2015/index.html. [10 October 2016].

Kang, S., 2014. Factors influencing intention of mobile application use. *International Journal of Mobile Communications*, 12(4), pp. 360–379.

Kannan, P.K., Chang, A.M. and Whinston, A.B., 2001, January. Wireless commerce: Marketing issues and possibilities. In *Proceedings of the 34th Annual Hawaii International Conference on System Sciences, 2001*. IEEE.

Katz, E., Blumler, J.G. and Gurevitch, M., 1974. *The uses and gratifications approach to mass communication.* Beverly Hills: Sage.

Kim, S.J., Wang, R.J.H. and Malthouse, E.C., 2015. The effects of adopting and using a brand's mobile application on customers' subsequent purchase behavior. *Journal of Interactive Marketing*, 31, pp. 28–41.

Kim, S.C., Yoon, D. and Han, E.K., 2014. Antecedents of mobile app usage among smartphone users. *Journal of Marketing Communications*, 22(6), pp. 1–18.

Kimes, S.E., 2011. Customer perceptions of electronic ordering. *Cornell Hospitality Report*, 11(9), pp. 4–18.

Kotler, P., 2000. *Marketing management: The millennium edition.* International edition. London: Prentice Hall.

Krcmar, M. and Strizhakova, Y., 2009. Uses and gratifications as media choice. In T. Hartman (ed.), *Media choice: A theoretical and empirical overview* (pp. 53–69). New York: Routledge.

Larivière, B., Joosten, H., Malthouse, E.C., van Birgelen, M., Aksoy, L., Kunz, W.H. and Huang, M.H., 2013. Value fusion: The blending of consumer and firm value in the distinct context of mobile technologies and social media. *Journal of Service Management*, 24(3), pp. 268–293.

Lewis, R., Brown, K. and Watkins, B., 2014, January. Identifying gratifications sought that drive positive attitudes toward mobile apps and intent to download mobile apps: Using gender as a moderating variable. In *American Academy of Advertising. Conference. Proceedings*, p. 70.

Lin, Y.H., Fang, C.H. and Hsu, C.L., 2014. Determining uses and gratifications for mobile phone apps. In *Future Information Technology* (pp. 661–668). Berlin, Heidelberg: Springer.

Morosan, C. and DeFranco, A., 2016. Modeling guests' intentions to use mobile apps in hotels: The roles of personalization, privacy, and involvement. *International Journal of Contemporary Hospitality Management*, 28(9), pp. 1968–1991.

Marriott International, 2015. Annual report. Available from: http://files.shareholder.com/downloads/MAR/0x0x884644/934434D3-0551-4E9D-94EF-687390A5AE6F/2015_AR.pdf. [10 October 2016].

Nyheim, P., Xu, S., Zhang, L. and Mattila, A.S., 2015. Predictors of avoidance towards personalization of restaurant smartphone advertising: A study from the Millennials' perspective. *Journal of Hospitality and Tourism Technology*, 6(2), pp. 145–159.

Paragas, F., Clara, D.Y., Main, L.T. and Rahman, N.B., 2010. Mobile telephony uses and gratifications among elderly Singaporeans. *Media Asia*, 37(4), p. 215.

Peng, K.F., Chen, Y. and Wen, K.W., 2014. Brand relationship, consumption values and branded app adoption. *Industrial Management & Data Systems*, 114(8), pp. 1131–1143.

Picoto, W.N., Palma-dos-Reis, A. and Bélanger, F., 2010, June. How does mobile business create value for firms? In *2010 Ninth International Conference on Mobile Business and 2010 Ninth Global Mobility Roundtable (ICMB-GMR)*, (pp. 9–16). IEEE.

Rafaeli, S., 1988. From new media to communication. *Sage Annual Review of Communication Research: Advancing Communication Science*, 16, pp. 110–134.

Sangle, P.S. and Awasthi, P., 2011. Consumer's expectations from mobile CRM services: A banking context. *Business Process Management Journal*, 17(6), pp. 898–918.

Shen, G.C.C., 2015. Users' adoption of mobile applications: Product type and message framing's moderating effect. *Journal of Business Research*, 68(11), pp. 2317–2321.

Skift, 2016. Hotel CEOs won't back down when it comes to pushing direct bookings. Available from: https://skift.com/2016/05/16/hotel-ceos-wont-back-down-when-it-comes-to-pushing-direct-bookings/. [15 October 2016].

Speller III, T.H., 2012. *The business and dynamics of free-to-play social-casual game apps* (Doctoral dissertation, Massachusetts Institute of Technology). Available from: http://dspace.mit.edu/handle/1721.1/70824. [15 October 2016].

Statista, 2016. Number of mobile app downloads worldwide from 2009 to 2017 (in millions). Available from: www.statista.com/statistics/266488/forecast-of-mobile-app-downloads/. [15 October 2016].

Stout, P.A., Villegas, J. and Kim, H., 2001. Enhancing learning through use of interactive tools on health-related websites. *Health Education Research*, 16(6), pp. 721–733.

Sundar, S.S., 2008. The MAIN model: A heuristic approach to understanding technology effects on credibility. In M.J. Metzger and A.J. Flanagin (eds.), *Digital media, youth, and credibility*. The John D. and Catherine T. MacArthur Foundation Series on Digital Media and Learning (pp. 73–100). Cambridge, MA: The MIT Press.

Venkatesh, V. and Bala, H., 2008. Technology acceptance model 3 and a research agenda on interventions. *Decision Sciences*, 39(2), pp. 273–315.

Venkatesh, V. and Davis, F.D., 2000. A theoretical extension of the technology acceptance model: Four longitudinal field studies. *Management Science*, 46(2), pp. 186–204.

Wang, B., Kim, S. and Malthouse, E.C., 2016. Branded apps and mobile platforms as new tools for advertising. *The new advertising: Branding, content, and consumer relationships in the data-driven social media era*. Santa Barbara, CA: ABC-CLIO.

Wang, H., Chung, J.E., Park, N., McLaughlin, M.L. and Fulk, J., 2012. Understanding online community participation: A technology acceptance perspective. *Communication Research*, 39(6), 781–801.

Wang, H.Y. and Wang, S.H., 2010. Predicting mobile hotel reservation adoption: Insight from a perceived value standpoint. *International Journal of Hospitality Management*, 29(4), pp. 598–608.

Wei, H.L., Lin, K.Y., Lu, H.P. and Chuang, I.H., 2015. Understanding the intentions of users to 'stick' to social networking sites: A case study in Taiwan. *Behaviour & Information Technology*, 34(2), pp. 151–162.

Weiser, M., 1991. The computer for the 21st century. *Scientific American*, 265(3), pp. 94–104.

Yang, H.C., 2013. Bon appétit for apps: Young american consumers' acceptance of mobile applications. *Journal of Computer Information Systems*, 53(3), pp. 85–96.

Zhao, Z. and Balagué, C., 2015. Designing branded mobile apps: Fundamentals and recommendations. *Business Horizons*, 58(3), pp. 305–315.

Further reading

Ask, J., Johnson, C., Drego, V.L., Harteveldt, H.H., Mulpuru, S. and Wiramihardja, L. 2011. Mobile is not just another channel. *Forrest Research*. Available from: www.forrester.com/report/Mobile+Is+Not+Jus t+Another+Channel/-/E-RES58676 [15 October 2016]. (Explaining the unique attributes of mobile phones and how marketers can leverage them to create new experiences for consumers.)

Furner, C.P., Racherla, P. and Babb, J.S., 2014. Mobile app stickiness (MASS) and mobile interactivity: A conceptual model. *The Marketing Review*, 14(2), pp. 163–188. (A discussion on how app features affect consumers' perceptions of interactivity.)

King, W.R. and He, J., 2006. A meta-analysis of the technology acceptance model. *Information & Management*, 43(6), pp. 740–755. (A detailed analysis of research using the TAM model.)

Krum, C., 2010. *Mobile marketing: Finding your customers no matter where they are*. Indianapolis, IN: Pearson Education. (A comprehensive guide for marketers on how to integrate mobile marketing with their existing on- and offline marketing campaigns.)

McQuail, D., 1985. Gratifications research and media theory: four models or one. In K.E. Rosengren, L.A. Wenner, and Palmer, P. (eds.), *Media gratification research: Current perspectives* (pp. 149–167). Beverly Hills, CA: Sage. (An introduction to U&G theory.)

Sundar, S.S., Jia, H., Waddell, T.F. and Huang, Y., 2015. Toward a theory of interactive media effects (TIME). In S. Sundart (ed.), *The handbook of the psychology of communication technology* (pp. 47–86). Chichester, UK: John Wiley & Sons, Ltd. (Explaining how interface features affect user psychology.)

43

Personalized hotel recommendations based on social networks

Shaowu Liu and Gang Li

Introduction

Recommender Systems (RecSys) aim to suggest items (hotels, books, movies, tourism attractions, etc.) that are potentially going to be liked by users. To identify the appropriate items, RecSys use various sources of information, such as the historical ratings given by users and the content of the items. RecSys were originally designed for users with insufficient personal experience or with limited knowledge of the items. However, with the rapid expansion of Web 2.0 and e-commerce, an overwhelming number of items are offered, and every user can benefit from RecSys.

Hotel recommendation is a well-studied topic in hospitality research (Chen and Chuang, 2016; Jannach et al., 2012). Most travelers used to receive similar recommendations via static methods, such as newspapers and television. Advances in Internet technology have made hotel recommendation more interactive, where travelers can now read reviews and recommendations shared by other travelers on social network, such as Twitter, TripAdvisor and Yelp. However, in all of these recommendation scenarios, travelers receive the same recommendation without personalization. For example, a traveler with a limited budget may still be recommended an expensive hotel because of its high average rating. Considering that there are thousands of hotels in popular destinations, it is impractical for travelers to find the hotel they really need by simply sorting the hotels via a criterion. Consequently, personalized hotel recommendation is needed to identify a small set of hotels which are potentially going to be liked by travelers.

Over the last decade there have been rapid advances in RecSys, in both academia and industry (Bennett and Lanning, 2007; Knijnenburg et al., 2012; Li et al., 2015). Numerous recommendation techniques have been proposed to achieve personalized recommendation. However, there has been limited work on personalized hotel recommendation (Garbers et al., 2006; Saga et al., 2008; Yu and Chang, 2009; Xiong and Geng, 2010) due to issues such as cold-start and non-rating data. This paper aims to review recommendation techniques in the context of hospitality and identify issues presented in personalized hotel recommendation.

Personalized hotel recommendation for individuals

Hotel recommendation is not a new thing, and it overlaps with hotel selection. Traditionally, the preferences of travelers were unknown or known only to a limited extent; thus, all travelers received similar recommendations derived from measuring the overall quality of hotels. Fortunately, social networks have made it possible to obtain a better understanding of travelers by analyzing the information they share on social networks, such as reviews, ratings, profiles, and social connections. With the availability of this rich information, personalized hotel recommendation becomes possible. In this section, we review how personalized hotel recommender systems can be built using information shared over social networks.

Recommendation using Explicit Feedback

Social network websites such as TripAdvisor and Yelp provide travelers with a virtual place to share their opinions on hotels. While other options are possible, ratings are the most commonly used format of review. For example, TripAdvisor allows travelers to rate a hotel from 1 to 5 stars, and optionally to rate different dimensions of the hotel, such as *cleanliness*, *location*, and *service*. Despite the popularity of star ratings, some websites tend to use other formats, such as thumbs up and thumbs down on Facebook. These kinds of feedback provided by travelers are called *Explicit Feedback*, where the travelers explicitly tell us whether they like or dislike the hotel. In general, explicit feedback-based recommender systems can be categorized into content-based filtering and collaborative filtering.

Content-based filtering

Content-based methods (Lops et al., 2011; Pazzani and Billsus, 2007) generate recommendations by exploiting regularities in the item content. For example, *actors*, *directors*, and *genres* can be extracted as the content of movies. In the context of hotel recommendation, the content could be *location, price, star rating*, etc. To make recommendations for a traveler u, we just need to find out which hotels are similar to the hotels the traveler liked before, i.e., highly rated by traveler u. The similarity between two hotels t_x and t_y can be computed by popular measures such as the Pearson Correlation Coefficient (PCC) and Vector Space Similarity.

Despite their simplicity, content-based methods have limitations. Firstly, it can be difficult to define features or extract content from some hotels. Secondly, travelers will always be recommended hotels that are highly similar to the hotels he/she liked, which leads to a lack of diversity (Bradley and Smyth, 2001) and a potentially better hotel may never be recommended.

Collaborative filtering

Collaborative filtering methods generate recommendations by analyzing preferences provided by travelers, e.g., ratings. One of the most popular and accurate collaborative filtering methods is Matrix Factorization (MF) (Koren et al., 2009). This approach discovers the latent factor spaces shared between travelers and hotels, where the latent factors can be used to describe both the taste of travelers and the characteristics of hotels. The attractiveness of a hotel to a traveler is then measured by the inner product of their latent feature vectors.

Formally, each traveler u is associated with a latent feature vector $p_u \in \mathbb{R}^k$ and each item i is associated with a latent feature vector $q_i \in \mathbb{R}^k$, where k is the number of factors. The aim of MF is then to estimate $\hat{r}_{ui} = b_{ui} + p_u^T q_i$ such that $\hat{r}_{ui} \cong r_{ui}$. The bias term $b_{ui} = \mu + b_u + b_i$ takes the biases into consideration, where μ is the overall average rating, b_u is the traveler bias, and b_i is the hotel bias. The latent feature vectors are learned by minimizing regularized squared error with respect to all known preferences:

$$\min_{p_u, q_u \in \mathbb{R}^k} \sum_{r_{ui} \in R} (r_{ui} - b_{ui} - p_u^T q_i)^2 + \lambda(||p_u||^2 + ||q_i||^2)$$

λ is the regularization coefficient. The optimization can be done with Stochastic Gradient Descent for the sake of speed on sparse data, or with Alternating Least Squares for the sake of parallelization on dense data.

Recommendation using Implicit Feedback

Not all users are willing to rate their preferences, where collecting feedback implicitly delivers a more user-friendly RecSys. Examples of implicit feedback include the time a user stayed on a webpage, the number of clicks a user performed on an item, and location information of users. The importance of implicit feedback has been recognized recently, and it provides an opportunity to utilize the vast amount of implicit data that have already been collected over the years, such as activity logs. In this section, we review implicit feedback-based recommender systems in the context of hotel recommendation.

Relative preference-based filtering

A preference relation (PR) encodes user preferences in form of pairwise ordering between items, i.e., is item X is better than item Y? This representation is a useful alternative to explicit ratings as it can be inferred from implicit data. For example, the PR over two web pages can be inferred by the browsing time, and consequently applies to the displayed hotels.

PR is formally defined as follows. Let $U = \{u\}^n$ and $I = \{i\}^m$ denote the set of n travelers and m hotels, respectively. The PR of a traveler $u \in U$ between hotels i and j is encoded as π_{uij}, which indicates the strength of traveler u's PR for the ordered hotel pair (i, j). A higher value of π_{uij} indicates a stronger preference for the first hotel over the second hotel (Desarkar et al., 2012; Liu et al., 2015):

$$\pi_{uij} = \begin{cases} \left(\dfrac{2}{3}, 1\right] & if \ i \succ j \ (u \ prefers \ i \ over \ j) \\[2mm] \left[\dfrac{1}{3}, \dfrac{2}{3}\right] & if \ i \simeq j \ (equally \ preferable) \\[2mm] \left[0, \dfrac{1}{3}\right) & if \ i \prec j \ (u \ prefers \ j \ over \ i) \end{cases}$$

The PR can be converted into user-wise preferences for hotels:

$$p_{ui} = \frac{\sum_{j \in I_u} \left[\!\left[\pi_{uij} > \dfrac{2}{3} \right]\!\right] - \sum_{j \in I_u} \left[\!\left[\pi_{uij} < \dfrac{1}{3} \right]\!\right]}{\left| \prod_{ui} \right|}$$

Where $[\![\cdot]\!]$ gives 1 for true and 0 for false, and $\prod_{ui}$ is the set of traveler u's PR related t hotel i.

Once the user-wise preferences are computed from implicit feedback, they can be set as input for model-based collaborative filtering methods (Brun et al., 2010; Desarkar et al., 2012; Liu et al., 2015).

Text-based filtering

Online reviews may contain both ratings and text-based comments. While ratings are easy to process, it remains a challenge to extract useful information from textual reviews. However, textual reviews can be particularly useful when travelers do not provide enough ratings. For example, TripAdvisor allows travelers to rate hotels on several optional dimensions such as *cleanliness* and *service*. When the rating of a dimension is missing from the traveler, it can be filled by extracting the traveler's opinion from textual reviews. Extracting opinions from text is the task of sentiment analysis and opinion mining (Liu 2012), which can be further divided into two sub-tasks: topic identification and opinion extraction.

In general, the first step is to identify topics from the text. For example, review comments may contain many sentences, and a method is required to classify which topic a sentence belongs to, e.g., *cleanliness*. This can be done using a simple keywords matching method (Liu et al., 2013) or advanced techniques such as topic models (Mei et al., 2007).

Once the topics are identified, the second task is to extract positive, negative, and subjective opinions from the associated text. One method is to look up words and/or phrases in sentiment dictionaries, such as SentiWordNet 3.0 (Baccianella et al., 2010). Having extracted the opinions, missing ratings can be filled and a denser dataset is obtained for better recommendation performance.

Evaluation of hotel recommender systems

The evaluation metrics are essential for building successful recommender systems. Efforts have been made to identify the correct way of measuring the quality of recommendations. This section reviews common evaluation metrics in hotel recommender systems.

Accuracy metrics

Two popular metrics are Mean Absolute Error (MAE) and Root Mean Squared Error (RMSE), which measure the differences between the predicted preferences and true preferences. Let N be the number of unrated items by user u_a, and $\hat{r}_i$ be the predicted rating of item t_i, the definition of MAE and RMSE are as follows:

$$\text{MAE} = \frac{\sum_{a,i} |\hat{r}_{a,i} - r_{a,i}|}{N}$$

$$\text{RMSE} = \sqrt{\frac{\sum_{a,i} (\hat{r}_{a,i} - r_{a,i})^2}{N}}$$

Diversity

Traditionally, the evaluation of RecSys is mainly based on accuracy metrics such as RMSE. However, the accuracy metrics fail to evaluate some properties of the hotels other than preferences, such as Serendipity (Ge et al., 2010) and Diversity (Zhou et al., 2008). For example, a hotel recommendation list should contain both budget hotels and luxury hotels even if a traveler prefers budget hotels in most cases.

One diversity metric is Personalization, in which the uniqueness of each user's recommendation list is measured. Personalization refers to the inter-user diversity (Zhou et al., 2008):

$$\text{Personalization} = \frac{2}{m(m-1)} \sum_{x \neq y} \left(1 - \frac{|L_k(u_x) \cap L_k(u_y)|}{L_k(u_x)} \right)$$

Where m is the number of users, and $\left(1 - \dfrac{|L_k(u_x) \cap L_k(u_y)|}{L_k(u_x)} \right)$ is the Hamming distance between recommendation lists $L_k(u_x)$ and $L_k(u_y)$.

Coverage

Coverage refers to the percentage of hotels out of all hotels a RecSys can recommend. This metric is based on the observation that some hotels may not have the chance to be recommended to any traveler if it is not popular, e.g., a new hotel.

Let N be the length of recommendation list, L_d be the number of distinct hotels in all Top-N recommendation lists, and L be the number of distinct hotels in all recommendation lists. The N-dependent coverage is defined as (Ge et al., 2010):

$$\text{Coverage}(N) = L_d / L$$

A low coverage means that the RecSys can only make recommendations out of a small number of distinct hotels, in other words, it always recommends the popular hotels. Note that RecSys with high coverage implies higher diversity (Lü and Liu, 2011).

Stability

Stability measures the consistency of recommendations for the same traveler (Adomavicius and Zhang, 2012). The recommendations generated by a stable RecSys should be similar after some new preferences are added. For example, the first recommendation of an unstable RecSys predicts hotel X as 5-star and hotel Y as 1-star. Then the traveler stayed in hotel X and rated it as 5-star. With this new preference added to the preferences data, an unstable RecSys may generate the second recommendation that predicts hotel Y as 5-star. The 5-star hotel Y, which was previously 1-star, may lead to user confusion and reduce the trust of the RecSys. The stability property has been studied in detail in Adomavicius and Zhang (2012).

Personalized hotel recommendation for groups

In real-world applications, there are many scenarios where recommendations are made for a group of travelers, such as holiday packages (McCarthy et al., 2007) and tourist promotions (Garcia et al., 2009). Group Recommender Systems (G-RecSys) focuse on making recommendations that fit the needs of a group of travelers, instead of individuals. In classic RecSys, the goal is to maximize the satisfaction of a single traveler. However, G–RecSys need to make a trade-off among travelers in the group, where the optimal recommendations that satisfy everyone often do not exist.

Recent developments in social networks and interactive media (e.g. interactive TV) have further linked users into groups (Gartrell et al, 2010; Jameson and Smyth, 2007; Masthoff, 2011; Vasuki et al, 2010; Yu et al, 2006), and therefore have heightened the need for G–RecSys. However, personalized G–RecSys have only been discussed in limited literature compared to classic RecSys, and this is particularly true in the context of hospitality. A few survey papers have tried to summarize related research. For example:

(1)   The influential survey by Jameson and Smyth (2007) divided group recommendation into four sub-tasks: Group Preference Specification, Group Recommendation Generation, Explaining Recommendations, and Achieving Consensus. Descriptions are given on how existing G–RecSys handle these tasks.
(2)   Boratto and Carta (2010) classified user groups into four types: Established Group, Occasional Group, Random Group, and Automatically Identified Group. Existing G–RecSys are examined with a focus on how the type of group affects the design of G–RecSys.
(3)   More recently, Masthoff (2011) surveyed techniques used in the Group Recommendation Generation sub-task. Eleven aggregation strategies inspired by Social Choice Theory are summarized with discussions on existing G–RecSys.

Current G–RecSys research mainly focus on answering the following four questions: (1) How to collect and represent preferences? (2) How to generate recommendations by aggregating preferences of individuals? (3) How to explain the recommendations? (4) How to help group users arriving at a final decision?

Group recommendation generation

Group recommendation generation refers to the process of aggregating group users' preferences and making recommendations based on the aggregated preferences. Regardless of preference specification, individual users' preferences have to be aggregated in some way, and identifying the proper aggregation approach has been the main focus in the literature (Arrow 2012; Jameson and Smyth, 2007). In general, there are three approaches to generating group recommendations, and all require preference aggregations (Jameson and Smyth, 2007):

(1)   Merging Recommendations of Individuals: In this approach, the classic RecSys is applied to make recommendations for individuals. The recommendations for a group are then computed by merging the recommended items for each individual in the group. The merging is controlled by a selected aggregation function and in the simplest case the items with the highest predicted ratings for individuals are selected.
(2)   Aggregating Preferences of Individuals: This approach also relies on the ratings of individuals predicted by the classic RecSys. The difference is that instead of making a list of recommendations for each individual, the ratings for each item are aggregated. In other words, each item receives a rating aggregated from the preferences of all group users. The group recommendation is made by selecting the items with the highest ratings.
(3)   Constructing Group Preference Models: This approach does not require predictions of ratings for individual users. Instead, the known preferences of individual users are

aggregated into a single profile for the whole group. After the aggregation, the group looks no different from a normal user, and recommendations are made for this group using classic RecSys.

Basically, G-RecSys either aggregate preferences of individuals or construct a Group Preference Model. The main advantage of Group Preference Models over preference aggregations is the privacy benefits. When users' preferences are aggregated into a Group Preference Model, the individual user's preferences are hidden. However, preference aggregation methods can make better recommendations in some cases. For example, items recommended by preference aggregation approaches will not be disliked by all group users, where it is possible, though unlikely, that no group user likes the items recommended by Group Preference Models. No matter which approach is selected, the main issue involved is how to perform aggregation. Most aggregation methods discussed in existing surveys are inspired by strategies from Social Choice Theory (Arrow, 2012). For example, the Maximizing Average strategy will recommend an item that can achieve the highest average rating from group members. On the other hand, the Minimizing Misery will discard items that are very disliked by any group member even if the average rating is high. These kinds of strategies are very intuitive but selecting which one to use is a manual process. The choice of aggregation methods is often left as an open question or very basic methods are used (Amer-Yahia et al., 2009). However, a lot of established aggregation methods have been developed in communities other than RecSys and Social Choice Theory, such as Fuzzy Integrals (Beliakov et al., 2007). These techniques are powerful tools to aggregate data, and are often less context dependent.

Explaining Recommendations

Explaining Recommendations (Knijnenburg et al., 2012; McSherry, 2005) is the task of making the recommendation process more transparent to the users, i.e. why are these items recommended? how confident are you that the recommendations will be liked? For example, a RecSys could make the following explanation (O'Donovan and Smyth, 2005): "the items are recommended to you because they have been successfully recommended to users A, B, and C who are similar to you. In addition, we have made X, Y, and Z times recommendations to them in the past, which received P, Q, and R likes." In the context of group recommendations, the Explaining Recommendations task refers to making group users fully understand the recommendations. However, the primary goal of explanation is not to convince the users about the proposed recommendations, but helping the users to understand other group users' feelings about the recommendations. This process will help the group users to adjust the proposed recommendations to arrive at a final decision. Unlike classic RSs, debate and negotiation are often necessary for group users, and this calls for understanding of not only the pros but also the cons of the proposed recommendations. While existing explanation approaches focus on determining how good the recommendation is for the user, it is now desirable to know how bad the recommendation is for each group user.

Achieving consensus

The proposed recommendations can be promising but may eventually be rejected by the group. Making the final decision is a complex process that may involve extensive debate and negotiation. Typical G-RecSys assume that group users are independent and consider each user equally.

Technically, G-RecSys is able to identify the recommendations that maximize the overall satisfaction of the group; however, the true maximized satisfaction may not be achieved when interactions exist among group users. For example, when recommending a travel destination for a family, the recommended destination may maximize the average satisfaction of all family members. However, the parents may prefer another destination over their favorites because they care about their children's satisfaction, but on the other hand, the children may not consider their parents' satisfaction too much. In this case, one of the children's favorite destinations that is not disliked by the parents may be the final decision. Ideally, G-RecSys should take such in-group interactions into consideration, either prior to the recommendation generation, or make an adjustment after receiving the feedback on the proposed recommendations. Considering user interactions in recommendation generation has been studied by Amer-Yahia et al. (2009), where a consensus function is defined as maximizing item relevance and minimizing disagreements between group users. However, modeling complex user interactions remains an unsolved research problem. Another way to consider user interactions is to make an adjustment by evaluating feedback on proposed recommendations. This kind of process is called Reinforcement Learning, and has been applied in the context of classic RecSys (Mahmood and Ricci, 2009; Taghipour et al., 2007).

Recommender systems software packages

Although many companies have implemented their own recommender systems to accommodate their specific business needs, there are still many free/open source recommender system software packages available. In this section, we review some popular software packages for practitioners to build their hotel recommender systems.

MyMediaLite

MyMediaLite (http://mymedialite.net/) is a recommender system library for the Microsoft. NET platform, and it runs on Linux and Mac OS X through the Mono platform. It implements common RecSys algorithms to build models from both explicit ratings and implicit feedback. The software is free and open source, and can be used, modified, and distributed under the terms of the GNU General Public License (GPL).

Apache Mahout

Apache Mahout (http://mahout.apache.org/) is a scalable machine learning library which implements a few standard recommender system algorithms. This software is particularly useful for building recommender systems on a large amount of data, e.g., 100 million records. The software is implemented in the Java programming language and is free/open source under Apache License.

Recommenderlab

Recommenderlab (https://cran.r-project.org/web/packages/recommenderlab/index.html) is a package for the R programming language. It provides a research infrastructure to test and develop recommender algorithms including UBCF, IBCF, FunkSVD, and association rule-based algorithms. The software is free/open source under GPL-2 license.

Easyrec

Easyrec (http://easyrec.org/) is a free/open source software package that can easily integrate recommender systems into websites though plugins and Javascript code. This is particularly useful for hotels who want to add simple recommendation functions to their website with limited resources.

waffles_recommend

waffles_recommend (http://uaf46365.ddns.uark.edu/waffles/command/recommend.html) is a command-line tool for predicting missing values in incomplete data, or for testing collaborative filtering recommendation systems. It provides simple recommender system algorithms and is computationally efficient.

LensKit

LensKit (http://lenskit.org/) is a software package that implements many popular collaborative filtering algorithms and provides a set of tools to benchmark them. The software is implemented in the Java programming language. The software is free and open source under General Public License (GNU).

GraphLab (Turi)

GraphLab (Turi) (https://turi.com/) is a sophisticated machine learning platform. It implements recommender system algorithms and provides commercial support. In addition, a one-year free subscription is available for academic use.

Conclusions

This chapter aimed to present the state of the art recommender systems for the purpose of hotel recommendation. This has included recommendation techniques using explicit feedback, such as ratings. We also reviewed recommendation techniques using implicit feedback, such as *clicks* and *page views*, which are gaining in popularity in recent years. To evaluate recommender systems, we reviewed commonly used metrics, including accuracy metrics, diversity, coverage, and stability. In addition, we provided a list of free and open source software packages for practitioners to create their own recommender systems.

There has been extensive research on the topic of recommender systems, some of which have been applied to hotel recommendation. As this chapter provides only an introduction to this topic, we recommend a list of books and papers under *Further Reading* for readers.

References

Adomavicius, G., & Zhang, J. (2012). Stability of recommendation algorithms. *ACM Transactions on Information Systems (TOIS)*, 30(4), 23.

Amer-Yahia, S., Roy, S. B., Chawlat, A., Das, G., & Yu, C. (2009). Group recommendation: Semantics and efficiency. *Proceedings of the VLDB Endowment*, 2(1), 754–765.

Arrow, K. J. (2012). *Social choice and individual values (Vol. 12).* Yale University Press.

Baccianella, S., Esuli, A., & Sebastiani, F. (2010, May). SentiWordNet 3.0: An enhanced lexical resource for sentiment analysis and opinion mining. *LREC*, 10, pp. 2200–2204.

Beliakov, G., Pradera, A., & Calvo, T. (2007). *Aggregation functions: A guide for practitioners* (Vol. 221). Heidelberg: Springer.

Bennett, J., & Lanning, S. (2007, August). The netflix prize. In *Proceedings of KDD cup and workshop* (Vol. 2007, p. 35).

Boratto, L. & Carta, S. (2010). State-of-the-art in group recommendation and new approaches for automatic identification of groups. In *Information retrieval and mining in distributed environments* (pp. 1–20). Springer Berlin Heidelberg.

Bradley, K., & Smyth, B. (2001). Improving recommendation diversity. In *Proceedings of the Twelfth Irish Conference on Artificial Intelligence and Cognitive Science*, Maynooth, Ireland (pp. 85–94).

Brun, A., Hamad, A., Buffet, O., & Boyer, A. (2010, September). Towards preference relations in recommender systems. In *Preference Learning (PL 2010) ECML/PKDD 2010 Workshop*.

Chen, T., & Chuang, Y. H. (2016). Fuzzy and nonlinear programming approach for optimizing the performance of ubiquitous hotel recommendation. *Journal of Ambient Intelligence and Humanized Computing*, 1–10.

Desarkar, M. S., Saxena, R., & Sarkar, S. (2012, July). Preference relation based matrix factorization for recommender systems. In *International Conference on User Modeling, Adaptation, and Personalization* (pp. 63–75). Springer Berlin Heidelberg.

Garbers, J., Niemann, M., & Mochol, M. (2006). A personalized hotel selection engine. In *Proceedings of the Third European Semantic Web Conference*.

Garcia, I., Sebastia, L., Onaindia, E., & Guzman, C. (2009, September). A group recommender system for tourist activities. In *International Conference on Electronic Commerce and Web Technologies* (pp. 26–37). Springer Berlin Heidelberg.

Gartrell, M., Xing, X., Lv, Q., Beach, A., Han, R., Mishra, S., & Seada, K. (2010, November). Enhancing group recommendation by incorporating social relationship interactions. In *Proceedings of the 16th ACM International Conference on Supporting Group Work* (pp. 97–106). ACM.

Ge, M., Delgado-Battenfeld, C., & Jannach, D. (2010, September). Beyond accuracy: Evaluating recommender systems by coverage and serendipity. In *Proceedings of the Fourth ACM Conference on Recommender systems* (pp. 257–260). ACM.

Jameson, A., & Smyth, B. (2007). Recommendation to groups. In *The adaptive web* (pp. 596–627). Springer Berlin Heidelberg.

Jannach, D., Gedikli, F., Karakaya, Z., & Juwig, O. (2012). Recommending hotels based on multi-dimensional customer ratings. *Information and communication technologies in tourism*. Springer-Verlag/Wien.

Knijnenburg, B. P., Willemsen, M. C., Gantner, Z., Soncu, H., & Newell, C. (2012). Explaining the user experience of recommender systems. *User Modeling and User-Adapted Interaction*, 22(4–5), 441–504.

Knijnenburg, B. P., Willemsen, M. C., Gantner, Z., Soncu, H., & Newell, C. (2012). Explaining the user experience of recommender systems. *User Modeling and User-Adapted Interaction*, 22(4–5), 441–504.

Koren, Y., Bell, R., & Volinsky, C. (2009). Matrix factorization techniques for recommender systems. *Computer*, 42(8), 30–37.

Li, X., Xu, G., Chen, E., & Zong, Y. (2015). Learning recency based comparative choice towards point-of-interest recommendation. *Expert Systems with Applications*, 42(9), 4274–4283.

Liu, B. (2012). Sentiment analysis and opinion mining. *Synthesis Lectures on Human Language Technologies*, 5(1), 1–167.

Liu, S., Law, R., Rong, J., Li, G., & Hall, J. (2013). Analyzing changes in hotel customers' expectations by trip mode. *International Journal of Hospitality Management*, 34, 359–371.

Liu, S., Li, G., Tran, T., & Jiang, Y. (2015). Preference relation-based Markov random fields for recommender systems. In *Proceedings of the 7th Asian Conference on Machine Learning* (pp. 157–172).

Lops, P., De Gemmis, M., & Semeraro, G. (2011). Content-based recommender systems: State of the art and trends. In *Recommender systems handbook* (pp. 73–105). Springer US.

Lü, L., & Liu, W. (2011). Information filtering via preferential diffusion. *Physical Review E*, 83(6), 066119.

Mahmood, T., & Ricci, F. (2009, June). Improving recommender systems with adaptive conversational strategies. In *Proceedings of the 20th ACM Conference on Hypertext and hypermedia* (pp. 73–82). ACM.

Masthoff, J. (2011). Group recommender systems: Combining individual models. In *Recommender systems handbook* (pp. 677–702). Springer US.

McCarthy, K., McGinty, L., & Smyth, B. (2007, August). Case-based group recommendation: Compromising for success. In *International Conference on Case-Based Reasoning* (pp. 299–313). Springer Berlin Heidelberg.

McSherry, D. (2005). Explanation in recommender systems. *Artificial Intelligence Review*, 24(2), 179–197.

Mei, Q., Ling, X., Wondra, M., Su, H., & Zhai, C. (2007, May). Topic sentiment mixture: Modeling facets and opinions in weblogs. In *Proceedings of the 16th International Conference on World Wide Web* (pp. 171–180). ACM.

O'Donovan, J., & Smyth, B. (2005, January). Trust in recommender systems. In *Proceedings of the 10th International Conference on Intelligent User Interfaces* (pp. 167–174). ACM.

Pazzani, M. J., & Billsus, D. (2007). Content-based recommendation systems. In *The adaptive web* (pp. 325–341). Springer Berlin Heidelberg.

Saga, R., Hayashi, Y., & Tsuji, H. (2008, October). Hotel recommender system based on user's preference transition. In IEEE International Conference on Systems, Man and Cybernetics, 2008. SMC 2008. (pp. 2437–2442). IEEE.

Taghipour, N., Kardan, A., & Ghidary, S. S. (2007, October). Usage-based web recommendations: A reinforcement learning approach. In *Proceedings of the 2007 ACM Conference on Recommender Systems* (pp. 113–120). ACM.

Vasuki, V., Natarajan, N., Lu, Z., & Dhillon, I. S. (2010, September). Affiliation recommendation using auxiliary networks. In *Proceedings of the Fourth ACM Conference on Recommender Systems* (pp. 103–110). ACM.

Xiong, Y. N., & Geng, L. X. (2010, August). Personalized Intelligent Hotel Recommendation System for Online Reservation—A Perspective of product and user characteristics. In *2010 International Conference on Management and Service Science (MASS)*. IEEE.

Yu, C. C., & Chang, H. P. (2009, September). Personalized location-based recommendation services for tour planning in mobile tourism applications. In *International Conference on Electronic Commerce and Web Technologies* (pp. 38–49). Springer Berlin Heidelberg.

Yu, Z., Zhou, X., Hao, Y., & Gu, J. (2006). TV program recommendation for multiple viewers based on user profile merging. *User Modeling and User-adapted Interaction*, 16(1), 63–82.

Zhou, T., Jiang, L. L., Su, R. Q., & Zhang, Y. C. (2008). Effect of initial configuration on network-based recommendation. *EPL (Europhysics Letters)*, 81(5), article no. 58004.

Further reading

Bobadilla, J., Ortega, F., Hernando, A., & Gutiérrez, A. (2013). Recommender systems survey. *Knowledge-Based Systems*, 46, 109–132. (An extensive survey of recommender systems.)

Chen, L., Chen, G., & Wang, F. (2015). Recommender systems based on user reviews: The state of the art. *User Modeling and User-Adapted Interaction*, 25(2), 99–154. (Create recommender systems from user reviews.)

Gavalas, D., Konstantopoulos, C., Mastakas, K., & Pantziou, G. (2014). Mobile recommender systems in tourism. *Journal of Network and Computer Applications*, 39, 319–333. (Recommender systems in the mobile environment.)

Liu, B. (2012). Sentiment analysis and opinion mining. *Synthesis Lectures on Human Language Technologies*, 5(1), 1–167. (Explains how to extract opinions from text-based reviews.)

Lü, L., Medo, M., Yeung, C. H., Zhang, Y. C., Zhang, Z. K., & Zhou, T. (2012). Recommender systems. *Physics Reports*, 519(1), 1–49. (An extensive survey of recommender systems.)

Park, D. H., Kim, H. K., Choi, I. Y., & Kim, J. K. (2012). A literature review and classification of recommender systems research. *Expert Systems with Applications*, 39(11), 10059–10072. (An extensive survey of recommender systems.)

Ricci, F., Rokach, L., & Shapira, B. (2011). *Introduction to recommender systems handbook* (pp. 1–35). Springer US. (This handbook covers most topics concerning recommender systems.)

44

The impact of smartphones on hospitality consumer behavior

Colin Mang, Natalya Brown and Linda Piper

Introduction

> Anything can change, because the smartphone revolution is still in the early stages.
> — *Tim Cook, CEO, Apple Inc.*

Smartphones provide users with mobile Internet connectivity, allowing users to perform functions on a hand-held device that previously required a computer. When Yelp, a leading publisher of crowd-sourced reviews of local businesses, launched a new filter to help users find check-in points near local restaurants for Pokémon Go, a smartphone game whose popularity exploded in the summer of 2016, the firm was exploiting a powerful trend ushered in by the rise of smartphones and their applications that has transformed tourism and hospitality marketing. Smartphone owners represented 79 percent of the US mobile market in 2015 (comScore 2016), while the median ownership rate was 68 percent across eleven advanced economies and 37 percent and rising in emerging and developing economies in 2015 (Pew Research Centre 2016).

The number of "connected" travelers, those with mobile Internet access while traveling, is on the rise and the hospitality industry is beginning to take note. A 2015 Ipsos study, "The TripBarometer Connected Traveler," released by travel review firm TripAdvisor, claims that, across the globe, 42 percent of travelers use their smartphones to plan or book a trip (TripAdvisor 2015b). Further, almost 75 percent of these connected travelers use their smartphone to search for restaurants while traveling and 34 percent of them want hotels or other types of accommodation to offer mobile check-in services. The majority of Chinese travelers can be considered connected while just under half of American travelers currently utilize their mobile devices to plan, book, navigate and/or search for activities and services while touring. According to emarketer. com, in 2016 close to 52 percent of travelers will use a mobile device to book their trips, and of the 48.5 million American adults who book trips using a mobile device, almost 80 percent of them will specifically use a smartphone to do so (emarketer.com 2016). They estimate that travel booked through mobile devices (which accounted for 52.08 billion USD in 2015) will represent close to 50 percent of the market value of travel bookings by 2019. The tourism and hospitality industry has experienced a tremendous increase in mobile activity in recent years, as mobility affords a new communication channel, allowing enterprises to market to their patrons and guests in a more personalized way.

As Birenboim (2016) notes, the fast pace of modern life has focused our attention on "episodic occurrences and immediate experiences." Experiences are central to the tourism and hospitality industry, and smartphones improve users' ability to document, share, and investigate these momentary experiences. In this chapter, we consider how smartphones and mobile technology have transformed the tourist experience. First, we examine the nature and habits of the connected traveler. Then, in order to understand how smartphones have transformed the tourist experience, we explore how hospitality consumers perceive and use smartphones. Finally, we discuss the responses of hospitality providers to the proliferation of smartphones and the new behaviors of the connected hospitality consumer.

The connected traveler and the "tourist gaze"

Tourism can be seen as an encounter between people, space, and contexts (Crouch 2005). The tourism experience encompasses the consumption of the physical, social, and cultural, their subjective interpretation and meaning, and involves multi-sensory dimensions, that is, sights, sounds, smells, tastes, and emotions (Tussyadiah and Zach 2012). Throughout the tourism experience, the traveler's attention is influenced by tales heard from returned travelers, the research that the traveler conducts, and the types of marketing messages that reach the traveler and help shape the experience. John Urry, who in the early 1990s coined the phrase "tourist gaze" to describe the focus of the traveler's interest, posited that there are three "notes" that shape the gaze (see Urry 1990, 2008). First, the gaze can be *organized* by professional sources – such as travel publications, travel agencies, hotel owners, photographers, television programs, tourism boards, tour operators. Second, gazes are *authorized* by different discourses – talk and interest in educational, health-based, group-based, and leisure and play activities. Third, the gaze can be *characterized* as either romantic or collective in nature. The tourist's gaze may center on being a part of happenings, events, and a sense of carnival, or it may focus on privacy and solitude and even a type of communion with nature, religion, or art.

The hospitality experience, whether based on a hotel or accommodation booking, a restaurant visited, an art gallery explored, a mode of transportation or a cruise enjoyed, will be organized, authorized, and characterized by the traveler's gaze. Over time the tourist gaze has become more mediated with new information sources, shifting both the traveler's interest and their perception of the travel experience (Beeton, Bowen and Santos 2005; Lagerkvist 2008). Smartphones, utilized directly and constantly by a connected traveler, are the mediators of the tourism experience *du jour*. At present, that gaze is now being organized for many connected travelers by smartphones, with the traveler exerting greater control over the information she or he receives.

The ubiquity of smartphones and other mobile devices in everyday life has translated to their increasing prevalence in traveler decision-making and experiences. Smartphones allow travelers to access location-specific services and they facilitate en-route decision-making; they reduce the amount of pre-trip planning required, and have subsequently become a growing marketing platform (Kennedy-Eden and Gretzel 2012; Kim and Law 2015; No and Kim 2014; Tussyadiah 2012). They also allow travelers to cope with unexpected situations and to conduct their travel with greater efficiency (Wang, Park and Fesenmaier 2012). The experience and the ability of the visitor to capture and alter the hospitality and travel experience has undergone a kind of revolution – from passive to more active, from less reactive to more proactive, and more personal. The focus of travelers' attention and their perception of their travel experience, the tourist gaze, is being shifted by the introduction of the smartphone. In the next section, we explore further the ways in which travelers are using their phones as well as the impact such usage is having on the travel experience.

Consumer use of smartphones in the hospitality context

> The same regions of the brain light up when someone touches their smartphone as when they touch a family member or a pet.
>
> – *Matt Cohler, Vice President, Facebook*

Smartphone users have described their devices as an extension of their personality and individuality, a companion, an assistant, a friend, and a source of security, and have attributed feeling more connected, informed, entertained, and productive with their use (Grant and O'Donohoe 2007; Wang, Xiang and Fesenmaier 2016). Within the hospitality context, smartphone technology has the ability to affect all three "stages" of the tourist experience, from the planning phase to the experiential phase to the post-trip reflection phase (Gretzel, Fesenmaier and O'Leary 2006; Wang et al. 2012; Wang, Xiang and Fesenmaier 2014). Also, smartphones can be used by travelers to find and share information, problem solve, make purchases, access social networks, and access entertainment, among other uses (Tussyadiah and Wang 2016). Travel decisions often require more pre-travel information processing than other types of consumer product decisions as travel is considered riskier (Huang, Chou and Lin 2010); smartphones provide a powerful new tool to enhance this process.

The prime category of information needs for a traveler is functional. These needs include the need for information to learn, to improve efficiency, and to reduce uncertainty and stress during travel. Smartphones can also satisfy the traveler's hospitality information needs in terms of novelty, creativity, and hedonic pleasure. Finally, the social networking capabilities provided by smartphones, which allow travelers to share and interpret their experiences with friends or connect with other travelers, satisfy travelers' social information needs. The outcome of this mediation is seen through the changes in travelers' behaviors/activities and emotional states (see Figure 44.1).

Earlier research examined the way in which mobile and social technologies have expanded and modified the traditional forms of tourism (e.g. Germann Molz 2012; Paris 2012; Wang et al. 2012). With mobile technology, travelers are engrossed in a hybrid middle ground, as the lines between the traditional binaries of home/away, authentic/inauthentic, leisure/work, host/guest, extraordinary/mundane, and present/absent on which tourism has been characterized are blurred (Hannam and Knox 2010; Hannam, Butler and Paris 2014). The tourist experience was often associated with an escape from the mundane, and was distinct from daily norms and values (Uriely 2005); however, smartphones blur the distinction by linking tourists to their home lives (Wang et al. 2016). MacKay and Vogt (2012) and Wang et al. (2016) show how advancements in information and communication technology have increased the spillover between the tourism context and the everyday context. Smartphones appear to be hastening the demise of the separation of the tourist experience and everyday life, long predicted and suggested by scholars such as Lash and Urry (1994) and Uriely (2005).

The instantaneous access to information that smartphones provide reduces a traveler's decision-making time frame, resulting in more instantaneous decisions and more micro-moments, as well as a shift in information needs towards more hedonic/creative needs (Lamsfus, Wang, Alzua-Sorzabal and Xiang 2015). Because smartphones enable en-route booking of hotels, transportation, tickets, and restaurant reservations (Wang et al. 2016), they allow for greater spontaneity and less pre-planning of travel arrangements (Huang et al. 2014). Kim, Xiang and Fesenmaier

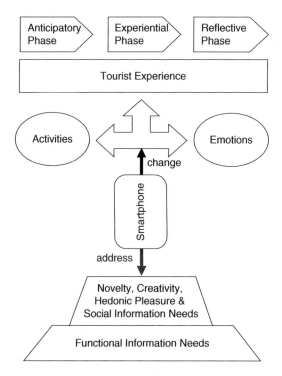

Figure 44.1 Mediation mechanisms of smartphones in the touristic experience

(2015) report that 60 percent of same-day bookings are made by mobile buyers, with bookings for airlines, hotels, and restaurants accounting for the majority of tourism purchases made from mobile phones.

Much of travelers' information and purchasing activities take place via software applications or "apps." Wang et al. (2012) identify twelve categories of travel "apps" including: *flight information* apps, which allow searching and tracking of flights; *destination guides*, which provide information about a particular locale; *online travel agencies*, which allow searching and booking of hotels, transportation, and attraction tickets; *facilitator* apps, which provide quick facts such as locations for local WiFi hotspots, gas stations, etc.; *attraction guides*, which provide travel tips and information regarding a particular attraction such as a theme park; *entertainment* apps, which provide amusement during the journey; *food finder* apps, which provide restaurant information; *language* translation apps; *local transportation* apps; *augmented reality* apps, which allow the user to view live spaces from a different perspective or from a different locale; *currency converter* apps for finding exchange rates; and *tip calculators*.

Both Kennedy-Eden and Gretzel (2012) and Pedrana (2013) note that travel apps have empowered individuals. Nevertheless, in a study reported in Lu, Mao, Wang, and Hu (2015), although 60 percent of travelers with a smartphone downloaded travel apps, only 45 percent of them used the apps for their travel decision-making. Consumer adoption of smartphone apps is hindered by the need to search in restricted app-stores and by the need to wait for a download and sometimes pay for the app (Dickinson et al. 2014; Lu et al. 2015), and as a result, consumers may opt to access websites from their phones instead. However, Budiu and Nielsen (2010) have found that an individual's ability to use mobile websites is significantly lower than the ability to use websites on a computer, with the average success rate for a given task being 80 percent on a PC but only 59 percent on a phone, with the smaller screen, awkward input, and slower data connection among the contributors to smartphone users' poorer performance. A further barrier to smartphone usage is the availability of data services; cellular data plans are often expensive for international travel and free WiFi hotspots may not always be readily available, thus limiting travelers' use of their phones. Mang, Piper and Brown (2016) found that less than half of international travelers have non-WiFi data access while traveling. Among those with continuous data access, they found that 63 percent use their phone to search for transportation, 55 percent of travelers use their phone to look at maps, 51 percent use it to search for restaurants and shops, and 48 percent use it to access information about a particular tourist attraction. In contrast, for those with data access only in WiFi zones, the figures are 28 percent, 23 percent, 21 percent, and 16 percent, respectively. The issue of data service availability also factors into decision-making with respect to accommodation, as a recent study by TripAdvisor found that 46 percent of travelers would look elsewhere if an accommodation did not provide free in-room WiFi (TripAdvisor 2015a). Several factors have been put forward to explain travelers' use and intention to use smartphones to retrieve these types of information. No and Kim (2014) found that travelers' intentions to use their mobile phones for this purpose is influenced by the perceived usefulness of the information, the ease of use of the phone, and prior satisfaction with travel websites. In addition, Mang et al. (2016) and Wang et al. (2014) found that greater use of one's phone in everyday contexts also increases the likelihood of use while traveling, while Kim, Chung, Lee and Preis (2015) emphasize the time-saving feature of mobile purchasing as an important driver of adoption.

Besides the transactional functions of information retrieval and purchasing, smartphones also facilitate social functions among connected travelers. One's use of a smartphone to communicate with others changes the organization of co-presence in both temporal and positional terms (see, for example, Campbell and Kwak 2011; Kwan, 2007; Line, Jain and Lyons 2011; Ling 2004; Neutens, Schwanen and Witloz 2011). This allows for rendezvous among separated members of a travel party or among independent travelers to be spontaneously arranged or renegotiated, leading to what Kwan (2007) refers to as an "extempore lifestyle." Similar to the information feature of smartphones, this communication feature both expands the choices available to the traveler and also enhances flexibility in travel scheduling and experience. The use of a smartphone's communication capabilities during travel has been associated with feeling more connected to friends and family, and even feeling safer. The feeling of improved personal security associated with the use of smartphones should not be understated in the tourism context. Travelers may often experience feelings of vulnerability because of language barriers and a lack of familiarity with their surroundings and emergency resources available (Schroeder, Pennington-Gray, Donohoe and Kiousis 2013).

The combination of the camera feature and data connectivity of smartphones facilitates the creation and sharing of consumer-generated media (CGM) such as photographs, videos, and online comments and reviews. These are becoming both an increasingly important source of information for other travelers (Cox, Burgess, Sellitto and Buultjens 2009; Gretzel, Kang, and Lee 2008; Jeong and Jeon 2008), and an increasingly important part of the reflective phase of the tourist experience (Leask, Fyall and Barron 2014). In a study, CGM on social media was perceived by travelers as more trustworthy in comparison to the content found on official tourism websites, from travel agents, and mass media advertising (Fotis, Buhalis and Rossides 2012). Of great importance to the hospitality industry in particular is the finding that this trustworthiness or perceived authenticity can have a significant impact on restaurant decision choices (Amaral, Tiago and Tiago 2014).

The discussion of smartphones is integrally linked to social media use by consumers as smartphone users are more frequent users of social media (Schroeder et al. 2013). Online social networks have become a key source of information for those seeking to learn about a destination prior to traveling, and have become an important outlet for travelers to both share and reflect on their travel experiences, and to inform friends and family about their adventure (Amaro, Duarte and Henriques 2016; Pudliner, 2007; Tussyadiah and Fesenmaier 2009; White and White 2007), and in particular to share photographs (Lo et al. 2011). The shift in the focus of personal photography from memory creation to communication (Sarvas and Froehlich 2011; Sontag 2004) and identity formation (Shanks and Svabo 2014; Van Dijck 2008) has been facilitated by online social networks (Dinhopl and Gretzel 2016). The use of smartphones accelerates the sharing process, providing digital immediacy (Bell and Lyall 2005) by allowing users to immediately capture and upload pictures or videos and share comments or reviews of their experiences at tourist sites or local businesses as they occur; furthermore, the use of a smartphone's location-based services capability allows for geo-tagging to broadcast one's location in real-time, so that smartphone users are not constrained to simply expressing the message "I was here" but have the option to communicate "I am here now" (Dinhopl and Gretzel 2016). While self-taken photos of oneself, "selfies," have become omnipresent on social media (Senft and Baym 2015; Wendt 2014), largely facilitated by the smartphone's integration of camera, data access, and portability, Dinhopl and Gretzel (2016, p. 126) found that selfies have important implications in the tourist context, as they allow tourists to "ascribe the characteristics they otherwise associate with tourist sights onto themselves," shifting the focus of the travel experience from the destination to oneself, and changing the very meaning of the excursion. Mang et al. (2016) found that using social networks is a key use of smartphones among travelers and that more than 60 percent of travelers use their phones to take photos while travelling.

From the perspective of the tourist, the use of smartphones has fundamentally altered the tourism experience. Smartphones have been associated with easier planning, including the ability to search for a broader range of information and the flexibility to search while traveling so that all aspects of a trip do not need to be preplanned. Using a smartphone affords more flexibility during trips to alter plans or undertake unplanned/spontaneous activities as well as less after-trip follow-up because photos and reviews can be uploaded during the trip. Smartphones create a feeling among travelers of being more connected with others; a sense of being better informed while traveling; feeling more secure; experiencing less stress; and having more fun. Smartphones allow connected travelers to feel more confident about travel; and enhance the perception of gaining greater value from the travel experience (Wang et al. 2014, 2016). As a result of these benefits, Lalicic and Weismayer (2016a, 2016b) found that tourists actually exhibit "passion" towards their phones, seeing their phones not only as devices but also as travel companions. Dickinson et al. (2014) identify new competencies developing among travelers as a result of smartphone use in the areas of space-time; the interactions of information, people, and objects encountered while traveling; and in relationships.

For many travelers, the smartphone has refocused the tourist gaze, through its information features and recommendations, and because it acts as a conduit to social media encouraging users to search out experiences and photo opportunities explicitly for the purpose of sharing online. In part, the smartphone itself has become an object of their gaze. Nevertheless, the degree to which a smartphone can shift the tourist gaze will depend on a traveler's position along Basala and Klenosky's (2001) novelty–familiarity continuum. Novelty-seeking, adventurous, allocentric explorers have the most to gain from smartphone usage as they can use their phones to locate new experiences, adjust their plans to take advantage of newly discovered opportunities after arriving in their destination, and share their experiences widely and in real-time with others. However, familiarity-seeking, psychocentric, mass tourists who seek the comfort and predictability of familiar travel activities such as visiting chain-hotels, chain-restaurants, and well-known attractions can still benefit from smartphones if the information provided encourages them to try a new activity or at the very least helps them to choose from among familiar alternatives. In the next section, we explore how hospitality providers have responded to consumer adoption of the smartphone and the actions they have undertaken to capture and retain the traveler's interest.

The reaction of hospitality providers to the change in consumer behavior

Businesses, service providers, and governments have begun to adapt to the growing adoption of smartphones by travelers, with changes seen across the transport, hospitality, tourist attraction, and destination marketing industries. Public transit services have begun to provide mobile applications showing the real-time location of buses and trains so that travelers can not only find the schedule, but can find out whether the buses and trains are running on schedule or not (Dickinson et al. 2014). Private transportation providers such as taxis and ride-sharing services allow travelers to order personal transport from their phones and track a driver's progress in real-time, providing greater convenience to smartphone users. Airlines have begun to make extensive use of mobile technology, not only providing basic information and transactional services such as allowing passengers to search for and book tickets and check-in and retrieve boarding passes, but also providing personalization services such as allowing customers to choose and upgrade seats, select meal options, purchase in-flight amenities, and access loyalty programs from their mobile devices. These options have opened new avenues for revenue generation (Morosan 2015). Wattanacharoensil and Schuckert (2015) also found that airports can use social media effectively to both communicate travel information such as flight delays and also market products and services available at the airport directly to visitors while they are on-site.

In the hospitality industry, Adukaite, Reimann, Marchiori and Cantoni (2014) found that, among hotels that have adopted the use of smartphone apps, the most common use has been for providing information services to potential customers, with 89 percent of hotel apps featuring an indicator of hotel location, 84 percent featuring a restaurant menu, 81 percent featuring room description, 78 percent containing contact information, 74 percent containing a description of room amenities, 73 percent having a photo gallery, and 60 percent providing information regarding conference facilities. However, they found that the provision of transactional functions is growing, with 69 percent providing mobile booking capabilities. Other functions include offering mobile check-in/check-out, allowing guests to arrange for wake-up calls and access to housekeeping and room service from their phones, allowing access to loyalty programs, and providing mobile concierge services. Although less common, these provisions have been found to both greatly increase the degree of satisfaction of a travelers' experience and save the traveler time (Adukaite et al. 2014; Chen, Knecht and Murphy 2015; Walsh 2014; Verma, Stock and McCarthy 2012). Gibbs, Gretzel and Saltzman (2016) discuss the variety of hotel mobile offerings while Neuhofer, Buhalis and Ladkin (2014) describe a situation in which a hotel offered a high degree of personalization by inviting visitors to input preferences for room temperature, favourite beverages, and preferred newspapers which can be retrieved by staff, also on mobile devices, for provision to the customer. Restaurants have also begun to embrace mobile technology, not only providing information about menu items and allowing reservations to be made from mobile devices, but in some instances allowing customers to order items and/or pay using their mobile phones, representing great convenience for smartphone-equipped patrons (see Neuhofer et al. 2014).

Theme parks have also begun to provide mobile apps, allowing visitors to book tickets, navigate within the park, check wait-times for rides, and make reservations at restaurants. Brown, Kappes and Marks (2013) experimented with "pushing" incentives such as preferred show seating and dining coupons to park visitors' smartphones; they found that both allowing park guests to view wait-times on their phones and providing incentives to undertake specific activities in the park could greatly improve crowd management and distribution, encouraging guests to move from congested attractions to less crowded areas of the park, thus improving overall utilization of the park facilities and reducing guest queuing time. Interestingly, tour operators have been slow to invest in mobile technology for a number of reasons, not least of which is that the booking of tour itineraries is a complicated process not easily conducted on a smartphone (Baran 2013). Recently, however, tour operators have begun to see the potential benefits of utilizing mobile technology and a few have created their own apps, such as myTrafalgar – an app that allows users to access all their trip information, connect with their trip director and other guests, view images, and learn about future trips (Baran 2015).

The traditional means to support travelers and visitors include guides, signage, and paper menus and maps; however, smartphones can overcome restrictions associated with physical places and materials. For example, in their examination of how smartphones may be used to enhance the experience of visiting cultural heritage sites, Garau and Ilardi (2014, p. 79) found that the "geographical and material boundaries of cultural artifacts are being broken down and the cultural artifacts are being projected into socio-cultural platforms that integrate learning, play, and simulation." The traditional communication transmission model for cultural sites is authoritarian and uni-directional, does not allow for dialogue, and limits interpretation. Smartphones and mobile technology facilitate broader participation, interaction, and sharing. This technology can give rise to open-ended experiences tailored to the users, and make it easier for guests and patrons to provide and share feedback. Guests and patrons can contribute to the development and transmission of content and are no longer merely passive receptors (Garau and Ilardi 2014).

One common way in which smartphones are used as facilitators are augmented reality (AR) systems. AR systems augment the surroundings of the user by providing virtual information registered in 3D space, that is, visitors view virtual overlays at the site or destination. Information ranges from descriptions of attractions, restaurants, and monuments to the location of Wi-Fi hotspots, banks, and parking to local news and weather. AR functionality includes search and browse capabilities, context-aware push recommendations, m-commerce, feedback mechanisms, routing and navigation, tour generation, map services, communication, exploration of visible surroundings, interactive AR, and filtering AR. AR systems are interactive, flexible, and easy to update, provide immediate access in context, and can be personalized and relevant (Yovcheva, Buhalis and Gatzidis 2012).

The overnight success of Pokémon Go, a location-based augmented reality game, and its exploitation by hospitality providers (who can pay a fee to increase the number of Pokémon characters at their location to lure in players), is an example of the marketing possibilities of AR systems. Xu et al. (2016) identify mobile gaming as a powerful new marketing tool to reach tourists. However, tom Dieck and Jung (2015) note that more research into travelers' acceptance of AR is still needed. Among museums, Kuflik, Wecker, Lanir and Stock (2015) found that mobile technology can not only enhance the experiences of visitors onsite, but can also help with pre-arrival planning by informing visitors about exhibits and activities. Likewise, mobile technology can assist with post-visit reflection by allowing visitors to view images and descriptions of the exhibits to share reviews of their experiences. Museums, like other attractions, can also connect directly with visitors through social media. Nevertheless, guests still seem to prefer the tactility of paper-based guidebooks and thus the full potential of AR systems has not been adequately exploited (Yovcheva et al. 2012) by this sector within the hospitality industry.

The location-based services (LBS) feature of smartphones has allowed for a range of location-specific apps provided by travel companies, local business associations, and city governments. By providing mobile games, AR, and navigation assistance to enhance the tourist experience in cities such as Bangkok, Cape Town, Dublin, London, and Nanjing (Dickinson et al. 2014; Han, Jung and Gibson 2014; Xu et al. 2016), promoters and providers of travel products and services can enhance tourist engagement with the destination (Waltz and Ballagas 2007). LBS combined with push notifications have been used by app providers to make recommendations to tourists as they pass within proximity of certain attractions or businesses (Chu, Kansal, Liu and Zhao 2011; Dickinson et al. 2014). This technology presents a new marketing channel for local attractions and businesses to draw tourists, particularly as Tussyadiah and Wang (2016) found that tourists are generally confident in the proactive recommendations received from their smartphones. Tussyadiah (2012) recommends incorporating merchant rewards such as discounts as well as competition-based or connection-based rewards, such as social recognition for visiting certain attractions, visiting locations more frequently, or visiting a chainstore's branches in many cities.

From the marketer's perspective, promotion via smartphones is a relatively cheap and easy way to connect with tourists. However, this does not automatically translate to travelers wishing to receive recommendations, advertisements, and offers on their phones. Interestingly, a high degree of skepticism and defensiveness among consumers has emerged in tandem with developments in mobile marketing communication strategies (Izquierdo-Yusta, Olarte-Pascual and Reinares-Lara 2015). Tussyadiah and Wang (2016) argue that there exists a conflict over the perceived agency of mobile technology. On the one hand, mobile technology is perceived as a means to enhance the traveler experience. On the other hand, the use of mobile technology can be perceived as a loss of control and, therefore, a reduction in the traveler experience. Using projective techniques, Tussyadiah and Wang (2016) studied tourists' feelings towards smartphones in order to examine the perceived agency of smartphones and to understand how the perceived behavioral qualities of smartphones might impact tourists' attitudes towards push recommendations (i.e. context-aware and pro-active contextual recommendations). The authors found that the majority of participants were likely to adopt and follow push recommendations. In addition, smartphones garnered confidence and trust among the majority of tourists as they believed that smartphone applications would generate reliable recommendations, that smartphones can be reliable travel partners, and that they would benefit from following the recommendations. Smartphones generated anxiety and fear among the minority of participants who were likely to reject push recommendations as they did not want to be overly reliant on technology, felt the smartphone was exerting control, and stripped them of making their own decisions. This *mediation paradox* stems from the fact that "planning and decision-making are an essential part of the tourism experience" (Tussyadiah and Wang 2016, p. 503). Those participants who associated smartphones with intelligence and social ability were more likely to have feelings of confidence or trust and less likely to exhibit fear and anxiety towards smartphones. Meanwhile, those participants who associated smartphones with control and reactivity had the highest proportion of feelings of fear and anxiety.

For mobile advertising in general, entertainment, credibility, perceived interactivity, ease of use, trust, and perceived utility have been identified as the factors that most affect consumers' attitudes towards smartphone applications (Izquierdo-Yusta et al. 2015). In a study involving Millennials in the US and restaurant smartphone advertising, Nyheim, Xu, Zhang and Mattila (2015) investigated the main factors that influence smartphone advertising avoidance and found that advertising irritation was directly related to advertising avoidance, while perceived personalization in advertising appeared to reduce resistance to advertisements. Interestingly, Nyheim et al. (2015) found that concerns about privacy had no significant effect on advertising avoidance.

Based on the growing importance of smartphones to their users while traveling (see for example Lalicic and Weismayer 2016a, 2016b), Tussyadiah (2014) recommends that features of the technology should be designed to encourage consumers to view their device as a travel companion/travel assistant. This concept of the smartphone as travel companion may increase the persuasive power of the information it provides to the user. Given the importance of CGM in shaping tourists' attitudes towards businesses and attractions, Burgess, Sellitto, Cox and Buultjens (2015) recommend that all businesses, particularly small and medium-sized local enterprises who lack widely recognized brand power and are thus more affected by positive and negative CGM, should ensure they have a CGM strategy and make effective use of social media and travel review platforms. The use of social media and mobile technology with LBS permits the real-time integration of tourist behaviors into strategic marketing activities (Gretzel 2010; Mistilis et al. 2014). Tussyadiah and Wang (2016) note that developing further understanding of how tourists respond to contextual recommendations will help tourist destinations in developing strategies to induce the patterns of tourist mobility that will benefit all tourism stakeholders.

Summary

Smartphones satisfy the functional, creative, and social informational needs of the hospitality consumer and provide an inexpensive marketing channel for hospitality providers. However, barriers remain regarding the adoption and acceptance of smartphones in the hospitality context, including lack of accessible data services when traveling, the cost of applications, limited ease of use, and a relative lack of mobile-friendly sites and applications (in comparison to PCs). By far the most transformative functions of smartphones for travelers are the communication and social networking functions. The smartphone's camera and data capabilities have led to a proliferation of consumer-generated media which has transformed not only the way that tourists experience, document, and share their travel experiences but also the way that prospective travelers form expectations and perceptions of destinations.

Regardless of the size of the hospitality enterprise, a mobile strategy is now necessary to do business in an increasingly connected world, in no small part because of traveler expectations being at least partially formed by the increasing proliferation of mobile reservation systems, travel guides and information systems, and augmented reality (AR) systems which have rendered the communication channel two-way and personalized. The evidence suggests that hospitality providers should integrate real-time consumer insights and behaviors into their strategic marketing efforts.

The response of hospitality consumers to the smartphone marketing strategies of hospitality providers has been generally positive and has encouraged further adoption and exploitation. One caveat for hospitality marketers and smartphone application developers is to be aware of the mediation paradox – the association of both confidence/trust and fear/anxiety with smartphone usage in the hospitality context. Comfort with the smartphone is far from universal. So while there is strong support for proactive and personalized recommendations to influence hospitality consumer behavior, hospitality providers must consider the attributes that inspire confidence/ trust and those that instill fear/anxiety as part of the development and design process. The issue of control is important, particularly in the tourism experience; therefore, applications that foster collaboration and negotiation will ease customer concerns over control.

It is clear that the benefits of smartphones for the hospitality industry have not been fully exploited. Hospitality organizations have just begun to design and adopt new business models that exploit the strengths of the mobile environment. Given the importance of perceived utility and credibility to consumer adoption and attitudes, hospitality organizations must provide accurate, reliable, abundant, and up-to-date information to patrons. Often, the search and decision process for restaurants, tours, theme parks, and transportation is group-based. Smartphone applications that support coordination, allow for the sharing of results and facilitate group decision-making can further enhance the community aspects of tourism and hospitality. Finally, guidelines and standardization for smartphone applications in the hospitality context would go a long way in facilitating wider adoption and proliferation among hospitality consumers and in encouraging greater content and service delivery.

Urry's (1990) tourist "gaze" has been altered and dramatized by the advent of the connected traveler and the adoption of the smartphone. The connected tourist gaze is now organized largely by the individual's use of searches and apps; it is a gaze authorized by enhanced discourses and activities, and it can be characterized simultaneously as either a solo or collective experience.

Notes

1   The top applications used by travelers are not travel-specific applications (Facebook, Google Maps, Skype) (Pew Research Centre 2016).
2   Hannam et al. (2014) argue that the convergence of tourism and technology, through smartphones, mobile applications, and social media, has exacerbated the "digital divide," as those on the disadvantaged side of the digital divide are deprived of the enhancement of experiences provided by mobile technology.

References

Adukaite, A., Reimann, A., Marchiori, E., and Cantoni, L. (2014) "Hotel mobile apps: The case of 4 and 5 star hotels in European German-speaking countries," in Z. Xiang and I. Tussyadiah (eds.) *Information and Communication Technologies in Tourism*, New York: Springer International Publishing, 45–57.

Amaral, F., Tiago, T. and Tiago, F. (2014) "User-generated content: Tourists' profiles on TripAdvisor," *International Journal of Strategic Innovative Marketing* 1(3), 137–145.

Amaro, S., Duarte, P. and Henriques, C. (2016) "Travelers' use of social media: A clustering approach," *Annals of Tourism Research* 59(1), 1–15.

Baran, M. (2013) "Tour operators cautious in embracing technology for smartphones, tablets: Seeing limited demand for mobile from travel professionals," *Travel Weekly*, 8 July.

Baran, M. (2015) "Apps and ops: Tour operators step up mobile efforts," *Travel Weekly*, 12 August.

Basala, S.L. and Klenosky, D.B. (2001) "Travel-style preferences for visiting a novel destination: A conjoint investigation across the novelty-familiarity continuum," *Journal of Travel Research* 40(2), 172–182.

Beeton, S., Bowen, H. and Santos, C.A. (2005) "State of knowledge: Mass media and its relationship to perceptions of quality," in G. Jennings and N. Nickerson (eds.) *Quality Tourism Experiences*, Oxford: Elsevier Butterworth-Heinemann, 25–37.

Bell, C. and Lyall, J. (2005) "'I was here': Pixilated evidence," in D. Crouch, R. Jackson, and F. Thompson (eds.) *The Media & the Tourist Imagination: Converging Cultures*, London: Routledge, 135–142.

Birenboim, A. (2016). "New approaches to the study of tourist experiences in time and space," *Tourism Geographies* 18(1), 9–17.

Brown, A., Kappes, J. and Marks, J. (2013) "Mitigating theme park crowding with incentives and information on mobile devices," *Journal of Travel Research* 52(4), 426–436.

Budiu, R. and Nielsen, J. (2010) *Usability of Mobile Websites: 85 Design Guidelines for Improving Access to Web-based Content and Services through Mobile Devices*, Fremont, CA: Nielsen Norman Group.

Burgess, S., Sellitto, C., Cox, C. and Buultjens, J. (2015) "Strategies for adopting consumer-generated media in small-sized to medium-sized tourism enterprises," *International Journal of Tourism Research* 17(5), 432–441.

Campbell, S.W. and Kwak, N. (2011) "Mobile communication and civil society: Linking patterns and places of use to engagement with others in public," *Human Communication Research* 37(2), 207–222.

Chen, M., Knecht, S. and Murphy, H.C. (2015) *An Investigation of Features and Functions of Smartphone Applications for Hotel Chains.* Paper presented at ENTER2015, Lugano, Switzerland.

Chu, D., Kansal, A., Liu, J., and Zhao, F. (2011) *Mobile Apps: It's Time to Move up to CondOS.* Paper presented at the 13th Workshop on Hot Topics in Operating Systems, Napa, California.

comScore. (2016) *January 2016 US Smartphone Subscriber Market Share.* Retrieved 6 August, 2016 from www.comscore.com/Insights/Rankings/comScore-Reports-January-2016-US-Smartphone-Subscriber-Market-Share

Cox, C., Burgess, S., Sellitto, C., and Buultjens, J. (2009) "The role of user-generated content in tourists' travel planning behavior," *Journal of Hospitality, Marketing and Management* 18(8), 743–764.

Crouch, D. (2005) "Flirting with space: Tourism geographies as sensuous/expressive practice," in C. Cartier and A. Lew (eds.) *Seductions of Places: Geographical Perspectives on Globalization and Touristed Landscapes,* London: Routledge, 23–35.

Dickinson, J.E., Ghali, K., Cherrett, T., Speed, C., Davies, N. and Norgate, S. (2014) "Tourism and the smartphone app: Capabilities, emerging practice and scope in the travel domain," *Current Issues in Tourism* 17(1), 84–101.

Dinhopl, A. and Gretzel, U. (2016) "Selfie-taking as touristic looking," *Annals of Tourism Research* 57, 126–139.

emarketer.com. (2015) *By 2016, Most Digital Travel Bookers Will Use Mobile Devices,* 19 November, 2015. Retrieved 25 August, 2016 from www.emarketer.com/Article/By-2016-Most-Digital-Travel-Bookers-Will-Use-Mobile-Devices/1013248

Fotis, J., Buhalis, D. and Rossides, N. (2012) "Social media use and impact during the holiday travel planning process," in M. Fuchs, F. Ricci, and L. Cantoni (eds.) *Information and Communication Technologies in Tourism 2012.* Vienna, Austria: Springer-Verlag, 13–24.

Garau, C. and Ilardi, E. (2014) "The 'non-places' meet the 'places': Virtual tours on smartphones for the enhancement of cultural heritage," *Journal of Urban Technology* 21(1), 77–89.

Germann Molz, J. (2012) *Travel Connections: Tourism, Technology and Togetherness in a Mobile World,* London: Routledge.

Gibbs, C., Gretzel, U. and Saltzman, J. (2016) "An experience-based taxonomy of branded hotel mobile application features," *Information Technology & Tourism* 16(2), 175–199.

Grant, I. and O'Donohoe, S. (2007) "Why young consumers are not open to mobile marketing communication," *International Journal of Advertising* 26(2), 223–246.

Gretzel, U. (2010) "Travel in the network: Redirected gazes, ubiquitous connections and new frontiers," in M. Levina and G. Kien (eds.) *Post-global Network and Everyday Life,* New York: Peter Lang, 41–58.

Gretzel, U., Fesenmaier, D.R. and O'Leary, J.T. (2006) "The transformation of consumer behavior," in D. Buhalis and C. Costa (eds.) *Tourism Business Frontier,* Oxford, UK: Elsevier, 9–18.

Gretzel, U., Kang, M. and Lee, W. (2008) "Differences in consumer-generated media adoption and use: A cross-national perspective," *Journal of Hospitality and Leisure Marketing* 17(1–2), 99–120.

Han, D., Jung, T., and Gibson, A. (2014) "Dublin AR: Implementing augmented reality (AR) in tourism," in Z. Xiang and I. Tussyadiah (eds.) *Information and Communication Technologies in Tourism,* Wien: Springer Computer Science, 511–523.

Hannam, K., Butler, G. and Paris, C.M. (2014) "Development and key issues in tourism mobility," *Annals of Tourism Research* 44(1), 171–185.

Hannam, K. and Knox, D. (2010) *Understanding Tourism,* London: Sage.

Huang, C-Y., Chou, C-J. and Lin, P-C. (2010) "Involvement theory in constructing bloggers' intention to purchase travel products," *Tourism Management* 31(4), 513–526.

Huang, W-J., Norman, W.C., Hallo, J.C., McGehee, N.G., McGee, J. and Goetcheus, C.L. (2014) "Serendipity and independent travel," *Tourism Recreation Research* 39(2), 169–183.

Izquierdo-Yusta, A., Olarte-Pascual, C. and Reinares-Lara, E. (2015) "Attitudes toward mobile advertising among users versus non-users of the mobile Internet," *Telematics and Informatics* 32(2), 355–366.

Jeong, M. and Jeon, M.M. (2008) "Customer reviews of hotel experiences through consumer generated media (CGM)," *Journal of Hospitality and Leisure Marketing* 17(1–2), 121–138.

Kennedy-Eden, H. and Gretzel, U. (2012) "A taxonomy of mobile applications in tourism," *e-Review of Tourism Research* 10(2), 47–50.

Kim, H.H. and Law, R. (2015) "Smartphones in tourism and hospitality marketing: A literature review," *Journal of Travel and Tourism Marketing,* 32(6), 692–711.

Kim, H., Xiang, Z., and Fesenmaier, D.R. (2015) "Use of the internet for trip planning: A generational analysis," *Journal of Travel & Tourism Marketing*, 32(3), 276–289.

Kim, M.J., Chung, N., Lee, C-K. and Preis, M.W. (2015) "Motivations and use context in mobile tourism shopping: Applying contingency and task – technology fit theories," *International Journal of Tourism Research* 17(1), 13–24.

Kuflik, T., Wecker, A.J., Lanir, J. and Stock, O. (2015) "An integrative framework for extending the boundaries of the museum visit experience: Linking the pre, during and post visit phases," *Information Technology & Tourism*, 15(1), 17–47.

Kwan, M-P. (2007) "Mobile communications, social networks, and urban travel: Hypertext as a new metaphor for conceptualizing spatial interaction," *The Professional Geographer* 59(4), 434–446.

Lagerkvist, A. (2008) "Travels in thirdspace: Experiential suspense in mediaspace – the case of America (un)known," *European Journal of Communication*, 23(3), 343–363.

Lalicic, L. and Weismayer, C. (2016a) "The passionate use of mobiles phones among tourists," *Information Technology & Tourism* 16(2), 153–173.

Lalicic, L. and Weismayer, C. (2016b) "Being passionate about the mobile while travelling," *Current Issues in Tourism*. doi:10.1080/13683500.2016.1141179.

Lamsfus, C., Wang, D., Alzua-Sorzabal, A. and Xiang, Z. (2015) "Going mobile: Defining context for on-the-go travelers," *Journal of Travel Research* 54(6), 691–701.

Lash, S. and Urry, J. (1994) *Economies of Signs and Space*. London: Sage.

Leask, A., Fyall, A. and Barron, P. (2014) "Generation Y: An agenda for future visitor attraction research," *International Journal of Tourism Research* 16(5), 462–471.

Line, T., Jain, J. and Lyons, G. (2011) "The role of ICTS in everyday mobile lives," *Journal of Transport Geography* 19(6), 1490–1499.

Ling, R. (2004) *The Mobile Connection: The Cell Phone's Impact on Society*, San Francisco: Morgan Kaufmann.

Lo, I.S., McKercher, B., Lo, A., Cheung, C. and Law, R. (2011) "Tourism and online photography," *Tourism Management* 32(4), 725–731.

Lu, J., Mao, Z., Wang, M. and Hu, L. (2015) "Goodbye maps, hello apps? Exploring the influential determinants of travel app adoption," *Current Issues in Tourism* 18(11), 1059–1079.

MacKay, K. and Vogt, C. (2012). "Information technology in the everyday and vacation contexts," *Annals of Tourism Research* 39(3), 1380–1401.

Mang, C.F., Piper, L.A. and Brown, N.R. (2016) "The incidence of smartphone usage among tourists," *International Journal of Tourism Research* 18(6), 591–601.

Mistilis, N., Buhalis, D. and Gretzel, U. (2014) "Future eDestination marketing: Perspective on an Australian tourism stakeholder network," *Journal of Travel Research* 53(6), 778–790.

Morosan, C. (2015) "Understanding the benefit of purchasing ancillary air travel services via mobile phones," *Journal of Travel & Tourism Marketing* 32(3), 227–240.

Neuhofer, B., Buhalis, D. and Ladkin, A. (2014) "A typology of technology-enhanced tourism experiences," *International Journal of Tourism Research* 16(4), 340–350.

Neutens, T., Schwanen, T., and Witloz, F. (2011) "The prism of everyday life: Towards a new research agenda for time geography," *Transport Reviews* 31(1), 25–47.

No, E. and Kim, J. (2014) "Determinants of the adoption for travel information on smartphone," *International Journal of Tourism Research* 16(6), 534–545.

Nyheim, P., Xu, S., Zhang, L. and Mattila, A.S. (2015) "Predictors of avoidance towards personalization of restaurant smartphone advertising: A study from the Millennials' perspective," *Journal of Hospitality and Tourism Technology* 6(2), 145–159.

Paris, C. (2012) "Flashpackers: An emerging subculture?" *Annals of Tourism Research* 39(2), 1094–1115.

Pedrana, M. (2013) "Location-based services and tourism: Possible implications for destination," *Current Issues in Tourism* 17(9), 753–762.

Pew Research Centre. (2016) *Smartphone Ownership and Internet Usage Continues to Climb in Emerging Economies: But Advanced Economies Still Have Higher Rates of Technology Use*. Retrieved 6 August, 2016 from www.pewglobal.org/files/2016/02/pew_research_center_global_technology_report_final_february_22__2016.pdf

Pudliner, B.A. (2007) Alternative literature and the tourist experience: Travel and tourist weblogs," *Journal of Tourism and Cultural Change* 5(1), 46–59.

Sarvas, R. and Froehlich, D.M. (2011) *From Snapshots to Social Media: The Changing Picture of Domestic Photography*, London: Springer.

Schroeder, A., Pennington-Gray, L., Donohoe, H. and Kiousis, S. (2013) "Using social media in times of crisis," *Journal of Travel and Tourism Marketing* 30(1–2), 126–143.

Senft, T.M. and Baym, N.K. (2015) "What does the selfie say? Investigating a global phenomenon," *International Journal of Communication* 9(19), 1588–1606.

Shanks, M. and Svabo, C. (2014) "Mobile-media photography: New modes of engagement," in J. Larsen and M. Sandbye (eds.) *Digital Snaps: The New Face of Photography*, London: I.B. Tauris & Co., 227–246.

Sontag, S. (2004) "Regarding the torture of others," *The New York Times Magazine*, 23 May, 25–29.

tom Dieck, M.C. and Jung, T. (2015) "A theoretical model of mobile augmented reality acceptance in urban heritage tourism," *Current Issues in Tourism.* doi:10.1080/13683500.2015.1070801.

TripAdvisor. (2015a). *TripAdvisor Study Reveals 42% of Travelers Worldwide Use Smartphones to Plan or Book Their Trips*, 3 June. Retrieved 6 September, 2016 from http://ir.tripadvisor.com/releasedetail.cfm?ReleaseID=919990

TripAdvisor. (2015b) *TripBarometer 2015 (Global) – Global Travel Economy*, 10 March. Retrieved 1 September, 2016 from www.tripadvisor.com/TripAdvisorInsights/n2580/tripbarometer-2015-global-global-travel-economy

Tussyadiah, I.P. (2012) "A concept of location-based social network marketing," *Journal of Travel & Tourism Marketing* 29(3), 205–220.

Tussyadiah, I.P. (2014) "Social actor attribution to mobile phones: The case of tourists," *Information Technology & Tourism* 14(1), 21–47.

Tussyadiah, I.P. and Fesenmaier, D.R. (2009) "Mediating the tourist experiences: Access to places via shared videos," *Annals of Tourism Research* 36(1), 24–40.

Tussyadiah, I.P. and Wang, D. (2016) "Tourists' attitudes toward proactive smartphone systems," *Journal of Travel Research* 55(4), 493–508.

Tussyadiah, I.P. and Zach, F.J. (2012) "The role of geo-based technology in place experiences," *Annals of Tourism Research* 39(2), 780–800.

Uriely, N. (2005) "The tourist experience: Conceptual developments," *Annals of Tourism Research* 32(1), 199–216.

Urry, J. (1990) *The Tourist Gaze*, London: Sage Publications.

Urry, J. (2008) "Globalising the tourist gaze," in B.S. Sutheeshna, S. Mishra and B.B. Parida (eds.) *Tourism Development Revisited: Concepts, Issues and Paradigms*, London: Sage Publications, 150–160.

Van Dijck, J. (2008) "Digital photography: Communication, identity, memory," *Visual Communication* 7(1), 57–76.

Verma, R., Stock, D. and McCarthy, L.M. (2012) "Customer preferences for online, social media, and mobile innovations in the hospitality industry," *Cornell Hospitality Quarterly* 53(3), 183–186.

Walsh, C.S. (2014) *The Mobile Travel Landscape: A Multi-region Spotlight*, New York, NY: PhoCusWright Inc.

Waltz, S.P. and Ballagas, R. (2007) "Pervasive persuasive: A rhetorical design approach to a location-based spell-casting game for tourists," in *Proceedings of DiGRA 2007 – The 3rd International Digital Games Research Conference*, Tokyo, 489–497.

Wang, D., Park, S. and Fesenmaier, D.R. (2012) "The role of smartphones in mediating the touristic experience," *Journal of Travel Research* 51(4), 371–387.

Wang, D., Xiang, Z. and Fesenmaier, D.R. (2014) "Adapting to the mobile world: A model of smartphone use," *Annals of Tourism Research* 48(1), 11–26.

Wang, D., Xiang, Z. and Fesenmaier, D.R. (2016) "Smartphone use in everyday life and travel," *Journal of Travel Research* 55(1), 52–63.

Wattanacharoensil, W. and Schuckert, M. (2015) "How global airports engage social media users: A study of Facebook use and its role in stakeholder communication," *Journal of Travel & Tourism Marketing* 32(6), 656–676.

Wendt, B. (2014) *The Allure of the Selfie: Instagram and the New Self-portrait*, Amsterdam: Network Notebooks.

White, N.R. and White, P.B. (2007) "Home and away tourists in a connected world," *Annals of Tourism Research* 34(1), 88–104.

Xu, F., Tian, F., Buhalis, D., Weber, J. and Zhang, H. (2016) "Tourists as mobile gamers: Gamification for tourism marketing," *Journal of Travel & Tourism Marketing* 33(8), 1124–1142.

Yovcheva, Z., Buhalis, D. and Gatzidis, C. (2012) "Overview of smartphone augmented reality applications for tourism," *eReview of Tourism Research* 10(2), 63–66.

Colin Mang, Natalya Brown and Linda Piper

Further reading

Choe, Y., Kim, J. and Fesenmaier, D.R. (2016) "Use of social media across the trip experience: An application of latent transition analysis," *Journal of Travel and Tourism Marketing* 34(4), 431–443. (Distinct traveler repertoires of social media use across the stages of the trip experience are identified and matched with strategies for destination marketers wishing to target them.)

Hudson, S. (2014) "Challenges of tourism marketing in the digital, global economy," in S. McCabe (ed.) *The Routledge Handbook of Tourism Marketing*, New York, NY: Routledge, 475–490. (A description of the digital marketing environment and the key changes in tourism consumer behavior due to information and computing technology.)

Karaniosis, S., Burgess, S. and Sellitto, C. (2012) "A classification of mobile tourism applications," in P. Ordonez de Pablos, R. Tennyson and J. Zhao (eds.) *Global Hospitality and Tourism Management Technologies*, Hershey, PA: ICI Global, 165–177. (A framework for evaluating mobile tourism applications.)

Urry, J. (1990) *The Tourist Gaze*, London: Sage Publications. (A treatise on the construction, transformation, and variability of the tourist gaze.)

Zheng, X., Tussyadiah, I. and Buhalis, D. (eds.) (2015) *Journal of Destination Marketing & Management: Special Issue on Smart Destinations* 4(3), 143–201. (The latest research on smart destinations in which information and communication technology is the driver and foundation for destination innovation and competitiveness.)

45

The effect of user-generated content on consumer responses in hotels and restaurants

A social communication framework

Lawrence Hoc Nang Fong

Introduction

Early online communication between businesses and consumers primarily relied on corporate websites for which businesses were the sole contributor to website content. With the emergence of Web 2.0 technology, the generation of website content is shifting toward a co-creation process between businesses and consumers. Consumers are free and even encouraged to publicize their opinions on business performance. Businesses, in turn, are allowed to respond to these opinions and other consumers can actively participate; interactions between businesses and consumers have become more vivid and transparent. The opinions raised by consumers are one type of user-generated content (UGC), "media content created or produced by the general public rather than by paid professionals and primarily distributed on the Internet" (Daugherty, Eastin and Bright 2008: 16). As this chapter focuses on the role of UGC in the business domain, the term is used here to denote online content generated by customers (Ayeh, Au and Law 2013; Lu and Stepchenkova 2015). Although "UGC" has been used interchangeably with "online review," this chapter considers UGC as a general description, and uses online review to indicate UGC contributed by individual customers.

The emergence of UGC has reduced the importance of marketers' communication in the consumer decision-making process (Goh, Heng and Lin 2013). Consumers believe that marketing information is disseminated to businesses' own advantage, and hence consider UGC to be more credible, relevant, and empathic (Bickart and Schindler 2001). The boom of UGC in the marketplace has led to a spiraling of research about its effect on consumer decisions and behavior. Among a variety of products and services, hotels and restaurants have been widely studied to investigate the effects of UGC.

Researchers have synthesized previous findings in the sizable literature on UGC in hospitality and tourism to provide insights for future research directions (Leung et al. 2013; Lu and Stepchenkova 2015; Schuckert, Liu and Law 2015; Serra Cantallops and Salvi 2014; Zeng and Gerritsen 2014). These review studies are essential as they save researchers time and effort in identifying the gaps in the literature. More importantly, the research directions suggested by these studies help to reduce redundancy in the literature. Review studies are especially important for online phenomena because as information technology changes, so do the research trends.

Although review studies about UGC in hospitality and tourism are not scant, some observations in these studies provide support to this chapter. First, earlier review studies only covered publications up to 2013, which does not allow the audience to understand the recent findings in the field. Second, although these studies have presented a critical review of the literature, none of them has based their review on an established theoretical framework or aimed to develop a framework that fits the hospitality and tourism domains. A framework is important for clarifying the relationship among constructs and providing a solid foundation for future studies. To fill in these gaps, this chapter adopts Cheung and Thadani's (2012) social communication framework to present a critical review of recent empirical evidence about the effect of UGC on consumer responses in the hotel and restaurant sectors. Their framework is adopted because of its theoretical foundation (social communication theory). Recent empirical evidence is useful to examine the robustness of this framework. This chapter focuses on UGC studies about hotels and restaurants and identifies research gaps for future investigations.

Effect of UGC on consumer responses

According to Cheung and Thadani (2012), the influence of UGC on consumer behavior is a social communication process that comprises five components: a response (receiver's reaction to the stimulus), a stimulus (UGC), a communicator (person who generates UGC), a receiver (person who responds to UGC), and a contextual factor (the environment in which the UGC is placed). A critical review of the literature based on these components is presented in the following subsections.

Response

Response is an outcome component in the social communication process. It refers to consumers' cognitive responses such as attitude and intention, along with behavioral responses (e.g., purchase behavior) after reading UGC (Cheung and Thadani 2012). Previous findings and theory suggest that these responses are interrelated. In particular, attitude predicts intention and then behavior (Ajzen 1991). Cognitive responses target either UGC (Ayeh, Au and Law 2013; Filieri and McLeay 2014) or service providers (i.e., hotels and restaurants) (Ladhari and Michaud 2015; Tsao et al. 2015). The latter has received more scholarly attention, which is understandable if researchers aim to provide practical suggestions for shaping purchase behavior.

Attitude is not directly influenced by UGC; other cognitive responses have a role. The perceived credibility and usefulness of UGC have been the commonly examined mediators. Perceived credibility denotes the extent to which individuals perceive UGC as believable, true, or factual (Cheung et al. 2009). It affects not only attitude toward service providers (Lim and van der Heide 2015) and purchase intention (Xie et al. 2011), but also perceived usefulness (Cheng and Ho 2015). Perceived usefulness refers to the extent to which individuals consider that the UGC will provide them with benefits that cannot be obtained elsewhere (Casaló, Flavián and Guinalíu 2011). Useful UGC fosters favorable attitudes toward customers' advice (Casaló, Flavián and Guinalíu 2011; Salehi-Esfahani et al. 2016). This attitude is translated into expectations of service providers and subsequently influences purchase intention (Shin et al. 2016).

The social psychology literature suggest that emotion, in addition to cognition, has an important role in shaping consumer behavior (Cohen, Pham and Andrade 2008). Customer emotions are readily identified in UGC (Magnini, Crotts and Zehrer 2011). Interestingly, little has been done on the effect of UGC on emotional response; prior studies have only considered a single feeling, namely enjoyment (Liu and Park 2015; Park and Nicolau 2015). Emotion is a broad and complicated notion that encompasses a variety of conflicting and complementary feelings such as fear, anger, sadness, shame, contentment, and happiness (Laros and Steenkamp 2005). These feelings are always explicitly expressed in UGC and are contagious to the audience (Kramer, Guillory and Hancock 2014). To date, the role of emotion in the relationship between UGC and behavior remains unexamined. More research effort should be devoted to emotion.

In line with businesses' desire to convert UGC readers to customers, researchers have examined the influence of UGC on behavioral responses such as booking volume (Cezar and Ögüt 2016; Ye et al. 2011). Others have focused on the UGC effect on sales volume (Kim, Lim and Brymer 2015; Phillips et al. 2016; Xie, Zhang and Zhang 2014), which can be considered a proxy of behavioral response. A major strength of these studies is that their findings were based on data extracted from online travel agents. However, behavior in the real world is influenced by a variety of environmental factors and the causal relationship between UGC and behavior cannot be examined using field data. Experimental studies in a controlled environment (e.g., a laboratory) are necessary to validate the findings from the field (Fong et al. 2016). For this reason, numerous studies about the effect of UGC have adopted an experimental design in a controlled environment (Casaló et al. 2015; Mauri and Minazzi 2013; Sparks and Browning 2011; Zhang, Wu and Mattila 2014). However, their operationalization of responses ceased at "intention," which has limited predicting power for actual behavior (Sheeran 2002). Future research should examine the UGC effect using experimental designs in controlled environments but with behavior as the endogenous variable.

Stimulus

Stimulus is the source component that shapes responses. In the context of this chapter, UGC is the stimulus. In the marketplace, UGC is characterized by two elements: rating and commentary (Fong, Lei and Law 2016). They exist in most (if not all) social media and booking platforms for hotels and restaurants including TripAdvisor.com, Expedia.com, Booking.com, Hotels.com, Agoda.com, Ctrip.com, Yelp.com, Airbnb.com, Opentable.com, and others. Rating represents a customer's quantitative evaluation of the supplier. It signals not only the valence of an online review (i.e., a positive or negative evaluation), but also its degree (e.g., extremely or moderately positive). Each online review is characterized by a rating given by the customer and these ratings are then aggregated to form an average rating of the supplier. An average rating above the midpoint signals that the supplier possesses more positive than negative evaluations, and vice versa. Using ratings, consumers can easily compare the performance of suppliers and they are likely to patronize those with higher average ratings. Rating is important because people inherently rely on heuristics to make decisions when they are overwhelmed by a large number of choices (Park and Nicolau 2015). The rating serves as a filter at the initial stage of a consumer's decision process. After this filtering process, consumers shift their attention to commentary (the second UGC element), which is unstructured text and thus more demanding of consumers' cognitive resources.

Although the positive relationships between rating and consumer responses are evident (Kim, Lim and Brymer 2015; Liu and Park 2015; Xie, Zhang and Zhang 2014), recent studies have shifted attention toward the degree of evaluation. Drawing data from UGC about restaurants, Park and Nicolau (2015) found that online reviews with extreme ratings, irrespective of whether they are positive or negative, are perceived as more useful and enjoyable than those with moderate ratings. The authenticity of extreme ratings is perceived as more suspect by consumers, who assume that these online reviews are manipulated by service providers, competitors or overly critical customers (Filieri 2016). A recent study using UGC data about hotels examined the relationship between the degree of evaluations and "recommendation sidedness" (Fong, Lei and Law 2016). Recommendation sidedness denotes whether the comments contain only one-sided opinions (positive or negative) or two-sided opinions (both positive and negative). The study showed that online reviews with moderately positive ratings have more two-sided comments than those with moderately negative ratings, whereas online reviews with extremely positive ratings have more one-sided comments than those with extremely negative ratings. These findings indicate that research on the effect of degree of evaluation is promising and more attempts should be made to investigate its relationship with other unexamined variables.

Compared with rating, commentary is more informative. The relevance, accuracy and value of information in commentary influence consumers' adoption of the information (Filieri and McLeay 2014). Higher readability and longer commentaries increase the perceived usefulness of online reviews (Fang et al. 2016; Liu and Park 2015). High-quality argument strengthens the trustworthiness of the commentary (Shan 2016). As with recommendation sidedness, commentary can contain a mixture of positive and negative opinions. To determine the overall valence of commentary, content analysis is necessary. As a manual approach is time-consuming and unreliable, sentiment analysis prevails. This analytical technique allows automated extraction of opinions and classification of opinion valence (Chiu et al. 2015). Application of sentiment analysis is not unusual in the hospitality literature (Chiu et al. 2015; Duan et al. 2015; Philander and Zhong 2016). Future hospitality research could go further by adding to the methodological aspects of sentiment analysis.

The literature indicates that valence is a seminal construct in UGC research. In addition to the positive relationship between valence and consumer responses such as trust in the online reviews, expectations of service, and purchase intention (Ladhari and Michaud 2015; Mauri and Minazzi 2013; Sparks and Browning 2011), the asymmetrical effect of positive and negative online reviews is also of interest to scholars. Owing to people's negativity bias, a negative stimulus has a stronger effect on responses than does a positive stimulus (Baumeister et al. 2001). Evidence of bias in the UGC domain, however, remains inconclusive. In some studies, negative online reviews were perceived as more useful (Salehi-Esfahani et al. 2016) and credible (Kusumasondjaja, Shanka and Marchegiani 2012). They have been shown to have a more important role in affecting booking intention (Sparks and Browning 2011; Tsao et al. 2015). In contrast, Pentina, Bailey and Zhang (2015) revealed that positive online reviews are more influential in terms of perceptions of helpfulness, trustworthiness, and credibility than are negative online reviews. Ong (2012) showed that negative and positive online reviews are equally important in consumers' choice of hotels and restaurants. It is worth revisiting asymmetry of valence to unveil the underlying reasons for these differences.

In addition to rating and commentary, researchers have also considered the effect of the online review set. Suppliers with more online reviews have been shown to be more favorable from customers' perspectives (Viglia, Furlan and Ladrón-de-Guevara 2014) and have higher sales volumes (Xie, Zhang and Zhang 2014). However, no effects on sales were found in Kim, Lim and Brymer (2015). A balanced set of reviews (e.g., four positive and four negative online reviews) is perceived as less useful than an unbalanced set, irrespective of whether it is positive (e.g., six positive reviews plus two negative reviews) or negative (e.g., six negative reviews plus two negative reviews) (Purnawirawan, de Pelsmacker and Dens 2012). Coherent with the primacy-recency reinforcement theory, the same study also discovered that a set of positively (negatively) unbalanced online reviews featuring positive (negative) online reviews wrapping negative (positive) ones is perceived as more useful than other sequences. To date, no studies have examined the effect of individual online reviews within a set of reviews, for example by investigating whether the effect of an individual review varies with its position in a set of reviews. This area presents many research possibilities.

Given the influence of UGC on consumer behavior, it is plausible to assume the existence of fake online reviews that favor some suppliers and hurt others. This phenomenon has been examined in prior studies. Apart from giving an overall rating of a supplier, customers can also rate individual aspects of their experience (e.g., location, sleep quality, rooms, cleanliness, and service on TripAdvisor.com). Previous studies have found a low correlation between overall ratings and individual ratings (Racherla, Connolly and Christodoulidou 2013; Schuckert, Liu and Law 2015). The discrepancies could be due to input error. However, these findings also hint that these online reviews were not based on real experiences (Schuckert, Liu and Law 2016). Using an experimental design, Yoo and Gretzel (2009) found that fake online reviews tend to be lengthy and have more recommendations about a hotel brand, greater self-expression (e.g., using the word "I"), and more positive words. It is important to discover additional clues and develop techniques that are effective in identifying fake UGC.

Suppliers' responses are increasingly important in shaping consumer behavior, especially if the online review is negative (Levy, Duan and Boo 2013). Such responses can suggest a service failure of the supplier and adversely affect purchase intention (Mauri and Minazzi 2013) and sales volume (Xie, Zhang and Zhang 2014). In their responses to negative online reviews, suppliers should be alert to their communication style (Park and Allen 2013). Good practice is to respond with an empathetic statement and paraphrase the complaint if the supplier wants potential customers to form a positive evaluation (Min, Lim and Magnini 2014). Moreover, a timely response is recommended to give an impression that the supplier is concerned about customer problems and to soothe complainers' dissatisfaction if they write their complaints during their stay in a hotel (Min, Lim and Magnini 2014). An active response to customers' comments is important to generate customer satisfaction (Liang, Schuckert and Law 2016). Responses should cater not only to negative online reviews, but also to positive ones (Lee and Blum 2015). In the existing literature, responses to customer commentary are still an emerging topic. More research effort is needed in this area.

Communicator

The communicator is the individual who produces the stimulus. As communicators are generally strangers to other consumers, there is doubt about their UGC and informational cues are needed to determine their credibility. The communicator's personal characteristics are a major cue that has a significant effect on consumer responses (Cheung and Thadani 2012). The credibility of communicators, including their trustworthiness and expertise, nurtures consumers' positive attitude toward them and increases the intention to adopt the views expressed in their UGC (Ayeh, Au and Law 2013; Ring Tkaczynski and Dolnicar 2016). It is therefore important for UGC platforms to provide information about the credibility of UGC contributors to increase the popularity of the platforms. Ratings of the communicator can be one indicator, and this information has been revealed to increase consumers' perceived usefulness of UGC (Fang et al. 2016; Liu and Park 2015). Furthermore, perceived usefulness can be enhanced by the disclosure of personal identity by communicators (Liu and Park 2015; Park and Nicolau 2015). Personal identity is not limited to textual information. Communicators' photos also influence their credibility, which in turn affects consumers' decisions about accommodation (Ert, Fleischer and Magen 2016).

Consumers' similarity with communicators influences their judgment of UGC, and similarity has a positive influence on consumer responses to suppliers (Ayeh, Au and Law 2013; Pentina, Bailey and Zhang 2015). A typical example of similarity is the sharing of socio-demographic characteristics (Shan 2016). However, the similarity effect may not be robust across all situations. Although incidental similarity (e.g., communicators and consumers share initials) enhances positive attitude and intention to patronize a restaurant, the effect is contingent on information load (the number of online reviews to which consumers are exposed) (Zhang, Wu and Mattila 2014) and the power concept in consumers' minds (Zhang 2015). As the similarity effect is tentative, investigations of the effect of other similarity variables will add knowledge to the hospitality literature and provide significant implications for practitioners. A plausible variable is preference similarity (He and Bond, 2013).

In Cheung and Thadani's (2012) framework, the communicator's motive to post UGC, in the eyes of consumers, is a communicator aspect that has not been found in studies about hotels and restaurants. Its effect on consumers' perceived credibility could be worthy of hospitality researchers' attention.

Receiver

The receiver is the consumer who responds to the UGC. According to Cheung and Thadani (2012), the effect of a stimulus on the response is contingent on the importance of the product/service to the consumer and the consumer's knowledge about the reviewed topic. In the literature about hotels and restaurants, these two receiver characteristics have not been examined. Instead, hospitality researchers have investigated the effects of other receiver-related constructs. The positive effect of valence on hotel booking intention is stronger if the consumer is a conformist with a tendency toward thinking and acting with the goal of seeking group approval (Tsao et al. 2015). The UGC effect on intention to visit a restaurant is stronger if the consumer is promotion-focused (i.e., focusing on gains in the pursuit of goals) (Pentina, Bailey and Zhang 2015). Compared with the response, stimulus, and communicator components of Cheung and Thadani's (2012) framework, the receiver has been given less attention by hospitality researchers. More research effort should be devoted to this aspect of the subject.

Contextual factor

The contextual factor is the environment in which consumers are exposed to UGC. Cheung and Thadani (2012) specifically related this component to platforms (i.e., UGC websites). Park and Lee (2009) found that UGCs on an established (versus newly initiated) website are more influential in generating purchases of educational products. Their findings have yet to be validated in the hotel and restaurant sectors. Moreover, UGC platforms for hotels and restaurants can be differentiated according to the reservation function. Some require communicators to make reservations on their websites before posting reviews (e.g., Expedia.com, OpenTable.com), whereas others do not have this requirement (e.g., TripAdvisor.com, Yelp.com). This difference may influence consumer responses. In addition to platforms/websites, product/service types can also be a contextual factor. Park and Lee (2009) also revealed that UGC about experience goods (versus search goods) has a greater effect on consumer responses. The difference between experience and search goods is that the quality of an experience good is more difficult to evaluate before purchase (Viglia, Furlan and Ladrón-de-Guevara 2014). Both hotels and restaurants were classified as experience goods but restaurants were considered to have more evaluable qualities

User-generated content and user responses

(i.e., they were closer to search goods). Given this difference, restaurant UGC is perceived as more trustworthy (Ong, 2012). In sum, the contextual factor is under-researched in the hotel and restaurant sectors and knowledge has yet to be accumulated in this area.

Conclusion

The effect of UGC on consumer responses in the hotel and restaurant sectors has been extensively examined in recent years (Kim and Tang 2016). The findings are rather scattered and an integrative framework that consolidates these findings in a systematic manner is lacking. This chapter has therefore presented a state-of-the-art review of related literature using Cheung and Thadani's (2012) social communication framework, which comprises five components: response, stimulus, communicator, receiver, and contextual factor. A modified framework is shown in Figure 45.1. Although some sub-components (e.g., involvement, attribution, prior knowledge, and platform) were not identified in the hotel- and restaurant-related UGC studies, other sub-components were identified and added to the framework, which makes it more comprehensive.

Within response, emotion is the sub-component that is not in Cheung and Thadani's (2012) framework. The dynamic between emotional and behavioral responses has yet to be examined. The usefulness and credibility of UGC remain the major antecedents of attitude and intention, which then shape actual behavior, for which sales volume is considered a proxy.

The body of literature about stimulus is large for the hotel and restaurant sectors. This chapter has enriched the understanding of the stimulus effect by introducing a number of subcomponents to Cheung and Thadani's (2012) framework. Although most scholarly attention has been devoted to rating and commentary, recent years have seen a growing interest in the effect of suppliers' responses. The sub-components of stimulus in Figure 45.1 were identified from

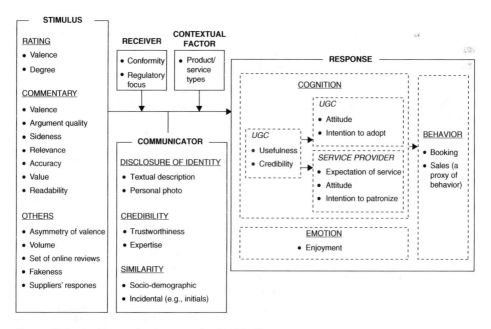

Figure 45.1   An integrative framework of UGC effect on consumer responses
Source: Modified from Cheung and Thadani (2012).

separate studies. Future research could examine their combined effects on responses. As some of the sub-components (e.g., valence and volume) have been widely examined, a meta-analysis of their effects is a promising topic.

As per Cheung and Thadani (2012), the credibility of the communicator has a significant effect on responses. Disclosure of identity is important. In addition to textual description of the communicators, photos of the communicators have also been shown to affect responses, although empirical evidence is still scant. Similarity is another salient sub-component of the communicator. Future research on the similarity effect should go beyond socio-demographic and incidental variables. Preference similarity is one option.

Both the receiver and contextual factors have moderating effects on the stimulus–response relationship. However, there is relatively little literature in this area for the hotel and restaurant sectors. The identified sub-components differ from those in Cheung and Thadani (2012). More research could be conducted on these two components.

Practitioners are recommended to improve their offerings based on the framework presented here. To improve their websites, especially by enhancing the usefulness and credibility of UGC, platform operators could consider the effect of the stimulus and communicator sub-components on consumer responses and should strive to prevent fake UGC. Hotel and restaurant operators are recommended to encourage credible communicators to experience their service and post online reviews, as these communicators' UGC is more persuasive. Furthermore, hotel and restaurant operators' responses to customers' comments should be timely and communication style should be effective. Although information communications technology is ever-changing, UGC will remain an influential factor that shapes consumer behavior for the foreseeable future. It is important to keep this body of literature growing.

References

Ajzen, I. (1991) "The Theory of Planned Behavior," *Organizational Behavior and Human Decision Processes*, 50(2), 179–211.

Ayeh, J. K., Au, N. and Law, R. (2013) "Do We Believe in TripAdvisor?" Examining Credibility Perceptions and Online Travelers' Attitude Toward Using User-generated Content," *Journal of Travel Research* 52(4), 437–52.

Baumeister, R. F., Bratslavsky, E., Finkenauer, C. and Vohs, K. D. (2001), "Bad Is Stronger Than Good," *Review of General Psychology* 5(4), 323–70.

Bickart, B. and Schindler, R. M. (2001) "Internet Forums as Influential Sources of Consumer Information," *Journal of Interactive Marketing* 15(3), 31–40.

Casaló, L. V. Flavián, C. and Guinalíu, M. (2011) "Understanding the Intention to Follow the Advice Obtained in an Online Travel Community," *Computers in Human Behavior* 27(2), 622–33.

Casaló, L. V., Flavián, C., Guinalíu, M. and Ekinci, Y. (2015) "Do Online Hotel Rating Schemes Influence Booking Behaviors?" *International Journal of Hospitality Management* 49, 28–36.

Cezar, A. and Öğüt, H. (2016) "Analyzing Conversion Rates in Online Hotel Booking: The Role of Customer Reviews, Recommendations and Rank Order in Search Listings," *International Journal of Contemporary Hospitality Management* 28(2), 286–304.

Cheng, Y. H. and Ho, H. Y. (2015) "Social Influence's Impact on Reader Perceptions of Online Reviews," *Journal of Business Research* 68(4), 883–87.

Cheung, C. M. K. and Thadani, D. R. (2012) "The Impact of Electronic Word-of-mouth Communication: A Literature Analysis and Integrative Model," *Decision Support Systems* 54(1), 461–70.

Cheung, M. Y., Luo, C., Sia, C. L. and Chen, H. (2009) "Credibility of Electronic Word-of-mouth: Informational and Normative Determinants of On-line Consumer Recommendations," *International Journal of Electronic Commerce* 13(4), 9–38.

Chiu, C., Chiu, N. H., Sung, R. J. and Hsieh, P. Y. (2015) "Opinion Mining of Hotel Customer-generated Contents in Chinese Weblogs," *Current Issues in Tourism* 18(5), 477–95.

Cohen, J. B., Pham, M. T. and Andrade, E. B. (2008) "The Nature and Role of Affect in Consumer Behavior," in C. P. Haugtvedt, P. Herr and F. Kardes (eds). *Handbook of Consumer Psychology*, New York, NY: Lawrence Erlbaum Associates, 297–348.

Daugherty, T., Eastin, M. S. and Bright, L. (2008) "Exploring Consumer Motivations for Creating User-generated Content," *Journal of Interactive Advertising* 8(2), 16–25.

Duan, W., Yu, Y., Cao, Q. and Levy, S. (2015) "Exploring the Impact of Social Media on Hotel Service Performance: A Sentimental Analysis Approach," *Cornell Hospitality Quarterly*. doi:10.1177/1938965515620483.

Ert, E., Fleischer, A. and Magen, N. (2016) "Trust and Reputation in the Sharing Economy: The Role of Personal Photos in Airbnb," *Tourism Management* 55, 62–73.

Filieri, R. (2016) "What Makes an Online Consumer Review Trustworthy?" *Annals of Tourism Research* 58, 46–64.

Filieri, R. and McLeay, F. (2014) "E-WOM and Accommodation: An Analysis of the Factors that Influence Travelers' Adoption of Information from Online Reviews," *Journal of Travel Research* 53(1), 44–57.

Fang, B., Ye, Q., Kucukusta, D. and Law, R. (2016) "Analysis of the Perceived Value of Online Tourism Reviews: Influence of Readability and Reviewer Characteristics," *Tourism Management* 52, 498–506.

Fong, L. H. N., Law, R., Tang, C. M. F. and Yap, M. H. T. (2016) "Experimental Research in Hospitality and Tourism: A Critical Review," *International Journal of Contemporary Hospitality Management* 28(2), 246–66.

Fong, L. H. N., Lei, S. S. I. and Law, R. (2016) "Asymmetry of Hotel Ratings on TripAdvisor: Evidence from Single-Versus Dual-Valence Reviews," *Journal of Hospitality Marketing & Management*. doi:10.1080/19368623.2016.1178619.

Goh, K. Y., Heng, C. S. and Lin, Z. (2013) "Social Media Brand Community and Consumer Behavior: Quantifying the Relative Impact of User- and Marketer-Generated Content," *Information Systems Research* 24(1), 88–107.

He, S. X. and Bond, S. D. (2013) "Word-of-mouth and the Forecasting of Consumption Enjoyment," *Journal of Consumer Psychology* 23(4), 464–82.

Kim, E. and Tang, R. (2016) "Rectifying Failure of Service: How Customer Perceptions of Justice Affect Their Emotional Response and Social Media Testimonial," *Journal of Hospitality Marketing & Management*, 25(8), 897–924.

Kim, W. G., Lim, H. and Brymer, R. A. (2015) "The Effectiveness of Managing Social Media on Hotel Performance," *International Journal of Hospitality Management* 44, 165–71.

Kramer, A. D. I., Guillory, J. E. and Hancock, J. T. (2014) "Experimental Evidence of Massive-scale Emotional Contagion Through Social Networks," *Proceedings of the National Academy of Sciences* 111(29), 8788–90.

Kusumasondjaja, S., Shanka, T. and Marchegiani, C. (2012) "Credibility of Online Reviews and Initial Trust: The Roles of Reviewer's Identity and Review Valence," *Journal of Vacation Marketing* 18(3), 185–95.

Ladhari, R. and Michaud, M. (2015) "eWOM Effects on Hotel Booking Intentions, Attitudes, Trust, and Website Perceptions," *International Journal of Hospitality Management* 46, 36–45.

Laros, F. J. M. and Steenkamp, J. B. E. M. (2005) "Emotions in Consumer Behavior: A Hierarchical Approach," *Journal of Business Research* 58(10), 1437–45.

Lee, H. and Blum, S. C. (2015) "How Hotel Responses to Online Reviews Differ by Hotel Rating: An Exploratory Study," *Worldwide Hospitality and Tourism Themes* 7(3), 242–50.

Leung, D., Law, R., van Hoof, H. and Buhalis, D. (2013) "Social Media in Tourism and Hospitality: A Literature Review," *Journal of Travel & Tourism Marketing* 30(1–2), 3–22.

Levy, S. E., Duan, W. and Boo, S. (2013) "An Analysis of One-Star Online Reviews and Responses in the Washington, D.C., Lodging Market," *Cornell Hospitality Quarterly* 54(1), 49–63.

Liang, S., Schuckert, M. and Law, R. (2016) "Multilevel Analysis of the Relationship Between Type of Travel, Online Ratings, and Management Response: Empirical Evidence from International Upscale Hotels," *Journal of Travel & Tourism Marketing*. doi:10.1080/10548408.2016.1156613.

Lim, Y. S. and Van Der Heide, B. (2015) "Evaluating the Wisdom of Strangers: The Perceived Credibility of Online Consumer Reviews on Yelp," *Journal of Computer-Mediated Communication* 20(1), 67–82

Liu, Z. and Park, S. (2015) "What Makes a Useful Online Review? Implication for Travel Product Websites," *Tourism Management* 47, 140–51.

Lu, W. and Stepchenkova, S. (2015) "User-generated Content as a Research Mode in Tourism and Hospitality Applications: Topics, Methods, and Software," *Journal of Hospitality Marketing & Management* 24(2), 119–54.

Magnini, V. P., Crotts, J. C. and Zehrer, A. (2011) "Understanding Customer Delight: An Application of Travel Blog Analysis," *Journal of Travel Research* 50(5), 535–45.

Mauri, A. G. and Minazzi, R. (2013) "Web Reviews Influence on Expectations and Purchasing Intentions of Hotel Potential Customers," *International Journal of Hospitality Management* 34, 99–107.

Min, H., Lim, Y. and Magnini, V. P. (2014) "Factors Affecting Customer Satisfaction in Responses to Negative Online Hotel Reviews: The Impact of Empathy, Paraphrasing, and Speed," *Cornell Hospitality Quarterly* 56(2), 223–31.

Ong, B. S. (2012) "The Perceived Influence of User Reviews in the Hospitality Industry," *Journal of Hospitality Marketing & Management* 21(5), 463–85.

Park, C. and Lee, T. M. (2009) "Information Direction, Website Reputation and eWOM Effect: A Moderating Role of Product Type," *Journal of Business Research* 62(1), 61–7.

Park, S. Y. and Allen, J. P. (2013) "Responding to Online Reviews: Problem Solving and Engagement in Hotels," *Cornell Hospitality Quarterly* 54(1), 64–73.

Park, S. and Nicolau, J. L. (2015) "Asymmetric Effects of Online Consumer Reviews," *Annals of Tourism Research* 50, 67–83.

Pentina, I., Bailey, A. A. and Zhang, L. (2015) "Exploring Effects of Source Similarity, Message Valence, and Receiver Regulatory Focus on Yelp Review Persuasiveness and Purchase Intentions," *Journal of Marketing Communications*. doi: 10.1080/13527266.2015.1005115.

Philander, K. and Zhong, Y. (2016) "Twitter Sentiment Analysis: Capturing Sentiment from Integrated Resort Tweets," *International Journal of Hospitality Management* 55, 16–24.

Phillips, P., Barnes, S., Zigan, K. and Schegg, R. (2016) "Understanding the Impact of Online Reviews on Hotel Performance: An Empirical Analysis," *Journal of Travel Research*. doi:10.1177/0047287516636481

Purnawirawan, N., De Pelsmacker, P. and Dens, N. (2012) "Balance and Sequence in Online Reviews: How Perceived Usefulness Affects Attitudes and Intentions," *Journal of Interactive Marketing* 26(4), 244–55.

Racherla, P., Connolly, D. J. and Christodoulidou, N. (2013) "What Determines Consumers' Ratings of Service Providers? An Exploratory Study of Online Traveler Reviews," *Journal of Hospitality Marketing & Management* 22(2), 135–61.

Ring, A., Tkaczynski, A. and Dolnicar, S. (2016) "Word-of-Mouth Segments: Online, Offline, Visual or Verbal?" *Journal of Travel Research* 55(4), 481–92.

Salehi-Esfahani, S., Ravichandran, S., Israeli, A. and Bolden Iii, E. (2016) "Investigating Information Adoption Tendencies Based on Restaurants' User-generated Content Utilizing a Modified Information Adoption Model," *Journal of Hospitality Marketing & Management*. doi: 10.1080/19368623.2016.1171190.

Schuckert, M., Liu, X. and Law, R. (2015) "Hospitality and Tourism Online Reviews: Recent Trends and Future Directions," *Journal of Travel & Tourism Marketing* 32(5), 608–21.

Serra Cantallops, A. and Salvi, F. (2014) "New Consumer Behavior: A Review of Research on eWOM and Hotels," *International Journal of Hospitality Management* 36, 41–51.

Shan, Y. (2016) "How Credible are Online Product Reviews? The Effects of Self-generated and System-generated Cues on Source Credibility Evaluation," *Computers in Human Behavior* 55, Part B, 633–41.

Sheeran, P. (2002) "Intention—Behavior Relations: A Conceptual and Empirical Review," *European Review of Social Psychology* 12(1), 1–36.

Shin, S., Chung, N., Kang, D. and Koo, C. (2016) "How Far, How Near Psychological Distance Matters in Online Travel Reviews: A Test of Construal-level Theory," in A. Inversini and R. Schegg (eds). *Information and Communication Technologies in Tourism 2016*, Cham: Springer International Publishing, 355–68.

Sparks, B. A. and Browning, V. (2011) "The Impact of Online Reviews on Hotel Booking Intentions and Perception of Trust," *Tourism Management* 32(6), 1310–23.

Tsao, W. C., Hsieh, M. T., Shih, L. W. and Lin, T. M. Y. (2015) "Compliance with eWOM: The Influence of Hotel Reviews on Booking Intention from the Perspective of Consumer Conformity," *International Journal of Hospitality Management* 46, 99–111.

Viglia, G., Furlan, R. and Ladrón-de-Guevara, A. (2014) "Please, Talk About It! When Hotel Popularity Boosts Preferences," *International Journal of Hospitality Management* 42, 155–64.

Xie, H., Miao, L., Kuo, P. J. and Lee, B. Y. (2011) "Consumers' Responses to Ambivalent Online Hotel Reviews: The Role of Perceived Source Credibility and Pre-decisional Disposition," *International Journal of Hospitality Management* 30(1), 178–83.

Xie, K. L., Zhang, Z. and Zhang, Z. (2014) "The Business Value of Online Consumer Reviews and Management Response to Hotel Performance," *International Journal of Hospitality Management* 43, 1–12.

Ye, Q., Law, R., Gu, B. and Chen, W. (2011) "The Influence of User-generated Content on Traveler Behavior: An Empirical Investigation on the Effects of E-word-of-mouth to Hotel Online Bookings," *Computers in Human Behavior* 27(2), 634–39.

Yoo, K. H. and Gretzel, U. (2009) "Comparison of Deceptive and Truthful Travel Reviews," in W. Hopken, U. Gretzel and R. Law (eds). *Information and Communication Technologies in Tourism 2009*. New York, NY: Springer, 37–48.

Zeng, B. and Gerritsen, R. (2014) "What Do We Know About Social Media in Tourism? A Review," *Tourism Management Perspectives* 10, 27–36.

Zhang, L. (2015) "Online Reviews: The Impact of Power and Incidental Similarity," *Journal of Hospitality Marketing & Management* 24(6), 633–51.

Zhang, L., Wu, L. and Mattila, A. S. (2014) "Online Reviews: The Role of Information Load and Peripheral Factors," *Journal of Travel Research* 55(3), 299–310.

Further reading

Babić Rosario, A., Sotgiu, F., De Valck, K. and Bijmolt, T. H. A. (2016) "The Effect of Electronic Word of Mouth on Sales: A Meta-Analytic Review of Platform, Product, and Metric Factors," *Journal of Marketing Research* 53(3), 297–318. (Moderators of UGC effect on sales.)

Floyd, K., Freling, R., Alhoqail, S., Cho, H.Y. and Freling, T. (2014) "How Online Product Reviews Affect Retail Sales: A Meta-analysis," *Journal of Retailing* 90(2), 217–32. (The UGC factors related to sales.)

Gopaldas, A. (2014) "Marketplace Sentiments," *Journal of Consumer Research* 41(4), 995–1014. (Conceptualization of marketplace sentiments.)

Liu, B. (2015) *Sentiment Analysis: Mining Opinions, Sentiments, and Emotions*, New York, NY: Cambridge University Press. (Sentiment analysis and its application.)

You, Y., Vadakkepatt, G. G. and Joshi, A. M. (2015) "A Meta-Analysis of Electronic Word-of-Mouth Elasticity," *Journal of Marketing* 79(2), 19–39. (Factors related to online review valence and volume elasticities.)

Part IX
Future of hospitality marketing
Trends and analysis

46

An overview of trends and challenges in the hospitality industry

Chris Ryan

Introduction

What will hotels look like in say, two decades hence? In a world where it might be said that change is the only constant, answers to such a question can at best be only speculative, regardless of the statisticians' attempts to establish trends, introduce dummy variables to account for exogenous factors, or to adopt alternative probability-based methods such as Bayesian theorems. This chapter aims to simply consider some possible trends and to introduce some ideas that the reader may reject, but even such a rejection would serve the purpose of initiating thinking about the challenges that face the industry. It is a chapter based on the author's experiences, and thus is anecdotal and speculative. In its defence, it might be said that the writer is someone who has spent almost four decades in tourism research, and has travelled to many countries, and taught in four, and given talks and presentations in many more. So, while not meeting the conventional standards of 'research science' it is offered as an 'informed piece of writing' that seeks to set the tone for much that will follow in this book, while additionally, it seeks to be future focused.

A brief history of the past and notes on the present

However, to explore the future, a short history and statement of the present is possibly required. Without such a starting point, it becomes difficult to assess the potential enormity of the changes that can occur – and each change represents a challenge.

Hospitality itself has a long history, dating from the time when one person invited a guest to share a 'home', and possibly a meal, or indeed offered overnight accommodation. The commercial hospitality industry commenced, it is thought, a little later, when payments were then made, even if as in the medieval period, an offering was made in the name of charity, and that became an expected custom. This chapter relates to the commercial industry, and in an age of Airbnb, couchsurfer and other examples of the internet-based sharing economy, has become something beyond what was previously understood to be the 'hospitality' sector of the economy. Consequently, if one adopts a definition of the hospitality industry simply being a situation when a market transaction occurs in the making of a payment for overnight accommodation, then the nature of that industry is extremely wide. It ranges from hotels to the individual householder offering a bed-space in their home to someone making a payment for just one night. According to Julian Persaud (Regional Director of Airbnb), and his presentation at the 2016 PATA conference held in Auckland in October 2016, in New Zealand alone the average number of nights each householder was obtaining was 38 per annum, with a revenue of approximately US$3,800. As an aside, he also noted that Airbnb was operating in 191 countries involving 2.5 million households – a significant growth from 2008 when the company was founded.

The hotel sector is itself heavily segmented. On the one hand there are four and five-star properties being operated (if not owned) by internationally well-known hotel groups such as Marriott or Accor, and on the other hand many budget-style hotels, some indeed offering access to rooms through the use of credit cards, phone-based apps, or similar means of access that reduce the costs of sustaining a 24-hour reception service. One (possibly extreme) example of this latter low-cost approach is the Jucy Snooze hotel (nicknamed the Pod hotel) operated by the New Zealand Jucy Campervan company at Christchurch International Hotel. Pictures of these sleeping pods can be seen on www.stuff.co.nz/business/84984258/new-zealands-first-pod-hotel-could-halt-sleepovers-at-christchurch-airport, and essentially the 'hotel' offers sleeping pods arranged in 'pods' of eight with an additional shared communal relaxation area. They are priced at NZ$39 (US$27.6) a night, and of course, many readers will recognise their origins in the Japanese capsule hotels (カプセルホテル *kapuseru hoteru*) that have long been part of the Japanese hotel portfolio. These too are aimed at price-conscious travellers and often come with fully equipped WiFi connections for game playing, internet surfing and the like.

Nibbling at the edge of the hotel sector, with its range of star-based hotels and loyalty schemes, are the motels that also provide accommodation, but often without offering restaurant facilities, and which have become a feature of motorway systems around the world. Additionally, there are camping grounds that also offer permanent cabin-serviced accommodation of a good standard. These are a feature of several countries that first provided camp grounds originating in the traditions of hiking and camping, and are not uncommon in countries such as Australia and New Zealand. In some European countries such as France and Germany, camping grounds will also offer a range of additional facilities that include spas, children's playgrounds and other sources of entertainment.

Camping itself has changed. Today, the verb 'glamping' has entered the lexicon, and tents are available that mimic the high end luxury of hotel rooms but in natural settings. The Pacific Islands also offer hotel rooms that are in traditional architectural styles by beaches but offer very high levels of comfort.

Thus today's hospitality industry offers a very wide range of accommodation appealing to many different segments. The examples include airport-based hotels that offer convenience and ease of access for those who arrive on a late flight or need to check in early for morning departures, to theme park based hotels that offer fantasy-style accommodation to, on the other hand, economy-based accommodation whose appeal rests primarily on low price. There are spa hotels seeking to become destinations in themselves through the offering of wellness breaks, to Buddhist meditation centres in China (a fast-growing sector at the commencement of the second decade of the twenty-first century) to some hotels that specifically seek to be a destination and thus offer products that are unique in the experiences they offer. One example of the latter would be the Al Maha resort in the United Arab Emirates – a hotel offering private chalets in a desert reclamation zone with an architecture and style of furnishing based on Bedouin traditions. It also offers its guests a range of traditional Arab-based experiences such as falconry, but possibly its primary marketing proposition is its involvement in the restoration of a desert made sterile by two centuries of camel grazing. Hence its support of a major replanting programme that has supported the re-introduction of reptiles, small mammals and notably gazelle and the Arabian oryx.

One might say that hotels offer products in varying modes of architecture, style, fantasy, and levels of service that can meet the requirements of the different parts of the travelling public.

The constant of change

So, what are the trends and challenges of the future? One constant challenge is the continuing change induced by information technologies. In 2006 the author spent six months in Charleston, South Carolina. The major sports and conference centre in that city was the Charleston Coliseum. In one tour of the facility, a comment was made that, in the building of the centre, one signifi-cant cost was that of installing miles of wiring to ensure that a full suite of telecommunication services were available in many points of the building. This statement was then followed by the wry comment that if they had waited a few years that cost would have been totally unnecessary in a world of mobile telephones.

In 2012–13 the author undertook some research into Chinese visitors' experiences of New Zealand for differing tourism authorities. It was found that Chinese visitors complained about the need to pay for internet connections in New Zealand hotels, because, in China, it was, and at the time of writing, is still generally true, that such a service is free to guests. In 2015–16 the complaints had all but disappeared. Had the hotels changed their policies? No! In the interven-ing years, smartphones had developed, and the New Zealand telcos were, for the most part, all offering 4G services and many were able to offer unlimited broadband capacity at prices far cheaper than previously. Technology had 'solved' the problem. Paradoxically, in late 2015 in a conversation with a General Manager of a five-star property in Sanya, Hainan Island, China, a comment was made that Chinese hotels are being faced with increasing telco charges and are changing their policies. Free internet access is being permitted in the hotels' public areas, but charges are being introduced for in-room internet connections because of a changing demand that consumes more broadband capacity. In short, hotel guests no longer simply look at their emails but are wanting to download films. Such a practice increases costs and of course threatens to downgrade the speed of the systems within the hotel.

Many responses are possible. One response that has attracted significant attention has been that of the Hotel Icon in Hong Kong. Based on an analysis of guest habits and usage patterns they have now introduced an additional service for guests, which is the offer of a free smart-phone for guests that can not only be used within the hotel but also taken anywhere in Hong Kong. Their analysis has indicated that the costs can be covered by the rates charged for a room and that the service is not generally abused. Equally, of course, software apps permit the tracing of telephones should that be required.

Change and hotel architecture

Thus, responses are being made to the changes induced by technology. But what of future technologies, and what of changes in the wider socio-demographic and natural environment? Readers may remember a television advertising campaign by Samsung for its high definition television sets where the windows of a train were replaced by such television sets so that the train passengers could gaze upon a differing series of landscapes only to complete their sightseeing by being in space. Many of us will have attended sports events where the critical moments of a match may be replayed on very large screens within the stadia, and indeed such replays have become part of the refereeing process in some sports such as rugby union. In various lectures,

I have speculated that it is quite possible that in the future when a guest checks in at reception they will be asked which landscape they would like to see from their room. The guest can then select from underwater scapes to mountains, lakes or urban settings according to their choice. That this may be possible is because potentially the hotel window may be replaced by the large screen and thus the view from the window can not only show the landscape selected but through information technology, portray the hourly or seasonal changes. Now consider the architectural implications of applying such technologies. Conventionally many hotels locate their rooms around the perimeter walls, looking outward so as to offer some natural light to a room, and a view, even if possibly just a view toward another wall of windows. Freed from the convention of locating rooms around the perimeter of a hotel, the internal design of the hotel can change, and equally the outer shape and dimensions of the hotel. Hotels need no longer be built on the principles of rectangles but can be of many different shapes.

It is a cliché that travelers from developing countries once went to the USA to see the future, but often today in order to see the architecture of the future, one travels to the Gulf countries or China. An examination of architecture in the United Arab Emirates, Qatar, or China, indicates the innovation that today is being shown by architects, including the development of airports such as Beijing Capital International Airport or Guangzhou (even if they are designed by architects whose head offices are in cities such as London or New York).

One challenge of building such innovatively shaped buildings is that such constructions do not come cheap, and one reason why many of them occur in developing countries is due to the easier access to green field (or desert) locations. The costs of building in an existing city centre or built-up area is, of course, higher. Access may be limited to the site. Construction may bring additional costs due to the potential disruption of water, sewage and electricity supplies for neighbours, who may well have their own 24-hour a day businesses, meaning there is no 'quiet, non-business' period of which the construction companies can take advantage. In turn, this creates a series of other challenges, some of which may threaten the current understanding of what constitutes a central business district.

Reference has been made to the innovative architecture of airport terminuses. Conventionally airports were seen as transport nodes, but particularly over the last two decades or so they have become accommodation and retail hubs. Initially much of the retailing was open to travellers who may have had access only after passing through customs controls, but today airports are seeking to develop land for purposes of more general retail purposes and additionally as logistics nodes and indeed as centres for business in addition to freight services. They are also becoming entertainment hubs. One can go to an Imax cinema at, among others, Hong Kong Airport, while there are cinemas at Changi Airport, Singapore and Portland Airport in the USA. At Indira Gandhi Airport at Delhi, one can experience moving seats and bubbles among other things at the cinema complex. Zurich Airport advertises a range of services including the hire of bicycles and roller skates to better enjoy the landscape and woods around the airport complex.

Hence, while conventional business centres (CBDs) grew up based on public transport systems and the conveniences of working in near proximity with others, CBDs are having to move to new understandings of function and place in an age of congestion and higher costs. New uses of buildings are being sought, and of course, some of these mean that former warehouses and office blocks are being converted to hotels in the midst of new entertainment centres of clubs, restaurants, theatres and street entertainment, and residential areas are being made accessible by cycle ways and light railway systems. Airports, often also easily accessed by the means of purpose-built rail and road infrastructure completed in the last decades, are also becoming multi-purpose assets which also include commercial accommodation and entertainment.

This emergence of new areas often requires and is based upon conference and meeting centres and again such developments require attached hotels of the required standard. Around the world for many decades now, the former port areas of the nineteenth century have become accommodation, marina, museum and restaurant areas, whether it be Liverpool, Boston, or Sydney and Auckland. Such developments mean that the hospitality industry is becoming increasingly involved in urban city renewals, the entertainment industry, city and town planning, and its management is having to increasingly engage in interactions with other site stakeholders. Management need to adopt holistic visions of the places within which their hotels are sited. Housekeeping, reception and food provision are now only part of the General Manager's concerns and GMs of the major hotels around the world, whether the Burj Al Arab in Dubai or the Hyatt Grand in Guangzhou, are often not simply a hotel manager but are playing much larger roles within their companies and in their locales – often at a regional level.

Yet, in the search for innovation of design and function, hotels are also having to meet an increasing need to develop sustainable buildings. Part of the innovation in design is the way in which hotels are sympathetic to their natural surroundings and environments. The aforementioned Al Maha comprises forty separate units, each lying below the sky-line of a ridge within the desert, and located within palm trees. They are not visible from a distance, and each has separate sightlines so that none look into the other. Water recycling and solar panels are also used. As also noted, the architecture is consistent with traditional styles for that part of the world. Any search on the internet for eco-hotels will reveal an array of accommodation. For example, the Eco Hotels of the World website provides details and a rating system for energy supplies, water usage, waste disposal and environmental protection participation. In more urban locations increasingly hotels will note the use of natural materials as being anti-allergenic, identify their waste disposal methods and, for example, the use of waste food disposal for fertiliser generation. While critics will comment about 'greenwashing' very slowly, there is an appreciation that if claims are made, there is a need to substantiate the claims with something tangible. Those who build in ways consistent with LEED (Leadership in Energy and Environmental Design) guidelines will often feature such adherence within their promotional materials. The more hotels undertake such things, the greater becomes the market awareness of the existence of such good practice. Using the (possibly) simplistic AIDA marketing model of awareness, intention, decision and action, one can hope that increased awareness influences consumer actions in that while possibly other components such as location, price, and convenience may determine accommodation choice (all other things being equal), the potential guest may select that hotel which adheres to such practices. In the view of the author, such promotion is akin to the common tourism awards schemes, which over a period arguably lift the performance of the industry as prize winners gain additional business, but also act as benchmarks against which other businesses seek to match themselves. Over a period of time, good practice is slowly spread over a region, or indeed a country.

Change and corporate good citizenship

These concerns are with us now, and it is to be expected that they will continue to be with us as the industry increasingly strives to provide choice to a market that increasingly becomes more discerning as (hopefully) incomes grow while accompanying the growing numbers of those achieving middle-class status. It has been a clichéd statement to argue that concern with the environment is a concern for the wealthy. The less well-off have many other things with which to contend regarding personal and family well-being before taking on responsibilities from a wider perspective. Among these new concerns are the ethical concerns relevant to corporate social responsibility (CSR). Historically, within the hospitality industry, it is suggested that environmental concerns were the first to be recognised as requiring special attention. Two reasons provided an impetus in this direction. The first was the growing concern over environmental matters that arguably emanated from the 1991 Rio Declaration on the Environment and Development as determined by the Earth Summit of that year in Rio de Janeiro. Prompted in part by the growth of environmental groups such as Greenpeace and others, many businesses from different sectors began to look at production processes. Such businesses quickly learned that cost savings could emerge from the adoption of such practices, even if the expected market demand often failed to materialise. The establishment of grading systems such as the Green Globe 21, the PATA Green Leaf and others gave a further impetus in terms of offering an external form of accreditation that could be used to meet criticisms of 'green washing'. In time, some of these systems were themselves criticised as establishing corporate ventures dependent upon the revenues gained from the accreditation processes, thereby raising suspicions that possibly the methods of evaluation were not as rigorous as one might have hoped. Nonetheless, companies, including hotel companies, sought to gain such accreditation and appointed staff to conduct and monitor environmental practice, and once promises are made public, a need for tangible delivery for the public becomes a necessity.

Many companies that did adopt such processes with integrity quickly realised that it was essential to obtain staff 'buy in' for these practices, and in turn that meant providing not simply exhortation but also training and empowerment of staff. Historically this move supplemented the interest of the 1990s in staff empowerment as a means of reducing labour turnover and improving job satisfaction and the provision of services to guests. A virtuous rather than vicious circle was being envisaged where empowered staff were more happy staff, who provided a better service to guests. In those guest interactions staff not only supported guest loyalty (thereby making repeat sales easier) but also obtained further job satisfaction, therefore reducing costs associated with labour turnover by improving staff retention.

The advent of communication technologies directly enhanced this 'virtuous circle' when companies introduced computer and internet-based knowledge management systems. These evolved beyond stock control and purchasing systems into marketing systems that kept details of guests, their preferences and usage of hotel chains and loyalty schemes into bulletin boards easily accessible by staff. Such bulletin boards could provide staff with information about training opportunities, posts for promotion, and posts at other properties, while all the time informing staff about news of new products, marketing campaigns, and good practice. Beyond this, hotel companies developed the notion that being a good corporate citizen also implied being a good employer. Such a notion led to further good practices.

Slowly, in many hotel companies, a more holistic understanding of employee needs emerged. Employees had lives beyond their time at the workplace. Discussion of work–life balance emerged, and equally, employees were seen as having a role within their communities. Companies such as Accor adopted 'Earth days' when employees participated in wider 'good citizenship' activities outside of the company – and often these actions were local in action where the hotel sought to establish itself as a good neighbour with the immediate community it served. It must be noted that hotels not only offer accommodation for the out of town or village visitor but also offer facilities used by local communities as a meeting or conference venue and as a banqueting centre for social events including marriage celebration, anniversaries and birthdays.

The core of job satisfaction, however, rests in the employee having confidence that the hotel or accommodation company is providing a service or product that possesses integrity; that it is a product that the employee him or herself can agree with from an ethical stance. This perspective takes the hotel company beyond its own walls into the need to ensure that its supplies come from trusted sources. Hotel CSR practices then began to be involved with a more holistic understanding of business where the property and the wider company seeks to be environmentally friendly for marketing, environmental and cost reduction reasons; where it seeks to be a good employer for various motives; where it concerns itself with the locale it serves as a neighbour; and where it seeks to ensure its suppliers are also ethical – if only to ensure that the products it purchases will not endanger its own employees and guests.

These concerns are particularly relevant, it is suggested, in societies that have been characterised by past poor and corrupt practices. In a society such as China, its history has led to governments proactively leading these types of practices – perhaps thereby illustrating the concept of a Chinese socialist market system. China's concern with environmental issues emerged in 2003 with the planning processes required for the 2008 Beijing Olympics that adopted a LEED-accredited Olympic Village. The Chinese Ministry of Commerce also announced plans to build 10,000 green hotels between 2008 and 2012. The National Hotel Rating System that determines star ratings of hotels in China did, in 2011, incorporate 'green measures' as one of the five core criteria for grading. Under the scheme, up to 300 points can be gained under the headings of green design, environmental policy, green consumption, green action, clean production and hazardous waste treatment. Also, the overarching goals of the scheme emphasise maximum resource efficiency, minimum environmental impacts, and the health and safety of customers and staff, including adherence to food, safety and hygiene regulations. In subsequent years further legislation has reinforced these measures by, for example, reference to employee rights under the China Labour Law. For example, Article 36 provides for an eight-hour working day and a 44-hour working week and lays down requirements that give employees rights to obtain over-time pay (Labour Law, Article 41). The Labour Law was updated with the Labour Contract Law of 2008, which was further updated with effect from 1 July 2013. China is no longer a low-waged labour force, and legislation has reinforced worker rights and when considered with other laws has brought about many significant improvements for China's hotel employees.

Further into the future

The industry of today has evolved into a heterogeneous market place of various products as described above. It is an industry that has embraced information technologies even while it is challenged by them. One such challenge has been the arrival of online travel agencies (OTAs) that has largely bypassed the old system of using travel agencies to make bookings. Today many guests will have made a booking through an OTA such as Booking.com, TripAdvisor.com or Expedia.com. This practice means that a hotel no longer retains the whole of the revenue derived from a booking, but many today have created loyalty schemes and have launched their own web pages to compete and enhance revenue. Today the sharing economy of room provision has emerged as a rival to these new systems. This has required hotels to more carefully consider yield management policies and so determine how many rooms they may provide an OTA with, and at what price. But these are app-based functions and technologies are now beginning to move beyond these to intelligent cloud-based systems. The cloud may again mean that a potential guest can make direct contact with the provider of the room and even bypass the apps of companies such as Booking.com. The competition will be based on which entity best reads the algorithms that reads an enquirer's past searchers. The global industry's primary cloud-based site booking system is SiteMinder, which in 2016 reported that direct bookings through SiteMinder averaged a value of US$600 as against the US$340 of OTAs (Siteminder, 2016). This was through the SiteMinder's internet booking engine, TheBookingButton, that hotels can use for direct booking. As the report noted:

> Our data shows that hotels globally are achieving 1.8 times more, on average, for accommodation booked via their own direct website than via OTAs and other third-party channels. While we can't forget the reach these third-party sites provide to hotels, it's important to note that direct bookings are not only achieving higher value overall but there is no commission payable on them, so they are much more profitable
>
> *(SiteMinder, 2016, p. 1)*

In short, the technology that created OTAs has permitted other services to emerge that compete with the OTAs. Continuing migration onto cloud computing is seen as the future of accessing the internet. Anderson and Rainie (2010) estimated that within a matter of a few years (by 2020), while desktops will retain a role, increasingly access to the internet will be through providers such as Google being accessed from a range of available devices, of which the smartphone will be dominant. Equally, an emergent 'internet of things' will be promising a greater accessibility and merger of functions. In a sense hotels initially promised a degree of luxury and services not available at home, but as personal incomes have increased and homes became acquainted with satellite television and high definition television, hotels offering such services were in effect merely saying that you can continue to do your favourite leisure things while away. The 'promise' switched from a promise of an 'extra' to the promise of not missing out on favourite screen viewing. The hotel of the future will, it is suggested, not only have to offer accommodation but also a means of accessing that accommodation prior to arrival as the guest will be able to set the room temperature, select their lighting scheme, switch on the jug or kettle for their hot drink, and, as indicated above, possibly set the view from their 'window' prior to their arrival by accessing the 'internet of things'.

The impact of technologies on hotels will not cease at that stage. Documents internal to the hotel companies are indicating a revived interest in obtaining feedback on hotel and room design from potential clientele through the use of simulation software that is becoming more sophisticated than the earlier versions of 'Second Life'. Beds are envisaged as being offered to massage the body, and toilets may be installed that can provide the guest with a medical check based on an analysis of urine and faeces. Variable patterns of lighting to set a mood are already a feasibility, and robotic check in at reception is making an appearance. Indeed, as the very embryonic experiment at one of the hotels at Huis Ten Bosch near Nagasaki, Japan, has indicated, such 'receptionists' need not have a human form but can add to the fantasy element of the hotel stay by adopting (in this instance) the form of a dinosaur.

Such introductions of technology may also be mindful of the changing nature of the market place. Taking the forecasts of bodies such as the United Nations World Tourism Organization (UNWTO), PATA, and the World Travel and Tourism Council (WTTC) as possessing credibility, all point to a growing demand for travel at a rate faster than global increases in GDP. Much of this, in the immediate future, is premised on a growing number of people in countries such as China and India joining the middle classes and possessing both a hunger and a means to meet the demand for increased amounts of travel. It should be noted that the IATA (International Air Transport Association) and IACO (International Civil Aviation Organization), at the time of the 2015 Paris United Nations Environmental Summit, gave an undertaking to eventually cap carbon emissions from the growth of air traffic from 2020. That is, air transport growth from that date should be carbon neutral, and carbon emissions should be held at 2020 levels. The aviation industry is fully aware of the need to achieve such goals. Certainly, the new technologies that lie behind aircraft such as the Dreamliner (the Boeing 787) and the new generation of single-aisle A320 Neo and Boeing 737 MAX continue to offer lower significant carbon emissions per passenger kilometre flown even when compared to aircraft developed just a decade ago. Thus it is expected that the demand for travel will continue to depend on the availability of the means of transportation, but accessibility and an over-crowding of air space and airports is a concern for the air industry. Air traffic control remains primarily a national affair and new initiatives for a more global or even regional air space control remain embryonic. If the experience of the ASEAN Air Traffic Management initiative is representative, progress will remain slow in the near future due to a reluctance to surrender national control to a multi-national entity.

But while such constraints of airport capacity and air space control may impact indirectly on the growth in the hotel industry, demand for hotel and other sources of accommodation is expected to continue to grow. As an indicator, domestic Chinese tourist demand grew from the movement of 1 billion people in 2012 to 4 billion just four years later according to the China Tourism Academy, and intra-Asian travel demand is being met not only by an expansion of air services but also by the new generations of fast rail services. It is recognised that these are competitive with air transport for distances of approximately 300 kilometres.

So who are these new travellers? The profile of world travellers by 2050 will be much more complex than at the start of the century. While the developed nations and some developing nations such as China are being characterised as an ageing population, those of emergent markets such as India, and many of the African countries are currently the opposite. For several African countries, 50 per cent of their populations are below the age of 25 to 30 years. The tourist market of the near future will comprise well-experienced travellers with income who wish for good value for money, but who are able and willing to pay for that value. At the other extreme will be new generations, increasingly 'tech savvy' and able to undertake long-haul travel as the first generation of their families to do so. The old profile of the European Caucasian tourists is already giving way to the middle-aged and younger Asian traveller. In the case of Chinese and other Asians such as the Vietnamese, Laotians, Indonesians and Cambodians, the younger generation have had very different life histories to those of their parents and grandparents who lived through periods of significant upheaval characterised by periods of war. These younger generations share much with their Western millennials and post-millennials in being used to a constant change in computer-based technologies. By 2050 these waves will be joined by an increasing number of Africans as the inheritors of current economic growth rates being obtained by some of the countries on that continent. While in 2015, World Global GDP grew at about 2.5%, several African countries such as Kenya and the Ivory Coast significantly performed better, although it is recognised that some have had fluctuating performances such as Botswana, which has yo-yoed from being one of the fastest growing nations in 2013 with an economic growth rate of 9.6% to record a slight negative fall in 2015 (World Bank, 2016).

As a response the hotel industry will continue to offer the very diversified products noted above, but accompanied by a growing dependency on new technologies, and meeting the demand for new urban experiences and equally meeting the demand for more 'natural' and 'authentic' experiences, however 'authentic' is defined. However, in a world where social relationships are increasingly based on electronic communications, the tourism experience may come to emphasise the role of inter-human communication. This phenomon will, in turn, raise interesting questions as to how the hotel industry will recruit its labour in the future as a series of counter-balancing trends exist. These are listed below:

a) In the developed world the population is ageing, thereby increasing the demand for younger-aged labour, implying higher labour costs.

b) In much of the developing world, the age pyramid reflects that a significant proportion of the total population are in the younger age groups, thereby implying the availability of a labour force.

c) A growing debate about the future of employment has emerged based on the work of Frey and Osborne (2013) at Oxford University. They noted that 47% of jobs in 702 occupational groups are at high risk of disappearing in two decades due to improvements in robotics and algorithms. While it might be argued that the hotel industry requires high levels of human contact, it should be noted that Bone (2015, p. 881) states "More surprisingly, we find that a substantial share of employment in service occupations, where most US job growth has occurred over the past decades (Autor and Dorn, 2013), are highly susceptible to computerisation. Additional support for this finding is provided by the recent growth in the market for service robots (MGI, 2013) and the gradual diminishment of the comparative advantage of human labour in tasks involving mobility and dexterity (Robotics-VO, 2013)." Their report lists the occupations examined, and it will be noted that while the hotel sector is not explicitly studied, many of the occupational groups listed include functions undertaken in hotels from administrative posts to floral arrangements and beauty salons. This pattern of employment creates an opportunity for capital replacements for human labour that can lower costs, although equally, it opens job opportunities for those high in empathetic intelligence who can think creatively to support the higher end of the market.

Just as an indication of trends to come, in September 2016 it was announced by the company Zume Pizzas that it was to replace its chefs by robots. Such a move was estimated to save significant labour costs. Indeed, the company employs only fifty people in its pizza delivery service in California (CNBC, 2016).

d) An implicit threat of the report of the future of employment (Frey and Osborne, 2013) is that if a large number of the middle-class administrative posts disappear, then this represents a threat to a major segment of the current tourism market. Tourism's secret is that its growth is primarily based upon the growing incomes of a growing number of middle-class occupations. If these occupations vanish, then bluntly put, so too might much of tourism.

e) Even under this scenario, high-end tourism will continue. In a report from Credit Suisse Bank, Stierli et al. (2015) report that the top 0.7% of the world's population controlled 45.2% of the world's total wealth. By the same token, 71% of the global population had but 3% of the world's wealth. Tourism is thus primarily dependent upon 29% of the world's population. Arguably given that most of that proportion have less than US$100,000 in assets, tourism (and the hotel industry) is perhaps mainly dependent upon the top 15% or so of the world's population. And, of course as just noted, many of these according to Frey and Osborne (2013) may be vulnerable to a loss of jobs, and hence income.

f) The implications for the hotel industry are, under these scenarios, uncertain. Regarding future employment, much may rest on human ingenuity to create jobs that as yet do not exist, but these will probably require high levels of skill and education. The hotel industry may again be faced with differing capital–labour ratios as it seeks to provide services thought to represent value for money, while for the highest market segment, money is no object and hence the unique, high-priced hotel accommodation complete with private transport arrangements and security guards will represent a key target market.

To conclude from these competing scenarios, it appears that over the next decade or so, the hotel industry will continue to experience growth as the new emergent markets of Asia and the Indian sub-continent, alongside those of the Gulf region, will create a new supply of tourists. However, in the next period from approximately the mid-2030s, the newer trends of advanced automation will reverse the trends of a growing expenditure by the middle classes. Indeed, in 2015 Stierli et al. (2015) commented on the phenomenon of declining middle-class incomes. Whether computer automation will usher in a new world of leisure for the masses is uncertain. There are straws in the wind that indicate subtle changes are already occurring in the global economy. Eberstadt (2016) noted that despite 88 months of continued expansion in the American economy since 2009, in 2015, the participation rate of American males in the workforce who were aged between 25 and 54 years of age had declined. Indeed, it appears that 32 percent of American males over the age of 20 years are without paid work. Their primary leisure occupation appears to be watching television as they average 5.5 hours a day of viewing, almost some 70 percent higher than mean daily viewing figures. Of these, Eberstadt (2016) notes in his research that a large majority are simply not looking for work. Paradoxically, this group of men have higher expenditures than the lowest quintile of income earners – a fact that points to the role of the state in supporting not only this new group of the 'leisured' but also the importance of the State in sustaining income and expenditure for the products of the future. This in turn has implications for the taxation policies of the future, and hence the growing concerns of the world's governments about the tax avoidance schemes of the world's major companies. Thus, as an example, Apple, in New Zealand, paid taxation of $6.8 million on a total revenue of $568 million. Apple accounts filed with the tax authorities in that company showed sales expenses of $551 million, yet the broadcaster, John Campbell, was unable to obtain responses from the company's Auckland offices that appeared to be closed (Campbell/Radio New Zealand, 2015).

Apart from the above, there remain many other challenges for the hotel industry. The threat of terrorism and war is perhaps a constant, but despite the headlines that attract so much attention, the Human Security Report of 2013 noted a continuing decline in deaths from war. While the Syrian conflict and the rise of ISIS may well have inhibited this decline, generally it is hoped this factor will become of less importance as ISIS continues to lose control of territory. For their part, civil aviation authorities are actively seeking to better target travellers to reduce the bottlenecks that occur at airports because of security checks, and it is expected that frequent travellers may see some easing of inspections over the next few years.

Of a longer-term concern issues of climate change may well become more urgent as 2016 looks to be again another year when global temperatures increased. Reference was made above to the role of aviation. Another major source of greenhouse gas emissions is that of transport, but hardly a day seems to pass when there are not reports of advances being made in solar panels, electric and driverless vehicles. These reports are embryonic but, for the optimist at least, they hold out hope for a smaller dependency on fossil fuels. Indeed, in the last two or three years, while the global economy continues a fragile recovery from the 2008 global financial crisis, it is notable that petroleum prices in real terms have remained relatively low because of a lack of growth in demand. Meanwhile, the search continues for alternative liquid fuels. In 2016 it was announced that LanzaTech had supplied Virgin Airlines with some 5700 litres of low-carbon ethanol produced from waste gases generated during the steel-making process for use in that airlines' planes as a further testing of an alternative to conventional aviation fuel derived from fossil sources.

Again, for the optimist, these straws in the wind offer hope for the wider tourism industry, and hence, in turn, for the hotel industry, but broader concerns remain over environmental degradation from other aspects of human activity. Hotels have their role to play in the attempts to address these issues. Some offer free parking to those driving hybrid and electric vehicles, and it is suggested that such vehicles will become more commonplace. Over the horizon lies a challenge to the whole concept of the private ownership of cars in a world of driverless, electric vehicles that can be summoned by some app or cloud-based application based on artificial intelligence.

Applications such as VIV hold the promise of bypassing the need to download and use apps. The scenario of the intelligent smartphone or computer-based 'assistant' envisaged in the film *Her* – an assistant based on artificial intelligence with emotional intelligence who certainly passes the Turing test in being able to converse with humans intelligently may well be present in a matter of a few decades. In 1991 I referenced the film *WestWorld* (made in 1973) as a harbinger of the possible theme park of the future, and remain of that opinion. That indeed would mean that the hotel of the future could well be served by the robots of the fiction of the past.

Conclusions

The hotel industry is today truly global and heavily segmented as to its offerings. For the most part, the demand for hotels remains a derived demand. That is, it is characterised by a demand derived from a need for accommodation at a destination – where destination is the primary reason for the travel. Yet hotels contribute to the attractiveness and the convenience of the destination. Some hotels do, currently, strive to be a destination in themselves such as the above-mentioned Al Maha or the Burj Al Arab in Dubai. Many more will seek similar status and destinations such as Macau and Las Vegas 'work' because of the hotels being combined places of gaming, entertainment (think of shows such as Macau's *Dancing Waters*) and retailing (again Macau's *Venetian Palace*). Yet as examples of unadulterated hedonism, even these latter hotels pay some attention to environmental matters, and the growing concerns of a public that require corporate citizenship.

The industry is and will remain dynamic. It is exciting and faces challenges that are inherent to the industry. Any unsold room today is a revenue lost for ever, and thus yield management remains a core weapon in management armoury as hotels struggle to fill rooms, offer discounts, compete with each other; all the while seeking to be profitable. In seeking to do this, the industry will increasingly turn to algorithms that will not only examine the individual property but will work across properties in a coherent pattern across a region. Equally those algorithms will allocate rooms across different parts of the chain of distribution that increasingly through AI programs such as VIV will attempt to bypass intermediaries to be easily accessible to the individual purchaser. Such developments may well be commonplace within two decades.

The architecture of hotels will become more innovative and environmentally friendly as new materials and construction methods involving the use of pre-modularised blocks reduce the costs of building while also permitting new designs. Design features of the buildings will become increasingly featured as hotels promise accommodation and an experience. Sensual if not sexual promise will cater for increasingly individually designed and selected services and room features. Each guest will create a series of cloud-based records that note preferences that the hotel will provide. These are unlikely to exist within the next decade or two – but by the middle of the century, they will become increasingly offered. Here the greater data collection of individual choice will feature in arguments that seek balances between the needs of privacy and security, but it is suggested that among post-millennials who live an increasing amount of their social life on apps, the meanings of privacy will change. Lives will become more transparent, and less judgemental.

Hotel management will need to become increasingly sophisticated, balancing the traditional functions of reception, accommodation and restaurant management with facilities management, retail leasing, landscaping, computer network and cloud management – all with different requirements for personnel management. Not to mention the potential for robot maintenance! Some of these skills will be delegated to algorithms, necessitating a continuing tension between retaining control, understanding the algorithms and drawing boundaries of delegation. In addition to empowering staff, debate may emerge about enabling algorithms. The hotel of the next two decades will evolve from current practices, but in creating new opportunities, the hotels of the latter part of the twenty-first century will be very different from those of today. But they may be fewer in number if indeed incomes of the middle classes become squeezed, and equally greater differentiation will exist to reflect the disparities in income and asset ownership unless governments can meet this particular challenge. As ever, hotels exist in a socio-economic-political environment, and will need to engage with that environment, and be very much influenced by it. The more things change, the more they stay the same.

References

Anderson, J.Q. & Rainie, L. (2010). The future of social relations. *Pew Internet and American Life Project.* http://pewinternet.org/Reports/2010/The-future-of-social-relations.aspx. Accessed 7 June 2017.

Autor, D.H. & Dorn, D. (2013). The growth of low-skill service jobs and the polarization of the US labor market. *The American Economic Review*, 103(5), 1553–1597.

Bone, J. (2015). False economy: Financialization, crises and socio-economic polarisation. *Sociology Compass*, 9(10), 876–886.

Campbell, J/Radio New Zealand (2015). *First Person with John Campbell: Apple's high ideals and low tax bill.* Podcast. www.radionz.co.nz/programmes/first-person/story/201776580/first-person-with-john-campbell-apple's-high-ideals-and-low-tax-bill. 29 October 2015. Accessed 11 October 2016.

CNBC (2016). *Inside the pizza chain that's replacing chefs with robots.* www.cnbc.com/2016/09/29/inside-the-pizza-chain-thats-replacing-chefs-with-robots.html. Accessed 11 October 2016.

Eberstadt, N. (2016). *Men Without Work: America's Invisible Crisis (New Threats to Freedom Series)*, West Conshohocken, PA: Templeton Press.

Frey, C.B. & Osborne, M.A. (2013). *The Future of Employment: How Susceptible are Jobs to Computerisation?* Oxford: Oxford Martin School, University of Oxford.

Human Security Report Project (2013). *Human Security Report 2013: The Decline in Global Violence: Evidence, Explanation, and Contestation*, Vancouver: Human Security Press.

Persaud, J. (2016). *The Airbnb Story.* Presentation at PATA Global Insights Conference, 2016. Exploring Connectivity. Sky City Convention Centre, Auckland, New Zealand.

Robotics-VO (2013). *A Roadmap for US Robotics. From Internet to Robotics.* 2013 Edition. Robotics in the United States of America.

SiteMinder (2016). *SiteMinder report: Average booking value on direct hotel websites nearly double that on third-party channels.* www.siteminder.com/news/average-booking-value-direct-hotel-websites-nearly-double-third-party-channels/. Posted 16 August 2016. Accessed 10 October 2016.

Stierli, M., Shorrocks, A., Davies, J.B., Lluberas, R., & Koutsoukis, A. (2015). *Global Wealth Report.* Zurich: Credit Suisse Bank.

World Bank (2016). *Data.* http://data.worldbank.org/indicator/NY.GDP.MKTP.KD.ZG. Accessed 10 October 2016.

47

Changes in hospitality consumers' needs and wants

James Arthur Williams and Stefanie Benjamin

Changes in hospitality consumers' needs and wants: An introduction

Change is a necessary evil for life, innovation, and predicative successes. Hospitality businesses face constant pressure to compete, and in order to compete, many businesses in this particular industry must be willing to adjust their marketing tactics and promotion schemes to appeal to existing and potential consumers. This stratagem seems simple in theory, but requires in-depth understanding of consumers' needs and wants prior to successful implementation. For instance, productive hospitality firms must grasp their targeted consumers' likes and dislikes, trends (e.g., Millennials desiring unique experiences) impacting their consumers' attitudes and behaviours, and challenges (i.e., income or location) that might skew consumers' decision-making about a particular hospitality establishment.

Hospitality establishments need to be proactive to assuage issues that might potentially impact their businesses in a negative fashion. However, the hospitality industry is doomed to repeat failed schemes if this industry cannot understand and predict the needs of current and prospective consumers. This prompts rudimentary and crucial questions: Who are our consumers? What are his or her needs? Can we meet those needs? How can we prepare to meet and to exceed stated needs?

What is a hospitality consumer?

The proverbial definition of a *consumer* is an individual who purchases goods or services. Yet, hospitality businesses (i.e., hotels, restaurants, casinos, and amusement parks) are housed in a very unique industry that is frequently misunderstood or unacknowledged by your average consumer, prompting the need to provide a detailed definition of the typical hospitality consumer. *Hospitality consumers* are individuals who pay for services that provide them with intangible experiences, positive or negative, that can alter their willingness to revisit a hospitality establishment in the future. Positive hospitality experiences encourage happy patrons to engage in word-of-mouth marketing, leading to revisits, thus making consumers the crucial component of any hospitality business. Without consumers, the hospitality industry would not exist.

Learning the terminology of hospitality consumers

Hospitality consumers become *transients* or *tenants* who are seeking pleasant accommodation while traversing terrains away from home. *Transients* are individuals pursuing short-term accommodation, renting real property (fixed property, principally land and buildings) for days or weeks at a time. Conversely, *tenants* are individuals seeking more permanent accommodations, renting real property for 30 days or longer. Transients and tenants are both considered guests, but vastly different guests, with different wants, needs, and expectations. These unique guests have needs, wants, and expectations that must be met, or they will eventually take their business to other companies. When we refer to transients and tenants, our minds quickly assume lodging; so we must also address *patrons* of the hospitality industry.

Patrons are customers who pay for a service, and they can be seen as a new or frequent visitor of an entity. Patrons can also be grouped as a guest, depending on the hospitality jargon. Patrons visit sporting or tourism events, restaurants, casinos, nightclubs, cruise ships, amusement parks, and hotels or resorts. Patrons encompass the term *guest* at any hospitality business, so this word will remain a hospitable term. These terms help us to identify the external customers, but analytics provide us with the required data to access, understand, and meet our guests' needs and wants.

Understanding the differences and trends of four niche market travellers

This understanding challenges hospitality organizations with the task of comprehending patrons' needs, wants, likes, and dislikes. Hospitality patrons demand quality customer service and experiences that create comfort, acceptance, and fun. In order to know hospitality patrons, hospitality decision-makers must become well versed in the demographics of its patrons. It is imperative to understand the generations of people. *Millennials* and *Generation Xers* are the top contributors to spending income in this economy, proving to be lucrative populations to the hospitality industry.

Millennials provide the voice of new patrons in the hospitality industry, considered by many researchers as the fastest growing travellers in the hospitality sector. By 2025, over 50 per cent of hospitality consumers will be considered Millennials. This drastic shift will occur within the next 10 years. *Millennials* are people born from 1977 to 1995 and researchers have cited Millennials as adventurous, technology-driven, culture sensitive, and passionate, to name a few.

Millennials seek unique experiences and are known to choose boutique hotels and authentic restaurants over chain establishments, prompting businesses to alter their tactics to cater to the needs and wants of this distinctive population. Prior to the proliferation of Millennials, *Generation Xers* ruled the hospitality consumer market. *Generation Xers* were raised to think in an individualistic manner and developed a survivor's mentality. Millennials and Generation X individuals require distinctive services to placate their specific needs and wants. Even though Millennials are the fastest growing consumer segment, Generation Xers are the biggest buyers, spending about $561 million in a three-month span online compared to Millennials, the second-largest consumer group, who spent about $489 million in a three-month span online (GEN HQ, 2016).

Baby Boomers consist of individuals born from 1946 to 1964, who became known as the first generation of television, birth of rock-n-roll, and free love movements. This unique generation partied hard, and those moments of nostalgia are being relived on celebrity cruise ships and tourism attractions. The Baby Boomers generation is one of the largest generations in history, with about 77 million people, becoming a niche that must be addressed and catered to. This "me" generation requires specific amenities and resources when traveling to locales away from their usual habitat. Baby Boomers are considered the oldest population of travellers that have a significant impact on the hospitality industry, while Generation Z/Centennials consist of new travellers born in the 2000s.

Centennials include a record number of Hispanics, comprising 49 percent of all babies born in 2001 (GEN HQ, 2016). This generation appear to be more interested in technology devices (e.g., video games, DVD players, and cell phones). It is projected that over 4 million Centennials will have their own cell phones, which creates a lack of peer-to-peer interaction and interpersonal communication. Centennials were raised during a more diverse population, and they have been inundated with an abundance of information, being disseminated via the Internet. They use the Internet and cell phones to transform into savvy consumers who know their interests and disinterests, making them unwilling to compromise. This new demographic contributes about $51 billion every year to the economy, while their parents contribute about $170 billion each year for them. Hospitality industries must forecast or prognosticate to appeal to these distinct demographics.

Black and LGBT travellers represent a niche within the market that must be addressed among hospitality businesses. Mandala research (Chideya, 2016) suggests that black or African American travellers account for $48 billion of the United States travel market; LGBT travellers account for a respectable $70 billion of revenue in the domestic market. Proactive hospitality companies should find strategic ways to accommodate and appeal to these distinct travellers, while noting that many of these travellers are included in the Baby Boomers, Generation Xers, Millennials, and Centennials demographics.

Meeting the demands of unique travellers

More and more generations of people are living for experiences, but peoples' needs and wants have a way of making those experiences drastically disparate. Many Millennials are motivated by environmental sustainability, so they are motivated to seek the usage of renewable resources in today's society. This demand enables hospitality businesses to adopt *corporate social responsibility (CSR)* into their governance plan as a significant initiative. *CSR* is a corporation's plans to assess and take responsibility for the company's impact on social wellbeing. Millennials are committed to organizations that promote sustainability and an overall obligation to a healthier society and a renewable planet. Millennials embrace personal wellbeing, choosing Panera Bread and Chipotle over the typical McDonald's and Burger King that Generation Xers overindulged in.

Millennials' demands are vastly different when compared to Baby Boomers, Centennials, and Generation Xers. Hospitality entities will need to individualize services provided to Generation Xers, whereas Baby Boomers prefer peaceful events and specialized tourism attractions, and Centennials are partial to technology-induced features or applications in the hospitality industry. Even though Millennials is the most researched generation, mainly due to the fact that Millennials will comprise 75 per cent of the workforce by 2020, future generations must be thoroughly researched. Hospitality businesses should understand the consumers' wants, needs, and special interests.

Diverse communication among consumers must be mirrored by the hospitality industry

Older generations may utilize technology; however, they functioned during a time when word-of-mouth and face-to-face interaction ruled their communication experiences. Hospitality firms should pander to Baby Boomers and Generation Xers by communicating in a fashion that relates to their discourse, while Millennials and Centennials might favor online communication (i.e.

Twitter, Facebook, Instagram, Snapchat, Yelp, and TripAdvisor). Marketing tactics should embody multiple streams that accommodate all consumers rather than employing a single perspective that appease one demographic or generation. Single perspectives have a propensity to exclude other demographics from an organization's strategic goals.

Social initiatives might not appeal to many Generation Xers, but Millennials are keen to broach trending topics, such as *Black Lives Matter (BLM)* and *HB2 Bill*. All of these sensitive topics have impacted our hospitality and tourism industries. For example, BLM caused the University of Missouri football players to refrain from playing in a game, which motivated legislators to terminate the tenure of the president, Tim Wolfe, on the campus. More than 50 organizations have decided to support the BLM movement; consequently, consumers supporting this agenda will be more willing to invest in these businesses, making this a beneficial business move.

Google, Twitter, Instagram, and Facebook have openly supported this movement, and Millennials, Centennials, and Generation Xers use those social media mediums extensively to make purchasing decisions in regard to services and products. If hospitality businesses choose to support issues that might be unpopular for some consumers, they must couch a message that is inclusive rather than divisive.

The HB2 Bill discriminates against the rights of transgendered individuals in regard to access to public restrooms, often referred to as the "Bathroom Bill". This bill could cost North Carolina $5 billion a year, and Charlotte is projected to lose $100 due to the NBA removal of their All-Star Game from their city; this forecasted cost encompasses losses from hotels, restaurants, tourism transportation, and general spending. Hospitality establishments cannot afford to communicate ineffectively, with direct rhetoric or indirect discourse that implies a lack of support or biased support for controversial issues. Most consumers are requesting authentic and honest communication from hospitality firms of their interest.

Finding ways to market to unique consumers

The *marketing mix* consists of four Ps: product/service, place, price, and promotion. Hospitality firms place a strategic emphasis on the services they can offer current and prospective consumers. *Product/service* require hospitality managers to understand how their services meet the needs of invested consumers. This prompts constant analysis of their work environment, while evaluating necessary modes of improvement, to keep capturing the interests of consumers. *Place* gives hospitality a venue to sell its services; for example, hoteliers attempt to target Millennials and Centennials through the Internet and target business travellers by reaching out to their companies. This approach enables hospitality businesses to reach the customer prior to consumers stumbling into their organization.

Price is created and controlled by the location of a hospitality business and consumers' interests. *Executive-level management* observe and understand market needs, enabling them to adjust prices to events in their target market. It is pertinent to set reasonable prices if businesses expect to maintain their market positioning. Growth occurs when hospitality businesses devote their time, efforts, and finances to *promotion*. Promotion is utilized to reach consumers in effective and efficient modes. Hospitality businesses need to learn the best times and modes for promoting their services. It is also important to note that successful hospitality entities *benchmark* to learn the best practices of their competition.

Hospitality firms should study their opponents' promotion strategies, giving them a blueprint and cheap technique to learn what works or does not work in their special market. Executive-level management must stay invested in their opponents and information retrieved from the *grass roots* of their business.

Strategic planning and implementation of marketing practices

Strategic planning requires an *action plan* developed at the executive level of hospitality organizations. Action plans will fail if they do not take the consumers' interests into consideration, more specifically, their wants and needs. In order to appeal to consumers, they must understand the distinct generational differences of their consumers. However, the comprehension of their consumer-base should not narrow the scope or aim of their consumers. Hospitality firms have to consider the interests of Baby Boomers, Generation Xers, Millennials, and Centennials. Managers should remain proactive by constantly assessing their consumers and forecasting their needs and wants, to devise and to implement services and experiences that are tailored to their interests.

Executive-level managers should converse with employees who work in the trenches or grass roots level of their hospitality business. At the grass roots level, top-level management has the ability to understand the needs and wants of *internal stakeholders*. Internal stakeholders comprehend the needs and wants of consumers, so they can provide beneficial information that empower executive-level managers to plan and to implement decisions that placate the needs and desires of consumers. Internal stakeholders become invested when executive-level managers appear to value their responses. Internal stakeholders can develop advantageous relationships with *external stakeholders*, discovering patterns and interests that might be missed by top-level management.

External stakeholders are consumers who frequent amusement parks, restaurants, hotels, casinos, etc., so in essence, everyone is an external stakeholder if they visit any of these types of businesses. This information is crucial because executive-level managers and grass roots-level employees must think as a consumer, servicing consumers from this perspective and functioning from this outlook as well. When employees operate as a consumer visiting a hospitality entity, they have a higher propensity to conduct themselves in an appropriate fashion. Consumers are the valued assets of any hospitality establishment because no establishment exists without consumers.

Summary

Consumers dictate the market and set the price for specific services in the hospitality industry. Without their patronage, hospitality businesses would cease to exist. The conundrum is that new hotels, restaurants, and tourist attractions are being built every day, motivating hospitality entities to augment their services and customer services. In order to have impeccable customer service and repeat guests, hospitality firms have to appeal to new consumers and pander to their needs by focusing on developing a level of happiness and comfort that match current and prospective consumers' needs. Effective communication is a boon and positions hospitality establishments in advantageous situations. Hospitality businesses should utilize communication that mirrors consumers' vernacular if they aim to remain a success in their distinct target market.

Successful strategic planning requires a detailed action plan that values employees at the grass roots level. This level of involvement extracts favorable data needed to devise a plan at the executive-level management, so that executive-level managers can understand the intricate needs and wants of consumers. Consumers are constantly changing within capricious hospitality environments. Today's hospitality businesses must remain proactive and ahead of the market if businesses plan to sustain growth and plan to attract new consumers.

This can only occur by understanding the marketing mix, the generations of consumers, and the special niche demographic within those generations; and the strategic plan at the executive level of management. It is also important to know how their business must invest in internal and external stakeholders. Hospitality businesses should mold their thinking to the thoughts of consumers, so that they operate and function from a consumer's frame of reference. Consumers are fickle, so hospitality businesses must be more pliable by adapting a more flexible paradigm.

References

Chideya, F. (2016). *Traveling While Black*. [online] Available at: www.nytimes.com/2014/01/05/travel/traveling-while-black.html?_r=1 [Accessed 1 Oct. 2016].

City-data.com. (2016). *Wilson, North Carolina (NC 27896) Profile: Population, Maps, Real Estate, Averages, Homes, Statistics, Relocation, Travel, Jobs, Hospitals, Schools, Crime, Moving, Houses, News, Sex Offenders*. [online] Available at: www.city-data.com/city/Wilson-North-Carolina.html [Accessed 15 Aug. 2016].

Forbes.com. (2016). *Forbes Welcome*. [online] Available at: www.forbes.com/sites/maurybrown/2016/07/22/the-economic-impact-of-charlotte-losing-nba-all-star-game-and-potentially-super-bowls-due-to-hb2/#61c4d86c3f60 [Accessed 7 Oct. 2016].

GEN HQ. (2016). *Generational Breakdown: Info About All of the Generations-GEN HQ*. [online] Available at http://genhq.com/faq-info-about-generations/ [Accessed 5 Sept. 2016].

Hospitality Net. (2016). *New Report: Consumer Mega-Trends Impacting Hospitality in 2016*. [online] Available at: www.hospitalitynet.org/news/4075712.html [Accessed 11 Sept. 2016].

Marketing Teacher. (2016). *The Six Living Generations in America*. [online] Available at: www.marketingteacher.com/the-six-living-generations-in-america/ [Accessed 8 Aug. 2016].

Mindtools.com. (2016). [online] Available at: www.mindtools.com/pages/article/newSTR_94.htm [Accessed 30 Sept. 2016].

Rutherford, J. (2016). *Why Your Online Selling Ideas Should Cater to Gen X | SaleHoo*. [online] Available at: www.salehoo.com/blog/why-your-online-selling-ideas-should-cater-to-generation-x [Accessed 5 Sept. 2016].

Review questions

1. What is a consumer?
2. What makes a hospitality consumer different from a typical consumer? Compare and contrast between a transient and a tenant.
3. Define patron in the hospitality industry and why is this word significant to hospitality businesses?
4. Name the generations travelling within the hospitality industry and elaborate on the impact of these generations on marketing plans.
5. Discuss ways to market to these intricate generations and explain tactics for attracting these unique consumers.
6. What are some threats that preclude hospitality firms from marketing to all consumers? How can hospitality businesses mitigate these threats?
7. Explore the role of internal and external stakeholders. What is the relevancy of these individuals within the hospitality sector?
8. How will you use lessons learned to maintain current consumers and to attract new consumers?
9. In what way would you employ the marketing mix to target one specific demographic without excluding other demographics?
10. Discuss the importance of hospitality businesses remaining flexible and open to new marketing tactics.

Case application

After 10 years of restaurant success, Unmaskytp Chicken World (UCW) closed its doors. UCW was located in Wilson, NC, with a population of 49,628 residents. Within Wilson's demographic, 46.6 per cent is male and 53.4 per cent is female, and is made up of 45.9 per cent Black residents, 41.7 per cent White residents, 8.7 per cent Hispanic residents, and 3.68 per cent other residents. UCW restaurant was located in East Wilson, where the demographic was 80 per cent Black. The restaurant demographic was about 65 per cent Black, 30 per cent White, and 5 per cent other. Most business occurred between 11:00 am and 2:00 pm, Monday–Friday. Another noticeable peak time was Sunday between 2:00 pm and 7:00 pm. It did not appear that UCW had a specific marketing plan; it focused on a unique flavored chicken and spicy barbeque. Other products were used to support their staple products.

Business was very productive for UCW, considering their low factory overheads due to the ownership of their respective real property. This leverage gave UCW the opportunity to keep product prices low, enabling them to remain competitive against franchise establishments and other local southern-style cooking restaurants. However, in the last five years of their tenure, UCW started receiving catering requests from businesses that catered to a White demographic. This proliferated business started appealing to a White clientele, so UCW started marketing to this demographic. The conundrum is that the restaurant never truly marketed its brand.

Some Black consumers appeared visibly upset about UCW's marketing stratagem, prompting some Black supporters to speak negatively about the restaurant. UCW decided to take their new catering business and White population interest as a sign to relocate to the west side of Wilson, which targeted a more upscale and White populous. UCW increased expenses by adding a new real property, and they never attracted the numbers to sustain and to grow their consumer appeal. UCW's business on the east side suffered because they lost the Black support and had to raise prices to attempt to break even. This impacted the overall quality of their product because they had to choose different venders.

UCW was forced to close their doors and enter the world of catering. This profitable restaurant vanquished in Wilson's southern-style cooking market after its relocation, leaving many in the community to wonder what had happened and how could this establishment have survived?

Based on what you have learned from changes in hospitality consumers' needs and wants, what advice would you give Unmaskytp Chicken World?

48

Future of hospitality marketing
Trends and challenges

Sergio Moreno Gil and J.R. Brent Ritchie

This chapter first establishes a conceptual framework for the integration of hospitality and its relationship with destination, as a determinant factor in the future of hospitality marketing and in the design of marketing strategies. Subsequently, the chapter proceeds to analyze the major trends affecting this industry, integrated into a dynamic diagnosis that highlights the main implications of these for the future of hospitality marketing. This chapter is not intended to perform a thorough analysis of the extensive literature on the subject or to establish a detailed analysis of the state of the art. It focuses instead on raising a series of reflections of an exploratory nature of the challenges we must face and need to consider in order to establish appropriate work plans and specific projects to succeed in such an increasingly changing and competitive industry. With this aim, the chapter draws on some of the seminal texts and basic hospitality literature, combined with current references.

The hidden force of change in hospitality marketing: The greater integration of hospitality within the destination

Hospitality must be conceptualized and analyzed as a system whose interactions cannot be separated from the tourist destination where the activity occurs. Thus, relationships occurring in the destination between different agents, and between these and the destination itself (e.g., relationship between accommodation and destination) are the key to understanding the phenomenon (Jafari 1989; Moreno-Gil and Martín-Santana 2015) and thus to be able to guide the destination's marketing actions.

Following Laws (2000), a mechanical and linear approach still persists in research on hospitality and tourism, despite the complexity of the system recommending alternative approaches. This situation is mainly the result of two factors: (1) the influence developed by the industry of products of mass consumption and the economic treatment of tourism issues, which makes intensive use of mathematical tools in search of stability and balance. In contrast, the tourism and hospitality industry has great complexity and diversity, driven by dynamic and heterogeneous forces, whose modeling could be made more realistic, among other methods, through the use of chaos theory (Gleick 1987; Russell and Faulkner 2004), and (2) the lack of consideration of the so-called equifinality which characterizes tourism system transactions, i.e., the fact that some inputs in a complex biological or social transaction process may result in different outputs (Bertalanffy 1968).

For this reason, this chapter adopts this alternative approach to analyze trends and their potential impact on the strategic and operational management of hospitality marketing. But before addressing these trends, the systemic hospitality marketing relationship with the destination where tourist activity occurs is discussed first.

An initial aspect to note is that a tourist destination can be perceived, among others, from a representative perspective (Carballo et al., 2015, Ritchie 1992). Destination is a perceptual, representative concept which is subjectively interpreted by the tourist. In this sense, a destination offers a mix of tourism products and services that are consumed under a destination brand. In this approach, hospitality marketing must have a direct and profound link with those destinations where its activities are located.

Dissociation between hospitality and tourism

The separation between hospitality marketing and destination marketing is largely explained by the dissociation existing between hospitality and tourism. While the conceptual and analytical perspective of hospitality has evolved from a production-focused perspective towards a more general, open market view (Brotherton 1999), this process still has a wide progress margin ahead, characterized by a more holistic and client-centered point of view (Lusch and Vargo 2006). This evolution margin is explained below, taking accommodation as an example under a traditional definition of hospitality around four basic features (Hepple, Kipps and Thomson 1990; King 1995). Accommodation is regarded as a main tourist product, since normally it is the first tourist decision made once a destination is chosen. In fact, accommodation is the tourism system product with the greatest interaction with the tourist during their holiday (Ottenbacher, Harrington and Parsa 2009).

The definition of hospitality product illustrates itself its impact on marketing: (1) it is conceived as the hosting of a guest who is away from home; (2) it is interactive between the provider and the recipient of the service; (3) it is composed of a mixture of tangible and intangible elements; and (4) the service provider seeks customer safety through both psychological and sociological comfort. This first categorization can draw some initial implications for marketing management: (1) the need to enhance product development and communication directly related to the destination (the tourist's place of residence as a reference) and compared to the tourist's living place (home as reference); (2) the importance of permanently interacting with the client (24/7), during but also before and after his/her stay; (3) the need for strengthening intangible aspects and their emotional connotations; and (4) the crucial role that both risk management and comprehensive security are reaching not only in physical terms, but also regarding tourist emotional balance.

Based on this more systemic and global, customer-focused approach to hospitality, we can think of it as an integrated system in a more general framework of analysis, namely the destination and the tourism system. In this respect, disregarding the internal composition of the accommodation system, there is a relationship between accommodation as a basic production unit and the destination, through the most important complementary services for accommodation. Taking as an example a vacation resort property, these are restoration (F&B), leisure and recreation, which can be provided directly by the housing itself or by other companies at the destination. In addition, there is a relationship between housing and destination resources (e.g., beaches, natural attractions) and other complementary services (e.g., shops, personal services), which again can be provided directly by the accommodation itself or not. In this sense, when a customer assesses the accommodation, this assessment is portrayed through the location attribute perceived by the client of the relationship between accommodation and destination resources and other services (Moreno-Gil, Martín and León 2012).

Therefore, the challenge is to establish a common philosophy which shares values, language and a coherent conceptual framework, and brings an interdisciplinary approach to the matter (Jones 1996; Keiser 1998; Airey and Tribe 2000), contextualizing hospitality marketing as a specialized field within an open system (Morrison 2002; Hemmington 2007). Hospitality cannot be considered in isolation from key drivers that will shape the destinations and the global business environments in which they are competing.

Considering the level of integration between tourism and hospitality, both in research and academic contexts, we can talk about different views that can lead to perceptual differences. Chen and Groves (1999) suggested three different philosophical models (see Figure 48.1), each involving different consequences for hospitality marketing management. In the first model, both subjects overlap to a variable degree for each individual case. This approach involves recognizing the independent peculiarities of each element, which has a symbiotic relationship with the others where no supremacy or hierarchy attribute is considered, but it raises the uncertainty of determining as a target the necessary overlapping degree.

Meanwhile, the second model features an overview of tourism that accommodates hospitality as one of its components. Both the size and centrality at which hospitality is represented make specific reference to the importance to be granted within the tourism system. The main problem of this model is the difficulty of determining both relative levels of importance and the position that should be granted to hospitality within tourism, as well as the role to be performed by destination marketing organizations or DMOs (Choy 1992).

Finally, the third model gives primacy to hospitality as unit of analysis, which incorporates tourism as a system component, varying again its inner "circle" radius and relative location in the figure according to its granted importance. This is the most used model in the hospitality literature, as it incorporates approaches for both accommodation management and service analysis. These useful features provide practical tools to address studies on customer behavior within the hospitality system, but they lack a wider perspective which can place such tourists in the more general context of their vacation trip, which is the approach that hospitality marketing needs.

Under this marketing perspective of integrating hospitality and tourism (and the destinations), the challenge lies in how to make tourists happier, safer, and healthier, all while creating new customized experiences for them. Thus, there is a need to inspire researchers to undertake

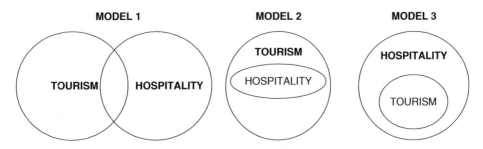

Figure 48.1   Marketing integration between tourism and accommodation
Source: Own work, adapted from Chen and Groves (1999).

further research related to other sectors in the economy and to attract other managers' attention to this field, where consumer needs should be the main source of inspiration (Hjalager 2015). In this process, the residents, the local culture, and the sense of place are the main ingredients and must be melded with the use of new technologies, tourism and hospitality knowledge, and marketing strategies. As an example, the *Michelin Guide*, introduced in 1900, was an innovation, as it provided information to help tourists with their trips (from how to inflate tires to where to purchase gas to where to eat and stay overnight). The hospitality industry should make this reverse trip, connecting its products with the destinations and the tourists' interests.

The challenges and suggested approaches above may seem at first glance too general, even poorly pragmatic. Thus, we further provide an applied example to illustrate a case where the integration between the hospitality and tourism system is clearly exposed, and where the prevailing paradigm is to strengthen destination identity in relation to the subjective comparison made by the tourist with his/her living place, the interactive relationships between transactions (Li and Petrick 2008), intangible assets (knowledge) over tangible assets (goods and capital), and the co-creation of value around client security through psychological and sociological comfort. The implications for hospitality marketing are clear. Thus, success is not solely based on the hospitality system, and not primarily on its available resources, but on systems integration and on how these resources are competitively used (Pearce 2014).

The sun experience in the Canary Islands

Toward a new business and marketing model

Taking the transformative approach and applying it to the principal touristic product of many destinations (i.e., sun and beach) results in betting on knowledge, that is, welfare, health, and comfort, and the environment around those resources. Applying knowledge, training, and research results in proposing a development linked to healthy leisure in natural environments. Today, the greatest competitive advantage is the knowledge the hospitality system possesses rather than the ownership of natural resources or their access to cheap labor. A project devised by researchers at the Spanish University of Las Palmas de Gran Canaria illustrates this change in connection with the industry.

Traditionally, sun beds and parasol beach areas are managed in some cases by the hotels themselves, or by external companies through public concession contracts. The current business model is disassociated from the destination. It uses low-skilled, non-intensive knowledge which generates precarious employment and disallows its scalability and internationalization. Moreover, the spa model (and even the thalassotherapy model) tends to develop indoors, disconnected from the destination. The proposed alternative approach for the Canary Islands project focuses on the main destination resource (climatic conditions) as the source, and links it with the hospitality system as well as tourist onsite motivations (e.g., body tanning and beauty, wanted physical well-being), where staff is provided with the required training, equipment, knowledge, and capabilities in order to implement it.

The project is about recreating a unique atmosphere and servicescape, whose design comes from the tourist. Thus, the process begins with an identification process to assess the tourist phototype (skin type), his/her current solar capital, and current weather conditions (e.g., ultraviolet radiation). According to these parameters, a custom-tailored enjoyment plan is designed for the tourist, including sunbathing time and exposure modes, nutritional supplements that enhance the objective (e.g., local product smoothies), possible additional treatments (e.g., massage), and other complementary activities (Moreno-Gil and Picazo-Peral 2015).

This model is fully portable (from the software developed with these features, to the business model itself, or specific training for specialists). As it can be guessed, the transition from the current traditional model to this approach implies a trans-disciplinary, multi-sectorial vision, with the participation of engineers, doctors, nutritionists, physical therapists, designers, software developers, etc. Thus, the traditional model of intensive, low-skilled labor is replaced by high-level specialized staff.

This simple example, applicable to the entire value chain and all hospitality processes, illustrates the conceptual framework previously presented, which has profound implications for the development of marketing. Thus, the destination and companies thereof can lead a value proposition focused not on the climate, as is the case with any other sun and beach destination, but on leadership in the category, building on the benefits of the climate and the products developed to take advantage of these benefits. Finally, the self-promotion of businesses and the destination is aligned with this proposal, where even the scientific argument can be easily integrated. An illustrative example is the promotional video from the Danish tour operator Spies (https://goo.gl/svorQr), which takes the Gran Canaria island as a model, using a scientific argument in a humorous tone, where the benefits of the sun are conveyed through a solar-cell powered charging experiment using two dummies.

The lack of adaptation to this new approach may involve some successful renowned brands in the hospitality industry being put off the market or relegated to the background. This has been the case with other leader companies in their sectors such as Nokia and Kodak in recent years. In this sense, both identifying and emphasizing the correct approach in hospitality and tourism research are crucial.

Current and future research in hospitality marketing

Evolution implies change (Xiao and Smith 2006), and the increasingly competitive market in which the sector is immersed, along with the continuing economic and social changes occurring worldwide, make the continued development of research necessary to provide new insights, ideas and resources to academia, destinations and businesses. These are continuously facing new challenges and the specific complexities of the industry (Silva, Rodrigues, Mendes and Pereira 2010). Furthermore, the hospitality industry is not particularly innovative (Abreu et al. 2010), and adaptation to new trends mainly takes place under external inspiration and alliances.

The need to continue emphasizing the interconnected research on tourism and hospitality becomes evident (Kim et al. 2009). In this way, the research focus on hospitality, which is a more recent topic than tourism (Ottenbacher et al. 2009), as required by the industry and the skills of its managers (Airey and Tribe 2000), suffers from a wider, interdisciplinary approach (Shaw and Nightingale 1995), taking into account the complex relationship between multiple interconnected, interdependent elements in the system (Morrison and O'Gorman 2008) and their related exchange functions and roles.

In this sense, it is necessary to develop research that generates new theory, or adjustments of existing theories and models, while also being applicable to solving problems in the sector (Sturman 2003), since theoretical research without practical applications, disregarding its uselessness, should not be validated (Van Scotter and Culligan 2003). Thus, a joint multidisciplinary research scenario emerges as a priority, where disciplines and areas involved are related to environmental and personal relationship management, physical and emotional wellness of the client, etc.

Especially in hospitality marketing research, the following conclusion can be drawn. The number of articles published on hospitality in the specialized literature on marketing and business is still very limited (King, Funk and Wilkins 2011). Moreover, the study by Park et al. (2011) on hospitality research published in the first decade of the new millennium highlights marketing as one of the most important topics of future research. Furthermore, King et al. (2011) focus on specific aspects such as internal marketing, marketing research, technology and brand management.

More specifically, in a paper published by Line and Runyan (2012), the authors review the hospitality marketing research in four top hospitality journals over three years in order to identify significant trends and gaps in the literature. The results showed that (1) topics related to the marketing environment represented 37% of the papers, while those related to marketing functions represented 62%; (2) within the marketing functions, management, planning, and strategy is the first category (19.7%), where branding is also a key topic; and (3) the main target industry analysis has been by and large related to hotels and lodging (40.1%), followed by restaurants and food service (31.8%) and festivals and events (6.6%).

Finally, in addition to explicit proposals from several authors on the need to emphasize research on specific areas of hospitality marketing, such as generational shift, brand management (including development, proliferation and competition, loyalty and brand promise delivery), and technology and social media management; the following section addresses some of the major trends, and how these must be integrated into hospitality marketing considering the tourist experience in the hospitality system.

As has become abundantly clear over the past years, this period is proving dramatically different from that of previous decades. As a global community, we are living through widespread changes whose scope and significance we are barely able to perceive at this point in time. Some of the dimensions of this evolution are already recognizable, and indeed, some are easily predictable. Others are as yet embryonic, where the nature of the changes they may bring about is still very uncertain. New research must provide answers to and guidelines for these new challenges.

Trends and new horizons for hospitality marketing

We live in a new paradigm, where constant change is the new normal. Although it is an interesting exercise to identify the main trends that are likely to influence hospitality marketing, using for instance a traditional PEST or even SWOT analysis, the exercise does not serve a full purpose unless it can provide some coherent and organized insights into the possible implications of these trends. Toward this end, instead of listing the main trends that could affect hospitality marketing, the following sections unify these trends into specific units in order to provide more guided insights, including the most significant implications for the future. As no single trend will dominate the global future, sometimes they are mutually reinforcing or work across purposes (Dwyer 2011). While it would be pretentious to think that these trends are exhaustive (they are not), it is expected that they will provide a useful starting point for further reflection and analysis.

A detailed understanding of these implications would require soliciting input from a broad range of sources and analyzing the results in depth. However, employing existing knowledge to draw some conclusions that could be of value to make practical decisions related to hospitality marketing is useful. These conclusions do not represent a definitive position but rather a dynamic diagnosis, where the inputs can be reorganized in different ways and where evolving and new forces will shape the nature of hospitality marketing.

The goal is to provide academics, students, policymakers, and senior executives in hospitality with a useful starting point for identifying some of the major forces with which they will have to cope in the coming years. But despite the value of this effort, it is incomplete, considering the rapid pace of change, and regardless of the best of intentions, it tends to view global trends from a limited perspective. However, it is hoped it helps to show new horizons, thus presenting some opportunities for the hospitality marketing of tomorrow.

After a review of some of the main global forces and trends that will shape the nature and scope of hospitality marketing, the next sections organize those trends together into three dynamics: brand management, trade management, and in-house experience management. This exercise helps to easily identify the new horizons and opportunities that will emerge in the coming decades.

Main trends related to brand management

Although it is speculative at this point, there is some evidence that, as a reaction to these trends, brand management will have to evolve. The following main forces have been identified, with many specific trends influencing the future of hospitality branding and its promotion.

Increasing online communication

- Touristic and generic apps have an intensive and widespread use by tourists.
- SoLoMo: social, local and mobile. Tourists have mobile access to local information on the same location, making social media contributions related to this local information.
- Multimedia content is king, and video content is queen, and both are becoming increasingly important. YouTube is currently the second search engine after Google. New ways of communicating via pictures and videos are developed every day (drones, 360-degree videos, virtual reality, augmented reality, etc.).
- R2T (resident-to-tourist) communication is a must (both online and face-to-face) in order to differentiate the experience.
- T2T (tourist-to-tourist) communication is boosting. New platforms related to reputation (e.g., TripAdvisor) are playing major roles in the hospitality industry, as social media are becoming of paramount importance. Social capital and online reputation are of crucial importance.
- The application of P2P technology is transforming the sector, extending its use on each product and combination of these, e.g., accommodation (Airbnb, Couchsurfing, HomeAway), transport (Uber, Blablacar), food (EatWith, ShareYourMeal), co-working spaces, etc. In addition, local society integrates into the business model and communications to be performed (e.g., Spotted By Locals).
- In the past, the elevator, first introduced in the hospitality industry by The Brighton Hotel in 1865, allowed hotels to profitably rent rooms at floors above the ground and first-floor levels (Hjalager 2015). Today, B2B connections through websites such as Airbnb allow hotels to sell rooms outside their buildings. For instance, the Spanish hotel chain Room Mate is renting external properties (flats and condos) through a new brand: Be Mate (https://es.bemate.com/), while providing all services through their staff in the cities where they also offer their standard hotel services. In particular, the global offer from Airbnb comprising 330,000 rooms (none of them in property) puts this company in the top 10 of lodging brands, next to traditional hotel companies.
- Crisis management communication is gaining importance in brand management.
- Online communication provides a means of approach and contact with niche segments and specific communities such as pets, panks (professional aunts, no kids), and multigenerational groups.

591

- Classical dimensions of space (now also in origin and not only at the destination) and time (lifetime customer relationship, instead of vacation-time) are reconfigured.
- Electronic marketing is now mainstream. Thus, besides the traditional SEO and SEM strategies, there is also remarketing, programmatic marketing campaigns, vertical portals, online reputation, optimization in virtual assistants (Siri), customer analysis and tracking through multiple devices, and company and industry performance "chatbots" monitoring. Brands are more digital than ever before.

Increasing competitive rivalry and tourists become more demanding

- Competition is now global, "new markets" such as Asia Pacific and Latin America take center stage from the point of view of supply, demand, and industry transformation.
- New markets bring cultural issues and challenges, requiring an adaptation of company policies in both national and regional contexts, but also generating new dynamics from those places as they will become global.
- Joint promotional effort (co-branding and rebranding) is increased by integrating multiple sectors and agents.
- Private public advocacy is needed to impact the economy in this competitive environment.
- There is an increasing demand for communication platforms that allow combining promotional actions from small and large companies.
- Improving promotional effectiveness is even more important than in past decades.
- A functional brand does not sell. It needs to improve its affective, authentic and emotional perceptions.
- Brand management and assignment formulas (e.g., franchising) become more complicated. "Glocal" brands will emerge, with a global focus but local sense of place, learning the best practices from other sectors and most successful companies.

Increasing tourist "non-touristic" communication (tourists don't perceive themselves as tourists)

- Communication is more sensory, but also more tangible, thus impacting on intangible assets.
- Experiential content increases over generic content.
- Further development of storytelling aimed at the citizen, not the "tourist," as a communication strategy.
- Generalization of "Bleisure," where the client cannot distinguish between leisure and business. Thus gastronomy, new urban spaces, creativity and the value added by the resident are of increasing importance in this new scenario.
- Events make up a new wave of more emotional and experiential communication.
- Testimonies from visitors and non-tourists are a strategic axis of communication.

Sustainability is now at center stage. The triple bottom-line approach includes: social, economic, and environmental dimensions

- Brands and tourism communication style are linked more to health, welfare, sustainability, food, sport, and technology, rather than to purely touristic themes.
- Tourists committed to socially supported causes (e.g., climate change, loss of biodiversity, ethnic conflicts, poverty alleviation) generate a greater impact on the businesses and destinations they interact with.

Traditional and new tourist integration

- Tourists grow older (Chris Paxson 2009). The population in developed countries is aging, and this has profound implications for the service, including its needs and motivations, and also for brand management and the communication to be performed.
- Millennials break in to the market, changing the ways of getting informed, making decisions and experiencing tourism.
- R2N (Repetitor to New customer) relationship obtains a greater role.
- The power of tourist prescription plays a yet more prominent role, whereas the challenges of integrating multigenerational groups and generational shift still remain.
- The need to link communication with the tourist life cycle and concerns is stressed.
- Loyalty programs will change, enhancing alliances with other sectors, with themed benefits for specific targets, fostering specific advocacy of niche markets, crowdsourcing, and recommendations from customer to customer.
- Customer relationship management will become more complicated and evolve to connect the customer's entire online interaction moments with the customer relationship management and to generate a network relationship management, integrating different stakeholders at the same time.

Research and knowledge will assume greater prominence in brand success and promotion

- Research not only provides information for strategic planning. The research process also becomes a part of the message content.
- The use of new analytical techniques helps research to address more sensory, emotional and intangible issues.
- Street marketing, pop-up spaces and experimentation become everyday actions in a permanent living labs environment.
- There is increased research on new products and the development of novel organizational capabilities.
- The analysis and strategic use of Big Data becomes a priority.

Main trends related to trade management

Although it is too early to reach firm conclusions regarding the changes that the relationship with trade will face, it seems that the spread of multiple channels, both on- and offline, and more media and communication platforms will influence the distribution process.

Greater polarization is envisioned between attractive deals with very competitive prices (both low cost and trusted brand offers) and experience and thematic customized proposals (all-inclusive vs. all-exclusive).

Increase of the influence of personal real-time price and quality comparisons on tourist decision-making:

- There is a need to increase real-time customer "excuses" and sales arguments to enhance sales conversion.
- The development of permanent "micro-events" in a company's own headquarters enhances the "special moment" that facilitates sales closing as well as promotion of its principal value proposal.

- A new kind of luxury is promoted, namely the freedom to do whatever you want, whenever you want.
- The classic discount coupon has evolved to flash sales offered by different websites, besides their own providers, while collaboration among supply providers remains less developed.
- Average stays decrease in favor of short breaks, thus increasing the focus on the "time-poor money-rich" segment, as well as the power of Now.
- A need for a more strategic use of market information has emerged, e.g., daily price yield management policies (Emeksiz et al. 2006) on assets such as stay, added products (spa, casinos, restaurants, etc.), groups, clients through their life cycle; and social media ratings knowledge for how and when to perform engagement actions on satisfied customers.
- Channel manager and its strategic management will be a priority, given the relentless rise of new marketing possibilities (channels, segments, markets), and their different operational features and returns.
- New comparative indicator tools will gain value, as they provide an alternative to classic price and customer satisfaction, related to transformation power, generated emotions (e.g., platforms such as Facebook have already incorporated the variable "emotion" into content sorting algorithms, making "matchmaking" more similar to natural human search), spiritual rejuvenation, and environmental and social aspects.
- Novel technology-based intermediation models will continue to emerge, orientated to those tourist decision processes both prior to booking and during the booking itself.

Direct marketing as pursued challenge

- A growth in marketing through agreements with other companies is expected, in order to provide unique experiences, combining direct marketing capabilities.
- The use of Information and Communication Technology (ICT) and alternative solutions are exponentially increasing.
- A higher integration of micro-offer marketing at the destination (products and services of all kinds) with traditional product marketing in markets of origin is also expected.
- Dynamic packages and customized bundles will be boosted.
- An increased emphasis on booking process integration (either by themselves or through intermediaries) linking the customer with the brand through the development of experiences.

Main trends related to the in-house experience management

The hospitality industry, with some exceptions (fast food restaurants), has generally opted to keep wages low, avoiding the need for technological innovation. However, the time has come to adopt technology more widely, as it will be difficult for the industry to maintain current price levels or to render new travel experiences without using new ICTs. Technology will radically change the customer experience and the communication process (Carballo et al. 2015). In addition to the impact of ICT in communication, safety and security and the power of locality and time suitability are major trends to take into account.

Increase of customized tourist online communication and service at home

- There is a growing need to be able to establish a permanent, real-time communication link with the tourist at home. Microblogging tools, such as Twitter, and instant messaging software allow customers to be in touch 24 hours a day, with personalized questions, suggestions and interactive messaging.

- The participation of staff and residents in tourist communications is enhanced.
- The use of ICT in tourism is endorsed, in order to facilitate tourist general feature recognition (e.g., video marketing for general categories, sex and age, context-based), and specific personal features for client identification (e.g., RFID, wearables, smart bracelets and beacons). This will allow a custom-tailored communication model.
- As "sunglasses replaced or supplemented hats with large shades and allowed tourists to experience attractions in sunny and snowy environments" (Hjalager 2015, p. 12), virtual reality glasses will replace ordinary settings with extraordinary alternatives.
- In addition to their intended standard service, robots will allow for a more personalized service and more custom-tailored communication in some aspects.
- Linking tourist communication to instant payment through alternative formats is intensively increasing. Credit cards have been improved with the introduction of new digital payment systems which allow firms to increase their instant selling, while product placement becomes increasingly important.
- Aromas and scents will play a prominent role in hospitality marketing.
- Wearables will play an outstanding leading role in tourist communication, as well as the Internet of Things (IoT), i.e., the set of devices and objects connected to the Internet, especially those with application in home automation and sensing.
- As industry once brought nature inwards (e.g., indoor pools, the first one having opened in London in 1837), other elements of nature can be interiorized through virtual reality, whereas actual experiences can be taken outside the hotel.
- Traveling brings stress to the body as well as cognitive and social challenges. The bed will be transformed into a "healthy rest station." Although the Westin Heavenly Bed introduced in 1999 was an innovation in promoting the core benefit of the hotel product (the rest), new resting-stations must be created that integrate body and mind care and bed and sauna in order to integrate an overall health benefit.
- In-house entertainment is competing with home entertainment, and strategic partnerships are needed to succeed in that battle. Customers are seeing more individualized experiences related to "special interests" that are aimed at enriching their lives with new experiences rather than traditional entertainment. Finally, augmented reality allows visitors to be less dependent on real life, facilitating the design of new entertainment possibilities.

The quest for safety and security will continue

- The so-called cocooning phenomenon represents the effort by many people to deny or escape from what has become a somewhat frightening world (terrorism, wars, health threats, etc.). Thus, for instance, it implies that hotel rooms should be able to provide the proper "cocooning environment," with better facilities and extra value than that obtained at home. Thus, the traditional air-conditioning feature is no longer enough. In addition, the creation of a customized atmosphere (temperature, views, emotions) and overall comfort is needed. The industry must also facilitate a "streaming environment" to connect with the destination and the customer's social world, in addition to teleconferencing. Finally, both environments (cocooning and streaming) must be integrated into a space of virtual reality where clients can flow and connect with others and where tourists can "experience" the destination before actually visiting it.

- There is a conflict between security and privacy and between security and discovering the outside that generates different alternative proposals (hotels as safety boxes, hotels as safe areas integrated into the region, open hotels, hotels as expedition campgrounds, etc.).
- There will be a higher demand for services related to specialized products that protect the traveler's health and facilitate access to reliable and reassuring medical services.

The power of locality and time suitability

- Micro-events, along with their programming schedules, will take place within company areas (e.g., in the hotel room through ICT), as well as in the company environment (i.e., its surroundings).
- Spending generated in different traditional business units, particularly in new products and services, assumes greater relevance.
- Both the resident and destination aspects such as gastronomy and authenticity become key *drivers* of the tourist experience, based on onsite resources and the impact of these resources on the contribution to the significance of the tourist and his/her transformation.
- It is important that residents of a tourism destination will accept all (or any) forms of hospitality development. In some important tourism destinations, such as Barcelona, new hotel projects have stagnated as a result of the residents' pressure against tourism development. Thus, hospitality marketing must actively seek the support and commitment of local communities.
- Despite the global trend of "sameness" around any destination, there are strong counterpressures to maintain individual and cultural distinctiveness and to provide the capacity to communicate in every place at the right time.
- *Product placement* will assume increasing prominence.
- Indoor environments will gain greater importance as new regulations control the quality of indoor air, the effects of building materials, water and energy issues, and the like (Dwyer et al. 2009). Regulations considering the industry's environmental, social, and economic influences are expected to be more restrictive.

The trends and new horizons that have emerged from this reflection and that are identified in this chapter are by no means exhaustive. However, they do provide some general insights into the challenges and opportunities in hospitality marketing for the future. These trends and their proactive actions will help the hospitality industry to adapt to the new scenarios and to design a new future in hospitality marketing. Undoubtedly, these new challenges will involve changes in the organizational chart, and in particular within the hospitality marketing structure.

References

Abreu, M., Grinevich, V., Kitson, M., & Savona, M. (2010). "Policies to enhance the 'hidden innovation' in services: Evidence and lessons from the UK". *The Service Industries Journal*, 30(1), 99–118.

Airey, D. & Tribe, J. (2000). "Education for hospitality". In *Search of Hospitality: Theoretical Perspectives and Debates*, C. Lashley, A. Morrison (eds). Butterworth-Heinemann: Oxford, pp. 192–276.

Bertalanffy, L. (1968). *General systems theory*. New York: Brazillier.

Brotherton, B. (1999). "Towards a definitive view of the nature of hospitality and hospitality management". *International Journal of Contemporary Hospitality Management*, 11(4), 165–173.

Carballo, M.M., Araña, J.E., León, C.J., & Moreno-Gil, S. (2015). "Economic valuation of tourism destination image". *Tourism Economics*, 21(4), 741–759.

Carballo-Fuentes, R.C., Moreno-Gil, S., González, C.L., & Ritchie, J.B. (2015). "Designing and promoting experiences in a tourist destination: An analysis of research and action needs". *Cuadernos de turismo*, 35, 71–94.

Chen, K.C. & Groves, D. (1999). "The importance of examining philosophical relationships between tourism and hospitality curricula". *International Journal of Contemporary Hospitality Management*, 11(1), 37–42.

Choy, D.J.L. (1992). "Alternative roles of national tourism organizations". *Tourism Management*, October, 357–365.

Chris Paxson, M. (2009). "Boomer boom for hospitality: Opportunities and challenges". *Journal of Hospitality Marketing & Management*, 18(1), 89–98.

Dwyer, L. (2011). "Trends underpinning global tourism in the coming decade". In *Global Tourism* (Third Edition), W.F. Theobald (ed). Taylor & Francis, pp. 529–545.

Dwyer, L., Edwards, D., Mistilis, N., Roman, D.C., & Scott, N. (2009). "Destination and enterprise management for a tourism future". *Tourism Management*, 30, 63–74.

Emeksiz, M., Gursoy, D., & Icoz, O. (2006). "A yield management model for five-star hotels: Computerized and non-computerized implementation". *International Journal of Hospitality Management*, 25(4), 536–551.

Gleick, J. (1987). *Chaos*. London: SphereBooks.

Hemmington, N. (2007). "From service to experience: Understanding and defining the hospitality business". *The Service Industries Journal*, 27(6).

Hepple, J., Kipps, M., & Thomson, J. (1990). "The concept of hospitality and an evaluation of its applicability to the experience of hospital patients". *International Journal of Hospitality Management*, 9(4), 305–317.

Hjalager, A.M. (2015). "100 innovations that transformed tourism". *Journal of Travel Research*, 54(1), 3–21.

Jafari, J. (1989). "Structure of tourism". In *Tourism marketing and management handbook*, S.F. Witt, L. Moutinho (eds). Prentice Hall.

Jones, P. (1996). "Viewpoint. Hospitality-research. Where have we got to?" *International Journal of Hospitality Management*, 15(1), 5–10.

Keiser, J. (1998). "Hospitality and tourism: A theoretical analysis and conceptual framework for identifying industry meanings". *Journal of Hospitality and Tourism Research*, 22(2), 115–128.

Kim, Y., Savage, K., Howey, R., & Van Hoof, H. (2009). "Academic foundations for hospitality and tourism research: A reexamination of citations". *Tourism Management*, 30, 752–758.

King, C., Funk, D.C., & Wilkins, H. (2011). "Bridging the gap: An examination of the relative alignment of hospitality research and industry priorities". *International Journal of Hospitality Management*, 30(1), 157–166.

King, C.A. (1995). "Viewpoint. What is hospitality?" *International Journal of Hospitality Management*, 14(3/4), 219–234.

Kotler, P., Heider, D.H., & Rein, I. (1993). *Marketing places: Attracting investment, industry, and tourism to cities, states and nations*. New York: The Free Press.

Laws, E. (2000). "Service quality in tourism research: Are we walking tall (yet)?" *Journal of Quality Assurance in Hospitality & Tourism*, 1(1), 31–56.

Li, X.R. & Petrick, J.F. (2008). "Tourism marketing in an era of paradigm shift". *Journal of Travel Research*, 46(3), 235–244.

Line, N.D. & Runyan, R.C. (2012). "Hospitality marketing research: Recent trends and future directions". *International Journal of Hospitality Management*, 31(2), 477–488.

Lusch, R.F. & Vargo, S.L. (2006). "Service-dominant logic: Reactions, reflections and refinements". *Marketing Theory*, 6, 281–288.

Moreno-Gil, S. & Martín Santana, J.D. (2015). "Understanding the image of self-contained and serviced apartments: The case of sun and beach destinations". *Journal of Hospitality & Tourism Research*, 39, 373–400.

Moreno-Gil, S.M. & Picazo-Peral, P. (2015). "La formación, la investigación y la exportación de conocimiento en el sector turístico". In *20 retos para el turismo en España*. Pirámide. Madrid, pp. 335–350

Moreno-Gil, S., Martín, S.J., & León L.J. (2012). "Key success factors for understanding the image of a tourist accommodation: An empirical study in the Canary Islands". *INNOVAR, Journal of Administrative and Social Sciences*, 22(44), 139–152.

Morrison, A. (2002). "Hospitality research: A pause for reflection". *International Journal of Tourism Research*, 4(3), 161–169.

Morrison, A. & O'Gorman (2008). "Hospitality studies and hospitality management: A symbiotic relationship". *International Journal of Hospitality Management*, 27, 214–221.

Ottenbacher, M., Harrington, R., & Parsa, H.G. (2009). "Defining the hospitality discipline: A discussion of pedagogical and research implications". *Journal of Hospitality & Tourism Research*, 33(3), 263–283.

Park, K., Phillips, W.J., Canter, D., & Abbott, J. (2011). "Hospitality and tourism research rankings by author, university, and country using six major journals: The first decade of the new millennium". *Journal of Hospitality and Tourism Research*, 35(3), 381–416.

Pearce, D.G. (2014). "The internationalization of tourism research". *Journal of Travel Research*, 53(3), 267–280.

Ritchie, J.R.B (1992). "New realities, new horizons: Leisure, tourism and society in the third millennium". *Annual Review of Travel*, 13–26.

Russell, R. & Faulkner, B. (2004). "Entrepreneurship, chaos and the tourism area lifecycle". Annals of Tourism Research, 31(3), 556–579.

Shaw, M. & Nightingale, M. (1995). "Scholarship reconsidered: Implications for hospitality education". *Hospitality Research Journal*, 19(1), 81–93.

Silva, J., Rodrigues, P., Mendes, J., & Pereira, L. (2010). "A tourism research Agenda for Portugal". *International Journal of Tourism Research*, 12, 90–101.

Sturman, M. (2003). "Building a bridge from the other bank: This issue's focus on research methods and tools for hospitality management". *Cornell Hotel and Restaurant Administration Quarterly*, April, 9–13.

Van Scotter, J. & Culligan, P.E. (2003). "The value of theoretical research and applied research for the hospitality industry". *Cornell Hotel and Restaurant Administration Quarterly*, April, 14–27.

Xiao, H. & Smith, S.L.J. (2006). "The making of tourism research: Insights from a social sciences journal". *Annals of Tourism Research*, 33(2), 490–507.

49

The evolving future of sales

Richard G. McNeill

Introduction

Pity the human! Trapped by *Nature's* marvelous gift of *Reason*. Trapped to ever ponder the future. Trapped to incessantly progress, regress, or alternatingly spiral in both directions, humans plunge into the unknown of time. Does a sparkling utopian world of unimagined delight await or a dark one, as sinister as that revealed in the 1999 film, *The Matrix*, where machines became the masters (*Matrix*, 1999)?

The human mind demands knowing the future; a quest which is a source of both fear and excitement. These simultaneous emotions mark human efforts to foresee, predict, and control. Both fortunately and unfortunately, the human's insatiable quest to see and to control the future has produced both undreamed positive progressive societal change, as well as generated periods of negative and regressive darkness. As tomorrow becomes today, reality either verifies, debunks, or partially substantiates yesterday's musings. Thus, the human stumbles into the future

Technological evolution has always advanced *Homo Sapiens'* progress over about the last 200,000 to 250,000-year history since this species first appeared. With the rise of agrarian civilizations about 5000 years ago, technological advancements significantly accelerated and altered the future. However, today's accelerating technological advancement developments are unprecedented and are driving such disrupting change as to render future forecasts nearly impossible. Today, mankind is in uncharted territory.

Long-term future speculation is not the focus of this chapter. The more pedestrian aim is to approximate the short-term evolving future of sales. This chapter tells the focused and evolving story of change in the world of sales: Beginning with the past, the story moves the narrative to the present state of sales and then, from the present, the story tells of unfolding disrupting forces altering this present which morphs into a new, albeit speculative, future. Such an ambitious task!

Indeed, who has an accurate crystal ball? Like most attempts to see the future, those who say that they are gifted with such foresight – don't. We are all trapped in *Presentism*, a common human paradigm which either imposes realities of the present onto the past or projects our limited knowledge into the future. Though there is an effort to guard against this bias, arguably, most of the best researchers often, unintentionally and unconsciously, fall victim to their inherent human nature. This author wants to make very clear his humility and awareness of his shared human limitations; especially those concerning wrestling with the future. Thus, within this context, the author takes on the task of gazing into a dusty, slightly cracked, and occluded orb.

What is the evolving future of sales? As stated, such speculation is risky business, yet, we can make some educated guesses. The author does so with the help of some reasoned and recognized fortune-tellers.

Overview: Disrupting technology, perspectives and change

Disrupting Technology. What's going on? Google's driverless cars are simply amazing! How can this be? Aren't these machines acting like human beings? Apple's Siri converses with humans as a friendly personal assistant and through a portable handheld smartphone that contains computing capabilities multiple times more powerful than the technology that carried humans to the moon and back in 1969. IBM's Watson buried the best human *Jeopardy* players and defeated world Grand Master chess champions. Digital technologies are rivaling the accuracy of doctors in diagnosing diseases. Machines and technology seem to be replacing tasks once only believed capable of being performed by the wet human brain. Avalanching technological marvels are astounding the average human every day. What's going on?

In 2014, Erik Brynjolfsson and Andrew McAfee authored, *The Second Machine Age: Work, Progress, and Prosperity in a Time of Brilliant Technologies* (Brynjolfsson and McAfee, 2014). The authors focus on the forces driving the reinvention of our lives and our economy. They argue that as technology advances exponentially and synergistically combines, it is taking society into an entirely new era. As the full effect of these rapidly advancing digital technologies is felt, human societies will realize both positive and negative outcomes.

The authors label positive outcomes as *Bounty*. This comes in the form of mind-stunning developments in personal technology, beneficial and advanced societal infrastructure, and almost unlimited access to personally enriching cultural items. In the future both consumer and business buyers can expect more of everything, including both tangible goods and digital products and services, at lower and lower prices.

Negative outcomes, labeled by the authors as *Spread*, envision dramatic and disrupting changes to human life; for example, professions of all types will be overturned. White-collar jobs and careers are not exempt, even though most people once could never believe that lawyers or accountants could be supplanted, at least at the rudimentary levels, by today's electronic software packages that are available. Other work such as the assembly line employee has long been replaced by robotics; and replacement of the workforce is accelerating. Recent economic indicators reflect this shift: fewer people are working, and wages are falling even as productivity and corporate profits advance (Brynjolfsson and McAfee, 2014).

Disruptive forces have affected the hotel salesforce. Lalia Rach is the Associate Dean at the College of Management and Director of the School of Hospitality Leadership at the University of Wisconsin-Stout. In her white paper, *The Evolution of Sales*, sponsored by the *Hospitality Sales and Marketing International (HSMAI) Foundation* (Rach, 2015), she states:

> The hotel industry is grappling with the changes in the consumer, technology, and local economies, as well as organizational changes at the unit level of hotels, corporate offices of hotel brands, management companies and ownership groups. Many of the changes have emerged as a result of disruption from multiple new technologies and intermediaries which have made information more transparent and added new value propositions for different types of customers. Disruption can cause chaos within a business or an industry segment but it can also create opportunity. The traditional processes of hotel sales need to be questioned and validated in this new environment. Customer engagement needs to be redefined at all

levels. There is a need for hotel companies to transform the concept of loyalty, shift the engagement with buyers and fashion a different sense of collaboration with customers.

(Rach, 2015 p. viii)

To better appreciate accelerating disruptive forces, knowledge of the rapidity of technological development and size is needed. Global data storage capacity grew from a 1986, 2.06 Exabyte – a mix of 99% analog data and 1% digital data – to a 2007, 299 Exabyte – a mix of 6% analog data and 94% digital data. The mix between analog data and digital data reached a 50/50 balance in 2002, causing some observers to label 2002 as *The Beginning of the Digital Age* (Hilbert and Lopez, 2011). In twenty-one years, global data storage capacity increased more than 100-fold. And, simultaneously, analog data was almost completely supplanted by digital data.

Moving forward, digital storage capacity has continued to explode. Reported by Cisco's *Visual Networking Index Initiative*, the Internet is now in the "zettabyte era." A zettabyte equals 1 sextillion bytes (a "1" followed by 27 zeros), or 1,000 exabyte. By the end of 2016, global Internet traffic will reach 1.1 zettabytes per year and by 2019, global traffic is expected to hit 2 zettabytes per year (Pappas, 2016).

How big is big? Size in the digital world is measured in bytes of information. What is an *Exabyte*? One *Exabyte* is one quintillion bytes (a "1" followed by 18 zeros) and could hold one fifth of all words ever spoken by human beings (Highscalability.com, 2016). Compare this with the familiar, *Gigabyte*, one billion bytes (a "1" followed by nine zeros). An *Exabyte* is one billion *Gigabytes*.

To bring this size down to human conceptualization, here is a more down-to-earth comparison. The universe is estimated to be 13.799 billion years old; its age as calculated from the Big Bang to the present day (Kragh, 1996). Translating the age of the universe from years to seconds and then to bytes, the resulting number is the equivalent of 43.52 exabyte.

With some perspective on the rapidity of technological disruption, the chapter turns to a discussion of *change*. Here a simple model that will organize this chapter is examined.

On Change. Change is life! Without change, there is no growth. Thus, all things are born, grow, and die. This cycle is the nature of the cosmos, of human beings, and organizations. Death leaves space for and informs (leaves legacy remnants and wisdom) the next generation to be born. So, change is a spiraling cycle. It cycles between birth and death, but is directional in that the spiral is either moving positively upward or negatively downward. Change over time is not unidirectional, but either up or down or simultaneously bidirectional.

This chapter references a simplified version of the *Hegelian Dialectic*. German philosopher, Georg Wilhelm Friedrich Hegel (1770–1861), building upon fellow German philosopher, Johann Gottlieb Fichte (1762–1814), posited that all things move in a cyclical and directional way; a triad of abstract concepts. *Thesis* is the culturally accepted state of the way things are; this state can be thought of as a traditional state. *Antithesis* represents the forces of disruption that upset thesis. The outcome of the clash with thesis by antithesis results in a new form of existence, *Synthesis*. Over time, synthesis becomes the new thesis and the cycle, once again, repeats itself continuously into the future. Here, the author uses this model to organize how sales is evolving into the future.

Purpose

The purpose of this chapter is to speculate upon the evolutionary path of hotel sales approximately five to ten years into the future. Further, the chapter aims to provide key reference points and a source for critical reflection on some evolving ideas and debates in the field of hospitality/hotel sales. The aim is to explore key issues that are, today, disrupting and perplexing both academic and industry practitioner observers.

Research questions

Question One. What is the current situation in hotel sales? This question will be answered by providing a brief history of sales and marketing eras that led to today's sales situation. Then, under the section title, *Thesis*, the most recent period, 1920 to 2002, is examined in detail.

Question Two. What are the disrupting forces that are propelling change in today's salesforce? This question is answered within the section titled *Antithesis*. This period of 2002 to 2016 (the present) features external disruptive forces beyond the control of salespeople, which are driving internal organizational management changes to rethink and reorganize their salesforces.

Question Three. What does the intermediate five to ten-year future possibly look like for sales? This question is answered within the section titled *Synthesis* and will be a speculative answer. As external disrupting forces – especially technological change – accelerate, the author remains humble in forecasting the future, even for this brief a period.

Methodology

Secondary research. Numerous articles were consulted and when coupled with the author's 18 years of sales and marketing industry experience and 27 years of academic teaching and research in hospitality sales and marketing, synthesized into a conceptual model. With a conceptual model as a guide, the author held verification interviews with industry professionals to compare secondarily gained concepts with primary practice of industry professionals.

Primary research. A small unpublished qualitative study was conducted among industry practitioners in the late summer of 2016 (McNeill, 2016). Interviews were conducted with 15 industry professionals. Interviewed participants were stratified: They were roughly divided into three cohorts representing perspectives from the converging functions of: (a) hospitality marketing, (b) sales, and (c) revenue management. Guiding questions for these interviews were developed as derived from the secondary research conducted by the author. Digitally captured interviews were converted to text and analyzed by *NVivo11*, a qualitative research software package (*NVivo 11 Plus*, 2016).

Limitations

Predicting the Future is Speculative. Here, the clarity of crystal ball speculation contained in this chapter is limited to an estimated five to ten-year forecast. Further, this chapter's title contains the word *Evolving*. This single word allows one to freeze present topical events and contextual changes and speculate at any point found along a continuum timeline proceeding from the present to approximately 10 years into the future.

Sales and Top-Line Revenue. A clear understanding of the word "sales" is mandatory. The author speaks of sales as a very limited definition: Hotel group sales generated by living, breathing salespeople. The ubiquitous and confusing word "sales" is frequently misunderstood and often loosely thrown about; thus, the reader may conflate this general use of the word with total top-line revenue flowing from all possible channels and markets. Here, the word "sales" has a very narrow meaning.

Salesforce and Target Markets. "Salesforce" is another term that needs clarity. In this chapter, the salesforce is a group of people selling products and services to a *Business-to-Business* (B2B) market.

Further, "salesforce" refers to a local or property-level group of people working on behalf of their employing hotel and selling to a B2B market of meeting and convention planners and decision-makers. This market, meeting planners, purchase meeting space and services from hotels and other venues.

Multiple-brand hotel corporations are globally dispersed and organized into various traditional levels: local/property, regional, national, and multinational. Further, hotel corporations are reengineering this traditional organizational schema. However, as stated, this chapter specifically limits its discussion of the evolving future of sales to the effect upon the local or property-level salesperson based in the U.S. national market.

Hospitality and Hotel Industries. Here, for purposes of focus, "hospitality industry," a broader term, is limited and narrowly defined in this chapter as the "hotel industry." The hotel industry and its salesforce structures and practices are arguably the progenitor of other salesforces within the broader hospitality industry and thus, representative and instructional for purposes of a reader's extrapolation into a broader scope of interests such as tourism sales.

Significance

Does the U.S. hotel industry exemplify the global tourism industry? How does a study of U.S.-based and local/property-level hotel salesforces have significance for a wider global hotel group business market? Are the findings of this narrowly focused study transferable to a broader geographic or to other sub-industries of the tourism industry or even to industries external to hospitality/tourism? The author believes the answer to this question is, "yes."

This chapter examines increasingly expanding and sophisticated technological forces that will affect most human-delivered jobs. This is especially true in B2B market sales – of all stripes – where the traditional key to success is communications and information transfer. But, let's return to a focus on the tourism/hospitality industry. Why is the microcosm of local/property-level selling significant to broader hospitality or tourism industries?

First, within the global travel and tourism industry, hotel meetings and convention sales is huge business. Second, U.S. hotel corporations will undoubtedly influence global sales and marketing trends.

To the first point of significance, global travel and tourism is a huge business. Global direct revenue contributions of travel and tourism in 2015 were reported by *The World Travel & Tourism Council* (WTTC) as totaling 9.8% of global GDP or US$7.2 trillion as compiled from 184 countries. Further, in its mid-year report in August 2016, the WTTC adjusted the 2016 growth rate to date at 3.1% and forecasted the second half of 2016 to slow to 2.3% (WTTC, 2016).

In the United States, direct contribution of travel and tourism was 6.77% of global 2015 tourism direct spending, US$488 billion, and 2.7% of U.S. GDP in 2015. This is forecast to rise to 2.8% in 2016 and rise from 2016 to 2026 to US$722.3 billion or 3.2% of total U.S. GDP (WTTC, 2016).

The direct spending size of meeting business, a sub-set of the larger travel and tourism industry, is substantial; approximately 57%. As today, living salespeople in hotels and other meeting venues capture this business, the relative importance of and future of salespeople is significant.

Direct total spending for meetings within the U.S. economy in 2012 was estimated at over $280 billion. Almost one half of the total spending, $130 billion (46%), was spent on travel and tourism commodities such as lodging, food service, and transportation. The majority, $150 billion (54%), was not travel-related, although related to the meeting: meeting planning and production costs, venue rental, and other (PWC, 2012).

Total meetings held in the U.S. in 2012 – best numbers available without the author purchasing a costly, privately available report – totaled more than an estimated 1.8 million meetings (PWC, 2012). Categorized by types of meetings, percentages were: Corporate/business meetings (50%), followed by conventions/conferences/congresses (27%), and trade shows (12%) (PWC, 2012).

To the second point of significance, U.S.-based hotel corporations have historically set the pace for the global hotel industry and its underlying sales and marketing technologies. Arguably most hospitality scholars would agree that U.S.-based hotel corporations dominate both geographic presence and exert a disproportionate influence on worldwide hotel management best practices. For example, in 2014 global rankings of global hotel corporations by rooms was: First, *Intercontinental Group* of Denham, England; second, *Hilton Worldwide*; third, *Marriott International*; fourth, *Wyndham Hotel Group*; fifth, *Choice Hotels International*; sixth, *Accor*, a French corporation; and seventh, *Starwood Hotels & Resorts*. Of the top seven hotel corporations, five were U.S. based (Hotel Online, 2014). On September 23, 2016, *Marriott International* completed acquisition of *Starwood Hotels & Resorts Worldwide*, thus creating the world' largest hotel company. Marriott International now has 30 brands and over 5,700 properties (Marriott, 2016).

Does a limited focus on local/property-level salesforce inform? Yes, this chapter closely examines the rapid changes occurring today at the local/property level of the hotel salesforce. From this basic level, one might extrapolate the effects of change as it cascades through the larger hotel corporate salesforce structure.

Back to the future: Hegelian *Thesis – Antithesis – Synthesis*

The following section, *Thesis*, presents a historical journey from the past to the present. *Thesis* provides answers to the first research question of this chapter: What is the current situation in hotel sales?

Hegelian Thesis: A brief journey from the distant past to the present

From antiquity to 2016, this journey briefly describes how sales and marketing arrived at today's state. The present status of sales in 2016, *Thesis*, is the beginning base upon which the chapter discusses disruptions – *Antithesis*.

Antiquity to 2016 (The Present). Sales and marketing is commonly believed to have progressed and is currently progressing through distinct phases of evolution. White (2010) presents seven phases. From his research, this author has modified the phase dates and has speculatively forecasted an eighth phase, which he names *The TraDigital Era*. Here is a quick overview of these eras:

1. ***Simple Trade Era*** – Antiquity – 1860s. Pre-Industrial Revolution. Transactional selling.
2. ***Production Era*** – 1860s–1920s. The Industrial Revolution. Transactional selling.
3. ***Sales Era*** – 1920s–1940s. Aggressive push selling as the pent-up demand existing in the previous phase is now satiated. Transactional selling.

4. *Marketing Department Era* – 1940s–1960s. Marketing-related activities consolidated into a unified department: The 4Ps and the promotion mix, advertising, personal sales, public relations, and sales promotion. Transactional selling begins to evolve to Consultative selling.

5. *Marketing Company Era* – 1960s–1990s. In the universities, the *Marketing Concept* was envisioned: The company exists to satisfy customer needs. Marketing was no longer compartmentalized – marketing became the goal of the entire business. Consultative selling.

6. *Relationship Marketing Era* – 1990s–2002. Focus on customer lifetime value – repeat and referral business. Consultative and Collaborative selling. Consultative selling begins to evolve to Collaborative selling. 2002 is the year that global data storage capacity reached a mix of 50% analog data and 50% digital data. Some observers view this as the beginning of the *Digital Age* (Hilbert and Lopez, 2011).

7. *Social/Mobile Marketing Era* –2002–2016 (The Present). Builds upon past phases, but focuses on real-time connections and customer controlled, permission-based and opt-in relations with customers. The author has read several – uncited – sources that show that *Traditional Marketing* (Outbound) and *Digital Marketing* (Inbound) is at an approximate 50%/50% mix. Notes: (1) Digital marketing is dependent on social media and other electronic variations; (2) *LinkedIn* was founded in 2002, *Facebook*, 2004, and *Twitter*, 2006; (3) Estimated global data storage capacity reaches 299 exabytes in 2007 and is projected to reach 1.1 zetabytes in 2016 and two zetabytes in 2019 (Pappas, 2016).

8. *TraDigital Marketing Era* – (The Present) 2016–2026 (A Ten-year Future) – *TraDigital* is a neologism. It is a word combination of *Traditional* and *Digital* marketing, signifying today's marketing transitional period. This is the author's vision of the evolving future of sales. Declining dominance of traditional marketing tools – print, live salespeople etc. The rise of digital marketing tools and the rise of *Big Data* predictive correlations to target markets.

The Triad – evolution of three distinctive selling strategies. In the late-1980s, Neil Rackham and his consulting firm looked at the history of sales and coalesced findings into three distinctive selling strategies.

The Rackham team studied more than 35,000 salesperson/client encounters in 27 countries. He concluded in his book, *Major Account Sales Strategy* (Rackham, 1989), that the traditional selling model taught in most educational programs and industry training did not represent actual practices of salespeople selling large accounts in the business to business (B2B) markets.

In 1996, and recognizing the growing importance of partnerships and customer/supplier alliances, Neil Rackham, Lawrence Friedman, and Richard Ruff thoroughly examined this topic in *Getting Partnering Right* (Rackham, Friedman, and Ruff, 1996). Here they described how market leaders were creating long-term competitive advantage through a new way of providing value to customers. Rackham incorporated these insights into his next contribution to the study of evolving go-to-market systems. In the influential book, *Rethinking the Sales Force* (Rackham and DeVincentis, 1999), the authors refined Rackham's earlier research and theorized the emergence of three distinct selling strategies:

Transactional selling strategy. This strategy is the oldest form of selling. It evolved in the earliest history of selling and became prominent in the *Sales Era* (White, 2010). Transactional selling has become more sophisticated over the years; however, it retains many historic characteristics. Transactional salespeople continue to sell low to medium-priced and simple products/services. A transactional salesperson's investment in long-term relationships with customers is a costly luxury since achieving sales revenue volume in this strategy is dependent upon a large volume of sales transactions with individual and usually unrelated buyers.

Richard G. McNeill

The traditional transactional salesperson is being replaced by technology. He or she has become a cost that is no longer supportable in selling/marketing simple and commoditized products and services. From the advancements of the quality and reengineering eras of the 1980s and 1990s, many of today's products are of similar quality and can generally perform the same function. They are perceived as commodities. Simultaneously, buyers have become more sophisticated and knowledgeable and have easy access to product/service specifications. The salesperson is no longer necessary to inform or educate buyers.

Since today's buyers know what they want, where to get it, and have access to many product suppliers (ease of the Internet), they are primarily interested in one thing price. The traditional salesperson involved in a transactional selling strategy has become a cost that is relatively high to the selling price. So, a competitor who sells without salespeople (over the Internet, for example) can offer a lower price.

In other words, a transactional selling strategy is a quantitative game of selling transactions to large numbers of individual and generally unrelated buyers. This strategy is distinguished from a consultative selling strategy, which is a *qualitative* approach based on repeat and referral business (McNeill, 2003).

Today, the hotel industry continues to employ property-level salespeople who utilize a transactional strategy. For example, many limited service/select service properties are generally similar in quality and services; thus, they are essentially commodities. Marriott, in the mid-1990s, reorganized its entire corporate salesforce and located many salespeople into centralized group reservation-like centers where primarily transactional sales strategies were practiced (MARRWEB, 2003). In 2008, Marriott again reorganized its salesforce, *SalesForce One*, and has salespeople selling from, what this author's qualitative study related to using a derisive term, *Cubicle Farms* (McNeill, 2016).

In general, all living salespeople who sell using transaction strategies, are incrementally being replaced by the Internet. They still exist but they add cost to product/services and most buyers find all the information necessary to purchase a simple product online. Thus, one must ask the question, what value does a transactional salesperson contribute? If none, then the price of the product can be reduced by the salesperson's salary and other costs. And, this is happening in the hotel business.

Consultative Selling Strategy. This form is the second oldest of the three basic forms. It theoretically fully evolved by the mid-1980s during the *Marketing Company Era* – 1960s to 1990s (White, 2010). Essentially, the basic approach of consultative selling was based on identifying the prospect/buyer needs and then matching those needs to a benefit solution offered by the seller. The early approach was clearly aligned with the overarching *Marketing Company Era* philosophy. By the late 1980s, Neil Rackham had modified this approach to include a significant amount of partnering with the customer; this added a new dimension to the basic customer *needs fulfillment* model. Today, this expanded version of consultative selling is still advocated, but as will be seen in the next section, a similar, transitional form called *Collaborative Selling* is prescribed (Rach, 2015).

Consultative salespeople sell high-priced and complex products/services. Long-term relationships with customers are a distinguishing and mandatory characteristic. The goal of consultative selling is repeat and referral business. Thus, supplier firms target customer firms with a high and long-term spending potential and attempt to convert them to preferred accounts. Generally, hotel salesforces sell consultatively at the local and property level and are capable of accommodating complex group business. Local property salespeople are currently selling consultatively and moving toward a more nuanced, *collaborative* strategy, which adds partnering practices to the general consultative strategy approach (Rach, 2015).

In general, consultative salespeople who have adopted collaborative partnering skills are the ideal salespeople for an earlier sales and marketing era. And, this selling strategy characterizes most of today's personal salespeople. However, as will be discussed in the section *Antithesis*, buyers have changed and no longer want to interact with salespeople, even with these advanced skills. Thus, frustration exists within today's consultative salesforce (McNeill, 2016).

Since today's consultative salesforce have advanced selling skills, they are potentially the talent pool to evolve to a higher form of selling strategy – *Alliance/Partnership Selling Strategy*. McNeill (2016) believes that local/property-level salespeople, despite their advanced selling and relationship-building skills, will be gradually replaced at the property level and migrate to a more advanced level. This is discussed in the section *Antithesis*.

Alliance/Partnership Selling Strategy. This form of selling is the newest and at the "cutting edge" of the three selling strategies. In its most complete form, there is no visible distinction between the seller and the buyer. In fact, the selling company forms a selling team that exactly matches the buying team. Teams are represented by cross-functional areas: for example, both teams include a technology person and/or financial person as the situation dictates. These teams are as permanent as is the partnership. These strategic alliances are characterized by such arrangements as the buyer and seller sharing the same warehouse and/or computer purchasing system. The seller may even have a permanent office located at the buyer's facility. The "vendor/buyer" distinction found in both the transactional sale and the consultative sale is blurred in alliance/partnership selling. This strategy is represented in corporate-wide salesforce organization – *Strategic Account Management* (SAM) and its sub-category, *Global Account Management* (GAM) as represented by the Marriott exemplar discussed below (McNeill, 2003).

In the mid-1990s hotel industry, the innovative and pioneering Marriott International reorganized its corporate salesforce. The reorganization effort was called *Marriott 2000* (MARRWEB, 2002). Traditionally, most hotels were corporations organized geographically by (a) National markets, (b) Regional, and (c) Local. When operating in several countries, the assembled national markets were held under a multinational umbrella.

Marriott needed to manage its many brands and its growing global hotel markets. First, as mentioned in the transactional selling section above, Marriott brought most of its transactional business into regionalized "group reservation centers" where small to medium-size business (measured by meeting room nights) would be handled by both inbound salespeople taking Internet inquiries and outbound salespeople proactively making cold-calls to prospects.

Second, at the local level, they moved consultative salespeople out of local properties; these salespeople were responsible for cluster selling (representing all of Marriott's several brands located in that locale).

Third, Marriott retained its traditional national salesforce (consultative salespeople) organized into sub-divided regions. But, they added new innovations to address growing global markets. They segmented customer accounts by size and commitment. Paralleling Rackham's (1989) Alliance/Partnering Selling Strategy, large national key accounts were handled by very experienced and skilled salespeople. Large global accounts with operations worldwide were targeted to enter special contract relationships with Marriott to contractually deliver a majority of the meetings required by the customer account (MARRWEB, 2003).

With the launch of *Marriott's Salesforce One* in 2008, this author is not informed as to the organizational details. Yet, he believes that given Marriott's September 23, 2016 merger with Starwood and becoming the world's largest hotel corporation, even *Salesforce One* will likely be revised. The recent merger clearly presents a reorganization issue as it created a corporation of 30 brands, more than 5,700 hotels, and located in more than 110 countries (Marriott, 2016).

Hegelian Antithesis: 2002–2016 – Disruptions affecting the hotel salesforce

This section, *Antithesis*, discusses a historical journey from the past to the present. *Antithesis* provides answers to the third research question of this chapter: What does the intermediate five to ten-year future possibly look like for sales?

Secondary source observations. In his book, *Revenue Disruptions* (Fernandez, 2012), Phil Fernandez, co-founder of *Marketo*, a global leader in revenue performance solutions, reflected on digital disruptions as affecting sales and marketing. He argues that given the global technological, cultural, and media changes, today's dominant sales and marketing model is at best obsolete and at worst totally dysfunctional. These disruptions have forever transformed the process of buying and selling.

In her recent book, *The Analytical Marketer* (Sweetwood, 2016), Adele Sweetwood, head of Global Marketing for SAS, the world's largest independent analytics company, described the turmoil of change affecting sales and marketing organizations. Analytics are driving big changes. Gone are the days of pure marketing art. Science now rules sales and marketing organizations. Leaders are grappling with issues that range from building an analytically driven marketing organization to determining the kinds of structure, talent, and tools that are needed to reinvent the new world of sales and marketing.

Primary source observations. In the late summer of 2016, the author conducted a small qualitative study. Interviews were conducted with 15 industry professionals. Interviewed participants were stratified: They were roughly divided into three cohorts representing perspectives from the converging functions of: (a) hospitality marketing, (b) sales, and (c) revenue management. The results are unpublished (McNeill, 2016).

The following are significant findings from this study. Collected data were categorized and analyzed by *NVivo11*, a qualitative research software package (*NVivo 11 Plus*, 2016).

The interviewees of the McNeill (2016) study expressed many misgivings and concerns about the future of hotel sales. These are organized into two categories: (a) General technological developments and (b) Developments directly affecting the hotel salesforce.

General technological developments

Artificial Intelligence (AI) is intelligence exhibited by machines; computers. The term generally applies when a machine mimics the cognitive functions normally associated with human beings. These mimicked human traits include: understanding human speech, competing in strategic games such as chess, self-driving cars, and interpreting complex data (Clark, 2015). AI is a general term and includes some of the other technological developments discussed below.

Interviewees noted that rapid *Business to Consumer* (B2C) technological developments seemed to leak rapidly into *Business to Business* (B2B) areas. Not long ago, it was unheard of that business buyers were comfortable making big purchases over the Internet. Today, that seems to be changing. What will happen to salespeople if this accelerates?

Transactional salespeople – those selling commodity-like products – are being replaced by the Internet. Will this happen to consultative salespeople should complex hotel products – such as resorts and full-service properties – continue to become commodity-like? More and more mega-hotel firms are benchmarking and emulating one another. Their product classes such as luxury, upscale, resort, etc. are beginning to look alike; they seem to all be trying to comply with the *Smith Travel Star Report* classifications (which calculates *RevPar* – Revenue per available room).

Will this cause me to lose my job like the transactional sales jobs currently being lost?

Salespeople know their properties very well. So, this gives them the power to customize it to buyers. AI is driving the rise of powerful databases which can be accessed by buyers.

Will my information base be taken over and will I become irrelevant?

Natural Language Processing (NLP) gives machines the ability to read and understand languages that humans speak. Computers derive meaning from human language input. They then access a sophisticated database to generate responses to the voice input. These databases are closed or open. For example, a closed database contains specific data such as generating responses to inquiries about law, medicine, etc. Open systems must have wider content databases as inquiries or interactions with the NLP system will be more varied and of wider scope (Johnson, 2009). Think of today's intelligent personal assistants such as Apple's *Siri*, Microsoft's *Cortana*, Google's *Assistant*, and Amazon's *Alexa*.

The interviewees were highly aware of the unique contributions made by living breathing salespeople. In traditional marketing, personal sales has historically been regarded as an irreplaceable two-way communication channel between buyer and seller. For example, print advertising is one-way; thus, if two-way interactions were needed to sell a product, a salesperson was used.

Interestingly, the interviewees were only concerned with personal assistants like Siri. Siri is an open database. Closed databases that focus specifically on industries – such as a meeting hotel – can be more sophisticated.

Will this real-time conversation between buyer and Siri or Cortana representing my hotel replace me?

Online sales chats (this roughly falls into this NLP category) by live salespeople at B2B business websites are aware when a buyer is viewing their website and can text chat with them in real time. The interviewees recognized that a meeting planner viewing the salesperson's hotel could have many of their questions answered. Pre-Web 2.0, this was only possible to do with a conversation by phone or in person.

Am I being replaced?

Facial Recognition Systems are computer applications capable of identifying or verifying a person from a digital image or a video frame. One way to do this is by comparing selected facial features from the image and facial database. Typically used in security systems, it is also used to compare other biometrics such as fingerprint or eye iris recognition. More recently, it has become popular as a marketing tool (Consumer Reports, 2015).

Interviewees only touched upon this technological development. It was not the highest concern, but addressed another important traditional salesperson's unique trait: Only people can read the subtleties of other people – see the emotion underneath. In truth, machines reading a person's emotions – like a salesperson does – are in the early stages of development. Marketers are using machines in focus-group like settings to determine a person's likes or dislikes regarding products.

Virtual Reality (VR) refers to computer technologies that use software to generate realistic images, sounds, and other sensations that replicate a real environment and simulate a user's physical presence in the environment, by enabling the user to interact with this space and any objects depicted there (Schnipper, 2017).

Recently, Marriott International set up VR kiosks in New York City. Here people could put VR googles on and take a VR tour of Marriott hotel properties. This appears to be part of its Travel Brilliantly campaign to attract Millennials; however, it has ramifications for meeting planners seeking hotel venues.

Traditionally, meeting planners arranged to tour a potential hotel meeting site face to face and with the hotel salesperson. What happens when the price of VR goggles drops and they become simple tools for meeting planners to use? Of course, any meeting site that is being very seriously considered by a meeting planner for use will be site-visited face to face.

Two interviewees were video gamers. They brought up this question and concern about virtual site visits. And, as usual, the concern was about salespeople being replaced.

The digital-mediated culture seems to have developed among the general population. Salespeople develop person-to-person relationships. Relationship building is a staple of salespeople. Millennials, as well as many others, are tethered, glued to smartphones. They don't want to talk with people on the phone; they would rather text them. Social media seems to intermediate face-to-face interactions. Relationships seem to be centered more around technology than face-to-face communication.

While the interviewees all talked about the power of relationships, they seemed to forget that today they are being intermediated by technology. And, people are seeing this development as normal. Certainly, the Millennial buyers of tomorrow will most probably feel this way.

So, the author is speaking for the interviewees: "Are personal face-to-face relationships only selectively valuable, while most people prefer to interact digitally?" If so, a salesperson's key value has been undermined.

Developments directly affecting the hotel salesforce

These are interviewee concerns that are current and continuing to develop.

Convergence is a term that refers to the merging of marketing, sales, and revenue management functions within a local hotel property. This is a positive development as these three elements align and work together. But, tension continues to exist.

Sales and marketing people have traditionally been responsible for price. Now, and for many years, this power has shifted to the revenue management people. Unless each of these three functions better understands the other, tensions will continue. But, pricing control is generally good for the business owner and will continue.

Interviewees had a quiet peace on this issue, but one salesperson referred to the revenue manager as a *bean-counter*. And, there were some comments about how the art of sales and marketing was continuing to be run by impersonal algorithms and the hospitality was being driven out of *hospitality*.

Third-party intermediation is a huge issue and deserves a more extensive introduction. Disrupting intermediation forces are separating traditional hotel sellers from meeting planner buyers. Third-party and other intermediary forces, such as *HelmsBriscoe* and *Cvent*, are significantly increasing in global reach and influence.

Founded in 1992, *Helmsbriscoe* is the highest volume purchaser in the meetings and event industry. The company is a type of contracted private salesforce who work on behalf of the meeting planner buyer as expert consultants. One could think of these experts as a private attorney or other consultant who helps locate meeting venues and then often accompanies the buyer to negotiation sessions with hotel and other venue salespeople. As of 2015, *HelmsBriscoe* worldwide had 1,200 associates, operated in 55 countries and was involved in an estimated US$1.8 billion in hotel spending (HelmsBriscoe, 2015).

Founded in 1999, *Cvent* is the largest event technology firm in the world; the analogy for its business is a technological platform similar to a consumer dating platform where meeting planners are matched with meeting venues. At the end of 2015, worldwide, it had more than 1,900 employers and 15,800 customers (Cvent, 2015).

The two third-party intermediation companies mentioned above focus on the hotel B2B (business) markets; primarily meeting business markets. The two third-party firms discussed above are the largest in their categories and serve as representatives of this new phenomenon. There are many other smaller firms in these categories.

These are different from intermediation companies such as *Expedia* and *Travelocity*, also known as OTAs or Online Travel Agencies which specialize in B2C (consumer) markets.

Here are some interviewee concerns regarding *Cvent* and *Helmsbriscoe*:

> *Cvent* daily generates a deluge of RFPs (requests for proposals). My management forces me to answer each within 24 hours. Even if I don't, Cvent sends me a reminder to answer it every four hours. I am buried with this paper work. Cvent gives me plenty of leads, but some of these meeting planners are simply sending this stuff out to anybody – they are often a waste of time.
>
> *Helmsbriscoe's* highly experienced salespeople often accompany their meeting planner client to a sales negotiation. Then they sometimes try to leverage their affiliations with other properties to drive an even lower price. They already take 10% of the meetings' value.
>
> What's amazing is that *Helmsbriscoe* also uses *Cvent* as a venue screening tool.
>
> I generally like them, but they are a private salesforce working for meeting planners for a fee. And, I am not sure where this whole intermediation thing is going.

Related to the above discussion on intermediation concerns intermediation in the B2C markets with the launch of *Travelocity* in 1986. *Travelocity*, also known as an OTA or Online Travel Agency, specialized in B2C (consumer) markets. After this launch, travel agents (essentially consumer travel salespeople) were decimated. In 1990 (shortly after the Travelocity launch in 1986), there were approximately 132,000 travel agents. In 2014, there were 74,100, which is forecast to drop to 65,400 in 2024 (Bujarski, 2006).

Interviewees noted the loss of sales jobs with the rise of many OTAs which serve B2C markets. Intermediation from *Cvent* and *Helmsbriscoe* serves B2B markets in which the meeting and convention business is included. The concern coming from the interviewees was that they have noted that developments in B2C markets often leak over and is replicated in B2B markets. Will the massive loss of hotel sales jobs follow the historical loss of travel agent jobs.

Truncated sales funnel

The sales funnel or sales pipeline is the traditional journey a customer takes in the sales process. Traditionally, at the local hotel, salespeople would cold-call prospective customers and enter them into this funnel. The salespeople would send printed information, make phone calls, and attempt to nurture these prospects to a point in the funnel where a face-to-face interview could be set up and a sale attempted. This point of the interview was approximately 50% to 60% in the middle of the funnel/pipeline.

Today, prospects don't take phone calls and cold-calling is essentially dead. Potential buyers gather information about potential meeting venues in the hidden space of the Internet. Hotel people don't even know they exist unless the buyer contacts them – usually by a *Cvent* RFP or through a hired *Helmsbriscoe* agent. Thus, old-fashioned relationship building is short-circuited.

Further, when the buyer contacts the seller, the buyer usually has plenty of information to have generally pre-decided. All that is left to do is negotiate a few details and write up the paperwork.

Here are some interviewees' concerns.

> Since the buyer already knows most of the information and only needs details, why can't the hotel's CSM (Conference Services Manager) perform this function? CSMs are cheaper in salary than salespeople. Will the CSM or someone like them replace me?

Summarizing the preceding section, *Antithesis*, it should be noted that the major concern facing local/ property-level salespeople is will they become obsolete? Will they lose their jobs? This will be addressed in the next section, Synthesis, which takes a speculative look at the immediate, five to ten-year evolving future of sales and the salesforce.

Hegelian Synthesis: 2016–2026 – A speculative future forecast of the hotel salesforce

Effects of external and internal forces. External forces were discussed in the previous section, *Antithesis*. These forces are generally uncontrollable and appear to be accelerating. Digital advancement will continue to drive change for the next five to ten years and, most likely, into the unforeseeable future.

External forces are responded to by organizational management – internal (to the entity) forces. Certainly, there is corporate motivation for sales and marketing innovation: Within the *marketing mix* (4Ps) and the sub-component, *promotional mix* (advertising, personal sales, publicity, and sales promotion), personal sales is the most expensive component. There also seems to be a pattern of sales and marketing innovation to drive increased effectiveness and efficiencies. New and cheaper ways of exchanging with *Business to Consumer* (B2C) markets have benefited by advancing technology. Management has quickly adapted many of these innovations to *Business to Business* (B2B) markets as technology permits.

Triad effects. Rackham's Triad of selling strategies (Rackham, 1989) guides the following general comments regarding the evolving future of sales.

For Transactional hotel salespeople selling commodity-like products and services such as limited-service hotels: They will disappear. They will be replaced by administrative clerks that simply handle logistic details and write-up standardized contracts.

For Consultative hotel salespeople selling complex products and services such as resorts or full-service hotels: They will be replaced by CSMs or other detailed coordinators who answer and negotiate minor contract issues. As a note, Marriott has already created a specialized *Destination Associate* to meet and greet site-visiting meeting planners – this was a former hotel salesperson function. And, remember, the meeting planner buyer already has *Cvent* and Internet-generated information and is often accompanied by a third-party intermediary such as a *Helmsbriscoe* sales agent.

For Alliance/Partnership hotel salespeople, in 2016 they were organizationally uncommon, but as mega-mergers continue in the hotel corporate world and global coverage continues, more Alliance/Partnering agreements will emerge. Who will be their salespeople (now under a new title such as *Key Account Director*)? The answer is former *Rock Star* Consultative salespeople migrating upward. This new breed, formerly known as salespeople and operating as a consultative team, will develop and maintain key global and contracted accounts.

Conclusions of this chapter

Back to the future

The title of the entire previous section, indeed the theme of this entire chapter, has been *Back to the Future*. This theme reflects on the fact that sales and marketing began in antiquity as an economic exchange between people; face-to-face or *People-to-People* (P2P) interactions. Beginning about 100 years ago, P2P interactions were replaced by scientific and objectified notions of B2C and B2B buyers. Beginning in the early 2000s, technology has potentially allowed a return (*Back to the Future*) of customized P2P sales and marketing.

To reiterate the above: P2P interactions began in White's (2010) *Simple Trade Era* – antiquity to about 1860 – where traders/peddlers and merchants physically interacted with buyers throughout the countryside or in town square marketplaces. B2C and B2B objectified sales and marketing then took place until again beginning to return to P2P interactions in the *Social/Mobile Era* – 2002–2016 and forecast to continue into the *TraDigital Era* – 2016–2026. Sales and marketing thinking began to objectify customers (B2C and B2B buyers).

Purpose of the chapter

The purpose of this chapter was to speculate upon the evolutionary path of hotel sales approximately five to ten years into the future. Three questions were asked and, hopefully adequately, answered: (1) What is the current situation in hotel sales? (2) What are the disrupting forces that are propelling change in today's salesforce? and (3) What does the intermediate five to ten-year future possibly look like for sales?

The chapter's argument

1. Change, especially disruptive technological change, will accelerate.
2. Change can be understood through many models, but this chapter uses the cyclical Hegelian model: *Thesis* is effected by *Antithesis* (disruptions), which creates a new state, *Synthesis*, and synthesis then becomes the new thesis. The cycle begins afresh and spirals into the future.
3. Disruptive change affects both general civilization and the hotel sales and marketing function.
4. The now evolving marketing era is the *TraDigital Era*. Traditional sales and marketing practices simultaneously combined with digital marketing practices.
5. Salespeople, specifically, are being replaced by technology because their unique human capabilities are being subsumed by technology. For example, a living salesperson's ability to read the buyer's emotions (facial recognition software), their ability to answer questions in a two-way dialogue (Natural Processing Language – NPL), their ability to form relationships (people today are comfortable with and tethered to mobile devices 24/7 and form relationships with texting and social media).

Conclusions

Finally, this chapter concludes the argument with this speculation into the immediate future: In the next five to ten-year period, hotel salespeople, as we currently know them:

a. At corporate branded local hotel properties, salesforces will generally no longer reside within an individual hotel. Exceptions will be larger group business properties retaining traditional consultative salespeople while smaller property salesforces are replaced by either or both: (1) Local area non-property based salespeople, employed by and selling for hotel corporations which own multiple hotel brands operating within the local area and/or (2) Regional area inbound group business hubs (similar to current B2C inbound reservation hubs) responding to smaller group leads attracted and generated by digital marketing efforts – these inbound small group hubs direct incoming leads to appropriate corporate hotels brands. Non-branded hotel properties will, most probably, continue to operate with traditional in-house salesforces.

b. At the local hotel properties that lose salesforces, salesperson functions formerly handled by in-house traditional salesforces will be subsumed at the local/property level by lower administrative level clerks; sales people will not be obsolete, only transformed and will probably carry a new appellation/title. For example, hotels will assign a type of group concierge to conduct site visits or provide details for leads directed to the local property by local area salespeople, inbound group hubs, or third-party intermediaries such as *Cvent* and *HelmsBriscoe*.

c. And, at the larger multi-brand hotel corporations, while smaller group business is addressed by non-traditional means as described in "b" above, growing and highly paid marketing/sales/service teams will systematically focus on developing targeted key accounts both nationally and globally. These key account developers may no longer be accurately labelled as "salespeople" as they are involved in developing and sustaining systematic long-term exchange relationships between large hotel corporations and large general corporations and key association entities. These systematically developed accounts will generate leads that will be directed to appropriate local hotel properties within the hotel corporate brand family. This account-based marketing/sales/service strategy will be a realization of Neil Rackham's 1996 hypothesized, alliance/partnering selling (Rackham, Friedman, and Ruff, 1996).

References

Bujarski, L. (2006). "The travel agent of the future." *Skift*. Online: https://skift.com/2016/10/13/new-skift-trends-report-the-travel-agent-of-the-future/.

Brynjolfsson. E and McAfee, A. (2014). *The second machine age: Work, progress, and prosperity in a time of brilliant technologies*. New York: W.W. Norton & Company, Inc.

Clark, J. (2015, December 8). "Why 2015 was a breakthrough year in artificial intelligence." *Bloomberg News*. Online: www.bloomberg.com/news/articles/2015-12-08/why-2015-was-a-breakthrough-year-in-artificial-intelligence.

Consumer Reports. (2015, December 30). "Facial recognition: Who's tracking you in public." Online: www.consumerreports.org/privacy/facial-recognition-who-is-tracking-you-in-public1/.

Cvent. (2015, December 31). "Company overview." Online: www.cvent.com/?cid=70100000000RqL9AAK&src=c_gppc&gclid=Cj0KEQjwp4fABRCer93Klpaki94BEiQAsXJMGvI3QrT_3OJ15MOGwP-szjkbxVTw0dwPUXf2lC_r_KkaAn9Z8P8HAQ.

Fernandez, P. (2012). *Revenue disruption: Game-changing sales and marketing strategies to accelerate growth*. Hoboken, NJ: John Wiley & Sons.

Helmsbriscoe. (2015). "Who we are." Online: www.helmsbriscoe.com/our-company.html.

Highscalability.com. (2016). "How big is a petabyte, exabyte, zettabyte, or a yottabyte?" Online: http://highscalability.com/blog/2012/9/11/how-big-is-a-petabyte-exabyte-zettabyte-or-a-yottabyte.html.

Hilbert, M. and Lopez, P. (2011). "Global information storage capacity." Online: https://commons.m.wikimedia.org/wiki/File:Hilbert_InfoGrowth.png#mw-jump-to-license.

Hotel Online. (2014, June 23). "2014 global hotel rankings: The leaders grow stronger; IHG retains top spot." Online: www.hotel-online.com/press_releases/release/global-hotel-rankings-the-leaders-grow-stronger-ihg-retains-top-spot.

Johnson, M. (2009). "How the statistical revolution changes (computational linguistics)." *Proceedings of the EACL 2009 Workshop on the Interaction between Linguistics and Computational Linguistics*. Online: www.aclweb.org/anthology/W09-0103.

Kragh, H. (1996). *Cosmology and controversy*. Princeton, NJ: Princeton University Press.

MARRWEB. (2003, May). "Global sale organization fact sheet." Online. Retrieved May 6, 2003, from https://extranet.marriott.com/.

Marriott. (2016, September 23). "Marriott International completes acquisition of Starwood Hotels & Resorts Worldwide." *Marriott International News Center*. Online: http://news.marriott.com/2016/09/marriotts-acquisition-of-starwood-complete/.

Matrix. (1999). *The Matrix*. Online: https://en.wikipedia.org/wiki/The_Matrix.

McNeill, R.G. (2003). "The 'go-to-market' frontier: Global account management (GAM)," *Global Business and Technology Association (GBATA), Annual Conference,* July 8 – July 12, 2003, Budapest, Hungry. Online: http://gbata.org/wp-content/uploads/2013/02/JGBAT_Vol1-1-p3.pdf.

McNeill, R.G. (2016). *What's going on: Hotel sales professionals in an age of disruption.* Unpublished qualitative study.

NVivo 11 Plus. (2016). *NVivo 11 plus: Qualitative research software for windows.* Melbourne, Australia: QSR International Pty Ltd.

Pappas, S. (2016, March 18). "How big is the internet, really?" *LiveScience.* Online: www.livescience.com/54094-how-big-is-the-internet.html.

PWC. (2012). "The economic significance of meetings to the U.S. economy: Interim study update for 2012." *Pricewaterhousecoopers LLP.* Online: www.conventionindustry.org/Files/2012%20ESS/CIC%20Meetings%20ESS%20Update%20EXECUTIVE%20SUMMARY-FINAL.pdf.

Rach, L. (2015). *The evolution of sales: Perspectives and realities defining the modern sales professional.* HSMAI Foundation Special Report. Online: www.hsmai.org/knowledge/whitepapersales.cfm?ItemNumber=21599.

Rackham, N. (1989). *Major account sales strategy.* New York: McGraw-Hill.

Rackham, N, Friedman, L.G, and Ruff, R. (1996). *Getting partnering right.* New York: McGraw-Hill.

Rackham, N. and De Vincentis, J. (1999). *Rethinking the sales force: Redefining selling to create and capture customer value.* New York: McGraw-Hill.

Schnipper, M. (2017, March 13). "Seeing is believing: The state of virtual reality." *The Verge.* Retrieved March 13, 2017. Online: www.theverge.com/a/virtual-reality/intro.

Sweetwood, A. (2016). *The analytical marketer: How to transform your marketing organization.* Boston, MA: Harvard Review Press.

White, S. (2010, June 18). "The evolution of marketing." Online: http://dstevenwhite.com/2010/06/18/the-evolution-of-marketing/.

WTTC. (2016). "Travel & tourism economic impact 2016. United States." *World Travel & Tourism Council (WTTC).* Online: www.wttc.org/-/media/files/reports/economic-impact-research/countries-2016/unitedstates2016.pdf.

Index

References to figures are in *italics* and tables in **bold**